THE NEW AMERICAN BIB
REVISED EDITION
CONCISE CONCORDANC

THE NEW AMERICAN BIBLE
REVISED EDITION
CONCISE CONCORDANCE

JOHN R. KOHLENBERGER III

EDITOR

NEW YORK   •   OXFORD

OXFORD UNIVERSITY PRESS

OXFORD
UNIVERSITY PRESS

Oxford New York Auckland Cape Town Dar es Salaam Hong Kong Karachi Kuala Lumpur Madrid
Melbourne Mexico City Nairobi New Dehli Shanghai Taipei Toronto

With offices in:

Argentina Austria Brazil Chile Czech Republic France Greece Guatemala Hungary Italy Japan Poland
Portugal Singapore South Korea Switzerland Thailand Turkey Ukraine Vietnam

Published by Oxford University Press, Inc.
198 Madison Avenue, New York, New York 10016

http://www.oup.com

Interior design and typesetting by Blue Heron Bookcraft, Battle Ground, WA.

Printed in the United States of America

3 5 7 9 8 6 4 2

INTRODUCTION

A concordance is an index to a book. It is usually arranged in alphabetical order and shows the location of each word in the book. In addition, it often supplies several words of the context in which each word is found.

The New American Bible Revised Edition Concise Concordance (NABRECC) is an selective concordance to the New American Bible. It covers all 73 books contained in the New American Bible Revised Edition (NABRE). However, it does not exhaustively index all the words of the NABRE. Rather, nearly 40,000 references to almost 6,000 key words provide access to texts most significant to personal and professional Bible research.

FEATURES OF THE NABRE CONCISE CONCORDANCE

The *NABRECC* indexes the Bible in two formats: (1) traditional concordance entries and (2) capsule biographies.

CONCORDANCE ENTRIES
Below is a traditional concordance entry:

> **LOVE** → BELOVED, LOVED, LOVER, LOVERS, LOVES, LOVING
> Gn   29: 20   a few days because of his **l** for her.

Headings:
   The heading consists of:
      (1) the indexed word: **LOVE**;
      (2) the list of related words following an arrow (→).
   The *NABRECC* indexes 5,890 words. Since contexts represent words spelled exactly as the entry headword, the key word is abbreviated and bold. If an indexed word occurs more than once in a context, it is abbreviated as many times as necessary within the context, as under the heading HOLY:

> Is   6: 3   "**H, h, h** is the LORD of hosts!"
> Rev   4: 8   "**H, h, h,** is the LORD God almighty,

Related words point to other spellings and forms of the headword (LOVED, LOVING) as well as cognate terms (BELOVED). Rather than listing all related words after each headword, the editor chose one indexed word to act as the "group heading." All related words are listed after the group heading, and each of the related word headings points back to the group heading. In the example above, LOVE serves as the group heading for six related words.

Context Lines:
   The context lines consist of:
      (1) the book-chapter-verse reference;
      (2) the context for the indexed word.
   37,139 context lines represent 38,177 occurrences of the 5,890 headwords. Books of the Bible are abbreviated according to the table on page viii. The book abbreviation is listed on each context line. Context lines are listed in the canonical order of the New American Bible Revised Edition.

   Taken by themselves, context lines can and do misrepresent the teaching of Scripture by taking statements out of the larger context. "There is no God" is a context taken straight from Psalm 14:1. Of course the Bible does not teach this; it is what "Fools say in their hearts"! Similarly, a context for

Leviticus 24:16 might read, "the LORD shall be put to death" while the text actually says, "One who blasphemes the name of the LORD shall be put to death."

Great care has been taken by the editor and programmer of the *NABRECC* to create contexts that are informative and accurate. But the reader should always check word contexts by looking them up in the NABRE itself. "The Wicked Bible," a KJV edition of 1631, accidentally omitted the word "not" from the seventh commandment, for which the printers were fined 300 pounds sterling! Though there are no longer such fines for misleading contexts, the editor and publisher are still deeply concerned that the *NABRECC* be used discerningly.

CAPSULE BIOGRAPHIES

435 prominent personalities are given capsule biographies:

> **SIMON** → =PETER, =SIMEON
> 1. See Peter.
> 2. Apostle, called the Zealot (Mt 10:4; Mk 3:18; Lk 6:15; Acts 1:13).
> 3. Samaritan sorcerer (Acts 8:9-24).

It is easier to represent and to locate key events in an individual's life in such an entry rather than by using context lines—especially in the entry on Jesus. As in the example above, different individuals of the same name are distinguished by separately numbered biographies. These entries index more than 2,220 biblical texts.

SPECIAL SYMBOLS AND TYPOGRAPHY

When a person or place is known by more than one name in the biblical text, the cross-reference indicates this by using the equal sign (=):

> **SIMON** → =PETER, =SIMEON

The equal sign does *not* mean that Peter is always the same individual as Simon, for there are twelve men named Simon in the NABRE.

Special typefaces. There are two headings apiece for GOD, LORD, and LORD's. *LORD and *LORD'S represent the proper name of God, *Yahweh*, which is typeset in the NABRE as "LORD" and "LORD's." This distinguishes "LORD" from "Lord" and "lord" (which are indexed under the heading LORD), and "LORD's" from "Lord's" and "lord's" (indexed under LORD'S). In contexts where the Hebrew words for "Lord" (*Adonay*) and "LORD" (*Yahweh*) appear in a compound name, the NABRE translates Lord GOD. Therefore the heading *GOD is used for "GOD" and GOD for "God" and "god."

Some words are set in italic type in the NABRE. These include *Selah* and *maskil* throughout the Psalms and *"Talitha koum,"* in Mark 5:41. The italic type usually represents words transliterated, rather than translated from Hebrew or Aramaic. These typefaces are reflected in the context lines, as under the headings ETHAN and TALITHA:

> Mk   5: 41   hand and said to her, "***T*** *koum*,"
> Ps   89: 1   A *maskil* of **E** the Ezrahite.

Note in the Mark 5:41 context that the abbreviated word is both bold and italic.

Brackets. In the preface to the revised edition of the New Testament, the translators note, "The editors of the Greek text placed square brackets around words or portions of words of which the authenticity is questionable because the evidence of textual witnesses is inconclusive. The same has been done in the translation insofar as it is possible to reproduce this convention in English." Whenever square brackets appear in the NABRE text, they also appear in the context line, as under the heading BELIEVE:

> Mk   9: 42   of these little ones who **b** [in me]
> Mk   11: 31   '[Then] why did you not **b** him?'

Books of One Chapter. Five books have only one chapter: Obadiah, Philemon, 2 John, 3 John, and Jude. Therefore some reference books refer only to the verse number (e.g., Jude 1). In the *NABRECC* all contexts from these books refer to chapter 1 in addition to the verse number (e.g., Jude 1:1).

Prologue to Ben Sira. The Wisdom of Ben Sira (or Ecclesiasticus) has a three-paragraph prologue or foreword preceding chapter 1. The abbreviation "Pr" is used as the "chapter" number of the prologue; the numbers 1, 2, and 3 are used as "verse" designations for the three paragraphs, as under the heading HEBREW:

> Sir   Pr: 2   in **H** do not have the same effect

The Shorter Ending of Mark. The NABRE is one of the few translations to include the "shorter ending" of Mark. However, it places this ending at the end of Mark 16, following the traditional "longer ending," verses 9 to 20. Rather than index this passage as part of verse 20, the letter "S" is used as the verse designation for the "shorter ending," as under the heading ETERNAL:

> Mk   16:   S   [proclamation of **e** salvation. Amen.]

ABBREVIATIONS

THE BOOKS OF THE BIBLE

Old Testament

Gn . . . . Genesis
Ex . . . . Exodus
Lv . . . . .Leviticus
Nm . . . . Numbers
Dt . . . . Deuteronomy
Jos . . . . .Joshua
Jgs . . . . .Judges
Ru . . . . Ruth
1 Sm . . . . .1 Samuel
2 Sm . . . . .2 Samuel
1 Kgs . . . . 1 Kings
2 Kgs . . . . 2 Kings
1 Chr . . . . .1 Chronicles
2 Chr . . . . .2 Chronicles
Ezr . . . . .Ezra
Neh . . . . Nehemiah
Tb . . . . Tobit
Jdt . . . . Judith
Est . . . . Esther
1 Mc . . . . .1 Maccabees
2 Mc . . . . .2 Maccabees
Jb . . . . .Job
Ps . . . . Psalms
Prv . . . . Proverbs
Eccl . . . . Ecclesiastes

Sg . . . . Song of Songs
Wis . . . . Wisdom
Sir . . . . Ben Sira (Ecclesiasticus)
Is . . . . Isaiah
Jer . . . . .Jeremiah
Lam . . . . Lamentations
Bar . . . . Baruch
Ez . . . . Ezekiel
Dn . . . . .Daniel
Hos . . . . Hosea
Jl . . . . Joel
Am . . . . .Amos
Ob . . . . Obadiah
Jon . . . . .Jonah
Mi . . . . Micah
Na . . . . Nahum
Hb . . . . Habakkuk
Zep . . . . Zephaniah
Hg . . . . Haggai
Zec . . . . .Zechariah
Mal . . . . Malachi

New Testament

Mt .Matthew
Mk . . . . .Mark
Lk . . . . Luke
Jn . . . . .John
Acts . . . . Acts of the Apostles

Rom . . . . Romans
1 Cor . . . . 1 Corinthians
2 Cor . . . . 2 Corinthians
Gal . . . . Galatians
Eph . . . . .Ephesians
Phil . . . . .Philippians
Col . . . . Colossians
1 Thes . . . . 1 Thessalonians
2 Thes . . . . 2 Thessalonians
1 Tm . . . . 1 Timothy
2 Tm . . . . 2 Timothy
Ti . . . . Titus
Phlm . . . . Philemon
Heb . . . . Hebrews
Jas . . . . .James
1 Pt .1 Peter
2 Pt .2 Peter
1 Jn . . . . .1 John
2 Jn . . . . .2 John
3 Jn . . . . .3 John
Jude . . . . .Jude
Rev . . . . Revelation

OTHER ABBREVIATIONS

Pr . . . . .Prologue to Ben Sira
S . . . . .Shorter Ending of Mark

SPECIAL SYMBOLS

*GOD, *LORD and *LORD'S index the proper name of God (*Yahweh*) typeset in small capital letters (GOD, LORD, LORD's) in the NABRE.

→ An arrow following an entry heading points to related words for additional study.

= An equals sign marks an alternate proper name for additional study (e.g., ISRAEL =JACOB).

DEDICATION

To Father Jon Buffington

Artist, Scholar, Friend

THE NEW AMERICAN BIBLE
REVISED EDITION
CONCISE CONCORDANCE

A

AARON
Genealogy of (Ex 6:16-20; Jos 21:4, 10; 1 Chr 5:29-41).

Priesthood of (Ex 28:1; Nm 17; Heb 5:1-4; 7), vestments of (Ex 28; 39), consecration of (Ex 29), ordination of (Lv 8).

Spokesman for Moses (Ex 4:14-16, 27-31; 7:1-2). Supported Moses' hands in battle (Ex 17:8-13). Built golden calf (Ex 32; Dt 9:20). Spoke against Moses (Nm 12). Priesthood opposed (Nm 16); staff budded (Nm 17). Forbidden to enter the promised land (Nm 20:1-12). Death of (Nm 20:22-29; 33:38-39). Praise of (Sir 45:6-22).

ABADDON → =APOLLYON
Jb	28:22	A and Death say, "Only by rumor
Rev	9:11	whose name in Hebrew is A

ABANDON → ABANDONED
Dt	4:31	God, he will not a or destroy you,
Jos	10: 6	"Do not a your servants.
1 Chr	28: 9	but if you a him, he will cast you
2 Chr	15: 2	but if you a him, he will a you.
Tb	4: 3	do not a her as long as she lives.
Ps	94:14	his people, nor a his inheritance.
Acts	2:27	because you will not a my soul

ABANDONED → ABANDON
Jgs	2:13	Because they had a the LORD
2 Chr	12: 5	You have a me, and so I have a you
Sir	49: 4	They a the Law of the Most High,
Is	54: 7	For a brief moment I a you,
Acts	2:31	neither was he a to the netherworld

ABBA
Mk	14:36	he said, "A, Father, all things are
Rom	8:15	through which we cry, "A, Father!"
Gal	4: 6	our hearts, crying out, "A, Father!"

ABDON
A judge of Israel (Jgs 12:13-15).

ABEDNEGO → =AZARIAH
Deported to Babylon with Daniel (Dn 1:1-6). Name changed from Azariah (Dn 1:7). Refused defilement by food (Dn 1:8-20). Refused idol worship (Dn 3:1-18); saved from furnace (Dn 3:19-97).

ABEL
Second son of Adam (Gn 4:2). Offered acceptable sacrifice (Gn 4:4; Heb 11:4; 12:24). Murdered by Cain (Gn 4:8; Mt 23:35; Lk 11:51; 1 Jn 3:12).

ABHOR → ABHORRED, ABHORS
Dt	7:26	a it utterly for it is under the ban.
Dt	23: 8	Do not a the Edomite: he is your
Dt	23: 8	Do not a the Egyptian: you were
Ps	119:163	Falsehood I hate and a; your law I
Am	5:10	a those who speak with integrity;
Am	6: 8	I a the pride of Jacob, I hate his
Mi	3: 9	You who a justice, and pervert all

ABHORRED → ABHOR
Ps	106:40	with his people, a his own heritage.

ABHORS → ABHOR
Ps	5: 7	and fraudulent man the LORD a.

ABIATHAR
High priest in days of Saul and David (1 Sm 22; 2 Sm 15; 1 Kgs 1–2; Mk 2:26). Escaped Saul's slaughter of priests (1 Sm 22:18-23). Supported David in Absalom's revolt (2 Sm 15:24-29). Supported Adonijah (1 Kgs 1:7-42); deposed by Solomon (1 Kgs 2:22-35; cf. 1 Sm 2:31-35).

ABIB
The month of the Exodus and Passover (Ex 13:4; 23:15; 34:18; Dt 16:1).

ABIDE → ABODE
Ps	15: 1	LORD, who may a in your tent?
Ps	91: 1	who a in the shade of the Almighty,
Wis	3: 9	the faithful shall a with him in love:

ABIGAIL
1. Sister of David (1 Chr 2:16-17).
2. Wife of Nabal (1 Sm 25:30); pled for his life with David (1 Sm 25:14-35). Became David's wife after Nabal's death (1 Sm 25:36-43); bore him Kileab (2 Sm 3:3) also known as Daniel (1 Chr 3:1).

ABIHU
Son of Aaron (Ex 6:23; 24:1, 9); killed for offering illicit fire (Lv 10; Nm 3:2-4; 1 Chr 24:1-2).

ABIJAH
1. Second son of Samuel (1 Chr 6:13); a corrupt judge (1 Sm 8:1-5).
2. An Aaronic priest (1 Chr 24:10; Lk 1:5).
3. Son of Jeroboam I of Israel; died as prophesied by Ahijah (1 Kgs 14:1-18).
4. Son of Rehoboam, also called Abijam; king of Judah who fought Jeroboam I attempting to reunite the kingdom (1 Kgs 14:31–15:8; 2 Chr 12:16–14:1; Mt 1:7).

ABILITY → ABLE
Mt	25:15	to each according to his a.
Acts	11:29	according to a, each should send

ABIMELECH
1. King of Gerar who took Abraham's wife Sarah, believing her to be his sister (Gn 20). Later made a covenant with Abraham (Gn 21:22-33).
2. King of Gerar who took Isaac's wife Rebekah, believing her to be his sister (Gn 26:1-11). Later made a covenant with Isaac (Gn 26:12-31).
3. Son of Gideon (Jgs 8:31). Attempted to make himself king (Jgs 9).

ABIRAM
Sided with Dathan in rebellion against Moses and Aaron (Nm 16; 26:9; Dt 11:6; Sir 45:18).

ABISHAG
Shunammite virgin; attendant of David in his old age (1 Kgs 1:1-15; 2:17-22).

ABISHAI
Son of Zeruiah, David's sister (1 Sm 26:6; 1 Chr 2:16). One of David's chief warriors (1 Chr 11:15-21): against Edom (1 Chr 18:12-13), Ammon (2 Sm 10), Absalom (2 Sm 18), Sheba (2 Sm 20). Wanted to kill Saul (1 Sm 26), killed Abner (2 Sm 2:18-27; 3:22-39), wanted to kill Shimei (2 Sm 16:5-13; 19:16-23).

ABLAZE
Jas	3: 5	small a fire can set a huge forest a.

ABLE → ABILITY, ENABLES
Ex	18:25	He picked out a men from all Israel
Nm	14:16	'The LORD was not a to bring this
Dt	7:24	No one will be a to stand up against
1 Kgs	3: 9	For who is a to give judgment
2 Chr	2: 5	Yet who is really a to build him
2 Chr	32:15	or kingdom has been a to rescue his
Jdt	11:18	of them will be a to withstand you.
1 Mc	3:53	How shall we be a to resist them
Dn	5:16	if you are a to read the writing
Dn	6:21	you serve so constantly been a
Acts	5:39	you will not be a to destroy them;
Acts	15:10	our ancestors nor we have been a
Rom	4:21	had promised he was also a to do.
Rom	8:39	nor any other creature will be a
Rom	14: 4	for the Lord is a to make him stand.
2 Cor	1: 4	that we may be a to encourage those
2 Cor	9: 8	God is a to make every grace
Eph	3:20	to him who is a to accomplish far
Eph	6:11	you may be a to stand firm against
2 Tm	1:12	that he is a to guard what has been
Heb	2:18	he is a to help those who are being
Heb	4:12	and a to discern reflections
Heb	5: 2	He is a to deal patiently
Heb	7:25	he is always a to save those who
Heb	11:19	that God was a to raise even
Jas	3: 2	a to bridle his whole body also.
Jas	4:12	lawgiver and judge who is a to save
Jude	1:24	To the one who is a to keep you
Rev	5: 3	or under the earth was a to open

ABNER
Cousin of Saul and commander of his army (1 Sm 14:50; 17:55-57; 26). Made Ishbaal king after Saul (2 Sm 2:8-10), but later defected to

David (2 Sm 3:6-21). Killed Asahel (2 Sm 2:18-32), for which he was killed by Joab and Abishai (2 Sm 3:22-39).

ABODE → ABIDE

Dt	26:15	Look down, then, from heaven, your holy **a**,

ABOLISH → ABOLISHED, ABOLISHING

Mt	5:17	think that I have come to **a** the law
Mt	5:17	I have come not to **a** but to fulfill.

ABOLISHED → ABOLISH

1 Mc	6:59	laws, which we **a**, that they became
2 Mc	2:22	laws that were in danger of being **a**,

ABOLISHING → ABOLISH

Dn	11:31	**a** the daily sacrifice and setting

ABOMINABLE → ABOMINATION

2 Chr	28: 3	accordance with the **a** practices
2 Chr	33: 2	following the **a** practices
2 Mc	6: 5	covered with **a** offerings prohibited
Sir	15:13	A wickedness the LORD hates
Ez	7:20	of them they made their **a** images,
Rev	21:27	nor any[one] who does **a** things

ABOMINATION → ABOMINABLE, ABOMINATIONS

Lv	18:22	with a woman; such a thing is an **a**.
1 Mc	6: 7	they had pulled down the **a**
Prv	6:16	hates, yes, seven are an **a** to him;
Prv	11: 1	False scales are an **a** to the LORD,
Prv	11:20	in heart are an **a** to the LORD,
Prv	12:22	Lying lips are an **a** to the LORD,
Dn	9:27	be the desolating **a** until the ruin
Dn	11:31	and setting up the desolating **a**.
Dn	12:11	and the desolating **a** is set up,
Lk	16:15	of human esteem is an **a** in the sight

ABOMINATIONS → ABOMINATION

Ezr	9: 1	peoples of the lands and their **a**—
Prv	26:25	them, for seven **a** are in their hearts.
Is	66: 3	and taken pleasure in their own **a**.
Ez	7: 3	and hold against you all your **a**.
Ez	8: 6	You shall see even greater **a**!
Ez	44: 7	broken my covenant by all your **a**.
Rev	17: 5	of harlots and of the **a** of the earth."

ABOUND → ABOUNDING

Rom	6: 1	we persist in sin that grace may **a**?
Rom	15:13	so that you may **a** in hope
2 Cor	3: 9	of righteousness will **a** much more
1 Thes	3:12	and **a** in love for one another

ABOUNDING → ABOUND

Ps	103: 8	LORD, slow to anger, **a** in mercy.
Ps	145: 8	slow to anger and **a** in mercy.
Col	2: 7	you were taught, **a** in thanksgiving.

ABOVE

Dt	4:39	the LORD is God in the heavens **a**
Jdt	13:18	God, **a** all the women on earth;
Ps	8: 2	sing of your majesty **a** the heavens
Ps	18:49	have elevated me **a** my opponents,
Ps	57: 6	your glory appear **a** all the earth.
Sir	32:13	A all, bless your Maker,
Is	6: 2	Seraphim were stationed **a**;
Is	40:22	one who is enthroned **a** the vault
Ez	1:26	up **a**, a figure that looked like
Ez	10:19	of the God of Israel was up **a** them.
Mt	10:24	No disciple is **a** his teacher, no slave **a** his master.
Jn	3: 7	you, 'You must be born from **a**.'
Jn	3:31	The one who comes from **a** is **a** all.
Jn	8:23	what is below, I belong to what is **a**.
Eph	1:21	far **a** every principality, authority,
Eph	4:10	who ascended far **a** all the heavens,
Phil	2: 9	him the name that is **a** every name,
Col	3: 2	Think of what is **a**, not of what is
2 Thes	2: 4	exalts himself **a** every so-called god
Jas	1:17	and every perfect gift is from **a**,
Jas	3:17	But the wisdom from **a** is first of all
1 Pt	4: 8	A all, let your love for one another

ABRAHAM → =ABRAM

Abram, son of Terah (Gn 11:26-27), husband of Sarah (Gn 11:29).

Covenant relation with the LORD (Gn 12:1-3; 13:14-17; 15; 17; 22:15-18; Ex 2:24; Neh 9:8; Ps 105; Mi 7:20; Lk 1:68-75; Rom 4; Heb 6:13-15). Called from Ur, via Haran, to Canaan (Gn 12:1; Acts 7:2-4; Heb 11:8-10). Moved to Egypt, nearly lost Sarah to Pharoah (Gn 12:10-20). Divided the land with Lot; settled in Hebron (Gn 13). Saved Lot from four kings (Gn 14:1-16); blessed by Melchizedek (Gn 14:17-20; Heb 7:1-20). Declared righteous by faith (Gn 15:6; 1 Mc 2:52; Rom 4:3; Gal 3:6-9). Fathered Ishmael by Hagar (Gn 16).

Name changed from Abram (Gn 17:5; Neh 9:7). Circumcised (Gn 17; Rom 4:9-12). Entertained three visitors (Gn 18); promised a son by Sarah (Gn 17:16; 18:9-15). Questioned destruction of Sodom and Gomorrah (Gn 18:16-33). Moved to Gerar; nearly lost Sarah to Abimelech (Gn 20). Fathered Isaac by Sarah (Gn 21:1-7; Acts 7:8; Heb 11:11-12); sent away Hagar and Ishmael (Gn 21:8-21; Gal 4:22-30). Covenant with Abimelech (Gn 21:22-32). Tested by offering Isaac (Gn 22; Heb 11:17-19; Jas 2:21-24). Sarah died; bought field of Ephron for burial (Gn 23). Secured wife for Isaac (Gn 24). Fathered children by Keturah (Gn 25:1-6; 1 Chr 1:32-33). Death (Gn 25:7-11).

Called servant of God (Gn 26:24), friend of God (2 Chr 20:7; Is 41:8; Jas 2:23), prophet (Gn 20:7), father of Israel (Ex 3:15; Is 51:2; Mt 3:9; Jn 8:39-58). Praised (Sir 44:19-23).

ABRAM → =ABRAHAM

Gn	17: 5	No longer will you be called **A**;

ABSALOM

Son of David by Maacah (2 Sm 3:3; 1 Chr 3:2). Killed Amnon for rape of his sister Tamar; banished by David (2 Sm 13). Returned to Jerusalem; received by David (2 Sm 14). Rebelled against David (2 Sm 15–17). Killed (2 Sm 18).

ABSENT

1 Cor	5: 3	although **a** in body but present
Col	2: 5	For even if I am **a** in the flesh, yet I

ABSTAIN → ABSTAINS, ABSTINENCE

Acts	15:29	to **a** from meat sacrificed to idols,
Acts	21:25	that they **a** from meat sacrificed

ABSTAINS → ABSTAIN

Rom	14: 3	eats must not despise the one who **a**, and the one who **a** must not pass

ABSTINENCE → ABSTAIN

1 Tm	4: 3	and require **a** from foods that God

ABUNDANCE → ABUNDANT, ABUNDANTLY

Jb	36:31	the nations, and gives food in **a**.
Lam	3:32	according to the **a** of his mercy;
2 Cor	9: 8	you may have an **a** for every good
1 Pt	1: 2	may grace and peace be yours in **a**.
2 Pt	1: 2	be yours in **a** through knowledge
Jude	1: 2	peace, and love be yours in **a**.

ABUNDANT → ABUNDANCE

Ps	51: 3	in your **a** compassion blot out my
2 Cor	9: 8	God is able to make every grace **a** for you,

ABUNDANTLY → ABUNDANCE

Jn	10:10	might have life and have it more **a**.

ABUSE → ABUSED, ABUSIVE

Heb	10:33	you were publicly exposed to **a**

ABUSED → ABUSE

Jgs	19:25	and **a** her all night until morning,

ABUSIVE → ABUSE

Sir	23:15	using **a** language will never acquire
2 Tm	3: 2	haughty, **a**, disobedient to their

ABYSS

Sir	1: 3	earth's extent, the **a** and wisdom—
Lk	8:31	not to order them to depart to the **a**.
Rom	10: 7	or 'Who will go down into the **a**?'
Rev	9: 1	the key for the passage to the **a**.
Rev	11: 7	the **a** will wage war against them
Rev	17: 8	It will come up from the **a** and is
Rev	20: 1	holding in his hand the key to the **a**

ACACIA → ACACIA-WOOD

Ex	25:10	You shall make an ark of **a** wood,
Ex	25:23	shall also make a table of **a** wood,
Ex	27: 1	You shall make an altar of **a** wood,

ACACIA-WOOD → ACACIA
Ex   26:15 make frames for the tabernacle, a uprights.

ACCEPT → ACCEPTABLE, ACCEPTANCE, ACCEPTED, ACCEPTING, ACCEPTS
Ps   119:108 **A** my freely offered praise;
Ez   20:40 there in the land I will a them all,
Zep   3: 7 will fear me, you will a correction;
Mal   1:10 I will not a any offering from your
Mt   11:14 And if you are willing to a it, he is
Mt   19:11 "Not all can a [this] word, but only
Jn   1:11 but his own people did not a him.
Jn   5:41 "I do not a human praise;
Jn   5:43 of my Father, but you do not a me;
Jn   6:60 saying is hard; who can a it?"
Acts   22:18 they will not a your testimony

ACCEPTABLE → ACCEPT
Lv   1: 4 that it may be a to make atonement
Prv   21: 3 just is more a to the LORD than
Is   58: 5 call a fast, a day a to the LORD?
2 Cor   6: 2 Behold, now is a very a time;
Phil   4:18 "a fragrant aroma," an a sacrifice,
1 Pt   2: 5 to offer spiritual sacrifices a to God

ACCEPTANCE → ACCEPT
Rom   11:15 what will their a be but life
1 Tm   1:15 is trustworthy and deserves full a:
1 Tm   4: 9 is trustworthy and deserves full a.

ACCEPTED → ACCEPT
Dt   26:18 today the LORD has a your agreement:
Lk   4:24 no prophet is a in his own native
2 Cor 11: 4 different gospel from the one you a,

ACCEPTING → ACCEPT
3 Jn   1: 7 and are a nothing from the pagans.

ACCEPTS → ACCEPT
Prv   10: 8 A wise heart a commands, but a babbling
Jn   3:32 heard, but no one a his testimony.

ACCESS
Rom   5: 2 through whom we have gained a
Eph   2:18 through him we both have a in one
Eph   3:12 and confidence of a through faith

ACCOMPLISH → ACCOMPLISHED, ACCOMPLISHES
Is   60:22 will swiftly a these things
Eph   3:20 is able to a far more than all we ask

ACCOMPLISHED → ACCOMPLISH
Rom   15:18 what Christ has a through me

ACCOMPLISHES → ACCOMPLISH
Eph   1:11 the One who a all things according

ACCORDANCE → ACCORDING
Mk   12:14 the way of God in a with the truth.
1 Cor 15: 3 for our sins in a with the scriptures;
1 Cor 15: 4 raised on the third day in a

ACCORDING → ACCORDANCE
Ex   26:30 set up the tabernacle a to its plan,
2 Chr   6:30 to each and all a to their ways,
Prv   26: 4 Do not answer fools a to their folly,
Prv   26: 5 Answer fools a to their folly,
Sir   16:12 judges people, each a to their deeds.
Sir   50:22 womb, fashioning it a to his will!
Ez   7: 3 you, judge you a to your ways,
Mt   9:29 it be done for you a to your faith."
Jn   19: 7 and a to that law he ought to die,
Rom   2: 6 who will repay everyone a to his
Rom   8: 4 who live not a to the flesh but a to the spirit.
Rom   8:13 For if you live a to the flesh,
2 Tm   1: 9 not a to our works but a to his own
2 Tm   2: 5 except by competing a to the rules.
Heb   2: 4 gifts of the holy Spirit a to his will.
Heb   5: 6 "You are a priest forever a
Jas   2: 8 if you fulfill the royal law a
1 Jn   5:14 that if we ask anything a to his will,
2 Jn   1: 6 we walk a to his commandments;
Rev   20:12 The dead were judged a to their

Rev   22:12 I will give to each a to his deeds.

ACCOUNT → ACCOUNTABLE
Ps   69: 8 For it is on your a I bear insult,
Mt   12:36 of judgment people will render an a
Rom   14:12 each of us shall give an a of himself
Heb   4:13 him to whom we must render an a.

ACCOUNTABLE → ACCOUNT
Rom   3:19 and the whole world stand a to God,

ACCURATELY
Acts   18:25 spoke and taught a about Jesus,

ACCURSED → CURSE
Wis   14: 8 but the handmade idol is a, and its
Mt   25:41 you a, into the eternal fire prepared
Rom   9: 3 I could wish that I myself were a
1 Cor 16:22 does not love the Lord, let him be a.
Gal   1: 8 preached to you, let that one be a!
2 Pt   2:14 are trained in greed. A children!
Rev   22: 3 Nothing a will be found there

ACCUSATION → ACCUSE
1 Tm   5:19 not accept an a against a presbyter

ACCUSE → ACCUSATION, ACCUSED, ACCUSER, ACCUSERS, ACCUSES
Dt   19:16 witness rises against someone to a
Ps   50:21 I a you, I lay out the matter before
Zec   3: 1 stood at his right side to a him.
Mt   12:10 so that they might a him.
Rom   2:15 their conflicting thoughts a or even

ACCUSED → ACCUSE
Mk   15: 3 The chief priests a him of many
Acts   22:30 why he was being a by the Jews,
Ti   1: 6 believing children who are not a

ACCUSER → ACCUSE
Ps   109: 6 him, an a to stand at his right hand,
Rev   12:10 For the a of our brothers is cast out,

ACCUSERS → ACCUSE
Ps   109:20 reward for my a from the LORD,

ACCUSES → ACCUSE
Rev   12:10 who a them before our God day

ACCUSTOMED → CUSTOM
Jer   13:23 able to do good, a to evil as you are.
Mt   27:15 of the feast the governor was a

ACHAN
    Sin at Jericho caused defeat at Ai; stoned (Jos 7; 22:20; 1 Chr 2:7).

ACHIEVE
Jb   5:12 so that their hands a no success;

ACHIOR
    Ammonite mercenary (Jdt 5:5–6:20); converted to Judaism after Judith's victory (Jdt 14:5-10).

ACHISH
    King of Gath before whom David feigned insanity (1 Sm 21:11-16). Later "ally" of David (2 Sm 27–29).

ACHOR
Jos   7:26 the place is called the Valley of A
Hos   2:17 the valley of A as a door of hope.

ACKNOWLEDGE → ACKNOWLEDGED, ACKNOWLEDGES
Ps   38:19 I a my guilt and grieve over my sin.
Mt   10:32 others I will a before my heavenly
Lk   12: 8 Son of Man will a before the angels
Rom   1:28 since they did not see fit to a God,
3 Jn   1: 9 loves to dominate, does not a us.

ACKNOWLEDGED → ACKNOWLEDGE
Lk   7:29 of John, a the righteousness of God;

ACKNOWLEDGES → ACKNOWLEDGE
Mt   10:32 Everyone who a me before others I
Lk   12: 8 everyone who a me before others

ACQUIT
Ex   23: 7 to death, for I will not a the guilty.

ACT → ACTED, ACTION, ACTIVE, ACTS
Gn   4: 7 If you a rightly, you will be accepted;
Dt   12: 4 not how you are to a toward the Lord,
Ps   37: 5 trust in him and he will a
Ps   119:126 It is time for the Lord to a;
Dn   9:19 be attentive and a without delay,
Jn   8: 4 the very a of committing adultery.

ACTED → ACT
Ez   20: 9 I a for the sake of my name, that it
Acts   3:17 that you a out of ignorance, just as
1 Tm   1:13 been mercifully treated because I a

ACTION → ACT
Dn   11:32 to their God shall take strong a.

ACTIVE → ACT
Jas   2:22 faith was a along with his works,

ACTS → ACT
Ex   6: 6 arm and with mighty a of judgment.
Ex   7: 4 mighty a of judgment I will bring
Ps   71:15 day after day your a of deliverance,
Mt   7:24 a on them will be like a wise man
Jas   1:25 who forgets but a doer who a,

ADAM
1. First man (Gn 1:26–2:25; Tb 8:6; Rom 5:14; 1 Tm 2:13). Sin of (Gn 3; Rom 5:12-21). Children of (Gn 4:1–5:5). Death of (Gn 5:5; Rom 5:12-21; 1 Cor 15:22).
2. Town (Jos 3:16).

ADAR
Month in which temple was rebuilt (Ezr 6:15); celebration of Purim (Est 3:7; 9:1-21); of victory over Nicanor (1 Mc 7:43-49).

ADD → ADDED, ADDING, ADDS
Dt   4: 2 you shall not a to what I command
2 Kgs   20: 6 I will a to your life fifteen years.
Prv   30: 6 A nothing to his words, lest he
Mt   6:27 you by worrying a a single moment
Lk   12:25 of you by worrying a a moment
Rev   22:18 them, God will a to him the plagues

ADDED → ADD
Acts   2:41 three thousand persons were a
Acts   2:47 And every day the Lord a to their
Acts   5:14 of men and women, were a to them.
Gal   3:19 It was a for transgressions,

ADDER
Prv   23:32 like a serpent, and stings like an a.

ADDING → ADD
Dt   13: 1 neither a to it nor subtracting
Eccl   7:27 a one to one to find the sum.

ADDRESSED
Lk   23:20 Again Pilate a them, still wishing
Acts   21:40 all was quiet he a them in Hebrew.
Heb   12: 5 forgotten the exhortation a to you as

ADDS → ADD
Rev   22:18 if anyone a to them, God will add

ADJURE
Sg   5: 8 I a you, Daughters of Jerusalem,
Mk   5: 7 I a you by God, do not torment
Acts   19:13 "I a you by the Jesus whom Paul

ADMAH
Dt   29:22 and Gomorrah, A and Zeboiim,
Hos   11: 8 How could I treat you as A, or make

ADMONISH → ADMONITION
1 Cor   4:14 but to a you as my beloved children.
Col   3:16 you teach and a one another,
1 Thes   5:12 you in the Lord and who a you,

ADMONITION → ADMONISH
Neh   1: 8 remember the a which you addressed

ADONIJAH
1. Son of David by Haggith (2 Sm 3:4; 1 Chr 3:2). Attempted to be king after David; killed at Solomon's order (1 Kgs 1–2).
2. Levite; teacher of the Law (2 Chr 17:8).

ADOPT → ADOPTED, ADOPTION
Acts   16:21 are not lawful for us Romans to a

ADOPTED → ADOPT
2 Kgs   17: 9 a unlawful practices toward the Lord,
Acts   7:21 Pharaoh's daughter a him

ADOPTION → ADOPT
Rom   8:23 within ourselves as we wait for a,
Rom   9: 4 theirs the a, the glory,
Gal   4: 5 the law, so that we might receive a.
Eph   1: 5 he destined us for a to himself

ADORNED → ADORNMENT
2 Kgs   9:30 she shadowed her eyes, a her hair,
Ez   16:11 I a you with jewelry,
Lk   21: 5 how the temple was a with costly
Rev   17: 4 purple and scarlet and a with gold,
Rev   21: 2 God, prepared as a bride a for her

ADORNMENT → ADORNED
Ex   28: 2 the glorious a of your brother Aaron
Prv   3:22 to your soul, and an a for your neck.
1 Pt   3: 3 Your a should not be an external

ADULLAM
1 Sm   22: 1 Gath and escaped to the cave of A.
1 Chr   11:15 cave of A while the Philistines were
Mi   1:15 glory of Israel shall come even to A.

ADULTERER → ADULTERY
Jb   24:15 The eye of the a watches

ADULTERERS → ADULTERY
Jer   23:10 The land is filled with a;
Mal   3: 5 to bear witness Against sorcerers, a,
1 Cor   6: 9 nor idolaters nor a nor boy
Heb   13: 4 God will judge the immoral and a.

ADULTERESS → ADULTERY
Lv   20:10 and the a shall be put to death.
Rom   7: 3 she will be called an a if she

ADULTERIES → ADULTERY
Jer   3: 8 all the a rebel Israel had committed,
Ez   23:43 worn-out one still has a in her!

ADULTERY → ADULTERER, ADULTERERS, ADULTERESS, ADULTERIES
Ex   20:14 You shall not commit a.
Dt   5:18 You shall not commit a.
Prv   6:32 those who commit a have no sense;
Jer   3: 9 committing a with stone and wood.
Ez   23:37 They committed a with their idols;
Hos   2: 4 her a from between her breasts,
Hos   3: 1 is loved by her spouse but commits a;
Mt   5:27 was said, 'You shall not commit a.'
Mt   5:28 lust has already committed a
Mt   5:32 is unlawful) causes her to commit a,
Mt   5:32 a divorced woman commits a.
Mt   15:19 evil thoughts, murder, a, unchastity,
Mt   19: 9 and marries another commits a."
Mt   19:18 you shall not commit a;
Mk   7:22 a, greed, malice, deceit,
Mk   10:11 another commits a against her;
Mk   10:12 marries another, she commits a."
Mk   10:19 you shall not commit a;
Lk   16:18 and marries another commits a,
Lk   18:20 'You shall not commit a;
Jn   8: 3 a woman who had been caught in a
Rom   2:22 You who forbid a, do you commit a?
Rom   13: 9 "You shall not commit a;
Jas   2:11 "You shall not commit a,"
Jas   2:11 Even if you do not commit a
2 Pt   2:14 Their eyes are full of a

ADVANCE → ADVANCED
1 Pt   1:11 it testified in a to the sufferings

ADVANCED → ADVANCE
Gn   18:11 and Sarah were old, a in years,

ADVANTAGE
Eccl   3:19 beings have no a over beasts, but all
Rom   3: 1 What a is there then in being a Jew?

1 Cor	10:24	No one should seek his own **a**,
Jude	1:16	as they fawn over people to gain **a**.

ADVERSARIES → ADVERSARY

2 Sm	22:49	you have exalted me above my **a**,
Na	1: 2	LORD takes vengeance on his **a**,
Heb	10:27	fire that is going to consume the **a**.

ADVERSARY → ADVERSARIES

1 Kgs	11:14	raised up an **a** against Solomon:
Zec	3: 2	the angel of the LORD said to the **a**, "May the LORD rebuke you, O **a**;
1 Tm	5:14	so as to give the **a** no pretext

ADVICE

Nm	31:16	who on Balaam's **a** were behind
1 Kgs	12: 8	he ignored the **a** the elders had given
2 Chr	10:13	Ignoring the **a** the elders had given
Tb	4:18	do not think lightly of any useful **a**.
Prv	8:14	Mine are counsel and **a**;
Prv	12:15	those who listen to **a** are the wise.
Prv	20:18	Plans made with **a** succeed;
Sir	37:11	Seek no **a** from a woman about her

ADVOCATE

Jn	14:16	and he will give you another **A** to be
Jn	14:26	The **A**, the holy Spirit
Jn	15:26	the **A** comes whom I will send you
Jn	16: 7	not go, the **A** will not come to you.
1 Jn	2: 1	sin, we have an **A** with the Father,

AENEAS

Paralytic healed by Peter (Acts 9:33-34).

AFFAIRS

Ps	112: 5	who conducts his **a** with justice.

AFFECTION

Gn	43:30	he was so overcome with **a** for his
Rom	12:10	love one another with mutual **a**;
2 Pt	1: 7	devotion with mutual **a**, mutual **a**

AFFLICT → AFFLICTED, AFFLICTING, AFFLICTION, AFFLICTIONS

Ex	15:26	I will not **a** you with any of the diseases
Tb	13: 5	He will **a** you for your iniquities,
Lam	3:33	He does not willingly **a** or bring grief

AFFLICTED → AFFLICT

Ps	9:13	does not forget the cry of the **a**.
Ps	25:16	pity on me, for I am alone and **a**.
Ps	119:107	I am very much **a**, LORD;
Is	53: 4	stricken, struck down by God and **a**,
2 Cor	1: 6	If we are **a**, it is for your
2 Cor	4: 8	We are **a** in every way, but not

AFFLICTING → AFFLICT

2 Thes	1: 6	afflictions those who are **a** you,

AFFLICTION → AFFLICT

Dt	16: 3	the bread of **a**, so that you may
Dt	26: 7	heard our cry and saw our **a**, our toil
Jb	36:15	saves the afflicted through their **a**,
Ps	25:18	Look upon my **a** and suffering;
2 Cor	1: 4	who encourages us in our every **a**,
2 Cor	4:17	this momentary light **a** is producing
2 Cor	7: 4	all the more because of all our **a**.

AFFLICTIONS → AFFLICT

Acts	7:10	and rescued him from all his **a**.
2 Cor	6: 4	much endurance, in **a**, hardships,
Col	1:24	what is lacking in the **a** of Christ

AFFORD

Lv	5: 7	the person cannot **a** an animal
Lv	5:11	is unable to **a** even two turtledoves
Lv	12: 8	however, she cannot **a** a lamb,

AFRAID → FEAR

Gn	3:10	but I was **a**, because I was naked,
Ex	2:14	Then Moses became **a** and thought,
Ex	3: 6	face, for he was **a** to look at God.
Ex	20:20	"Do not be **a**, for God has come
Ex	34:30	they were **a** to come near him.
Dt	2: 4	Though they are **a** of you, be very
Dt	20: 3	Do not be weakhearted or **a**,

Jos	10:25	to them, "Do not be **a** or dismayed,
1 Kgs	19: 3	Elijah was **a** and fled for his life;
1 Chr	13:12	David was **a** of God that day,
Ps	27: 1	of whom should I be **a**?
Ps	56: 4	when I am **a**, in you I place my
Prv	3:24	you will not be **a**, when you rest,
Mt	1:20	do not be **a** to take Mary your wife
Mt	10:31	So do not be **a**; you are worth more
Mt	14:27	"Take courage, it is I; do not be **a**."
Mt	28: 5	the women in reply, "Do not be **a**!
Mt	28:10	Jesus said to them, "Do not be **a**.
Lk	1:13	to him, "Do not be **a**, Zechariah,
Lk	1:30	said to her, "Do not be **a**, Mary,
Lk	2:10	angel said to them, "Do not be **a**;
Lk	12:32	Do not be **a** any longer, little flock,
Jn	14:27	not let your hearts be troubled or **a**.
Acts	9:26	but they were all **a** of him,
Acts	27:24	and said, 'Do not be **a**, Paul.
Rom	13: 4	be **a**, for it does not bear the sword
Heb	13: 6	is my helper, [and] I will not be **a**.
2 Pt	2:10	they are not **a** to revile glorious

AFTERNOON → NOON

Mk	15:33	the whole land until three in the **a**.
Acts	10: 3	One **a** about three o'clock, he saw

AGABUS

A Christian prophet (Acts 11:28; 21:10).

AGAG → AGAGITE

King of Amalekites; not killed by Saul (1 Sm 15).

AGAGITE → AGAG

Est	8: 3	the harm done by Haman the **A**

AGAIN

Gn	8:21	Never **a** will I curse the ground
Dt	30: 9	God, will **a** take delight in your
Jb	14:14	to die, and live **a**, all the days of my
Ps	42: 6	for I shall **a** praise him, my savior
Ps	78:41	**A** and **a** they tested God,
Ps	85: 7	Certainly you will **a** restore our life,
Jer	12:15	I will have compassion on them **a**
Jer	31: 4	**A** I will build you, and you shall
Ez	37:22	They shall never **a** be two nations, never **a** be divided into two
Zec	1:17	the LORD will **a** comfort Zion, and will **a** choose Jerusalem.
Jn	14: 3	I will come back **a** and take you
Rom	11:23	for God is able to graft them in **a**.
Heb	5:12	have someone teach you **a** the basic
Heb	6: 1	laying the foundation all over **a**:
Heb	6: 6	to bring them to repentance **a**,

AGE → AGED, AGES

Gn	21: 2	bore Abraham a son in his old **a**,
Gn	37: 3	for he was the child of his old **a**;
Mt	13:39	The harvest is the end of the **a**,
Mt	28:20	you always, until the end of the **a**."
Lk	18:30	return in this present **a** and eternal life in the **a** to come."
Gal	1: 4	us from the present evil **a** in accord
1 Tm	6:17	rich in the present **a** not to be proud
Ti	2:12	justly, and devoutly in this **a**,

AGED → AGE

Lv	19:32	Stand up in the presence of the **a**,
Sir	25: 5	How appropriate is wisdom in the **a**,

AGES → AGE

Tb	13: 1	because his kingship lasts for all **a**.
Rom	16:25	of the mystery kept secret for long **a**
1 Cor	2: 7	God predetermined before the **a**
Eph	2: 7	in the **a** to come he might show
Eph	3: 9	of the mystery hidden from **a** past
Col	1:26	the mystery hidden from **a**
1 Tm	1:17	To the king of the **a**, incorruptible,

AGREE → AGREEMENT

Mt	18:19	you, if two of you **a** on earth
Mk	14:56	him, but their testimony did not **a**.
2 Cor	13:11	one another, **a** with one another,

1 Tm   6: 3 does not a with the sound words

AGREEMENT → AGREE
Dt   26:17 you have accepted the LORD's a:
2 Cor 6:16 What a has the temple of God

AGRIPPA
Descendant of Herod; king before whom Paul argued his case in Caesarea (Acts 25:13–26:32).

AGUR
Prv   30: 1 The words of A, son of Jakeh

AHAB
1. Son of Omri; king of Israel (1 Kgs 16:28–22:40), husband of Jezebel (1 Kgs 16:31). Promoted Baal worship (1 Kgs 16:31-33); opposed by Elijah (1 Kgs 17:1; 18; 21), a prophet (1 Kgs 20:35-43), Micaiah (1 Kgs 22:1-28). Defeated Ben-Hadad (1 Kgs 20). Killed for failing to kill Ben-Hadad and for murder of Naboth (1 Kgs 20:35–21:40).
2. A false prophet (Jer 29:21-22).

AHASUERUS → =ARTAXERXES
King of Persia (Ezr 4:6), husband of Esther. Deposed Vashti; replaced her with Esther (Est 1–2). Sealed Haman's edict to annihilate the Jews (Est 3). Received Esther without having called her (Est 5:1-8). Honored Mordecai (Est 6). Hanged Haman (Est 7). Issued edict allowing Jews to defend themselves (Est 8). Promoted Mordecai (Est 8:1-2, 15; 9:4; 10). Called Artaxerxes in Ezra and Nehemiah.

AHAZ
Son of Jotham; king of Judah, (2 Kgs 16; 2 Chr 28; Mt 1:9). Idolatry of (2 Kgs 16:3-4, 10-18; 2 Chr 28:1-4, 22-25). Defeated by Aram and Israel (2 Kgs 16:5-6; 2 Chr 28:5-15). Sought help from Assyria rather than the LORD (2 Kgs 16:7-9; 2 Chr 28:16-21; Is 7).

AHAZIAH
1. Son of Ahab; king of Israel (1 Kgs 22:52–2 Kgs 1:18; 2 Chr 20:35-37). Made an unsuccessful alliance with Jehoshaphat (2 Chr 20:35-37). Died for seeking Baal rather than the LORD (2 Kgs 1).
2. Son of Jehoram; king of Judah (2 Kgs 8:25-29; 9:14-29), also called Jehoahaz (2 Chr 21:17–22:9; 25:23). Killed by Jehu while visiting Joram (2 Kgs 9:14-29; 2 Chr 22:1-9).

AHEAD
Nm   22:26 angel of the LORD again went a,
Dt   1:22 "Let us send men a to spy
Jos   24:12 I sent the hornets a of you
Mt   11:10 I am sending my messenger a
Jn   1:15 after me ranks a of me because he
1 Cor 11:21 each one goes a with his own
Phil   3:13 but straining forward to what lies a,

AHIJAH
1. Priest during Saul's reign (1 Sm 14:3,18).
2. Prophet of Shiloh (1 Kgs 11:29-39; 14:1-18).

AHIKAM
Father of Gedaliah (2 Kgs 25:22), protector of Jeremiah (Jer 26:24).

AHIMAAZ
1. Father-in-law of Saul (1 Sm 14:50).
2. Son of Zadok, the high priest, loyal to David (2 Sm 15:27,36; 17:17-20; 18:19-33).

AHIMELECH
1. Priest who helped David in his flight from Saul (1 Sm 21–22).
2. One of David's warriors (1 Sm 26:6).

AHINOAM
1. Wife of Saul (1 Sm 14:50).
2. Wife of David (1 Sm 25:43; 30:5; 1 Chr 3:1).

AHITHOPHEL
One of David's counselors who sided with Absalom (2 Sm 15:12, 31-37; 1 Chr 27:33-34); committed suicide when his advice was ignored (2 Sm 16:15–17:23).

AI
Gn   12: 8 Bethel to the west and A to the east.
Jos   7: 4 but they fled before the army at A,
Jos   8:26 the ban on all the inhabitants of A.

AIJALON
Jos   10:12 at Gibeon, Moon, in the valley of A!

AIM → AIMLESSLY
Ps   21:13 you will a at their faces with your
1 Tm   1: 5 The a of this instruction is love

AIMLESSLY → AIM
1 Cor 9:26 Thus I do not run a; I do not fight as

AIR
Dn   3:80 All you birds of the a,
Acts   22:23 cloaks and flinging dust into the a,
1 Cor 14: 9 For you will be talking to the a.
Eph   2: 2 the ruler of the power of the a,
1 Thes 4:17 the clouds to meet the Lord in the a.
Rev   16:17 poured out his bowl into the a.

AKELDAMA
Acts   1:19 was called in their language 'A,'

ALABASTER
Mt   26: 7 up to him with an a jar of costly
Mk   14: 3 a woman came with an a jar
Lk   7:37 Bringing an a flask of ointment,

ALARM → ALARMED
Nm   10: 9 you shall sound the a on the trumpets,
Jl   2: 1 sound the a on my holy mountain!

ALARMED → ALARM
Mk   13: 7 and reports of wars do not be a;
2 Thes 2: 2 or to be a either by a "spirit,"

ALCIMUS
A high priest in the time of the Maccabees (1 Mc 7:5-25; 9; 2 Mc 14).

ALERT
Mk   13:33 Be a! You do not know

ALEXANDER
1 Mc   1: 1 After A the Macedonian,
1 Mc 10: 1 and sixtieth year, A Epiphanes,
Acts   19:33 and A signaled with his hand that he
1 Tm   1:20 among them Hymenaeus and A,
2 Tm   4:14 A the coppersmith did me a great

ALIEN → ALIENS
Ex   12:19 for anyone, a resident a or a native,
Ex   22:20 not oppress or afflict a resident a,
Lv   19:34 you shall love the a as yourself;
Lv   23:22 shall leave for the poor and the a.
Dt   24:17 You shall not deprive the resident a

ALIENATED
Eph   4:18 a from the life of God because

ALIENS → ALIEN
Gn   15:13 your descendants will reside as a
Ex   23: 9 since you were once a yourselves
1 Pt   2:11 I urge you as a and sojourners

ALIKE → LIKE
Nm   15:15 alien will be a before the LORD;
Ps   14: 3 have gone astray; all a are perverse.
Eccl 11: 6 or whether both a will turn out well.
Rom 14: 5 another person considers all days a.

ALIVE → LIVE
Gn   6:19 to keep them a along with you.
Gn   16:13 and remained a after he saw me?"
Lv   16:10 he shall place before the LORD a,
Nm   16:30 and they go down a to Sheol,
2 Sm 12:18 "When the child was a, we spoke
Ps   55:16 let them go down a to Sheol,
Prv   1:12 Let us swallow them a, like Sheol,
Lk   24:23 who announced that he was a.
Acts   1: 3 He presented himself a to them
Acts   9:41 and the widows, he presented her a.
Rom   7: 9 commandment came, sin became a;
1 Thes 4:17 Then we who are a, who are left,
Rev   1:18 but now I am a forever and ever.
Rev   3: 1 you have the reputation of being a,
Rev   19:20 The two were thrown a

ALL
Gn   2: 3 rested from a the work he had done

Gn	3:20	she was the mother of a the living.
Gn	6:13	that the end of a mortals has come,
Gn	7:21	A creatures that moved on earth
Gn	7:21	the earth, as well as a humankind.
Gn	11: 6	and a have the same language,
Gn	12: 3	A the families of the earth will find
Gn	13:15	a the land that you see I will give
Gn	45: 9	God has made me lord of a Egypt;
Gn	46: 6	a his descendants came to Egypt.
Ex	3:15	this is my title for a generations.
Ex	12:12	executing judgment on a the gods
Ex	20: 1	Then God spoke a these words:
Ex	24: 4	then wrote down a the words
Ex	24: 7	"A that the LORD has said,
Ex	33:19	I will make a my goodness pass
Ex	35:21	a, as their hearts moved them
Lv	20:22	Be careful to observe a my statutes and a my decrees;
Nm	3:13	I struck down a the firstborn
Nm	11:29	If only a the people of the LORD
Nm	27:16	the God of the spirits of a humanity,
Dt	8: 3	a that comes forth from the mouth of the LORD.
Dt	10:12	to follow in a his ways, to love
Dt	28: 2	A these blessings will come
Dt	28:15	a these curses shall come upon you
Jos	8:34	were read aloud a the words
Jos	21:44	the LORD gave a their enemies
1 Sm	12:20	have indeed committed a this evil!
2 Sm	5: 1	A the tribes of Israel came to David
1 Kgs	5:10	the East and a the wisdom of Egypt.
2 Kgs	17:16	they bowed down to a the host
Est	2:15	the admiration of a who saw her.
Est	3: 6	he sought to destroy a the Jews,
Est	4:13	palace, you alone of a the Jews.
Jb	1:22	In a this Job did not sin, nor did he
Jb	2:10	Through a this, Job did not sin
Ps	8: 2	is your name through a the earth!
Ps	8: 7	your hands, put a things at his feet:
Ps	34: 2	I will bless the LORD at a times;
Ps	34:21	He watches over a his bones;
Ps	47: 8	For God is king over a the earth;
Ps	57: 6	your glory appear above a the earth.
Ps	72:17	may a the nations regard him as
Ps	135: 5	that our Lord is greater than a gods.
Ps	145: 9	The LORD is good to a, compassionate toward a your
Ps	145:17	The LORD is just in a his ways, merciful in a his works.
Prv	3: 5	in the LORD with a your heart,
Prv	3:17	ways, and a her paths are peace;
Prv	8:36	a who hate me love death."
Eccl	1: 2	A things are vanity!
Sg	8: 7	Were one to offer a the wealth
Wis	12:15	you govern a things righteously;
Wis	16: 7	seen, but by you, the savior of a.
Sir	1: 1	A wisdom is from the Lord
Sir	7:29	With a your soul fear God
Is	2: 2	A nations shall stream toward it.
Is	25: 8	wipe away the tears from a faces;
Is	44: 9	who fashion idols are a nothing;
Is	53: 6	We had a gone astray like sheep,
Is	53: 6	laid upon him the guilt of us a.
Jer	3:17	A nations will gather together there
Jer	29:13	you seek me with a your heart,
Ez	36:33	When I cleanse you of a your guilt,
Jl	3: 1	will pour out my spirit upon a flesh.
Jl	4: 2	I will gather a the nations and bring
Mt	6:29	a his splendor was clothed like one
Mt	6:33	and a these things will be given you
Mt	12:15	followed him, and he cured them a,
Mt	28:18	"A power in heaven and on earth
Mk	7:19	(Thus he declared a foods clean.)
Mk	7:23	A these evils come from within
Mk	10:27	A things are possible for God."
Mk	14:36	Father, a things are possible to you.
Lk	10:27	with a your heart, with a your strength,
Jn	1: 3	A things came to be through him,
Jn	1: 7	so that a might believe through him.
Jn	1:16	his fullness we have a received,
Jn	16:13	of truth, he will guide you to a truth.
Jn	17:21	so that they may a be one, as you,
Acts	2: 4	And they were a filled with the holy
Acts	2:17	a portion of my spirit upon a flesh.
Acts	2:44	A who believed were together
Acts	2:44	and had a things in common;
Acts	10:44	fell upon a who were listening
Rom	2:12	A who sin outside the law will
Rom	2:12	and a who sin under the law will be
Rom	3:23	a have sinned and are deprived
Rom	5:12	and thus death came to a, inasmuch as a sinned—
Rom	6:10	death, he died to sin once and for a;
Rom	10:12	the same Lord is Lord of a, enriching a who call upon him.
Rom	14:10	For we shall a stand before
1 Cor	9:22	I have become a things to a, to save
1 Cor	12:12	and a the parts of the body,
1 Cor	12:29	Are a apostles? Are a prophets?
1 Cor	15:22	For just as in Adam a die, so too in Christ shall a be brought
1 Cor	15:28	to him, so that God may be a in a.
1 Cor	15:51	We shall not a fall asleep, but we will a be changed,
2 Cor	5:14	to the conviction that one died for a; therefore, a have died.
Eph	1:22	And he put a things beneath his feet
Eph	1:22	gave him as head over a things
Eph	1:23	the one who fills a things in every
Eph	4: 6	one God and Father of a, who is over a and through a and in a.
Phil	4: 7	that surpasses a understanding will
Col	1:15	God, the firstborn of a creation.
Col	1:16	a things were created through him
Col	1:19	in him a the fullness was pleased
Col	2: 3	whom are hidden a the treasures
Col	3:11	but Christ is a and in a.
1 Thes	5:18	In a circumstances give thanks,
1 Tm	4:10	who is the savior of a,
1 Tm	6:10	love of money is the root of a evils,
2 Tm	3:12	a who want to live religiously
2 Tm	3:16	A scripture is inspired by God and is
Ti	1:15	To the clean a things are clean,
Heb	1: 2	whom he made heir of a things
Heb	1: 3	who sustains a things by his mighty
Heb	8:11	for a shall know me, from least
Heb	9:26	now once for a he has appeared
1 Pt	1:24	for: "A flesh is like grass, and a its glory
1 Pt	5: 7	Cast a your worries upon him
2 Pt	3: 9	that a should come to repentance.
Rev	4:11	and power, for you created a things;
Rev	15: 4	A the nations will come and worship
Rev	21: 5	"Behold, I make a things new."

ALLEGORY
Gal	4:24	Now this is an a.

ALLELUIA → HALLELUJAH
Rev	19: 1	multitude in heaven, saying: "A!
Rev	19: 3	They said a second time: "A!
Rev	19: 4	on the throne, saying, "Amen. A."
Rev	19: 6	peals of thunder, as they said: "A!

ALLOW → ALLOWED
Lk	4:41	and did not a them to speak because
Acts	16: 7	the Spirit of Jesus did not a them,

ALLOWED → ALLOW
Mt	19: 8	your hearts Moses a you to divorce
Acts	28:16	Paul was a to live by himself,

ALLURE
Hos	2:16	Therefore, I will a her now;

ALLY
2 Mc	8:24	With the Almighty as their a,

ALMIGHTY → MIGHT
Gn	17: 1	to Abram and said: I am God the A.
Gn	35:11	I am God A; be fruitful

Ex	6: 3	As God the **A** I appeared
Nm	24: 4	Of one who sees what the **A** sees,
Ru	1:20	the **A** has made my life very bitter.
Jdt	16: 5	"But the Lord **A** thwarted them,
Jb	6: 4	For the arrows of the **A** are in me,
Jb	11: 7	or find out the perfection of the **A**?
Jb	21:15	What is the **A** that we should serve
Jb	33: 4	the breath of the **A** keeps me alive.
Ps	91: 1	who abide in the shade of the **A**,
Is	13: 6	as destruction from the **A** it comes.
Bar	3: 1	"Lord **A**, God of Israel,
Jl	1:15	destruction from the **A** it is coming!
Rev	1: 8	was and who is to come, the **a**."
Rev	4: 8	holy is the Lord God **a**, who was,
Rev	19: 6	his reign, [our] God, the **a**.
Rev	21:22	for its temple is the Lord God **a**

ALMOND → ALMONDS

Ex	25:33	shaped like a blossoms,

ALMONDS → ALMOND

Nm	17:23	blossoms, and borne ripe **a**!

ALMS → ALMSGIVING

Tb	4:16	you have left over, give away as **a**;
Tb	4:16	do not let your eye begrudge the **a**
Tb	12: 8	It is better to give **a** than to store
Mt	6: 2	When you give **a**, do not blow
Lk	12:33	Sell your belongings and give **a**.
Acts	3: 2	to beg for a from the people who

ALMSGIVING → ALMS

Tb	4:10	For **a** delivers from death and keeps
Sir	7:10	Do not be impatient in prayer or neglect **a**.

ALONE

Gn	2:18	It is not good for the man to be **a**.
Ex	18:18	heavy for you; you cannot do it **a**.
Dt	6: 4	Lord is our God, the Lord **a**!
Dt	8: 3	it is not by bread **a** that people live,
1 Kgs	19:10	I **a** remain, and they seek to take my
Tb	8: 6	'It is not good for the man to be **a**;
Ps	51: 6	Against you, you **a** have I sinned;
Ps	62: 2	My soul rests in God **a**, from whom
Ps	136: 4	Who **a** has done great wonders,
Ps	148:13	name, for his name **a** is exalted,
Eccl	4:11	How can one **a** keep warm?
Is	2:11	and the Lord **a** will be exalted,
Dn	13:14	when they could find her **a**.
Mt	4: 4	'One does not live by bread **a**,
Mk	2: 7	Who but God **a** can forgive sins?"
Mk	10:18	No one is good but God **a**.
Jn	16:32	own home and you will leave me **a**.
Jn	16:32	But I am not **a**, because the Father
Rom	11: 3	and I **a** am left, and they are seeking
Jas	2:24	by works and not by faith **a**.
Rev	15: 4	For you **a** are holy. All the nations

ALOUD → LOUD

Ez	9: 1	Then he cried **a** for me to hear:
Rev	1: 3	Blessed is the one who reads **a**

ALPHA

Rev	1: 8	"I am the **A** and the Omega,"
Rev	21: 6	I [am] the **A** and the Omega,
Rev	22:13	I am the **A** and the Omega, the first

ALREADY

Mt	17:12	but I tell you that Elijah has **a** come,
Jn	3:18	not believe has **a** been condemned,
Jn	19:33	to Jesus and saw that he was **a** dead,
Phil	3:12	It is not that I have **a** taken hold of it
Phil	3:12	or have **a** attained perfect maturity,
2 Thes	2: 7	mystery of lawlessness is **a** at work.
2 Tm	2:18	[the] resurrection has **a** taken place
1 Jn	2: 8	away, and the true light is **a** shining.

ALTAR → ALTARS

Gn	8:20	Noah built an **a** to the Lord,
Gn	8:20	he offered burnt offerings on the **a**.
Gn	12: 7	So Abram built an **a** there
Gn	13:18	There he built an **a** to the Lord.

Gn	22: 9	Abraham built an **a** there
Gn	22: 9	put him on top of the wood on the **a**.
Gn	26:25	So Isaac built an **a** there
Gn	35: 1	and build an **a** there to the God who
Ex	17:15	Moses built an **a** there, which he
Ex	20:24	An **a** of earth make for me,
Ex	24: 4	at the foot of the mountain an **a**
Ex	27: 1	You shall make an **a** of acacia
Ex	30: 1	burning incense you shall make an **a**
Ex	32: 5	Aaron built an **a** in front of the calf
Ex	37:25	The **a** of incense was made
Ex	38: 1	The **a** for burnt offerings was made
Lv	8:11	the oil seven times on the **a**, and anointed the **a**,
Lv	9:24	burnt offering and the fat on the **a**.
Dt	27: 5	an **a** made of stones that no iron tool
Jos	8:30	the Lord, the God of Israel, an **a**
Jos	22:10	they built an **a** there at the Jordan, an impressively large **a**.
Jgs	6:24	So Gideon built there an **a**
Jgs	13:20	rose to the heavens from the **a**,
Jgs	21: 4	next day the people built an **a** there
1 Sm	7:17	Israel and built an **a** to the Lord.
1 Sm	14:35	and Saul built an **a** to the Lord—
2 Sm	24:25	David built an **a** to the Lord
1 Kgs	3: 4	its a Solomon sacrificed a thousand
1 Kgs	12:33	went up to the **a** he built in Bethel
1 Kgs	13: 2	"**A**, **a**, thus says the Lord:
1 Kgs	16:32	Ahab set up an **a** to Baal
1 Kgs	18:30	he repaired the **a** of the Lord
2 Kgs	16:10	When he saw the **a** in Damascus,
1 Chr	21:26	then built an **a** there to the Lord.
2 Chr	4: 1	made a bronze **a** twenty cubits long,
2 Chr	4:19	the golden **a**, the tables
2 Chr	15: 8	and to restore the **a** of the Lord
2 Chr	32:12	shall bow down before one **a** only,
2 Chr	33:16	He restored the **a** of the Lord,
Ezr	3: 2	began building the **a** of the God
Neh	10:35	to be burnt on the **a** of the Lord,
Jdt	4:12	The **a**, too, they draped in sackcloth;
1 Mc	1:54	upon the **a** of burnt offerings,
1 Mc	1:59	on the pagan **a** that was over the **a**
1 Mc	2:24	forward and killed him upon the **a**.
1 Mc	4:45	so they tore down the **a**.
1 Mc	4:47	built a new **a** like the former one.
1 Mc	4:56	celebrated the dedication of the **a**
2 Mc	1:19	took some of the fire from the **a**
2 Mc	1:32	in the brilliance coming from the **a**.
Ps	43: 4	That I may come to the **a** of God,
Ps	51:21	will offer up young bulls on your **a**.
Ps	118:27	branches up to the horns of the **a**.
Sir	35: 8	The offering of the just enriches the **a**:
Is	6: 6	he had taken with tongs from the **a**.
Is	60: 7	be acceptable offerings on my **a**,
Lam	2: 7	The Lord has rejected his **a**,
Ez	8:16	between the porch and the **a**,
Ez	40:47	with the **a** standing in front
Ez	47: 1	of the temple to the south of the **a**.
Jl	1:13	wail, ministers of the **a**!
Am	2: 8	in pledge they recline beside any **a**.
Am	9: 1	saw the Lord standing beside the **a**.
Mal	1: 7	By offering defiled food on my **a**!
Mt	5:24	leave your gift there at the **a**,
Mt	23:18	'If one swears by the **a**, it means
Mt	23:18	if one swears by the gift on the **a**,
Lk	11:51	Zechariah who died between the **a**
Acts	17:23	I even discovered an **a** inscribed,
1 Cor	10:18	the sacrifices participants in the **a**?
Heb	13:10	We have an **a** from which those
Jas	2:21	he offered his son Isaac upon the **a**?
Rev	6: 9	I saw underneath the **a** the souls
Rev	8: 3	angel came and stood at the **a**,
Rev	11: 1	the temple of God and the **a**,

ALTARS → ALTAR

Ex	34:13	Tear down their **a**;
Nm	3:31	the **a**, the utensils of the sanctuary

Nm	23: 1	"Build me seven **a** here, and here
Dt	7: 5	Tear down their **a**, smash their
Jgs	2: 2	you must pull down their **a**.
2 Kgs	23:20	upon the **a** all the priests of the high
2 Chr	33: 3	He set up **a** to the Baals,
2 Chr	34: 4	the **a** of the Baals were torn down;
1 Mc	2:45	about and tore down the pagan **a**;
Is	36: 7	places and **a** Hezekiah has removed,
Ez	6: 5	scatter your bones around your **a**.
Hos	8:11	Ephraim made many **a** to expiate sin, they became a for sinning.

ALTER
Ps	89:35	the promise of my lips I will not **a**.

ALWAYS
Dt	5:29	that they might **a** be of such a mind,
Dt	14:23	you may learn **a** to fear the LORD,
Ps	16: 8	I keep the LORD **a** before me;
Ps	103: 9	He will not **a** accuse, and nurses no
Prv	5:19	and by her ardor **a** be intoxicated.
Prv	6:21	them fastened over your heart **a**,
Prv	23:17	only those who **a** fear the LORD;
Is	57:16	not accuse forever, nor **a** be angry;
Mt	26:11	The poor you will **a** have with you;
Mt	26:11	but you will not **a** have me.
Mt	28:20	I am with you **a**, until the end
Lk	18: 1	to pray **a** without becoming weary.
Jn	6:34	to him, "Sir, give us this bread **a**."
Jn	11:42	I know that you **a** hear me;
2 Cor	2:14	who **a** leads us in triumph in Christ
2 Cor	5: 6	So we are **a** courageous,
2 Cor	6:10	as sorrowful yet **a** rejoicing;
Phil	4: 4	Rejoice in the Lord **a**. I shall say it
1 Thes	5:15	**a** seek what is good [both] for each
1 Thes	5:16	Rejoice **a**.
Phlm	1: 4	I give thanks to my God **a**,
Heb	7:25	he is **a** able to save those who
1 Pt	3:15	**A** be ready to give an explanation

AMALEK → AMALEKITE, AMALEKITES
Ex	17: 8	Then **A** came and waged war
Ex	17:14	out the memory of **A** from under
Nm	24:20	Upon seeing **A**, Balaam recited his
Dt	25:17	Bear in mind what **A** did to you
1 Sm	15: 3	attack **A**, and put under the ban
1 Sm	15: 8	He took Agag, king of **A**, alive,
1 Sm	28:18	carry out his fierce anger against **A**,

AMALEKITE → AMALEK
2 Sm	1: 8	and I replied, 'An **A**.'

AMALEKITES → AMALEK
Nm	14:43	For there the **A** and Canaanites will

AMASA
Nephew of David (1 Chr 2:17). Commander of Absalom's forces (2 Sm 17:24-27). Returned to David (2 Sm 19:14). Killed by Joab (2 Sm 20:4-13).

AMAZED → AMAZEMENT
Mt	8:27	The men were **a** and said,
Mt	9:33	The crowds were **a** and said,
Mt	15:31	The crowds were **a** when they saw
Mk	6: 6	He was **a** at their lack of faith.
Mk	15: 5	further answer, so that Pilate was **a**.
Rev	17: 8	the world shall be **a** when they see

AMAZEMENT → AMAZED
Acts	3:10	and they were filled with **a**

AMAZIAH
1. Son of Joash; king of Judah (2 Kgs 14; 2 Chr 25). Defeated Edom (2 Kgs 14:7; 2 Chr 25:5-13); defeated by Israel for worshiping Edom's gods (2 Kgs 14:8-14; 2 Chr 25:14-24).
2. Idolatrous priest who opposed Amos (Am 7:10-17).

AMBASSADOR → AMBASSADORS
Eph	6:20	for which I am an **a** in chains,

AMBASSADORS → AMBASSADOR
2 Cor	5:20	So we are **a** for Christ, as if God

AMBITION
Phil	1:17	proclaim Christ out of selfish **a**,
Jas	3:14	and selfish **a** in your hearts, do not
Jas	3:16	where jealousy and selfish **a** exist,

AMBUSH
Jos	8: 2	Set an **a** behind the city.
Jgs	20:29	Israel set men in **a** around Gibeah.
2 Chr	20:22	the LORD laid an **a** against
Prv	12: 6	words of the wicked are a deadly **a**,

AMEN
Dt	27:15	all the people shall answer, "**A**!"
1 Chr	16:36	Let all the people say, **A**!
Neh	5:13	the whole assembly answered, "**A**,"
Neh	8: 6	raised high, answered, "**A**, a!"
Tb	8: 8	They said together, "**A**, a!"
Jdt	13:20	And all the people answered, "**A**!
Jdt	13:20	all the people answered, "**A**! A!"
Ps	89:53	be the LORD forever! **A** and a!
Rom	1:25	creator, who is blessed forever. **A**.
Rom	9: 5	is over all be blessed forever. **A**.
Rom	11:36	To him be glory forever. **A**.
1 Cor	14:16	the uninstructed say the "**A**"
2 Cor	1:20	the **A** from us also goes through him
Rev	3:14	" 'The **A**, the faithful and true
Rev	5:14	living creatures answered, "**A**,"
Rev	19: 4	who sat on the throne, saying, "**A**.
Rev	22:20	says, "Yes, I am coming soon." **A**!

AMENDS
Lv	26:41	and they make **a** for their iniquity,

AMMON → AMMONITE, AMMONITES
Neh	13:23	Jews who had married women of Ashdod, **A**,

AMMONITE → AMMON
Dt	23: 4	No **A** or Moabite may ever come
Neh	2:10	Tobiah the **A** official had heard
Neh	13: 1	"No **A** or Moabite may ever be
Jdt	6: 5	you, Achior, you **A** mercenary,

AMMONITES → AMMON
Gn	19:38	He is the ancestor of the **A** of today.
Dt	2:19	you possession of any land of the **A**,
Jgs	11: 4	later, the **A** went to war with Israel.
2 Sm	10: 1	the king of the **A** died, and Hanun
1 Kgs	11: 5	Milcom, the abomination of the **A**.
Jer	49: 6	I will restore the fortunes of the **A**—
Ez	25: 2	turn toward the **A** and prophesy
Ez	25:10	along with the **A**, to the people

AMNON
Firstborn of David (2 Sm 3:2; 1 Chr 3:1). Killed by Absalom for raping his sister Tamar (2 Sm 13).

AMON
1. Son of Manasseh; king of Judah (2 Kgs 21:18-26; 1 Chr 3:14; 2 Chr 33:21-25).
2. Ruler of Samaria under Ahab (1 Kgs 22:26; 2 Chr 18:25).

AMORITE → AMORITES
Gn	14:13	camping at the oak of Mamre the **A**,
Ez	16: 3	your father was an **A**, your mother

AMORITES → AMORITE
Gn	15:16	of the **A** is not yet complete.
Ex	34:11	about to drive out before you the **A**,
Nm	21:31	So Israel settled in the land of the **A**.
Jgs	6:10	gods of the **A** in whose land you are
1 Sm	7:14	also peace between Israel and the **A**.
Am	2: 9	I who destroyed the **A** before them,

AMOS
1. Prophet from Tekoa (Tb 2:6; Am 1:1; 7:10-17).
2. Ancestor of Jesus (Lk 3:25).

AMRAM
Ex	6:20	**A** married his aunt Jochebed,
1 Chr	5:29	The children of **A** were Aaron,

AMULETS
Is	3:20	cinctures, perfume boxes, and **a**;

ANAK → ANAKIM
Jos   15:13 (Arba was the father of **A**), that is,

ANAKIM → ANAK
Nm   13:28 we saw descendants of the **A** there.
Dt   1:28 besides, we saw the **A** there.' "
Jos   11:22 so that no **A** were left in the land

ANANIAS
   1. Husband of Sapphira; died for lying to God (Acts 5:1-11).
   2. Disciple who baptized Saul (Acts 9:10-19).
   3. High priest at Paul's arrest (Acts 22:30–24:1).

ANATHOTH
Jer   32: 7 "Purchase my field in **A**, since you,

ANCESTOR → ANCESTORS
Rom   4: 1 found, our **a** according to the flesh?

ANCESTORS → ANCESTOR
Ps   106: 6 We have sinned like our **a**;
Lk   11:48 give consent to the deeds of your **a**,
Jn   4:20 Our **a** worshiped on this mountain;
Jn   6:31 Our **a** ate manna in the desert, as it
Acts   5:30 The God of our **a** raised Jesus,
Heb   1: 1 ways to our **a** through the prophets;

ANCHOR
Heb   6:19 This we have as an **a** of the soul,

ANCIENT
Ps   24: 7 be lifted, you **a** portals, that the king
Ps   68:34 rides the heights of the **a** heavens,
Prv   22:28 Do not remove the **a** landmark
Is   58:12 people shall rebuild the **a** ruins;
Dn   7: 9 and the **A** of Days took his throne.
Dn   7:13 When he reached the **A** of Days
Dn   7:22 until the **A** of Days came,
Mi   5: 1 origin is from of old, from **a** times.
Hb   3: 6 **A** mountains were shattered, the age-old
Rev   12: 9 The huge dragon, the **a** serpent,
Rev   20: 2 He seized the dragon, the **a** serpent,

ANDREW
   Apostle; brother of Simon Peter (Mt 4:18; 10:2; Mk 1:16-18, 29; 3:18; 13:3; Lk 6:14; Jn 1:35-41; 6:8-9; 12:22; Acts 1:13).

ANEW → NEW
Wis   19: 6 was being made over **a**,
1 Pt   1:23 You have been born **a**,

ANGEL → ANGELS, ARCHANGEL; see also MESSENGER
Gn   48:16 The **a** who has delivered me
Ex   3: 2 There the **a** of the LORD appeared
Ex   14:19 The **a** of God, who had been leading
Ex   23:20 I am sending an **a** before you,
Ex   32:34 See, my **a** will go before you.
Ex   33: 2 I will send an **a** before you
Nm   20:16 sent an **a** who led us out of Egypt.
Nm   22:22 and the **a** of the LORD took
Jgs   13: 3 An **a** of the LORD appeared
2 Sm   14:17 my lord the king is like an **a** of God,
2 Sm   19:28 my lord the king is like an **a** of God.
2 Sm   24:16 the **a** causing the destruction among
1 Kgs   13:18 and an **a** told me by the word
1 Kgs   19:35 That night the **a** of the LORD went
1 Chr   21:15 sent an **a** to Jerusalem to destroy it;
Tb   5: 4 found the **a** Raphael standing before
Tb   5: 4 not know that this was an **a** of God).
Tb   12:22 because an **a** of God appeared
1 Mc   7:41 your **a** went out and killed
2 Mc   11: 6 tears to send a good **a** to save Israel.
Ps   34: 8 The **a** of the LORD encamps
Ps   35: 5 the **a** of the LORD driving them
Is   37:36 the **a** of the LORD went forth
Dn   3:49 the **a** of the Lord went down
Dn   3:95 who sent his **a** to deliver
Dn   6:23 My God sent his **a** and closed
Dn   13:59 "for the **a** of God waits
Dn   14:34 when an **a** of the Lord told him,
Hos   12: 5 He contended with an **a**
Zec   1:11 they answered the **a** of the LORD,

Zec   3: 1 the high priest standing before the **a**
Mt   1:20 the **a** of the Lord appeared to him
Mt   2:13 the **a** of the Lord appeared to Joseph
Mt   28: 2 for an **a** of the Lord descended
Lk   1:11 the **a** of the Lord appeared to him,
Lk   1:26 the **a** Gabriel was sent from God
Lk   2: 9 The **a** of the Lord appeared to them
Lk   22:43 to strengthen him an **a** from heaven
Jn   12:29 said, "An **a** has spoken to him."
Acts   5:19 the **a** of the Lord opened the doors
Acts   6:15 his face was like the face of an **a**.
Acts   7:30 an **a** appeared to him in the desert
Acts   8:26 the **a** of the Lord spoke to Philip,
Acts   10: 3 plainly in a vision an **a** of God come
Acts   12: 7 Suddenly the **a** of the Lord stood
Acts   27:23 For last night an **a** of the God
2 Cor   11:14 even Satan masquerades as an **a**
Gal   1: 8 an **a** from heaven should preach
Gal   4:14 rather you received me as an **a**
Rev   1: 1 by sending his **a** to his servant John,
Rev   2: 1 "To the **a** of the church in Ephesus,
Rev   5: 2 I saw a mighty **a** who proclaimed
Rev   7: 2 I saw another **a** come
Rev   8: 3 Another **a** came and stood
Rev   9:11 They had as their king the **a**
Rev   14: 6 Then I saw another **a** flying high
Rev   16: 2 The first **a** went and poured out his
Rev   19:17 I saw an **a** standing on the sun.
Rev   22:16 sent my **a** to give you this testimony

ANGELS → ANGEL
Gn   19: 1 The two **a** reached Sodom
Tb   11:14 name, and blessed be all his holy **a**.
Ps   91:11 For he commands his **a** with regard
Ps   103:20 all you his **a**, mighty in strength,
Ps   148: 2 Praise him, all you his **a**;
Wis   16:20 your people with food of **a**
Mt   4: 6 command his **a** concerning you'
Mt   4:11 **a** came and ministered to him.
Mt   13:39 of the age, and the harvesters are **a**.
Mt   16:27 with his **a** in his Father's glory,
Mt   18:10 that their **a** in heaven always look
Mt   24:36 one knows, neither the **a** of heaven,
Mt   25:41 fire prepared for the devil and his **a**.
Mt   26:53 with more than twelve legions of **a**?
Mk   1:13 beasts, and the **a** ministered to him.
Mk   8:38 his Father's glory with the holy **a**."
Mk   12:25 but they are like the **a** in heaven.
Mk   13:32 one knows, neither the **a** in heaven,
Lk   2:15 When the **a** went away from them
Lk   4:10 will command his **a** concerning you,
Lk   12: 8 Man will acknowledge before the **a**
Lk   15:10 there will be rejoicing among the **a**
Lk   16:22 he was carried away by **a**
Lk   20:36 no longer die, for they are like **a**;
Jn   1:51 opened and the **a** of God ascending
Jn   20:12 and saw two **a** in white sitting there,
Acts   7:53 the law as transmitted by **a**, but you
Acts   23: 8 say that there is no resurrection or **a**
Rom   8:38 nor life, nor **a**, nor principalities,
1 Cor   4: 9 world, to **a** and human beings alike.
1 Cor   6: 3 you not know that we will judge **a**?
1 Cor   11:10 on her head, because of the **a**.
Gal   3:19 it was promulgated by **a** at the hand
Col   2:18 in self-abasement and worship of **a**,
2 Thes   1: 7 from heaven with his mighty **a**,
1 Tm   3:16 spirit, seen by **a**,
1 Tm   5:21 and the elect **a** to keep these rules
Heb   1: 4 the **a** as the name he has inherited is
Heb   1: 6 "Let all the **a** of God worship
Heb   1: 7 Of the **a** he says: "He makes his **a** winds
Heb   2: 2 announced through **a** proved firm,
Heb   2: 7 for a little while lower than the **a**;
Heb   2: 9 was made "lower than the **a**,"
Heb   12:22 and countless **a** in festal gathering,
Heb   13: 2 have unknowingly entertained **a**.
1 Pt   1:12 things into which **a** longed to look.

1 Pt	3:22	hand of God, with a, authorities,
2 Pt	2: 4	if God did not spare the a when they
Jude	1: 6	The a too, who did not keep to their
Rev	1:20	the seven stars are the a of the seven
Rev	3: 5	presence of my Father and of his a.
Rev	5:11	many a who surrounded the throne
Rev	7: 1	this I saw four a standing at the four
Rev	8: 2	the seven a who stood before God
Rev	9:14	"Release the four a who are bound
Rev	12: 7	and his a battled against the dragon.
Rev	12: 7	The dragon and its a fought back,
Rev	15: 1	seven a with the seven last plagues,
Rev	21:12	gates where twelve a were stationed

ANGER → ANGRY

Gn	27:45	until your brother's a against you
Ex	34: 6	slow to a and abounding in love
Nm	14:18	'The LORD is slow to a
Nm	22:22	now God's a flared up at him
Nm	25: 3	the LORD's a flared up against
Dt	9:19	I dreaded the fierce a of the LORD
Dt	29:27	uprooted them from their soil in a,
Jos	7: 1	and the a of the LORD flared
Jos	7:26	Then the LORD turned from his a.
Jos	23:16	the a of the LORD will flare
Jgs	14:19	he went off to his own family in a,
1 Kgs	16:13	the God of Israel, to a by their idols.
Neh	9:17	slow to a and rich in mercy;
Ps	6: 2	Do not reprove me in your a,
Ps	30: 6	For his a lasts but a moment;
Ps	37: 8	Refrain from a; abandon wrath;
Ps	78:38	and again he turned back his a,
Ps	86:15	slow to a, abounding in mercy
Ps	90: 7	Truly we are consumed by your a,
Ps	95:11	Therefore I swore in my a:
Ps	103: 8	slow to a, abounding in mercy.
Ps	103: 9	accuse, and nurses no lasting a;
Ps	145: 8	slow to a and abounding in mercy.
Prv	12:16	Fools immediately show their a,
Prv	15: 1	wrath, but a harsh word stirs up a.
Prv	19:11	It is good sense to be slow to a,
Prv	29:11	Fools give vent to all their a;
Prv	30:33	the churning of a produces strife.
Sir	30:24	Envy and a shorten one's days,
Is	48: 9	sake of my name I restrain my a,
Is	63: 6	trampled down the peoples in my a,
Lam	4:11	The LORD has exhausted his a,
Dn	9:16	let your a and your wrath be turned
Hos	11: 9	I will not give vent to my blazing a,
Jl	2:13	slow to a, abounding in steadfast
Jon	4: 2	slow to a, abounding in kindness,
Mi	7:18	Who does not persist in a forever,
Na	1: 3	The LORD is slow to a, yet great
Mk	3: 5	Looking around at them with a
Eph	4:26	do not let the sun set on your a,
Eph	6: 4	do not provoke your children to a,
Col	3: 8	a, fury, malice, slander,
1 Tm	2: 8	holy hands, without a or argument.

ANGRY → ANGER

1 Kgs	11: 9	The LORD became a with Solomon,
Ps	2:11	Accept correction lest he become a
Ps	79: 5	Will you be a forever?
Prv	25:23	and a backbiting tongue, a looks.
Jer	3:12	I will not remain a with you;
Jon	4: 4	asked, "Are you right to be a?"
Zec	1: 2	The LORD was very a with your
Mt	5:22	whoever is a with his brother will
Lk	15:28	He became a, and when he refused
Jn	7:23	are you a with me because I made
Eph	4:26	Be a but do not sin; do not let
Rev	12:17	Then the dragon became a

ANGUISH

Jb	7:11	I will speak in the a of my spirit;
Zep	1:15	a day of distress and a, a day of ruin
Jn	16:21	is in a because her hour has arrived;
Rom	9: 2	sorrow and constant a in my heart.

ANIMAL → ANIMALS

Gn	1:25	God made every kind of wild a, every kind of tame a,
Ex	22:18	who lies with an a shall be put
Lv	18:23	not have sexual relations with an a,
Lv	20:15	man has sexual relations with an a,
Lv	20:15	put to death, and you shall kill the a.
Ps	50:10	For every a of the forest is mine,
Lk	10:34	Then he lifted him up on his own a,
Heb	12:20	"If even an a touches the mountain,

ANIMALS → ANIMAL

Gn	2:19	out of the ground all the wild a
Gn	3: 1	all the wild a that the LORD God
Gn	3:14	this, cursed are you among all the a,
Gn	7: 2	and of the unclean a, one pair,
Gn	8:19	and all the a, all the birds, and all
Gn	9: 2	come upon all the a of the earth
Dt	14: 4	These are the a you may eat:
Dt	14: 6	Any among the a that has divided
Ps	147: 9	Who gives a their food and young
Is	40:16	fuel, nor its a be enough for burnt
Acts	11: 6	saw the four-legged a of the earth,
Jude	1:10	know by nature like irrational a.

ANNA

1. Wife of Tobit (Tb 1:20; 2:1, 11).
2. Prophetess who spoke about the child Jesus (Lk 2:36-38).

ANNAS

High priest A.D. 6–15 (Lk 3:2; Jn 18:13, 24; Acts 4:6).

ANNUL

Gal	3:17	does not a a covenant previously

ANOINT → ANOINTED, ANOINTING

Ex	28:41	A and install them,
Ex	30:26	you shall a the tent of meeting
Ex	30:30	and his sons you shall also a
1 Sm	9:16	whom you are to a as ruler of my
1 Sm	15: 1	to a you king over his people Israel.
1 Kgs	1:34	the prophet shall a him king over
1 Kgs	19:16	You shall also a Jehu,
2 Kgs	9: 3	I a you king over Israel.'
Ps	23: 5	You a my head with oil;
Mk	16: 1	so that they might go and a him.
Lk	7:46	You did not a my head with oil,

ANOINTED → ANOINT

Gn	31:13	where you a a sacred pillar
Lv	4: 3	If it is the a priest who thus does
1 Sm	2:10	king, and exalt the horn of his a!"
1 Sm	10: 1	the LORD has a you ruler over his
1 Sm	16:13	a him in the midst of his brothers,
1 Sm	26: 9	can lay a hand on the LORD's a
2 Sm	1:14	hand to desecrate the LORD's a?"
2 Sm	2: 4	and a David king over the house
2 Sm	5: 3	and they a David king over Israel.
2 Sm	19:22	He cursed the a of the LORD."
1 Kgs	1:39	of oil from the tent and a Solomon.
1 Chr	16:22	"Do not touch my a, to my
2 Chr	6:42	do not reject the plea of your a,
Ps	2: 2	the LORD and against his a one:
Ps	18:51	and shown mercy to his a, to David
Ps	89:21	with my holy oil I have a him.
Ps	105:15	"Do not touch my a ones, to my
Is	61: 1	me, because the LORD has a me;
Dn	9:24	and a holy of holies will be a.
Dn	9:26	sixty-two weeks an a one shall be
Hb	3:13	your people, to save your a one.
Zec	4:14	are the two a ones who stand
Mk	6:13	they a with oil many who were sick
Lk	4:18	because he has a me to bring glad
Lk	7:46	oil, but she a my feet with ointment.
Jn	1:41	Messiah" (which is translated A).
Jn	12: 3	nard and a the feet of Jesus
Acts	10:38	how God a Jesus of Nazareth
2 Cor	1:21	you in Christ and who a us is God;
Heb	1: 9	a you with the oil of gladness

ANOINTING → ANOINT
Ex	30:25	and blend them into sacred a oil,
1 Jn	2:27	the a that you received from him
1 Jn	2:27	his a teaches you about everything

ANOTHER → ANOTHER'S
Prv	27: 2	Let a praise you, not your own
Is	48:11	My glory I will not give to a.
Lk	19:44	a within you because you did not
Jn	4:37	that 'One sows and a reaps.'
Jn	5:43	yet if a comes in his own name,
Jn	13:34	a new commandment: love one a.
Jn	13:34	so you also should love one a.
Jn	14:16	he will give you a Advocate to be
Jn	18:15	Peter and a disciple followed Jesus.
Rom	12:10	love one a with mutual affection;
Rom	12:10	anticipate one a in showing honor.
1 Cor	7: 5	but then return to one a,
1 Cor	12: 9	to a faith by the same Spirit; to a gifts of healing
1 Cor	16:20	Greet one a with a holy kiss.
Gal	1: 7	(not that there is a).
Eph	4: 2	bearing with one a through love,
Eph	4:25	for we are members one of a.
Eph	4:32	[And] be kind to one a,
Eph	4:32	forgiving one a as God has forgiven
Col	3:16	you teach and admonish one a,
1 Thes	4:18	console one a with these words.
Heb	10:24	consider how to rouse one a to love
Jas	4:11	Do not speak evil of one a, brothers.
1 Pt	1:22	love one a intensely from a [pure]
1 Pt	4: 8	let your love for one a be intense,
1 Jn	3:11	we should love one a,
1 Jn	3:23	love one a just as he commanded
Rev	20:12	Then a scroll was opened, the book

ANOTHER'S → ANOTHER
Jn	13:14	feet, you ought to wash one a feet.
Gal	6: 2	Bear one a burdens, and so you will

ANSWER → ANSWERED, ANSWERS
1 Kgs	18:26	to noon, saying, "Baal, a us!"
1 Kgs	18:37	A me, LORD! A me, that this
Jb	30:20	I cry to you, but you do not a me;
Ps	4: 2	A me when I call, my saving God.
Ps	20:10	a when we call upon you.
Prv	15: 1	A mild a turns back wrath,
Prv	26: 5	A fools according to their folly,
Is	46: 7	They cry out to it, but it cannot a;
Is	58: 9	and the LORD will a, you shall cry
Is	65:24	Before they call, I will a;
Mt	22:46	No one was able to a him a word,
Mt	27:14	But he did not a him one word,
Lk	23: 9	him at length, but he gave him no a.

ANSWERED → ANSWER
1 Chr	21:26	who a him by sending down fire
Ps	118:21	I thank you for you a me;

ANSWERS → ANSWER
1 Kgs	18:24	The God who a with fire is God."
Prv	18:13	Whoever a before listening, theirs is

ANT → ANTS
Prv	6: 6	Go to the a, O sluggard, study her

ANTICHRIST → ANTICHRISTS
1 Jn	2:18	as you heard that the a was coming,
1 Jn	2:22	the Father and the Son, this is the a.
1 Jn	4: 3	This is the spirit of the a that, as you
2 Jn	1: 7	such is the deceitful one and the a.

ANTICHRISTS → ANTICHRIST
1 Jn	2:18	so now many a have appeared.

ANTIOCH
Acts	11:26	it was in A that the disciples were
Acts	13: 1	were in the church at A prophets
Gal	2:11	And when Cephas came to A,

ANTIOCHUS
Antiochus IV Epiphanes, king of the Syrian Greeks B.C.E. 175-164 (1 Mc 1:10-19). Plundered the temple in Jerusalem (1 Mc 1:20-28). At-

tempted to force the Hellenization of the Jewish people (1 Mc 1:41-53), including defiling the altar and holy place (1 Mc 1:54-63). His policies sparked the Maccabean revolt.

ANTIPAS
Rev	2:13	in me, not even in the days of A,

ANTS → ANT
Prv	30:25	A—a species not strong, yet they

ANXIETIES → ANXIETY
1 Cor	7:32	I should like you to be free of a.

ANXIETY → ANXIETIES, ANXIOUS
Sir	11:10	My son, why increase your a,

ANXIOUS → ANXIETY
1 Cor	7:32	An unmarried man is a

ANYTHING → THING
Gn	18:14	Is a too marvelous for the LORD
Jer	32:27	Is a too difficult for me?
Mt	18:19	of you agree on earth about a
Mk	2:12	"We have never seen a like this."
Jn	1:46	to him, "Can a good come
Jn	14:14	If you ask a of me in my name,
Jn	16:23	you will not question me about a.
2 Cor	13: 8	we cannot do a against the truth,

APART
Rom	1: 1	and set a for the gospel of God,
Rom	3:21	God has been manifested a

APOLLOS
Christian from Alexandria, learned in the Scriptures; instructed by Aquila and Priscilla (Acts 18:24-28). Ministered at Corinth (Acts 19:1; 1 Cor 1:12; 3; Ti 3:13).

APOLLYON → =ABADDON
Rev	9:11	Hebrew is Abaddon and in Greek A.

APOSTASY
1 Mc	2:15	of enforcing the a came to the city

APOSTLE → APOSTLES, APOSTLES', APOSTLESHIP, SUPERAPOSTLES
Rom	1: 1	called to be an a and set apart
Rom	11:13	then as I am the a to the Gentiles,
1 Cor	1: 1	called to be an a of Christ Jesus
1 Cor	9: 1	Am I not an a? Have I not seen
1 Cor	15: 9	not fit to be called an a, because I
2 Cor	12:12	of an a were performed among you
1 Tm	2: 7	and a (I am speaking the truth, I am
2 Tm	1:11	I was appointed preacher and a
Heb	3: 1	Jesus, the a and high priest of our
1 Pt	1: 1	Peter, an a of Jesus Christ,
2 Pt	1: 1	a slave and a of Jesus Christ,

APOSTLES → APOSTLE
See also Andrew, Bartholomew, Barnabas, James, John, Judas, Matthew, Matthias, Nathanael, Paul, Peter, Philip, Simon, Thaddaeus, Thomas.
Mt	10: 2	names of the twelve a are these:
Mk	3:14	[named a] that they might be
Lk	6:13	Twelve, whom he also named a:
Lk	11:49	'I will send to them prophets and a;
Acts	1:26	he was counted with the eleven a.
Acts	2:42	themselves to the teaching of the a
Acts	2:43	and signs were done through the a.
Acts	4:33	great power the a bore witness
Acts	4:35	and put them at the feet of the a,
Acts	5:18	laid hands upon the a and put them
Acts	8: 1	of Judea and Samaria, except the a.
Acts	14:14	The a Barnabas and Paul tore their
Rom	16: 7	they are prominent among the a
1 Cor	12:28	in the church to be, first, a;
1 Cor	15: 9	For I am the least of the a, not fit
2 Cor	11:13	For such people are false a,
2 Cor	11:13	who masquerade as a of Christ.
Eph	2:20	built upon the foundation of the a
Eph	3: 5	has now been revealed to his holy a
Eph	4:11	And he gave some as a, others as
Jude	1:17	by the a of our Lord Jesus Christ,
Rev	2: 2	tested those who call themselves a

Rev 21:14 names of the twelve **a** of the Lamb.

APOSTLES' → APOSTLE
Acts 8:18 conferred by the laying on of the **a** hands,

APOSTLESHIP → APOSTLE
Rom 1: 5 we have received the grace of **a**,
1 Cor 9: 2 you are the seal of my **a** in the Lord.

APPALLED
Jer 50:13 who passes by Babylon will be **a**

APPEAL → APPEALING
Acts 25:11 me over to them. I **a** to Caesar."
1 Pt 3:21 an **a** to God for a clear conscience,

APPEALING → APPEAL
2 Cor 5:20 Christ, as if God were **a** through us.

APPEAR → APPEARANCE, APPEARANCES, APPEARED, APPEARING, APPEARS
Gn 1: 9 basin, so that the dry land may **a**.
Ex 23:15 No one shall **a** before me
Sir 35: 6 Do not **a** before the Lord empty-handed,
Mt 24:30 of the Son of Man will **a** in heaven,
Lk 19:11 of God would **a** there immediately.
2 Cor 5:10 we must all **a** before the judgment
Heb 9:24 he might now **a** before God on our
Heb 9:28 sins of many, will **a** a second time,

APPEARANCE → APPEAR
Nm 9:15 on the **a** of fire over the tabernacle.
1 Sm 16: 7 Do not judge from his **a** or from his
1 Sm 16: 7 not see as a mortal, who sees the **a**.
Sir 19:29 People are known by their **a**; the sensible
Is 52:14 beyond that of mortals his **a**,
Jl 2: 4 Their **a** is that of horses;
Mt 28: 3 His **a** was like lightning and his
Lk 12:56 how to interpret the **a** of the earth
2 Cor 5:12 who boast of external **a** rather than
2 Tm 1:10 now made manifest through the **a**
2 Tm 4: 8 but to all who have longed for his **a**.
Rev 9: 7 The **a** of the locusts was like

APPEARANCES → APPEAR
Jn 7:24 Stop judging by **a**, but judge

APPEARED → APPEAR
Gn 12: 7 The LORD **a** to Abram and said:
Gn 17: 1 the LORD **a** to Abram and said:
Gn 18: 1 The LORD **a** to Abraham
Gn 26: 2 The LORD **a** to him and said:
Gn 35: 9 God **a** to him again and blessed
Ex 3: 2 the LORD **a** to him as fire flaming
Ex 6: 3 As God the Almighty I **a**
Ex 16:10 glory of the LORD **a** in the cloud!
Nm 14:10 the glory of the LORD **a** at the tent
Nm 16:19 glory of the LORD **a** to the entire
Nm 20: 6 the glory of the LORD **a** to them,
Jgs 6:12 messenger of the LORD **a** to him
Jgs 13: 3 of the LORD **a** to the woman
1 Kgs 9: 2 the LORD **a** to Solomon a second
2 Chr 1: 7 That night God **a** to Solomon
Ps 102:17 has rebuilt Zion and **a** in glory,
Dn 5: 5 the fingers of a human hand **a**,
Mt 1:20 the angel of the Lord **a** to him
Mt 2:13 the angel of the Lord **a** to Joseph
Mt 2:19 the angel of the Lord **a** in a dream
Mk 9: 4 Elijah **a** to them along with Moses,
Lk 1:11 the angel of the Lord **a** to him,
Lk 22:43 him an angel from heaven **a** to him.
Lk 24:34 been raised and has **a** to Simon!"
Acts 2: 3 there **a** to them tongues as of fire,
1 Cor 15: 5 that he **a** to Cephas,
Ti 2:11 For the grace of God has **a**,
Heb 9:26 now once for all he has **a** at the end
Rev 12: 1 A great sign **a** in the sky, a woman

APPEARING → APPEAR
Acts 1: 3 **a** to them during forty days

APPEARS → APPEAR
Mal 3: 2 Who can stand firm when he **a**?

Jas 4:14 are a puff of smoke that **a** briefly

APPETITE → APPETITES
Prv 6:30 hunger they steal to satisfy their **a**.
Prv 16:26 The **a** of workers works for them,

APPETITES → APPETITE
Rom 16:18 our Lord Christ but their own **a**,

APPLE → APPLES
Dt 32:10 guarded them as the **a** of his eye,
Ps 17: 8 Keep me as the **a** of your eye;
Prv 7: 2 my teaching as the **a** of your eye;
Sg 2: 3 Like an **a** tree among the trees
Sg 8: 5 Beneath the **a** tree I awakened you;

APPLES → APPLE
Prv 25:11 Golden **a** in silver settings are
Sg 2: 5 refresh me with **a**, for I am sick
Sg 7: 9 the fragrance of your breath like **a**,

APPLIED → APPLY
Eccl 1:17 yet when I **a** my mind to know
Eccl 8:16 I **a** my heart to know wisdom
1 Cor 4: 6 I have **a** these things to myself

APPLY → APPLIED
Ex 12:22 **a** some of this blood to the lintel
Prv 23:12 **A** your heart to instruction, and your

APPOINT → APPOINTED, APPOINTS
1 Sm 8: 5 your example, **a** a king over us,
1 Sm 13:14 a man after his own heart to **a** as ruler
Is 60:17 I will **a** peace your governor,
Hos 2: 2 They will **a** for themselves one head
Ti 1: 5 and **a** presbyters in every town, as I

APPOINTED → APPOINT
Ex 31: 6 assistant I myself have **a** Oholiab,
Neh 5:14 that King Artaxerxes **a** me governor
Est 9:31 for their **a** time, these days of Purim
Dn 8:19 for it is for the **a** time of the end.
Dn 11:27 because the **a** end is not yet.
Hb 1:12 LORD, you have **a** them for judgment,
Mk 3:16 [he **a** the twelve:] Simon, whom he
Lk 10: 1 this the Lord **a** seventy [-two] others
Jn 15:16 but I who chose you and **a** you to go
Acts 3:20 send you the Messiah already **a**
Heb 9:27 Just as it is **a** that human beings die

APPOINTS → APPOINT
Heb 7:28 For the law **a** men subject
Heb 7:28 was taken after the law, **a** a son,

APPORTION → PORTION
Nm 33:54 You will **a** the land among

APPROACH → APPROACHED, APPROACHES
Lv 18: 6 None of you shall **a** a close relative
Heb 4:16 So let us confidently **a** the throne
Heb 7:25 save those who **a** God through him,

APPROACHED → APPROACH
Lk 22:47 a crowd **a** and in front was one

APPROACHES → APPROACH
Nm 17:28 Anyone who **a** the tabernacle

APPROVED
Rom 16:10 Greet Apelles, who is **a** in Christ.
2 Cor 10:18 who recommends himself who is **a**,

AQUILA
Husband of Priscilla; co-worker with Paul, instructor of Apollos (Acts 18; Rom 16:3; 1 Cor 16:19; 2 Tm 4:19).

ARAB → ARABIA, ARABIANS, ARABS
Neh 2:19 Geshem the **A** mocked and ridiculed

ARABAH
Dt 3:17 Chinnereth to the Salt Sea of the **A**,
Jos 11:16 the **A**, as well as the mountain
Ez 47: 8 runs down into the **A** and empties

ARABIA → ARAB
2 Chr 9:14 All the kings of **A** also,
Gal 1:17 I went into **A** and then returned

Gal   4:25   represents Sinai, a mountain in **A**;

ARABIANS → ARAB
1 Mc   5:39   they have also hired **A** to help them,

ARABS → ARAB
Neh   4: 1   Tobiah, the **A**, the Ammonites,
Acts   2:11   Cretans and **A**, yet we hear them

ARAM → ARAMAIC, ARAMEAN, ARAMEANS
Gn   10:23   The descendants of **A**:
Gn   24:10   to the city of Nahor in **A** Naharaim.
Nm   23: 7   From **A** Balak has led me here,
Jgs   3: 8   king of **A** Naharaim;
Jgs   10: 6   the gods of **A**, the gods of Sidon,
1 Kgs   19:15   shall anoint Hazael as king of **A**.
2 Kgs   13: 3   king of **A**, and of Ben-hadad,
2 Chr   16: 7   you relied on the king of **A** and did

ARAMAIC → ARAM
2 Kgs   18:26   "Please speak to your servants in **A**;
Ezr   4: 7   The document was written in **A**
2 Mc   15:36   month, called Adar in **A**, the eve
Is   36:11   "Please speak to your servants in **A**;
Dn   2: 4   Chaldeans answered the king in **A**:

ARAMEAN → ARAM
Gn   31:20   Jacob had hoodwinked Laban the **A**
Dt   26: 5   was a refugee **A** who went down

ARAMEANS → ARAM
2 Sm   8: 6   and the **A** became David's subjects,
2 Kgs   7: 6   the army of the **A** to hear the sound
2 Kgs   8:28   where the **A** wounded Joram.

ARARAT
Gn   8: 4   came to rest on the mountains of **A**.
2 Kgs   19:37   sword and fled into the land of **A**.
Tb   1:21   him and fled to the mountains of **A**.
Jer   51:27   **A**, Minni, and Ashkenaz;

ARAUNAH → =ORNAN
2 Sm   24:16   the threshing floor of **A** the Jebusite.

ARBA
Jos   14:15   Hebron was formerly called Kiriath-arba, for **A**,

ARBITRATOR
Lk   12:14   appointed me as your judge and a?"

ARCHANGEL → ANGEL
1 Thes   4:16   with the voice of an a
Jude   1: 9   Yet the a Michael, when he argued

ARCHELAUS
Mt   2:22   heard that **A** was ruling over Judea

ARCHER → ARCHERS
Prv   26:10   An a wounding all who pass by is

ARCHERS → ARCHER
Gn   49:23   and shooting, the a opposed him;
1 Sm   31: 3   Then the a hit him, and he was
2 Chr   35:23   Then the a shot King Josiah,
Jdt   2:15   and twelve thousand mounted a,
1 Mc   9:11   the a came on ahead of the army,
Jer   50:29   Call a out against Babylon, all who

ARCHIPPUS
Co-worker of Paul (Col 4:17; Phlm 2).

ARCHITE
2 Sm   16:16   David's friend Hushai the **A** came

ARCHITECT
Heb   11:10   whose a and maker is God.

ARCHIVES
Ezr   5:17   be made in the royal a of Babylon
1 Mc   14:23   copy of their words in the public a,

AREOPAGUS
Acts   17:19   him and led him to the **A** and said,
Acts   17:22   Paul stood up at the **A** and said:
Acts   17:34   a member of the Court of the **A**,

ARGUE → ARGUING, ARGUMENT, ARGUMENTS
Mk   8:11   forward and began to a with him,

ARGUING → ARGUE
Mk   9:14   them and scribes a with them.

ARGUMENT → ARGUE
Lk   9:46   An a arose among the disciples
1 Tm   2: 8   up holy hands, without anger or a.

ARGUMENTS → ARGUE
Acts   2:40   He testified with many other a,
2 Cor   10: 4   We destroy a
Col   2: 4   one may deceive you by specious a.

ARIEL
Is   29: 1   **A**, **A**, city where David encamped!

ARIMATHEA
Jn   19:38   Joseph of **A**, secretly a disciple

ARIOCH
Dn   2:15   He asked **A**, the officer of the king,

ARISE → RISE
Nm   10:35   Moses would say, "**A**, O LORD,
Sg   2:10   lover speaks and says to me, "**A**,
Dn   7:17   kings which shall a on the earth.
Dn   12: 1   "At that time there shall a Michael,
Mi   4:13   **A** and thresh, O daughter Zion;
Mt   24:11   Many false prophets will a

ARISEN → RISE
Dt   34:10   then no prophet has a in Israel like
Lk   9: 8   of the ancient prophets has a."

ARISES → RISE
1 Mc   14:41   until a trustworthy prophet a.

ARISTARCHUS
Companion of Paul (Acts 19:29; 20:4; 27:2; Col 4:10; Phlm 24).

ARK
Gn   6:14   Make yourself an a of gopherwood,
Gn   7: 1   Go into the a, you and all your
Gn   8:16   Go out of the a, together with your
Ex   25:10   You shall make an a of acacia
Ex   25:16   In the a you are to put the covenant
Ex   37: 1   Bezalel made the a of acacia wood,
Ex   40:20   the covenant and put it in the a;
Nm   3:31   Their responsibility was the a,
Nm   10:35   Whenever the a set out,
Dt   10: 5   the tablets in the a I had made.
Jos   3: 3   you see the a of the covenant
Jgs   20:27   LORD (for the a of the covenant
1 Sm   3: 3   of the LORD where the a of God
1 Sm   4:11   The a of God was captured,
1 Sm   5: 2   They then took the a of God
1 Sm   6: 3   intend to send back the a of the God
1 Sm   7: 2   From the day the a came to rest
2 Sm   6:17   brought in the a of the LORD
1 Kgs   8: 9   There was nothing in the a
1 Chr   13: 9   out his hand to steady the a,
2 Chr   35: 3   "Put the holy a in the house built
2 Mc   2: 4   and the a should accompany him,
Ps   132: 8   place, you and your mighty a.
Jer   3:16   say, "The a of the covenant
Lk   17:27   to the day that Noah entered the a,
Heb   9: 4   and the a of the covenant entirely
Heb   11: 7   with reverence built an a
1 Pt   3:20   Noah during the building of the a,
Rev   11:19   the a of his covenant could be seen

ARM → ARMED, ARMIES, ARMOR, ARMOR-BEARER, ARMS, ARMY
Ex   6: 6   redeem you by my outstretched a
Dt   4:34   with strong hand and outstretched a,
Dt   7:19   and outstretched a
1 Kgs   8:42   hand and your outstretched a),
2 Chr   32: 8   He has only an a of flesh, but we
Jb   40: 9   Have you an a like that of God,
Ps   10:15   Break the a of the wicked and depraved;
Ps   44: 4   your own a, the light of your face
Ps   89:14   You have a mighty a. Your hand is
Sg   8: 6   your heart, as a seal upon your a;
Is   40:10   GOD, who rules by his strong a;
Is   52:10   The LORD has bared his holy a

Is	53: 1	whom has the **a** of the Lord been
Jer	27: 5	power, with my outstretched **a**;
Zec	11:17	May the sword fall upon his **a**
Zec	11:17	His **a** will surely wither, and his
Lk	1:51	He has shown might with his **a**,
1 Pt	4: 1	**a** yourselves also with the same

ARMED → ARM

Lk	11:21	a strong man fully **a** guards his

ARMIES → ARM

1 Sm	17:36	because he has insulted the **a**
Ps	60:12	Do you no longer march with our **a**?
Lk	21:20	you see Jerusalem surrounded by **a**,
Rev	19:14	The **a** of heaven followed him,

ARMOR → ARM

1 Sm	31: 9	head and stripped him of his **a**;
1 Kgs	20:11	puts on a boast like one who takes it
1 Chr	10:10	They put his **a** in the temple of their
Wis	5:17	He shall take his zeal for **a** and arm
Rom	13:12	darkness [and] put on the **a** of light;
Eph	6:11	Put on the **a** of God so that you may
Eph	6:13	put on the **a** of God, that you may

ARMOR-BEARER → ARM, BEAR

1 Sm	31: 4	Saul said to his **a**, "Draw your
1 Sm	31: 4	But the **a**, badly frightened, refused,

ARMS → ARM

Gn	49:24	taut, and his **a** were nimble,
Jgs	15:14	ropes around his **a** became like flax
Jgs	16:12	the ropes off his **a** like thread.
2 Sm	22:35	my **a** to bend even a bow of bronze.
Ps	37:17	The **a** of the wicked will be broken,
Prv	31:17	she exerts her **a** with vigor.
Sg	5:14	His **a** are rods of gold adorned
Is	40:11	in his **a** he gathers the lambs,
Dn	2:32	its chest and **a** were silver, its belly
Dn	10: 6	his **a** and feet looked like burnished
Hos	11: 3	to walk, who took them in my **a**;

ARMY → ARM

Ex	14:17	glory through Pharaoh and all his **a**,
Ex	15: 4	and **a** he hurled into the sea;
2 Kgs	25:11	led into exile the last of the **a** remaining
Ps	27: 3	Though an **a** encamp against me,
Ps	33:16	A king is not saved by a great **a**,
Ez	38:15	a great company, a mighty **a**?
Jl	2:11	raises his voice at the head of his **a**;
Rev	19:19	riding the horse and against his **a**.

ARNON

Nm	21:13	for the **A** forms Moab's boundary,
Jos	12: 1	from the River **A** to Mount Hermon,
Jer	48:20	and cry out, Proclaim it at the **A**:

AROMA

2 Cor	2:15	For we are the **a** of Christ for God

AROUND

Jos	6: 4	seventh day march **a** the city seven
Ps	3: 4	But you, Lord, are a shield **a** me;
Ps	48:13	walk all **a** it, note the number of its
Prv	3: 3	bind them **a** your neck;
Is	11: 5	Justice shall be the band **a** his waist,
Ez	1:18	eyes filled the four rims all **a**.
Ez	10:12	with eyes all **a** like the four wheels.
Lk	2: 9	the glory of the Lord shone **a** them,
Jn	13: 4	took a towel and tied it **a** his waist.
1 Pt	5: 8	the devil is prowling **a** like a roaring
Rev	4: 3	**A** the throne was a halo as brilliant
Rev	7:11	All the angels stood **a** the throne and **a** the elders

ARPAD

Is	36:19	are the gods of Hamath and **A**?
Jer	49:23	Hamath and **A** are shamed, for they

ARPHAXAD

Jdt	1: 1	time **A** was ruling over the Medes

ARRAYED

Jb	6: 4	the terrors of God are **a** against me.

ARREST → ARRESTED

Mt	21:46	they were attempting to **a** him,
Mk	14: 1	scribes were seeking a way to **a** him
Acts	12: 3	Jews he proceeded to **a** Peter also.

ARRESTED → ARREST

Mt	14: 3	Now Herod had **a** John,
Mt	26:50	they laid hands on Jesus and **a** him.

ARROGANCE → ARROGANT, ARROGANTLY

1 Sm	2: 3	longer, Do not let **a** issue from your
1 Mc	1:24	much blood and spoke with great **a**.
Prv	8:13	Pride, **a**, the evil way,
Is	9: 8	those who say in **a** and pride

ARROGANT → ARROGANCE

2 Chr	32:25	generosity, for he had become **a**.
Ps	73: 3	of the **a** when I saw the prosperity
Ps	101: 5	eyes and **a** hearts I cannot endure.
Dn	7:11	the first of the **a** words
Ti	1: 7	be blameless, not **a**, not irritable,

ARROGANTLY → ARROGANCE

Dn	7: 8	eyes, and a mouth that spoke **a**.

ARROW → ARROWS

1 Sm	20:36	the boy ran, he shot an **a** past him.
2 Kgs	9:24	so that the **a** went through his heart
2 Kgs	13:17	"An **a** of victory for the Lord!
Ps	64: 8	God shoots an **a** at them; in a moment
Ps	91: 5	terror of the night nor the **a** that flies
Prv	25:18	A club, sword, or sharp **a**—
Is	49: 2	He made me a sharpened **a**, in his
Jer	9: 7	A murderous **a** is their tongue,

ARROWS → ARROW

Ex	19:13	be stoned to death or killed with **a**.
Dt	32:42	I will make my **a** drunk with blood,
1 Sm	20:20	the month I will shoot **a** to the side
2 Kgs	13:15	"Take bow and **a**," and he took
Jb	6: 4	For the **a** of the Almighty are in me,
Ps	38: 3	Your **a** have sunk deep in me;
Ps	127: 4	Like **a** in the hand of a warrior are
Prv	26:18	scattering firebrands and deadly **a**,
Eph	6:16	to quench all [the] flaming **a**

ART → ARTISAN, ARTISANS, ARTS

Acts	17:29	stone by human **a** and imagination.

ARTAXERXES → =AHASUERUS

1. King of Persia; allowed rebuilding of temple under Ezra (Ezr 4; 7), and of walls of Jerusalem under his cupbearer Nehemiah (Neh 2; 5:14; 13:6).
2. See Ahasuerus.

ARTEMIS

Acts	19:27	of the great goddess **A** will be of no

ARTISAN → ART

Jer	10: 9	The work of the **a** and the handiwork
Hos	8: 6	An **a** made it, it is no god at all.

ARTISANS → ART

Hos	13: 2	their skill, all of them the work of **a**.

ARTS → ART

Ex	7:11	did the same thing by their magic **a**.
Ex	8:14	to produce gnats by their magic **a**,

ASA

King of Judah (1 Kgs 15:8-24; 1 Chr 3:10; 2 Chr 14–16). Godly reformer (2 Chr 15); in later years defeated Israel with help of Aram, not the Lord (1 Kgs 15:16-22; 2 Chr 16).

ASAHEL

1. Nephew of David, one of his warriors (2 Sm 23:24; 1 Chr 2:16; 11:26; 27:7). Killed by Abner (2 Sm 2); avenged by Joab (2 Sm 3:22-39).

2. Levite; teacher (2 Chr 17:8).

ASAPH

1. Recorder to Hezekiah (2 Kgs 18:18, 37; Is 36:3, 22).

2. Levitical musician (1 Chr 6:24; 15:17-19; 16:4-7, 37), seer (2 Chr 29:30). Sons of (1 Chr 25; 2 Chr 5:12; 20:14; 29:13; 35:15; Ezr 2:41; 3:10; Neh 7:44; 11:17; 12:27-47). Psalms of (2 Chr 29:30; Ps 50; 73–83).

ASCEND → ASCENDED, ASCENDING, ASCENTS
Ps   139: 8 If I a to the heavens, you are there;
Is   14:14 I will a above the tops of the clouds;

ASCENDED → ASCEND
Jgs   13:20 angel of the LORD a in the flame
Jn   20:17 for I have not yet a to the Father.
Eph   4: 8 "He a on high and took prisoners

ASCENDING → ASCEND
Jn   1:51 the angels of God a and descending
Jn   6:62 of Man a to where he was before?

ASCENTS → ASCEND
   Songs of ascents (Ps 120–134).

ASH → ASHES
1 Sm   2: 8 from the a heap lifts up the poor,
Ps   113: 7 dust, lifts the poor from the a heap,

ASHAMED → SHAME
Ezr   9: 6 I am too a and humiliated to raise
Is   29:22 No longer shall Jacob be a,
Ez   43:10 of Israel so they are a for their sins.
Zec   13: 4 all prophets will be a of the visions
Mk   8:38 Whoever is a of me and of my
Mk   8:38 the Son of Man will be a
Rom   1:16 For I am not a of the gospel.
Rom   6:21 the things of which you are now a?
2 Tm   1: 8 So do not be a of your testimony
Heb   2:11 he is not a to call them "brothers,"
Heb   11:16 God is not a to be called their God,

ASHDOD
Jos   13: 3 lords of the Philistines in Gaza, A,
1 Sm   5: 1 transferred it from Ebenezer to A.

ASHER
   Son of Jacob by Zilpah (Gn 30:13; 35:26; 46:17; Ex 1:4; 1 Chr 2:2). Tribe of blessed (Gn 49:20; Dt 33:24-25), numbered (Nm 1:40-41; 26:44-47), allotted land (Jos 10:24-31; Ez 48:2), failed to fully possess (Jgs 1:31-32), failed to support Deborah (Jgs 5:17), supported Gideon (Jgs 6:35; 7:23) and David (1 Chr 12:37), 12,000 from (Rev 7:6).

ASHERAH → ASHERAHS, ASTARTE
Dt   16:21 not plant an a of any kind of wood
Jgs   6:25 As for the a beside it, cut it down
1 Kgs 16:33 and also made an a. Ahab did more
1 Kgs 18:19 four hundred prophets of A who eat
2 Chr 15:16 had made an obscene object for A;

ASHERAHS → ASHERAH
Dt   12: 3 burn up their a, and chop down the idols
Jgs   3: 7 and served the Baals and the A,
2 Kgs 17:10 They set up pillars and a for themselves

ASHES → ASH
Gn   18:27 Lord, though I am only dust and a!
1 Kgs 13: 5 the a from the altar were scattered,
Jdt   4:11 and sprinkled a on their heads,
Est   4: 1 put on sackcloth and a, and went
1 Mc   3:47 they sprinkled a on their heads
Jb   42: 6 have said, and repent in dust and a.
Ps   102:10 I eat a like bread, mingle my drink
Sir   17:32 while all mortals are dust and a.
Is   44:20 He is chasing a! A deluded mind
Is   61: 3 in Zion a diadem instead of a,
Jer   6:26 dress in sackcloth, roll in the a.
Dn   9: 3 with fasting, sackcloth, and a.
Dn   14:14 his servants to bring some a,
Jon   3: 6 himself with sackcloth, and sat in a.
Mt   11:21 have repented in sackcloth and a.

ASHIMA
2 Kgs 17:30 those from Hamath made A;

ASHKELON
Jgs   1:18 with its territory, A with its territory,
Zec   9: 5 A will see it and be afraid;
Zec   9: 5 from Gaza, A will not be inhabited,

ASIA
Acts   2: 9 and Cappadocia, Pontus and A,
Acts 16: 6 the message in the province of A.

Rom   16: 5 who was the firstfruits in A
1 Cor 16:19 churches of A send you greetings.
Rev   1: 4 John, to the seven churches in A:

ASIDE → SIDE
Ex   32: 8 They have quickly turned a
Dt   28:14 not turning a, either to the right

ASK → ASKED, ASKING, ASKS
Ex   3:13 and they a me, 'What is his name?'
Ex   12:26 When your children a you,
Dt   4:32 A now of the days of old,
Dt   32: 7 A your father, he will inform you,
Jos   4: 6 When your children a you,
Jgs   13:18 Why do you a my name?
Ps   2: 8 A it of me, and I will give you
Prv   30: 7 Two things I a of you, do not deny
Is   7:11 A for a sign from the LORD,
Is   65: 1 to respond to those who did not a,
Jer   6:16 roads, a the pathways of old,
Mt   6: 8 what you need before you a him.
Mt   7: 7 "A and it will be given to you;
Mk   6:23 "I will grant you whatever you a
Mk   11:24 tell you, all that you a for in prayer,
Lk   11:13 holy Spirit to those who a him?"
Jn   14:14 If you a anything of me in my
Jn   15: 7 a for whatever you want and it will
Jn   16:24 a and you will receive, so that your
1 Cor 14:35 they should a their husbands
Eph   3:20 accomplish far more than all we a
Jas   1: 5 he should a God who gives to all
Jas   4: 3 You a but do not receive,
Jas   4: 3 because you a wrongly, to spend it
1 Jn   3:22 receive from him whatever we a,
1 Jn   5:14 if we a anything according to his

ASKED → ASK
Ps   21: 5 He a life of you; you gave it to him,
Ps   106:15 So he gave them what they a
Jn   16:24 Until now you have not a anything
Jn   19:38 a Pilate if he could remove the body

ASKING → ASK
Mt   20:22 "You do not know what you are a.
Rom   10:20 to those who were not a for me."

ASKS → ASK
Lk   11:10 For everyone who a, receives;

ASLEEP → SLEEP
Ps   4: 9 In peace I will lie down and fall a,
Jon   1: 5 hold of the ship, and lay there fast a.
Mt   8:24 swamped by waves; but he was a.
Mt   28:13 and stole him while we were a.'
Mk   14:37 When he returned he found them a.
Mk   14:37 said to Peter, "Simon, are you a?
Jn   11:11 "Our friend Lazarus is a, but I am

ASS
Gn   16:12 He shall be a wild a of a man,
Jgs   15:15 upon the fresh jawbone of an a,
Hos   8: 9 a wild a off on its own—
Mt   21: 5 meek and riding on an a,

ASSEMBLE → ASSEMBLED, ASSEMBLY
Is   48:14 All of you a and listen:
Jl   2:16 A the elderly;
Zep   3: 8 to a kingdoms, In order to pour
Rev   16:14 of the whole world to a them

ASSEMBLED → ASSEMBLE
Nm   16:19 Korah had a all the community
Rev   16:16 then a the kings in the place that is

ASSEMBLY → ASSEMBLE
Ex   12:16 first day you will hold a sacred a,
2 Chr 29:28 The entire a bowed down,
Neh   8: 2 priest brought the law before the a,
Ps   22:23 my brethren; in the a I will praise you:
Ps   26: 5 I hate an evil a; with the wicked
Ps   149: 1 his praise in the a of the faithful.

Jl   1:14   Call an a! Gather the elders, all who
Jl   2:15   Proclaim a fast, call an a!
Lk   23: 1 Then the whole a of them arose
Heb   12:23   and the a of the firstborn enrolled
Jas   2: 2   in fine clothes comes into your a,

ASSHUR
Gn   10:22   Elam, **A**, Arpachshad,

ASSIGN → ASSIGNED
Nm   4:19   go in and a to each of them his task
Ez   47:23   lives, there you shall a his heritage—

ASSIGNED → ASSIGN
1 Cor   3: 5   just as the Lord a each one.
1 Cor   7:17   should live as the Lord has a, just as

ASSIST → ASSISTANCE
1 Tm   5:16   widowed relatives, she must a them;

ASSISTANCE → ASSIST
1 Cor   12:28   gifts of healing, a, administration,

ASSOCIATE → ASSOCIATED
Sir   37:12   Instead, a with a religious person,
Zec   13: 7   against the one who is my a—
Acts   10:28   for a Jewish man to a with, or visit,
Rom   12:16   not be haughty but a with the lowly;
1 Cor   5: 9   in my letter not to a with immoral
1 Cor   5:11   to you not to a with anyone named

ASSOCIATED → ASSOCIATE
Eph   5: 7   So do not be a with them.

ASSURED
Col   2: 2   richness of fully a understanding,
Col   4:12   and fully a in all the will of God.

ASSYRIA → ASSYRIAN, ASSYRIANS
2 Kgs   15:29   deporting the inhabitants to **A**.
2 Kgs   18:11   deported the Israelites to **A** and
2 Kgs   19:10   be handed over to the king of **A**.'
Is   10: 5   **A**, the rod of my wrath, the staff I
Is   36: 1   king of **A**, went up against all
Is   37:37   the king of **A**, broke camp, departed,
Jer   50:18   as I once punished the king of **A**;
Hos   14: 4   **A** will not save us, nor will we
Na   3:18   O king of **A**, your nobles have gone
Zec   10:10   of Egypt, and gather them from **A**.

ASSYRIAN → ASSYRIA
Jdt   2:14   and officers of the **A** forces.

ASSYRIANS → ASSYRIA
Jdt   15: 6   swept down on the camp of the **A**,
Sir   48:21   God struck the camp of the **A**
Ez   23: 5   and lusted after her lovers, the **A**:

ASTARTE → ASHERAH, ASTARTES
1 Sm   31:10   put his armor in the temple of **A**
1 Kgs   11: 5   Solomon followed **A**, the goddess

ASTARTES → ASTARTE
Jgs   2:13   the Lord and served Baal and the **A**,
1 Sm   7: 4   the Israelites removed their Baals and **A**,
1 Sm   12:10   the Lord and served the Baals and **A**.

ASTONISHED
Lk   2:48   they were a, and his mother said

ASTOUNDED
Lk   24:22   from our group, however, have a us:
Acts   10:45   who had accompanied Peter were a

ASTRAY → STRAY
Nm   5:12   If a man's wife goes a and becomes
Dt   30:17   but are led a and bow down to other
Ps   14: 3   All have gone a; all alike are
Ps   58: 4   from the womb, they have gone a.
Ps   119:67   Before I was afflicted I went a,
Prv   10:17   whoever disregards reproof goes a.
Sir   31: 5   pursues money will be led a by it.
Is   53: 6   We had all gone a like sheep,
Jer   23:13   by Baal and led my people Israel a.
Am   2: 4   ancestors followed have led them a,
Mt   18:12   sheep and one of them goes a,

1 Pt   2:25   For you had gone a like sheep,
2 Pt   2:15   they have gone a,

ASUNDER
Ps   107:14   of death and broke their chains a.
Is   24:19   The earth will burst a, the earth will

ASYLUM
Nm   35:11   cities to serve as cities of a,

ATE → EAT
Gn   3: 6   she took some of its fruit and a it;
Gn   3: 6   who was with her, and he a it.
Gn   3:13   "The snake tricked me, so I a it."
Gn   27:25   Jacob served it to him, and Isaac a;
Ex   16:35   The Israelites a the manna for forty
Ex   16:35   they a the manna until they came
Nm   25: 2   and the people a of the sacrifices
Ru   2:14   some roasted grain and she a her fill
2 Sm   9:11   so Meribbaal a at David's table like
2 Kgs   6:29   So we boiled my son and a him.
Ps   78:25   Man a the bread of the angels;
Ez   3: 3   I a it, and it was as sweet as honey
Dn   14:27   and when the dragon a them,
Mt   14:20   They all a and were satisfied,
Mt   15:37   They all a and were satisfied.
Mk   6:42   They all a and were satisfied.
Lk   9:17   They all a and were satisfied.
Jn   6:58   Unlike your ancestors who a
1 Cor   10: 3   All a the same spiritual food,

ATHALIAH
    Granddaughter of Omri; wife of Jehoram and mother of Ahaziah;
encouraged their evil ways (2 Kgs 8:18, 27; 2 Chr 22:2). At death of
Ahaziah she made herself queen, killing all his sons but Joash (2 Kgs
11:1-3; 2 Chr 22:10-12); killed six years later when Joash revealed
(2 Kgs 11:4-16; 2 Chr 23:1-15).

ATHENS
Acts   17:16   Paul was waiting for them in **A**,

ATHLETE
1 Cor   9:25   Every a exercises discipline
2 Tm   2: 5   an a cannot receive the winner's

ATONE → ATONEMENT, ATONES
Sir   3: 3   Those who honor their father a for sins;

ATONEMENT → ATONE
Ex   29:36   as a purification offering, to make a.
Ex   32:30   be able to make a for your sin."
Lv   4:31   Thus the priest shall make a,
Lv   5: 6   Thus the priest shall make a
Lv   5:18   make a on the offerer's behalf
Lv   5:26   The priest shall make a
Lv   23:28   because it is the Day of **A**, when a is made
Nm   8:21   made a for them to cleanse them.
1 Chr   6:34   of holies and of making a for Israel,
Neh   10:34   sin offerings to make a for Israel,
Sir   35: 5   and to avoid injustice is a.

ATONES → ATONEMENT
Sir   3:30   so almsgiving a for sins;

ATTACK → ATTACKED, ATTACKING, ATTACKS
1 Sm   15: 3   now, a Amalek, and put under
1 Sm   24: 8   would not permit them to a Saul.

ATTACKED → ATTACK
1 Mc   2:38   and soldiers a them on the sabbath,

ATTACKING → ATTACK
Ps   109: 3   surround me, a me without cause.

ATTACKS → ATTACK
1 Mc   2:41   us fight against anyone who a us
Lk   11:22   when one stronger than he a

ATTAIN → ATTAINED
Phil   3:11   if somehow I may a the resurrection

ATTAINED → ATTAIN
Phil   3:16   with regard to what we have a,

ATTEMPTED
Heb   11:29   when the Egyptians a it they were

ATTEND → ATTENTION
Prv   22:17   and let your mind a to my teaching;

ATTENDANT
Lk   4:20   he handed it back to the a and sat

ATTENTION → ATTEND, ATTENTIVE
Lam   2:20   "Look, O Lord, and pay a:
1 Tm   4: 1   faith by paying a to deceitful spirits
Ti   1:14   instead of paying a to Jewish myths
3 Jn   1:10   I will draw a to what he is doing,

ATTENTIVE → ATTENTION
2 Chr   6:40   your ears be a to the prayer of this
Neh   1:11   may your ears be a to the prayer
Ps   130: 2   May your ears be a to my cry
Prv   4:20   to my words be a, to my sayings
2 Pt   1:19   You will do well to be a to it,

ATTIRE
Jdt   10: 3   the festive a she had worn while her
Est   D: 1   arrayed herself in her splendid a.

AUGUSTUS
Lk   2: 1   from Caesar A that the whole world

AUTHOR
Acts   3:15   The a of life you put to death,

AUTHORITIES → AUTHORITY
Lk   12:11   synagogues and before rulers and a,
Jn   7:26   Could the a have realized that he is
Jn   12:42   even among the a, believed in him,
Acts   16:19   the public square before the local a.
Rom   13: 1   be subordinate to the higher a,
Rom   13: 6   for the a are ministers of God,
Eph   3:10   principalities and a in the heavens.
Ti   3: 1   the control of magistrates and a,
1 Pt   3:22   with angels, a, and powers subject

AUTHORITY → AUTHORITIES
Mt   7:29   for he taught them as one having a,
Mt   9: 6   the Son of Man has a on earth
Mk   1:27   A new teaching with a.
Mk   11:28   what a are you doing these things?
Mk   11:28   who gave you this a to do them?"
Lk   4:32   teaching because he spoke with a.
Lk   5:24   the Son of Man has a on earth
Lk   7: 8   For I too am a person subject to a,
Acts   1: 7   Father has established by his own a.
Rom   13: 1   for there is no a except from God,
Rom   13: 2   whoever resists a opposes what God
1 Cor   7: 4   wife does not have a over her own
1 Cor   7: 4   does not have a over his own body,
1 Cor   11:10   a woman should have a sign of a
1 Cor   15:24   sovereignty and every a and power.
2 Cor   10: 8   boast a little too much of our a,
Eph   1:21   far above every principality, a,
1 Tm   2:12   to teach or to have a over a man.
Ti   2:15   Exhort and correct with all a.
Rev   2:26   end, I will give a over the nations.
Rev   12:10   our God and the a of his Anointed.
Rev   13: 4   the dragon because it gave its a

AUTUMN
Jude   1:12   fruitless trees in late a, twice dead

AVENGE → VENGEANCE
Nm   31: 2   A the Israelites on the Midianites,
Dt   32:43   For he will a the blood of his servants,
Jgs   16:28   I may a myself on the Philistines
2 Kgs   9: 7   thus will I a the blood of my
1 Mc   2:67   observe the law, and a your people.
Jl   4:21   I will a their blood, and I will not
Rev   6:10   a our blood on the inhabitants

AVENGED → VENGEANCE
Gn   4:24   If Cain is a seven times,
Rev   19: 2   He has a on her the blood of his

AVENGER → VENGEANCE
Nm   35:12   of asylum from the a of blood,
Jos   20: 3   flee for asylum from the a of blood.
Ps   8: 3   your foes, to silence enemy and a.
1 Thes   4: 6   the Lord is an a in all these things,

AVENGING → VENGEANCE
1 Sm   25:26   and from a yourself by your own hand.
Na   1: 2   A jealous and a God is the Lord,

AVERTED
Jdt   13:20   and you a our disaster,

AVOID → AVOIDED
1 Tm   6:20   A profane babbling
2 Tm   2:16   A profane, idle talk, for such people
Ti   3: 9   A foolish arguments, genealogies,

AVOIDED → AVOID
Prv   16: 6   and by the fear of the Lord evil is a.
Is   53: 3   He was spurned and a by men,

AWAKE → AWAKEN, AWAKENED, AWOKE
Jgs   5:12   A, a, Deborah! A, a,
Ps   44:24   A! Why do you sleep, O Lord?
Ps   57: 9   A, my soul; a, lyre and harp!
Is   51: 9   A, a, put on strength,
Is   52: 1   A, a! Put on your strength, Zion;
Dn   12: 2   sleep in the dust of the earth shall a;
Zec   13: 7   A, O sword, against my shepherd,
Mt   24:42   Therefore, stay a! For you do not
Eph   5:14   "A, O sleeper, and arise
1 Thes   5:10   so that whether we are a or asleep

AWAKEN → AWAKE
Jn   11:11   is asleep, but I am going to a him."

AWAKENED → AWAKE
1 Kgs   18:27   he is asleep and must be a."
Sg   8: 5   Beneath the apple tree I a you;

AWARE
Mk   5:30   a at once that power had gone

AWAY
Nm   22:33   she turned a from me these three
Jb   1:21   gave and the Lord has taken a;
Prv   3: 7   the Lord and turn a from evil;
Eccl   3: 6   a time to keep, and a time to cast a.
Jon   1: 3   flee to Tarshish, a from the Lord.
Zep   1: 2   I will completely sweep a all things
Zep   3:15   you, he has turned a your enemies;
Hg   1: 9   what you brought home, I blew a.
Mt   4:10   Jesus said to him, "Get a, Satan!
Mk   13:31   Heaven and earth will pass a, but my words will not pass a.
Lk   8:13   for a time and fall a in time of trial.
Lk   24: 2   They found the stone rolled a
Jn   1:29   who takes a the sin of the world.
Jn   14:28   'I am going a and I will come back
1 Cor   7:31   in its present form is passing a.
2 Cor   5:17   the old things have passed a;
Heb   2: 1   so that we may not be carried a.
Heb   6: 6   and then have fallen a, to bring
2 Pt   3:10   then the heavens will pass a
1 Jn   2: 8   for the darkness is passing a,
1 Jn   2:17   and its enticement are passing a.
Rev   7:17   and God will wipe a every tear
Rev   21: 1   and the former earth had passed a,

AWE → AWESOME
1 Kgs   3:28   had given, they were in a of him,
Is   29:23   Jacob, be in a of the God of Israel.
Mal   2: 5   for me, standing in a of my name.
Mt   9: 8   saw this they were struck with a
Lk   5:26   and, struck with a, they said,
Acts   2:43   A came upon everyone, and many
Rom   11:20   not become haughty, but stand in a.
Heb   12:28   pleasing to God in reverence and a.

AWESOME → AWE
Gn   28:17   "How a this place is!
Dt   7:21   in your midst, is a great and a God.

Dt	10:17	mighty and **a**, who has no favorites,
Dt	28:58	and to fear this glorious and **a** name,
Neh	1: 5	great and **a** God, you preserve your
Neh	9:32	and **a** God, who preserves
Jb	37:22	surrounding God's **a** majesty!
Ps	65: 6	You answer us with **a** deeds
Ps	66: 3	Say to God: "How **a** your deeds!
Ps	66: 5	**a** in deeds before the children
Ps	68:36	**A** is God in his holy place, the God
Ps	89: 8	more **a** than all those around him!
Ps	99: 3	them praise your great and **a** name:
Is	64: 2	While you worked **a** deeds we could
Dn	9: 4	great and **a** God, you who keep your

AWL

Ex	21: 6	he shall pierce his ear with an **a**,
Dt	15:17	you shall take an **a** and put it

AWOKE → AWAKE

1 Kgs	3:15	Solomon **a**; it was a dream!
Ps	78:65	Then the Lord **a** as from sleep,
Mt	1:24	When Joseph **a**, he did as the angel

AX

Is	10:15	Will the **a** boast against the one who hews
Mt	3:10	now the **a** lies at the root of the trees.

AZARIAH → =ABEDNEGO, =UZZIAH
1. King of Judah; see Uzziah (2 Kgs 15:1-7).
2. Prophet (2 Chr 15:1-8).
3. Opponent of Jeremiah (Jer 43:2).
4. Jewish exile; see Abednego (Dn 1:6-19).

AZAZEL

Lv	16: 8	is for the Lord and which for **A**.

AZEKAH

Jos	10:10	slope, attacking them as far as **A**

B

BAAL → BAALS

Nm	25: 3	attached itself to the **B** of Peor,
Dt	4: 3	midst everyone who followed the **B**
Jgs	2:13	and served **B** and the Astartes,
1 Kgs	16:32	set up an altar to **B** in the house of **B**
1 Kgs	18:25	Elijah then said to the prophets of **B**,
1 Kgs	19:18	every knee that has not bent to **B**,
2 Kgs	3: 2	the pillar of **B** that his father had
2 Kgs	10:28	Thus Jehu destroyed **B** in Israel.
2 Chr	23:17	the people went to the temple of **B**
Ps	106:28	joined in the rites of **B** of Peor,
Jer	2: 8	The prophets prophesied by **B**,
Jer	19: 5	children in fire as offerings to **B**—
Hos	2:18	shall never again call me "My **b**."
Hos	13: 1	but he became guilty through **B**
Rom	11: 4	men who have not knelt to **B**."

BAALS → BAAL

Jgs	3: 7	and served the **B** and the Asherahs,
Jgs	8:33	themselves by following the **B**,
Jgs	10:10	our God and served the **B**."
1 Sm	7: 4	So the Israelites removed their **B**
2 Chr	17: 3	his father, and did not seek the **B**.
2 Chr	34: 4	the altars of the **B** were torn down;
Hos	2:19	from her mouth the names of the **B**;

BAALZEBUB

2 Kgs	1: 2	"Go and inquire of **B**, the god

BAASHA
King of Israel (1 Kgs 15:16–16:7; 2 Chr 16:1-6).

BABBLER → BABBLERS

Prv	20:19	so have nothing to do with a **b**!

BABBLERS → BABBLER

Is	44:25	I bring to nought the omens of **b**,

BABEL → BABYLON

Gn	11: 9	That is why it was called **B**,

BABES

Ps	8: 3	with the mouths of **b** and infants.

BABYLON → BABEL, BABYLONIANS

2 Kgs	24:15	He deported Jehoiachin to **B**,
2 Kgs	24:15	he led captive from Jerusalem to **B**.
1 Chr	9: 1	Judah had been exiled to **B** because
2 Chr	36:18	princes, all these he brought to **B**.
2 Chr	36:20	the sword he carried captive to **B**,
Ezr	7: 6	this Ezra came up from **B**. He was
Ps	137: 1	the rivers of **B** there we sat weeping
Ps	137: 8	Desolate Daughter **B**, you shall be
Is	13: 1	An oracle concerning **B**; a vision
Is	14: 4	taunt-song against the king of **B**:
Is	21: 9	out and says, 'Fallen, fallen is **B**!
Is	47: 1	sit in the dust, virgin daughter **B**;
Jer	25:11	nations shall serve the king of **B**;
Jer	50: 1	word the Lord spoke against **B**,
Jer	51:37	**B** shall become a heap of ruins,
Jer	52:11	and the King of **B** brought him to **B**
Bar	2:24	or serve the king of **B**, and you
Bar	6: 1	to those led captive to **B** by the king
Dn	2:48	ruler of the whole province of **B**
Dn	2:48	prefect over all the wise men of **B**.
Dn	14:36	he set him down in **B** above the den.
1 Pt	5:13	chosen one at **B** sends you greeting,
Rev	14: 8	"Fallen, fallen is **B** the great,
Rev	17: 5	which is a mystery, "**B** the great,
Rev	18: 2	"Fallen, fallen is **B** the great.

BABYLONIANS → BABYLON

Dn	14: 3	The **B** had an idol called Bel,

BACCHIDES

1 Mc	7: 8	So the king chose **B**,
1 Mc	9:11	the army of **B** moved out of camp

BACK → BACKS

Gn	8:11	the evening the dove came **b** to him,
Gn	19:26	But Lot's wife looked **b**, and she
Nm	10:36	"Bring **b**, O Lord, the myriads of Israel's
Ru	1:11	replied, "Go **b**, my daughters.
2 Sm	12:23	Can I bring him **b** again? I shall go
Ps	114: 5	Jordan, that you turned **b**?
Ps	137: 8	one who pays you **b** what you have
Is	38: 8	So the sun came **b** the ten steps it
Is	38:17	Behind your **b** you cast all my sins.
Is	49: 5	That Jacob may be brought **b** to him
Jer	29:14	bring you **b** to the place
Mt	28: 2	approached, rolled **b** the stone,
Heb	10:39	are not among those who draw **b**

BACKS → BACK

Neh	9:26	they cast your law behind their **b**.
Prv	19:29	and blows for the **b** of fools.

BAD → WORSE

Gn	37: 2	Joseph brought their father **b** reports
Prv	20:14	"**B**, **b**!" says the buyer, then goes
Jer	24: 2	other basket contained very **b** figs, so **b** they could not be eaten.
Mt	7:17	fruit, and a rotten tree bears **b** fruit.
1 Cor	15:33	"**B** company corrupts good

BAG → BAGGAGE, BAGS

1 Sm	17:49	David put his hand into the **b**
Prv	16:33	Into the **b** the lot is cast,
Ez	12: 7	During the day I brought out my **b**, an exile's **b**.
Hg	1: 6	the hired worker labors for a **b** full
Lk	10: 4	Carry no money **b**, no sack,

BAGGAGE → BAG

1 Sm	10:22	He is hiding among the **b**.

BAGS → BAG

Mi	6:11	crooked scales, **b** of false weights?

BAKE → BAKED, BAKER

Ex	16:23	Whatever you want to **b**, **b**;

BAKED → BAKE

Ex	12:39	out of Egypt they **b** into unleavened
Lv	2: 4	you offer a grain offering **b**

BAKER → BAKE

Gn	40: 1	cupbearer and **b** offended their lord,

BALAAM
Prophet who attempted to curse Israel (Nm 22–24; Dt 23:5-6; 2 Pt 2:15; Jude 11; Rev 2:14). Killed in Israel's vengeance on Midianites (Nm 31:8; Jos 13:22).

BALAK
Moabite king who hired Balaam to curse Israel (Nm 22–24; Jos 24:9; Mi 6:5).

BALANCE → BALANCES
Prv	16:11	**B** and scales belong to the LORD;
Sir	6:15	price, no amount can **b** their worth.
Is	40:12	in scales and the hills in a **b**?

BALANCES → BALANCE
Sir	28:25	gold, so make **b** and scales for your

BALDY
2 Kgs	2:23	jeered at him: "Go away, **b**; go away, **b**!"

BALL
Is	22:18	toss you like a **b** into a broad land.

BALM
Jer	8:22	Is there no **b** in Gilead, no healer
Jer	46:11	procure **b**, Virgin daughter Egypt!

BAND → BANDS
1 Sm	10: 5	city, you will meet a **b** of prophets

BANDAGE → BANDAGED
1 Kgs	20:38	himself with a **b** over his eyes.

BANDAGED → BANDAGE
Lk	10:34	wine over his wounds and **b** them.

BANDITS
Hos	7: 1	Thieves break in, **b** roam outside.

BANDS → BAND
Hos	11: 4	with human cords, with **b** of love;

BANK → BANKS
Gn	41:17	I was standing on the **b** of the Nile,
Ex	2: 3	the reeds on the **b** of the Nile.
Ex	7:15	yourself by the **b** of the Nile,
2 Kgs	2:13	and stood at the **b** of the Jordan.
Ez	47:12	Along each **b** of the river every kind
Mt	25:27	have put my money in the **b** so
Mk	5:13	two thousand rushed down a steep **b**

BANKS → BANK
Jos	3:15	overflows all its **b** during the entire
1 Chr	12:16	when it was overflowing both its **b**,

BANNERS
Ps	20: 6	raise the **b** in the name of our God.

BANQUET → BANQUETS
Jdt	12:10	the fourth day Holofernes gave a **b**
Est	5: 5	to the **b** Esther had prepared.
Est	6:14	off to the **b** Esther had prepared.
Sg	2: 4	He brought me to the **b** hall and his
Lk	5:29	Levi gave a great **b** for him in his
Lk	14:13	when you hold a **b**, invite the poor,

BANQUETS → BANQUET
Mk	12:39	and places of honor at **b**.

BAPTISM → BAPTIZE
Mt	3: 7	and Sadducees coming to his **b**,
Mt	21:25	Where was John's **b** from?
Mk	1: 4	in the desert proclaiming a **b**
Mk	10:38	be baptized with the **b** with which I
Mk	10:39	and with the **b** with which I am
Mk	11:30	Was John's **b** of heavenly
Lk	3: 3	proclaiming a **b** of repentance
Lk	7:29	were baptized with the **b** of John,
Lk	12:50	There is a **b** with which I must be
Lk	20: 4	was John's **b** of heavenly
Acts	1:22	from the **b** of John until the day
Acts	10:37	after the **b** that John preached,
Acts	13:24	by proclaiming a **b** of repentance
Acts	18:25	although he knew only the **b**
Acts	19: 3	They replied, "With the **b** of John."
Acts	19: 4	baptized with a **b** of repentance,

Rom	6: 4	with him through **b** into death,
Eph	4: 5	one Lord, one faith, one **b**;
Col	2:12	You were buried with him in **b**,
1 Pt	3:21	This prefigured **b**, which saves you

BAPTISMS → BAPTIZE
Heb	6: 2	instruction about **b** and laying

BAPTIST → BAPTIZE
Mt	3: 1	In those days John the **B** appeared,
Mt	11:11	been none greater than John the **B**;
Mt	14: 8	on a platter the head of John the **B**."
Mt	16:14	"Some say John the **B**,

BAPTIZE → BAPTISM, BAPTISMS, BAPTIST, BAPTIZED, BAPTIZING
Mt	3:11	He will **b** you with the holy Spirit
Mk	1: 8	he will **b** you with the holy Spirit."
Lk	3:16	He will **b** you with the holy Spirit
Jn	1:26	answered them, "I **b** with water;
Jn	1:33	the one who sent me to **b** with water
Jn	1:33	he is the one who will **b**
1 Cor	1:17	For Christ did not send me to **b**

BAPTIZED → BAPTIZE
Mt	3: 6	were being **b** by him in the Jordan
Mt	3:13	to John at the Jordan to be **b** by him.
Mt	3:14	"I need to be **b** by you, and yet you
Mt	3:16	After Jesus was **b**, he came
Mk	1: 5	were being **b** by him in the Jordan
Mk	1: 8	I have **b** you with water;
Mk	1: 9	and was **b** in the Jordan by John.
Mk	10:38	be **b** with the baptism with which I am **b**?"
Mk	10:39	with the baptism with which I am **b**, you will be **b**;
Mk	16:16	believes and is **b** will be saved;
Lk	3: 7	who came out to be **b** by him,
Lk	3:12	Even tax collectors came to be **b**
Lk	3:21	After all the people had been **b**
Lk	3:21	also had been **b** and was praying,
Lk	7:29	and who were **b** with the baptism
Lk	7:30	of the law, who were not **b** by him,
Lk	12:50	is a baptism with which I must be **b**,
Jn	3:23	there, and people came to be **b**,
Acts	1: 5	for John **b** with water, but in a few days you will be **b** with
Acts	2:38	"Repent and be **b**, every one
Acts	2:41	who accepted his message were **b**,
Acts	8:12	men and women alike were **b**.
Acts	8:13	after being **b**, became devoted
Acts	8:16	they had only been **b** in the name
Acts	8:36	What is to prevent my being **b**?"
Acts	8:38	down into the water, and he **b** him.
Acts	9:18	He got up and was **b**,
Acts	10:48	He ordered them to be **b** in the name
Acts	11:16	'John **b** with water but you will be **b** with
Acts	16:15	she and her household had been **b**,
Acts	16:33	he and all his family were **b** at once.
Acts	18: 8	who heard believed and were **b**.
Acts	19: 3	He said, "How were you **b**?"
Acts	19: 4	then said, "John **b** with a baptism
Acts	19: 5	they were **b** in the name of the Lord
Acts	22:16	and have yourself **b** and your sins
Rom	6: 3	we who were **b** into Christ Jesus were **b** into his death?
1 Cor	1:13	Or were you **b** in the name of Paul?
1 Cor	1:14	[to God] that I **b** none of you except
1 Cor	1:15	no one can say you were **b** in my
1 Cor	1:16	(I **b** the household of Stephanas
1 Cor	1:16	not know whether I **b** anyone else.)
1 Cor	10: 2	all of them were **b** into Moses
1 Cor	12:13	in one Spirit we were all **b** into one
1 Cor	15:29	having themselves **b** for the dead?
Gal	3:27	of you who were **b** into Christ have

BAPTIZING → BAPTIZE
Mt	28:19	**b** them in the name of the Father,
Jn	1:28	the Jordan, where John was **b**.
Jn	1:31	the reason why I came **b** with water
Jn	3:23	was also **b** in Aenon near Salim,
Jn	3:26	here he is **b** and everyone is coming
Jn	4: 1	and **b** more disciples than John

Acts   10:47 the water for **b** these people,

BAR → BARS
Jgs   16: 3 and tore them loose, **b** and all.
Neh   7: 3 they shall shut and **b** the doors.

BAR-JESUS → =ELYMAS
Acts   13: 6 met a magician named **B** who was

BARABBAS
Prisoner released by Pilate instead of Jesus (Mt 27:16-26; Mk 15:7-15; Lk 23:18-19; Jn 18:40).

BARAK
Judge who fought with Deborah against Canaanites (Jgs 4–5; 1 Sm 12:11; Heb 11:32).

BARBARIAN
2 Mc   2:21 land, put to flight the **b** hordes,
Col   3:11 circumcision and uncircumcision, **b**,

BARBS
Nm   33:55 remain will become **b** in your eyes

BARE → BARED, BAREFOOT
Ps   18:16 the world's foundations lay **b**,

BARED → BARE
Is   52:10 The LORD has **b** his holy arm
Ez   4: 7 **b** arm you shall prophesy against it.

BAREFOOT → BARE, FOOT
Is   20: 3 naked and **b** for three years as a sign
Mi   1: 8 lament and wail, go **b** and naked;

BARGAINED
Hos   8: 9 on its own—Ephraim **b** for lovers.

BARLEY
Ex   9:31 Now the flax and the **b** were ruined,
Ru   1:22 at the beginning of the **b** harvest.
2 Kgs   7: 1 and two seahs of **b** for a shekel,
Jdt   8: 2 had died at the time of the **b** harvest.
Jn   6: 9 is a boy here who has five **b** loaves
Rev   6: 6 three rations of **b** cost a day's pay.

BARN → BARNS
Mt   13:30 gather the wheat into my **b**." ' "
Lk   12:24 they have neither storehouse nor **b**,

BARNABAS → =JOSEPH
Disciple, originally Joseph (Acts 4:36), prophet (Acts 13:1), apostle (Acts 14:14). Brought Paul to apostles (Acts 9:27), Antioch (Acts 11:22-29; Gal 2:1-13), on the first missionary journey (Acts 13–14). Together at Jerusalem Council, they separated over John Mark (Acts 15). Later co-workers (1 Cor 9:6; Col 4:10).

BARNS → BARN
Dt   28: 8 upon you, on your **b** and on all your
Ps   144:13 May our **b** be full with every kind
Prv   3:10 will your **b** be filled with plenty,
Mt   6:26 they gather nothing into **b**, yet your
Lk   12:18 I shall tear down my **b** and build

BARREN
Gn   11:30 Sarai was **b**; she had no child.
Gn   29:31 her fruitful, while Rachel was **b**.
Ex   23:26 no woman in your land will be **b**
Jgs   13: 2 His wife was **b** and had borne no
1 Sm   2: 5 The **b** wife bears seven sons,
Prv   30:16 Sheol, a **b** womb, land that never
Is   49:21 me these, when I was bereft and **b**?
Is   54: 1 you **b** one who never bore a child,
Lk   1: 7 because Elizabeth was **b** and both
Lk   23:29 'Blessed are the **b**, the wombs

BARS → BAR
Ex   26:26 Also make **b** of acacia wood;
Nm   3:36 of the tabernacle, its **b**, columns,
Ps   147:13 he has strengthened the **b** of your
Lam   2: 9 he smashed her **b** to bits.

BARSABBAS → =JOSEPH, =JUDAS, =JUSTUS
Acts   1:23 two, Joseph called **B**, who was
Acts   15:22 Judas, who was called **B**, and Silas,

BARTHOLOMEW → =NATHANAEL?
Apostle (Mt 10:3; Mk 3:18; Lk 6:14; Acts 1:13). Possibly also called Nathanael (Jn 1:45-49; 21:2).

BARTIMAEUS
Blind man healed by Jesus (Mk 10:46-52).

BARUCH
Jeremiah's secretary (Jer 32:12-16; 36; 43:1-6; 45:1-2). Book of Baruch ascribed to him (Bar 1:1, 3, 8).

BARZILLAI
1. Gileadite who aided David during Absalom's revolt (2 Sm 17:27; 19:31-39).
2. Son-in-law of 1. (Ezr 2:61; Neh 7:63).

BASE → BASED
Ex   29:12 shall pour out at the **b** of the altar.
2 Kgs 18:19 what do you **b** this trust of yours?

BASED → BASE
Phil   3: 9 of my own **b** on the law

BASHAN
Nm   21:33 Og, king of **B**, advanced against them
Jos   13:30 all of **B**, the entire kingdom of Og, king of **B**,
Jos   22: 7 Moses had assigned land in **B**;
Ps   22:13 fierce bulls of **B** encircle me.
Am   4: 1 you cows of **B**, who live
Mi   7:14 Let them feed in **B** and Gilead,
Zec   11: 2 oaks of **B**, for the dense forest is cut

BASIC
Heb   5:12 teach you again the **b** elements
Heb   6: 1 let us leave behind the **b** teaching

BASIN → BASINS
Jn   13: 5 he poured water into a **b** and began

BASINS → BASIN
1 Kgs   7:38 He made ten bronze **b**, each four

BASKET → BASKETS
Ex   2: 3 she took a papyrus **b**, daubed it
Jer   24: 2 One **b** contained excellent figs,
Jer   24: 2 the other **b** contained very bad figs,
Am   8: 1 a **b** of end-of-summer fruit.
Mt   5:15 and then put it under a bushel **b**;
Acts   9:25 in the wall, lowering him in a **b**.
2 Cor 11:33 lowered in a **b** through a window

BASKETS → BASKET
Mk   6:43 up twelve wicker **b** full of fragments
Mk   8: 8 up the fragments left over—seven **b**.
Mk   8:19 how many wicker **b** full

BATCH
Rom   11:16 are holy, so is the whole **b** of dough;
1 Cor   5: 7 you may become a fresh **b** of dough,
Gal   5: 9 A little yeast leavens the whole **b**

BATHE → BATHED, BATHING
Ex   2: 5 Pharaoh's daughter came down to **b**
Ps   58:11 and **b** their feet in the blood
Dn   13:15 only, wanting to **b** in the garden,
Lk   7:38 began to **b** his feet with her tears.

BATHED → BATHE
Sg   5: 3 I have **b** my feet, am I then to soil
Ez   16: 9 Then I **b** you with water,
Jn   13:10 "Whoever has **b** has no need except

BATHING → BATHE
2 Sm   11: 2 From the roof he saw a woman **b**;
Jdt   12: 8 After **b**, she prayed to the Lord,

BATHSHEBA
Wife of Uriah who committed adultery with and became wife of David (2 Sm 11; Ps 51), mother of Solomon (2 Sm 12:24; 1 Kgs 1–2; 1 Chr 3:5).

BATTLE → BATTLES
Ex   13:18 of the land of Egypt arrayed for **b**.
Jos   4:13 equipped for **b**, crossed over before
1 Sm   17:47 For the **b** belongs to the LORD,
1 Sm   31: 3 the fury of the **b** converged on Saul.

2 Sm   1:25   have fallen in the thick of **b**!
1 Kgs 22:30   will disguise myself and go into **b**,
2 Chr 20:15   for the **b** is not yours but God's.
Eccl   9:11   the swift, nor the **b** by the valiant,
Jer   4:19   heard the blast of the horn, the **b** cry.
1 Cor   14: 8   sound, who will get ready for **b**?
Rev   16:14   them for the **b** on the great day
Rev   20: 8   and Magog, to gather them for **b**;

BATTLES → BATTLE
1 Sm   8:20   lead us in warfare, and fight our **b**."
1 Sm   18:17   and fight the **b** of the LORD."
1 Sm   25:28   because my lord fights the **b**
2 Chr   32: 8   God, to help us and to fight our **b**."

BEAM
Ezr   6:11   a **b** is to be taken from his house,

BEAR → ARMOR-BEARER, BEARING, BEARS, BIRTH, BIRTHDAY,
   BIRTHRIGHT, BORE, BORN, BORNE, CHILDBEARING, CUPBEARER,
   FIRSTBORN, NEWBORN, REBIRTH, STILLBORN
Gn   4:13   "My punishment is too great to **b**.
Gn   17:19   your wife Sarah is to **b** you a son,
Ex   28:12   Thus Aaron shall **b** their names
Jgs   13: 3   you will conceive and **b** a son.
1 Sm   17:36   has killed both a lion and a **b**.
Jb   9: 9   He made the **B** and Orion,
Is   7:14   pregnant and about to **b** a son,
Is   11: 7   The cow and the **b** shall graze,
Is   53:11   the many, their iniquity he shall **b**.
Ez   47:12   Every month they will **b** fresh fruit
Dn   7: 5   The second beast was like a **b**;
Am   5:19   fled from a lion and a **b** met him;
Mt   1:23   shall be with child and **b** a son,
Mt   7:18   A good tree cannot **b** bad fruit,
Mt   7:18   nor can a rotten tree **b** good fruit.
Lk   1:13   wife Elizabeth will **b** you a son,
Jn   15: 2   branch in me that does not **b** fruit,
Jn   15: 8   that you **b** much fruit and become
Jn   15:16   to go and **b** fruit that will remain,
Acts   15:10   nor we have been able to **b**?
Rom   7: 4   order that we might **b** fruit for God.
1 Cor   15:49   **b** the image of the heavenly one.
Gal   6: 2   **B** one another's burdens, and so you

BEARD → BEARDS
Ezr   9: 3   plucked hair from my head and **b**,
Is   50: 6   cheeks to those who tore out my **b**;
Jer   48:37   been shaved bald, every **b** cut off;

BEARDS → BEARD
2 Sm   10: 4   shaved off half their **b**, cut away

BEARING → BEAR
Is   53: 2   He had no majestic **b** to catch our eye,
Eph   4: 2   **b** with one another through love,
Col   1: 6   as in the whole world it is **b** fruit
Col   1:10   in every good work **b** fruit
Col   3:13   **b** with one another and forgiving

BEARS → BEAR
Gn   1:11   every kind of plant that **b** seed
1 Cor   13: 7   It **b** all things, believes all things,

BEAST → BEASTS
Is   35: 9   there, nor any **b** of prey approach,
Dn   7: 6   this I looked and saw another **b**,
Dn   7: 6   To this **b** dominion was given.
Rev   11: 7   the **b** that comes up from the abyss
Rev   13: 1   I saw a **b** come out of the sea
Rev   13: 2   The **b** I saw was like a leopard,
Rev   13:11   I saw another **b** come
Rev   13:18   can calculate the number of the **b**,
Rev   16: 2   on those who had the mark of the **b**
Rev   17: 3   on a scarlet **b** that was covered
Rev   19:20   The **b** was caught and with it
Rev   19:20   who had accepted the mark of the **b**
Rev   20: 4   who had not worshiped the **b** or its

BEASTS → BEAST
Dn   7: 3   which emerged four immense **b**,
Mk   1:13   He was among wild **b**,

BEAT → BEATEN, BEATING, BEATINGS
Prv   23:35   they **b** me, but I did not feel it.
Is   2: 4   They shall **b** their swords
Jl   4:10   **B** your plowshares into swords,
Mi   4: 3   They shall **b** their swords
Lk   10:30   They stripped and **b** him and went
Acts   22:19   and **b** those who believed in you.

BEATEN → BEAT
Ex   5:16   Look how your servants are **b**!
Acts   16:22   and ordered them to be **b** with rods.
2 Cor   11:25   Three times I was **b** with rods,
1 Pt   2:20   if you are patient when **b** for doing

BEATING → BEAT
Lk   22:63   custody were ridiculing and **b** him.

BEATINGS → BEAT
2 Cor   6: 5   **b**, imprisonments, riots, labors,

BEAUTIFUL → BEAUTY
Gn   12:11   "I know that you are a **b** woman.
Gn   12:14   saw that the woman was very **b**.
Gn   29:17   eyes, but Rachel was shapely and **b**.
Jos   7:21   I saw a **b** Babylonian mantle,
2 Sm   11: 2   a woman bathing; she was very **b**.
2 Sm   13: 1   son Absalom had a **b** sister named
2 Sm   14:27   named Tamar, who was a **b** woman.
1 Kgs   1: 3   for a **b** girl throughout the territory
1 Kgs   1: 4   The girl was very **b** indeed, and she
Tb   6:12   girl is wise, courageous, and very **b**;
Jdt   10: 4   Thus she made herself very **b**,
Jdt   10:14   appeared marvelously **b** to them,
Jdt   11:21   of the earth to the other looks so **b**
Est   2: 2   "Let **b** young virgins be sought
Est   2: 3   realm to gather all **b** young virgins
Jb   42:15   women were as **b** as the daughters
Prv   11:22   swine's snout is a **b** woman without
Sg   1:15   How **b** you are, my friend, how **b**!
Sg   1:16   How **b** you are, my lover—
Sg   4: 1   How **b** you are, my friend, how **b**
Sg   6: 4   **B** as Tirzah are you, my friend;
Is   52: 7   How **b** upon the mountains are
Jer   3:19   land, the most **b** heritage among
Ez   16:13   were very, very **b**, fit for royalty.
Ez   31: 9   I made it **b** with abundant foliage,
Dn   13: 2   who married a very **b**
Dn   13:31   Susanna, very delicate and **b**,
Hos   10:11   I myself laid a yoke upon her **b** neck;
Mt   23:27   which appear **b** on the outside,
Acts   3: 2   temple called "the **B** Gate" every
Acts   3:10   to sit begging at the **B** Gate
Acts   7:20   was born, and he was extremely **b**.
Rom   10:15   "How **b** are the feet of those who
Heb   11:23   they saw that he was a **b** child,

BEAUTY → BEAUTIFUL
2 Sm   14:25   praised for his **b** than Absalom,
Jdt   10: 7   were very much astounded at her **b**
Jdt   10:19   They marveled at her **b**,
Jdt   10:23   all marveled at the **b** of her face.
Jdt   16: 6   the **b** of her face brought him down.
Jdt   16: 9   his eyes, her **b** captivated his mind,
Est   1:11   that he might display her **b**
Est   D: 5   She glowed with perfect **b** and her
1 Mc   1:26   and the **b** of the women faded.
1 Mc   2:12   laid waste, our **b**, our glory.
Ps   27: 4   To gaze on the LORD's **b**, to visit
Ps   45:12   that the king might desire your **b**.
Ps   50: 2   the perfection of **b**, God shines
Prv   6:25   Do not lust in your heart after her **b**,
Prv   31:30   Charm is deceptive and **b** fleeting;
Wis   8: 2   bride and was enamored of her **b**.
Wis   13: 3   in their **b** they thought them gods,
Wis   13: 3   original source of **b** fashioned them.
Wis   13: 5   the **b** of created things their original
Sir   9: 8   do not gaze upon **b** that is not yours;
Sir   26:16   the **b** of a good wife in her
Sir   36:27   A woman's **b** makes her husband's face

Sir	40:22	Grace and **b** delight the eye,
Sir	43: 9	The **b** of the heavens and the glory
Is	3:24	Then, instead of **b**, shame.
Is	28: 1	Fading blooms of his glorious **b**,
Is	28: 4	blooms of his glorious **b** at the head
Ez	16:14	among the nations for your **b**,
Ez	16:15	you trusted in your own **b** and used
Ez	16:25	so that you could degrade your **b**
Ez	27: 3	you said, "I am a ship, perfect in **b**;
Ez	27: 4	your builders perfected your **b**.
Ez	27:11	walls, they made your **b** perfect.
Ez	28:12	full of wisdom, perfect in **b**.
Ez	28:17	grown haughty because of your **b**;
Ez	31: 8	the garden of God could match its **b**.
Ez	32:19	Whom do you excel in **b**? Go down!
Dn	13:32	so as to sate themselves with her **b**.
Dn	13:56	said to him, "**b** has seduced you,
Jas	9:17	the **b** of its appearance vanishes.
1 Pt	3: 4	in the imperishable **b** of a gentle

BECAME → BECOME

Gn	2: 7	of life, and the man **b** a living being.
Ex	15:25	it into the water, the water **b** fresh.
Dt	26: 5	But there he **b** a nation great,
2 Kgs	17:15	followed emptiness and **b** empty;
1 Chr	11: 9	David **b** ever more powerful,
Dn	2:35	struck the statue **b** a great mountain
Hos	9:10	they **b** as abhorrent as the thing they
Mt	17: 2	sun and his clothes **b** white as light.
Lk	6:16	and Judas Iscariot, who **b** a traitor.
Jn	1:14	And the Word **b** flesh and made his
1 Cor	9:20	To the Jews I **b** like a Jew to win
1 Cor	9:20	under the law I **b** like one under
2 Cor	8: 9	for your sake he **b** poor although he
Heb	5: 9	he **b** the source of eternal salvation

BECOME → BECAME

Gn	2:24	and the two of them **b** one body.
Gn	9:15	the waters will never again **b** a flood
Ps	118:22	rejected has **b** the cornerstone.
Mt	19: 5	wife, and the two shall **b** one flesh'?
Mk	12:10	rejected has **b** the cornerstone;
Lk	4: 3	command this stone to **b** bread."
Jn	1:12	him he gave power to **b** children
Acts	4:11	which has **b** the cornerstone.'
1 Cor	9:22	I have **b** all things to all, to save
Eph	5:31	and the two shall **b** one flesh."
Heb	2:17	he had to **b** like his brothers in every
Heb	7:22	**b** the guarantee of an [even] better
1 Pt	2: 7	rejected has **b** the cornerstone,"

BED → BEDS, SICKBED

Gn	47:31	Israel bowed at the head of the **b**.
Gn	48: 2	rallied his strength and sat up in **b**.
1 Kgs	1:47	And the king in his **b** did homage.
Jdt	13: 4	Judith stood by Holofernes' **b**
Ps	36: 5	On his **b** he hatches plots;
Ps	63: 7	I think of you upon my **b**,
Sg	3: 1	my **b** at night I sought him whom
Is	28:20	For the **b** shall be too short
Dn	7: 1	as Daniel lay in **b** he had a dream,
Mt	8:14	saw his mother-in-law lying in **b**
Lk	11: 7	my children and I are already in **b**.
Lk	17:34	there will be two people in one **b**;
Acts	9:34	Get up and make your **b**."
Heb	13: 4	the marriage **b** be kept undefiled,

BEDS → BED

Ps	4: 5	your hearts, wail upon your **b**,
Prv	26:14	its hinges and sluggards, on their **b**.

BEE → BEES

Sir	11: 3	The **b** is least among winged
Is	7:18	and for the **b** in the land of Assyria.

BEER-LAHAI-ROI

Gn	16:14	That is why the well is called **B**.

BEER-SHEBA

Gn	21:31	This is why the place is called **B**;

Gn	26:33	the name of the city is **B** to this day.
1 Sm	3:20	Israel from Dan to **B** came to know
2 Sm	24:15	Dan to **B** seventy thousand
1 Kgs	5: 5	vine and fig tree from Dan to **B**,

BEES → BEE

Dt	1:44	and put you to flight the way **b** do,
Jgs	14: 8	there was a swarm of **b** in the lion's
Ps	118:12	They surrounded me like **b**;

BEFALL → BEFALLS

Dt	31:29	so that evil will **b** you in time
Ps	91:10	No evil shall **b** you, no affliction
Am	3: 6	Does disaster **b** a city unless the LORD

BEFALLS → BEFALL

Eccl	2:14	Yet I knew that the same lot **b** both.

BEFORE

Gn	18:22	remained standing **b** the LORD.
Gn	27: 4	eat, so that I may bless you **b** I die."
Ex	4:21	that you perform **b** Pharaoh all
Ex	23:15	shall appear **b** me empty-handed.
Ex	33: 2	Jebusites, I will send an angel **b** you
Nm	17:22	deposited the staffs **b** the LORD
Dt	1:30	who goes **b** you, is the one who will
Dt	7:22	remove these nations **b** you little
Dt	11:26	I set **b** you this day a blessing
Dt	30:15	I have today set **b** you life and good,
1 Sm	4: 7	This has never happened **b**.
Jb	26: 6	Naked **b** him is Sheol, and Abaddon
Ps	16: 8	I keep the LORD always **b** me;
Ps	37: 7	Be still **b** the LORD; wait for him.
Ps	97: 5	melt like wax **b** the LORD,
Ps	97: 7	all gods bow down **b** him.
Ps	139: 4	Even **b** a word is on my tongue,
Prv	8:23	was formed, at the first, **b** the earth.
Prv	16:18	Pride goes **b** disaster, and a haughty spirit **b** a fall.
Prv	18:12	**B** disaster the heart is haughty,
Prv	18:13	Whoever answers **b** listening,
Sir	1: 4	**B** all other things wisdom was
Sir	18:19	**B** you speak, learn; **b** you get sick,
Is	43:10	**B** me no god was formed,
Is	48: 5	**b** they took place I informed you,
Is	49:16	your walls are ever **b** me.
Is	53: 7	or a sheep silent **b** shearers, he did
Is	65:24	**B** they call, I will answer;
Jer	1: 5	**B** I formed you in the womb I knew
Jer	1: 5	**b** you were born I dedicated you,
Mal	3: 1	he will prepare the way **b** me;
Mal	3:23	**B** the day of the LORD comes,
Mt	5:16	your light must shine **b** others,
Mt	6: 8	what you need **b** you ask him.
Mt	7: 6	or throw your pearls **b** swine,
Mt	11:10	he will prepare your way **b** you.'
Mt	24:38	In [those] days **b** the flood,
Lk	12: 8	who acknowledges me **b** others
Lk	12: 8	Man will acknowledge **b** the angels
Lk	22:61	to him, "**B** the cock crows today,
Jn	1:15	of me because he existed **b** me.' "
Jn	8:58	I say to you, **b** Abraham came to be,
Jn	10: 8	All who came [**b** me] are thieves
Jn	13:19	on I am telling you **b** it happens,
Jn	17: 5	I had with you **b** the world began.
Acts	2:25	'I saw the Lord ever **b** me, with him
Acts	8:32	and as a lamb **b** its shearer is silent,
Rom	14:10	shall all stand **b** the judgment seat
Col	1:17	He is **b** all things, and in him all
Ti	1: 2	does not lie, promised **b** time began,
Heb	12: 2	that lay **b** him he endured the cross,
1 Pt	1:20	He was known **b** the foundation
Rev	7: 9	They stood **b** the throne and **b** the Lamb,

BEG → BEGGAR, BEGGED, BEGGING

Lk	16: 3	to dig and I am ashamed to **b**.
Jn	9: 8	this the one who used to sit and **b**?"

BEGAN → BEGIN

Gn	4:26	time people **b** to invoke the LORD
Lk	3:23	When Jesus **b** his ministry he was

Lk   14:30   'This one **b** to build but did not have

BEGGAR → BEG
Sir   40:28   My son, do not live the life of a **b**;
Jn   9: 8   had seen him earlier as a **b** said,

BEGGED → BEG
Mk   6:56   **b** him that they might touch only

BEGGING → BEG
Ps   37:25   or his offspring **b** for bread.

BEGIN → BEGAN, BEGINNING, BEGUN
1 Pt   4:17   time for the judgment to **b**

BEGINNING → BEGIN
Gn   1: 1   In the **b**, when God created
Ps   111:10   of the Lord is the **b** of wisdom;
Prv   1: 7   the Lord is the **b** of knowledge;
Prv   4: 7   The **b** of wisdom is: get wisdom;
Prv   9:10   The **b** of wisdom is fear
Eccl   3:11   they cannot find out, from **b** to end,
Eccl   7: 8   is the end of a thing than its **b**;
Is   40:21   Was it not told you from the **b**?
Is   46:10   At the **b** I declare the outcome;
Mt   19: 8   wives, but from the **b** it was not so.
Mt   24: 8   All these are the **b** of the labor
Mt   24:21   such as has not been since the **b**
Mk   1: 1   The **b** of the gospel of Jesus Christ
Lk   1: 2   who were eyewitnesses from the **b**
Jn   1: 1   In the **b** was the Word,
Jn   8:44   He was a murderer from the **b**
Jn   15:27   you have been with me from the **b**.
Acts   1:22   **b** from the baptism of John until
Col   1:18   He is the **b**, the firstborn
Heb   7: 3   without **b** of days or end of life,
1 Jn   1: 1   What was from the **b**, what we have
1 Jn   3: 8   the devil has sinned from the **b**.
2 Jn   1: 6   as you heard from the **b**,
Rev   21: 6   and the Omega, the **b** and the end.
Rev   22:13   and the last, the **b** and the end."

BEGOT → BEGOTTEN
Dt   32: 6   Is he not your father who **b** you,

BEGOTTEN → BEGOT
Ps   2: 7   are my son; today I have **b** you.
Acts   13:33   are my son; this day I have **b** you.'
Heb   1: 5   are my son; this day I have **b** you"?
Heb   5: 5   are my son; this day I have **b** you";

BEGUILE
Jdt   16: 8   and put on a linen robe to **b** him.

BEGUN → BEGIN
Dt   3:24   you have **b** to show to your servant

BEHALF
Jer   7:16   not raise a cry or prayer in their **b**!
Jn   5:32   is another who testifies on my **b**,
Jn   5:32   testimony he gives on my **b** is true.
Jn   8:14   "Even if I do testify on my own **b**,
Heb   6:20   has entered on our **b** as forerunner,

BEHAVE → BEHAVING, BEHAVIOR
1 Tm   3:15   you should know how to **b**

BEHAVING → BEHAVE
1 Cor   7:36   thinks he is **b** improperly toward his

BEHAVIOR → BEHAVE
Ti   2: 3   should be reverent in their **b**,

BEHEADED → HEAD
Lk   9: 9   But Herod said, "John I **b**.
Rev   20: 4   of those who had been **b** for their

BEHEMOTH
Jb   40:15   Look at **B**, whom I made along

BEHIND
Ps   50:17   you cast my words **b** you!
Ps   139: 5   **B** and before you encircle me
Is   38:17   **B** your back you cast all my sins.
Ez   3:12   I heard **b** me a loud rumbling noise
Mt   16:23   turned and said to Peter, "Get **b** me,

Lk   2:43   the boy Jesus remained **b**
Lk   8:44   came up **b** him and touched
Phil   3:13   forgetting what lies **b** but straining
Heb   6: 1   let us leave **b** the basic teaching
Rev   1:10   and heard **b** me a voice as loud as

BEHOLD
Nm   23: 9   I see him, from the heights I **b** him.
Jb   19:27   own eyes, not another's, will **b** him:

BEING → BEINGS
Gn   2: 7   life, and the man became a living **b**.
Dt   6: 5   your whole heart, and with your whole **b**,
Dt   10:12   your whole heart and with your whole **b**,
Dt   30: 6   with your whole heart and your whole **b**,
2 Kgs   23:25   he did, with his whole heart, his whole **b**,
1 Cor   15:45   became a living **b**," the last Adam
Heb   1: 3   the very imprint of his **b**, and who

BEINGS → BEING
Mt   9: 8   given such authority to human **b**.

BEL
     Babylonian deity (Is 46:1; Jer 50:2; 51:44; Bar 6:40; Dan 14:3-28).

BELIAR
2 Cor   6:15   What accord has Christ with **B**?

BELIEF → BELIEVE
2 Mc   15:11   kind of waking vision, worthy of **b**.
2 Thes   2:13   by the Spirit and **b** in truth.

BELIEVE → BELIEF, BELIEVED, BELIEVER, BELIEVERS, BELIEVES, BELIEVING
Gn   45:26   unmoved, for he did not **b** them.
Ex   4: 1   "suppose they do not **b** me or listen
Ex   4: 5   is so they will **b** that the Lord,
Ex   4: 8   If they do not **b** you or pay attention
Ex   4: 9   if they do not **b** even these two signs
1 Kgs   10: 7   "I did not **b** the report until I came
2 Chr   9: 6   "I did not **b** the report until I came
2 Chr   32:15   Do not **b** him! Since no other god
Tb   2:14   Yet I would not **b** her and told her
Tb   10: 7   mother do not **b** they will ever see
Tb   14: 4   **b** that whatever God has said will be
Jb   9:16   I could not **b** that he would listen
Ps   27:13   I **b** I shall see the Lord's
Ps   78:32   they did not **b** in his wonders.
Prv   14:15   The naive **b** everything, but the shrewd
Is   43:10   I have chosen To know and **b** in me
Jer   12: 6   Do not **b** them, even when they
Lam   4:12   The kings of the earth did not **b**,
Mt   9:28   "Do you **b** that I can do this?"
Mt   18: 6   one of these little ones who **b** in me
Mt   21:25   us, 'Then why did you not **b** him?'
Mt   21:32   of righteousness, you did not **b** him;
Mt   21:32   later change your minds and **b** him.
Mt   24:23   or, 'There he is!' do not **b** it.
Mt   24:26   is in the inner rooms,' do not **b** it.
Mt   27:42   the cross now, and we will **b** in him.
Mk   1:15   Repent, and **b** in the gospel."
Mk   9:24   out, "I do **b**, help my unbelief!"
Mk   9:42   of these little ones who **b** [in me]
Mk   11:24   **b** that you will receive it and it shall
Mk   11:31   '[Then] why did you not **b** him?'
Mk   13:21   Look, there he is!' do not **b** it.
Mk   15:32   the cross that we may see and **b**."
Mk   16:11   been seen by her, they did not **b**.
Mk   16:13   but they did not **b** them either.
Mk   16:16   whoever does not **b** will be
Mk   16:17   signs will accompany those who **b**:
Lk   1:20   because you did not **b** my words,
Lk   8:12   their hearts that they may not **b**
Lk   8:13   they **b** only for a time and fall away
Lk   20: 5   will say, 'Why did you not **b** him?'
Lk   22:67   them, "If I tell you, you will not **b**,
Lk   24:11   nonsense and they did not **b** them.
Lk   24:25   of heart to **b** all that the prophets
Jn   1: 7   so that all might **b** through him.
Jn   1:50   "Do you **b** because I told you that I

Jn	3:12	earthly things and you do not **b**, how will you **b** if I tell you
Jn	3:18	but whoever does not **b** has already
Jn	4:21	Jesus said to her, "**B** me, woman,
Jn	4:42	"We no longer **b** because of your
Jn	4:48	signs and wonders, you will not **b**."
Jn	5:38	because you do not **b** in the one
Jn	5:44	How can you **b**, when you accept
Jn	5:47	But if you do not **b** his writings,
Jn	5:47	how will you **b** my words?"
Jn	6:29	God, that you **b** in the one he sent."
Jn	6:30	do, that we may see and **b** in you?
Jn	6:36	you have seen [me], you do not **b**.
Jn	6:64	are some of you who do not **b**."
Jn	6:64	beginning the ones who would not **b**
Jn	6:69	We have come to **b** and are
Jn	7: 5	For his brothers did not **b** in him.
Jn	8:24	For if you do not **b** that I AM,
Jn	8:45	I speak the truth, you do not **b** me.
Jn	8:46	the truth, why do you not **b** me?
Jn	9:18	Now the Jews did not **b** that he had
Jn	9:35	"Do you **b** in the Son of Man?"
Jn	9:36	is he, sir, that I may **b** in him?"
Jn	9:38	He said, "I do **b**, Lord," and he
Jn	10:25	them, "I told you and you do not **b**.
Jn	10:26	But you do not **b**, because you are
Jn	10:37	my Father's works, do not **b** me;
Jn	10:38	them, even if you do not **b** me,
Jn	11:15	that I was not there, that you may **b**.
Jn	11:26	me will never die. Do you **b** this?"
Jn	11:27	I have come to **b** that you are
Jn	11:42	that they may **b** that you sent me."
Jn	11:48	leave him alone, all will **b** in him,
Jn	12:36	you have the light, **b** in the light,
Jn	12:37	their presence they did not **b** in him,
Jn	12:39	For this reason they could not **b**,
Jn	13:19	it happens you may **b** that I AM.
Jn	14:10	Do you not **b** that I am in the Father
Jn	14:11	**B** me that I am in the Father
Jn	14:11	**b** because of the works themselves.
Jn	14:29	so that when it happens you may **b**.
Jn	16: 9	sin, because they do not **b** in me;
Jn	16:30	Because of this we **b** that you came
Jn	16:31	answered them, "Do you **b** now?
Jn	17:20	those who will **b** in me through their
Jn	17:21	the world may **b** that you sent me.
Jn	19:35	so that you also may [come to] **b**.
Jn	20:25	my hand into his side, I will not **b**."
Jn	20:27	and do not be unbelieving, but **b**."
Jn	20:29	to **b** because you have seen me?
Jn	20:31	you may [come to] **b** that Jesus is
Acts	13:41	you will never **b** even if someone
Acts	15:11	we **b** that we are saved through
Acts	16:31	"**B** in the Lord Jesus and you
Acts	19: 4	telling the people to **b** in the one
Acts	26:27	Agrippa, do you **b** the prophets? I know you **b**."
Acts	28:24	he had said, while others did not **b**.
Rom	3:22	faith in Jesus Christ for all who **b**.
Rom	4:11	of all the uncircumcised who **b**,
Rom	4:24	who **b** in the one who raised Jesus
Rom	6: 8	we **b** that we shall also live
Rom	10: 9	**b** in your heart that God raised him
Rom	10:14	how can they **b** in him of whom
1 Cor	11:18	among you, and to a degree I **b** it;
2 Cor	4:13	we too **b** and therefore speak,
Gal	3:22	might be given to those who **b**.
Eph	1:19	greatness of his power for us who **b**,
1 Thes	4:14	For if we **b** that Jesus died and rose,
2 Thes	2:11	power so that they may **b** the lie,
1 Tm	1:16	those who would come to **b** in him
1 Tm	4: 3	with thanksgiving by those who **b**
1 Tm	4:10	of all, especially of those who **b**.
Heb	11: 6	anyone who approaches God must **b**
Jas	2:19	You **b** that God is one. You do well.
Jas	2:19	Even the demons **b** that and tremble.
1 Pt	1: 8	you do not see him now yet **b**

1 Jn	3:23	we should **b** in the name of his Son,
1 Jn	4:16	and to **b** in the love God has for us.
1 Jn	5:10	Whoever does not **b** God has made
1 Jn	5:13	you who **b** in the name of the Son
Jude	1: 5	later destroyed those who did not **b**.

BELIEVED → BELIEVE

Ex	4:31	The people **b**, and when they heard
Ex	14:31	They **b** in the LORD and in Moses
Jdt	14:10	of Israel had done, **b** firmly in God.
Ps	106:12	Then they **b** his words and sang his
Dn	13:41	The assembly **b** them, since they
Jon	3: 5	the people of Nineveh **b** God;
Mk	16:14	they had not **b** those who saw him
Lk	1:45	Blessed are you who **b** that what
Jn	3:18	because he has not **b** in the name
Jn	4:50	The man **b** what Jesus said to him
Jn	5:46	For if you had **b** Moses, you would have **b** me,
Jn	7:48	or the Pharisees **b** in him?
Jn	8:31	said to those Jews who **b** in him,
Jn	12:38	"Lord, who has **b** our preaching,
Jn	12:42	among the authorities, **b** in him,
Jn	17: 8	and they have **b** that you sent me.
Jn	20: 8	at the tomb first, and he saw and **b**.
Jn	20:29	who have not seen and have **b**."
Acts	2:44	All who **b** were together and had all
Acts	8:13	Even Simon himself **b** and,
Acts	22:19	and beat those who **b** in you.
Rom	4: 3	"Abraham **b** God, and it was
Rom	4:17	in whom he **b**, who gives life
Rom	4:18	He **b**, hoping against hope, that he
Rom	10:14	on him in whom they have not **b**?
Rom	10:16	who has **b** what was heard
2 Cor	4:13	is written, "I **b**, therefore I spoke,"
Gal	3: 6	Thus Abraham "**b** God, and it was
Eph	1:13	and have **b** in him, were sealed
2 Thes	1:10	on that day among all who have **b**, for our testimony to you was **b**.
2 Thes	2:12	that all who have not **b** the truth
1 Tm	3:16	Gentiles, **b** in throughout the world,
2 Tm	3:14	to what you have learned and **b**,
Heb	4: 3	For we who **b** enter into [that] rest,
Jas	2:23	that says, "Abraham **b** God, and it

BELIEVER → BELIEVE

Acts	16: 1	of a Jewish woman who was a **b**,
2 Cor	6:15	Or what has a **b** in common

BELIEVERS → BELIEVE

Acts	5:14	Yet more than ever, **b** in the Lord,
Acts	10:45	The circumcised **b** who had
Acts	11: 2	the circumcised **b** confronted him,
Acts	15: 5	Pharisees who had become **b** stood
Acts	17:34	some did join him, and became **b**.
Acts	19: 2	holy Spirit when you became **b**?"
Acts	19:18	who had become **b** came forward
Acts	21:20	how many thousands of **b** there are
1 Thes	1: 7	a model for all the **b** in Macedonia
1 Thes	2:10	we behaved toward you **b**.
1 Tm	6: 2	whose masters are **b** must not take

BELIEVES → BELIEVE

Sir	34: 2	wind, so anyone who **b** in dreams.
Mk	11:23	but **b** that what he says will happen,
Mk	16:16	Whoever **b** and is baptized will be
Jn	3:15	everyone who **b** in him may have
Jn	3:16	everyone who **b** in him might not
Jn	3:36	Whoever **b** in the Son has eternal
Jn	5:24	**b** in the one who sent me has eternal
Jn	6:35	whoever **b** in me will never thirst.
Jn	6:40	and **b** in him may have eternal life,
Jn	6:47	to you, whoever **b** has eternal life.
Jn	7:38	Whoever **b** in me, as scripture says:
Jn	11:25	whoever **b** in me, even if he dies,
Jn	11:26	lives and **b** in me will never die.
Jn	12:44	"Whoever **b** in me **b** not only in me
Jn	12:46	everyone who **b** in me might not
Jn	14:12	whoever **b** in me will do the works
Acts	10:43	everyone who **b** in him will receive

Rom 9:33 whoever **b** in him shall not be put
Rom 10:10 For one **b** with the heart and so is
Rom 10:11 "No one who **b** in him will be put
Rom 14: 2 One person **b** that one may eat
1 Cor 13: 7 It bears all things, **b** all things,
1 Pt 2: 6 whoever **b** in it shall not be put
1 Jn 5: 1 Everyone who **b** that Jesus is
1 Jn 5: 5 the one who **b** that Jesus is the Son

BELIEVING → BELIEVE
Jn 12:11 away and **b** in Jesus because of him.
Rom 15:13 fill you with all joy and peace in **b**,
1 Jn 5:10 not **b** the testimony God has given

BELL → BELLS
Ex 28:34 a gold **b**, a pomegranate, a gold **b**,

BELLS → BELL
Zec 14:20 will be written on the horses' **b**.

BELLY
Gn 3:14 On your **b** you shall crawl, and dust
Lv 11:42 Whether it crawls on its **b**,
Jgs 3:21 thigh, and thrust it into Eglon's **b**.
Prv 13:25 but the **b** of the wicked suffers want.
Jon 2: 1 in the **b** of the fish three days
Jon 2: 2 his God, from the **b** of the fish:
Mt 12:40 was in the **b** of the whale three days

BELONG → BELONGED, BELONGS
Dt 10:14 highest heavens, **b** to the LORD,
Ps 47:10 the shields of the earth **b** to God,
Jn 10:16 sheep that do not **b** to this fold.
Jn 15:19 because you do not **b** to the world,
Jn 17:14 because they do not **b** to the world
Jn 17:14 the world any more than I **b**
Rom 1: 6 who are called to **b** to Jesus Christ;
Rom 7: 4 so that you might **b** to another,
Rom 8: 9 Spirit of Christ does not **b** to him.
1 Cor 1:12 of you is saying, "I **b** to Paul,"
1 Cor 1:12 "I **b** to Cephas," or "I **b** to Christ."
1 Cor 12:15 "Because I am not a hand I do not **b**
1 Cor 12:15 it does not for this reason **b** any less
1 Cor 15:23 his coming, those who **b** to Christ;
Gal 3:29 And if you **b** to Christ, then you are

BELONGED → BELONG
Jn 15:19 If you **b** to the world, the world
Acts 9: 2 men or women who **b** to the Way,

BELONGS → BELONG
Ps 22:29 For kingship **b** to the LORD,
Ps 62:12 I have heard: Strength **b** to God;
Mt 19:14 of heaven **b** to such as these."
Jn 18:37 Everyone who **b** to the truth listens
2 Cor 10: 7 consider that as he **b** to Christ, so do
Col 2:17 the reality **b** to Christ.

BELOVED → LOVE
Dt 33:12 The **b** of the LORD, he abides
2 Sm 1:23 Saul and Jonathan, **b** and dear,
Neh 13:26 and though he was **b** of his God
Tb 3:10 'You had only one **b** daughter,
Ps 127: 2 all this God gives to his **b** in sleep.
Sir 46:13 B of his people, dear to his Maker,
Jer 11:15 What right has my **b** in my house,
Jer 12: 7 The **b** of my soul I have delivered
Dn 3:35 your **b**, Isaac your servant,
Dn 9:23 to announce, because you are **b**.
Dn 10:11 "Daniel, **b**," he said to me,
Dn 10:19 "Do not fear, **b**. Peace!
Mt 3:17 "This is my **b** Son, with whom I am
Mt 12:18 chosen, my **b** in whom I delight;
Mt 17: 5 "This is my **b** Son, with whom I am
Mk 1:11 the heavens, "You are my **b** Son;
Mk 9: 7 came a voice, "This is my **b** Son.
Mk 12: 6 He had one other to send, a **b** son.
Lk 3:22 from heaven, "You are my **b** Son;
Lk 20:13 I shall send my **b** son;
Acts 15:25 to you along with our **b** Barnabas
Rom 1: 7 to all the **b** of God in Rome,

Rom 9:25 her who was not **b** I will call 'b.'
Rom 11:28 they are **b** because of the patriarchs.
Rom 12:19 **B**, do not look for revenge but leave
Rom 16: 5 Greet my **b** Epaenetus, who was
Rom 16: 8 Greet Ampliatus, my **b** in the Lord.
Rom 16: 9 in Christ, and my **b** Stachys.
Rom 16:12 Greet the **b** Persis, who has worked
1 Cor 4:14 to admonish you as my **b** children.
1 Cor 4:17 who is my **b** and faithful son
1 Cor 15:58 Therefore, my **b** brothers, be firm,
2 Cor 7: 1 Since we have these promises, **b**,
2 Cor 12:19 and all for building you up, **b**.
Eph 1: 6 his grace that he granted us in the **b**.
Eph 5: 1 be imitators of God, as **b** children,
Phil 2:12 my **b**, obedient as you have always
Phil 4: 1 this way stand firm in the Lord, **b**.
Col 1: 7 it from Epaphras our **b** fellow slave,
Col 1:13 us to the kingdom of his **b** Son,
Col 3:12 holy and **b**, heartfelt compassion,
Col 4: 7 Tychicus, my **b** brother,
Col 4: 9 a trustworthy and **b** brother, who is
Col 4:14 Luke the **b** physician sends
1 Tm 6: 2 their work are believers and are **b**.
Phlm 1:16 a brother, **b** especially to me,
Heb 6: 9 But we are sure in your regard, **b**,
Jas 1:16 Do not be deceived, my **b** brothers:
Jas 2: 5 Listen, my **b** brothers. Did not God
1 Pt 2:11 **B**, I urge you as aliens
1 Pt 4:12 **B**, do not be surprised that a trial
2 Pt 1:17 Son, my **b**, with whom I am well
2 Pt 3: 1 This is now, **b**, the second letter I
2 Pt 3: 8 But do not ignore this one fact, **b**,
2 Pt 3:14 Therefore, **b**, since you await these
2 Pt 3:15 as salvation, as our **b** brother Paul,
2 Pt 3:17 Therefore, **b**, since you are
1 Jn 2: 7 **B**, I am writing no new
1 Jn 3: 2 **B**, we are God's children now;
1 Jn 3:21 **B**, if [our] hearts do not condemn
1 Jn 4: 1 **B**, do not trust every spirit but test
1 Jn 4: 7 **B**, let us love one another,
1 Jn 4:11 **B**, if God so loved us, we also must
3 Jn 1: 1 to the **b** Gaius whom I love in truth.
3 Jn 1: 2 **B**, I hope you are prospering
3 Jn 1: 5 **B**, you are faithful in all you do
3 Jn 1:11 **B**, do not imitate evil but imitate
Jude 1: 1 **b** in God the Father and kept safe
Jude 1: 3 **B**, although I was making every
Jude 1:17 But you, **b**, remember the words
Jude 1:20 But you, **b**, build yourselves
Rev 20: 9 of the holy ones and the **b** city.

BELOW
Jos 2:11 in heaven above and on earth **b**.
Jn 8:23 "You belong to what is **b**, I belong
Acts 2:19 above and signs on the earth **b**:

BELSHAZZAR
King of Babylon in days of Daniel (Bar 1:11-12; Dn 5).

BELT → BELTS
1 Sm 18: 4 dress, even his sword, bow, and **b**.
Is 11: 5 and faithfulness a **b** upon his hips.
Dn 10: 5 a **b** of fine gold around his waist.
Mk 1: 6 with a leather **b** around his waist.
Acts 21:11 took Paul's **b**, bound his own feet

BELTESHAZZAR → =DANIEL
Dn 1: 7 Daniel to B, Hananiah to Shadrach,

BELTS → BELT
Mk 6: 8 food, no sack, no money in their **b**.

BEN-HADAD
1. King of Syria in time of Asa (1 Kgs 15:18-20; 2 Chr 16:2-4).
2. King of Syria in time of Ahab (1 Kgs 20; 2 Kgs 6:24; 8:7-15).
3. King of Syria in time of Jehoahaz (2 Kgs 13:3, 24-25; Jer 49:27; Am 1:4).

BEN-HINNOM
2 Kgs 23:10 defiled Topheth in the Valley of B,

2 Chr 28: 3 offered sacrifice in the Valley of **B**,
Jer 32:35 in the Valley of **B** to sacrifice their

BEN-ONI → =BENJAMIN
Gn 35:18 she named him **B**; but his father

BENAIAH
    A commander of David's army (2 Sm 8:18; 20:23; 23:20-30); loyal to Solomon (1 Kgs 1:8–2:46; 4:4).

BENCH
Jn 19:13 on the judge's **b** in the place called

BEND → BENT
2 Sm 22:35 my arms to **b** even a bow of bronze.
Phil 2:10 name of Jesus every knee should **b**,

BENEATH
Dt 5: 8 below or in the waters **b** the earth;

BENEFACTOR → BENEFACTORS
Est E:13 our savior and constant **b**,
2 Mc 4: 2 government the man who was the **b**
Rom 16: 2 for she has been a **b** to many

BENEFACTORS → BENEFACTOR
Est E: 3 begin plotting against their own **b**.
Lk 22:25 over them are addressed as 'B';

BENEFICIAL → BENEFIT
1 Cor 6:12 for me," but not everything is **b**.
1 Cor 10:23 is lawful," but not everything is **b**.

BENEFIT → BENEFICIAL
Gal 5: 2 Christ will be of no **b** to you.

BENJAMIN → =BEN-ONI, BENJAMINITE
    Twelfth son of Jacob by Rachel (Gn 35:16-24; 46:19-21; 1 Chr 2:2). Jacob refused to send him to Egypt, but relented (Gn 42–45). Tribe of blessed (Gn 49:27; Dt 33:12), numbered (Nm 1:37; 26:41), allotted land (Jos 18:11-28; Ez 48:23), failed to fully possess (Jgs 1:21), nearly obliterated (Jgs 20–21), sided with Ishbaal (2 Sm 2) but turned to David (1 Chr 12:2, 30). 12,000 from (Rev 7:8).

BENJAMINITE → BENJAMIN
Jgs 3:15 of Gera, a **B** who was left-handed.
1 Sm 9:21 "Am I not a **B**, from the smallest
2 Sm 19:17 son of Gera, the **B** from Bahurim,
Est 2: 5 son of Shimei, son of Kish, a **B**,

BENT → BEND
Lk 13:11 she was **b** over,
Jn 8: 6 Jesus **b** down and began to write
Jn 20: 5 he **b** down and saw the burial cloths
Rom 11:10 and keep their backs **b** forever."

BEOR
Nm 22: 5 son of **B**, at Pethor on the river,
Nm 31: 8 Balaam, son of **B**, with the sword.

BERAKAH
2 Chr 20:26 the Valley of **B**—for there they blessed

BEREAVES
Lam 1:20 Outside the sword **b**—

BERNICE
Acts 25:13 **B** arrived in Caesarea on a visit

BEROEA
Acts 17:10 Paul and Silas to **B** during the night.

BERYL
Rev 21:20 the eighth, **b**, the ninth topaz,

BESIDES
Wis 12:13 is there any god **b** you who have
Is 45:21 **b** whom there is no other God?
Dn 14:41 and there is no other **b** you!"

BESIEGED → SIEGE
2 Kgs 17: 5 Samaria, which he **b** for three years.

BEST → GOOD
Gn 45:18 I will assign you the **b** land
Nm 18:29 from their **b** parts, that is the part
Dt 33:21 He saw that the **b** should be his,
Mi 7: 4 The **b** of them is like a brier,

BESTOW → BESTOWER
Prv 4: 9 a glorious crown will she **b**

BESTOWER → BESTOW
Is 23: 8 thing against Tyre, the **b** of crowns,

BETH-SHAN
1 Sm 31:10 but impaled his body on the wall of **B**.

BETHANY
Mt 26: 6 when Jesus was in **B** in the house
Mk 11:12 they were leaving **B** he was hungry.
Jn 1:28 happened in **B** across the Jordan,
Jn 11: 1 Lazarus from **B**, the village of Mary

BETHEL → =LUZ
Gn 12: 8 pitching his tent with **B** to the west
Gn 28:19 He named that place **B**,
Gn 31:13 I am the God of **B**, where you
Gn 35: 8 was buried under the oak below **B**,
Jos 8: 9 position to the west of Ai, toward **B**.
Jgs 20:18 They went up to **B** and consulted
1 Sm 7:16 passing through **B**,
1 Kgs 12:29 And he put one in **B**, the other
1 Kgs 13:11 was an old prophet living in **B**,
2 Kgs 2: 2 The LORD has sent me on to **B**."
2 Kgs 10:29 the golden calves at **B** and at Dan.
2 Kgs 23:15 Likewise the altar which was at **B**,
Tb 2: 6 by the prophet Amos against **B**:
Am 4: 4 Come to **B** and sin, to Gilgal and sin
Am 7:10 the priest of **B**, sent word

BETHLEHEM → BETHLEHEM-EPHRATHAH, EPHRATH
Gn 35:19 on the road to Ephrath (now **B**).
Ru 1: 1 so a man from **B** of Judah left home
Ru 1:19 on together until they reached **B**.
Ru 4:11 Bestow a name in **B**!
1 Sm 17:12 an Ephrathite named Jesse from **B**
2 Sm 23:15 from the cistern by the gate of **B**!"
Mt 2: 1 When Jesus was born in **B** of Judea,
Mt 2: 6 'And you, **B**, land of Judah,
Mt 2:16 the massacre of all the boys in **B**
Lk 2:15 to **B** to see this thing that has taken
Jn 7:42 of David's family and come from **B**,

BETHLEHEM-EPHRATHAH → BETHLEHEM
Mi 5: 1 **B** least among the clans of Judah,

BETHPHAGE
Mt 21: 1 came to **B** on the Mount of Olives,

BETHSAIDA
Mt 11:21 Woe to you, **B**! For if the mighty
Jn 1:44 Now Philip was from **B**, the town

BETHUEL
Gn 22:23 **B** became the father of Rebekah.
Gn 24:24 "I am the daughter of **B** the son

BETRAY → BETRAYER, BETRAYING
Mt 24:10 they will **b** and hate one another.
Mt 26:21 I say to you, one of you will **b** me."
Jn 13:11 For he knew who would **b** him;

BETRAYER → BETRAY
Mk 14:42 up, let us go. See, my **b** is at hand."

BETRAYING → BETRAY
Lk 22:48 are you **b** the Son of Man

BETROTH → BETROTHED
Dt 28:30 Though you **b** a wife, another will

BETROTHED → BETROTH
Dt 20: 7 Is there anyone who has **b** a woman
Mt 1:18 his mother Mary was **b** to Joseph,
Lk 1:27 a virgin **b** to a man named Joseph,

BETTER → GOOD
1 Sm 15:22 Obedience is **b** than sacrifice,
Tb 3: 6 It is **b** for me to die than to live,
Tb 12: 8 with righteousness is **b** than wealth
Tb 12: 8 It is **b** to give alms than to store
Ps 37:16 **B** the meagerness of the righteous
Ps 63: 4 For your love is **b** than life;

Ps	118: 8	B to take refuge in the LORD than
Prv	3:14	Her profit is b than profit in silver,
Prv	8:11	[For Wisdom is b than corals,]
Prv	8:19	My fruit is b than gold, even pure
Prv	12: 9	B to be slighted and have a servant
Prv	15:16	B a little with fear of the LORD
Prv	15:17	B a dish of herbs where love is than
Prv	16: 8	B a little with justice, than a large
Prv	16:16	How much b to get wisdom than
Prv	16:19	It is b to be humble with the poor
Prv	16:32	The patient are b than warriors,
Prv	17: 1	B a dry crust with quiet than a house
Prv	19: 1	B to be poor and walk in integrity
Prv	21: 9	It is b to dwell in a corner
Prv	21:19	It is b to dwell in a wilderness than
Prv	25:24	It is b to dwell in a corner
Prv	27: 5	B is an open rebuke than a love
Prv	27:10	B a neighbor near than kin far away.
Prv	28: 6	B to be poor and walk in integrity
Eccl	2:24	There is nothing b for mortals than
Eccl	3:12	there is nothing b than to rejoice
Eccl	3:22	there is nothing b for mortals than
Eccl	4: 3	b off than both is the yet unborn,
Eccl	4: 6	B is one handful with tranquility
Eccl	4: 9	Two are b than one: They get
Eccl	4:13	B is a poor but wise youth than
Eccl	5: 4	It is b not to make a vow than make
Eccl	6: 9	the eyes see is b than what
Eccl	7: 1	good name is b than good ointment,
Eccl	7: 2	It is b to go to the house
Eccl	7: 3	Sorrow is b than laughter;
Eccl	7: 5	It is b to listen to the rebuke
Eccl	7: 8	B is the end of a thing than its
Eccl	7: 8	b is a patient spirit than a lofty one.
Eccl	9: 4	"A live dog is b off than a dead
Eccl	9:16	said, "Wisdom is b than force,"
Sir	16: 3	For one can be b than a thousand;
Sir	23:27	That nothing is b than the fear
Sir	40:20	but b than either, love of friends.
Sir	40:23	but b than either, a sensible wife.
Sir	40:26	exult, but b than either, fear of God.
Sir	40:28	life of a beggar; b to die than to beg.
Dn	1:20	he found them ten times b than any
Jon	4: 3	for it is b for me to die than
Mt	5:29	It is b for you to lose one of your
Mt	18: 6	it would be b for him to have a great
Mt	19:10	with his wife, it is b not to marry."
Mt	26:24	It would be b for that man if he had
Mk	14:21	It would be b for that man if he had
Lk	10:42	Mary has chosen the b part and it
Jn	11:50	do you consider that it is b for you
1 Cor	7: 9	for it is b to marry than to be
Phil	1:23	be with Christ, [for] that is far b.
Heb	6: 9	of b things related to salvation,
Heb	7:19	other hand, a b hope is introduced,
Heb	7:22	guarantee of an [even] b covenant.
Heb	8: 6	as he is mediator of a b covenant, enacted on b promises.
Heb	9:23	by b sacrifices than these.
Heb	10:34	knowing that you had a b
Heb	11:16	But now they desire a b homeland,
Heb	11:35	in order to obtain a b resurrection.
Heb	11:40	God had foreseen something b
1 Pt	3:17	For it is b to suffer for doing good,
2 Pt	2:21	it would have been b for them not

BETWEEN

Gn	3:15	I will put enmity b you
Gn	3:15	and b your offspring and hers;
Gn	9:13	serve as a sign of the covenant b me
Gn	16: 5	May the LORD decide b you
Gn	17: 2	B you and me I will establish my
Gn	17:11	be the sign of the covenant b me
Gn	31:44	it will be a treaty b you and me."
Ex	8:19	will make a distinction b my people
Ex	31:17	B me and the Israelites it is to be
Jgs	11:10	"The LORD is witness b us

1 Sm	7:12	placed it b Mizpah and Jeshanah;
Is	2: 4	He shall judge b the nations, and set
Is	5: 3	Judah, judge b me and my vineyard:
Ez	20:12	them my sabbaths to be a sign b me
Ez	34:17	I will judge b one sheep and another, b rams and goats.
Mi	4: 3	He shall judge b many peoples
Lk	11:51	of Zechariah who died b the altar
Rom	10:12	For there is no distinction b Jew
Phil	1:23	I am caught b the two. I long
1 Tm	2: 5	one mediator b God and the human

BEWARE

Eccl	12:12	As to more than these, my son, b.
Mt	7:15	"B of false prophets, who come
Phil	3: 2	B of the dogs! B of the evil workers! B of the mutilation!

BEWITCHED

Gal	3: 1	Who has b you, before whose eyes

BEYOND

Gn	31:52	I may not pass b this mound
Gn	31:52	nor may you pass b it into mine.
Jos	24: 2	lived b the River and served other
Ps	147: 5	in power, with wisdom b measure.
Sir	6:15	Faithful friends are b price,
Sir	8:13	Do not give collateral b your means;
Is	52:14	b that of mortals his appearance,
1 Cor	4: 6	from us not to go b what is written,
1 Cor	10:13	not let you be tried b your strength;
2 Cor	4:17	weight of glory b all comparison,
2 Cor	10:16	may preach the gospel even b you,

BEZALEL

Judahite craftsman in charge of building the tabernacle (Ex 31:1-11; 35:30–39:31).

BIG

Lv	8:23	and on the b toe of his right foot.
Lv	14:14	and the b toe of the right foot

BILDAD

One of Job's friends (Jb 2:11; 8; 18; 25; 42:9).

BILHAH

Servant of Rachel, mother of Jacob's sons Dan and Naphtali (Gn 30:1-7; 35:25; 46:23-25).

BILL

Dt	24: 1	and he writes out a b of divorce
Dt	24: 3	and he writes out a b of divorce
Is	50: 1	Where is the b of divorce
Mt	5:31	divorces his wife must give her a b
Mt	19: 7	that the man give the woman a b
Mk	10: 4	him to write a b of divorce

BILLOWS

Jon	2: 4	breakers and your b passed over me.

BIND → BINDING, BINDS, BOUND

Dt	6: 8	B them on your arm as a sign
Dt	11:18	B them on your arm as a sign,
Prv	3: 3	b them around your neck;
Prv	7: 3	B them on your fingers, write them
Ez	34:16	the injured I will b up, and the sick I
Mt	16:19	Whatever you b on earth shall be
Mt	18:18	whatever you b on earth shall be

BINDING → BIND

Ps	147: 3	brokenhearted, and b up their wounds.

BINDS → BIND

Jb	5:18	For he wounds, but he b up;
Is	30:26	On the day the LORD b

BIRD → BIRD'S, BIRDS

Gn	7: 3	of every b of the air, seven pairs,
Gn	7:14	on the earth, and every kind of b.
Lv	20:25	detestable through any beast or b
Dt	4:17	the form of any b that flies
Ps	11: 1	me, "Flee like a b to the mountains!
Ps	124: 7	our lives like a b from the fowler's
Prv	6: 5	like a b from the hand of the fowler.
Prv	7:23	Like a b that rushes into a snare,

Prv 27: 8 Like a **b** far from the nest so is
Is 46:11 I summon from the east a **b** of prey,
Rev 18: 2 a cage for every unclean **b**, [a cage]

BIRD'S → BIRD
Dt 22: 6 you come across a **b** nest

BIRDS → BIRD
Gn 1:21 teems, and all kinds of winged **b**.
Gn 1:22 and let the **b** multiply on the earth.
Dt 14:11 You may eat all clean **b**.
Eccl 10:20 For the **b** of the air may carry your
Jer 7:33 will be food for the **b** of the sky
Ez 17:23 all kinds of winged **b** will dwell
Mt 6:26 Look at the **b** in the sky; they do not
Mt 8:20 dens and **b** of the sky have nests,
Mt 13: 4 the path, and **b** came and ate it up.
Acts 10:12 and reptiles and the **b** of the sky.
Rom 1:23 or of **b** or of four-legged animals
Rev 19:21 all the **b** gorged themselves on their

BIRTH → BEAR
Dt 32:18 you forgot the God who gave you **b**.
Ps 58: 4 wicked have been corrupt since **b**;
Ps 71: 6 On you I have depended since **b**;
Eccl 3: 2 A time to give **b**, and a time to die;
Eccl 7: 1 the day of death than the day of **b**.
Is 26:18 in pain, giving **b** only to wind;
Jer 2:27 and to a stone, "You gave me **b**."
Jer 30: 6 Inquire and see: does a male give **b**?
Mt 1:18 Now this is how the **b** of Jesus
Lk 1:14 and many will rejoice at his **b**,
Lk 1:57 have her child she gave **b** to a son.
Jn 9: 1 by he saw a man blind from **b**.
Acts 3: 2 a man crippled from **b** was carried
Acts 14: 8 man, lame from **b**, who had never
1 Cor 1:26 powerful, not many were of noble **b**.
Jas 1:15 sin reaches maturity it gives **b**
Jas 1:18 He willed to give us **b** by the word
1 Pt 1: 3 his great mercy gave us a new **b**
Rev 12: 5 She gave **b** to a son, a male child,

BIRTHDAY → BEAR, DAY
Mt 14: 6 But at a **b** celebration for Herod,

BIRTHRIGHT → BEAR, RIGHT
1 Chr 5: 1 of his father his **b** was given
1 Chr 5: 2 though the **b** had been Joseph's.)
Heb 12:16 who sold his **b** for a single meal.

BISHOP
1 Tm 3: 1 the office of **b** desires a noble task.
1 Tm 3: 2 a **b** must be irreproachable,
Ti 1: 7 For a **b** as God's steward must be

BIT → BITE, BITS
2 Kgs 19:28 your nose and my **b** in your mouth,
Ps 32: 9 with **b** and bridle their temper is

BITE → BIT, BITES, BITING, BITTEN
Sir 21: 2 a serpent that will **b** you if you go
Jer 8:17 charm will work when they **b** you—
Am 9: 3 command the serpent to **b** them.

BITES → BITE
Prv 23:32 but in the end it **b** like a serpent,

BITING → BITE
Gal 5:15 if you go on **b** and devouring one

BITS → BIT
Jas 3: 3 If we put **b** into the mouths

BITTEN → BITE
Nm 21: 8 everyone who has been **b** will look

BITTER → BITTERLY, BITTERNESS
Ex 1:14 making life **b** for them with hard
Ex 12: 8 with unleavened bread and **b** herbs.
Ex 15:23 drink its water, because it was too **b**.
Nm 5:24 may enter into her to her **b** hurt.
Ru 1:13 daughters, my lot is too **b** for you,
Ru 1:20 Call me Mara ['**B**'],
Prv 5: 4 to the hungry, any **b** thing is sweet.

Eccl 7:26 More **b** than death I find the woman
Is 5:20 who change **b** to sweet, and sweet into **b**!
Rev 8:11 this water, because it was made **b**.

BITTERLY → BITTER
Lk 22:62 He went out and began to weep **b**.

BITTERNESS → BITTER
Prv 14:10 The heart knows its own **b**, and its
Eph 4:31 All **b**, fury, anger, shouting,

BITUMEN
Gn 11: 3 bricks for stone, and **b** for mortar.
Gn 14:10 Valley of Siddim was full of **b** pits;
Ex 2: 3 basket, daubed it with **b** and pitch,

BLACK → BLACKNESS
Zec 6: 2 horses, the second chariot **b** horses,
Mt 5:36 make a single hair white or **b**.
Rev 6: 5 and there was a **b** horse, and its
Rev 6:12 sun turned as **b** as dark sackcloth

BLACKNESS → BLACK
Jb 3: 5 settle upon it, **b** of day affright it!

BLAMELESS
Gn 6: 9 man and **b** in his generation;
Gn 17: 1 Walk in my presence and be **b**.
Est E:13 and of Esther, our **b** royal consort,
1 Mc 4:42 He chose **b** priests,
Jb 1: 1 In the land of Uz there was a **b**
Jb 1: 8 one on earth like him, **b** and upright,
Ps 19:14 Then shall I be **b**, innocent of grave
Ps 37:18 LORD knows the days of the **b**;
Ps 119: 1 Blessed those whose way is **b**,
Prv 28:10 pit, but the **b** will attain prosperity.
Wis 10: 5 man, kept him **b** before God,
Wis 10:15 people and their **b** descendants—
Wis 18:21 For the **b** man hastened to be their
Sir 11:10 is greedy for wealth will not be **b**?
Ez 28:15 **B** were you in your ways
Phil 1:10 be pure and **b** for the day of Christ,
Phil 2:15 that you may be **b** and innocent,
Phil 3: 6 based on the law I was **b**.
1 Thes 3:13 to be **b** in holiness before our God
1 Thes 5:23 be preserved **b** for the coming
Ti 1: 6 on condition that a man be **b**,
Ti 1: 7 bishop as God's steward must be **b**,

BLASPHEME → BLASPHEMED, BLASPHEMER, BLASPHEMERS, BLASPHEMES, BLASPHEMIES, BLASPHEMING, BLASPHEMOUS, BLASPHEMY
Acts 26:11 in an attempt to force them to **b**;
1 Tm 1:20 over to Satan to be taught not to **b**.
Jas 2: 7 Is it not they who **b** the noble name

BLASPHEMED → BLASPHEME
Lv 24:11 the LORD's name in a curse and **b**.
Ez 20:27 this way also your ancestors **b** me,
Mt 26:65 tore his robes and said, "He has **b**!

BLASPHEMER → BLASPHEME
1 Tm 1:13 I was once a **b** and a persecutor

BLASPHEMERS → BLASPHEME
Sir 3:16 who neglect their father are like **b**;

BLASPHEMES → BLASPHEME
Lv 24:15 Anyone who **b** God shall bear the penalty;
Mk 3:29 whoever **b** against the holy Spirit
Lk 12:10 but the one who **b** against the holy

BLASPHEMIES → BLASPHEME
Tb 1:18 because of the **b** he had uttered;
1 Mc 7:38 Remember their **b**, and do not let
2 Mc 8: 4 and the **b** uttered against his name;
2 Mc 10:35 angered over such **b**,
Mk 3:28 and all **b** that people utter will be
Lk 5:21 "Who is this who speaks **b**?
Rev 13: 6 its mouth to utter **b** against God,

BLASPHEMING → BLASPHEME
1 Sm 3:13 he knew his sons were **b** God,
Mt 9: 3 to themselves, "This man is **b**."

Rev   13: 6 **b** his name and his dwelling

BLASPHEMOUS → BLASPHEME
2 Mc   10: 4 and not hand them over to **b**
2 Mc   13:11 to be subjected again to **b** Gentiles.
Acts   6:11 heard him speaking **b** words against
Rev   13: 1 and on its heads **b** name[s].
Rev   17: 3 that was covered with **b** names,

BLASPHEMY → BLASPHEME
Mt   12:31 sin and **b** will be forgiven people,
Mt   12:31 but **b** against the Spirit will not be
Mt   26:65 You have now heard the **b**;
Mk   14:64 You have heard the **b**. What do you
Jn   10:33 you for a good work but for **b**.

BLAST → BLASTS
Ex   19:16 and a very loud **b** of the shofar,
Jos   6: 5 they give a long **b** on the ram's
Jb   4: 9 and by the **b** of his wrath they are

BLASTS → BLAST
Lv   23:24 rest, with trumpet **b** as a reminder,
Rev   8:13 the trumpet **b** that the three angels

BLAZING
Ez   21: 3 The **b** flame shall not be quenched
Heb   12:18 which could be touched and a **b** fire

BLEACH
Mk   9: 3 as no fuller on earth could **b** them.

BLEATING
1 Sm   15:14 is this **b** of sheep that comes to my

BLEMISH → BLEMISHES
Ex   12: 5 be a year-old male and without **b**.
Lv   1: 3 offering must be a male without **b**.
Nm   19: 2 free from every **b** and on which no
Eph   5:27 she might be holy and without **b**.
Phil   2:15 of God without **b** in the midst
2 Pt   3:14 found without spot or **b** before him,

BLEMISHES → BLEMISH
Jude   1:12 These are **b** on your love feasts,

BLESS → BLESSED, BLESSEDNESS, BLESSES, BLESSING, BLESSINGS
Gn   12: 2 you a great nation, and I will **b** you;
Gn   12: 3 I will **b** those who **b** you and curse
Gn   17:16 I will **b** her, and I will give you
Gn   17:16 Her also will I **b**; she will give rise
Gn   17:20 I will heed you: I hereby **b** him.
Gn   22:17 I will **b** you and make your
Gn   26: 3 and I will be with you and **b** you;
Gn   26:24 I will **b** you and multiply your
Gn   27: 4 so that I may **b** you before I die."
Gn   27:34 and said, "Father, **b** me too!"
Gn   28: 3 May God Almighty **b** you and make
Gn   32:27 will not let you go until you **b** me."
Gn   48: 9 his father, "that I may **b** them."
Ex   20:24 I will come to you and **b** you.
Ex   23:25 then he will **b** your food and drink,
Nm   6:24 The Lord **b** you and keep you!
Nm   22: 6 know that whoever you **b** is blessed
Nm   23:20 I was summoned to **b**; I will **b**;
Nm   24: 1 the Lord was pleased to **b** Israel,
Nm   24: 9 Blessed are those who **b** you,
Dt   1:11 over, and **b** you as he promised!
Dt   7:13 He will love and **b** and multiply
Dt   7:13 he will **b** the fruit of your womb
Dt   8:10 satisfied, you must **b** the Lord,
Dt   14:29 may **b** you in all that you undertake.
Dt   15: 4 will **b** you abundantly in the land
Dt   21: 5 and to **b** in the name of the Lord,
Dt   23:21 may **b** you in all your undertakings
Dt   24:19 may **b** you in all your undertakings.
Dt   26:15 and **b** your people Israel
Dt   27:12 stand on Mount Gerizim to **b** the people:
Dt   30:16 God, will **b** you in the land you are
Dt   33:11 **B**, Lord, his strength, be pleased
Jgs   5: 2 rallied for duty—**b** the Lord!
Ru   2: 4 they replied, "The Lord **b** you."

1 Sm   2:20 Eli would **b** Elkanah and his wife,
2 Sm   7:29 then, **b** the house of your servant,
2 Sm   21: 3 that you may **b** the heritage
1 Chr   4:10 that you may truly **b** me and extend
1 Chr 16:43 David returned to **b** his household.
1 Chr 29:20 "Now **b** the Lord your God!"
Neh   9: 5 "Arise, **b** the Lord, your God,
Neh   9: 5 may they **b** your glorious name,
Tb   4:19 At all times **b** the Lord, your God,
Tb   8:15 all your chosen ones **b** you forever!
Tb   12: 6 "**B** God and give him thanks before all
Ps   5:13 For you, Lord, **b** the just one;
Ps   16: 7 I **b** the Lord who counsels me;
Ps   26:12 in assemblies I will **b** the Lord.
Ps   28: 9 your people, **b** your inheritance;
Ps   29:11 may the Lord **b** his people
Ps   34: 2 I will **b** the Lord at all times;
Ps   62: 5 they **b** with their mouths,
Ps   63: 5 I will **b** you as long as I live;
Ps   66: 8 **B** our God, you peoples;
Ps   67: 2 God be gracious to us and **b** us;
Ps   68:27 In your choirs, **b** God;
Ps   96: 2 Sing to the Lord, **b** his name;
Ps   100: 4 Give thanks to him, **b** his name;
Ps   103: 1 **B** the Lord, my soul;
Ps   103: 2 **B** the Lord, my soul; and do not
Ps   103:20 **B** the Lord, all you his angels,
Ps   103:21 **B** the Lord, all you his hosts,
Ps   103:22 **B** the Lord, all his creatures,
Ps   104: 1 **B** the Lord, my soul!
Ps   104:35 be no more. **B** the Lord, my soul!
Ps   109:28 Though they curse, may you **b**;
Ps   115:12 remembers us and will **b** us,
Ps   115:18 It is we who **b** the Lord,
Ps   118:26 We **b** you from the house
Ps   128: 5 May the Lord **b** you from Zion;
Ps   129: 8 We **b** you in the name
Ps   132:15 I will **b** Zion with provisions;
Ps   134: 1 O come, **b** the Lord, all you
Ps   135:19 House of Israel, **b** the Lord!
Ps   135:19 House of Aaron, **b** the Lord!
Ps   135:20 House of Levi, **b** the Lord!
Ps   135:20 fear the Lord, **b** the Lord!
Ps   145: 2 Every day I will **b** you; I will praise
Ps   145:10 Lord and your faithful **b** you.
Ps   145:21 all flesh will **b** his holy name
Sir   39:35 and voice proclaim and **b** his name!
Jer   31:23 "May the Lord **b** you,
Dn   3:57 **B** the Lord, all you works
Hg   2:19 From this day, I will **b** you.
Lk   6:28 **b** those who curse you;
Acts   3:26 sent him to **b** you by turning each
Rom   12:14 **B** those who persecute [you],
1 Cor   4:12 When ridiculed, we **b**;
1 Cor 10:16 The cup of blessing that we **b**, is it
Heb   6:14 "I will indeed **b** you and multiply"
Jas   3: 9 With it we **b** the Lord and Father,

BLESSED → BLESS
Gn   1:22 and God **b** them, saying:
Gn   2: 3 God **b** the seventh day and made it
Gn   5: 2 created, he **b** them and named them
Gn   9: 1 God **b** Noah and his sons and said
Gn   9:26 "**B** be the Lord, the God
Gn   14:19 He **b** Abram with these words:
Gn   24: 1 the Lord had **b** him in every way.
Gn   39: 5 the Lord **b** the Egyptian's house
Gn   48:20 So he **b** them that day and said,
Ex   20:11 the Lord has **b** the sabbath day
Ex   39:43 had commanded, he **b** them.
Lv   9:22 hands over the people and **b** them.
Nm   22: 6 I know that whoever you bless is **b**
Nm   24: 9 **B** are those who bless you,
Dt   7:14 You will be **b** above all peoples;
Dt   12: 7 the Lord, your God, has **b** you.
Dt   16:15 has **b** you in all your crops and in all
Dt   28: 3 May you be **b** in the city, and **b** in the country!

Dt	33:13	**B** by the Lord is his land
Jos	22: 6	Joshua then **b** them and sent them
Jgs	5:24	Most **b** of women is Jael, the wife
Jgs	13:24	the boy grew up the Lord **b** him.
Ru	2:19	one who took notice of you be **b**!"
1 Sm	25:33	**B** is your good judgment and **b** are
1 Sm	26:25	"**B** are you, my son David!
2 Sm	22:47	The Lord lives! **B** be my rock!
1 Kgs	1:48	'B be the Lord, the God of Israel,
1 Kgs	2:45	But King Solomon shall be **b**,
1 Chr	16: 2	he **b** the people in the name
1 Chr	17:27	Lord, who **b** it, it is **b** forever."
2 Chr	2:11	"B be the Lord, the God
2 Chr	31:10	for the Lord has **b** his people.
Tb	3:11	"B are you, merciful God!
Tb	8:15	"B are you, God, with every pure
Jdt	13:17	saying with one accord, "B are you,
Jb	1:21	**b** be the name of the Lord!"
Jb	29:11	The ear that heard **b** me; the eye
Jb	42:12	Thus the Lord **b** the later days
Ps	1: 1	**B** is the man who does not walk in
Ps	2:11	**B** are all who take refuge in him!
Ps	18:47	The Lord lives! **B** be my rock!
Ps	28: 6	**B** be the Lord, who has heard
Ps	31:22	**B** be the Lord, marvelously he
Ps	32: 1	**B** is the one whose fault is removed,
Ps	33:12	**B** is the nation whose God is the Lord,
Ps	34: 9	**b** is the stalwart one who takes refuge
Ps	40: 5	**B** the man who sets his security in the Lord,
Ps	41: 2	**B** the one concerned for the poor;
Ps	41:14	**B** be the Lord, the God of Israel,
Ps	66:20	**B** be God, who did not reject my
Ps	68:20	**B** be the Lord day by day, God,
Ps	72:19	**B** be his glorious name forever;
Ps	84:13	**b** the man who trusts in you!
Ps	89:53	**B** be the Lord forever!
Ps	106:48	**B** be the Lord, the God of Israel,
Ps	112: 1	**B** the man who fears the Lord,
Ps	113: 2	**B** be the name of the Lord both
Ps	118:26	**B** is he who comes in the name
Ps	119: 2	**B** those who keep his testimonies,
Ps	128: 1	**B** are all who fear the Lord,
Ps	135:21	**B** be the Lord from Zion,
Ps	137: 8	**b** the one who pays you back
Ps	144: 1	**B** be the Lord, my rock,
Prv	22: 9	The generous will be **b**, for they
Jer	17: 7	**B** are those who trust
Dn	2:20	"B be the name of God forever
Mt	5: 3	"B are the poor in spirit, for theirs
Mt	5: 4	**B** are they who mourn, for they will
Mt	5: 5	**B** are the meek, for they will inherit
Mt	5: 6	**B** are they who hunger and thirst
Mt	5: 7	**B** are the merciful, for they will be
Mt	5: 8	**B** are the clean of heart, for they
Mt	5: 9	**B** are the peacemakers, for they will
Mt	5:10	**B** are they who are persecuted
Mt	5:11	**B** are you when they insult you
Mt	11: 6	**b** is the one who takes no offense
Mk	10:16	Then he embraced them and **b** them,
Mk	11: 9	**B** is he who comes in the name
Lk	1:42	"Most **b** are you among women,
Lk	1:42	and **b** is the fruit of your womb.
Lk	1:48	from now on will all ages call me **b**.
Lk	6:20	"B are you who are poor,
Lk	6:21	**B** are you who are now hungry,
Lk	6:21	**B** are you who are now weeping,
Lk	6:22	**B** are you when people hate you,
Jn	12:13	**B** is he who comes in the name
Jn	13:17	this, **b** are you if you do it.
Jn	20:29	**B** are those who have not seen
Acts	3:25	the families of the earth shall be **b**.'
Acts	20:35	said, 'It is more **b** to give than
Rom	1:25	than the creator, who is **b** forever.
Rom	4: 7	"B are they whose iniquities are
Rom	9: 5	God who is over all be **b** forever.
Gal	3: 8	you shall all the nations be **b**."

Eph	1: 3	**B** be the God and Father of our Lord
Eph	1: 3	who has **b** us in Christ with every
1 Tm	6:15	that the **b** and only ruler will make
Ti	2:13	as we await the **b** hope,
Heb	7: 7	a lesser person is **b** by a greater.
Jas	1:12	**B** is the man who perseveres
Jas	5:11	Indeed we call **b** those who have
1 Pt	3:14	because of righteousness, **b** are you.
1 Pt	4:14	for the name of Christ, **b** are you,
Rev	1: 3	**B** is the one who reads aloud and **b**
Rev	14:13	**B** are the dead who die in the Lord
Rev	16:15	**B** is the one who watches and keeps
Rev	19: 9	**B** are those who have been called
Rev	20: 6	**B** and holy is the one who shares
Rev	22: 7	**B** is the one who keeps
Rev	22:14	**B** are they who wash their robes so

BLESSEDNESS → BLESS

Rom	4: 6	David declares the **b** of the person

BLESSES → BLESS

Prv	3:33	but the dwelling of the just he **b**;

BLESSING → BLESS

Gn	12: 2	name great, so that you will be a **b**.
Gn	26: 4	the nations of the earth will find **b**—
Gn	27:36	and now he has taken away my **b**."
Gn	27:36	"Have you not saved a **b** for me?"
Gn	28: 4	and your descendants the **b** of Abraham,
Ex	32:29	to bring a **b** upon yourselves this
Lv	25:21	I will command such a **b** for you
Dt	11:26	I set before you this day a **b**
Dt	23: 6	but turned his curse into a **b** for you,
Dt	28: 8	The Lord will affirm the **b**
Dt	30: 1	the **b** and the curse which I have set
Dt	33: 1	This is the **b** with which Moses,
Jos	8:33	commanded for the **b** of the people
2 Sm	7:29	by your **b** the house of your servant
Neh	13: 2	our God turned the curse into a **b**."
Tb	8:15	are you, God, with every pure **b**!
Tb	12: 6	by **b** and extolling his name in song.
Ps	3: 9	May your **b** be upon your people!
Prv	10:22	It is the Lord's **b** that brings
Sir	11:22	God's **b** is the lot of the righteous,
Is	44: 3	my **b** upon your descendants.
Ez	34:26	in its season, the **b** of abundant rain.
Jl	2:14	again relent and leave behind a **b**,
Zec	8:13	will I save you that you may be a **b**.
Mal	3:10	down upon you **b** without measure!
Mk	14:22	he took bread, said the **b**, broke it,
Rom	15:29	come in the fullness of Christ's **b**.
1 Cor	10:16	The cup of **b** that we bless, is it not
1 Cor	14:16	you pronounce a **b** [with] the spirit,
Gal	3:14	that the **b** of Abraham might be
Eph	1: 3	every spiritual **b** in the heavens,
Heb	6: 7	whom it is cultivated receives a **b**
Heb	12:17	he wanted to inherit his father's **b**,
Heb	12:17	even though he sought the **b**
Jas	3:10	From the same mouth come **b**
1 Pt	3: 9	a **b**, because to this you were called, that you might inherit a **b**.
Rev	5:12	strength, honor and glory and **b**."
Rev	7:12	"Amen. **B** and glory,

BLESSINGS → BLESS

Gn	48:20	the people of Israel pronounce **b**,
Gn	49:26	the **b** of fresh grain and blossoms,
Gn	49:26	the **b** of the everlasting mountains,
Dt	28: 2	All these **b** will come upon you
Jos	8:34	of the law, the **b** and the curses,
Ps	21: 7	make him the pattern of **b** forever,
Ps	24: 5	He will receive **b** from the Lord,
Ps	72:17	tribes of the earth give **b** with his name;
Prv	10: 6	**B** are for the head of the just;
Sir	40:27	The fear of God is a paradise of **b**;
Rom	15:27	come to share in their spiritual **b**,
Rom	15:27	also to serve them in material **b**.

BLEW → BLOW
Ex 15:10 When you **b** with your breath,
Tb 11:11 gall in his hand and **b** into his eyes.
Hg 1: 9 what you brought home, I **b** away.
Mt 7:25 the winds **b** and buffeted the house.
Rev 8: 7 When the first one **b** his trumpet,

BLIGHT
Dt 28:22 and drought, with **b** and mildew,
1 Kgs 8:37 or if **b** comes, or mildew, or locusts,
Am 4: 9 I struck you with **b** and mildew;
Hg 2:17 with searing wind, **b**, and hail,

BLIND → BLINDED, BLINDFOLDED, BLINDNESS, BLINDS
Ex 4:11 another mute or deaf, seeing or **b**?
Lv 19:14 a stumbling block in front of the **b**,
Lv 21:18 he who is **b**, or lame, or who has
Lv 22:22 One that is **b** or lame or maimed,
Dt 27:18 be anyone who misleads the **b**
2 Sm 5: 8 "The **b** and the lame shall not enter
Jb 29:15 I was eyes to the **b**, and feet
Ps 146: 8 the LORD gives sight to the **b**.
Is 35: 5 Then the eyes of the **b** shall see,
Is 42: 7 To open the eyes of the **b**, to bring
Is 42:19 Who is **b** but my servant, or deaf
Is 56:10 All the sentinels of Israel are **b**,
Mal 1: 8 you offer a **b** animal for sacrifice,
Mt 9:27 there, two **b** men followed [him],
Mt 11: 5 the **b** regain their sight, the lame
Mt 15:14 they are **b** guides [of the **b**].
Mt 15:14 If a **b** person leads a **b** person,
Mt 23:16 "Woe to you, **b** guides, who say,
Mk 10:46 Bartimaeus, a **b** man, the son
Lk 6:39 "Can a **b** person guide a **b** person?
Lk 14:13 poor, the crippled, the lame, the **b**;
Jn 9: 1 by he saw a man **b** from birth.
Jn 9:25 One thing I do know is that I was **b**
Rom 2:19 that you are a guide for the **b**
2 Pt 1: 9 Anyone who lacks them is **b**
Rev 3:17 pitiable, poor, **b**, and naked.

BLINDED → BLIND
Jn 12:40 "He **b** their eyes and hardened their
2 Cor 4: 4 of this age has **b** the minds

BLINDFOLDED → BLIND
Mk 14:65 They **b** him and struck him and said
Lk 22:64 They **b** him and questioned him,

BLINDNESS → BLIND
Dt 28:28 you with madness, **b** and panic,

BLINDS → BLIND
Ex 23: 8 for a bribe **b** the clear-sighted
Dt 16:19 for a bribe **b** the eyes even

BLOCK
Lv 19:14 or put a stumbling **b** in front
Is 44:19 Shall I worship a **b** of wood?"
Ez 3:20 I place a stumbling **b** before them,
Sir 31: 7 It is a stumbling **b** for fools;
Rom 11: 9 a stumbling **b** and a retribution
Rom 14:13 resolve never to put a stumbling **b**
1 Cor 1:23 crucified, a stumbling **b** to Jews
1 Cor 8: 9 in no way becomes a stumbling **b**
Rev 2:14 to put a stumbling **b** before

BLOOD → BLOODSHED, BLOODTHIRSTY
Gn 4:10 Your brother's **b** cries out to me
Gn 9: 6 Anyone who sheds the **b** of a human
Gn 9: 6 being shall that one's **b** be shed;
Ex 4:25 "Surely you are a spouse of **b**
Ex 7:17 Nile and it will be changed into **b**.
Ex 12:13 for you the **b** will mark the houses
Ex 12:13 Seeing the **b**, I will pass over you;
Ex 24: 8 he took the **b** and splashed it
Ex 24: 8 "This is the **b** of the covenant
Lv 1: 5 shall offer its **b** by splashing it on all
Lv 3:17 You shall not eat any fat or any **b**.
Lv 17:11 since the life of the flesh is in the **b**,
Lv 17:14 You shall not consume the **b** of any

Lv 17:14 Since the life of all flesh is its **b**,
Nm 35:19 of **b** is the one who will kill
Nm 35:33 can have no expiation for the **b** shed
Dt 12:23 that you do not eat of the **b**; for **b** is life;
1 Sm 14:32 and eating the meat with the **b** in it.
1 Kgs 21:19 the dogs licked up the **b** of Naboth,
1 Kgs 21:19 the dogs shall lick up your **b**, too."
1 Kgs 22:38 the dogs licked up his **b**
2 Kgs 9:33 of her **b** spurted against the wall
1 Mc 1:24 He shed much **b** and spoke
Ps 50:13 of bulls or drink the **b** of he-goats?
Ps 72:14 for precious is their **b** in his sight.
Ps 78:44 God turned their rivers to **b**;
Ps 106:38 Shedding innocent **b**, the **b** of their
Prv 6:17 tongue, hands that shed innocent **b**,
Sir 34:27 to deny a laborer wages is to shed **b**.
Is 1:11 In the **b** of calves, lambs, and goats
Is 9: 4 every cloak rolled in **b**, will be
Is 34: 6 LORD has a sword sated with **b**,
Is 66: 3 neck, Making an offering of pig's **b**,
Jl 3: 3 in the heavens and on the earth, **b**,
Zec 9:11 by the **b** of your covenant, I have
Mt 23:30 them in shedding the prophets' **b**.'
Mt 26:28 for this is my **b** of the covenant,
Mt 27: 6 treasury, for it is the price of **b**."
Mt 27: 8 even today is called the Field of B.
Mt 27:24 "I am innocent of this man's **b**.
Mk 14:24 "This is my **b** of the covenant,
Lk 11:51 from the **b** of Abel to the **b** of Zechariah
Lk 22:20 cup is the new covenant in my **b**,
Lk 22:44 sweat became like drops of **b** falling
Jn 6:53 of the Son of Man and drink his **b**,
Jn 19:34 immediately **b** and water flowed
Acts 1:19 'Akeldama,' that is, Field of B.
Acts 2:20 and the moon to **b**,
Acts 15:20 meat of strangled animals, and **b**.
Acts 18: 6 to them, "Your **b** be on your heads!
Acts 20:26 I am not responsible for the **b** of any
Rom 3:25 by his **b**, to prove his righteousness
Rom 5: 9 since we are now justified by his **b**,
1 Cor 10:16 a participation in the **b** of Christ?
1 Cor 11:25 cup is the new covenant in my **b**.
Eph 1: 7 him we have redemption by his **b**,
Eph 2:13 become near by the **b** of Christ.
Eph 6:12 our struggle is not with flesh and **b**
Col 1:20 by the **b** of his cross [through him],
Heb 9: 7 year, not without **b** that he offers
Heb 9:12 not with the **b** of goats and calves but with his own **b**,
Heb 9:20 "This is 'the **b** of the covenant
Heb 9:22 almost everything is purified by **b**,
Heb 9:22 of **b** there is no forgiveness.
Heb 10: 4 it is impossible that the **b** of bulls
Heb 12: 4 resisted to the point of shedding **b**.
Heb 12:24 and the sprinkled **b** that speaks more
Heb 13:12 consecrate the people by his own **b**.
Heb 13:20 by the **b** of the eternal covenant,
1 Pt 1:19 with the precious **b** of Christ as
1 Jn 1: 7 the **b** of his Son Jesus cleanses us
1 Jn 5: 6 one who came through water and **b**,
1 Jn 5: 6 by water alone, but by water and **b**.
1 Jn 5: 8 and the **b**, and the three are of one
Rev 1: 5 has freed us from our sins by his **b**,
Rev 5: 9 with your **b** you purchased for God
Rev 6:10 avenge our **b** on the inhabitants
Rev 6:12 and the whole moon became like **b**.
Rev 7:14 them white in the **b** of the Lamb.
Rev 11: 6 have power to turn water into **b**
Rev 12:11 conquered him by the **b** of the Lamb
Rev 14:20 **b** poured out of the wine press
Rev 16: 4 These also turned to **b**.
Rev 16: 6 For they have shed the **b** of the holy
Rev 16: 6 you [have] given them **b** to drink;
Rev 17: 6 was drunk on the **b** of the holy ones
Rev 17: 6 on the **b** of the witnesses to Jesus.
Rev 18:24 In her was found the **b** of prophets
Rev 19:13 a cloak that had been dipped in **b**,

BLOODSHED → BLOOD, SHED
Lv 17: 4 shall be judged guilty of **b**—
Is 5: 7 He waited for judgment, but see, **b**!
Ez 9: 9 the land is filled with **b**, the city
Hos 4: 2 and adultery break out; **b** follows **b**.
Hb 2:12 you who build a city by **b**, and who

BLOODTHIRSTY → BLOOD
Ps 55:24 These **b** liars will not live half their
Ps 59: 3 from the **b** save me.
Ps 139:19 O God, the **b** depart from me!
Prv 29:10 The **b** hate the blameless,

BLOSSOM → BLOSSOMS
Is 27: 6 Israel shall sprout and **b**,
Hos 14: 6 he will **b** like the lily;
Hb 3:17 For though the fig tree does not **b**,

BLOSSOMS → BLOSSOM
Ex 25:33 shaped like almond **b**, each with its
Nm 17:23 sprouts, produced **b**, and borne ripe

BLOT → BLOTTED
Ex 17:14 I will completely **b** out the memory
Dt 9:14 and **b** out their name from under
Ps 51: 3 your abundant compassion **b** out my
Jer 18:23 and their sin do not **b** out from your

BLOTTED → BLOT
Dt 25: 6 that his name may not be **b**
Ps 9: 6 their name you **b** out for all time.

BLOW → BLEW, BLOWING, BLOWS
Sg 4:16 **B** upon my garden that its perfumes
Ez 33: 6 coming and does not **b** the trumpet,
Jl 2: 1 **B** the horn in Zion, sound the alarm
Rev 7: 1 so that no wind could **b** on land
Rev 8: 6 seven trumpets prepared to **b** them.

BLOWING → BLOW
Jos 6:13 the ark of the Lord, **b** their horns.
2 Chr 23:13 of the land rejoicing and **b** trumpets,
Tb 6: 9 has white scales, **b** right into them,
Lk 12:55 the wind is **b** from the south you say

BLOWS → BLOW
Prv 27: 6 Trustworthy are the **b** of a friend,
Is 40: 7 breath of the Lord **b** upon it."
Jn 3: 8 The wind **b** where it wills, and you

BLUSH
Is 1:29 **b** on account of the gardens
Jer 6:15 they do not know how to **b**.
Jer 8:12 they do not know how to **b**.

BOANERGES
Mk 3:17 James, whom he named **B**, that is,

BOAST → BOASTED, BOASTFUL, BOASTING, BOASTS
Ps 75: 5 I say to the boastful: "Do not **b**!"
Prv 20:14 the buyer, then goes away only to **b**.
Prv 27: 1 Do not **b** about tomorrow, for you
Rom 2:23 You who **b** of the law, do you
Rom 5: 3 but we even **b** of our afflictions,
Rom 11:18 do not **b** against the branches.
1 Cor 1:31 boasts, should **b** in the Lord."
1 Cor 13: 3 I hand my body over so that I may **b**
2 Cor 1:14 that we are your **b** as you also are
2 Cor 5:12 giving you an opportunity to **b**
2 Cor 5:12 those who **b** of external appearance
2 Cor 10: 8 even if I should **b** a little too much
2 Cor 10:17 boasts, should **b** in the Lord."
2 Cor 11:30 If I must **b**, I will **b** of the things
Gal 6:14 may I never **b** except in the cross
Eph 2: 9 is not from works, so no one may **b**.
Phil 2:16 so that my **b** for the day of Christ

BOASTED → BOAST
Ps 44: 9 In God we have **b** all the day long;

BOASTFUL → BOAST
Ps 75: 5 So I say to the **b**: "Do not boast!"
Rom 1:30 haughty, **b**, ingenious in their

BOASTING → BOAST
1 Cor 4: 7 it, why are you **b** as if you did not
1 Cor 5: 6 Your **b** is not appropriate.
Jas 4:16 now you are **b** in your arrogance. All such **b** is evil.

BOASTS → BOAST
1 Cor 1:31 "Whoever **b**, should boast
2 Cor 10:17 "Whoever **b**, should boast

BOAT → BOATS
Sir 33: 2 is tossed about like a **b** in a storm.
Mt 4:21 They were in a **b**, with their father
Mt 8:23 He got into a **b** and his disciples
Mt 13: 2 around him that he got into a **b**
Mt 14:13 withdrew in a **b** to a deserted place
Mt 14:29 Peter got out of the **b** and began
Lk 5: 3 and taught the crowds from the **b**.
Jn 21: 6 the net over the right side of the **b**

BOATS → BOAT
Lk 5: 7 filled both **b** so that they were

BOAZ
Wealthy Bethlehemite who showed favor to Ruth (Ru 2), married her (Ru 4). Ancestor of David (Ru 4:18-22; 1 Chr 2:12-15), Jesus (Mt 1:5-16; Lk 3:23-32).

BODIES → BODY
Nm 14:29 wilderness your dead **b** shall fall.
Is 66:14 your **b** shall flourish like the grass;
Dn 3:94 the fire had had no power over the **b**
Mt 27:52 the **b** of many saints who had fallen
Rom 1:24 the mutual degradation of their **b**.
Rom 8:23 adoption, the redemption of our **b**.
Rom 12: 1 to offer your **b** as a living sacrifice,
1 Cor 6:15 not know that your **b** are members
Eph 5:28 love their wives as their own **b**.
Heb 10:22 and our **b** washed in pure water.

BODILY → BODY
Lk 3:22 upon him in **b** form like a dove.
Col 2: 9 the whole fullness of the deity **b**,

BODY → BODIES, BODILY
Ps 16: 9 my **b** also dwells secure,
Ez 1:23 each had two wings covering the **b**.
Mi 6: 7 the fruit of my **b** for the sin of my
Mt 6:22 "The lamp of the **b** is the eye.
Mt 10:28 not be afraid of those who kill the **b**
Mt 10:28 destroy both soul and **b** in Gehenna.
Mt 26:26 said, "Take and eat; this is my **b**."
Mt 27:58 Pilate and asked for the **b** of Jesus;
Mk 14:22 and said, "Take it; this is my **b**."
Lk 11:34 The lamp of the **b** is your eye.
Lk 11:34 it is bad, then your **b** is in darkness.
Lk 12: 4 not be afraid of those who kill the **b**
Lk 12:23 food and the **b** more than clothing.
Lk 22:19 "This is my **b**, which will be given
Lk 24: 3 they did not find the **b** of the Lord
Jn 2:21 speaking about the temple of his **b**.
Rom 6: 6 our sinful **b** might be done away
Rom 7:24 will deliver me from this mortal **b**?
Rom 8:10 although the **b** is dead because
Rom 12: 4 For as in one **b** we have many parts,
1 Cor 5: 3 although absent in **b** but present
1 Cor 6:13 the Lord, and the Lord is for the **b**;
1 Cor 6:18 a person commits is outside the **b**,
1 Cor 6:18 person sins against his own **b**.
1 Cor 6:19 not know that your **b** is a temple
1 Cor 6:20 Therefore, glorify God in your **b**.
1 Cor 7: 4 not have authority over her own **b**,
1 Cor 7: 4 not have authority over his own **b**,
1 Cor 9:27 No, I drive my **b** and train it,
1 Cor 10:16 a participation in the **b** of Christ?
1 Cor 11:24 said, "This is my **b** that is for you.
1 Cor 12:12 As a **b** is one though it has many
1 Cor 12:12 many, are one **b**, so also Christ.
1 Cor 12:13 we were all baptized into one **b**,
1 Cor 12:15 a hand I do not belong to the **b**,"

1 Cor	12:15	this reason belong any less to the **b**.
1 Cor	15:44	It is sown a natural **b**; it is raised a spiritual **b**.
2 Cor	4:10	about in the **b** the dying of Jesus,
2 Cor	5: 8	we would rather leave the **b** and go
2 Cor	12: 2	fourteen years ago (whether in the **b** or out of the **b** I do not know,
Gal	6:17	I bear the marks of Jesus on my **b**.
Eph	1:23	which is his **b**, the fullness
Eph	2:16	God, in one **b**, through the cross,
Eph	4: 4	one **b** and one Spirit, as you were
Eph	4:12	for building up the **b** of Christ,
Eph	5:30	because we are members of his **b**.
Phil	1:20	Christ will be magnified in my **b**,
Phil	3:21	He will change our lowly **b**
Phil	3:21	with his glorified **b** by the power
Col	1:18	He is the head of the **b**, the church.
Col	1:24	of Christ on behalf of his **b**,
1 Thes	5:23	and **b**, be preserved blameless
Heb	10: 5	desire, but a **b** you prepared for me;
Jas	2:26	just as a **b** without a spirit is dead,
1 Pt	2:24	our sins in his **b** upon the cross,
Jude	1: 9	in a dispute over the **b** of Moses,

BOIL → BOILED, BOILING, BOILS

Ex	23:19	You shall not **b** a young goat in its
Is	38:21	apply it to the **b** for his recovery."

BOILED → BOIL

Lam	4:10	women have **b** their own children!

BOILING → BOIL

Jer	1:13	"I see a **b** kettle whose mouth is

BOILS → BOIL

Ex	9: 9	cause festering **b** on human being
Dt	28:27	will strike you with Egyptian **b**

BOLDLY → BOLDNESS

Acts	9:28	spoke out **b** in the name of the Lord.
Acts	14: 3	period, speaking out **b** for the Lord,

BOLDNESS → BOLDLY

Acts	4:13	Observing the **b** of Peter and John
Acts	4:29	to speak your word with all **b**,
Eph	3:12	in whom we have **b** of speech

BOND → BONDAGE, BONDS

Eph	4: 3	of the spirit through the **b** of peace:
Col	3:14	on love, that is, the **b** of perfection.

BONDAGE → BOND

Ex	2:23	The Israelites groaned under their **b** and cried out, and from their **b** their cry
Ps	69:34	the poor, and does not spurn those in **b**.

BONDS → BOND

Ps	116:16	you have loosed my **b**.
Is	52: 2	Loose the **b** from your neck,

BONE → BONES

Gn	2:23	is **b** of my bones and flesh of my
Ez	37: 7	bones came together, **b** joining to **b**.

BONES → BONE

Gn	50:25	you must bring my **b** up from this
Ex	12:46	You shall not break any of its **b**.
Ex	13:19	also took Joseph's **b** with him,
Jos	24:32	The **b** of Joseph,
2 Kgs	13:21	came in contact with the **b** of Elisha,
Ps	22:15	all my **b** are disjointed.
Ps	22:18	I can count all my **b**. They stare
Ps	34:21	He watches over all his **b**;
Prv	14:30	to the body, but jealousy rots the **b**.
Sir	28:17	a blow from the tongue will break **b**.
Jer	20: 9	in my heart, imprisoned in my **b**;
Ez	37: 4	Prophesy over these **b**, and say
Ez	37: 4	Dry **b**, hear the word
Mt	23:27	inside are full of dead men's **b**

BOOK → BOOKS

Ex	24: 7	Taking the **b** of the covenant,
Ex	32:33	against me will I blot out of my **b**.
Dt	29:19	curse written in this **b** will pounce

Jos	1: 8	Do not let this **b** of the law depart
Jos	10:13	This is recorded in the B of Jashar.
Jos	23: 6	that is written in the **b** of the law
2 Kgs	22: 8	"I have found the **b** of the law
Neh	8: 8	read clearly from the **b** of the law
Ps	69:29	they be blotted from the **b** of life;
Is	34:16	Search through the **b** of the LORD
Dn	12: 1	who is found written in the **b**.
Mk	12:26	you not read in the B of Moses,
Jn	20:30	that are not written in this **b**.
Acts	1: 1	In the first **b**, Theophilus, I dealt
Phil	4: 3	whose names are in the **b** of life.
Rev	3: 5	erase his name from the **b** of life
Rev	13: 8	of the world in the **b** of life,
Rev	17: 8	have not been written in the **b** of life
Rev	20:12	scroll was opened, the **b** of life.
Rev	20:15	written in the **b** of life was thrown
Rev	21:27	are written in the Lamb's **b** of life.
Rev	22: 7	the prophetic message of this **b**.
Rev	22:18	hears the prophetic words in this **b**:
Rev	22:18	the plagues described in this **b**,

BOOKS → BOOK

Eccl	12:12	making of many **b** there is no end,
Dn	7:10	convened, and the **b** were opened.
Jn	21:25	whole world would contain the **b**

BOOTHS

Lv	23:34	month is the LORD's feast of B,
Dt	16:13	You shall celebrate the feast of B
2 Chr	8:13	feast of Weeks, and the feast of B.
Ezr	3: 4	kept the feast of B in the manner
Neh	8:14	should dwell in **b** during the feast
1 Mc	10:21	and sixtieth year at the feast of B,
2 Mc	1: 9	celebrate the feast of B in the month
Zec	14:16	and to celebrate the feast of B.

BOOTY

Prv	1:13	gain, we shall fill our houses with **b**;

BORDER → BORDERS

2 Chr	9:26	and down to the **b** of Egypt.

BORDERS → BORDER

Ex	16:35	until they came to the **b** of Canaan.
Ps	147:14	He brings peace to your **b**,
Ez	47:15	These are the **b** of the land:

BORE → BEAR

Gn	6: 4	of human beings, who **b** them sons.
Gn	16:15	Hagar **b** Abram a son, and Abram
Gn	16:15	the son whom Hagar **b** him Ishmael.
Ex	19: 4	how I **b** you up on eagles' wings
Ps	22:11	since my mother **b** me you are my God.
Is	53: 4	Yet it was our pain that he **b**,
Mt	8:17	our infirmities and **b** our diseases."
1 Pt	2:24	He himself **b** our sins in his body

BORN → BEAR

Gn	17:17	"Can a child be **b** to a man who is
Ex	1:22	into the Nile every boy that is **b**,
Jb	14: 1	Man **b** of woman is short-lived
Prv	17:17	and a brother is **b** for the time
Is	9: 5	For a child is **b** to us, a son is given
Is	66: 8	or a nation be **b** in a single moment?
Jer	1: 5	before you were **b** I dedicated you,
Mt	1:16	Of her was **b** Jesus who is called
Mt	2: 1	When Jesus was **b** in Bethlehem
Mk	14:21	that man if he had never been **b**."
Lk	1:35	the child to be **b** will be called holy,
Lk	2:11	of David a savior has been **b** for you
Lk	7:28	I tell you, among those **b** of women,
Jn	1:13	who were **b** not by natural
Jn	3: 3	God without being **b** from above."
Jn	3: 5	of God without being **b** of water
Jn	3: 7	you, 'You must be **b** from above.'
Jn	3: 8	everyone who is **b** of the Spirit."
Jn	18:37	For this I was **b** and for this I came
Rom	9:11	before they had yet been **b** or had
1 Cor	15: 8	as to one **b** abnormally, he appeared

Gal   4: 4   God sent his Son, **b** of a woman,
1 Pt   1:23   You have been **b** anew,

BORNE → BEAR
Gn   21: 7   Yet I have **b** him a son in his old
Nm   17:23   produced blossoms, and **b** ripe almonds!

BORROW → BORROWED, BORROWER
Dt   15: 6   to many nations, and **b** from none;
Dt   28:12   to many nations but **b** from none.
2 Kgs   4: 3   **b** vessels from all your neighbors—
Mt   5:42   your back on one who wants to **b**.

BORROWED → BORROW
Neh   5: 4   pay the king's tax we have **b** money

BORROWER → BORROW
Prv   22: 7   and the **b** is the slave of the lender.
Sir   29: 6   curses and insults the **b** will repay,
Is   24: 2   Lender and **b**, creditor and debtor.

BOSOM
Prv   6:27   Can a man take embers into his **b**,

BOTHER → BOTHERING
Lk   11: 7   in reply from within, 'Do not **b** me;

BOTHERING → BOTHER
Lk   18: 5   this widow keeps **b** me I shall

BOTTOM
Am   9: 3   from my gaze at the **b** of the sea,
Mk   15:38   was torn in two from top to **b**.

BOUGHS
Lv   23:40   and **b** of leafy trees and valley
Ez   31: 6   Under its **b** all the wild animals

BOUGHT → BUY
Gn   33:19   he had pitched his tent he **b**
Gn   50:13   Abraham had **b** for a burial ground
2 Sm   24:24   So David **b** the threshing floor
Neh   5: 8   we **b** back our Jewish kindred who

BOUND → BIND, BOUNDARY
Nm   30: 5   which she **b** herself remains valid.
Jgs   16:21   Gaza and **b** him with bronze fetters,
2 Kgs   25: 7   put out his eyes, **b** him with fetters,
Jer   39: 7   and **b** him in chains to bring him
Dn   3:21   They were **b** and cast
Mt   16:19   bind on earth shall be **b** in heaven;
Mt   18:18   bind on earth shall be **b** in heaven,
Mk   15: 1   They **b** Jesus, led him away,
Lk   13:16   whom Satan has **b** for eighteen
Rom   7: 2   Thus a married woman is **b** by law
1 Cor   7:15   or sister is not **b** in such cases;
1 Cor   7:39   A wife is **b** to her husband as long
Rev   9:14   "Release the four angels who are **b**

BOUNDARIES → BOUNDARY
Nm   34:12   land, with the **b** that surround it.
Dt   32: 8   He set up the **b** of the peoples
Ez   47:13   These are the **b** of the land

BOUNDARY → BOUND, BOUNDARIES
Nm   34: 3   Your southern **b** will be

BOUNTIFULLY → BOUNTY
2 Cor   9: 6   whoever sows **b** will also reap **b**.

BOUNTY → BOUNTIFULLY
1 Kgs   10:13   gave her from Solomon's royal **b**.
Ps   65:12   You adorn the year with your **b**;
Wis   16:25   your all-nourishing **b** according

BOW → BOWED, BOWS, BOWSTRINGS, RAINBOW
Gn   9:13   I set my **b** in the clouds to serve as
Gn   27:29   you, and nations **b** down to you;
Gn   27:29   may your mother's sons **b** down
Gn   49: 8   of your father shall **b** down to you.
Ex   20: 5   you shall not **b** down before them
Ex   34:14   You shall not **b** down to any other god,
Dt   5: 9   you shall not **b** down before them
Dt   26:10   and you shall **b** down before
1 Sm   18: 4   dress, even his sword, **b**, and belt.
2 Sm   22:35   my arms to bend even a **b** of bronze.

1 Kgs   22:34   But someone drew his **b** at random,
2 Kgs   13:15   said to him, "Take **b** and arrows,"
1 Chr   16:29   **b** down to the LORD, splendid in holiness.
Est   3: 2   would kneel and **b** down to Haman,
Est   3: 2   would not kneel and **b** down.
Ps   44: 7   Not in my **b** do I trust, nor does my
Ps   95: 6   Enter, let us **b** down in worship;
Ps   97: 7   all gods **b** down before him.
Ps   138: 2   I **b** low toward your holy temple;
Hos   1: 7   I will not save them by **b** or sword,
Zec   9:13   For I have bent Judah as my **b**,
Zec   14:17   up to Jerusalem to **b** down to the King,
Rev   6: 2   a white horse, and its rider had a **b**.

BOWED → BOW
Gn   37: 7   around my sheaf and **b** down to it."
Gn   47:31   Then Israel **b** at the head of the bed.
Ex   12:27   Then the people knelt and **b** down,
Ex   34: 8   knelt and **b** down to the ground.
Jdt   10: 9   Judith **b** down to God.
Jdt   13:17   They **b** down and worshiped God,
Ps   38: 7   I am stooped and deeply **b**;
Ps   145:14   and raises up all who are **b** down.
Ps   146: 8   raises up those who are **b** down;

BOWELS
2 Chr   21:15   pains from a disease in your **b**,
2 Mc   9: 5   with excruciating pains in his **b**

BOWL → BOWLS
Dt   28: 5   grain basket and your kneading **b**!
Dt   28:17   grain basket and your kneading **b**!
Eccl   12: 6   snapped and the golden **b** is broken,
Sg   7: 3   a round **b** that should never lack
Rev   16: 2   and poured out his **b** on the earth.

BOWLS → BOWL
Ezr   1:10   golden **b**, thirty; silver **b**,
Jer   52:19   the basins, fire holders, **b**, pots,
Jer   52:19   the sacrificial **b** made of gold
Rev   5: 8   harp and gold **b** filled with incense,
Rev   16: 1   pour out the seven **b** of God's fury
Rev   21: 9   angels who held the seven **b** filled

BOWS → BOW
1 Sm   2: 4   "The **b** of the mighty are broken,
Ps   37:15   their **b** will be broken.
Is   46: 1   Bel **b** down, Nebo stoops, their idols

BOWSTRINGS → BOW
Jgs   16: 7   seven fresh **b** that have not dried,"

BOY → BOYS
Gn   22:12   "Do not lay your hand on the **b**,"
Gn   44:22   lord, 'The **b** cannot leave his father;
Ex   1:22   into the Nile every **b** that is born,
Jgs   13: 5   for the **b** is to be a nazirite for God
Ru   4:16   Naomi took the **b**, cradled him against
Mt   17:18   and from that hour the **b** was cured.
Lk   2:43   the **b** Jesus remained behind
Jn   6: 9   "There is a **b** here who has five

BOYS → BOY
Ex   1:18   done this, allowing the **b** to live?"
1 Mc   2:46   any uncircumcised **b** whom they

BOZRAH
Is   34: 6   For the LORD has a sacrifice in **B**,
Jer   49:13   **B** shall become an object of horror,

BRACELETS
Gn   24:22   two gold **b** weighing ten shekels
Jdt   10: 4   feet, and put on her anklets, **b**, rings,
Is   3:19   the pendants, **b**, and veils;
Ez   16:11   jewelry, putting **b** on your arms,

BRAIDED
1 Tm   2: 9   not with **b** hairstyles and gold

BRAMBLES
Lk   6:44   nor do they gather grapes from **b**.

BRANCH → BRANCHES
Nm   13:23   where they cut down a **b**

1 Mc	13:37	crown and the palm **b** that you sent.
Is	4: 2	The **b** of the Lord will be beauty
Jer	1:11	"I see a **b** of the almond tree,"
Mal	3:19	fire, leaving them neither root nor **b**,
Jn	15: 2	He takes away every **b** in me
Jn	15: 4	Just as a **b** cannot bear fruit on its

BRANCHES → BRANCH

Gn	2:10	there it divides and becomes four **b**.
Gn	40:10	and on the vine were three **b**.
Ex	25:32	Six **b** are to extend from its sides,
Ex	25:32	from its sides, three **b** on one side,
Lv	23:40	fruit of majestic trees, **b** of palms,
2 Sm	18: 9	as the mule passed under the **b**
Neh	8:15	hill country and bring in **b** of olive,
1 Mc	13:51	the waving of palm **b**, the playing
Ps	118:27	in procession with leafy **b**
Ez	17: 6	produced **b**, and put forth shoots.
Lk	13:19	birds of the sky dwelt in its **b**.' "
Jn	12:13	they took palm **b** and went
Jn	15: 5	I am the vine, you are the **b**.
Rom	11:21	if God did not spare the natural **b**,
Rev	7: 9	and holding palm **b** in their hands.

BRAND

Am	4:11	you were like a **b** plucked
Zec	3: 2	Is this not a **b** plucked

BREACH → BREACHED, BREACHES

Jgs	21:15	had made a **b** among the tribes
Ps	106:23	in the **b** to turn back his destroying
Ps	144:14	May there be no **b** in the walls,
Ez	22:30	stand in the **b** before me to keep me

BREACHED → BREACH

2 Kgs	25: 4	the city walls were **b**. That night,

BREACHES → BREACH

Am	9:11	I will wall up its **b**, raise up its

BREAD → SHOWBREAD

Gn	3:19	sweat of your brow you shall eat **b**,
Gn	14:18	of Salem, brought out **b** and wine.
Ex	12: 8	eating it roasted with unleavened **b**
Ex	12:17	the custom of the unleavened **b**,
Ex	16: 4	going to rain down **b** from heaven
Ex	23:15	keep the feast of Unleavened **B**.
Ex	23:15	you must eat unleavened **b** for seven
Lv	7:13	loaves of leavened **b** along
Dt	8: 3	it is not by **b** alone that people live,
Dt	16: 3	You shall not eat leavened **b** with it.
Dt	16: 3	shall eat with it only unleavened **b**, the **b** of affliction,
Dt	29: 5	it was not **b** that you ate, nor wine
Jgs	7:13	a round loaf of barley **b** was rolling
1 Sm	21: 5	"I have no ordinary **b** on hand, only holy **b**;
1 Kgs	17: 6	Ravens brought him **b** and meat
1 Kgs	22:27	and feed him scanty rations of **b**
Ps	37:25	or his offspring begging for **b**.
Ps	42: 4	My tears have been my **b** day and night,
Ps	53: 5	my people as they feed upon **b**?
Ps	80: 6	You have fed them the **b** of tears,
Ps	136:25	gives **b** to all flesh, for his mercy
Ps	146: 7	oppressed, who gives **b** to the hungry.
Prv	6:26	a harlot may be scarcely a loaf of **b**,
Prv	9:17	and **b** taken secretly is pleasing!"
Prv	20:17	**B** earned by deceit is sweet,
Eccl	9: 7	eat your **b** with joy and drink your
Eccl	11: 1	Send forth your **b** upon the face
Wis	16:20	and furnished them **b** from heaven,
Sir	15: 3	will feed him with the **b** of learning,
Sir	23:17	To the unchaste all **b** is sweet;
Is	55: 2	spend your money for what is not **b**;
Am	8:11	Not a hunger for **b**, or a thirst
Ob	1: 7	who eat your **b** will replace you
Mt	4: 3	these stones become loaves of **b**."
Mt	6:11	Give us today our daily **b**;
Mt	15:33	"Where could we ever get enough **b**
Mt	16: 5	disciples had forgotten to bring **b**.
Mt	26:26	Jesus took **b**, said the blessing,
Mk	2:26	ate the **b** of offering that only

Lk	4: 4	'One does not live by **b** alone.' "
Lk	11: 3	Give us each day our daily **b**
Lk	22:19	Then he took the **b**,
Lk	24:35	to them in the breaking of the **b**.
Jn	6:33	For the **b** of God is
Jn	6:35	said to them, "I am the **b** of life;
Jn	6:41	"I am the **b** that came down
Jn	6:48	I am the **b** of life.
Jn	6:51	I am the living **b** that came down
Jn	6:51	whoever eats this **b** will live
Jn	6:51	the **b** that I will give is my flesh
Jn	21:13	and took the **b** and gave it to them,
Acts	2:42	to the breaking of the **b**
1 Cor	5: 8	with the unleavened **b** of sincerity
1 Cor	10:16	The **b** that we break, is it not
1 Cor	11:23	night he was handed over, took **b**,
1 Cor	11:26	For as often as you eat this **b**

BREADTH

Gn	13:17	across its length and **b**, for I give it
Eph	3:18	with all the holy ones what is the **b**

BREAK → BREAKING, BREAKS, BROKE, BROKEN, BROKENHEARTED, DAYBREAK

Ex	12:46	You shall not **b** any of its bones.
Ex	19:21	warn the people not to **b** through
Ex	34:20	not redeem it, you must **b** its neck.
Jgs	2: 1	I will never **b** my covenant
Ps	3: 8	you **b** the teeth of the wicked.
Ps	10:15	**B** the arm of the wicked
Prv	25:15	and a soft tongue can **b** a bone.
Is	42: 3	A bruised reed he will not **b**,
Ez	17:15	Can he **b** a covenant and go free?
Mt	6:19	destroy, and thieves **b** in and steal.
Mt	12:20	A bruised reed he will not **b**,
Mt	15: 3	why do you **b** the commandment
Jn	19:33	dead, they did not **b** his legs,
Acts	20: 7	week when we gathered to **b** bread,
Rom	2:25	but if you **b** the law,
1 Cor	10:16	The bread that we **b**, is it not
Rev	5: 2	to open the scroll and **b** its seals?"

BREAKFAST

Jn	21:12	said to them, "Come, have **b**."

BREAKING → BREAK

Dt	31:20	despising me and **b** my covenant,
Ez	16:59	despised an oath by **b** a covenant.
Acts	2:42	life, to the **b** of the bread
Rom	2:23	do you dishonor God by **b** the law?

BREAKS → BREAK

Ps	46:10	to the ends of the earth, **b** the bow,
Mt	5:19	whoever **b** one of the least of these

BREAST → BREASTPIECE, BREASTPLATE, BREASTPLATES, BREASTS

Lk	18:13	to heaven but beat his **b** and prayed,

BREASTPIECE → BREAST, PIECE

Ex	28:15	The **b** of decision you shall
Ex	28:30	this **b** of decision you shall put
Lv	8: 8	He then set the **b** on him,

BREASTPLATE → BREAST

Wis	5:18	Shall put on righteousness for a **b**,
Is	59:17	He put on justice as his **b**, victory as
Eph	6:14	clothed with righteousness as a **b**,
1 Thes	5: 8	putting on the **b** of faith and love

BREASTPLATES → BREAST

Rev	9: 9	and they had chests like iron **b**.
Rev	9:17	and yellow **b**, and the horses' heads

BREASTS → BREAST

Gn	49:25	The blessings of **b** and womb,
Ps	22:10	made me safe at my mother's **b**.
Sg	4: 5	Your **b** are like two fawns,
Is	32:12	Beat your **b** for the pleasant fields,
Is	66:11	with delight at her abundant **b**!
Ez	23: 3	There the Egyptians fondled their **b**
Na	2: 8	Moaning like doves, beating their **b**.
Lk	11:27	and the **b** at which you nursed."

Lk   23:29 bore and the **b** that never nursed.'

BREATH → BREATHED, BREATHING
Gn   2: 7 blew into his nostrils the **b** of life,
Gn   6:17 sky in which there is the **b** of life;
2 Sm 22:16 the LORD, at the storming **b** of his nostrils.
Jb   27: 3 So long as I still have life **b** in me, the **b** of God in my nostrils,
Ps   39:12 Every man is but a **b**.
Eccl 12: 7 the life **b** returns to God who gave
Is   40: 7 when the **b** of the LORD blows
Jer   10:14 molded a fraud, without **b** of life.
Acts 17:25 he who gives to everyone life and **b**
2 Thes 2: 8 will kill with the **b** of his mouth
Rev   11:11 a **b** of life from God entered them.

BREATHED → BREATH
Mk   15:37 Jesus gave a loud cry and **b** his last.
Jn   20:22 this, he **b** on them and said to them,

BREATHING → BREATH
Acts   9: 1 still **b** murderous threats against

BRIBE → BRIBES
Ex   23: 8 Never take a **b**, for a **b** blinds
Dt   16:19 you shall not take a **b**, for a **b** blinds
1 Sm 12: 3 From whom have I accepted a **b**
Eccl   7: 7 the wise, and a **b** corrupts the heart.
Mi   3:11 Its leaders render judgment for a **b**,

BRIBES → BRIBE
1 Sm   8: 3 accepting **b** and perverting justice.
Prv   15:27 but those who hate **b** will live.
Is   5:23 Those who acquit the guilty for **b**,
Ez   22:12 in you who take **b** to shed blood.

BRICK → BRICKS
Ex   1:14 at mortar and **b** and all kinds of field

BRICKS → BRICK
Gn   11: 3 let us mold **b** and harden them
Ex   5: 8 levy upon them the same quota of **b**

BRIDE → BRIDEGROOM
Sg   4: 8 With me from Lebanon, my **b**!
Is   49:18 as jewels, bedeck yourself like a **b**.
Is   62: 5 in his **b** so shall your God rejoice
Jer   2: 2 how you loved me as a **b**,
Jn   3:29 who has the **b** is the bridegroom;
Rev   19: 7 come, his **b** has made herself ready.
Rev   21: 2 prepared as a **b** adorned for her
Rev   21: 9 I will show you the **b**, the wife
Rev   22:17 The Spirit and the **b** say, "Come."

BRIDEGROOM → BRIDE
Ps   19: 6 it comes forth like a **b** from his
Jer   25:10 the voice of the **b** and the voice
Bar   2:23 the voice of the **b** and the voice
Mt   9:15 guests mourn as long as the **b** is
Mt   9:15 will come when the **b** is taken away
Mt   25: 1 lamps and went out to meet the **b**.
Mk   2:20 will come when the **b** is taken away
Jn   3:29 The one who has the bride is the **b**;

BRIDLE
Ps   32: 9 bit and **b** their temper is curbed,
Is   30:28 **b** the jaws of the peoples to send
Jas   3: 2 man, able to **b** his whole body also.
Rev   14:20 a horse's **b** for two hundred miles.

BRIEF → BRIEFLY
Is   54: 7 For a **b** moment I abandoned you,

BRIEFLY → BRIEF
Heb   13:22 for I have written to you rather **b**.

BRIER → BRIERS
Mi   7: 4 The best of them is like a **b**,

BRIERS → BRIER
Is   7:24 for all the country shall be **b**

BRIGHT → BRIGHTER, BRIGHTNESS
Mt   17: 5 a **b** cloud cast a shadow over them,
Ez   1: 4 with flashing fire, a **b** glow all around it,

Rev   19: 8 She was allowed to wear a **b**,
Rev   22:16 of David, the **b** morning star."

BRIGHTER → BRIGHT
Acts 26:13 a light from the sky, **b** than the sun,

BRIGHTNESS → BRIGHT
Is   59: 9 for **b**, and we walk in gloom!
Is   60:19 Nor shall the **b** of the moon give
Am   5:20 not light, gloom without any **b**!
Acts 22:11 see nothing because of the **b**

BRIM
Jn   2: 7 So they filled them to the **b**.

BRING → BRINGING, BRINGS, BROUGHT
Gn   6:17 to **b** the flood waters on the earth,
Gn   6:19 all living creatures you shall **b** two
Gn   28:15 you go, and **b** you back to this land.
Ex   13:19 you must **b** my bones up with you from here."
Lv   1: 2 you shall **b** your offering
Nm   20: 5 only to **b** us to this wretched place?
Dt   24: 4 you shall not **b** such guilt
2 Sm 12:23 Can I **b** him back again?
2 Kgs 22:16 I am about to **b** evil upon this place
Ps   25:17 **b** me out of my distress.
Prv   25: 8 have seen do not **b** forth too quickly
Eccl 11: 9 that God will **b** you to judgment.
Eccl 12:14 because God will **b** to judgment
Is   60:17 Instead of bronze I will **b** gold, instead of iron I will **b** silver;
Jer   24: 6 good and **b** them back to this land,
Ez   5:17 I will **b** the sword against you.
Zec   3: 8 I will surely **b** my servant
Zec   4: 7 He will **b** forth the first stone amid
Mt   10:34 I have come to **b** peace
Mt   10:34 I have come to **b** not peace
Lk   4:18 he has anointed me to **b** glad tidings
Rom   8:33 Who will **b** a charge against God's
Rom   10: 6 (that is, to **b** Christ down)
Rom   10:15 of those who **b** [the] good news!"
1 Cor 8: 8 Now food will not **b** us closer
2 Jn   1:10 to you and does not **b** this doctrine,
Rev   21:24 of the earth will **b** their treasure.

BRINGING → BRING
Nm   14: 3 Why is the LORD **b** us into this
Dt   8: 7 God, is **b** you into a good country,
1 Kgs 21:21 I am **b** evil upon you:
Is   52: 7 the feet of the one **b** good news,
Lk   18:15 People were **b** even infants to him
Heb   2:10 exist, in **b** many children to glory,
2 Pt   2: 1 **b** swift destruction on themselves.

BRINGS → BRING
Sir   26: 2 A loyal wife **b** joy to her husband,
Mt   12:35 A good person **b** forth good
Mt   12:35 an evil person **b** forth evil
Lk   11:26 and **b** back seven other spirits more
Jas   5:20 know that whoever **b** back a sinner

BRISKET
Ex   29:26 take the **b** of Aaron's installation ram
Lv   7:30 shall bring the fat together with the **b**,
Nm   6:20 along with the **b** of the elevated offering

BROKE → BREAK
Ex   32:19 **b** them on the base of the mountain.
Ex   34: 1 on the former tablets that you **b**.
Dt   32:51 because both of you **b** faith with me
2 Kgs 23:14 He **b** to pieces the pillars, cut down
2 Kgs 25:13 the Chaldeans **b** into pieces;
Jer   31:32 They **b** my covenant, though I was
Ez   17:19 And my covenant which he **b**, I will
Mt   14:19 he said the blessing, **b** the loaves,
Mt   26:26 said the blessing, **b** it, and giving it
Mk   14:22 said the blessing, **b** it, and gave it
1 Cor 11:24 he had given thanks, **b** it and said,

BROKEN → BREAK
Gn   17:14 he has **b** my covenant.
1 Sm   4:18 of a **b** neck since he was an old man

2 Kgs	18:21	trust in Egypt, that **b** reed of a staff,
Ps	34:21	not one of them shall be **b**.
Prv	18:14	ill, but a **b** spirit who can bear?
Eccl	4:12	A three-ply cord is not easily **b**.
Eccl	12: 6	is snapped and the golden bowl is **b**,
Wis	4: 5	Their twigs shall be **b** off untimely,
Jer	33:21	with my servant David be **b**,
Ez	44: 7	Thus you have **b** my covenant by all
Jn	7:23	that the law of Moses may not be **b**,
Jn	19:36	"Not a bone of it will be **b**."
Rom	11:20	They were **b** off because

BROKENHEARTED → BREAK, HEART

Ps	34:19	The Lord is close to the **b**,
Ps	109:16	poor and brought death to the **b**.
Ps	147: 3	Healing the **b**, and binding up their
Is	61: 1	to bind up the **b**, To proclaim liberty

BRONZE

Gn	4:22	of all who forge instruments of **b**
Ex	26:11	make fifty **b** clasps and put them
Ex	27: 2	You shall then plate it with **b**.
Ex	27:10	columns and twenty pedestals of **b**;
Ex	30:18	shall make a **b** basin with a **b** stand.
Nm	17: 4	So taking the **b** censers which had
Nm	21: 9	Moses made a **b** serpent
Dt	28:23	over your heads will be like **b**
1 Sm	17: 5	He had a **b** helmet on his head
1 Kgs	7:15	He fashioned two **b** columns,
1 Kgs	7:27	He also made ten stands of **b**,
2 Kgs	16:14	The **b** altar that stood before
2 Kgs	25:13	The **b** columns that belonged
2 Kgs	25:13	they carried away the **b** to Babylon.
1 Mc	14:48	should be engraved on **b** tablets,
Ps	18:35	war, my arms to string a bow of **b**.
Is	60:17	Instead of **b** I will bring gold,
Is	60:17	Instead of wood, **b**;
Dn	2:32	were silver, its belly and thighs **b**,
Dn	7:19	with its iron teeth and **b** claws,
Dn	10: 6	and feet looked like burnished **b**,
Dn	14: 7	"it is only clay inside and **b** outside;
Zec	6: 1	and the mountains were of **b**.

BROOD

Mt	3: 7	he said to them, "You **b** of vipers!
Mt	12:34	You **b** of vipers, how can you say
Mt	23:33	You serpents, you **b** of vipers,
Lk	13:34	a hen gathers her **b** under her wings,

BROOK

Jer	15:18	To me you are like a deceptive **b**,

BROOM

1 Kgs	19: 4	until he came to a solitary **b** tree
Is	14:23	sweep it with the **b** of destruction,

BROTH

Jgs	6:19	meat in a basket and the **b** in a pot,
Is	65: 4	pigs, with **b** of unclean meat in their

BROTHER → BROTHER'S, BROTHER-IN-LAW, BROTHERS

Gn	4: 8	Cain said to his **b** Abel, "Let us go
Gn	4: 8	Cain attacked his **b** Abel and killed
Gn	20:13	we come to, say: He is my **b**.' "
Gn	27:35	"Your **b** came here by a ruse
Gn	27:41	so that I may kill my **b** Jacob."
Gn	32:12	Save me from the hand of my **b**,
Gn	42:20	you must bring me your youngest **b**.
Gn	43:30	affection for his **b** that he was
Gn	45: 4	"I am your **b** Joseph, whom you
Ex	7: 1	Aaron your **b** will be your prophet.
Dt	13: 7	If your **b**, your father's child or your
Dt	25: 5	her husband's **b** shall come to her,
2 Sm	13:12	But she answered him, "No, my **b**!
Sg	8: 1	Would that you were a **b** to me,
Am	1:11	Because he pursued his **b**
Ob	1:10	of violence to your **b** Jacob,
Mt	5:22	is angry with his **b** will be liable
Mt	5:22	and whoever says to his **b**, 'Raqa,'
Mt	5:24	first and be reconciled with your **b**,

Mt	10:21	B will hand over **b** to death,
Mk	3:35	does the will of God is my **b**
Lk	20:28	'If someone's **b** dies leaving a wife
Lk	20:28	and raise up descendants for his **b**.'
Rom	14:15	If your **b** is being hurt by what you
Rom	14:21	that causes your **b** to stumble.
1 Cor	5:11	to associate with anyone named a **b**,
Phlm	1:16	slave, a **b**, beloved especially to me,
Jas	2:15	If a **b** or sister has nothing to wear
1 Jn	2:10	Whoever loves his **b** remains
1 Jn	3:15	who hates his **b** is a murderer,
1 Jn	3:17	who has worldly means sees a **b**
1 Jn	4:20	God," but hates his **b**, he is a liar;
1 Jn	4:20	does not love a **b** whom he has seen
1 Jn	5:16	If anyone sees his **b** sinning,

BROTHER'S → BROTHER

Gn	4: 9	do not know. Am I my **b** keeper?"
Lv	20:21	If a man takes his **b** wife, it is severe
Dt	25: 7	does not want to marry his **b** wife,
Mk	6:18	for you to have your **b** wife."

BROTHER-IN-LAW → BROTHER

Gn	38: 8	in fulfillment of your duty as **b**,

BROTHERS → BROTHER

Gn	9:25	of slaves shall he be to his **b**."
Gn	27:29	Be master of your **b**, and may your
Gn	37:11	So his **b** were furious at him but his
Gn	42:13	"are twelve **b**, sons of a certain man
Jgs	9: 5	and killed his **b**, the seventy sons
2 Chr	21:13	because you have killed your **b**
1 Mc	3:25	Judas and his **b** began to be feared,
Mt	5:47	And if you greet your **b** only,
Mt	12:49	"Here are my mother and my **b**.
Mt	19:29	who has given up houses or **b**
Mt	20:24	they became indignant at the two **b**.
Mk	3:33	"Who are my mother and [my] **b**?"
Mk	12:20	Now there were seven **b**.
Lk	21:16	even be handed over by parents, **b**,
Lk	22:32	back, you must strengthen your **b**."
Jn	7: 5	For his **b** did not believe in him.
2 Cor	11:26	at sea, dangers among false **b**;
1 Thes	4:10	for all the **b** throughout Macedonia.
1 Thes	5:26	Greet all the **b** with a holy kiss.
1 Tm	5: 1	as a father. Treat younger men as **b**,
Heb	2:11	he is not ashamed to call them "**b**,"
Heb	2:17	to become like his **b** in every way,

BROUGHT → BRING

Gn	2:19	he **b** them to the man to see what he
Gn	2:22	When he **b** her to the man,
Gn	15: 7	I am the Lord who **b** you
Ex	13: 9	a strong hand the Lord **b** you
Ex	32: 1	that man Moses who **b** us
Nm	21: 5	"Why have you **b** us up from Egypt
Jgs	2: 1	I **b** you up from Egypt and led you
Ru	1:21	the Lord has **b** me back empty.
Ru	1:21	since the Lord has **b** me to trial,
2 Chr	36:18	princes, all these he **b** to Babylon.
Ezr	1: 7	the house of the Lord **b** forth
Ezr	6: 5	and **b** to Babylon be sent back;
Ps	30: 4	you **b** my soul up from Sheol;
Ps	105:43	He **b** his people out with joy,
Prv	8:25	place, before the hills, I was **b** forth;
Ez	11: 1	**b** me to the east gate of the house
Dn	5:13	Daniel was **b** into the presence
Jon	2: 7	But you **b** my life up from the pit,
Hg	1: 6	sown much, but have **b** in little;
Mt	4:24	they **b** to him all who were sick
Mk	6:28	He **b** in the head on a platter
Mk	8:22	they **b** to him a blind man
Mk	15:22	They **b** him to the place of Golgotha
1 Tm	6: 7	For we **b** nothing into the world,
Heb	13:20	who **b** up from the dead the great

BRUISED

Is	42: 3	A **b** reed he will not break,
Mt	12:20	A **b** reed he will not break,

BRUTE
Ps   73:22 I was like a **b** beast in your

BUCKET
Is   40:15 the nations count as a drop in the **b**,
Jn   4:11 you do not even have a **b**

BUCKLER
Ps   35: 2 Take up the shield and **b**;

BUDDED
Gn   40:10 It had barely **b** when its blossoms

BUGLE
1 Cor 14: 8 if the **b** gives an indistinct sound,

BUILD → BUILDER, BUILDERS, BUILDING, BUILDINGS, BUILDS,
    BUILT, REBUILD, REBUILT
Gn   11: 4 let us **b** ourselves a city and a tower.
Ex   20:25 for me, do not **b** it of cut stone,
Nm   23: 1 to Balak, "**B** me seven altars here,
Dt   6:10 fine, large cities that you did not **b**,
Dt   27: 5 and you shall **b** there an altar
2 Sm   7: 5 Is it you who would **b** me a house
Ps   127: 1 Unless the LORD **b** the house, they labor in vain who **b**.
Eccl   3: 3 a time to tear down, and a time to **b**.
Sir   21: 8 Those who **b** their houses with someone else's
Is   57:14 **B** up, **b** up, prepare the way,
Is   62:10 **B** up, **b** up the highway, clear it
Jer   18: 9 kingdom that I will **b** up and plant
Mi   3:10 Who **b** up Zion with bloodshed,
Zep   1:13 They will **b** houses, but not dwell
Hg   1: 8 **b** the house that I may be pleased
Zec   6:12 he will **b** the temple of the LORD.
Mt   16:18 upon this rock I will **b** my church,
Mt   23:29 You **b** the tombs of the prophets
Mk   14:58 three days I will **b** another not made
Acts   20:32 word of his that can **b** you
1 Thes 5:11 one another and **b** one another up,
Jude   1:20 **b** yourselves up in your most holy

BUILDER → BUILD
1 Cor 3:10 to me, like a wise master **b** I laid

BUILDERS → BUILD
1 Kgs 5:32 Solomon's and Hiram's **b**,
Ezr   3:10 While the **b** were laying
Ps   118:22 The stone the **b** rejected has become
Mt   21:42 that the **b** rejected has become
Mk   12:10 that the **b** rejected has become
Lk   20:17 which the **b** rejected has become
Acts   4:11 by you, the **b**, which has become
1 Pt   2: 7 which the **b** rejected has become

BUILDING → BUILD
Jos   22:16 by **b** an altar of your own you have
1 Kgs 9: 1 After Solomon finished **b** the house
Ezr   4: 1 the exiles were **b** a temple
Neh   2:18 They replied, "Let us begin **b**!"
Mi   7:11 It is the day for **b** your walls;
Lk   6:48 That one is like a person **b** a house,
Rom   15: 2 our neighbor for the good, for **b** up.
1 Cor 3: 9 you are God's field, God's **b**.
1 Cor 14:26 Everything should be done for **b** up.
2 Cor 5: 1 destroyed, we have a **b** from God,
2 Cor 10: 8 which the Lord gave for **b** you
2 Cor 12:19 and all for **b** you up, beloved.
Eph   4:12 for **b** up the body of Christ,

BUILDINGS → BUILD
Mk   13: 1 teacher, what stones and what **b**!"

BUILDS → BUILD
Prv   14: 1 Wisdom **b** her house, but Folly tears
Prv   29: 4 By justice a king **b** up the land;
Jer   22:13 Woe to him who **b** his house
1 Cor 3:10 each one must be careful how he **b**
1 Cor 3:12 If anyone **b** on this foundation
1 Cor 8: 1 inflates with pride, but love **b** up.
1 Cor 10:23 is lawful," but not everything **b** up.
1 Cor 14: 4 speaks in a tongue **b** himself up, but whoever
        prophesies **b** up

BUILT → BUILD
Gn   8:20 Noah **b** an altar to the LORD,
Gn   12: 7 So Abram **b** an altar there
Gn   22: 9 him, Abraham **b** an altar there
Gn   26:25 So Isaac **b** an altar there
Gn   35: 7 There he **b** an altar and called
Ex   17:15 Moses **b** an altar there, which he
Ex   32: 5 Aaron **b** an altar in front of the calf
Jos   8:30 Ebal, Joshua **b** to the LORD,
Jos   22:11 of Manasseh have **b** an altar"
Jgs   6:24 So Gideon **b** there an altar
1 Sm   7:17 Israel and **b** an altar to the LORD.
1 Sm   14:35 and Saul **b** an altar to the LORD—
2 Sm   24:25 David **b** an altar to the LORD
1 Mc   4:47 **b** a new altar like the former one.
Ps   122: 3 Jerusalem, **b** as a city, walled round
Prv   9: 1 Wisdom has **b** her house, she has set
Prv   24: 3 By wisdom a house is **b**,
Is   5: 2 Within it he **b** a watchtower,
Hos   10: 1 his fruit, the more altars he **b**;
Mt   7:24 be like a wise man who **b** his house
Mk   12: 1 it, dug a wine press, and **b** a tower.
Lk   6:49 act is like a person who **b** a house
1 Cor 3:14 that someone **b** upon the foundation,
1 Cor 14:17 very well, but the other is not **b** up.
Eph   2:20 **b** upon the foundation
Col   2: 7 rooted in him and **b** upon him
Heb   11: 7 seen, with reverence **b** an ark
1 Pt   2: 5 let yourselves be **b** into a spiritual

BULL → BULLS
Ex   29: 1 Procure a young **b** and two
Lv   1: 5 The **b** shall then be slaughtered
Lv   4: 3 the LORD an unblemished **b**

BULLS → BULL
1 Chr 29:21 a thousand **b**, a thousand rams,
Ezr   6:17 they offered one hundred **b**,
Ps   22:13 Many **b** surround me; fierce **b**
Ps   50:13 Do I eat the flesh of **b** or drink
Heb   10: 4 it is impossible that the blood of **b**

BURDEN → BURDENED, BURDENS, BURDENSOME
Gn   49:15 He bent his shoulder to the **b**
Ex   18:22 Lighten your **b** by letting them bear
Nm   11:11 with me that you **b** me with all this
Ps   38: 5 me, a **b** too heavy for me.
Is   10:27 day, His **b** shall be taken from your
Jer   23:33 "What is the **b** of the LORD?"
Jer   23:33 "You are the **b**, and I cast you
Mt   11:30 my yoke is easy, and my **b** light."
Acts   15:28 you any **b** beyond these necessities,
2 Cor 11: 9 I did not anyone, for the brothers
2 Cor 12:14 And I will not be a **b**, for I want not
2 Thes 3: 8 worked, so as not to **b** any of you.
Rev   2:24 on you I will place no further **b**,

BURDENED → BURDEN
Is   43:24 Instead, you **b** me with your sins,
1 Tm   5:16 the church is not to be **b**, so that it

BURDENS → BURDEN
Wis   9:15 For the corruptible body **b** the soul
Lk   11:46 You impose on people **b** hard
Gal   6: 2 Bear one another's **b**, and so you

BURDENSOME → BURDEN
1 Jn   5: 3 And his commandments are not **b**,

BURIAL → BURY
Gn   23: 6 dead in the choicest of our **b** sites.
Gn   23: 6 us would deny his his **b** ground
Gn   49:30 Ephron the Hittite for a **b** ground.
Dt   34: 6 day no one knows the place of his **b**.
Mt   26:12 body, she did it to prepare me for **b**.

BURIED → BURY
Gn   15:15 you will be **b** at a ripe old age.
Ru   1:17 you die I will die, and there be **b**.
Acts   2:29 David that he died and was **b**,
Rom   6: 4 We were indeed **b** with him through

1 Cor 15: 4 that he was **b**; that he was raised
Col   2:12 You were **b** with him in baptism,

BURN → BURNED, BURNING, BURNS, BURNT
Ex   3: 3 Why does the bush not **b** up?"
Ex   21:25 **b** for **b**, wound for wound,
Lk   3:17 his barn, but the chaff he will **b**

BURNED → BURN
Gn   38:24 said, "Bring her out; let her be **b**."
Lv   20:14 the two women as well shall be **b**
Lv   21: 9 she shall be **b** with fire.
Nm   11: 3 fire of the LORD **b** among them.
2 Kgs 23:20 and **b** human bones upon them.
Jer   36:29 You are the one who **b** that scroll,
Mt   13:40 are collected and **b** [up] with fire,
Jn   15: 6 them into a fire and they will be **b**.
1 Cor   3:15 But if someone's work is **b** up,
Heb   6: 8 it will soon be cursed and finally **b**.
Rev   8: 7 A third of the land was **b** up,

BURNING → BURN
Lv   6: 2 while the fire is kept **b** on the altar.
Ps   79: 5 your jealous anger keep **b** like fire?
Ps   140:11 Drop **b** coals upon them;
Ez   1:13 living creatures seemed like **b** coals
Dn   7: 9 flames of fire, with wheels of **b** fire.
Lk   24:32 not our hearts **b** [within us] while he
Jn   5:35 He was a **b** and shining lamp,
Acts   7:30 Sinai in the flame of a **b** bush.
Rom   12:20 so doing you will heap **b** coals
Rev   8: 8 like a large **b** mountain was hurled

BURNISHED
1 Kgs   7:45 of the LORD were of **b** bronze.
Dn   10: 6 arms and feet looked like **b** bronze,

BURNS → BURN
Sir   23:16 not to be quenched till it **b** itself out;
Is   44:16 Half of it he **b** in the fire, on its

BURNT → BURN
Gn   8:20 he offered **b** offerings on the altar.
Gn   22: 2 There offer him up as a **b** offering
Gn   22: 8 "God will provide the sheep for the **b** offering."
Ex   10:25 also must give us sacrifices and **b** offerings
Ex   18:12 brought a **b** offering and sacrifices for God,
Ex   29:18 ram on the altar, since it is a **b** offering,
Ex   40: 6 Put the altar for **b** offerings in front of
Lv   1: 3 If a person's offering is a **b** offering
Dt   12: 6 bringing your **b** offerings and sacrifices,
Jos   8:31 On this altar they sacrificed **b** offerings
Jos   22:26 altar of our own'—not for **b** offerings
Jgs   13:16 But if you want to prepare a **b** offering,
1 Sm   15:22 "Does the LORD delight in **b** offerings
1 Kgs   3: 4 Solomon sacrificed a thousand **b** offerings.
1 Kgs 10: 5 and the **b** offerings he offered in the house
2 Chr   7: 1 down from heaven and consumed the **b** offerings
Ezr   3: 2 the **b** offerings prescribed in the law of Moses,
Ezr   8:35 offered as **b** offerings to the God of Israel
Jdt   16:18 were purified, they offered their **b** offerings,
1 Mc   1:45 to prohibit **b** offerings, sacrifices,
1 Mc   1:54 abomination upon the altar of **b** offerings,
1 Mc   4:44 ought to be done with the altar for **b** offerings
1 Mc   4:56 joyfully offered **b** offerings and sacrifices
Ps   51:18 a **b** offering you would not accept.
Ps   66:15 B offerings of fatlings I will offer
Is   40:16 nor its animals be enough for **b** offerings.
Jer   6:20 Your **b** offerings find no favor with me,
Ez   43:18 set up for sacrificing **b** offerings
Ez   46:13 Every day you shall bring as a **b** offering
Hos   6: 6 knowledge of God rather than **b** offerings.
Mi   6: 6 Shall I come before him with **b** offerings,
Mk   12:33 is worth more than all **b** offerings

BURST → BURSTS
Gn   7:11 fountains of the great abyss **b** forth,
Jb   32:19 wine, like wineskins ready to **b**.
Dn   14:27 and when the dragon ate them, he **b**.
Lk   5:37 the new wine will **b** the skins, and it

Lk   6:48 the river **b** against that house
Acts   1:18 headlong, he **b** open in the middle,

BURSTS → BURST
Jer   23:19 In a whirling storm that **b**

BURY → BURIAL, BURIED
Gn   23: 4 that I may **b** my deceased wife."
Gn   50: 7 So Joseph went up to **b** his father;
2 Kgs   9:10 Jezebel so that no one can **b** her."
Mt   8:22 me, and let the dead **b** their dead."
Lk   9:60 him, "Let the dead **b** their dead.

BUSH → THORNBUSH
Ex   3: 3 to him as fire flaming out of a **b**.
Ex   3: 2 looked, although the **b** was on fire,
Mk   12:26 in the passage about the **b**, how God
Lk   20:37 known in the passage about the **b**,
Acts   7:35 angel who appeared to him in the **b**.

BUSHEL
Mt   5:15 and then put it under a **b** basket;

BUSINESS
Jas   4:13 spend a year there doing **b**,

BUSYBODIES
1 Tm   5:13 idlers but gossips and **b** as well,

BUY → BOUGHT, BUYER, BUYING, BUYS
2 Sm   24:21 "To **b** the threshing floor from you,
Jer   13: 1 Go **b** yourself a linen loincloth;
Jer   19: 1 Go, **b** a potter's earthenware flask.
Mt   27: 7 **b** the potter's field as a burial place
Jn   6: 5 "Where can we **b** enough food
Rev   3:18 I advise you to **b** from me gold
Rev   3:18 **b** ointment to smear on your eyes so
Rev   13:17 so that no one could **b** or sell except

BUYER → BUY
Dt   28:68 slaves, but there will be no **b**.
Prv   20:14 says the **b**, then goes away only

BUYING → BUY
Mt   21:12 those engaged in selling and **b** there.
Lk   17:28 were eating, drinking, **b**, selling,

BUYS → BUY
Mt   13:44 sells all that he has and **b** that field.

BYWORD → WORD
2 Chr   7:20 a proverb and a **b** among all nations.
Jb   17: 6 I am made a **b** of the people;
Ps   44:15 You make us a **b** among the nations;
Ez   23:10 She became a **b** for women because

C

CAESAR
Mt   22:17 it lawful to pay the census tax to **C**
Mk   12:17 "Repay to **C** what belongs to **C**
Jn   19:12 him, you are not a Friend of **C**.
Acts   17: 7 act in opposition to the decrees of **C**
Acts   25:11 me over to them. I appeal to **C**."

CAESAREA
Mt   16:13 of **C** Philippi he asked his disciples,
Acts   10: 1 Now in **C** there was a man named
Acts   12:19 left Judea to spend some time in **C**.
Acts   25: 4 Paul was being held in custody in **C**

CAIAPHAS
  High priest at trial of Jesus (Mt 26:3, 57; Lk 3:2; Jn 11:49; 18:13-28);
at trial of disciples (Acts 4:6).

CAIN
  Firstborn of Adam (Gn 4:1), murdered brother Abel (Gn 4:1-25; Heb
11:4; 1 Jn 3:12; Jude 11).

CAKE → CAKES
1 Kgs 17:13 first make me a little **c** and bring it
Hos   7: 8 nations, Ephraim is an unturned **c**.

CAKES → CAKE
Ex   29: 2 flour make unleavened **c** mixed
Ex   29:23 of bread, one of the **c** made with oil,

Jgs	6:21	touched the meat and unleavened c,
Jdt	10: 5	grain, dried fig c, and pure bread.
Jer	7:18	dough to make c for the Queen
Jer	44:19	did we bake c in her image and pour
Dn	14:27	he boiled together and made into c.
Hos	3: 1	turn to other gods and love raisin c.

CALAMITIES → CALAMITY

1 Sm	10:19	saves you from all your evils and c,

CALAMITY → CALAMITIES

Prv	22: 8	Those who sow iniquity reap c,

CALCULATE

Rev	13:18	who understands can c the number

CALEB

Judahite who spied out Canaan (Nm 13:6); allowed to enter land because of faith (Nm 13:30–14:38; Dt 1:36; 1 Mc 2:56; Sir 46:7-9). Given Hebron (Jos 14:6–15:19).

CALF → CALVES

Ex	32: 4	it with a tool, made a molten c.
Lv	9: 2	Aaron, "Take a c of the herd
Dt	9:16	making for yourselves a molten c.
Neh	9:18	made for themselves a molten c,
Is	11: 6	The c and the young lion shall
Jer	31:18	I was like an untamed c.
Hos	8: 5	He has rejected your c, Samaria!
Lk	15:23	Take the fattened c and slaughter it.
Acts	7:41	So they made a c in those days,

CALL → CALLED, CALLING, CALLS, SO-CALLED

Gn	2:19	man to see what he would c them;
Gn	30:13	women will c me fortunate!"
Dt	4:26	I c heaven and earth this day
Ru	1:20	"Do not c me Naomi ['Sweet'].
1 Sm	3: 5	"I did not c you," Eli answered.
1 Kgs	18:24	You shall c upon the name of your
1 Kgs	18:24	and I will c upon the name
Ps	4: 2	Answer me when I c, my saving
Ps	28: 1	To you, Lord, I c; my Rock,
Ps	50:15	Then c on me on the day of distress;
Ps	61: 3	From the ends of the earth I c;
Ps	116:13	and c on the name of the Lord.
Ps	145:18	is near to all who c upon him, to all who c upon him in truth.
Prv	1:28	Then they will c me, but I will not
Prv	8: 1	Does not Wisdom c,
Is	5:20	Those who c evil good, and good
Is	55: 6	found, c upon him while he is near.
Is	60:14	They shall c you "City
Is	64: 6	There are none who c upon your name,
Is	65:24	Before they c, I will answer;
Jer	33: 3	C to me, and I will answer you;
Lam	3:21	But this I will c to mind;
Hos	2:18	You shall c me "My husband,"
Hos	2:18	shall never again c me "My baal."
Jon	1: 6	Get up, c on your god!
Zep	3: 9	That they all may c upon the name
Zec	13: 9	They will c upon my name, and I
Mt	9:13	I did not come to c the righteous
Mt	23: 9	C no one on earth your father;
Mk	10:18	him, "Why do you c me good?
Lk	6:46	"Why do you c me, 'Lord, Lord,'
Jn	13:13	You c me 'teacher' and 'master,'
Jn	15:15	I no longer c you slaves,
Acts	10:15	clean, you are not to c profane."
Rom	9:25	not my people I will c 'my people,'
Rom	9:25	was not beloved I will c 'beloved.'
Rom	10:12	of all, enriching all who c upon him.
1 Cor	1: 2	all those everywhere who c
1 Thes	4: 7	For God did not c us to impurity
2 Tm	2:22	along with those who c on the Lord
Heb	2:11	not ashamed to c them "brothers,"
2 Pt	1:10	be all the more eager to make your c

CALLED → CALL

Gn	1: 5	God c the light "day,"
Gn	1: 5	and the darkness he c "night."

Gn	1: 8	God c the dome "sky."
Gn	1:10	God c the dry land "earth,"
Gn	1:10	and the basin of water he c "sea."
Gn	2:19	whatever the man c each living
Gn	2:23	This one shall be c 'woman,'
Gn	3: 9	The Lord God then c to the man
Gn	21:17	and God's angel c to Hagar
Gn	22:11	the angel of the Lord c to him
Ex	3: 4	God c out to him from the bush:
Ex	19: 3	Then the Lord c to him
1 Sm	3: 4	The Lord c to Samuel,
2 Sm	22: 7	In my distress I c out: Lord!
1 Kgs	18:26	c upon Baal from morning to noon,
1 Chr	21:26	He c upon the Lord,
Ps	116: 4	I c on the name of the Lord,
Prv	1:24	'Because I c and you refused,
Is	1:26	that you shall be c city of justice,
Is	42: 6	the Lord, have c you for justice,
Is	43: 1	I have c you by name:
Is	49: 1	Before birth the Lord c me,
Is	56: 7	For my house shall be c a house
Is	65:12	Because I c and you did not answer,
Lam	3:55	I have c upon your name,
Hos	11: 1	loved him, out of Egypt I c my son.
Mt	1:16	born Jesus who is c the Messiah.
Mt	2:15	"Out of Egypt I c my son."
Mt	2:23	and dwelt in a town c Nazareth,
Mt	2:23	"He shall be c a Nazorean."
Mt	5: 9	for they will be c children of God.
Mt	5:19	do so will be c least in the kingdom
Mt	5:19	commandments will be c greatest
Mt	23: 8	As for you, do not be c 'Rabbi.'
Lk	1:32	and will be c Son of the Most High,
Lk	1:35	the child to be born will be c holy,
Lk	1:76	will be c prophet of the Most High,
Lk	15:19	I no longer deserve to be c your son;
Jn	15:15	I have c you friends, because I have
Jn	19:17	to what is c the Place of the Skull,
Rom	1: 1	c to be an apostle and set apart
Rom	1: 6	who are c to belong to Jesus Christ;
Rom	1: 7	of God in Rome, c to be holy.
Rom	8:28	who are c according to his purpose.
Rom	8:30	And those he predestined he also c;
Rom	8:30	and those he c he also justified;
1 Cor	1: 9	by him you were c to fellowship
1 Cor	1:24	but to those who are c,
1 Cor	7:15	God has c you to peace.
1 Cor	7:17	assigned, just as God c each one.
1 Cor	7:24	God in the state in which he was c.
Gal	5:13	For you were c for freedom,
Eph	4: 4	also c to the one hope of your call;
Col	3:15	which you were also c in one body.
2 Thes	2:14	c you through our gospel to possess
1 Tm	6:12	you were c when you made
2 Tm	1: 9	He saved us and c us to a holy life,
Heb	9:15	those who are c may receive
Heb	11:16	is not ashamed to be c their God,
Jas	2:23	and he was c "the friend of God."
1 Pt	1:15	but, as he who c you is holy,
1 Pt	2: 9	the praises" of him who c you
1 Pt	3: 9	because to this you were c, that you
1 Pt	5:10	of all grace who c you to his eternal
2 Pt	1: 3	of him who c us by his own glory
1 Jn	3: 1	we may be c the children of God.
Jude	1: 1	to those who are c, beloved in God
Rev	12: 9	who is c the Devil and Satan,
Rev	17:14	and those with him are c, chosen,
Rev	19:11	its rider was [c] "Faithful
Rev	19:13	his name was c the Word of God.

CALLING → CALL

1 Sm	3: 8	that the Lord was c the youth.
Is	40:26	numbers them, c them all by name.
Mt	27:47	it said, "This one is c for Elijah."
Mk	10:49	get up, he is c you."
Acts	22:16	washed away, c upon his name.'
1 Cor	1:26	Consider your own c, brothers.

Phil 3:14 the prize of God's upward c,
Heb 3: 1 sharing in a heavenly c,

CALLS → CALL

Ps 42: 8 Deep c to deep in the roar of your
Prv 9: 3 she c from the heights out over
Hos 7: 7 none of them c upon me.
Jl 3: 5 everyone who c upon the name
Mt 22:45 If David c him 'lord,' how can he
Jn 10: 3 as he c his own sheep by name
Acts 2:21 everyone shall be saved who c
Rom 4:17 and c into being what does not exist.
Rom 10:13 For "everyone who c on the name
1 Thes 2:12 of the God who c you into his
1 Thes 5:24 The one who c you is faithful,
2 Tm 2:19 and, "Let everyone who c
Rev 2:20 Jezebel, who c herself a prophetess,

CALM

Mk 4:39 wind ceased and there was great c.

CALVES → CALF

1 Kgs 12:28 took counsel, made two c of gold,
2 Kgs 10:29 the golden c at Bethel and at Dan.
Hos 13: 2 sacrifice," they say. People kiss c!
Mi 6: 6 burnt offerings, with c a year old?
Mal 3:20 go out leaping like c from the stall
Heb 9:12 not with the blood of goats and c

CAME → COME

Gn 7: 6 old when the flood c upon the earth.
Gn 11: 5 The LORD c down to see the city
Gn 15: 1 the word of the LORD c to Abram
Gn 20: 3 God c to Abimelech in a dream one
Ex 13: 3 day on which you c out of Egypt,
Ex 32:24 it into the fire, and this calf c out."
Lv 9:24 Fire c forth from the LORD's
Nm 11:25 LORD then c down in the cloud
Nm 11:25 and as the spirit c to rest on them,
Nm 12: 5 the LORD c down in a column
Nm 16:35 the LORD c forth which consumed
Nm 24: 2 tribe, the spirit of God c upon him,
Jgs 3:10 spirit of the LORD c upon him,
Jgs 11:29 of the LORD c upon Jephthah.
1 Sm 3:10 the LORD c and stood there,
1 Sm 19: 9 the LORD c upon Saul as he was
1 Sm 19:23 the spirit of God c upon him also,
2 Kgs 1:10 And fire c down from heaven
2 Chr 15: 1 The spirit of God c upon Azariah,
2 Chr 20:14 of the LORD c upon Jahaziel,
Ps 18:10 He parted the heavens and c down,
Eccl 5:15 evil, that they go just as they c.
Dn 3:93 and Abednego c out of the fire.
Mt 7:25 the floods c, and the winds blew
Mk 1:11 And a voice c from the heavens,
Jn 1: 3 All things c to be through him,
Jn 1: 3 and without him nothing c to be.
Jn 1:11 He c to what was his own, but his
Jn 1:17 and truth c through Jesus Christ.
Jn 6:41 "I am the bread that c down
Jn 6:51 I am the living bread that c down
Jn 10:10 I c so that they might have life
Acts 19: 6 them, the holy Spirit c upon them,
Rom 5:12 and thus death c to all, inasmuch as
1 Cor 11:12 For just as woman c from man,
1 Tm 1:15 Christ Jesus c into the world to save
1 Jn 5: 6 This is the one who c through water
Rev 2: 8 who once died but c to life,
Rev 20: 4 They c to life and they reigned
Rev 20: 9 But fire c down from heaven

CAMEL → CAMEL'S, CAMELS

Mt 19:24 easier for a c to pass through the eye
Mt 23:24 out the gnat and swallow the c!
Mk 10:25 for a c to pass through [the] eye
Lk 18:25 easier for a c to pass through the eye

CAMEL'S → CAMEL

Mk 1: 6 John was clothed in c hair,

CAMELS → CAMEL

Gn 24:14 'Drink, and I will water your c, too,'

CAMP → ENCAMP, ENCAMPS

Ex 16:13 quail came up and covered the c.
Ex 16:13 was a layer of dew all about the c,
Ex 33: 7 to the tent of meeting outside the c.
Lv 24:14 Take the blasphemer outside the c;
Nm 9:17 tent, the Israelites would break c;
Nm 9:17 settled, the Israelites would pitch c.
Nm 11:26 and so they prophesied in the c.
Dt 23:15 over to you, your c must be holy,
1 Sm 4: 7 out, "Gods have come to their c.
Heb 13:13 Let us then go to him outside the c,

CAN → CANNOT

Gn 17:17 "C a child be born to a man who is
Gn 17:17 C Sarah give birth at ninety?"
Gn 41:15 hears a dream he c interpret it.' "
Nm 23: 8 How c I lay a curse on the one
Nm 35:33 the land c have no expiation
Jb 4:17 "C anyone be more in the right than
Jb 4:17 C mortals be more blameless than
Jb 11: 7 C you find out the depths of God?
Jb 34:29 who then c behold him,
Jb 38:35 C you send forth the lightnings
Jb 40: 9 c you thunder with a voice like his?
Jb 42: 2 I know that you c do all things,
Jb 42: 2 no purpose of yours c be hindered.
Ps 19:13 Who c detect trespasses?
Ps 22:18 I c count all my bones. They stare
Ps 56: 5 What c mere flesh do to me?
Ps 139: 7 Where c I go from your spirit?
Ps 139: 7 From your presence, where c I flee?
Prv 20: 6 but who c find someone worthy
Eccl 7:13 Who c make straight what God has
Sir 15:15 you c keep the commandments;
Is 43:13 There is none who c deliver
Is 43:13 I act and who c cancel it?
Jer 18: 6 C I not do to you, house of Israel,
Ez 37: 3 c these bones come back to life?
Dn 2: 9 there c be but one decree for you.
Dn 5:16 heard that you c give interpretations
Jl 2:11 Utterly terrifying! Who c survive it?
Mal 3: 2 But who c endure the day of his
Mt 5:13 its taste, with what c it be seasoned?
Mt 6:24 "No one c serve two masters.
Mk 2: 7 Who but God alone c forgive sins?"
Lk 18:26 this said, "Then who c be saved?"
Jn 3: 4 "How c a person once grown old be
Jn 3: 9 said to him, "How c this happen?"
Jn 6:44 No one c come to me unless
Jn 10:29 and no one c take them
Jn 15: 5 without me you c do nothing.
Rom 9:19 For who c oppose his will?"
Heb 13: 6 What c anyone do to me?"
Jas 2:14 C that faith save him?
Jas 3: 8 no human being c tame the tongue.
Rev 13: 4 "Who c compare with the beast or who c fight against it?"

CANA

Jn 2: 1 third day there was a wedding in C

CANAAN → CANAANITE, CANAANITES

Gn 9:18 Ham was the father of C.
Gn 9:25 "Cursed be C! The lowest of slaves
Gn 13:12 Abram settled in the land of C,
Gn 42: 5 there was famine in the land of C.
Ex 6: 4 to give them the land of C, the land
Nm 13: 2 men to reconnoiter the land of C,
Nm 33:51 across the Jordan into the land of C,
Nm 34: 2 When you enter the land of C,
Dt 32:49 and view the land of C, which I am
1 Chr 16:18 "To you will I give the land of C,
Ps 106:38 they sacrificed to the idols of C,
Dn 13:56 "Offspring of C, not of Judah,"
Acts 13:19 seven nations in the land of C,

CANAANITE → CANAAN

Gn 28: 1 "You shall not marry a C woman!
Mt 15:22 a C woman of that district came

CANAANITES → CANAAN

Gn 10:18 the clans of the C spread out,
Gn 12: 6 The C were then in the land.
Ex 3: 8 the country of the C, the Hittites,
Ex 33: 2 Driving out the C, Amorites,
Jos 16:10 they did not dispossess the C living
Jos 17:12 the C continued to inhabit this
Jgs 1: 1 be first among us to attack the C
Jgs 1:27 The C continued to live in this
Jgs 3: 5 the Israelites settled among the C,

CANDACE

Acts 8:27 a court official of the C, that is,

CANNOT → CAN

Ex 33:20 But you c see my face, for no one
Nm 23:20 I will bless; I c revoke it!
1 Kgs 8:27 the highest heavens c contain you,
Jb 23: 8 or west, I c perceive him;
Jb 37:23 We c find him, preeminent in power
Eccl 1:15 What is crooked c be made straight,
Eccl 1:15 and you c count what is not there.
Sg 8: 7 Deep waters c quench love,
Sir 9:10 new ones c equal them.
Is 45:20 idols and pray to gods that c save.
Mt 5:14 city set on a mountain c be hidden.
Mt 16: 3 [you c judge the signs of the times.]
Mt 27:42 he c save himself.
Mk 3:24 against itself, that kingdom c stand.
Lk 16:13 You c serve God and mammon."
Jn 7:34 [me], and where I am you c come."
Jn 13:33 'Where I go you c come,' so now I
Jn 15: 4 Just as a branch c bear fruit on its
Jn 16:12 to tell you, but you c bear it now.
Rom 8: 8 who are in the flesh c please God.
1 Cor 10:21 You c drink the cup of the Lord
1 Cor 10:21 You c partake of the table
1 Cor 15:50 blood c inherit the kingdom of God,

CANOPY

Ps 18:12 his c, water-darkened stormclouds.
Jer 43:10 set up, and stretch his c above them.

CAPERNAUM

Mt 4:13 and went to live in C by the sea,
Mt 11:23 And as for you, C: 'Will you be
Jn 4:46 official whose son was ill in C.
Jn 6:59 teaching in the synagogue in C.

CAPITALS

Ex 36:38 with their hooks as well as their c
1 Kgs 7:16 He also made two c cast in bronze,

CAPTAIN

2 Kgs 1: 9 the king sent a c with his company
Jon 1: 6 The c approached him and said,

CAPTIVATED → CAPTURE

Jdt 16: 9 his eyes, her beauty c his mind,

CAPTIVE → CAPTURE

2 Kgs 24:16 of Babylon brought c to Babylon.
1 Mc 1:32 And they took c the women
Ps 106:46 from all who held them c.
Is 52: 2 from your neck, c daughter Zion!
Rom 7:23 taking me c to the law of sin
2 Cor 10: 5 take every thought c in obedience
Eph 4: 8 on high and took prisoners c;

CAPTIVES → CAPTURE

Ps 68:19 you took c, received slaves as
Is 61: 1 To proclaim liberty to the c,
Lk 4:18 has sent me to proclaim liberty to c
2 Tm 3: 6 make c of women weighed down

CAPTIVITY → CAPTURE

Dt 28:41 with you, for they will go into c.
Ezr 3: 8 had come from the c to Jerusalem,
Ezr 8:35 those who had returned from the c,

Neh 1: 2 the remnant preserved after the c,
Tb 13: 6 In the land of my c I give thanks,
Ps 53: 7 When God reverses the c of his people
Jer 15: 2 whoever is marked for c, to c.
Rev 13:10 Anyone destined for c goes into c.

CAPTORS → CAPTURE

1 Kgs 8:50 them mercy in the sight of their c,
Ps 137: 3 For there our c asked us
Is 14: 2 they will take captive their c

CAPTURE → CAPTIVATED, CAPTIVE, CAPTIVES, CAPTIVITY, CAPTORS, CAPTURED

1 Sm 23:26 and his men in order to c them.

CAPTURED → CAPTURE

1 Sm 4:11 The ark of God was c, and Eli's two

CARAVAN → CARAVANS

Gn 37:25 they saw a c of Ishmaelites coming

CARAVANS → CARAVAN

Jgs 5: 6 Anath, in the days of Jael, c ceased:

CARCASS → CARCASSES

Jgs 14: 9 scooped the honey from the lion's c.

CARCASSES → CARCASS

Gn 15:11 of prey swooped down on the c,

CARCHEMISH

2 Chr 35:20 up to fight at C on the Euphrates,

CARE → CARED, CAREFUL, CARELESS, CARES

Ps 8: 5 a son of man that you c for him?
1 Tm 3: 5 how can he take c of the church
Heb 2: 6 the son of man that you c for him?
Jas 1:27 to c for orphans and widows in their

CARED → CARE

Dt 32:10 He shielded them, c for them,
Ru 4:16 against her breast, and c for him.

CAREFUL → CARE

Dt 2: 4 they are afraid of you, be very c
Dt 5:32 Be c, therefore, to do as
Dt 6:12 be c not to forget the LORD,
Dt 12:28 Be c to heed all these words I
Dt 24: 8 of scaly infection you shall be c
Jgs 13: 4 be c to drink no wine or beer
2 Kgs 10:31 Jehu was not c to walk in the law
2 Kgs 17:37 You must be c always to observe
2 Kgs 21: 8 that they are c to observe all I have
1 Chr 22:13 if you are c to observe the statutes
2 Chr 33: 8 that they are c to observe all I
Ez 18: 9 and is c to observe my ordinances,
Ez 18:19 and has been c to observe all my
Ez 20:19 and be c to observe my ordinances;
Ti 3: 8 in God be c to devote themselves

CARELESS → CARE

Mt 12:36 for every c word they speak.

CARES → CARE

Ps 94:19 When c increase within me,
Ps 142: 5 no one c for me.
Eccl 5: 2 As dreams come along with many c,
1 Pt 5: 7 upon him because he c for you.

CARGO

Jon 1: 5 they threw its c into the sea.
Acts 27:18 the next day they jettisoned some c,

CARMEL

1 Sm 25: 2 of Maon who had property in C;
1 Kgs 18:20 the prophets gather on Mount C.
Na 1: 4 Laid low are Bashan and C,

CARNELIAN

Ex 28:17 in the first row, a c, a topaz,
Rev 4: 3 sparkled like jasper and c.
Rev 21:20 the sixth c, the seventh chrysolite,

CAROUSING

1 Pt 4: 3 orgies, c, and wanton idolatry.

CARPENTER → CARPENTER'S, CARPENTERS
Mk   6: 3   Is he not the c, the son of Mary,

CARPENTER'S → CARPENTER
Mt   13:55   Is he not the c son? Is not his

CARPENTERS → CARPENTER
1 Chr 14: 1   masons and c to build him a house.
2 Chr 24:12   c to restore the LORD's house,
Ezr   3: 7   Then they hired stonecutters and c,

CARRIED → CARRY
Dt   1:31   your God, c you, as one carries his
Jer   10: 5   They must be c about, for they
Jn   20:15   if you c him away, tell me where
Heb   13: 9   Do not be c away by all kinds
Rev   17: 3   he c me away in spirit to a deserted

CARRIES → CARRY
Dt   1:31   carried you, as one c his own child,
Is   40:24   and the stormwind c them away like

CARRY → CARRIED, CARRIES, CARRYING
Nm   1:50   It is they who shall c the tabernacle
Dt   10: 8   of Levi to c the ark of the covenant
1 Chr 15: 2   said, "No one may c the ark of God
1 Chr 15: 2   the LORD chose them to c the ark
Is   46: 4   lift you up, I will c you to safety.
Mt   3:11   I am not worthy to c his sandals.
Mt   27:32   pressed into service to c his cross.
Lk   14:27   Whoever does not c his own cross

CARRYING → CARRY
Jos   6: 6   seven of the priests c ram's horns
Is   40:11   the lambs, C them in his bosom,
Lk   22:10   city, a man will meet you c a jar
Jn   19:17   c the cross himself he went
2 Cor   4:10   always c about in the body

CART
1 Sm   6:11   the ark of the LORD on the c,
1 Chr 13: 7   Uzzah and Ahio were guiding the c,

CARVED
1 Kgs   6:29   and the outer rooms had c figures

CASE → CASES
Jos   20: 4   shall plead his c in the hearing
Prv   18:17   Those who plead the c first seem
Prv   25: 9   Argue your own c with your
Is   41:21   Present your c, says the LORD;
Jer   12: 1   so, I must lay out the c against you.
Acts   25:14   Festus referred Paul's c to the king,

CASES → CASE
Ex   18:26   The more difficult c they referred
Ex   18:26   but all the lesser c they settled

CAST → CASTING, CASTS, DOWNCAST
Lv   16: 8   he shall c lots to determine
Jos   18: 6   then c lots for you here before
1 Sm   14:42   "C lots between me and my son
Est   3: 7   or lot, was c in Haman's presence
Est   9:24   to destroy them and had c the *pur*,
Ps   22:19   for my clothing they c lots.
Ps   55:23   C your care upon the LORD,
Ps   71: 9   Do not c me aside in my old age;
Prv   16:33   Into the bag the lot is c,
Is   38:17   Behind your back you c all my sins.
Jer   7:15   I will c you out of my sight, as I c away
Jer   14:19   Have you really c Judah off? Is Zion
Jl   4: 3   For my people they c lots,
Ob   1:11   his gates and c lots for Jerusalem,
Jon   1: 7   let us c lots to discover on whose
Jon   1: 7   So they c lots, and the lot fell
Jn   19:24   c lots for it to see whose it will be,"
Jn   19:24   and for my vesture they c lots."
Jn   21: 6   "C the net over the right side
Jn   21: 6   So they c it, and were not able
1 Pt   5: 7   C all your worries upon him

CASTING → CAST
Mt   4:18   brother Andrew, c a net into the sea;

Mt   27:35   they divided his garments by c lots;
Mk   1:16   his brother Andrew c their nets

CASTLE
Prv   18:19   strife is more daunting than c gates.

CASTRATE
Gal   5:12   you might also c themselves!

CASTS → CAST
Ps   147: 6   but c the wicked to the ground.

CATAPULTS
1 Mc   6:51   c and mechanical bows for shooting

CATCH → CATCHES, CATCHING, CAUGHT
Sg   2:15   C us the foxes, the little foxes
Lk   5: 4   water and lower your nets for a c."
Lk   11:54   for they were plotting to c him

CATCHES → CATCH
1 Cor   3:19   "He c the wise in their own ruses,"

CATCHING → CATCH
Lk   5:10   from now on you will be c men."

CATERPILLAR → CATERPILLARS
Ps   78:46   He gave their harvest to the c,

CATERPILLARS → CATERPILLAR
2 Chr   6:28   or mildew, or locusts swarm, or c;

CATTLE
Ps   104:14   You make the grass grow for the c

CAUGHT → CATCH
Gn   22:13   saw a single ram c by its horns
Ex   22: 6   if c, must make twofold restitution.
Dt   24: 7   If anyone is c kidnapping a fellow
2 Sm   18: 9   oak tree, his hair c fast in the tree.
Prv   6: 2   lips, c by the words of your mouth;
Sg   7: 6   like purple; a king is c in its locks.
Sir   27:26   and whoever lays a snare is c in it.
Lk   5: 5   hard all night and have c nothing,
Jn   8: 3   brought a woman who had been c
2 Cor   12: 2   was c up to the third heaven.
1 Thes   4:17   will be c up together with them

CAUSE → CAUSED, CAUSES
1 Kgs   8:45   and petition, and uphold their c.
Ps   9: 5   For you upheld my right and my c,
Ps   35: 7   Without c they set their snare
Ps   35: 7   without c they dug a pit for me.
Ps   45: 5   In the c of truth, meekness,
Ps   74:22   Arise, God, defend your c;
Ps   109: 3   me, attacking me without c.
Ps   119:86   Help me! I am pursued without c.
Ps   119:154   Take up my c and redeem me;
Jer   11:20   for to you I have entrusted my c!
Jer   51:36   I will certainly defend your c, I will
Lk   17: 2   for him to c one of these little ones
Jn   15:25   fulfilled, 'They hated me without c.'
1 Cor   8:13   that I may not c my brother to sin.
1 Jn   2:10   there is nothing in him to c a fall.

CAUSED → CAUSE
Ex   21:13   but God c death to happen by his hand,
1 Kgs   14:16   committed and c Israel to commit."
2 Kgs   23:15   son of Nebat, who c Israel to sin—

CAUSES → CAUSE
Mt   5:29   If your right eye c you to sin, tear it
Mt   5:30   And if your right hand c you to sin,
Mt   5:32   the marriage is unlawful) c her
Mt   18: 8   If your hand or foot c you to sin,

CAUTIOUS
Prv   14:16   The wise person is c and turns

CAVE → CAVES
Gn   19:30   lived with his two daughters in a c.
Gn   23: 9   he will sell me the c of Machpelah,
Gn   25: 9   buried him in the c of Machpelah,
Gn   49:29   my ancestors in the c that lies
Gn   50:13   buried him in the c in the field
Jos   10:16   had fled hid in the c at Makkedah.

1 Sm 22: 1 and escaped to the c of Adullam.
1 Sm 24: 4 the inmost recesses of the c.
1 Kgs 19: 9 There he came to a c, where he took
Ps 57: 1 when he fled from Saul into a c.
Ps 142: 1 of David, when he was in the c.
Jn 11:38 It was a c, and a stone lay across it.

CAVERNS
Is 2:21 And they shall go into c in the rocks

CAVES → CAVE
Jgs 6: 2 the c, and the strongholds.
1 Sm 13: 6 they hid themselves in c, thickets,
2 Mc 6:11 nearby c to observe the seventh day
Is 2:19 People will go into c in the rocks
Heb 11:38 in c and in crevices in the earth.
Rev 6:15 free person hid themselves in c

CEASE → CEASED
Gn 8:22 and day and night shall not c.
Prv 22:10 discord goes too; strife and insult c.
Jer 31:36 of Israel c as a people before me
1 Cor 13: 8 if tongues, they will c;

CEASED → CEASE
1 Mc 9:73 Then the sword c from Israel.
Ps 77: 9 Has God's mercy c forever?
Lam 5:15 The joy of our hearts has c,

CEDAR → CEDARS
2 Sm 7: 2 "Here I am living in a house of c,
1 Kgs 7: 7 it was paneled with c from floor
2 Chr 25:18 sent word to a c of Lebanon,
Ezr 3: 7 that they might ship c trees
Jb 40:17 He carries his tail like a c;
Ps 92:13 tree, shall grow like a c of Lebanon.
Sg 8: 9 will board her up with c planks."
Sir 24:13 "Like a c in Lebanon I grew tall,
Is 41:19 In the wilderness I will plant the c,
Ez 17: 3 He plucked the crest of the c,
Ez 31: 3 A c of Lebanon—

CEDARS → CEDAR
Jgs 9:15 and devour the c of Lebanon.'
1 Kgs 5:24 to provide Solomon with all the c
Ps 29: 5 voice of the LORD cracks the c; the LORD splinters the c
Is 37:24 To cut down its lofty c, its choice

CELEBRATE → CELEBRATED
Ex 12:14 you will c it as a statute forever.
Ex 12:48 among you would c the Passover
Nm 29:12 days you will c a pilgrimage feast
Dt 16:15 seven days you shall c this feast
Neh 12:27 to Jerusalem to c a joyful dedication
Sg 1: 4 let us c your love: it is beyond wine!
Na 2: 1 C your feasts, Judah, fulfill your
Lk 15:23 Then let us c with a feast,
Lk 15:32 But now we must c and rejoice,
1 Cor 5: 8 Therefore let us c the feast,

CELEBRATED → CELEBRATE
1 Mc 4:56 eight days they c the dedication

CELL
Acts 12: 7 by him and a light shone in the c.
Acts 16:24 he put them in the innermost c

CENSER → CENSERS
2 Chr 26:19 who was holding a c for burning
Ez 8:11 of Shaphan, each with c in hand;
Rev 8: 3 stood at the altar, holding a gold c.

CENSERS → CENSER
Lv 10: 1 Nadab and Abihu took their c and,
Nm 16:18 So each of them took their c,
Nm 17: 3 the c of those who sinned at the cost
1 Mc 1:22 bowls, the golden c, and the curtain.

CENSUS
Ex 30:12 you take a c of the Israelites who
Nm 1: 2 Take a c of the whole community
Nm 26: 2 Take a c, by ancestral houses,

CENTER
Rev 7:17 in the c of the throne will shepherd

CENTURION → CENTURIONS
Mt 8: 5 a c approached him and appealed
Mt 27:54 The c and the men with him who
Mk 15:39 the c who stood facing him saw
Lk 23:47 The c who witnessed what had
Acts 10: 1 a c of the Cohort called the Italica,
Acts 22:25 Paul said to the c on duty, "Is it
Acts 27: 1 prisoners over to a c named Julius

CENTURIONS → CENTURION
Acts 23:17 called one of the c and requested,

CEPHAS → =PETER
Name given to the apostle Peter (Jn 1:42; 1 Cor 1:12; 3:22; 9:5; 15:5; Gal 1:18; 2:9, 11, 14).

CHAFF
Jb 21:18 wind, like c the storm carries away!
Ps 1: 4 They are like c driven by the wind.
Ps 35: 5 Make them like c before the wind,
Jer 13:24 I will scatter them like c that flies
Dn 2:35 fine as the c on the threshing floor
Hos 13: 3 dawn, Like c storm-driven
Zep 2: 2 driven away, like c that disappears;
Mt 3:12 his barn, but the c he will burn
Lk 3:17 his barn, but the c he will burn

CHAIN → CHAINED, CHAINS
Gn 41:42 and put a gold c around his neck.
Mk 5: 3 him any longer, even with a c.
Rev 20: 1 the key to the abyss and a heavy c.

CHAINED → CHAIN
2 Tm 2: 9 But the word of God is not c.

CHAINS → CHAIN
Ex 28:14 as well as two c of pure gold,
Ex 28:14 fasten the cordlike c to the filigree
1 Kgs 6:21 he drew golden c across in front
Ps 107:10 and gloom, imprisoned in misery and c.
Lam 3: 7 escape, weighed me down with c;
Mk 5: 4 been bound with shackles and c,
Mk 5: 4 the c had been pulled apart by him
Acts 12: 7 The c fell from his wrists.
Acts 16:26 and the c of all were pulled loose.
Acts 28:20 hope of Israel that I wear these c."
Eph 6:20 for which I am an ambassador in c,
Col 4:18 Remember my c. Grace be
Heb 11:36 even c and imprisonment.
2 Pt 2: 4 them to the c of Tartarus
Jude 1: 6 he has kept in eternal c, in gloom,

CHALDEA → CHALDEAN, CHALDEANS, CHALDEES
Jer 50:10 C shall become plunder;
Ez 23:16 she sent messengers to them in C.

CHALDEAN → CHALDEA
Ezr 5:12 them into the power of the C,
Dn 5:30 very night Belshazzar, the C king,

CHALDEANS → CHALDEA
Gn 11:31 brought them out of Ur of the C,
Gn 15: 7 of the C to give you this land as
2 Chr 36:17 up against them the king of the C,
Jdt 5: 7 who were in the land of the C.
Is 47: 5 daughter of the C, No longer shall
Jer 50:35 A sword upon the C—
Bar 1: 2 at the time the C took Jerusalem
Ez 1: 3 land of the C by the river Chebar.
Dn 1: 4 the language and literature of the C.
Dn 5:11 enchanters, C, and diviners.
Hb 1: 6 For now I am raising up the C,

CHALDEES → CHALDEA
Neh 9: 7 Who brought him from Ur of the C,

CHAMBER → CHAMBERS
Tb 6:14 that they have died in the bridal c.
Jb 37: 9 Out of its c the tempest comes forth;
Am 9: 6 Who has built his upper c in heaven,

CHAMBERS → CHAMBER
1 Chr 9:26 had charge of the c and treasures
1 Chr 23:28 courts, the c, and the preservation
Sg   1: 4 king has brought me to his bed c.

CHAMPION
1 Sm 17: 4 A c named Goliath of Gath came

CHANGE → CHANGED, CHANGERS, CHANGES
1 Kgs 8:47 they have a c of heart in the land
Jer   4:28 I have spoken, I will not c my mind,
Jer   13:23 Can Ethiopians c their skin,
Mal   3: 6 the LORD, do not c, and you,
Mt   21:32 you did not later c your minds
Heb   7:12 When there is a c of priesthood,
Heb   7:12 there is necessarily a c of law as
Jas   1:17 no alteration or shadow caused by c.

CHANGED → CHANGE
Gn   31: 7 me and c my wages ten times.
Jer   2:11 But my people have c their glory
Lk   9:29 While he was praying his face c
1 Cor 15:51 all fall asleep, but we will all be c,
Heb   1:12 and like a garment they will be c.

CHANGERS → CHANGE
Mt   21:12 overturned the tables of the money c
Mk   11:15 overturned the tables of the money c

CHANGES → CHANGE
Dn   2:21 He causes the c of the times

CHANNELS
Is   8: 7 It shall rise above all its c,

CHARACTER
Rom   5: 4 endurance, proven c, and proven c,

CHARGE → CHARGES
Gn   39: 4 he put him in c of his household
Nm   4:16 shall be in c of the oil for the light,
Nm   4:16 He shall be in c of the whole
Nm   9:23 they kept the c of the LORD,
Dt   11: 1 therefore, and keep his c, statutes,
Mt   24:47 to you, he will put him in c of all his
Mk   15:26 of the c against him read,
Rom   8:33 will bring a c against God's chosen
1 Cor 9:18 I offer the gospel free of c so as not
2 Cor 11: 7 the gospel of God to you without c?
Phlm   1:18 or owes you anything, c it to me.

CHARGES → CHARGE
Lk   23:14 the c you have brought against him,
Acts 25: 7 brought many serious c against him,

CHARIOT → CHARIOTS
Gn   41:43 then had him ride in his second c,
Ex   14:25 he so clogged their c wheels
Jgs   4:15 himself dismounted from his c
1 Kgs 7:33 were constructed like c wheels;
2 Kgs 2:11 a fiery c and fiery horses came
1 Chr 28:18 and, finally, gold to fashion the c:
2 Chr 1:17 A c imported from Egypt cost six hundred
Ps   104: 3 You make the clouds your c;
Sir   48: 9 whirlwind, in a c with fiery horses.
Zec   6: 2 The first c had red horses, the second c black horses,
Acts   8:28 Seated in his c, he was reading

CHARIOTS → CHARIOT
Ex   14:28 it covered the c and the horsemen.
Ex   15:19 When Pharaoh's horses and c
Jos   11: 4 with a multitude of horses and c.
Jos   17:18 if, despite their strength and iron c,
Jgs   4: 3 nine hundred iron c Jabin harshly
2 Sm   8: 4 but left one hundred for his c.
2 Kgs 6:17 mountainside was filled with fiery c
2 Chr 1:14 Solomon amassed c and horses:
Jdt   7:20 army, infantry, c, and cavalry,
1 Mc   1:17 force, with c, elephants and cavalry,
Ps   20: 8 Some rely on c, others on horses,
Is   36: 9 you do, in Egypt for c and horses?
Jl   2: 5 c they hurtle across mountaintops;
Na   2: 4 of the c on the day he prepares

Hg   2:22 I will overthrow the c and their
Zec   6: 1 and saw four c coming
Rev   9: 9 of many horse-drawn c racing

CHARITABLE
Tb   1:16 I had performed many c deeds

CHARM → CHARMED, CHARMER
Prv   31:30 C is deceptive and beauty fleeting;
Jer   8:17 Against them no c will work

CHARMED → CHARM
Eccl 10:11 If the snake bites before it is c,

CHARMER → CHARM
Sir   12:13 Who pities a snake c when he is

CHASM
Lk   16:26 us and you a great c is established

CHASTE
2 Cor 11: 2 present you as a c virgin to Christ.
Ti   2: 5 to be self-controlled, c,

CHASTENED → CHASTISE
Jb   33:19 Or he is c on a bed of pain,

CHASTISE → CHASTENED
Jer   30:11 I will c you as you deserve, I will

CHATTER
Sir   21:16 A fool's c is like a load

CHEATED
Gn   31: 7 yet your father c me and changed

CHEBAR
Ez   1: 1 was among the exiles by the river C,
Ez   10:15 creatures I had seen by the river C.

CHEEK → CHEEKS
1 Kgs 22:24 up and struck Micaiah on the c,
Jb   16:10 They strike me on the c with insults;
Lam   3:30 To offer one's c to be struck, to be
Mi   4:14 the rod they strike on the c the ruler
Mt   5:39 strikes you on [your] right c,
Lk   6:29 the person who strikes you on one c,

CHEEKS → CHEEK
Sg   1:10 Your c lovely in pendants,
Sg   5:13 His c are like beds of spices
Is   50: 6 me, my c to those who tore out my
Lam   1: 2 in the night, her c damp with tears.
Hos   11: 4 those who raise an infant to their c;

CHEERFUL → CHEERFULNESS, CHEERS
Sir   35:11 With each contribution show a c countenance,
2 Cor 9: 7 compulsion, for God loves a c giver.

CHEERFULNESS → CHEERFUL
Rom   12: 8 if one does acts of mercy, with c.

CHEERS → CHEERFUL
Jgs   9:13 'Must I give up my wine that c gods

CHEESE
2 Sm 17:29 and butter and c from the flocks
Jb   10:10 out like milk, and thicken me like c?

CHEMOSH
Nm   21:29 You are no more, people of C!
1 Kgs 11: 7 then built a high place to C,
2 Kgs 23:13 horror, of C, the Moabite horror,
Jer   48: 7 C shall go into exile, his priests

CHERETHITES
2 Sm 15:18 As all the C and Pelethites,
1 Kgs 1:38 and the C and Pelethites went down,
Ez   25:16 I will cut off the C and wipe

CHERISHED
Ps   66:18 Had I c evil in my heart, the Lord

CHERUB → CHERUBIM
Ex   25:19 make one c at one end,
Ps   18:11 Mounted on a c he flew,
Ez   28:14 With a c I placed you; I put you
Ez   41:18 Each c had two faces:

CHERUBIM → CHERUB
Gn 3:24 man, stationing the c and the fiery
Ex 25:18 Make two c of beaten gold
Ex 26: 1 yarn, with c embroidered on them.
Nm 7:89 covenant, from between the two c;
1 Sm 4: 4 hosts, who is enthroned upon the c.
2 Sm 6: 2 of hosts enthroned above the c."
1 Kgs 6:23 the inner sanctuary he made two c,
2 Kgs 19:15 God of Israel, enthroned on the c!
1 Chr 13: 6 "LORD enthroned upon the c."
2 Chr 3: 7 and he engraved c upon the walls.
2 Chr 3:11 of the c spanned twenty cubits:
Ps 80: 2 Seated upon the c, shine forth
Ps 99: 1 he is enthroned on the c, the earth
Is 37:16 God of Israel, enthroned on the c!
Ez 10: 1 the c was something like a sapphire,
Ez 10: 4 the LORD had moved off the c
Ez 41:18 were figures of c and palm trees:
Ez 41:18 a palm tree between each pair of c.
Heb 9: 5 Above it were the c of glory

CHEST → CHESTS
2 Kgs 12:10 Jehoiada the priest then took a c,
Dn 2:32 gold, its c and arms were silver,
Zec 13: 6 are these wounds on your c?"
Rev 1:13 robe, with a gold sash around his c.

CHESTS → CHEST
Rev 15: 6 with a gold sash around their c.

CHEW → CHEWS
Dt 14: 7 any of the following that c the cud
Dt 14: 7 which indeed c the cud, but do not

CHEWS → CHEW
Lv 11: 3 it is cloven-footed and c the cud.

CHIEF
Gn 39:21 by making the c jailer well-disposed
Gn 40: 2 the c cupbearer and the c baker,
Gn 41: 9 the c cupbearer said to Pharaoh:
1 Sm 21: 8 Edomite, the c of Saul's shepherds.
Dn 5:11 father, made him c of the magicians,
Dn 10:13 one of the c princes, came to help
Mt 20:18 will be handed over to the c priests
Mt 27: 6 The c priests gathered
Mk 15: 3 The c priests accused him of many
Acts 9:14 he has authority from the c priests
Acts 26:10 I received from the c priests,
1 Pt 5: 4 when the c Shepherd is revealed,

CHILD → CHILD'S, CHILDBEARING, CHILDHOOD, CHILDISH, CHILDLESS, CHILDREN, CHILDREN'S, GRANDCHILDREN
Gn 17:17 "Can a c be born to a man who is
Ex 2: 3 and putting the c in it, placed it
Dt 1:31 as one carries his own c, all along
Jgs 11:34 She was his only c: he had neither
1 Sm 1:22 husband, "Once the c is weaned,
1 Sm 1:27 I prayed for this c, and the LORD
2 Sm 12:16 pleaded with God on behalf of the c.
Tb 3:15 and he has no other c to be his heir,
Ps 131: 2 soul, Like a weaned c to its mother,
Eccl 6: 3 I proclaim that the c born dead,
Sir 4:10 Then God will call you his c, and he
Sir 6:18 My c, from your youth choose discipline;
Sir 30: 9 Pamper a c and he will be a terror
Is 9: 5 For a c is born to us, a son is given
Is 11: 6 with a little c to guide them.
Is 49:15 tenderness for the c of her womb?
Is 66:13 As a mother comforts her c, so I will
Jer 4:31 of a mother bearing her first c—
Jer 6:26 as for an only c with bitter wailing:
Hos 11: 1 When Israel was a c I loved him,
Mt 1:18 with c through the holy Spirit.
Mt 2:11 on entering the house they saw the c
Mt 18: 2 He called a c over, placed it in their
Mk 5:39 The c is not dead but asleep."
Mk 10:15 of God like a c will not enter it."
Lk 1:80 The c grew and became strong
Lk 2:40 The c grew and became strong,

Lk 9:48 "Whoever receives this c in my
1 Cor 13:11 When I was a c, I used to talk as a c, think as a c, reason as a c;
Gal 4: 7 So you are no longer a slave but a c, and if a c then also an heir,
Heb 11:23 they saw that he was a beautiful c,
Rev 12: 4 to devour her c when she gave birth.

CHILD'S → CHILD
Ex 2: 8 went and called the c own mother.

CHILDBEARING → CHILD, BEAR
Gn 3:16 I will intensify your toil in c;

CHILDHOOD → CHILD
Prv 29:21 are pampered from c they will turn

CHILDISH → CHILD
1 Cor 13:11 I became a man, I put aside c things.

CHILDLESS → CHILD
Gn 15: 2 if I die c and have only a servant
1 Sm 15:33 your sword has made women c,
1 Sm 15:33 your mother be c among women."
Sir 16: 3 rather die c than have impious
Sir 42: 9 when she is married, lest she be c;

CHILDREN → CHILD
Gn 3:16 in pain you shall bring forth c.
Gn 21: 7 added, "that Sarah would nurse c!
Gn 30: 1 Jacob, "Give me c or I shall die!"
Ex 2: 6 said, "It is one of the Hebrews' c."
Ex 12:26 When your c ask you, 'What does
Ex 20: 5 on the c of those who hate me,
Dt 4: 9 make them known to your c and to your children's c,
Dt 6: 7 Keep repeating them to your c.
Dt 11:19 Teach them to your c,
Dt 14: 1 You are c of the LORD, your God.
Dt 24:16 shall not be put to death for their c,
Dt 24:16 nor shall c be put to death for their
Dt 32:46 words you should command your c,
Jos 4: 6 When your c ask you, 'What do
1 Sm 1: 2 Peninnah had c, but Hannah had no c.
Ezr 10:44 away, both the women and their c.
Neh 13:24 Of their c, half spoke the language
1 Mc 1:60 who had their c circumcised,
Ps 33:13 looks down and observes the c of Adam,
Ps 34:12 Come, c, listen to me; I will teach
Ps 78: 5 ancestors, they were to teach their c;
Ps 103:13 As a father has compassion on his c,
Prv 7:24 So now, c, listen to me, be attentive
Prv 14:26 defense, a refuge even for one's c.
Prv 17: 6 Children's c are the crown
Prv 17: 6 and the glory of c is their parentage.
Prv 20: 7 happy are their c after them!
Prv 31:28 Her c rise up and call her blessed;
Eccl 6: 3 Should one have a hundred c
Sir 4:11 Wisdom teaches her c
Is 1: 4 evil offspring, corrupt c!
Is 30: 1 Rebellious c, oracle of the LORD,
Is 54:13 All your c shall be taught
Jer 4:22 They are senseless c,
Jer 31:15 Rachel mourns for her c, she refuses to be consoled for her c—
Ez 23:37 even the c they bore for me they
Hos 1: 2 of prostitution and c of prostitution,
Hos 2: 6 I will have no pity on her c, for they are c of prostitution.
Jl 1: 3 Report it to your c. Have your c report it to their c,
Zec 10: 7 Their c will see and rejoice—
Mt 2:18 Rachel weeping for her c, and she
Mt 3: 9 you, God can raise up c to Abraham
Mt 5: 9 for they will be called c of God.
Mt 7:11 how to give good gifts to your c,
Mt 13:38 the good seed the c of the kingdom.
Mt 13:38 The weeds are the c of the evil one,
Mt 15:26 is not right to take the food of the c
Mt 18: 3 unless you turn and become like c,
Mt 19:14 Jesus said, "Let the c come to me,
Mt 27:25 blood be upon us and upon our c."
Mk 10:14 to them, "Let the c come to me;

Mk	10:30	sisters and mothers and c and lands,
Mk	13:12	c will rise up against parents
Lk	18:16	"Let the c come to me and do not
Jn	1:12	he gave power to become c of God,
Jn	8:39	"If you were Abraham's c,
Acts	2:39	and to your c and to all those far off,
Rom	8:14	by the Spirit of God are c of God.
Rom	8:16	with our spirit that we are c of God,
Rom	9: 8	it is not the c of the flesh who are the c of God,
Rom	9:26	there they shall be called c
2 Cor	12:14	C ought not to save for their parents, but parents for their c.
Gal	3:26	through faith you are all c of God
Gal	4:28	like Isaac, are c of the promise.
Eph	2: 3	and we were by nature c of wrath,
Eph	5: 8	light in the Lord. Live as c of light,
Eph	6: 1	C, obey your parents [in the Lord],
Eph	6: 4	do not provoke your c to anger,
Phil	2:15	c of God without blemish
Col	3:20	C, obey your parents in everything,
Col	3:21	do not provoke your c, so they may
1 Thes	2: 7	as a nursing mother cares for her c.
1 Tm	3: 4	keeping his c under control
1 Tm	3:12	and must manage their c and their
1 Tm	5:10	that she has raised c,
1 Tm	5:14	marry, have c, and manage a home,
Ti	1: 6	believing c who are not accused
Ti	2: 4	to love their husbands and c,
Heb	2:13	I and the c God has given me."
1 Pt	1:14	Like obedient c, do not act
1 Jn	3: 1	that we may be called the c of God.
1 Jn	3:10	the c of God and the c of the devil
2 Jn	1: 1	and to her c whom I love in truth—
3 Jn	1: 4	to hear that my c are walking

CHILDREN'S → CHILD

Prv	13:22	an inheritance to their c children,
Jer	31:29	and the c teeth are set on edge,"
Ez	18: 2	but the c teeth are set on edge"?

CHOICE → CHOOSE

Prv	8:10	and knowledge rather than c gold.
Prv	10:20	C silver is the tongue of the just;
Jer	2:21	But I had planted you as a c vine,

CHOKE → CHOKED

Mt	13:22	the lure of riches c the word and it

CHOKED → CHOKE

Mk	4: 7	the thorns grew up and c it and it
Lk	8: 7	and the thorns grew with it and c it.
Lk	8:14	they are c by the anxieties

CHOOSE → CHOICE, CHOOSES, CHOSE, CHOSEN

Dt	30:19	C life, then, that you and your
1 Kgs	18:25	"C one young bull and prepare it
Prv	3:31	the violent and c none of their ways:
Sir	15:15	If you c, you can keep
Is	7:15	may learn to reject evil and c good;
Is	14: 1	take pity on Jacob and again c Israel,
Zec	2:16	the LORD will again c Jerusalem.
Jn	6:70	them, "Did I not c you twelve?

CHOOSES → CHOOSE

Nm	16: 7	the LORD then c is the holy one.
Dt	12:14	place which the LORD c in one

CHORAZIN

Mt	11:21	"Woe to you, C! Woe to you,
Lk	10:13	"Woe to you, C! Woe to you,

CHOSE → CHOOSE

Gn	13:11	c for himself the whole Jordan Plain
Dt	4:37	ancestors he c their descendants
1 Sm	2:28	I c them out of all the tribes
Neh	9: 7	are the LORD God who c Abram,
Ps	47: 5	Who c our heritage for us, the glory
Ps	78:68	God c the tribe of Judah,
Ps	78:70	He c David his servant, took him
Ez	20: 5	The day I c Israel, I swore
Mk	13:20	for the sake of the elect whom he c,

Lk	6:13	and from them he c Twelve,
Jn	15:16	It was not you who c me, but I who c you
Acts	6: 5	so they c Stephen, a man filled
Acts	15:40	But Paul c Silas and departed
1 Cor	1:27	God c the foolish of the world
1 Cor	1:27	and God c the weak of the world
Eph	1: 4	as he c us in him,
2 Thes	2:13	because God c you as the firstfruits

CHOSEN → CHOOSE

Dt	7: 6	has c you from all the peoples
Dt	18: 5	has c him out of all your tribes to be
Jos	24:22	you have c to serve the LORD."
Jgs	10:14	and cry out to the gods you have c;
1 Sm	8:18	of the king whom you have c,
1 Kgs	8:44	LORD toward the city you have c
Neh	1: 9	to the place I have c as the dwelling
Ps	89: 4	made a covenant with my c one;
Ps	105: 6	offspring of Jacob the c one!
Ps	119:30	The way of loyalty I have c;
Is	41: 8	Jacob, whom I have c,
Is	42: 1	my c one with whom I am pleased.
Is	43:10	my servant whom I have c To know
Hg	2:23	like a signet ring, for I have c you—
Zec	3: 2	who has c Jerusalem rebuke you!
Mt	12:18	my servant whom I have c,
Mt	22:14	Many are invited, but few are c."
Lk	9:35	voice that said, "This is my c Son;
Lk	10:42	Mary has c the better part and it will
Lk	23:35	him save himself if he is the c one,
Jn	15:19	and I have c you out of the world,
Acts	1: 2	to the apostles whom he had c.
Acts	9:15	this man is a c instrument of mine
Rom	11: 5	time there is a remnant, c by grace.
Col	3:12	as God's c ones, holy and beloved,
1 Thes	1: 4	loved by God, how you were c.
1 Pt	2: 6	a cornerstone, c and precious,
1 Pt	2: 9	But you are "a c race, a royal
Rev	17:14	and those with him are called, c,

CHRIST → CHRIST'S, CHRISTIAN, CHRISTIANS, MESSIAH

Mk	1: 1	of the gospel of Jesus C [the Son]
Jn	1:17	and truth came through Jesus C.
Acts	3: 6	the name of Jesus C the Nazorean,
Acts	4:10	of Jesus C the Nazorean whom you
Acts	9:34	to him, "Aeneas, Jesus C heals you.
Rom	1: 4	from the dead, Jesus C our Lord.
Rom	3:22	faith in Jesus C for all who believe.
Rom	5: 1	with God through our Lord Jesus C,
Rom	5: 6	For C, while we were still helpless,
Rom	5: 8	while we were still sinners C died
Rom	5:11	of God through our Lord Jesus C,
Rom	5:17	life through the one person Jesus C.
Rom	6: 4	just as C was raised from the dead
Rom	6:23	is eternal life in C Jesus our Lord.
Rom	7: 4	to the law through the body of C,
Rom	8: 1	for those who are in C Jesus.
Rom	8: 9	have the Spirit of C does not belong
Rom	8:17	heirs of God and joint heirs with C,
Rom	8:35	will separate us from the love of C?
Rom	10: 4	For C is the end of the law
Rom	12: 5	are one body in C and individually
Rom	13:14	But put on the Lord Jesus C,
Rom	14: 9	For this is why C died and came
Rom	15: 3	For C did not please himself;
Rom	15: 5	another, in keeping with C Jesus,
Rom	15: 7	then, as C welcomed you,
Rom	16:18	such people do not serve our Lord C
1 Cor	1: 2	have been sanctified in C Jesus,
1 Cor	1: 7	the revelation of our Lord Jesus C.
1 Cor	1:13	Is C divided? Was Paul crucified
1 Cor	1:17	For C did not send me to baptize
1 Cor	1:17	the cross of C might not be emptied
1 Cor	1:23	but we proclaim C crucified,
1 Cor	1:30	due to him that you are in C Jesus,
1 Cor	2: 2	I was with you except Jesus C,
1 Cor	2:16	But we have the mind of C.

1 Cor	3:11	one that is there, namely, Jesus **C**.
1 Cor	5: 7	For our paschal lamb, **C**, has been
1 Cor	6:15	that your bodies are members of **C**?
1 Cor	8: 6	Jesus **C**, through whom all things
1 Cor	8:12	they are, you are sinning against **C**.
1 Cor	10: 4	them, and the rock was the **C**.
1 Cor	11: 1	Be imitators of me, as I am of **C**.
1 Cor	11: 3	to know that **C** is the head of every
1 Cor	11: 3	of his wife, and God the head of **C**.
1 Cor	15: 3	that **C** died for our sins
1 Cor	15:14	And if **C** has not been raised,
1 Cor	15:22	so too in **C** shall all be brought
1 Cor	15:57	victory through our Lord Jesus **C**.
2 Cor	1: 5	to us, so through **C** does our
2 Cor	2:14	who always leads us in triumph in **C**
2 Cor	3: 3	be a letter of **C** administered by us,
2 Cor	3:14	because through **C** it is taken away.
2 Cor	4: 4	light of the gospel of the glory of **C**,
2 Cor	4: 5	ourselves but Jesus **C** as Lord,
2 Cor	4: 6	of God on the face of [Jesus] **C**.
2 Cor	5:10	before the judgment seat of **C**,
2 Cor	5:14	For the love of **C** impels us,
2 Cor	5:17	whoever is in **C** is a new creation:
2 Cor	6:15	What accord has **C** with Beliar?
2 Cor	10: 1	the gentleness and clemency of **C**,
2 Cor	11: 2	present you as a chaste virgin to **C**.
2 Cor	11:13	who masquerade as apostles of **C**.
Gal	1: 7	and wish to pervert the gospel of **C**.
Gal	2:16	the law but through faith in Jesus **C**,
Gal	2:16	we may be justified by faith in **C**
Gal	2:16	the law but through faith in Jesus **C**,
Gal	3:28	for you are all one in **C** Jesus.
Gal	5: 1	For freedom **C** set us free;
Gal	6: 2	and so you will fulfill the law of **C**.
Eph	1: 3	who has blessed us in **C** with every
Eph	2: 5	life with **C** (by grace you have been
Eph	2:10	created in **C** Jesus for the good
Eph	2:12	were at that time without **C**,
Eph	2:20	**C** Jesus himself as the capstone.
Eph	3: 8	Gentiles the inscrutable riches of **C**,
Eph	3:17	and that **C** may dwell in your hearts
Eph	4:13	to the extent of the full stature of **C**,
Eph	4:15	way into him who is the head, **C**,
Eph	4:32	as God has forgiven you in **C**.
Eph	5: 2	as **C** loved us and handed himself
Eph	5:21	one another out of reverence for **C**.
Eph	5:23	of his wife just as **C** is head
Eph	5:25	even as **C** loved the church
Phil	1: 6	complete it until the day of **C** Jesus.
Phil	1:18	or in truth, **C** is being proclaimed?
Phil	1:21	For to me life is **C**, and death is
Phil	1:23	to depart this life and be with **C**,
Phil	1:27	in a way worthy of the gospel of **C**,
Phil	1:29	for the sake of **C**, not only
Phil	2: 5	attitude that is also yours in **C** Jesus,
Phil	2:11	tongue confess that Jesus **C** is Lord,
Phil	3: 7	to consider a loss because of **C**.
Phil	3:18	as enemies of the cross of **C**.
Phil	4:19	with his glorious riches in **C** Jesus.
Col	1: 4	have heard of your faith in **C** Jesus
Col	1:27	it is **C** in you, the hope for glory.
Col	1:28	may present everyone perfect in **C**.
Col	2: 2	of the mystery of God, **C**,
Col	2: 6	as you received **C** Jesus the Lord,
Col	2:17	the reality belongs to **C**.
Col	3: 1	If then you were raised with **C**,
Col	3: 3	the peace of **C** control your hearts,
Col	3:16	Let the word of **C** dwell in you
1 Thes	4:16	and the dead in **C** will rise first.
1 Thes	5: 9	salvation through our Lord Jesus **C**,
1 Thes	5:18	the will of God for you in **C** Jesus.
2 Thes	2: 1	to the coming of our Lord Jesus **C**
2 Thes	2:14	the glory of our Lord Jesus **C**.
1 Tm	1:15	**C** Jesus came into the world to save
1 Tm	1:16	**C** Jesus might display all his
1 Tm	2: 5	God and the human race, **C** Jesus,
1 Tm	4: 6	will be a good minister of **C** Jesus,
1 Tm	6:14	the appearance of our Lord Jesus **C**
2 Tm	1: 9	on us in **C** Jesus before time began,
2 Tm	1:10	appearance of our savior **C** Jesus,
2 Tm	2: 1	in the grace that is in **C** Jesus.
2 Tm	2: 3	me like a good soldier of **C** Jesus.
2 Tm	2: 8	Remember Jesus **C**,
2 Tm	2:10	the salvation that is in **C** Jesus,
2 Tm	3:12	in **C** Jesus will be persecuted.
2 Tm	3:15	salvation through faith in **C** Jesus.
Ti	2:13	great God and of our savior Jesus **C**,
Phlm	1: 6	good there is in us that leads to **C**.
Phlm	1:20	in the Lord. Refresh my heart in **C**.
Heb	3: 6	**C** was faithful as a son placed over
Heb	3:14	We have become partners of **C**
Heb	5: 5	it was not **C** who glorified himself
Heb	6: 1	behind the basic teaching about **C**
Heb	9:11	when **C** came as high priest
Heb	9:24	For **C** did not enter into a sanctuary
Heb	9:28	so also **C**, offered once to take away
Heb	10:10	of the body of Jesus **C** once for all.
Heb	13: 8	Jesus **C** is the same yesterday,
1 Pt	1: 2	with the blood of Jesus **C**:
1 Pt	1:11	Spirit of **C** within them indicated
1 Pt	1:11	to the sufferings destined for **C**
1 Pt	1:19	with the precious blood of **C** as
1 Pt	2:21	because **C** also suffered for you,
1 Pt	3:15	sanctify **C** as Lord in your hearts.
1 Pt	3:18	For **C** also suffered for sins once,
1 Pt	3:21	through the resurrection of Jesus **C**,
1 Pt	4: 1	since **C** suffered in the flesh,
1 Pt	4:14	you are insulted for the name of **C**,
2 Pt	1: 1	of our God and savior Jesus **C**:
2 Pt	1:16	and coming of our Lord Jesus **C**,
2 Pt	3:18	of our Lord and savior Jesus **C**.
1 Jn	2: 1	Father, Jesus **C** the righteous one.
1 Jn	2:22	Whoever denies that Jesus is the **C**.
1 Jn	3:23	Jesus **C**, and love one another just
1 Jn	4: 2	acknowledges Jesus **C** come
1 Jn	5: 1	Jesus is the **C** is begotten by God,
1 Jn	5: 6	blood, Jesus **C**, not by water alone,
1 Jn	5:20	one who is true, in his Son Jesus **C**.
2 Jn	1: 7	not acknowledge Jesus **C** as coming
2 Jn	1: 9	of the **C** does not have God;
Jude	1: 1	a slave of Jesus **C** and brother
Jude	1: 1	the Father and kept safe for Jesus **C**:
Jude	1: 4	our only Master and Lord, Jesus **C**.
Jude	1:17	by the apostles of our Lord Jesus **C**,
Rev	1: 1	The revelation of Jesus **C**,
Rev	1: 5	and from Jesus **C**, the faithful
Rev	20: 4	they reigned with **C** for a thousand
Rev	20: 6	they will be priests of God and of **C**,

CHRIST'S → CHRIST

Eph	4: 7	according to the measure of **C** gift.

CHRISTIAN → CHRIST

Acts	26:28	soon persuade me to play the **C**."
1 Pt	4:16	suffer as a **C** should not be ashamed

CHRISTIANS → CHRIST

Acts	11:26	that the disciples were first called **C**.

CHRYSOLITE

Ez	28:13	topaz, and beryl, **c**, onyx,
Rev	21:20	the seventh **c**, the eighth beryl,

CHURCH → CHURCHES

Mt	16:18	and upon this rock I will build my **c**,
Mt	18:17	refuses to listen to them, tell the **c**.
Mt	18:17	If he refuses to listen even to the **c**,
Acts	5:11	great fear came upon the whole **c**
Acts	8: 1	persecution of the **c** in Jerusalem,
Acts	8: 3	was trying to destroy the **c**;
Acts	12: 1	members of the **c** to harm them.
Acts	14:23	presbyters for them in each **c** and,
Acts	15: 4	they were welcomed by the **c**,
Acts	20:28	which you tend the **c** of God that he
Rom	16: 5	greet also the **c** at their house.

1 Cor	4:17	I teach them everywhere in every c.
1 Cor	6: 4	people of no standing in the c?
1 Cor	10:32	to Jews or Greeks or the c of God,
1 Cor	11:18	you meet as a c there are divisions
1 Cor	12:28	God has designated in the c to be,
1 Cor	14: 4	whoever prophesies builds up the c.
1 Cor	14:12	of them for building up the c.
1 Cor	14:35	for a woman to speak in the c.
1 Cor	15: 9	because I persecuted the c of God.
Gal	1:13	how I persecuted the c of God
Eph	1:22	him as head over all things to the c,
Eph	3:10	now be made known through the c
Eph	3:21	to him be glory in the c
Eph	5:23	wife just as Christ is head of the c,
Eph	5:25	even as Christ loved the c
Phil	3: 6	in zeal I persecuted the c,
Col	1:18	He is the head of the body, the c.
Col	1:24	behalf of his body, which is the c,
1 Tm	3: 5	can he take care of the c of God?
1 Tm	3:15	which is the c of the living God,
Jas	5:14	summon the presbyters of the c,
3 Jn	1: 9	I wrote to the c, but Diotrephes,
Rev	2: 1	"To the angel of the c in Ephesus,

CHURCHES → CHURCH

Acts	15:41	Cilicia bringing strength to the c.
Acts	16: 5	Day after day the c grew stronger
1 Cor	7:17	I give this order in all the c.
1 Cor	11:16	such a custom, nor do the c of God.
1 Cor	14:34	women should keep silent in the c,
2 Cor	11: 8	I plundered other c by accepting
1 Thes	2:14	become imitators of the c of God
2 Thes	1: 4	you in the c of God regarding your
Rev	1: 4	John, to the seven c in Asia:
Rev	1:20	stars are the angels of the seven c,
Rev	1:20	seven lampstands are the seven c.
Rev	2: 7	to hear what the Spirit says to the c.
Rev	22:16	to give you this testimony for the c.

CILICIA

Jdt	2:25	He seized the territory of C, and cut
Acts	15:41	C bringing strength to the churches.
Acts	21:39	of Tarsus in C, a citizen of no mean

CIRCLE → ENCIRCLE

Jos	6:11	the ark of the LORD c the city,
Jb	26:10	has marked out a c on the surface

CIRCUMCISE → CIRCUMCISED, CIRCUMCISION

Gn	17:11	C the flesh of your foreskin.
Dt	10:16	C therefore the foreskins of your
Dt	30: 6	will c your hearts and the hearts
Jos	5: 2	and c Israel for the second time.
Lk	1:59	on the eighth day to c the child,
Jn	7:22	and you c a man on the sabbath.
Acts	21:21	telling them not to c their children

CIRCUMCISED → CIRCUMCISE

Gn	17:10	every male among you shall be c.
Gn	17:26	and his son Ishmael were c;
Gn	21: 4	was eight days old, Abraham c him,
Gn	34:15	by having every male among you c.
Jos	5: 3	c the Israelites at Gibeath-haaraloth.
Jdt	14:10	He c the flesh of his foreskin and he
1 Mc	1:60	women who had their children c,
1 Mc	2:46	forcibly c any uncircumcised boys
2 Mc	6:10	for having c their children were
Acts	10:45	The c believers who had
Acts	11: 2	Jerusalem the c believers confronted
Acts	15: 1	"Unless you are c according
Acts	16: 3	Paul had him c, for they all knew
Rom	3:30	and will justify the c on the basis
Rom	4: 9	this blessedness apply only to the c,
1 Cor	7:18	someone called after he had been c?
1 Cor	7:18	He should not be c.
Gal	2: 3	was a Greek, was compelled to be c,
Gal	2: 7	uncircumcised, just as Peter to the c,
Gal	6:13	having themselves c observe
Gal	6:13	they only want you to be c so

Phil	3: 5	C on the eighth day, of the race
Col	2:11	were also c with a circumcision not

CIRCUMCISION → CIRCUMCISE

Ex	4:26	spouse of blood," in regard to the c.
1 Mc	1:15	They disguised their c
Acts	7: 8	Then he gave him the covenant of c,
Rom	2:25	C, to be sure, has value if you
Rom	2:25	your c has become uncircumcision.
Rom	2:29	and c is of the heart, in the spirit,
1 Cor	7:19	C means nothing,
Gal	5: 6	neither c nor uncircumcision counts
Eph	2:11	by those called the c, which is done
Phil	3: 3	For we are the c, we who worship
Col	2:11	with a c not administered by hand,
Col	2:11	carnal body, with the c of Christ.

CIRCUMSTANCES

Phil	4:12	indeed how to live in humble c;
1 Thes	5:18	In all c give thanks, for this is

CISTERN → CISTERNS

Prv	5:15	Drink water from your own c,
Jer	38: 6	him into the c of Prince Malchiah,

CISTERNS → CISTERN

Dt	6:11	garner, with c that you did not dig,
Neh	9:25	with all good things, C already dug,
Jer	2:13	They have dug themselves c, broken c that cannot hold water.

CITADEL → CITADELS

1 Mc	1:33	strong towers, and it became their c.
1 Mc	4:41	men to attack those in the c,

CITADELS → CITADEL

Ps	48:14	examine its c, that you may tell

CITIES → CITY

Gn	13:12	while Lot settled among the c
Gn	19:25	He overthrew those c and the whole
Ex	1:11	for Pharaoh the garrison c of Pithom
Lv	25:32	levitical c the Levites shall always
Nm	35:11	select for yourselves c to serve as c of asylum,
Dt	6:10	fine, large c that you did not build,
Jos	20: 2	for yourselves the c of refuge
Ps	69:36	Zion, and rebuild the c of Judah.
Is	6:11	Until the c are desolate,
Is	64: 9	Your holy c have become
Jer	4:16	shouting their war cry against the c
Zec	1:17	My c will again overflow
Lk	19:17	take charge of ten c.'
2 Pt	2: 6	if he condemned the c of Sodom
Rev	16:19	three parts, and the gentile c fell.

CITIZEN → CITIZENS, CITIZENSHIP

Acts	21:39	in Cilicia, a c of no mean city;
Acts	22:25	to scourge a man who is a Roman c
Acts	23:27	I learned that he was a Roman c.

CITIZENS → CITIZEN

Acts	16:38	they heard that they were Roman c.
Eph	2:19	you are fellow c with the holy ones

CITIZENSHIP → CITIZEN

Acts	22:28	"I acquired this c for a large sum
Phil	3:20	But our c is in heaven, and from it

CITY → CITIES

Gn	4:17	Cain also became the founder of a c,
Gn	11: 4	let us build ourselves a c
Gn	18:24	were fifty righteous people in the c;
Gn	19:14	LORD is about to destroy the c."
Dt	28: 3	May you be blessed in the c,
Dt	28:16	May you be cursed in the c,
Jos	6:16	for the LORD has given you the c.
Jgs	16: 3	seized the doors of the c gate
2 Sm	5: 9	which he called the C of David.
1 Kgs	8:44	the LORD toward the c you have
1 Chr	11: 7	therefore was called the C of David.
Neh	11: 1	the holy c, while the other nine
1 Mc	1:31	He plundered the c and set fire to it,
1 Mc	2:31	king who were in the C of David,

Ps   46: 5 of the river gladden the c of God,
Ps   48: 2 highly praised in the c of our God:
Ps   60:11 will bring me to the fortified c?
Ps   122: 3 built as a c, walled round about.
Ps   127: 1 Unless the LORD guard the c,
Prv   11:10 the just prosper, the c rejoices;
Prv   31:23 is prominent at the c gates as he sits
Prv   31:31 her deeds praise her at the c gates.
Is   1:21 prostitute, the faithful c, so upright!
Is   1:26 shall be called c of justice, faithful c.
Is   62:12 "Cared For," "A C Not Forsaken."
Jer   34: 2 I am handing this c over to the king
Jer   34:22 to bring them back to this c.
Lam   1: 1 How solitary sits the c, once filled
Ez   4: 1 you, and draw on it a c, Jerusalem.
Ez   11: 3 The c is the pot, and we are
Dn   9:24 for your people and for your holy c:
Am   5: 3 The c that marched
Jon   1: 2 Set out for the great c of Nineveh,
Jon   3: 2 Set out for the great c of Nineveh,
Jon   4:11 I not be concerned over the great c
Na   3: 1 Ah! The bloody c, all lies,
Hb   2:12 you who build a c by bloodshed,
Zep   2:15 Is this the exultant c that dwelt
Zec   8: 3 will be called the faithful c,
Zec   14: 2 half the c will go into exile.
Mt   4: 5 the devil took him to the holy c,
Mt   5:14 A c set on a mountain cannot be
Lk   2: 4 to the c of David that is called
Lk   19:41 near, he saw the c and wept over it,
Acts   18:10 for I have many people in this c."
Heb   11:10 forward to the c with foundations,
Heb   12:22 Zion and the c of the living God,
Heb   13:14 For here we have no lasting c,
Rev   3:12 and the name of the c of my God,
Rev   11: 2 who will trample the holy c
Rev   16:19 The great c was split into three
Rev   17:18 you saw represents the great c
Rev   18:10 alas, great c, Babylon, mighty c.
Rev   20: 9 of the holy ones and the beloved c.
Rev   21: 2 I also saw the holy c, a new
Rev   21:22 I saw no temple in the c, for its

CLAIM → CLAIMED, CLAIMING
Neh   2:20 neither share nor c nor memorial

CLAIMED → CLAIM
Acts   4:32 no one c that any of his possessions

CLAIMING → CLAIM
Acts   5:36 c to be someone important,
Rom   1:22 While c to be wise, they became

CLAN → CLANS
Nm   27: 4 his c merely because he had no son?

CLANS → CLAN
Gn   36:15 These are the c of the sons of Esau.
Nm   1: 2 Israelites, by c and ancestral houses,
Mi   5: 1 least among the c of Judah,

CLAP → CLAPPING
Ps   47: 2 All you peoples, c your hands;
Ps   98: 8 Let the rivers c their hands,
Is   55:12 trees of the field shall c their hands.
Lam   2:15 by on the road, c their hands at you;
Ez   6:11 C your hands, stamp your feet,
Na   3:19 news of you c their hands over you;

CLAPPING → CLAP
Ez   25: 6 c your hands and stamping your feet,

CLASPS
Ex   26: 6 Then make fifty c of gold and join
Ex   36:13 Then fifty c of gold were made,

CLAUDIUS
Acts   11:28 the world, and it happened under C.
Acts   18: 2 Priscilla because C had ordered all
Acts   23:26 "C Lysias to his excellency

CLAWS
Dn   7:19 with its iron teeth and bronze c,

CLAY
Jb   10: 9 that you fashioned me from c!
Jb   33: 6 God, I too was pinched from c.
Wis   15: 7 class the worker in c is the judge.
Sir   33:13 Like c in the hands of a potter, to be
Is   29:16 the potter were taken to be the c:
Is   41:25 like mud, like a potter treading c.
Is   45: 9 Shall the c say to the potter,
Is   64: 7 we are the c and you our potter:
Jer   18: 6 like c in the hand of the potter,
Lam   4: 2 How they are treated like c jugs,
Dn   14: 7 "it is only c inside and bronze
Rom   9:21 the potter have a right over the c,
2 Tm   2:20 and silver but also of wood and c,

CLEAN → CLEANSE, CLEANSED, CLEANSES, CLEANSING
Gn   7: 2 Of every c animal, take with you
Lv   10:10 and between what is c and what is
Lv   20:25 the c animals from the unclean,
Lv   20:25 and the c birds from the unclean,
Dt   14:11 You may eat all c birds.
2 Kgs   5:10 flesh will heal, and you will be c."
Ps   24: 4 "The c of hand and pure of heart,
Prv   20: 9 say, "I have made my heart c, I am
Eccl   9: 2 the good, for the c and the unclean,
Wis   15: 7 the vessels that serve for c purposes
Ez   36:25 I will sprinkle c water over you to make you c;
Zec   3: 5 "Let them put a c turban on his
Mt   8: 2 if you wish, you can make me c."
Mt   27:59 body, Joseph wrapped it [in] c linen
Mk   7:19 (Thus he declared all foods c.)
Jn   13:10 for he is c all over; so you are c, but not all."
Acts   10:15 "What God has made c, you are not
Rom   14:20 Everything is indeed c, but it is
Heb   10:22 our hearts sprinkled c from an evil

CLEANSE → CLEAN
2 Chr   29:15 LORD, to c the LORD's house.
Jb   9:30 with soap and c my hands with lye,
Ps   51: 4 and from my sin c me.
Sir   38:10 c your heart of every sin.
Ez   36:25 and from all your idols I will c you.
Mt   10: 8 raise the dead, c lepers,
2 Cor   7: 1 let us c ourselves from every
Jas   4: 8 C your hands, you sinners,
1 Jn   1: 9 and c us from all wrongdoing.

CLEANSED → CLEAN
Neh   13:30 So I c them of all foreign
Mt   8: 3 His leprosy was c immediately.
Mt   11: 5 walk, lepers are c, the deaf hear,
Lk   4:27 yet not one of them was c, but only
Heb   10: 2 once c, would no longer have had

CLEANSES → CLEAN
2 Tm   2:21 If anyone c himself of these things,
1 Jn   1: 7 of his Son Jesus c us from all sin.

CLEANSING → CLEAN
Mk   1:44 for your c what Moses prescribed;
Lk   5:14 for your c what Moses prescribed;
Eph   5:26 c her by the bath of water
2 Pt   1: 9 forgetful of the c of his past sins.

CLEAR → CLEARED, CLEARLY
Nm   15:34 there was no c decision as to what
Ps   19: 9 The command of the LORD is c,
Mt   3:12 He will c his threshing floor
Acts   23: 1 a perfectly c conscience before God
1 Tm   3: 9 of the faith with a c conscience.
2 Tm   1: 3 a c conscience as my ancestors did,
Heb   13:18 that we have a c conscience,
1 Pt   3:16 keeping your conscience c, so that,
Rev   21:11 stone, like jasper, c as crystal.
Rev   21:18 the city was pure gold, c as glass.

CLEARED → CLEAR
Ps   80:10 You c out what was before it;

Is 5: 2 He spaded it, c it of stones,

CLEARLY → CLEAR
Mk 8:25 his eyes a second time and he saw c;
Lk 6:42 you will see c to remove the splinter

CLEFT → CLEFTS
Jer 13: 4 hide it there in a c of the rock.

CLEFTS → CLEFT
Sg 2:14 My dove in the c of the rock,

CLEVERLY
2 Pt 1:16 We did not follow c devised myths

CLIMB → CLIMBED
Sg 7: 9 I thought, "Let me c the date-palm!
Am 9: 2 Though they c to the heavens,

CLIMBED → CLIMB
Lk 19: 4 and c a sycamore tree in order to see

CLING → CLINGS, CLUNG
Ps 119:31 I c to your testimonies, LORD;

CLINGS → CLING
Gn 2:24 father and mother and c to his wife,
Ps 63: 9 My soul c fast to you;
Heb 12: 1 of every burden and sin that c to us

CLOAK → CLOAKS
Ex 22:25 take your neighbor's c as a pledge,
Dt 22:12 the c that you wrap around yourself.
Ru 3: 9 wing of your c over your servant,
Ez 16: 8 I spread the corner of my c over you
Mt 5:40 your tunic, hand him your c as well.
Mt 9:21 "If only I can touch his c, I shall be
Heb 1:12 You will roll them up like a c,

CLOAKS → CLOAK
Ex 12:34 in their c on their shoulders.
Mk 11: 8 Many people spread their c
Acts 22:23 and throwing off their c and flinging

CLOSED → CLOSER
Gn 2:21 his ribs and c up its place with flesh.
Gn 20:18 the LORD had c every womb
Lk 12: 3 have whispered behind c doors will

CLOSER → CLOSED
1 Cor 8: 8 Now food will not bring us c

CLOTH → CLOTHS, SACKCLOTH
Nm 4: 6 on top of this spread an all-violet c
Dt 22:17 spread out the c before the elders
Mt 9:16 cloak with a piece of unshrunken c,
Mk 14:51 nothing but a linen c about his body.
Acts 16:14 a dealer in purple c, from the city

CLOTHE → CLOTHED, CLOTHES, CLOTHING
Ps 132:16 I will c its priests with salvation;
Ps 132:18 His foes I will c with shame,
1 Pt 5: 5 c yourselves with humility in your

CLOTHED → CLOTHE
Gn 3:21 of skin, with which he c them.
Lv 8: 7 with the sash, c him with the robe,
2 Chr 6:41 God, will be c with salvation,
Ps 30:12 sackcloth and c me with gladness.
Ps 104: 1 You are c with majesty
Ps 132: 9 Your priests will be c with justice;
Is 61:10 For he has c me with garments
Zec 3: 5 c him with the garments while
Lk 24:49 the city until you are c with power
2 Cor 5: 2 to be further c with our heavenly
Gal 3:27 into Christ have c yourselves
Rev 12: 1 in the sky, a woman c with the sun,

CLOTHES → CLOTHE
Dt 29: 4 Your c did not fall from you
Mt 17: 2 sun and his c became white as light.
Lk 12:28 If God so c the grass in the field
1 Tm 2: 9 or pearls, or expensive c,
Jas 2: 2 in fine c comes into your assembly,
Jas 2: 2 and a poor person in shabby c

CLOTHING → CLOTHE
Ex 3:22 for silver and gold articles and for c,
Ex 12:35 articles of silver and gold and for c.
Ex 21:10 food, her c, or her conjugal rights.
Ps 22:19 for my c they cast lots.
Ps 102:27 Like c you change them and they
Sir 29:21 and c, and also a house for decent
Dn 7: 9 His c was white as snow, the hair
Mt 3: 4 John wore c made of camel's hair
Mt 7:15 who come to you in sheep's c,
1 Tm 6: 8 If we have food and c, we shall be

CLOTHS → CLOTH
Lk 24:12 down, and saw the burial c alone;

CLOUD → CLOUDS
Ex 13:21 of a column of c to show them
Ex 16:10 of the LORD appeared in the c!
Ex 19: 9 am coming to you now in a dense c,
Ex 24:18 entered into the midst of the c
Ex 40:34 the c covered the tent of meeting,
Lv 16: 2 myself in a c above the ark's cover.
Nm 9:15 the c covered the tabernacle,
Dt 1:33 and by day in the c, to show you
1 Kgs 8:10 the c filled the house of the LORD
1 Kgs 18:44 "There is a c as small as a man's
Neh 9:19 day the column of c did not cease
Ps 105:39 He spread a c out as a cover,
Is 19: 1 is riding on a swift c on his way
Ez 1: 4 North, a large c with flashing fire,
Ez 10: 4 the temple was filled with the c,
Mk 9: 7 Then a c came, casting a shadow
Mk 9: 7 then from the c came a voice,
Lk 21:27 of Man coming in a c with power
Acts 1: 9 and a c took him from their sight.
1 Cor 10: 2 were baptized into Moses in the c
Heb 12: 1 by so great a c of witnesses, let us
Rev 10: 1 down from heaven wrapped in a c,
Rev 11:12 in a c as their enemies looked on.
Rev 14:14 I looked and there was a white c,
Rev 14:14 on the c one who looked like a son

CLOUDS → CLOUD
Gn 9:13 my bow in the c to serve as a sign
Jgs 5: 4 heavens poured, the c poured rain,
1 Kgs 18:45 All at once the sky grew dark with c
Jb 38:37 Who counts the c with wisdom?
Ps 36: 6 your fidelity, to the c.
Ps 68: 5 exalt the rider of the c.
Ps 77:18 The c poured down their rains;
Ps 104: 3 You make the c your chariot;
Prv 25:14 C and wind but no rain—
Is 14:14 will ascend above the tops of the c;
Dn 3:73 Lightnings and c, bless the Lord;
Dn 7:13 with the c of heaven One like a son
Jl 2: 2 and gloom, a day of thick c!
Na 1: 3 comes, and c are the dust at his feet;
Zep 1:15 and gloom, a day of thick black c,
Mt 24:30 Man coming upon the c of heaven
Mt 26:64 'coming on the c of heaven.'
1 Thes 4:17 them in the c to meet the Lord
Jude 1:12 They are waterless c blown
Rev 1: 7 he is coming amid the c, and every

CLUB → CLUBS
Prv 25:18 A c, sword, or sharp arrow—
Dn 14:26 this dragon without sword or c."

CLUBS → CLUB
Mk 14:43 and c who had come from the chief

CLUNG → CLING
Acts 3:11 As he c to Peter and John,

CLUSTER → CLUSTERS
Nm 13:23 a branch with a single c of grapes
Mi 7: 1 There is no c to eat, no early fig

CLUSTERS → CLUSTER
Rev 14:18 and cut the c from the earth's vines,

CO-WORKER → WORK
Rom 16:21 Timothy, my c, greets you;

CO-WORKERS → WORK
3 Jn 1: 8 so that we may be c in the truth.

COALS
Ps 11: 6 rains upon the wicked fiery c
Ps 18: 9 it kindled c into flame.
Ps 140:11 Drop burning c upon them;
Prv 6:28 Or can a man walk on live c, and his
Prv 25:22 For live c you will heap on their
Ez 1:13 creatures seemed like burning c
Ez 10: 2 burning c from the place among
Rom 12:20 by so doing you will heap burning c

COAST → COASTLANDS
Nm 34: 6 will have the Great Sea with its c;

COASTLANDS → COAST, LAND
Is 42: 4 the c will wait for his teaching.
Is 66:19 the distant c which have never heard

COCK
Jn 13:38 the c will not crow before you deny
Jn 18:27 And immediately the c crowed.

COFFIN
Gn 50:26 and laid to rest in a c in Egypt.

COHORT
Mk 15:16 and assembled the whole c.
Acts 10: 1 centurion of the C called the Italica,
Acts 27: 1 named Julius of the C Augusta.

COIN → COINS
Mt 17:27 you will find a c worth twice
Mt 22:19 Show me the c that pays the census
Mt 22:19 Then they handed him the Roman c.
Lk 15: 9 me because I have found the c that I

COINS → COIN
Lk 15: 8 "Or what woman having ten c
Lk 21: 2 poor widow putting in two small c.
Jn 2:15 spilled the c of the money-changers

COLD
Gn 8:22 seedtime and harvest, c and heat,
Ps 147:17 Who can withstand his c?
Zec 14: 6 that day there will no longer be c
Mt 10:42 whoever gives only a cup of c water
Mt 24:12 the love of many will grow c.
Rev 3:16 neither hot nor c, I will spit you

COLLECT → COLLECTION, COLLECTOR, COLLECTORS
Mt 13:30 "First c the weeds and tie them

COLLECTION → COLLECT
1 Cor 16: 1 in regard to the c for the holy ones,

COLLECTOR → COLLECT
Mt 10: 3 Thomas and Matthew the tax c;
Lk 5:27 saw a tax c named Levi sitting
Lk 18:10 a Pharisee and the other was a tax c.
Lk 19: 2 who was a chief tax c

COLLECTORS → COLLECT
Mt 5:46 Do not the tax c do the same?
Mt 9:10 many tax c and sinners came and sat
Mt 11:19 a friend of tax c and sinners.'
Mt 17:24 the c of the temple tax approached
Mt 21:32 but tax c and prostitutes did.

COLONY
Acts 16:12 of Macedonia and a Roman c.

COLT
Zec 9: 9 donkey, on a c, the foal of a donkey.
Mt 21: 5 ass, and on a c, the foal of a beast
Jn 12:15 comes, seated upon an ass's c."

COME → CAME, COMES, COMING, OUTCOME
Gn 38:16 to her at the roadside and said, "C,
Ex 3: 5 God said: Do not c near!
Ex 19:11 third day the LORD will c down
Ex 24: 1 C up to the LORD, you and Aaron,

Dt 28: 2 All these blessings will c upon you
Dt 28:45 All these curses will c upon you,
1 Sm 4: 7 out, "Gods have c to their camp.
Ps 14: 7 from Zion might c the salvation
Ps 17: 2 From you let my vindication c;
Ps 88: 3 Let my prayer c before you;
Ps 91:10 you, no affliction c near your tent.
Ps 119:41 Let your mercy c to me, LORD,
Ps 121: 1 From whence shall c my help?
Ps 144: 5 incline your heavens and c down;
Prv 2: 6 from his mouth c knowledge
Prv 24:34 Then poverty will c upon you like
Sg 2:13 my friend, my beautiful one, and c!
Is 1:18 C now, let us set things right,
Is 13: 5 They c from a far-off country,
Is 41:22 Or declare to us the things to c,
Is 55: 1 you who are thirsty, c to the water!
Is 55: 1 You who have no money, c,
Is 55: 1 C, buy grain without money,
Is 59:20 Then for Zion shall c a redeemer,
Hos 3: 5 They will c trembling
Mi 6: 6 Shall I c before him with burnt
Hb 2: 3 it, it will surely c, it will not be late.
Zec 10: 4 From them will c the tower,
Zec 14: 5 will c, and all his holy ones
Mt 2: 2 and have c to do him homage."
Mt 5:17 think that I have c to abolish the law
Mt 5:17 I have c not to abolish but to fulfill.
Mt 6:10 your kingdom c, your will be done,
Mt 10:34 think that I have c to bring peace
Mt 10:34 I have c to bring not peace
Mt 11:14 it, he is Elijah, the one who is to c.
Mt 12:28 the kingdom of God has c upon you.
Mt 15:19 For from the heart c evil thoughts,
Mt 17:12 I tell you that Elijah has already c,
Mt 19:14 said, "Let the children c to me,
Mt 24: 5 For many will c in my name,
Mt 27:40 God, [and] c down from the cross!"
Mk 13:33 do not know when the time will c.
Lk 5:32 I have not c to call the righteous
Lk 7:20 ask, 'Are you the one who is to c,
Jn 2: 4 My hour has not yet c."
Jn 6:37 the Father gives me will c to me,
Jn 12:23 "The hour has c for the Son of Man
Jn 14: 3 I will c back again and take you
Gal 4: 4 But when the fullness of time had c,
Col 2:17 These are shadows of things to c;
Heb 10: 9 says, "Behold, I c to do your will."
1 Pt 2: 4 C to him, a living stone,
2 Pt 3: 9 but that all should c to repentance.
1 Jn 4: 2 acknowledges Jesus Christ c
Rev 1: 4 is and who was and who is to c,
Rev 3: 3 are not watchful, I will c like a thief,
Rev 3: 3 at what hour I will c upon you.
Rev 4: 1 "C up here and I will show you
Rev 4: 8 was, and who is, and who is to c."
Rev 22:17 The Spirit and the bride say, "C."
Rev 22:17 Let the one who thirsts c forward,
Rev 22:20 Amen! C, Lord Jesus!

COMES → COME
Dt 8: 3 by all that c forth from the mouth
1 Chr 16:33 who c, who c to rule the earth.
Jb 3:25 what I dreaded c upon me.
Ps 30: 6 At dusk weeping c for the night;
Ps 62: 2 alone, from whom c my salvation
Ps 118:26 Blessed is he who c in the name
Ps 121: 2 My help c from the LORD,
Prv 11: 2 When pride c, disgrace c;
Is 40:10 Here c with power the Lord GOD,
Mt 4: 4 by every word that c forth
Mk 7:20 "But what c out of a person, that is
Mk 11: 9 Blessed is he who c in the name
Lk 18: 8 But when the Son of Man c, will he
Lk 19:38 "Blessed is the king who c
Jn 3:31 But the one who c from heaven [is]

Jn	6:33	is that which c down from heaven
Jn	10:10	A thief c only to steal and slaughter
Jn	14: 6	No one c to the Father except
Jn	15:26	the Advocate c whom I will send
Jn	16:13	But when he c, the Spirit of truth,
Acts	1: 8	when the holy Spirit c upon you,
Rom	10:17	Thus faith c from what is heard,
Rom	10:17	what is heard c through the word
Gal	2:21	for if justification c through the law,
Gal	3:18	if the inheritance c from the law,
Phil	3: 9	that which c through faith in Christ,
2 Jn	1:10	If anyone c to you and does not
Rev	3:12	which c down out of heaven
Rev	11: 7	the beast that c up from the abyss

COMFORT → COMFORTED, COMFORTERS, COMFORTING, COMFORTS

Jb	2:11	to give him sympathy and c.
Jb	7:13	"My bed shall c me, my couch shall
Ps	71:21	Restore my honor; turn and c me,
Ps	119:50	This is my c in affliction,
Ps	119:76	May your mercy c me in accord
Ps	119:82	When will you c me?
Eccl	4: 1	of the victims with none to c them!
Is	22: 4	Do not try to c me for the ruin
Is	40: 1	C, give c to my people, says your
Is	51: 3	the Lord shall c Zion, shall c all
Is	51:19	Who is there to c you?
Is	57:18	lead them and restore full c to them
Is	61: 2	by our God; To c all who mourn;
Is	66:13	comforts her child, so I will c you;
Lam	2:13	can I give in order to c you,
Zec	1:17	the Lord will again c Zion,
Col	4:11	God, and they have been a c to me.

COMFORTED → COMFORT

Ru	2:13	You have c me. You have spoken
1 Chr	7:22	his relatives had come and c him,
Est	D: 8	and c her with reassuring words.
Jb	42:11	c him for all the evil the Lord
Ps	119:52	recite your judgments of old I am c,
Mt	5: 4	they who mourn, for they will be c.
Lk	16:25	but now he is c here, whereas you
Acts	20:12	alive and were immeasurably c.

COMFORTERS → COMFORT

Jb	16: 2	Troublesome c, all of you!
Ps	69:21	was none, for c, but found none.

COMFORTING → COMFORT

Zec	1:13	replied favorably, with c words.

COMFORTS → COMFORT

Is	66:13	As a mother c her child, so I will

COMING → COME

Ez	43: 2	of the God of Israel c from the east!
Dn	7:13	I saw c with the clouds of heaven
Jl	2: 1	for the day of the Lord is c!
Mal	3: 2	who can endure the day of his c?
Mal	3:19	For the day is c, blazing like
Mk	13:26	see 'the Son of Man c in the clouds'
Jn	1:27	the one who is c after me,
Jn	4:25	"I know that the Messiah is c,
Jn	17:13	But now I am c to you. I speak this
1 Thes	1:10	who delivers us from the c wrath.
1 Thes	4:15	who are left until the c of the Lord,
2 Thes	2: 1	to the c of our Lord Jesus Christ
Jas	5: 8	because the c of the Lord is at hand.
2 Pt	1:16	and c of our Lord Jesus Christ,
2 Pt	3: 4	"Where is the promise of his c?
2 Pt	3:12	hastening the c of the day of God,
1 Jn	2:18	you heard that the antichrist was c,
Rev	1: 7	Behold, he is c amid the clouds,
Rev	3:11	I am c quickly. Hold fast to what
Rev	16:15	("Behold, I am c like a thief."
Rev	21: 2	c down out of heaven from God,
Rev	21:10	me the holy city Jerusalem c down
Rev	22: 7	"Behold, I am c soon."
Rev	22:20	says, "Yes, I am c soon." Amen!

COMMAND → COMMANDED, COMMANDERS, COMMANDMENT, COMMANDMENTS, COMMANDS

Ex	7: 2	You will speak all that I c you.
Ex	25:22	I will tell you all that I c you
Dt	1:26	you defied the c of the Lord,
Dt	4: 2	not add to what I c you nor subtract
Dt	13: 1	Every word that I c you, you shall
Jos	1: 9	I c you: be strong and steadfast!
2 Mc	7:30	I will not obey the king's c.
2 Mc	7:30	I obey the c of the law given to our
Prv	8:29	waters should not transgress his c;
Jer	1: 7	whatever I c you, you shall speak.
Jer	1:17	up and tell them all that I c you.
Jer	7:23	Walk exactly in the way I c you,
Jer	11: 4	to my voice and do all that I c you.
Jer	26: 2	whatever I c you, tell them,
Dn	3:95	they disobeyed the royal c
Mt	4: 3	c that these stones become loaves
Mt	4: 6	'He will c his angels concerning
Jn	10:18	This c I have received from my
Jn	15:14	my friends if you do what I c you.
1 Cor	7: 6	of concession, however, not as a c.
2 Cor	8: 8	I say this not by way of c, but to test

COMMANDED → COMMAND

Gn	7: 5	complied, just as the Lord had c.
Ex	7: 6	exactly as the Lord had c them.
Ex	40:32	altar, as the Lord had c Moses.
Lv	8:36	the Lord had c through Moses.
Dt	6:24	The Lord c us to observe all
Dt	18:20	word in my name that I have not c,
Jos	1:16	"We will do all you have c us,
Jos	22: 2	the servant of the Lord, c you,
2 Kgs	21: 8	careful to observe all I have c them
2 Chr	33: 8	are careful to observe all I c them,
Ps	33: 9	and it came to be, c, and it stood
Ps	78: 5	Which he c our ancestors, they were
Ps	148: 5	for he c and they were created,
Is	13: 3	I have c my consecrated ones,
Am	2:12	wine, and c the prophets, "Do not
Mt	28:20	to observe all that I have c you.
Jn	14:31	that I do just as the Father has c me.
1 Jn	3:23	and love one another just as he c us.
2 Jn	1: 4	in the truth just as we were c

COMMANDERS → COMMAND

Nm	31:14	the c of thousands and the c of hundreds,

COMMANDMENT → COMMAND

Dt	6: 1	This then is the c, the statutes
Dt	7:11	Therefore carefully observe the c,
Mt	22:36	which c in the law is the greatest?"
Mt	22:38	This is the greatest and the first c.
Mk	7: 8	You disregard God's c but cling
Mk	12:31	is no other c greater than these."
Lk	23:56	on the sabbath according to the c.
Jn	13:34	I give you a new c:
Rom	7: 8	sin, finding an opportunity in the c,
Rom	7: 9	but when the c came, sin became
Rom	7:10	the c that was for life turned
Rom	7:11	sin, seizing an opportunity in the c,
Rom	7:12	and the c is holy and righteous
Rom	13: 9	and whatever other c there may be,
Eph	6: 2	This is the first c with a promise,
1 Tm	6:14	to keep the c without stain
Heb	7:18	a former c is annulled because of its
Heb	9:19	When every c had been proclaimed
1 Jn	2: 7	I am writing no new c to you
1 Jn	2: 7	The old c is the word that you have
1 Jn	3:23	And his c is this: we should believe
2 Jn	1: 5	not as though I were writing a new c

COMMANDMENTS → COMMAND

Gn	26: 5	my mandate, my c, my ordinances,
Ex	20: 6	those who love me and keep my c,
Lv	26: 3	and are careful to observe my c,
Lv	26:14	heed me and do not keep all these c,
Dt	5:10	those who love me and keep my c.

Dt	7: 9	those who love him and keep his c,
Dt	11:13	to my c which I give you today,
Dt	11:27	for obeying the c of the LORD,
Dt	28:13	if you obey the c of the LORD,
Dt	30:16	If you obey the c of the LORD,
Jos	22: 5	ways, keep his c, hold fast to him,
Jgs	3: 4	would obey the c the LORD had
2 Kgs	17:16	They abandoned all the c
Ezr	9:10	For we have abandoned your c,
Neh	1: 5	who love you and keep your c.
Tb	3: 4	and disobeyed your c.
Eccl	12:13	Fear God and keep his c, for this
Sir	15:15	If you choose, you can keep the c;
Dn	9: 4	and keep your c and your precepts!
Mt	5:19	breaks one of the least of these c
Mt	19:17	wish to enter into life, keep the c."
Mt	22:40	prophets depend on these two c."
Mk	10:19	You know the c: 'You shall not kill;
Lk	1: 6	observing all the c and ordinances
Lk	18:20	You know the c, 'You shall not
Jn	14:15	you love me, you will keep my c.
Jn	15:10	If you keep my c, you will remain
Jn	15:10	just as I have kept my Father's c
Rom	13: 9	The c, "You shall not commit
1 Cor	7:19	what matters is keeping God's c.
Eph	2:15	abolishing the law with its c
1 Jn	2: 3	that we know him is to keep his c.
1 Jn	5: 2	when we love God and obey his c.
1 Jn	5: 3	of God is this, that we keep his c. And his c are not burdensome,
2 Jn	1: 6	that we walk according to his c;
Rev	12:17	those who keep God's c and bear
Rev	14:12	the holy ones who keep God's c

COMMANDS → COMMAND

Ps	91:11	For he c his angels with regard
Mk	1:27	He c even the unclean spirits
Lk	8:25	who c even the winds and the sea,

COMMEMORATED

Est	9:28	These days were to be c and kept

COMMEND → COMMENDED

Lk	23:46	into your hands I c my spirit";
2 Cor	3: 1	we beginning to c ourselves again?
2 Cor	4: 2	of the truth we c ourselves

COMMENDED → COMMEND

Lk	16: 8	the master c that dishonest steward

COMMIT → COMMITS, COMMITTED, COMMITTING

Ex	20:14	You shall not c adultery.
Dt	5:18	You shall not c adultery.
1 Kgs	14:16	committed and caused Israel to c."
2 Kgs	17:21	causing them to c a great sin.
Ps	37: 5	C your way to the LORD;
Prv	6:32	those who c adultery have no sense;
Jer	7: 9	and murder, c adultery and perjury,
Mt	5:27	was said, 'You shall not c adultery.'
Mt	5:32	unlawful) causes her to c adultery;
Mt	19:18	you shall not c adultery;
Mk	10:19	you shall not c adultery;
Lk	18:20	'You shall not c adultery;
Rom	2:22	forbid adultery, do you c adultery?
Rom	13: 9	"You shall not c adultery;
Jas	2:11	"You shall not c adultery,"
Jas	2:11	Even if you do not c adultery
Rev	2:22	plunge those who c adultery

COMMITS → COMMIT

Mt	5:32	a divorced woman c adultery.
Mt	19: 9	and marries another c adultery."
Mk	10:11	marries another c adultery against
Mk	10:12	marries another, she c adultery."
Lk	16:18	wife and marries another c adultery,
Lk	16:18	from her husband c adultery.
Jn	8:34	everyone who c sin is a slave of sin.
1 Cor	6:18	other sin a person c is outside
1 Jn	3: 4	Everyone who c sin c lawlessness,

COMMITTED → COMMIT

2 Kgs	17:22	Jeroboam in all the sins he c;
2 Kgs	24: 3	for the sins Manasseh had c in all
1 Mc	2: 6	that were being c in Judah
Mt	5:28	lust has already c adultery with her
Rom	3:25	the forgiveness of sins previously c,
Jas	5:15	If he has c any sins, he will be
1 Pt	2:22	"He c no sin, and no deceit was

COMMITTING → COMMIT

Jer	3: 9	c adultery with stone and wood.
Jn	8: 4	caught in the very act of c adultery.

COMMON

2 Chr	1:15	and gold as c in Jerusalem as stones,
2 Chr	9:27	The king made silver as c
Prv	22: 2	Rich and poor have a c bond:
Acts	2:44	together and had all things in c;
Acts	4:32	own, but they had everything in c.

COMMUNITY

Ex	12: 3	Tell the whole c of Israel:
Lv	4:13	If the whole c of Israel errs
Nm	1: 2	of the whole c of the Israelites,

COMPANION → COMPANIONS

Jb	30:29	a brother to jackals, a c to ostriches
Prv	13:20	wise, but the c of fools fares badly.
Mal	2:14	faith, though she is your c,

COMPANIONS → COMPANION

Ps	38:12	Friends and c shun my disease;
Sir	9:16	Take the righteous for your table c;
Dn	2:13	Daniel and his c were also sought
Acts	4:13	they recognized them as the c
Heb	1: 9	the oil of gladness above your c";

COMPANY

Ex	6:26	out from the land of Egypt, c by c."
Ex	12:51	out of the land of Egypt c by c.
Ps	14: 5	God is with the c of the just.
1 Cor	15:33	"Bad c corrupts good morals."

COMPARE → COMPARED

Prv	3:15	no treasure of yours can c with her.
Prv	8:11	[and no treasures can c with her.]
Is	46: 5	you liken me as an equal, c me,
Lam	2:13	To what can I c you—to what can I
Mt	11:16	"To what shall I c this generation?
Lk	7:31	to what shall I c the people of this
Lk	13:20	what shall I c the kingdom of God?
2 Cor	10:12	and c themselves with one another,

COMPARED → COMPARE

Bar	3:36	no other is to be c to him:
Rom	8:18	of this present time are as nothing c

COMPASSION → COMPASSIONATE

2 Kgs	13:23	them with c because of his covenant
2 Chr	36:15	for he had c on his people and his
1 Mc	3:44	and to pray and ask for mercy and c.
2 Mc	7: 6	saying, 'And God will have c on his
Ps	77:10	mercy, in anger withheld his c?"
Ps	79: 8	let your c move quickly ahead of us,
Ps	103:13	As a father has c on his children,
Ps	103:13	so the LORD has c on those who
Jer	13:14	showing no c, I will neither spare
Ez	16: 5	c to do any of these things for you.
Hos	2:21	with loyalty and with c;
Hos	13:14	C is hidden from my eyes.
Mi	7:19	And will again have c on us,
Lk	15:20	sight of him, and was filled with c.
Phil	2: 1	in the Spirit, any c and mercy,
Col	3:12	and beloved, heartfelt c, kindness,

COMPASSIONATE → COMPASSION

Ex	22:26	out to me, I will listen; for I am c.
Sir	2:11	For the Lord is c and merciful;
Lam	4:10	of c women have boiled their own
Jas	5:11	Lord, because "the Lord is c

COMPEL → COMPELLED, COMPULSION

Gal	2:14	how can you c the Gentiles to live

COMPELLED → COMPEL
Gal 6:12 the flesh who are trying to c you

COMPELLED → COMPEL
Gal 2: 3 a Greek, was c to be circumcised,

COMPETING
2 Tm 2: 5 crown except by c according

COMPLACENT
Is 32: 9 You women so c, rise up and hear

COMPLAIN → COMPLAINED, COMPLAINING, COMPLAINT
Jb 7:11 I will c in the bitterness of my soul.
Lam 3:39 What should the living c about?

COMPLAINED → COMPLAIN
Nm 11: 1 Now the people c bitterly
Acts 6: 1 the Hellenists c against the Hebrews

COMPLAINING → COMPLAIN
1 Pt 4: 9 hospitable to one another without c.

COMPLAINT → COMPLAIN
Jb 10: 1 I will give myself up to c;
Ps 142: 3 Before him I pour out my c,
Sir 35:17 the widow when she pours out her c.
Hb 2: 1 what answer he will give to my c.

COMPLETE → COMPLETED, COMPLETELY
Jn 15:11 be in you and your joy may be c.
Jn 16:24 receive, so that your joy may be c.
2 Cor 10: 6 once your obedience is c.
Phil 2: 2 c my joy by being of the same
Ti 2:10 but exhibiting c good faith, so as
Jas 1: 4 so that you may be perfect and c,
1 Jn 1: 4 this so that our joy may be c.
2 Jn 1:12 to face so that our joy may be c.

COMPLETED → COMPLETE
Gn 2: 2 On the seventh day God c the work

COMPLETELY → COMPLETE
2 Chr 12:12 from him so as not to destroy him c;

COMPREHEND → COMPREHENDED
Eph 3:18 may have strength to c with all

COMPREHENDED → COMPREHEND
Jb 38:18 Have you c the breadth of the earth?

COMPULSION → COMPEL
2 Cor 9: 7 without sadness or c, for God loves

CONCEAL → CONCEALING, CONCEALS
Prv 12:23 The shrewd c knowledge, but the hearts
Prv 25: 2 It is the glory of God to c a matter,
Prv 28:13 Those who c their sins do not prosper,

CONCEALING → CONCEAL
Gn 37:26 killing our brother and c his blood?

CONCEALS → CONCEALING
Prv 10:11 the mouth of the wicked c violence.

CONCEIT → CONCEITED
2 Cor 12:20 slander, gossip, c, and disorder.

CONCEITED → CONCEIT
Gal 5:26 Let us not be c, provoking one
1 Tm 3: 6 so that he may not become c
1 Tm 6: 4 is c, understanding nothing, and has
2 Tm 3: 4 reckless, c, lovers of pleasure rather

CONCEIVE → CONCEIVED, CONCEIVES
Jb 15:35 They c malice, bring forth deceit,
Is 33:11 You c dry grass, bring forth stubble;
Lk 1:31 you will c in your womb and bear

CONCEIVED → CONCEIVE
1 Sm 2:21 favored Hannah so that she c
Ps 51: 7 in guilt, in sin my mother c me.
Is 8: 3 prophetess and she c and bore a son.
Mt 1:20 that this child has been c in her.
Lk 1:24 After this time his wife Elizabeth c,

CONCEIVES → CONCEIVE
Ps 7:15 Consider how one c iniquity;

CONCERN → CONCERNED
Phil 4:10 at last you revived your c for me.

CONCERNED → CONCERN
Jon 4:10 "You are c over the gourd plant
1 Cor 9: 9 out the grain." Is God c about oxen,
Phil 4:10 of course, c about me but lacked

CONCESSION
1 Cor 7: 6 This I say by way of c, however,

CONCUBINE → CONCUBINES
Gn 35:22 and lay with Bilhah, his father's c.
Jgs 19:25 So the man seized his c and thrust
Jgs 20: 6 I took my c and cut her up and sent
2 Sm 3: 7 have you slept with my father's c?"

CONCUBINES → CONCUBINE
2 Sm 5:13 David took more c and wives
2 Sm 16:21 "Go to your father's c, whom he
1 Kgs 11: 3 princesses and three hundred c,

CONDEMN → CONDEMNATION, CONDEMNED, CONDEMNING, CONDEMNS, SELF-CONDEMNED
Jb 9:20 right, my own mouth might c me;
Jb 34:17 will you c the supreme Just One,
Jb 34:29 If he is silent, who then can c?
Jb 40: 8 Would you c me that you may be
Ps 94:21 the just and c the innocent to death?
Dn 13:48 to c a daughter of Israel without
Mt 12:41 arise with this generation and c it,
Mt 12:42 arise with this generation and c it,
Mt 20:18 and they will c him to death,
Mk 10:33 and they will c him to death
Lk 11:31 this generation and she will c them,
Lk 11:32 arise with this generation and c it,
Jn 3:17 Son into the world to c the world,
Jn 8:11 Jesus said, "Neither do I c you.
Rom 2: 1 you judge another you c yourself,
Rom 8:34 Who will c? It is Christ [Jesus] who
Rom 14:22 is the one who does not c himself
1 Jn 3:20 in whatever our hearts c, for God is
1 Jn 3:21 if [our] hearts do not c us, we have

CONDEMNATION → CONDEMN
Mk 12:40 They will receive a very severe c."
Jn 5:29 deeds to the resurrection of c.
Rom 5:16 was the judgment that brought c;
Rom 5:18 as through one transgression c came
Rom 8: 1 now there is no c for those who are
2 Cor 3: 9 if the ministry of c was glorious,
1 Tm 5:12 will incur c for breaking their first
Jas 5:12 "No," that you may not incur c.
2 Pt 2: 3 from of old their c has not been idle
Jude 1: 4 long ago were designated for this c,

CONDEMNED → CONDEMN
1 Mc 1:57 law, was c to death by royal decree.
Ps 34:22 those who hate the righteous are c.
Ps 34:23 none are c who take refuge in him.
Ps 37:33 power, nor let him be c when tried.
Dn 13:41 the people, and they c her to death.
Dn 13:43 things for which these men have c me."
Mt 12: 7 you would not have c these innocent
Mt 12:37 and by your words you will be c."
Mt 27: 3 seeing that Jesus had been c,
Mk 14:64 They all c him as deserving to die.
Mk 16:16 whoever does not believe will be c.
Lk 6:37 condemning and you will not be c.
Lk 23:41 we have been c justly,
Jn 3:18 believes in him will not be c,
Jn 3:18 does not believe has already been c,
Jn 8:10 Has no one c you?"
Jn 16:11 the ruler of this world has been c.
Rom 3: 7 why am I still being c as a sinner?
Rom 8: 3 the sake of sin, he c sin in the flesh,
Rom 14:23 whoever has doubts is c if he eats,
1 Cor 11:32 that we may not be c along
2 Thes 2:12 approved wrongdoing may be c.
Heb 11: 7 Through this he c the world

Jas 5: 6 You have c; you have murdered
2 Pt 2: 6 and if he c the cities of Sodom

CONDEMNING → CONDEMN
Dn 13:53 unjust sentences, c the innocent,
Acts 13:27 by c him they fulfilled the oracles

CONDEMNS → CONDEMN
Jb 15: 6 Your own mouth c you, not I;
Prv 17:15 the wicked, whoever c the just—

CONDUCT → CONDUCTS
Tb 4:14 and discipline yourself in all your c.
Prv 21: 8 but one's c is blameless and right.
Eccl 6: 8 in knowing how to c themselves
Sir 37:17 The root of all c is the heart;
Rom 13: 3 are not a cause of fear to good c,
Col 4: 5 C yourselves wisely toward
1 Pt 1:15 in every aspect of your c,
1 Pt 3: 1 without a word by their wives' c

CONDUCTS → CONDUCT
Ps 112: 5 who c his affairs with justice.

CONFESS → CONFESSED, CONFESSES, CONFESSING, CONFESSION
Lv 5: 5 person shall c the wrong committed,
Lv 16:21 he shall c over it all the iniquities
Lv 26:40 They will c their iniquity
Nm 5: 7 that person shall c the wrong
Ps 32: 5 I said, "I c my transgression
Prv 28:13 who c and forsake them obtain mercy.
Rom 10: 9 if you c with your mouth that Jesus
Phil 2:11 every tongue c that Jesus Christ is
Heb 13:15 is, the fruit of lips that c his name.
Jas 5:16 c your sins to one another and pray

CONFESSED → CONFESS
Neh 9: 2 stood forward and c their sins

CONFESSES → CONFESS
Rom 10:10 and one c with the mouth and so is
1 Jn 2:23 whoever c the Son has the Father as

CONFESSING → CONFESS
Neh 1: 6 c the sins we have committed
Dn 9:20 c my sin and the sin of my people

CONFESSION → CONFESS
Neh 9: 3 another fourth they made their c
2 Cor 9:13 for your obedient c of the gospel
1 Tm 6:12 when you made the noble c
1 Tm 6:13 under Pontius Pilate for the noble c,
Heb 3: 1 the apostle and high priest of our c,
Heb 4:14 Son of God, let us hold fast to our c.
Heb 10:23 to our c that gives us hope, for he

CONFIDENCE → CONFIDENT
Jb 4: 6 Is not your piety a source of c,
Jb 8:14 His c is but a gossamer thread,
Prv 3:26 For the LORD will be your c,
Prv 11:13 but a trustworthy person keeps a c.
2 Cor 3: 4 Such c we have through Christ
2 Cor 7:16 because I have c in you in every
2 Cor 8:22 because of his great c in you.
Eph 3:12 and c of access through faith in him.
Phil 3: 3 Jesus and do not put our c in flesh,
Phil 3: 4 I myself have grounds for c even
Heb 3: 6 if [only] we hold fast to our c
Heb 10:19 of Jesus we have c of entrance
Heb 10:35 do not throw away your c;
Heb 13: 6 Thus we may say with c:
1 Jn 2:28 when he appears we may have c

CONFIDENT → CONFIDENCE
Jb 6:20 disappointed, though they were c;
2 Cor 10: 7 Whoever is c of belonging to Christ
Phil 1: 6 I am c of this, that the one who
Phil 3: 4 If anyone else thinks he can be c

CONFINED
Gn 40: 3 the same jail where Joseph was c.

CONFIRM → CONFIRMATION, CONFIRMED
2 Sm 7:25 c the promise that you have spoken

Rom 15: 8 to c the promises to the patriarchs,

CONFIRMATION → CONFIRM
Phil 1: 7 in the defense and c of the gospel.

CONFIRMED → CONFIRM
1 Kgs 8:26 your servant, David my father, be c.
2 Chr 35: 2 and c them in the service of the LORD's

CONFLICTING → CONFLICTS
Rom 2:15 witness and their c thoughts accuse

CONFLICTS → CONFLICTING
Jas 4: 1 where do the c among you come

CONFORMED
Rom 8:29 predestined to be c to the image

CONFOUNDED
Ps 35: 4 against me be turned back and c.
Acts 9:22 and c [the] Jews who lived

CONFRONT
Ps 17:13 O LORD, c and cast them down;

CONFUSE → CONFUSED, CONFUSION
Gn 11: 7 go down and there c their language,
Ps 55:10 Lord, check and c their tongues.

CONFUSED → CONFUSE
Gn 11: 9 there the LORD c the speech of all

CONFUSION → CONFUSE
1 Sm 7:10 into such c that they were defeated
Neh 4: 2 Jerusalem and to throw us into c.
Mi 7: 4 now is the time of your c.
Acts 19:29 The city was filled with c,

CONIAH → =JEHOIACHIN
Jer 22:28 Is this man C a thing despised, to be

CONQUER → CONQUERED, CONQUEROR, CONQUERS
Rom 8:37 these things we c overwhelmingly
Rev 11: 7 wage war against them and c them
Rev 13: 7 against the holy ones and c them,
Rev 17:14 but the Lamb will c them, for he is

CONQUERED → CONQUER
Jn 16:33 take courage, I have c the world."
Heb 11:33 who by faith c kingdoms, did what
1 Jn 2:13 because you have c the evil one.
1 Jn 4: 4 and you have c them, for the one
Rev 12:11 They c him by the blood

CONQUEROR → CONQUER
Mi 1:15 Again I will bring the c to you,

CONQUERS → CONQUER
1 Jn 5: 4 is begotten by God c the world.
1 Jn 5: 4 victory that c the world is our faith.

CONSCIENCE → CONSCIENCES
1 Sm 25:31 any regrets or burdens on your c,
Acts 23: 1 a perfectly clear c before God
Acts 24:16 strive to keep my c clear before God
Rom 2:15 while theirs c also bears witness
Rom 9: 1 my c joins with the holy Spirit
Rom 13: 5 of the wrath but also because of c.
1 Cor 8: 7 to idols, their c, which is weak,
1 Cor 8:10 idol, may not his c too, weak as it is,
1 Cor 10:25 raising questions on grounds of c,
1 Cor 10:27 raising questions on grounds of c.
1 Cor 10:28 attention to it and on account of c;
1 Cor 10:29 be determined by someone else's c?
2 Cor 1:12 of our c that we have conducted
2 Cor 4: 2 to everyone's c in the sight of God.
1 Tm 1: 5 heart, a good c, and a sincere faith.
1 Tm 1:19 by having faith and a good c.
1 Tm 1:19 Some, by rejecting c, have made
1 Tm 3: 9 mystery of the faith with a clear c.
2 Tm 1: 3 with a clear c as my ancestors did,
Heb 9: 9 cannot perfect the worshiper in c
Heb 10:22 hearts sprinkled clean from an evil c
Heb 13:18 are confident that we have a clear c,
1 Pt 3:16 keeping your c clear, so that,
1 Pt 3:21 but an appeal to God for a clear c,

CONSCIENCES → CONSCIENCE
1 Cor   8:12   your brothers and wound their c,
1 Tm   4: 2   hypocrisy of liars with branded c.
Ti   1:15   their minds and their c are tainted.
Heb   9:14   cleanse our c from dead works

CONSECRATE → CONSECRATED
Ex   13: 2   C to me every firstborn;

CONSECRATED → CONSECRATE
Lv   8:15   Thus he c it so that atonement could
1 Kgs   9: 3   I have c this house which you have
2 Chr   7:16   c this house that my name may be

CONSENT
Phlm   1:14   want to do anything without your c,

CONSEQUENCES
Nm   9:13   person shall bear the c of this sin.

CONSIDER → CONSIDERED
Jb   37:14   Stand and c the marvels of God!
Eccl   7:13   C the work of God. Who can make
Is   43:18   past, the things of long ago c not;
Heb   10:24   We must c how to rouse one
Heb   12: 3   C how he endured such opposition
Jas   1: 2   C it all joy, my brothers, when you

CONSIDERED → CONSIDER
Prv   17:28   fools, keeping silent, are c wise;

CONSIST
Lk   12:15   may be rich, one's life does not c

CONSISTENT
Ti   2: 1   you must say what is c with sound

CONSOLATION → CONSOLATIONS, CONSOLED
Jb   6:10   I should still have c and could exult
Jb   21: 2   and let that be the c you offer.
Jb   21:34   How empty the c you offer me!
Lk   2:25   and devout, awaiting the c of Israel,
Lk   6:24   rich, for you have received your c.

CONSOLATIONS → CONSOLE
Jb   15:11   Are the c of God not enough

CONSOLED → CONSOLE
Mt   2:18   and she would not be c, since they

CONSPIRACY → CONSPIRED
2 Sm   15:12   So the c gained strength,

CONSPIRED → CONSPIRACY
1 Sm   22:13   "Why have you c against me

CONSTANTLY
Acts   10: 2   Jewish people and pray to God c.

CONSTRUCTED → CONSTRUCTION
Heb   9: 2   For a tabernacle was c, the outer

CONSTRUCTION → CONSTRUCTED
Ex   38:24   used in the entire c of the sanctuary,
Jn   2:20   "This temple has been under c

CONSULT → CONSULTED, CONSULTS
Is   40:14   Whom did he c to gain knowledge?
Ez   20: 3   Have you come to c me?
Hos   4:12   My people c their piece of wood,

CONSULTED → CONSULT
Ez   20: 3   not allow myself to be c by you!—

CONSULTS → CONSULT
Dt   18:11   casts spells, c ghosts and spirits,

CONSUME → CONSUMED, CONSUMING
Nm   16:21   that I may c them at once.
Dt   5:25   For this great fire will c us.
Ps   21:10   the LORD in his anger will c them,
Eccl   10:12   favor, but the lips of fools c them.
Is   26:11   prepared for your enemies c them.
Is   43: 2   be burned, nor will flames c you.
Jn   2:17   "Zeal for your house will c me."
Heb   10:27   that is going to c the adversaries.

CONSUMED → CONSUME
Ex   3: 2   bush was on fire, it was not being c.

Lv   9:24   presence and c the burnt offering
Nm   11: 1   and c the outskirts of the camp.
Nm   16:35   came forth which c the two hundred
2 Kgs   1:10   came down from heaven and c him
2 Chr   7: 1   heaven and c the burnt offerings
Ps   90: 7   Truly we are c by your anger,
Is   1:28   who desert the LORD shall be c.
Lam   4:11   in Zion that has c her foundations.
Zep   3: 8   of my passion all the earth will be c.
Gal   5:15   that you are not c by one another.
Rev   20: 9   down from heaven and c them.

CONSUMING → CONSUME
Heb   12:29   For our God is a c fire.

CONTAIN
1 Kgs   8:27   the highest heavens cannot c you,
2 Chr   2: 5   the highest heavens cannot c him?
2 Chr   6:18   the highest heavens cannot c you,
Jn   21:25   the whole world would c the books

CONTEMPT
1 Mc   1:39   sabbaths to shame, her honor to c.
Ps   107:39   But he poured out c on princes,
Ps   123: 3   us favor, for we have our fill of c.
Prv   18: 3   With wickedness comes c,
Mk   9:12   suffer greatly and be treated with c?
1 Cor   11:22   Or do you show c for the church
Heb   6: 6   themselves and holding him up to c.

CONTEND → CONTENDED
Jb   9: 3   Should one wish to c with him,
Jude   1: 3   to encourage you to c for the faith

CONTENDED → CONTEND
Dt   33: 8   c against him at the waters

CONTENT → CONTENTMENT
Jos   7: 7   Would that we had been c to dwell
Sir   26: 4   his heart is c, a smile ever on his
Sir   29:23   or much, be c with what you have:
2 Cor   12:10   Therefore, I am c with weaknesses,
1 Tm   6: 8   clothing, we shall be c with that.
Heb   13: 5   money but be c with what you have,

CONTENTMENT → CONTENT
1 Tm   6: 6   religion with c is a great gain.

CONTINUAL → CONTINUE
Prv   15:15   evil, but a good heart is a c feast.

CONTINUALLY → CONTINUE
Lk   24:53   they were c in the temple praising
Heb   13:15   let us c offer God a sacrifice

CONTINUE → CONTINUAL, CONTINUALLY, CONTINUED
Ps   89:37   His dynasty will c forever,
2 Cor   1:10   of death, and he will c to rescue us;
Heb   13: 1   Let mutual love c.

CONTINUED → CONTINUE
Gn   7:17   The flood c upon the earth for forty
Tb   14: 2   he c to fear God and give thanks
Acts   6: 7   The word of God c to spread,
Acts   12:24   But the word of God c to spread
Acts   14: 7   where they c to proclaim the good

CONTRADICTED
Acts   13:45   with violent abuse c what Paul said.

CONTRARY
Acts   18:13   to worship God c to the law."
Rom   3:31   On the c, we are supporting the law.
Rom   11:24   tree, and grafted, c to nature,

CONTRIBUTE → CONTRIBUTED
Rom   12:13   C to the needs of the holy ones,

CONTRIBUTED → CONTRIBUTE
Mk   12:44   they have all c from their surplus
Mk   12:44   from her poverty, has c all she had,

CONTRITE
Ps   51:19   My sacrifice, O God, is a c spirit; a c, humbled heart,
Dn   3:39   with c heart and humble spirit let us

CONTROL → SELF-CONTROL, SELF-CONTROLLED
Sir 21:11 Those who keep the Law c their thoughts;
Col 3:15 let the peace of Christ c your hearts,

CONTROVERSIES
Acts 26: 3 in all the Jewish customs and c.

CONVERSATION
Sir 9:15 let all your c be about the law

CONVERSION → CONVERT
Acts 15: 3 telling of the c of the Gentiles,

CONVERT → CONVERSION, CONVERTS
Mt 23:15 traverse sea and land to make one c,
1 Tm 3: 6 He should not be a recent c,

CONVERTS → CONVERT
Tb 1: 8 and c who had joined the Israelites.
Acts 13:43 worshipers who were c to Judaism

CONVICT → CONVICTED, CONVICTION
Jude 1:15 and to c everyone for all the godless

CONVICTED → CONVICT
Dn 13:61 their own words Daniel had c them
Jas 2: 9 are c by the law as transgressors.

CONVICTION → CONVICT
1 Thes 1: 5 in the holy Spirit and [with] much c.

CONVINCE → CONVINCED
Acts 18: 4 attempting to c both Jews
Acts 28:23 trying to c them about Jesus
2 Tm 4: 2 c, reprimand, encourage through all

CONVINCED → CONVINCE
Acts 28:24 Some were c by what he had said,
Rom 4:21 and was fully c that what he had
Rom 8:38 For I am c that neither death,

COOL
Jgs 3:20 he sat alone in his c upper room.
Lk 16:24 his finger in water and c my tongue,

COPPER
Mt 10: 9 gold or silver or c for your belts;

COPY
Dt 17:18 he shall write a c of this law
Heb 9:24 made by hands, a c of the true one,

CORD → CORDS
Gn 38:18 "Your seal and c, and the staff
Nm 15:38 fastening a violet c to each corner.
Jos 2:18 you tie this scarlet c in the window
Eccl 4:12 A three-ply c is not easily broken.
Eccl 12: 6 Before the silver c is snapped

CORDS → CORD
2 Sm 22: 6 The c of Sheol tightened;
Hos 11: 4 I drew them with human c,
Jn 2:15 He made a whip out of c and drove

CORIANDER
Ex 16:31 It was like c seed, white, and it
Nm 11: 7 Manna was like c seed and had

CORINTH → CORINTHIANS
Acts 18: 1 this he left Athens and went to C.
1 Cor 1: 2 to the church of God that is in C,
2 Cor 1: 1 to the church of God that is in C,

CORINTHIANS → CORINTH
Acts 18: 8 many of the C who heard believed
2 Cor 6:11 We have spoken frankly to you, C;

CORNELIUS
Roman to whom Peter preached; first Gentile Christian (Acts 10).

CORNER → CORNERS, CORNERSTONE
Prv 7:12 lurking in ambush at every c.
Prv 21: 9 dwell in a c of the housetop than
Acts 26:26 this was not done in a c.

CORNERS → CORNER
Dt 22:12 put tassels on the four c of the cloak
Ez 7: 2 comes upon the four c of the land!
Mt 6: 5 on street c so that others may see

Acts 10:11 lowered to the ground by its four c.
Rev 7: 1 standing at the four c of the earth,
Rev 20: 8 the nations at the four c of the earth,

CORNERSTONE → CORNER, STONE
Jb 38: 6 pedestals sunk, and who laid its c,
Ps 118:22 builders rejected has become the c.
Is 28:16 A precious c as a sure foundation;
Mt 21:42 builders rejected has become the c;
Mk 12:10 builders rejected has become the c;
Lk 20:17 builders rejected has become the c'?
Acts 4:11 builders, which has become the c.'
1 Pt 2: 6 in Zion, a c, chosen and precious,

CORPSE
Lv 22: 4 become unclean by contact with a c,
Mt 24:28 Wherever the c is, there the vultures

CORRECTING → CORRECTION
2 Tm 2:25 c opponents with kindness.

CORRECTION → CORRECTING, CORRECTS
Jer 2:30 c they did not take.
Jer 5: 3 laid them low, but they refused c;
Zep 3: 2 It listens to no voice, accepts no c;
Zep 3: 7 you will fear me, you will accept c;
2 Tm 3:16 refutation, for c, and for training

CORRECTS → CORRECT
Prv 9: 7 Whoever c the arrogant earns

CORRESPONDS
Gal 4:25 it c to the present Jerusalem, for she

CORRUPT → CORRUPTED, CORRUPTION, CORRUPTS
Gn 6:11 the earth was c in the view of God
Ps 14: 1 Their deeds are loathsome and c;
Acts 2:40 yourselves from this c generation."

CORRUPTED → CORRUPT
Eph 4:22 of life, c through deceitful desires,
Rev 19: 2 the great harlot who c the earth

CORRUPTION → CORRUPT
Acts 2:31 netherworld nor did his flesh see c.
Acts 13:35 not suffer your holy one to see c.'
2 Pt 1: 4 escaping from the c that is

CORRUPTS → CORRUPT
Eccl 7: 7 of the wise, and a bribe c the heart.

COST → COSTLY
Nm 17: 3 who sinned at the c of their lives.
1 Chr 21:24 burnt offerings that c me nothing."
Lk 14:28 and calculate the c to see if there is

COSTLY → COST
Mt 26: 7 an alabaster jar of c perfumed oil,

COTS
Acts 5:15 and laid them on c and mats so

COUCH → COUCHES
Est 7: 8 had thrown himself on the c

COUCHES → COUCH
Am 6: 4 of ivory, and lounge upon their c;

COUNCIL
Ps 82: 1 God takes a stand in the divine c,
Ps 89: 8 dreaded in the c of the holy ones,
Jer 23:18 has stood in the c of the LORD,
Mk 15:43 a distinguished member of the c,

COUNSEL → COUNSELOR, COUNSELORS, COUNSELS
2 Sm 15:34 thwart for me the c of Ahithophel.
2 Sm 17:23 saw that his c was not acted upon,
Tb 4:18 "Seek c from every wise person,
Jb 12:13 his are c and understanding.
Ps 73:24 With your c you guide me,
Ps 107:11 and scorned the c of the Most High,
Prv 12:20 but those who c peace have joy.
Prv 15:22 Plans fail when there is no c,
Wis 9:17 Or who can know your c,
Sir 25: 4 and good c in the elderly!
Is 11: 2 A spirit of c and of strength, a spirit

Is   28:29   wonderful is his c and great his

COUNSELOR → COUNSEL
Sir   37: 7   Every c points out a way, but some
Is   40:13   Lord, or instructed him as his c?
Rom   11:34   of the Lord or who has been his c?"

COUNSELORS → COUNSEL
Jb   12:17   He sends c away barefoot,
Ps   119:24   are my delight; they are my c.
Prv   11:14   security lies in many c.
Prv   24: 6   and victory depends on many c.

COUNSELS → COUNSEL
Ps   16: 7   I bless the Lord who c me;

COUNT → COUNTED, COUNTING, COUNTS
Gn   15: 5   Look up at the sky and c the stars,
Dt   16: 9   You shall c off seven weeks;
Ps   22:18   I can c all my bones. They stare
Ps   33:18   fear him, upon those who c on his mercy,
Ps   90:12   Teach us to c our days aright,
Ps   139:18   Were I to c them, they would
Rev   7: 9   which no one could c, from every

COUNTED → COUNT
Gn   13:16   your descendants too might be c.
Nm   23:10   Who has ever c the dust of Jacob,
Mt   10:30   all the hairs of your head are c.

COUNTERFEITS
Wis   15: 9   and takes pride in fashioning c.

COUNTING → COUNT
2 Cor   5:19   not c their trespasses against them

COUNTRIES → COUNTRY
Ez   20:34   gather you from the c over which you

COUNTRY → COUNTRIES, COUNTRYSIDE
Lk   15:13   a distant c where he squandered his

COUNTRYSIDE → COUNTRY
Mk   1: 5   People of the whole Judean c

COUNTS → COUNT
Gal   5: 6   circumcision nor uncircumcision c

COURAGE → COURAGEOUS
2 Sm   7:27   your servant now finds the c
Ezr   7:28   I therefore took c and, with the hand
Tb   5:10   "Take c! God's healing is near; so take c!"
Tb   7:17   "Take c, my daughter!
Jn   16:33   but take c, I have conquered
Acts   23:11   stood by him and said, "Take c.
Acts   27:22   I urge you now to keep up your c;
Acts   27:25   Therefore, keep up your c, men;

COURAGEOUS → COURAGE
1 Mc   2:64   be c and strong in keeping the law,
1 Cor   16:13   firm in the faith, be c, be strong.

COURIERS
2 Chr   30: 6   the c, with the letters written
Est   3:15   The c set out in haste at the king's
Est   8:10   by mounted c riding thoroughbred

COURSE
Ps   19: 6   and like a hero joyfully runs its c.
Eccl   1: 6   the wind, constantly shifting its c.

COURT → COURTS, COURTYARD
Ex   27: 9   also make a c for the tabernacle.
Nm   3:26   the c enclosing both the tabernacle
1 Kgs   7: 8   in which he lived was in another c,
Ez   10: 3   in and a cloud filled the inner c.
Dn   7:10   The c was convened, and the books
Mt   5:25   while on the way to c with him.
1 Cor   6: 6   brother goes to c against brother,
Jas   2: 6   themselves not haul you off to c?

COURTS → COURT
1 Chr   28: 6   who shall build my house and my c,
Ps   65: 5   choose and bring to dwell in your c.
Ps   84:11   in your c than a thousand elsewhere.
Ps   96: 8   Bring gifts and enter his c;

Ps   100: 4   with thanksgiving, his c with praise.

COURTYARD → COURT
Mk   14:66   While Peter was below in the c,

COUSIN
Est   2: 7   foster father to his c Hadassah,
Col   4:10   as does Mark the c of Barnabas

COVENANT → COVENANTS
Gn   6:18   I will establish my c with you.
Gn   9: 9   I am now establishing my c
Gn   15:18   that day the Lord made a c
Gn   17: 2   you and me I will establish my c,
Ex   2:24   was mindful of his c with Abraham,
Ex   6: 5   to slavery, I am mindful of my c.
Ex   19: 5   obey me completely and keep my c,
Ex   23:32   You shall not make a c with them
Ex   24: 7   Taking the book of the c, he read it
Ex   34:28   on the tablets the words of the c,
Lv   26:42   I will remember my c with Jacob, and also my c with Isaac;
Lv   26:42   and also my c with Abraham I will
Dt   4:13   He proclaimed to you his c,
Dt   28:69   words of the c which the Lord
Dt   28:69   addition to the c he made with them
Jos   3: 6   "Take up the ark of the c and cross
Jgs   2: 1   I will never break my c with you,
1 Kgs   8: 1   ark of the Lord's c from the city
1 Kgs   8:21   which is the c of the Lord that he
1 Kgs   8:23   you keep c and love toward your
2 Kgs   23: 2   book of the c that had been found
1 Chr   16:15   He remembers forever his c the pact
2 Chr   34:30   book of the c that had been found
Ezr   10: 3   enter into a c before our God
Neh   1: 5   you preserve your c of mercy
Neh   9:32   God, who preserves the c of mercy,
Jdt   9:13   planned dire things against your c,
1 Mc   1:15   and abandoned the holy c;
1 Mc   1:57   was found with a scroll of the c,
1 Mc   2:27   who stands by the c follow me!"
Ps   25:14   and his c instructs them.
Ps   44:18   you, nor been disloyal to your c.
Ps   78:37   they were not faithful to his c.
Ps   89: 4   I have made a c with my chosen
Ps   105: 8   He remembers forever his c,
Ps   111: 9   him, he remembers his c forever.
Ps   132:12   If your sons observe my c, and my
Sir   28: 7   remember the c of the Most High,
Is   28:15   "We have made a c with death,
Is   42: 6   and set you as a c for the people,
Is   61: 8   an everlasting c I will make
Jer   31:31   I will make a new c with the house
Jer   32:40   them I will make an everlasting c,
Ez   16:60   set up an everlasting c with you.
Ez   17:15   Can he break a c and go free?
Ez   37:26   I will make a c of peace with them;
Ez   37:26   it shall be an everlasting c
Dn   11:28   his mind set against the holy c;
Hos   6: 7   But they, at Adam, violated the c;
Mal   2: 4   that my c with Levi might endure,
Mal   3: 1   of the c whom you desire—
Mt   26:28   for this is my blood of the c,
Mk   14:24   "This is my blood of the c,
Lk   1:72   and to be mindful of his holy c
Lk   22:20   "This cup is the new c in my blood,
Acts   7: 8   he gave him the c of circumcision,
Rom   11:27   this is my c with them when I take
1 Cor   11:25   "This cup is the new c in my blood.
2 Cor   3: 6   qualified us as ministers of a new c,
2 Cor   3:14   unlifted when they read the old c,
Gal   3:17   not annul a c previously ratified
Heb   7:22   the guarantee of an [even] better c.
Heb   8: 8   I will conclude a new c
Heb   9:15   reason he is mediator of a new c:
Heb   12:24   the mediator of a new c,
Heb   13:20   sheep by the blood of the eternal c,
Rev   11:19   the ark of his c could be seen

COVENANTS → COVENANT

Wis	12:21	ancestors you gave the sworn c
Rom	9: 4	glory, the c, the giving of the law,
Gal	4:24	These women represent two c.
Eph	2:12	and strangers to the c of promise,

COVER → COVERED, COVERING, COVERS

Gn	6:14	and c it inside and out with pitch.
Ex	33:22	will c you with my hand until I have
Nm	4: 5	c the ark of the covenant with it.
Hos	10: 8	cry out to the mountains, "C us!"
Mal	2:13	of the LORD you c with tears,
Lk	23:30	and to the hills, 'C us!'
Jas	5:20	death and will c a multitude of sins.

COVERED → COVER

Ex	14:28	it c the chariots and the horsemen.
Ex	16:13	quail came up and c the camp.
Ex	24:15	Then the cloud c the mountain.
Ex	40:34	the cloud c the tent of meeting,
Nm	9:15	erected, the cloud c the tabernacle,
Ez	10:12	were c with eyes all around like the four
Jon	3: 8	beast alike must be c with sackcloth
Rom	4: 7	are forgiven and whose sins are c.

COVERING → COVER

Ex	35:11	with its tent, its c, its clasps,
1 Cor	11:15	hair has been given [her] for a c?

COVERS → COVER

Prv	10:12	up disputes, but love c all offenses.
Is	11: 9	of the LORD, as water c the sea.
Hb	2:14	glory, just as the water c the sea.
Mal	2:16	the one who c his garment with violence,
1 Pt	4: 8	because love c a multitude of sins.

COVET → COVETOUSNESS

Ex	20:17	You shall not c your neighbor's
Ex	34:24	no one will c your land when you
Dt	5:21	You shall not c your neighbor's
Dt	7:25	Do not c the silver or gold on them,
Mi	2: 2	You c fields, and seize them;
Rom	7: 7	I did not know what it is to c except
Rom	13: 9	you shall not c," and whatever
Jas	4: 2	You c but do not possess.

COVETOUSNESS → COVET

Rom	7: 8	produced in me every kind of c.

COW → COWS

Is	11: 7	The c and the bear shall graze,

COWARDICE → COWARDS

2 Tm	1: 7	For God did not give us a spirit of c

COWARDS → COWARDICE

Rev	21: 8	But as for c, the unfaithful,

COWS → COW

Gn	41: 2	up out of the Nile came seven c,
1 Sm	6: 7	take two milk c that have not borne
Am	4: 1	Hear this word, you c of Bashan,

CRAFT → CRAFTINESS, CRAFTY

Ex	31: 3	and knowledge in every c:

CRAFTINESS → CRAFT

Lk	20:23	Recognizing their c he said to them,

CRAFTY → CRAFT

Jb	15: 5	and you choose to speak like the c.
Sir	11:29	for many are the snares of the c.
2 Cor	12:16	yet I was c and got the better of you

CRAGS

Nm	23: 9	For from the top of the c I see him,
Dt	32:13	He suckled them with honey from the c

CRAVED → CRAVING

Ps	78:18	hearts, demanding the food they c.
Ps	78:29	he gave them what they had c.

CRAVES → CRAVING

Prv	13: 4	The appetite of the sluggard c

CRAVING → CRAVED, CRAVES, CRAVINGS

Prv	10: 3	but the c of the wicked he thwarts.

CRAVINGS → CRAVING

Ps	106:14	In the desert they gave in to their c,

CREATE → CREATED, CREATING, CREATION, CREATOR

Ps	51:12	A clean heart c for me, God;
Is	4: 5	Then will the LORD c,
Is	45: 7	and c the darkness, I make weal and c woe;
Eph	2:15	that he might c in himself one new

CREATED → CREATE

Gn	1: 1	when God c the heavens
Gn	1:21	God c the great sea monsters and all
Gn	1:27	God c mankind in his image; in the image of God he c them; male and female he c them.
Gn	5: 1	When God c human beings,
Gn	5: 2	he c them male and female.
Gn	5: 2	When they were c, he blessed them
Gn	6: 7	the earth the human beings I have c,
Dt	4:32	ever since God c humankind
Ps	89:13	Zaphon and Amanus you c;
Ps	89:48	frail the sons of man you have c!
Ps	104:30	they are c and you renew the face
Ps	148: 5	for he commanded and they were c,
Sir	1: 4	all other things wisdom was c;
Is	40:26	eyes on high and see who c these:
Is	41:20	this, the Holy One of Israel has c it.
Is	42: 5	who c the heavens and stretched
Is	43: 1	thus says the LORD, who c you,
Is	43: 7	called by my name I c for my glory;
Is	45: 8	I, the LORD, have c this.
Is	45:12	the earth and c the people upon it;
Is	54:16	I have c the smith who blows
Is	54:16	who have c the destroyer to work
Jer	31:22	The LORD has c a new thing
Ez	21:35	In the place you were c, In the land
Ez	28:13	for you the day you were c.
Ez	28:15	your ways from the day you were c,
Mal	2:10	Has not one God c us?
1 Cor	11: 9	nor was man c for woman,
Eph	2:10	c in Christ Jesus for the good works
Eph	3: 9	ages past in God who c all things
Eph	4:24	c in God's way in righteousness
Col	1:16	in him were c all things in heaven
Col	1:16	all things were c through him
1 Tm	4: 3	foods that God c to be received
1 Tm	4: 4	For everything c by God is good,
Heb	1: 2	through whom he c the universe,
Heb	12:27	to [the] removal of shaken, c things,
Rev	4:11	and power, for you c all things;
Rev	4:11	will they came to be and were c."
Rev	10: 6	who c heaven and earth and sea

CREATING → CREATE

Is	65:17	I am c new heavens and a new earth;
Is	65:18	I am c Jerusalem to be a joy

CREATION → CREATE

Gn	2: 3	from all the work he had done in c.
Tb	8: 5	and all your c bless you forever.
Mk	10: 6	But from the beginning of c,
Mk	13:19	the beginning of God's c until now,
Rom	1:20	Ever since the c of the world,
Rom	8:19	For c awaits with eager expectation
Rom	8:20	for c was made subject to futility,
Rom	8:21	that c itself would be set free
Rom	8:22	We know that all c is groaning
2 Cor	5:17	So whoever is in Christ is a new c:
Col	1:15	invisible God, the firstborn of all c.
Heb	9:11	that is, not belonging to this c,
2 Pt	3: 4	as it was from the beginning of c."
Rev	3:14	the source of God's c, says this:

CREATOR → CREATE

Jdt	9:12	heaven and earth, C of the waters,
2 Mc	1:24	Lord God, c of all things,
2 Mc	7:23	since it is the C of the universe who
2 Mc	13:14	the outcome to the C of the world,

Eccl	12: 1	Remember your C in the days
Sir	24: 8	the C of all gave me his command,
Is	40:28	of old, c of the ends of the earth.
Is	43:15	your Holy One, the c of Israel,
Rom	1:25	the creature rather than the c, who is
Col	3:10	for knowledge, in the image of its c.
1 Pt	4:19	over to a faithful c as they do good.

CREATURE → CREATURES

Gn	1:24	earth bring forth every kind of living c:
Gn	9:10	with every living c that was
Lv	11:43	by any swarming c nor defile
Rom	1:25	and worshiped the c rather than
Rev	4: 7	The first c resembled a lion,
Rev	5:13	Then I heard every c in heaven

CREATURES → CREATURE

Gn	1:20	teem with an abundance of living c,
Ps	104:24	the earth is full of your c.
Wis	9: 2	to rule the c produced by you,
Ez	1: 5	likeness of four living c appeared.
Ez	10:15	were indeed the living c I had seen
Jas	1:18	may be a kind of firstfruits of his c.
Rev	4: 6	there were four living c covered
Rev	5: 6	and the four living c and the elders,
Rev	8: 9	a third of the c living in the sea
Rev	19: 4	and the four living c fell down

CREDIT → CREDITOR, CREDITORS

Lk	6:33	good to you, what c is that to you?
1 Pt	2:20	But what c is there if you are patient

CREDITOR → CREDIT

Lk	7:41	people were in debt to a certain c;

CREDITORS → CREDIT

Dt	15: 2	C shall remit all claims on loans
Is	50: 1	to which of my c have I sold you?

CREEPING

Ez	8:10	figures of all kinds of c things

CRETANS → CRETE

Acts	2:11	converts to Judaism, C and Arabs,
Ti	1:12	said, "C have always been liars,

CRETE → CRETANS

Acts	27:12	a port in C facing west-northwest,
Ti	1: 5	this reason I left you in C so

CREVICES

Ob	1: 3	who dwell in mountain c, in your lofty

CRIED → CRY

Ex	2:23	under their bondage and c out,
Ex	14:10	the Israelites c out to the LORD.
Nm	20:16	When we c to the LORD, he heard
Jos	24: 7	When they c out to the LORD,
Jgs	3: 9	But when the Israelites c
Jgs	4: 3	the Israelites c out to the LORD;
Jgs	6: 6	and so the Israelites c
Jgs	10:12	Yet when you c out to me, and I
Jdt	7:19	The Israelites c to the Lord,
Jb	29:12	For I rescued the poor who c
Ps	18: 7	LORD! I c out to my God.
Ps	22: 6	To you they c out and they escaped;
Ps	107:13	their distress they c to the LORD,
Jon	1: 5	afraid and each one c to his god.
Jon	1:14	Then they c to the LORD:
Mt	14:30	beginning to sink, he c out, "Lord,
Mt	27:46	about three o'clock Jesus c

CRIES → CRY

Prv	1:20	Wisdom c aloud in the street,
Prv	8: 3	city, in the entryways she c aloud:
Heb	5: 7	supplications with loud c and tears

CRIME → CRIMINAL, CRIMINALS

Gn	50:17	So now please forgive the c that we,

CRIMINAL → CRIME

Jn	18:30	"If he were not a c, we would not
2 Tm	2: 9	even to the point of chains, like a c.

CRIMINALS → CRIME

Lk	23:32	both c, were led away with him

CRIMSON → CRIMSONED

Gn	38:28	took and tied a c thread on his hand,
Is	1:18	Though they be red like c, they may

CRIMSONED → CRIMSON

Is	63: 1	Edom, in c garments, from Bozrah?

CRIPPLED

2 Sm	9: 3	son, the one whose feet are c."
Lk	14:13	invite the poor, the c, the lame,
Acts	14: 8	At Lystra there was a c man,

CRITICIZE

Sir	11: 7	not find fault; examine first, then c.

CROOKED

Dt	32: 5	basely, a twisted and c generation!
Ps	125: 5	c ways may the LORD send down
Prv	2:15	Whose ways are c, whose paths are
Prv	8: 8	are sincere, none of them wily or c;
Eccl	1:15	What is c cannot be made straight,
Eccl	7:13	straight what God has made c?
Is	59: 8	Their roads they have made c,
Phil	2:15	without blemish in the midst of a c

CROP → CROPS

2 Tm	2: 6	to have the first share of the c.

CROPS → CROP

Heb	6: 7	and brings forth c useful to those

CROSS → CROSSED, CROSSING, CROSSROADS

Nm	32: 5	Do not make us c the Jordan."
Dt	4:22	I shall not c the Jordan; but you are
Dt	30:13	"Who will c the sea to get it for us
Dt	31: 3	(It is Joshua who will c before you,
Jos	3:14	out from their tents to c the Jordan,
Mt	10:38	whoever does not take up his c
Mt	16:24	take up his c, and follow me.
Mt	27:32	pressed into service to carry his c.
Mk	15:30	by coming down from the c."
Lk	14:27	Whoever does not carry his own c
Jn	19:17	carrying the c himself he went
Jn	19:25	by the c of Jesus were his mother
1 Cor	1:17	the c of Christ might not be emptied
1 Cor	1:18	The message of the c is foolishness
Gal	5:11	block of the c has been abolished.
Gal	6:14	in the c of our Lord Jesus Christ,
Eph	2:16	through the c, putting that enmity
Phil	2: 8	obedient to death, even death on a c.
Phil	3:18	as enemies of the c of Christ.
Col	1:20	by the blood of his c [through him],
Col	2:14	it from our midst, nailing it to the c;
Heb	12: 2	lay before him he endured the c,

CROSSED → CROSS

Dt	12:10	But after you have c the Jordan
Jos	4: 7	the LORD when it c the Jordan.'
2 Kgs	2: 8	and the two of them c over on dry

CROSSING → CROSS

Gn	48:14	But Israel, c his hands, put out his

CROSSROADS → CROSS, ROAD

Prv	8: 2	road, at the c she takes her stand;

CROW → CROWED, CROWS

Jn	13:38	the cock will not c before you deny

CROWD → CROWDS

Ex	12:38	A c of mixed ancestry also went
Mt	21: 8	The very large c spread their cloaks
Mk	8: 2	heart is moved with pity for the c,
Mk	14:43	accompanied by a c with swords
Jn	7:31	many of the c began to believe

CROWDS → CROWD

Mt	4:25	And great c from Galilee,
Mt	7:28	words, the c were astonished at his
Lk	3: 7	He said to the c who came out to be

Acts   8: 6 the c paid attention to what was said
Acts   14:19 Iconium arrived and won over the c.
Acts   17:13 cause a commotion and stir up the c.

CROWED → CROW
Mt   26:74 And immediately a cock c.

CROWN → CROWNED, CROWNS
Ps   21: 4 placed on his head a c of pure gold.
Prv   4: 9 a glorious c will she bestow
Prv   12: 4 of worth is the c of her husband,
Prv   14:24 The c of the wise is wealth;
Prv   16:31 Gray hair is a c of glory; it is gained
Prv   17: 6 Children's children are the c
Prv   27:24 nor even a c from age to age.
Sir   1:18 The c of wisdom is the fear of the Lord,
Is   62: 3 You shall be a glorious c
Zec   9:16 like gemstones of a c they will shine
Mt   27:29 Weaving a c out of thorns,
Mk   15:17 purple and, weaving a c of thorns,
Jn   19: 2 the soldiers wove a c out of thorns
Jn   19: 5 out, wearing the c of thorns
Phil   4: 1 my joy and c, in this way stand firm
1 Thes 2:19 c to boast of in the presence of our
2 Tm   4: 8 on the c of righteousness awaits me,
Jas   1:12 been proved he will receive the c
1 Pt   5: 4 you will receive the unfading c
Rev   2:10 and I will give you the c of life.
Rev   3:11 so that no one may take your c.
Rev   6: 2 He was given a c, and he rode forth
Rev   12: 1 and on her head a c of twelve stars.
Rev   14:14 man, with a gold c on his head

CROWNED → CROWN
Jdt   15:13 the other women c themselves
Ps   8: 6 a god, c him with glory and honor.
Sg   3:11 his mother has c him on the day
Heb   2: 7 you c him with glory and honor,
Heb   2: 9 but we do see Jesus "c with glory

CROWNS → CROWN
Is   23: 8 the bestower of c, Whose merchants
Zec   6:11 take silver and gold, and make c;
Rev   4: 4 and with gold c on their heads.
Rev   4:10 They throw down their c before
Rev   9: 7 heads they wore what looked like c

CROWS → CROW
Lk   22:34 before the cock c this day, you will

CRUCIFIED → CRUCIFY
Mt   20:19 to be mocked and scourged and c,
Mt   26: 2 Man will be handed over to be c."
Mt   27:22 They all said, "Let him be c!"
Mt   27:23 shouted the louder, "Let him be c!"
Mt   27:26 he handed him over to be c.
Mt   27:35 After they had c him, they divided
Mt   27:38 Two revolutionaries were c
Mt   27:44 The revolutionaries who were c
Mt   28: 5 that you are seeking Jesus the c.
Mk   15:15 scourged, handed him over to be c.
Mk   15:24 Then they c him and divided his
Mk   15:25 in the morning when they c him.
Mk   15:27 him they c two revolutionaries,
Mk   15:32 Those who were c with him
Mk   16: 6 You seek Jesus of Nazareth, the c.
Lk   23:33 they c him and the criminals there,
Lk   24: 7 be handed over to sinners and be c,
Lk   24:20 to a sentence of death and c him.
Jn   19:16 he handed him over to them to be c.
Jn   19:18 There they c him, and with him two
Jn   19:20 where Jesus was c was near the city;
Jn   19:23 When the soldiers had c Jesus,
Jn   19:32 the other one who was c with Jesus.
Jn   19:41 where he had been c there was
Acts   2:36 Messiah, this Jesus whom you c."
Acts   4:10 Christ the Nazorean whom you c,
Rom   6: 6 that our old self was c with him,
1 Cor   1:13 Was Paul c for you?
1 Cor   1:23 but we proclaim Christ c,

1 Cor   2: 2 you except Jesus Christ, and him c.
1 Cor   2: 8 they would not have c the Lord
2 Cor 13: 4 For indeed he was c
Gal   2:19 I have been c with Christ;
Gal   3: 1 Christ was publicly portrayed as c?
Gal   5:24 Christ [Jesus] have c their flesh
Gal   6:14 which the world has been c to me,
Rev   11: 8 where indeed their Lord was c.

CRUCIFY → CRUCIFIED
Mt   23:34 some of them you will kill and c,
Mt   27:31 clothes, and led him off to c him.
Mk   15:13 They shouted again, "C him."
Mk   15:14 only shouted the louder, "C him."
Mk   15:20 clothes, and led him out to c him.
Lk   23:21 continued their shouting, "C him!
Jn   19: 6 saw him they cried out, "C him,
Jn   19: 6 "Take him yourselves and c him.
Jn   19:10 you and I have power to c you?"
Jn   19:15 him away, take him away! C him!"
Jn   19:15 said to them, "Shall I c your king?"

CRUEL
Is   13: 9 the day of the LORD comes, c,

CRUMBS
Ps   147:17 He disperses hail like c.

CRUSH → CRUSHED, CRUSHES
Jdt   9:10 C their arrogance by the hand
1 Mc   3:22 He will c them before us; so do not
Jb   6: 9 that God would decide to c me,
Ps   89:11 You c Rahab with a mortal blow;
Ps   89:24 I will c his foes before him,
Is   53:10 it was the LORD's will to c him
Rom   16:20 of peace will quickly c Satan under

CRUSHED → CRUSH
Jgs   5:26 She hammered Sisera, c his head;
Ps   34:19 saves those whose spirit is c.
Ps   51:10 the bones you have c will rejoice.
Ps   74:14 You c the heads of Leviathan,
Is   53: 5 for our sins, c for our iniquity.

CRUSHES → CRUSH
Jdt   16: 2 for the Lord is a God who c wars;

CRY → CRIED, CRIES, CRYING
Ex   2:23 their bondage their c for help went
Jgs   10:14 c out to the gods you have chosen;
1 Mc   4:10 So now let us c to Heaven
Ps   5: 3 Attend to the sound of my c,
Ps   28: 2 of my pleading when I c to you
Ps   34:16 and his ears toward their c.
Ps   40: 2 bends down to me and hears my c,
Ps   88: 3 incline your ear to my c.
Prv   21:13 to the c of the poor will themselves
Sir   4: 6 Rock will hear the sound of their c.
Jer   4:31 The c of daughter Zion gasping,
Lam   2:18 C out to the Lord from your heart,
Hb   1: 2 must I c for help and you do not
Hb   2:11 For the stone in the wall shall c out,
Mk   15:37 Jesus gave a loud c and breathed his
Rom   8:15 through which we c, "Abba,

CRYING → CRY
Ps   69: 4 I am weary with c out; my throat is
Mt   3: 3 "A voice of one c out in the desert,
Mk   1: 3 A voice of one c out in the desert:
Gal   4: 6 of his Son into our hearts, c out,

CRYSTAL
Ez   1:22 upwards like shining c over their
Rev   4: 6 that resembled a sea of glass like c.
Rev   21:11 stone, like jasper, clear as c.
Rev   22: 1 sparkling like c,

CUBS
2 Sm   17: 8 as a bear in the wild robbed of her c.
Prv   17:12 Face a bear robbed of her c,

CUCUMBERS
Nm   11: 5 cost in Egypt, and the c, the melons,

CUD
Lv   11: 3   it is cloven-footed and chews the c.
Dt   14: 6   and that chews the c you may eat.

CULTIVATED
Rom   11:24   into a c one, how much more will
Heb   6: 7   for whom it is c receives a blessing

CUMMIN
Mt   23:23   pay tithes of mint and dill and c,

CUNNING
2 Cor   11: 3   the serpent deceived Eve by his c,

CUP → CUPBEARER, CUPS
Gn   40:11   Pharaoh's c was in my hand;
2 Sm   12: 3   from his own c she drank;
1 Kgs   7:26   and its brim resembled that of a c,
Ps   23: 5   my head with oil; my c overflows.
Ps   75: 9   Yes, a c is in the LORD's hand,
Is   51:22   from your hand the c of staggering;
Jer   25:15   Take this c of the wine of wrath
Lam   4:21   Uz, The c will pass to you as well;
Ez   23:31   path, I will put her c into your hand.
Hb   2:16   The c from the LORD's right hand
Mt   10:42   And whoever gives only a c of cold
Mt   20:22   Can you drink the c that I am going
Mt   23:25   You cleanse the outside of c
Mt   23:26   cleanse first the inside of the c,
Mt   26:27   Then he took a c, gave thanks,
Mt   26:39   is possible, let this c pass from me;
Mk   9:41   Anyone who gives you a c of water
Mk   10:38   Can you drink the c that I drink
Mk   14:23   Then he took a c, gave thanks,
Mk   14:36   Take this c away from me, but not
Lk   11:39   you cleanse the outside of the c
Lk   22:17   Then he took a c, gave thanks,
Lk   22:20   "This c is the new covenant in my
Lk   22:42   willing, take this c away from me;
Jn   18:11   Shall I not drink the c
1 Cor   10:16   The c of blessing that we bless, is it
1 Cor   10:21   You cannot drink the c of the Lord
1 Cor   10:21   the Lord and also the c of demons.
1 Cor   11:25   In the same way also the c,
1 Cor   11:25   "This c is the new covenant in my
1 Cor   11:27   drinks the c of the Lord unworthily
Rev   14:10   full strength into the c of his wrath,
Rev   17: 4   in her hand a gold c that was filled
Rev   18: 6   her c pour double what she poured.

CUPBEARER → BEAR, CUP
Gn   40: 1   the royal c and baker offended their
Gn   41: 9   Then the chief c said to Pharaoh:
Neh   1:11   for I was c to the king.
Tb   1:22   Ahiqar had been chief c,

CUPS → CUP
Ex   25:33   one branch there are to be three c,
1 Mc   1:22   the offering table, the c and bowls,
Mk   7: 4   the purification of c and jugs

CURDS
Gn   18: 8   Then he got some c and milk,
Is   7:15   C and honey he will eat so that he

CURE → CURED, CURING
2 Kgs   5: 3   He would c him of his leprosy."
2 Chr   21:18   of the bowels for which there was no c.
Mt   8: 7   to him, "I will come and c him."
Mk   3: 2   if he would c him on the sabbath so
Lk   9: 1   over all demons and to c diseases,

CURED → CURE
Mt   8:16   spirits by a word and c all the sick,
Mt   12:15   followed him, and he c them all,
Lk   6:18   tormented by unclean spirits were c.
Acts   5:16   unclean spirits, and they were all c.
Acts   28: 9   the island came to Paul and were c.

CURING → CURE
Mt   4:23   and c every disease and illness.
Mt   9:35   and c every disease and illness.

Lk   9: 6   news and c diseases everywhere.

CURSE → ACCURSED, CURSED, CURSES, CURSING
Gn   12: 3   bless you and c those who c you.
Gn   27:13   "Let any c against you, my son,
Ex   22:27   God, nor c a leader of your people.
Lv   24:16   utters the name of the LORD in a c
Nm   5:18   water of bitterness that brings a c.
Nm   22: 6   Now come, c this people for me,
Nm   22: 6   and whoever you c is cursed."
Nm   22:12   with them and do not c this people,
Nm   24: 9   and cursed are those who c you!
Dt   11:26   you this day a blessing and a c:
Dt   11:28   a c if you do not obey
Dt   21:23   anyone who is hanged is a c of God.
Dt   23: 6   turned his c into a blessing for you,
Dt   30: 1   the blessing and the c which I have set
Jos   24: 9   Balaam, son of Beor, to c you,
2 Sm   16: 9   should this dead dog c my lord
Neh   10:30   the sanction of a c take this oath
Neh   13: 2   but they hired Balaam to c them,
Neh   13: 2   though our God turned the c
Jb   2: 9   C God and die!"
Ps   62: 5   their mouths, but inwardly they c.
Ps   109:28   Though they c, may you bless;
Prv   3:33   The c of the LORD is on the house
Prv   20:20   Those who c father or mother—their lamp
Prv   30:11   There are some who c their fathers,
Sir   4: 5   do not give them reason to c you.
Sir   21:27   When the godless c their adversary, they really c themselves.
Is   24: 6   Therefore a c devours the earth,
Lam   3:65   your c be upon them;
Mal   2: 2   I will send a c upon you and your
Mal   2: 2   upon you and your blessing I will c.
Mk   14:71   He began to c and to swear, "I do
Lk   6:28   bless those who c you,
Rom   12:14   [you], bless and do not c them.
Gal   3:10   on works of the law are under a c;
Gal   3:13   ransomed us from the c of the law by becoming a c for us,
Jas   3: 9   it we c human beings who are made

CURSED → CURSE
Gn   3:17   it, C is the ground because of you!
Gn   9:25   he said: "C be Caanan!
Gn   27:29   C be those who curse you,
Nm   22: 6   and whoever your curse is c."
Nm   23: 8   on the one whom God has not c?
Nm   24: 9   you, and c are those who curse you!
Dt   27:15   "C be anyone who makes a carved
Dt   27:16   "C be anyone who dishonors father
Dt   27:17   "C be anyone who moves
Dt   27:18   "C be anyone who misleads
Dt   27:19   "C be anyone who deprives
Dt   27:20   "C be anyone who has relations
Dt   27:21   "C be anyone who has relations
Dt   27:22   "C be anyone who has relations
Dt   27:23   "C be anyone who has relations
Dt   27:24   "C be anyone who strikes down
Dt   27:25   "C be anyone who accepts payment
Dt   27:26   "C be anyone whose actions do not
Dt   28:16   May you be c in the city, and c in the country!
Jos   6:26   C before the LORD be the man
1 Sm   17:43   the Philistine c David by his gods
2 Sm   16: 7   Shimei was saying as he c:
2 Sm   19:22   He c the anointed of the LORD."
1 Kgs   21:13   "Naboth has c God and king."
Jb   3: 1   Job opened his mouth and c his day.
Jer   11: 3   C be anyone who does not observe
Jer   17: 5   C is the man who trusts in human
Mal   1:14   C is the cheat who has in his flock
Mk   11:21   fig tree that you c has withered."
Gal   3:10   "C be everyone who does not
Gal   3:13   "C be everyone who hangs
Heb   6: 8   it will soon be c and finally burned.

CURSES → CURSE
Ex   21:17 Whoever c father or mother shall be
Dt   28:15 all these c shall come upon you
Jos   8:34 the blessings and the c, exactly as
2 Chr 34:24 all the c written in the book that was

CURSING → CURSE
Ps   109:18 May c clothe him like a robe;
Rom   3:14 their mouths are full of bitter c.
Jas   3:10 same mouth come blessing and c.

CURTAIN → CURTAINS
1 Mc   1:22 the golden censers, and the c.

CURTAINS → CURTAIN
1 Mc   4:51 on the table and hung up the c.

CUSH → CUSHITE
Gn   2:13 that winds all through the land of C.
Gn   10: 6 C, Mizraim, Put and Canaan.

CUSHITE → CUSH
Nm   12: 1 he had in fact married a C woman.
2 Sm 18:21 The C bowed to Joab and ran off.

CUSTODY
Lv   24:12 he was kept in c till a decision
Nm   15:34 But they put him in c, for there was
Acts   4: 3 and put them in c until the next day,
Acts 24:23 centurion that he should be kept in c

CUSTOM → ACCUSTOMED, CUSTOMS
Ru   4: 7 it used to be the c in Israel that,
1 Mc   1:14 according to the Gentile c.
Mk   10: 1 as was his c, he again taught them.
Lk   4:16 to his c into the synagogue
Jn   18:39 But you have a c that I release one
Jn   19:40 according to the Jewish burial c.
Acts 17: 2 Following his usual c, Paul joined
1 Cor 11:16 we do not have such a c, nor do

CUSTOMS → CUSTOM
1 Mc   1:42 and abandon their particular c.
Acts 16:21 are advocating c that are not lawful

CUT → CUTTING
Gn   15:10 but the birds he did not c up.
Gn   17:14 such a one will be c off from his
Ex   34:13 stones, and c down their asherahs.
Jgs   21: 6 "Today one tribe has been c off
1 Sm 17:51 he killed him, and c off his head.
1 Sm 24: 5 and stealthily c off an end of Saul's
2 Chr 15:16 Asa c down this object, smashed it,
Jdt   13: 8 his neck twice and c off his head.
Ps   37: 9 Those who do evil will be c off,
Prv   2:22 the wicked will be c off
Prv   10:31 the perverse tongue will be c off.
Prv   23:18 and your hope will not be c off.
Is   14:22 and c off from Babylon name
Is   53: 8 For he was c off from the land
Jer   34:18 they c in two so they could pass
Ez   37:11 our hope is lost, and we are c off."
Dn   9:26 an anointed one shall be c down
Mt   3:10 not bear good fruit will be c down
Mk   9:43 your hand causes you to sin, c it off.
Jn   18:26 the one whose ear Peter had c off,
Acts   2:37 heard this, they were c to the heart,
Rom 11:22 otherwise you too will be c off.
1 Cor 11: 6 she may as well have her hair c off.
1 Cor 11: 6 for a woman to have her hair c off

CUTTING → CUT
Mt   26:51 high priest's servant, c off his ear.

CYMBAL → CYMBALS
1 Cor 13: 1 a resounding gong or a clashing c.

CYMBALS → CYMBAL
2 Sm   6: 5 harps, tambourines, sistrums, and c.
1 Chr 15:16 and c, to make a loud sound
2 Chr 5:12 clothed in fine linen, with c, harps,
2 Chr 29:25 in the LORD's house with c,
Ezr   3:10 with c to praise the LORD

Neh   12:27 hymns and the music of c, harps,
Ps   150: 5 Give praise with crashing c,

CYPRESS
Is   55:13 of the thornbush, the c shall grow,
Hos   14: 9 I am like a verdant c tree.

CYPRUS
Acts 13: 4 Seleucia and from there sailed to C.

CYRENIAN
Mt   27:32 out, they met a C named Simon;

CYRUS
    Persian king who allowed exiles to return (2 Chr 36:22–Ezr 1:8), to rebuild temple (Ezr 5:13–6:14), as appointed by the LORD (Is 44:28–45:13).

D

DAGON
Jgs   16:23 offer a great sacrifice to their god D
1 Sm   5: 2 brought it into the temple of D, placing it beside D.
1 Chr 10:10 they impaled at the temple of D.

DAILY → DAY
Mt   6:11 Give us today our d bread;
Lk   9:23 take up his cross d and follow me.
Lk   11: 3 Give us each day our d bread

DAMASCUS
2 Sm   8: 5 The Arameans of D came to help
2 Kgs 8: 7 Elisha came to D at a time
2 Kgs 16:10 When he saw the altar in D,
Is   7: 8 The head of Aram is D, and the head of D is Rezin;
Is   17: 1 Oracle on D: See, D shall cease
Am   1: 3 For three crimes of D, and now
Acts   9: 3 as he was nearing D, a light
Acts 22: 6 that journey as I drew near to D,

DAN
    1. Son of Jacob by Bilhah (Gn 30:4-6; 35:25; 46:23). Tribe of blessed (Gn 49:16-17; Dt 33:22), numbered (Nm 1:39; 26:43), allotted land (Jos 19:40-48; Ez 48:1), failed to fully possess (Jgs 1:34-35), failed to support Deborah (Jgs 5:17), possessed Laish/Dan (Jgs 18).
    2. Northernmost city in Israel (Gn 14:14; Jgs 18; 20:1).

DANCE → DANCERS, DANCES, DANCING
Jdt   15:12 her and performed a d in her honor.
Ps   149: 3 Let them praise his name in d,
Ps   150: 4 Give praise with tambourines and d,
Eccl   3: 4 a time to mourn, and a time to d.
Jer   31:13 women shall make merry and d,
Mt   11:17 but you did not d, we sang a dirge
Mt   14: 6 Herodias performed a d before
Mk   6:22 performed a d that delighted Herod
Lk   7:32 the flute for you, but you did not d.

DANCERS → DANCE
Jgs   21:23 of them from the d they had seized,
Ps   87: 7 singers and d: "All my springs are in you."

DANCES → DANCE
1 Sm 21:12 that during their d they sing out,
1 Sm 29: 5 for whom they sing during their d,

DANCING → DANCE
Ex   15:20 out after her with tambourines, d;
Ex   32:19 the camp, he saw the calf and the d.
Jgs   11:34 with tambourine-playing and d.
1 Sm 18: 6 singing and d, with tambourines,
2 Sm   6:14 David came d before the LORD
2 Sm   6:16 jumping and d before the LORD,
2 Sm   6:21 "I was d before the LORD.
1 Chr 15:29 she saw King David leaping and d,
Ps   30:12 You changed my mourning into d;
Lam   5:15 ceased, d has turned into mourning;
Lk   15:25 he heard the sound of music and d.

DANGER → DANGERS
Lk   8:23 were taking in water and were in d.
Acts 19:40 is, we are in d of being charged

DANGERS → DANGER

2 Cor	11:26	in **d** from rivers, **d** from robbers,
2 Cor	11:26	**d** from Gentiles, **d** in the city,
2 Cor	11:26	**d** in the wilderness, **d** at sea,

DANIEL → =BELTESHAZZAR

1. Hebrew exile to Babylon, name changed to Belteshazzar (Dn 1:6-7). Refused to eat unclean food (Dn 1:8-21). Interpreted Nebuchadnezzar's dreams (Dn 2; 4), writing on the wall (Dn 5). Thrown into lion's den (Dn 6; 14:30-42). Visions of (Dn 7-12). Saves Susanna (Dn 13:45-64). Destroys idol and temple of Bel (Dn 14:1-22). Destroys a dragon (Dn 14:23-28).

2. Son of David (1 Chr 3:1).

DARE → DARED

Mt	22:46	did anyone **d** to ask him any more
Acts	7:32	trembling, did not **d** to look at it.
1 Cor	6: 1	a case against another **d** to bring it

DARED → DARE

Mk	12:34	And no one **d** to ask him any more
Jn	21:12	none of the disciples **d** to ask him,
Acts	5:13	None of the others **d** to join them,

DARIUS

1. King of Persia (Ezr 4:5), allowed rebuilding of temple (Ezr 5–6).

2. Mede who conquered Babylon (Dn 6:1).

DARK → DARKEN, DARKENED, DARKENS, DARKNESS

Gn	15:12	a great, **d** dread descended upon him.
Gn	15:17	When the sun had set and it was **d**,
Jos	2: 5	At **d**, when it was time to close
Ps	35: 6	Make their way slippery and **d**,
Ps	139:12	Darkness is not **d** for you, and night
2 Pt	1:19	it, as to a lamp shining in a **d** place,

DARKEN → DARK

Jl	3: 4	The sun will **d**, the moon turn blood-red,

DARKENED → DARK

Jl	2:10	Sun and moon are **d**, and the stars
Jl	4:15	Sun and moon are **d**, and the stars
Mt	24:29	the sun will be **d**, and the moon will
Rom	1:21	and their senseless minds were **d**.
Eph	4:18	**d** in understanding,
Rev	9: 2	the air were **d** by the smoke

DARKENS → DARK

Am	5: 8	into dawn, and **d** day into night;

DARKNESS → DARK

Gn	1: 2	with **d** over the abyss and a mighty
Gn	1: 4	then separated the light from the **d**.
Ex	10:22	there was dense **d** throughout
Dt	5:23	the voice from the midst of the **d**,
Jos	24: 7	he put **d** between you
2 Sm	22:29	My God brightens the **d** about me.
Tb	5:10	but must remain in **d**, like the dead
Jb	12:22	He uncovers deep things from the **d**,
Ps	18:12	He made **d** his cloak around him;
Ps	18:29	my God brightens my **d**.
Ps	91: 6	Nor the pestilence that roams in **d**,
Ps	97: 2	Cloud and **d** surround him;
Ps	112: 4	Light shines through the **d**
Ps	139:12	**D** is not dark for you, and night
Ps	139:12	as the day. **D** and light are but one.
Prv	4:19	The way of the wicked is like **d**;
Eccl	2:13	profit over folly as light has over **d**.
Is	5:20	good evil, who change **d** to light,
Is	5:20	and light into **d**, who change bitter
Is	9: 1	walked in **d** have seen a great light;
Is	42:16	I will turn **d** into light before them,
Is	45: 7	and create the **d**, I make weal
Is	58:10	Then your light shall rise in the **d**,
Jer	13:16	your God, before he brings **d**;
Jer	13:16	the light you look for turns to **d**,
Am	5:18	mean for you? It will be **d**, not light!
Am	5:20	the day of the Lord will be **d**,
Na	1: 8	and pursues his enemies into **d**.
Zep	1:15	desolation, A day of **d** and gloom,
Mt	4:16	who sit in **d** have seen a great light,

Mt	6:23	bad, your whole body will be in **d**.
Mt	6:23	And if the light in you is **d**, how great will the **d** be.
Mt	22:13	feet, and cast him into the **d** outside,
Lk	1:79	to shine on those who sit in **d**
Lk	11:34	it is bad, then your body is in **d**.
Lk	23:44	**d** came over the whole land until
Jn	1: 5	the light shines in the **d**, and the **d** has not overcome it.
Jn	3:19	but people preferred **d** to light,
Jn	8:12	follows me will not walk in **d**,
Jn	12:35	so that **d** may not overcome you.
Acts	2:20	The sun shall be turned to **d**,
Rom	2:19	the blind and a light for those in **d**,
Rom	13:12	throw off the works of **d** [and] put
2 Cor	4: 6	said, "Let light shine out of **d**,"
2 Cor	6:14	fellowship does light have with **d**?
Eph	5: 8	For you were once **d**, but now you
Eph	5:11	no part in the fruitless works of **d**;
Col	1:13	He delivered us from the power of **d**
1 Thes	5: 5	We are not of the night or of **d**.
Heb	12:18	blazing fire and gloomy **d** and storm
1 Pt	2: 9	out of **d** into his wonderful light.
2 Pt	2:17	the gloom of **d** has been reserved.
1 Jn	1: 5	light, and in him there is no **d** at all.
1 Jn	2: 8	for the **d** is passing away,
1 Jn	2: 9	yet hates his brother, is still in the **d**.
Jude	1:13	of **d** has been reserved forever.
Rev	16:10	Its kingdom was plunged into **d**,

DASH → DASHED

2 Kgs	8:12	you will **d** their little children
Jdt	16: 4	sword, **D** my infants to the ground,
Lk	4:11	you, lest you **d** your foot against

DASHED → DASH

Is	13:16	Their infants shall be **d** to pieces
Na	3:10	Even her little ones were **d** to pieces

DATHAN

Involved in Korah's rebellion against Moses and Aaron (Nm 16:1-27; 26:9; Dt 11:6; Ps 106:17; Sir 45:18).

DAUGHTER → DAUGHTER-IN-LAW, DAUGHTERS, DAUGHTERS-IN-LAW

Gn	24:24	"I am the **d** of Bethuel the son
Gn	29:10	the **d** of his mother's brother Laban,
Gn	34: 3	attracted to Dinah, **d** of Jacob,
Gn	38: 2	There Judah saw the **d**
Ex	2: 5	Pharaoh's **d** came down to bathe
Ex	21: 7	When a man sells his **d** as a slave,
Nm	27: 8	shall transfer his heritage to his **d**;
Jgs	11:34	it was his **d** who came out to meet
Ru	2: 2	said to her, "Go ahead, my **d**."
Ru	3:10	"May the Lord bless you, my **d**!
1 Sm	18:20	Now Saul's **d** Michal loved David.
2 Sm	6:16	Michal, **d** of Saul, looked down
1 Kgs	11: 1	many foreign women besides the **d**
Jdt	10:12	"I am a **d** of the Hebrews, and I am
Est	2: 7	Mordecai adopted her as his own **d**.
Ps	9:15	salvation in the gates of **d** Zion.
Is	47: 1	sit in the dust, virgin **d** Babylon;
Is	52: 2	from your neck, captive **d** Zion!
Is	62:11	Say to **d** Zion, "See, your savior
Jer	6: 2	Lovely and delicate **d** Zion, you are
Jer	46:11	procure balm, Virgin **d** Egypt!
Lam	2: 1	in his wrath has abhorred **d** Zion,
Ez	16:45	you are truly the **d** of your mother
Mi	7: 6	the **d** rises up against her mother,
Zep	3:14	Shout for joy, **d** Zion!
Zep	3:14	with all your heart, **d** Jerusalem!
Zec	9: 9	Exult greatly, O **d** Zion!
Zec	9: 9	Shout for joy, O **d** Jerusalem!
Mt	9:18	him, and said, "My **d** has just died.
Mt	14: 6	the **d** of Herodias performed a dance
Mt	15:28	her **d** was healed from that hour.
Mk	5:35	arrived and said, "Your **d** has died;
Mk	7:29	demon has gone out of your **d**."
Lk	12:53	a mother against her **d** and a **d** against her mother,
Heb	11:24	be known as the son of Pharaoh's **d**;

DAUGHTER-IN-LAW → DAUGHTER
Gn   11:31 and his **d** Sarai, the wife of his son
Gn   38:16 he did not realize that she was his **d**.
Ru   1:22 came back with her Moabite **d** Ruth,
Ru   4:15 his mother is the **d** who loves you.
1 Chr 2: 4 Judah's **d** Tamar bore him Perez
Mi   7: 6 The **d** against her mother-in-law,
Mt   10:35 and a **d** against her mother-in-law;

DAUGHTERS → DAUGHTER
Gn   6: 4 with the **d** of human beings,
Gn   19:36 Thus the two **d** of Lot became
Gn   29:16 Now Laban had two **d**;
Ex   2:16 the priest of Midian had seven **d**,
Nm   27: 1 The **d** of Zelophehad,
Nm   36:10 The **d** of Zelophehad did exactly as
Dt   7: 3 neither giving your **d** to their sons nor taking their **d** for
              your
Dt   12:31 their sons and **d** to their gods.
Ru   1:11 Naomi replied, "Go back, my **d**.
Ezr   9:12 then, give your **d** to their sons
Ezr   9:12 do not take their **d** for your sons.
Neh   5: 5 to reduce our sons and **d** to slavery,
Jb   42:15 women were as beautiful as the **d**
Ps 144:12 youth, Our **d**, like carved columns,
Prv 30:15 The leech has two **d**:
Sg   1: 5 and beautiful, **D** of Jerusalem—
Sir   7:24 Do you have **d**? Keep them chaste,
Ez   23: 2 two women, **d** of the same mother.
Jl   3: 1 Your sons and **d** will prophesy,
Lk   23:28 to them and said, "**D** of Jerusalem,
Acts 2:17 sons and your **d** shall prophesy,
Acts 21: 9 He had four virgin **d** gifted
2 Cor 6:18 and you shall be sons and **d** to me,

DAUGHTERS-IN-LAW → DAUGHTER
Ru   1: 8 Naomi said to her **d**, "Go back,

DAVID
Son of Jesse (Ru 4:17-22; 1 Chr 2:13-15), ancestor of Jesus (Mt 1:1-17; Lk 3:31). Wives and children (1 Sm 18; 25:39-44; 2 Sm 3:2-5; 5:13-16; 11:27; 1 Chr 3:1-9).
   Anointed king by Samuel (1 Sm 16:1-13). Musician to Saul (1 Sm 16:14-23; 18:10). Killed Goliath (1 Sm 17). Relation with Jonathan (1 Sm 18:1-4; 19–20; 23:16-18; 2 Sm 1). Disfavor of Saul (1 Sm 18:6–23:29). Spared Saul's life (1 Sm 24; 26). Among Philistines (1 Sm 21:11-16; 27–30). Lament for Saul and Jonathan (2 Sm 1).
   Anointed king of Judah (2 Sm 2:1-11). Conflict with house of Saul (2 Sm 2–4). Anointed king of Israel (2 Sm 5:1-4; 1 Chr 11:1-3). Conquered Jerusalem (2 Sm 5:6-10; 1 Chr 11:4-9). Brought ark to Jerusalem (2 Sm 6; 1 Chr 13; 15–16). The LORD promised eternal dynasty (2 Sm 7; 1 Chr 17; Ps 132). Showed kindness to Mephibosheth (2 Sm 9). Adultery with Bathsheba, murder of Uriah (2 Sm 11–12). Son Amnon raped daughter Tamar; killed by Absalom (2 Sm 13). Absalom's revolt (2 Sm 14–17); death (2 Sm 18). Sheba's revolt (2 Sm 20). Victories: Philistines (2 Sm 5:17-25; 21:15-22; 1 Chr 14:8-17; 20:4-8), Ammonites (2 Sm 10; 1 Chr 19), various (2 Sm 8; 1 Chr 18). Mighty men (2 Sm 23:8-39; 1 Chr 11–12). Punished for numbering army (2 Sm 24; 1 Chr 21). Appointed Solomon king (1 Kgs 1:28–2:9). Prepared for building of temple (1 Chr 22–29). Last words (2 Sm 23:1-7). Death (1 Kgs 2:10-12; 1 Chr 29:28).
   Psalmist (Mt 22:43-45), musician (Am 6:5), prophet (2 Sm 23:2-7; Acts 1:16; 2:30).
   Psalms of: 2 (Acts 4:25), 3–32, 34–41, 51–65, 68–70, 86, 95 (Heb 4:7), 101, 103, 108–110, 122, 124, 131, 133, 138-145.

DAWN → DAWNS
Jb   38:12 morning and shown the **d** its place
Ps   57: 9 lyre and harp! I will wake the **d**.
Sg   6:10 is this that comes forth like the **d**,
Sir 24:32 make my teachings shine forth like the **d**;
Is   14:12 O Morning Star, son of the **d**!
Is   58: 8 light shall break forth like the **d**,
Is   62: 1 vindication shines forth like the **d**
Hos   6: 3 as certain as the **d** is his coming.
Zep   3: 5 judgment unfailingly, at **d**;

DAWNS → DAWN
Ps   97:11 Light **d** for the just, and gladness

2 Pt 1:19 until day **d** and the morning star

DAY → BIRTHDAY, DAILY, DAY'S, DAYBREAK, DAYLIGHT, DAYS
Gn   1: 5 God called the light "**d**,"
Gn   1: 5 and morning followed—the first **d**.
Gn   1: 8 the second **d**.
Gn   1:13 and morning followed—the third **d**.
Gn   1:19 the fourth **d**.
Gn   1:23 and morning followed—the fifth **d**.
Gn   1:31 and morning followed—the sixth **d**.
Gn   2: 2 On the seventh **d** God completed
Gn   8:22 and **d** and night shall not cease.
Ex   12:17 must observe this **d** throughout your
Ex   13:21 Thus they could travel both **d**
Ex   16:30 the people rested on the seventh **d**.
Ex   20: 8 Remember the sabbath **d**—
Ex   40: 2 On the first **d** of the first month you
Nm   14:14 and you go before them by **d**
Dt   1:33 and by **d** in the cloud, to show you
Dt   34: 6 to this **d** no one knows the place
Jos   1: 8 Recite it by **d** and by night, that you
Jos 10:14 or since was there a **d** like this,
2 Kgs 7: 9 This is a **d** of good news, and we are
1 Chr 16:23 announce his salvation, **d** after **d**.
Neh   8:10 Do not be saddened this **d**,
Neh   8:18 the book of the law of God **d** after **d**,
Tb   12:18 So bless God every **d**;
1 Mc 4:54 that very **d** it was rededicated
1 Mc 7:48 observed that **d** as a **d** of much joy.
2 Mc 15:36 never to let this **d** pass unobserved,
2 Mc 15:36 Aramaic, the eve of Mordecai's **D**.
Ps   1: 2 on his law he meditates **d** and night.
Ps   19: 3 **D** unto **d** pours forth speech;
Ps   37:13 he sees that their **d** is coming.
Ps   84:11 Better one **d** in your courts than
Ps   96: 2 proclaim his salvation **d** after **d**.
Ps 118:24 This is the **d** the LORD has made;
Ps 119:97 your law, Lord! I study it all **d** long.
Ps 119:164 Seven times a **d** I praise you
Prv 11: 4 Wealth is useless on a **d** of wrath,
Prv 27: 1 know what any **d** may bring forth.
Eccl 7: 1 the **d** of death than the **d** of birth.
Sir   5: 8 it will be no help on the **d** of wrath.
Is   2:12 hosts will have his **d** against all
Is   13: 9 Indeed, the **d** of the LORD comes,
Is   49: 8 on the **d** of salvation I help you;
Is   60:19 shall the sun be your light by **d**,
Is   66: 8 a land be brought forth in one **d**,
Jer 30: 7 How mighty is that **d**—there is none
Jer 46:10 GOD of hosts, a **d** of vengeance,
Jer 50:31 For your **d** has come, the time
Ez   4: 6 I allot you one **d** for each year.
Ez   7: 7 The time has come, near is the **d**:
Ez   30: 2 Wail: "Alas the **d**!"
Dn   6:14 three times a **d** he offers his
Jl   1:15 O! The **d**! For near is the **d**
Jl   3: 4 Before the **d** of the LORD arrives, that great and
              terrible **d**.
Am   3:14 On the **d** when I punish Israel for its
Am   5:20 Truly, the **d** of the LORD will be
Mi   7: 4 The **d** announced by your sentinels!
Hb   3:16 I await the **d** of distress that will
Zep   1:14 Near is the great **d** of the LORD,
Zec   2:15 themselves to the LORD on that **d**.
Zec 14: 1 A **d** is coming for the LORD
Zec 14: 7 There will be one continuous **d**—
Zec 14: 7 not **d** and night, for in the evening
Mal   3: 2 But who can endure the **d** of his
Mal   3:23 Before the **d** of the LORD comes, the great and terrible **d**;
Mt   10:15 on the **d** of judgment than
Mt   12:36 the **d** of judgment people will render
Mt   20:19 he will be raised on the third **d**."
Mt   24:38 to the **d** that Noah entered the ark.
Mt   25:13 you know neither the **d** nor the hour.
Mt   28: 1 as the first **d** of the week was
Lk   1:59 the eighth **d** to circumcise the child,
Lk   11: 3 Give us each **d** our daily bread

Lk	17:24	so will the Son of Man be [in his **d**].
Lk	24:46	and rise from the dead on the third **d**
Jn	6:40	I shall raise him [on] the last **d**."
Acts	2:20	the great and splendid **d** of the Lord,
Acts	2:46	Every **d** they devoted themselves
Acts	5:42	And all **d** long, both at the temple
Acts	17:31	because he has established a **d**
Rom	2: 5	wrath for yourself for the **d** of wrath
Rom	14: 5	considers one **d** more important
1 Cor	5: 5	may be saved on the **d** of the Lord.
1 Cor	15: 4	raised on the third **d** in accordance
1 Cor	15:31	Every **d** I face death; I swear it
2 Cor	4:16	inner self is being renewed **d** by **d**.
2 Cor	6: 2	on the **d** of salvation I helped you."
2 Cor	6: 2	behold, now is the **d** of salvation.
2 Cor	11:25	I passed a night and a **d** on the deep;
Eph	4:30	were sealed for the **d** of redemption.
Eph	6:13	be able to resist on the evil **d** and,
Phil	1: 6	to complete it until the **d** of Christ
1 Thes	5: 2	the **d** of the Lord will come like
1 Thes	5: 8	But since we are of the **d**, let us be
2 Thes	2: 2	the effect that the **d** of the Lord is
Heb	7:27	to offer sacrifice **d** after **d**,
2 Pt	3: 8	the Lord one **d** is like a thousand
2 Pt	3: 8	and a thousand years like one **d**.
2 Pt	3:10	the **d** of the Lord will come like
1 Jn	4:17	the **d** of judgment because as he is,
Jude	1: 6	for the judgment of the great **d**.
Rev	1:10	caught up in spirit on the Lord's **d**
Rev	6:17	because the great **d** of their wrath
Rev	8:12	The **d** lost its light for a third
Rev	16:14	on the great **d** of God the almighty.
Rev	20:10	There they will be tormented **d**
Rev	21:25	During the **d** its gates will never be

DAY'S → DAY

Nm	11:31	to a distance of a **d** journey
1 Kgs	19: 4	and went a **d** journey
Jon	3: 4	only a single **d** walk announcing,
Acts	1:12	a sabbath **d** journey away.
Rev	6: 6	"A ration of wheat costs a **d** pay,

DAYBREAK → DAY, BREAK

Lk	4:42	At **d**, Jesus left and went

DAYLIGHT → DAY, LIGHT

Am	8: 9	and in broad **d** cover the land

DAYS → DAY

Gn	1:14	the seasons, the **d** and the years,
Gn	3:14	dust you shall eat all the **d** of your
Gn	3:17	toil you shall eat its yield all the **d**
Gn	7: 4	rain down on the earth for forty **d**
Ex	24:18	He was on the mountain for forty **d**
Ex	34:28	there with the LORD for forty **d**
Nm	13:25	reconnoitering the land forty **d** later.
Nm	14:34	forty **d**—you shall bear your
Dt	32: 7	Remember the **d** of old,
Jgs	17: 6	In those **d** there was no king
Jgs	21:25	In those **d** there was no king
1 Sm	17:16	morning and evening for forty **d**.
2 Sm	7:12	when your **d** have been completed
1 Kgs	19: 8	he walked forty **d** and forty nights
Tb	4: 5	Perform righteous deeds all the **d**
Jdt	16:24	of Israel mourned her for seven **d**.
1 Mc	4:56	For eight **d** they celebrated
Ps	21: 5	gave it to him, length of **d** forever.
Ps	23: 6	mercy will pursue me all the **d**
Ps	23: 6	house of the LORD for endless **d**.
Ps	34:13	in life, who loves to see the good **d**?
Ps	39: 6	you establish the expanse of my **d**;
Ps	90:12	Teach us to count our **d** aright,
Ps	103:15	As for man, his **d** are like the grass;
Ps	128: 5	see Jerusalem's prosperity all the **d**
Prv	9:11	For by me your **d** will be multiplied
Prv	31:12	profit, not loss, all the **d** of her life.
Eccl	9: 9	all the **d** of the vain life granted you
Eccl	12: 1	your Creator in the **d** of your youth,
Eccl	12: 1	before the evil **d** come

Dn	12:11	thousand two hundred and ninety **d**.
Dn	12:12	three hundred and thirty-five **d**.
Hos	3: 5	and to his bounty, in the last **d**.
Jl	3: 2	in those **d**, I will pour out my spirit.
Mt	4: 2	He fasted for forty **d** and forty
Mk	1:13	remained in the desert for forty **d**,
Mk	10:34	but after three **d** he will rise."
Lk	4: 2	for forty **d**, to be tempted
Lk	4: 2	He ate nothing during those **d**,
Lk	19:43	For the **d** are coming upon you
Acts	1: 3	appearing to them during forty **d**
Acts	2:17	'It will come to pass in the last **d**,'
Eph	5:16	opportunity, because the **d** are evil.
2 Tm	3: 1	will be terrifying times in the last **d**.
Heb	1: 2	in these last **d**, he spoke to us
2 Pt	3: 3	in the last **d** scoffers will come
Rev	11: 3	those twelve hundred and sixty **d**,
Rev	11:11	But after the three and a half **d**,
Rev	12: 6	of for twelve hundred and sixty **d**.

DAZZLING

Mk	9: 3	and his clothes became **d** white,
Lk	24: 4	two men in **d** garments appeared
Acts	10:30	a man in **d** robes stood before me

DEACONS

1 Tm	3: 8	Similarly, **d** must be dignified,
1 Tm	3:10	against them, let them serve as **d**.
1 Tm	3:12	**D** may be married only once
1 Tm	3:13	serve well as **d** gain good standing

DEAD → DEATH, DIE, DIED, DIES, DYING

Ex	12:30	there was not a house without its **d**.
Nm	17:13	there between the living and the **d**.
Dt	18:11	spirits, or seeks oracles from the **d**.
1 Kgs	3:22	one is my son, the **d** one is yours."
Ps	115:17	The **d** do not praise the LORD,
Eccl	9: 4	live dog is better off than a **d** lion."
Is	8:19	consulting the **d** on behalf
Is	26:19	But your **d** shall live, their corpses
Mt	8:22	and let the **d** bury their **d**."
Mt	9:24	The girl is not **d** but sleeping."
Mt	10: 8	the sick, raise the **d**, cleanse lepers,
Mt	11: 5	the deaf hear, the **d** are raised,
Mt	14: 2	He has been raised from the **d**;
Mt	28: 7	'He has been raised from the **d**,
Mk	12:27	He is not God of the **d**
Lk	15:24	because this son of mine was **d**,
Lk	16:31	should rise from the **d**.' "
Lk	20:37	the **d** will rise even Moses made
Lk	24: 5	seek the living one among the **d**?
Lk	24:46	and rise from the **d** on the third day
Jn	5:21	For just as the Father raises the **d**
Jn	11:44	The **d** man came out, tied hand
Jn	20: 9	that he had to rise from the **d**.
Jn	21:14	after being raised from the **d**.
Rom	6: 4	was raised from the **d** by the glory
Rom	6:11	of yourselves as [being] **d** to sin
Rom	14: 9	that he might be Lord of both the **d**
1 Cor	15:12	say there is no resurrection of the **d**?
1 Cor	15:12	is preached as raised from the **d**,
1 Cor	15:29	themselves baptized for the **d**?
Eph	2: 1	You were **d** in your transgressions
Eph	5:14	and arise from the **d**, and Christ will
Phil	3:11	attain the resurrection from the **d**.
Col	1:18	the firstborn from the **d**, that in all
Col	2:13	when you were **d** [in] transgressions
1 Thes	4:16	and the **d** in Christ will rise first.
2 Tm	4: 1	who will judge the living and the **d**,
Heb	11:19	was able to raise even from the **d**,
Jas	2:26	just as a body without a spirit is **d**, so also faith without works is **d**.
1 Pt	4: 5	ready to judge the living and the **d**.
Rev	1: 5	the firstborn of the **d** and ruler
Rev	1:18	Once I was **d**, but now I am alive
Rev	11:18	and the time for the **d** to be judged,
Rev	14:13	Blessed are the **d** who die
Rev	20:12	I saw the **d**, the great and the lowly,

Rev 20:12 The **d** were judged according

DEAF

Ex 4:11 Who makes another mute or **d**,
Lv 19:14 You shall not insult the **d**, or put
Is 29:18 that day the **d** shall hear the words
Is 35: 5 see, and the ears of the **d** be opened;
Is 42:19 or **d** like the messenger I send?
Mk 7:32 to him a **d** man who had a speech
Lk 7:22 lepers are cleansed, the **d** hear,

DEAL → DEALT

Ex 1:10 let us **d** shrewdly with them to stop
Ez 16:59 I will **d** with you for what you did;
Heb 5: 2 He is able to **d** patiently

DEALT → DEAL

Ex 1:20 Therefore God **d** well

DEAR

Ps 102:15 Its stones are **d** to your servants;

DEATH → DEAD

Ex 21:12 a mortal blow must be put to **d**.
Ex 21:15 father or mother shall be put to **d**.
Ex 21:16 in his possession, shall be put to **d**.
Ex 21:17 father or mother shall be put to **d**.
Ex 22:18 lies with an animal shall be put to **d**.
Ex 31:14 desecrates it shall be put to **d**.
Ex 31:15 on the sabbath day shall be put to **d**.
Nm 23:10 May I die the **d** of the just, may my
Nm 35:16 and the murderer must be put to **d**.
Dt 13: 6 or that dreamer shall be put to **d**,
Dt 17: 6 witnesses shall a person be put to **d**;
Dt 30:19 I have set before you life and **d**,
Ru 1:17 if even **d** separates me from you!"
2 Chr 23:15 the royal palace, they put her to **d**.
2 Chr 25: 4 "Parents shall not be put to **d**
2 Chr 25: 4 nor shall children be put to **d**
Jb 3:21 They wait for **d** and it does not
Ps 13: 4 light to my eyes lest I sleep in **d**,
Ps 18: 5 The cords of **d** encompassed me;
Ps 22:16 you lay me in the dust of **d**.
Ps 23: 4 through the valley of the shadow of **d**,
Ps 49:15 Sheol, and **D** will shepherd them.
Ps 89:49 that he should live and not see **d**?
Ps 116:15 the LORD is the **d** of his devoted.
Prv 5: 5 Her feet go down to **d**, her steps
Prv 8:36 all who hate me love **d**."
Prv 10: 2 nothing, but justice saves from **d**.
Prv 14:12 right, but the end of it leads to **d**!
Prv 16:25 right, but the end of it leads to **d**!
Prv 18:21 **D** and life are in the power
Eccl 7: 1 the day of **d** than the day of birth.
Sg 8: 6 For Love is strong as **D**, longing is
Wis 1:12 Do not court **d** by your erring way
Sir 4:28 Even to the **d**, fight for what is right,
Sir 15:17 Before everyone are life and **d**,
Is 28:15 "We have made a covenant with **d**,
Is 53:12 he surrendered himself to **d**,
Jer 26:16 man does not deserve a **d** sentence;
Ez 18:23 pleasure in the **d** of the wicked—
Ez 18:32 in the **d** of anyone who dies—
Ez 33:11 no pleasure in the **d** of the wicked,
Dn 3:88 and saved us from the power of **d**;
Dn 13:28 lawless intent to put Susanna to **d**.
Dn 13:62 law of Moses they put them to **d**.
Hos 13:14 Where are your plagues, O **d**!
Hb 2: 5 and is insatiable as **d**, Who gathers
Mt 10:21 Brother will hand over brother to **d**,
Mt 10:21 parents and have them put to **d**.
Mt 16:28 who will not taste **d** until they see
Mk 10:33 and they will condemn him to **d**
Jn 5:24 but has passed from **d** to life.
Jn 8:51 keeps my word will never see **d**."
Jn 11:13 But Jesus was talking about his **d**,
Acts 2:24 releasing him from the throes of **d**,
Rom 5:12 and through sin, **d**, and thus **d** came
Rom 6: 3 Jesus were baptized into his **d**?

Rom 6:23 For the wages of sin is **d**,
Rom 8:13 the spirit you put to **d** the deeds
1 Cor 15:21 For since **d** came through a human
1 Cor 15:26 The last enemy to be destroyed is **d**,
1 Cor 15:55 Where, O **d**, is your victory?
1 Cor 15:55 Where, O **d**, is your sting?"
2 Cor 2:16 latter an odor of **d** that leads to **d**,
2 Cor 3: 7 Now if the ministry of **d**,
Phil 2: 8 becoming obedient to **d**, even **d** on a cross.
Col 1:22 in his fleshly body through his **d**,
2 Tm 1:10 who destroyed **d** and brought life
Heb 2:14 through **d** he might destroy the one who has the power of **d**,
Jas 5:20 of his way will save his soul from **d**
1 Jn 3:14 that we have passed from **d** to life
1 Jn 3:14 does not love remains in **d**.
Rev 1:18 I hold the keys to **d**
Rev 2:11 not be harmed by the second **d**." '
Rev 6: 8 Its rider was named **D**, and Hades
Rev 9: 6 that time these people will seek **d**
Rev 9: 6 long to die but **d** will escape them.
Rev 20: 6 The second **d** has no power over
Rev 20:14 Then **D** and Hades were thrown
Rev 20:14 (This pool of fire is the second **d**)
Rev 21: 4 and there shall be no more **d**
Rev 21: 8 and sulfur, which is the second **d**."

DEBATE → DEBATER

Acts 15: 2 no little dissension and **d** by Paul
Acts 15: 7 After much **d** had taken place,

DEBATER → DEBATE

1 Cor 1:20 Where is the **d** of this age?

DEBAUCHERIES → DEBAUCHERY

Na 3: 4 For the many **d** of the prostitute,

DEBAUCHERY → DEBAUCHERIES

2 Mc 6: 4 Gentiles filled the temple with **d**
Eph 5:18 in which lies **d**, but be filled

DEBIR

Jos 12:13 the king of **D**, one; the king
Jgs 1:11 there against the inhabitants of **D**,

DEBORAH

1. Prophetess who led Israel to victory over Canaanites (Jgs 4–5).
2. Rebekah's nurse (Gn 35:8).

DEBT → DEBTOR, DEBTORS, DEBTS

1 Sm 22: 2 by all those in difficulties or in **d**,
Neh 10:32 and forgive every kind of **d**.
1 Mc 10:43 or because of any other **d**, shall be
Mt 18:30 in prison until he paid back the **d**.
Mt 18:32 you your entire **d** because you
Mt 18:34 he should pay back the whole **d**.
Lk 7:43 whose larger **d** was forgiven."

DEBTOR → DEBT

Is 24: 2 and borrower, creditor and **d**.

DEBTORS → DEBT

Hb 2: 7 Will your **d** not rise suddenly?
Mt 6:12 us our debts, as we forgive our **d**;
Lk 16: 5 called in his master's **d** one by one.
Rom 8:12 brothers, we are not **d** to the flesh,

DEBTS → DEBT

Dt 15: 1 you shall have a remission of **d**,
1 Mc 15: 8 All **d**, present or future,
Prv 22:26 those who become surety for **d**;
Mt 6:12 and forgive us our **d**, as we forgive

DECAPOLIS

Mt 4:25 from Galilee, the **D**, Jerusalem,

DECAYS

Sir 10: 9 Even during life the body **d**.

DECEIT → DECEITFUL, DECEITFULLY, DECEIVE, DECEIVED, DECEIVERS

Dt 32: 4 without **d**, just and upright is he!
Jb 27: 4 falsehood, nor my tongue utter **d**!
Ps 32: 2 no guilt, in whose spirit is no **d**.

Ps	101: 7	No one who practices **d** can remain
Prv	26:24	but inwardly they maintain **d**;
Mk	7:22	greed, malice, **d**, licentiousness,
Acts	13:10	full of every sort of **d** and fraud.
1 Pt	2:22	and no **d** was found in his mouth."

DECEITFUL → DECEIT

Ps	35:20	in the land they fashion **d** speech.
Prv	12:17	but the **d** make lying witnesses.
Zep	3:13	be found in their mouths a **d** tongue;
2 Cor	11:13	people are false apostles, **d** workers,
Eph	4:14	in the interests of **d** scheming.
1 Tm	4: 1	faith by paying attention to **d** spirits

DECEITFULLY → DECEIT

1 Mc	1:30	spoke to them **d** in peaceful terms,

DECEIVE → DECEIT

2 Kgs	18:29	Do not let Hezekiah **d** you, for he
Prv	26:19	Such are those who **d** their neighbor,
Is	3:12	My people, your leaders **d** you,
Jer	37: 9	Do not **d** yourselves, saying:
Rom	16:18	flattering speech they **d** the hearts
1 Cor	3:18	Let no one **d** himself. If any one
Eph	5: 6	Let no one **d** you with empty
Col	2: 4	that no one may **d** you by specious
2 Thes	2: 3	Let no one **d** you in any way.
1 Jn	1: 8	are without sin," we **d** ourselves,
1 Jn	3: 7	Children, let no one **d** you.
Rev	20: 8	to **d** the nations at the four corners

DECEIVED → DECEIT

Dn	14: 7	"Do not be **d**, O king," he said;
Ob	1: 3	The pride of your heart has **d** you—
Jn	7:47	them, "Have you also been **d**?
Rom	7:11	**d** me and through it put me to death.
1 Cor	6: 9	Do not be **d**; neither fornicators nor
2 Cor	11: 3	as the serpent **d** Eve by his cunning,
1 Tm	2:14	Adam was not **d**, but the woman was **d** and transgressed.
2 Tm	3:13	from bad to worse, deceivers and **d**.
Jas	1:16	Do not be **d**, my beloved brothers:

DECEIVERS → DECEIT

Ti	1:10	idle talkers and **d**,
2 Jn	1: 7	Many **d** have gone

DECIDE → DECIDED, DECISION

Is	11: 3	he judge, nor by hearsay shall he **d**,
Acts	24:22	comes down, I shall **d** your case."

DECIDED → DECIDE

Lk	1: 3	I too have **d**, after investigating

DECISION → DECIDE

Lv	24:12	in custody till a **d** from the LORD
Nm	27:21	who will seek for him the **d** of the Urim
Prv	16:33	from the LORD comes every **d**.
Jl	4:14	of the LORD in the Valley of D.
Zep	3: 8	For it is my **d** to gather nations,

DECLARE → DECLARED

Lv	23: 4	holy days which you shall **d** at their proper time.
Jn	16:14	from what is mine and **d** it to you.

DECLARED → DECLARE

2 Kgs	17:23	just as he had **d** through all his servants,
Is	43: 9	Who among them could have **d** this, or announced
Mk	7:19	(Thus he **d** all foods clean.)

DECREASE

Ps	107:38	and their livestock did not **d**.
Jer	29: 6	Increase there; do not **d**.
Jn	3:30	He must increase; I must **d**."

DECREE → DECREED, DECREES

Ezr	5: 3	"Who issued the **d** for you to build
Est	3: 9	let a **d** be issued to destroy them;
1 Mc	1:57	was condemned to death by royal **d**.
Ps	2: 7	I will proclaim the **d** of the LORD,
Ps	81: 6	He made it a **d** for Joseph when he
Dn	2:13	When the **d** was issued that the wise
Lk	2: 1	In those days a **d** went
Rom	1:32	Although they know the just **d**

DECREED → DECREE

1 Kgs	22:23	LORD himself has **d** evil against
2 Kgs	24:13	house of the LORD, as the LORD had **d**.
Ps	122: 4	the LORD, As it was **d** for Israel,
Is	10:22	their destruction is **d**,
Dn	9:24	"Seventy weeks are **d** for your

DECREES → DECREE

2 Kgs	23: 3	and **d** with his whole heart and soul,
Is	10: 1	statutes, who write oppressive **d**,
Acts	17: 7	act in opposition to the **d** of Caesar

DEDICATED → DEDICATION

Nm	18: 6	**d** to the LORD for the labor they
1 Kgs	8:63	all the Israelites **d** the house

DEDICATION → DEDICATED

Nm	7:10	For the **d** of the altar also, the tribal
2 Chr	7: 9	they had celebrated the **d** of the altar
Ezr	6:16	celebrated the **d** of this house
Neh	12:27	At the **d** of the wall of Jerusalem,
1 Mc	4:56	eight days they celebrated the **d**
Dn	3: 2	be summoned to the **d** of the statue
Jn	10:22	The feast of the D was then taking

DEED → DO

Sir	3: 8	In word and **d** honor your father,
Jer	32:10	I had written and sealed the **d**,
Mk	6: 5	able to perform any mighty **d** there,
Lk	24:19	who was a prophet mighty in **d**
Col	3:17	in word or in **d**, do everything

DEEDS → DO

Dt	3:24	or on earth can perform **d**
Dt	11: 7	your own eyes all these great **d**
Ezr	9:13	that has come upon us for our evil **d**
Ps	9: 2	I will declare all your wondrous **d**.
Ps	26: 7	and recount all your wondrous **d**.
Ps	28: 4	Repay them for their **d**, for the evil
Ps	45: 5	right hand show your wondrous **d**.
Ps	65: 6	us with awesome **d** of justice,
Ps	66: 3	"How awesome your **d**!
Ps	71:17	day I proclaim your wondrous **d**.
Ps	75: 2	name, we declare your wonderful **d**.
Ps	77:12	I will recall the **d** of the LORD;
Ps	78: 4	The praiseworthy **d** of the LORD
Ps	145: 6	acts and recount your great **d**.
Prv	31:31	let her **d** praise her at the city gates.
Sir	16:12	people, each according to their **d**.
Is	63: 7	The loving **d** of the LORD I will
Is	63: 7	to his mercy and his many loving **d**.
Jer	50:29	Repay them for their **d**;
Lam	3:64	LORD, according to their **d**;
Hos	5: 4	Their **d** do not allow them to return
Mt	13:58	work many mighty **d** there because
Lk	10:13	the mighty **d** done in your midst had
Acts	2:22	to you by God with mighty **d**,
Rom	8:13	you put to death the **d** of the body,
1 Cor	12:28	then, mighty **d**; then,
Col	1:21	hostile in mind because of evil **d**
2 Tm	4:14	will repay him according to his **d**.
Rev	18: 6	Pay her back double for her **d**.
Rev	19: 8	linen represents the righteous **d**

DEEP → DEPTH, DEPTHS

Gn	2:21	So the LORD God cast a **d** sleep
Gn	15:12	to set, a **d** sleep fell upon Abram,
1 Sm	26:12	because a **d** slumber
Ps	36: 7	your judgments, like the mighty **d**;
Ps	42: 8	D calls to **d** in the roar of your
Prv	22:14	of the foreign woman is a **d** pit;
Prv	23:27	For the harlot is a **d** pit,
Is	7:11	let it be **d** as Sheol, or high as
Is	29:10	out on you a spirit of **d** sleep.
Ez	23:32	sister you shall drink, **d** and wide;
Dn	2:22	He reveals **d** and hidden things
Jon	2: 4	You cast me into the **d**,
Lk	5: 4	"Put out into **d** water and lower
Acts	20: 9	sinking into a **d** sleep as Paul talked
Rev	2:24	of the so-called **d** secrets of Satan:

DEER
Ps   42: 2 As the **d** longs for streams of water,

DEFEAT
Dt   7: 2 them over to you and you **d** them,

DEFECT
Nm   19: 2 for you a red heifer without **d**
Dt   15:21 But if a firstling has any **d,**
Dt   17: 1 an ox or a sheep with any serious **d;**
Dn   1: 4 should be young men without any **d,**

DEFEND → DEFENDED, DEFENSE, DEFENSES
Est   8:11 city to gather and **d** their lives,
Jb   13:15 I will **d** my conduct before him.
Ps   72: 4 he may **d** the oppressed among
Prv   31: 9 justly, **d** the needy and the poor!
Is   1:17 hear the orphan's plea, **d** the widow.
Is   1:23 The fatherless they do not **d,**
Jer   5:28 justice they do not **d** By advancing
Jer   51:36 I will certainly **d** your cause, I will

DEFENDED → DEFEND
Est   9:16 also mustered and **d** themselves,

DEFENSE → DEFEND
Ps   35:23 be vigilant in my **d,** in my cause,
Lk   21:14 not to prepare your **d** beforehand,
Acts   22: 1 I am about to say to you in my **d."**
Phil   1:16 I am here for the **d** of the gospel;

DEFENSES → DEFEND
Ps   60: 3 God, you rejected us, broke our **d;**

DEFERRED
Prv   13:12 Hope **d** makes the heart sick,

DEFILE → DEFILED, DEFILES
Nm   35:34 Do not **d** the land in which you live
Jdt   9: 8 **d** the tent where your glorious name
Ez   20: 7 do not **d** yourselves with the idols
Dn   1: 8 was resolved not to **d** himself
Mt   15:20 These are what **d** a person,
Mt   15:20 with unwashed hands does not **d."**
Mk   7:15 one from outside can **d** that person;
Mk   7:15 come out from within are what **d."**
Jude   1: 8 nevertheless also **d** the flesh,

DEFILED → DEFILE
Gn   34: 5 Shechem had **d** his daughter Dinah;
1 Mc   1:37 they **d** the sanctuary.
Ps   79: 1 they have **d** your holy temple;
Ez   22: 4 idols you made you have become **d.**
Ez   23:13 I saw that she had **d** herself—
Ez   39: 7 never again allow my holy name to be **d.**
Rev   14: 4 These are they who were not **d**

DEFILES → DEFILE
Mt   15:11 not what enters one's mouth that **d**
Mt   15:11 out of the mouth is what **d** one."

DEFRAUD
Mk   10:19 you shall not **d;** honor your father

DEFY
1 Sm   17:10 "I **d** the ranks of Israel today.

DEGENERATE
Dt   32: 5 Yet his **d** children have treated him

DEGRADING
Rom   1:26 handed them over to **d** passions.

DEITY
Col   2: 9 the whole fullness of the **d** bodily,

DELAY → DELAYED, DELAYS
Ps   40:18 my God, do not **d!**
Ps   70: 6 LORD, do not **d!**
Eccl   5: 3 a vow to God, **d** not its fulfillment.
Sir   35:22 God indeed will not **d,**
Dn   9:19 be attentive and act without **d,**
Heb   10:37 to come shall come; he shall not **d.**
Rev   10: 6 in them, "There shall be no more **d.**

DELAYED → DELAY
Mt   25: 5 Since the bridegroom was long **d,**
Lk   12:45 'My master is **d** in coming,'

DELAYS → DELAY
Hb   2: 3 If it **d,** wait for it, it will surely

DELICACIES
Prv   23: 3 Do not desire his **d;** it is food

DELIGHT → DELIGHTED, DELIGHTS
Dt   28:63 Just as the LORD once took **d**
Dt   28:63 so will the LORD now take **d**
Dt   30: 9 will again take **d** in your prosperity,
Dt   30: 9 just as he took **d** in your ancestors,
1 Sm   15:22 "Does the LORD **d** in burnt
Jb   22:26 then you shall **d** in the Almighty,
Ps   16: 3 they are noble, in whom is all my **d.**
Ps   37: 4 Find your **d** in the LORD who will
Ps   40: 9 I **d** to do your will, my God;
Ps   68:31 silver scatter the peoples that **d**
Ps   111: 2 the LORD, studied by all who **d** in them.
Ps   119:16 In your statutes I take **d;** I will never
Ps   119:24 Your testimonies are my **d;**
Ps   119:35 commandments, for that is my **d.**
Ps   119:47 I **d** in your commandments, which I
Ps   119:70 as for me, your law is my **d.**
Ps   119:77 I may live, for your law is my **d.**
Ps   119:92 Had your law not been my **d,**
Ps   119:143 me, your commandments are my **d.**
Ps   119:174 your law is my **d.**
Ps   147:10 He takes no **d** in the strength
Prv   2:14 Who **d** in doing evil and celebrate
Prv   8:30 I was his **d** day by day,
Prv   8:31 having my **d** with human beings.
Prv   11: 1 but an honest weight, his **d.**
Prv   29:17 comfort, and give **d** to your soul.
Sg   2: 3 In his shadow I **d** to sit, and his fruit
Sir   40:20 Wine and strong drink **d** the soul,
Is   11: 3 and his **d** shall be the fear
Is   13:17 of silver and take no **d** in gold.
Is   55: 2 eat well, you shall **d** in rich fare.
Is   58:13 If you call the sabbath a **d,**
Is   62: 4 But you shall be called "My **D** is
Is   65:18 to be a joy and its people to be a **d;**
Is   66:11 That you may drink with **d** at her
Jer   31:20 favored son, the child in whom I **d?**
Ez   24:16 away from you the **d** of your eyes,
Ez   24:21 of your strength, the **d** of your eyes,
Ez   24:25 glorious joy, the **d** of their eyes,
Zec   11: 7 I took two staffs: one I called **D,**
Mk   12:37 [The] great crowd heard this with **d.**
Rom   7:22 For I take **d** in the law of God,

DELIGHTED → DELIGHT
Jon   4: 6 Jonah was greatly **d** with the plant.

DELIGHTS → DELIGHT
Jb   27:10 If he **d** in the Almighty and calls
Ps   5: 5 You are not a god who **d** in evil;
Ps   35:27 "Exalted be the LORD who **d**
Ps   112: 1 who greatly **d** in his commands.
Sir   26:13 A gracious wife **d** her husband;
Mi   7:18 forever, but instead **d** in mercy,

DELILAH
Philistine who betrayed Samson (Jgs 16:4-22).

DELIVER → DELIVERANCE, DELIVERED, DELIVERER, DELIVERS
Ps   22: 9 let him **d** him; if he loves him,
Ps   89:49 can **d** his soul from the power of Sheol?
Is   50: 2 Have I not the strength to **d?**
Jer   1: 8 them, for I am with you to **d** you—
Mt   27:43 let him **d** him now if he wants him.

DELIVERANCE → DELIVER
Est   4:14 and **d** will come to the Jews
1 Mc   4:25 Thus Israel experienced a great **d**
Jon   2:10 I will pay: **d** is from the LORD.
Phil   1:19 this will result in **d** for me through

DELIVERED → DELIVER
1 Mc	2:60	was **d** from the mouths of lions.
Ps	33:16	nor a warrior **d** by great strength.
Ps	34: 5	me, **d** me from all my fears.
Dn	3:88	For he has **d** us from Sheol,
Dn	3:88	raging flame and **d** us from the fire.

DELIVERER → DELIVER
2 Sm	22: 2	my rock, my fortress, my **d**,
Ps	18: 3	my fortress, my **d**, My God,
Ps	40:18	You are my help and **d**; my God,
Ps	70: 6	You are my help and **d**.
Ps	144: 2	my stronghold, my **d**, My shield,
Rom	11:26	"The **d** will come out of Zion,

DELIVERS → DELIVER
Ps	41: 2	of misfortune, the LORD **d** him.

DEMAND → DEMANDED, DEMANDING
1 Cor	1:22	For Jews **d** signs and Greeks look

DEMANDED → DEMAND
Lk	12:20	this night your life will be **d** of you;
Lk	12:48	still more will be **d** of the person
Lk	22:31	behold Satan has **d** to sift all of you

DEMANDING → DEMAND
Ps	78:18	their hearts, **d** the food they craved.

DEMAS
Associate of Paul (Col 4:14; 2 Tm 4:10; Phlm 24).

DEMETRIUS
1 Mc	10: 2	When King **D** heard of it,
Acts	19:24	a silversmith named **D** who made
3 Jn	1:12	**D** receives a good report from all,

DEMOLISH
Nm	33:52	images, and **d** all their high places.

DEMON → DEMONIAC, DEMONIACS, DEMONIC, DEMONS
Tb	3: 8	the wicked **d** Asmodeus kept killing
Tb	3:17	rid her of the wicked **d** Asmodeus.
Tb	6: 8	a woman who is afflicted by a **d**
Tb	6:14	said that it was a **d** that killed them.
Tb	6:16	do not worry about that **d**.
Tb	6:18	As soon as the **d** smells the odor,
Tb	8: 3	The odor of the fish repulsed the **d**,
Mt	9:33	when the **d** was driven out the mute
Mt	11:18	they said, 'He is possessed by a **d**.'
Mt	15:22	My daughter is tormented by a **d**."
Mt	17:18	him and the **d** came out of him,
Mk	7:26	she begged him to drive the **d**
Mk	7:29	The **d** has gone out of your
Mk	7:30	child lying in bed and the **d** gone.
Lk	4:33	man with the spirit of an unclean **d**,
Lk	4:35	the **d** threw the man down in front
Lk	7:33	you said, 'He is possessed by a **d**.'
Lk	8:29	by the **d** into deserted places.)
Lk	9:42	the **d** threw him to the ground
Lk	11:14	was driving out a **d** [that was] mute,
Jn	10:21	surely a **d** cannot open the eyes

DEMONIAC → DEMON
Mt	9:32	out, a **d** who could not speak was
Mt	12:22	brought to him a **d** who was blind

DEMONIACS → DEMON
Mt	8:28	two **d** who were coming
Mt	8:33	what had happened to the **d**.

DEMONIC → DEMON
Rev	16:14	These were **d** spirits who performed

DEMONS → DEMON
Dt	32:17	They sacrificed to **d**, to "no-gods,"
Bar	4: 7	your Maker with sacrifices to **d**
Bar	4:35	to be inhabited by **d** for a long time.
Mt	7:22	Did we not drive out **d** in your
Mt	8:16	many who were possessed by **d**,
Mt	8:31	The **d** pleaded with him, "If you
Mt	9:34	drives out **d** by the prince of **d**."
Mt	10: 8	the dead, cleanse lepers, drive out **d**.
Mt	12:24	"This man drives out **d** only

Mt	12:24	of Beelzebul, the prince of **d**."
Mt	12:27	And if I drive out **d** by Beelzebul,
Mt	12:28	the Spirit of God that I drive out **d**,
Mk	1:32	all who were ill or possessed by **d**.
Mk	1:34	and he drove out many **d**,
Mk	1:39	driving out **d** throughout the whole
Mk	3:15	and to have authority to drive out **d**:
Mk	3:22	the prince of **d** he drives out **d**."
Mk	6:13	They drove out many **d**, and they
Mk	9:38	we saw someone driving out **d**
Mk	16: 9	out of whom he had driven seven **d**.
Mk	16:17	in my name they will drive out **d**,
Lk	4:41	And **d** also came out from many,
Lk	8: 2	from whom seven **d** had gone out,
Lk	8:27	who was possessed by **d** met him.
Lk	8:30	because many **d** had entered him.
Lk	8:33	The **d** came out of the man
Lk	8:35	the man from whom the **d** had come
Lk	8:38	man from whom the **d** had come
Lk	9: 1	and authority over all **d** and to cure
Lk	9:49	we saw someone casting out **d**
Lk	10:17	even the **d** are subject to us because
Lk	11:15	the prince of **d**, he drives out **d**."
Lk	11:18	it is by Beelzebul that I drive out **d**.
Lk	11:19	I, then, drive out **d** by Beelzebul,
Lk	11:20	finger of God that [I] drive out **d**,
Lk	13:32	I cast out **d** and I perform healings
1 Cor	10:20	[they sacrifice] to **d**, not to God,
1 Cor	10:20	you to become participants with **d**.
1 Cor	10:21	of the Lord and also the cup of **d**.
Jas	2:19	Even the **d** believe that and tremble.
Rev	9:20	to give up the worship of **d**
Rev	18: 2	She has become a haunt for **d**.

DEMONSTRATION
1 Cor	2: 4	but with a **d** of spirit and power,

DEN
Is	11: 8	The baby shall play by the viper's **d**,
Jer	7:11	become in your eyes a **d** of thieves?
Dn	6: 8	shall be thrown into a **d** of lions.
Dn	14:31	They threw Daniel into a lions' **d**,
Na	2:12	Where is the lionesses' **d**, the young
Mt	21:13	you are making it a **d** of thieves."
Mk	11:17	you have made it a **d** of thieves."
Lk	19:46	prayer, but you have made it a **d**

DENARIUS
Mk	12:15	Bring me a **d** to look at."
Lk	20:24	"Show me a **d**; whose image

DENIED → DENY
Mt	26:70	But he **d** it in front of everyone,
Jn	18:25	He **d** it and said, "I am not."
1 Tm	5: 8	family members has **d** the faith
Rev	3: 8	my word and have not **d** my name.

DENIES → DENY
Mt	10:33	But whoever **d** me before others,
Lk	12: 9	whoever **d** me before others will be
1 Jn	2:22	Whoever **d** that Jesus is the Christ.
1 Jn	2:22	Whoever **d** the Father and the Son,
1 Jn	2:23	No one who **d** the Son has

DENOUNCE → DENOUNCED
Nm	23: 7	curse for me Jacob, come, **d** Israel."

DENOUNCED → DENOUNCE
Nm	23: 8	one whom the LORD has not **d**?

DENY → DENIED, DENIES, DENYING
Sir	14: 4	What they **d** themselves they collect for
Mt	16:24	to come after me must **d** himself,
Mt	26:34	crows, you will **d** me three times."
Mk	8:34	to come after me must **d** himself,
Lk	9:23	he must **d** himself and take up his
Acts	4:16	through them, and we cannot **d** it.
2 Tm	2:12	But if we **d** him he will **d** us.
2 Tm	2:13	faithful, for he cannot **d** himself.
Ti	1:16	God, but by their deeds they **d** him.
2 Pt	2: 1	even **d** the Master who ransomed

Jude 1: 4 and who **d** our only Master

DENYING → DENY
Is 59:13 and **d** the LORD, turning back

DEPART → DEPARTED, DEPARTURE
Gn 49:10 The scepter shall never **d**
2 Sm 12:10 the sword shall never **d** from your
Is 52:11 D, **d**, go out from there,
Mt 25:41 say to those on his left, 'D from me,
Phil 1:23 I long to **d** this life and be

DEPARTED → DEPART
1 Sm 16:14 of the LORD had **d** from Saul,

DEPARTURE → DEPART
2 Tm 4: 6 and the time of my **d** is at hand.
2 Pt 1:15 remember these things after my **d**.

DEPEND → DEPENDS
Jdt 9:11 nor does your might **d**

DEPENDS → DEPEND
Rom 4:16 For this reason, it **d** on faith,
Rom 9:16 So it **d** not upon a person's will

DEPRAVED → DEPRAVITY
2 Pt 2:10 follow the flesh with its **d** desire

DEPRAVITY → DEPRAVED
Ez 16:58 The penalty of your **d** and your abominations—
Ez 23:48 Thus I will put an end to **d** in the land,
Ez 23:48 women will be warned not to imitate your **d**.

DEPRIVE
1 Cor 7: 5 Do not **d** each other, except perhaps

DEPTH → DEEP
Rom 8:39 nor **d**, nor any other creature will be
Rom 11:33 the **d** of the riches and wisdom
Eph 3:18 breadth and length and height and **d**,

DEPTHS → DEEP
Ex 15: 5 they sank into the **d** like a stone.
Ps 86:13 rescued me from the **d** of Sheol.
Ps 130: 1 Out of the **d** I call to you, LORD;
Prv 9:18 that her guests are in the **d** of Sheol!
1 Cor 2:10 everything, even the **d** of God.

DESCENDANT → DESCENDANTS, DESCENDED, DESCENDING
Lv 21:21 No **d** of Aaron the priest who has
2 Tm 2: 8 raised from the dead, a **d** of David:

DESCENDANTS → DESCENDANT
Gn 9: 9 with you and your **d** after you
Gn 15:18 To your **d** I give this land,
Ex 28:43 ordinance for him and for his **d**.
Dt 4:37 your ancestors he chose their **d**
Ps 112: 2 His **d** shall be mighty in the land,
Is 44: 3 offspring, my blessing upon your **d**.
Lk 1:55 to Abraham and to his **d** forever."
Acts 2:30 set one of his **d** upon his throne,
Rom 9: 7 of Abraham because they are his **d**;

DESCENDED → DESCENDANT
Lk 3:22 the holy Spirit **d** upon him in bodily
Rom 1: 3 **d** from David according to the flesh,
Eph 4: 9 also **d** into the lower [regions]

DESCENDING → DESCENDANT
Mt 3:16 saw the Spirit of God **d** like a dove
Mk 1:10 the Spirit, like a dove, **d** upon him.
Jn 1:51 and **d** on the Son of Man."

DESERT → DESERTED, DESERTS
Dt 32:10 a wasteland of howling **d**.
Ps 78:17 against the Most High in the **d**.
Ps 106:14 In the **d** they gave in to their

DESERTED → DESERT
Mk 8: 4 satisfy them here in this **d** place?"
2 Tm 4:10 **d** me and went to Thessalonica,

DESERTS → DESERT
Heb 11:38 They wandered about in **d**

DESERVE → DESERVED, DESERVES, DESERVING
1 Sm 26:16 you people **d** death because you

1 Kgs 2:26 Though you **d** to die, I will not put
Ps 94: 2 give the proud what they **d**!
Jer 26:16 man does not **d** a death sentence;
Rom 1:32 all who practice such things **d** death,
Rev 2:23 give each of you what your works **d**.
Rev 16: 6 blood to drink; it is what they **d**."

DESERVED → DESERVE
Ezr 9:13 made less of our sinfulness than it **d**

DESERVES → DESERVE
Dt 25: 2 if the one in the wrong **d** whipping,
Mt 26:66 They said in reply, "He **d** to die!"
Lk 10: 7 you, for the laborer **d** his payment.
Acts 26:31 is doing nothing [at all] that **d** death
1 Tm 5:18 and, "A worker **d** his pay."

DESERVING → DESERVE
Mk 14:64 They all condemned him as **d** to die.
Acts 23:29 law and not of any charge **d** death
Acts 25:25 that he had done nothing **d** death,

DESIRE → DESIRED, DESIRES
Dt 5:21 You shall not **d** your neighbor's
2 Sm 23: 5 all my salvation and my every **d**?
Ps 21: 3 You have granted him his heart's **d**;
Ps 40:15 in disgrace those who **d** my ruin.
Ps 70: 3 Let those who **d** my ruin turn back
Prv 10:24 but the **d** of the just will be granted.
Prv 11:23 The **d** of the just ends only in good;
Prv 24: 1 the wicked, nor **d** to be with them;
Sir 6:37 mind, and make you wise as you **d**.
Is 26: 8 your memory are the **d** of our souls.
Hos 6: 6 For it is loyalty that I **d**,
Mt 9:13 meaning of the words, 'I **d** mercy,
Mt 12: 7 knew what this meant, 'I **d** mercy,
Rom 10: 1 my heart's **d** and prayer to God
Heb 11:16 But now they **d** a better homeland,
Jas 1:14 is lured and enticed by his own **d**.
Jas 1:15 Then **d** conceives and brings forth

DESIRED → DESIRE
Eccl 2:10 that my eyes **d** did I deny them,
Lk 22:15 them, "I have eagerly **d** to eat this

DESIRES → DESIRE
Ps 140: 9 do not grant the **d** of the wicked
Sir 18:30 guide, but keep your **d** in check.
Lk 5:39 has been drinking old wine **d** new,
Jn 8:44 willingly carry out your father's **d**.
Rom 13:14 no provision for the **d** of the flesh,
Eph 2: 3 among them in the **d** of our flesh,
1 Tm 3: 1 the office of bishop **d** a noble task.
1 Tm 6: 9 into many foolish and harmful **d**,
2 Tm 3: 6 down by sins, led by various **d**,
2 Tm 4: 3 following their own **d** and insatiable
1 Pt 1:14 with the **d** of your former ignorance
1 Pt 2:11 worldly **d** that wage war against
1 Pt 4: 2 one's life in the flesh on human **d**,
2 Pt 2:18 licentious **d** of the flesh those who

DESOLATE → DESOLATING, DESOLATION
Ex 23:29 lest the land become **d** and the wild
1 Mc 1:39 Her sanctuary became **d** as
1 Mc 4:38 They found the sanctuary **d**,
Mt 23:38 your house will be abandoned, **d**.
Rev 17:16 they will leave her **d** and naked;

DESOLATING → DESOLATE
Mt 24:15 you see the **d** abomination spoken
Mk 13:14 you see the **d** abomination standing

DESOLATION → DESOLATE
Na 2:11 Emptiness, **d**, waste;
Lk 21:20 armies, know that its **d** is at hand.

DESPAIR → DESPAIRED
Jdt 9:11 protector of those in **d**, savior of
2 Cor 4: 8 perplexed, but not driven to **d**;

DESPAIRED → DESPAIR
2 Cor 1: 8 strength, so that we **d** even of life.

DESPISE → DESPISED, DESPISING
Ex	22:27	shall not **d** God, nor curse a leader
Prv	1: 7	fools **d** wisdom and discipline.
Prv	23:22	do not **d** your mother when she is
Mt	6:24	be devoted to one and **d** the other.
Lk	16:13	be devoted to one and **d** the other.

DESPISED → DESPISE
2 Sm	6:16	the LORD, she **d** him in her heart.
Ps	22: 7	scorned by men, **d** by the people.
Ps	106:24	Next they **d** the beautiful land;
Prv	12: 8	but the perverse of heart are **d**.
Eccl	9:16	yet the wisdom of the poor man is **d**
1 Cor	1:28	chose the lowly and **d** of the world,

DESPISING → DESPISE
Dt	31:20	**d** me and breaking my covenant,

DESTINE → DESTINED, DESTINY
Is	65:12	You I will **d** for the sword;

DESTINED → DESTINE
Lk	2:34	this child is **d** for the fall and rise
Acts	13:48	All who were **d** for eternal life came
Eph	1: 5	he **d** us for adoption to himself
Eph	1:11	**d** in accord with the purpose
1 Thes	3: 3	know that we are **d** for this.
1 Pt	1:11	to the sufferings **d** for Christ

DESTINY → DESTINE
Ps	31:16	My **d** is in your hands; rescue me
Is	65:11	and fill cups of mixed wine for **D**,

DESTITUTE
Prv	31: 8	the mute, and for the rights of the **d**;

DESTROY → DESTROYED, DESTROYER, DESTROYING, DESTROYS, DESTRUCTION, DESTRUCTIVE
Gn	6:13	So I am going to **d** them
Gn	18:28	Will you **d** the whole city because
Gn	18:28	I will not **d** it, he answered, if I find
Dt	6:15	and he **d** you from upon the land.
2 Kgs	8:19	LORD was unwilling to **d** Judah.
2 Kgs	13:23	He was unwilling to **d** them
1 Chr	21:15	sent an angel to Jerusalem to **d** it;
Est	3: 6	he sought to **d** all the Jews,
Is	65:25	harm or **d** on all my holy mountain,
Jer	1:10	to tear down, to **d** and to demolish,
Hos	11: 9	anger, I will not **d** Ephraim again;
Mt	2:13	to search for the child to **d** him."
Mt	10:28	of the one who can **d** both soul
Mk	14:58	say, 'I will **d** this temple made
Lk	4:34	Have you come to **d** us?
Jn	10:10	only to steal and slaughter and **d**;
1 Cor	1:19	"I will **d** the wisdom of the wise,
1 Cor	3:17	temple, God will **d** that person;
Jas	4:12	judge who is able to save or to **d**.
1 Jn	3: 8	God was revealed to **d** the works
Rev	11:18	and to **d** those who **d** the earth."

DESTROYED → DESTROY
Gn	9:11	never again shall all creatures be **d**
Gn	19:29	When God **d** the cities of the Plain,
Dt	28:20	until you are speedily **d** and perish
Jos	24: 8	land, and I **d** them at your approach.
1 Mc	1:30	and **d** many of the people in Israel.
Ps	37:38	Sinners will be **d** together;
Dn	2:44	up a kingdom that shall never be **d**
Dn	6:27	whose kingdom shall not be **d**,
Dn	14:28	"he has **d** Bel, killed the dragon,
Lk	17:27	and the flood came and **d** them all.
1 Cor	15:24	when he has **d** every sovereignty
1 Cor	15:26	The last enemy to be **d** is death,
2 Cor	4: 9	struck down, but not **d**;
2 Cor	5: 1	should be **d**, we have a building
2 Pt	2:12	their destruction they will also be **d**,
Jude	1: 5	of Egypt later **d** those who did not

DESTROYER → DESTROY
Ex	12:23	not let the **d** come into your houses
Jer	6:26	"How suddenly the **d** comes

1 Cor	10:10	did, and suffered death by the **d**.
Heb	11:28	that the **D** of the firstborn might not

DESTROYING → DESTROY
Ps	106:23	the breach to turn back his **d** anger.

DESTROYS → DESTROY
Ps	145:20	love him, but all the wicked he **d**.
Prv	1:32	them, the smugness of fools **d** them.
1 Cor	3:17	If anyone **d** God's temple, God will

DESTRUCTION → DESTROY
Sir	36:11	and your people's oppressors meet **d**.
Is	10:22	their **d** is decreed, as overflowing
Is	13: 6	as **d** from the Almighty it comes.
Is	14:23	I will sweep it with the broom of **d**,
Hb	2:17	and the **d** of the animals shall terrify
Mt	7:13	and the road broad that leads to **d**,
Rom	9:22	the vessels of wrath made for **d**?
1 Cor	5: 5	man to Satan for the **d** of his flesh,
Phil	1:28	This is proof to them of **d**,
Phil	3:19	Their end is **d**. Their God is their
1 Tm	6: 9	which plunge them into ruin and **d**.
2 Pt	2: 1	bringing swift **d** on themselves.
2 Pt	2: 3	been idle and their **d** does not sleep.
2 Pt	3: 7	of judgment and of **d** of the godless.
2 Pt	3:16	and unstable distort to their own **d**,
Rev	17: 8	from the abyss and is headed for **d**.
Rev	17:11	to the seven and is headed for **d**.

DESTRUCTIVE → DESTROY
2 Pt	2: 1	who will introduce **d** heresies

DETAIL
Heb	9: 5	not the time to speak of these in **d**.

DETERMINED
Ru	1:18	for she saw she was **d** to go
Jb	38: 5	Who **d** its size? Surely you know?
Dn	11:36	for what is **d** must take place.

DEVIATED
1 Tm	1: 6	Some people have **d** from these

DEVIL
Wis	2:24	But by the envy of the **d**,
Mt	4: 1	the desert to be tempted by the **d**.
Mt	4: 5	the **d** took him to the holy city,
Mt	4: 8	the **d** took him up to a very high
Mt	4:11	Then the **d** left him and, behold,
Mt	13:39	the enemy who sows them is the **d**.
Mt	25:41	the eternal fire prepared for the **d**
Lk	4: 2	forty days, to be tempted by the **d**.
Lk	4: 3	The **d** said to him, "If you are
Lk	4: 6	The **d** said to him, "I shall give
Lk	4:13	the **d** had finished every temptation,
Lk	8:12	but the **d** comes and takes away
Jn	6:70	Yet is not one of you a **d**?"
Jn	8:44	You belong to your father the **d**
Jn	13: 2	The **d** had already induced Judas,
Acts	10:38	healing all those oppressed by the **d**,
Acts	13:10	"You son of the **d**, you enemy of all
Eph	4:27	and do not leave room for the **d**.
Eph	6:11	firm against the tactics of the **d**.
Heb	2:14	the power of death, that is, the **d**,
Jas	4: 7	Resist the **d**, and he will flee
1 Pt	5: 8	Your opponent the **d** is prowling
1 Jn	3: 8	Whoever sins belongs to the **d**, because the **d** has sinned
1 Jn	3: 8	to destroy the works of the **d**.
1 Jn	3:10	the children of the **d** are made plain;
Jude	1: 9	with the **d** in a dispute over the body
Rev	2:10	the **d** will throw some of you
Rev	12: 9	who is called the **D** and Satan,
Rev	12:12	for the **D** has come down to you
Rev	20: 2	serpent, which is the **D** or Satan,
Rev	20:10	The **D** who had led them astray was

DEVIOUS
Prv	3:32	To the LORD the **d** are an abomination,
Prv	2:15	are crooked, whose paths are **d**;
Prv	14: 2	those who are **d** in their ways spurn

DEVISED
2 Pt   1:16   We did not follow cleverly **d** myths

DEVOID
Jude   1:19   on the natural plane, **d** of the Spirit.

DEVOTE → DEVOTED, DEVOTION
Mi   4:13   You shall **d** their spoils
Ti   3: 8   in God be careful to **d** themselves
Ti   3:14   learn to **d** themselves to good works

DEVOTED → DEVOTE
1 Mc   4:42   blameless priests, **d** to the law;
Ps   52:11   good,—in the presence of those **d** to you.
Ps   79: 2   those **d** to you for the beasts of the earth.
Ps   116:15   eyes of the LORD is the death of his **d**.
Mt   6:24   or be **d** to one and despise the other.
Acts   2:42   They **d** themselves to the teaching
1 Cor   16:15   that they have **d** themselves

DEVOTION → DEVOTE
Jer   2: 2   I remember the **d** of your youth,

DEVOUR → DEVOURED, DEVOURING, DEVOURS
2 Chr   7:13   I command the locust to **d** the land,
Dn   14:32   so that they would **d** Daniel.
Hos   13: 8   I will **d** them on the spot like a lion,
Mk   12:40   They **d** the houses of widows and,
1 Pt   5: 8   lion looking for [someone] to **d**.
Rev   12: 4   to **d** her child when she gave birth.

DEVOURED → DEVOUR
Gn   37:20   could say that a wild beast **d** him.
Gn   41: 4   gaunt cows **d** the seven fine-looking, fat cows.
1 Kgs   18:38   fire came down and **d** the burnt offering,
Jer   30:16   Yet all who devour you shall be **d**,

DEVOURING → DEVOUR
Ps   18: 9   his nostrils, a **d** fire from his mouth;
Ps   50: 3   **D** fire precedes him, it rages
Gal   5:15   you go on biting and **d** one another,

DEVOURS → DEVOUR
2 Sm   11:25   for the sword **d** now here and now
Jer   46:10   The sword **d** and is sated,

DEVOUT
Jdt   8:31   But now, since you are a **d** woman,
Ps   16:10   Sheol, nor let your **d** one see the pit.
Ps   132: 9   with justice; your **d** will shout for joy."
Ps   132:16   with salvation; its **d** shall shout for joy.
Lk   2:25   This man was righteous and **d**,
Acts   10: 2   **d** and God-fearing along with his
Acts   10: 7   and a **d** soldier from his staff,
Acts   22:12   Ananias, a **d** observer of the law,

DEW
Gn   27:28   give to you of the **d** of the heavens
Ex   16:13   morning there was a layer of **d** all
Dt   32: 2   and my utterance drench like the **d**,
Jgs   6:37   and if **d** is on the fleece alone,
2 Sm   1:21   upon you be neither **d** nor rain,
Jb   38:28   Who has begotten the drops of **d**?
Prv   19:12   but his favor, like **d** on the grass.
Is   26:19   For your **d** is a **d** of light,
Dn   3:64   Every shower and **d**, bless the Lord;
Hos   6: 4   like the **d** that disappears early.
Hos   14: 6   I will be like the **d** for Israel:
Hg   1:10   the heavens withheld the **d**,
Zec   8:12   and the heavens will yield their **d**.

DIADEM → DIADEMS
Ex   39:30   The plate of the sacred **d** was made
Is   62: 3   a royal **d** in the hand of your God.

DIADEMS → DIADEM
Rev   12: 3   and on its heads were seven **d**.
Rev   13: 1   on its horns were ten **d**, and on its
Rev   19:12   and on his head were many **d**.

DICTATE
Jer   36:18   "Yes, he would **d** all these words to me,"

DIE → DEAD
Gn   2:17   when you eat from it you shall **d**.
Gn   3: 3   touch it, or else you will **d**.' "
Gn   3: 4   "You certainly will not **d**!
Ex   11: 5   firstborn in the land of Egypt will **d**,
Ex   14:11   that you brought us to **d**
Nm   23:10   May I **d** the death of the just,
Ru   1:17   Where you **d** I will **d**, and there be
Tb   3: 6   It is better for me to **d** than to live,
Jb   2: 9   Curse God and **d**!"
Jb   12: 2   people with whom wisdom shall **d**!
Ps   118:17   I shall not **d** but live and declare
Prv   5:23   They will **d** from lack of discipline.
Prv   10:21   many, but fools **d** for want of sense.
Prv   15:10   one who hates reproof will **d**.
Prv   23:13   them with the rod, they will not **d**.
Eccl   3: 2   A time to give birth, and a time to **d**;
Sir   40:28   of a beggar; better to **d** than to beg.
Is   22:13   and drink, for tomorrow we **d**!"
Is   66:24   For their worm shall not **d**, their fire
Jer   31:30   but all shall **d** because of their own
Ez   3:18   then they shall **d** for their sin, but I
Ez   18: 4   Only the one who sins shall **d**!
Ez   18:31   Why should you **d**, house of Israel?
Ez   33: 8   their ways, they shall **d** in their sins,
Jon   4: 3   it is better for me to **d** than to live."
Mt   26:35   "Even though I should have to **d**
Jn   6:50   so that one may eat it and not **d**.
Jn   8:21   for me, but you will **d** in your sin.
Jn   11:26   and believes in me will never **d**.
Jn   11:50   that one man should **d** instead
Jn   12:33   the kind of death he would **d**.
Jn   18:14   one man should **d** rather than
Jn   21:23   that that disciple would not **d**.
Rom   5: 7   one might even find courage to **d**.
Rom   14: 8   and if we **d**, we **d** for the Lord;
1 Cor   15:22   For just as in Adam all **d**, so too
1 Cor   15:32   eat and drink, for tomorrow we **d**."
Heb   9:27   that human beings **d** once,
Rev   9: 6   they will long to **d** but death will
Rev   14:13   Blessed are the dead who **d**

DIED → DEAD
Nm   14: 2   "If only we had **d** in the land
Nm   17:14   to those who **d** because of Korah.
2 Sm   24:15   seventy thousand of the people **d**.
1 Kgs   3:19   This woman's son **d** during
1 Chr   10:13   Thus Saul **d** because of his treason
Lk   16:22   When the poor man **d**, he was
Lk   16:22   The rich man also **d** and was buried,
Jn   6:58   your ancestors who ate and still **d**,
Rom   5: 6   yet **d** at the appointed time
Rom   5: 8   while we were still sinners Christ **d**
Rom   6: 2   How can we who **d** to sin yet live
Rom   6: 8   If, then, we have **d** with Christ,
Rom   6:10   death, he **d** to sin once and for all;
Rom   14: 9   For this is why Christ **d** and came
1 Cor   8:11   the brother for whom Christ **d**.
1 Cor   15: 3   that Christ **d** for our sins
2 Cor   5:15   He indeed **d** for all, so that those
2 Cor   5:15   but for him who for their sake **d**
Gal   2:19   For through the law I **d** to the law,
Col   2:20   If you **d** with Christ to the elemental
Col   3: 3   For you have **d**, and your life is
1 Thes   4:14   For if we believe that Jesus **d**
1 Thes   5:10   who **d** for us, so that whether we are
2 Tm   2:11   If we have **d** with him we shall
Heb   11:13   All these **d** in faith. They did not
Rev   8: 9   of the creatures living in the sea **d**,
Rev   8:11   Many people **d** from this water,
Rev   16: 3   every creature living in the sea **d**.

DIES → DEAD
Dt   25: 5   and one of them **d** without a son,
Eccl   2:16   that the wise person **d** like the fool!
Eccl   3:19   The one **d** as well as the other.
Sir   8: 7   Do not rejoice when someone **d**;

Sir 14:18 one **d** and another flourishes.
Mt 22:24 'If a man **d** without children,
Jn 12:24 of wheat falls to the ground and **d**,
Jn 12:24 but if it **d**, it produces much fruit.
Rom 7: 2 but if her husband **d**, she is released
1 Cor 7:39 But if her husband **d**, she is free
1 Cor 15:36 sow is not brought to life unless it **d**.

DIFFER → DIFFERED, DIFFERENCE, DIFFERENT, DIFFERS
Rom 12: 6 Since we have gifts that **d** according

DIFFERED → DIFFER
Dn 7: 7 It **d** from the beasts that preceded it.

DIFFERENCE → DIFFER
Ez 22:26 nor teach the **d** between unclean
Ez 44:23 known to them the **d** between clean

DIFFERENT → DIFFER
Lv 19:19 animals with others of a **d** species;
Lv 19:19 of yours with two **d** kinds of seed;
Lv 19:19 a garment woven with two **d** kinds
Nm 14:24 Caleb, because he has a **d** spirit
Dn 7: 3 beasts, each **d** from the others.
Dn 7:19 very terrible and **d** from the others,
Dn 7:23 on earth, **d** from all the others;
Dn 7:24 them, **D** from those before him,
2 Cor 11: 4 if you receive a **d** spirit from the one
2 Cor 11: 4 or a **d** gospel from the one you
Gal 1: 6 [the] grace [of Christ] for a **d** gospel

DIFFERS → DIFFER
1 Cor 15:41 For star **d** from star in brightness.

DIFFICULT
Ez 3: 5 and **d** language am I sending you,
Dn 2:11 What you demand, O king, is too **d**;

DIG → DIGS, DUG
Ez 8: 8 man, he ordered, **d** through the wall.

DIGNITY
Prv 31:25 She is clothed with strength and **d**,
1 Tm 2: 2 tranquil life in all devotion and **d**.

DIGS → DIG
Ex 21:33 someone uncovers or **d** a cistern
Prv 26:27 Whoever **d** a pit falls into it;
Eccl 10: 8 Whoever **d** a pit may fall into it,
Sir 27:26 Whoever **d** a pit falls into it,

DILIGENCE → DILIGENT
Rom 12: 8 if one is over others, with **d**;

DILIGENT → DILIGENCE, DILIGENTLY
Prv 12:24 The **d** hand will govern, but sloth
Prv 12:27 but the wealth of the **d** is splendid.
Prv 13: 4 appetite of the **d** is amply satisfied.
Prv 21: 5 The plans of the **d** end in profit,

DILIGENTLY → DILIGENT
Mt 2: 8 "Go and search **d** for the child.

DIM
Gn 48:10 Now Israel's eyes were **d** from age;
Lam 5:17 grow sick, at this our eyes grow **d**:

DINAH
Only daughter of Jacob, by Leah (Gn 30:21; 46:15). Raped by Shechem; avenged by Simeon and Levi (Gn 34).

DINE → DINNER
Lk 11:37 a Pharisee invited him to **d** at his

DINNER → DINE
Lk 14:12 "When you hold a lunch or a **d**,

DIONYSIUS
Acts 17:34 Among them were **D**, a member

DIONYSUS
2 Mc 6: 7 the festival of **D** was celebrated,
2 Mc 14:33 erect here a splendid temple to **D**."

DIOTREPHES
3 Jn 1: 9 but **D**, who loves to dominate,

DIP → DIPPED
Lk 16:24 Send Lazarus to **d** the tip of his

DIPPED → DIP
Gn 37:31 a goat, **d** the tunic in its blood.
Mt 26:23 "He who has **d** his hand
Rev 19:13 a cloak that had been **d** in blood,

DIRECT → DIRECTED, DIRECTIONS, DIRECTS
Jdt 12: 8 to **d** her way for the triumph of her
2 Thes 3: 5 May the Lord **d** your hearts

DIRECTED → DIRECT
Is 40:13 Who has **d** the spirit of the LORD,
Acts 7:44 the One who spoke to Moses **d** him
Ti 1: 5 presbyters in every town, as I **d** you,

DIRECTIONS → DIRECT
Ez 1:17 of the four **d** without veering as they
Ez 10:11 of the four **d** without veering as they

DIRECTS → DIRECT
Prv 16: 9 the way, but the LORD **d** the steps.
Jer 10:23 their course nor **d** their own step.

DIRT
2 Sm 1: 2 torn and his head covered with **d**.
1 Pt 3:21 It is not a removal of **d**

DISAGREEMENT
Acts 15:39 So sharp was their **d** that they

DISAPPEAR → DISAPPEARING
Ps 37:20 fattened lambs; like smoke they **d**.

DISAPPEARING → DISAPPEAR
Heb 8:13 and has grown old is close to **d**.

DISAPPOINT → DISAPPOINTED
Rom 5: 5 and hope does not **d**,

DISAPPOINTED → DISAPPOINT
Sir 2:10 trusted in the Lord and been **d**?

DISCERN → DISCERNING, DISCERNMENT
Jb 6:30 or cannot my taste **d** falsehood?

DISCERNING → DISCERN
Gn 41:33 let Pharaoh seek out a **d** and wise
Gn 41:39 there is no one as **d** and wise as you
1 Cor 11:29 eats and drinks without **d** the body,

DISCERNMENT → DISCERN
Prv 16:21 The wise of heart is esteemed for **d**,
1 Cor 12:10 to another **d** of spirits;

DISCIPLE → DISCIPLES, DISCIPLES'
Mt 10:24 No **d** is above his teacher, no slave
Lk 14:26 his own life, he cannot be my **d**.
Lk 14:27 and come after me cannot be my **d**.
Lk 14:33 all his possessions cannot be my **d**.
Jn 9:28 and said, "You are that man's **d**;
Jn 19:26 and the **d** there whom he loved,
Jn 19:38 secretly a **d** of Jesus for fear
Jn 20: 2 to the other **d** whom Jesus loved,
Jn 21: 7 So the **d** whom Jesus loved said
Jn 21:20 saw the **d** following whom Jesus
Jn 21:24 It is this **d** who testifies to these
Acts 9:10 There was a **d** in Damascus named
Acts 16: 1 there was a **d** named Timothy,

DISCIPLES → DISCIPLE
Is 8:16 seal the instruction with my **d**.
Mt 9:10 came and sat with Jesus and his **d**.
Mt 10: 1 he summoned his twelve **d** and gave
Mt 12: 2 your **d** are doing what is unlawful
Mt 26:56 Then all the **d** left him and fled.
Mt 28:19 and make **d** of all nations,
Mk 3: 7 withdrew toward the sea with his **d**.
Mk 6:29 When his **d** heard about it,
Mk 7: 5 him, "Why do your **d** not follow
Mk 9:18 I asked your **d** to drive it out,
Mk 14:14 eat the Passover with my **d**?" '
Lk 6:13 day came, he called his **d** to himself,
Lk 11: 1 to pray just as John taught his **d**."
Lk 22:45 from prayer and returned to his **d**,

Jn	2:11	and his **d** began to believe in him.
Jn	6:66	many [of] his **d** returned to their
Jn	8:31	in my word, you will truly be my **d**,
Jn	9:28	we are **d** of Moses!
Jn	12:16	His **d** did not understand this at first,
Jn	13:35	all will know that you are my **d**,
Jn	15: 8	bear much fruit and become my **d**.
Jn	18:17	"You are not one of this man's **d**,
Jn	20:20	The **d** rejoiced when they saw
Jn	20:30	of [his] **d** that are not written in this
Acts	6: 1	as the number of **d** continued
Acts	9: 1	murderous threats against the **d**
Acts	11:26	the **d** were first called Christians.
Acts	13:52	The **d** were filled with joy
Acts	14:22	strengthened the spirits of the **d**
Acts	18:23	bringing strength to all the **d**.

DISCIPLES' → DISCIPLE

Jn	13: 5	and began to wash the **d** feet

DISCIPLINARIAN → DISCIPLINE

Gal	3:24	the law was our **d** for Christ, that we
Gal	3:25	come, we are no longer under a **d**.

DISCIPLINE → DISCIPLINARIAN, DISCIPLINED, DISCIPLINES

Dt	4:36	he let you hear his voice to **d** you;
Dt	11: 2	have neither known nor seen the **d**
Prv	3:11	The **d** of the LORD, my son,
Prv	5:23	They will die from lack of **d**,
Prv	6:23	a way to life are the reproofs that **d**,
Prv	22:15	but the rod of **d** will drive it out.
Sir	6:18	child, from your youth choose **d**;
Heb	12: 5	do not disdain the **d** of the Lord
Heb	12: 7	Endure your trials as "**d**";
Heb	12: 7	is there whom his father does not **d**?
Heb	12: 8	If you are without **d**, in which all
Heb	12:11	all **d** seems a cause not for joy

DISCIPLINED → DISCIPLINE

1 Cor	11:32	we are being **d** so that we may not
Heb	12:10	They **d** us for a short time as

DISCIPLINES → DISCIPLINE

Dt	8: 5	that, even as a man **d** his son,
Dt	8: 5	so the LORD, your God, **d** you.
2 Mc	6:16	Although he **d** us with misfortunes,
Sir	30: 2	Whoever **d** a son will benefit
Heb	12: 6	for whom the Lord loves, he **d**;

DISCLOSE → DISCLOSED

Prv	25: 9	but the secrets of others do not **d**;
1 Cor	3:13	come to light, for the Day will **d** it.

DISCLOSED → DISCLOSE

1 Cor	14:25	the secrets of his heart will be **d**,

DISCORD

Prv	6:14	always plotting evil, sowing **d**.
Prv	6:19	the one who sows **d** among kindred.
Sir	28: 9	and sows **d** among those who are

DISCOURAGE → DISCOURAGED

Nm	32: 7	Why do you wish to **d** the Israelites
Ez	13:22	Because you **d** the righteous with lies

DISCOURAGED → DISCOURAGE

Nm	32: 9	so **d** the Israelites that they would
2 Sm	17: 2	upon him when he is weary and **d**,
1 Mc	4:27	he heard it he was disturbed and **d**,
2 Cor	4: 1	the mercy shown us, we are not **d**.
2 Cor	4:16	Therefore, we are not **d**;

DISCOURSE

Sir	6:35	Be eager to hear every **d**;
Sir	8: 8	Do not neglect the **d** of the wise,

DISCREDITED

Ti	2: 5	that the word of God may not be **d**.

DISCUSSED → DISCUSSIONS

Lk	6:11	**d** together what they might do

DISCUSSING → DISCUSSIONS

Lk	24:17	them, "What are you **d** as you walk

DISCUSSIONS → DISCUSSED, DISCUSSING

Acts	18:19	and held **d** with the Jews.

DISDAIN

Mal	1: 6	O priests, who **d** my name.

DISEASE → DISEASES

2 Chr	16:12	reign, Asa contracted **d** in his feet;
2 Chr	21:15	pains from a **d** in your bowels,
Ps	106:15	and sent a wasting **d** against them.
Mt	4:23	curing every **d** and illness among
Mt	9:35	and curing every **d** and illness.
Mt	10: 1	to cure every **d** and every illness.

DISEASES → DISEASE

Ex	15:26	any of the **d** with which I afflicted
Dt	7:15	of the malignant **d** that you know
Dt	28:60	back upon you all the **d** of Egypt
Mt	4:24	all who were sick with various **d**
Mt	8:17	our infirmities and bore our **d**."
Mk	1:34	many who were sick with various **d**,
Mk	3:10	those who had **d** were pressing
Lk	4:40	sick with various **d** brought them
Lk	6:18	hear him and to be healed of their **d**;
Lk	7:21	that time he cured many of their **d**,
Lk	9: 1	over all demons and to cure **d**,
Lk	9: 6	news and curing **d** everywhere.
Acts	19:12	their **d** left them and the evil spirits

DISGRACE → DISGRACED

1 Mc	4:58	the people now that the **d** brought
Ps	44:16	All day long my **d** is before me;
Prv	11: 2	When pride comes, **d** comes;
Prv	18: 3	comes contempt, and with **d**, scorn.
Sir	22: 3	An undisciplined child is a **d** to
Is	4: 1	be given us, put an end to our **d**!"
Lam	5: 1	to us, pay attention, and see our **d**:
Lk	1:25	to take away my **d** before others."
1 Tm	3: 7	so that he may not fall into a **d**,

DISGRACED → DISGRACE

Ps	71:24	my ruin have been shamed and **d**.

DISGUISE → DISGUISED

1 Kgs	14: 2	and **d** yourself so that no one will

DISGUISED → DISGUISE

1 Sm	28: 8	So he **d** himself, putting on other

DISH

2 Kgs	21:13	Jerusalem clean as one wipes a **d**,
Prv	19:24	The sluggard buries a hand in the **d**;
Lk	11:39	the outside of the cup and the **d**,

DISHONEST

Ex	18:21	trustworthy men who hate **d** gain,
Lk	16: 8	master commended that **d** steward
Lk	16:10	the person who is **d** in very small matters is also **d** in great ones.

DISHONOR → DISHONORED, DISHONORS

1 Mc	1:40	glory had been, so great was her **d**:
Lam	2: 2	to the ground in **d** a kingdom and its
Jn	8:49	I honor my Father, but you **d** me.
Acts	5:41	worthy to suffer **d** for the sake
Rom	2:23	do you **d** God by breaking the law?
2 Cor	6: 8	through glory and **d**,

DISHONORED → DISHONOR

Jas	2: 6	But you **d** the poor person.

DISHONORS → DISHONOR

Dt	27:16	"Cursed be anyone who **d** father
Sir	23:18	The man who **d** his marriage bed says

DISMAYED

Dt	31: 8	So do not fear or be **d**."
Jos	1: 9	Do not fear nor be **d**,
Jos	8: 1	Do not be afraid or **d**.

DISOBEDIENCE → DISOBEY

Rom	5:19	just as through the **d** of one person
Rom	11:30	received mercy because of their **d**,
Rom	11:32	For God delivered all to **d**, that he

2 Cor 10: 6 and we are ready to punish every **d**,
Heb 2: 2 and **d** received its just recompense,
Heb 4: 6 news did not enter because of **d**,
Heb 4:11 fall after the same example of **d**.

DISOBEDIENT → DISOBEY
Bar 1:19 day, we have been **d** to the LORD,
Lk 1:17 the **d** to the understanding
Acts 26:19 I was not **d** to the heavenly vision.
Rom 10:21 long I stretched out my hands to a **d**
Eph 2: 2 spirit that is now at work in the **d**.
Eph 5: 6 wrath of God is coming upon the **d**.
Col 3: 6 of God is coming [upon the **d**].
2 Tm 3: 2 haughty, abusive, **d** to their parents,
Ti 1:16 They are vile and **d** and unqualified
Ti 3: 3 we ourselves were once foolish, **d**,
Heb 3:18 rest," if not to those who were **d**?
Heb 11:31 the harlot did not perish with the **d**,

DISOBEY → DISOBEDIENCE, DISOBEDIENT, DISOBEYING, DISOBEYS
Lv 26:27 If, despite all this, you **d**
Est 3: 3 "Why do you **d** the king's order?"

DISOBEYING → DISOBEY
1 Pt 2: 8 They stumble by **d** the word, as is

DISOBEYS → DISOBEY
Jn 3:36 whoever **d** the Son will not see life,

DISORDER
1 Cor 14:33 since he is not the God of **d**
2 Cor 12:20 slander, gossip, conceit, and **d**.
Jas 3:16 there is **d** and every foul practice.

DISPERSE → DISPERSED, DISPERSION
Ps 106:27 the nations, **d** them in foreign lands.
Ez 12:15 when I **d** them among the nations

DISPERSED → DISPERSE
Is 11:12 The **d** of Judah he shall assemble
Jn 11:52 into one the **d** children of God.

DISPERSION → DISPERSE
Jn 7:35 not going to the **d** among the Greeks
Jas 1: 1 Christ, to the twelve tribes in the **d**,
1 Pt 1: 1 sojourners of the **d** in Pontus,

DISPLAY
Ez 39:21 I will **d** my glory among the nations,
1 Tm 1:16 Christ Jesus might **d** all his patience

DISPLEASED
Prv 24:18 the LORD see it, be **d** with you,
Jon 4: 1 But this greatly **d** Jonah, and he

DISPOSSESS → DISPOSSESSED
Nm 33:52 **d** all the inhabitants of the land
Dt 11:23 the LORD will **d** all these nations
Jos 23:13 will no longer **d** these nations at your

DISPOSSESSED → DISPOSSESS
Jos 23: 9 the LORD has **d** great and strong nations;
Ob 1:17 possession of those who **d** them.

DISPUTES
Prv 18:18 The lot puts an end to **d**,

DISQUALIFIED → DISQUALIFY
1 Cor 9:27 to others, I myself should be **d**.

DISQUALIFY → DISQUALIFIED
Col 2:18 Let no one **d** you,

DISREGARDED
Is 40:27 and my right is **d** by my God"?

DISREPUTE
1 Cor 4:10 you are held in honor, but we in **d**.

DISSENSION → DISSENSIONS
Acts 15: 2 Because there arose no little **d**

DISSENSIONS → DISSENSION
Rom 16:17 to watch out for those who create **d**
Gal 5:20 fury, acts of selfishness, **d**, factions,

DISSOLVED
2 Pt 3:10 and the elements will be **d** by fire,

DISTANCE → DISTANT
Ex 2: 4 sister stationed herself at a **d** to find
Ex 20:21 So the people remained at a **d**,
Dt 32:52 may indeed see the land from a **d**,
Mk 14:54 a **d** into the high priest's courtyard
Mk 15:40 also women looking on from a **d**.

DISTANT → DISTANCE
Jer 4:16 are coming from the **d** land,

DISTINCTION → DISTINCTIONS
Ex 8:19 I will make a **d** between my people
Acts 15: 9 He made no **d** between us and them,
Rom 3:22 all who believe. For there is no **d**;
Rom 10:12 For there is no **d** between Jew

DISTINCTIONS → DISTINCTION
Jas 2: 4 you not made **d** among yourselves

DISTINGUISH → DISTINGUISHED
Lv 10:10 be able to **d** between what is sacred

DISTINGUISHED → DISTINGUISH
Lk 14: 8 A more **d** guest than you may have

DISTRESS → DISTRESSED
Dt 4:30 In your **d**, when all these things
Jgs 2:15 and they were in great **d**.
2 Sm 22: 7 In my **d** I called out: LORD!
2 Chr 15: 4 in their **d** they turned to the LORD,
Neh 9:37 as they please. We are in great **d**!"
Ps 18: 7 In my **d** I called out: LORD!
Ps 25:17 of my heart; bring me out of my **d**.
Ps 86: 7 On the day of my **d** I call to you,
Ps 81: 8 In **d** you called and I rescued you;
Ps 107: 6 In their **d** they cried to the LORD,
Ps 120: 1 answered me when I called in my **d**:
Prv 1:27 when **d** and anguish befall you.'
Is 25: 4 a refuge to the needy in their **d**;
Is 37: 3 A day of **d** and rebuke, a day
Jer 30: 7 A time of **d** for Jacob, though he
Ob 1:12 not speak haughtily on the day of **d**!
Jon 2: 3 Out of my **d** I called to the LORD,
Rom 2: 9 and **d** will come upon every human
Rom 8:35 Will anguish, or **d**, or persecution,

DISTRESSED → DISTRESS
Mk 14:33 and began to be troubled and **d**.

DISTRIBUTE → DISTRIBUTED, DISTRIBUTION
Mk 8: 6 and gave them to his disciples to **d**,
Lk 18:22 that you have and **d** it to the poor,

DISTRIBUTED → DISTRIBUTE
Acts 4:35 they were **d** to each according

DISTRIBUTION → DISTRIBUTE
Acts 6: 1 were being neglected in the daily **d**.

DISTURBANCE → DISTURBED
Acts 19:23 that time a serious **d** broke
Acts 24:18 in the temple without a crowd or **d**.

DISTURBED → DISTURBANCE
Acts 15:24 teachings and **d** your peace of mind,

DIVIDE → DIVIDED, DIVIDING, DIVISION, DIVISIONS
Ps 22:19 they **d** my garments among them;
Is 53:12 and he shall **d** the spoils

DIVIDED → DIVIDE
Gn 10:25 for in his time the world was **d**;
Neh 9:11 The sea you **d** before them, on dry
Is 63:12 is the one who **d** the waters before
Dn 2:41 mean that it shall be a **d** kingdom,
Dn 5:28 your kingdom has been **d** and given
Mt 12:25 "Every kingdom **d** against itself
Mk 6:41 also **d** the two fish among them all.
Mk 15:24 **d** his garments by casting lots
Lk 11:18 And if Satan is **d** against himself,
1 Cor 1:13 Is Christ **d**? Was Paul crucified

DIVIDING → DIVIDE
Eph 2:14 broke down the **d** wall of enmity,

DIVINATION → DIVINE
Gn   44: 5 drinks and which he uses for **d**?
1 Sm   15:23 For a sin of **d** is rebellion,
2 Kgs 17:17 They practiced augury and **d**.
Sir   34: 5 **D**, omens, and dreams are unreal;
Ez   13:23 see false visions or practice **d** again.

DIVINE → DIVINATION, DIVINERS
Ex   31: 3 I have filled him with a **d** spirit
Ps   82: 1 God takes a stand in the **d** council,
2 Pt   1: 3 His **d** power has bestowed on us
2 Pt   1: 4 may come to share in the **d** nature,

DIVINERS → DIVINE
Is   44:25 make fools of **d**, Turn back the wise
Jer   29: 8 prophets and **d** who are among you;
Mi   3: 7 put to shame, and the **d** confounded;
Zec   10: 2 the **d** have seen false visions;

DIVISION → DIVIDE
Lk   12:51 No, I tell you, but rather **d**.
Jn   7:43 So a **d** occurred in the crowd

DIVISIONS → DIVIDE
1 Cor   1:10 and that there be no **d** among you,
1 Cor   11:18 as a church there are **d** among you,
Jude   1:19 These are the ones who cause **d**;

DIVORCE → DIVORCED, DIVORCES
Dt   22:19 he may not **d** her as long as he lives.
Dt   22:29 He may not **d** her as long as he
Dt   24: 1 he writes out a bill of **d** and hands it
Dt   24: 3 he writes out a bill of **d** and hands it
Is   50: 1 Where is the bill of **d** with which I
Jer   3: 8 her away and gave her a bill of **d**,
Mal   2:16 For I hate **d**, says the LORD,
Mt   5:31 his wife must give her a bill of **d**.'
Mt   19: 3 a man to **d** his wife for any cause
Mt   19: 7 the man give the woman a bill of **d**
Mt   19: 8 Moses allowed you to **d** your wives,
Mk   10: 2 lawful for a husband to **d** his wife?"
Mk   10: 4 permitted him to write a bill of **d**
1 Cor   7:11 and a husband should not **d** his wife.
1 Cor   7:12 living with him, he should not **d** her;
1 Cor   7:13 her, she should not **d** her husband.

DIVORCED → DIVORCE
Lv   21: 7 nor a woman who has been **d** by her
Lv   21:14 or a woman who has been **d** or one
Lv   22:13 daughter is widowed or **d** and,
Nm   30:10 vow of a widow or of a **d** woman,
Ez   44:22 as wives either widows or **d** women,
Mt   5:32 marries a **d** woman commits
Lk   16:18 and the one who marries a woman **d**

DIVORCES → DIVORCE
Mt   5:31 'Whoever **d** his wife must give her
Mt   5:32 you, whoever **d** his wife (unless
Mt   19: 9 you, whoever **d** his wife (unless
Mk   10:11 "Whoever **d** his wife and marries
Mk   10:12 if she **d** her husband and marries
Lk   16:18 "Everyone who **d** his wife

DO → DEED, DEEDS, DOER, DOERS, DOES, DOING, DONE,
         EVILDOERS, WRONGDOER, WRONGDOING
Gn   18:25 Far be it from you to **d** such a thing,
Ex   19: 8 the LORD has said, we will **d**."
Ps   37: 3 **d** good that you may dwell
Ps   143:10 Teach me to **d** your will, for you are
Sir   12: 1 If you **d** good, know for whom you
Sir   15:11 for what he hates he does not **d**.
Jer   22: 3 **D** what is right and just.
Jer   22: 3 **D** not wrong or oppress the resident
Mt   23: 3 you, but **d** not follow their example.
Mt   23: 3 they preach but they **d** not practice.
Mk   3: 4 them, "Is it lawful to **d** good
Mk   3: 4 on the sabbath rather than to **d** evil,
Lk   6:31 **D** to others as you would have them **d** to you.
Jn   6:28 "What can we **d** to accomplish
Jn   7:17 to **d** his will shall know whether my
Acts   16:30 "Sirs, what must I **d** to be saved?"

Acts   22:10 I asked, 'What shall I **d**, sir?'
Rom   7:15 What I **d**, I **d** not understand. For I **d** not **d** what I want,
Col   3:17 **d** everything in the name
1 Pt   3:11 must turn from evil and **d** good,

DOCTRINE → DOCTRINES
2 Tm   4: 3 people will not tolerate sound **d** but,
Ti   1: 9 be able both to exhort with sound **d**
Ti   2: 1 say what is consistent with sound **d**,
Ti   2:10 as to adorn the **d** of God our savior

DOCTRINES → DOCTRINE
Mt   15: 9 teaching as **d** human precepts.' "
Mk   7: 7 me, teaching as **d** human precepts.'
1 Tm   1: 3 certain people not to teach false **d**

DOE
Prv   5:19 your lovely hind, your graceful **d**.

DOEG
         Edomite; Saul's chief shepherd; murdered 85 priests at Nob (1 Sm
         21:8; 22:6-23; Ps 52).

DOER → DO
Jas   4:11 law, you are not a **d** of the law

DOERS → DO
Jas   1:22 Be **d** of the word and not hearers

DOES → DO
Ps   135: 6 Whatever the LORD desires he **d**
Eccl   3:14 whatever God **d** will endure forever;
Mk   3:35 [For] whoever **d** the will of God is
Jn   5:19 for what he **d**, his son will do also.
Rom   10: 5 "The one who **d** these things will
3 Jn   1:11 Whoever **d** what is good is of God;
3 Jn   1:11 whoever **d** what is evil has never

DOG → DOGS
Jgs   7: 5 the water as a **d** does with its tongue
1 Sm   17:43 "Am I a **d** that you come against
1 Sm   24:15 A dead **d**! A single flea!
Eccl   9: 4 "A live **d** is better off than a dead
2 Pt   2:22 "The **d** returns to its own vomit,"

DOGS → DOG
Ex   22:30 you must throw it to the **d**.
1 Kgs   21:19 the **d** shall lick up your blood, too."
2 Kgs   9:10 the **d** shall devour Jezebel so that no
Ps   22:17 **D** surround me; a pack of evildoers
Prv   26:11 As **d** return to their vomit, so fools
Is   56:11 Yes, the **d** have a ravenous appetite;
Mt   7: 6 "Do not give what is holy to **d**,
Mt   15:26 the children and throw it to the **d**."
Phil   3: 2 Beware of the **d**! Beware of the evil
Rev   22:15 Outside are the **d**, the sorcerers,

DOING → DO
Zep   3: 5 in its midst is just, **d** no wrong;
Mk   11:28 authority are you **d** these things?
1 Pt   3:17 For it is better to suffer for **d** good,

DOME
Gn   1: 6 Let there be a **d** in the middle

DOMINATED → DOMINION
1 Cor   6:12 but I will not let myself be **d**

DOMINION → DOMINATED, DOMINIONS
Gn   1:26 Let them have **d** over the fish
Jb   25: 2 **D** and dread are his who brings
Ps   110: 2 from Zion. Have **d** over your enemies!
Ps   103:19 in heaven; his **d** extends over all.
Dn   7:14 His **d** is an everlasting **d** that shall
Zec   9:10 His **d** will be from sea to sea,
Eph   1:21 and **d**, and every name that is named

DOMINIONS → DOMINION
Dn   7:27 whom all **d** shall serve and obey."
Col   1:16 invisible, whether thrones or **d**

DONE → DO
Gn   4:10 God then said: What have you **d**?
Est   6: 6 him, "What should be **d** for the man
Jb   21:31 what he has **d** who will repay him?

Ps 71:19 You have **d** great things;
Ps 98: 1 for he has **d** marvelous deeds.
Ps 105: 5 Recall the wondrous deeds he has **d**,
Eccl 1: 9 what has been **d**, that will be **d**.
Jer 50:29 what they have **d**, do to them,
Jl 2:21 for the LORD has **d** great things!
Ob 1:15 As you have **d**, so will it be **d**
Mi 6: 3 My people, what have I **d** to you?
Mt 6:10 come, your will be **d**, on earth as
Mt 26:42 my drinking it, your will be **d**!"
Lk 19:17 He replied, 'Well **d**, good servant!
Lk 23:41 this man has **d** nothing criminal."
Rev 16:17 from the throne, saying, "It is **d**."

DONKEY
Nm 22:30 the **d** said to Balaam, "Am I not your **d**,
Dt 22:10 not plow with an ox and a **d** harnessed together.
Zec 9: 9 savior is he, Humble, and riding on a **d**,

DOOM → DOOMED
Dt 32:35 and their **d** is rushing upon them!

DOOMED → DOOM
Ps 79:11 of your arm preserve those **d** to die.
Ps 102:21 prisoners, to release those **d** to die."
Zec 14:11 never again will it be **d**.

DOOR → DOORPOST, DOORPOSTS, DOORS
Gn 4: 7 but if not, sin lies in wait at the **d**:
Gn 19: 9 in closer to break down the **d**.
Dt 15:17 and put it through his ear into the **d**,
Jgs 19:22 the house and beat on the **d**.
Prv 5: 8 do not go near the **d** of her house,
Prv 9:14 She sits at the **d** of her house
Prv 26:14 The **d** turns on its hinges
Dn 14:11 shut the **d** and seal it with your ring.
Mt 6: 6 close the **d**, and pray to your Father
Mt 7: 7 and the **d** will be opened to you.
Acts 14:27 how he had opened the **d** of faith
1 Cor 16: 9 because a **d** has opened for me wide
2 Cor 2:12 although a **d** was opened for me
Col 4: 3 that God may open a **d** to us
Rev 3: 8 I have left an open **d** before you,
Rev 3:20 I stand at the **d** and knock.
Rev 3:20 hears my voice and opens the **d**,
Rev 4: 1 had a vision of an open **d** to heaven,

DOORPOST → DOOR
Ex 21: 6 at the door or **d**, he shall pierce his

DOORPOSTS → DOOR
Ex 12: 7 apply it to the two **d** and the lintel

DOORS → DOOR
Jgs 16: 3 seized the **d** of the city gate
1 Kgs 6:31 sanctuary, **d** of pine were made;
Neh 3: 1 They consecrated it and set up its **d**,
Jn 20:26 came, although the **d** were locked,
Acts 5:19 the Lord opened the **d** of the prison,
Acts 16:26 all the **d** flew open, and the chains

DORCAS → =TABITHA
Disciple, also known as Tabitha, whom Peter raised from the dead (Acts 9:36-43).

DOUBLE → DOUBLE-TONGUED
Dt 21:17 giving him a **d** share of whatever he
1 Sm 1: 5 but he would give a **d** portion
2 Kgs 2: 9 "May I receive a **d** portion of your
Is 40: 2 of the LORD **d** for all her sins.
1 Tm 5:17 who preside well deserve **d** honor,
Rev 18: 6 Pay her back **d** for her deeds.

DOUBLE-TONGUED → DOUBLE, TONGUE
Sir 28:13 Cursed be gossips and the **d**,

DOUBT → DOUBTED, DOUBTING, DOUBTS
Mt 14:31 you of little faith, why did you **d**?"
Mk 11:23 sea,' and does not **d** in his heart

DOUBTED → DOUBT
Mt 28:17 him, they worshiped, but they **d**.

DOUBTING → DOUBT
Jas 1: 6 not **d**, for the one who doubts is like

DOUBTS → DOUBT
Rom 14:23 whoever has **d** is condemned if he
Jas 1: 6 for the one who **d** is like a wave

DOUGH
Ex 12:39 The **d** they had brought out of Egypt
1 Cor 5: 6 that a little yeast leavens all the **d**?
Gal 5: 9 yeast leavens the whole batch of **d**.

DOVE → DOVES
Gn 8: 8 Then he released a **d**, to see
Ps 55: 7 "If only I had wings like a **d** that I
Sg 5: 2 my friend, my **d**, my perfect one!
Hos 7:11 Ephraim is like a **d**,
Mk 1:10 like a **d**, descending upon him.

DOVES → DOVE
Sg 4: 1 Your eyes are **d** behind your veil.
Is 59:11 like **d** we moan without ceasing.
Ez 7:16 moaning like **d** of the valley
Mt 10:16 shrewd as serpents and simple as **d**.
Mt 21:12 seats of those who were selling **d**.

DOWN → DOWNCAST, DOWNFALL
Gn 11: 5 The LORD came **d** to see the city
Gn 18:21 that I must go **d** to see whether
Gn 46: 3 Do not be afraid to go **d** to Egypt,
Ex 3: 8 Therefore I have come **d** to rescue
Ex 19:11 third day the LORD will come **d**
Nm 11:25 LORD then came **d** in the cloud
2 Sm 22:10 He parted the heavens and came **d**,
Neh 9:13 On Mount Sinai you came **d**,
Ps 18:17 He reached **d** from on high
Ps 113: 6 looking **d** on heaven and earth?
Prv 5: 5 Her feet go **d** to death, her steps
Eccl 3: 3 a time to tear **d**, and a time to build.
Dn 8:10 so that it cast **d** to earth some
Mk 15:30 by coming **d** from the cross."
Lk 4: 9 of God, throw yourself **d** from here,
Jn 6:41 bread that came **d** from heaven,"
Jn 10:11 A good shepherd lays **d** his life
1 Jn 3:16 know love was that he laid **d** his life
1 Jn 3:16 so we ought to lay **d** our lives
Rev 3:12 which comes **d** out of heaven
Rev 12: 9 whole world, was thrown **d** to earth,
Rev 12: 9 and its angels were thrown **d** with it.
Rev 21: 2 coming **d** out of heaven from God,
Rev 21:10 the holy city Jerusalem coming **d**

DOWNCAST → DOWN, CAST
2 Cor 7: 6 who encourages the **d**,

DOWNFALL → DOWN, FALL
Prv 29:16 but the just will behold their **d**.
Sir 25: 7 lives to see the **d** of his enemies.

DRAG → DRAGGED, DRAGGING
Ps 28: 3 Do not **d** me off with the wicked,

DRAGGED → DRAG
Acts 14:19 Paul and **d** him out of the city,

DRAGGING → DRAG
Jn 21: 8 yards, **d** the net with the fish.
Acts 8: 3 house after house and **d** out men

DRAGON → DRAGONS
Is 27: 1 he will slay the **d** in the sea.
Is 51: 9 Rahab, you who pierced the **d**?
Dn 14:23 There was a great **d**
Rev 12: 3 it was a huge red **d**, with seven
Rev 13: 2 To it the **d** gave its own power
Rev 16:13 frogs come from the mouth of the **d**,
Rev 20: 2 He seized the **d**, the ancient serpent,

DRAGONS → DRAGON
Est F: 4 The two **d** are myself and Haman.
Ps 74:13 the heads of the **d** on the waters.

DRANK → DRINK
Gn 9:21 He **d** some of the wine,

Jgs	15:19	and Samson **d** till his spirit returned
Jdt	12:20	by her, **d** a great quantity of wine,
Jer	51: 7	The nations **d** its wine, thus they
Mk	14:23	it to them, and they all **d** from it.
1 Cor	10: 4	and all **d** the same spiritual drink,
1 Cor	10: 4	for they **d** from a spiritual rock

DRAW → DRAWS, DREW

Gn	24:11	when women go out to **d** water,
Ex	2:16	and they came to **d** water and fill
1 Sm	31: 4	"**D** your sword and run me through;
Is	12: 3	With joy you will **d** water
Jn	2: 8	"**D** some out now and take it
Jn	4: 7	woman of Samaria came to **d** water.
Jn	12:32	earth, I will **d** everyone to myself."
Jas	4: 8	**D** near to God, and he will **d** near

DRAWS → DRAW

Ps	40: 3	**D** me up from the pit of destruction,

DREAD

Gn	9: 2	and **d** of you shall come upon all
Gn	15:12	and a great, dark **d** descended upon him.
Dt	31: 6	have no fear or **d** of them, for it is
Jos	2: 9	that a **d** of you has come upon us,
1 Sm	11: 7	The **d** of the LORD came

DREAM → DREAMER, DREAMERS, DREAMS

Gn	20: 3	came to Abimelech in a **d** one night
Gn	28:12	Then he had a **d**: a stairway rested
Gn	31:11	In the **d** God's angel said to me,
Gn	37: 5	Once Joseph had a **d**, and when he
Gn	37: 6	said to them, "Listen to this **d** I had.
Gn	40: 5	each his own **d** and each **d** with its
Gn	41: 1	lapse of two years, Pharaoh had a **d**.
Jgs	7:13	man was telling another about a **d**.
1 Kgs	3: 5	appeared to Solomon in a **d** at night.
Est	F: 2	I recall the **d** I had about these very
Dn	2: 1	reign, King Nebuchadnezzar had a **d**
Dn	2: 3	"I had a **d** which will allow my
Dn	7: 1	as Daniel lay in bed he had a **d**,
Dn	7: 1	Then he wrote down the **d**;
Jl	3: 1	your old men will **d** dreams,
Mt	1:20	of the Lord appeared to him in a **d**
Mt	2:12	having been warned in a **d** not
Mt	2:13	the Lord appeared to Joseph in a **d**
Mt	2:19	the Lord appeared in a **d** to Joseph
Mt	2:22	because he had been warned in a **d**,
Mt	27:19	suffered much in a **d** today because
Acts	2:17	your old men shall **d** dreams.

DREAMER → DREAM

Gn	37:19	to one another: "Here comes that **d**!

DREAMERS → DREAM

Jer	27: 9	to your diviners and **d**, to your
Jude	1: 8	these **d** nevertheless also defile

DREAMS → DREAM

Nm	12: 6	to them, in **d** I speak to them;
1 Sm	28: 6	neither in **d** nor by Urim nor
Sir	34: 7	For **d** have led many astray,
Jer	23:28	the prophets who have **d** tell their **d**;
Jl	3: 1	your old men will dream **d**,
Acts	2:17	visions, your old men shall dream **d**.

DREGS

Ps	75: 9	out, they will drain it even to the **d**;
Is	51:17	Who drained to the **d** the bowl

DRESSED

1 Sm	17:38	Then Saul **d** David in his own tunic,
Jdt	10: 7	in looks and differently **d**, they were
Lk	7:25	Someone **d** in fine garments?
Rev	3: 4	they will walk with me **d** in white,
Rev	4: 4	**d** in white garments and with gold

DREW → DRAW

Ex	2:10	said, "I **d** him out of the water."
Ps	18:17	**d** me out of the deep waters.

DRIED → DRY

Jos	5: 1	that the LORD had **d** up the waters

Is	51:10	Was it not you who **d** up the sea,
Rev	16:12	Its water was **d** up to prepare

DRIES → DRY

Prv	17:22	a depressed spirit **d** up the bones.
Na	1: 4	it dry, and all the rivers he **d** up.

DRINK → DRANK, DRINKING, DRINKS, DRUNK, DRUNKARD, DRUNKARDS, DRUNKENNESS

Gn	24:14	that I may **d**,' and she answers, 'D, and I will
Ex	15:23	where they could not **d** its water,
Ex	17: 1	was no water for the people to **d**,
Ex	32: 6	Then they sat down to eat and **d**,
Ex	32:20	the water and made the Israelites **d**.
Nm	6: 3	abstain from wine and strong **d**; they may neither **d** wine vinegar,
Nm	20: 5	And there is no water to **d**!"
Jgs	7: 5	kneels down to **d** raising his hand
Jgs	13: 4	be careful to **d** no wine or beer
2 Sm	23:15	only someone would give me a **d**
Tb	4:15	Do not **d** wine till you become
Jdt	12:17	to her, "**D** and be happy with us!"
Ps	50:13	of bulls or **d** the blood of he-goats?
Ps	80: 6	made them **d** tears in great measure.
Prv	5:15	**D** water from your own cistern,
Prv	31: 7	When they **d**, they will forget their
Eccl	2:24	better for mortals than to eat and **d**
Eccl	9: 7	and **d** your wine with a merry heart,
Sir	15: 3	him the water of understanding to **d**.
Is	22:13	"Eat and **d**, for tomorrow we die!"
Jer	8:14	he has given us poisoned water to **d**,
Jer	25:15	to whom I will send you **d** it.
Jer	35: 2	there, and give them wine to **d**.
Ez	23:32	The cup of your sister you shall **d**,
Dn	1:12	vegetables to eat and water to **d**.
Am	2:12	But you made the nazirites **d** wine,
Hb	2:15	the cup of your wrath to **d**,
Mt	20:22	Can you **d** the cup that I am going to **d**?"
Mt	26:27	them, saying, "**D** from it, all of you,
Mt	27:34	they gave Jesus wine to **d** mixed
Mt	27:34	he had tasted it, he refused to **d**.
Lk	1:15	He will **d** neither wine nor strong **d**.
Lk	12:19	years, rest, eat, **d**, be merry!" '
Lk	22:18	this time on I shall not **d** of the fruit
Jn	4: 7	Jesus said to her, "Give me a **d**."
Jn	18:11	Shall I not **d** the cup that the Father
Rom	14:17	of God is not a matter of food and **d**,
1 Cor	10: 4	and all drank the same spiritual **d**,
1 Cor	10:21	You cannot **d** the cup of the Lord
1 Cor	12:13	we were all given to **d** of one Spirit.
1 Cor	15:32	"Let us eat and **d**, for tomorrow we
Col	2:16	on you in matters of food and **d**
Heb	9:10	only in matters of food and **d**
Rev	14: 8	made all the nations **d** the wine
Rev	14:10	will also **d** the wine of God's fury,
Rev	16: 6	you [have] given them blood to **d**;

DRINKING → DRINK

Est	5: 6	During the **d** of the wine, the king
Est	7: 2	as they were **d** wine, the king said
Jb	1:13	**d** wine in the house of their eldest
Is	5:22	who are champions at **d** wine,
Mt	11:19	The Son of Man came eating and **d**
Lk	17:27	they were eating and **d**,
1 Tm	5:23	Stop **d** only water, but have a little

DRINKS → DRINK

Jn	4:13	"Everyone who **d** this water will be
Jn	6:54	and **d** my blood has eternal life,
1 Cor	11:27	or **d** the cup of the Lord unworthily

DRIP → DRIPPINGS

Prv	5: 3	the lips of the stranger **d** honey,
Jl	4:18	day the mountains will **d** new wine,
Am	9:13	The mountains shall **d** with the juice

DRIPPINGS → DRIP

Ps	19:11	also than honey or **d** from the comb.

DRIVE → DRIVEN, DRIVING, DROVE
Ex   6: 1 hand, he will **d** them from his land.
Ex   23:30 little I will **d** them out before you,
Mk   11:15 the temple area he began to **d**

DRIVEN → DRIVE
Jn   12:31 the ruler of this world will be **d** out.
Jas   1: 6 is like a wave of the sea that is **d**

DRIVING → DRIVE
Lv   20:23 of the nations whom I am **d**
Ps   35: 5 the angel of the LORD **d** them on.
Acts   26:24 much learning is **d** you mad."

DROP → DROPPINGS, DROPS
Dt   28:40 ointment, for your olives will **d** off.
Is   40:15 See, the nations count as a **d**

DROPPINGS → DROP
Tb   2:10 their warm **d** settled in my eyes,

DROPS → DROP
Lk   22:44 his sweat became like **d** of blood

DROSS
Ps   119:119 Like **d** you regard all the wicked
Prv   25: 4 Remove the **d** from silver, and it
Is   1:22 Your silver is turned to **d**, your wine
Is   1:25 and refine your **d** in the furnace,
Ez   22:18 house of Israel has become **d** to me.

DROUGHT
Dt   28:22 with fiery heat and **d**, with blight
Sir   35:26 as rain clouds in time of **d**.
Jer   14: 1 came to Jeremiah concerning the **d**:
Jer   17: 8 In the year of **d** it shows no distress,

DROVE → DRIVE
Jos   24:18 our approach the LORD **d** out all
Mt   21:12 **d** out all those engaged in selling
Mk   1:12 At once the Spirit **d** him

DROWNED
Mt   18: 6 and to be **d** in the depths of the sea.
Lk   8:33 steep bank into the lake and was **d**.
Heb   11:29 Egyptians attempted it they were **d**.

DROWSY
Mt   25: 5 they all became **d** and fell asleep.

DRUNK → DRINK
Gn   9:21 became **d**, and lay naked inside his
Dt   32:42 I will make my arrows **d** with blood,
1 Sm   1:13 Eli, thinking she was **d**,
1 Sm   25:36 was in a festive mood and very **d**.
2 Sm   11:13 drank with David, who got him **d**.
Sir   31:28 wine enough, **d** at the proper time.
Is   29: 9 You who are **d**, but not from wine,
Jer   13:13 all the inhabitants of this land **d**,
Jn   2:10 and then when people have **d** freely,
Acts   2:15 These people are not **d**, as you
1 Cor 11:21 goes hungry while another gets **d**.
Eph   5:18 And do not get **d** on wine,
1 Thes 5: 7 and those who are **d** get **d** at night.
Rev   17: 6 that the woman was **d** on the blood
Rev   18: 3 all the nations have **d** the wine

DRUNKARD → DRINK
Dt   21:20 listen to us; he is a glutton and a **d**."
Is   19:14 does, as a **d** staggers in his vomit.
Is   24:20 The earth will reel like a **d**,
Mt   11:19 he is a glutton and a **d**, a friend
1 Cor   5:11 a slanderer, a **d**, or a robber,
1 Tm   3: 3 not a **d**, not aggressive, but gentle,

DRUNKARDS → DRINK
Ps   107:27 They reeled, staggered like **d**;
Prv   23:21 For **d** and gluttons come to poverty,
Jl   1: 5 Wake up, you **d**, and weep;
Mt   24:49 servants, and eat and drink with **d**,
1 Cor   6:10 the greedy nor **d** nor slanderers nor

DRUNKENNESS → DRINK
Tb   4:15 let **d** accompany you on your way.

Lk   21:34 drowsy from carousing and **d**
Rom   13:13 the day, not in orgies and **d**,
1 Pt   4: 3 debauchery, evil desires, **d**, orgies,

DRUSILLA
Acts   24:24 later Felix came with his wife **D**,

DRY → DRIED, DRIES
Gn   1: 9 basin, so that the **d** land may appear.
Gn   7:22 Everything on **d** land
Ex   14:16 may pass through the sea on **d** land.
Jos   3:17 while all Israel crossed on **d** ground,
Jgs   6:37 while all the ground is **d**, I shall
2 Kgs   2: 8 of them crossed over on **d** ground.
Ps   66: 6 He changed the sea to **d** land;
Ps   95: 5 The sea and **d** land belong to God,
Ez   37: 4 **D** bones, hear the word
Na   1: 4 He roars at the sea and leaves it **d**,
Heb   11:29 the Red Sea as if it were **d** land,

DUE
Lv   10:13 your sons' **d** from the oblations
1 Chr 16:29 to the LORD the glory **d** his name!
Mal   1: 6 father, where is the honor **d** to me?
Mal   1: 6 a master, where is the fear **d** to me?
Rom   1:27 their own persons the **d** penalty
Rom   13: 7 taxes to whom taxes are **d**,
Rom   13: 7 honor to whom honor is **d**.
1 Pt   5: 6 that he may exalt you in **d** time.

DUG → DIG
Ps   57: 7 They have **d** a pit before me.
Mt   21:33 hedge around it, **d** a wine press in it,

DULL
Is   6:10 **d** their ears and close their eyes;
Is   59: 1 to save, nor his ear too **d** to hear.

DUNG
Lam   4: 5 reclined on crimson now embrace **d** heaps.
Mal   2: 3 I will spread **d** on your faces,

DUNGEON
Gn   40:15 they should have put me into a **d**."
Is   42: 7 and from the **d**, those who live

DUST
Gn   13:16 make your descendants like the **d**
Gn   28:14 Your descendants will be like the **d**
Nm   23:10 Who has ever counted the **d**
1 Sm   2: 8 He raises the needy from the **d**;
Jb   42: 6 have said, and repent in **d** and ashes.
Ps   22:16 you lay me in the **d** of death.
Ps   72: 9 before him, his enemies lick the **d**.
Ps   90: 3 You turn humanity back into **d**,
Ps   103:14 formed, remembers that we are **d**.
Eccl   3:20 both were made from the **d**, and to the **d** they both
                  return.
Is   65:25 but the serpent's food shall be **d**.
Mi   7:17 They will lick the **d** like a snake,
Na   1: 3 and clouds are the **d** at his feet;
Mt   10:14 and shake the **d** from your feet.
Acts   13:51 So they shook the **d** from their feet
Rev   18:19 They threw **d** on their heads

DUTIES → DUTY
Nm   8:26 are to regulate the **d** of the Levites.

DUTY → DUTIES
Gn   38: 8 of your **d** as brother-in-law,
Dt   25: 5 her and performing the **d**

DWELL → DWELLING, DWELLINGS, DWELLS
Ex   25: 8 for me, that I may **d** in their midst.
1 Kgs   6:13 I will **d** in the midst of the Israelites
1 Kgs   8:27 "Is God indeed to **d** on earth?
Ps   23: 6 I will **d** in the house of the LORD
Ps   24: 1 the world and those who **d** in it.
Is   57:15 I **d** in a high and holy place,
Zec   2:15 people, and I will **d** in your midst.
Acts   7:48 Yet the Most High does not **d**
2 Cor 12: 9 the power of Christ may **d** with me.
Eph   3:17 Christ may **d** in your hearts through

Col	1:19	all the fullness was pleased to **d**,
Col	3:16	the word of Christ **d** in you richly,
Rev	12:12	heavens, and you who **d** in them.
Rev	21: 3	He will **d** with them and they will

DWELLING → DWELL

Dt	12:11	chooses as the **d** place for his name
Ez	37:27	My **d** shall be with them; I will be
Jl	4:17	LORD am your God, **d** on Zion,
Jn	14: 2	house there are many **d** places.
Eph	2:22	being built together into a **d** place
Rev	13: 6	and his **d** and those who dwell

DWELLINGS → DWELL

Ps	49:12	their **d** through all generations,

DWELLS → DWELL

Is	8:18	of hosts, who **d** on Mount Zion.
Jl	4:21	The LORD **d** in Zion.
Jn	14:10	The Father who **d** in me is doing his
Rom	7:17	I who do it, but sin that **d** in me.
Rom	8: 9	if only the Spirit of God **d** in you.
1 Cor	3:16	and that the Spirit of God **d** in you?
Col	2: 9	in him **d** the whole fullness
1 Tm	6:16	who **d** in unapproachable light,

DYING → DEAD

2 Cor	6: 9	as **d** and behold we live;

E

EACH

Gn	49:28	To **e** he gave a suitable blessing.
Ex	12: 3	a lamb, one apiece for **e** household.
Nm	1: 4	there shall be a man from **e** tribe,
Nm	17:17	Write **e** man's name on his staff;
Is	6: 2	**e** of them had six wings:
Ez	10:14	E living creature had four faces:
Lk	11: 3	Give us **e** day our daily bread
Acts	2: 6	were confused because **e** one heard
Rom	14:12	**e** of us shall give an account
1 Cor	7: 7	but **e** has a particular gift from God,
1 Cor	12: 7	To **e** individual the manifestation
1 Pt	4:10	As **e** one has received a gift, use it
Rev	2:23	I will give **e** of you what your works
Rev	4: 8	creatures, **e** of them with six wings,
Rev	6:11	E of them was given a white robe,
Rev	21:21	**e** of the gates made from a single
Rev	22: 2	twelve times a year, once **e** month;

EAGER → EAGERLY

Rom	8:19	with **e** expectation the revelation
2 Pt	1:10	be all the more **e** to make your call

EAGERLY → EAGER

Lk	22:15	them, "I have **e** desired to eat this

EAGLE → EAGLE'S, EAGLES'

Dt	32:11	As an **e** incites its nestlings,
Prv	30:19	The way of an **e** in the sky, the way
Jer	48:40	Like an **e** he swoops, spreading his
Jer	49:16	you build your nest high as the **e**,
Ez	1:10	an ox, and each had the face of an **e**.
Ez	17: 3	The great **e**, with wide wingspan
Rev	4: 7	the fourth looked like an **e** in flight.
Rev	8:13	heard an **e** flying high overhead cry
Rev	12:14	given the two wings of the great **e**,

EAGLE'S → EAGLE

Ps	103: 5	so your youth is renewed like the **e**.
Dn	7: 4	was like a lion, but with **e** wings.

EAGLES' → EAGLE

Ex	19: 4	how I bore you up on **e** wings
Is	40:31	strength, they will soar on **e** wings;

EAR → EARRINGS, EARS

Ex	21: 6	he shall pierce his **e** with an awl,
Dt	15:17	put it through his **e** into the door,
2 Kgs	19:16	Incline your **e**, LORD, and listen!
Jb	12:11	Does not the **e** judge words as
Ps	116: 2	Who turned an **e** to me on the day I
Prv	2: 2	Turning your **e** to wisdom,

Prv	25:12	gives wise reproof to a listening **e**.
Eccl	1: 8	by seeing nor has the **e** enough
Is	59: 1	to save, nor his **e** too dull to hear.
Is	64: 3	No **e** has ever heard, no eye ever
Dn	9:18	Give **e**, my God, and listen;
Mk	14:47	priest's servant, and cut off his **e**.
Lk	22:51	Then he touched the servant's **e**
1 Cor	2: 9	and **e** has not heard, and what has

EARLY

Dt	11:14	land, the **e** rain and the late rain,
Ps	127: 2	It is vain for you to rise **e** and put
Prv	27:14	with a loud voice in the **e** morning,
Hos	6: 4	mist, like the dew that disappears **e**.
Jl	2:23	has faithfully given you the **e** rain,
Lk	24:22	were at the tomb **e** in the morning
Jas	5: 7	patient with it until it receives the **e**

EARNEST → EARNESTNESS

Rev	3:19	Be **e**, therefore, and repent.

EARNESTNESS → EARNEST

2 Cor	7:11	behold what **e** this godly sorrow has

EARRINGS → EAR, RING

Ex	35:22	them, brought brooches, **e**, rings,

EARS → EAR

Gn	41: 5	He saw seven **e** of grain,
Dt	29: 3	to see, or **e** to hear until this day.
Neh	1:11	may your **e** be attentive
Ps	34:16	righteous and his **e** toward their cry.
Ps	115: 6	They have **e** but do not hear,
Prv	26:17	who grabs a passing dog by the **e**.
Wis	15:15	to breathe the air, Nor **e** to hear,
Is	6:10	dull their **e** and close their eyes;
Is	35: 5	see, and the **e** of the deaf be opened;
Jer	6:10	See! their **e** are uncircumcised,
Bar	2:31	give them a heart and **e** that listen;
Mt	11:15	Whoever has **e** ought to hear.
Mk	8:18	eyes and not see, **e** and not hear?
Acts	7:51	uncircumcised in heart and **e**,
Acts	28:27	they will not hear with their **e**;
1 Pt	3:12	and his **e** turned to their prayer,
Rev	2: 7	" ' "Whoever has **e** ought to hear
Rev	13: 9	Whoever has **e** ought to hear these

EARTH → EARTHEN, EARTHLY, EARTHQUAKE, EARTHQUAKES

Gn	1: 1	God created the heavens and the **e**—
Gn	1: 2	and the **e** was without form
Gn	1:28	fill the **e** and subdue it.
Gn	4:12	a constant wanderer on the **e**.
Gn	6:11	the **e** was corrupt in the view of God
Gn	6:17	to bring the flood waters on the **e**,
Gn	6:17	everything on **e** shall perish.
Gn	7:24	swelled on the **e** for one hundred
Gn	9:13	the covenant between me and the **e**.
Gn	12: 3	families of the **e** will find blessing
Gn	14:19	High, the creator of heaven and **e**;
Gn	24: 3	the God of heaven and the God of **e**,
Gn	28:14	will be like the dust of the **e**,
Gn	28:14	families of the **e** will find blessing.
Ex	19: 5	all peoples, though all the **e** is mine.
Dt	5: 8	or on the **e** below or in the waters beneath the **e**;
Jos	3:13	the Lord of the whole **e**,
1 Kgs	8:27	"Is God indeed to dwell on **e**?
1 Chr	16:23	all the **e**, announce his salvation,
1 Chr	16:30	Tremble before him, all the **e**;
Jdt	2: 5	the great king, the lord of all the **e**:
Jdt	13:18	God, above all the women on **e**;
Jdt	13:18	the creator of heaven and **e**,
Jb	26: 7	suspends the **e** over nothing at all;
Ps	8: 2	is your name through all the **e**!
Ps	24: 1	The **e** is the LORD's and all it
Ps	37:11	But the poor will inherit the **e**,
Ps	37:29	The righteous will inherit the **e**
Ps	46: 7	he utters his voice and the **e** melts.
Ps	47: 3	feared, the great king over all the **e**,
Ps	73:25	None beside you delights me on **e**.
Ps	90: 2	the **e** and the world brought forth,

Ps	97: 1	let the e rejoice; let the many
Ps	108: 6	your glory above all the e.
Prv	8:26	When the e and the fields were not
Sir	40:11	All that is of e returns to e, and what
Is	6: 3	All the e is filled with his glory!"
Is	24:20	The e will reel like a drunkard,
Is	37:16	God over all the kingdoms of the e.
Is	37:16	who made the heavens and the e.
Is	40:22	enthroned above the vault of the e,
Is	51: 6	the e wear out like a garment and its
Is	55: 9	as the heavens are higher than the e,
Is	65:17	creating new heavens and a new e;
Is	66: 1	are my throne, the e, my footstool.
Jer	10:10	Before whose anger the e quakes,
Jer	23:24	Do I not fill heaven and e?—
Jer	33:25	establish statutes for heaven and e,
Dn	2:39	which shall rule over the whole e.
Dn	3:74	Let the e bless the Lord,
Dn	12: 2	in the dust of the e shall awake;
Jl	3: 3	signs in the heavens and on the e,
Am	9: 5	Who melts the e with his touch,
Hb	2:20	silence before him, all the e!
Hg	2: 6	I will shake the heavens and the e,
Hg	2:21	I will shake the heavens and the e;
Zec	14: 9	will be king over the whole e;
Mt	5:13	"You are the salt of the e.
Mt	5:18	until heaven and e pass away,
Mt	5:35	nor by the e, for it is his footstool;
Mt	6:10	will be done, on e as in heaven.
Mt	16:19	you bind on e shall be bound
Mt	16:19	you loose on e shall be loosed
Mt	24:35	Heaven and e will pass away,
Mt	28:18	and on e has been given to me.
Lk	2:14	on e peace to those on whom his
Lk	5:24	of Man has authority on e to forgive
Jn	12:32	And when I am lifted up from the e,
Acts	2:19	above and signs on the e below:
Acts	4:24	maker of heaven and e and the sea
Acts	7:49	are my throne, the e is my footstool.
1 Cor	10:26	for "the e and its fullness are
1 Cor	15:47	The first man was from the e,
Eph	1:10	things in Christ, in heaven and on e.
Eph	3:15	family in heaven and on e is named,
Phil	2:10	in heaven and on e and under the e,
Heb	1:10	Lord, you established the e,
Heb	12:26	His voice shook the e at that time,
2 Pt	3:13	and a new e in which righteousness
Rev	5: 3	on e or under the e was able to open
Rev	6: 8	authority over a quarter of the e,
Rev	8: 7	which was hurled down to the e.
Rev	12:12	But woe to you, e and sea,
Rev	20:11	The e and the sky fled from his
Rev	21: 1	I saw a new heaven and a new e.
Rev	21: 1	and the former e had passed away,

EARTHEN → EARTH

2 Cor	4: 7	we hold this treasure in e vessels,

EARTHLY → EARTH

Jn	3:12	If I tell you about e things and you
2 Cor	5: 1	For we know that if our e dwelling,
Phil	3:19	minds are occupied with e things.
Col	3: 5	then, the parts of you that are e:
Jas	3:15	not come down from above but is e,

EARTHQUAKE → EARTH, QUAKE

1 Kgs	19:11	after the wind, an e—but the Lord was not in the e;
Est	A: 4	noise and tumult, thunder and e—
Is	29: 6	With thunder, e, and great noise,
Mt	28: 2	And behold, there was a great e;
Acts	16:26	there was suddenly such a severe e
Rev	6:12	sixth seal, and there was a great e;
Rev	11:13	people were killed during the e;
Rev	16:18	It was such a violent e that there has

EARTHQUAKES → EARTH, QUAKE

Mt	24: 7	famines and e from place to place.

EASIER → EASY

Mt	9: 5	Which is e, to say, 'Your sins are
Lk	16:17	It is e for heaven and earth to pass
Lk	18:25	For it is e for a camel to pass

EAST

Gn	2: 8	in the e, and placed there the man
Ex	14:21	with a strong e wind all night long
Ps	103:12	As far as the e is from the west,
Ez	11:23	to rest on the mountain e of the city.
Ez	43: 2	God of Israel coming from the e!
Hos	13:15	his brothers, an e wind will come,
Jon	4: 8	God provided a scorching e wind;
Zec	14: 4	will be split in two from e to west
Mt	2: 1	behold, magi from the e arrived
Mt	8:11	many will come from the e
Rev	16:12	the way for the kings of the E.

EASY → EASIER

Mt	11:30	For my yoke is e, and my burden

EAT → ATE, EATEN, EATER, EATING, EATS

Gn	2:16	You are free to e from any
Gn	2:17	From that tree you shall not e; when you e from it you shall die.
Gn	3:19	of your brow you shall e bread,
Gn	9: 4	lifeblood still in it you shall not e.
Ex	12:11	This is how you are to e it:
Ex	12:20	You shall e nothing leavened;
Ex	16:12	evening twilight you will e meat,
Ex	32: 6	Then they sat down to e and drink,
Lv	11: 4	you shall not e any of the following
Dt	14: 4	These are the animals you may e:
2 Sm	9: 7	you shall e at my table always."
1 Mc	1:62	hearts not to e anything unclean;
Ps	22:27	The poor will e their fill;
Ps	50:13	Do I e the flesh of bulls or drink
Prv	31:27	and does not e the bread of idleness.
Eccl	2:24	nothing better for mortals than to e
Eccl	5:17	It is appropriate to e and drink
Is	11: 7	the lion shall e hay like the ox.
Is	55: 1	no money, come, buy grain and e;
Is	65:25	and the lion shall e hay like the ox—
Jer	19: 9	they shall e one another's flesh
Lam	2:20	Must women e their own offspring,
Ez	3: 1	Son of man, e what you find here:
Dn	1:12	Let us be given vegetables to e
Mt	15: 2	[their] hands when they e a meal."
Mt	26:26	it to his disciples said, "Take and e;
Mk	2:26	only the priests could lawfully e,
Mk	14:14	room where I may e the Passover
Lk	10: 8	you, e what is set before you,
Lk	12:19	up for many years, rest, e, drink,
Lk	12:29	do not seek what you are to e
Jn	4:32	"I have food to e of which you do
Jn	6:31	them bread from heaven to e.' "
Jn	6:53	unless you e the flesh of the Son
Acts	10:13	"Get up, Peter. Slaughter and e."
Rom	14: 2	believes that one may e anything,
Rom	14:15	brother is being hurt by what you e,
1 Cor	5:11	not even to e with such a person.
1 Cor	8:13	I will never e meat again, so that I
1 Cor	10:25	E anything sold in the market,
1 Cor	10:31	So whether you e or drink,
1 Cor	11:26	For as often as you e this bread
2 Thes	3:10	to work, neither should that one e.
Rev	2: 7	the victor I will give the right to e

EATEN → EAT

Gn	3:11	Have you e from the tree of which I
Ez	4:14	myself nor have I e carrion flesh
Dn	14:12	you do not find that Bel has e it all
Acts	10:14	For never have I e anything profane
Acts	12:23	to God, and he was e by worms
Rev	10:10	but when I had e it, my stomach

EATER → EAT

Jgs	14:14	"Out of the e came food,

EATING → EAT
Tb	1:11	I refrained from e that Gentile food.
Lk	7:34	The Son of Man came e
Rom	14:20	to become a stumbling block by e;
1 Cor	8: 4	So about the e of meat sacrificed

EATS → EAT
Gn	3:22	and e of it and lives forever?
Ex	12:15	For whoever e leavened bread
Lv	7:18	Anyone who e of it shall bear
Lk	15: 2	sinners and e with them."
Jn	6:51	whoever e this bread will live
1 Cor	11:27	Therefore whoever e the bread

EBAL
Dt	11:29	the blessing, on Mount E, the curse.
Jos	8:30	on Mount E, Joshua built

EBED-MELECH
An Ethiopian eunuch; saved Jeremiah from the cistern (Jer 38:1-13; 39:16).

EBENEZER
1 Sm	4: 1	them in battle and camped at E,
1 Sm	5: 1	transferred it from E to Ashdod.
1 Sm	7:12	he named it E, explaining, "As far

EBER
Ancestor of Abraham (Gn 11:14-17), of Jesus (Lk 3:35).

ECBATANA
Ezr	6: 2	a scroll was found in E,
Tb	3: 7	On that very day, at E in Media,
Jdt	1: 1	was ruling over the Medes in E.

EDEN
Gn	2: 8	LORD God planted a garden in E,
Is	51: 3	wilderness he shall make like E,
Ez	28:13	In E, the garden of God, you lived;
Ez	31: 9	So that all the trees in E were envious of it.
Jl	2: 3	before it is like the garden of E,

EDGE → TWO-EDGED
Jos	3: 8	you come to the e of the waters
Jer	31:29	the children's teeth are set on e,"

EDICT
Heb	11:23	they were not afraid of the king's e.

EDOM → =ESAU, EDOMITE, EDOMITES
Gn	25:30	That is why he was called E.
Gn	36: 1	the descendants of Esau (that is, E).
Nm	20:18	But E answered him, "You shall
1 Kgs	11:16	they had killed off every male in E.
Ps	60:10	upon E I cast my sandal.
Is	63: 1	Who is this that comes from E,
Jer	49: 7	Concerning E. Thus says
Lam	4:21	daughter E, dwelling in the land
Ez	25:12	Because E took vengeance
Am	1:11	For three crimes of E, and now
Ob	1: 1	says the Lord GOD concerning E:
Mal	1: 4	If E says, "We have been crushed,

EDOMITE → EDOM
1 Sm	22: 9	Then Doeg the E, who was standing
Ps	52: 2	when Doeg the E entered and reported

EDOMITES → EDOM
2 Sm	8:13	defeating eighteen thousand E
1 Chr	18:13	all the E became David's subjects.

EDUCATED
Acts	22: 3	of Gamaliel I was e strictly in our

EFFECT → EFFECTIVE
Heb	9:17	For a will takes e only at death;

EFFECTIVE → EFFECT
Phlm	1: 6	in the faith may become e

EFFORT
2 Pt	1: 5	make every e to supplement your
2 Pt	1:15	make every e to enable you always

EGG → EGGS
Lk	11:12	a scorpion when he asks for an e?

EGGS → EGG
Dt	22: 6	nest with young birds or e in it,
Is	59: 5	They hatch adders' e, and weave
Is	59: 5	Whoever eats the e will die, if one

EGLAH
A wife of David (2 Sm 3:5; 1 Chr 3:3).

EGLON
1. King of Moab killed by Ehud (Jgs 3:12-30).
2. City in Canaan (Jos 10).

EGYPT → EGYPTIAN, EGYPTIANS
Gn	12:10	so Abram went down to E
Gn	26: 2	Do not go down to E, but camp
Gn	37:28	the Ishmaelites, who took him to E.
Gn	41:41	in charge of the whole land of E."
Gn	42: 3	went down to buy grain from E.
Gn	45: 9	God has made me lord of all E;
Gn	45:20	whole land of E shall be yours.' "
Gn	46: 6	and all his descendants came to E.
Gn	47:27	Thus Israel settled in the land of E,
Ex	1: 8	of Joseph, rose to power in E.
Ex	3:11	and bring the Israelites out of E?"
Ex	7: 3	that I work in the land of E,
Ex	12:12	judgment on all the gods of E—
Ex	12:40	had stayed in E was four hundred
Ex	12:41	of the LORD left the land of E.
Ex	32: 1	who brought us out of the land of E,
Nm	11:18	Oh, how well off we were in E!'
Nm	14: 4	appoint a leader and go back to E."
Nm	24: 8	God who brought them out of E.
Dt	6:21	were once slaves of Pharaoh in E,
Dt	6:21	us out of E with a strong hand
Dt	16:12	that you too were slaves in E,
Jos	15:47	as far as the Wadi of E and the coast
1 Kgs	11:40	Jeroboam fled to Shishak, king of E.
1 Kgs	14:25	king of E, attacked Jerusalem.
2 Chr	35:20	Neco, king of E, came up to fight
2 Chr	36: 3	The king of E deposed him
Neh	9:18	God who brought you up from E,'
Ps	78:51	He struck all the firstborn of E,
Ps	80: 9	You brought a vine out of E;
Is	19: 1	Oracle on E: See, the LORD is
Is	19: 1	The idols of E tremble before him,
Jer	42:19	Do not go to E! Mark well that I am
Jer	44: 1	the Judahites who were living in E,
Jer	46: 2	king of E, defeated at Carchemish
Lam	5: 6	We extended a hand to E
Ez	29: 2	king of E, and prophesy against him and against all E.
Ez	30: 4	A sword will come against E,
Hos	11: 1	loved him, out of E I called my son.
Mt	2:15	"Out of E I called my son."
Heb	11:27	By faith he left E, not fearing
Rev	11: 8	names "Sodom" and "E,"

EGYPTIAN → EGYPT
Gn	16: 1	she had an E maidservant named
Ex	1:19	women are not like the E women.
Ex	2:11	he saw an E striking a Hebrew,
Ex	14:24	of fiery cloud upon the E army
Dt	11: 4	what he did to the E army
Acts	7:24	man by striking down the E.

EGYPTIANS → EGYPT
Ex	1:12	so that the E began to loathe
Ex	3:22	So you will plunder the E.
Ex	12:36	had made the E so well-disposed
Ex	12:36	And so they despoiled the E.
Ex	14: 4	and the E will know that I am
Ex	15:26	with which I afflicted the E;
Nm	14:13	"The E will hear of this,
Ez	16:26	served as a prostitute with the E,
Acts	7:22	[in] all the wisdom of the E and was
Heb	11:29	when the E attempted it they were

EHUD
Left-handed judge who delivered Israel from Moabite king, Eglon (Jgs 3:12-30).

EIGHT → EIGHTH

Gn	17:12	you, when he is e days old, shall be
Gn	21: 4	When his son Isaac was e days old,
2 Kgs	22: 1	Josiah was e years old when he
1 Pt	3:20	ark, in which a few persons, e in all,

EIGHTEEN

Lk	13:11	who for e years had been crippled

EIGHTH → EIGHT

Lv	12: 3	On the e day, the flesh of the boy's
Lv	23:39	and the e day shall be days of rest.
Lv	25:22	and when you sow in the e year,
Lk	1:59	When they came on the e day
Phil	3: 5	Circumcised on the e day,
Rev	17:11	but exists no longer is an e king,

EIGHTY

Ex	7: 7	Moses was e years old, and Aaron
2 Sm	19:36	I am now e years old.
Ps	90:10	of our years, or e, if we are strong;

EIGHTY-FIVE

Jos	14:10	and now I am e years old,

EITHER

Sir	40:18	but better than e, finding a treasure.
Sir	40:26	exult, but better than e, fear of God.
Lk	16:13	He will e hate one and love
Rev	3:15	I wish you were e cold or hot.

EKRON

Jos	13: 3	Ashdod, Ashkelon, Gath, and E);
1 Sm	5:10	The ark of God was next sent to E;
1 Sm	6:17	one for Gath, and one for E.
2 Kgs	1: 2	the god of E, whether I shall recover
Am	1: 8	I will turn my hand against E,

EL

Gn	33:20	up an altar there and invoked "E,

EL-BERITH

Jgs	9:46	into the crypt of the temple of E.

ELAH

1. Son of Baasha; king of Israel (1 Kgs 16:6-14).
2. Valley in which David fought Goliath (1 Sm 17:2, 19; 21:9).

ELAM

1 Chr	1:17	The sons of Shem were E, Asshur,
Jer	49:34	Jeremiah the prophet concerning E

ELDAD

Nm	11:27	"E and Medad are prophesying

ELDER → ELDERS

Is	3: 2	judge and prophet, diviner and e,
Ez	16:46	Your e sister was Samaria with her

ELDERS → ELDER

Ex	3:16	Go and gather the e of the Israelites.
Ex	24: 1	and seventy of the e of Israel.
Dt	25: 7	she shall go up to the e at the gate
Jos	24: 1	summoning the e, leaders, judges,
Jgs	2: 7	of those e who outlived Joshua
Ru	4: 2	picked out ten of the e of the town
Ps	105:22	as he desired, to teach his e wisdom.
Prv	31:23	as he sits with the e of the land.
Is	3:14	into judgment with the people's e
Ez	8:11	stood seventy of the e of the house
Dn	13:50	To Daniel the e said, "Come,
Mt	15: 2	break the tradition of the e?
Mt	27:12	accused by the chief priests and e,
Mk	7: 3	hands, keeping the tradition of the e.
Lk	9:22	greatly and be rejected by the e,
Acts	4: 5	their leaders, e, and scribes were
Acts	23:14	They went to the chief priests and e
Acts	24: 1	Ananias came down with some e
Acts	25:15	the e of the Jews brought charges
Rev	4: 4	thrones on which twenty-four e sat,
Rev	4:10	the twenty-four e fall down before
Rev	5: 6	the four living creatures and the e,
Rev	7:11	and around the e and the four living
Rev	11:16	The twenty-four e who sat on their

Rev	14: 3	the four living creatures and the e.
Rev	19: 4	The twenty-four e and the four

ELEAZAR

1. Third son of Aaron (Ex 6:23-25). Succeeded Aaron as high priest (Nm 20:26; Dt 10:6). Allotted land to tribes (Jos 14:1). Death (Jos 24:33).
2. Father of the writer of Sirach (Sir 50:27).
3. Brother of Judas Maccabeus (1 Mc 2:5; 6:43-46).

ELECT → ELECTION

Wis	3: 9	holy ones, and his care is with the e.
Mt	24:22	sake of the e they will be shortened.
Mt	24:24	if that were possible, even the e.
Mt	24:31	they will gather his e from the four
Mk	13:20	the sake of the e whom he chose,
Mk	13:22	mislead, if that were possible, the e.
Mk	13:27	gather [his] e from the four winds,
Rom	11: 7	it did not attain, but the e attained it;
1 Tm	5:21	and the e angels to keep these rules

ELECTION → ELECT

Rom	11:28	but in respect to e, they are beloved
2 Pt	1:10	eager to make your call and e firm,

ELEMENTAL → ELEMENTS

Gal	4: 3	were enslaved to the e powers
Gal	4: 9	to the weak and destitute e powers?
Col	2: 8	according to the e powers
Col	2:20	Christ to the e powers of the world,

ELEMENTS → ELEMENTAL

Wis	7:17	the universe and the force of its e,
Heb	5:12	someone teach you again the basic e
2 Pt	3:10	and the e will be dissolved by fire,
2 Pt	3:12	in flames and the e melted by fire.

ELEPHANT → ELEPHANTS

1 Mc	6:46	He ran under the e, stabbed it

ELEPHANTS → ELEPHANT

1 Mc	1:17	with chariots, e and cavalry,

ELEVEN

Gn	32:23	two maidservants and his e children,
Gn	37: 9	e stars were bowing down to me."
Ex	26: 8	all e sheets shall be of the same
Dt	1: 2	It is a journey of e days from Horeb
Mt	28:16	The e disciples went to Galilee,
Lk	24: 9	announced all these things to the e
Lk	24:33	they found gathered together the e
Acts	1:26	he was counted with the e apostles.
Acts	2:14	Then Peter stood up with the E,

ELI → ELOI

1. High priest in youth of Samuel (1 Sm 1-4). Blessed Hannah (1 Sm 1:12-18); raised Samuel (1 Sm 2:11-26). Prophesied against because of wicked sons (1 Sm 2:27-36). Death of Eli and sons (1 Sm 4:11-22).
2. "*Eli, Eli, lema sabachthani?*" (Mt 27:46).

ELIAKIM → =JEHOIAKIM

1. Original name of king Jehoiakim (2 Kgs 23:34; 2 Chr 36:4).
2. Hezekiah's palace administrator (2 Kgs 18:17-37; 19:2; Is 36:1-22; 37:2).

ELIASHIB

Neh	3: 1	E the high priest and his priestly

ELIEZER

1. Servant of Abraham (Gn 15:2).
2. Son of Moses (Ex 18:4; 1 Chr 23:15-17).

ELIHU

A friend of Job (Jb 32–37).

ELIJAH

Prophet; predicted famine in Israel (1 Kgs 17:1; Jas 5:17). Fed by ravens (1 Kgs 17:2-6). Raised Sidonian widow's son (1 Kgs 17:7-24). Defeated prophets of Baal at Carmel (1 Kgs 18:16-46). Ran from Jezebel (1 Kgs 19:1-9). Prophesied death of Azariah (2 Kgs 1). Succeeded by Elisha (1 Kgs 19:19-21; 2 Kgs 2:1-18). Taken to heaven in whirlwind (2 Kgs 2:11-12; 1 Mc 2:58; Sir 48:1-12).

Return prophesied (Mal 3:23-24); equated with John the Baptist (Mt

17:9-13; Mk 9:9-13; Lk 1:17). Appeared with Moses in transfiguration of Jesus (Mt 17:1-8; Mk 9:1-8).

ELIM
Ex 15:27 Then they came to E, where there
Nm 33: 9 at E there were twelve springs

ELIMELECH
Ru 1: 3 E, the husband of Naomi, died,
Ru 4: 9 from Naomi all the holdings of E,

ELIPHAZ
1. Firstborn of Esau (Gn 36).
2. A friend of Job (Jb 4–5; 15; 22; 42:7, 9).

ELISHA
Prophet; successor of Elijah (1 Kgs 19:16-21; Sir 48:12-14); inherited his mantle (2 Kgs 2:1-18). Purified bad water (2 Kgs 2:19-22). Cursed young men (2 Kgs 2:23-25). Aided Israel's defeat of Moab (2 Kgs 3). Provided widow with oil (2 Kgs 4:1-7). Raised Shunammite woman's son (2 Kgs 4:8-37). Purified food (2 Kgs 4:38-41). Fed 100 men (2 Kgs 4:42-44). Healed Naaman's leprosy (2 Kgs 5). Made axhead float (2 Kgs 6:1-7). Captured Arameans (2 Kgs 6:8-23). Political adviser to Israel (2 Kgs 6:24–8:6; 9:1-3; 13:14-19), Aram (2 Kgs 8:7-15). Death (2 Kgs 13:20).

ELIZABETH
Mother of John the Baptist (Lk 1:5-58).

ELKANAH
Husband of Hannah, father of Samuel (1 Sm 1–2).

ELOI → ELI
Mk 15:34 voice, "*E, E, lema sabachthani?*"

ELON
Judge of Israel (Jgs 12:11-12).

ELOQUENT
Ex 4:10 I have never been e,
Acts 18:24 a native of Alexandria, an e speaker,

ELSE
Ex 4:13 please, my Lord, send someone e!"
Acts 4:12 is no salvation through anyone e,

ELYMAS → =BAR-JESUS
Acts 13: 8 E the magician (for that is what his

EMBALMED
Gn 50: 2 When the physicians e Israel,
Gn 50:26 He was e and laid to rest in a coffin

EMBRACE → EMBRACED
Prv 4: 8 will bring you honors if you e her;
Prv 5:20 with a stranger, and e another woman?
Eccl 3: 5 a time to e, and a time to be far

EMBRACED → EMBRACE
Gn 48:10 close to him, he kissed and e them.
2 Chr 7:22 they e other gods, bowing down to them

EMBROIDERED
Ez 16:10 I clothed you with an e gown,
Ez 26:16 robes, and strip off their e garments.

EMERALD
Ex 28:17 row, a carnelian, a topaz, and an e;
Rev 4: 3 was a halo as brilliant as an e.
Rev 21:19 the third chalcedony, the fourth e,

EMMANUEL
Is 7:14 about to bear a son, shall name him E.
Is 8: 8 will fill the width of your land, E!
Mt 1:23 and they shall name him E,"

EMMAUS
Lk 24:13 miles from Jerusalem called E,

EMPTIED → EMPTY
Neh 5:13 may he thus be shaken out and e!"
1 Cor 1:17 cross of Christ might not be e of its
Phil 2: 7 Rather, he e himself,

EMPTY → EMPTIED, EMPTY-HANDED
2 Kgs 4: 3 as many e vessels as you can.
Ru 3:17 'Do not go back to your mother-in-law e.' "
Lk 1:53 the rich he has sent away e.

Eph 5: 6 one deceive you with e arguments,
Col 2: 8 that no one captivate you with an e,

EMPTY-HANDED → EMPTY, HAND
Gn 31:42 would now have sent me away e.
Ex 3:21 when you go, you will not go e.
Ex 23:15 No one shall appear before me e.
Dt 15:13 you shall not send him away e,
Sir 35: 6 Do not appear before the Lord e,
Mk 12: 3 him, beat him, and sent him away e.

ENABLES → ABLE
Phil 3:21 body by the power that e him

ENCAMP → CAMP
Ps 27: 3 Though an army e against me,
Is 29: 3 I will e like David against you;

ENCAMPS → CAMP
Ps 34: 8 the LORD e around those who fear

ENCHANTERS
Dn 1:20 the magicians and e in his kingdom.
Dn 5: 7 The king shouted for the e,

ENCIRCLE → CIRCLE
Ps 22:13 fierce bulls of Bashan e me.

ENCOURAGE → ENCOURAGED, ENCOURAGEMENT, ENCOURAGES, ENCOURAGING
Dt 1:38 E him, for he is the one who is
Dt 3:28 Joshua, and e and strengthen him,
2 Sm 11:25 on the city and destroy it.' E him."
Ez 13:22 and e the wicked so they do not turn
Eph 6:22 us and that he may e your hearts.
Col 4: 8 us and that he may e your hearts,
1 Thes 3: 2 strengthen and e you in your faith,
1 Thes 5:11 e one another and build one another
2 Tm 4: 2 e through all patience and teaching.

ENCOURAGED → ENCOURAGE
Acts 16:40 where they saw and e the brothers,
Acts 18:27 the brothers e him and wrote
Acts 27:36 They were all e, and took some food
Rom 1:12 you and I may be mutually e by one
1 Cor 14:31 so that all may learn and all be e.
Col 2: 2 that their hearts may be e as they are
Heb 6:18 taken refuge might be strongly e

ENCOURAGEMENT → ENCOURAGE
1 Mc 12: 9 we have for our e the holy books
Acts 4:36 (which is translated "son of e"),
Acts 20: 2 he provided many words of e
Rom 15: 4 by the e of the scriptures we might
Rom 15: 5 and e grant you to think in harmony
1 Cor 14: 3 for their building up, e, and solace.
Phil 2: 1 If there is any e in Christ,
Phlm 1: 7 much joy and e from your love,

ENCOURAGES → ENCOURAGE
Is 41: 7 The woodworker e the goldsmith,

ENCOURAGING → ENCOURAGE
1 Mc 5:53 and e the people the whole way,
2 Mc 15: 9 By e them with words from the law
Acts 20: 1 after e them, he bade them farewell
1 Thes 2:12 exhorting and e you and insisting

END → ENDS
Gn 6:13 that the e of all mortals has come,
Ex 12:41 At the e of four hundred and thirty
Dt 8:16 also make you prosperous in the e.
Prv 5: 4 the e she is as bitter as wormwood,
Prv 5:11 And you groan in the e, when your
Prv 14:12 right, but the e of it leads to death!
Prv 14:13 sad, and the e of joy may be sorrow.
Prv 16:25 right, but the e of it leads to death!
Prv 20:21 outset will not be blessed in the e.
Prv 21: 5 The plans of the diligent e in profit,
Eccl 3:11 out, from beginning to e, the work
Eccl 7: 8 Better is the e of a thing than its
Eccl 12:12 making of many books there is no e,
Sir 11:28 for how they e, they are known.

Sir	21: 9	they will e in a flaming fire.
Ez	7: 2	The e comes upon the four corners
Dn	6:27	whose dominion shall be without e,
Dn	8:17	that the vision refers to the e time."
Dn	9:26	His e shall come in a flood;
Dn	9:26	until the e of the war, which is
Dn	12:13	for your reward at the e of days."
Mt	10:22	endures to the e will be saved.
Mt	13:39	The harvest is the e of the age,
Mt	24:13	perseveres to the e will be saved.
Mt	24:14	nations, and then the e will come.
Mt	28:20	you always, until the e of the age."
Lk	21: 9	it will not immediately be the e."
Jn	13: 1	world and he loved them to the e.
Rom	6:21	For the e of those things is death.
Rom	10: 4	For Christ is the e of the law
1 Cor	15:24	then comes the e, when he hands
Phil	3:19	Their e is destruction. Their God is
Heb	3:14	of the reality firm until the e,
1 Pt	4: 7	The e of all things is at hand.
Rev	2:26	who keeps to my ways until the e,
Rev	21: 6	the Omega, the beginning and the e.
Rev	22:13	the last, the beginning and the e."

ENDOR
1 Sm	28: 7	is a woman in E who is a medium."

ENDOWED
Ex	28: 3	the various artisans whom I have e

ENDS → END
Ps	2: 8	your possession, the e of the earth.
Ps	67: 8	the e of the earth may revere him.
Prv	30: 4	who has established all the e
Is	40:28	of old, creator of the e of the earth.
Mi	5: 3	shall reach to the e of the earth:
Lk	11:31	she came from the e of the earth
Acts	13:47	salvation to the e of the earth.' "
Rom	10:18	their words to the e of the world."

ENDURANCE → ENDURE
Rom	5: 3	knowing that affliction produces e,
2 Cor	6: 4	God, through much e, in afflictions,
Ti	2: 2	sound in faith, love, and e.
Heb	10:36	You need e to do the will of God
2 Pt	1: 6	self-control with e, e with devotion,
Rev	1: 9	and the e we have in Jesus,
Rev	13:10	Such is the faithful e of the holy

ENDURE → ENDURANCE, ENDURED, ENDURES, ENDURING
Jb	20:21	therefore his prosperity shall not e.
Ps	72:17	as long as the sun, may his name e.
Ps	104:31	the glory of the LORD e forever;
Prv	12:19	Truthful lips e forever, the lying
Jer	10:10	whose wrath the nations cannot e.
Mal	3: 2	who can e the day of his coming?
1 Cor	4:12	when persecuted, we e;
Heb	12: 7	E your trials as "discipline";

ENDURED → ENDURE
Rom	9:22	power, has e with much patience
2 Tm	3:11	and Lystra, persecutions that I e.
Heb	12: 2	that lay before him he e the cross,
Heb	12: 3	Consider how he e such opposition

ENDURES → ENDURE
1 Chr	16:41	LORD, "whose love e forever,"
1 Mc	4:24	is good, whose mercy e forever."
Ps	136: 1	he is good; for his mercy e forever.
Sir	40:17	cut off, and righteousness e forever.
Bar	4: 1	of God, the law that e forever;
Dn	3:89	is good, whose mercy e forever.
Jn	6:27	for the food that e for eternal life,
1 Cor	13: 7	things, hopes all things, e all things.
2 Cor	9: 9	his righteousness e forever."

ENDURING → ENDURE
Ps	19:10	of the LORD is pure, e forever.
Dn	6:27	"For he is the living God, e forever,

ENEMIES → ENEMY
Ex	1:10	war they too may join our e to fight

Ex	23:22	I will be an enemy to your e
Dt	6:19	driving all your e out of your way,
Jos	21:44	the LORD gave all their e
Jgs	2:14	no longer able to withstand their e.
2 Sm	7: 1	him rest from his e on every side,
Jdt	8:35	you to take vengeance upon our e!"
Est	9: 5	The Jews struck down all their e
Est	9:22	the Jews obtained rest from their e
1 Mc	4:36	"Now that our e have been crushed,
Ps	23: 5	a table before me in front of my e;
Ps	110: 1	I make your e your footstool."
Prv	16: 7	he makes even e be at peace
Is	59:18	to their deeds he repays his e
Mi	7: 6	and your e are members of your
Mt	5:44	love your e, and pray for those who
Mk	12:36	I place your e under your feet." '
Lk	6:35	love your e and do good to them,
Lk	20:43	I make your e your footstool." '
Acts	2:35	I make your e your footstool." '
Rom	5:10	if, while we were e, we were
Rom	11:28	gospel, they are e on your account;
1 Cor	15:25	he has put all his e under his feet.
Phil	3:18	conduct themselves as e of the cross
Heb	1:13	until I make your e your footstool"?
Heb	10:13	he waits until his e are made his

ENEMY → ENEMIES, ENMITY
Ex	15: 6	hand, O LORD, shattered the e.
Ex	23:22	I will be an e to your enemies
Dt	33:27	He drove the e out of your way
1 Sm	18:29	the more and was his e ever after.
2 Sm	22:18	He rescued me from my mighty e,
Est	3:10	the Agagite, the e of the Jews.
Est	7: 6	"The e oppressing us is this wicked
Ps	8: 3	your foes, to silence e and avenger.
Ps	18:18	He rescued me from my mighty e,
Ps	74:10	How long, O God, will the e jeer?
Prv	27: 6	friend, dangerous, the kisses of an e.
Jer	30:14	I struck you as an e would strike,
Lam	2: 5	The Lord has become the e, he has
Mi	2: 8	rise up against my people as an e:
Mt	5:43	love your neighbor and hate your e.'
Mt	13:39	the e who sows them is the devil.
Lk	10:19	and upon the full force of the e
1 Cor	15:26	The last e to be destroyed is death,
Jas	4: 4	of the world makes himself an e

ENGEDI
1 Sm	24: 1	and stayed in the strongholds of E.

ENGRAVE → ENGRAVED, ENGRAVES
Zec	3: 9	seven facets I will e its inscription—

ENGRAVED → ENGRAVE
Ex	32:16	the writing of God, e on the tablets.
Jer	17: 1	E with a diamond point

ENGRAVES → ENGRAVE
Ex	28:11	As a gem-cutter e a seal, so shall

ENJOY → ENJOYMENT
Eccl	9: 9	E life with the wife you love,
Heb	11:25	of God rather than e the fleeting

ENJOYMENT → ENJOY
1 Tm	6:17	provides us with all things for our e.

ENLARGE → LARGE
Is	54: 2	E the space for your tent,

ENLARGES → LARGE
Dt	19: 8	your God, e your territory, as he

ENLIGHTENED → LIGHT
Eph	1:18	May the eyes of [your] hearts be e,
Heb	6: 4	case of those who have once been e
Heb	10:32	after you had been e, you endured

ENLIGHTENING → LIGHT
Ps	19: 9	of the LORD is clear, e the eye.

ENLIGHTENS → LIGHT
Jn   1: 9 which e everyone, was coming

ENMITY → ENEMY
Gn   3:15 I will put e between you
Jas   4: 4 of the world means e with God?

ENOCH
   1. Son of Cain (Gn 4:17-18).
   2. Descendant of Seth; walked with God and taken by him (Gn 5:18-24; Heb 11:5). Prophet (Jude 14).

ENOUGH
Dt   1: 6 You have stayed long e at this
Prv   30:15 get their fill, four never say, "E!"

ENRICHED → RICH
Prv   11:25 confers benefits will be amply e,
1 Cor   1: 5 in him you were e in every way,
2 Cor   9:11 You are being e in every way for all

ENROLL → ENROLLMENT
Nm   1: 3 Aaron shall e in companies all

ENROLLMENT → ENROLL
Nm   1:45 The total e of the Israelites of twenty

ENSIGNS
Nm   2: 2 under the e of their ancestral

ENSLAVE → SLAVE
Gal   2: 4 Christ Jesus, that they might e us—

ENSNARED → SNARE
Dt   7:25 it for yourselves, lest you be e by it;

ENTANGLED
2 Pt   2:20 again become e and overcome

ENTER → ENTERED, ENTERING, ENTERS, ENTRANCE, ENTRY
Ex   40:35 Moses could not e the tent
Nm   20:24 he shall not e the land I have given
Dt   1:37 said, You shall not e there either,
Ps   95:11 "They shall never e my rest."
Ps   100: 4 E his gates with thanksgiving,
Ps   118:20 own gate, through it the righteous e.
Prv   4:14 The path of the wicked do not e,
Jl   4: 2 There I will e into judgment
Mt   5:20 you will not e into the kingdom
Mt   7:13 "E through the narrow gate;
Mt   7:21 will e the kingdom of heaven,
Mt   18: 3 you will not e the kingdom
Mt   18: 8 better for you to e into life maimed
Mt   19:17 If you wish to e into life,
Mk   10:15 of God like a child will not e it."
Mk   10:23 who have wealth to e the kingdom
Lk   13:24 to e through the narrow door,
Lk   13:24 will attempt to e but will not be
Lk   24:26 these things and e into his glory?"
Jn   3: 5 no one can e the kingdom of God
Acts   14:22 many hardships to e the kingdom
Heb   3:11 wrath, "They shall not e into my
Heb   4: 3 For we who believed e
Heb   4:11 let us strive to e into that rest,
Rev   15: 8 that no one could e it until the seven
Rev   21:27 but nothing unclean will e it,
Rev   21:27 Only those will e whose names are

ENTERED → ENTER
2 Chr   26:16 He e the temple of the LORD
Ez   43: 4 glory of the LORD e the temple
Lk   9:34 frightened when they e the cloud.
Lk   22: 3 Then Satan e into Judas, the one
Jn   13:27 he took the morsel, Satan e him.
Acts   11: 8 or unclean has ever e my mouth.'
Heb   6:20 where Jesus has e on our behalf as
Heb   9:12 he e once for all into the sanctuary,
Rev   11:11 a breath of life from God e them.

ENTERING → ENTER
Heb   4: 1 on our guard while the promise of e

ENTERS → ENTER
Jn   10: 2 whoever e through the gate is

Jn   10: 9 Whoever e through me will be

ENTERTAINED
Heb   13: 2 it some have unknowingly e angels.

ENTHRONED → THRONE
1 Sm   4: 4 hosts, who is e upon the cherubim.
2 Sm   6: 2 of hosts e above the cherubim."
2 Kgs   19:15 God of Israel, e on the cherubim!
1 Chr   13: 6 by the name "LORD e
Ps   22: 4 Yet you are e as the Holy One;
Ps   29:10 The LORD sits e above the flood!
Ps   55:20 who sits e forever, will hear me
Ps   99: 1 he is e on the cherubim, the earth
Ps   102:13 But you, LORD, are e forever;
Ps   123: 1 I raise my eyes, to you e in heaven.
Is   37:16 God of Israel, e on the cherubim!
Is   40:22 The one who is e above the vault of

ENTICE → ENTICED, ENTICES
Prv   1:10 My son, should sinners e you,

ENTICED → ENTICE
Jb   31: 9 heart has been e toward a woman,
Jb   31:27 And had my heart been secretly e
Jas   1:14 he is lured and e by his own desire.

ENTICES → ENTICE
Dt   13: 7 your intimate friend e you secretly,

ENTIRE
Acts   2: 2 it filled the e house in which they
Gal   5: 3 he is bound to observe the e law.

ENTRANCE → ENTER
Ex   26:36 the e of the tent make a variegated
Mk   16: 3 for us from the e to the tomb?"

ENTRAP → TRAP
Mt   22:15 and plotted how they might e him

ENTREAT → ENTREATED
1 Kgs   13: 6 to the man of God, "E the LORD,

ENTREATED → ENTREAT
1 Kgs   13: 6 So the man of God e the LORD,

ENTRUST → TRUST
2 Tm   2: 2 me through many witnesses e

ENTRUSTED → TRUST
Lk   12:48 required of the person e with much,
Rom   3: 2 they were e with the utterances
Rom   6:17 of teaching to which you were e.
1 Cor   9:17 I have been e with a stewardship.
Gal   2: 7 that I had been e with the gospel
1 Thes   2: 4 by God to be e with the gospel,
1 Tm   1:11 God, with which I have been e.
1 Tm   6:20 guard what has been e to you.
2 Tm   1:12 to guard what has been e to me until
Ti   1: 3 which I was e by the command

ENTRY → ENTER
2 Pt   1:11 e into the eternal kingdom of our

ENVIOUS → ENVY
Ez   31: 9 that all the trees in Eden were e of it.

ENVOY
Prv   13:17 a trustworthy e is a healing remedy.

ENVY → ENVIOUS
Prv   3:31 Do not e the violent and choose
Wis   2:24 But by the e of the devil,
Sir   9:11 Do not e the wicked for you do not
Is   11:13 Ephraim shall not e Judah, and Judah
Mk   7:22 deceit, licentiousness, e, blasphemy,
Rom   1:29 full of e, murder, rivalry, treachery,
Gal   5:21 occasions of e, drinking bouts,
Phil   1:15 some preach Christ from e
1 Tm   6: 4 From these come e, rivalry, insults,
Ti   3: 3 living in malice and e,
1 Pt   2: 1 insincerity, e, and all slander;

EPAPHRAS
   Associate of Paul (Col 1:7; 4:12; Phlm 23).

EPAPHRODITUS
Associate of Paul (Phil 2:25; 4:18).

EPHAH
Ex   16:36 (An omer is one tenth of an e.)
Ez   45:10 an honest e, and an honest bath.

EPHESIANS → EPHESUS
Acts 19:28 shout, "Great is Artemis of the E!"

EPHESUS → EPHESIANS
Acts 18:19 When they reached E, he left them
Acts 19: 1 to E where he found some disciples.
Acts 20:17 of the church at E summoned.
1 Cor 15:32 If at E I fought with beasts,
Eph   1: 1 the holy ones who are [in E] faithful
Rev   2: 1 "To the angel of the church in E,

EPHOD
Ex   28: 6 The e they shall make of gold
Lv   8: 7 with the robe, placed the e on him,
Jgs   8:27 Gideon made an e out of the gold
Jgs   17: 5 and he made an e and teraphim,
1 Chr 15:27 David was also wearing a linen e.
Hos   3: 4 pillar, without e or household gods.

EPHPHATHA
Mk   7:34 groaned, and said to him, "E!"

EPHRAIM
1. Second son of Joseph (Gn 41:52; 46:20). Blessed as firstborn by Jacob (Gn 48). Tribe of numbered (Nm 1:33; 26:37), blessed (Dt 33:17), allotted land (Jos 16:4-9; Ez 48:5), failed to fully possess (Jos 16:10; Jgs 1:29).
2. A term for the Northern Kingdom of Israel (Is 7:17; Hos 5).

EPHRATH → BETHLEHEM, EPHRATHAH
Gn   35:19 on the road to E (now Bethlehem).

EPHRATHAH → EPHRATH
Ru   4:11 Prosper in E! Bestow a name

EPHRON
Hittite who sold Abraham a field (Gn 23).

EPICUREAN
Acts 17:18 Even some of the E and Stoic

EPIPHANES
1 Mc   1:10 offshoot, Antiochus E, son of King

EQUAL → EQUALITY
Jb   28:17 Gold or crystal cannot e her, nor can
Sir   9:10 new ones cannot e them.
Is   40:25 To whom can you liken me as an e?
Is   46: 5 whom would you liken me as an e,
Jn   5:18 father, making himself e to God.

EQUALITY → EQUAL
Phil   2: 6 of God, did not regard e with God

EQUIP → EQUIPPED
Eph   4:12 to e the holy ones for the work

EQUIPPED → EQUIP
2 Tm   3:17 competent, e for every good work.

ER
Gn   38: 6 named Tamar for his firstborn, E.

ERASTUS
Associate(s) of Paul (Acts 19:22; Rom 16:23; 2 Tm 4:20).

ERECT → ERECTED
Heb   8: 5 he was about to e the tabernacle.

ERECTED → ERECT
1 Mc   1:54 the king e the desolating abomination

ERROR
2 Pt   2:18 escaped from people who live in e.
2 Pt   3:17 be led into the e of the unprincipled
Jude   1:11 to Balaam's e for the sake of gain,

ESAU → =EDOM
Firstborn of Isaac, twin of Jacob (Gn 25:21-26). Also called Edom (Gn 25:30). Sold Jacob his birthright (Gn 25:29-34); lost blessing (Gn 27). Married Hittites (Gn 26:34), Ishmaelites (Gn 28:6-9). Reconciled

to Jacob (Gn 33). Genealogy (Gn 36). The LORD chose Jacob over Esau (Mal 1:2-3), but gave Esau land (Dt 2:2-12). Descendants eventually obliterated (Ob 1-21; Jer 49:7-22).

ESCAPE → ESCAPED, ESCAPES
2 Sm   15:14 or none of us will e from Absalom.
Jb   11:20 E shall be cut off from them,
Ps   68:21 e from death is the LORD God's.
Prv   12:13 ensnared, but the just e from a tight spot.
Sir   16:13 Criminals do not e with their
Jer   11:11 upon them a disaster they cannot e.
Ez   17:15 Can he e if he does this?
Dn   13:22 if I refuse, I cannot e your power.
Rom   2: 3 that you will e the judgment
1 Thes 5: 3 woman, and they will not e.
Heb   2: 3 how shall we e if we ignore so great
Heb   12:25 they did not e when they refused

ESCAPED → ESCAPE
1 Sm   22: 1 Gath and e to the cave of Adullam.
Ps   124: 7 We e with our lives like a bird
Jn   10:39 but he e from their power.
Heb   11:34 raging fires, e the devouring sword;
2 Pt   2:20 they, having e the defilements

ESCAPES → ESCAPE
Sir   42:20 no single thing e him.

ESHCOL
Nm   13:23 They also reached the Wadi E,

ESTABLISH → ESTABLISHED
Gn   6:18 I will e my covenant with you.
Dt   28: 9 The LORD will e you as a holy
1 Kgs 9: 5 I will e your royal throne over Israel
1 Chr 28: 7 I will e his kingdom forever, if he
Ps   89: 5 and e your throne through all ages."
Rom   10: 3 to e their own [righteousness],
Heb   10: 9 takes away the first to e the second.

ESTABLISHED → ESTABLISH
Gn   9:17 the covenant I have e between me
Ex   6: 4 I also e my covenant with them,
1 Kgs 2:12 his father, and his kingship was e.
Ps   89: 3 For I said, "My mercy is e forever;
Prv   8:27 When he e the heavens, there was I,
Is   2: 2 house shall be e as the highest
Is   54:14 In justice shall you be e,
Jer   10:12 power, e the world by his wisdom,
2 Pt   1:12 and are e in the truth you have.

ESTEEM → ESTEEMED
Prv   3: 4 Then will you win favor and e before God

ESTEEMED → ESTEEM
Acts   5:13 to join them, but the people e them.

ESTHER → HADASSAH
Jewess, originally named Hadassah, who lived in Persia; cousin of Mordecai (Est 2:7). Chosen queen of Ahasuerus (Est 2:8-18). Persuaded by Mordecai to foil Haman's plan to exterminate the Jews (Est 3-4). Revealed Haman's plans to Ahasuerus, resulting in Haman's death (Est 7), the Jews' preservation (Est 8-9), Mordecai's exaltation (Est 8:15; 9:4; 10). Decreed celebration of Purim (Est 9:18-32).

ESTRANGED
Ez   14: 5 e from me because of all their idols.

ETERNAL → ETERNITY
Gn   49:26 the delights of the e hills.
2 Mc   1:25 and e, Israel's savior from all evil,
Wis   7:26 For she is the reflection of e light,
Wis   17: 2 as exiles from the e providence.
Dn   13:42 "E God, you know what is hidden
Mt   18: 8 or two feet to be thrown into e fire.
Mt   19:16 what good must I do to gain e life?"
Mt   19:29 times more, and will inherit e life.
Mt   25:41 into the e fire prepared for the devil
Mt   25:46 these will go off to e punishment,
Mt   25:46 but the righteous to e life."
Mk   10:17 what must I do to inherit e life?"
Mk   10:30 and e life in the age to come.

Mk	16: S	[proclamation of e salvation. Amen.]
Lk	10:25	what must I do to inherit e life?"
Lk	16: 9	will be welcomed into e dwellings.
Lk	18:18	what must I do to inherit e life?"
Lk	18:30	age and e life in the age to come."
Jn	3:15	believes in him may have e life."
Jn	3:16	not perish but might have e life.
Jn	3:36	believes in the Son has e life,
Jn	4:14	of water welling up to e life."
Jn	4:36	and gathering crops for e life,
Jn	5:24	in the one who sent me has e life
Jn	5:39	think you have e life through them;
Jn	6:27	for the food that endures for e life,
Jn	6:40	and believes in him may have e life,
Jn	6:47	to you, whoever believes has e life.
Jn	6:54	flesh and drinks my blood has e life,
Jn	6:68	You have the words of e life.
Jn	10:28	I give them e life, and they shall
Jn	12:25	this world will preserve it for e life.
Jn	12:50	that his commandment is e life.
Jn	17: 2	he may give e life to all you gave
Jn	17: 3	Now this is e life, that they should
Acts	13:46	yourselves as unworthy of e life,
Acts	13:48	who were destined for e life came
Rom	1:20	his invisible attributes of e power
Rom	2: 7	e life to those who seek glory,
Rom	5:21	e life through Jesus Christ our Lord.
Rom	6:22	sanctification, and its end is e life.
Rom	6:23	of God is e life in Christ Jesus our
Rom	16:26	to the command of the e God,
2 Cor	4:17	us an e weight of glory beyond all
2 Cor	4:18	is transitory, but what is unseen is e.
2 Cor	5: 1	not made with hands, e in heaven.
Gal	6: 8	the spirit will reap e life
Eph	3:11	This was according to the e purpose
2 Thes	1: 9	These will pay the penalty of e ruin,
1 Tm	6:12	Lay hold of e life, to which you
1 Tm	6:16	To him be honor and e power.
2 Tm	2:10	Christ Jesus, together with e glory.
Ti	1: 2	in the hope of e life that God,
Ti	3: 7	and become heirs in hope of e life.
Heb	5: 9	he became the source of e salvation
Heb	6: 2	of the dead and e judgment.
Heb	9:12	blood, thus obtaining e redemption.
Heb	9:14	who through the e spirit offered
Heb	9:15	receive the promised e inheritance.
Heb	13:20	by the blood of the e covenant,
1 Pt	5:10	to his e glory through Christ [Jesus]
2 Pt	1:11	entry into the e kingdom of our
1 Jn	1: 2	proclaim to you the e life that was
1 Jn	2:25	the promise that he made us: e life.
1 Jn	3:15	no murderer has e life remaining
1 Jn	5:11	God gave us e life, and this life is
1 Jn	5:13	you may know that you have e life,
1 Jn	5:20	He is the true God and e life.
Jude	1: 6	he has kept in e chains, in gloom,
Jude	1: 7	undergoing a punishment of e fire.
Jude	1:21	Lord Jesus Christ that leads to e life.

ETERNITY → ETERNAL

Sir	1: 2	sea, the drops of rain, the days of e—
Sir	1: 4	and prudent understanding, from e.
Sir	42:21	he is from all e one and the same,
2 Pt	3:18	be glory now and to the day of e.

ETHAN

1 Kgs	5:11	wiser than E the Ezrahite,
1 Chr	15:19	and E, sounded brass cymbals.
Ps	89: 1	A *maskil* of E the Ezrahite.

ETHIOPIA → ETHIOPIAN, ETHIOPIANS

Jdt	1:10	of Egypt as far as the borders of E.
Est	1: 1	provinces from India to E—
Ps	87: 4	with E, "This one was born there."
Is	18: 1	insects, beyond the rivers of E,
Ez	30: 4	there will be anguish in E,

ETHIOPIAN → ETHIOPIA

Jer	38: 7	Now Ebed-melech, an E, a court official

Acts	8:27	Now there was an E eunuch, a court

ETHIOPIANS → ETHIOPIA

Jer	13:23	Can E change their skin,
Am	9: 7	Are you not like the E to me,

EUNICE
  Mother of Timothy (2 Tm 1:5).

EUNUCH → EUNUCHS

Est	2:14	the care of the royal e Shaashgaz,
Is	56: 3	Nor should the e say, "See, I am
Acts	8:27	Now there was an Ethiopian e,

EUNUCHS → EUNUCH

Is	56: 4	To the e who keep my sabbaths,

EUODIA

Phil	4: 2	I urge E and I urge Syntyche

EUPHRATES

Gn	2:14	The fourth river is the E.
Gn	15:18	of Egypt to the Great River, the E,
Dt	11:24	from the E River to the Western
2 Kgs	24: 7	the wadi of Egypt to the E River.
Rev	9:14	at the banks of the great river E."
Rev	16:12	his bowl on the great river E.

EUTYCHUS

Acts	20: 9	and a young man named E who was

EVANGELIST → EVANGELISTS

Acts	21: 8	we went to the house of Philip the e,
2 Tm	4: 5	perform the work of an e;

EVANGELISTS → EVANGELIST

Eph	4:11	others as e, others as pastors

EVE

Gn	3:20	man gave his wife the name "E,"
Gn	4: 1	had intercourse with his wife E,
Tb	8: 6	you made his wife E to be his helper
2 Cor	11: 3	as the serpent deceived E by his
1 Tm	2:13	For Adam was formed first, then E.

EVENING → EVENINGS

Gn	1: 5	E came, and morning followed—
Gn	8:11	In the e the dove came back to him,
Gn	24:11	Near e, at the time when women go
Eccl	11: 6	at e do not let your hand be idle:
Zec	14: 7	night, for in the e there will be light.

EVENINGS → EVENING

Dn	8:14	"For two thousand three hundred e
Dn	8:26	As for the vision of the e

EVER → EVERLASTING, FOREVER

Ex	11: 6	has never been, nor will e be again.
Ex	15:18	the LORD reign forever and e!
Dt	4:32	anything so great e happen before?
Ps	25:15	My eyes are e upon the LORD,
Ps	111: 8	Established forever and e, to be
Jer	31:36	e this fixed order gives way before
Dn	7:18	to possess it forever and e."
Mi	4: 5	the LORD, our God, forever and e.
Jn	1:18	No one has e seen God.
Gal	1: 5	to whom be glory forever and e.
Eph	3:21	to all generations, forever and e.
Phil	4:20	God and Father, glory forever and e.
1 Tm	1:17	God, honor and glory forever and e.
2 Tm	4:18	To him be glory forever and e.
Heb	1: 8	throne, O God, stands forever and e;
Heb	13:21	to whom be glory forever [and e].
1 Pt	4:11	glory and dominion forever and e.
1 Jn	4:12	No one has e seen God. Yet, if we
Rev	1: 6	be glory and power forever [and e].
Rev	1:18	but now I am alive forever and e.
Rev	4: 9	the throne, who lives forever and e,
Rev	7:12	might be to our God forever and e.
Rev	10: 6	by the one who lives forever and e,
Rev	11:15	and he will reign forever and e."
Rev	14:11	them will rise forever and e,
Rev	20:10	day and night forever and e.
Rev	22: 5	and they shall reign forever and e.

EVERLASTING → EVER, LAST

Gn	9:16	remember the **e** covenant between
Gn	17: 7	the ages as an **e** covenant, to be
Gn	17:13	be in your flesh as an **e** covenant.
Gn	17:19	my covenant as an **e** covenant
1 Chr	16:17	for Jacob, an **e** covenant for Israel:
1 Mc	6:44	and win an **e** name for himself.
Ps	78:66	**e** shame he dealt them.
Ps	105:10	for Jacob, an **e** covenant for Israel:
Ps	106:48	the God of Israel, from **e** to **e**!
Sir	15: 6	find, and an **e** name he will inherit.
Is	33:14	who of us can live with **e** flames?"
Is	35:10	Zion singing, crowned with **e** joy;
Is	51:11	Zion singing, crowned with **e** joy;
Is	55: 3	I will make with you an **e** covenant,
Is	55:13	as an **e** sign that shall not fail.
Is	61: 7	their own land; **e** joy shall be theirs.
Jer	25: 9	of horror, of hissing, of **e** reproach.
Jer	50: 5	to the Lord in an **e** covenant,
Ez	16:60	I will set up an **e** covenant with you.
Ez	37:26	it shall be an **e** covenant with them.
Dn	3:100	his kingship is an **e** kingship,
Dn	7:14	His dominion is an **e** dominion
Dn	7:27	kingship shall be an **e** kingship,
Dn	9:24	E justice will be introduced,
Dn	12: 2	Some to **e** life, others to reproach and **e** disgrace.

EVERY → EVERYONE, EVERYTHING, EVERYWHERE

Gn	1:29	I give you **e** seed-bearing plant
Gn	1:29	**e** tree that has seed-bearing fruit
Gn	7: 4	the earth **e** being that I have made.
Gn	7:23	The Lord wiped out **e** being
Ex	11: 5	E firstborn in the land of Egypt will
Tb	12:18	So bless God **e** day; give praise
Ps	7:12	patient, not exercising anger **e** day.
Ps	50:10	For **e** animal of the forest is mine,
Ps	145: 2	E day I will bless you; I will praise
Prv	30: 5	E word of God is tested; he is
Eccl	3: 1	time for **e** affair under the heavens.
Eccl	12:14	God will bring to judgment **e** work,
Sir	6:35	Be eager to hear **e** discourse;
Is	40: 4	E valley shall be lifted up,
Is	45:23	To me **e** knee shall bend; by me **e** tongue shall swear,
Jer	2:20	On **e** high hill, under **e** green tree,
Ez	21:12	When it comes **e** heart shall melt,
Ez	21:12	**e** spirit will grow faint, and **e** knee
Mt	4: 4	by **e** word that comes forth
Mt	7:17	Just so, **e** good tree bears good fruit,
Mt	9:35	and curing **e** disease and illness.
Mt	12:25	"E kingdom divided against itself
Lk	4:13	the devil had finished **e** temptation,
Jn	15: 2	He takes away **e** branch in me
Rom	3:19	so that **e** mouth may be silenced
Rom	14:11	Lord, **e** knee shall bend before me,
Rom	14:11	**e** tongue shall give praise to God."
1 Cor	15:24	he has destroyed **e** sovereignty and **e** authority
2 Cor	10: 5	take **e** thought captive in obedience
Eph	1: 3	in Christ with **e** spiritual blessing
Eph	1:21	far above **e** principality, authority,
Eph	1:21	**e** name that is named not only
Phil	2:10	name of Jesus **e** knee should bend,
Phil	2:11	**e** tongue confess that Jesus Christ is
1 Thes	5:22	Refrain from **e** kind of evil.
2 Tm	3:17	equipped for **e** good work.
Heb	12: 1	let us rid ourselves of **e** burden
1 Jn	4: 1	do not trust **e** spirit but test
Rev	1: 7	and **e** eye will see him, even those
Rev	7:17	and God will wipe away **e** tear
Rev	21: 4	He will wipe **e** tear from their eyes,

EVERYONE → EVERY, ONE

Jer	31:34	E, from least to greatest, shall know me—
Ez	20:11	**e** who keeps them has life through
Dn	12: 1	**e** who is found written in the book.
Jl	3: 5	**e** who calls upon the name
Mt	7: 8	For **e** who asks, receives;
Mt	7:21	"Not **e** who says to me, 'Lord,

Lk	11: 4	for we ourselves forgive **e** in debt
Jn	1: 9	which enlightens **e**, was coming
Jn	3:16	so that **e** who believes in him might
Acts	2:21	be that **e** shall be saved who calls
Rom	10:13	For "**e** who calls on the name
1 Cor	10:33	just as I try to please **e** in every way,
1 Tm	2: 4	who wills **e** to be saved and to come
1 Jn	3: 4	E who commits sin commits
1 Jn	4: 7	**e** who loves is begotten by God

EVERYTHING → EVERY, THING

Gn	1:31	God looked at **e** he had made,
Gn	6:17	**e** on earth shall perish.
Ex	19: 8	together, "E the Lord has said,
Ps	150: 6	Let **e** that has breath give praise
Eccl	3: 1	There is an appointed time for **e**,
Eccl	3:11	God has made **e** appropriate to its
Eccl	9: 2	E is the same for everybody:
Jer	10:16	for he is the maker of **e**!
Lk	1: 3	investigating **e** accurately anew,
Jn	6:37	E that the Father gives me will
Jn	14:26	he will teach you **e** and remind you
Acts	4:32	his own, but they had **e** in common.
Rom	14:20	E is indeed clean, but it is wrong
1 Cor	2:10	For the Spirit scrutinizes **e**,
1 Cor	10:31	you do, do **e** for the glory of God.
Col	3:17	do **e** in the name of the Lord Jesus,
1 Thes	5:21	Test **e**; retain what is good.
1 Tm	4: 4	For **e** created by God is good,
2 Pt	1: 3	has bestowed on us **e** that makes

EVERYWHERE → EVERY, WHERE

Lk	9: 6	good news and curing diseases **e**.
Acts	17:30	he demands that all people **e** repent

EVIDENCE

Nm	35:30	the **e** of witnesses is required to kill
Dt	22:15	the young woman shall take the **e**
2 Thes	1: 5	This is **e** of the just judgment

EVIL → EVILDOERS, EVILS

Gn	6: 5	was always nothing but **e**,
Gn	44: 4	'Why did you repay good with **e**?
Ex	32:22	know how the people are prone to **e**.
Nm	32:13	that had done **e** in the sight
Dt	1:35	one of this **e** generation shall look
Dt	13: 6	Thus shall you purge the **e**
Dt	28:20	perish for the **e** you have done
1 Sm	12:20	have indeed committed all this **e**!
1 Sm	16:14	and he was tormented by an **e** spirit
1 Sm	18:10	The next day an **e** spirit from God
1 Sm	19: 9	an **e** spirit from the Lord came
2 Sm	11:27	of the Lord what David had done was **e**.
1 Kgs	11: 6	Solomon did what was **e** in the sight
1 Kgs	16:25	But Omri did what was **e**
2 Kgs	15:24	He did what was **e** in the Lord's
Tb	6: 8	is afflicted by a demon or **e** spirit,
Tb	12: 7	good, and **e** will not overtake you.
Jb	1: 1	Job, who feared God and avoided **e**.
Jb	1: 8	fearing God and avoiding **e**."
Jb	2: 3	upright, fearing God and avoiding **e**.
Jb	28:28	and avoiding **e** is understanding.
Ps	5: 5	You are not a god who delights in **e**;
Ps	28: 4	their deeds, for the **e** that they do.
Ps	34:14	Keep your tongue from **e**, your lips
Ps	34:15	Turn from **e** and do good;
Ps	37:27	Turn from **e** and do good, that you
Ps	51: 6	I have done what is **e** in your eyes
Ps	53: 5	Do they not know better, those who do **e**,
Ps	97:10	hate **e**, he protects the souls
Ps	141: 4	Do not let my heart incline to **e**,
Prv	3: 7	the Lord and turn away from **e**;
Prv	4:27	to left, keep your foot far from **e**.
Prv	8:13	[fear of the Lord is hatred of **e**;]
Prv	11:19	life, but pursuit of **e**, toward death.
Prv	11:27	but those who pursue **e** will have **e**
Prv	14:16	person is cautious and turns from **e**;
Prv	14:22	Do not those who plan **e** go astray?
Prv	16: 6	the fear of the Lord **e** is avoided.

Prv	17:13	If you return e for good, e will not
Prv	20:30	E is cleansed away by bloody
Prv	24:20	For the e have no future, the lamp
Prv	28: 5	The e understand nothing of justice,
Sir	7: 1	Do no e, and e will not overtake
Is	5:20	Those who call e good, and good e,
Is	13:11	I will punish the world for its e
Jer	4:14	Cleanse your heart of e, Jerusalem,
Jer	18: 8	I have decreed turns from its e,
Jer	18:10	nation does what is e in my eyes,
Ez	7: 5	E upon e! See it coming!
Ez	33:11	Turn, turn from your e ways!
Dn	9:13	law of Moses, this e has come upon us.
Am	5:13	are struck dumb for it is an e time.)
Am	5:14	Seek good and not e, that you may
Jon	3: 8	they all must turn from their e way
Mi	3: 2	who hate what is good, and love e?
Hb	1:13	the sight of e you cannot endure.
Zec	8:17	none of you plot e against another
Mt	6:13	test, but deliver us from the e one.
Mt	12:35	an e person brings forth e out of a store of e.
Mt	13:38	weeds are the children of the e one,
Mt	15:19	For from the heart come e thoughts,
Mk	7:21	from their hearts, come e thoughts,
Jn	3:19	to light, because their works were e.
Jn	17:15	that you keep them from the e one.
Rom	2: 9	every human being who does e,
Rom	3: 8	we should do e that good may come
Rom	7:19	I want, but I do the e I do not want.
Rom	7:21	I want to do right, e is at hand.
Rom	12: 9	hate what is e, hold on to what is
Rom	12:17	Do not repay anyone e for e;
Rom	12:21	Do not be conquered by e but conquer e with good.
Rom	16:19	is good, and simple as to what is e;
1 Cor	10: 6	so that we might not desire e things,
1 Cor	14:20	In respect to e be like infants,
Eph	5:16	opportunity, because the days are e.
Eph	6:12	with the e spirits in the heavens.
Eph	6:16	[the] flaming arrows of the e one.
Col	1:21	hostile in mind because of e deeds
Col	3: 5	passion, e desire, and the greed
1 Thes	5:22	Refrain from every kind of e.
2 Thes	3: 3	you and guard you from the e one.
Heb	5:14	by practice to discern good and e.
Jas	1:13	is not subject to temptation to e,
Jas	2: 4	and become judges with e designs?
Jas	3: 8	It is a restless e, full of deadly
Jas	4:16	All such boasting is e.
1 Pt	2:16	using freedom as a pretext for e,
1 Pt	3: 9	Do not return e for e, or insult
1 Pt	3:10	days must keep the tongue from e
1 Pt	3:17	be the will of God, than for doing e.
1 Jn	2:13	you have conquered the e one.
1 Jn	2:14	and you have conquered the e one.
1 Jn	3:12	Cain who belonged to the e one
1 Jn	3:12	Because his own works were e,
1 Jn	5:18	and the e one cannot touch him.
1 Jn	5:19	is under the power of the e one.
2 Jn	1:11	greets him shares in his e works.
3 Jn	1:11	do not imitate e but imitate good.
3 Jn	1:11	does what is e has never seen God.

EVILDOERS → DO, EVIL

Jb	34: 8	Keeps company with e and goes
Jb	34:22	no darkness so dense that e can hide
Ps	14: 4	Will these e never learn?
Ps	34:17	The LORD's face is against e
Ps	36:13	There make the fall;
Ps	64: 3	the malicious crowd, the mob of e.
Ps	94: 4	go on boasting, all these e?
Ps	94:16	Who will stand up for me against e?
Ps	141: 9	set for me, from the snares of e.
Prv	10:29	who walk honestly, downfall for e.
Prv	21:15	is a joy for the just, downfall for e.
Prv	24:19	Do not be provoked at e, do not
Is	31: 2	and against those who help e.
Mal	3:15	for e not only prosper but even test

Mt	7:23	Depart from me, you e.'
Lk	13:27	Depart from me, all you e!'
1 Pt	2:12	so that if they speak of you as e,

EVILS → EVIL

Jer	2:13	Two e my people have done:
1 Tm	6:10	love of money is the root of all e,

EWE

2 Sm	12: 3	at all except one little e lamb that he

EXACT

Est	4: 7	as well as the e amount of silver

EXALT → EXALTED, EXALTING, EXALTS

Jos	3: 7	Today I will begin to e you
1 Sm	2:10	and e the horn of his anointed!"
Tb	13: 6	and e the King of the ages.
Tb	13: 7	As for me, I e my God, my soul
Ps	34: 4	and let us e his name together.
Prv	4: 8	Extol her, and she will e you;
Sir	1:30	Do not e yourself lest you fall
Is	33:10	now e myself, now lift myself up.
Dn	3:57	praise and e him above all forever.
Jas	4:10	before the Lord and he will e you.
1 Pt	5: 6	God, that he may e you in due time.

EXALTED → EXALT

Nm	24: 7	Agag and their dominion will be e.
Jos	4:14	day the LORD e Joshua
2 Sm	5:12	had e his kingdom for the sake
1 Chr	14: 2	his kingdom was greatly e
1 Chr	29:11	you are e as head over all.
1 Chr	29:25	the LORD e Solomon greatly
Neh	9: 5	which is e above all blessing
Jb	24:24	They are e for a while, and then are
Ps	18:47	be my rock! E be God, my savior!
Ps	46:11	I am e among the nations,
Ps	89:25	through my name his horn will be e.
Ps	89:43	You have e the right hand of his
Ps	97: 9	all the earth, e far above all gods.
Ps	99: 2	in Zion, e above all the peoples.
Ps	138: 2	For you have e over all your name
Ps	148:13	for his name alone is e, His majesty
Prv	11:11	blessing of the upright the city is e,
Is	2:11	and the LORD alone will be e,
Is	2:17	the LORD alone will be e
Is	5:16	of hosts shall be e by judgment,
Is	12: 4	deeds, proclaim how e is his name.
Is	33: 5	The LORD is e,
Is	52:13	he shall be raised high and greatly e.
Jer	17:12	of glory, e from the beginning,
Hos	13: 1	there was terror; he was e in Israel;
Mt	23:12	whoever humbles himself will be e.
Lk	14:11	who humbles himself will be e."
Lk	18:14	who humbles himself will be e."
Acts	2:33	E at the right hand of God,
Acts	5:31	God e him at his right hand as
Phil	2: 9	God greatly e him and bestowed

EXALTING → EXALT

Dn	11:36	wills, e himself and making himself

EXALTS → EXALT

1 Sm	2: 7	makes rich, humbles, and also e.
Prv	14:34	Justice e a nation, but sin is
Sir	7:11	there is One who e and humbles.
Lk	14:11	For everyone who e himself will be
Lk	18:14	for everyone who e himself will be
2 Thes	2: 4	e himself above every so-called god

EXAMINE → EXAMINED

Ps	26: 2	E me, Lord, and test me; search
Sir	11: 7	not find fault; e first, then criticize.
Lam	3:40	Let us search and e our ways,
1 Cor	11:28	A person should e himself, and so
2 Cor	13: 5	E yourselves to see whether you are

EXAMINED → EXAMINE

Acts	17:11	e the scriptures daily to determine

EXAMPLE 94 EXTOL

EXAMPLE → EXAMPLES
Jdt   8:24 let us set an e for our kindred.
1 Cor 10:11 things happened to them as an e,
1 Tm   1:16 display all his patience as an e
1 Tm   4:12 but set an e for those who believe,
Jas   5:10 Take as an e of hardship
1 Pt   2:21 leaving you an e that you should
2 Pt   2: 6 making them an e for the godless
Jude   1: 7 vice, serve as an e by undergoing

EXAMPLES → EXAMPLE
1 Cor 10: 6 These things happened as e for us,
1 Pt   5: 3 to you, but be e to the flock.

EXCEL → EXCELLENCE, EXCELLENT
Gn   49: 4 water, you shall no longer e, for you
2 Cor   8: 7 Now as you e in every respect,
2 Cor   8: 7 may you e in this gracious act also.

EXCELLENCE → EXCEL
Phil   4: 8 if there is any e and if there is

EXCELLENT → EXCEL
1 Cor 12:31 I shall show you a still more e way.
Ti   3: 8 these are e and beneficial to others.
Heb   1: 4 has inherited is more e than theirs.
Heb   8: 6 so much more e a ministry as he is

EXCEPT
Nm 14:30 swore to settle you, e Caleb,
2 Sm 22:32 Truly, who is God e the LORD?
1 Kgs 12:20 to the house of David e the tribe
1 Kgs 15: 5 e in the case of Uriah the Hittite.
Mt 11:27 No one knows the Son e the Father,
Mt 11:27 no one knows the Father e the Son
Lk 11:29 will be given it, e the sign of Jonah.
Jn   3:13 to heaven e the one who has come
Jn   6:46 has seen the Father e the one who is
Jn 14: 6 comes to the Father e through me.
Jn 17:12 none of them was lost e the son

EXCESSIVE
2 Cor   2: 7 may be overwhelmed by e pain.

EXCHANGED
Ps 106:20 They e their glory for the image
Rom   1:23 e the glory of the immortal God
Rom   1:25 They e the truth of God for a lie
Rom   1:26 Their females e natural relations

EXCLUDE → EXCLUDED
Lk   6:22 and when they e and insult you,

EXCLUDED → EXCLUDE
2 Chr 26:21 for he was e from the house

EXCUSE
Jn 15:22 as it is they have no e for their sin.
Rom   1:20 As a result, they have no e;
Rom   2: 1 you are without e, every one of you

EXECUTED → EXECUTES
Nm 33: 4 gods, too, the LORD e judgments.

EXECUTES → EXECUTED
Dt 10:18 who e justice for the orphan

EXERCISES
1 Cor 9:25 Every athlete e discipline in every

EXHIBITED
1 Cor 4: 9 God has e us apostles as the last

EXHORT → EXHORTATION
Ti   2:15 E and correct with all authority.

EXHORTATION → EXHORT
Acts 13:15 you has a word of e for the people,
Acts 15:31 it, they were delighted with the e.

EXILE → EXILED, EXILES
2 Kgs 25:11 guard, led into e the last of the army
Ezr   6:21 who had returned from the e and all
Ps 144:14 walls, no e, no outcry in our streets.
Is   5:13 Therefore my people go into e
Jer 13:19 Judah is taken into e—all of it—in total e.

Jer 48: 7 Chemosh shall go into e, his priests
Jer 49: 3 For Milcom is going into e,
Lam   1: 3 Judah has gone into e,

EXILED → EXILE
Sir 47:24 caused them to be e from their land.

EXILES → EXILE
Ezr   6:19 The returned e kept the Passover
Jer 24: 5 favor Judah's e whom I sent away
Ez 11:25 I told the e everything the LORD

EXIST → EXISTED, EXISTS
Rom   4:17 and calls into being what does not e.
1 Cor   8: 6 all things are and for whom we e,
Heb   2:10 and through whom all things e,

EXISTED → EXIST
2 Pt   3: 5 the fact that the heavens e of old

EXISTS → EXIST
Heb 11: 6 God must believe that he e

EXODUS
Heb 11:22 spoke of the E of the Israelites

EXORCISTS
Acts 19:13 some itinerant Jewish e tried

EXPECTATION → EXPECTING
Prv 10:28 but the e of the wicked perishes.
Lk   3:15 Now the people were filled with e,

EXPECTING → EXPECTATION
Lk   6:35 to them, and lend e nothing back;

EXPENSIVE
1 Tm   2: 9 ornaments, or pearls, or e clothes,

EXPERIENCE
Sir 25: 6 The crown of the elderly, wide e;
Gal   3: 4 Did you e so many things in vain?—

EXPIATE → EXPIATED, EXPIATION
Heb   2:17 high priest before God to e the sins

EXPIATED → EXPIATE
Prv 16: 6 By steadfast loyalty guilt is e,
Dn   9:24 guilt will be e, Everlasting justice

EXPIATION → EXPIATE
Nm 35:33 the land can have no e for the blood
Is 27: 9 shall be the e of Jacob's guilt,
Rom   3:25 whom God set forth as an e,
1 Jn   2: 2 He is e for our sins, and not for our
1 Jn   4:10 us and sent his Son as e for our sins.

EXPLAIN → EXPLAINED, EXPLAINING
2 Chr   9: 2 that Solomon could not e it to her.
Mt 13:36 "E to us the parable of the weeds
Mt 15:15 in reply, "E [this] parable to us."
Heb   5:11 and it is difficult to e, for you have

EXPLAINED → EXPLAIN
Jgs 14:17 and she e the riddle to her people.
Mk   4:34 his own disciples he e everything
Acts 18:26 and e to him the Way [of God] more

EXPLAINING → EXPLAIN
Dn   5:12 e riddles and solving problems,

EXPLOIT
Lv 19:13 You shall not e your neighbor.
2 Pt   2: 3 In their greed they will e you

EXPOSE → EXPOSED
Mt   1:19 yet unwilling to e her to shame,
Eph   5:11 works of darkness; rather e them,

EXPOSED → EXPOSE
Ez 23:29 so that your indecent nakedness is e.
Jn   3:20 so that his works might not be e.
Eph   5:13 everything e by the light becomes
Heb 10:33 times you were publicly e to abuse
Rev 16:15 not go naked and people see him e.)

EXTOL
Jb 36:24 Remember, you should e his work,

EXTORTION

Ps	62:11	Do not trust in e; in plunder put no
Ez	22:29	The people of the land practice e
Lk	3:14	"Do not practice e, do not falsely

EXTRAORDINARY

Acts	19:11	So e were the mighty deeds God

EXULT → EXULTS

Sg	1: 4	Let us e and rejoice in you;
Hb	3:18	LORD and e in my saving God.

EXULTS → EXULT

1 Sm	2: 1	"My heart e in the LORD,

EYE → EYES, EYEWITNESSES

Ex	21:24	e for e, tooth for tooth,
Lv	24:20	fracture for fracture, e for e,
Dt	19:21	Life for life, e for e, tooth for tooth,
Ps	17: 8	Keep me as the apple of your e;
Ps	94: 9	The one who formed the e not see?
Prv	7: 2	my teaching as the apple of your e;
Prv	30:17	The e that mocks a father, or scorns
Eccl	1: 8	The e is not satisfied by seeing nor
Sir	31:13	Remember that the greedy e is evil.
Is	64: 3	ear has ever heard, no e ever seen,
Zec	2:12	you strikes me directly in the e.
Mt	5:29	If your right e causes you to sin,
Mt	5:38	said, 'An e for an e and a tooth
Mt	6:22	"The lamp of the body is the e.
Mt	6:22	If your e is sound, your whole body
Mt	7: 3	the splinter in your brother's e,
Mt	7: 3	the wooden beam in your own e?
Mt	18: 9	And if your e causes you to sin,
Mk	10:25	to pass through [the] e of [a] needle
1 Cor	2: 9	"What e has not seen, and ear has
1 Cor	12:17	If the whole body were an e,
1 Cor	15:52	in the blink of an e, at the last
Rev	1: 7	and every e will see him, even those

EYES → EYE

Gn	3: 7	the e of both of them were opened,
Nm	15:39	desires of your hearts and your e.
Nm	22:31	the LORD opened Balaam's e,
Nm	33:55	remain will become barbs in your e
Dt	11:12	the e of the LORD, your God,
Dt	16:19	a bribe blinds the e even of the wise
Dt	29: 3	or e to see, or ears to hear until this
Dt	34: 4	have let you see it with your own e,
Jos	23:13	for your sides and thorns for your e,
Jgs	16:28	at one blow for my two e."
1 Kgs	10: 7	my own e that not even the half had
2 Kgs	6:17	And the LORD opened the e
2 Kgs	9:30	it, she shadowed her e, adorned her
2 Chr	16: 9	The e of the LORD roam over
Tb	2:10	warm droppings settled in my e,
Tb	6: 9	the e of one who has white scales,
Jb	31: 1	I made a covenant with my e not
Ps	13: 4	Give light to my e lest I sleep
Ps	25:15	My e are ever upon the LORD,
Ps	36: 2	his e are closed to the fear of God.
Ps	51: 6	I have done what is evil in your e
Ps	66: 7	His e are fixed upon the nations.
Ps	115: 5	but do not speak, e but do not see.
Ps	118:23	it is wonderful in our e.
Ps	119:18	Open my e to see clearly
Ps	119:37	Avert my e from what is worthless;
Ps	121: 1	I raise my e toward the mountains.
Ps	123: 1	To you I raise my e, to you
Ps	123: 2	So our e are on the LORD our
Ps	139:16	Your e saw me unformed;
Ps	141: 8	For my e are upon you, O LORD,
Prv	3: 7	Do not be wise in your own e,
Prv	4:25	Let your e look straight ahead
Prv	6:17	Haughty e, a lying tongue,
Prv	15: 3	The e of the LORD are in every
Prv	17:24	the e of a fool are on the ends
Prv	22:12	The e of the LORD watch over
Prv	23:29	Who have bleary e?

Prv	26: 5	they become wise in their own e.
Eccl	2:10	that my e desired did I deny them,
Sg	4: 1	Your e are doves behind your veil.
Is	1:15	hands, I will close my e to you;
Is	6: 5	and my e have seen the King,
Is	6:10	dull their ears and close their e;
Is	6:10	Lest they see with their e, and hear
Is	33:17	Your e will see a king in his
Is	42: 7	To open the e of the blind, to bring
Jer	8:23	of water, my e a fountain of tears,
Lam	3:48	My e stream with tears over
Ez	1:18	e filled the four rims all around.
Ez	24:16	from you the delight of your e,
Dn	7: 8	This horn had e like human e,
Dn	10: 6	his e were like fiery torches,
Hb	1:13	Your e are too pure to look
Zec	4:10	"These seven are the e
Mt	9:30	And their e were opened.
Mt	13:15	they have closed their e, lest they see with their e
Mt	21:42	done, and it is wonderful in our e'?
Mk	8:25	he laid hands on his e a second time
Lk	10:23	"Blessed are the e that see what
Lk	24:31	With that their e were opened
Jn	9:10	"[So] how were your e opened?"
Jn	10:21	surely a demon cannot open the e
Jn	12:40	"He blinded their e and hardened
Jn	12:40	that they might not see with their e
Acts	9: 8	when he opened his e he could see
Acts	28:27	they have closed their e, so they may not see with their e
Rom	11:10	let their e grow dim so that they
Eph	1:18	May the e of [your] hearts be
Heb	4:13	exposed to the e of him to whom we
1 Pt	3:12	For the e of the Lord are
1 Jn	1: 1	what we have seen with our e,
1 Jn	2:16	lust, enticement for the e,
Rev	1:14	and his e were like a fiery flame.
Rev	2:18	whose e are like a fiery flame
Rev	4: 6	four living creatures covered with e
Rev	5: 6	He had seven horns and seven e;
Rev	7:17	wipe away every tear from their e."
Rev	19:12	his e were [like] a fiery flame,
Rev	21: 4	He will wipe every tear from their e,

EYEWITNESSES → EYE, WITNESS

Lk	1: 2	just as those who were e
2 Pt	1:16	but we had been e of his majesty.

EZEKIEL

Priest called to be prophet to the exiles (Sir 49:8; Ez 1–3). Symbolically acted out destruction of Jerusalem (Ez 4–5; 12; 24).

EZION-GEBER

1 Kgs	9:26	King Solomon also built a fleet at E,
2 Chr	20:36	the fleet was built at E.

EZRA

Priest and teacher of the Law who led a return of exiles to Israel to reestablish temple and worship (Ezr 7–8). Corrected intermarriage of priests (Ezr 9–10). Read Law at celebration of Feast of Tabernacles (Neh 8). Participated in dedication of Jerusalem's walls (Neh 12).

F

FACE → FACES

Gn	32:31	"because I have seen God f to f,"
Ex	3: 6	Moses hid his f, for he was afraid
Ex	33:11	used to speak to Moses f to f,
Ex	33:20	But you cannot see my f, for no one
Ex	34:30	radiant the skin of his f had become,
Nm	6:25	The LORD let his f shine
Nm	12: 8	f to f I speak to him, plainly and not
Dt	5: 4	F to f, the LORD spoke with you
Dt	31:17	them and hide my f from them;
Dt	34:10	whom the LORD knew f to f,
Jgs	6:22	messenger of the LORD f to f!"
2 Kgs	14: 8	"Come, let us meet f to f."
2 Chr	25:17	saying, "Come, let us meet f to f."
2 Chr	30: 9	he will not turn away his f from you
Ezr	9: 6	and humiliated to raise my f to you,

Jdt	10:23	all marveled at the beauty of her f.
Jdt	16: 6	by the beauty of her f brought him down.
Est	7: 8	the f of Haman was covered over.
Jb	1:11	surely he will curse you to your f."
Ps	4: 7	show us the light of your f!"
Ps	13: 2	How long will you hide your f
Ps	21: 7	you gladden him with the joy of your f.
Ps	27: 8	says my heart, "seek his f"; your f,
Ps	31:17	Let your f shine on your servant;
Ps	51:11	Turn away your f from my sins;
Ps	51:13	Do not drive me from before your f,
Ps	67: 2	may his f shine upon us.
Ps	80: 4	light up your f and we shall be
Ps	104:29	When you hide your f, they panic.
Ps	119:135	Let your f shine upon your servant;
Eccl	8: 1	Wisdom illumines the f
Sir	13:25	The heart changes one's f, either for good
Is	8:17	who is hiding his f from the house
Is	50: 7	Therefore I have set my f like flint,
Is	54: 8	for a moment I hid my f from you;
Jer	32: 4	He shall speak with him f to f
Jer	44:11	I have set my f against you for evil,
Ez	1:10	each of the four had a human f,
Ez	1:10	and on the right the f of a lion,
Ez	1:10	and on the left, the f of an ox,
Ez	1:10	and each had the f of an eagle.
Ez	39:23	betrayed me, I hid my f from them,
Ez	39:29	I will no longer hide my f
Dn	10: 6	chrysolite, his f shone like lightning,
Mt	17: 2	his f shone like the sun and his
Mt	18:10	upon the f of my heavenly Father.
Mt	26:67	they spat in his f and struck him,
Lk	9:29	While he was praying his f changed
Acts	6:15	saw that his f was like the f of an angel.
1 Cor	13:12	as in a mirror, but then f to f.
2 Cor	3: 7	intently at the f of Moses because
2 Cor	4: 6	of God on the f of [Jesus] Christ.
2 Cor	10: 1	I who am humble when f to f
1 Pt	3:12	but the f of the Lord is against
2 Jn	1:12	to speak f to f so that our joy may be
3 Jn	1:14	you soon, when we can talk f to f.
Rev	1:16	and his f shone like the sun at its
Rev	4: 7	the third had a f like that of a human
Rev	10: 1	his f was like the sun and his feet
Rev	22: 4	They will look upon his f, and his

FACES → FACE

Ex	25:20	their f looking toward the cover.
Ps	34: 6	and your f may not blush for shame.
Ps	83:17	Cover their f with shame, till they
Is	6: 2	with two they covered their f,
Ez	1: 6	but each had four f and four wings,
Ez	10:14	Each living creature had four f:
Ez	41:18	Each cherub had two f:
Rev	9: 7	their f were like human f,

FACT

| 2 Pt | 3: 5 | They deliberately ignore the f |

FACTIONS

| 1 Cor | 11:19 | there have to be f among you |
| Gal | 5:20 | acts of selfishness, dissensions, f, |

FAIL → FAILED, FAILINGS, FAILS

Nm	15:22	If through inadvertence you f to do
Dt	31: 6	he will never f you or forsake you.
1 Chr	28:20	He will not f you or abandon you
Is	58:11	like a flowing spring whose waters never f.
Ez	47:12	will not wither, nor will their fruit f.
Lk	22:32	that your own faith may not f;
2 Cor	13: 5	unless, of course, you f the test.

FAILED → FAIL

| Rom | 9: 6 | it is not that the word of God has f. |
| 2 Cor | 13: 6 | you will discover that we have not f. |

FAILINGS → FAIL

| Rom | 15: 1 | to put up with the f of the weak |

FAILS → FAIL

| Ps | 143: 7 | for my spirit f me. |

FAINT

| Ps | 142: 4 | When my spirit is f within me, |
| Is | 40:31 | grow weary, walk and not grow f. |

FAIR → FAIRLY

| Mt | 16: 2 | 'Tomorrow will be f, for the sky is |

FAIRLY → FAIR

| Ps | 58: 2 | do you judge f you children |
| Col | 4: 1 | treat your slaves justly and f, |

FAITH → FAITHFUL, FAITHFULLY, FAITHFULNESS, FAITHLESS

Nm	5: 6	thus breaking f with the LORD,
Dt	32:51	of you broke f with me among
Jgs	9:15	'If you are anointing me in good f,
Jgs	9:16	then, if you have acted in good f
Jgs	9:19	then, you have acted in good f
1 Mc	10:27	to keep f with us, and we will
Ps	116:10	I kept f, even when I said, "I am
Ps	146: 6	that is in them, Who keeps f forever,
Sir	27:17	your friend, keep f with him;
Is	7: 9	Unless your f is firm, you shall not
Is	26: 2	nation may enter, one that keeps f.
Mi	7: 5	Put no f in a friend, do not trust
Hb	2: 4	is righteous because of f shall live.
Mt	6:30	provide for you, O you of little f?
Mt	8:10	no one in Israel have I found such f.
Mt	8:26	are you terrified, O you of little f?"
Mt	9: 2	When Jesus saw their f, he said
Mt	9:22	Your f has saved you."
Mt	9:29	done for you according to your f."
Mt	14:31	him, "O you of little f, why did you
Mt	15:28	in reply, "O woman, great is your f!
Mt	16: 8	he said, "You of little f, why do you
Mt	17:20	to them, "Because of your little f.
Mt	17:20	if you have f the size of a mustard
Mt	21:21	you, if you have f and do not waver,
Mt	21:22	you ask for in prayer with f,
Mk	2: 5	When Jesus saw their f, he said
Mk	4:40	Do you not yet have f?"
Mk	5:34	"Daughter, your f has saved you.
Mk	10:52	your f has saved you."
Mk	11:22	to them in reply, "Have f in God.
Lk	5:20	When he saw their f, he said,
Lk	7: 9	even in Israel have I found such f."
Lk	7:50	the woman, "Your f has saved you;
Lk	8:25	he asked them, "Where is your f?"
Lk	8:48	"Daughter, your f has saved you;
Lk	12:28	provide for you, O you of little f?
Lk	17: 5	said to the Lord, "Increase our f."
Lk	17: 6	"If you have f the size of a mustard
Lk	17:19	up and go; your f has saved you."
Lk	18: 8	comes, will he find f on earth?"
Lk	18:42	your f has saved you."
Lk	22:32	prayed that your own f may not fail;
Acts	3:16	And by f in his name, this man,
Acts	6: 5	a man filled with f and the holy
Acts	6: 7	were becoming obedient to the f.
Acts	11:24	filled with the holy Spirit and f.
Acts	13: 8	turn the proconsul away from the f.
Acts	14: 9	saw that he had the f to be healed,
Acts	14:22	exhorted them to persevere in the f,
Acts	14:27	how he had opened the door of f
Acts	15: 9	for by f he purified their hearts.
Acts	16: 5	day the churches grew stronger in f
Acts	20:21	God and to f in our Lord Jesus.
Acts	24:24	to him speak about f in Christ Jesus.
Acts	26:18	who have been consecrated by f
Rom	1: 5	to bring about the obedience of f,
Rom	1: 8	of you, because your f is heralded
Rom	1:12	encouraged by one another's f,
Rom	1:17	the righteousness of God from f to f;
Rom	1:17	one who is righteous by f will live."
Rom	3:22	of God through f in Jesus Christ
Rom	3:25	expiation, through f, by his blood,

Rom	3:26	justify the one who has f in Jesus.
Rom	3:27	No, rather on the principle of f.
Rom	3:28	a person is justified by f apart
Rom	3:30	the circumcised on the basis of f and the uncircumcised through f.
Rom	3:31	we then annulling the law by this f?
Rom	4: 5	his f is credited as righteousness.
Rom	4: 9	Now we assert that "f was credited
Rom	4:11	received through f while he was
Rom	4:12	follow the path of f that our father
Rom	4:13	the righteousness that comes from f.
Rom	4:14	f is null and the promise is void.
Rom	4:16	it depends on f, so that it may be
Rom	4:19	He did not weaken in f when he
Rom	4:20	he was empowered by f and gave
Rom	5: 1	since we have been justified by f,
Rom	9:30	is, righteousness that comes from f;
Rom	9:32	Because they did it not by f, but as
Rom	10: 6	that comes from f says, "Do not say
Rom	10: 8	is, the word of f that we preach),
Rom	10:17	Thus f comes from what is heard,
Rom	11:20	but you are there because of f.
Rom	12: 3	to the measure of f that God has
Rom	12: 6	if prophecy, in proportion to the f;
Rom	14: 1	Welcome anyone who is weak in f,
Rom	14:22	Keep the f [that] you have
Rom	14:23	if he eats, because this is not from f; for whatever is not from f is sin.
Rom	16:26	to bring about the obedience of f,
1 Cor	2: 5	so that your f might rest not
1 Cor	12: 9	to another f by the same Spirit;
1 Cor	13: 2	I have all f so as to move mountains
1 Cor	13:13	So f, hope, love remain, these three;
1 Cor	15:14	is our preaching; empty, too, your f.
1 Cor	15:17	has not been raised, your f is vain;
1 Cor	16:13	stand firm in the f, be courageous,
2 Cor	1:24	Not that we lord it over your f;
2 Cor	1:24	your joy, for you stand firm in the f.
2 Cor	4:13	then, we have the same spirit of f,
2 Cor	5: 7	for we walk by f, not by sight.
2 Cor	8: 7	in every respect, in f, discourse,
2 Cor	10:15	as your f increases, our influence
2 Cor	13: 5	to see whether you are living in f.
Gal	1:23	is now preaching the f he once tried
Gal	2:16	law but through f in Jesus Christ,
Gal	2:16	we may be justified by f in Christ
Gal	2:20	I live by f in the Son of God who
Gal	3: 8	God would justify the Gentiles by f,
Gal	3:11	one who is righteous by f will live."
Gal	3:12	But the law does not depend on f;
Gal	3:14	the promise of the Spirit through f.
Gal	3:22	sin, that through f in Jesus Christ
Gal	3:23	Before f came, we were held
Gal	3:23	confined for the f that was to be
Gal	3:24	that we might be justified by f.
Gal	3:25	But now that f has come, we are no
Gal	3:26	For through f you are all children
Gal	5: 5	the Spirit, by f, we await the hope
Gal	5: 6	but only f working through love.
Gal	6:10	who belong to the family of the f.
Eph	1:15	hearing of your f in the Lord Jesus
Eph	2: 8	you have been saved through f,
Eph	3:12	of access through f in him.
Eph	3:17	may dwell in your hearts through f;
Eph	4: 5	one Lord, one f, one baptism;
Eph	4:13	until we all attain to the unity of f
Eph	6:16	all circumstances, hold f as a shield,
Eph	6:23	and love with f, from God
Phil	1:25	for your progress and joy in the f,
Phil	1:27	together for the f of the gospel,
Phil	2:17	the sacrificial service of your f,
Phil	3: 9	which comes through f in Christ,
Col	1: 4	have heard of your f in Christ Jesus
Col	1:23	provided that you persevere in the f,
Col	2: 5	and the firmness of your f in Christ.
Col	2: 7	in the f as you were taught,
Col	2:12	with him through f in the power
1 Thes	1: 3	calling to mind your work of f
1 Thes	1: 8	every place your f in God has gone
1 Thes	3: 2	and encourage you in your f,
1 Thes	3: 5	I sent to learn about your f, for fear
1 Thes	3: 6	bringing us the good news of your f
1 Thes	3: 7	and affliction, through your f.
1 Thes	3:10	to remedy the deficiencies of your f.
1 Thes	5: 8	putting on the breastplate of f
2 Thes	1: 3	because your f flourishes ever more,
2 Thes	1: 4	and f in all your persecutions
2 Thes	1:11	good purpose and every effort of f,
2 Thes	3: 2	wicked people, for not all have f.
1 Tm	1: 2	to Timothy, my true child in f:
1 Tm	1: 4	of God that is to be received by f.
1 Tm	1: 5	a good conscience, and a sincere f.
1 Tm	1:14	along with the f and love that are
1 Tm	1:19	by having f and a good conscience.
1 Tm	1:19	have made a shipwreck of their f,
1 Tm	2: 7	teacher of the Gentiles in f
1 Tm	2:15	provided women persevere in f
1 Tm	3: 9	of the f with a clear conscience.
1 Tm	3:13	confidence in their f in Christ Jesus.
1 Tm	4: 1	away from the f by paying attention
1 Tm	4: 6	nourished on the words of the f
1 Tm	4:12	speech, conduct, love, f, and purity.
1 Tm	5: 8	family members has denied the f
1 Tm	6:10	desire for it have strayed from the f
1 Tm	6:11	righteousness, devotion, f, love,
1 Tm	6:12	Compete well for the f. Lay hold
1 Tm	6:21	people have deviated from the f.
2 Tm	1: 5	as I recall your sincere f that first
2 Tm	1:13	in the f and love that are in Christ
2 Tm	2:18	and are upsetting the f of some.
2 Tm	2:22	desires and pursue righteousness, f,
2 Tm	3: 8	depraved mind, unqualified in the f.
2 Tm	3:10	way of life, purpose, f, patience,
2 Tm	3:15	salvation through f in Christ Jesus.
2 Tm	4: 7	finished the race; I have kept the f.
Ti	1: 1	sake of the f of God's chosen ones
Ti	1: 4	my true child in our common f:
Ti	1:13	so that they may be sound in the f,
Ti	2: 2	self-controlled, sound in f, love,
Ti	3:15	Greet those who love us in the f.
Phlm	1: 5	and the f you have in the Lord Jesus
Phlm	1: 6	in the f may become effective
Heb	4: 2	they were not united in f with those
Heb	6: 1	from dead works and f in God,
Heb	6:12	those who, through f and patience,
Heb	10:38	But my just one shall live by f,
Heb	10:39	among those who have f and will
Heb	11: 1	F is the realization of what is hoped
Heb	11: 3	By f we understand that the universe
Heb	11: 4	By f Abel offered to God a sacrifice
Heb	11: 5	By f Enoch was taken up so that he
Heb	11: 6	without f it is impossible to please
Heb	11: 7	By f Noah, warned about what was
Heb	11: 7	righteousness that comes through f.
Heb	11: 8	By f Abraham obeyed when he was
Heb	11: 9	By f he sojourned in the promised
Heb	11:11	By f he received power to generate,
Heb	11:13	All these died in f. They did not
Heb	11:17	By f Abraham, when put to the test,
Heb	11:20	By f regarding things still to come
Heb	11:21	By f Jacob, when dying,
Heb	11:22	By f Joseph, near the end of his life,
Heb	11:23	By f Moses was hidden by his
Heb	11:24	By f Moses, when he had grown up,
Heb	11:27	By f he left Egypt, not fearing
Heb	11:28	By f he kept the Passover
Heb	11:29	By f they crossed the Red Sea as
Heb	11:30	By f the walls of Jericho fell
Heb	11:31	By f Rahab the harlot did not perish
Heb	11:33	who by f conquered kingdoms,
Heb	11:39	though approved because of their f,
Heb	12: 2	Jesus, the leader and perfecter of f.

Heb	13: 7	their way of life and imitate their f.
Jas	1: 3	of your f produces perseverance.
Jas	1: 6	But he should ask in f, not doubting,
Jas	2: 5	are poor in the world to be rich in f
Jas	2:14	if someone says he has f but does
Jas	2:14	Can that f save him?
Jas	2:17	So also f of itself, if it does not have
Jas	2:18	"You have f and I have works."
Jas	2:18	Demonstrate your f to me without
Jas	2:20	that f without works is useless?
Jas	2:22	You see that f was active along
Jas	2:22	and f was completed by the works.
Jas	2:24	by works and not by f alone.
Jas	2:26	so also f without works is dead.
Jas	5:15	prayer of f will save the sick person,
1 Pt	1: 5	of God are safeguarded through f,
1 Pt	1: 7	so that the genuineness of your f,
1 Pt	1: 9	as you attain the goal of [your] f,
1 Pt	1:21	so that your f and hope are in God.
1 Pt	5: 9	steadfast in f, knowing that your
2 Pt	1: 1	those who have received a f of equal
2 Pt	1: 5	to supplement your f with virtue,
1 Jn	5: 4	that conquers the world is our f.
Jude	1: 3	contend for the f that was once
Jude	1:20	yourselves up in your most holy f;
Rev	2:13	and have not denied your f in me,
Rev	2:19	your works, your love, f, service,
Rev	14:12	commandments and their f in Jesus.

FAITHFUL → FAITH

Dt	7: 9	the f God who keeps covenant
Dt	32: 4	A f God, without deceit,
1 Sm	2: 9	guards the footsteps of his f ones,
1 Sm	2:35	I will choose a f priest who shall do
2 Chr	6:41	your f ones rejoice in good things.
2 Chr	31:20	and f before the LORD, his God.
Neh	9: 8	You found his heart f in your sight,
1 Mc	2:52	Was not Abraham found f in trial,
1 Mc	3:13	an assembly of f men ready for war.
1 Mc	7: 8	in the kingdom, and f to the king.
2 Mc	1: 2	his covenant with his f servants,
Ps	4: 4	works wonders for his f one;
Ps	12: 2	the f have vanished
Ps	30: 5	Sing praise to the LORD, you f;
Ps	31:24	LORD, all you who are f to him.
Ps	37:28	justice and does not abandon the f
Ps	78: 8	and whose spirit was not f to God.
Ps	85: 9	of peace To his people and to his f.
Ps	89:20	to your f ones you said: "I have set
Ps	97:10	evil, he protects the souls of the f,
Ps	101: 6	I look to the f of the land to sit
Ps	145:10	LORD and your f bless you.
Ps	148:14	to the praise of all his f,
Ps	149: 1	his praise in the assembly of the f.
Ps	149: 5	Let the f rejoice in their glory,
Ps	149: 9	such is the glory of all God's f.
Prv	25:13	of the harvest are f messengers
Wis	3: 9	the f shall abide with him in love:
Sir	6:14	F friends are a sturdy shelter;
Sir	6:15	F friends are beyond price,
Sir	6:16	F friends are life-saving medicine;
Sir	34: 8	mouth of the f is complete wisdom.
Sir	39:13	Listen to me, my f children:
Is	1:21	has become a prostitute, the f city,
Is	1:26	shall be called city of justice, f city.
Is	25: 1	wonderful plans of old, f and true.
Is	49: 7	Because of the LORD who is f,
Hos	12: 1	with gods, and is f to holy ones.
Mi	7: 2	The f have vanished from the earth,
Zec	8: 3	Jerusalem will be called the f city,
Mt	24:45	then, is the f and prudent servant,
Lk	12:42	is the f and prudent steward whom
Acts	11:23	them all to remain f to the Lord
1 Cor	1: 9	God is f, and by him you were
1 Cor	4:17	is my beloved and f son in the Lord;
1 Cor	10:13	God is f and will not let you be tried
2 Cor	1:18	As God is f, our word to you is not

Eph	1: 1	are [in Ephesus] f in Christ Jesus:
Col	1: 2	and f brothers in Christ in Colossae:
1 Thes	5:24	The one who calls you is f, and he
2 Thes	3: 3	But the Lord is f; he will strengthen
1 Tm	3:11	but temperate and f in everything.
2 Tm	2: 2	to f people who will have the ability
2 Tm	2:13	If we are unfaithful he remains f,
Heb	2:17	f high priest before God to expiate
Heb	3: 2	who was f to the one who appointed
Heb	3: 2	just as Moses was "f in [all] his
Heb	3: 5	Moses was "f in all his house" as
Heb	3: 6	Christ was f as a son placed over his
1 Pt	4:19	over to a f creator as they do good.
1 Pt	5:12	whom I consider a f brother,
1 Jn	1: 9	he is f and just and will forgive our
Rev	1: 5	and from Jesus Christ, the f witness,
Rev	2:10	Remain f until death, and I will give
Rev	2:13	in the days of Antipas, my f witness,
Rev	3:14	Amen, the f and true witness,
Rev	17:14	with him are called, chosen, and f."
Rev	19:11	its rider was [called] "F and True."

FAITHFULLY → FAITH

1 Sm	12:24	and serve him f with all your heart,
2 Chr	31:15	who f made the distribution to their
2 Chr	34:12	The men worked f at their task;
Sir	7:20	not mistreat a servant who works f,
Is	61: 8	I will f give them their recompense,

FAITHFULNESS → FAITH

1 Sm	26:23	everyone's righteousness and f.
Ps	26: 3	I walk guided by your f.
Ps	30:10	give you thanks or declare your f?
Ps	54: 7	in your f, destroy them.
Ps	57:11	your f reaches to the skies.
Ps	71:22	praise you with the lyre for your f,
Ps	91: 4	his f is a protecting shield.
Ps	92: 3	love at daybreak, your f in the night,
Ps	100: 5	his f lasts through every generation.
Ps	108: 5	your f, to the skies.
Ps	115: 1	glory because of your mercy and f.
Ps	119:138	in righteousness and in surpassing f.
Ps	143: 1	in your f listen to my pleading;
Is	11: 5	his waist, and f a belt upon his hips.
Is	38:19	to their children, O God, your f.
Lam	3:23	great is your f!
Mi	7:20	You will show f to Jacob,
Zec	8: 8	I will be their God, in f and justice.
Gal	5:22	patience, kindness, generosity, f,

FAITHLESS → FAITH

Ps	119:158	I view the f with loathing because
Mt	17:17	reply, "O f and perverse generation,
Rom	1:31	They are senseless, f, heartless,

FALL → DOWNFALL, FALLEN, FALLING, FALLS, FELL

Nm	14:29	wilderness your dead bodies shall f.
1 Chr	21:13	But let me f into the hand
Ps	35: 8	let them f into the pit they have dug.
Ps	37:24	but he will never f, for the LORD
Ps	91: 7	Though a thousand f at your side,
Prv	16:18	and a haughty spirit before a f.
Eccl	4:10	If that one should f, there is no other
Eccl	10: 8	Whoever digs a pit may f into it,
Sir	28:23	who forsake the Lord will f victim
Is	40:30	weary, and youths stagger and f,
Jer	6:15	Therefore they will f among
Hos	10: 8	and to the hills, "F upon us!"
Mk	4:17	of the word, they quickly f away.
Lk	10:18	have observed Satan f like lightning
Lk	23:30	say to the mountains, 'F upon us!'
Acts	5:15	at least his shadow might f on one
Rom	9:33	and a rock that will make them f,
Rom	11:11	I ask, did they stumble so as to f?
1 Cor	10:12	secure should take care not to f.
Heb	10:31	It is a fearful thing to f
1 Pt	2: 8	and a rock that will make them f."
Rev	6:16	"F on us and hide us from the face

FALLEN → FALL

2 Sm	1:19	How can the warriors have f!
Sir	28:18	Many have f by the edge
Is	14:12	How you have f from the heavens,
Is	21: 9	He calls out and says, 'F, f is
Am	9:11	that day I will raise up the f hut
Acts	15:16	and rebuild the f hut of David;
Gal	5: 4	you have f from grace.
Heb	6: 6	and then have f away, to bring them
Rev	9: 1	I saw a star that had f from the sky
Rev	14: 8	"F, f is Babylon the great,
Rev	17:10	five have already f, one still lives,
Rev	18: 2	"F, f is Babylon the great.

FALLING → FALL

Sir	34:19	against stumbling, a help against f.
Lk	22:44	[like drops of blood f on the ground.]
1 Tm	6: 9	want to be rich are f into temptation

FALLS → FALL

Prv	11:14	For lack of guidance a people f;
Prv	26:27	Whoever digs a pit f into it;
Eccl	4:10	If the one f, the other will help
Mt	13:21	of the word, he immediately f away.
Lk	20:18	Everyone who f on that stone will
Lk	20:18	it will crush anyone on whom it f."
Jn	12:24	a grain of wheat f to the ground

FALSE → FALSEHOOD, FALSELY, FALSIFYING

Ex	20:16	shall not bear f witness against your
Ex	23: 1	You shall not repeat a f report.
Dt	19:18	If the witness is a f witness and has
Prv	19: 5	The f witness will not go
Prv	21:28	The f witness will perish, but one
Prv	25:18	one who bears f witness against
Mt	7:15	"Beware of f prophets, who come
Mt	15:19	theft, f witness, blasphemy.
Mt	24:11	Many f prophets will arise
Mt	24:24	F messiahs and f prophets will arise,
Mk	10:19	you shall not bear f witness;
Mk	13:22	F messiahs and f prophets will arise
Lk	6:26	their ancestors treated the f prophets
Lk	18:20	you shall not bear f witness;
Acts	6:13	They presented f witnesses who
Acts	13: 6	who was a Jewish f prophet.
2 Cor	11:13	For such people are f apostles,
2 Cor	11:26	at sea, dangers among f brothers;
2 Pt	2: 1	also f prophets among the people,
2 Pt	2: 1	there will be f teachers among you,
1 Jn	4: 1	because many f prophets have gone
Rev	16:13	and from the mouth of the f prophet.
Rev	19:20	it the f prophet who had performed
Rev	20:10	the beast and the f prophet were.

FALSEHOOD → FALSE

Jb	31: 5	If I have walked in f and my foot
Ps	119:163	F I hate and abhor; your law I love.
Prv	30: 8	Put f and lying far from me, give me
Is	28:15	f we have found a hiding place,"—
Rom	3: 7	redounds to his glory through my f,
Eph	4:25	putting away f, speak the truth,

FALSELY → FALSE

Lv	19:12	You shall not swear f by my name,
Prv	24:28	Do not testify f against your neighbor
Jer	5:31	The prophets prophesy f,
Mt	5:11	evil against you [f] because of me.

FALSIFYING → FALSE

2 Cor	4: 2	deceitfully or f the word of God,

FAME → FAMOUS

Jos	6:27	his f spread throughout the land.
1 Chr	14:17	Thus David's f was spread abroad
2 Chr	9: 1	heard a report of Solomon's f,
1 Mc	3:26	His f reached the king,
Is	66:19	which have never heard of my f,
Mk	1:28	His f spread everywhere throughout

FAMILIES → FAMILY

Ex	1:21	feared God, God built up f for them.

Jos	14: 1	and the heads of f in the tribes
Ps	107:41	and increased their f like flocks.
Am	3: 2	known, among all the f of the earth;
Acts	3:25	your offspring all the f of the earth
Ti	1:11	as they are upsetting whole f

FAMILY → FAMILIES

Gn	24:40	get a wife for my son from my own f
Lk	2: 4	he was of the house and f of David,
Acts	16:33	and all his f were baptized at once.
Gal	6:10	who belong to the f of the faith.
Eph	3:15	from whom every f in heaven
1 Tm	5: 4	their religious duty to their own f
1 Tm	5: 8	especially f members has denied

FAMINE → FAMINES

Gn	12:10	There was f in the land;
Gn	26: 1	There was a f in the land,
Gn	41:27	they are seven years of f.
Gn	42: 5	since there was f in the land
Gn	43: 1	Now the f in the land grew severe.
Ru	1: 1	the judges there was a f in the land;
2 Kgs	4:38	to Gilgal, there was a f in the land.
2 Kgs	6:25	of the siege the f in Samaria was so
2 Chr	6:28	"If there is f in the land
1 Mc	6:54	the sanctuary because the f was too
Jb	5:20	In f he will deliver you from death,
Ps	37:19	in days of f they will be satisfied.
Sir	39:29	Fire and hail, f and disease:
Jer	14:15	and f shall these prophets meet their
Am	8:11	when I will send a f upon the land:
Lk	4:25	and a severe f spread over the entire
Acts	11:28	would be a severe f all over
Rom	8:35	or persecution, or f, or nakedness,
Rev	18: 8	in one day, pestilence, grief, and f;

FAMINES → FAMINE

Lk	21:11	will be powerful earthquakes, f,

FAMISHED

Gn	25:29	came in from the open country, f.

FAMOUS → FAME

1 Kgs	1:47	Solomon's name more f than your

FAN

Mt	3:12	His winnowing f is in his hand.

FAR

Gn	18:25	F be it from you to do such a thing,
Jos	24:16	"F be it from us to forsake
1 Sm	12:23	f be it from me to sin against
Ps	22:12	Do not stay f from me, for trouble is
Ps	103:12	As f as the east is from the west, so f has he removed our sins
Ps	119:155	Salvation is f from sinners because
Prv	5: 8	Keep your way f from her, do not
Prv	31:10	F beyond jewels is her value.
Is	29:13	though their hearts are f from me,
Is	57:19	Peace to those who are f and near,
Jer	23:23	and not a God f off?
Mk	7: 6	lips, but their hearts are f from me;
Mk	12:34	"You are not f from the kingdom

FARMER

2 Tm	2: 6	The hardworking f ought to have
Jas	5: 7	See how the f waits for the precious

FASHION → FASHIONED

Jb	31:15	Did not the same One f us

FASHIONED → FASHION

1 Kgs	7:15	He f two bronze columns, each eighteen
Jb	10: 9	remember that you f me from clay!
Ps	119:73	Your hands made me and f me;

FAST → FASTED, FASTING, FASTS

Dt	10:20	to him hold f and by his name shall
Dt	11:22	ways exactly, and holding f to him,
Dt	13: 5	serve, and to him you shall hold f.
Dt	30:20	his voice, and holding f to him.
2 Chr	20: 3	He proclaimed a f throughout all

Ezr	8:21	Then I proclaimed a f,
Est	4:16	f on my behalf, all of you, not eating
Ps	139:10	me, your right hand holds me f.
Prv	4: 4	"Let your heart hold f my words:
Is	56: 4	me, and who hold f to my covenant,
Is	58: 5	Is this what you call a f, a day
Jl	1:14	Proclaim a holy f! Call an assembly!
Jon	3: 5	they proclaimed a f and all of them,
Mt	6:16	"When you f, do not look gloomy
Mt	9:14	do we and the Pharisees f [much],
Mt	9:14	but your disciples do not f?"
Lk	18:12	I f twice a week, and I pay tithes
2 Thes	2:15	hold f to the traditions that you were
1 Tm	3: 9	holding f to the mystery of the faith
Heb	4:14	God, let us hold f to our confession.
Rev	3:11	Hold f to what you have, so that no

FASTED → FAST

1 Kgs	21:27	He f, slept in the sackcloth,
Ezr	8:23	So we f, seeking this from our God,
Jdt	8: 6	She f all the days of her
1 Mc	3:47	That day they f and wore sackcloth;
Zec	7: 5	was it really for me that you f?
Mt	4: 2	He f for forty days and forty nights,

FASTING → FAST

Tb	12: 8	Prayer with f is good.
Ps	35:13	afflicted myself with f, sobbed my
Dn	9: 3	and petition, with f, sackcloth,
Mt	6:16	they may appear to others to be f.
Acts	13: 2	were worshiping the Lord and f,
Acts	14:23	with prayer and f, commended them

FASTS → FAST

Sir	34:31	So one who f for sins, but goes

FAT → FATLING, FATLINGS, FATTED, FATTENED

Lv	3:16	All the f belongs to the LORD.
Lv	7:23	You shall not eat the f of any ox
Jgs	3:17	now Eglon was a very f man.
Ez	34:20	Now I will judge between the f
Dn	14:27	Then Daniel took some pitch, f,

FATE

Nm	16:29	merely suffering the f common
Ps	81:16	but their f is fixed forever.

FATHER → FATHER'S, FATHER-IN-LAW, FATHERS

Gn	2:24	That is why a man leaves his f
Gn	17: 4	are to become the f of a multitude
Gn	19:32	let us ply our f with wine
Gn	19:32	we may ensure posterity by our f."
Gn	26:24	I am the God of Abraham, your f.
Gn	27:38	But Esau said to his f, "Have you only one blessing, f?
Gn	31: 5	the God of my f has been with me.
Gn	46: 3	I am God, the God of your f.
Ex	20:12	Honor your f and your mother,
Ex	21:15	Whoever strikes f or mother shall be
Ex	21:17	Whoever curses f or mother shall be
Ex	22:16	If her f refuses to give her to him,
Dt	5:16	Honor your f and your mother,
Dt	21:18	son who will not listen to his f
Dt	26: 5	"My f was a refugee Aramean who
Dt	32: 6	Is he not your f who begot you,
Jgs	17:10	"Be f and priest to me, and I will
Jgs	18:19	with us and be our f and priest.
2 Sm	7:14	I will be a f to him, and he shall be
1 Kgs	2:12	sat on the throne of David his f,
1 Chr	17:13	I will be a f to him, and he shall be
1 Chr	22:10	and I will be a f to him, and I will
1 Chr	28: 6	for my son, and I will be a f to him.
Jb	38:28	Has the rain a f? Who has begotten
Ps	27:10	Even if my f and mother forsake
Ps	68: 6	F of the fatherless,
Ps	89:27	cry to me, 'You are my f, my God,
Ps	103:13	As a f has compassion on his
Prv	10: 1	A wise son gives his f joy,
Prv	17:25	A foolish son is vexation to his f,
Prv	19:26	Whoever mistreats a f or drives
Prv	20:20	Those who curse f or mother—

Prv	23:22	Listen to your f who begot you,
Prv	23:24	The f of a just person will exult
Prv	28:24	Whoever defrauds f or mother
Wis	2:16	and boasts that God is his F.
Sir	3: 3	Those who honor their f atone
Sir	3:16	Those who neglect their f are like
Is	8: 4	learns to say, "My f, my mother,"
Is	45:10	Woe to anyone who asks a f,
Is	63:16	For you are our f.
Jer	2:27	"You are my f," and to a stone,
Jer	3:19	would call me, "My F," I thought,
Jer	31: 9	For I am a f to Israel, Ephraim is my
Ez	16: 3	your f was an Amorite, your mother
Ez	18:19	son charged with the guilt of his f?"
Mi	7: 6	For the son belittles his f,
Mal	1: 6	A son honors his f, and a servant
Mal	1: 6	I am a f, where is the honor due
Mal	2:10	Have we not all one f? Has not one
Mt	3: 9	'We have Abraham as our f.'
Mt	5:16	deeds and glorify your heavenly F.
Mt	6: 9	Our F in heaven, hallowed be your
Mt	6:14	your heavenly F will forgive you.
Mt	6:15	neither will your F forgive your
Mt	6:26	yet your heavenly F feeds them.
Mt	10:37	"Whoever loves f or mother more
Mt	11:27	been handed over to me by my F.
Mt	11:27	No one knows the Son except the F,
Mt	11:27	no one knows the F except the Son
Mt	15: 4	'Honor your f and your mother,'
Mt	15: 4	'Whoever curses f or mother shall
Mt	18:10	upon the face of my heavenly F.
Mt	19: 5	this reason a man shall leave his f
Mt	19:19	honor your f and your mother';
Mt	19:29	brothers or sisters or f or mother
Mt	23: 9	Call no one on earth your f; you have but one F in heaven.
Mt	28:19	baptizing them in the name of the F,
Mk	14:36	"Abba, F, all things are possible
Lk	6:36	just as [also] your F is merciful.
Lk	9:59	let me go first and bury my f."
Lk	11: 2	F, hallowed be your name,
Lk	12:30	your F knows that you need them.
Lk	12:53	a f will be divided against his son and a son against his f,
Lk	14:26	comes to me without hating his f
Lk	15:12	So the f divided the property
Lk	16:24	And he cried out, 'F Abraham,
Lk	18:20	honor your f and your mother.' "
Lk	23:34	[Then Jesus said, "F, forgive them,]
Jn	3:35	The F loves the Son and has given
Jn	4:23	true worshipers will worship the F
Jn	4:23	indeed the F seeks such people
Jn	5:17	them, "My F is at work until now,
Jn	5:18	but he also called God his own f,
Jn	5:20	For the F loves his Son and shows
Jn	6:44	me unless the F who sent me draw
Jn	6:46	has seen the F except the one who is from God; he has seen the F.
Jn	8:19	"You know neither me nor my F.
Jn	8:19	me, you would know my F also."
Jn	8:28	but I say only what the F taught me.
Jn	8:41	You are doing the works of your f!"
Jn	8:41	We have one F, God."
Jn	8:44	You belong to your f the devil
Jn	8:44	because he is a liar and the f of lies.
Jn	10:17	This is why the F loves me,
Jn	10:30	The F and I are one."
Jn	10:38	the F is in me and I am in the F."
Jn	12:27	'F, save me from this hour'?
Jn	14: 6	comes to the F except through me.
Jn	14: 9	has seen me has seen the F.
Jn	14: 9	How can you say, 'Show us the F'?
Jn	14:11	Believe me that I am in the F and the F is in me,
Jn	14:21	loves me will be loved by my F,
Jn	14:28	rejoice that I am going to the F; for the F is greater than I.
Jn	15: 9	As the F loves me, so I also love

Jn	15:23	Whoever hates me also hates my F.
Jn	20:17	for I have not yet ascended to the F.
Jn	20:17	'I am going to my F and your F,
Jn	20:21	As the F has sent me, so I send
Acts	1: 4	"the promise of the F
Rom	4:16	Abraham, who is the f of all of us,
Rom	8:15	through which we cry, "Abba, F!"
1 Cor	4:15	for I became your f in Christ Jesus
2 Cor	1: 3	God and F of our Lord Jesus Christ,
2 Cor	1: 3	the F of compassion and God of all
2 Cor	6:18	and I will be a f to you, and you
Gal	4: 6	our hearts, crying out, "Abba, F!"
Eph	5:31	this reason a man shall leave [his] f
Eph	6: 2	"Honor your f and mother."
Phil	2:11	is Lord, to the glory of God the F.
1 Thes	2:11	one of you as a f treats his children,
1 Tm	5: 1	older man, but appeal to him as a f.
Heb	1: 5	"I will be a f to him, and he shall be
Heb	12: 9	all the more to the F of spirits
Jas	1:17	coming down from the F of lights,
1 Jn	1: 3	for our fellowship is with the F
1 Jn	2:15	the love of the F is not in him.
1 Jn	2:22	Whoever denies the F and the Son,
1 Jn	3: 1	See what love the F has bestowed
2 Jn	1: 9	remains in the teaching has the F
Rev	3: 5	his name in the presence of my F
Rev	3:21	and sit with my F on his throne.

FATHER'S → FATHER

Gn	12: 1	from your f house to a land that I
Gn	27:34	As he heard his f words, Esau burst
Gn	31:19	had stolen her f household images.
Gn	49: 4	for you climbed into your f bed
Dt	23: 1	A man shall not marry his f wife, nor shall he dishonor his f bed.
2 Sm	16:21	"Go to your f concubines, whom he
Est	4:14	you and your f house will perish.
Prv	4: 1	Hear, O children, a f instruction,
Lk	2:49	that I must be in my F house?"
Jn	1:14	the glory as of the F only Son,
Jn	1:18	who is at the F side, has revealed
Jn	2:16	here, and stop making my F house
Jn	10:29	can take them out of the F hand.
Jn	14: 2	In my F house there are many
Rev	14: 1	and his F name written on their

FATHER-IN-LAW → FATHER

Ex	18: 8	told his f of all that the LORD had
Jn	18:13	He was the f of Caiaphas, who was

FATHERS → FATHER

Ps	22: 5	In you our f trusted; they trusted
Lam	5: 3	We have become orphans, without f;
1 Cor	4:15	yet you do not have many f, for I
Eph	6: 4	F, do not provoke your children
Col	3:21	F, do not provoke your children,
1 Jn	2:13	I am writing to you, f, because you

FATLING → FAT

2 Sm	6:13	six steps, he sacrificed an ox and a f.

FATLINGS → FAT

Ps	66:15	Burnt offerings of f I will offer you

FATTED → FAT

Prv	15:17	of herbs where love is than a f ox

FATTENED → FAT

Jas	5: 5	you have f your hearts for the day

FAULT → FAULTLESS

1 Sm	29: 3	me until now I have never found f
Sir	11: 7	Before investigating, do not find f;
Mt	18:15	tell him his f between you and him
Rom	9:19	"Why [then] does he still find f?

FAULTLESS → FAULT

Heb	8: 7	For if that first covenant had been f,

FAVOR → FAVORED, FAVORITE, FAVORITISM, FAVORS

Gn	6: 8	But Noah found f with the LORD.
Ex	33:12	You have found f with me.

Ex	34: 9	he said, "If I find f with you, Lord,
Lv	26: 9	I will look with f upon you,
Nm	11:15	please do me the f of killing me
Jgs	6:17	"If you look on me with f, give me
Neh	2: 8	Since I enjoyed the good f of my God,
Est	7: 3	"If I have found f with you, O king,
1 Mc	4:10	Heaven in the hope that he will f us,
Jb	42: 8	To him I will show f, and not punish
Ps	5:13	surround him with f like a shield.
Ps	30: 6	lasts but a moment; his f a lifetime.
Ps	90:17	May the f of the Lord our God be
Prv	8:35	life, and wins f from the LORD;
Prv	13:15	Good sense brings f, but the way
Prv	18: 5	It is not good to f the guilty,
Prv	18:22	a f granted by the LORD.
Prv	19: 6	Many curry f with a noble;
Eccl	9:11	by the shrewd, nor f by the experts;
Is	49: 8	In a time of f I answer you,
Is	61: 2	To announce a year of f
Dn	1: 9	Though God had given Daniel the f
Lk	1:30	for you have found f with God.
Lk	2:14	peace to those on whom his f rests."
Lk	2:40	and the f of God was upon him.
Lk	2:52	and age and f before God and man.
Acts	7:10	He granted him f and wisdom
Acts	7:46	who found f in the sight of God
2 Cor	1:15	so that you might receive a double f,

FAVORED → FAVOR

Ps	85: 2	You once f, LORD, your land,
Lk	1:28	coming to her, he said, "Hail, f one!

FAVORITE → FAVOR

2 Sm	23: 1	Jacob, f of the Mighty One of Israel.

FAVORITISM → FAVOR

Sir	4:22	Show no f to your own discredit;

FAVORS → FAVOR

Prv	3:34	he scoffs at, but the lowly he f.

FAWNS

Gn	49:21	loose, which brings forth lovely f.
Sg	4: 5	Your breasts are like two f,

FEAR → AFRAID, FEARED, FEARFUL, FEARING, FEARS, GOD-FEARING

Gn	9: 2	F and dread of you shall come
Gn	21:17	Do not f; God has heard the boy's voice
Ex	9:30	you do not yet f the LORD God."
Ex	20:20	put the f of him upon you so you do
Dt	2:25	This day I will begin to put a f
Dt	6:13	The LORD, your God, shall you f;
Dt	10:12	ask of you but to f the LORD,
Dt	31:12	hear and so learn to f the LORD,
Jos	2:24	the land tremble with f because
Jos	4:24	and that you may f the LORD,
1 Sm	12:14	If you f and serve the LORD,
1 Sm	12:24	But you must f the LORD
2 Sm	23: 3	justice, who rules in the f of God,
2 Chr	19: 7	let the f of the LORD be upon you.
2 Chr	26: 5	lived, who taught him to f God;
Est	8:17	for f of the Jews fell upon them.
Jb	6:14	though he has forsaken the f
Ps	2:11	Serve the LORD with f;
Ps	15: 4	but honors those who f the LORD;
Ps	19:10	The f of the LORD is pure,
Ps	23: 4	the shadow of death, I will f no evil,
Ps	27: 1	and my salvation; whom should I f?
Ps	33: 8	Let all the earth f the LORD;
Ps	34: 8	encamps around those who f him,
Ps	34:10	F the LORD, you his holy ones;
Ps	34:12	I will teach you f of the LORD.
Ps	46: 3	Thus we do not f, though earth be
Ps	55:20	they have no f of God.
Ps	90:11	Your wrath matches the f it inspires.
Ps	91: 1	You shall not f the terror
Ps	111:10	The f of the LORD is
Ps	118: 4	Let those who f the LORD say,
Ps	119:63	I am the friend of all who f you,

Ps	145:19	the desire of those who f him;
Prv	1: 7	F of the LORD is the beginning
Prv	1:29	and the f of the LORD they did not
Prv	2: 5	will you understand the f
Prv	3: 7	f the LORD and turn away
Prv	8:13	[The f of the LORD is hatred]
Prv	9:10	of wisdom is f of the LORD,
Prv	10:27	F of the LORD prolongs life,
Prv	14:27	The f of the LORD is a fountain
Prv	15:33	The f of the LORD is training
Prv	16: 6	the f of the LORD evil is avoided.
Prv	19:23	The f of the LORD leads to life;
Prv	22: 4	and f of the LORD is riches,
Prv	29:25	F of others becomes a snare,
Eccl	8:12	shall be well with those who f God,
Eccl	12:13	all is heard: F God and keep his
Sir	1:11	The f of the Lord is glory and exultation,
Sir	7:29	With all your soul f God and revere
Sir	40:26	but better than either, f of God.
Sir	40:26	In the f of the Lord there is no want;
Is	8:12	calls conspiracy, nor f what they f,
Is	11: 3	and his delight shall be the f
Is	33: 6	knowledge, is the f of the LORD,
Is	35: 4	fearful of heart: Be strong, do not f!
Is	41:10	Do not f: I am with you; do not be
Is	41:13	say to you, Do not f, I will help you.
Is	43: 1	Do not f, for I have redeemed you;
Is	43: 5	F not, for I am with you;
Is	51: 7	Do not f the reproach of others;
Is	54:14	you shall not f, from destruction,
Jer	5:22	Should you not f me—
Jer	17: 8	It does not f heat when it comes,
Jer	30:10	you, my servant Jacob, do not f!—
Jon	1: 9	"I f the LORD, the God of heaven,
Mi	6: 9	city (It is prudent to f your name!):
Zep	3:15	you have no further misfortune to f.
Lk	12: 5	I shall show you whom to f.
Lk	18: 4	that I neither f God nor respect any
Jn	19:38	a disciple of Jesus for f of the Jews,
Jn	20:19	the disciples were, for f of the Jews,
Acts	5:11	great f came upon the whole church
Rom	8:15	a spirit of slavery to fall back into f,
Rom	13: 3	rulers are not a cause of f to good
Rom	13: 3	you wish to have no f of authority?
2 Cor	5:11	since we know the f of the Lord,
Phil	2:12	work out your salvation with f
Heb	2:15	free those who through f of death
1 Pt	3:14	be afraid or terrified with f of them,
1 Jn	4:18	There is no f in love, but perfect love drives out f
Jude	1:23	on others have mercy with f,
Rev	14: 7	voice, "F God and give him glory,
Rev	15: 4	Who will not f you, Lord, or glorify

FEARED → FEAR

Ex	1:21	And because the midwives f God,
Ex	14:31	Egypt, the people f the LORD.
Jb	1: 1	Job, who f God and avoided evil.
Ps	76:12	bring gifts to the one to be f,
Hg	1:12	thus the people f the LORD.
Mk	6:20	Herod f John, knowing him to be

FEARFUL → FEAR

Heb	10:27	but a f prospect of judgment

FEARING → FEAR

Dt	8: 6	by walking in his ways and f him.
Col	3:22	but in simplicity of heart, f the Lord.

FEARS → FEAR

Jdt	16:16	one who f the Lord is forever great.
Ps	34: 5	me, delivered me from all my f.
Prv	31:30	the woman who f the LORD is
Eccl	7:18	but the one who f God will succeed
Sir	15: 1	Whoever f the LORD will do this;
2 Cor	7: 5	external conflicts, internal f.
1 Jn	4:18	so one who f is not yet perfect

FEAST → FEASTING, FEASTS

Ex	5: 1	that they may hold a f for me

Ex	23:14	a year you shall celebrate a pilgrim f
1 Mc	1:45	to profane the sabbaths and f days,
Ps	36: 9	They f on the rich food of your
Prv	15:15	but a good heart is a continual f.
Is	25: 6	for all peoples A f of rich food
1 Cor	5: 8	Therefore let us celebrate the f,

FEASTING → FEAST

Est	9:17	and made it a day of f and rejoicing.
Prv	17: 1	with quiet than a house full of f

FEASTS → FEAST

1 Mc	1:39	her f were turned into mourning,
Jb	1: 4	His sons used to take turns giving f,
Hos	2:13	all her seasonal f.
Am	8:10	I will turn your f into mourning
Na	2: 1	Celebrate your f, Judah, fulfill your
Jude	1:12	These are blemishes on your love f,

FED → FEED

Dt	8:16	f you in the wilderness with manna,
Ps	80: 6	You have f them the bread of tears,
1 Cor	3: 2	I f you milk, not solid food,

FEEBLE

Is	35: 3	Strengthen hands that are f,

FEED → FED, FEEDS

1 Kgs	17: 4	commanded ravens to f you there.
Jn	21:15	He said to him, "F my lambs."
Jn	21:17	[Jesus] said to him, "F my sheep.
Rom	12:20	"if your enemy is hungry, f him;

FEEDS → FEED

Is	40:11	Like a shepherd he f his flock;
Mt	6:26	yet your heavenly Father f them.

FEEL

Ps	115: 7	They have hands but do not f,

FEET → FOOT

Ex	3: 5	Remove your sandals from your f,
Ex	12:11	sandals on your f and your staff
Ex	24:10	Under his f there appeared to be
Ex	30:21	they must wash their hands and f,
Dt	8: 4	nor did your f swell these forty
Ru	3: 8	only to find a woman lying at his f.
2 Sm	22:34	Who made my f swift as a deer's,
Ps	8: 7	of your hands, put all things at his f:
Ps	22:17	have pierced my hands and my f
Ps	40: 3	muddy clay, Sets my f upon rock,
Ps	56:14	death, kept my f from stumbling,
Ps	66: 9	alive and not allowed our f to slip.
Ps	73: 2	for me, my f had almost stumbled;
Ps	115: 7	but do not feel, f but do not walk;
Ps	119:105	Your word is a lamp for my f,
Prv	1:16	[For their f run to evil, they hasten]
Prv	4:26	Survey the path for your f, and all
Prv	5: 5	Her f go down to death, her steps
Prv	6:18	f that are quick to run to evil,
Is	6: 2	with two they covered their f,
Is	52: 7	the mountains are the f of the one
Dn	2:33	iron, its f partly iron and partly clay.
Na	1: 3	and clouds are the f of the dust
Hb	3:19	he makes my f swift as those of deer
Zec	14: 4	that day God's f will stand
Mt	10:14	and shake the dust from your f
Mt	22:44	your enemies under your f" '?
Lk	1:79	to guide our f into the path
Lk	7:38	stood behind him at his f weeping
Lk	7:38	began to bathe his f with her tears,
Lk	8:35	had come out sitting at his f.
Lk	24:39	Look at my hands and my f, that it
Jn	13: 5	began to wash the disciples' f
Acts	4:35	and put them at the f of the apostles,
Acts	5: 2	and put it at the f of the apostles.
Rom	3:15	Their f are quick to shed blood;
Rom	10:15	"How beautiful are the f of those
Rom	16:20	quickly crush Satan under your f.
1 Cor	12:21	nor again the head to the f, "I do
1 Cor	15:25	has put all his enemies under his f.

Eph	1:22	he put all things beneath his f
Eph	6:15	and your f shod in readiness
1 Tm	5:10	washed the f of the holy ones,
Heb	2: 8	subjecting all things under his f."
Heb	12:13	Make straight paths for your f,
Rev	1:15	His f were like polished brass
Rev	12: 1	with the moon under her f,

FELIX
Governor before whom Paul was tried (Acts 23:23–24:27).

FELL → FALL

Gn	15:12	to set, a deep sleep f upon Abram,
1 Sm	4:18	Eli f backward from his chair
1 Sm	31: 4	took his own sword and f upon it.
Mt	7:25	The rain f, the floods came,
Mk	4: 8	And some seed f on rich soil
Jn	18: 6	turned away and f to the ground.
Acts	5: 5	he f down and breathed his last,
Heb	11:30	of Jericho f after being encircled
Rev	1:17	I f down at his feet as though dead.
Rev	5:14	the elders f down and worshiped.
Rev	6:13	the sky f to the earth like unripe figs
Rev	8:10	a large star burning like a torch f
Rev	8:10	It f on a third of the rivers

FELLOW → FELLOWSHIP

Lv	25:46	harshly over any of your f Israelites.
Mt	18:31	when his f servants saw what had
Rev	22: 9	I am a f servant of yours and of your

FELLOWSHIP → FELLOW

1 Cor	1: 9	by him you were called to f with his
2 Cor	6:14	Or what f does light have
2 Cor	13:13	the f of the holy Spirit be with all
1 Jn	1: 3	so that you too may have f with us;
1 Jn	1: 3	for our f is with the Father
1 Jn	1: 6	If we say, "We have f with him,"
1 Jn	1: 7	then we have f with one another,

FEMALE

Gn	1:27	male and f he created them.
Gn	5: 2	he created them male and f.
Gn	6:19	one male and one f , to keep them
Mt	19: 4	the Creator 'made them male and f'
Mk	10: 6	'God made them male and f.
Gal	3:28	free person, there is not male and f;

FERTILE

Is	5: 1	friend had a vineyard on a f hillside;

FERVENTLY → FERVOR

Jdt	4:12	one accord they cried out f
Acts	12: 5	the church was f being made to God

FERVOR → FERVENTLY

Jdt	4: 9	of Israel cried to God with great f

FESTAL → FESTIVAL

Heb	12:22	and countless angels in f gathering,

FESTIVAL → FESTAL, FESTIVALS

Ps	42: 5	thanksgiving, with the multitude keeping f.
Col	2:16	or with regard to a f or new moon

FESTIVALS → FESTIVAL

Lv	23: 2	declare holy days. These are my f:
Neh	10:34	and f, for the holy offerings and sin
Is	1:14	Your new moons and f I detest;

FESTUS
Governor who sent Paul to Caesar (Acts 25–26).

FEVER

Dt	28:22	will strike you with consumption, f,
Mk	1:30	mother-in-law lay sick with a f.
Lk	4:39	her, rebuked the f, and it left her.
Jn	4:52	told him, "The f left him yesterday,
Acts	28: 8	father of Publius was sick with a f

FEW

Gn	47: 9	F and hard have been these years
1 Chr	16:19	When they were f in number,
1 Mc	3:18	"Many are easily hemmed in by a f;

1 Mc	3:18	deliverance by many or by f;
Ps	105:12	When they were f in number,
Eccl	5: 1	therefore let your words be f.
Sir	32: 8	Be brief, say much in f words;
Mt	7:14	And those who find it are f.
Mt	22:14	Many are invited, but f are chosen."
Lk	10: 2	is abundant but the laborers are f;
Lk	13:23	will only a f people be saved?"

FIDELITY

Tb	3: 2	All your ways are mercy and f;
Ps	25: 5	Guide me by your f and teach me,

FIELD → FIELDS

Gn	4: 8	Abel, "Let us go out in the f."
Gn	23:17	Thus Ephron's f in Machpelah,
Gn	49:30	the cave in the f of Machpelah,
Gn	49:30	the f that Abraham bought
Lv	19: 9	that you reap the f to its very edge,
Ru	2: 3	The f she entered to glean
Ps	103:15	he blossoms like a flower in the f.
Prv	24:30	I passed by the f of a sluggard,
Prv	31:16	She picks out a f and acquires it;
Is	5: 8	to house, who connect f with f,
Is	40: 6	their loyalty like the flower of the f.
Jer	32: 7	"Purchase my f in Anathoth,
Mt	6:30	If God so clothes the grass of the f,
Mt	13:38	the f is the world, the good seed
Mt	13:44	is like a treasure buried in a f,
Mt	13:44	sells all that he has and buys that f.
Mt	24:40	Two men will be out in the f;
Mt	27: 8	why that f even today is called the F
1 Cor	3: 9	you are God's f, God's building.

FIELDS → FIELD

Neh	5: 3	"We are forced to pawn our f,
Ps	144:13	by tens of thousands in our f;
Mi	2: 2	You covet f, and seize them;
Lk	2: 8	in that region living in the f
Jn	4:35	up and see the f ripe for the harvest.

FIERCE

Gn	49: 7	Cursed be their fury so f, and their

FIERY → FIRE

Dn	3:49	drove the f flames

FIFTY

Gn	18:24	the f righteous people within it?
Jn	8:57	"You are not yet f years old

FIG → FIGS

Gn	3: 7	so they sewed f leaves together
Jgs	9:10	Then the trees said to the f tree,
1 Kgs	5: 5	and f tree from Dan to Beer-sheba,
Prv	27:18	Those who tend a f tree eat its fruit;
Hos	9:10	Like the first fruits of the f tree,
Mi	4: 4	under their own f trees, undisturbed;
Na	3:12	But all your fortresses are f trees,
Hb	3:17	though the f tree does not blossom,
Zec	3:10	under your vines and f trees."
Mt	21:19	immediately the f tree withered.
Mt	24:32	"Learn a lesson from the f tree.
Lk	13: 6	a person who had a f tree planted
Jn	1:48	you, I saw you under the f tree."
Jas	3:12	Can a f tree, my brothers,

FIGHT → FIGHTING, FIGHTS, FOUGHT

Ex	14:14	The LORD will f for you;
Dt	1:30	you, is the one who will f for you,
Neh	4:14	our God will f with us."
1 Mc	2:40	do not f against the Gentiles for our
Prv	18: 6	The lips of fools walk into a f,
Sir	4:28	to the death, f for what is right,
Jer	21: 5	and I myself will f against you
Zec	14: 3	go forth and f against those nations,
1 Tm	1:18	Through them may you f a good f

FIGHTING → FIGHT

Ex	2:13	and now two Hebrews were f!
Ex	14:25	because the LORD is f for them
Acts	5:39	find yourselves f against God."

FIGHTS → FIGHT
Jos 23:10 your God, himself who f for you,

FIGS → FIG
2 Kgs 20: 7 "Bring a poultice of f and apply it
Jer 24: 1 of f placed before the temple
Na 3:12 are fig trees, bearing early f;
Mk 11:13 it was not the time for f.
Lk 6:44 For people do not pick f
Jas 3:12 produce olives, or a grapevine f?
Rev 6:13 the earth like unripe f shaken loose

FIGURE → FIGURES
Dt 4:16 for yourselves to represent any f,
Jn 10: 6 Although Jesus used this f

FIGURES → FIGURE
Jn 16:25 "I have told you this in f of speech.
Jn 16:25 I will no longer speak to you in f

FILL → FILLED, FILLS, FULL, FULLNESS, FULLY
Gn 1:28 f the earth and subdue it.
Gn 9: 1 fertile and multiply and f the earth.
Ps 72:19 may he f all the earth with his glory.
Ps 81:11 wide your mouth that I may f it.'
Prv 30:15 Three things never get their f,
Jer 23:24 Do I not f heaven and earth?—
Ez 10: 2 f both your hands with burning
Hg 2: 7 And I will f this house with glory—
Jn 2: 7 told them, "F the jars with water."
Rom 15:13 May the God of hope f you with all
Eph 4:10 heavens, that he might f all things.

FILLED → FILL
Ex 1: 7 that the land was f with them.
Ex 31: 3 I have f him with a divine spirit
Ex 35:31 has f him with a divine spirit of skill
Ex 40:34 of the Lord f the tabernacle.
1 Kgs 8:11 of the Lord had f the house
2 Kgs 3:17 yet this wadi will be f with water
2 Chr 5:14 the Lord had f the house of God.
2 Chr 7: 1 the glory of the Lord f the house.
Ps 71: 8 My mouth shall be f with your
Ps 107: 9 f the hungry with good things.
Ps 127: 5 Blessed is the man who has f his quiver
Sir 2:16 those who love him are f with his
Sir 39: 6 he will be f with the spirit
Is 6: 4 and the house was f with smoke.
Ez 10: 4 the temple was f with the cloud,
Ez 43: 5 glory of the Lord f the temple!
Dn 2:35 mountain and f the whole earth.
Na 2:13 He f his lairs with prey, and his dens
Hb 2:14 But the earth shall be f
Lk 1:15 He will be f with the holy Spirit
Lk 1:41 and Elizabeth, f with the holy Spirit,
Lk 1:67 his father, f with the holy Spirit,
Lk 2:40 and became strong, f with wisdom;
Jn 6:26 you ate the loaves and were f.
Jn 12: 3 the house was f with the fragrance
Acts 2: 4 they were all f with the holy Spirit
Acts 4: 8 Then Peter, f with the holy Spirit,
Acts 4:31 they were all f with the holy Spirit
Acts 5: 3 why has Satan f your heart so
Acts 7:55 But he, f with the holy Spirit,
Acts 9:17 sight and be f with the holy Spirit."
Acts 13: 9 as Paul, f with the holy Spirit,
Acts 13:52 The disciples were f with joy
Eph 5:18 debauchery, but be f with the Spirit,
Rev 8: 5 f it with burning coals
Rev 15: 8 the temple became so f

FILLS → FILL
Eph 1:23 of the one who f all things in every

FILTH → FILTHY
Is 4: 4 the Lord washes away the f
Is 28: 8 tables are covered with vomit, with f,
Mt 23:27 men's bones and every kind of f.

FILTHY → FILTH
Zec 3: 3 before the angel, clad in f garments.

Rev 22:11 still act wickedly, and the f still be f.

FIND → FINDS, FOUND
Gn 18:26 If I f fifty righteous people
Ex 33:13 I may continue to f favor with you.
Dt 4:29 you shall indeed f him if you search
Jb 23: 3 Would that I knew how to f him,
Ps 132: 5 Till I f a place for the Lord,
Prv 2: 5 the knowledge of God you will f;
Prv 4:22 they are life to those who f them,
Prv 8:17 love, and those who seek me f me.
Prv 18:22 To f a wife is to f happiness,
Prv 20: 6 who can f someone worthy of trust?
Prv 24:14 If you f it, you will have a future,
Prv 31:10 Who can f a woman of worth?
Eccl 12:10 sought to f appropriate sayings,
Sir 11: 7 Before investigating, do not f fault;
Jer 6:16 thus you will f rest for yourselves.
Jer 29:13 you look for me, you will f me.
Dn 6: 5 and satraps tried to f grounds
Mt 7: 7 seek and you will f;
Mt 11:29 and you will f rest for your selves.
Mt 16:25 loses his life for my sake will f it.
Mt 22: 9 invite to the feast whomever you f.'
Lk 11: 9 seek and you will f;
Lk 18: 8 comes, will he f faith on earth?"
Lk 23: 4 crowds, "I f this man not guilty."
Lk 24: 3 they did not f the body of the Lord
Jn 10: 9 come in and go out and f pasture.
Acts 23: 9 "We f nothing wrong with this
Rom 9:19 "Why [then] does he still f fault?

FINDS → FIND
Prv 8:35 For whoever f me f life, and wins
Sir 25:10 How great is the one who f wisdom,
Mt 7: 8 and the one who seeks, f;
Mt 13:46 When he f a pearl of great price,
Lk 11:10 and the one who seeks, f;
Lk 12:37 servants whom the master f vigilant
Lk 15: 4 go after the lost one until he f it?
Lk 15: 8 searching carefully until she f it?

FINE
Lk 7:25 Someone dressed in f garments?
1 Pt 3: 3 jewelry, or dressing in f clothes,

FINGER → FINGERS
Ex 8:15 to Pharaoh, "This is the f of God."
Ex 31:18 tablets inscribed by God's own f.
Dt 9:10 by God's own f, with a copy of all
2 Chr 10:10 say, 'My little f is thicker than my
Mt 23: 4 they will not lift a f to move them.
Lk 11:20 if it is by the f of God that [I] drive
Lk 16:24 to dip the tip of his f in water
Jn 8: 6 to write on the ground with his f.
Jn 20:25 and put my f into the nailmarks

FINGERS → FINGER
2 Sm 21:20 who had six f on each hand and six
Ps 8: 4 the work of your f, the moon
Prv 7: 3 Bind them on your f, write them
Dn 5: 5 the f of a human hand appeared,

FINISH → FINISHED
Lk 14:30 but did not have the resources to f.'
Acts 20:24 if only I may f my course

FINISHED → FINISH
Gn 24:15 He had scarcely f speaking
Ex 40:33 Thus Moses f all the work.
Dt 32:45 Moses had f speaking all these
1 Kgs 8:54 After Solomon f offering this entire
Ezr 6:14 They f the building according
Neh 6:15 The wall was f on the twenty-fifth
Jn 19:30 taken the wine, he said, "It is f."
2 Tm 4: 7 I have f the race;
Rev 11: 7 When they have f their testimony,

FINS
Dt 14: 9 whatever has both f and scales you

FIRE → FIERY

Gn	19:24	f from the Lord out of heaven.
Ex	3: 2	appeared to him as f flaming
Ex	3: 2	although the bush was on f, it was
Ex	13:21	of a column of f to give them light.
Ex	19:18	had come down upon it in f.
Ex	40:38	and f in the cloud at night,
Lv	9:24	F came forth from the Lord's
Lv	10: 2	F therefore came forth
Nm	11: 1	the Lord's f burned among them
Nm	16:35	And f from the Lord came forth
Dt	4:12	spoke to you from the midst of the f.
Dt	4:24	is a consuming f, a jealous God.
Jgs	6:21	a f came up from the rock
1 Kgs	18:38	The Lord's f came down
1 Kgs	19:12	after the earthquake, f—but the Lord was not in the f;
2 Kgs	1:10	And f came down from heaven
2 Kgs	16: 3	he even immolated his child by f,
2 Chr	7: 1	f came down from heaven
2 Chr	28: 3	and immolated his children by f
2 Chr	33: 6	who immolated his children by f
Neh	1: 3	breached, its gates gutted by f."
Ps	50: 3	Devouring f precedes him, it rages
Ps	89:47	Must your wrath smolder like f?
Sir	2: 5	For in f gold is tested,
Is	5:24	as the tongue of f licks up stubble,
Is	10:17	The Light of Israel will become a f,
Is	30:27	fury, tongue like a consuming f,
Is	66:24	die, their f shall not be extinguished;
Jer	23:29	Is not my word like f—
Jer	36:23	and throw it into the f in the brazier,
Ez	1:13	The f gleamed intensely, and from it
Dn	3:92	walking in the f, and the fourth
Dn	7: 9	His throne was flames of f, with wheels of burning f.
Am	4:11	like a brand plucked from the f,
Zec	2: 9	I will be an encircling wall of f
Zec	3: 2	not a brand plucked from the f?"
Mal	3: 2	For he will be like a refiner's f,
Mt	3:11	you with the holy Spirit and f.
Mt	18: 8	two feet to be thrown into eternal f.
Mt	25:41	the eternal f prepared for the devil
Mk	9:43	Gehenna, into the unquenchable f.
Mk	9:48	not die, and the f is not quenched.'
Mk	9:49	"Everyone will be salted with f.
Lk	3:16	you with the holy Spirit and f.
Lk	12:49	"I have come to set the earth on f,
Jn	15: 6	throw them into a f and they will be
Acts	2: 3	appeared to them tongues as of f,
1 Cor	3:13	It will be revealed with f, and the f [itself] will test
Heb	10:27	a flaming f that is going to consume
Heb	12:29	For our God is a consuming f.
Jas	3: 6	The tongue is also a f.
Jas	3: 6	the entire course of our lives on f, itself set on f by Gehenna.
1 Pt	1: 7	perishable even though tested by f,
2 Pt	3:10	the elements will be dissolved by f,
Jude	1: 7	a punishment of eternal f.
Jude	1:23	by snatching them out of the f;
Rev	8: 7	came hail and f mixed with blood,
Rev	9:17	and out of their mouths came f,
Rev	11: 5	f comes out of their mouths
Rev	15: 2	like a sea of glass mingled with f.
Rev	20:14	were thrown into the pool of f.
Rev	20:14	(This pool of f is the second death.

FIRM → FIRMLY

Is	7: 9	Unless your faith is f, you shall not be f!
1 Cor	16:13	on your guard, stand f in the faith,
2 Cor	1:24	your joy, for you stand f in the faith.
Gal	5: 1	so stand f and do not submit again
Phil	1:27	that you are standing f in one spirit,
Phil	4: 1	in this way stand f in the Lord,
1 Thes	3: 8	now live, if you stand f in the Lord.
2 Thes	2:15	stand f and hold fast to the traditions
Heb	3:14	of the reality f until the end,

FIRMLY → FIRM

2 Chr	31: 4	might f adhere to the law of the Lord.

FIRST → FIRSTBORN, ONE

Gn	1: 5	and morning followed—the f day.
Gn	9:20	soil, was the f to plant a vineyard.
Gn	13: 4	site where he had f built the altar;
Ex	12: 2	you will reckon it the f month
Ex	23:19	The choicest f fruits of your soil you
Ex	40:17	On the f day of the f month
Prv	3: 9	with f fruits of all your produce;
Prv	18:17	Those who plead the case f seem
Sir	11: 7	examine f, then criticize.
Is	41: 4	am the f, and at the last I am he.
Is	44: 6	I am the f, I am the last;
Is	48:12	I, it is I who am the f, and am I
Dn	7: 4	The f was like a lion,
Mt	5:24	go f and be reconciled with your
Mt	6:33	But seek f the kingdom [of God]
Mt	7: 5	the wooden beam from your eye f;
Mt	8:21	let me go f and bury my father."
Mt	19:30	But many who are f will be last, and the last will be f.
Mt	22:38	greatest and the f commandment.
Mk	9:11	say that Elijah must come f?"
Mk	9:35	"If anyone wishes to be f, he shall
Mk	10:31	But many that are f will be last, and [the] last will be f."
Mk	10:44	to be f among you will be the slave
Mk	13:10	the gospel must f be preached to all
Mk	16: 2	had risen, on the f day of the week,
Lk	11:26	of that person is worse than the f."
Jn	8: 7	you who is without sin be the f
Acts	11:26	disciples were f called Christians.
Rom	1:16	for Jew f, and then Greek.
1 Cor	12:28	has designated in the church to be, f,
1 Cor	15:45	it is written, "The f man, Adam,
2 Cor	8: 5	they gave themselves f to the Lord
Eph	1:12	his glory, we who f hoped in Christ.
Eph	6: 2	This is the f commandment
1 Thes	4:16	and the dead in Christ will rise f.
1 Tm	2:13	For Adam was formed f, then Eve.
Heb	8:13	he declares the f one obsolete.
Heb	10: 9	He takes away the f to establish
Jas	3:17	wisdom from above is f of all pure,
2 Pt	2:20	last condition is worse than their f.
1 Jn	4:19	We love because he f loved us.
Rev	1:17	not be afraid. I am the f and the last,
Rev	2: 4	you have lost the love you had at f.
Rev	4: 7	The f creature resembled a lion,
Rev	8: 7	When the f one blew his trumpet,
Rev	9:12	The f woe has passed, but there are
Rev	13:12	all the authority of the f beast in its
Rev	13:12	its inhabitants worship the f beast,
Rev	20: 5	This is the f resurrection.
Rev	22:13	and the Omega, the f and the last,

FIRSTBORN → BEAR, FIRST

Gn	25:34	Esau treated his right as f with disdain.
Gn	27:36	First he took away my right as f,
Gn	27:19	"I am Esau, your f. I did as you told me.
Gn	48:18	the other one is the f; lay your right hand
Ex	4:22	Thus says the Lord: Israel is my son, my f.
Ex	11: 5	Every f in the land of Egypt will die,
Ex	12:29	so at midnight the Lord struck down every f
Ex	13: 2	Consecrate to me every f;
Ex	34:20	The f among your sons you shall redeem.
Nm	3:41	in place of all the f of the Israelites,
Dt	21:17	he shall recognize as his f the son
Jos	6:26	At the cost of his f will he lay its foundation,
1 Kgs	16:34	At the cost of Abiram, his f son, he laid
Ps	78:51	He struck all the f of Egypt, the first fruits
Ps	89:28	I myself make him the f, Most High
Sir	36:17	Israel, whom you named your f.
Ez	20:26	make a fiery offering of every womb's f,
Mi	6: 7	Shall I give my f for my crime,
Zec	12:10	grieve for him as one grieves over a f.
Lk	2: 7	and she gave birth to her f son.
Rom	8:29	that he might be the f among many brothers.

Col	1:15	the invisible God, the f of all creation.
Col	1:18	He is the beginning, the f from the dead,
Heb	12:23	the assembly of the f enrolled in heaven,
Rev	1: 5	the faithful witness, the f of the dead

FISH → FISHERMEN

Gn	1:26	Let them have dominion over the f
Ex	7:18	The f in the Nile will die,
Nm	11: 5	We remember the f we used to eat
Tb	8: 3	odor of the f repulsed the demon,
Tb	11: 8	Apply the f gall to his eyes,
Ez	47: 9	of living creature; f will abound.
Jon	2: 1	But the Lord sent a great f
Jon	2: 1	in the belly of the f three days
Jon	2: 2	his God, from the belly of the f:
Mt	7:10	or a snake when he asks for a f?
Mt	14:17	and two f are all we have here."
Mk	8: 7	They also had a few f. He said
Lk	5: 6	they caught a great number of f
Jn	6: 9	has five barley loaves and two f;
Jn	21:11	of one hundred fifty-three large f.

FISHERMEN → FISH, MAN

Mk	1:16	their nets into the sea; they were f.

FIT → FITTING

Lk	9:62	to what was left behind is f

FITTING → FIT

Ps	147: 1	how pleasant to give f praise.
Heb	2:10	For it was f that he, for whom

FIVE

1 Sm	6: 4	"F golden tumors and f golden mice to correspond
1 Sm	6:16	the f Philistine leaders returned
1 Sm	17:40	David selected f smooth stones
1 Mc	2: 2	He had f sons: John, who was called
Is	30:17	if f threaten, you shall flee.
Mt	14:19	Taking the f loaves and the two fish,
Mt	16: 9	do you not remember the f loaves for the f thousand,
Mt	25: 2	F of them were foolish and f were wise.
Mt	25:15	To one he gave f talents;
Jn	4:18	For you have had f husbands,
1 Cor	14:19	church I would rather speak f words
Rev	9: 5	only to torment them for f months;
Rev	17:10	f have already fallen, one still lives,

FIX

Am	9: 4	I will f my gaze upon them for evil

FLAME → FLAMES, FLAMING

Jgs	13:20	ascended in the f of the altar.
Is	10:17	a f, That burns and consumes its
Acts	7:30	Sinai in the f of a burning bush.
Rev	1:14	and his eyes were like a fiery f.
Rev	2:18	whose eyes are like a fiery f
Rev	19:12	His eyes were [like] a fiery f,

FLAMES → FLAME

Ps	106:18	f consumed the wicked.
Dn	3:22	the f devoured the men who threw
Dn	3:49	drove the fiery f out of the furnace,
Lk	16:24	I am suffering torment in these f.

FLAMING → FLAME

Ex	3: 2	appeared to him as fire f
Eph	6:16	quench all [the] f arrows of the evil

FLASH → FLASHED, FLASHES, FLASHING

Ps	144: 6	F forth lightning and scatter my
Ez	21:15	a slaughter, burnished to f lightning!

FLASHED → FLASH

Ps	77:18	your arrows f back and forth.
Acts	9: 3	from the sky suddenly f around him.

FLASHES → FLASH

Lk	17:24	For just as lightning f and lights
Rev	4: 5	From the throne came f of lightning,
Rev	8: 5	rumblings, f of lightning,
Rev	11:19	There were f of lightning,
Rev	16:18	Then there were lightning f,

FLASHING → FLASH

Dt	32:41	When I sharpen my f sword, and my

FLASK

2 Kgs	9: 1	Take this f of oil with you, and go
2 Kgs	9: 3	From the f you have, pour oil on his

FLATTERING → FLATTERY

Prv	26:28	enemy, and the f mouth works ruin.

FLATTERY → FLATTERING

Prv	29: 5	Those who speak f to their neighbor cast

FLAX

Jos	2: 6	them among her stalks of f spread
Jgs	15:14	ropes around his arms became like f
Prv	31:13	She seeks out wool and f

FLED → FLEE

Ex	2:15	But Moses f from Pharaoh and went
2 Sm	4: 4	his nurse took him and f, but in their
2 Sm	19:10	Now, he has f the country before
Ps	3: 1	when he f from his son Absalom.
Ps	57: 1	when he f from Saul into a cave.
Ps	114: 3	The sea saw and f; the Jordan turned
Mk	14:50	And they all left him and f.
Rev	12: 6	The woman herself f into the desert
Rev	16:20	Every island f, and mountains
Rev	20:11	and the sky f from his presence

FLEE → FLED

Gn	19:17	F to the hills at once, or you will be
Gn	27:43	f at once to my brother Laban
Tb	6:18	it will f and never again show itself
Ps	11: 1	me, "F like a bird to the mountains!
Ps	64: 9	by their own tongues; all who see them f.
Ps	68: 2	those who hate him f before him.
Ps	139: 7	From your presence, where can I f?
Sir	21: 2	F from sin as from a serpent
Is	30:17	if five threaten, you shall f.
Jer	46: 6	The swift cannot f, nor the warrior
Jer	51: 6	F from Babylon; each of you save
Jon	1: 3	Jonah made ready to f to Tarshish,
Zec	2:10	F from the land of the north—
Lk	3: 7	Who warned you to f
Jas	4: 7	the devil, and he will f from you.

FLEECE

Jgs	6:37	I am putting this woolen f
Jgs	6:37	and if dew is on the f alone,

FLEETING

Sir	41:11	The human body is a f thing,

FLESH

Gn	2:23	is bone of my bones and f of my f;
Gn	17:13	in your f as an everlasting covenant.
1 Sm	17:44	I will feed your f to the birds
2 Chr	32: 8	He has only an arm of f, but we
Jb	19:26	off, and from my f I will see God:
Ps	50:13	Do I eat the f of bulls or drink
Ps	73:26	Though my f and my heart fail,
Sir	17:31	worthless then the thoughts of f and blood!
Sir	41: 4	This decree for all f is from God;
Sir	44:20	his own f he incised the ordinance,
Is	31: 3	not God, their horses f, not spirit;
Jer	17: 5	beings, who makes f his strength,
Ez	37: 6	on you, make f grow over you,
Ez	44: 7	uncircumcised in heart and f,
Mal	2:15	make them one, with f and spirit?
Mt	16:17	For f and blood has not revealed this
Mt	19: 5	and the two shall become one f"?
Mt	26:41	spirit is willing, but the f is weak."
Lk	24:39	because a ghost does not have f
Jn	1:14	the Word became f and made his
Jn	3: 6	What is born of f is f and what is
Jn	6:51	that I will give is my f for the life
Jn	6:63	gives life, while the f is of no avail.
Acts	2:17	out a portion of my spirit upon all f.
Rom	7: 5	For when we were in the f,
Rom	8: 3	weakened by the f, was powerless

Rom   8: 3 own Son in the likeness of sinful **f**
Rom   8: 3 of sin, he condemned sin in the **f**,
Rom   8: 4 who live not according to the **f**
Rom   8: 9 But you are not in the **f**;
Rom   8:13 For if you live according to the **f**,
1 Cor   6:16 two," it says, "will become one **f**."
1 Cor 15:39 Not all **f** is the same, but there is one
1 Cor 15:50 **f** and blood cannot inherit
2 Cor 12: 7 a thorn in the **f** was given to me,
Gal   3: 3 are you now ending with the **f**?
Gal   5:17 the **f** has desires against the Spirit, and the Spirit against
                the **f**;
Gal   5:19 Now the works of the **f** are obvious:
Eph   2: 3 following the wishes of the **f**
Eph   5:31 and the two shall become one **f**."
Eph   6:12 For our struggle is not with **f**
Phil   1:22 If I go on living in the **f**, that means
Phil   3: 4 for confidence even in the **f**.
Phil   3: 4 else thinks he can be confident in **f**,
Col   1:24 and in my **f** I am filling up what is
1 Tm   3:16 Who was manifested in the **f**,
Heb   5: 7 In the days when he was in the **f**,
1 Pt   1:24 "All **f** is like grass, and all its glory
1 Jn   4: 2 Jesus Christ come in the **f** belongs
2 Jn   1: 7 Jesus Christ as coming in the **f**;
Jude   1: 8 nevertheless also defile the **f**,
Rev   19:18 to eat the **f** of kings, the **f** of military
Rev   19:18 and the **f** of all, free and slave,

FLEW → FLY
Ps   18:11 Mounted on a cherub he **f**,
Is   6: 6 Then one of the seraphim **f** to me,

FLIES → FLY
Ex   8:17 I will send swarms of **f** upon you
Ps   91: 5 of the night nor the arrow that **f**
Ps   105:31 spoke and there came swarms of **f**,

FLIGHT → FLY
Dt   1:44 and put you to **f** the way bees do,
Dt   32:30 or two put ten thousand to **f**,
Mt   24:20 Pray that your **f** not be in winter

FLINT
Ex   4:25 Zipporah took a piece of **f** and cut
Jos   5: 2 Make **f** knives and circumcise Israel
Is   50: 7 Therefore I have set my face like **f**,

FLOATED
Gn   7:18 but the ark **f** on the surface

FLOCK → FLOCKS
Gn   4: 4 fatty portion of the firstlings of his **f**.
Ex   2:17 in their defense and watered their **f**.
Ex   3: 1 Meanwhile Moses was tending the **f**
Ps   77:21 You led your people like a **f**
Ps   78:52 them like a **f** through the wilderness.
Ps   80: 2 ear, you who guide Joseph like a **f**!
Sg   4: 1 Your hair is like a **f** of goats
Sg   6: 6 Your teeth are like a **f** of ewes
Is   40:11 Like a shepherd he feeds his **f**;
Jer   31:10 he guards them as a shepherd his **f**.
Am   7:15 took me from following the **f**,
Zec   11: 7 So I shepherded the **f** to be
Mt   26:31 the sheep of the **f** will be dispersed';
Lk   2: 8 keeping the night watch over their **f**.
Lk   12:32 little **f**, for your Father is pleased
Jn   10:16 voice, and there will be one **f**,
Acts   20:28 over the whole **f** of which the holy
1 Cor   9: 7 Or who shepherds a **f** without using some of the milk
                from the **f**?
1 Pt   5: 2 Tend the **f** of God in your midst,
1 Pt   5: 3 to you, but be examples to the **f**.

FLOCKS → FLOCK
Jer   10:21 have failed, and all their **f** scattered.

FLOGGED
Acts   5:40 they had them **f**, ordered them

FLOOD → FLOODS
Gn   7: 7 ark because of the waters of the **f**.

Gn   9:15 waters will never again become a **f**
Ps   29:10 LORD sits enthroned above the **f**!
Is   28:18 When the raging **f** passes through,
Mt   24:38 In [those] days before the **f**,
Lk   6:48 when the **f** came, the river burst
2 Pt   2: 5 he brought a **f** upon the godless

FLOODS → FLOOD
Mt   7:25 The rain fell, the **f** came,

FLOOR
Dt   15:14 and threshing **f** and wine press;
Jgs   6:37 woolen fleece on the threshing **f**,
Ru   3: 3 and go down to the threshing **f**.
1 Chr 21:15 by the threshing **f** of Ornan
Dn   14:19 "Look at the **f** and consider whose
Mt   3:12 He will clear his threshing **f**

FLOUR
Nm   7:13 both filled with bran **f** mixed
Lk   13:21 of wheat **f** until the whole batch

FLOURISH
Ps   72: 7 That abundance may **f** in his days,
Ps   92: 8 Though the wicked **f** like grass
Ps   92:13 The just shall **f** like the palm tree,

FLOW → FLOWING
Lv   12: 7 be clean again after her **f** of blood.
Ps   78:16 He made streams **f** from crags,
Jl   4:18 and the hills **f** with milk,
Jl   4:18 streams of Judah will **f** with water.
Zec   14: 8 fresh water will **f** from Jerusalem,
Jn   7:38 of living water will **f** from within

FLOWER → FLOWERS
Jb   14: 2 Like a **f** that springs up and fades,
Ps   103:15 he blossoms like a **f** in the field.
Is   40: 7 The grass withers, the **f** wilts,
Jas   1:10 he will pass away "like the **f**
1 Pt   1:24 all its glory like the **f** of the field;
1 Pt   1:24 the grass withers, and the **f** wilts;

FLOWERS → FLOWER
1 Kgs   6:18 in the form of gourds and open **f**;

FLOWING → FLOW
Ex   3: 8 land, a land **f** with milk and honey,
Ex   33: 3 to a land **f** with milk and honey.
Nm   16:14 bringing us to a land **f** with milk
Jos   5: 6 us, a land **f** with milk and honey.
Jer   32:22 them, a land **f** with milk and honey.
Ez   20: 6 them, a land **f** with milk and honey,
Ez   47: 1 I saw water **f** out from under
Rev   22: 1 **f** from the throne of God

FLUTE → FLUTES
1 Mc   3:45 the **f** and the harp were silent.
Mt   11:17 'We played the **f** for you, but you
1 Cor 14: 7 how will what is being played on **f**

FLUTES → FLUTE
1 Sm   10: 5 by lyres, tambourines, **f**, and harps,

FLY → FLEW, FLIES, FLIGHT, FLYING
Gn   1:20 earth let birds **f** beneath the dome
Rev   12:14 so that she could **f** to her place

FLYING → FLY
Zec   5: 1 my eyes again and saw a **f** scroll.
Rev   14: 6 I saw another angel **f** high overhead,

FOAL
Zec   9: 9 donkey, on a colt, the **f** of a donkey.
Mt   21: 5 colt, the **f** of a beast of burden.' "

FOAM → FOAMING, FOAMS
Ps   46: 4 Though its waters rage and **f**
Mk   9:20 to roll around and **f** at the mouth.

FOAMING → FOAM
Ps   75: 9 cup is in the LORD's hand, **f** wine,
Jude   1:13 the sea, **f** up their shameless deeds,

FOAMS → FOAM
Lk   9:39 and it convulses him until he **f**

FOE → FOES
Ex	23:22	to your enemies and a f to your foes.
Ps	60:13	Give us aid against the f;
Ps	78:42	day he redeemed them from the f,
Lam	1: 5	gone away, captive before the f.

FOES → FOE
Ex	23:22	to your enemies and a foe to your f.
Lv	26:17	and your f will lord it over you.
Ps	3: 2	How many are my f, LORD!
Ps	44: 6	Through you we batter our f;
Lam	1: 5	Her f have come out on top,

FOLD → FOLDING, FOLDS
Jn	10:16	sheep that do not belong to this f.

FOLDING → FOLD
Prv	6:10	a little f of the arms to rest—
Prv	24:33	a little f of the arms to rest—

FOLDS → FOLD
Neh	5:13	I shook out the f of my garment,
Ps	50: 9	your house, or he-goats from your f.

FOLLOW → FOLLOWED, FOLLOWING, FOLLOWS
Ex	16: 4	see whether they f my instructions
1 Sm	8: 3	His sons did not f his example,
1 Kgs	11:10	this very thing, not to f other gods.
1 Kgs	18:21	If the LORD is God, f him; if Baal, f him."
1 Mc	1:44	ordering them to f customs foreign
Ez	13: 3	the fools who f their own spirit
Mt	8:19	I will f you wherever you go."
Mt	8:22	But Jesus answered him, "F me,
Mt	16:24	himself, take up his cross, and f me.
Lk	9:23	and take up his cross daily and f me.
Lk	9:61	another said, "I will f you, Lord,
Jn	10: 4	and the sheep f him, because they
Jn	10: 5	But they will not f a stranger,
Jn	10:27	I know them, and they f me.
Jn	12:26	Whoever serves me must f me,
Jn	13:36	I am going, you cannot f me now, though you will f later."
Jn	21:19	said this, he said to him, "F me."
1 Tm	5:15	have already turned away to f Satan.
1 Pt	2:21	that you should f in his footsteps.
2 Pt	1:16	We did not f cleverly devised myths
Rev	14: 4	the ones who f the Lamb wherever

FOLLOWED → FOLLOW
Nm	32:11	they have not f me unreservedly—
Jgs	2:12	They f other gods, the gods
Jer	9:13	but f instead their stubborn hearts
Mt	9: 9	And he got up and f him.
Mk	1:18	they abandoned their nets and f him.
Mk	14:54	Peter f him at a distance
Lk	18:28	up our possessions and f you."
Lk	18:43	received his sight and f him,
Rev	13: 3	the whole world f after the beast.

FOLLOWING → FOLLOW
Nm	32:15	If you turn away from f him, he will
Jgs	2:17	themselves by f other gods,
Sir	5: 2	your strength in f the desires of your
Lk	22:54	Peter was f at a distance.
Eph	2: 2	you once lived f the age of this
Eph	2: 2	f the ruler of the power of the air,
2 Pt	2:15	gone astray, f the road of Balaam,

FOLLOWS → FOLLOW
Prv	10:17	Whoever f instruction is in the path to life,
Jn	8:12	Whoever f me will not walk

FOLLY → FOOL
Prv	9:13	Woman F is raucous,
Prv	13:16	prudently but the foolish parade f.
Prv	14: 1	but F tears hers down with her own
Prv	14:18	The simple have f as an adornment,
Prv	14:24	the diadem of fools is f.
Prv	14:29	a short temper raises f high.
Prv	15:14	but the mouth of fools feeds on f.
Prv	16:22	have it, but f is the training of fools.

Prv	19: 3	Their own f leads people astray;
Prv	22:15	F is bound to the heart of a youth,
Prv	26: 4	answer fools according to their f,
Prv	26: 5	Answer fools according to their f,
Eccl	1:17	madness and f, I learned that this
Eccl	2:13	as much profit over f as light has
Eccl	10: 1	than wisdom or wealth is a little f!
Sir	41:15	Better is the person who hides his f than
Mk	7:22	envy, blasphemy, arrogance, f.

FOOD → FOODS
Gn	1:30	I give all the green plants for f.
Gn	3: 6	saw that the tree was good for f
Nm	21: 5	are disgusted with this wretched f!"
Tb	1:11	refrained from eating that Gentile f
1 Mc	1:63	to die rather than to be defiled with f
Ps	78:18	hearts, demanding the f they craved.
Ps	104:27	to you to give them f in due time.
Ps	111: 5	He gives f to those who fear him,
Prv	12:11	Those who till their own land have f
Prv	23: 3	it is f that deceives.
Prv	31:15	and distributes f to her household,
Is	65:25	but the serpent's f shall be dust.
Dn	1: 8	to defile himself with the king's f
Mt	3: 4	His f was locusts and wild honey.
Mt	6:25	Is not life more than f and the body
Jn	4:32	"I have f to eat of which you do not
Jn	4:34	"My f is to do the will of the one
Jn	6:27	Do not work for f that perishes
Jn	6:27	for the f that endures for eternal life,
Jn	6:55	For my flesh is true f, and my blood
1 Cor	3: 2	not solid f, because you were unable
1 Cor	6:13	"F for the stomach and the stomach for f,"
1 Cor	8: 8	Now f will not bring us closer
1 Cor	10: 3	All ate the same spiritual f,
1 Tm	6: 8	If we have f and clothing, we shall
Heb	5:14	But solid f is for the mature,
Jas	2:15	to wear and has no f for the day,

FOODS → FOOD
Mk	7:19	(Thus he declared all f clean.)
1 Tm	4: 3	require abstinence from f that God

FOOL → FOLLY, FOOL'S, FOOLISH, FOOLISHLY, FOOLISHNESS, FOOLS
Ps	14: 1	The f says in his heart, "There is no God."
Ps	49:11	the f will perish together
Ps	53: 2	The f says in his heart, "There is no God."
Prv	10:18	and whoever spreads slander is a f.
Prv	14:16	the f is reckless and gets embroiled.
Prv	15: 5	The f spurns a father's instruction,
Prv	19:10	Luxury is not befitting a f;
Prv	20: 3	strife, while every f starts a quarrel.
Prv	26: 7	in the mouth of a f hangs limp,
Prv	29:20	There is more hope for a f!
Sir		always wisdom, but the f changes like the moon.
Sir	31:30	Wine in excess is a snare for the f;
Hos	9: 7	"The prophet is a f, the man
Mt	5:22	says, 'You f,' will be liable to fiery
Lk	12:20	'You f, this night your life will be

FOOL'S → FOOL
Sir	21:16	A f chatter is like a load

FOOLISH → FOOL
Dt	32: 6	LORD, so f and unwise a people?
Prv	10: 1	but a f son is a grief to his mother.
Prv	17:25	A f son is vexation to his father,
Sir	42: 8	chastisement for the silly and the f,
Is	44:25	wise and make their knowledge f.
Jer	5:21	to this, you f and senseless people,
Mt	25: 2	Five of them were f and five were
Lk	24:25	said to them, "Oh, how f you are!
1 Cor	1:20	made the wisdom of the world f?
1 Cor	1:27	God chose the f of the world
Ti	3: 3	For we ourselves were once f,
1 Pt	2:15	silence the ignorance of f people.

FOOLISHLY → FOOL
2 Chr 16: 9 You have acted f in this matter,

FOOLISHNESS → FOOL
1 Cor 1:18 of the cross is f to those who are
1 Cor 1:21 the will of God through the f
1 Cor 1:23 block to Jews and f to Gentiles,
1 Cor 1:25 the f of God is wiser than human
1 Cor 2:14 God, for to him it is f, and he cannot
1 Cor 3:19 wisdom of this world is f in the eyes
2 Cor 11: 1 would put up with a little f from me!

FOOLS → FOOL
Ps   94: 8 You f, when will you be wise?
Prv   1: 7 f despise wisdom and discipline.
Prv   1:32 the smugness of f destroys them.
Prv   3:35 possess glory, but f will bear shame.
Prv 10:21 many, but f die for want of sense.
Prv 13:19 from evil is an abomination to f.
Prv 13:20 but the companion of f fares badly.
Prv 14:24 the diadem of f is folly.
Prv 16:22 have it, but folly is the training of f.
Prv 17:12 her cubs, but never f in their folly!
Prv 18: 2 F take no delight in understanding,
Prv 18: 6 The lips of f walk into a fight,
Prv 26: 4 Do not answer f according to their
Prv 26:11 to their vomit, so f repeat their folly.
Prv 27:22 Though you pound f with a pestle,
Prv 29:11 F give vent to all their anger;
Eccl 5: 3 For God has no pleasure in f;
Eccl 7: 4 but the heart of f is in the house
Eccl 7: 5 wise than to listen to the song of f;
Mt   23:17 Blind f, which is greater, the gold,
Rom   1:22 claiming to be wise, they became f
1 Cor 4:10 We are f on Christ's account,
2 Cor 11:19 For you gladly put up with f,

FOOT → BAREFOOT, FEET, FOOTHOLD, FOOTSTOOL
Ex   21:24 for tooth, hand for hand, f for f,
Dt   11:24 place where you set f shall be yours:
Jos   1: 3 place where you set f I have given
Ps   26:12 My f stands on level ground;
Ps   91:12 lest you strike your f against a stone.
Ps   94:18 When I say, "My f is slipping,"
Ps 121: 3 He will not allow your f to slip;
Prv   1:15 hold back your f from their path!
Prv   3:23 your f will never stumble;
Prv   4:27 nor to left, keep your f far from evil.
Prv 25:17 Let your f be seldom in your
Is   1: 6 of the f to the head there is no sound
Mt   18: 8 If your hand or f causes you to sin,
Lk   4:11 you dash your f against a stone.' "
1 Cor 12:15 If a f should say, "Because I am not
Rev 10: 2 He placed his right f on the sea and his left f on the land,

FOOTHOLD → FOOT
Ps   69: 3 of the deep, where there is no f.

FOOTSTOOL → FOOT
1 Chr 28: 2 the f for the feet of our God;
Ps   99: 5 bow down before his f; holy is he!
Ps 110: 1 while I make your enemies your f."
Is   66: 1 are my throne, the earth, my f.
Lam   2: 1 Not remembering his f on the day
Mt   5:35 nor by the earth, for it is his f;
Acts 7:49 are my throne, the earth is my f.
Heb   1:13 until I make your enemies your f"?
Heb 10:13 until his enemies are made his f.

FORBEARANCE
Rom   3:26 through the f of God—to prove his

FORBID
Rom   2:22 You who f adultery, do you commit
1 Cor 14:39 and do not f speaking in tongues,
1 Tm   4: 3 They f marriage and require

FORCE → FORCED
Gn   34: 2 he seized her and lay with her by f.
Jgs   8:12 and Zalmunna, terrifying the entire f.
1 Kgs 9:15 the conscript labor f King Solomon raised

Acts 26:11 an attempt to f them to blaspheme;

FORCED → FORCE
Ex   1:11 to oppress them with f labor.
1 Kgs 5:27 Solomon raised thirty thousand f laborers
Phlm 1:14 that the good you do might not be f

FORDS
Jos   2: 7 along the way to the f of the Jordan.

FOREHEAD → FOREHEADS
Ex   13: 9 your hand and a reminder on your f,
Ex   28:38 this plate must always be over his f,
Dt   6: 8 let them be as a pendant on your f.
Dt   11:18 let them be as a pendant on your f.
1 Sm 17:49 and struck the Philistine on the f.
Rev 17: 5 On her f was written a name,

FOREHEADS → FOREHEAD
Ez   9: 4 an X on the f of those who grieve
Rev   7: 3 put the seal on the f of the servants
Rev   9: 4 not have the seal of God on their f.
Rev 13:16 image on their right hands or their f,
Rev 14: 1 his Father's name written on their f.
Rev 20: 4 nor had accepted its mark on their f
Rev 22: 4 face, and his name will be on their f.

FOREIGN → FOREIGNER, FOREIGNERS
Gn   35: 2 "Get rid of the f gods among you;
1 Kgs 11: 1 loved many f women besides
2 Chr 33:15 He removed the f gods and the idol
Ps   81:10 There shall be no f god among you;
Prv   2:16 from a f woman with her smooth words,
Prv 23:27 and the f woman a narrow well;
Acts 17:18 sounds like a promoter of f deities,"

FOREIGNER → FOREIGN
Ex   12:43 No f may eat of it.
Dt   17:15 you may not set over you a f, who is
Dt   23:21 From a f you may demand interest,
Lk   17:18 but this f returned to give thanks
1 Cor 14:11 I shall be a f to one who speaks it, and one who speaks it a f to me.

FOREIGNERS → FOREIGN
1 Kgs 8:41 "To the f, likewise, who are not
Mt   27: 7 potter's field as a burial place for f.
1 Cor 14:21 by the lips of f I will speak to this

FOREKNEW → KNOW
Rom   8:29 For those he f he also predestined
Rom 11: 2 not rejected his people whom he f.

FOREKNOWLEDGE → KNOW
Jdt   9: 6 and your judgment is made with f.
Acts 2:23 up by the set plan and f of God,

FOREMOST
1 Tm   1:15 to save sinners. Of these I am the f.

FORERUNNER → RUN
Heb   6:20 Jesus has entered on our behalf as f,

FORESAW → SEE
Acts 2:31 he f and spoke of the resurrection

FORESKIN → FORESKINS
Gn   17:14 flesh of his f has not been cut away,
Ex   4:25 of flint and cut off her son's f and,

FORESKINS → FORESKIN
1 Sm 18:25 the bride than the f of one hundred
Jer   4: 4 remove the f of your hearts,

FOREST
1 Kgs 7: 2 of the F of Lebanon one hundred
1 Chr 16:33 of the f exult before the LORD,
Ps   50:10 For every animal of the f is mine,
Jas   3: 5 small a fire can set a huge f ablaze.

FORETOLD → TELL
Sir 48:25 He f what would happen till the end of time,

FOREVER → EVER
Gn   3:22 tree of life, and eats of it and lives f?
Gn   6: 3 shall not remain in human beings f,

Ex	3:15	This is my name f; this is my title
Dt	29:28	are for us and for our children f,
2 Sm	7:13	I will establish his royal throne f.
2 Sm	7:26	so that your name may be f great.
1 Kgs	2:33	there shall be peace f
1 Kgs	9: 3	have built and I set my name there f;
1 Chr	16:15	He remembers f his covenant
1 Chr	16:41	LORD, "whose love endures f,"
1 Chr	17:24	may be great and abide f,
2 Chr	5:13	whose love endures f," the cloud
2 Chr	33: 7	of Israel, I shall set my name f.
Ezr	3:11	for his love for Israel endures f";
Tb	3:11	be your holy and honorable name f! May all your works f bless you.
1 Mc	4:24	is good, whose mercy endures f."
Ps	9: 8	The LORD rules f, has set up his
Ps	19:10	of the LORD is pure, enduring f.
Ps	28: 9	pasture and carry them f!
Ps	29:10	The LORD reigns as king f!
Ps	33:11	But the plan of the LORD stands f,
Ps	44: 9	your name we will praise f.
Ps	44:24	Rise up! Do not reject us f!
Ps	72:19	Blessed be his glorious name f;
Ps	73:26	the rock of my heart, my portion f.
Ps	74:10	Will the enemy revile your name f?
Ps	77: 9	Has God's mercy ceased f?
Ps	79:13	pasture, will give thanks to you f;
Ps	81:16	him, but their fate is fixed f.
Ps	86:12	glorify your name f, Lord my God.
Ps	89: 2	I will sing of your mercy f,
Ps	92: 9	but you, LORD, are f on high.
Ps	100: 5	His mercy endures f, his faithfulness
Ps	102:13	But you, LORD, are enthroned f;
Ps	104:31	the glory of the LORD endure f;
Ps	107: 1	he is good, his mercy endures f!"
Ps	110: 4	"You are a priest f in the manner
Ps	111: 3	work, his righteousness endures f.
Ps	112: 6	the righteous shall be remembered f.
Ps	117: 2	the faithfulness of the LORD is f.
Ps	118: 1	for he is good, his mercy endures f.
Ps	119:111	Your testimonies are my heritage f;
Ps	119:152	that you have established them f.
Ps	136: 1	he is good; for his mercy endures f;
Ps	146: 6	that is in them, Who keeps faith f,
Prv	10:25	but the just are established f.
Prv	27:24	For wealth does not last f, nor even
Eccl	3:14	whatever God does will endure f;
Wis	5:15	But the righteous live f,
Sir	40:17	cut off, and righteousness endures f.
Is	26: 4	Trust in the LORD f!
Is	40: 8	but the word of our God stands f."
Is	51: 6	My salvation shall remain f and my
Is	51: 8	But my victory shall remain f,
Is	59:21	children from this time forth and f,
Jer	3:12	LORD, I will not keep my anger f.
Jer	33:11	God's love endures f."
Lam	5:19	But you, LORD, are enthroned f;
Bar	3: 3	for you are enthroned f, while we are perishing f.
Dn	2:44	an end to them, and it shall stand f.
Dn	3:57	praise and exalt him above all f.
Dn	6:27	enduring f, whose kingdom shall not
Hos	2:21	I will betroth you to me f;
Jn	6:51	whoever eats this bread will live f;
Rom	9: 5	God who is over all be blessed f.
Rom	16:27	through Jesus Christ be glory f
Heb	5: 6	"You are a priest f according
Heb	7:17	"You are a priest f according
Heb	7:24	but he, because he remains f,
Heb	13: 8	is the same yesterday, today, and f.
1 Pt	1:25	the word of the Lord remains f."
1 Jn	2:17	does the will of God remains f.
2 Jn	1: 2	dwells in us and will be with us f.
Rev	1:18	dead, but now I am alive f and ever.
Rev	4: 9	on the throne, who lives f and ever,
Rev	11:15	and he will reign f and ever."
Rev	20:10	tormented day and night f and ever.
Rev	22: 5	and they shall reign f and ever.

FOREWARNED → WARN

2 Pt	3:17	since you are f, be on your guard

FORFEIT

Prv	20: 2	who incur his anger f their lives.
Mk	8:36	gain the whole world and f his life?
Lk	9:25	whole world yet lose or f himself?

FORGAVE → FORGIVE

Ps	78:38	being compassionate f their sin;
Ps	85: 3	You f the guilt of your people,
Mt	18:27	let him go and f him the loan.
Mt	18:32	I f you your entire debt because you

FORGET → FORGETFUL, FORGETS, FORGETTING, FORGOT, FORGOTTEN

Gn	41:51	has made me f entirely my troubles
Dt	6:12	be careful not to f the LORD,
2 Kgs	17:38	I made with you, you must not f;
1 Mc	1:49	so that they might f the law
Ps	9:18	depart, all the nations that f God.
Ps	10:12	lift up your hand! Do not f the poor!
Ps	50:22	you who f God, lest I start ripping
Ps	78: 7	And not f God's deeds, but keep his
Ps	103: 2	and do not f all his gifts,
Ps	119:93	I will never f your precepts;
Ps	137: 5	If I f you, Jerusalem, may my right hand f.
Prv	3: 1	My son, do not f my teaching,
Prv	4: 5	Do not f or turn aside
Prv	31: 5	in drinking they f what has been
Is	49:15	Can a mother f her infant,
Is	49:15	Even should she f, I will never f
Jer	2:32	Does a young woman f her jewelry,

FORGETFUL → FORGET

2 Pt	1: 9	f of the cleansing of his past sins.

FORGETS → FORGET

Jb	8:13	is the end of everyone who f God,

FORGETTING → FORGET

Phil	3:13	f what lies behind but straining

FORGIVE → FORGAVE, FORGIVEN, FORGIVENESS, FORGIVES, FORGIVING

Gn	50:17	So now please f the crime that we,
Ex	10:17	now, do f me my sin only this once,
Ex	32:32	Now if you would only f their sin!
Jos	24:19	who will not f your transgressions
1 Sm	25:28	Please f the offense of your
1 Kgs	8:34	and f the sin of your people Israel,
1 Kgs	8:36	and f the sin of your servants,
1 Kgs	8:39	f and take action.
1 Kgs	8:50	F your people who have sinned
2 Chr	6:25	and f the sin of your people Israel,
2 Chr	6:27	and f the sin of your servants,
2 Chr	6:30	place of your enthronement, and f.
2 Chr	6:39	F your people who have sinned
Sir	5: 6	my many sins he will f."
Sir	28: 2	F your neighbor the wrong done
Sir	34:23	many sacrifices does he f their sins.
Jer	18:23	Do not f their crime, and their sin do
Jer	31:34	for I will f their iniquity and no
Jer	33: 8	I will f all their offenses
Jer	36: 3	then I can f their wickedness
Am	7: 2	the land, I said: F, O Lord GOD!
Mt	6:12	and f us our debts, as we f our
Mt	6:14	If you f others their transgressions,
Mt	6:14	your heavenly Father will f you.
Mt	6:15	But if you do not f others,
Mt	6:15	your Father f your transgressions.
Mt	9: 6	has authority on earth to f sins"—
Mt	18:21	against me, how often must I f him?
Mk	2: 7	Who but God alone can f sins?"
Mk	2:10	of Man has authority to f sins
Mk	11:25	f anyone against whom you have
Mk	11:25	in turn f you your transgressions.
Lk	5:21	Who but God alone can f sins?"
Lk	5:24	has authority on earth to f sins"—

Lk	6:37	F and you will be forgiven.
Lk	11: 4	and f us our sins for we ourselves f
Lk	17: 3	and if he repents, f him.
Lk	17: 4	'I am sorry,' you should f him."
Lk	23:34	said, "Father, f them, they know not
Jn	20:23	Whose sins you f are forgiven them,
2 Cor	2: 7	so that on the contrary you should f
2 Cor	2:10	Whomever you f anything, so do I.
2 Cor	12:13	not burden you? F me this wrong!
1 Jn	1: 9	just and will f our sins and cleanse

FORGIVEN → FORGIVE

Lv	4:20	on their behalf, that they may be f.
Lv	19:22	he will be f for the wrong he has
Nm	15:25	and they will be f, since it was
Ps	32: 1	fault is removed, whose sin is f.
Mt	9: 5	to say, 'Your sins are f,' or to say,
Mt	12:31	sin and blasphemy will be f people,
Mt	12:31	against the Spirit will not be f.
Mk	2: 9	'Your sins are f,' or to say, 'Rise,
Lk	6:37	Forgive and you will be f.
Lk	7:47	tell you, her many sins have been f;
Lk	7:47	But the one to whom little is f,
Rom	4: 7	are they whose iniquities are f
Eph	4:32	one another as God has f you
Col	3:13	as the Lord has f you, so must you
Jas	5:15	has committed any sins, he will be f.
1 Jn	2:12	because your sins have been f

FORGIVENESS → FORGIVE

Ps	130: 4	with you is f and so you are revered.
Sir	5: 5	Do not be so confident of f that you
Dn	9: 9	belong compassion and f, though we
Mt	26:28	on behalf of many for the f of sins.
Mk	1: 4	of repentance for the f of sins.
Mk	3:29	the holy Spirit will never have f,
Lk	1:77	salvation through the f of their sins,
Lk	3: 3	of repentance for the f of sins,
Lk	24:47	for the f of sins, would be preached
Acts	5:31	grant Israel repentance and f of sins.
Acts	10:43	in him will receive f of sins through
Acts	13:38	that through him f of sins is being
Acts	26:18	so that they may obtain f of sins
Eph	1: 7	by his blood, the f of transgressions,
Col	1:14	we have redemption, the f of sins.
Heb	9:22	the shedding of blood there is no f.
Heb	10:18	Where there is f of these, there is no

FORGIVES → FORGIVE

Sir	2:11	f sins and saves in time of trouble.
Sir	16:11	he remits and f, but also pours
Mt	18:35	you, unless each of you f his brother
Lk	7:49	"Who is this who even f sins?"

FORGIVING → FORGIVE

Ex	34: 7	and f wickedness, rebellion, and sin;
Nm	14:18	in kindness, f iniquity and rebellion;
Ps	86: 5	you are good and f, most merciful
Ps	99: 8	you were a f God to them,
Eph	4:32	f one another as God has forgiven

FORGOT → FORGET

Dt	32:18	you f the God who gave you birth.
1 Sm	12: 9	But they f the Lord their God;
Ps	78:11	They f his deeds, the wonders
Ps	106:13	But they soon f all he had done;
Ps	106:21	They f the God who had saved
Jer	23:27	just as their ancestors f my name
Hos	2:15	but me she f—oracle of the Lord.

FORGOTTEN → FORGET

Ps	9:19	For the needy will never be f,
Ps	44:21	If we had f the name of our God,
Ps	77:10	Has God f how to show mercy,
Sir	35: 9	of the just is accepted, never to be f.
Is	17:10	you have f the God who saves you,
Is	49:14	my Lord has f me."
Jer	2:32	my people have f me days without
Hos	8:14	Israel has f his maker and has built
Mt	16: 5	the disciples had f to bring bread.

Heb	12: 5	f the exhortation addressed to you as

FORM → FORMED, FORMLESS, FORMS

Gn	1: 2	and the earth was without f or shape,
Dt	4:15	Because you saw no f at all
Lk	3:22	upon him in bodily f like a dove.
Jn	5:37	never heard his voice nor seen his f,
Acts	14:11	have come down to us in human f."
1 Cor	7:31	in its present f is passing away.
Phil	2: 6	though he was in the f of God,

FORMED → FORM

Gn	2: 7	the Lord God f the man
Ps	94: 9	The one who f the eye not see?
Ps	139:13	You f my inmost being; you knit me
Is	43: 1	you, Jacob, and f you, Israel:
Is	43:10	Before me no god was f,
Is	44: 2	help, who f you from the womb:
Is	49: 5	Lord has spoken who f me as his
Jer	1: 5	Before I f you in the womb I knew
Gal	4:19	in labor until Christ be f in you!
1 Tm	2:13	For Adam was f first, then Eve.
2 Pt	3: 5	of old and earth was f out of water

FORMER

1 Mc	4:47	and built a new altar like the f one.
Eph	4:22	put away the old self of your f way

FORMLESS → FORM

Wis	11:17	the universe from f matter, to send

FORMS → FORM

Am	4:13	The one who f mountains and creates winds,

FORNICATION → FORNICATORS

Tb	4:12	guard, son, against every kind of f,

FORNICATORS → FORNICATION

1 Cor	6: 9	neither f nor idolaters nor adulterers

FORSAKE → FORSAKEN, FORSAKES, FORSAKING

Dt	31: 6	he will never fail you or f you.
Jos	1: 5	I will not leave you nor f you.
Jos	24:16	us to f the Lord to serve other
Ps	27:10	Even if my father and mother f me,
Ps	94:14	the Lord will not f his people,
Ps	138: 8	Never f the work of your hands!
Prv	4: 6	Do not f her, and she will preserve
Is	55: 7	Let the wicked f their way,
Jer	17:13	all who f you shall be put to shame;
Heb	13: 5	said, "I will never f you or abandon

FORSAKEN → FORSAKE

Is	1: 4	They have f the Lord,
Is	49:14	Zion said, "The Lord has f me;
Dn	14:38	"you have not f those who love
Mt	27:46	my God, why have you f me?"

FORSAKES → FORSAKE

Prv	2:17	One who f the companion of her

FORSAKING → FORSAKE

Hos	4:12	prostitute themselves, f their God.

FORTH

Ps	50: 2	perfection of beauty, God shines f.

FORTIFIED → FORTRESS

Nm	13:28	and the towns are f and very large.
Dt	9: 1	having large cities f to the heavens,

FORTRESS → FORTIFIED

2 Sm	22: 2	my rock, my f, my deliverer,
Ps	59:10	for you I watch; you, God, are my f,
Ps	71: 3	for you are my rock and f.

FORTUNE → FORTUNE-TELLING

Is	65:11	Who spread a table for F and fill

FORTUNE-TELLING → FORTUNE, TELL

Acts	16:16	profit to her owners through her f.

FORTY

Gn	7: 4	rain down on the earth for f days and f nights,
Gn	18:29	"What if only f are found there?"
Ex	16:35	Israelites ate the manna for f years,

Ex	24:18	He was on the mountain for f days and f nights.
Nm	14:34	reconnoitering the land—f days—
Nm	14:34	one year for each day: f years.
Dt	25: 3	F lashes may be given, but no more;
Jos	14: 7	I was f years old when Moses,
1 Sm	4:18	He had judged Israel for f years.
2 Sm	5: 4	king, and he reigned f years:
1 Kgs	19: 8	he walked f days and f nights
2 Chr	9:30	Jerusalem over all Israel for f years.
Neh	9:21	F years in the desert you sustained
Ez	29:12	among deserted cities for f years;
Am	2:10	you through the desert for f years,
Jon	3: 4	"F days more and Nineveh shall be
Mt	4: 2	He fasted for f days and f nights,
Lk	4: 2	for f days, to be tempted
2 Cor	11:24	Jews I received f lashes minus one.
Heb	3:17	was he "provoked for f years"?

FOUGHT → FIGHT

Jos	10:42	the God of Israel, f for Israel.
1 Cor	15:32	If at Ephesus I f with beasts,
Rev	12: 7	The dragon and its angels f back,

FOUND → FIND

Gn	6: 8	But Noah f favor with the LORD.
Ex	12:19	seven days no leaven may be f
Ex	33:12	You have f favor with me.
2 Kgs	22: 8	"I have f the book of the law
1 Chr	28: 9	If you search for him, he will be f;
1 Mc	1:56	of the law that they f they tore
Prv	10:13	lips of the intelligent is f wisdom,
Eccl	7:27	See, this have I f, says Qoheleth,
Is	55: 6	Seek the LORD while he may be f,
Is	65: 1	be f by those who did not seek me.
Jer	15:16	When I f your words, I devoured
Dn	1:19	of them, none was f equal to Daniel,
Dn	5:27	on the scales and f wanting;
Dn	12: 1	everyone who is f written
Mt	1:18	she was f with child through
Lk	1:30	for you have f favor with God.
Lk	7: 9	even in Israel have I f such faith."
Lk	15: 6	me because I have f my lost sheep.'
Lk	15: 9	me because I have f the coin that I
Lk	15:24	he was lost, and has been f.'
Rom	10:20	"I was f [by] those who were not
Phil	2: 7	and f human in appearance,
Rev	5: 4	tears because no one was f worthy
Rev	20:15	whose name was not f written

FOUNDATION → FOUNDATIONS, FOUNDED

Ezr	3: 6	though the f of the LORD's temple
Ps	97: 2	and right are the f of his throne.
Is	28:16	A precious cornerstone as a sure f;
Lk	14:29	after laying the f and finding
Rom	15:20	so that I do not build on another's f,
1 Cor	3:10	like a wise master builder I laid a f,
1 Cor	3:11	no one can lay a f other than the one
Eph	2:20	built upon the f of the apostles
2 Tm	2:19	God's solid f stands, bearing this
Heb	6: 1	without laying the f all over again:

FOUNDATIONS → FOUNDATION

1 Kgs	6:37	The f of the LORD's house were
Ps	82: 5	and all the world's f shake.
Ps	137: 7	"Level it, level it down to its f!"
Is	54:11	in carnelians, your f in sapphires;
Heb	11:10	looking forward to the city with f,

FOUNDED → FOUNDATION

Ps	78:69	like the earth which he f forever.
Prv	3:19	The LORD by wisdom f the earth,

FOUNTAIN → FOUNTAINS

Ps	36:10	For with you is the f of life,
Prv	10:11	The mouth of the just is a f of life,
Prv	13:14	teaching of the wise is a f of life,
Prv	14:27	The fear of the LORD is a f of life,
Prv	16:22	Good sense is a f of life to those
Sg	4:12	bride, a garden enclosed, a f sealed!
Jer	8:23	spring of water, my eyes a f of tears,

Bar	3:12	You have forsaken the f of wisdom!
Zec	13: 1	that day a f will be opened

FOUNTAINS → FOUNTAIN

Gn	7:11	day All the f of the great abyss burst

FOUR → FOURTH

Gn	2:10	it divides and becomes f branches.
1 Kgs	18:19	as well as the f hundred and fifty
1 Kgs	18:19	the f hundred prophets of Asherah
Prv	30:15	never get their fill, f never say,
Prv	30:18	for me, yes, f I cannot understand:
Prv	30:21	yes, under f it cannot bear up:
Prv	30:24	F things are among the smallest
Prv	30:29	yes, f are stately in their carriage:
Is	11:12	he shall assemble from the f corners
Ez	1: 5	of f living creatures appeared.
Ez	10: 9	saw f wheels beside the cherubim,
Ez	10:14	Each living creature had f faces:
Dn	1:17	To these f young men God gave
Dn	7: 3	which emerged f immense beasts,
Dn	8: 8	and in its place came up f others, facing the f winds of heaven.
Zec	2: 3	the LORD showed me f workmen.
Zec	6: 5	me, "These are the f winds
Mt	15:38	who ate were f thousand men,
Mk	8:20	the seven loaves for the f thousand,
Jn	4:35	f months the harvest will be here'?
Rev	4: 6	there were f living creatures covered
Rev	9:14	"Release the f angels who are

FOURTEEN

Mt	1:17	Abraham to David is f generations;
Mt	1:17	the Babylonian exile, f generations;
Mt	1:17	exile to the Messiah, f generations.
2 Cor	12: 2	f years ago (whether in the body

FOURTH → FOUR

Gn	15:16	In the f generation your descendants
Ex	20: 5	down to the third and f generation ;
Dn	3:92	and the f looks like a son of God."

FOWLER

Prv	6: 5	or like a bird from the hand of the f.

FOX → FOXES

Neh	3:35	if a f attacks it, it will breach their
Lk	13:32	"Go and tell that f, 'Behold, I cast

FOXES → FOX

Sg	2:15	Catch us the f, the little f
Lk	9:58	"F have dens and birds of the sky

FRAGRANCE → FRAGRANT

Jn	12: 3	was filled with the f of the oil.

FRAGRANT → FRAGRANCE

Ex	25: 6	anointing oil and for the f incense;
Ex	30: 7	On it Aaron shall burn f incense.
Eph	5: 2	offering to God for a f aroma.
Phil	4:18	through Epaphroditus, "a f aroma,"

FRANKINCENSE → INCENSE

Is	60: 6	shall come bearing gold and f,
Mt	2:11	and offered him gifts of gold, f,

FREE → FREED, FREEDOM, FREELY

Ps	146: 7	The LORD sets prisoners f;
Lk	13:12	you are set f of your infirmity."
Jn	8:32	truth, and the truth will set you f."
Jn	8:36	frees you, then you will truly be f.
1 Cor	12:13	slaves or f persons, and we were all
Gal	3:28	there is neither slave nor f person,
Gal	5: 1	For freedom Christ set us f;
Eph	6: 8	he does, whether he is slave or f.
Heb	13: 5	Let your life be f from love
1 Pt	2:16	Be f, yet without using freedom as

FREED → FREE

Rev	1: 5	has f us from our sins by his blood,

FREEDOM → FREE

Rom	8:21	in the glorious f of the children
1 Cor	7:21	even if you can gain your f,

2 Cor 3:17 the Spirit of the Lord is, there is **f**.
Gal 5: 1 For **f** Christ set us free;
1 Pt 2:16 yet without using **f** as a pretext
2 Pt 2:19 They promise them **f**, though they

FREELY → FREE
Hos 14: 5 their apostasy, I will love them **f**;

FRESH → FRESHEN
Zec 14: 8 On that day, **f** water will flow from Jerusalem,

FRESHEN → FRESH
Ez 47: 8 polluted waters of the sea to **f** them.

FRIEND → FRIENDLY, FRIENDS, FRIENDSHIP
Dt 13: 7 your intimate **f** entices you secretly,
2 Sm 16:17 "Is this your devotion to your **f**?
2 Chr 20: 7 descendants of Abraham, your **f**?
Ps 41:10 Even my trusted **f**, who ate my
Prv 17:17 A **f** is a **f** at all times, and a brother
Prv 27: 6 Trustworthy are the blows of a **f**,
Prv 27:10 Do not give up your own **f** and your father's **f**;
Sg 5:16 lover, and such my **f**,
Sir 7:18 Do not barter a **f** for money,
Sir 9:10 A new **f** is like new wine—
Sir 25: 9 Happy the one who finds a **f**,
Sir 27:17 Cherish your **f**, keep faith with him;
Is 41: 8 offspring of Abraham my **f**—
Mt 11:19 a **f** of tax collectors and sinners.'
Jn 19:12 him, you are not a **F** of Caesar.
Jas 2:23 and he was called "the **f** of God."

FRIENDLY → FRIEND
Sir 12: 9 is successful even an enemy is **f**;

FRIENDS → FRIEND
Jb 2:11 three of Job's **f** heard of all
Jb 42:10 of Job, after he had prayed for his **f**;
Prv 16:28 and talebearing separates bosom **f**.
Prv 18:24 There are **f** who bring ruin, but there are true **f** more loyal
Sir 6: 5 Pleasant speech multiplies **f**,
Sir 12: 8 In prosperity we cannot know our **f**;
Sir 37: 1 there are **f** who are **f** in name only.
Lam 1: 2 Her **f** have all betrayed her,
Jn 15:13 to lay down one's life for one's **f**.
Jn 15:14 You are my **f** if you do what I
3 Jn 1:15 The **f** greet you; greet the **f** there

FRIENDSHIP → FRIEND
Wis 7:14 who gain this treasure win the **f**

FRIGHTEN
Dt 28:26 the field, with no one to **f** them off.
2 Chr 32:18 on the wall, to **f** and terrify them

FROGS
Ex 7:27 a plague of **f** over all your territory.
Rev 16:13 saw three unclean spirits like **f** come

FRONT
Ex 14:19 moving from in **f** of them,
Ex 32:15 written on both sides, **f** and back.
Ez 2:10 it was covered with writing **f**
Rev 4: 6 creatures covered with eyes in **f**

FROST
Zec 14: 6 day there will no longer be cold or **f**.

FRUIT → FRUITFUL, FRUITS
Gn 1:11 every kind of **f** tree on earth that bears **f** with its seed in it.
Gn 3: 3 it is only about the **f** of the tree
Gn 3: 6 So she took some of its **f** and ate it;
Dt 28: 4 Blessed be the **f** of your womb,
Dt 28:53 you will eat the **f** of your womb,
Jgs 9:11 up my sweetness and my sweet **f**,
Ps 1: 3 of water, that yields its **f** in season;
Ps 92:15 They shall bear **f** even in old age,
Prv 8:19 My **f** is better than gold, even pure
Prv 11:30 The **f** of justice is a tree of life,
Prv 12:14 the **f** of their mouths people have

Prv 27:18 Those who tend a fig tree eat its **f**;
Is 27: 6 covering all the world with **f**.
Jer 17: 8 no distress, but still produces **f**.
Ez 47:12 river every kind of **f** tree will grow;
Ez 47:12 will not wither, nor will their **f** fail.
Am 8: 1 a basket of end-of-summer **f**.
Mt 3: 8 Produce good **f** as evidence of your
Mt 3:10 that does not bear good **f** will be cut
Mt 7:17 every good tree bears good **f**, and a rotten tree bears bad **f**.
Lk 6:44 every tree is known by its own **f**.
Lk 13: 6 when he came in search of **f** on it
Jn 15: 2 branch in me that does not bear **f**,
Jn 15: 2 he prunes so that it bears more **f**.
Jn 15:16 to go and bear **f** that will remain,
Rom 7: 4 order that we might bear **f** for God.
Col 1:10 in every good work bearing **f**
Heb 13:15 the **f** of lips that confess his name.
Rev 22: 2 that produces **f** twelve times a year,

FRUITFUL → FRUIT
Gn 35:11 be **f** and multiply.
Ex 1: 7 the Israelites were **f** and prolific.
Ps 128: 3 wife will be like a **f** vine within your
Phil 1:22 the flesh, that means **f** labor for me.

FRUITS → FRUIT
Lv 2:14 of first ripe **f** to the LORD,
Lv 23:17 your first-ripened **f** to the LORD,
Nm 28:26 On the day of first **f**, on your feast
1 Mc 3:49 garments, the first **f**, and the tithes;
Prv 3: 9 with first **f** of all your produce;
Jer 2: 3 LORD, the first **f** of his harvest;
Hos 9:10 Like the first **f** of the fig tree,
Mt 7:16 By their **f** you will know them.
Lk 3: 8 Produce good **f** as evidence of your

FRUSTRATES → FRUSTRATION
Jb 5:12 He **f** the plans of the cunning,
Ps 33:10 of nations, **f** the designs of peoples.

FRUSTRATION → FRUSTRATES
Dt 28:20 **f** in everything you set your hand to,

FUEL
Is 9:18 and the people are like **f** for fire;
Ez 21:37 You shall be **f** for the fire,

FULFILL → FULFILLED
Ps 119:166 and I **f** your commandments.
Eccl 5: 3 **f** what you have vowed.
Jer 33:14 when I will **f** the promise I made
Mt 1:22 **f** what the Lord had said through
Mt 3:15 fitting for us to **f** all righteousness."
Mt 5:17 I have come not to abolish but to **f**.
Mt 8:17 to **f** what had been said by Isaiah
Mt 12:17 to **f** what had been spoken through
Mt 13:35 to **f** what had been said through
Jn 18: 9 This was to **f** what he had said,
Gal 6: 2 and so you will **f** the law of Christ.
Jas 2: 8 if you **f** the royal law according

FULFILLED → FULFILL
2 Chr 10:15 the LORD **f** the word he had
Prv 13:12 sick, but a wish **f** is a tree of life.
Mt 2:15 said through the prophet might be **f**,
Mt 2:17 was **f** what had been said through
Mt 2:23 through the prophets might be **f**,
Mt 4:14 Isaiah the prophet might be **f**:
Mt 13:14 Isaiah's prophecy is **f** in them,
Mt 21: 4 through the prophet might be **f**:
Mt 26:54 how would the scriptures be **f**
Mt 26:56 writings of the prophets may be **f**."
Mt 27: 9 was **f** what had been said through
Mk 14:49 but that the scriptures may be **f**."
Lk 1: 1 events that have been **f** among us,
Lk 4:21 "Today this scripture passage is **f**
Lk 21:24 until the times of the Gentiles are **f**.
Lk 24:44 the prophets and psalms must be **f**."
Jn 12:38 Isaiah the prophet spoke might be **f**:

Jn	13:18	But so that the scripture might be f,
Jn	15:25	word written in their law might be f,
Jn	17:12	order that the scripture might be f.
Jn	18:32	word of Jesus might be f that he said
Jn	19:24	of scripture might be f [that says]:
Jn	19:28	order that the scripture might be f,
Jn	19:36	the scripture passage might be f:
Acts	1:16	to be f which the holy Spirit spoke
Rom	8: 4	decree of the law might be f in us,
Rom	13: 8	one who loves another has f the law.
Jas	2:23	Thus the scripture was f that says,
Rev	10: 7	mysterious plan of God shall be f,

FULL → FILL

Jb	14: 1	is short-lived and f of trouble,
Eccl	1: 7	yet never does the sea become f.
Is	1:15	Your hands are f of blood!
Mt	23:25	but inside they are f of plunder
Jn	1:14	only Son, f of grace and truth.
Eph	4:13	the extent of the f stature of Christ,
Jas	3:17	f of mercy and good fruits,
2 Jn	1: 8	for but may receive a f recompense.

FULLNESS → FILL

Dt	33:16	With the best of the earth and its f,
Jn	1:16	From his f we have all received,
1 Cor	10:26	"the earth and its f are the Lord's."
Gal	4: 4	But when the f of time had come,
Eph	1:23	the f of the one who fills all things
Eph	3:19	may be filled with all the f of God.
Col	1:19	him all the f was pleased to dwell,
Col	2: 9	him dwells the whole f of the deity
Col	2:10	and you share in this f in him,

FULLY → FILL

Lk	6:40	but when f trained, every disciple
Rom	4:21	was f convinced that what he had
Rom	14: 5	Let everyone be f persuaded in his
1 Cor	13:12	then I shall know f, as I am f known.

FURNACE

Ps	21:10	you will make them a fiery f.
Sir	31:26	As the f tests the work of the smith,
Is	48:10	I tested you in the f of affliction.
Dn	3: 6	be instantly cast into a white-hot f."
Dn	3:49	drove the fiery flames out of the f,
Mt	13:42	will throw them into the fiery f,
Rev	1:15	like polished brass refined in a f,
Rev	9: 2	passage like smoke from a huge f.

FURNISHED

| Mk | 14:15 | will show you a large upper room f |

FURY

Sir	40: 5	dread, terror of death, f and strife.
Hb	3:12	earth, in f you trampled the nations.
Rom	2: 8	f to those who selfishly disobey
Rev	16:19	the cup filled with the wine of his f
Rev	19:15	in the wine press the wine of the f

FUTILE → FUTILITY

| 1 Pt | 1:18 | were ransomed from your f conduct, |

FUTILITY → FUTILE

| Rom | 8:20 | for creation was made subject to f, |
| Eph | 4:17 | Gentiles do, in the f of their minds; |

FUTURE

Prv	23:18	For you will surely have a f,
Prv	24:20	For the evil have no f, the lamp
Jer	29:11	woe, so as to give you a f of hope.
Jer	31:17	There is hope for your f—
1 Cor	3:22	life or death, or the present or the f:
1 Tm	6:19	treasure a good foundation for the f,

G

GABBATHA

| Jn | 19:13 | Stone Pavement, in Hebrew, G. |

GABRIEL

Angel who interpreted Daniel's visions (Dn 8:16-26; 9:20-27); announced births of John (Lk 1:11-20), Jesus (Lk 1:26-38).

GAD

1. Son of Jacob by Zilpah (Gn 30:9-11; 35:26; 1 Chr 2:2). Tribe of blessed (Gn 49:19; Dt 33:20-21), numbered (Nm 1:25; 26:18), allotted land east of the Jordan (Nm 32; 34:14; Jos 18:7; 22), west (Ez 48:27-28), 12,000 from (Rev 7:5).

2. Prophet; seer of David (1 Sm 22:5; 2 Sm 24:11-19; 1 Chr 29:29).

GADARENES

| Mt | 8:28 | side, to the territory of the G, |

GAIN → GAINED

Gn	24:60	may your descendants g possession
1 Sm	8: 3	but looked to their own g,
Ps	90:12	that we may g wisdom of heart.
Prv	1: 5	intelligent will g sound guidance,
Prv	4: 1	that you may g understanding!
Prv	28:16	who hate ill-gotten g prolong their
Sir	6: 7	When you g friends, g them through
Mk	8:36	is there for one to g the whole world
Lk	9:25	one to g the whole world yet lose
1 Cor	13: 3	but do not have love, I g nothing.
Phil	1:21	to me life is Christ, and death is g.
Phil	3: 8	so much rubbish, that I may g Christ
1 Tm	3:13	well as deacons g good standing
1 Tm	6: 5	religion to be a means of g.
1 Tm	6: 6	with contentment is a great g.
Ti	1: 7	aggressive, not greedy for sordid g,
Ti	1:11	for sordid g what they should not.
Jude	1:11	to Balaam's error for the sake of g,

GAINED → GAIN

| Prv | 16:31 | it is g by a life that is just. |

GAIUS

| Rom | 16:23 | G, who is host to me |
| 3 Jn | 1: 1 | to the beloved G whom I love |

GALATIA → GALATIANS

| 1 Pt | 1: 1 | of the dispersion in Pontus, G, |

GALATIANS → GALATIA

| Gal | 3: 1 | O stupid G! Who has bewitched |

GALILEAN → GALILEE

Mt	26:69	"You too were with Jesus the G."
Mk	14:70	one of them; for you too are a G."
Lk	22:59	was with him, for he also is a G."
Lk	23: 6	this Pilate asked if the man was a G;
Acts	5:37	him came Judas the G at the time

GALILEANS → GALILEE

Lk	13: 1	about the G whose blood Pilate had
Jn	4:45	into Galilee, the G welcomed him,
Acts	2: 7	these people who are speaking G?

GALILEE → GALILEAN, GALILEANS

Tb	1: 5	on every hilltop in G to the calf
1 Mc	5:15	of Gentile G have joined forces
Mt	3:13	Jesus came from G to John
Mt	4:15	the Jordan, G of the Gentiles,
Mt	21:11	the prophet, from Nazareth in G."
Mt	26:32	up, I shall go before you to G."
Mt	28:10	Go tell my brothers to go to G,
Lk	23:49	who had followed him from G
Jn	2: 1	there was a wedding in Cana in G,
Jn	7:41	Messiah will not come from G,

GALL

Tb	11: 8	Apply the fish g to his eyes,
Jb	16:13	pours out my g upon the ground.
Mt	27:34	Jesus wine to drink mixed with g.

GALLIO

Proconsul of Achaia, who refused to hear complaints against Paul (Acts 18:12-17).

GAMALIEL

Prominent Pharisee (Acts 5:34-39); teacher of Paul (Acts 22:5).

GAME

| Gn | 25:28 | Esau, because he was fond of g; |
| Gn | 27: 3 | open country to hunt some g for me. |

GAMES
2 Mc   4:18 When the quinquennial **g** were held

GANGRENE
2 Tm   2:17 and their teaching will spread like **g**.

GAPS
Neh   4: 1 for the **g** were beginning to be

GARDEN → GARDENER, GARDENS
Gn   2: 8 The LORD God planted a **g**
Gn   2:15 and settled him in the **g** of Eden,
Gn   3:23 banished him from the **g** of Eden,
Gn   13:10 like the LORD's own **g**, or like
Sg   4:12 A **g** enclosed, my sister, my bride,
Is   58:11 And you shall be like a watered **g**,
Ez   28:13 In Eden, the **g** of God, you lived;
Dn   13:15 wanting to bathe in the **g**,
Jn   19:41 he had been crucified there was a **g**, and in the **g** a new tomb,

GARDENER → GARDEN
Lk   13: 7 he said to the **g**, 'For three years
Jn   20:15 She thought it was the **g** and said

GARDENS → GARDEN
Jer   31:12 themselves shall be like watered **g**,
Am   4: 9 locusts devoured your **g**

GARMENT → GARMENTS
Neh   5:13 I shook out the folds of my **g**,
Ps   102:27 they all wear out like a **g**;
Sir   14:17 All flesh grows old like a **g**;
Is   51: 6 the earth wear out like a **g** and its

GARMENTS → GARMENT
Gn   3:21 for the man and his wife **g** of skin,
Gn   37:29 Joseph was not in it, he tore his **g**,
Gn   44:13 At this, they tore their **g**.
2 Sm   13:31 tore his **g**, and lay on the ground.
2 Sm   13:31 standing by him also tore their **g**.
Jdt   10: 3 laid aside the **g** of her widowhood,
Prv   31:24 She makes **g** and sells them,
Is   52: 1 Put on your glorious **g**, Jerusalem,
Is   63: 1 in crimsoned **g**, from Bozrah?

GATE → GATES
Dt   21:19 the elders at the **g** of his home city,
Jos   2: 5 when it was time to close the **g**,
Ru   4:11 All those at the **g**,
Est   2:19 was passing his time at the king's **g**,
Jb   29: 7 I went out to the **g** of the city
Ps   69:13 Those who sit in the **g** gossip
Ps   118:20 This is the LORD's own **g**,
Mt   7:13 "Enter through the narrow **g**;
Mt   7:13 for the **g** is wide and the road broad
Jn   10: 2 enters through the **g** is the shepherd
Jn   10: 7 say to you, I am the **g** for the sheep.
Jn   10: 9 I am the **g**. Whoever enters through
Acts   3: 2 at the **g** of the temple called "the Beautiful **G**"
Heb   13:12 Jesus also suffered outside the **g**,

GATES → GATE
Gn   24:60 of the **g** of their enemies!'
Dt   6: 9 of your houses and on your **g**.
Neh   1: 3 been breached, its **g** gutted by fire."
1 Mc   4:38 the altar desecrated, the **g** burnt,
Ps   24: 7 Lift up your heads, O **g**;
Ps   87: 2 The LORD loves the **g** of Zion
Ps   100: Enter his **g** with thanksgiving,
Ps   118:19 Open the **g** of righteousness;
Is   60:11 Your **g** shall stand open constantly;
Is   60:18 "Salvation" and your **g** "Praise."
Is   62:10 pass through the **g**, prepare a way
Lam   4:12 foe or enemy could enter the **g**
Ez   48:31 the **g** are named after the tribes
Mt   16:18 the **g** of the netherworld shall not
Rev   21:12 twelve **g** where twelve angels were
Rev   21:21 The twelve **g** were twelve pearls,
Rev   21:21 each of the **g** made from a single
Rev   21:25 During the day its **g** will never be

Rev   22:14 life and enter the city through its **g**.

GATH
1 Sm   5: 8 the ark of the God of Israel to **G**.
1 Sm   17: 4 champion named Goliath of **G** came
1 Sm   21:11 Saul, going to Achish, king of **G**.
2 Sm   1:20 Do not report it in **G**, as good news
Mi   1:10 Do not announce it in **G**, do not

GATHER → GATHERED, GATHERS
Ex   16: 4 to go out and **g** their daily portion;
Dt   30: 4 will the LORD, your God, **g** you;
Ru   2: 7 'I would like to **g** the gleanings
Neh   1: 9 the world, I will **g** them from there,
Ps   106:47 **g** us from among the nations
Is   11:12 nations and **g** the outcasts of Israel;
Jer   3:17 All nations will **g** together to honor
Jer   23: 3 I myself will **g** the remnant of my
Zep   2: 1 **G**, **g** yourselves together, O nation
Zep   3:20 home, and at that time I will **g** you;
Zec   14: 2 And I will **g** all the nations against
Mt   12:30 and whoever does not **g** with me
Mt   13:30 but **g** the wheat into my barn." ' "
Mt   23:37 yearned to **g** your children together,
Mt   25:26 plant and **g** where I did not scatter?
Mk   13:27 **g** [his] elect from the four winds,
Lk   3:17 and to **g** the wheat into his barn,
Lk   11:23 and whoever does not **g** with me
Lk   13:34 to **g** your children together as a hen
Lk   17:37 is, there also the vultures will **g**."
Jn   11:52 to **g** into one the dispersed children
Rev   19:17 **G** for God's great feast,
Rev   20: 8 and Magog, to **g** them for battle;

GATHERED → GATHER
Gn   1: 9 Let the water under the sky be **g**
Ex   16:18 the one who had **g** a large amount
Ex   16:18 the one who had **g** a small amount
Ex   16:18 They **g** as much as each needed
Nm   11:32 one who got the least **g** ten homers
Mt   18:20 or three are **g** together in my name,
Rev   19:19 their armies **g** to fight against

GATHERS → GATHER
Ps   147: 2 and **g** the dispersed of Israel,
Is   56: 8 who **g** the dispersed of Israel—
Jer   31:10 who scattered Israel, now **g** them;
Mt   23:37 as a hen **g** her young under her

GAVE → GIVE
Gn   2:20 The man **g** names to all the tame
Gn   3: 6 and she also **g** some to her husband,
Gn   14:20 Abram **g** him a tenth of everything.
Gn   35:12 The land I **g** to Abraham and Isaac I
Ex   31:18 he **g** him the two tablets
Dt   3:12 I **g** Reuben and Gad the territory
Dt   9:10 The LORD **g** me the two stone
Dt   26: 9 and **g** us this land, a land flowing
Jos   11:23 Joshua **g** it to Israel as their
Jos   15:13 had commanded, Joshua **g** Caleb,
Jos   21:44 the LORD **g** them peace on every
Jos   24:13 I **g** you a land you did not till
Jgs   3: 6 **g** their own daughters to their sons
1 Sm   27: 6 That same day Achish **g** him Ziklag,
2 Sm   12: 8 I **g** you your lord's house and your
2 Sm   12: 8 I **g** you the house of Israel
1 Kgs   5: 9 Moreover, God **g** Solomon wisdom,
1 Kgs   5:26 The LORD **g** Solomon wisdom as
Neh   9:15 heaven you **g** them in their hunger,
Neh   9:20 and you **g** them water in their thirst.
Neh   9:22 You **g** them kingdoms and peoples,
Jb   1:21 The LORD **g** and the LORD has
Jb   42:10 the LORD even **g** to Job twice as
Ps   69:22 and for my thirst they **g** me vinegar.
Eccl   12: 7 life breath returns to God who **g** it.
Ez   3: 2 mouth, and he **g** me the scroll to eat.
Dn   1:17 four young men God **g** knowledge
Mt   25:35 I was hungry and you **g** me food,
Mt   25:35 I was thirsty and you **g** me drink,

Mt	25:42	I was hungry and you **g** me no food,
Mt	25:42	I was thirsty and you **g** me no drink,
Mk	6: 7	and **g** them authority over unclean
Mk	11:28	Or who **g** you this authority to do
Jn	1:12	who did accept him he **g** power
Jn	3:16	the world that he **g** his only Son,
Jn	17: 4	the work that you **g** me to do.
Jn	17: 6	name to those whom you **g** me
Acts	11:17	God **g** them the same gift he **g** to us
2 Cor	8: 5	they **g** themselves first to the Lord
Eph	4: 8	he **g** gifts to men."
Eph	4:11	And he **g** some as apostles, others as
1 Tm	2: 6	who **g** himself as ransom for all.
Ti	2:14	who **g** himself for us to deliver us
1 Jn	5:11	God **g** us eternal life, and this life is
Rev	11:13	and **g** glory to the God of heaven.
Rev	13: 2	To it the dragon **g** its own power
Rev	20:13	The sea **g** up its dead;
Rev	20:13	Death and Hades **g** up their dead.

GAZA

Jgs	16: 1	Once Samson went to **G**, where he
1 Sm	6:17	one for **G**, one for Ashkelon,
Am	1: 6	For three crimes of **G**, and now

GAZE

Sir	9: 8	do not **g** upon beauty that is not
Rev	11: 9	nation will **g** on their corpses

GAZELLE

2 Sm	2:18	fleet of foot as a **g** in the open field,
Sg	2: 9	My lover is like a **g** or a young stag.
Sg	7: 4	are like two fawns, twins of a **g**.

GEDALIAH

Governor of Judah appointed by Nebuchadnezzar (2 Kgs 25:22-26; Jer 39–41).

GEHAZI

Servant of Elisha (2 Kgs 4:12–5:27; 8:4-5).

GEHENNA

Mt	5:22	'You fool,' will be liable to fiery **G**.
Mt	5:29	your whole body thrown into **G**.
Mt	5:30	to have your whole body go into **G**.
Mt	10:28	destroy both soul and body in **G**.
Mt	18: 9	two eyes to be thrown into fiery **G**.
Mt	23:15	of **G** twice as much as yourselves.
Mt	23:33	you flee from the judgment of **G**?
Mk	9:43	than with two hands to go into **G**,
Mk	9:45	with two feet to be thrown into **G**.
Mk	9:47	with two eyes to be thrown into **G**,
Lk	12: 5	killing has the power to cast into **G**;
Jas	3: 6	lives on fire, itself set on fire by **G**.

GEMS → GEMSTONES

Ex	25: 7	other **g** for mounting on the ephod

GEMSTONES → GEMS

Zec	9:16	For like **g** of a crown they will shine

GENEALOGIES → GENEALOGY

1 Tm	1: 4	with myths and endless **g**,
Ti	3: 9	Avoid foolish arguments, **g**,

GENEALOGY → GENEALOGIES

Mt	1: 1	The book of the **g** of Jesus Christ,

GENERATION → GENERATIONS

Ex	1: 6	his brothers and that whole **g** died.
Ex	20: 6	the thousandth **g** of those who love
Ex	34: 7	children to the third and fourth **g**!
Nm	32:13	until the whole **g** that had done evil
Dt	1:35	a single one of this evil **g** shall look
Jgs	2:10	a later **g** arose that did not know
1 Mc	2:61	And so, consider this from **g** to **g**,
Ps	78: 4	we recount them to the next **g**,
Ps	102:19	Let this be written for the next **g**,
Ps	112: 2	a **g** of the upright will be blessed.
Ps	145: 4	One **g** praises your deeds to the next
Is	34:17	forever, and dwell in it from **g** to **g**.
Jl	1: 3	and their children to the next **g**.
Mt	12:39	evil and unfaithful **g** seeks a sign,

Mt	17:17	"O faithless and perverse **g**,
Mt	23:36	these things will come upon this **g**.
Mt	24:34	this **g** will not pass away until all
Mk	9:19	"O faithless **g**, how long will I be
Mk	13:30	this **g** will not pass away until all
Lk	7:31	shall I compare the people of this **g**?
Lk	11:29	said to them, "This **g** is an evil **g**;
Lk	11:50	in order that this **g** might be charged
Lk	21:32	this **g** will not pass away until all
Acts	2:40	yourselves from this corrupt **g**."
Phil	2:15	midst of a crooked and perverse **g**,
Heb	3:10	of this I was provoked with that **g**

GENERATIONS → GENERATION

Ex	12:17	day throughout your **g** as a statute
Ex	30:21	his descendants throughout their **g**.
Ex	31:13	you and me throughout the **g**,
Ex	40:15	priesthood throughout all future **g**.
1 Chr	16:15	the pact imposed for a thousand **g**—
Jb	8: 8	Inquire of the former **g**,
Ps	33:11	designs of his heart through all **g**.
Ps	45:18	your name renowned through all **g**;
Ps	48:14	citadels, that you may tell future **g**:
Ps	90: 1	have been our refuge through all **g**.
Ps	102:13	your renown is for all **g**.
Ps	105: 8	he commanded for a thousand **g**,
Ps	119:90	Through all **g** your truth endures;
Ps	145:13	for all ages, your dominion for all **g**.
Ps	146:10	your God, Zion, through all **g**!
Sir	2:10	Consider the **g** long past and see:
Is	41: 4	Who has called forth the **g**
Is	51: 8	forever, my salvation, for all **g**.
Dn	3:100	his dominion endures through all **g**.
Mt	1:17	Abraham to David is fourteen **g**;
Mt	1:17	to the Babylonian exile, fourteen **g**;
Mt	1:17	exile to the Messiah, fourteen **g**.
Eph	3: 5	other **g** as it has now been revealed
Eph	3:21	church and in Christ Jesus to all **g**,
Col	1:26	hidden from ages and from **g** past.

GENEROSITY → GENEROUS

Sir	37:11	from a miser about **g**, from a cruel
Rom	12: 8	if one contributes, in **g**; if one is
2 Cor	8: 2	in a wealth of **g** on their part.
2 Cor	9:11	enriched in every way for all **g**,
2 Cor	9:13	the **g** of your contribution to them
Gal	5:22	patience, kindness, **g**, faithfulness,

GENEROUS → GENEROSITY, GENEROUSLY

Sir	14: 5	whom will they be **g** that are stingy
Sir	35:10	With a **g** spirit pay homage to the Lord,
Mt	20:15	Are you envious because I am **g**?'
1 Tm	6:18	good works, to be **g**, ready to share,

GENEROUSLY → GENEROUS

Sir	35:12	Most High as he has given to you, **g**,
Acts	10: 2	to give alms **g** to the Jewish people
Jas	1: 5	should ask God who gives to all **g**

GENTILE → GENTILES

1 Mc	1:14	according to the **G** custom.
Mt	18:17	treat him as you would a **G** or a tax
Gal	2:14	are living like a **G** and not like

GENTILES → GENTILE

1 Mc	1:11	a covenant with the **G** all around us;
1 Mc	2:12	The **G** have defiled them!
1 Mc	4:54	on which the **G** had desecrated it,
1 Mc	13:41	the yoke of the **G** was removed
Mt	4:15	beyond the Jordan, Galilee of the **G**,
Lk	2:32	a light for revelation to the **G**,
Lk	21:24	be taken as captives to all the **G**;
Lk	21:24	until the times of the **G** are fulfilled.
Lk	22:25	kings of the **G** lord it over them
Acts	9:15	of mine to carry my name before **G**,
Acts	10:45	have been poured out on the **G** also,
Acts	11: 1	the **G** too had accepted the word
Acts	11:18	repentance to the **G** too."
Acts	13:46	of eternal life, we now turn to the **G**.
Acts	13:47	'I have made you a light to the **G**,

Acts 14:27 opened the door of faith to the **G**.
Acts 15:19 to stop troubling the **G** who turn
Acts 18: 6 From now on I will go to the **G**."
Acts 22:21 send you far away to the **G**.' "
Acts 26:20 and then to the **G**, I preached
Acts 28:28 of God has been sent to the **G**;
Rom 2:14 the **G** who do not have the law
Rom 3:29 Does he not belong to **G**, too? Yes, also to **G**,
Rom 9:24 from the Jews but also from the **G**.
Rom 11:11 salvation has come to the **G**, so as
Rom 11:12 number is enrichment for the **G**,
Rom 11:13 Now I am speaking to you **G**.
Rom 11:13 then as I am the apostle to the **G**,
Rom 15: 9 so that the **G** might glorify God
Rom 15: 9 I will praise you among the **G**
Rom 15:27 for if the **G** have come to share
1 Cor 1:23 block to Jews and foolishness to **G**,
2 Cor 11:26 dangers from **G**, dangers in the city,
Gal 1:16 that I might proclaim him to the **G**,
Gal 3: 8 God would justify the **G** by faith,
Eph 3: 6 that the **G** are coheirs,
Eph 3: 8 to the **G** the inscrutable riches
Eph 4:17 you must no longer live as the **G** do,
Col 1:27 glory of this mystery among the **G**;
1 Tm 2: 7 teacher of the **G** in faith and truth.
2 Tm 4:17 and all the **G** might hear it.

GENTLE → GENTLENESS, GENTLY
1 Thes 2: 7 Rather, we were **g** among you,
1 Tm 3: 3 aggressive, but **g**, not contentious,
Jas 3:17 pure, then peaceable, **g**, compliant,
1 Pt 3: 4 in the imperishable beauty of a **g**

GENTLENESS → GENTLE
Est D: 8 God changed the king's anger to **g**.
2 Cor 10: 1 Paul, urge you through the **g**
Gal 5:23 **g**, self-control. Against such there is
Eph 4: 2 with all humility and **g**,
1 Tm 6:11 faith, love, patience, and **g**.
1 Pt 3:16 but do it with **g** and reverence,

GENTLY → GENTLE
Jb 15:11 and speech that deals **g** with you?

GENUINENESS
2 Cor 8: 8 to test the **g** of your love by your
1 Pt 1: 7 so that the **g** of your faith,

GERAR
Gn 20: 2 king of **G**, sent and took Sarah.
Gn 26: 6 So Isaac settled in **G**.

GERASENES
Lk 8:26 they sailed to the territory of the **G**,

GERIZIM
Dt 27:12 on Mount **G** to bless the people:
Jos 8:33 Half of them were facing Mount **G**

GERSHOM
Son of Moses (Ex 2:22; 1 Chr 23:15).

GERSHON → GERSHONITES
Gn 46:11 **G**, Kohath, and Merari.
1 Chr 23: 6 **G**, Kohath, and Merari.

GERSHONITES → GERSHON
Nm 3:21 these were the clans of the **G**.
Jos 21: 6 the **G** obtained by lot thirteen cities.

GESHEM
Neh 6: 1 Tobiah, **G** the Arab, and our other

GESHUR
2 Sm 13:38 and stayed in **G** for three years.

GET
Gn 24: 4 my relatives to **g** a wife for my son
Dt 30:12 go up to the heavens to **g** it for us
Prv 4: 5 **G** wisdom, **g** understanding!
Mt 16:23 and said to Peter, "**G** behind me,
Mk 6: 2 "Where did this man **g** all this?
Mk 13:16 field must not return to **g** his cloak.

GETHSEMANE
Mt 26:36 came with them to a place called **G**,
Mk 14:32 Then they came to a place named **G**,

GEZER
Jos 16:10 the Canaanites living in **G**;
1 Chr 14:16 Philistine army from Gibeon to **G**.

GHOST → GHOSTS
Mt 14:26 "It is a **g**," they said, and they cried
Lk 24:39 because a **g** does not have flesh

GHOSTS → GHOST
Dt 18:11 casts spells, consults **g** and spirits,

GIANT → GIANTS
1 Mc 3: 3 and put on his breastplate like a **g**.
Sir 47: 4 As a youth he struck down the **g**

GIANTS → GIANT
Wis 14: 6 the proud **g** were being destroyed,
Bar 3:26 In it were born the **g**,

GIBEAH
Jgs 19:12 We will go on to **G**.
1 Sm 10:26 Saul also went home to **G**,
Hos 10: 9 the days of **G** you have sinned,

GIBEON → GIBEONITES
Jos 10:12 Sun, stand still at **G**, Moon,
2 Sm 2:13 encountered them at the pool of **G**.
1 Kgs 3: 5 In **G** the LORD appeared

GIBEONITES → GIBEON
2 Sm 21: 1 his family because he put the **G**

GIDEON → =JERUBBAAL
Judge, also called Jerubbaal; freed Israel from Midianites (Jgs 6–8; Heb 11:32). Given sign of fleece (Jgs 8:36-40).

GIFT → GIFTS
Nm 18: 7 I give you your priesthood as a **g**.
Prv 21:14 A secret **g** allays anger,
Eccl 3:13 of all their toil—this is a **g** of God.
Eccl 5:18 of their toil: This is a **g** from God.
Sir 18:16 So a word can be better than a **g**.
Mt 5:23 if you bring your **g** to the altar,
Mt 8: 4 offer the **g** that Moses prescribed;
Jn 4:10 "If you knew the **g** of God and who
Acts 2:38 you will receive the **g** of the holy
Acts 8:20 that you could buy the **g** of God
Acts 11:17 God gave them the same **g** he gave
Rom 1:11 you some spiritual **g** so that you
Rom 5:15 the **g** is not like the transgression.
Rom 6:23 the **g** of God is eternal life in Christ
1 Cor 7: 7 each has a particular **g** from God,
2 Cor 9:15 be to God for his indescribable **g**!
Eph 2: 8 is not from you; it is the **g** of God;
Eph 4: 7 to the measure of Christ's **g**.
Phil 4:17 It is not that I am eager for the **g**;
1 Tm 4:14 Do not neglect the **g** you have,
2 Tm 1: 6 stir into flame the **g** of God that you
Heb 6: 4 tasted the heavenly **g** and shared
Jas 1:17 and every perfect **g** is from above,
1 Pt 3: 7 we are joint heirs of the **g** of life,
1 Pt 4:10 As each one has received a **g**, use it
Rev 21: 6 the thirsty I will give a **g**
Rev 22:17 the one who wants it receive the **g**

GIFTS → GIFT
Ezr 1: 6 and many precious **g**, besides all
Est 9:22 to one another and **g** to the poor.
Ps 76:12 May all around him bring **g**
Prv 18:16 **G** clear the way for people,
Mt 2:11 treasures and offered him **g** of gold,
Lk 11:13 how to give good **g** to your children,
Rom 11:29 For the **g** and the call of God are
Rom 12: 6 Since we have **g** that differ
1 Cor 12: 1 Now in regard to spiritual **g**,
1 Cor 12: 4 are different kinds of spiritual **g**,
1 Cor 12:28 then, **g** of healing, assistance,
1 Cor 12:30 Do all have **g** of healing?
1 Cor 12:31 eagerly for the greatest spiritual **g**.

1 Cor	14: 1	but strive eagerly for the spiritual **g**,
Eph	4: 8	he gave **g** to men."
Heb	2: 4	of the **g** of the holy Spirit according
Heb	9: 9	in which **g** and sacrifices are offered

GIHON

Gn	2:13	name of the second river is the **G**;
2 Chr	32:30	the upper outlet for water from **G**

GILBOA

1 Chr	10: 8	and his sons fallen on Mount **G**.

GILEAD → GILEADITE

Nm	32:29	will give them **G** as a possession.
Jgs	11: 1	son of a prostitute, fathered by **G**.
2 Sm	2: 9	where he made him king over **G**,
1 Chr	27:21	for the half-tribe of Manasseh in **G**,
Jer	8:22	Is there no balm in **G**, no healer
Jer	46:11	Go up to **G**, procure balm,
Hos	6: 8	**G** is a city of evildoers,
Mi	7:14	Let them feed in Bashan and **G**,

GILEADITE → GILEAD

Jgs	11: 1	Jephthah the **G** was a warrior.
2 Sm	19:32	Barzillai the **G** also came down

GILGAL

Jos	4:20	At **G** Joshua set up the twelve
Jos	5: 9	Therefore the place is called **G**
Jgs	2: 1	LORD went up from **G** to Bochim
1 Sm	7:16	**G** and Mizpah and judging Israel

GIRD → GIRDED

1 Sm	2: 4	while the tottering **g** on strength.
Ps	45: 4	**G** your sword upon your hip,

GIRDED → GIRD

1 Kgs	18:46	He **g** up his clothing and ran before
Ps	18:33	This God who **g** me with might,
Ps	93: 1	the LORD is robed, **g** with might.

GIRGASHITES

Dt	7: 1	the Hittites, **G**, Amorites,

GIRL → GIRLS

Ex	1:16	but if it is a **g**, she may live."
2 Kgs	5: 2	the land of Israel in a raid a little **g**,
Tb	6:12	The **g** is wise, courageous, and very
Mk	5:41	means, "Little **g**, I say to you,
Mk	6:22	The king said to the **g**, "Ask of me

GIRLS → GIRL

Zec	8: 5	boys and **g** playing in its streets.

GIVE → GAVE, GIVEN, GIVER, GIVES, GIVING, LAWGIVER, LIFE-GIVING

Gn	9: 3	I **g** them all to you as I did the green
Gn	12: 7	your descendants I will **g** this land.
Gn	28:22	Of everything you **g** me, I will
Ex	13: 5	he swore to your ancestors to **g** you,
Ex	17: 2	and said, "**G** us water to drink."
Ex	30:15	The rich need not **g** more, nor shall the poor **g** less,
Nm	6:26	upon you kindly and **g** you peace!
Nm	11:13	Where can I get meat to **g** to all this
Dt	15:10	When you **g**, **g** generously and not
Jos	1: 6	you may **g** this people possession
1 Sm	1:11	you **g** your handmaid a male child,
1 Sm	1:11	I will **g** him to the LORD all
1 Kgs	3: 5	Whatever you ask I shall **g** you.
2 Chr	1:10	**G** me, therefore,
Neh	9: 6	To all of them you **g** life,
Tb	4:16	"**G** to the hungry some of your
Tb	4:16	eye begrudge the alms that you **g**.
Tb	12: 9	Those who **g** alms will enjoy a full
Jb	2: 4	that a man has he will **g** for his life.
Ps	13: 4	**G** light to my eyes lest I sleep
Ps	30:13	God, forever will I **g** you thanks.
Prv	21:26	all the day, but the just **g** unsparingly.
Prv	23:26	My son, **g** me your heart, and let
Prv	25:21	hungry, **g** them food to eat, if thirsty, **g** something to drink;
Prv	27:10	Do not **g** up your own friend and
Prv	28:27	Those who **g** to the poor have no lack,
Prv	30: 8	me, **g** me neither poverty nor riches;

Prv	30:15	has two daughters: "**G**," and "**G**."
Is	7:14	the Lord himself will **g** you a sign;
Is	42: 8	my glory I **g** to no other, nor my
Ez	36:26	I will **g** you a new heart, and a new
Hos	9:14	**G** them, LORD! **g** them what?
Hos	11: 8	How could I **g** you up, Ephraim,
Mt	5:42	**G** to the one who asks of you,
Mt	6: 2	When you **g** alms, do not blow
Mt	6:11	**G** us today our daily bread;
Mt	7: 6	"Do not **g** what is holy to dogs,
Mt	7:11	know how to **g** good gifts to your
Mt	7:11	your heavenly Father **g** good things
Mt	10: 8	without cost you are to **g**.
Mt	16:19	I will **g** you the keys to the kingdom
Mk	8:37	What could one **g** in exchange
Mk	10:45	to **g** his life as a ransom for many."
Lk	6:38	**G** and gifts will be given to you;
Lk	11: 3	**G** us each day our daily bread
Lk	11:13	know how to **g** good gifts to your
Lk	11:13	Father in heaven **g** the holy Spirit
Jn	4:14	the water I shall **g** will never thirst;
Jn	6:52	"How can this man **g** us [his] flesh
Jn	10:28	I **g** them eternal life, and they shall
Jn	13:34	I **g** you a new commandment:
Jn	14:16	he will **g** you another Advocate
Jn	14:27	leave with you; my peace I **g** to you.
Jn	14:27	Not as the world gives do I **g** it
Jn	17: 2	so that he may **g** eternal life to all
Acts	3: 6	gold, but what I do have I **g** you:
Acts	20:35	said, 'It is more blessed to **g** than
Rom	8:32	also **g** us everything else along
1 Cor	13: 3	If I **g** away everything I own,
Gal	6: 9	reap our harvest, if we do not **g** up.
Heb	13:17	you and will have to **g** an account,
Rev	2: 7	To the victor I will **g** the right to eat
Rev	2:10	and I will **g** you the crown of life.
Rev	2:17	To the victor I shall **g** some
Rev	2:17	also **g** a white amulet upon which is
Rev	2:26	I will **g** authority over the nations.
Rev	2:28	to him I will **g** the morning star.
Rev	3:21	I will **g** the victor the right to sit
Rev	14: 7	"Fear God and **g** him glory, for his

GIVEN → GIVE

Ex	16:15	which the LORD has **g** you to eat.
Dt	1:21	God, has **g** this land over to you.
Dt	26:11	the LORD, your God, has **g** you.
Ps	115:16	he has **g** the earth to the children
Sir	35:12	Give to the Most High as he has **g** to you,
Is	9: 5	a child is born to us, a son is **g** to us;
Dn	2:37	the God of heaven has **g** dominion
Am	9:15	From the land I have **g** them—
Mt	6:33	these things will be **g** you besides.
Mt	7: 7	"Ask and it will be **g** to you;
Mt	22:30	they neither marry nor are **g**
Mt	25:29	more will be **g** and he will grow
Mk	4:25	To the one who has, more will be **g**;
Mk	8:12	I say to you, no sign will be **g** to this
Lk	6:38	Give and gifts will be **g** to you;
Lk	22:19	is my body, which will be **g** for you;
Jn	1:17	while the law was **g** through Moses,
Jn	3:27	except what has been **g** him
Acts	5:32	God has **g** to those who obey him."
Rom	5: 5	the holy Spirit that has been **g** to us.
Rom	11:35	who has **g** him anything that he may
1 Cor	11:24	after he had **g** thanks, broke it
2 Cor	5: 5	who has **g** us the Spirit as a first
2 Cor	12: 7	a thorn in the flesh was **g** to me,
Eph	4: 7	grace was **g** to each of us according
1 Jn	4:13	in us, that he has **g** us of his Spirit.
1 Jn	5:20	has **g** us discernment to know
Rev	6: 2	He was **g** a crown, and he rode forth

GIVER → GIVE

2 Cor	9: 7	for God loves a cheerful **g**.

GIVES → GIVE

Ex	4:11	Who **g** one person speech?

Ps 119:130 light, **g** understanding to the simple.
Ps 136:25 And **g** bread to all flesh, for his
Prv 2: 6 For the LORD **g** wisdom, from his
Prv 14:30 A tranquil mind **g** life to the body,
Eccl 2:26 he **g** wisdom and knowledge
Eccl 2:26 God **g** the task of gathering
Sir 34:20 **g** health and life and blessing.
Sir 35: 4 who **g** alms presents a sacrifice of praise.
Is 40:29 He **g** power to the faint,
Mt 10:42 whoever **g** only a cup of cold water
Jn 5:21 the Father raises the dead and **g** life,
Jn 6:32 my Father **g** you the true bread
Jn 6:37 that the Father **g** me will come
Jn 6:63 It is the spirit that **g** life,
Jn 14:27 Not as the world **g** do I give it
Rom 4:17 who **g** life to the dead and calls
1 Cor 15:57 to God who **g** us the victory through
2 Cor 3: 6 brings death, but the Spirit **g** life.
1 Thes 4: 8 who [also] **g** his holy Spirit to you.
Jas 4: 6 proud, but **g** grace to the humble."

GIVING → GIVE
Mt 24:38 marrying and **g** in marriage,
Phil 4:15 shared with me in an account of **g**
Jas 1:17 all good **g** and every perfect gift is

GLAD → GLADDEN, GLADNESS
1 Chr 16:31 Let the heavens be **g** and the earth
Ps 14: 7 and Israel be **g** when the LORD
Ps 16: 9 Therefore my heart is **g**, my soul
Ps 32:11 Be **g** in the LORD and rejoice,
Ps 34: 3 let the poor hear and be **g**.
Ps 40:17 seek you rejoice and be **g** in you.
Ps 48:12 Mount Zion is **g**! The daughters
Ps 53: 7 will rejoice and Israel will be **g**.
Ps 67: 5 May the nations be **g** and rejoice;
Ps 69:33 "See, you lowly ones, and be **g**;
Ps 70: 5 seek you rejoice and be **g** in you,
Ps 90:15 Make us **g** as many days as you
Ps 96:11 Let the heavens be **g** and the earth
Ps 97: 1 let the many islands be **g**.
Ps 97: 8 Zion hears and is **g**,
Ps 118:24 let us rejoice in it and be **g**.
Ps 149: 2 Let Israel be **g** in its maker,
Prv 15:13 A **g** heart lights up the face,
Is 25: 9 and be **g** that he has saved us!"
Is 66:10 Jerusalem and be **g** because of her,
Mt 5:12 Rejoice and be **g**, for your reward
Jn 8:56 to see my day; he saw it and was **g**.
Jn 11:15 I am **g** for you that I was not there,
Acts 2:26 Therefore my heart has been **g**

GLADDEN → GLAD
Ps 86: 4 **G** the soul of your servant;
Ps 104:15 wine to **g** their hearts, oil to make

GLADNESS → GLAD
Ps 51:10 You will let me hear **g** and joy;
Ps 51:14 Restore to me the **g** of your salvation;
Ps 100: 2 serve the LORD with **g**;
Is 16:10 orchards are taken away joy and **g**,
Is 35:10 They meet with joy and **g**,
Is 51: 3 Joy and **g** shall be found in her,
Is 51:11 They will meet with joy and **g**,
Is 61: 3 To give them oil of **g** instead
Jer 7:34 of joy, the cry of **g**, the voice
Jer 16: 9 the song of joy and the song of **g**,
Jer 25:10 the song of joy and the song of **g**,
Jer 33:11 of joy, the song of **g**, the song
Jl 1:16 the house of our God, joy and **g**?
Zep 3:17 Who will rejoice over you with **g**,
Zec 8:19 will become occasions of joy and **g**,
Lk 1:14 And you will have joy and **g**,
Heb 1: 9 you with the oil of **g** above your

GLASS
Rev 4: 6 resembled a sea of **g** like crystal.
Rev 15: 2 something like a sea of **g** mingled

Rev 21:18 the city was pure gold, clear as **g**.
Rev 21:21 was of pure gold, transparent as **g**.

GLAZED
Prv 26:23 Like a **g** finish on earthenware are

GLEAM
Hb 3:11 at the **g** of your flashing spear.

GLEAN → GLEANED, GLEANER, GLEANING, GLEANINGS
Ru 2: 2 **g** grain in the field of anyone who

GLEANED → GLEAN
Ru 2:17 She **g** in the field until evening,
Mi 7: 1 fruit, when the vines have been **g**;

GLEANER → GLEAN
Sir 33:16 like a **g** following the grape-pickers;

GLEANING → GLEAN
Is 24:13 with a **g** when the vintage is done.

GLEANINGS → GLEAN
Ob 1: 5 you, would they not leave some **g**?

GLOAT
Ps 22:18 They stare at me and **g**;
Rev 11:10 of the earth will **g** over them and be

GLOOM
Jb 3: 5 May darkness and **g** claim it,
Ps 107:10 Some lived in darkness and **g**,
Is 8:23 There is no **g** where there had been
Jl 2: 2 a day of darkness and **g**, a day
Am 5:20 not light, **g** without any brightness!
Zep 1:15 A day of darkness and **g**, a day

GLORIFIED → GLORY
Is 60: 9 Holy One of Israel who has **g** you.
Mt 9: 8 **g** God who had given such authority
Mk 2:12 They were all astounded and **g** God,
Lk 5:26 seized them all and they **g** God, and,
Lk 7:16 all, and they **g** God, exclaiming,
Jn 7:39 because Jesus had not yet been **g**.
Jn 11: 4 Son of God may be **g** through it."
Jn 12:16 Jesus had been **g** they remembered
Jn 12:23 come for the Son of Man to be **g**.
Jn 12:28 "I have **g** it and will glorify it
Jn 13:31 "Now is the Son of Man **g**, and God is **g** in him.
Jn 13:32 [If God is **g** in him,] God will
Jn 14:13 that the Father may be **g** in the Son.
Jn 15: 8 By this is my Father **g**, that you bear
Jn 17: 4 I **g** you on earth by accomplishing
Jn 17:10 is mine, and I have been **g** in them.
Acts 3:13 has **g** his servant Jesus whom you
Rom 8:17 so that we may also be **g** with him.
Rom 8:30 and those he justified he also **g**.
Gal 1:24 So they **g** God because of me.
2 Thes 1:10 comes to be **g** among his holy ones
2 Thes 1:12 of our Lord Jesus may be **g** in you,
2 Thes 3: 1 Lord may speed forward and be **g**,
1 Pt 4:11 God may be **g** through Jesus Christ,

GLORIFIES → GLORY
Jn 8:54 but it is my Father who **g** me,

GLORIFY → GLORY
Ps 86:12 all my heart, **g** your name forever,
Jn 8:54 "If I **g** myself, my glory is worth
Jn 12:28 Father, **g** your name." Then a voice
Jn 12:28 glorified it and will **g** it again."
Jn 13:32 God will also **g** him in himself, and he will **g** him at once.
Jn 16:14 He will **g** me, because he will take
Jn 17: 1 son, so that your son may **g** you,
Jn 17: 5 Now **g** me, Father, with you,
Jn 21:19 what kind of death he would **g** God.
Rom 15: 6 you may with one voice **g** the God
Rom 15: 9 the Gentiles might **g** God for his
1 Cor 6:20 Therefore, **g** God in your body.
1 Pt 2:12 and **g** God on the day of visitation.
1 Pt 4:16 but **g** God because of the name.
Rev 15: 4 not fear you, Lord, or **g** your name?

GLORIFYING → GLORY

Lk	2:20	g and praising God for all they had
Lk	5:25	lying on, and went home, g God.
2 Cor	9:13	you are g God for your obedient

GLORIOUS → GLORY

Ex	28: 2	For the g adornment of your brother
Ex	28:40	for the g adornment of Aaron's sons
Dt	28:58	to fear this g and awesome name,
Neh	9: 5	"And may they bless your g name,
Jdt	16:13	great are you and g,
1 Mc	2: 9	her g vessels carried off as spoils,
Ps	66: 2	sing of his g name; give him g praise.
Ps	72:19	Blessed be his g name forever;
Ps	87: 3	G things are said of you, O city
Is	11:10	his dwelling shall be g.
Is	28: 1	Fading blooms of his g beauty,
Is	28: 4	The fading blooms of his g beauty
Is	42:21	to make his teaching great and g.
Is	63:12	Moses by the hand, with his g arm?
Is	63:15	us from your holy and g palace!
Jer	48:17	scepter is broken, the g staff!
Col	1:11	in accord with his g might, for all
1 Tm	1:11	according to the g gospel
Jas	2: 1	the faith in our g Lord Jesus Christ.
1 Pt	1: 8	with an indescribable and g joy,
2 Pt	2:10	are not afraid to revile g beings,
Jude	1: 8	scorn lordship, and revile g beings.

GLORIOUSLY → GLORY

Ex	15: 1	the LORD, for he is g triumphant;

GLORY → GLORIFIED, GLORIFIES, GLORIFY, GLORIFYING, GLORIOUS, GLORIOUSLY

Ex	14: 4	I will receive g through Pharaoh
Ex	14:17	I will receive g through Pharaoh
Ex	14:18	when I receive g through Pharaoh,
Ex	16: 7	in the morning you will see the g
Ex	16:10	there the g of the LORD appeared
Ex	24:16	The g of the LORD settled
Ex	24:17	the Israelites the g of the LORD
Ex	29:43	it will be made sacred by my g.
Ex	33:18	said, "Please let me see your g!"
Ex	33:22	When my g passes I will set you
Ex	40:34	and the g of the LORD filled
Lv	9:23	the g of the LORD appeared to all
Nm	14:10	the g of the LORD appeared
Nm	14:21	the LORD's g that fills the whole
Nm	14:22	all the people who have seen my g
Nm	16:19	the g of the LORD appeared
Nm	17: 7	it and the g of the LORD appeared.
Nm	20: 6	the g of the LORD appeared
Dt	5:24	has indeed let us see his g and his
Jos	7:19	"My son, give g to the LORD,
1 Sm	4:21	"Gone is the g from Israel,"
1 Sm	15:29	The G of Israel neither deceives nor
2 Sm	1:19	the g of Israel, slain upon your
1 Kgs	8:11	since the g of the LORD had filled
1 Chr	16:10	G in his holy name;
1 Chr	16:24	Tell his g among the nations;
1 Chr	16:28	give to the LORD g and might;
1 Chr	29:12	Riches and g are from you,
2 Chr	5:14	since the g of the LORD had filled
2 Chr	7: 1	and the g of the LORD filled
Tb	12:15	serve before the G of the Lord."
Jdt	15: 9	"You are the g of Jerusalem!
1 Mc	1:40	As her g had been, so great was her
Jb	29:20	My g is fresh within me, and my
Ps	3: 4	my g, you keep my head high.
Ps	8: 6	god, crowned him with g and honor.
Ps	19: 2	The heavens declare the g of God;
Ps	24: 7	portals, that the king of g may enter.
Ps	26: 8	site of the dwelling-place of your g.
Ps	29: 1	give to the LORD g and might;
Ps	29: 3	the God of g thunders, the LORD,
Ps	29: 9	All in his Temple say, "G!"
Ps	57: 6	may your g appear above all
Ps	63: 3	sanctuary to see your power and g.

Ps	72:19	may he fill all the earth with his g.
Ps	96: 3	Tell his g among the nations;
Ps	96: 8	to the LORD the g due his name!
Ps	97: 6	all peoples see his g.
Ps	102:16	all the kings of the earth, your g,
Ps	104:31	May the g of the LORD endure
Ps	108: 6	your g above all the earth.
Ps	138: 5	"How great is the g of the LORD!"
Ps	145:12	mighty acts, the majestic g of your rule.
Ps	149: 9	such is the g of all God's faithful.
Prv	3:35	The wise will possess g, but fools
Prv	20:29	The g of the young is their strength,
Prv	25: 2	It is the g of God to conceal
Prv	25: 2	the g of kings to fathom a matter.
Wis	7:25	emanation of the g of the Almighty;
Is	6: 3	All the earth is filled with his g!"
Is	35: 2	They will see the g of the LORD,
Is	40: 5	Then the g of the LORD shall be
Is	42: 8	my g I give to no other, nor my
Is	42:12	Let them give g to the LORD,
Is	43: 7	by my name I created for my g;
Is	48:11	My g I will not give to another.
Is	60:19	forever, your God will be your g.
Is	66:18	they shall come and see my g.
Is	66:19	heard of my fame, or seen my g;
Is	66:19	they shall proclaim my g among
Jer	2:11	my people have changed their g
Bar	5: 4	of justice, the g of God's worship.
Ez	1:28	the likeness of the g of the LORD.
Ez	3:23	The g of the LORD was standing
Ez	8: 4	There I saw the g of the God
Ez	10: 4	The g of the LORD had moved off
Ez	10: 4	brilliant with the g of the LORD.
Ez	10:18	Then the g of the LORD left
Ez	43: 2	there was the g of the God of Israel
Ez	43: 2	and the earth shone with his g.
Ez	43: 5	there the g of the LORD filled
Ez	44: 4	and the g of the LORD filled
Dn	2:37	and strength, power and g;
Hos	4: 7	I will change their g into shame.
Hb	2:14	the knowledge of the LORD's g,
Hb	3: 3	His g covered the heavens,
Zec	2: 9	and I will be the g in its midst."
Zec	12: 7	that the g of the house of David
Mt	16:27	with his angels in his Father's g,
Mt	24:30	of heaven with power and great g.
Mt	25:31	the Son of Man comes in his g,
Mk	8:38	in his Father's g with the holy
Mk	10:37	in your g we may sit one at your
Mk	13:26	the clouds' with great power and g,
Lk	2: 9	and the g of the Lord shone around
Lk	2:14	"G to God in the highest
Lk	2:32	and g for your people Israel."
Lk	9:26	ashamed of when he comes in his g
Lk	9:32	they saw his g and the two men
Lk	19:38	in heaven and g in the highest."
Lk	21:27	in a cloud with power and great g.
Lk	24:26	these things and enter into his g?"
Jn	1:14	we saw his g, the g as of the Father's only Son,
Jn	2:11	in Galilee and so revealed his g
Jn	7:18	speaks on his own seeks his own g,
Jn	7:18	whoever seeks the g of the one who
Jn	8:50	I do not seek my own g; there is one
Jn	8:54	myself, my g is worth nothing;
Jn	11: 4	but is for the g of God, that the Son
Jn	11:40	if you believe you will see the g
Jn	12:41	Isaiah said this because he saw his g
Jn	17: 5	with the g that I had with you before
Jn	17:22	have given them the g you gave me,
Jn	17:24	they may see my g that you gave
Acts	7: 2	The God of g appeared to our father
Acts	7:55	to heaven and saw the g of God
Rom	1:23	exchanged the g of the immortal
Rom	2: 7	eternal life to those who seek g,
Rom	2:10	But there will be g, honor,
Rom	3: 7	to his g through my falsehood,

Rom	3:23	and are deprived of the **g** of God.
Rom	4:20	by faith and gave **g** to God
Rom	5: 2	we boast in hope of the **g** of God.
Rom	8:18	compared with the **g** to be revealed
Rom	9: 4	the adoption, the **g**, the covenants,
Rom	9:23	he has prepared previously for **g**,
Rom	11:36	To him be **g** forever. Amen.
Rom	16:27	through Jesus Christ be **g** forever
1 Cor	2: 7	before the ages for our **g**,
1 Cor	2: 8	not have crucified the Lord of **g**.
1 Cor	10:31	do, do everything for the **g** of God.
1 Cor	11:15	if a woman has long hair it is her **g**,
2 Cor	1:20	also goes through him to God for **g**.
2 Cor	3: 7	because of its **g** that was going
2 Cor	3:10	what was endowed with **g** has come
2 Cor	3:10	because of the **g** that surpasses it.
2 Cor	3:18	unveiled face on the **g** of the Lord,
2 Cor	3:18	into the same image from **g** to **g**,
2 Cor	4: 4	light of the gospel of the **g** of Christ,
2 Cor	4: 6	light the knowledge of the **g** of God
2 Cor	4:15	to overflow for the **g** of God.
2 Cor	4:17	weight of **g** beyond all comparison,
Eph	1:12	might exist for the praise of his **g**,
Eph	1:14	possession, to the praise of his **g**.
Eph	3:13	afflictions for you; this is your **g**.
Eph	3:21	to him be **g** in the church
Phil	1:11	comes through Jesus Christ for the **g**
Phil	2:11	is Lord, to the **g** of God the Father.
Phil	3:19	their **g** is in their "shame."
Phil	4:20	God and Father, **g** forever and ever.
Col	1:27	of the **g** of this mystery among
Col	1:27	it is Christ in you, the hope for **g**.
Col	3: 4	you too will appear with him in **g**.
1 Thes	2:12	calls you into his kingdom and **g**.
1 Thes	2:20	For you are our **g** and joy.
2 Thes	2:14	to possess the **g** of our Lord Jesus
1 Tm	1:17	God, honor and **g** forever and ever.
1 Tm	3:16	throughout the world, taken up in **g**.
2 Tm	2:10	Christ Jesus, together with eternal **g**.
2 Tm	4:18	To him be **g** forever and ever.
Heb	1: 3	who is the refulgence of his **g**,
Heb	2: 7	you crowned him with **g** and honor,
Heb	2: 9	we do see Jesus "crowned with **g**
Heb	2:10	in bringing many children to **g**,
Heb	3: 3	is worthy of more "**g**" than Moses,
Heb	9: 5	of **g** overshadowing the place
Heb	13:21	to whom be **g** forever [and ever].
1 Pt	1: 7	may prove to be for praise, **g**,
1 Pt	1:24	all its **g** like the flower of the field;
1 Pt	4:11	to whom belong **g** and dominion
1 Pt	4:13	that when his **g** is revealed you may
1 Pt	4:14	for the Spirit of **g** and of God rests
1 Pt	5: 1	has a share in the **g** to be revealed.
1 Pt	5: 4	receive the unfading crown of **g**.
1 Pt	5:10	his eternal **g** through Christ [Jesus]
2 Pt	1: 3	of him who called us by his own **g**
2 Pt	1:17	**g** from God the Father
2 Pt	1:17	came to him from the majestic **g**,
2 Pt	3:18	To him be **g** now and to the day
Jude	1:25	through Jesus Christ our Lord be **g**,
Rev	1: 6	to him be **g** and power forever
Rev	4: 9	the living creatures give **g**
Rev	4:11	to receive **g** and honor and power,
Rev	5:12	honor and **g** and blessing."
Rev	5:13	be blessing and honor, **g** and might,
Rev	7:12	Blessing and **g**,
Rev	11:13	and gave **g** to the God of heaven.
Rev	14: 7	"Fear God and give him **g**, for his
Rev	15: 8	filled with the smoke from God's **g**
Rev	16: 9	they did not repent or give him **g**.
Rev	19: 1	Salvation, **g**, and might belong
Rev	19: 7	rejoice and be glad and give him **g**.
Rev	21:23	for the **g** of God gave it light, and its

GLUTTON → GLUTTONS
Sir	31:20	of nausea and colic are with the **g**!
Mt	11:19	'Look, he is a **g** and a drunkard,

Lk	7:34	'Look, he is a **g** and a drunkard,

GLUTTONS → GLUTTON
Prv	23:21	drunkards and **g** come to poverty,
Ti	1:12	liars, vicious beasts, and lazy **g**."

GNASH → GNASHED, GNASHES
Lam	2:16	They hiss and **g** their teeth, saying,

GNASHED → GNASH
Ps	35:16	me, **g** their teeth against me.

GNASHES → GNASH
Jb	16: 9	me, he **g** his teeth against me;
Ps	112:10	is angry; **g** his teeth and wastes away;

GNAT → GNATS
Mt	23:24	who strain out the **g** and swallow

GNATS → GNAT
Ex	8:12	will turn into **g** throughout the land
Ps	105:31	of flies, **g** through all their country.

GO → GOES, GOING, GONE
Gn	4: 8	Abel, "Let us **g** out in the field."
Gn	7: 1	**G** into the ark, you and all your
Gn	11: 7	let us **g** down and there confuse
Gn	18:21	that I must **g** down to see whether
Gn	46: 4	I will **g** down to Egypt with you
Ex	3:19	you to **g** unless his hand is forced.
Ex	5: 1	Let my people **g**, that they may hold
Ex	12:31	**G** and serve the LORD as you
Ex	13:15	stubbornly refused to let us **g**,
Ex	33: 3	But I myself will not **g** up in your
Nm	13:30	"We ought to **g** up and seize
Dt	1:26	But you refused to **g** up;
Dt	6:14	You shall not **g** after other gods,
Jos	1: 9	God, is with you wherever you **g**.
Ru	1:16	Wherever you **g** I will **g**,
Ps	122: 1	to me, "Let us **g** to the house
Prv	6: 6	**G** to the ant, O sluggard, study her
Is	2: 3	from Zion shall **g** forth instruction,
Ez	1:12	Wherever the spirit would **g**,
Mi	4: 2	from Zion shall **g** forth instruction,
Zec	14: 3	the LORD will **g** forth and fight
Mt	5:41	one mile, **g** with him for two miles.
Mt	6: 6	you pray, **g** to your inner room,
Mt	28:19	**G**, therefore, and make disciples
Lk	9:57	will follow you wherever you **g**."
Jn	6:68	him, "Master, to whom shall we **g**?
Jn	14: 3	if I **g** and prepare a place for you,

GOADS
Eccl	12:11	The sayings of the wise are like **g**;

GOAL
Phil	3:14	I continue my pursuit toward the **g**,

GOAT → GOATS, GOATS'
Gn	37:31	and after slaughtering a **g**,
Ex	26: 7	make sheets woven of **g** hair
Lv	16: 9	The **g** that is determined by lot
Nm	7:16	one **g** for a purification offering;
Tb	2:12	also gave her a young **g** for a meal.
Lk	15:29	you never gave me even a young **g**

GOATS → GOAT
Ez	34:17	and another, between rams and **g**.
Mt	25:32	separates the sheep from the **g**.
Heb	9:12	not with the blood of **g** and calves
Heb	10: 4	blood of bulls and **g** take away sins.

GOATS' → GOAT
Nm	31:20	everything made of **g** hair,

GOD → GOD'S, GOD-FEARING, GODDESS, GODLESS, GODLINESS, GODLY, GODS
Gn	1: 1	when **G** created the heavens
Gn	1: 3	Then **G** said: Let there be light,
Gn	1: 7	**G** made the dome, and it separated
Gn	1: 9	Then **G** said: Let the water under
Gn	1:11	Then **G** said: Let the earth bring
Gn	1:21	**G** saw that it was good,
Gn	1:22	and **G** blessed them, saying:

Gn	1:25	G saw that it was good.	Ex	8:15	Pharaoh, "This is the finger of G."
Gn	1:26	Then G said: Let us make human	Ex	10:16	Lord, your G, and against you,
Gn	1:27	G created mankind in his image;	Ex	13:19	"G will surely take care of you,
Gn	1:27	in the image of G he created them;	Ex	14:19	The angel of G, who had been
Gn	1:28	G blessed them and G said to them:	Ex	15: 2	This is my G, I praise him;
Gn	1:31	G looked at everything he had	Ex	16:12	that I, the Lord, am your G.
Gn	2: 3	G blessed the seventh day and made	Ex	17: 9	hill with the staff of G in my hand."
Gn	2: 4	When the Lord G made the earth	Ex	18: 4	"The G of my father is my help;
Gn	2: 7	the Lord G formed the man	Ex	18: 5	encamped at the mountain of G,
Gn	2: 8	The Lord G planted a garden	Ex	19: 3	went up to the mountain of G.
Gn	2:16	The Lord G gave the man this	Ex	20: 1	Then G spoke all these words:
Gn	2:22	The Lord G then built the rib	Ex	20: 2	I am the Lord your G,
Gn	3: 1	the woman, "Did G really say,	Ex	20: 5	Lord, your G, am a jealous G,
Gn	3: 5	G knows well that when you eat	Ex	20: 7	of the Lord, your G, in vain.
Gn	3: 8	the sound of the Lord G walking	Ex	20:10	is a sabbath of the Lord your G.
Gn	3: 9	The Lord G then called	Ex	20:12	the Lord your G is giving you.
Gn	3:13	The Lord G then asked	Ex	20:19	but do not let G speak to us, or we
Gn	3:14	the Lord G said to the snake:	Ex	22:19	Whoever sacrifices to any g,
Gn	3:21	The Lord G made for the man	Ex	22:27	You shall not despise G, nor curse
Gn	3:23	The Lord G therefore banished	Ex	23:19	to the house of the Lord, your G.
Gn	5: 1	he made them in the likeness of G;	Ex	24:10	and they beheld the G of Israel.
Gn	5:24	Enoch walked with G, and he was no longer here, for G took him.	Ex	29:46	their G, might dwell among them.
			Ex	34: 6	Lord, a G gracious and merciful,
Gn	6:12	G saw how corrupt the earth had	Ex	34:14	shall not bow down to any other g,
Gn	8: 1	G remembered Noah and all	Ex	34:14	"Jealous" his name—is a jealous G.
Gn	9: 1	G blessed Noah and his sons	Nm	15:40	and you will be holy to your G.
Gn	9: 6	of G have human beings been made.	Nm	16:22	"O G, G of the spirits of all living
Gn	9:16	the everlasting covenant between G	Nm	22: 9	Then G came to Balaam and said:
Gn	14:18	He was a priest of G Most High.	Nm	22:18	the command of the Lord, my G.
Gn	14:19	be Abram by G Most High,	Nm	22:38	I can speak only what G puts in my
Gn	16:13	saying, "You are G who sees me";	Nm	23:19	G is not a human being who speaks
Gn	16:13	"Have I really seen G and remained	Nm	23:19	Is G one to speak and not act,
Gn	17: 1	I am G the Almighty.	Nm	25:13	he was jealous on behalf of his G
Gn	17: 7	to be your G and the G of your	Nm	27:16	the G of the spirits of all humanity,
Gn	19:29	G overthrew the cities where Lot	Dt	1:21	your G, has given this land over
Gn	21: 2	at the set time that G had stated.	Dt	1:32	would not trust the Lord, your G,
Gn	21: 6	"G has given me cause to laugh,	Dt	3:22	your G, who will fight for you."
Gn	21:17	G has heard the boy's voice in this	Dt	3:24	What g in heaven or on earth can
Gn	21:20	G was with the boy as he grew up.	Dt	4: 7	our G, is to us whenever we call
Gn	21:22	"G is with you in everything you	Dt	4:24	your G, is a consuming fire, a jealous G.
Gn	21:33	by name the Lord, G the Eternal.	Dt	4:29	the Lord, your G, from there,
Gn	22: 1	G put Abraham to the test and said	Dt	4:31	Lord, your G, is a merciful G,
Gn	22: 8	"G will provide the sheep	Dt	4:39	that the Lord is G in the heavens
Gn	22:12	For now I know that you fear G,	Dt	5: 9	Lord, your G, am a jealous G,
Gn	25:11	Abraham, G blessed his son Isaac,	Dt	5:11	of the Lord, your G, in vain.
Gn	26:24	I am the G of Abraham, your father.	Dt	5:12	Lord, your G, commanded you.
Gn	28:17	is nothing else but the house of G,	Dt	5:14	is a sabbath of the Lord your G.
Gn	30: 2	"Can I take the place of G, who has	Dt	5:15	your G, brought you out from there
Gn	31:13	I am the G of Bethel, where you	Dt	5:16	the Lord your G is giving you.
Gn	31:42	But G saw my plight and the fruits	Dt	5:24	out that G may speak to a mortal
Gn	31:50	G will be a witness between you	Dt	5:26	of the living G speaking
Gn	32:31	"because I have seen G face	Dt	6: 2	the Lord, your G, by keeping,
Gn	33:11	G has been generous toward me,	Dt	6: 4	The Lord is our G, the Lord
Gn	35: 1	an altar there to the G who appeared	Dt	6: 5	your G, with your whole heart,
Gn	35:10	G said to him: Your name is Jacob.	Dt	6:13	The Lord your G, shall you fear;
Gn	35:11	Then G said to him: I am G	Dt	6:16	put the Lord, your G, to the test,
Gn	41:38	so endowed with the spirit of G?"	Dt	7: 6	people holy to the Lord, your G;
Gn	41:51	"G has made me forget entirely my	Dt	7: 9	that the Lord, your G, is G:
Gn	41:52	"G has made me fruitful in the land	Dt	7: 9	the faithful G who keeps covenant
Gn	46: 2	There G, speaking to Israel	Dt	7:21	midst, is a great and awesome G.
Gn	48:15	The G who has been my shepherd	Dt	8: 5	Lord, your G, disciplines you.
Gn	50:19	Can I take the place of G?	Dt	8:11	your G, by failing to keep his
Gn	50:20	harm to me, G meant it for good,	Dt	8:18	your G, for he is the one who gives
Gn	50:24	G will surely take care of you	Dt	10:12	your G, to follow in all his ways,
Ex	1:17	The midwives, however, feared G;	Dt	10:14	your G, as well as the earth
Ex	3: 4	G called out to him from the bush:	Dt	10:17	Lord, your G, is the G of gods,
Ex	3: 6	I am the G of your father,	Dt	10:21	he is your G, who has done for you
Ex	3: 6	the G of Abraham, the G of Isaac, and the G of Jacob.	Dt	11: 1	the Lord, your G, therefore,
Ex	3:12	G answered: I will be with you;	Dt	11:13	your G, with your whole heart
Ex	3:12	you will serve G at this mountain.	Dt	12:12	Lord, your G, with your sons
Ex	3:14	G replied to Moses: I am who I am.	Dt	12:28	in the sight of the Lord, your G.
Ex	3:18	The Lord, the G of the Hebrews,	Dt	13: 4	your G, is testing you to know
Ex	4:27	meeting him at the mountain of G,	Dt	14: 1	are children of the Lord, your G.
Ex	6: 7	own people, and I will be your G;	Dt	14: 2	people holy to the Lord, your G;
Ex	7: 1	I have made you a g to Pharaoh,	Dt	15: 6	your G, will bless you as he
Ex	8: 6	is none like the Lord, our G.	Dt	15:19	your G, every male firstling born

Dt	16:11	your **G**, will choose as the dwelling
Dt	16:17	LORD, your **G**, has given to you.
Dt	16:22	such as the LORD, your **G**, hates.
Dt	18:13	sincere with the LORD, your **G**.
Dt	18:15	your **G**, raise up for you
Dt	19: 9	your **G**, and ever walking in his
Dt	21:23	anyone who is hanged is a curse of **G**.
Dt	23: 6	your **G**, would not listen to Balaam
Dt	23: 6	the LORD, your **G**, loves you.
Dt	23:15	your **G**, journeys along in the midst
Dt	23:22	your **G**, will surely require it of you
Dt	25:16	abomination to the LORD, your **G**.
Dt	26: 5	your **G**, "My father was a refugee
Dt	27: 5	your **G**, an altar made of stones
Dt	28: 1	your **G**, will set you high above all
Dt	28:15	your **G**, carefully observing all his
Dt	29:12	as his people and he may be your **G**,
Dt	30: 2	LORD, your **G**, obeying his voice,
Dt	30: 4	the LORD, your **G**, gather you;
Dt	30: 6	your **G**, will circumcise your hearts
Dt	30:16	your **G**, will bless you in the land
Dt	30:20	LORD, your **G**, obeying his voice,
Dt	31: 6	your **G**, who marches with you;
Dt	32: 3	praise the greatness of our **G**!
Dt	32: 4	A faithful **G**, without deceit,
Dt	32:18	you, you forgot the **G** who gave you
Dt	32:39	am he, and there is no **g** besides me.
Jos	1: 9	your **G**, is with you wherever you
Jos	1:13	your **G**, is about to give you rest;
Jos	14: 8	loyal to the LORD, my **G**.
Jos	14:14	loyal to the LORD, the **G** of Israel.
Jos	22: 5	your **G**, follow him in all his ways,
Jos	22:22	"The LORD is the **G** of gods.
Jos	22:34	among them that the LORD is **G**.
Jos	23: 3	your **G**, who fought for you.
Jos	23: 8	your **G**, as you have done up to this
Jos	23:11	care to love the LORD, your **G**.
Jos	23:14	your **G**, made concerning you has
Jos	23:15	your **G**, made to you has come true
Jos	24:19	the LORD, for he is a holy **G**; he is a passionate **G**
Jgs	1: 7	I have done, so has **G** repaid me."
Jgs	5: 5	before the LORD, the **G** of Israel.
Jgs	6:20	The messenger of **G** said to him:
Jgs	6:31	If he is a **g**, let him act for himself,
Jgs	8:33	Baals, making Baal-berith their **g**.
Jgs	13: 6	husband, "A man of **G** came to me;
Jgs	13: 6	the appearance of an angel of **G**,
Jgs	16:23	a great sacrifice to their **g** Dagon
Jgs	16:23	"Our **g** has delivered Samson our
Jgs	16:28	and said, "Lord **G**, remember me!
Ru	1:16	shall be my people and your **G**, my **G**.
1 Sm	2: 2	there is no Rock like our **G**.
1 Sm	2: 3	an all-knowing **G** is the LORD,
1 Sm	2: 3	LORD, a **G** who weighs actions.
1 Sm	3: 3	lamp of **G** was not yet extinguished,
1 Sm	3: 3	the LORD where the ark of **G** was.
1 Sm	4:11	The ark of **G** was captured,
1 Sm	5:11	away the ark of the **G** of Israel.
1 Sm	10: 9	leave Samuel, **G** changed his heart.
1 Sm	11: 6	the spirit of **G** rushed upon him
1 Sm	12:12	the LORD your **G** is your king.
1 Sm	16:15	evil spirit from **G** is tormenting you.
1 Sm	17:36	insulted the armies of the living **G**."
1 Sm	17:45	the **G** of the armies of Israel whom
1 Sm	17:46	land shall learn that Israel has a **G**.
1 Sm	19:23	the spirit of **G** came upon him also,
1 Sm	28:13	"I see a **g** rising from the earth,"
1 Sm	28:15	me and **G** has turned away from me.
1 Sm	28:15	Since **G** no longer answers me
1 Sm	30: 6	took courage in the LORD his **G**
2 Sm	6: 7	**G** struck him on that spot, and he
2 Sm	7:23	What **g** has ever led a nation,
2 Sm	7:27	LORD of hosts, **G** of Israel,
2 Sm	14:14	though **G** does not bring back
2 Sm	14:17	lord the king is like an angel of **G**,
2 Sm	21:14	out, **G** granted relief to the land.
2 Sm	22: 3	my **G**, my rock of refuge!
2 Sm	22:32	Truly, who is **G** except the LORD?
2 Sm	22:32	Who but our **G** is the rock?
2 Sm	22:33	This **G** who girded me with might,
2 Sm	22:47	Exalted be **G**, the rock of my
1 Kgs	2: 3	your **G**, walking in his ways
1 Kgs	5: 9	**G** gave Solomon wisdom,
1 Kgs	5:19	my **G**, as the LORD said to David
1 Kgs	8:23	"LORD, **G** of Israel, there is no **G**
1 Kgs	8:27	"Is **G** indeed to dwell on earth?
1 Kgs	8:60	may know that the LORD is **G**
1 Kgs	8:61	our **G**, observing his statutes
1 Kgs	10:24	hear the wisdom **G** had put into his
1 Kgs	11: 4	his **G**, as the heart of David his
1 Kgs	11:33	Chemosh, **g** of Moab, and Milcom, **g** of the Ammonites.
1 Kgs	15:30	the LORD, the **G** of Israel,
1 Kgs	18:21	If the LORD is **G**, follow him;
1 Kgs	18:24	The **G** who answers with fire is **G**."
1 Kgs	18:36	"LORD, **G** of Abraham, Isaac,
1 Kgs	18:39	LORD is **G**! The LORD is **G**!"
1 Kgs	20:28	Aram has said the LORD is a **g** of mountains, not a **g** of plains,
2 Kgs	1: 2	of Baalzebub, the **g** of Ekron,
2 Kgs	5:15	that there is no **G** in all the earth,
2 Kgs	17: 7	their **G**, who had brought them
2 Kgs	19: 4	sent to taunt the living **G**, and will
2 Kgs	19: 4	the LORD, your **G**, has heard.
2 Kgs	19:15	You alone are **G** over all
2 Kgs	19:19	that you alone, LORD, are **G**."
1 Chr	12:19	may your **G** be your helper!"
1 Chr	13: 2	is so decreed by the LORD our **G**,
1 Chr	16:35	"Save us, O **G**, our savior, gather us
1 Chr	17:20	is no one like you, no **G** but you,
1 Chr	17:24	LORD of hosts, **G** of Israel,
1 Chr	21: 8	Then David said to **G**, "I have
1 Chr	21:15	**G** also sent an angel to Jerusalem
1 Chr	22:19	to seeking the LORD your **G**.
1 Chr	22:19	the sanctuary of the LORD **G**,
1 Chr	28: 2	the footstool for the feet of our **G**;
1 Chr	28: 9	know the **G** of your father and serve
1 Chr	28:20	dismayed, for the LORD **G**, my **G**,
1 Chr	29: 1	whom alone **G** has chosen, is still
1 Chr	29: 2	stored up for the house of my **G**,
1 Chr	29:10	LORD, **G** of Israel our father,
1 Chr	29:13	our **G**, we give you thanks and we
1 Chr	29:18	**G** of our ancestors Abraham, Isaac,
2 Chr	1: 7	That night **G** appeared to Solomon
2 Chr	2: 3	and festivals of the LORD, our **G**:
2 Chr	2: 4	our **G** is greater than all other gods.
2 Chr	5:14	LORD had filled the house of **G**.
2 Chr	6:14	"LORD, **G** of Israel, there is no **G**
2 Chr	6:18	"Is **G** indeed to dwell with human
2 Chr	13:12	See, **G** is with us, at our head,
2 Chr	15: 3	time Israel was without a true **G**,
2 Chr	15:12	LORD, the **G** of their ancestors,
2 Chr	18:13	I shall speak whatever my **G** says."
2 Chr	19: 3	and have set your heart to seek **G**."
2 Chr	19: 7	LORD, our **G**, there is no injustice.
2 Chr	20: 6	"LORD, **G** of our ancestors, are you not **G** in heaven,
2 Chr	20:20	in the LORD, your **G**, be firm,
2 Chr	25: 8	for with **G** is power to help
2 Chr	26: 5	seek **G** as long as Zechariah lived,
2 Chr	26: 5	the LORD, **G** made him prosper.
2 Chr	30: 9	your **G**, is gracious and merciful
2 Chr	30:19	who have set their heart to seek **G**,
2 Chr	31:21	for the service of the house of **G**
2 Chr	32:15	the less shall your **g** rescue you
2 Chr	32:17	deride the LORD, the **G** of Israel,
2 Chr	32:31	the land, **G** abandoned him as a test,
2 Chr	33:12	to appease the LORD, his **G**.
2 Chr	34:33	LORD, the **G** of their ancestors.
Ezr	1: 3	that is, the **G** who is in Jerusalem.
Ezr	2:68	offerings for the house of **G**,
Ezr	6:16	of this house of **G** with joy.
Ezr	7: 9	hand of his **G** was over him.

Ezr	7:18	the silver and gold, as your **G** wills.
Ezr	7:23	for the house of the **G** of heaven,
Ezr	8:22	of our **G** is over all who seek him,
Ezr	8:31	hand of our **G** remained over us,
Ezr	9: 6	"My **G**, I am too ashamed
Ezr	9: 9	life to raise again the house of our **G**
Ezr	10: 3	a covenant before our **G** to dismiss
Neh	1: 5	"Lord, **G** of heaven,
Neh	4:14	our **G** will fight with us."
Neh	5:15	because I feared **G**, did not do this.
Neh	8: 8	from the book of the law of **G**,
Neh	8:18	book of the law of **G** day after day,
Neh	9: 5	your **G**, from eternity to eternity!"
Neh	9:17	But you are a forgiving **G**,
Neh	9:31	you are a gracious and merciful **G**.
Neh	9:32	and awesome **G**, who preserves
Neh	10:30	the law of **G** given through Moses,
Neh	10:40	will not neglect the house of our **G**.
Neh	13: 2	though our **G** turned the curse
Neh	13:11	is the house of **G** neglected?"
Neh	13:26	though he was beloved of his **G**
Neh	13:31	Remember this in my favor, my **G**!
Tb	3:11	"Blessed are you, merciful **G**!
Tb	4:19	your **G**, and ask him that all your
Jdt	3: 8	and tribes should invoke him as a **g**.
Jdt	6: 2	Who is **G** beside Nebuchadnezzar?
Jdt	6: 2	Their **G** will not save them;
Jdt	8:20	since we acknowledge no other **g**
Jb	1: 1	Job, who feared **G** and avoided evil.
Jb	1:22	nor did he charge **G** with wrong.
Jb	2:10	We accept good things from **G**;
Jb	4:17	anyone be more in the right than **G**?
Jb	5:17	Happy the one whom **G** reproves!
Jb	8: 3	Does **G** pervert judgment,
Jb	8:20	**G** will not cast away the upright;
Jb	9: 2	can anyone be in the right before **G**?
Jb	11: 7	Can you find out the depths of **G**?
Jb	19:26	off, and from my flesh I will see **G**:
Jb	20:29	the heritage appointed him by **G**.
Jb	21:19	"**G** is storing up the man's misery
Jb	21:22	Can anyone teach **G** knowledge,
Jb	22:12	Does not **G**, in the heights
Jb	22:13	Yet you say, "What does **G** know?
Jb	31: 6	Let **G** weigh me in the scales
Jb	31:14	then should I do when **G** rises up?
Jb	32:13	**G** can vanquish him but no
Jb	33: 6	I am like you before **G**, I too was
Jb	33:14	For **G** does speak, once, even twice,
Jb	33:26	He shall pray and **G** will favor him;
Jb	34:10	far be it from **G** to do wickedness;
Jb	34:23	For no one has **G** set a time to come
Jb	36: 5	Look, **G** is great, not disdainful;
Jb	36:26	**G** is great beyond our knowledge,
Jb	40: 2	who would instruct **G** give answer?
Ps	5: 3	of my cry, my king and my **G**!
Ps	5: 5	You are not a **g** who delights in evil;
Ps	7:11	**G** is a shield above me saving
Ps	7:12	**G** is a just judge,
Ps	14: 5	**G** is with the company of the just.
Ps	18: 3	deliverer, My **G**, my rock of refuge,
Ps	18:22	I was not disloyal to my **G**.
Ps	18:29	my **G** brightens my darkness.
Ps	18:32	Truly, who is **G** except the Lord?
Ps	18:32	Who but our **G** is the rock?
Ps	18:33	This **G** who girded me with might,
Ps	18:47	Exalted be **G**, my savior!
Ps	19: 2	The heavens declare the glory of **G**;
Ps	22: 2	My **G**, my **G**, why have you
Ps	22:11	my mother bore me you are my **G**.
Ps	27: 9	do not forsake me, **G** my savior!
Ps	29: 3	the **G** of glory thunders,
Ps	31: 6	redeem me, Lord, **G** of truth.
Ps	31:15	I say, "You are my **G**."
Ps	33:12	the nation whose **G** is the Lord,
Ps	35:23	in my cause, my **G** and my Lord.

Ps	40: 4	song in my mouth, a hymn to our **G**.
Ps	40: 9	I delight to do your will, my **G**;
Ps	42: 2	so my soul longs for you, O **G**.
Ps	42: 3	My soul thirsts for **G**, the living **G**.
Ps	42: 3	can I enter and see the face of **G**?
Ps	42: 9	I will pray to the **G** of my life,
Ps	42:12	Wait for **G**, for I shall again praise
Ps	43: 4	That I may come to the altar of **G**,
Ps	44: 9	**G** we have boasted all the day long;
Ps	45: 7	Your throne, O **G**, stands forever;
Ps	45: 8	therefore **G**, your **G**, has anointed
Ps	46: 2	**G** is our refuge and our strength,
Ps	46: 6	**G** is in its midst; it shall not be
Ps	46: 6	**G** will help it at break of day.
Ps	46:11	"Be still and know that I am **G**!
Ps	47: 2	shout to **G** with joyful cries.
Ps	47: 7	Sing praise to **G**, sing praise;
Ps	47: 8	For **G** is king over all the earth;
Ps	48:10	O **G**, your mercy within your
Ps	48:15	That this is **G**, our **G** for ever
Ps	49: 8	or pay to **G** his own ransom.
Ps	50: 2	perfection of beauty, **G** shines forth.
Ps	50: 3	Our **G** comes and will not be silent!
Ps	51: 3	Have mercy on me, **G**, in accord
Ps	51:12	A clean heart create for me, **G**;
Ps	51:19	sacrifice, O **G**, is a contrite spirit;
Ps	53: 2	says in his heart, "There is no **G**."
Ps	53: 3	**G** looks out from the heavens
Ps	53: 3	discerning person who is seeking **G**.
Ps	54: 6	**G** is present as my helper;
Ps	55:20	**G**, who sits enthroned forever,
Ps	55:20	they have no fear of **G**.
Ps	56: 5	I praise the word of **G**; I trust in **G**,
Ps	56:14	I may walk before **G** in the light
Ps	57: 4	May **G** send help from heaven
Ps	57: 4	May **G** send fidelity and mercy.
Ps	57: 8	My heart is steadfast, **G**, my heart is
Ps	59:18	**G**, are my fortress, my loving **G**.
Ps	62: 2	My soul rests in **G** alone,
Ps	62: 8	deliverance and honor are with **G**,
Ps	62: 9	Trust **G** at all times, my people!
Ps	62:12	I have heard: Strength belongs to **G**,
Ps	63: 2	O **G**, you are my **G**—it is you I
Ps	65: 6	deeds of justice, O **G** our savior,
Ps	66: 2	Shout joyfully to **G**, all the earth;
Ps	66: 3	Say to **G**: "How awesome your
Ps	66: 5	Come and see the works of **G**,
Ps	66:16	all you who fear **G**, while I recount
Ps	66:20	Blessed be **G**, who did not reject my
Ps	68: 5	Sing to **G**, praise his name;
Ps	68:21	Our **G** is a **G** who saves;
Ps	68:27	In your choirs, bless **G**;
Ps	68:36	Awesome is **G** in his holy place,
Ps	69: 6	**G**, you know my folly; my faults are
Ps	70: 2	Graciously rescue me, **G**!
Ps	70: 5	help always say, "**G** be glorified!"
Ps	70: 6	**G**, come to me quickly!
Ps	71:17	**G**, you have taught me from my
Ps	71:18	do not forsake me, **G**, That I may
Ps	71:19	O **G**, who is your equal?
Ps	71:22	my **G**, And sing to you
Ps	73:17	Till I entered the sanctuary of **G**
Ps	73:26	heart fail, **G** is the rock of my heart,
Ps	76:12	keep vows to the Lord your **G**.
Ps	77:14	Your way, **G**, is holy; what **g** is as as great as our **G**?
Ps	77:15	You are the **G** who does wonders;
Ps	78:19	They spoke against **G**, and said,
Ps	78:59	**G** heard and grew angry;
Ps	79: 9	Help us, **G** our savior, on account
Ps	81: 2	Sing joyfully to **G** our strength;
Ps	82: 1	**G** takes a stand in the divine
Ps	84: 3	and flesh cry out for the living **G**.
Ps	84:11	the house of my **G** than a home
Ps	84:12	a sun and shield is the Lord **G**,
Ps	86:12	your name forever, Lord my **G**.

Ps	86:15	are a compassionate and gracious G,		Is	60:19	forever, your G will be your glory.
Ps	87: 3	things are said of you, O city of G!		Is	61: 2	and a day of vindication by our G;
Ps	89: 8	A G dreaded in the council		Is	61:10	LORD, my being exults in my G;
Ps	90: 2	from eternity to eternity you are G.		Is	62: 5	his bride so shall your G rejoice
Ps	91: 2	fortress, my G in whom I trust."		Jer	3:23	in the LORD our G is Israel's
Ps	94: 1	LORD, avenging G, avenging G,		Jer	7:23	I will be your G and you shall be
Ps	94:22	height, my G, my rock of refuge,		Jer	10:10	The LORD is truly G, he is the living G, the eternal King,
Ps	95: 3	For the LORD is the great G,		Jer	23:23	Am I a G near at hand only—
Ps	95: 7	For he is our G, we are the people		Jer	23:23	the LORD—and not a G far off?
Ps	99: 8	you were a forgiving G to them,		Jer	23:36	pervert the words of the living G,
Ps	99: 9	Exalt the LORD, our G;		Jer	31:33	I will be their G, and they shall be
Ps	100: 3	Know that the LORD is G,		Jer	32:27	the LORD, the G of all the living!
Ps	106:21	They forgot the G who had saved		Jer	42:13	the voice of the LORD, your G,
Ps	108: 2	My heart is steadfast, G; my heart is		Jer	51:10	what the LORD, our G, has done.
Ps	108: 6	on high over the heavens, G;		Jer	51:56	The LORD is a G of recompense,
Ps	113: 5	Who is like the LORD our G,		Bar	4: 8	forgot the eternal G who nourished
Ps	115: 3	Our G is in heaven and does		Ez	11:20	be my people, and I will be their G.
Ps	116: 5	yes, our G is merciful.		Ez	28: 2	of heart, you say, "I am a g!
Ps	123: 2	our eyes are on the LORD our G,		Ez	28: 2	But you are a man, not a g;
Ps	136: 2	Praise the G of gods; for his mercy		Ez	28: 2	yet you pretend you are a g at heart!
Ps	136:26	Praise the G of heaven, for his		Ez	28:13	In Eden, the garden of G, you lived;
Ps	139:17	to me are your designs, O G;		Ez	34:31	of my pasture, and I am your G—
Ps	139:23	Probe me, G, know my heart;		Ez	43: 2	the glory of the G of Israel coming
Ps	143:10	to do your will, for you are my G.		Dn	2:19	and he blessed the G of heaven:
Ps	145: 1	I will extol you, my G and king;		Dn	2:28	there is a G in heaven who reveals
Ps	147: 1	How good to sing praise to our G;		Dn	3:17	If our G, whom we serve, can save
Ps	150: 1	Praise G in his holy sanctuary;		Dn	3:45	know that you alone are the Lord G,
Prv	2: 5	the knowledge of G you will find;		Dn	3:96	there is no other G who can rescue
Prv	3: 4	esteem before G and human beings.		Dn	3:96	that whoever blasphemes the G
Prv	25: 2	It is the glory of G to conceal		Dn	6:17	said, "Your G, whom you serve so
Prv	30: 5	Every word of G is tested; he is		Dn	9: 4	the LORD, my G, and confessed,
Eccl	1:13	A bad business G has given		Dn	10:12	and humble yourself before G,
Eccl	2:26	For to the one who pleases G,		Dn	11:32	to their G shall take strong action.
Eccl	3:11	G has made everything appropriate		Dn	11:36	making himself greater than any g;
Eccl	3:14	that whatever G does will endure		Dn	11:36	dreadful blasphemies against the G
Eccl	5: 1	G is in heaven and you are on earth;		Dn	13:45	G stirred up the holy spirit
Eccl	5: 3	For G has no pleasure in fools;		Dn	14: 4	but Daniel worshiped only his G.
Eccl	5:18	their toil: This is a gift from G.		Dn	14: 6	"You do not think Bel is a living g?
Eccl	7:18	the one who fears G will succeed		Hos	2: 1	called, "Children of the living G."
Eccl	8:12	shall be well with those who fear G,		Hos	4: 6	have forgotten the law of your G,
Eccl	11: 5	So you do not know the work of G,		Hos	6: 6	of G rather than burnt offerings.
Eccl	12: 7	life breath returns to G who gave it.		Hos	9: 8	hostility in the house of his G.
Eccl	12:13	all is heard: Fear G and keep his		Hos	12: 7	You must return to your G.
Sir	32:14	Whoever seeks G must accept		Hos	13: 4	am your G, since the land of Egypt;
Wis	2:18	if the righteous one is the son of G, G will help him and deliver him		Jl	2:13	your G, For he is gracious
				Jl	2:23	and rejoice in the LORD, your G!
Is	5:16	by justice the Holy G shown holy.		Am	4:12	prepare to meet your G, O Israel!
Is	7:11	for a sign from the LORD, your G;		Am	4:13	the LORD, the G of hosts, is his
Is	12: 2	G indeed is my salvation;		Jon	1: 6	Get up, call on your g!
Is	17:10	you have forgotten the G who saves		Jon	1: 6	Perhaps this g will be mindful of us
Is	25: 9	"Indeed, this is our G; we looked		Jon	3: 5	the people of Nineveh believed G;
Is	29:23	Jacob, be in awe of the G of Israel.		Jon	4: 2	you are a gracious and merciful G,
Is	30:18	For the LORD is a G of justice:		Mi	3: 7	because there is no answer from G.
Is	35: 4	Here is your G, he comes		Mi	6: 8	and to walk humbly with your G.
Is	37:16	You alone are G over all		Mi	7: 7	I will wait for G my savior; my G
Is	40: 1	comfort to my people, says your G.		Mi	7:18	Who is a G like you, who removes
Is	40: 3	the wasteland a highway for our G!		Na	1: 2	and avenging G is the LORD,
Is	40: 8	the word of our G stands forever."		Hb	1:11	make their own strength their g!
Is	40:18	To whom can you liken G?		Hb	3:18	LORD and exult in my saving G.
Is	40:28	The LORD is G from of old,		Zep	3:17	LORD, your G, is in your midst,
Is	41:10	do not be anxious: I am your G.		Hg	1:14	of the LORD of hosts, their G,
Is	41:13	your G, who grasp your right hand;		Zec	9:16	the LORD their G will save them:
Is	43:10	Before me no g was formed,		Zec	14: 5	Then the LORD, my G, will come,
Is	44: 6	I am the last; there is no G but me.		Mal	2:10	Has not one G created us?
Is	44:15	Yet he makes a g and worships it,		Mal	3: 8	Can anyone rob G? But you are
Is	45:18	who is G, The designer and maker		Mt	1:23	which means "G is with us."
Is	48:17	your G, teaching you how		Mt	4: 4	forth from the mouth of G.' "
Is	49: 4	my recompense is with my G.		Mt	4: 7	the Lord, your G, to the test.' "
Is	52: 7	saying to Zion, "Your G is King!"		Mt	4:10	your G, shall you worship and him
Is	52:12	your rear guard is the G of Israel.		Mt	5: 8	clean of heart, for they will see G.
Is	53: 4	struck down by G and afflicted,		Mt	5: 9	for they will be called children of G.
Is	55: 7	to our G, who is generous		Mt	6:24	You cannot serve G and mammon.
Is	57:21	no peace for the wicked! says my G.		Mt	12:28	if it is by the Spirit of G that I drive
Is	59: 2	that separate you from your G, It is		Mt	12:28	the kingdom of G has come
				Mt	16:16	Messiah, the Son of the living G."

Mt	19: 6	what G has joined together,	Jn	20:28	said to him, "My Lord and my G!"
Mt	19:26	but for G all things are possible."	Jn	20:31	the Son of G, and that through this
Mt	22:21	and to G what belongs to G."	Acts	1: 3	speaking about the kingdom of G.
Mt	22:32	'I am the G of Abraham, the G of Isaac, and the G of Jacob'?	Acts	2:22	to you by G with mighty deeds,
			Acts	2:24	But G raised him up, releasing him
Mt	22:32	He is not the G of the dead	Acts	2:33	Exalted at the right hand of G,
Mt	22:37	Lord, your G, with all your heart,	Acts	2:36	that G has made him both Lord
Mt	27:40	if you are the Son of G, [and] come	Acts	3:15	but G raised him from the dead;
Mt	27:46	which means, "My G, my G,	Acts	4:31	speak the word of G with boldness.
Mk	1: 1	of Jesus Christ [the Son of G].	Acts	5: 4	lied not to human beings, but to G."
Mk	1:24	who you are—the Holy One of G!"	Acts	5:29	"We must obey G rather than men.
Mk	2: 7	Who but G alone can forgive sins?"	Acts	5:31	G exalted him at his right hand as
Mk	7:13	You nullify the word of G in favor	Acts	5:32	as is the holy Spirit that G has given
Mk	10: 6	'G made them male and female.	Acts	5:39	But if it comes from G, you will not
Mk	10: 9	Therefore what G has joined	Acts	5:39	find yourselves fighting against G."
Mk	10:18	No one is good but G alone.	Acts	6: 7	The word of G continued to spread,
Mk	10:24	hard it is to enter the kingdom of G!	Acts	7:55	standing at the right hand of G,
Mk	10:27	it is impossible, but not for G. All things are possible for G."	Acts	8:21	your heart is not upright before G.
			Acts	10:46	in tongues and glorifying G.
Mk	11:22	to them in reply, "Have faith in G.	Acts	11: 9	answered, 'What G has made clean,
Mk	12:17	and to G what belongs to G."	Acts	12:24	the word of G continued to spread
Mk	12:29	The Lord our G is Lord alone!	Acts	13:32	that what G promised our ancestors
Mk	12:30	You shall love the Lord your G	Acts	14:22	to enter the kingdom of G."
Mk	15:34	which is translated, "My G, my G,	Acts	15:10	are you now putting G to the test
Lk	1:19	"I am Gabriel, who stand before G.	Acts	17:23	altar inscribed, 'To an Unknown G.'
Lk	1:30	for you have found favor with G.	Acts	17:30	G has overlooked the times
Lk	1:35	will be called holy, the Son of G.	Acts	20:27	to you the entire plan of G.
Lk	1:37	nothing will be impossible for G."	Acts	20:32	now I commend you to G
Lk	1:47	my spirit rejoices in G my savior.	Acts	24:16	keep my conscience clear before G
Lk	2:14	"Glory to G in the highest	Acts	28: 6	and began to say that he was a g.
Lk	2:40	and the favor of G was upon him.	Rom	1: 4	established as Son of G in power
Lk	3:38	Seth, the son of Adam, the son of G.	Rom	1:16	It is the power of G for the salvation
Lk	4: 3	"If you are the Son of G,	Rom	1:17	it is revealed the righteousness of G
Lk	4: 8	your G, and him alone shall you	Rom	1:18	wrath of G is indeed being revealed
Lk	4:41	shouting, "You are the Son of G."	Rom	1:24	G handed them over to impurity
Lk	5:21	Who but G alone can forgive sins?"	Rom	1:26	G handed them over to degrading
Lk	8:39	recount what G has done for you."	Rom	2:11	There is no partiality with G.
Lk	9:20	said in reply, "The Messiah of G."	Rom	2:16	G will judge people's hidden works
Lk	10: 9	'The kingdom of G is at hand	Rom	3: 4	G must be true, though every
Lk	10:27	Lord, your G, with all your heart,	Rom	3:19	world stand accountable to G,
Lk	11:42	to judgment and to love for G.	Rom	3:23	and are deprived of the glory of G.
Lk	13:18	"What is the kingdom of G like?	Rom	3:29	Does G belong to Jews alone?
Lk	18:13	'O G, be merciful to me a sinner.'	Rom	4: 3	"Abraham believed G, and it was
Lk	18:19	No one is good but G alone.	Rom	4: 6	whom G credits righteousness apart
Lk	18:27	human beings is possible for G."	Rom	4:17	He is our father in the sight of G,
Lk	20:25	and to G what belongs to G."	Rom	5: 1	G through our Lord Jesus Christ,
Lk	20:37	he called 'Lord' the G of Abraham,	Rom	5: 8	But G proves his love for us
Lk	22:69	the right hand of the power of G."	Rom	6:22	sin and have become slaves of G,
Lk	22:70	"Are you then the Son of G?"	Rom	6:23	the gift of G is eternal life in Christ
Jn	1: 1	the Word was with G, and the Word was G.	Rom	7: 4	order that we might bear fruit for G.
Jn	1:12	power to become children of G,	Rom	8: 7	of the flesh is hostility toward G;
Jn	1:18	No one has ever seen G.	Rom	8: 7	it does not submit to the law of G,
Jn	1:18	The only Son, G, who is at the Father's	Rom	8: 8	are in the flesh cannot please G.
Jn	1:29	the Lamb of G, who takes away	Rom	8:17	heirs, heirs of G and joint heirs
Jn	1:49	him, "Rabbi, you are the Son of G;	Rom	8:28	for good for those who love G,
Jn	3: 2	are a teacher who has come from G,	Rom	8:31	If G is for us, who can be against
Jn	3:16	For G so loved the world that he	Rom	10: 9	in your heart that G raised him
Jn	3:34	one whom G sent speaks the words of G.	Rom	11: 2	G has not rejected his people whom
Jn	4:24	G is Spirit, and those who worship	Rom	11: 2	he pleads with G against Israel?
Jn	5:18	but he also called G his own father, making himself equal to G.	Rom	11:22	the kindness and severity of G:
			Rom	11:32	For G delivered all to disobedience,
Jn	5:44	praise that comes from the only G?	Rom	13: 1	there is no authority except from G,
Jn	6:29	"This is the work of G, that you	Rom	13: 1	exist have been established by G.
Jn	6:33	For the bread of G is	Rom	14:12	give an account of himself [to G].
Jn	6:69	that you are the Holy One of G."	Rom	16:20	the G of peace will quickly crush
Jn	7:17	whether my teaching is from G	1 Cor	1:18	are being saved it is the power of G.
Jn	8:42	"If G were your Father, you would	1 Cor	1:20	Has not G made the wisdom
Jn	8:42	for I came from G and am here;	1 Cor	1:24	Christ the power of G and the wisdom of G.
Jn	8:47	belongs to G hears the words of G;	1 Cor	1:27	G chose the foolish of the world
Jn	8:47	because you do not belong to G."	1 Cor	1:27	G chose the weak of the world
Jn	11:40	you will see the glory of G?"	1 Cor	2: 9	what G has prepared for those who
Jn	13: 3	that he had come from G and was returning to G,	1 Cor	2:11	pertains to G except the Spirit of G.
Jn	13:31	glorified, and G is glorified in him.	1 Cor	3: 6	watered, but G caused the growth.
Jn	14: 1	You have faith in G; have faith	1 Cor	3:16	know that you are the temple of G,
Jn	17: 3	the only true G, and the one whom	1 Cor	3:16	that the Spirit of G dwells in you?
Jn	20:17	Father, to my G and your G.' "	1 Cor	3:17	temple, G will destroy that person;

1 Cor	3:17	for the temple of **G**, which you are,
1 Cor	6:20	Therefore, glorify **G** in your body.
1 Cor	7: 7	each has a particular gift from **G**,
1 Cor	7:15	**G** has called you to peace.
1 Cor	8: 3	But if one loves **G**, one is known
1 Cor	8: 8	food will not bring us closer to **G**.
1 Cor	10:13	**G** is faithful and will not let you be
1 Cor	10:31	do, do everything for the glory of **G**.
1 Cor	12:24	**G** has so constructed the body as
1 Cor	14:25	so he will fall down and worship **G**,
1 Cor	14:25	"**G** is really in your midst."
1 Cor	14:33	since he is not the **G** of disorder
1 Cor	15:24	he hands over the kingdom to his **G**
1 Cor	15:28	to him, so that **G** may be all in all.
1 Cor	15:34	For some have no knowledge of **G**;
2 Cor	1: 9	but in **G** who raises the dead.
2 Cor	2:14	But thanks be to **G**, who always
2 Cor	3: 5	our qualification comes from **G**,
2 Cor	4: 2	or falsifying the word of **G**,
2 Cor	4: 4	in whose case the **g** of this age has
2 Cor	4: 4	of Christ, who is the image of **G**.
2 Cor	4: 7	the surpassing power may be of **G**
2 Cor	5: 5	prepared us for this very thing is **G**,
2 Cor	5:19	**G** was reconciling the world
2 Cor	5:20	as if **G** were appealing through us.
2 Cor	5:20	behalf of Christ, be reconciled to **G**.
2 Cor	5:21	become the righteousness of **G**
2 Cor	6:16	we are the temple of the living **G**;
2 Cor	9: 7	for **G** loves a cheerful giver.
2 Cor	10:13	to the limits **G** has apportioned us,
Gal	2: 6	**G** shows no partiality)—
Gal	6: 7	**G** is not mocked, for a person will
Eph	2: 8	is not from you; it is the gift of **G**;
Eph	2:10	the good works that **G** has prepared
Eph	2:22	a dwelling place of **G** in the Spirit.
Eph	4: 6	one **G** and Father of all, who is over
Eph	5: 1	So be imitators of **G**, as beloved
Eph	6: 6	doing the will of **G** from the heart,
Phil	2: 6	though he was in the form of **G**,
Phil	2: 6	regard equality with **G** something
Phil	2: 9	**G** greatly exalted him and bestowed
Phil	2:13	For **G** is the one who, for his good
Phil	3:19	Their **G** is their stomach;
Phil	4: 7	the peace of **G** that surpasses all
Phil	4:19	My **G** will fully supply whatever
Col	3: 1	is seated at the right hand of **G**.
1 Thes	2: 4	as we were judged worthy by **G**
1 Thes	2: 4	but rather **G**, who judges our hearts.
1 Thes	4: 7	For **G** did not call us to impurity
1 Thes	4: 9	yourselves have been taught by **G**
1 Thes	5: 9	For **G** did not destine us for wrath,
2 Thes	1: 8	on those who do not acknowledge **G**
1 Tm	1:17	the only **G**, honor and glory forever
1 Tm	2: 5	For there is one **G**. There is also one mediator between **G**
1 Tm	4: 4	everything created by **G** is good,
2 Tm	1: 6	flame the gift of **G** that you have
Ti	1: 2	in the hope of eternal life that **G**,
Ti	2:13	of the glory of the great **G**
Heb	1: 1	**G** spoke in partial and various ways
Heb	3: 4	but the founder of all is **G**.
Heb	4: 4	**G** rested on the seventh day from all
Heb	4:12	Indeed, the word of **G** is living
Heb	6:10	For **G** is not unjust so as to overlook
Heb	6:18	which it was impossible for **G** to lie,
Heb	7:19	through which we draw near to **G**.
Heb	7:25	those who approach **G** through him,
Heb	10: 7	I come to do your will, O **G**.' "
Heb	10:31	to fall into the hands of the living **G**.
Heb	11: 5	no more because **G** had taken him."
Heb	11: 5	he was attested to have pleased **G**.
Heb	11: 6	who approaches **G** must believe
Heb	11:16	**G** is not ashamed to be called their **G**,
Heb	12: 7	**G** treats you as sons.
Heb	12:29	For our **G** is a consuming fire.
Heb	13:15	let us continually offer **G** a sacrifice
Jas	1:13	say, "I am being tempted by **G**";
Jas	1:13	for **G** is not subject to temptation
Jas	1:27	undefiled before **G** and the Father is
Jas	2:19	You believe that **G** is one.
Jas	2:23	"Abraham believed **G**, and it was
Jas	2:23	he was called "the friend of **G**."
Jas	4: 4	of the world means enmity with **G**?
Jas	4: 6	"**G** resists the proud, but gives
Jas	4: 8	Draw near to **G**, and he will draw
1 Pt	1:21	him believe in **G** who raised him
1 Pt	1:21	so that your faith and hope are in **G**.
1 Pt	1:23	the living and abiding word of **G**,
1 Pt	3:18	that he might lead you to **G**.
1 Pt	4: 2	human desires, but on the will of **G**.
1 Pt	4:11	let it be with the words of **G**;
1 Pt	4:11	that in all things **G** may be glorified
1 Pt	4:17	to begin with the household of **G**;
1 Pt	4:17	who fail to obey the gospel of **G**?
1 Pt	5: 5	"**G** opposes the proud but bestows
2 Pt	1:21	spoke under the influence of **G**.
2 Pt	2: 4	if **G** did not spare the angels
1 Jn	1: 5	**G** is light, and in him there is no
1 Jn	2:14	and the word of **G** remains in you,
1 Jn	2:17	does the will of **G** remains forever.
1 Jn	3: 1	we may be called the children of **G**.
1 Jn	3: 9	who is begotten by **G** commits sin,
1 Jn	3: 9	sin because he is begotten by **G**.
1 Jn	3:10	the children of **G** and the children
1 Jn	3:10	to act in righteousness belongs to **G**,
1 Jn	3:20	for **G** is greater than our hearts
1 Jn	4: 2	how you can know the Spirit of **G**:
1 Jn	4: 2	come in the flesh belongs to **G**,
1 Jn	4: 7	one another, because love is of **G**;
1 Jn	4: 7	is begotten by **G** and knows **G**.
1 Jn	4: 8	is without love does not know **G**, for **G** is love.
1 Jn	4: 9	this way the love of **G** was revealed
1 Jn	4: 9	**G** sent his only Son into the world
1 Jn	4:11	if **G** so loved us, we also must love
1 Jn	4:12	No one has ever seen **G**. Yet, if we love one another, **G** remains in us,
1 Jn	4:15	that Jesus is the Son of **G**, **G** remains in him and he in **G**.
1 Jn	4:16	**G** is love, and whoever remains in love remains in **G**
1 Jn	4:20	"I love **G**," but hates his brother,
1 Jn	4:20	seen cannot love **G** whom he has
1 Jn	5: 2	that we love the children of **G** when we love **G**
1 Jn	5: 3	For the love of **G** is this, that we
1 Jn	5: 4	begotten by **G** conquers the world.
1 Jn	5:10	**G** has this testimony within himself.
1 Jn	5:11	**G** gave us eternal life, and this life
1 Jn	5:18	that no one begotten by **G** sins;
1 Jn	5:18	the one begotten by **G** he protects,
2 Jn	1: 9	of the Christ does not have **G**;
3 Jn	1:11	Whoever does what is good is of **G**;
3 Jn	1:11	does what is evil has never seen **G**.
Jude	1: 4	grace of our **G** into licentiousness
Jude	1:21	Keep yourselves in the love of **G**
Rev	2:18	" 'The Son of **G**, whose eyes are
Rev	3: 1	one who has the seven spirits of **G**
Rev	4: 5	which are the seven spirits of **G**.
Rev	4: 8	holy is the Lord **G** almighty,
Rev	6: 9	witness they bore to the word of **G**.
Rev	7: 2	holding the seal of the living **G**.
Rev	7:10	"Salvation comes from our **G**,
Rev	7:12	might be to our **G** forever and ever.
Rev	7:17	**G** will wipe away every tear
Rev	11:16	on their thrones before **G** prostrated themselves and worshiped **G**
Rev	12: 5	Her child was caught up to **G**
Rev	13: 6	to utter blasphemies against **G**,
Rev	14: 7	voice, "Fear **G** and give him glory,
Rev	15: 3	are your works, Lord **G** almighty.
Rev	15: 7	gold bowls filled with the fury of **G**,
Rev	16:14	on the great day of **G** the almighty.
Rev	17:17	For **G** has put it into their minds
Rev	17:17	the words of **G** are accomplished.
Rev	18:20	For **G** has judged your case against

Rev	19: 1	glory, and might belong to our **G**,
Rev	19: 6	his reign, [our] **G**, the almighty.
Rev	19: 9	words are true; they come from **G**."
Rev	19:13	his name was called the Word of **G**.
Rev	21: 3	**G** himself will always be with them [as their **G**].
Rev	21:11	It gleamed with the splendor of **G**.
Rev	21:23	for the glory of **G** gave it light,
Rev	22: 5	for the Lord **G** shall give them light,

*GOD → *LORD [This is the proper name of God, *Yahweh*, and is GOD in the NAB.]

Gn	15: 2	"Lord **G**, what can you give me,
Jgs	6:22	Lord **G**, that I have seen
Jgs	16:28	and said, "Lord **G**, remember me!
2 Sm	7:18	I, Lord **G**, and what is my house,
Ps	71:16	O **G**, I will tell of your singular
Ps	73:28	to make the Lord **G** my refuge.
Is	25: 8	The Lord **G** will wipe away
Is	40:10	comes with power the Lord **G**,
Is	50: 9	See, the Lord **G** is my help;
Is	61: 1	spirit of the Lord **G** is upon me,
Is	61:11	So will the Lord **G** make justice
Jer	32:17	Ah, my Lord **G**! You made
Hb	3:19	**G**, my Lord, is my strength;
Zep	1: 7	in the presence of the Lord **G**!

GOD'S → GOD

2 Chr	20:15	for the battle is not yours but **G**.
1 Cor	2: 7	we speak **G** wisdom, mysterious,
1 Cor	3: 9	For we are **G** co-workers; you are **G** field, **G** building.
1 Cor	9:21	though I am not outside **G** law
2 Tm	2:19	**G** solid foundation stands,
Ti	1: 7	For a bishop as **G** steward must be
Heb	4:10	And whoever enters into **G** rest,
1 Pt	2:10	people" but now you are **G** people;
1 Jn	3: 2	Beloved, we are **G** children now;
Rev	3:14	the source of **G** creation, says this:
Rev	11:19	**G** temple in heaven was opened,
Rev	14:10	will also drink the wine of **G** fury,

GOD-FEARING → FEAR, GOD

Jdt	11:17	Your servant is, indeed, a **G** woman,
Jb	1: 9	"Is it for nothing that Job is **G**?
Acts	10:22	an upright and **G** man,

GODDESS → GOD

1 Kgs	11: 5	Astarte, the **g** of the Sidonians,
1 Kgs	11:33	down to Astarte, **g** of the Sidonians,
2 Mc	1:13	of the **g** Nanea through a deceitful
Acts	19:27	of the great **g** Artemis will be of no
Acts	19:37	nor have they insulted our **g**.

GODLESS → GOD

Jb	8:13	so shall the hope of the **g** perish.
1 Tm	1: 9	lawless and unruly, the **g** and sinful,
2 Pt	3: 7	and of destruction of the **g**.

GODLINESS → GOD

2 Mc	12:45	those who had gone to rest in **g**,

GODLY → GOD

Sir	27:11	conversation of the **g** is always wisdom,
Sir	44: 1	I will now praise the **g**,
Sir	44:10	Yet these also were **g**;
Mal	2:15	does the One require? **G** offspring!
2 Cor	7: 9	for you were saddened in a **g** way,
2 Cor	7:10	For **g** sorrow produces a salutary
2 Cor	7:11	what earnestness this **g** sorrow has

GODS → GOD

Gn	35: 4	They gave Jacob all the foreign **g**
Ex	12:12	judgment on all the **g** of Egypt—
Ex	15:11	Who is like you among the **g**,
Ex	20: 3	shall not have other **g** beside me.
Dt	5: 7	shall not have other **g** beside me.
Dt	7:25	images of their **g** you shall destroy
Dt	13: 3	"Let us go after other **g**,"
Jos	24:14	the **g** your ancestors served beyond
Jgs	2:17	themselves by following other **g**,
1 Sm	4: 7	out, "**G** have come to their camp.
1 Sm	17:43	the Philistine cursed David by his **g**

1 Kgs	20:23	"Their **g** are mountain **g**.
2 Kgs	17: 7	They venerated other **g**,
1 Chr	16:26	the **g** of the nations all do nothing,
2 Chr	2: 4	our God is greater than all other **g**.
Jdt	3: 8	to destroy all the **g** of the land,
Est	C:18	because we worshiped their **g**.
1 Mc	5:68	burned the carved images of their **g**;
Ps	82: 6	"**G** though you be,
Ps	89: 7	LORD among the sons of the **g**?
Ps	97: 7	all **g** bow down before him.
Ps	135: 5	that our Lord is greater than all **g**.
Ps	136: 2	Praise the God of **g**; for his mercy
Wis	12:24	error, taking for **g** the worthless
Is	8:19	not a people inquire of their **g**,
Jer	2:11	even though they are not **g** at all!
Jer	10:11	The **g** that did not make heaven
Jer	16:20	make for themselves **g**? But these are not **g** at all!
Dn	5: 4	they praised their **g** of gold
Zep	2:11	he makes all the **g** of earth waste
Jn	10:34	your law, 'I said, "You are **g**" '?
Acts	19:26	saying that **g** made by hands are not **g** at all.
1 Cor	8: 5	even though there are so-called **g**

GOES → GO

Nm	5:12	If a man's wife **g** astray
Prv	16:18	Pride **g** before disaster,
Is	42:13	The LORD **g** forth like a warrior,
Mt	26:24	The Son of Man indeed **g**, as it is
Rev	14: 4	follow the Lamb wherever he **g**.

GOG

Ez	38: 2	turn your face against **G** of the land
Ez	38:18	day, the day **G** invades the land
Rev	20: 8	corners of the earth, **G** and Magog,

GOING → GO

Jn	8:21	Where I am **g** you cannot come."
Jn	13:36	to him, "Master, where are you **g**?"
Jn	16:10	because I am **g** to the Father

GOLAN

Dt	4:43	and **G** in Bashan for the Manassites.

GOLD → GOLDEN, GOLDSMITH, GOLDSMITHS

Ex	3:22	in her house for silver and **g** articles
Ex	12:35	Egyptians for articles of silver and **g**
Ex	20:23	you make for yourselves gods of **g**.
Ex	25:17	shall then make a cover of pure **g**,
Ex	25:31	make a menorah of pure beaten **g**—
Ex	28: 6	ephod they shall make of **g** thread
Ex	32:31	making a god of **g** for themselves!
Dt	17:17	a vast amount of silver and **g**.
Jos	7:21	a bar of **g** fifty shekels in weight;
1 Kgs	6:21	sanctuary, and covered it with **g**.
1 Kgs	20: 3	'Your silver and **g** are mine,
2 Chr	9:13	The **g** that came to Solomon in one
2 Chr	9:13	six hundred and sixty-six **g** talents,
Ezr	1: 6	in every way, with silver, **g**, goods,
Tb	12: 8	to give alms than to store up **g**,
1 Mc	1:23	he took away the silver and **g**
Jb	22:25	Almighty himself shall be your **g**
Jb	23:10	me, I should come forth like **g**.
Jb	28:15	Solid **g** cannot purchase her, nor can
Jb	31:24	Had I put my trust in **g** or called
Ps	19:11	More desirable than **g**, than a hoard
Ps	115: 4	Their idols are silver and **g**,
Ps	119:127	your commandments more than **g**,
Prv	3:14	and better than **g** is her revenue;
Prv	8:19	My fruit is better than **g**, even pure
Prv	22: 1	and high esteem, than **g** and silver.
Wis	3: 6	As **g** in the furnace, he proved them,
Sir	2: 5	For in fire **g** is tested,
Sir	30:15	have bodily health than any **g**,
Sir	31: 5	The lover of **g** will not be free
Is	60:17	Instead of bronze I will bring **g**,
Dn	2:32	Its head was pure **g**, its chest
Hg	2: 8	Mine is the silver and mine the **g**—
Zec	4: 2	"I see a lampstand all of **g**,
Zec	6:11	You will take silver and **g**,

Mt	2:11	treasures and offered him gifts of **g**,
Acts	3: 6	"I have neither silver nor **g**,
1 Pt	1: 7	faith, more precious than **g** that is
Rev	3:18	to buy from me **g** refined by fire so
Rev	9: 7	wore what looked like crowns of **g**;
Rev	21:18	while the city was pure **g**, clear as
Rev	21:21	the street of the city was of pure **g**,

GOLDEN → GOLD

1 Mc	1:21	sanctuary and took away the **g** altar,
Eccl	12: 6	is snapped and the **g** bowl is broken,
Dn	3: 5	worship the **g** statue which King

GOLDSMITH → GOLD

Is	46: 6	They hire a **g** to make it into a god

GOLDSMITHS → GOLD

Bar	6:45	produced by woodworkers and **g**;

GOLGOTHA

Mt	27:33	to a place called **G** (which means
Mk	15:22	the place of **G** (which is translated
Jn	19:17	Place of the Skull, in Hebrew, **G**.

GOLIATH

Philistine giant killed by David (1 Sm 17; 21:9; Sir 47:4).

GOMER

Hos	1: 3	So he went and took **G**,

GOMORRAH

Gn	13:10	had destroyed Sodom and **G**.
Gn	18:20	against Sodom and **G** is so great,
Gn	19:24	down sulfur upon Sodom and **G**,
Dt	29:22	the catastrophe of Sodom and **G**,
Is	1: 9	Sodom, would have resembled **G**.
Jer	23:14	like Sodom, its inhabitants like **G**.
Mt	10:15	**G** on the day of judgment than
Rom	9:29	and have been made like **G**."
Jude	1: 7	Sodom, **G**, and the surrounding

GONE → GO

Is	53: 6	We had all **g** astray like sheep,
Mk	5:30	once that power had **g** out from him,
1 Pt	3:22	who has **g** into heaven and is
1 Jn	4: 1	because many false prophets have **g**
2 Jn	1: 7	Many deceivers have **g**

GONG

1 Cor	13: 1	I am a resounding **g** or a clashing

GOOD → BEST, BETTER, GOODNESS, GOODS

Gn	1: 4	God saw that the light was **g**.
Gn	1:10	God saw that it was **g**.
Gn	1:12	its seed in it. God saw that it was **g**.
Gn	1:18	God saw that it was **g**.
Gn	1:21	God saw that it was **g**,
Gn	1:25	God saw that it was **g**.
Gn	1:31	he had made, and found it very **g**.
Gn	2: 9	delightful to look at and **g** for food,
Gn	2: 9	the tree of the knowledge of **g**
Gn	2:17	except the tree of knowledge of **g**
Gn	2:18	It is not **g** for the man to be alone.
Gn	3: 6	saw that the tree was **g** for food
Gn	3:22	like one of us, knowing **g** and evil!
Gn	50:20	God meant it for **g**, to achieve this
Ex	3: 8	lead them up from that land into a **g**
Dt	6:18	enter in and possess the **g** land
Dt	30:15	I have today set before you life and **g**,
Jos	23:15	to exterminate you from this **g** land
1 Sm	16:12	a youth with beautiful eyes, and **g** looking.
1 Sm	25:21	He has repaid **g** with evil.
2 Sm	14:17	angel of God, discerning **g** and evil.
2 Chr	7: 3	"who is so **g**, whose love endures
2 Chr	31:20	He did what was **g**, upright,
Neh	9:20	Your **g** spirit you bestowed
Tb	8: 6	'It is not **g** for the man to be alone;
1 Mc	4:24	"who is **g**, whose mercy endures
Jb	2:10	We accept **g** things from God;
Ps	34: 9	Taste and see that the LORD is **g**;
Ps	34:15	Turn from evil and do **g**;
Ps	37: 3	do **g** that you may dwell in the land

Ps	37:27	Turn from evil and do **g**, that you
Ps	52:11	for it is **g**,—in the presence of those
Ps	73: 1	How **g** God is to the upright,
Ps	84:12	The LORD withholds no **g** thing
Ps	103: 5	Who fills your days with **g** things,
Ps	109: 5	They repay me evil for **g**,
Ps	119:68	You are **g** and do what is **g**;
Ps	133: 1	How **g** and how pleasant it is,
Ps	145: 9	The LORD is **g** to all,
Ps	147: 1	How **g** to sing praise to our God;
Prv	11:27	Those who seek the **g** seek favor,
Prv	13:22	The **g** leave an inheritance to their
Prv	14:22	But those who plan **g** win steadfast
Prv	15: 3	keeping watch on the evil and the **g**.
Prv	15:23	a word in season, how **g** it is!
Prv	15:30	**g** news invigorates the bones.
Prv	19: 2	Desire without knowledge is not **g**;
Prv	22: 1	A **g** name is more desirable than
Eccl	12:14	hidden qualities, whether **g** or bad.
Sir	2: 9	hope for **g** things, for lasting joy
Sir	12: 1	If you do **g**, know for whom you are
Sir	26: 3	A **g** wife is a generous gift
Sir	39:27	For the **g** all these are **g**,
Sir	41:13	The **g** things of life last a number
Is	5:20	Those who call evil **g**, and **g** evil,
Is	40: 9	mountain, Zion, herald of **g** news!
Is	40: 9	voice, Jerusalem, herald of **g** news!
Is	52: 7	the feet of the one bringing **g** news,
Jer	6:16	of old, "Which is the way to **g**?"
Jer	13:23	As easily would you be able to do **g**,
Jer	32:39	for their own **g** and the **g** of their
Lam	3:26	It is **g** to hope in silence
Ez	34:14	In **g** pastures I will pasture them;
Dn	3:99	It has seemed **g** to me to publish
Hos	8: 3	But Israel has rejected what is **g**;
Am	5:14	Seek **g** and not evil, that you may
Mi	6: 8	what is **g**, and what the LORD
Na	2: 1	the footsteps of one bearing **g** news,
Mt	5:13	It is no longer **g** for anything
Mt	5:45	his sun rise on the bad and the **g**,
Mt	7:11	know how to give **g** gifts to your
Mt	7:11	your heavenly Father give **g** things
Mt	7:17	Just so, every **g** tree bears **g** fruit,
Mt	12:35	A **g** person brings forth **g**
Mt	13:24	to a man who sowed **g** seed in his
Mt	13:48	down to put what is **g** into buckets.
Mt	25:21	done, my **g** and faithful servant.
Mk	3: 4	to do **g** on the sabbath rather than
Mk	10:18	"Why do you call me **g**? No one is **g** but God alone.
Lk	2:10	I proclaim to you **g** news of great
Lk	3: 9	does not produce **g** fruit will be cut
Lk	6:27	do **g** to those who hate you,
Lk	6:35	love your enemies and do **g** to them,
Lk	6:43	"A **g** tree does not bear rotten fruit,
Lk	6:43	nor does a rotten tree bear **g** fruit.
Lk	7:22	poor have the **g** news proclaimed
Lk	8: 8	And some seed fell on **g** soil,
Lk	14:34	"Salt is **g**, but if salt itself loses its
Lk	18:19	"Why do you call me **g**? No one is **g** but God alone.
Lk	19:17	He replied, 'Well done, **g** servant!
Jn	1:46	to him, "Can anything **g** come
Jn	2:10	him, "Everyone serves **g** wine first,
Jn	2:10	have kept his **g** wine until now."
Jn	10:11	I am the **g** shepherd. A **g** shepherd
Jn	10:14	I am the **g** shepherd, and I know
Acts	8:12	Philip as he preached the **g** news
Rom	7:12	is holy and righteous and **g**.
Rom	7:16	not want, I concur that the law is **g**.
Rom	7:18	I know that **g** does not dwell in me,
Rom	8:28	all things work for **g** for those who
Rom	10:15	of those who bring [the] **g** news!"
Rom	12: 2	what is **g** and pleasing and perfect.
Rom	12: 9	what is evil, hold on to what is **g**;
Rom	12:21	by evil but conquer evil with **g**.
Rom	13: 4	for it is a servant of God for your **g**.
Rom	16:19	want you to be wise as to what is **g**,

1 Cor 15:33 "Bad company corrupts **g** morals."
2 Cor 9: 8 an abundance for every **g** work.
Gal 6:10 the opportunity, let us do **g** to all,
Eph 2:10 in Christ Jesus for the **g** works
Eph 6: 8 the Lord for whatever **g** he does,
Phil 1: 6 the one who began a **g** work in you
Phil 2:13 for his **g** purpose, works in you both
Col 1:10 in every **g** work bearing fruit
1 Thes 5:21 Test everything; retain what is **g**,
2 Thes 2:17 strengthen them in every **g** deed
1 Tm 1: 5 from a pure heart, a **g** conscience,
1 Tm 1: 8 We know that the law is **g**,
1 Tm 1:18 them may you fight a **g** fight
1 Tm 4: 4 For everything created by God is **g**,
1 Tm 6:18 Tell them to do **g**, to be rich in **g** works,
2 Tm 2: 3 me like a **g** soldier of Christ Jesus.
2 Tm 3:17 equipped for every **g** work.
Ti 2: 3 to drink, teaching what is **g**,
Ti 2: 7 yourself as a model of **g** deeds
Ti 2:14 as his own, eager to do what is **g**.
Heb 5:14 are trained by practice to discern **g**
Heb 10: 1 has only a shadow of the **g** things
Heb 10:24 one another to love and **g** works.
Heb 13:16 Do not neglect to do **g** and to share
1 Pt 2: 3 you have tasted that the Lord is **g**.
1 Pt 3:17 For it is better to suffer for doing **g**,
3 Jn 1: 2 in every respect and are in **g** health,
3 Jn 1:11 do not imitate evil but imitate **g**.
3 Jn 1:11 Whoever does what is **g** is of God;

GOODNESS → GOOD

Ps 23: 6 **g** and mercy will pursue me all
Ps 27:13 I believe I shall see the LORD's **g**
Ti 1: 8 hospitable, a lover of **g**, temperate,

GOODS → GOOD

Prv 3:27 Do not withhold any **g** from the owner
Sir 34:21 Ill-gotten **g** offered in sacrifice are tainted.

GOPHERWOOD

Gn 6:14 Make yourself an ark of **g**,

GORGED

Rev 19:21 all the birds **g** themselves on their

GORGIAS

1 Mc 4: 1 Now **G** took five thousand infantry
1 Mc 5:59 But **G** and his men came

GOSHEN

Gn 45:10 You can settle in the region of **G**,
Ex 8:18 make an exception of the land of **G**,

GOSPEL

Mk 8:35 sake and that of the **g** will save it.
Rom 1: 1 and set apart for the **g** of God,
Rom 1:16 For I am not ashamed of the **g**.
Rom 15:16 the priestly service of the **g** of God,
1 Cor 1:17 me to baptize but to preach the **g**,
1 Cor 9:12 place an obstacle to the **g** of Christ.
1 Cor 9:14 those who preach the **g** should live by the **g**.
1 Cor 9:16 If I preach the **g**, this is no reason
2 Cor 4: 3 And even though our **g** is veiled,
2 Cor 4: 4 not see the light of the **g** of the glory
2 Cor 9:13 confession of the **g** of Christ
2 Cor 11: 4 or a different **g** from the one you
Gal 1: 6 grace [of Christ] for a different **g**
Eph 1:13 of truth, the **g** of your salvation,
Eph 3: 6 in Christ Jesus through the **g**,
Eph 6:15 shod in readiness for the **g** of peace.
Phil 1: 7 defense and confirmation of the **g**.
Phil 1:27 in a way worthy of the **g** of Christ,
Col 1:23 the hope of the **g** that you heard,
1 Thes 2: 4 by God to be entrusted with the **g**,
2 Thes 1: 8 those who do not obey the **g** of our
2 Tm 1: 8 hardship for the **g** with the strength
Phlm 1:13 in my imprisonment for the **g**,
1 Pt 4: 6 this is why the **g** was preached even

GOSSIP → GOSSIPS

Sir 19: 6 and whoever repeats **g** has no sense.

2 Cor 12:20 selfishness, slander, **g**, conceit,

GOSSIPS → GOSSIP

Sir 28:13 Cursed be **g**
Rom 1:29 treachery, and spite. They are **g**
1 Tm 5:13 not only idlers but **g** and busybodies

GOURDS

1 Kgs 6:18 house was carved in the form of **g**
2 Kgs 4:39 a sackful of poisonous wild **g**.

GOVERN → GOVERNOR, GOVERNORS

2 Chr 1:10 wisdom and knowledge to **g** this people,

GOVERNOR → GOVERN

Gn 42: 6 Joseph, as **g** of the country,
Neh 5:14 King Artaxerxes appointed me **g**
Neh 12:26 in the time of Nehemiah the **g**
Hg 2:21 to Zerubbabel, the **g** of Judah:
Mal 1: 8 Present it to your **g**! Will he be
Mt 27: 2 handed him over to Pilate, the **g**.
Lk 3: 1 when Pontius Pilate was **g** of Judea,

GOVERNORS → GOVERN

Mk 13: 9 You will be arraigned before **g**

GRACE → GRACIOUS

Wis 3: 9 Because **g** and mercy are with his
Jn 1:14 only Son, full of **g** and truth.
Jn 1:16 have all received, **g** in place of **g**,
Jn 1:17 **g** and truth came through Jesus
Acts 6: 8 Stephen, filled with **g** and power,
Acts 11:23 he arrived and saw the **g** of God,
Acts 13:43 to remain faithful to the **g** of God.
Acts 14: 3 word about his **g** by granting signs
Acts 14:26 been commended to the **g** of God
Acts 15:11 we are saved through the **g**
Acts 15:40 by the brothers to the **g** of the Lord.
Acts 18:27 who had come to believe through **g**.
Acts 20:24 witness to the gospel of God's **g**.
Rom 1: 5 him we have received the **g**
Rom 1: 7 **G** to you and peace from God our
Rom 3:24 by his **g** through the redemption
Rom 5: 2 [faith] to this **g** in which we stand,
Rom 5:15 how much more did the **g** of God
Rom 5:17 who receive the abundance of **g**
Rom 5:20 **g** overflowed all the more,
Rom 5:21 in death, **g** also might reign through
Rom 6: 1 we persist in sin that **g** may abound?
Rom 6:14 are not under the law but under **g**.
Rom 6:15 are not under the law but under **g**?
Rom 11: 5 there is a remnant, chosen by **g**.
Rom 11: 6 otherwise **g** would no longer be **g**.
Rom 12: 3 by the **g** given to me I tell everyone
Rom 12: 6 differ according to the **g** given to us,
Rom 15:15 because of the **g** given me by God
Rom 16:20 The **g** of our Lord Jesus be
1 Cor 1: 3 **G** to you and peace from God our
1 Cor 1: 4 account for the **g** of God bestowed
1 Cor 3:10 According to the **g** of God given
1 Cor 15:10 But by the **g** of God I am what I am,
1 Cor 15:10 his **g** to me has not been ineffective.
1 Cor 16:23 The **g** of the Lord Jesus be
2 Cor 1: 2 **g** to you and peace from God our
2 Cor 1:12 human wisdom but by the **g** of God.
2 Cor 4:15 so that the **g** bestowed in abundance
2 Cor 6: 1 to you not to receive the **g** of God
2 Cor 8: 1 of the **g** of God that has been given
2 Cor 9:14 because of the surpassing **g** of God
2 Cor 12: 9 to me, "My **g** is sufficient for you,
2 Cor 13:13 The **g** of the Lord Jesus Christ
Gal 1: 3 **g** to you and peace from God our
Gal 1: 6 called you by [the] **g** [of Christ]
Gal 1:15 apart and called me through his **g**,
Gal 2: 9 they recognized the **g** bestowed
Gal 2:21 I do not nullify the **g** of God;
Gal 5: 4 you have fallen from **g**.
Gal 6:18 The **g** of our Lord Jesus Christ be
Eph 1: 2 **g** to you and peace from God our
Eph 1: 6 the glory of his **g** that he granted us

Eph	1: 7	in accord with the riches of his **g**
Eph	2: 5	Christ (by **g** you have been saved),
Eph	2: 7	riches of his **g** in his kindness to us
Eph	2: 8	by **g** you have been saved through
Eph	3: 2	of God's **g** that was given to me
Eph	3: 7	gift of God's **g** that was granted me
Eph	3: 8	all the holy ones, this **g** was given,
Eph	4: 7	**g** was given to each of us according
Eph	4:29	it may impart **g** to those who hear.
Eph	6:24	**G** be with all who love our Lord
Phil	1: 2	**g** to you and peace from God our
Phil	1: 7	who are all partners with me in **g**,
Phil	4:23	The **g** of the Lord Jesus Christ be
Col	1: 2	**g** to you and peace from God our
Col	1: 6	came to know the **g** of God in truth,
Col	4:18	**G** be with you.
1 Thes	1: 1	**g** to you and peace.
1 Thes	5:28	The **g** of our Lord Jesus Christ be
2 Thes	1: 2	**g** to you and peace from God [our]
2 Thes	1:12	in accord with the **g** of our God
2 Thes	2:16	and good hope through his **g**,
2 Thes	3:18	The **g** of our Lord Jesus Christ be
1 Tm	1: 2	**g**, mercy, and peace from God
1 Tm	1:14	Indeed, the **g** of our Lord has been
1 Tm	6:21	from the faith. **G** be with all of you.
2 Tm	1: 2	**g**, mercy, and peace from God
2 Tm	1: 9	the **g** bestowed on us in Christ Jesus
2 Tm	2: 1	be strong in the **g** that is in Christ
2 Tm	4:22	**G** be with all of you.
Ti	1: 4	**g** and peace from God the Father
Ti	2:11	For the **g** of God has appeared,
Ti	3: 7	that we might be justified by his **g**
Ti	3:15	us in the faith. **G** be with all of you.
Phlm	1: 3	**G** to you and peace from God our
Phlm	1:25	The **g** of the Lord Jesus Christ be
Heb	2: 9	by the **g** of God he might taste death
Heb	4:16	confidently approach the throne of **g**
Heb	4:16	mercy and to find **g** for timely help.
Heb	10:29	and insults the spirit of **g**?
Heb	12:15	no one be deprived of the **g** of God,
Heb	13: 9	to have our hearts strengthened by **g**
Heb	13:25	**G** be with all of you.
Jas	4: 6	But he bestows a greater **g**;
Jas	4: 6	proud, but gives **g** to the humble."
1 Pt	1: 2	may **g** and peace be yours
1 Pt	1:10	who prophesied about the **g** that was
1 Pt	1:13	completely on the **g** to be brought
1 Pt	4:10	as good stewards of God's varied **g**.
1 Pt	5:10	The God of all **g** who called you
1 Pt	5:12	that this is the true **g** of God.
2 Pt	1: 2	may **g** and peace be yours
2 Pt	3:18	grow in **g** and in the knowledge
2 Jn	1: 3	**G**, mercy, and peace will be with us
Jude	1: 4	who pervert the **g** of our God
Rev	1: 4	**g** to you and peace from him who is
Rev	22:21	The **g** of the Lord Jesus be with all.

GRACEFUL

Prv	5:19	your lovely hind, your **g** doe.
Sir	24:16	my branches so glorious and so **g**.

GRACIOUS → GRACE

Gn	43:29	said to him, "May God be **g** to you,
Ex	34: 6	the LORD, a God **g** and merciful,
Nm	6:25	shine upon you, and be **g** to you!
Dt	7: 2	with them and do not be **g** to them.
Neh	9:17	are a forgiving God, **g** and merciful,
2 Mc	10:26	they begged him to be **g** to them,
2 Mc	14: 9	the same **g** consideration that you
Ps	26:11	redeem me, be **g** to me!
Ps	31:10	Be **g** to me, LORD, for I am
Ps	67: 2	May God be **g** to us and bless us;
Ps	86:15	are a compassionate and **g** God,
Ps	103: 8	Merciful and **g** is the LORD.
Ps	111: 4	**g** and merciful is the LORD.
Ps	112: 4	**g**, compassionate, and righteous.
Ps	116: 5	**G** is the LORD and righteous;

Ps	119:132	Turn to me and be **g**,
Ps	145: 8	The LORD is **g** and merciful,
Prv	11:16	A **g** woman gains esteem,
Sir	6: 5	and **g** lips, friendly greetings.
Is	30:19	He will be most **g** to you when you
Jl	2:13	your God, For he is **g** and merciful,
Jon	4: 2	I knew that you are a **g** and merciful
Mt	11:26	Father, such has been your **g** will.
Lk	4:22	and were amazed at the **g** words
Lk	10:21	Father, such has been your **g** will.
Col	4: 6	Let your speech always be **g**,

GRAFT → GRAFTED

Rom	11:23	for God is able to **g** them in again.

GRAFTED → GRAFT

Rom	11:17	were **g** in their place and have come

GRAIN → GRAINS

Gn	41: 5	He saw seven ears of **g**,
Gn	41:57	came to Egypt to Joseph to buy **g**,
Dt	25: 4	muzzle an ox when it treads out **g**.
Ru	2: 2	glean **g** in the field of anyone who
Jl	2:19	I am sending you **g**, new wine,
Mk	2:23	a path while picking the heads of **g**.
Lk	6: 1	were picking the heads of **g**,
1 Cor	9: 9	an ox while it is treading out the **g**."

GRAINS → GRAIN

Is	48:19	the offspring of your loins like its **g**,

GRANDCHILDREN → CHILD

1 Tm	5: 4	But if a widow has children or **g**,

GRANDMOTHER → MOTHER

2 Tm	1: 5	faith that first lived in your **g** Lois

GRANT → GRANTED

Ps	85: 8	**g** us your salvation.
Ps	140: 9	do not **g** the desires of the wicked
Sir	45:26	May he **g** you wisdom of heart

GRANTED → GRANT

1 Sm	1:27	child, and the LORD **g** my request.
Est	7: 2	ask, Queen Esther, shall be **g** you.
Prv	10:24	but the desire of the just will be **g**.
Jn	6:65	come to me unless it is **g** him by my
Phil	1:29	For to you has been **g**, for the sake

GRAPE → GRAPES, GRAPEVINE

Nm	6: 3	or any kind of **g** juice, nor eat either

GRAPES → GRAPE

Gn	40:11	so I took the **g**, pressed them
Nm	13:23	with a single cluster of **g** on it,
Dt	32:32	Their **g** are **g** of poison, and their
Is	5: 2	Then he waited for the crop of **g**, but it yielded rotten **g**.
Jer	31:29	"The parents ate unripe **g**,
Ez	18: 2	"Parents eat sour **g**,
Mi	6:15	oil, crush the **g**, yet drink no wine.
Mt	7:16	Do people pick **g** from thornbushes,
Rev	14:18	the earth's vines, for its **g** are ripe."

GRAPEVINE → GRAPE, VINE

Jas	3:12	brothers, produce olives, or a **g** figs?

GRASPED

Jgs	16:29	Samson **g** the two middle columns

GRASS

Ps	37: 2	Like **g** they wither quickly;
Ps	103:15	As for man, his days are like the **g**;
Ps	104:14	You make the **g** grow for the cattle
Prv	19:12	but his favor, like dew on the **g**.
Is	40: 6	"All flesh is **g**, and all their loyalty
Mt	6:30	If God so clothes the **g** of the field,
1 Pt	1:24	"All flesh is like **g**, and all its glory
1 Pt	1:24	the **g** withers, and the flower wilts;
Rev	8: 7	a third of the trees and all green **g**.

GRASSHOPPERS

Nm	13:33	own eyes we seemed like mere **g**,
Is	40:22	its inhabitants like **g**, Who stretches

GRATIFY
Gal   5:16 you will certainly not **g** the desire

GRATITUDE
Col   3:16 spiritual songs with **g** in your hearts

GRAVE → GRAVES
Nm   19:16 who touches a human bone or a **g**,
Ps   5:10 Their throat is an open **g**;
Ps   49:15 Straight to the **g** they descend,
Ps   88:12 Is your mercy proclaimed in the **g**,
Is   53: 9 was given a **g** among the wicked,

GRAVEL
Prv 20:17 afterward the mouth is filled with **g**.
Lam   3:16 He has made me eat **g**, trampled me

GRAVES → GRAVE
Ez   37:12 make you come up out of your **g**,
Lk   11:44 You are like unseen **g** over
Rom   3:13 Their throats are open **g**;

GRAY
Ps   71:18 Now that I am old and **g**, do not
Prv 16:31 **G** hair is a crown of glory;
Prv 20:29 and the dignity of the old is **g** hair.
Sir   6:18 when you have **g** hair you will find wisdom.

GREAT → GREATER, GREATEST, GREATNESS
Gn   1:16 God made the two **g** lights,
Gn   6: 5 LORD saw how **g** the wickedness
Gn   12: 2 I will make of you a **g** nation,
Gn   12: 2 I will make your name **g**,
Gn   15: 1 I will make your reward very **g**.
Gn   15:18 the Wadi of Egypt to the **G** River,
Gn   21:18 for I will make of him a **g** nation."
Gn   46: 3 for there I will make you a **g** nation.
Ex   32:10 Then I will make of you a **g** nation.
Ex   32:11 of the land of Egypt with **g** power
Dt   4:32 Did anything so **g** ever happen
Dt   7:21 midst, is a **g** and awesome God.
Dt 10:17 the Lord of lords, the **g** God,
Jos   7: 9 will you do for your **g** name?"
Jgs 16: 5 out where he gets his **g** strength,
2 Sm 7:22 Therefore, **g** are you, Lord GOD!
2 Sm 22:36 and your help has made me **g**.
1 Chr 16:25 For **g** is the LORD and highly
1 Chr 17:19 purpose, you have done this **g** thing.
Neh 1: 5 of heaven, **g** and awesome God,
Neh 8: 6 blessed the LORD, the **g** God,
Tb 11:14 May his **g** name be with us,
Jdt   2: 5 "Thus says the **g** king, the lord
Jdt 16:13 O Lord, **g** are you and glorious,
Jdt 16:16 one who fears the Lord is forever **g**.
1 Mc 4:25 Israel experienced a **g** deliverance
Ps 18:36 your favor made me **g**.
Ps 25:11 pardon my guilt, though it is **g**.
Ps 47: 3 feared, the **g** king over all the earth,
Ps 48: 3 of Zaphon, the city of the **g** king.
Ps 77:14 what god is as **g** as our God?
Ps 95: 3 For the LORD is the **g** God, the **g** king over all gods,
Ps 145: 3 **G** is the LORD and worthy
Prv 22: 1 is more desirable than **g** riches,
Sir 17:29 How **g** is the mercy of the Lord,
Sir 25:10 How **g** is the one who finds
Jer 10: 6 you are **g**, **g** and mighty is your
Jer 27: 5 the earth, by my **g** power, with my
Jer 32:19 **g** in counsel, mighty in deed,
Lam 3:23 **g** is your faithfulness!
Ez 17: 3 The **g** eagle, with wide wingspan
Dn 2:45 The **g** God has revealed to the king
Dn 9: 4 Lord, **g** and awesome God, you who
Dn 14:23 There was a **g** dragon
Jl   2:11 How **g** is the day of the LORD!
Jon 2: 1 the LORD sent a **g** fish to swallow Jonah,
Na   1: 3 is slow to anger, yet **g** in power;
Zep 1:14 Near is the **g** day of the LORD,
Mal 1:11 my name is **g** among the nations;
Mal 3:23 comes, the **g** and terrible day;
Mt   4:16 sit in darkness have seen a **g** light,

Mt 13:46 When he finds a pearl of **g** price,
Mt 20:26 to be **g** among you shall be your
Mk 13:26 coming in the clouds' with **g** power
Lk   2:10 you good news of **g** joy that will be
Lk   6:23 your reward will be **g** in heaven.
Lk   6:35 your reward will be **g** and you will
Lk 21:27 in a cloud with power and **g** glory.
Eph 1:19 with the exercise of his **g** might,
Eph 2: 4 because of the **g** love he had for us,
1 Tm 3:16 Undeniably **g** is the mystery
1 Tm 6: 6 with contentment is a **g** gain.
Ti   2:13 of the glory of the **g** God and of our
Heb 2: 3 if we ignore so **g** a salvation?
Heb 10:21 since we have "a **g** priest over
Heb 12: 1 we are surrounded by so **g** a cloud
Heb 13:20 the dead the **g** shepherd of the sheep
1 Pt 1: 3 in his **g** mercy gave us a new birth
Jude 1: 6 for the judgment of the **g** day.
Rev 6:17 because the **g** day of their wrath has
Rev 7:14 have survived the time of **g** distress;
Rev 14: 8 fallen is Babylon, the **g**, that made
Rev 16:14 the battle on the **g** day of God
Rev 17: 1 the **g** harlot who lives near the many
Rev 18:10 "Alas, alas, **g** city, Babylon,

GREATER → GREAT
Gn   1:16 lights, the **g** one to govern the day,
2 Chr 2: 4 for our God is **g** than all other gods.
Mt 11:11 there has been none **g** than John
Mt 12: 6 something **g** than the temple is here.
Mk 12:31 other commandment **g** than these."
Lk 11:31 there is something **g** than Solomon
Lk 11:32 and there is something **g** than Jonah
Jn   1:50 You will see **g** things than this."
Jn 14:12 I do, and will do **g** ones than these,
Jn 15:13 No one has **g** love than this, to lay
Jn 15:20 you, 'No slave is **g** than his master.'
Heb 11:26 of the Anointed **g** wealth than
1 Jn 3:20 for God is **g** than our hearts
1 Jn 4: 4 is in you is **g** than the one who is
1 Jn 5: 9 the testimony of God is surely **g**.

GREATEST → GREAT
2 Sm 7: 9 your name like that of the **g** on earth.
Mt 18: 4 himself like this child is the **g**
Mt 22:38 This is the **g** and the first
Mt 23:11 The **g** among you must be your
Lk   9:48 all of you is the one who is the **g**."
Lk 22:24 of them should be regarded as the **g**.
1 Cor 13:13 but the **g** of these is love.

GREATNESS → GREAT
Dt   3:24 to show to your servant your **g**
Dt 32: 3 LORD, praise the **g** of our God!
Ez 38:23 so I will show my **g** and holiness
Eph 1:19 and what is the surpassing **g** of his

GREECE → GREEK, GREEKS
1 Mc 1: 1 in his place, having first ruled in **G**.
Dn 10:20 I leave, the prince of **G** will come;

GREED → GREEDY
Lk 12:15 "Take care to guard against all **g**,
Eph 5: 3 or **g** must not even be mentioned
Col 3: 5 evil desire, and the **g** that is idolatry.
2 Pt 2: 3 In their **g** they will exploit you
2 Pt 2:14 and their hearts are trained in **g**.

GREEDY → GREED
Prv 1:19 This is the way of everyone **g** for loot:
Prv 15:27 The **g** tear down their own house,
Prv 28:25 The **g** person stirs up strife,
1 Cor 5:11 if he is immoral, **g**, an idolater,
1 Cor 6:10 thieves nor the **g** nor drunkards nor
Eph 5: 5 no immoral or impure or **g** person,
1 Tm 3: 8 to drink, not **g** for sordid gain,
Ti   1: 7 aggressive, not **g** for sordid gain,

GREEK → GREECE
2 Mc 4:10 his compatriots into the **G** way

Jn   19:20 written in Hebrew, Latin, and **G**.
Acts 16: 1 a believer, but his father was a **G**.
Acts 17:12 a few of the influential **G** women
Acts 21:37 He replied, "Do you speak **G**?
Rom   1:16 for Jew first, and then **G**.
Gal   3:28 There is neither Jew nor **G**, there is
Col   3:11 Here there is not **G** and Jew,

GREEKS → GREECE
1 Mc   6: 2 left there by the first king of the **G**,
Dn   8:21 The he-goat is the king of the **G**,
Jn   12:20 there were some **G** among those
Acts 18: 4 to convince both Jews and **G**.
Acts 20:21 and **G** to repentance before God
1 Cor 1:22 signs and **G** look for wisdom,
1 Cor 12:13 whether Jews or **G**, slaves or free

GREEN
Gn   1:30 I give all the **g** plants for food.
Gn   9: 3 them all to you as I did the **g** plants.
Ps   23: 2 In **g** pastures he makes me lie down;
Jer   17: 8 when it comes, its leaves stay **g**;
Mk   6:39 sit down in groups on the **g** grass.

GREET → GREETING, GREETINGS
Mt   5:47 And if you **g** your brothers only,
1 Cor 16:20 All the brothers **g** you. **G** one another with a holy kiss.

GREETING → GREET
Lk   1:29 what sort of **g** this might be.
1 Cor 16:21 write you this **g** in my own hand.
Col   4:18 The **g** is in my own hand, Paul's.
2 Thes 3:17 This **g** is in my own hand, Paul's.

GREETINGS → GREET
Mt   23: 7 **g** in marketplaces, and the salutation

GREW → GROW
Gn 21:20 God was with the boy as he **g** up.
Jgs 13:24 the boy **g** up the LORD blessed
1 Sm 2:21 while young Samuel **g**
1 Sm 3:19 Samuel **g** up, and the LORD was
2 Sm 3: 1 in which David **g** ever stronger,
Is   53: 2 He **g** up like a sapling before him,
Lk   1:80 The child **g** and became strong
Lk   2:40 the child **g** and became strong,

GRIEF → GRIEVE, GRIEVED, GRIEVOUS
Prv   10: 1 a foolish son is a **g** to his mother.
Jer   8:18 My joy is gone, **g** is upon me,

GRIEVE → GRIEF
Eph   4:30 And do not **g** the holy Spirit of God,
1 Thes 4:13 so that you may not **g** like the rest,

GRIEVED → GRIEF
Gn   6: 6 on the earth, and his heart was **g**.
Is   63:10 they rebelled and **g** his holy spirit;

GRIEVOUS → GRIEF
Eccl   5:12 This is a **g** evil which I have seen

GRIND → GRINDING
Jb   31:10 Then may my wife **g** for another,

GRINDING → GRIND
Is   3:15 and **g** down the faces of the poor?
Mt   8:12 will be wailing and **g** of teeth."
Mt 13:42 there will be wailing and **g** of teeth.
Mt 13:50 there will be wailing and **g** of teeth.
Mt 22:13 there will be wailing and **g** of teeth.'
Mt 24:51 there will be wailing and **g** of teeth.
Mt 25:30 there will be wailing and **g** of teeth.'
Lk 13:28 **g** of teeth when you see Abraham,
Lk 17:35 will be two women **g** meal together;

GROAN → GROANED, GROANING
Prv 29: 2 when the wicked rule, the people **g**.
Rom 8:23 **g** within ourselves as we wait
2 Cor 5: 2 For in this tent we **g**, longing to be
2 Cor 5: 4 For while we are in this tent we **g**

GROANED → GROAN
Ex   2:23 The Israelites **g** under their bondage

GROANING → GROAN
Ex   6: 5 I have heard the **g** of the Israelites,
Rom 8:22 all creation is **g** in labor pains even

GROPE
Dt   28:29 at midday you will **g** in the dark as
Is   59:10 who are blind we **g** along the wall,
Acts 17:27 even perhaps **g** for him and find

GROUND → GROUNDED, GROUNDS
Gn   2: 7 the man out of the dust of the **g**
Gn   3:17 it, Cursed is the **g** because of you!
Ex   3: 5 the place where you stand is holy **g**.
Jos   3:17 while all Israel crossed on dry **g**,
Jgs   6:37 while all the **g** is dry, I shall know
1 Sm 5: 3 face down on the **g** before the ark
2 Kgs 2: 8 two of them crossed over on dry **g**.
Ps   26:12 My foot stands on level **g**;
Ps 147: 6 poor, but casts the wicked to the **g**.
Mt 10:29 falls to the **g** without your Father's
Mt 13: 5 Some fell on rocky **g**, where it had
Mt 25:25 off and buried your talent in the **g**.
Mk   4:31 that, when it is sown in the **g**,
Lk 22:44 [like drops of blood falling on the **g**.]
Jn   8: 6 to write on the **g** with his finger.

GROUNDED → GROUND
Eph   3:17 that you, rooted and **g** in love,

GROUNDS → GROUND
Dn   6: 5 find **g** for accusation against Daniel

GROUP → GROUPS
2 Sm 2:13 one **g** on one side of the pool

GROUPS → GROUP
Mk   6:39 to have them sit down in **g**

GROVES
Dt   6:11 and olive **g** that you did not plant;

GROW → GREW, GROWING, GROWN, GROWTH
Gn   2: 9 the LORD God made **g** every tree
Nm   6: 5 the hair of their heads **g** freely.
Jgs 16:22 began to **g** as soon as it was shaved.
Ps 92:13 tree, shall **g** like a cedar of Lebanon.
Ez 47:12 river every kind of fruit tree will **g**;
Mt   6:28 from the way the wild flowers **g**.
Eph   4:15 we should **g** in every way into him
1 Pt   2: 2 through it you may **g** into salvation,
2 Pt   3:18 But **g** in grace and in the knowledge

GROWING → GROW
1 Sm 2:26 young Samuel was **g** in stature
Col   1: 6 world it is bearing fruit and **g**,
Col   1:10 fruit and **g** in the knowledge of God,

GROWL
Ex   11: 7 not even a dog will **g**, so that you
Jdt   11:19 and not even a dog will **g** at you.

GROWN → GROW
Ex   2:11 after Moses had **g** up, when he had
2 Chr 10:10 The young men who had **g**
Heb 11:24 when he had **g** up, refused to be

GROWTH → GROW
1 Cor 3: 7 but only God, who causes the **g**.
Eph   4:16 brings about the body's **g** and builds
Col   2:19 achieves the **g** that comes

GRUDGE
Gn 50:15 has been nursing a **g** against us
Lv 19:18 and cherish no **g** against your own
Mk   6:19 Herodias harbored a **g** against him

GRUMBLE → GRUMBLED
Lk   19: 7 all saw this, they began to **g**, saying,

GRUMBLED → GRUMBLE
Mt 20:11 on receiving it they **g** against

GUARANTEE → GUARANTEED
Gn 43: 9 I myself will serve as a **g** for him.
Heb 7:22 become the **g** of an [even] better

GUARANTEED → GUARANTEE
Rom 4:16 and the promise may be **g** to all his

GUARD → GUARDED, GUARDIAN, GUARDIANS, GUARDING, GUARDS, SAFEGUARD
Gn 3:24 to **g** the way to the tree of life.
Ps 91:11 to you, to **g** you wherever you go.
Ps 141: 3 Set a **g**, LORD, before my mouth,
Prv 2:11 over you, understanding will **g** you;
Sir 6:13 and be on **g** with your friends.
Sir 32:23 be on your **g**, for whoever does so
Is 52:12 and your rear **g** is the God of Israel.
Mt 27:66 a seal to the stone and setting the **g**.
Lk 12:15 "Take care to **g** against all greed,
Phil 4: 7 all understanding will **g** your hearts
2 Thes 3: 3 you and **g** you from the evil one.
1 Tm 6:20 **g** what has been entrusted to you.
2 Tm 1:12 is able to **g** what has been entrusted
2 Tm 1:14 **G** this rich trust with the help

GUARDED → GUARD
Jn 17:12 and I **g** them, and none of them was

GUARDIAN → GUARD
1 Pt 2:25 to the shepherd and **g** of your souls.

GUARDIANS → GUARD
Is 49:23 Kings shall be your **g**, their princesses
Gal 4: 2 he is under the supervision of **g**

GUARDING → GUARD
Prv 2: 8 **G** the paths of justice,

GUARDS → GUARD
1 Sm 2: 9 He **g** the footsteps of his faithful
Prv 13: 6 Justice **g** one who walks honestly,
Mt 28: 4 The **g** were shaken with fear of him

GUEST → GUESTS
Mk 14:14 "Where is my **g** room where I may

GUESTS → GUEST
Prv 9:18 that her **g** are in the depths of Sheol!
Mt 9:15 "Can the wedding **g** mourn as long
Lk 5:34 make the wedding **g** fast while

GUIDANCE → GUIDE
Prv 11:14 For lack of **g** a people falls;

GUIDE → GUIDANCE, GUIDED, GUIDES
Ps 31: 4 your name's sake lead me and **g** me.
Ps 67: 5 you **g** the nations upon the earth.
Ps 73:24 With your counsel you **g** me,
Is 58:11 the LORD will **g** you always
Lk 1:79 to **g** our feet into the path
Lk 6:39 a blind person **g** a blind person?
Jn 16:13 of truth, he will **g** you to all truth.

GUIDED → GUIDE
Ps 78:72 with skilled hands he **g** them.

GUIDES → GUIDE
Prv 11: 3 The honesty of the upright **g** them;
Mt 15:14 they are blind **g** [of the blind].
Mt 23:16 "Woe to you, blind **g**, who say,
Mt 23:24 Blind **g**, who strain out the gnat

GUILT → GUILTY; for GUILT OFFERING see also REPARATION
Gn 44:16 has uncovered your servants' **g**.
Ezr 9: 6 and our **g** reaches up to heaven.
Ps 32: 5 my sin to you; my **g** I did not hide.
Ps 32: 5 and you took away the **g** of my sin.
Ps 51: 7 Behold, I was born in **g**, in sin
Prv 14: 9 The wicked scorn a **g** offering,
Jer 2:22 stain of your **g** is still before me,
Zec 3: 9 I will take away the **g** of that land

GUILTY → GUILT
Ex 23: 7 to death, for I will not acquit the **g**.
Ex 34: 7 yet not declaring the **g** guiltless,
Nm 14:18 not declaring the **g** guiltless,
Is 5:23 Those who acquit the **g** for bribes,
Dn 13:53 and freeing the **g**, although the Lord
Na 1: 3 will not leave the **g** unpunished.

Mk 3:29 but is **g** of an everlasting sin."

GUSHED
Ps 78:20 he struck the rock, water **g** forth,
Ps 105:41 He split the rock and water **g** forth;

GYMNASIUM
1 Mc 1:14 Thereupon they built a **g**
2 Mc 4: 9 was given authority to establish a **g**

H

HABAKKUK
Prophet to Judah (Hb 1:1; 3:1). In Bel and the Dragon (Dn 14:33-39).

HABIT
Nm 22:30 in the **h** of treating you this way

HAD → HAVE
Nm 11: 4 again, "If only we **h** meat for food!
Jgs 1:19 plain, because they **h** iron chariots.
1 Sm 2:12 they **h** respect neither
Jb 42:10 to Job twice as much as he **h** before.
Ps 55: 7 "If only I **h** wings like a dove that I
Is 5: 1 My friend **h** a vineyard on a fertile
Ez 1: 6 form, but each **h** four faces and four
Ez 10:14 Each living creature **h** four faces:
Ez 41:18 Each cherub **h** two faces:
Mk 10:22 sad, for he **h** many possessions.
Acts 1:16 the scripture **h** to be fulfilled
Acts 2:44 and **h** all things in common;
Acts 14: 9 saw that he **h** the faith to be healed,
2 Cor 8:15 "Whoever **h** much did not have
2 Cor 8:15 whoever **h** little did not have less."
Rev 13:11 it **h** two horns like a lamb's

HADAD
Edomite adversary of Solomon (1 Kgs 11:14-25).

HADADEZER
2 Sm 8: 3 David then defeated H,

HADASSAH → =ESTHER
Est 2: 7 foster father to his cousin H, that is,

HADES
Tb 4:19 cast down is cast down to the recesses of H.
Rev 6: 8 Death, and H accompanied him.
Rev 20:13 Death and H gave up their dead.
Rev 20:14 H were thrown into the pool of fire.

HAGAR
Servant of Sarah, wife of Abraham, mother of Ishmael (Gn 16:1-6; 25:12). Driven away by Sarah while pregnant (Gn 16:5-16); after birth of Isaac (Gn 21:9-21; Gal 4:21-31).

HAGGAI
Postexilic prophet who encouraged rebuilding of the temple (Ezr 5:1; 6:14; Hg 1–2).

HAIL → HAILSTONES
Ex 9:19 will die when the **h** comes down
Ex 9:26 the Israelites were, was there no **h**.
Ps 78:47 He killed their vines with **h**,
Ps 147:17 He disperses **h** like crumbs.
Sir 39:29 Fire and **h**, famine and disease:
Jn 19: 3 and they came to him and said, "H,
Rev 8: 7 there came **h** and fire mixed
Rev 16:21 **h** because this plague was so severe.

HAILSTONES → HAIL
Jos 10:11 these **h** than the Israelites killed
Ez 13:11 **h** shall fall, and a stormwind shall
Rev 16:21 Large **h** like huge weights came

HAIR → HAIRS, HAIRY
Ex 26: 7 goat **h** for a tent over the tabernacle.
Jgs 16:22 the **h** of his head began to grow as
Jgs 20:16 sling a stone at a **h** without missing.
2 Sm 14:26 because his **h** became too heavy
Prv 16:31 Gray **h** is a crown of glory;
Prv 20:29 and the dignity of the old is gray **h**.
Sir 6:18 when you have gray **h** you will find

Dn	7: 9	the **h** on his head like pure wool;
Dn	14:27	Daniel took some pitch, fat, and **h**;
Mt	3: 4	wore clothing made of camel's **h**
Lk	7:44	her tears and wiped them with her **h**.
Lk	21:18	but not a **h** on your head will be
Jn	11: 2	oil and dried his feet with her **h**;
Jn	12: 3	of Jesus and dried them with her **h**;
1 Cor	11: 6	she may as well have her **h** cut off.
1 Cor	11:14	that if a man wears his **h** long it is
1 Cor	11:15	a woman has long **h** it is her glory,
1 Pt	3: 3	braiding the **h**, wearing gold
Rev	1:14	The **h** of his head was as white as
Rev	9: 8	and they had **h** like women's **h**.

HAIRS → HAIR

Ps	40:13	They are more numerous than the **h**
Mt	10:30	Even all the **h** of your head are
Lk	12: 7	Even the **h** of your head have all

HAIRY → HAIR

Gn	27:11	my brother Esau is a **h** man and I

HALAH

2 Kgs	18:11	to Assyria and led them off to H,

HALF → HALF-TRIBE

Gn	15:10	placed each **h** opposite the other;
Ex	24: 6	Moses took **h** of the blood and put it
Ex	24: 6	the other **h** he splashed on the altar.
Jos	8:33	H of them were facing Mount Gerizim and **h** Mount Ebal,
2 Sm	10: 4	servants, shaved off **h** their beards,
1 Kgs	3:25	and give **h** to one woman and **h**
1 Kgs	10: 7	not even the **h** had been told me.
Neh	4:10	only **h** my work force took a hand
Neh	13:24	**h** spoke the language of Ashdod,
Est	5: 3	Even if it is **h** of my kingdom,
Is	44:19	"H the wood I burned in the fire,
Ez	16:51	did not commit **h** the sins you did.
Mk	6:23	of me, even to **h** of my kingdom."
Lk	19: 8	"Behold, **h** of my possessions,
Rev	8: 1	in heaven for about **h** an hour.
Rev	11:11	But after the three and a **h** days,

HALF-TRIBE → HALF, TRIBE

Jos	4:12	Gadites, and **h** of Manasseh, armed,

HALL

Dn	5:10	she entered the banquet **h** and said,
Mt	22:10	and the **h** was filled with guests.
Acts	19: 9	in the lecture **h** of Tyrannus.

HALLELUJAH → ALLELUIA

1 Chr	16:36	Let all the people say, Amen! H.
Tb	13:18	all its houses will cry out, H!
Ps	111: 1	H! I will praise the LORD
Ps	149: 1	H! Sing to the LORD a new song,

HALLOWED

Mt	6: 9	Father in heaven, **h** be your name,
Lk	11: 2	Father, **h** be your name,

HALO

Rev	4: 3	the throne was a **h** as brilliant as
Rev	10: 1	in a cloud, with a **h** around his head;

HAM

Son of Noah (Gn 5:32; 1 Chr 1:4), father of Canaan (Gn 9:18; 10:6-20; 1 Chr 1:8-16). Saw Noah's nakedness (Gn 9:20-27).

HAMAN

Agagite nobleman honored by Ahasuerus (Est 3:1-2). Plotted to exterminate the Jews because of Mordecai (Est 3:3-15). Forced to honor Mordecai (Est 5–6). Plot exposed by Esther (Est 5:1-8; 7:1-8). Hanged (Est 7:9-10).

HAMATH

2 Sm	8: 9	Toi, king of H, heard that David had
2 Kgs	14:28	regained Damascus and H for Israel,
2 Kgs	18:34	Where are the gods of H

HAMMERS

Jer	10: 4	With nails and **h** they are fastened,

HAMOR

Gn	34: 2	son of H the Hivite, the leader

HAMSTRING → HAMSTRUNG

Jos	11: 6	You must **h** their horses and burn

HAMSTRUNG → HAMSTRING

Jos	11: 9	he **h** their horses and burned their
1 Chr	18: 4	David **h** all the chariot horses,

HANAMEL

Jer	32: 7	H, son of your uncle Shallum,

HANANEL

Neh	3: 1	of the Hundred, the Tower of H.
Jer	31:38	the Tower of H to the Corner Gate.

HANANI

Neh	7: 2	Over Jerusalem I placed H,

HANANIAH → =SHADRACH

1. False prophet; adversary of Jeremiah (Jer 28).
2. Original name of Shadrach (Dn 1:6-19; 2:17).

HAND → EMPTY-HANDED, HANDED, HANDFUL, HANDS, LEFT-HANDED

Gn	3:22	reaches out his **h** to take fruit
Gn	4:11	your brother's blood from your **h**.
Gn	16:12	of a man, his **h** against everyone,
Gn	16:12	and everyone's **h** against him;
Gn	22:12	"Do not lay your **h** on the boy,"
Gn	24: 2	"Put your **h** under my thigh,
Gn	47:29	put your **h** under my thigh as a sign
Gn	48:14	put out his right **h** and laid it
Gn	48:14	his left **h** on the head of Manasseh,
Ex	4: 6	Put your **h** into the fold of your
Ex	4: 6	there was his **h** covered with scales,
Ex	6: 1	by a strong **h**, he will drive them
Ex	13: 3	a strong **h** that the LORD brought
Ex	15: 6	in power, your right **h**, O LORD,
Ex	21:24	tooth for tooth, **h** for **h**, foot for foot,
Ex	33:22	with my **h** until I have passed by.
Dt	4:34	with strong **h** and outstretched arm,
Dt	19:21	tooth for tooth, **h** for **h**, and foot
Dt	32:39	and from my **h** no one can deliver.
1 Sm	24:11	delivered you into my **h** in the cave.
1 Sm	24:11	will not raise a **h** against my master,
1 Sm	26: 9	who can lay a **h** on the LORD's anointed
2 Sm	1:14	to put forth your **h** to desecrate
1 Kgs	8:42	your mighty **h** and your outstretched
1 Kgs	13: 4	Jeroboam stretched forth his **h**
1 Kgs	18:44	a cloud as small as a man's **h** rising
2 Chr	6:15	your **h** has fulfilled this very day.
2 Chr	32:15	your god rescue you from my **h**!"
2 Chr	32:22	from the **h** of Sennacherib,
Ezr	7: 9	the favoring **h** of his God was over
Neh	4:11	each worked with one **h** and held
Jdt	9:10	their arrogance by the **h** of a female.
Jdt	13:15	him down by the **h** of a female!
Jb	40: 4	I put my **h** over my mouth.
Ps	32: 4	night your **h** was heavy upon me;
Ps	37:24	fall, for the LORD holds his **h**.
Ps	44: 4	It was your right **h**, your own arm,
Ps	45:10	gold comes to stand at your right **h**.
Ps	63: 9	fast to you; your right **h** upholds me.
Ps	74:11	Why draw back your **h**, why hold
Ps	75: 9	a cup is in the LORD's **h**,
Ps	80:18	May your **h** be with the man
Ps	91: 7	ten thousand at your right **h**,
Ps	95: 4	Whose **h** holds the depths
Ps	109:31	he stands at the right **h** of the poor
Ps	110: 1	"Sit at my right **h**, while I make
Ps	137: 5	Jerusalem, may my right **h** forget.
Ps	139:10	Even there your **h** guides me,
Ps	145:16	You open wide your **h** and satisfy
Prv	3:16	Long life is in her right **h**, in her left
Prv	19:24	The sluggard buries a **h** in the dish;
Prv	21: 1	water in the **h** of the LORD;
Eccl	2:24	this, I saw, is from the **h** of God.
Eccl	9:10	Anything you can turn your **h** to,

Sir	7:32	To the poor also extend your **h**,
Is	1:25	I will turn my **h** against you,
Is	5:25	back, his **h** is still outstretched.
Is	11: 8	the child lay his **h** on the adder's
Is	41:13	your God, who grasp your right **h**;
Is	44: 5	And this one shall write on his **h**,
Is	48:13	my **h** laid the foundations
Is	48:13	my right **h** spread out the heavens.
Is	64: 7	our potter: we are all the work of your **h**.
Jer	22:24	were a signet ring on my right **h**,
Jer	31:32	I took them by the **h** to lead them
Jer	51: 7	in the **h** of the LORD making
Lam	3: 3	Against me alone he turns his **h**—
Ez	1: 3	There the **h** of the LORD came
Ez	2: 9	then I saw a **h** stretched out to me;
Dn	5: 5	the fingers of a human **h** appeared,
Dn	10:10	But then a **h** touched me, raising me
Am	7: 7	plummet in **h**, by a wall built
Jon	4:11	who cannot know their right **h**
Hb	2:16	the LORD's right **h** shall come
Mt	3:12	His winnowing fan is in his **h**.
Mt	5:30	if your right **h** causes you to sin,
Mt	6: 3	not let your left **h** know what your
Mt	12:10	a man there who had a withered **h**.
Mt	18: 8	If your **h** or foot causes you to sin,
Mt	22:44	"Sit at my right **h** until I place your
Mt	26:64	seated at the right **h** of the Power'
Mk	1:31	grasped her **h**, and helped her up.
Mk	3: 1	a man there who had a withered **h**.
Mk	5:41	He took the child by the **h** and said
Mk	9:43	If your **h** causes you to sin, cut it
Mk	12:36	"Sit at my right **h** until I place your
Mk	14:62	seated at the right **h** of the Power
Lk	5:13	Jesus stretched out his **h**,
Lk	9:62	"No one who sets a **h** to the plow
Lk	20:42	said to my lord, "Sit at my right **h**
Lk	22:69	be seated at the right **h** of the power
Jn	10:28	No one can take them out of my **h**.
Jn	20:27	bring your **h** and put it into my side,
Acts	2:34	said to my Lord, "Sit at my right **h**
Acts	7:55	Jesus standing at the right **h** of God,
Rom	8:34	who also is at the right **h** of God,
1 Cor	12:15	I am not a **h** I do not belong
Eph	1:20	him at his right **h** in the heavens,
Col	3: 1	is seated at the right **h** of God.
Heb	1:13	"Sit at my right **h** until I make your
Heb	8: 1	his seat at the right **h** of the throne
Heb	10:12	seat forever at the right **h** of God;
1 Pt	3:22	heaven and is at the right **h** of God,
Rev	1:16	In his right **h** he held seven stars.
Rev	5: 1	in the right **h** of the one who sat

HANDED → HAND

Mt	26: 2	Man will be **h** over to be crucified."
Mt	27:26	he **h** him over to be crucified.
Acts	3:13	his servant Jesus whom you **h** over
Rom	4:25	who was **h** over for our
1 Cor	15: 3	For I **h** on to you as of first

HANDFUL → HAND

Eccl	4: 6	Better is one **h** with tranquility than

HANDLE

Col	2:21	"Do not **h**! Do not taste!

HANDS → HAND

Gn	5:29	from our work and the toil of our **h**,
Gn	27:22	voice is Jacob's, the **h** are Esau's."
Gn	37:22	was to save him from their **h**
Ex	29:10	his sons shall lay their **h** on its head.
Ex	32:15	two tablets of the covenant in his **h**,
1 Sm	5: 4	his head and **h** broken off and lying
2 Sm	18:12	pieces of silver in my two **h**,
2 Kgs	11:12	him, clapping their **h** and shouting,
2 Kgs	22:17	me by all the works of their **h**,
1 Mc	2:48	the law from the **h** of the Gentiles
Ps	18:25	the cleanness of my **h** in his sight.
Ps	22:17	They have pierced my **h** and my
Ps	47: 2	All you peoples, clap your **h**;

Ps	63: 5	I will lift up my **h**, calling on your
Ps	90:17	Prosper the work of our **h**!
Ps	115: 7	They have **h** but do not feel,
Ps	138: 8	Never forsake the work of your **h**!
Prv	21:25	them, for their **h** refuse to work.
Prv	31:13	and flax and weaves with skillful **h**.
Prv	31:20	She reaches out her **h** to the poor,
Sir	33:13	Like clay in the **h** of a potter, to be
Sir	33:13	are people in the **h** of their Maker,
Is	5:12	the work of his **h** they do not see!
Is	35: 3	Strengthen **h** that are feeble,
Is	37:19	at all, but the work of human **h**—
Is	45:12	It was my **h** that stretched
Is	49:16	palms of my **h** I have engraved you;
Is	55:12	trees of the field shall clap their **h**.
Is	65: 2	I have stretched out my **h** all day
Jer	26:14	As for me, I am in your **h**;
Ez	1: 8	Human **h** were under their wings,
Dn	3:17	white-hot furnace and from your **h**,
Hos	14: 4	say, 'Our god,' to the work of our **h**;
Mi	7: 3	Their **h** succeed at evil;
Zec	8:13	Do not fear; let your **h** be strong.
Mal	1:10	not accept any offering from your **h**!
Mk	7: 5	instead eat a meal with unclean **h**?"
Mk	10:16	blessed them, placing his **h** on them.
Lk	23:46	into your **h** I commend my spirit";
Lk	24:40	he showed them his **h** and his feet.
Jn	20:27	"Put your finger here and see my **h**,
Acts	6: 6	who prayed and laid **h** on them.
Acts	8:18	by the laying on of the apostles' **h**,
Acts	13: 3	they laid **h** on them and sent them
Acts	19: 6	And when Paul laid [his] **h** on them,
Acts	28: 8	laid his **h** on him and healed him.
Rom	10:21	I stretched out my **h** to a disobedient
1 Cor	15:24	when he **h** over the kingdom to his
1 Thes	4:11	and to work with your [own] **h**,
1 Tm	2: 8	lifting up holy **h**, without anger
1 Tm	4:14	word with the imposition of **h**
2 Tm	1: 6	through the imposition of my **h**.
Heb	6: 2	about baptisms and laying on of **h**,
Heb	10:31	to fall into the **h** of the living God.
1 Jn	1: 1	with our **h** concerns the Word
Rev	13:16	a stamped image on their right **h**
Rev	20: 4	its mark on their foreheads or **h**.

HANDSOME

Gn	39: 6	Now Joseph was well-built and **h**.
1 Sm	17:42	and **h** in appearance, he began
1 Kgs	1: 6	Adonijah was also very **h**, and next
2 Mc	3:26	young men, remarkably strong, strikingly **h**,
Dn	1: 4	be young men without any defect, **h**,

HANG → HANGED, HANGING, HUNG

Jdt	14: 1	and **h** it on the parapet of your wall.

HANGED → HANG

2 Sm	17:23	his household, he **h** himself.
Mt	27: 5	and went off and **h** himself.

HANGING → HANG

Acts	10:39	put him to death by **h** him on a tree.

HANNAH

Wife of Elkanah, mother of Samuel (1 Sm 1). Prayer at dedication of Samuel (1 Sm 2:1-10). Blessed (1 Sm 2:18-21).

HAPPEN → HAPPENED, HAPPENING, HAPPENS

Gn	49: 1	I may tell you what is to **h** to you
Ex	2: 4	to find out what would **h** to him.
Dn	10:14	make you understand what shall **h**
Mk	10:32	to tell them what was going to **h**
Jn	18: 4	that was going to **h** to him,

HAPPENED → HAPPEN

1 Sm	4: 7	Woe to us! This has never **h** before.
Jl	1: 2	Has anything like this ever **h** in your

HAPPENING → HAPPEN

1 Pt	4:12	if something strange were **h** to you.

HAPPENS → HAPPEN
Sir 2: 4 Accept whatever **h** to you;

HAPPINESS → HAPPY
Sir 8:19 to no one, do not banish your **h**.
Lam 3:17 of peace, I have forgotten what **h** is;

HAPPY → HAPPINESS
1 Kgs 10: 8 **H** are your servants, **h** these
Tb 13:16 H too will I be if a remnant of my
Est 5: 9 That day Haman left **h** and in good
Jb 5:17 **H** the one whom God reproves!
Prv 3:13 H the one who finds wisdom,
Prv 8:34 H the one who listens to me,
Sir 14: 1 H those whose mouth causes them
Sir 14:20 H those who meditate on Wisdom,
Sir 25: 9 H the one who finds a friend,
Sir 26: 1 H the husband of a good wife;
Sir 34:17 H the soul that fears the Lord!
Is 30:18 **h** are all who wait for him!
Is 56: 2 H is the one who does this,

HARAN
Gn 11:27 Nahor, and H, and H begot Lot.
Gn 11:31 But when they reached H,

HARD → HARDEN, HARDENED, HARDENING, HARDENS, HARDER, HARDSHIPS
Ex 1:14 life bitter for them with **h** labor,
Mt 19:23 it will be **h** for one who is rich
Rom 16:12 who has worked **h** in the Lord.
2 Pt 3:16 In them there are some things **h**

HARDEN → HARD
Ex 4:21 But I will **h** his heart and he will
Ex 14: 4 I will so **h** Pharaoh's heart that
Ex 14:17 I will **h** the hearts of the Egyptians
Ps 95: 8 Do not **h** your hearts as at Meribah,
Heb 3: 8 'H not your hearts as
Heb 4: 7 'H not your hearts.' "

HARDENED → HARD
Ex 7:13 Pharaoh, however, **h** his heart and
Ex 7:22 So Pharaoh **h** his heart and would not
Ex 8:15 Yet Pharaoh **h** his heart and would not
Ex 9:12 But the LORD **h** Pharaoh's heart,
Ex 10:20 Yet the LORD **h** Pharaoh's heart,
Ex 10:27 But the LORD **h** Pharaoh's heart,
Ex 11:10 the LORD **h** Pharaoh's heart, and he
Mk 8:17 Are your hearts **h**?
Jn 12:40 blinded their eyes and **h** their heart,
Rom 11: 7 the elect attained it; the rest were **h**,
Heb 3:13 of you may grow **h** by the deceit

HARDENING → HARD
Rom 11:25 a **h** has come upon Israel in part,

HARDENS → HARD
Rom 9:18 he wills, and he **h** whom he wills.

HARDER → HARD
Jer 5: 3 They set their faces **h** than stone,
1 Cor 15:10 I have toiled **h** than all of them;

HARDSHIPS → HARD
2 Cor 6: 4 in afflictions, **h**, constraints,
2 Cor 12:10 weaknesses, insults, **h**, persecutions,

HAREM
Est 2: 9 her maids to the best place in the **h**.

HARM → HARMED, HARMFUL
Gn 31: 7 did not let him do me any **h**.
Gn 48:16 who has delivered me from all **h**,
Gn 50:20 Even though you meant **h** to me,
1 Sm 26:21 I will not **h** you again, because you
1 Chr 16:22 anointed, to my prophets do no **h**."
Neh 6: 2 They were planning to do me **h**.
Prv 12:21 No **h** befalls the just, but the wicked
Eccl 8: 9 one person tyrannizes over another for **h**.
1 Pt 3:13 Now who is going to **h** you if you
Rev 9:19 like snakes, with heads that inflict **h**.
Rev 11: 5 If anyone wants to **h** them,

HARMED → HARM
Rev 2:11 The victor shall not be **h**

HARMFUL → HARM
2 Kgs 4:41 there was no longer anything **h**
1 Tm 6: 9 and into many foolish and **h** desires,

HARP → HARPISTS, HARPS
Ps 33: 2 Give thanks to the LORD on the **h**;
Ps 108: 3 Awake, lyre and **h**! I will wake
Ps 150: 3 the horn, praise him with **h** and lyre,
Is 5:12 Banqueting on wine with **h** and lyre,
Rev 5: 8 Each of the elders held a **h** and gold

HARPISTS → HARP
Rev 14: 2 like that of **h** playing their harps.
Rev 18:22 No melodies of **h** and musicians,

HARPS → HARP
1 Sm 10: 5 and **h**, and will be in prophetic
1 Chr 15:16 to play on musical instruments, **h**,
1 Chr 25: 1 to the accompaniment of lyres and **h**
Neh 12:27 hymns and the music of cymbals, **h**,
1 Mc 4:54 it was rededicated with songs, **h**,
Ps 137: 2 in its midst we hung up our **h**.
Rev 15: 2 They were holding God's **h**,

HARSH
Prv 15: 1 wrath, but a **h** word stirs up anger.
Jude 1:15 all the **h** words godless sinners have

HARVEST
Gn 8:22 earth, seedtime and **h**, cold and heat,
Ex 23:16 of the grain **h** with the first fruits
Prv 10: 5 a son who slumbers during **h**,
Prv 20: 4 when they look for the **h**, it is not
Jer 8:20 "The **h** is over, the summer ended,
Jl 4:13 Wield the sickle, for the **h** is ripe;
Mt 9:37 "The **h** is abundant but the laborers
Mt 13:39 The **h** is the end of the age,
Lk 10: 2 "The **h** is abundant but the laborers
Lk 10: 2 so ask the master of the **h** to send out laborers for his **h**.
Jn 4:35 'In four months the **h** will be here'?
Jn 4:35 and see the fields ripe for the **h**.
2 Cor 9:10 increase the **h** of your righteousness.
Rev 14: 5 "Use your sickle and reap the **h**,
Rev 14:15 because the earth's **h** is fully ripe."

HAS → HAVE
Jb 1:12 well, all that he **h** is in your power;
Jb 42: 7 concerning me, as **h** my servant Job.
Is 34: 8 For the LORD **h** a day
Jer 23:28 What **h** straw to do with wheat?—
Mt 8:20 the Son of Man **h** nowhere to rest
Mt 9: 6 the Son of Man **h** authority on earth
Mk 3:30 had said, "He **h** an unclean spirit."
Jn 3:36 believes in the Son **h** eternal life,
Jn 4:44 testified that a prophet **h** no honor
Jn 15:13 No one **h** greater love than this,
Rom 6: 9 death no longer **h** power over him.
1 Cor 7: 7 each **h** a particular gift from God,
1 Cor 7:13 if any woman **h** a husband who is
1 Cor 11:15 a woman **h** long hair it is her glory,
1 Jn 2:23 who denies the Son **h** the Father,
1 Jn 2:23 confesses the Son **h** the Father as
1 Jn 5:12 Whoever possesses the Son **h** life;
Rev 20: 6 The second death **h** no power over

HASIDEANS
1 Mc 2:42 they were joined by a group of H,
1 Mc 7:13 The H were the first among
2 Mc 14: 6 "Those Jews called H, led by Judas

HASTENING
2 Pt 3:12 and **h** the coming of the day of God,

HATE → HATED, HATES, HATING, HATRED
Ex 18:21 men who **h** dishonest gain, and set
2 Chr 18: 7 but I **h** him, because he prophesies
Ps 5: 6 You **h** all who do evil;
Ps 45: 8 You love justice and **h** wrongdoing;
Ps 97:10 You who love the LORD, **h** evil,

Ps	119:104	therefore I h all false ways.
Ps	119:163	Falsehood I h and abhor; your law I
Ps	129: 5	recoil in disgrace, all who h Zion.
Ps	139:21	Do I not h, LORD, those who h
Prv	8:13	way, and the perverse mouth I h.
Prv	9: 8	the arrogant, lest they h you;
Prv	13: 5	The just h deceitful words, but the wicked
Prv	15:32	who disregard discipline h themselves,
Prv	25:17	have their fill of you—and h you.
Prv	29:10	The bloodthirsty h the blameless,
Eccl	3: 8	A time to love, and a time to h;
Sir	7:15	Do not h hard work;
Is	61: 8	justice, I h robbery and wrongdoing;
Jer	44: 4	commit this abominable deed I h,"
Am	5:15	H evil and love good, and let justice
Mal	2:16	For I h divorce, says the LORD,
Mt	5:43	your neighbor and h your enemy.'
Lk	6:22	Blessed are you when people h you,
Lk	6:27	do good to those who h you,
Lk	16:13	He will either h one and love
Jn	7: 7	The world cannot h you, but it hates
Rom	7:15	do what I want, but I do what I h.
Rom	12: 9	h what is evil, hold on to what is

HATED → HATE

Gn	37: 4	they h him so much that they could
Prv	1:29	Because they h knowledge,
Mt	10:22	You will be h by all because of my
Jn	15:18	hates you, realize that it h me first.
Rom	9:13	"I loved Jacob but h Esau."
Heb	1: 9	loved justice and h wickedness;

HATES → HATE

Prv	6:16	There are six things the LORD h,
Sir	15:11	for what he h he does not do.
Sir	15:13	wickedness the LORD h and he
Sir	33: 2	Whoever h the law is without
Jn	15:19	out of the world, the world h you.
Jn	15:23	Whoever h me also h my Father.
Eph	5:29	For no one h his own flesh

HATING → HATE

2 Tm	3: 3	licentious, brutal, h what is good,
Ti	3: 3	hateful ourselves and h one another.

HATRED → HATE

Ps	139:22	With fierce h I hate them, enemies I
Prv	10:12	H stirs up disputes, but love covers
Prv	15:17	love is than a fatted ox and h with it.

HAUGHTINESS → HAUGHTY

Prv	29:23	H brings humiliation, but the humble

HAUGHTY → HAUGHTINESS

Ps	18:28	h eyes you bring low.
Prv	6:17	H eyes, a lying tongue,
Prv	16:18	disaster, and a h spirit before a fall.
Prv	18:12	Before disaster the heart is h,
Rom	12:16	do not be h but associate

HAUNT

Rev	18: 2	She has become a h for demons.

HAVE → HAD, HAS, HAVING

Gn	1:26	Let them h dominion over the fish
Gn	18:10	year, and Sarah will then h a son."
Gn	27:38	father, "H you only one blessing,
Ex	16:12	the morning you will h your fill
Ex	20: 3	You shall not h other gods beside
Dt	5: 7	You shall not h other gods beside
Jos	22:25	You h no share in the LORD.'
Jb	40: 9	H you an arm like that of God,
Ps	73:25	Whom else h I in the heavens?
Ps	115: 5	They h mouths but do not speak,
Ps	119:99	I h more insight than all my
Jer	2:28	Jerusalem are the altars you h set
Jer	5:21	people, Who h eyes and do not see,
Jer	5:21	not see, who h ears and do not hear.
Mal	2:10	H we not all one father?
Mt	3: 9	'We h Abraham as our father.'

Mt	21:21	you, if you h faith and do not waver,
Mk	10:21	sell what you h, and give
Mk	10:21	and you will h treasure in heaven;
Mk	14: 7	The poor you will always h
Mk	14: 7	but you will not always h me.
Jn	3:16	not perish but might h eternal life.
Jn	4:32	"I h food to eat of which you do not
Jn	8:12	but will h the light of life."
Jn	16:12	"I h much more to tell you, but you
Jn	16:33	In the world you will h trouble,
Acts	3: 6	said, "I h neither silver nor gold, but what I do I give you:
Rom	5: 1	we h peace with God through our
Rom	8: 9	Whoever does not h the Spirit
Rom	12: 6	Since we h gifts that differ
1 Cor	2:16	But we h the mind of Christ.
1 Cor	13: 1	angelic tongues but do not h love,
2 Cor	8:15	had much did not h more,
2 Cor	8:15	whoever had little did not h less."
Eph	1: 7	him we h redemption by his blood,
Eph	2:18	for through him we both h access
Heb	4:14	since we h a great high priest who
Heb	6:19	This we h as an anchor of the soul,
1 Jn	2:20	you h the anointing that comes
1 Jn	2:20	holy one, and you all h knowledge.
1 Jn	5:12	the Son of God does not h life.
Rev	22:14	wash their robes so as to h the right

HAVILAH

Gn	2:11	winds through the whole land of H,

HAVING → HAVE

Mt	7:29	he taught them as one h authority,

HAY

1 Cor	3:12	precious stones, wood, h, or straw,

HAZAEL

1 Kgs	19:15	you shall anoint H as king of Aram.
2 Kgs	8: 9	H went to visit him,

HAZOR

Jos	11:11	was left alive. H itself he burned.
Jer	49:33	H shall become a haunt for jackals,

HEAD → BEHEADED, HEADLONG, HEADS, HOTHEADED

Gn	3:15	They will strike at your h, while you
Gn	28:18	stone that he had put under his h,
Gn	48:18	lay your right hand on his h!"
Dt	28:13	will make you the h not the tail,
Jgs	16:17	"No razor has touched my h, for I
1 Sm	1:11	No razor shall ever touch his h."
1 Sm	9: 2	he stood h and shoulders
1 Sm	17:51	he killed him, and cut off his h.
Jdt	13: 8	his neck twice and cut off his h.
1 Mc	7:47	they cut off Nicanor's h and his
Ps	23: 5	You anoint my h with oil;
Ps	133: 2	Like fine oil on the h, running down
Prv	1: 9	diadem will they be for your h;
Prv	10: 6	Blessings are for the h of the just;
Is	59:17	victory as a helmet on his h;
Jer	8:23	that my h were a spring of water,
Dn	2:32	Its h was pure gold, its chest
Dn	7: 9	the hair on his h like pure wool;
Mt	8:20	of Man has nowhere to rest his h."
Mk	6:28	He brought in the h on a platter
Jn	19: 2	out of thorns and placed it on his h,
1 Cor	11: 3	that Christ is the h of every man, and a husband the h of his wife, and God the h of Christ.
1 Cor	11: 4	with his h covered brings shame upon his h.
1 Cor	11: 5	with her h unveiled brings shame upon her h,
1 Cor	11: 5	as if she had had her h shaved.
1 Cor	12:21	you," nor again the h to the feet,
Eph	1:22	gave him as h over all things
Eph	5:23	the husband is h of his wife just as Christ is h of the church,
Col	1:18	He is the h of the body, the church.
Rev	1:14	of his h was as white as white wool
Rev	10: 1	in a cloud, with a halo around his h;

Rev   12: 1 on her **h** a crown of twelve stars.
Rev   14:14 with a gold crown on his **h**
Rev   19:12 and on his **h** were many diadems.

HEADLONG → HEAD
Acts   1:18 and falling **h**, he burst open

HEADS → HEAD
Nm   6: 5 the hair of their **h** grow freely.
Neh   3:36 their reproach upon their own **h**
1 Mc   3:47 they sprinkled ashes on their **h**
Ps   22: 8 they shake their **h** at me:
Ps   24: 7 Lift up your **h**, O gates;
Ez   11:21 their conduct down upon their **h**—
Dn   7: 6 those of a bird, and it had four **h**.
Mt   27:39 by reviled him, shaking their **h**
Mk   2:23 make a path while picking the **h**
Lk   21:28 erect and raise your **h** because your
Acts   18: 6 to them, "Your blood be on your **h**!
Rev   4: 4 and with gold crowns on their **h**.
Rev   12: 3 dragon, with seven **h** and ten horns,
Rev   12: 3 and on its **h** were seven diadems.
Rev   17: 9 The seven **h** represent seven hills

HEAL → HEALED, HEALING, HEALS, HEALTH
Nm   12:13 "Please, not this! Please, **h** her!"
Dt   32:39 I who inflict wounds and **h** them,
2 Kgs 20: 8 the sign that the LORD will **h** me
Tb   3:17 So Raphael was sent to **h** them both:
Tb   12:14 God sent me to **h** you and your
Ps   6: 3 **h** me, LORD, for my bones are
Ps   41: 5 **h** me, although I have sinned
Eccl   3: 3 A time to kill, and a time to **h**;
Is   19:22 moved by their entreaty and **h** them.
Is   57:18 I saw their ways, but I will **h** them.
Is   57:19 says the LORD; and I will **h** them.
Jer   17:14 **H** me, LORD, that I may be
Jer   30:17 I will **h** your injuries—
Jer   33: 6 I will **h** them and reveal to them
Jer   51: 9 "We have tried to **h** Babylon,
Lam   2:13 is vast as the sea; who could **h** you?
Hos   5:13 But he cannot **h** you, nor take away
Hos   6: 1 is he who has torn, but he will **h** us;
Hos   14: 5 I will **h** their apostasy, I will love
Zec   11:16 seek the strays, nor **h** the injured,
Mt   13:15 and be converted, and I **h** them.'
Lk   9: 2 kingdom of God and to **h** [the sick].
Jn   4:47 him to come down and **h** his son,
Jn   12:40 be converted, and I would **h** them."
Acts   4:30 you stretch forth [your] hand to **h**,
Acts   28:27 and be converted, and I **h** them.'

HEALED → HEAL
Lv   13:18 on a person's skin which later **h**,
Lv   13:37 grown in it, the disease has been **h**;
Lv   14: 3 that the scaly infection has **h**
Lv   14:48 since the infection has been **h**.
1 Sm   6: 3 Then you will be **h**, and will learn
2 Kgs   8:29 Jezreel to be **h** of the wounds
2 Kgs   9:15 to be **h** of the wounds the Arameans
2 Chr 22: 6 to Jezreel to be **h** of the wounds
Tb   12: 3 led me back safe and sound, **h** my wife,
Ps   30: 3 out to you for help and you **h** me.
Is   6:10 understand, and they turn and be **h**.
Is   53: 5 us whole, by his wounds we were **h**.
Jer   15:18 wound incurable, refusing to be **h**?
Jer   17:14 Heal me, LORD, that I may be **h**;
Jer   51: 8 her wounds, in case she can be **h**.
Jer   51: 9 heal Babylon, but she cannot be **h**.
Hos   7: 1 when I would have **h** Israel,
Mt   8: 8 the word and my servant will be **h**.
Mt   8:13 at that very hour [his] servant was **h**.
Mt   14:36 and as many as touched it were **h**.
Mt   15:28 her daughter was **h** from that hour.
Mk   5:29 that she was **h** of her affliction.
Mk   6:56 and as many as touched it were **h**;
Lk   6:18 him and to be **h** of their diseases;
Lk   6:19 came forth from him and **h** them all.
Lk   7: 7 the word and let my servant be **h**.

Lk   8:47 how she had been **h** immediately.
Lk   9:11 he **h** those who needed to be cured.
Lk   9:42 the unclean spirit, **h** the boy,
Lk   14: 4 after he had **h** him, dismissed him.
Lk   17:15 realizing he had been **h**, returned,
Lk   22:51 touched the servant's ear and **h** him.
Jn   5:13 The man who was **h** did not know
Acts   14: 9 saw that he had the faith to be **h**,
Heb   12:13 is lame may not be dislocated but **h**.
Jas   5:16 for one another, that you may be **h**.
1 Pt   2:24 By his wounds you have been **h**.
Rev   13: 3 but this mortal wound was **h**.
Rev   13:12 whose mortal wound had been **h**.

HEALING → HEAL
2 Kgs 20: 5 Now I am **h** you. On the third day
Tb   5:10 God's **h** is near; so take courage!"
Jb   5:18 he strikes, but his hands give **h**.
Ps   147: 3 **H** the brokenhearted, and binding up
Prv   12:18 but the tongue of the wise is **h**.
Prv   13:17 a trustworthy envoy is a **h** remedy.
Sir   21: 1 when it cuts, there is no **h**.
Sir   28: 3 and expect **h** from the LORD?
Jer   8:15 for a time of **h**, but terror comes
Jer   14:19 for a time of **h**, but terror comes
Jer   30:13 for your running sore, no **h** for you.
Ez   30:21 It has not been immobilized for **h**,
Mal   3:20 justice will arise with **h** in its wings;
Lk   5:17 the power of the Lord was with him for **h**.
Acts   4:22 of **h** had been done was over forty
Acts   10:38 **h** all those oppressed by the devil,
1 Cor 12: 9 another gifts of **h** by the one Spirit;
1 Cor 12:28 then, gifts of **h**, assistance,
1 Cor 12:30 Do all have gifts of **h**? Do all speak

HEALS → HEAL
Ps   103: 3 all your sins, and **h** all your ills,
Sir   38: 9 but pray to God, for it is he who **h**.
Acts   9:34 him, "Aeneas, Jesus Christ **h** you.

HEALTH → HEAL
Tb   5:16 In good **h** we will leave you,
Tb   5:16 and in good **h** we will return to you,
Tb   5:21 Our son will leave in good **h** and come back to us in good **h**.
2 Mc   9:19 and best wishes for their **h**
2 Mc   11:28 We too are in good **h**.
Wis   7:10 Beyond **h** and beauty I loved her,
Sir   30:15 rather have bodily **h** than any gold,
Sir   34:20 gives **h** and life and blessing.
Is   38:16 You have given me **h** and restored
Jer   30:17 For I will restore your **h**; I will heal
Lk   7:10 they found the slave in good **h**.
Acts   3:16 it has given him this perfect **h**,
3 Jn   1: 2 in every respect and are in good **h**,

HEAP
1 Sm   2: 8 from the ash **h** lifts up the poor,
Prv   25:22 live coals you will **h** on their heads,
Rom   12:20 so doing you will **h** burning coals

HEAR → HEARD, HEARERS, HEARING, HEARS
Nm   14:13 "The Egyptians will **h** of this,
Dt   1:17 for you bring to me and I will **h** it."
Dt   4:36 the heavens he let you **h** his voice
Dt   5: 1 all Israel and said to them, **H**,
Dt   6: 3 **H** then, Israel, and be careful
Dt   6: 4 **H**, O Israel! The LORD is our
Dt   9: 1 **H**, O Israel! You are now
Dt   13:12 all Israel shall **h** of it and fear,
Dt   19:20 The rest shall **h** and be afraid, and never
Dt   20: 3 and say to them, "**H**, O Israel!
Dt   31:13 shall **h** and learn to fear the LORD,
Jos   7: 9 other inhabitants of the land **h** of it,
2 Kgs 19:16 **H** the words Sennacherib has sent
2 Chr   7:14 I will **h** them from heaven
Jb   20: 3 A rebuke that puts me to shame I **h**,
Jb   26:14 a whisper of a word we **h** of him:
Jb   31:35 Oh, that I had one to **h** my case:

Ps	30:11	H, O Lᴏʀᴅ, have mercy on me;
Ps	51:10	You will let me **h** gladness and joy;
Ps	94: 9	the one who shaped the ear not **h**?
Ps	135:17	They have ears but do not **h**;
Eccl	7:21	you may **h** your servant cursing
Sir	21:15	When the intelligent **h** a wise saying,
Is	1:10	H the word of the Lᴏʀᴅ,
Is	21: 3	I am too bewildered to **h**,
Is	29:18	day the deaf shall **h** the words
Is	59: 1	to save, nor his ear too dull to **h**.
Jer	5:21	not see, who have ears and do not **h**.
Ez	33: 7	when you **h** a word from my mouth,
Ez	37: 4	bones, **h** the word of the Lᴏʀᴅ!
Mi	6: 2	H, O mountains, the Lᴏʀᴅ's case,
Mt	11: 5	the deaf **h**, the dead are raised,
Mt	13:17	and to **h** what you **h** but did not **h** it.
Mk	12:29	"The first is this: 'H, O Israel!
Lk	7:22	the deaf **h**, the dead are raised,
Jn	5:25	the dead will **h** the voice of the Son of God, and those who **h** will live.
Acts	13: 7	and wanted to **h** the word of God.
Acts	13:44	whole city gathered to **h** the word
Acts	17:32	"We should like to **h** you on this
Rom	10:14	how can they **h** without someone
Heb	3: 7	that today you would **h** his voice,
Rev	9:20	which cannot see or **h** or walk.

HEARD → HEAR

Gn	3: 8	When they **h** the sound the Lᴏʀᴅ God
Gn	21:17	God has **h** the boy's voice in this
Ex	2:24	God **h** their moaning and God was
Ex	6: 5	Now that I have **h** the groaning
Nm	12: 2	And the Lᴏʀᴅ **h** this.
Nm	14:27	I have **h** the grumblings
Dt	4:32	Was it ever **h** of?
Jos	24:27	for it has **h** all the words
2 Sm	7:22	God but you, as we have always **h**.
1 Kgs	5:14	the earth who had **h** of his wisdom.
1 Kgs	10: 1	having **h** a report of Solomon's
Jb	42: 5	By hearsay I had **h** of you, but now
Ps	18: 7	From his temple he **h** my voice;
Ps	62:12	two things I have **h**:
Ps	78:59	God **h** and grew angry;
Sir	3: 5	and when they pray they are **h**.
Is	40:21	Have you not **h**? Was it not told you
Is	40:28	Have you not **h**? The Lᴏʀᴅ is
Is	66: 8	Who ever **h** of such a thing, or who
Jer	18:13	who has ever **h** the like?
Lam	3:56	You **h** me call, "Do not let your ear
Ez	10: 5	of the cherubim could be **h** as far as
Dn	10:12	before God, your prayer was **h**.
Dn	12: 8	I **h**, but I did not understand;
Dn	13:44	The Lᴏʀᴅ **h** her prayer.
Mt	2: 3	When King Herod **h** this, he was
Mt	5:21	"You have **h** that it was said to your
Mt	5:27	"You have **h** that it was said,
Mt	5:33	"Again you have **h** that it was said
Mt	5:38	"You have **h** that it was said,
Mt	5:43	"You have **h** that it was said,
Mk	6: 2	many who **h** him were astonished.
Mk	14:64	You have **h** the blasphemy.
Lk	12: 3	in the darkness will be **h** in the light,
Jn	8:26	what I **h** from him I tell the world."
Acts	2: 6	because each one **h** them speaking
Rom	10:14	in him of whom they have not **h**?
1 Cor	2: 9	and ear has not **h**, and what has not
2 Cor	12: 4	into Paradise and **h** ineffable things,
2 Tm	1:13	sound words that you **h** from me,
Heb	4: 2	word that they **h** did not profit them,
2 Pt	1:18	We ourselves **h** this voice come
1 Jn	1: 3	seen and **h** we proclaim now to you,
1 Jn	3:11	this is the message you have **h**
2 Jn	1: 6	as you **h** from the beginning,
Rev	1:10	**h** behind me a voice as loud as
Rev	22: 8	I, John, who **h** and saw these things,

HEARERS → HEAR

Jas	1:22	doers of the word and not **h** only,

HEARING → HEAR

Nm	11: 1	bitterly in the **h** of the Lᴏʀᴅ;
Sir	4: 8	Give a **h** to the poor, and return
Bar	1: 3	of this scroll in the **h** of Jeconiah,
Am	8:11	but for **h** the word of the Lᴏʀᴅ.
Lk	4:21	passage is fulfilled in your **h**."
1 Cor	12:17	were an eye, where would the **h** be?
1 Cor	12:17	If the whole body were **h**,

HEARS → HEAR

Ps	69:34	For the Lᴏʀᴅ **h** the poor,
Prv	15:29	wicked, but **h** the prayer of the just.
Is	30:19	as soon as he **h** he will answer you.
Jn	5:24	whoever **h** my word and believes
Jn	8:47	belongs to God **h** the words of God;
1 Jn	5:14	according to his will, he **h** us.
Rev	22:18	warn everyone who **h** the prophetic

HEART → BROKENHEARTED, HEART'S, HEARTLESS, HEARTS, WHOLEHEARTED

Gn	6: 6	on the earth, and his **h** was grieved.
Ex	28:30	may be over Aaron's **h** whenever he
Dt	4:29	you search after him with all your **h**
Dt	6: 5	with your whole **h**, and with your
Dt	10:12	with your whole **h** and with your
Dt	11:13	with your whole **h** and your whole
Dt	13: 4	your God, with all your **h** and soul.
Dt	26:16	to observe them with your whole **h**
Dt	29: 3	the Lᴏʀᴅ has not given you a **h** to understand,
Dt	29:17	whose **h** is now turning away from the Lᴏʀᴅ,
Dt	30: 2	with your whole **h** and your whole
Dt	30: 6	with your whole **h** and your whole
Dt	30:10	with your whole **h** and your whole
Dt	30:14	in your mouth and in your **h**, to do it.
Jos	22: 5	serve him with your whole **h**
1 Sm	10: 9	to leave Samuel, God changed his **h**.
1 Sm	12:20	but serve him with your whole **h**.
1 Sm	12:24	serve him faithfully with all your **h**,
1 Sm	13:14	his own **h** to appoint as ruler over
1 Sm	16: 7	The Lᴏʀᴅ looks into the **h**.
2 Sm	6:16	Lᴏʀᴅ, she despised him in her **h**.
1 Kgs	2: 4	in faithfulness with their whole **h**
1 Kgs	8:39	to their ways, you who know every **h**;
1 Kgs	8:48	if with their whole **h** and soul they
1 Kgs	9: 3	eyes and my **h** shall be there always.
1 Kgs	11: 4	was old his wives had turned his **h**
1 Kgs	14: 8	and followed me with his whole **h**,
1 Kgs	15:14	yet Asa's **h** was entirely
2 Kgs	23: 3	and decrees with his whole **h** and soul,
1 Chr	28: 9	and serve him with a whole **h**
2 Chr	6:38	if with all their **h** and soul they turn
2 Chr	7:16	eyes and my **h** shall be there always.
2 Chr	15:12	ancestors, with all their **h** and soul;
2 Chr	15:17	yet Asa's **h** was undivided as long
2 Chr	22: 9	the Lᴏʀᴅ with his whole **h**."
2 Chr	34:31	decrees with his whole **h** and soul,
2 Chr	36:13	hardened his **h** rather than return
Tb	1:12	I was mindful of God with all my **h**,
1 Mc	1: 3	him, and his **h** became proud
1 Mc	2:24	his **h** was moved and his just fury
Jb	22:22	and place his words in your **h**.
Jb	31: 7	and my **h** has followed my eyes,
Jb	37: 1	At this my **h** trembles and leaps
Ps	7:11	above me saving the upright of **h**.
Ps	9: 2	praise you, Lᴏʀᴅ, with all my **h**;
Ps	16: 9	Therefore my **h** is glad, my soul
Ps	19:15	the thoughts of my **h** before you,
Ps	20: 5	Grant what is in your **h**, fulfill your
Ps	26: 2	and test me; search my **h** and mind.
Ps	28: 7	and my shield, in whom my **h** trusts.
Ps	28: 7	I am helped, so my **h** rejoices;
Ps	44:22	who knows the secrets of the **h**?
Ps	51:12	A clean **h** create for me, God;
Ps	51:19	a contrite, humbled **h**, O God,
Ps	66:18	Had I cherished evil in my **h**,

Ps	73: 1	upright, to those who are pure of **h**!
Ps	73:26	Though my flesh and my **h** fail,
Ps	73:26	God is the rock of my **h**, my portion
Ps	81:13	away to the hardness of their **h**;
Ps	90:12	that we may gain wisdom of **h**.
Ps	97:11	and gladness for the honest of **h**.
Ps	108: 2	My **h** is steadfast, God; my **h** is
Ps	109:22	my **h** is pierced within me.
Ps	111: 1	with all my **h** in the assembled
Ps	119: 2	who seek him with all their **h**.
Ps	119:10	With all my **h** I seek you; do not let
Ps	119:11	In my **h** I treasure your promise,
Ps	119:34	law, to observe it with all my **h**.
Ps	119:36	Direct my **h** toward your
Ps	119:58	I entreat you with all my **h**:
Ps	119:69	I keep your precepts with all my **h**.
Ps	119:111	they are the joy of my **h**.
Ps	119:112	My **h** is set on fulfilling your
Ps	119:145	I call with all my **h**, O Lord;
Ps	119:161	but my **h** reveres only your word.
Ps	138: 1	I thank you, Lord, with all my **h**;
Ps	139:23	Probe me, God, know my **h**;
Ps	141: 4	Do not let my **h** incline to evil,
Prv	2: 2	inclining your **h** to understanding;
Prv	3: 5	Trust in the Lord with all your **h**,
Prv	4: 4	"Let your **h** hold fast my words:
Prv	4:21	your sight, keep them within your **h**;
Prv	4:23	With all vigilance guard your **h**,
Prv	6:21	them fastened over your **h** always,
Prv	6:25	not lust in your **h** after her beauty,
Prv	7: 3	write them on the tablet of your **h**.
Prv	12:25	Worry weighs down the **h**,
Prv	13:12	Hope deferred makes the **h** sick,
Prv	14:13	Even in laughter the **h** may be sad,
Prv	15:13	A glad **h** lights up the face,
Prv	15:13	but an anguished **h** breaks the spirit.
Prv	15:30	cheerful glance brings joy to the **h**;
Prv	17:22	A joyful **h** is the health of the body,
Prv	20: 9	say, "I have made my **h** clean, I am
Prv	21: 1	A king's **h** is channeled water
Prv	22:11	The Lord loves the pure of **h**;
Prv	22:15	Folly is bound to the **h** of a youth,
Prv	23:15	son, if your **h** is wise, my **h** also will
Prv	23:17	Do not let your **h** envy sinners,
Prv	23:26	give me your **h**, and let your eyes
Prv	24:17	stumble, do not let your **h** exult,
Prv	27:19	water, so the **h** reflects the person.
Eccl	2:10	my **h** rejoiced in the fruit of all my
Eccl	5: 1	and let not your **h** be quick to utter
Eccl	7: 7	the wise, and a bribe corrupts the **h**.
Eccl	7:21	not give your **h** to every word that is spoken;
Eccl	9: 7	and drink your wine with a merry **h**,
Sg	4: 9	You have ravished my **h**, my sister,
Sg	5: 2	was sleeping, but my **h** was awake.
Sg	8: 6	Set me as a seal upon your **h**,
Sir	2: 2	Be sincere of **h** and steadfast,
Sir	21: 6	fears the Lord repents in his **h**.
Sir	37:17	The root of all conduct is the **h**;
Is	40: 2	Speak to the **h** of Jerusalem,
Is	51: 7	people who have my teaching at **h**:
Is	57:15	lowly, to revive the **h** of the crushed.
Is	66:14	You will see and your **h** shall exult,
Jer	3:15	for you shepherds after my own **h**,
Jer	4:14	Cleanse your **h** of evil, Jerusalem,
Jer	9:25	of Israel is uncircumcised at **h**.
Jer	17: 9	than anything is the human **h**,
Jer	17:10	explore the mind and test the **h**,
Jer	24: 7	I will give them a **h** to know me,
Jer	24: 7	return to me with their whole **h**.
Jer	29:13	when you seek me with all your **h**,
Jer	32:39	I will give them one **h** and one way,
Jer	32:41	in this land, with all my **h** and soul.
Bar	2:31	I will give them a **h** and ears that listen;
Ez	11:19	I will give them another **h**
Ez	18:31	make for yourselves a new **h**

Ez	28: 2	Because you are haughty of **h**,
Ez	28: 2	yet you pretend you are a god at **h**!
Ez	36:26	I will give you a new **h**, and a new
Ez	36:26	I will remove the **h** of stone
Ez	36:26	and give you a **h** of flesh.
Ez	44: 7	uncircumcised in **h** and flesh,
Dn	3:39	with contrite **h** and humble spirit let
Hos	11: 8	My **h** is overwhelmed, my pity is
Jl	2:12	return to me with your whole **h**,
Zep	3:14	Be glad and exult with all your **h**,
Mal	2: 2	you do not take to **h** giving honor
Mal	3:24	He will turn the **h** of fathers to their sons, and the **h** of sons
Mt	5: 8	Blessed are the clean of **h**, for they
Mt	5:28	adultery with her in his **h**.
Mt	6:21	treasure is, there also will your **h** be.
Mt	11:29	me, for I am meek and humble of **h**;
Mt	12:34	fullness of the **h** the mouth speaks.
Mt	13:15	and understand with their **h** and be
Mt	15:19	For from the **h** come evil thoughts,
Mt	18:35	forgives his brother from his **h**."
Mt	22:37	with all your **h**, with all your soul,
Mk	11:23	does not doubt in his **h** but believes
Mk	12:30	the Lord your God with all your **h**,
Lk	2:19	things, reflecting on them in her **h**.
Lk	2:51	mother kept all these things in her **h**.
Lk	6:45	of goodness in his **h** produces good,
Lk	6:45	fullness of the **h** the mouth speaks.
Lk	8:15	it with a generous and good **h**,
Lk	10:27	with all your **h**, with all your being,
Lk	12:34	treasure is, there also will your **h** be.
Lk	24:25	How slow of **h** to believe all
Acts	2:46	with exultation and sincerity of **h**,
Acts	4:32	of believers was of one **h** and mind,
Acts	5: 3	why has Satan filled your **h** so
Acts	8:21	for your **h** is not upright before God.
Acts	15: 8	who knows the **h**, bore witness
Acts	16:14	and the Lord opened her **h** to pay
Acts	28:27	and understand with their **h** and be
Rom	2:29	and circumcision is of the **h**,
Rom	10: 8	your mouth and in your **h**" (that is,
Rom	10: 9	in your **h** that God raised him
1 Cor	14:25	secrets of his **h** will be disclosed,
2 Cor	2: 4	and anguish of **h** I wrote to you
Eph	6: 5	in sincerity of **h**, as to Christ,
Eph	6: 6	doing the will of God from the **h**,
Phil	1: 7	because I hold you in my **h**,
1 Tm	1: 5	instruction is love from a pure **h**,
2 Tm	2:22	call on the Lord with purity of **h**.
Phlm	1:12	him, that is, my own **h**, back to you.
Heb	3:12	may have an evil and unfaithful **h**,
Heb	4:12	reflections and thoughts of the **h**.
Heb	10:22	let us approach with a sincere **h**
Heb	12: 5	or lose **h** when reproved by him;
1 Pt	1:22	another intensely from a [pure] **h**.

HEART'S → HEART

Ps	37: 4	who will give you your **h** desire.
Rom	10: 1	my **h** desire and prayer to God

HEARTLESS → HEART

Rom	1:31	are senseless, faithless, **h**, ruthless.

HEARTS → HEART

Ex	35:21	all, as their **h** moved them and their
Jos	24:23	you and turn your **h** to the Lord,
1 Sm	10:26	warriors whose **h** the Lord had
1 Chr	29:18	and direct their **h** toward you.
1 Mc	1:62	and resolved in their **h** not to eat
Jb	1: 5	sinned and cursed God in their **h**."
Ps	7:10	O just God, who tries **h** and minds.
Ps	33:15	fashioned together their **h** is the One
Ps	95: 8	Do not harden your **h** as at Meribah,
Ps	104:15	wine to gladden their **h**, oil to make
Prv	17: 3	but the tester of **h** is the Lord.
Prv	21: 2	but it is the Lord who weighs **h**.
Eccl	9: 3	madness is in their **h** during life;

Sir	48:10	To turn back the **h** of parents toward
Is	29:13	though their **h** are far from me,
Jer	4: 4	remove the foreskins of your **h**,
Jer	17: 1	point upon the tablets of their **h**,
Jer	31:33	them, and write it upon their **h**;
Lam	5:15	The joy of our **h** has ceased,
Ez	14: 3	of their idols alive in their **h**,
Ez	24:25	the pride of their **h**, their sons
Mt	15: 8	lips, but their **h** are far from me;
Mk	6:52	the contrary, their **h** were hardened.
Mk	7: 6	lips, but their **h** are far from me;
Lk	1:17	turn the **h** of fathers toward children
Lk	16:15	of others, but God knows your **h**;
Lk	24:32	"Were not our **h** burning [within]
Jn	14: 1	"Do not let your **h** be troubled.
Jn	14:27	Do not let your **h** be troubled
Acts	1:24	Lord, who know the **h** of all,
Acts	15: 9	for by faith he purified their **h**.
Rom	2:15	of the law are written in their **h**,
Rom	5: 5	into our **h** through the holy Spirit
2 Cor	1:22	Spirit in our **h** as a first installment.
2 Cor	3: 2	written on our **h**, known and read
2 Cor	3: 3	but on tablets that are **h** of flesh.
2 Cor	4: 6	has shone in our **h** to bring to light
Eph	1:18	the eyes of [your] **h** be enlightened,
Eph	3:17	may dwell in your **h** through faith;
Phil	4: 7	all understanding will guard your **h**
Col	3:15	the peace of Christ control your **h**,
Col	3:16	with gratitude in your **h** to God.
1 Thes	2: 4	but rather God, who judges our **h**.
1 Thes	3:13	so as to strengthen your **h**, to be
2 Thes	2:17	encourage your **h** and strengthen
Phlm	1: 7	because the **h** of the holy ones have
Heb	3: 8	'Harden not your **h** as
Heb	8:10	and I will write them upon their **h**.
Heb	10:16	'I will put my laws in their **h**, and I
Heb	10:22	with our **h** sprinkled clean
Jas	4: 8	and purify your **h**, you of two
1 Pt	3:15	sanctify Christ as Lord in your **h**.
2 Pt	1:19	and the morning star rises in your **h**.
2 Pt	2:14	and their **h** are trained in greed.
1 Jn	3:20	in whatever our **h** condemn, for God is greater than our **h**
Rev	2:23	to know that I am the searcher of **h**

HEAT → HEATED

Gn	8:22	cold and **h**, Summer and winter,
Ps	19: 7	to the other; nothing escapes its **h**.
Dn	3:66	Fire and **h**, bless the Lord;
Hg	1:11	proclaimed a devastating **h** upon the land
Rev	16: 9	were burned by the scorching **h**

HEATED → HEAT

Dn	3:19	to be **h** seven times more than usual

HEAVEN → HEAVENLY, HEAVENS

Gn	14:19	High, the creator of **h** and earth;
Gn	21:17	God's angel called to Hagar from **h**:
Gn	22:11	of the LORD called to him from **h**,
Gn	24: 3	the God of **h** and the God of earth,
Ex	16: 4	to rain down bread from **h** for you.
Ex	20:22	that I have spoken to you from **h**.
Dt	3:24	What god in **h** or on earth can
Dt	4:26	I call **h** and earth this day to witness
Dt	26:15	then, from **h**, your holy abode,
Dt	31:28	so may call **h** and earth to witness
Jos	2:11	God, is God in **h** above and on earth
1 Kgs	8:23	there is no God like you in **h**
1 Kgs	8:30	the place of your enthronement, **h**,
1 Kgs	22:19	the whole host of **h** standing to his
2 Kgs	1:10	may fire come down from **h**
2 Kgs	2: 1	take Elijah up to **h** in a whirlwind,
2 Chr	6:14	there is no God like you in **h**
2 Chr	7:14	I will hear them from **h** and pardon
Ezr	7:12	scribe of the law of the God of **h**,
Jdt	5: 8	and worshiped the God of **h**,
1 Mc	2:58	zeal for the law, was taken up to **h**.
1 Mc	3:50	And they cried aloud to **H**:

Jb	16:19	Even now my witness is in **h**,
Ps	121: 2	LORD, the maker of **h** and earth.
Prv	30: 4	Who has gone up to **h** and come
Jer	10:11	The gods that did not make **h** and earth—
Jer	23:24	Do I not fill **h** and earth?—
Dn	2:19	vision, and he blessed the God of **h**:
Dn	7:13	the clouds of **h** One like a son
Dn	14: 5	but only the living God who made **h**
Mt	3: 2	for the kingdom of **h** is at hand!"
Mt	4:17	for the kingdom of **h** is at hand."
Mt	5:12	for your reward will be great in **h**.
Mt	5:19	be called least in the kingdom of **h**.
Mt	5:19	called greatest in the kingdom of **h**.
Mt	6: 9	Our Father in **h**, hallowed be your
Mt	6:10	your will be done, on earth as in **h**.
Mt	6:20	But store up treasures in **h**,
Mt	7:21	will enter the kingdom of **h**,
Mt	7:21	who does the will of my Father in **h**.
Mt	16:19	you the keys to the kingdom of **h**.
Mt	16:19	bind on earth shall be bound in **h**;
Mt	16:19	loose on earth shall be loosed in **h**."
Mt	18: 3	you will not enter the kingdom of **h**.
Mt	18:18	bind on earth shall be bound in **h**,
Mt	18:18	loose on earth shall be loosed in **h**.
Mt	19:14	the kingdom of **h** belongs to such as
Mt	19:21	and you will have treasure in **h**.
Mt	19:23	is rich to enter the kingdom of **h**.
Mt	23:13	kingdom of **h** before human beings.
Mt	24:35	**H** and earth will pass away, but my
Mt	26:64	and 'coming on the clouds of **h**.' "
Mt	28:18	"All power in **h** and on earth has
Mk	8:11	from **h** a sign from **h** to test him.
Mk	10:21	and you will have treasure in **h**;
Mk	13:31	**H** and earth will pass away, but my
Mk	14:62	coming with the clouds of **h**.' "
Lk	3:21	and was praying, **h** was opened
Lk	9:54	to call down fire from **h** to consume
Lk	10:20	your names are written in **h**."
Lk	12:33	an inexhaustible treasure in **h**
Lk	15: 7	**h** over one sinner who repents than
Lk	18:22	and you will have a treasure in **h**.
Lk	19:38	Peace in **h** and glory
Lk	21:33	**H** and earth will pass away, but my
Lk	24:51	from them and was taken up to **h**.
Jn	3:13	the one who has come down from **h**,
Jn	6:31	'He gave them bread from **h**
Jn	6:38	because I came down from **h** not
Jn	12:28	Then a voice came from **h**, "I have
Acts	1:11	as you have seen him going into **h**."
Acts	7:55	looked up intently to **h** and saw
Rom	10: 6	your heart, 'Who will go up into **h**?'
1 Cor	15:47	the second man, from **h**.
2 Cor	12: 2	was caught up to the third **h**.
Eph	1:10	things in Christ, in **h** and on earth.
Phil	2:10	of those in **h** and on earth and under
Phil	3:20	But our citizenship is in **h**,
Col	1: 5	of the hope reserved for you in **h**.
Col	1:16	in him were created all things in **h**
Col	4: 1	that you too have a Master in **h**.
1 Thes	1:10	and to await his Son from **h**,
1 Thes	4:16	will come down from **h**,
Heb	9:24	one, but **h** itself, that he might now
Heb	12:23	of the firstborn enrolled in **h**,
1 Pt	1: 4	and unfading, kept in **h** for you
1 Pt	3:22	who has gone into **h** and is
2 Pt	1:18	voice come from **h** while we were
Rev	4: 1	I had a vision of an open door to **h**,
Rev	5:13	I heard every creature in **h**
Rev	11:19	God's temple in **h** was opened,
Rev	12: 7	Then war broke out in **h**;
Rev	19: 1	loud voice of a great multitude in **h**,
Rev	19:14	The armies of **h** followed him,
Rev	21: 1	Then I saw a new **h** and a new earth.
Rev	21: 2	coming down out of **h** from God,
Rev	21:10	coming down out of **h** from God.

HEAVENLY → HEAVEN

Mt	5:48	just as your **h** Father is perfect.
Lk	2:13	there was a multitude of the **h** host
2 Cor	5: 2	further clothed with our **h** habitation
2 Tm	4:18	will bring me safe to his **h** kingdom.
Heb	3: 1	sharing in a **h** calling,
Heb	6: 4	tasted the **h** gift and shared
Heb	9:23	for the copies of the **h** things to be
Heb	12:22	of the living God, the **h** Jerusalem,

HEAVENS → HEAVEN

Gn	1: 1	when God created the **h**
Gn	2: 1	Thus the **h** and the earth and all
Gn	28:12	with its top reaching to the **h**;
Dt	10:14	Look, the **h**, even the highest **h**,
Dt	28:12	the **h**, to give your land rain in due
Dt	28:23	The **h** over your heads will be like bronze
Dt	33:26	who rides the **h** in his power,
2 Sm	22:10	He parted the **h** and came down,
1 Kgs	8:27	If the **h** and the highest **h** cannot
2 Kgs	19:15	It is you who made the **h**
Neh	9: 6	You made the **h**, the highest **h**
Jb	38:33	you know the ordinances of the **h**;
Jb	41: 3	Everything under the **h** is mine.
Ps	8: 4	When I see your **h**, the work of your
Ps	19: 2	The **h** declare the glory of God;
Ps	33: 6	Lord's word the **h** were made;
Ps	57: 6	Be exalted over the **h**, God;
Ps	73:25	Whom else have I in the **h**?
Ps	102:26	the **h** are the work of your hands.
Ps	103:11	For as the **h** tower over the earth,
Ps	108: 5	your mercy is greater than the **h**;
Ps	115:16	The **h** belong to the Lord, but he
Ps	136: 5	Who skillfully made the **h**, for his
Ps	148: 1	Praise the Lord from the **h**;
Prv	3:19	established the **h** by understanding;
Eccl	3: 1	a time for every affair under the **h**.
Is	1: 2	Hear, O **h**, and listen, O earth,
Is	14:12	How you have fallen from the **h**,
Is	45: 8	you **h**, like dew from above,
Is	51: 6	Though the **h** vanish like smoke,
Is	55: 9	as the **h** are higher than the earth,
Is	65:17	See, I am creating new **h** and a new
Is	66: 1	The **h** are my throne, the earth,
Jer	31:37	If the **h** on high could be measured,
Ez	1: 1	by the river Chebar, the **h** opened,
Jl	3: 3	I will set signs in the **h**
Mt	3:16	the **h** were opened [for him], and he
Acts	7:49	'The **h** are my throne, the earth is
Acts	7:56	I see the **h** opened and the Son
Eph	4:10	who ascended far above all the **h**,
Heb	4:14	priest who has passed through the **h**,
Heb	7:26	from sinners, higher than the **h**.
2 Pt	3: 5	ignore the fact that the **h** existed
2 Pt	3:10	the **h** will pass away with a mighty
Rev	19:11	Then I saw the **h** opened, and there

HEAVIER → HEAVY

Prv	27: 3	a fool's provocation is **h** than both.

HEAVY → HEAVIER

Ex	18:18	The task is too **h** for you;
Dt	25:13	differing weights in your bag, one **h**
1 Kgs	12: 4	"Your father put a **h** yoke on us.
Ps	88: 8	Your wrath lies **h** upon me;
Sir	30:13	your son and make **h** his yoke,
Is	47: 6	the aged you laid a very **h** yoke.
Mt	23: 4	They tie up **h** burdens [hard]

HEBREW → HEBREWS, HEBREWS'

Gn	14:13	brought the news to Abram the **H**,
Gn	41:12	There was a **H** youth with us,
Ex	1:19	"The **H** women are not like
Ex	2:11	he saw an Egyptian striking a **H**,
Ex	21: 2	When you purchase a **H** slave, he is
Sir	Pr: 2	in **H** do not have the same effect
Jer	34: 9	Everyone must free their **H** slaves,
Jon	1: 9	"I am a **H**," he replied; "I fear

Jn	19:20	and it was written in **H**, Latin,
Acts	21:40	was quiet he addressed them in **H**.
Phil	3: 5	of Benjamin, a **H** of **H** parentage,

HEBREWS → HEBREW

Ex	3:18	the God of the **H**, has come to meet
Ex	9: 1	says the Lord, the God of the **H**:
Jdt	10:12	"I am a daughter of the **H**, and I am
2 Cor	11:22	Are they **H**? So am I.

HEBREWS' → HEBREW

Ex	2: 6	and said, "It is one of the **H** children."

HEBRON → =MAMRE

Gn	13:18	the oak of Mamre, which is at **H**.
Gn	23: 2	now **H**—in the land of Canaan,
Jos	14:13	and gave him **H** as his heritage.
Jos	20: 7	**H**) in the mountain region of Judah.
Jos	21:13	city of refuge for homicides at **H**,
Jgs	16: 3	to the top of the ridge opposite **H**.
2 Sm	2:11	David was king in **H** over the house
2 Sm	3: 2	Sons were born to David in **H**:
1 Chr	2:43	The sons of **H** were Korah,
1 Chr	11: 1	Israel gathered around David in **H**,

HEDGE

Is	5: 5	Take away its **h**, give it to grazing,
Hos	2: 8	I will **h** in her way with thorns
Mi	7: 4	brier, the most honest like a thorn **h**.

HEED → HEEDING, HEEDS

Ex	23:13	Give **h** to all that I have told you.
Prv	17: 4	The evildoer gives **h** to wicked lips,

HEEDING → HEED

Dt	7:12	your reward for **h** these ordinances

HEEDS → HEED

Prv	15: 5	but whoever **h** reproof is prudent.

HEEL

Gn	3:15	head, while you strike at their **h**.
Gn	25:26	brother came out, gripping Esau's **h**;
Jb	18: 9	A trap seizes him by the **h**, a snare
Jn	13:18	food has raised his **h** against me.'

HEIFER

Gn	15: 9	Bring me a three-year-old **h**,
Nm	19: 2	for you a red **h** without defect
Jgs	14:18	"If you had not plowed with my **h**,

HEIGHT → HIGH

Nm	23: 3	And so he went out on the barren **h**.
Sir	1: 3	Heaven's **h**, earth's extent,
Rom	8:39	nor **h**, nor depth, nor any other
Eph	3:18	breadth and length and **h** and depth,
Rev	21:16	miles in length and width and **h**.

HEIGHTS → HIGH

Ps	18:34	like a deer's, and set me on the **h**,
Ps	148: 1	praise him in the **h**.
Hb	3:19	and enables me to tread upon the **h**.

HEIR → HEIRS

Gn	15: 4	your own offspring will be your **h**.
Lk	20:14	said to one another, 'This is the **h**.
Gal	4: 7	a child, and if a child then also an **h**,
Heb	1: 2	whom he made **h** of all things

HEIRS → HEIR

Rom	4:14	who adhere to the law are the **h**,
Rom	8:17	then **h**, of God and joint **h** with Christ,
Gal	3:29	**h** according to the promise.
Ti	3: 7	become **h** in hope of eternal life.
Heb	11: 9	and Jacob, **h** of the same promise;
Jas	2: 5	**h** of the kingdom that he promised
1 Pt	3: 7	since we are joint **h** of the gift

HELD → HOLD

2 Kgs	3: 3	still **h** fast unceasingly to the sins
Col	2:19	and **h** together by its ligaments
Rev	1:16	In his right hand he **h** seven stars,
Rev	6: 5	and its rider **h** a scale in his hand.
Rev	10: 2	In his hand he **h** a small scroll

HELDAI
Zec   6:14 as a gracious reminder to H,

HELIODORUS
2 Mc   3:40 was how the matter concerning H

HELLENISTS
Acts   6: 1 grow, the H complained against
Acts   9:29 also spoke and debated with the H,

HELMET
Ps   108: 9 Ephraim is the h for my head,
Wis   5:18 wear sure judgment for a h,
Is   59:17 victory as a h on his head;
Eph   6:17 And take the h of salvation
1 Thes 5: 8 and the h that is hope for salvation.

HELP → HELPED, HELPER, HELPLESS, HELPS
Gn   4: 1 child with the h of the LORD."
Ex   23: 5 you must h him with it.
1 Sm   7:12 far as this place the LORD has been our h."
1 Chr 12:23 to David's h until there was a vast
2 Chr 28:16 time King Ahaz sent an appeal for h
Neh   6:16 our God's h that this work had been
Jdt   6:21 called upon the God of Israel for h.
Ps   22:20 my strength, come quickly to h me.
Ps   33:20 the LORD, he is our h and shield.
Ps   40:18 You are my h and deliverer;
Ps   46: 2 an ever-present h in distress.
Ps   79: 9 H us, God our savior, on account
Ps 108:13 worthless is human h.
Ps 115: 9 LORD, who is their h and shield.
Ps 121: 1 From whence shall come my h?
Ps 146: 5 Blessed the one whose h is the God
Sir   2: 6 Trust in God, and he will h you;
Sir   29: 9 of the commandment, h the poor,
Is   41:10 I will h you, I will uphold you
Lam   1: 7 and she had no h, Her foes looked
Mk   9:24 out, "I do believe, h my unbelief!"
Acts 16: 9 over to Macedonia and h us."
Acts 26:22 I have enjoyed God's h to this very
Heb   2:18 able to h those who are being tested.
Heb   4:16 and to find grace for timely h.

HELPED → HELP
Lk   1:54 He has h Israel his servant,
2 Cor 6: 2 on the day of salvation I h you."

HELPER → HELP
Ps   30:11 mercy on me; LORD, be my h."
Heb 13: 6 "The Lord is my h, [and] I will not

HELPLESS → HELP
Ps   10:14 To you the h can entrust their cause;

HELPS → HELP
Ps   37:40 The LORD h and rescues them,

HEM
Lk   19:43 you and h you in on all sides.

HEMAN
1 Chr 15:19 The singers, H, Asaph, and Ethan,
Ps   88: 1 a *maskil* of H the Ezrahite.

HEMORRHAGES
Lk   8:43 a woman afflicted with h for twelve

HEN
Mt   23:37 as a h gathers her young under her
Lk   13:34 together as a h gathers her brood

HERALD
Is   40: 9 mountain, Zion, h of good news!
Is   40: 9 voice, Jerusalem, h of good news!
2 Pt   2: 5 Noah, a h of righteousness,

HERBS
Ex   12: 8 with unleavened bread and bitter h.
Nm   9:11 with unleavened bread and bitter h,

HERD → HERDS
Mt   8:31 us out, send us into the h of swine."

HERDS → HERD
Dt   8:13 your h and flocks have increased,

Dt   12: 6 the firstlings of your h and flocks.
2 Sm 12: 4 h to prepare a meal for the traveler

HERE
Ex   3: 4 Moses! He answered, "H I am."
1 Sm 3: 4 Samuel, who answered, "H I am."
Prv   9: 4 "Let whoever is naive turn in h;
Is   6: 8 "H I am," I said; "send me!"
Is   40: 9 the cities of Judah: H is your God!
Mt   12:42 something greater than Solomon h.
Mt   24:23 you then, 'Look, h is the Messiah!'
Mk   16: 6 He has been raised; he is not h.
Rev   4: 1 "Come up h and I will show you
Rev 11:12 heaven say to them, "Come up h."

HERITAGE
Jdt   9:12 God of the h of Israel,
Ps 119:111 Your testimonies are my h forever;

HERMON
Dt   3: 8 from the Wadi Arnon to Mount H
Ps 133: 3 Like dew of H coming down

HEROD → HERODIANS
1. King of Judea who tried to kill Jesus (Mt 2; Lk 1:5).
2. Son of 1. Tetrarch of Galilee who arrested and beheaded John the Baptist (Mt 14:1-12; Mk 6:14-29; Lk 3:1, 19-20; 9:7-9); tried Jesus (Lk 23:6-15).
3. Grandson of 1. King of Judea who killed James (Acts 12:2); arrested Peter (Acts 12:3-19). Death (Acts 12:19-23).

HERODIANS → HEROD
Mt   22:16 disciples to him, with the H, saying,
Mk   3: 6 took counsel with the H against him
Mk   12:13 and H to him to ensnare him in his

HERODIAS
Wife of Herod the Tetrarch who persuaded her daughter to ask for John the Baptist's head (Mt 14:1-12; Mk 6:14-29; Lk 3:19).

HEROES
Gn   6: 4 They were the h of old, the men

HESHBON
Nm   21:26 For H was the city of Sihon,
Dt   3: 6 king of H, so also here we put all

HEWN
Is   51: 1 to the rock from which you were h,
Mk   15:46 in a tomb that had been h

HEZEKIAH
King of Judah (Sir 48:17-25). Restored the temple and worship (2 Chr 29–31). Sought the LORD for help against Assyria (2 Kgs 18–19; 2 Chr 32:1-23; Is 36–37). Illness healed (2 Kgs 20:1-11; 2 Chr 32:24-26; Is 38). Judged for showing Babylonians his treasures (2 Kgs 20:12-21; 2 Chr 32:31; Is 39).

HEZRON
Ru   4:18 Perez was the father of H,
Mt   1: 3 Perez became the father of H,

HID → HIDE
Gn   3: 8 and his wife h themselves
Ex   2: 2 he was, she h him for three months.
Ex   3: 6 Moses h his face, for he was afraid
Jos   6:17 because she h the messengers we
1 Kgs 18:13 that I h a hundred of the prophets
2 Mc 1:19 h it secretly in the hollow of a dry
Is   49: 2 arrow, in his quiver he h me.
Is   54: 8 for a moment I h my face from you;
Ez   39:23 me, I h my face from them,

HIDDEN → HIDE
Jos   2: 6 and h them among her stalks of flax
Jos   7:22 and there they were, h in the tent,
2 Kgs 11: 3 six years he remained h with her
Jb   28:11 streams, and brings h things to light.
Ps   69: 6 my faults are not h from you.
Ps 142: 4 this path, they have h a trap for me.
Prv   2: 4 and like h treasures search her out,
Prv 27: 5 rebuke than a love that remains h.
Is   40:27 "My way is h from the LORD,
Dn   2:22 He reveals deep and h things

Mt	13:35	I will announce what has lain **h**
Mk	4:22	there is nothing **h** except to be made
Lk	10:21	for although you have **h** these things
Lk	18:34	the word remained **h** from them
1 Cor	2: 7	wisdom, mysterious, **h**, which God
1 Cor	4: 5	bring to light what is **h** in darkness
Eph	3: 9	plan of the mystery **h** from ages past
Col	1:26	the mystery **h** from ages
Col	2: 3	in whom are **h** all the treasures
Col	3: 3	your life is **h** with Christ in God.
Rev	2:17	I shall give some of the **h** manna;

HIDE → HID, HIDDEN

Gn	18:17	Shall I **h** from Abraham what I am
Ex	2: 3	when she could no longer **h** him,
Dt	31:17	them and **h** my face from them;
Ps	13: 2	How long will you **h** your face
Ps	17: 8	**h** me in the shadow of your wings
Ps	27: 5	For God will **h** me in his shelter
Sir	4:23	time, and do not **h** your wisdom;
Ez	39:29	I will no longer **h** my face
Rev	6:16	**h** us from the face of the one who

HIGH → HEIGHT, HEIGHTS, HIGHER, HIGHEST, HIGHLY, HIGHWAY

Gn	14:18	He was a priest of God Most **H**.
Gn	14:22	God Most **H**, the creator of heaven
1 Kgs	3: 2	were sacrificing on the **h** places,
1 Kgs	11: 7	then built a **h** place to Chemosh,
1 Kgs	12:31	built temples on the **h** places
Ps	7: 8	and return on **h** above them,
Ps	21: 8	through the mercy of the Most **H**.
Ps	46: 5	the holy dwelling of the Most **H**.
Ps	82: 6	offspring of the Most **H** all of you,
Ps	91: 1	dwell in the shelter of the Most **H**,
Ps	113: 5	Lᴏʀᴅ our God, enthroned on **h**,
Wis	5:15	thought of them is with the Most **H**.
Sir	35:12	Give to the Most **H** as he has given to you,
Is	14:14	I will be like the Most **H**!"
Jer	2:20	On every **h** hill, under every green
Mt	4: 8	took him up to a very **h** mountain,
Mt	17: 1	and led them up a **h** mountain
Mk	5: 7	me, Jesus, Son of the Most **H** God?
Mk	14:53	They led Jesus away to the **h** priest,
Jn	18:22	the way you answer the **h** priest?"
Acts	23: 4	you revile God's **h** priest?"
Eph	4: 8	"He ascended on **h** and took
Heb	2:17	and faithful **h** priest before God
Heb	7: 1	Salem and priest of God Most **H**,"
Heb	7:26	that we should have such a **h** priest:

HIGHER → HIGH

Dt	28:43	will rise above you **h** and **h**,

HIGHEST → HIGH

1 Kgs	8:27	the **h** heavens cannot contain you,
Mt	21: 9	of the Lord; hosanna in the **h**."
Lk	2:14	"Glory to God in the **h** and on earth
Lk	19:38	in heaven and glory in the **h**."

HIGHLY → HIGH

Rom	12: 3	of himself more **h** than one ought

HIGHWAY → HIGH, WAY

Is	40: 3	in the wasteland a **h** for our God!

HILKIAH

2 Kgs	22:10	king, "**H** the priest has given me
2 Chr	34:14	**H** the priest found the book

HILL → HILLS

Ex	17: 9	on top of the **h** with the staff of God
Is	40: 4	every mountain and **h** made low;
Lk	3: 5	mountain and **h** shall be made low.

HILLS → HILL

Ps	114: 6	You **h**, like lambs?
Prv	8:25	before the **h**, I was brought forth;
Is	2: 2	mountain and raised above the **h**.
Hos	10: 8	and to the **h**, "Fall upon us!"
Jl	4:18	and the **h** flow with milk,
Am	9:13	and all the **h** shall run with it.
Lk	23:30	and to the **h**, 'Cover us!'

HINDER → HINDERED, HINDRANCE

Acts	11:17	who was I to be able to **h** God?"

HINDERED → HINDER

1 Pt	3: 7	so that your prayers may not be **h**.

HINDRANCE → HINDER

Acts	28:31	and without **h** he proclaimed
Rom	14:13	block or **h** in the way of a brother.

HINGES

Prv	26:14	The door turns on its **h**

HIP

Gn	32:26	he struck Jacob's **h** at its socket,

HIRAM → =HURAM, =HURAM-ABI

King of Tyre; helped David build his palace (2 Sm 5:11-12; 1 Chr 14:1); helped Solomon build the temple (1 Kgs 5; 2 Chr 2) and his navy (1 Kgs 9:10-27; 2 Chr 8).

HIRE → HIRED, HIRES

Mt	20: 1	dawn to **h** laborers for his vineyard.

HIRED → HIRE

Dt	23: 5	and because they **h** Balaam,
1 Mc	5:39	have also **h** Arabians to help them,
Lk	15:15	So he **h** himself out to one
Jn	10:12	A **h** man, who is not a shepherd

HIRES → HIRE

Prv	26:10	by is anyone who **h** a drunken fool.

HITTITE → HITTITES

Gn	23:10	So Ephron the **H** replied
Gn	27:46	with life because of the **H** women.
2 Sm	11: 3	and wife of Uriah the **H**,
2 Sm	11:17	fell, and Uriah the **H** also died.
Ez	16: 3	was an Amorite, your mother a **H**.

HITTITES → HITTITE

Gn	25:10	Abraham had bought from the **H**;
Dt	20:17	the **H**, Amorites, Canaanites,
Ezr	9: 1	Canaanites, **H**, Perizzites, Jebusites,
Neh	9: 8	give the land of the Canaanites, **H**,

HIVITE → HIVITES

Gn	34: 2	son of Hamor the **H**, the leader

HIVITES → HIVITE

Ex	23:28	I will send hornets to drive the **H**,
Jos	9: 7	But the Israelites replied to the **H**,

HOBAB

Nm	10:29	Moses said to **H**, son of Reuel
Jgs	4:11	Cain, the descendants of **H**,

HOLD → HELD, HOLDING, HOLDS

Dt	13: 5	serve, and to him you shall **h** fast.
Ps	73:23	you take **h** of my right hand.
Prv	3:18	and those who **h** fast are happy.
Prv	4: 4	"Let your heart **h** fast my words:
Prv	13:18	those who **h** on to reproof receive honor.
Sir	21:14	it cannot **h** any knowledge at all.
Zec	8:23	will take **h** of the cloak of every
Acts	7:60	do not **h** this sin against them";
1 Cor	15: 2	if you **h** fast to the word I preached
Phil	2:16	as you **h** on to the word of life,
Col	1:17	and in him all things **h** together.
2 Thes	2:15	**h** fast to the traditions that you were
1 Tm	6:12	Lay **h** of eternal life, to which you
Heb	3:14	Christ if only we **h** the beginning
Heb	4:14	God, let us **h** fast to our confession.
Heb	10:23	Let us **h** unwaveringly to our

HOLDING → HOLD

Ex	9: 2	to let them go and persist in **h** them,
1 Kgs	11:36	that David my servant may always have a **h**
1 Kgs	15: 4	his God, gave him a **h** in Jerusalem,
2 Kgs	8:19	promised David that he would leave him a **h**
Jn	20:17	Jesus said to her, "Stop **h** on to me,
Col	2:19	and not **h** closely to the head,
1 Tm	3: 9	**h** fast to the mystery of the faith

HOLDS → HOLD

Ps	37:24	fall, for the Lᴏʀᴅ **h** his hand.

Ps	139:10	your right hand **h** me fast.
Rev	2: 1	" 'The one who **h** the seven stars

HOLE → HOLES

Ps	7:16	He digs a **h** and bores it deep, but he

HOLES → HOLE

Hg	1: 6	worker labors for a bag full of **h**.

HOLIES → HOLY

Heb	9: 3	the tabernacle called the Holy of H,

HOLINESS → HOLY

Ps	89:36	By my **h** I swore once for all:
Ps	93: 5	**h** befits your house, LORD, for all
Wis	9: 3	And to govern the world in **h**
Ez	20:41	through you I will manifest my **h**
Ez	36:23	I will show the **h** of my great name,
Ez	38:23	so I will show my greatness and **h**
Am	4: 2	Lord GOD has sworn by his **h**:
Lk	1:75	in **h** and righteousness before him
Rom	1: 4	the spirit of **h** through resurrection
2 Cor	7: 1	making **h** perfect in the fear of God.
Eph	4:24	way in righteousness and **h** of truth.
1 Thes	4: 7	did not call us to impurity but to **h**.
1 Tm	2:15	persevere in faith and love and **h**,
Heb	12:10	in order that we may share his **h**.
Heb	12:14	that **h** without which no one will see
2 Pt	3:11	be, conducting yourselves in **h**

HOLLOW

Ex	27: 8	altar itself in the form of a **h** box.

HOLOCAUST → HOLOCAUSTS; see also BURNT [OFFERING]

Ps	40: 7	**H** and sin-offering you do not request;

HOLOCAUSTS → HOLOCAUST; see also BURNT [OFFERINGS]

Heb	10: 6	**h** and sin offerings you took no delight in.

HOLOFERNES

Assyrian general (Jdt 2:4). Beguiled and beheaded by Judith (Jdt 10–13).

HOLY → HOLIES, HOLINESS

Ex	3: 5	place where you stand is **h** ground.
Ex	15:11	like you, magnificent among the **h** ones?
Ex	19: 6	me a kingdom of priests, a **h** nation.
Ex	20: 8	the sabbath day—keep it **h**.
Ex	26:33	which divides the **h** place from the **h**
Lv	11:44	shall make and keep yourselves **h**, because I am **h**.
Lv	19: 2	Be **h**, for I, the LORD your God, am **h**.
Nm	16: 7	LORD then chooses is the **h** one.
Dt	5:12	keep it **h**, as the LORD, your God,
Dt	23:15	your camp must be **h**, so that he
Dt	26:15	from heaven, your **h** abode,
Jos	5:15	on which you are standing is **h**."
Jos	24:19	serve the LORD, for he is a **h** God;
1 Sm	2: 2	There is no **H** One like the LORD;
1 Sm	6:20	of the LORD, this **H** God?
2 Kgs	4: 9	"I know that he is a **h** man of God.
1 Chr	16:10	Glory in his **h** name;
1 Chr	16:35	we may give thanks to your **h** name
1 Chr	29: 3	all that I stored up for the **h** house,
2 Chr	3: 8	made the room of the **h** of holies.
2 Chr	30:27	reached heaven, God's **h** dwelling.
Ezr	9: 2	thus intermingling the **h** seed
Neh	11: 1	to reside in Jerusalem, the **h** city,
Tb	11:14	and blessed be all his **h** angels.
1 Mc	1:15	and abandoned the **h** covenant;
Jb	6:10	the commands of the **H** One.
Ps	2: 6	my king on Zion, my **h** mountain."
Ps	5: 8	bow down toward your **h** sanctuary
Ps	11: 4	The LORD is in his **h** temple;
Ps	22: 4	you are enthroned as the **H** One;
Ps	24: 3	Who can stand in his **h** place?
Ps	30: 5	give thanks to his **h** memory.
Ps	33:21	in his **h** name we trust.
Ps	47: 9	God sits upon his **h** throne.
Ps	77:14	Your way, God, is **h**; what god is as
Ps	78:54	he brought them to his **h** mountain,
Ps	89: 6	in the assembly of the **h** ones.

Ps	89:19	is our shield, the **H** One of Israel,
Ps	99: 3	great and awesome name: **H** is he!
Ps	99: 9	bow down before his **h** mountain;
Ps	105: 3	Glory in his **h** name; let hearts
Ps	111: 9	**h** and fearsome is his name.
Prv	9:10	of the **H** One is understanding.
Wis	3: 9	grace and mercy are with his **h** ones,
Wis	6:10	who keep the **h** precepts hallowed will be found **h**,
Is	1: 4	spurned the **H** One of Israel,
Is	5:16	by justice the **H** God shown **h**.
Is	6: 3	"H, h, h is the LORD of hosts!
Is	6:13	**H** offspring is the trunk.
Is	29:23	they shall sanctify the **H** One
Is	40:25	me as an equal? says the **H** One.
Is	43: 3	am your God, the **H** One of Israel,
Is	52:10	The LORD has bared his **h** arm
Is	54: 5	Your redeemer, the **H** One of Israel,
Is	57:15	whose name is **h**: I dwell in a high and **h** place,
Is	58:13	your own pursuits on my **h** day;
Is	58:13	the LORD's **h** day glorious;
Jer	17:22	but keep **h** the sabbath day, as I
Ez	22:26	law and desecrate what I consider **h**;
Ez	36:20	they desecrated my **h** name,
Dn	3:52	blessed is your **h** and glorious name,
Dn	8:13	I heard a **h** one speaking,
Dn	9:24	for your people and for your **h** city:
Dn	9:24	and a **h** of holies will be anointed.
Dn	11:28	his mind set against the **h** covenant;
Jon	2: 5	I again look upon your **h** temple?"
Hb	2:20	But the LORD is in his **h** temple;
Zec	8: 3	LORD of hosts, the **h** mountain.
Zec	14: 5	come, and all his **h** ones with him.
Zec	14:20	"H to the LORD" will be written
Mt	1:18	with child through the **h** Spirit.
Mt	3:11	He will baptize you with the **h** Spirit
Mt	4: 5	the devil took him to the **h** city,
Mt	24:15	in the **h** place (let the reader
Mt	28:19	and of the Son, and of the **h** Spirit,
Mk	1:24	who you are—the **H** One of God!"
Mk	3:29	blasphemes against the **h** Spirit will
Lk	1:15	will be filled with the **h** Spirit even
Lk	1:35	"The **h** Spirit will come upon you,
Lk	1:35	the child to be born will be called **h**,
Lk	1:49	things for me, and **h** is his name.
Lk	3:22	the **h** Spirit descended upon him
Lk	4: 1	Filled with the **h** Spirit,
Lk	10:21	moment he rejoiced [in] the **h** Spirit
Lk	11:13	in heaven give the **h** Spirit to those
Jn	6:69	that you are the **H** One of God."
Jn	14:26	the **h** Spirit that the Father will send
Jn	20:22	said to them, "Receive the **h** Spirit.
Acts	1: 5	will be baptized with the **h** Spirit."
Acts	2: 4	they were all filled with the **h** Spirit
Acts	2:27	nor will you suffer your **h** one to see
Acts	2:38	will receive the gift of the **h** Spirit.
Acts	4:27	this city against your **h** servant Jesus
Acts	5: 3	heart so that you lied to the **h** Spirit
Acts	8:15	that they might receive the **h** Spirit,
Acts	10:44	the **h** Spirit fell upon all who were
Acts	13:35	'You will not suffer your **h** one
Acts	15: 8	granting them the **h** Spirit just as he
Acts	19: 2	"Did you receive the **h** Spirit
Acts	19: 2	even heard that there is a **h** Spirit."
Rom	1: 2	his prophets in the **h** scriptures,
Rom	7:12	So then the law is **h**, and the commandment is **h**
Rom	11:16	If the firstfruits are **h**, so is
Rom	11:16	and if the root is **h**, so are
Rom	12: 1	sacrifice, **h** and pleasing to God,
Rom	15:16	sanctified by the **h** Spirit.
Rom	16:16	Greet one another with a **h** kiss.
1 Cor	7:14	husband is made **h** through his wife,
1 Cor	7:14	wife is made **h** through the brother.
1 Cor	16:20	Greet one another with a **h** kiss.
Eph	1: 4	to be **h** and without blemish before
Eph	3: 5	now been revealed to his **h** apostles
Eph	4:30	do not grieve the **h** Spirit of God,

Col	1:22	to present you h, without blemish,
Col	3:12	God's chosen ones, h and beloved,
1 Tm	2: 8	lifting up h hands, without anger
2 Tm	1: 9	He saved us and called us to a h life,
Ti	3: 5	rebirth and renewal by the h Spirit,
Heb	2: 4	the gifts of the h Spirit according
Heb	6: 4	gift and shared in the h Spirit
Heb	7:26	h, innocent, undefiled,
Heb	9: 2	this is called the H Place.
1 Pt	1:15	but, as he who called you is h, be h
1 Pt	1:16	is written, "Be h because I [am] h."
1 Pt	2: 5	be a h priesthood to offer spiritual
1 Pt	2: 9	a royal priesthood, a h nation,
1 Pt	3: 5	how the h women who hoped
2 Pt	1:21	by the h Spirit spoke under
1 Jn	2:20	that comes from the h one, and you
Jude	1:14	has come with his countless h ones
Jude	1:20	in your most h faith; pray in the h Spirit.
Rev	3: 7	" 'The h one, the true, who holds
Rev	4: 8	"H, h, h is the Lord God almighty,
Rev	11: 2	who will trample the h city
Rev	15: 4	For you alone are h. All the nations
Rev	20: 6	h is the one who shares in the first
Rev	21: 2	I also saw the h city, a new
Rev	21:10	and showed me the h city Jerusalem
Rev	22:11	still do right, and the h still be h."
Rev	22:19	in the h city described in this book.

HOME → HOMELAND, HOMELESS, HOMES

Dt	6: 7	Recite them when you are at h
Dt	11:19	speaking of them when you are at h
Ps	68: 7	God gives a h to the forsaken,
Ps	84: 4	As the sparrow finds a h
Ps	84: 4	My h is by your altars,
Ps	113: 9	Gives the childless wife a h,
Prv	7:11	and unruly, her feet cannot stay at h;
Prv	27: 8	the nest so is anyone far from h.
Eccl	12: 5	mortals go to their lasting h,
Is	55:12	in peace you shall be brought h;
Hg	1: 9	and what you brought h, I blew
Mk	2:11	rise, pick up your mat, and go h."
Mk	5:19	"Go h to your family and announce
Jn	19:27	hour the disciple took her into his h.
Acts	16:15	come and stay at my h," and she
1 Cor	11:34	he should eat at h, so that your
2 Cor	5: 8	leave the body and go h to the Lord.

HOMELAND → HOME, LAND

Heb	11:14	thus show that they are seeking a h.

HOMELESS → HOME

Is	58: 7	afflicted and the h into your house;
1 Cor	4:11	roughly treated, we wander about h

HOMES → HOME

Nm	32:18	to our h until all the Israelites have
1 Chr	16:43	each to their own h, and David
Neh	4: 8	daughters, your wives and your h."
Ps	49:12	Their tombs are their h forever,
Hos	11:11	And I will resettle them in their h,

HOMICIDE

Dt	4:42	a h might flee who killed a neighbor

HONEST → HONESTY

Lv	19:36	weights, an h ephah and an h hin.
Eccl	7:29	God made humankind h, but they have

HONESTY → HONEST

Gn	30:33	my wages, my h will testify for me:

HONEY → HONEYCOMB

Ex	3: 8	a land flowing with milk and h,
Ex	16:31	it tasted like wafers made with h.
Nm	14: 8	a land which flows with milk and h.
Jgs	14: 8	of bees in the lion's carcass, and h.
Ps	19:11	than h or drippings from the comb.
Ps	119:103	sweeter than h to my mouth!
Prv	5: 3	the lips of the stranger drip h,
Prv	25:16	If you find h, eat only what you
Sg	4:11	Your lips drip h, my bride,

Is	7:15	h he will eat so that he may learn
Ez	3: 3	it was as sweet as h in my mouth.
Mt	3: 4	His food was locusts and wild h.
Rev	10: 9	mouth it will taste as sweet as h."

HONEYCOMB → HONEY

Prv	16:24	Pleasing words are a h,

HONOR → HONORABLE, HONORED, HONORING, HONORS

Ex	20:12	H your father and your mother,
Dt	5:16	H your father and your mother,
1 Sm	2:30	I will h those who h me, but those
2 Sm	10: 3	these consolers—to h your father?
Tb	4: 3	H your mother, and do not abandon
Ps	8: 6	god, crowned him with glory and h.
Ps	112: 9	his horn shall be exalted in h.
Prv	3: 9	H the LORD with your wealth,
Prv	13:18	those who hold on to reproof receive h.
Prv	18:12	is haughty, but before h is humility.
Prv	19:11	to anger, and an h to overlook an offense.
Prv	22: 4	of the LORD is riches, h and life.
Prv	25:27	is not good; nor to seek h after h.
Prv	29:23	but the humble of spirit acquire h.
Sir	3: 3	Those who h their father atone for sins;
Sir	7:31	H God and respect the priest;
Mal	1: 6	a father, where is the h due to me?
Mal	2: 2	do not take to heart giving h to my name,
Mt	13:57	"A prophet is not without h except
Mt	15: 4	'H your father and your mother,'
Mt	19:19	h your father and your mother';
Mt	23: 6	They love places of h at banquets, seats of h in synagogues,
Mk	6: 4	"A prophet is not without h except
Lk	14: 8	not recline at table in the place of h.
Jn	4:44	that a prophet has no h in his native
Jn	5:23	Whoever does not h the Son does not h the Father
Jn	8:49	I h my Father, but you dishonor me.
Jn	12:26	The Father will h whoever serves
Rom	12:10	anticipate one another in showing h.
Rom	13: 7	respect is due, h to whom h is due.
1 Cor	12:23	we surround with greater h, and our
Eph	6: 2	"H your father and mother."
1 Tm	5:17	who preside well deserve double h,
Heb	2: 7	you crowned him with glory and h,
Heb	3: 3	house has more "h" than the house
1 Pt	1: 7	h at the revelation of Jesus Christ.
2 Pt	1:17	For he received h and glory
Rev	4: 9	the living creatures give glory and h
Rev	4:11	to receive glory and h and power,
Rev	5:12	strength, h and glory and blessing."
Rev	7:12	wisdom and thanksgiving, h, power,

HONORABLE → HONOR

Phil	4: 8	true, whatever is h, whatever is just,

HONORED → HONOR

1 Cor	12:26	if one part is h, all the parts share its

HONORING → HONOR

Sir	3:12	My son, be steadfast in h your father;

HONORS → HONOR

Prv	15:33	and humility goes before h.
Is	29:13	only and h me with their lips alone,
Mal	1: 6	A son h his father, and a servant
Mt	15: 8	'This people h me with their lips,

HOOFS → HOOVES

Lv	11: 3	Any animal that has h you may eat,

HOOK → HOOKS

Is	37:29	I will put my h in your nose and my
Mt	17:27	drop in a h, and take the first fish

HOOKS → HOOK

Ex	26:37	them with gold, with their h of gold;
Is	2: 4	and their spears into pruning h;
Mi	4: 3	and their spears into pruning h;

HOOVES → HOOFS

Dt	14: 6	Any among the animals that has divided h,

HOPE → HOPED, HOPES, HOPING

Ru	1:12	Even if I had any such h, or if tonight
Ezr	10: 2	this there still remains a h for Israel.
Jdt	9:11	in despair, savior of those without h.
Jb	17:15	Where then is my h, my happiness,
Ps	9:19	nor will the h of the afflicted ever
Ps	39: 8	what do I wait? You are my only h.
Ps	62: 6	alone, from whom comes my h.
Ps	65: 6	The h of all the ends of the earth
Ps	71:14	I will always h in you and add to all
Ps	119:43	for in your judgments is my h.
Ps	146: 5	of Jacob, whose h is in the LORD,
Prv	11: 7	When a person dies, h is destroyed;
Prv	13:12	H deferred makes the heart sick,
Prv	23:18	and your h will not be cut off.
Prv	24:14	and your h will not be cut off.
Prv	26:12	There is more h for fools than
Eccl	9: 4	is chosen among all the living has h:
Sir	34:16	for their h is in their savior.
Jer	14: 8	H of Israel, LORD, our savior
Jer	29:11	woe, so as to give you a future of h.
Lam	3:21	will call to mind; therefore I will h:
Ez	37:11	bones are dried up, our h is lost,
Dn	13:60	God who saves those who h in him.
Mt	12:21	in his name the Gentiles will h."
Jn	5:45	in whom you have placed your h.
Acts	2:26	my flesh, too, will dwell in h,
Acts	23: 6	am on trial for h in the resurrection
Rom	4:18	hoping against h, that he would
Rom	5: 4	character, and proven character, h,
Rom	5: 5	and h does not disappoint,
Rom	8:20	of the one who subjected it, in h
Rom	8:24	For in h we were saved. Now h that sees for itself is not h.
Rom	12:12	Rejoice in h, endure in affliction,
Rom	15: 4	of the scriptures we might have h.
Rom	15:12	in him shall the Gentiles h."
Rom	15:13	May the God of h fill you with all
Rom	15:13	you may abound in h by the power
1 Cor	13:13	So faith, h, love remain, these three;
2 Cor	1:10	him we have put our h [that] he will
2 Cor	3:12	since we have such h, we act very
Eph	2:12	without h and without God
Eph	4: 4	also called to the one h of your call;
Col	1: 5	because of the h reserved for you
Col	1:23	not shifting from the h of the gospel
Col	1:27	it is Christ in you, the h for glory.
1 Thes	1: 3	endurance in h of our Lord Jesus
1 Thes	4:13	grieve like the rest, who have no h.
1 Thes	5: 8	the helmet that is h for salvation.
2 Thes	2:16	and good h through his grace,
1 Tm	1: 1	our savior and of Christ Jesus our h,
1 Tm	4:10	because we have set our h
Ti	1: 2	in the h of eternal life that God,
Ti	2:13	as we await the blessed h,
Ti	3: 7	become heirs in h of eternal life.
Heb	3: 6	to our confidence and pride in our h.
Heb	6:11	for the fulfillment of h until the end,
Heb	7:19	other hand, a better h is introduced,
Heb	10:23	to our confession that gives us h.
1 Pt	1: 3	a living h through the resurrection
1 Pt	1:21	so that your faith and h are in God.
1 Pt	3:15	asks you for a reason for your h,
1 Jn	3: 3	Everyone who has this h based

HOPED → HOPE

Heb	11: 1	is the realization of what is h
1 Pt	3: 5	how the holy women who h in God

HOPES → HOPE

Rom	8:24	For who h for what one sees?
1 Cor	13: 7	believes all things, h all things,

HOPHNI

A wicked priest (1 Sm 1:3; 2:34; 4:4-17).

HOPING → HOPE

Rom	4:18	He believed, h against hope, that he

HOR

Nm	33:38	Aaron the priest ascended Mount H
Dt	32:50	brother Aaron died on Mount H

HOREB → =SINAI

Ex	3: 1	he came to the mountain of God, H.
Ex	17: 6	in front of you on the rock in H.
Dt	5: 2	God, made a covenant with us at H;
1 Kgs	19: 8	nights to the mountain of God, H.
Ps	106:19	At H they fashioned a calf,

HORMAH

Nm	14:45	them, beating them back as far as H.
Nm	21: 3	Hence that place was named H.

HORN → HORNS

1 Sm	16: 1	Fill your h with oil, and be on your
Ps	18: 3	shield, my saving h, my stronghold!
Ps	148:14	He has lifted high the h of his
Dn	7: 8	a little h, sprang out of their midst,
Dn	7: 8	This h had eyes like human eyes,
Dn	8: 5	with a prominent h on its forehead
Jl	2:15	Blow the h in Zion! Proclaim a fast,
Zec	9:14	The Lord GOD will sound the ram's h,

HORNETS

Jos	24:12	And I sent the h ahead of you

HORNS → HORN

Gn	22:13	ram caught by its h in the thicket.
Ex	27: 2	At the four corners make h that are
Jos	6: 4	seven priests carrying ram's h ahead
Dn	7:24	The ten h shall be ten kings rising
Dn	8: 3	by the river a ram with two great h,
Zec	2: 1	and looked and there were four h.
Rev	5: 6	He had seven h and seven eyes;
Rev	9:13	the [four] h of the gold altar before
Rev	12: 3	with seven heads and ten h,
Rev	13: 1	beast come out of the sea with ten h
Rev	13: 1	on its h were ten diadems, and on its
Rev	13:11	it had two h like a lamb's but spoke
Rev	17: 3	names, with seven heads and ten h.

HORRIBLE → HORROR

Jer	5:30	and h has happened in the land:
Jer	18:13	Truly h things virgin Israel has
Hos	6:10	of Israel I have seen a h thing:

HORROR → HORRIBLE

Jer	15: 4	I will make them an object of h
Ez	32:10	I will fill many nations with h;

HORSE → HORSE'S, HORSEMEN, HORSES

Ex	15: 1	h and chariot he has cast
Est	6: 8	the h the king rode with the royal
Ps	32: 9	Do not be like a h or mule, without
Ps	33:17	Useless is the h for safety;
Prv	26: 3	The whip for the h, the bridle
Jer	51:21	With you I shatter h and rider,
Zec	1: 8	on a red h standing in the shadows
Rev	6: 2	and there was a white h, and its
Rev	19:11	opened, and there was a white h;

HORSE'S → HORSE

Rev	14:20	to the height of a h bridle for two

HORSEMEN → HORSE, MAN

Is	31: 1	and in h because of their combined
Hos	1: 7	sword, by warfare, by horses or h.

HORSES → HORSE

Gn	47:17	them food in exchange for their h,
Ex	14:23	all Pharaoh's h and chariots
Dt	17:16	shall not have a great number of h;
Jos	11: 6	You must hamstring their h
1 Kgs	5: 6	had forty thousand stalls for h
2 Kgs	2:11	and fiery h came between the two
2 Kgs	6:17	fiery chariots and h around Elisha
2 Kgs	18:24	in Egypt for chariots and h?
Ps	20: 8	others on h, but we on the name
Ps	147:10	takes no delight in the strength of h,
Is	31: 3	not God, their h flesh, not spirit;
Jer	12: 5	you, how will you race against h?

Jl	2: 4	Their appearance is that of h;
Zec	6: 2	The first chariot had red h, the second chariot black h,
Rev	9: 7	was like that of h ready for battle.
Rev	19:14	mounted on white h and wearing

HOSANNA

Mt	21: 9	"H to the Son of David;
Mt	21: 9	name of the Lord; h in the highest."
Mt	21:15	area, "H to the Son of David,"
Mk	11: 9	following kept crying out: "H!
Mk	11:10	that is to come! H in the highest!"
Jn	12:13	out to meet him, and cried out: "H!

HOSEA

Prophet whose wife and family pictured the unfaithfulness of Israel (Hos 1–3).

HOSHEA → =JOSHUA

1. Original name of Joshua (Nm 13:8, 16).
2. Last king of Israel (2 Kgs 15:30; 17:1-6).

HOSPITABLE → HOSPITALITY

1 Tm	3: 2	decent, h, able to teach,
Ti	1: 8	but h, a lover of goodness,
1 Pt	4: 9	Be h to one another without

HOSPITALITY → HOSPITABLE

Rom	12:13	needs of the holy ones, exercise h.
1 Tm	5:10	practiced h, washed the feet
Heb	13: 2	Do not neglect h, for through it

HOST → HOSTS

Dt	4:19	the whole heavenly h, do not be led astray
1 Kgs	22:19	with the whole h of heaven standing
2 Kgs	17:16	bowed down to all the h of heaven;
2 Kgs	23: 5	and to the whole h of heaven.
Neh	9: 6	the highest heavens and all their h,
Is	34: 4	All the h of heaven shall rot;
Dn	8:10	it cast down to earth some of the h
Lk	2:13	of the heavenly h with the angel,

HOSTILE → HOSTILITY

Col	1:21	and h in mind because of evil deeds

HOSTILITY → HOSTILE

Hos	9: 8	his ways, h in the house of his God.

HOSTS → HOST

1 Sm	1: 3	to the LORD of h at Shiloh,
1 Kgs	19:10	the God of h, but the Israelites have
Ps	46: 8	The LORD of h is with us;
Ps	59: 6	LORD God of h, are the God
Ps	103:21	all you his h, his ministers who
Is	48: 2	whose name is the LORD of h.
Jer	23:36	God, the LORD of h, our God.

HOT → HOTHEADED

Ex	11: 8	left Pharaoh's presence in h anger.
Rev	3:15	that you are neither cold nor h.
Rev	3:15	I wish you were either cold or h.

HOTHEADED → HEAD, HOT

Prv	29:22	up strife, and the h cause many sins.

HOUR

Mt	8:13	that very h [his] servant was healed.
Mt	24:36	of that day and h no one knows,
Mk	14:35	it were possible the h might pass
Mk	14:37	you not keep watch for one h?
Lk	12:40	for at an h you do not expect,
Jn	2: 4	My h has not yet come."
Jn	7:30	because his h had not yet come.
Jn	8:20	because his h had not yet come.
Jn	12:23	"The h has come for the Son
Jn	12:27	'Father, save me from this h'?
Jn	12:27	this purpose that I came to this h.
Jn	13: 1	Jesus knew that his h had come
Jn	17: 1	and said, "Father, the h has come.
1 Jn	2:18	Children, it is the last h; and just as
1 Jn	2:18	Thus we know this is the last h.
Rev	8: 1	in heaven for about half an h.
Rev	17:12	along with the beast for one h.
Rev	18:10	In one h your judgment has come."

HOUSE → HOUSEHOLD, HOUSES, HOUSETOP, HOUSETOPS, STOREHOUSE

Gn	19: 2	into your servant's h for the night,
Gn	24:23	a place in your father's h for us
Ex	20:17	shall not covet your neighbor's h.
Nm	12: 7	Throughout my h he is worthy
Dt	5:21	shall not desire your neighbor's h
Jos	2: 1	the h of a prostitute named Rahab,
Jos	6:22	said, "Go into the prostitute's h
2 Sm	3: 1	a long war between the h of Saul and the h of David,
2 Sm	7: 5	Is it you who would build me a h
2 Sm	7:11	the LORD will make a h for you:
2 Sm	23: 5	Is not my h firm before God?
1 Kgs	6: 7	The h was built of stone dressed at
2 Kgs	15: 5	He lived in a h apart, while Jotham,
1 Chr	9:23	the h which was then a tent.
1 Chr	17:12	He it is who shall build me a h,
Ezr	1: 5	up to build the h of the LORD
Ezr	3:11	of the LORD's h had been laid.
Neh	10:40	We will not neglect the h of our
Tb	14: 5	They will build the h again, but it will
1 Mc	7:37	"You have chosen this h to bear
1 Mc	7:37	to be a h of prayer and supplication
Ps	23: 6	I will dwell in the h of the LORD
Ps	27: 4	dwell in the LORD's h all the days
Ps	52:10	tree flourishing in the h of God,
Ps	69:10	zeal for your h has consumed me,
Ps	84:11	of the h of my God than a home
Ps	122: 1	"Let us go to the h of the LORD."
Ps	127: 1	Unless the LORD build the h,
Prv	7:27	Her h is a highway to Sheol,
Prv	9: 1	Wisdom has built her h, she has set
Prv	14: 1	Wisdom builds her h, but Folly
Prv	14:11	The h of the wicked will be
Eccl	10:18	when hands are slack, the h leaks.
Is	5: 8	Those who join h to h, who connect
Is	7:13	Then he said: Listen, h of David!
Is	56: 7	make them joyful in my h of prayer;
Is	56: 7	For my h shall be called a h of prayer for all peoples.
Jer	3:18	those days the h of Judah will walk
Jer	7:11	Has this h which bears my name
Jer	18: 2	Arise and go down to the potter's h;
Jer	31:31	a new covenant with the h of Israel and the h of Judah.
Jer	32:34	in the h which bears my name
Ez	2: 8	do not rebel like this rebellious h.
Ez	33: 7	you as a sentinel for the h of Israel;
Ez	39:29	out my spirit upon the h of Israel—
Jl	4:18	will rise from the h of the LORD,
Hg	1: 4	paneled houses while this h lies
Hg	2: 7	And I will fill this h with glory—
Zec	8: 9	foundation of the h of the LORD
Zec	13: 6	wounds in the h of my friends."
Mt	7:24	be like a wise man who built his h
Mt	12:29	can anyone enter a strong man's h
Mt	12:29	Then he can plunder his h.
Mt	13:57	his native place and in his own h."
Mt	21:13	'My h shall be a h of prayer,'
Mk	3:25	And if a h is divided against itself,
Mk	3:25	that h will not be able to stand.
Lk	6:48	one is like a person building a h,
Lk	6:48	the river burst against that h
Lk	10: 7	Stay in the same h and eat and drink
Lk	11:17	laid waste and h will fall against h.
Lk	15: 8	not light a lamp and sweep the h,
Lk	19: 9	to this h because this man too is
Jn	2:16	my Father's h a marketplace."
Jn	2:17	for your h will consume me."
Jn	12: 3	the h was filled with the fragrance
Jn	14: 2	In my Father's h there are many
Rom	16: 5	greet also the church at their h.
Heb	3: 2	Moses was "faithful in [all] his h."
Heb	8: 8	a new covenant with the h of Israel and the h of Judah.
Heb	10:21	we have "a great priest over the h
1 Pt	2: 5	a spiritual h to be a holy priesthood
2 Jn	1:10	do not receive him in your h or even

HOUSEHOLD → HOUSE

Gn	7: 1	you and all your **h**, for you alone
Gn	31:19	had stolen her father's **h** images.
Ex	12: 3	itself a lamb, one apiece for each **h**.
Jos	24:15	As for me and my **h**, we will serve
Prv	31:21	concerned for her **h** when it snows—
Prv	31:27	watches over the affairs of her **h**,
Mi	7: 6	enemies are members of your **h**.
Mt	10:36	enemies will be those of his **h**.'
Jn	4:53	he and his whole **h** came to believe.
Acts	16:31	and you and your **h** will be saved."
Eph	2:19	ones and members of the **h** of God,
1 Tm	3: 4	He must manage his own **h** well,
1 Tm	3:15	how to behave in the **h** of God,
1 Pt	4:17	to begin with the **h** of God;

HOUSES → HOUSE

Ex	12:27	passed over the **h** of the Israelites
1 Mc	1:31	demolished its **h** and its surrounding
Is	65:21	They shall build **h** and live in them,
Jer	29:28	be a long time; build **h** to live in;
Ez	11: 3	are saying, "No need to build **h**!
Mt	19:29	everyone who has given up **h**
Mk	12:40	They devour the **h** of widows and,
Acts	4:34	property or **h** would sell them,

HOUSETOP → HOUSE

Prv	21: 9	better to dwell in a corner of the **h**
Mt	24:17	a person on the **h** must not go down

HOUSETOPS → HOUSE

Mt	10:27	hear whispered, proclaim on the **h**.

HOVERING

Dt	32:11	its nestlings, **h** over its young, So he
Is	31: 5	Like **h** birds, so the LORD of hosts

HOW

Gn	6:15	This is **h** you shall build it:
Gn	28:17	"**H** awesome this place is!
Ex	12:11	This is **h** you are to eat it:
Nm	23: 8	**H** can I lay a curse on the one
Nm	23: 8	**H** denounce the one whom
Dt	31:27	For I already know **h** rebellious
2 Sm	1:19	**H** can the warriors have fallen!
1 Kgs	3: 7	youth, not knowing at all **h** to act—
2 Chr	6:18	**h** much less this house which I have
Jb	25: 4	**H** can anyone be in the right against
Ps	6: 4	and you, LORD, **h** long . . . ?
Ps	8: 2	**h** awesome is your name through all
Ps	31:20	**H** great is your goodness, Lord,
Ps	36: 8	**H** precious is your mercy, O God!
Ps	92: 6	**H** great are your works, LORD!
Ps	119: 9	**H** can the young keep his way
Ps	147: 1	**H** good to sing praise to our God;
Prv	15:23	a word in season, **h** good it is!
Is	1:21	**H** she has become a prostitute,
Is	14:12	**H** you have fallen from the heavens,
Jer	1: 6	I said, "I do not know **h** to speak.
Lam	1: 1	**H** solitary sits the city, once filled
Ez	33:10	**H** can we survive?"
Hos	11: 8	**H** could I give you up, Ephraim,
Mal	1: 2	but you say, "**H** do you love us?"
Mk	10:23	"**H** hard it is for those who have
Lk	12:27	Notice **h** the flowers grow.
Lk	20:44	him 'lord,' **h** can he be his son?"
Jn	3: 4	"**H** can a person once grown old be
Jn	7:15	"**H** does he know scripture without
Eph	5:15	Watch carefully then **h** you live,
1 Tm	3: 5	if a man does not know **h** to manage
1 Tm	3: 5	**h** can he take care of the church
Heb	2: 3	**h** shall we escape if we ignore so
2 Pt	2: 9	then the Lord knows **h** to rescue

HUGE

Rev	16:21	hailstones like **h** weights came

HULDAH

Prophetess inquired by Hilkiah for Josiah (2 Kgs 22; 2 Chr 34:14-28).

HUMAN

Gn	1:26	Let us make **h** beings in our image,
Nm	19:16	or who touches a **h** bone or a grave,
Nm	23:19	God is not a **h** being who speaks falsely,
1 Kgs	13: 2	they shall burn **h** bones upon you."
2 Kgs	23:14	where they had been with **h** bones.
Jdt	8:16	God is not like a **h** being to be
Is	37:19	at all, but the work of **h** hands—
Ez	1:10	each of the four had a **h** face,
Dn	5: 5	the fingers of a **h** hand appeared,
Hos	11: 4	I drew them with **h** cords,
Mt	9: 8	given such authority to **h** beings.
Mt	15: 9	as doctrines **h** precepts.' "
Lk	16:15	is of **h** esteem is an abomination
Lk	20: 6	'Of **h** origin,' then all the people
Jn	5:41	"I do not accept **h** praise;
Jn	5:34	accept testimony from a **h** being,
Acts	5:38	or this activity is of **h** origin, it will
1 Cor	1:26	of you were wise by **h** standards,
1 Cor	2:13	not with words taught by **h** wisdom,
Phil	2: 7	of a slave, coming in **h** likeness;
Col	2: 8	philosophy according to **h** tradition,
Col	2:22	they accord with **h** precepts
1 Thes	4: 8	disregards not a **h** being but God,
1 Tm	2: 5	between God and the **h** race, Christ Jesus, himself **h**,
Rev	4: 7	had a face like that of a **h** being,
Rev	9: 7	their faces were like **h** faces,
Rev	14: 4	as the firstfruits of the **h** race

HUMBLE → HUMBLED, HUMBLES, HUMBLY

2 Chr	7:14	pronounced, **h** themselves and pray,
2 Chr	33:23	he did not **h** himself before
2 Chr	36:12	and he did not **h** himself before
Ps	18:28	For **h** people you save;
Ps	25: 9	and teaches the **h** his way.
Prv	11: 2	but with the **h** is wisdom.
Dn	10:12	and **h** yourself before God,
Zep	2: 3	the LORD, all you **h** of the land,
Zep	3:12	a remnant in your midst a people **h**
Mt	11:29	me, for I am meek and **h** of heart;
Jas	4: 6	the proud, but gives grace to the **h**."
Jas	4:10	**H** yourselves before the Lord and he
1 Pt	3: 8	one another, compassionate, **h**.
1 Pt	5: 5	proud but bestows favor on the **h**."
1 Pt	5: 6	So **h** yourselves under the mighty

HUMBLED → HUMBLE

Lv	26:41	their uncircumcised hearts are **h**
1 Kgs	21:29	how Ahab has **h** himself before me?
2 Kgs	22:19	have **h** yourself before the LORD
2 Chr	12: 7	saw that they had **h** themselves,
2 Chr	33:12	He **h** himself abjectly before
2 Chr	34:27	have **h** yourself before God
Dn	5:22	Belshazzar, have not **h** your heart,
Mt	23:12	Whoever exalts himself will be **h**;
Lk	14:11	who exalts himself will be **h**,
Phil	2: 8	he **h** himself, becoming obedient

HUMBLES → HUMBLE

Lk	14:11	but the one who **h** himself will be

HUMBLY → HUMBLE

Mi	6: 8	and to walk **h** with your God.

HUMILIATION → HUMILITY

Prv	29:23	Haughtiness brings **h**,
Acts	8:33	In [his] **h** justice was denied him.

HUMILITY → HUMILIATION

Prv	15:33	wisdom, and **h** goes before honors.
Prv	18:12	is haughty, but before honor is **h**.
Prv	22: 4	The result of **h** and fear
Sir	3:17	conduct your affairs with **h**, and you
Zep	2: 3	Seek justice, seek **h**;
Acts	20:19	I served the Lord with all **h**
Eph	4: 2	with all **h** and gentleness,
Col	3:12	kindness, **h**, gentleness,
1 Pt	5: 5	clothe yourselves with **h** in your

HUNDRED → HUNDREDFOLD

Gn	6: 3	Their days shall comprise one **h**
Gn	15:13	and oppressed for four **h** years.
Gn	17:17	born to a man who is a **h** years old?
1 Kgs	18:13	that I hid a **h** of the prophets
Is	65:20	at a **h** years shall be considered
Mt	13: 8	fruit, a **h** or sixty or thirtyfold.
Mt	18:12	If a man has a **h** sheep and one
Lk	7:41	one owed five **h** days' wages
Acts	1:15	(there was a group of about one **h**
Rom	4:19	(for he was almost a **h** years old)
1 Cor	15: 6	to more than five **h** brothers at once,
Rev	7: 4	seal, one **h** and forty-four thousand
Rev	13:18	His number is six **h** and sixty-six.

HUNDREDFOLD → HUNDRED

Gn	26:12	region and reaped a **h** the same year.

HUNG → HANG

Ps	137: 2	in its midst we **h** up our harps.

HUNGER → HUNGRY

Dt	8: 3	therefore let you be afflicted with **h**,
Neh	9:15	heaven you gave them in their **h**,
Is	49:10	They shall not **h** or thirst;
Mt	5: 6	Blessed are they who **h** and thirst
Rev	7:16	They will not **h** or thirst anymore,

HUNGRY → HUNGER

Tb	4:16	"Give to the **h** some of your food,
Ps	50:12	Were I **h**, I would not tell you,
Ps	107: 9	thirsty, filled the **h** with good things.
Ps	146: 7	oppressed, who gives bread to the **h**.
Prv	25:21	If your enemies are **h**, give them
Sir	4: 2	Do not grieve the **h**, nor anger
Is	29: 8	when a **h** man dreams he is eating
Is	58: 7	it not sharing your bread with the **h**,
Ez	18: 7	gives food to the **h** and clothes
Mt	12: 1	His disciples were **h** and began
Mt	15:32	I do not want to send them away **h**,
Mt	25:35	For I was **h** and you gave me food,
Mt	25:42	For I was **h** and you gave me no
Mk	11:12	were leaving Bethany he was **h**.
Lk	1:53	The **h** he has filled with good
Rom	12:20	"if your enemy is **h**, feed him;
1 Cor	4:11	To this very hour we go **h**
1 Cor	11:34	If anyone is **h**, he should eat
Phil	4:12	of being well fed and of going **h**,

HUNT → HUNTER

Gn	27: 3	the open country to **h** some game

HUNTER → HUNT

Gn	10: 9	He was a mighty **h** in the eyes
Gn	25:27	Esau became a skillful **h**, a man

HUR

Ex	17:12	Aaron and **H** supported his hands,

HURAM → =HIRAM

2 Chr	4:11	When **H** had made the pots, shovels,
2 Chr	4:11	When **H** had made the pots, shovels,

HURAM-ABI → =HIRAM

2 Chr	2:12	sending you a craftsman of great skill, **H**,

HURRY

Gn	19:22	**H**, escape there! I cannot do

HURT

Dn	6:23	mouths so that they have not **h** me.

HUSBAND → HUSBAND'S, HUSBANDS

Gn	3: 6	and she also gave some to her **h**,
Gn	3:16	Yet your urge shall be for your **h**,
Gn	16: 3	gave her to her **h** Abram to be his
Nm	30: 9	the day her **h** learns of it he opposes
Dt	24: 4	then her former **h**, who dismissed
Prv	6:34	For passion enrages the **h**,
Prv	7:19	For my **h** is not at home, he has
Prv	31:11	Her **h** trusts her judgment;
Prv	31:23	Her **h** is prominent at the city gates
Prv	31:28	her **h**, too, praises her:

Sir	26: 1	Happy the **h** of a good wife;
Is	54: 5	For your **h** is your Maker;
Hos	2:18	You shall call me "My **h**," and you
Mt	1:19	Joseph her **h**, since he was
Mk	10:12	if she divorces her **h** and marries
Jn	4:17	said to him, "I do not have a **h**."
Jn	4:17	right in saying, 'I do not have a **h**.'
Rom	7: 2	is bound by law to her living **h**; but if her **h** dies, she is released
1 Cor	7: 2	wife, and every woman her own **h**.
1 Cor	7: 3	The **h** should fulfill his duty toward
1 Cor	7: 3	and likewise the wife toward her **h**.
1 Cor	7:10	wife should not separate from her **h**
1 Cor	7:11	or become reconciled to her **h**—
1 Cor	7:11	and a **h** should not divorce his wife.
1 Cor	7:14	For the unbelieving **h** is made holy
1 Cor	7:39	is bound to her **h** as long as he lives.
1 Cor	7:39	But if her **h** dies, she is free to be
2 Cor	11: 2	to one **h** to present you as a chaste
Eph	5:23	For the **h** is head of his wife just as
Eph	5:33	and the wife should respect her **h**.
Rev	21: 2	as a bride adorned for her **h**.

HUSBAND'S → HUSBAND

Dt	25: 5	but her **h** brother shall come to her,

HUSBANDS → HUSBAND

Tb	3: 8	been given in marriage to seven **h**,
Tb	3: 8	"You are the one who kills your **h**!
Jn	4:18	For you have had five **h**,
1 Cor	14:35	they should ask their **h** at home.
Eph	5:22	should be subordinate to their **h** as
Eph	5:25	**H**, love your wives, even as Christ
Eph	5:28	**h** should love their wives as their
Col	3:18	be subordinate to your **h**, as is
Col	3:19	**H**, love your wives, and avoid any
Ti	2: 4	train younger women to love their **h**
Ti	2: 5	under the control of their **h**,
1 Pt	3: 1	be subordinate to your **h** so that,
1 Pt	3: 7	you **h** should live with your wives

HUSHAI

Wise man of David who frustrated Ahithophel's advice and foiled Absalom's revolt (2 Sm 15:32-37; 16:15–17:16; 1 Chr 27:33).

HUT

Is	24:20	reel like a drunkard, sway like a **h**;

HYMENAEUS

A false teacher (1 Tm 1:20; 2 Tm 2:17).

HYMN → HYMNS

Mt	26:30	after singing a **h**, they went
Mk	14:26	after singing a **h**, they went

HYMNS → HYMN

Tb	13:18	of Jerusalem will sing **h** of gladness,
1 Mc	4:24	they were singing **h** and glorifying
Acts	16:25	singing **h** to God as the prisoners
Eph	5:19	one another [in] psalms and **h**
Col	3:16	singing psalms, **h**, and spiritual

HYPOCRISY → HYPOCRITE, HYPOCRITES

Mt	23:28	but inside you are filled with **h**
Mk	12:15	Knowing their **h** he said to them,
1 Tm	4: 2	through the **h** of liars with branded

HYPOCRITE → HYPOCRISY

Sir	32:15	it, but the **h** will be ensnared by it.
Mt	7: 5	**h**, remove the wooden beam
Lk	6:42	You **h**! Remove the wooden beam

HYPOCRITES → HYPOCRISY

Ps	26: 4	men, nor with **h** do I mingle.
Mt	6: 2	as the **h** do in the synagogues
Mt	6: 5	do not be like the **h**, who love
Mt	6:16	fast, do not look gloomy like the **h**.
Mt	15: 7	**H**, well did Isaiah prophesy
Mt	22:18	"Why are you testing me, you **h**?
Mt	23:13	to you, scribes and Pharisees, you **h**.
Mt	23:15	to you, scribes and Pharisees, you **h**.
Mt	23:23	to you, scribes and Pharisees, you **h**.

Mt	23:25	to you, scribes and Pharisees, you **h**.
Mt	23:27	to you, scribes and Pharisees, you **h**.
Mt	23:29	to you, scribes and Pharisees, you **h**.
Mt	24:51	and assign him a place with the **h**,
Mk	7: 6	did Isaiah prophesy about you **h**,
Lk	12:56	You **h**! You know how to interpret
Lk	13:15	The Lord said to him in reply, "**H**!

HYSSOP

Ex	12:22	Then take a bunch of **h**, and dipping
Nm	19: 6	**h** and scarlet yarn and throw them
Ps	51: 9	Cleanse me with **h**, that I may be
Jn	19:29	soaked in wine on a sprig of **h**
Heb	9:19	with water and crimson wool and **h**,

I

I AM

Gn	15: 1	**I am** your shield; I will make your reward
Gn	17: 1	**I am** God the Almighty. Walk in my presence
Ex	3:14	God replied to Moses: **I am** who **I am**.
Ps	46:11	"Be still and know that **I am** God!
Is	41:10	Do not fear: **I am** with you;
Is	43:15	**I am** the LORD, your Holy One, the creator
Is	44: 6	**I am** the first, **I am** the last;
Jer	32:27	**I am** the LORD, the God of all the living!
Hos	1: 9	are not my people, and I am not "**I am**" for you.
Mt	16:15	to them, "But who do you say that **I am**?"
Mt	28:20	And behold, **I am** with you always,
Mk	8:29	asked them, "But who do you say that **I am**?"
Mk	14:62	Jesus answered, "**I am**; and 'you will see
Jn	6:35	Jesus said to them, "**I am** the bread of life;
Jn	6:41	"**I am** the bread that came down from heaven,"
Jn	6:51	**I am** the living bread that came down from heaven;
Jn	8:12	saying, "**I am** the light of the world.
Jn	8:24	if you do not believe that **I AM**, you will die
Jn	8:28	the Son of Man, then you will realize that **I AM**,
Jn	8:58	before Abraham came to be, **I AM**."
Jn	9: 5	**I am** the light of the world."
Jn	10: 7	I say to you, **I am** the gate for the sheep.
Jn	10:11	**I am** the good shepherd.
Jn	10:36	because I said, '**I am** the Son of God '?
Jn	11:25	"**I am** the resurrection and the life;
Jn	13:19	when it happens you may believe that **I AM**.
Jn	14: 6	"**I am** the way and the truth and the life.
Jn	14:10	Do you not believe that **I am** in the Father
Jn	15: 1	"**I am** the true vine, and my Father
Jn	15: 5	**I am** the vine, you are the branches.
Jn	18: 5	He said to them, "**I AM**."
Acts	9: 5	"**I am** Jesus, whom you are persecuting.
Acts	18:10	for **I am** with you.
Rev	1: 8	"**I am** the Alpha and the Omega,"
Rev	1:17	**I am** the first and the last,
Rev	1:18	but now **I am** alive forever and ever.
Rev	3:11	**I am** coming quickly. Hold fast
Rev	21: 6	I [am] the Alpha and the Omega,
Rev	22: 7	"Behold, **I am** coming soon."
Rev	22:12	"Behold, **I am** coming soon.
Rev	22:13	**I am** the Alpha and the Omega,
Rev	22:16	**I am** the root and offspring of David,
Rev	22:20	"Yes, **I am** coming soon."

IBZAN

Judge of Israel (Jgs 12:8-10).

ICHABOD

1 Sm	4:21	She named the child I, saying,

ICONIUM

Acts	14: 1	I they entered the Jewish synagogue
2 Tm	3:11	as happened to me in Antioch, I,

IDDO

2 Chr	9:29	of I the seer concerning Jeroboam,
2 Chr	12:15	and of I the seer (his family record).
2 Chr	13:22	in the midrash of the prophet I.

IDLE → IDLENESS

Eccl	11: 6	at evening do not let your hand be **i**:
Sir	33:28	Force him to work that he be not **i**,

1 Thes	5:14	brothers, admonish the **i**,
Ti	1:10	many rebels, **i** talkers and deceivers,

IDLENESS → IDLE

Prv	31:27	and does not eat the bread of **i**.
Sir	33:29	for **i** teaches much mischief.

IDOL → IDOLATER, IDOLATERS, IDOLATRY, IDOLS

Ex	20: 4	You shall not make for yourself an **i**
Dt	27:15	who makes a carved or molten **i**,
Wis	14: 8	but the handmade **i** is accursed,
Is	40:19	An **i**? An artisan casts it, the smith
Dn	14: 3	Babylonians had an **i** called Bel,
1 Cor	8: 4	that "there is no **i** in the world,"
1 Cor	10:19	Or that an **i** is anything?

IDOLATER → IDOL

1 Cor	5:11	greedy, an **i**, a slanderer, a drunkard,
Eph	5: 5	is, an **i**, has any inheritance

IDOLATERS → IDOL

1 Cor	5:10	or the greedy and robbers or **i**;
1 Cor	6: 9	fornicators nor **i** nor adulterers nor
1 Cor	10: 7	And do not become **i**, as some

IDOLATRY → IDOL

1 Sm	15:23	and arrogance, the crime of **i**.
Ez	23:49	and you shall pay for your sins of **i**.
Col	3: 5	evil desire, and the greed that is **i**.
1 Pt	4: 3	orgies, carousing, and wanton **i**.

IDOLS → IDOL

Dt	7: 5	asherahs, and destroy their **i** by fire.
1 Kgs	15:12	removing all the **i** his ancestors had
1 Mc	1:43	they sacrificed to **i** and profaned
Ps	31: 7	hate those who serve worthless **i**,
Ps	78:58	with their **i** provoked him to jealous
Ps	115: 4	Their **i** are silver and gold, the work
Wis	14:12	of wantonness is the devising of **i**;
Is	2: 8	Their land is full of **i**;
Is	42: 8	give to no other, nor my praise to **i**.
Ez	14: 3	keep the memory of their **i** alive
Ez	23:37	committed adultery with their **i**;
Ez	23:39	slaughtered their children for their **i**,
Dn	14: 5	"Because I do not revere **i** made
Hb	2:18	should trust in it, and make mute **i**?
Acts	15:20	by letter to avoid pollution from **i**,
1 Cor	8: 1	in regard to meat sacrificed to **i**:
2 Cor	6:16	has the temple of God with **i**?
1 Thes	1: 9	to God from **i** to serve the living
1 Jn	5:21	be on your guard against **i**.
Rev	2:14	to eat food sacrificed to **i**

IF

Gn	4: 7	I you act rightly, you will be
Gn	4: 7	but **i** not, sin lies in wait at the door:
Ex	19: 5	**i** you obey me completely and keep
Ex	33:15	"I you are not going yourself,
1 Kgs	18:21	I the LORD is God, follow him;
1 Chr	28: 9	I you search for him, he will be
1 Chr	28: 9	but **i** you abandon him, he will cast
Jer	18: 8	I that nation against whom I have
Ez	18:21	**i** the wicked man turns away
Ez	18:21	**i** he keeps all my statutes and does
Mt	4: 3	to him, "I you are the Son of God,
Mt	27:40	yourself, **i** you are the Son of God,
Mk	3:24	I a kingdom is divided against itself,
Mk	5:28	She said, "I I but touch his clothes,
Lk	6:32	For **i** you love those who love you,
Jn	13:17	I you understand this, blessed are you **i** you do it.
Jn	14:15	"I you love me, you will keep my
Jn	15:10	I you keep my commandments,
Rom	6: 8	I, then, we have died with Christ,
Rom	8:31	I God is for us, who can be against
Jas	1: 5	But **i** any of you lacks wisdom,
1 Jn	1: 9	I we acknowledge our sins, he is
Rev	3:20	I anyone hears my voice and opens

IGNORANCE → IGNORE

Acts	3:17	that you acted out of **i**, just as your
Acts	17:30	God has overlooked the times of **i**,

1 Tm   1:13 I acted out of i in my unbelief.
1 Pt   2:15 doing good you may silence the i

IGNORANT → IGNORE
Heb   5: 2 is able to deal patiently with the i
2 Pt   3:16 things hard to understand that the i

IGNORE → IGNORANCE, IGNORANT, IGNORED
2 Pt   3: 5 They deliberately i the fact

IGNORED → IGNORE
Prv   1:25 my counsel, and my reproof you i—

ILL → ILLNESS
Jn   11: 1 Now a man was i,
1 Cor 11:30 That is why many among you are i

ILLEGITIMATE
Hos   5: 7 for they have borne i children;
Jn   8:41 they said to him, "We are not i.

ILLNESS → ILL
Jn   11: 4 said, "This i is not to end in death,

IMAGE → IMAGES
Gn   1:26 Let us make human beings in our i,
Gn   1:27 God created mankind in his i; in the i of God he created them;
Gn   9: 6 in the i of God have human beings
Ps 106:20 glory for the i of a grass-eating bull.
Wis   2:23 the i of his own nature he made us.
Is   44:17 a god, an i to worship and adore.
Rom   8:29 to be conformed to the i of his Son,
1 Cor 11: 7 because he is the i and glory
1 Cor 15:49 Just as we have borne the i
1 Cor 15:49 also bear the i of the heavenly one.
2 Cor   4: 4 glory of Christ, who is the i of God.
Col   1:15 He is the i of the invisible God,
Col   3:10 knowledge, in the i of its creator.
Rev   13:14 to make an i for the beast who had
Rev   14:11 or its i or accept the mark of its
Rev   20: 4 or its i nor had accepted its mark

IMAGES → IMAGE
Nm   33:52 destroy all their molten i,
Is   42:17 Who say to molten i, "You are our

IMAGINATION → IMAGINE
Acts 17:29 silver, or stone by human art and i.

IMAGINE → IMAGINATION
Eph   3:20 far more than all we ask or i,

IMITATE → IMITATORS
Dt   18: 9 shall not learn to i the abominations
Heb   13: 7 of their way of life and i their faith.
3 Jn   1:11 Beloved, do not i evil but i good.

IMITATORS → IMITATE
1 Cor 4:16 Therefore, I urge you, be i of me.
1 Cor 11: 1 Be i of me, as I am of Christ.
Eph   5: 1 So be i of God, as beloved children,
1 Thes 1: 6 And you became i of us
1 Thes 2:14 have become i of the churches
Heb   6:12 but i of those who, through faith

IMMORAL → IMMORALITY
1 Cor 5: 9 letter not to associate with i people,
1 Cor 5:10 at all referring to the i of this world
1 Cor 5:11 named a brother, if he is i, greedy,
Heb 12:16 that no one be an i or profane

IMMORALITY → IMMORAL
1 Cor 5: 1 reported that there is i among you,
1 Cor 5: 1 i of a kind not found even among
1 Cor 6:13 is not for i, but for the Lord,
1 Cor 7: 2 of i every man should have his own
1 Cor 10: 8 Let us not indulge in i as some
2 Cor 12:21 have not repented of the impurity, i,
Gal   5:19 i, impurity, licentiousness,
Eph   5: 3 I or any impurity or greed must not
Col   3: 5 i, impurity, passion, evil desire,
1 Thes 4: 3 that you refrain from i,

IMMORTAL → IMMORTALITY
Wis   4: 1 for i is the memory of virtue,
Sir 17:30 since human beings are not i.
Rom   1:23 exchanged the glory of the i God

IMMORTALITY → IMMORTAL
Wis   8:13 Because of her I shall have i
Rom   2: 7 and i through perseverance in good
1 Cor 15:53 is mortal must clothe itself with i.
1 Cor 15:54 which is mortal clothes itself with i,
1 Tm   6:16 who alone has i, who dwells
2 Tm   1:10 life and i to light through the gospel,

IMPALE → IMPALED
Est   7: 9 The king answered, "I him on it."

IMPALED → IMPALE
Ezr   6:11 and he is to be lifted up and i on it;
Est   2:23 and both of them were i on stakes;
Est   7:10 they i Haman on the stake he had set up

IMPARTIALLY
1 Pt   1:17 Father him who judges i according

IMPEDIMENT
Mk   7:32 him a deaf man who had a speech i

IMPENITENT
Rom   2: 5 By your stubbornness and i heart,

IMPERISHABLE
Wis   18: 4 through whom the i light of the law
Mk   16: S i proclamation of eternal salvation.
1 Cor 9:25 a perishable crown, but we an i one.
1 Pt   1: 4 to an inheritance that is i, undefiled,
1 Pt   1:23 not from perishable but from i seed,

IMPLORE → IMPLORED
Mal   1: 9 So now i God's favor, that he may

IMPLORED → IMPLORE
Ex   32:11 But Moses i the Lord, his God,

IMPORTANCE → IMPORTANT
1 Cor 15: 3 handed on to you as of first i what I

IMPORTANT → IMPORTANCE
Ex   18:22 Every i case they should refer

IMPOSSIBLE
Zec   8: 6 should it seem i in my eyes also?—
Mt   17:20 Nothing will be i for you."
Mt   19:26 "For human beings this is i,
Mk   10:27 "For human beings it is i, but not
Lk   1:37 for nothing will be i for God."
Lk 18:27 said, "What is i for human beings is
Acts   2:24 because it was i for him to be held
Heb   6: 4 For it is i in the case of those who
Heb   6:18 in which it was i for God to lie,
Heb 10: 4 for it is i that the blood of bulls
Heb 11: 6 without faith it is i to please him,

IMPOSTOR
Mt 27:63 that this i while still alive said,

IMPRINT
Heb   1: 3 of his glory, the very i of his being,

IMPRISONMENT → PRISON
Acts 23:29 of any charge deserving death or i.
Acts 26:31 [at all] that deserves death or i."
Heb 11:36 scourging, even chains and i.

IMPRISONMENTS → PRISON
2 Cor 6: 5 beatings, i, riots, labors, vigils,
2 Cor 11:23 far more i, far worse beatings,

IMPUDENT
Prv   7:13 him, and with an i look says to him:

IMPURE → IMPURITY
Eph   5: 5 this, that no immoral or i or greedy
1 Thes 2: 3 was not from delusion or i motives,

IMPURITY → IMPURE
Rom   1:24 them over to i through the lusts
Rom   6:19 parts of your bodies as slaves to i

2 Cor 12:21 and have not repented of the i,
Gal   5:19 immorality, i, licentiousness,
Eph   4:19 practice of every kind of i to excess.
Eph   5: 3 or any i or greed must not even be
Col   3: 5 immorality, i, passion, evil desire,
1 Thes 4: 7 For God did not call us to i

IMPUTES
Ps   32: 2 man to whom the LORD i no guilt,

INCENSE → FRANKINCENSE
Ex   25: 6 anointing oil and for the fragrant i;
Ex   30: 1 burning i you shall make an altar
Ex   40: 5 Put the golden altar of i in front
Nm   16:17 you take his own censer, put i in it,
2 Chr 26:16 to make an offering on the altar of i.
Ps   141: 2 Let my prayer be i before you;
Is   1:13 i is an abomination to me.
Hos   2:15 for whom she burnt i, When she
Lk   1:10 outside at the hour of the i offering,
Heb   9: 4 in which were the gold altar of i
Rev   5: 8 a harp and gold bowls filled with i,
Rev   8: 4 The smoke of the i along

INCITED
Acts   13:50 i the women of prominence who

INCLINE
Prv   4:20 attentive, to my sayings i your ear;
Is   37:17 I your ear, LORD, and listen!

INCREASE → INCREASED, INCREASES
Dt   1:11 i you a thousand times over,
Mt   24:12 and because of the i of evildoing,
Lk   17: 5 said to the Lord, "I our faith."
Jn   3:30 He must i; I must decrease."
1 Thes 3:12 and may the Lord make you i

INCREASED → INCREASE
Gn   7:17 As the waters i, they lifted the ark,
Acts   6: 7 the disciples in Jerusalem i greatly;
Rom   5:20 where sin i, grace overflowed all

INCREASES → INCREASE
Ps   62:11 On wealth that i, do not set your
Prv   29:16 When the wicked increase, crime i;

INCUR → INCURRING
Lv   19:17 so that you do not i sin because
1 Tm   5:12 will i condemnation for breaking

INCURABLE
Jer   15:18 my wound i, refusing to be healed?
Jer   30:12 I is your wound, grievous your

INCURRING → INCUR
Nm   18:22 meeting, thereby i the penalty of death.

INDEPENDENT
1 Cor 11:11 Woman is not i of man or man

INDESCRIBABLE
2 Cor   9:15 Thanks be to God for his i gift!

INDIA
Est   1: 1 twenty-seven provinces from I

INDICTMENT
Jer   25:31 LORD has an i against the nations,

INDIGNANT
Mk   10:14 When Jesus saw this he became i
Lk   13:14 i that Jesus had cured

INDULGE → INDULGED, SELF-INDULGENCE
1 Cor 10: 8 Let us not i in immorality as some

INDULGED → INDULGE
Jude   1: 7 as they, i in sexual promiscuity

INFANT → INFANTS
Is   65:20 shall there be in it an i who lives

INFANTS → INFANT
Ps   8: 3 with the mouths of babes and i.
Mt   21:16 the text, 'Out of the mouths of i
1 Cor   3: 1 but as fleshly people, as i in Christ.
1 Cor 14:20 In respect to evil be like i,

1 Pt   2: 2 like newborn i, long for pure

INFERIOR
2 Cor 12:11 no way i to these "superapostles,"

INFIRMITIES
Mt   8:17 "He took away our i and bore our
Lk   8: 2 had been cured of evil spirits and i,

INHABITANTS → INHABITED
Nm   33:55 if you do not dispossess the i
Neh   10:31 not marry our daughters to the local i,
Jos   9:24 that all its i be destroyed before you.
1 Mc   1:28 the land quaked on account of its i,
Is   6:11 are desolate, without i, Houses,
Rev   6:10 our blood on the i of the earth?"
Rev   8:13 Woe to the i of the earth
Rev   13: 8 All the i of the earth will worship it,

INHABITED → INHABITANTS
Jer   17:25 This city will remain i forever.

INHERIT → INHERITANCE, INHERITED
Sir   4:16 their descendants too will i me.
Mt   5: 5 the meek, for they will i the land.
Mt   19:29 times more, and will i eternal life.
Mk   10:17 what must I do to i eternal life?"
Lk   10:25 what must I do to i eternal life?"
Lk   18:18 what must I do to i eternal life?"
1 Cor   6: 9 the unjust will not i the kingdom
1 Cor 15:50 blood cannot i the kingdom of God,
1 Cor 15:50 nor does corruption i incorruption.
Heb   1:14 sake of those who are to i salvation?
1 Pt   3: 9 called, that you might i a blessing.
Rev   21: 7 The victor will i these gifts, and I

INHERITANCE → INHERIT
Prv   13:22 The good leave an i to their
Eccl   7:11 Wisdom is as good as an i
Lk   12:13 my brother to share the i with me."
Gal   3:18 For if the i comes from the law, it is
Gal   4:30 slave woman shall not share the i
Eph   1:14 of our i toward redemption as God's
Eph   5: 5 has any i in the kingdom of Christ
Col   1:12 to share in the i of the holy ones
Col   3:24 the Lord the due payment of the i;
Heb   9:15 may receive the promised eternal i.
1 Pt   1: 4 to an i that is imperishable,

INHERITED → INHERIT
Heb   1: 4 the name he has i is more excellent

INIQUITIES
Lv   16:22 The goat will carry off all their i
Rom   4: 7 are they whose i are forgiven

INJURED → INJURY
Ez   34:16 will bring back, the i I will bind up,

INJURY → INJURED
Lv   24:20 The same i that one gives another

INJUSTICE
Prv   16: 8 justice, than a large income with i.
Sir   7: 3 Do not sow in the furrows of i,
Rom   9:14 Is there i on the part of God?

INK
Jer   36:18 "while I wrote them down with i
2 Cor   3: 3 written not in i but by the Spirit
2 Jn   1:12 I do not intend to use paper and i.
3 Jn   1:13 do not wish to write with pen and i.

INMOST → INNER
Prv   20:27 it searches through the i being.

INN
Lk   2: 7 there was no room for them in the i.
Lk   10:34 took him to an i and cared for him.

INNER → INMOST, INWARDLY
Ez   10: 3 in and a cloud filled the i court.
Mt   24:26 say, 'He is in the i rooms,' do not
2 Cor   4:16 our i self is being renewed day
Eph   3:16 through his Spirit in the i self,

INNOCENCE → INNOCENT
Ps   26: 6 I will wash my hands in i so that I
Hos   8: 5 long will they be incapable of i

INNOCENT → INNOCENCE
Ex   23: 7 The i and the just you shall not put
Dt   19:10 i blood will not be shed and you
1 Mc 1:37 They shed i blood around
Jb   34: 5 "I am i, but God has taken away
Ps   19:14 shall I be blameless, i of grave sin.
Prv   6:17 tongue, hands that shed i blood,
Prv 17:26 It is wrong to fine an i person,
Is   59: 7 and they hasten to shed i blood;
Dn   13:53 condemning the i, and freeing
Mt   27: 4 have sinned in betraying i blood."
Mt   27:24 saying, "I am i of this man's blood.
Lk   23:47 "This man was i beyond doubt."
Phil   2:15 that you may be blameless and i,

INQUIRE
Dt   12:30 Do not i regarding their gods,
2 Kgs 1: 2 "Go and i of Baalzebub, the god

INSCRIBE → INSCRIBED, INSCRIPTION
Is   30: 8 tablet they can keep, i it on a scroll;

INSCRIBED → INSCRIBE
Dn   5:25 "This is the writing that was i:
Rev 19:12 He had a name i that no one knows

INSCRIPTION → INSCRIBE
Mk   15:26 The i of the charge against him
2 Tm 2:19 bearing this i, "The Lord knows

INSCRUTABLE
Rom 11:33 How i are his judgments and how

INSECTS
Dt   14:19 All winged i are also unclean

INSIDE
Gn   6:14 and cover it i and out with pitch.
Dn   14: 7 "it is only clay i and bronze
Mt   23:26 cleanse first the i of the cup,
Mt   23:27 but i are full of dead men's bones

INSIGHT
Dn   11:35 Some of those with i shall stumble so
Dn   12: 3 But those with i shall shine brightly
Eph   1: 8 In all wisdom and i,

INSINCERITY
1 Pt   2: 1 of all malice and all deceit, i, envy,

INSIST
Ti   3: 8 I want you to i on these points,

INSOLENT
Rom   1:30 They are i, haughty, boastful,

INSPIRED
2 Tm 3:16 All scripture is i by God and is

INSTALL → INSTALLATION, INSTALLMENT
Ex   29: 9 and thus shall you i Aaron and his sons.

INSTALLATION → INSTALL
Ex   29:22 since this is the ram for i;

INSTALLMENT → INSTALL
2 Cor 1:22 the Spirit in our hearts as a first i.

INSTANT
Lk   4: 5 kingdoms of the world in a single i.

INSTEAD
Is   60:17 I of bronze I will bring gold,
Mk   15:11 him release Barabbas for them i.

INSTITUTION
1 Pt   2:13 every human i for the Lord's sake,

INSTRUCT → INSTRUCTED, INSTRUCTION, INSTRUCTIONS,
    INSTRUCTORS
Ps   32: 8 I will i you and show you the way
Ps   105:22 To i his princes as he desired,
1 Cor 14:19 mind, so as to i others also, than ten

INSTRUCTED → INSTRUCT
Ps 119:102 I do not turn, for you have i me.
Is   40:13 LORD, or i him as his counselor?
Acts 18:25 He had been i in the Way

INSTRUCTION → INSTRUCT
Ex   24:12 commandments intended for their i.
Prv   1: 8 your father's i, and reject not your
Prv   4: 1 O children, a father's i, be attentive,
Prv   4:13 Hold fast to i, never let it go;
Prv   8:10 Take my i instead of silver,
Prv   8:33 Listen to i and grow wise, do not
Prv 15: 5 The fool spurns a father's i,
Prv 19:20 Listen to counsel and receive i,
Prv 23:12 Apply your heart to i, and your ear
Prv 28: 9 who turn their ears from hearing i,
Prv 29:18 but happy is the one who follows i.
Wis   3:11 despise wisdom and i are doomed.
Is   29:24 those who find fault shall receive i.
Mi   4: 2 For from Zion shall go forth i,
Rom 15: 4 previously was written for our i,
Eph   6: 4 with the training and i of the Lord.
1 Tm 1: 5 The aim of this i is love from a pure

INSTRUCTIONS → INSTRUCT
Acts   1: 2 after giving i through the holy Spirit

INSTRUCTORS → INSTRUCT
Prv   5:13 my teachers, incline my ear to my i!

INSTRUMENT → INSTRUMENTS
Acts   9:15 for this man is a chosen i of mine

INSTRUMENTS → INSTRUMENT
1 Chr 15:16 as singers and to play on musical i,
1 Chr 23: 5 praise the LORD with the i

INSULT → INSULTED, INSULTS
Mt   5:11 Blessed are you when they i you

INSULTED → INSULT
Lk   18:32 he will be mocked and i and spat

INSULTS → INSULT
Rom 15: 3 "The i of those who insult you fall
2 Cor 12:10 I am content with weaknesses, i,

INTEGRITY
Jb   4: 6 and your i of life your hope?
Ps   41:13 In my i may you support me and let
Ps 101: 2 I study the way of i; when will you
Prv 19: 1 walk in i than rich and crooked
Prv 20: 7 The just walk in i; happy are their
Prv 28: 6 walk in i than rich and crooked
Sir   7: 6 of the prominent and mar your i.
Am   5:10 and abhor those who speak with i;
Mal   2: 6 He walked with me in i
Ti   2: 7 respect, with i in your teaching,

INTELLIGENT
Prv 11:12 lacks sense, but the i keep silent.
Prv 18:15 heart of the i acquires knowledge,

INTELLIGIBLE
1 Cor 14: 9 do not utter i speech, how will

INTENT
Ex   32:12 'With evil i he brought them out,

INTENTLY
Acts   6:15 sat in the Sanhedrin looked i at him

INTERCEDE → INTERCEDES, INTERCESSION
1 Sm 2:25 anyone can i for the sinner
1 Sm 2:25 LORD, who can i for the sinner?"
Jer   7:16 now, must not i for this people!

INTERCEDES → INTERCEDE
Rom   8:26 the Spirit itself i with inexpressible
Rom   8:27 Spirit, because it i for the holy ones
Rom   8:34 hand of God, who indeed i for us.

INTERCESSION → INTERCEDE
Heb   7:25 he lives forever to make i for them.

INTEREST → INTERESTS

Ex	22:24	you must not demand i from them.
Dt	23:20	You shall not demand i from your
Dt	23:21	a foreigner you may demand i,
Dt	23:21	you may not demand i from your
Ps	15: 5	lends no money at i, accepts no
Lk	19:23	I would have collected it with i.'

INTERESTS → INTEREST

Is	58:13	seeking your own i, or pursuing
Phil	2: 4	each looking out not for his own i,
Phil	2:21	For they all seek their own i,

INTERMARRY → MARRY

Dt	7: 3	You shall not i with them,

INTERMARRYING → MARRY

Jos	23:12	by i and intermingling with them,
Ezr	9:14	violate your commandments by i

INTERPRET → INTERPRETATION, INTERPRETATIONS, INTERPRETED, INTERPRETS

Gn	41:15	a dream but there was no one to i it.
Gn	41:15	'If he hears a dream he can i it.' "
1 Cor	12:30	Do all speak in tongues? Do all i?
1 Cor	14:13	a tongue should pray to be able to i.
1 Cor	14:27	and each in turn, and one should i.

INTERPRETATION → INTERPRET

Gn	40:16	that Joseph had given a favorable i,
1 Cor	12:10	to another i of tongues.
1 Cor	14:26	a revelation, a tongue, or an i.
2 Pt	1:20	that is a matter of personal i,

INTERPRETATIONS → INTERPRET

Gn	40: 8	to them, "Do i not come from God?
Dn	5:16	I have heard that you can give i and

INTERPRETED → INTERPRET

Lk	24:27	he i to them what referred to him

INTERPRETS → INTERPRET

1 Cor	14: 5	unless he i, so that the church may

INVADED

Jl	1: 6	For a nation i my land,

INVISIBLE

Rom	1:20	his i attributes of eternal power
Col	1:15	He is the image of the i God,
Col	1:16	earth, the visible and the i,
1 Tm	1:17	ages, incorruptible, i, the only God,
Heb	11:27	as if seeing the one who is i.

INVITE → INVITED, INVITES

Jdt	12:10	he did not i any of the officers.
Mt	22: 9	i to the feast whomever you find.'
Lk	14:13	you hold a banquet, i the poor,

INVITED → INVITE

Lk	11:37	a Pharisee i him to dine at his home.
Lk	14:10	when you are i, go and take

INVITES → INVITE

1 Cor	10:27	If an unbeliever i you and you want

INVOKE → INVOKED

Gn	4:26	time people began to i the Lord
Is	48: 1	i the God of Israel without sincerity,
1 Pt	1:17	if you i as Father him who judges

INVOKED → INVOKE

Gn	12: 8	Lord and i the Lord by name.
Dn	9:18	desolate city upon which your name is i.

INWARDLY → INNER

Ps	62: 5	with their mouths, but i they curse.
Rom	2:29	one is a Jew i, and circumcision is

IRON

Gn	4:22	forge instruments of bronze and i.
2 Kgs	6: 6	and brought the i to the surface.
Ps	2: 9	an i rod you will shepherd them,
Prv	27:17	I is sharpened by i;
Is	60:17	instead of i I will bring silver;
Dn	2:33	its legs i, its feet partly i and partly

Dn	7: 7	it had great i teeth with which it
Rev	2:27	He will rule them with an i rod.
Rev	12: 5	to rule all the nations with an i rod.
Rev	19:15	He will rule them with an i rod,

IRRATIONAL

2 Pt	2:12	like i animals born by nature
Jude	1:10	they know by nature like i animals.

IRREVOCABLE

Rom	11:29	the gifts and the call of God are i.

ISAAC

Son of Abraham by Sarah (Gn 17:19; 21:1-7; 1 Chr 1:28). Abrahamic covenant perpetuated with (Gn 17:21; 26:2-5). Offered up by Abraham (Gn 22; Heb 11:17-19). Rebekah taken as wife (Gn 24). Inherited Abraham's estate (Gn 25:5). Father of Esau and Jacob (Gn 25:19-26; 1 Chr 1:34). Nearly lost Rebekah to Abimelech (Gn 26:1-11). Covenant with Abimelech (Gn 26:12-31). Tricked into blessing Jacob (Gn 27). Death (Gn 35:27-29). Father of Israel (Ex 3:6; Dt 29:12; Rom 9:10).

ISAIAH

Prophet to Judah (Is 1:1). Called by the Lord (Is 6). Announced judgment to Ahaz (Is 7), deliverance from Assyria to Hezekiah (2 Kgs 19; Is 36–37), deliverance from death to Hezekiah (2 Kgs 20:1-11; Is 38). Chronicler of Judah's history (2 Chr 26:22; 32:32).

ISCARIOT

Mt	10: 4	and Judas I who betrayed him.
Lk	22: 3	Judas, the one surnamed I, who was

ISHBAAL

Son of Saul who attempted to succeed him as king (2 Sm 2:8–4:12).

ISHMAEL → ISHMAELITES

Son of Abraham by Hagar (Gn 16; 1 Chr 1:28). Blessed, but not son of covenant (Gn 17:18-21; Gal 4:21-31). Sent away by Sarah (Gn 21:8-21). Children (Gn 25:12-18; 1 Chr 1:29-31). Death (Gn 25:17).

ISHMAELITES → ISHMAEL

Gn	37:27	let us sell him to these I,

ISLAND

Rev	1: 9	on the i called Patmos because I
Rev	16:20	Every i fled, and mountains

ISRAEL → ISRAELITE, ISRAELITES, =JACOB

1. Name given to Jacob (Gn 32:29; 35:10; see Jacob).

2. Corporate name of Jacob's descendants; often specifically Northern Kingdom.

Gn	49:24	of the Shepherd, the Rock of I,
Gn	49:28	All these are the twelve tribes of I,
Ex	28:11	with the names of the sons of I
Ex	28:29	of the sons of I on the breastpiece
Nm	19:13	these persons shall be cut off from I.
Nm	24:17	and a scepter shall rise from I,
Dt	6: 4	Hear, O I! The Lord is our God,
Dt	10:12	therefore, I, what does the Lord,
Dt	18: 1	have no hereditary portion with I;
Jos	4:22	'I crossed the Jordan here on dry
Jos	24:31	the work the Lord had done for I.
Jgs	17: 6	In those days there was no king in I;
Jgs	21: 3	one tribe of I should be lacking?"
Ru	4:14	May he become famous in I!
1 Sm	3:20	Thus all I from Dan to Beer-sheba
1 Sm	4:21	saying, "Gone is the glory from I,"
1 Sm	14:23	Thus the Lord saved I that day.
1 Sm	15:26	has rejected you as king of I."
1 Sm	17:46	land shall learn that I has a God.
1 Sm	18:16	But all I and Judah loved David,
2 Sm	5: 2	You shall shepherd my people I; you shall be ruler over I."
2 Sm	5: 3	they anointed David king over I.
2 Sm	7:26	Lord of hosts is God over I,'
2 Sm	14:25	all I there was no man more praised
1 Kgs	1:35	him I designate ruler of I
1 Kgs	8:25	to sit before me on the throne of I,
1 Kgs	10: 9	to place you on the throne of I.
1 Kgs	12:19	so I has been in rebellion against
1 Kgs	18:17	him, "Is it you, you disturber of I?"
2 Kgs	5: 8	the king of I had torn his garments,
2 Kgs	5: 8	find out that there is a prophet in I."

2 Kgs	17:20	rejected the entire people of I:
1 Chr	17:22	You made your people I your own
1 Chr	21: 1	A satan rose up against I, and he
1 Chr	29:25	Solomon greatly in the eyes of all I,
2 Chr	9: 8	In the love your God has for I,
Tb	1: 4	that all I might offer sacrifice there.
Jdt	8:33	the Lord will deliver I by my hand.
Jdt	15:10	You have done good things for I,
1 Mc	4:25	Thus I experienced a great
Ps	22: 4	you are the glory of I.
Ps	78:21	anger flared up against I.
Ps	81: 9	If only you will listen to me, I!
Ps	98: 3	faithfulness toward the house of I.
Ps	125: 5	with the evildoers. Peace upon I!
Is	1: 3	But I does not know, my people has
Is	11:12	nations and gather the outcasts of I;
Is	27: 6	root, I shall sprout and blossom,
Is	44:21	Jacob, I, for you are my servant!
Is	46:13	within Zion, give to I my glory.
Jer	2: 3	I was dedicated to the LORD,
Jer	23: 6	be saved, I shall dwell in security.
Jer	31: 2	As I comes forward to receive rest,
Jer	31:10	The One who scattered I,
Jer	31:31	a new covenant with the house of I
Jer	33:17	on the throne of the house of I,
Lam	2: 5	the enemy, he has devoured I:
Ez	3:17	you a sentinel for the house of I,
Ez	33: 7	you as a sentinel for the house of I;
Ez	34: 2	prophesy against the shepherds of I.
Ez	36: 1	prophesy to the mountains of I
Ez	37:28	the LORD, make I holy, by putting
Ez	39:23	that the house of I went into exile
Dn	9:20	my sin and the sin of my people I,
Hos	7: 1	when I would have healed I,
Hos	11: 1	When I was a child I loved him,
Am	4:12	you, prepare to meet your God, O I!
Am	7:11	and I shall surely be exiled from its
Am	8: 2	The end has come for my people I;
Am	9:14	I will restore my people I, they shall
Mi	5: 1	for me one who is to be ruler in I;
Zep	3:13	the remnant of I. They shall do no
Zec	11:14	the kinship between Judah and I.
Mal	1: 5	even beyond the territory of I."
Mt	2: 6	is to shepherd my people I.' "
Mt	10: 6	to the lost sheep of the house of I.
Mt	15:24	to the lost sheep of the house of I."
Mk	12:29	"The first is this: 'Hear, O I!
Mk	15:32	the King of I, come down now
Lk	1:54	He has helped I his servant,
Lk	2:34	for the fall and rise of many in I,
Lk	22:30	judging the twelve tribes of I.
Jn	12:13	of the Lord, [even] the king of I."
Acts	1: 6	going to restore the kingdom to I?"
Rom	9: 6	For not all who are of I are I,
Rom	9:31	but that I, who pursued the law
Rom	11: 7	What I was seeking it did not attain,
Rom	11:26	and thus all I will be saved, as it is
Eph	2:12	alienated from the community of I
Heb	8: 8	a new covenant with the house of I

ISRAELITE → ISRAEL

Ex	35:29	Every I man and woman brought
Neh	9: 2	of I descent separated themselves
Jn	1:47	and said of him, "Here is a true I.
Rom	11: 1	For I too am an I, a descendant

ISRAELITES → ISRAEL

Ex	1: 7	But the I were fruitful and prolific.
Ex	2:23	The I groaned under their bondage
Ex	3: 9	the outcry of the I has reached me,
Ex	12:35	the I did as Moses had commanded:
Ex	14:22	so that the I entered into the midst
Ex	16:12	I have heard the grumbling of the I.
Ex	16:35	The I ate the manna for forty years,
Ex	28:30	the decisions for the I over his heart
Ex	29:45	I will dwell in the midst of the I
Ex	31:16	So shall the I observe the sabbath,

Ex	33: 5	Speak to the I: You are
Ex	39:42	so the I had carried out all the work.
Nm	2:32	the enrollments of the I according
Nm	6:23	This is how you shall bless the I.
Nm	9: 2	Tell the I to celebrate the Passover
Nm	9:17	the tent, the I would break camp;
Nm	9:17	settled, the I would pitch camp.
Nm	14: 2	All the I grumbled against Moses
Nm	20:12	my holiness before the I,
Nm	27:12	the land that I have given to the I.
Nm	33: 3	after the Passover the I went forth
Nm	35:10	Speak to the I and say to them:
Dt	4:44	law which Moses set before the I.
Dt	33: 1	of God, blessed the I before he died.
Jos	1: 2	to the land that I will give the I.
Jos	5: 6	Now the I wandered forty years
Jos	7: 1	But the I acted treacherously
Jos	8:32	in the presence of the I,
Jos	18: 1	community of the I assembled
Jos	21: 3	the I gave the Levites the following
Jos	22: 9	Manasseh left the other I at Shiloh
Jgs	2:11	the I did what was evil in the sight
Jgs	3:12	Again the I did what was evil
Jgs	4: 1	The I again did what was evil
Jgs	6: 1	The I did what was evil in the sight
Jgs	10: 6	The I again did what was evil
Jgs	13: 1	The I again did what was evil
1 Sm	17: 2	Saul and the I rallied and camped
1 Kgs	9:22	made none of the I forced laborers,
1 Kgs	12:17	to reign over the I who lived
1 Chr	9: 2	cities and dwell there were certain I,
2 Cor	11:22	So am I. Are they I? So am I.

ISSACHAR

Son of Jacob by Leah (Gn 30:18; 35:23; 1 Chr 2:1). Tribe of blessed (Gn 49:14-15; Dt 33:18-19), numbered (Nm 1:29; 26:25), allotted land (Jos 19:17-23; Ez 48:25), assisted Deborah (Jgs 5:15), 12,000 from (Rev 7:7).

ITALICA → ITALY

Acts	10: 1	centurion of the Cohort called the I,

ITALY → ITALICA

Acts	27: 1	was decided that we should sail to I,
Heb	13:24	Those from I send you greetings.

ITHAMAR

Son of Aaron (Ex 6:23; 1 Chr 5:29). Duties at tabernacle (Ex 38:21; Nm 4:21-33; 7:8).

ITTAI

2 Sm	15:19	the king said to I the Gittite:

IVORY

1 Kgs	10:22	with a cargo of gold, silver, i, apes,
1 Kgs	22:39	including the i house he built and all
Am	3:15	The houses of i shall lie in ruin,
Rev	18:12	all articles of i and all articles

IVY

2 Mc	6: 7	procession, wearing wreaths of i.

J

JABBOK

Gn	32:23	and crossed the ford of the J.
Dt	3:16	and to the Wadi J, which is

JABESH

1 Sm	11: 1	All the people of J begged Nahash,
1 Sm	31:12	and, returning to J, burned them.
1 Chr	10:12	their bones under the oak of J,

JABIN

Jos	11: 1	When J, king of Hazor,
Jgs	4:23	God humbled the Canaanite king, J,

JACKALS

Jgs	15: 4	Samson went and caught three hundred j,
Ps	63:11	sword shall become the prey of j!
Is	35: 7	The abode where j crouch will be
Mal	1: 3	a waste, his heritage a desert for j.

JACOB → =ISRAEL
 1. Son of Isaac, younger twin of Esau (Gn 26:21-26; 1 Chr 1:34). Bought Esau's birthright (Gn 26:29-34); tricked Isaac into blessing him (Gn 27:1-37). Fled to Haran (Gn 28:1-5). Abrahamic covenant perpetuated through (Gn 28:13-15; Mal 1:2). Vision at Bethel (Gn 28:10-22). Served Laban for Rachel and Leah (Gn 29:1-30). Children (Gn 29:31-30:24; 35:16-26; 1 Chr 2–9). Flocks increased (Gn 30:25-43). Returned to Canaan (Gn 31). Wrestled with God; name changed to Israel (Gn 32:23-33). Reconciled to Esau (Gn 33). Returned to Bethel (Gn 35:1-15). Favored Joseph (Gn 37:3). Sent sons to Egypt during famine (Gn 42–43). Settled in Egypt (Gn 46). Blessed Ephraim and Manasseh (Gn 48). Blessed sons (Gn 49:1-28; Heb 11:21). Death (Gn 49:29-33). Burial (Gn 50:1-14).
 2. Corporate name of Jacob's descendants; often specifically Northern Kingdom.

1 Mc	1:28	all the house of J was clothed
Ps	53: 7	captivity of his people J will rejoice
Ps	59:14	people will know God rules over J,
Ps	135: 4	For the LORD has chosen J
Sir	36:13	Gather all the tribes of J,
Is	44: 1	Hear then, J, my servant, Israel,
Jer	30:10	you, my servant J, do not fear!—
Jer	30:10	J shall again find rest, secure,
Ez	39:25	Now I will restore the fortunes of J
Mi	7:20	You will show faithfulness to J,
Rom	9:13	"I loved J but hated Esau."

JAEL
 Woman who killed Canaanite general, Sisera (Jgs 4:17-22; 5:6, 24-27).

JAIL → JAILER
Gn   39:20 into the j where the king's prisoners

JAILER → JAIL
Gn   39:21 the chief j well-disposed toward
Acts   16:27 When the j woke up and saw

JAIR
 Judge from Gilead (Jgs 10:3-5).

JAIRUS
 Synagogue ruler whose daughter Jesus raised (Mk 5:22-43; Lk 8:41-56).

JAMBRES
2 Tm   3: 8 as Jannes and J opposed Moses,

JAMES
 1. Apostle; brother of John (Mt 4:21-22; 10:2; Mk 3:17; Lk 5:1-10). At transfiguration (Mt 17:1-13; Mk 9:1-13; Lk 9:28-36). Killed by Herod (Acts 12:2).
 2. Apostle; son of Alphaeus (Mt 10:3; Mk 3:18; Lk 6:15).
 3. Brother of Jesus (Mt 13:55; Mk 6:3; Lk 24:10; Gal 1:19) and Judas (Jude 1). With believers before Pentecost (Acts 1:13). Leader of church at Jerusalem (Acts 12:17; 15; 21:18; Gal 2:9, 12). Author of epistle (Jas 1:1).

JANNES
2 Tm   3: 8 Just as J and Jambres opposed

JAPHETH
 Son of Noah (Gn 5:32; 1 Chr 1:4-5). Blessed (Gn 9:18-28). Sons of (Gn 10:2-5).

JAR → JARS
1 Kgs 17:14 The j of flour shall not go empty,
Mk   14: 3 She broke the alabaster j and poured
Lk   22:10 a man will meet you carrying a j

JARS → JAR
Jgs   7:19 and broke the j they were holding.
Jn   2: 6 there were six stone water j there

JASHAR
Jos   10:13 This is recorded in the Book of J.
2 Sm   1:18 it is recorded in the Book of J):

JASON
2 Mc   4: 7 Onias' brother J obtained the high
Acts   17: 7 and J has welcomed them.

JASPER
Ex   28:20 row, a chrysolite, an onyx, and a j.

Ez	28:13	onyx, and j, sapphire, garnet,
Rev	4: 3	whose appearance sparkled like j
Rev	21:19	the first course of stones was j,

JAWBONE
Jgs   15:15 Coming upon the fresh j of an ass,

JAZER
Nm   21:32 Moses sent spies to J;
Nm   32: 1 Noticing that the land of J

JEALOUS → JEALOUSY
Ex	20: 5	am a j God, inflicting punishment
Ex	34:14	for the LORD—"J" his name—is a j God.
Nm	11:29	him, "Are you j for my sake?
Nm	25:11	by his being as j among them as I am;
Nm	25:13	everlasting priesthood, because he was j
Dt	4:24	God, is a consuming fire, a j God.
Dt	5: 9	am a j God, bringing punishment
Ez	36: 6	in my j fury I speak, because you
Na	1: 2	A j and avenging God is
Zec	8: 2	I am intensely j for Zion, stirred to j
Acts	7: 9	"And the patriarchs, j of Joseph,
Acts	17: 5	But the Jews became j and recruited
Rom	10:19	"I will make you j of those who are
Rom	11:11	the Gentiles, so as to make them j.

JEALOUSY → JEALOUS
Nm	5:14	by a feeling of j that makes him
Prv	27: 4	but before j who can stand?
Ez	8: 3	facing north where the statue of j that provokes j stood.
Acts	5:17	of the Sadducees, and, filled with j,
Acts	13:45	they were filled with j
Rom	13:13	licentiousness, not in rivalry and j.
1 Cor	3: 3	While there is j and rivalry among
2 Cor	11: 2	am jealous of you with the j of God,
2 Cor	12:20	that there may be rivalry, j, fury,
Gal	5:20	hatreds, rivalry, j, outbursts of fury,
Jas	4: 5	to dwell in us tends toward j"?

JEBUS → =JERUSALEM, JEBUSITE, JEBUSITES
1 Chr 11: 4 that is, J, where the inhabitants

JEBUSITE → JEBUS
2 Sm   24:18 threshing floor of Araunah the J."
2 Chr 3: 1 the threshing floor of Ornan the J.

JEBUSITES → JEBUS
Gn   15:21 the Girgashites, and the J.
Ex   3: 8 Girgashites, the Hivites and the J.
Jos   15:63 so the J dwell in Jerusalem beside
2 Sm   5: 6 against the J who inhabited

JECONIAH → =JEHOIACHIN
 A form of Jehoiachin (Jer 24:1).

JEDIDIAH → =SOLOMON
2 Sm   12:25 the prophet Nathan to name him J,

JEDUTHUN
1 Chr 16:41 With them were Heman and J
2 Chr 35:15 Heman, and J, the king's seer.
Ps   39: 1 For the leader, for J. A psalm

JEERED
2 Kgs 2:23 came out of the city and j at him:

JEHOAHAZ
 1. Son of Jehu; king of Israel (2 Kgs 13:1-9).
 2. Son of Josiah; king of Judah (2 Kgs 23:31-34; 2 Chr 36:1-4).

JEHOASH → =JOASH
 1. Son of Ahaziah, king of Judah (2 Kgs 12). See Joash, 1.
 2. Son of Jehoahaz; king of Israel. Defeat of Aram prophesied by Elisha (2 Kgs 13:10-25). Defeated Amaziah in Jerusalem (2 Kgs 14:1-16). See Joash, 2.

JEHOIACHIN → =CONIAH, =JECONIAH
 Son of Jehoiakim; king of Judah exiled by Nebuchadnezzar (2 Kgs 24:8-17; 2 Chr 36:8-10; Ez 1:2). Raised from prisoner status (2 Kgs 25:27-30; Jer 52:31-34).

JEHOIADA
 Priest who sheltered Joash from Athaliah (2 Kgs 11–12; 2 Chr 22:11-24:16).

JEHOIAKIM → =ELIAKIM
Son of Josiah; made king of Judah by Nebuchadnezzar (2 Kgs 23:34–24:6; 2 Chr 36:4-8; Jer 22:18-23). Burned scroll of Jeremiah's prophecies (Jer 36).

JEHORAM → =JORAM
1. Son of Jehoshaphat; king of Judah. Prophesied against by Elijah; killed by the LORD (2 Chr 21). See Joram, 1.
2. Son of Ahab; king of Israel (2 Chr 22:5). With Jehoshaphat fought against Moab (2 Kgs 3). See Joram, 2.

JEHOSHAPHAT
1. Son of Asa; king of Judah. Strengthened his kingdom (2 Chr 17). Joined with Ahab against Aram (2 Kgs 22; 2 Chr 18). Established judges (2 Chr 19). Joined Joram against Moab (2 Kgs 3; 2 Chr 20).
2. Valley of judgment (Jl 4:2, 12).

JEHOZADAK
1 Chr 5:41 J was one of those who went
Hg 1:12 son of J, and all the remnant

JEHU
1. Prophet against Baasha (2 Kgs 16:1-7).
2. King of Israel. Anointed by Elijah to obliterate house of Ahab (1 Kgs 19:16-17); anointed by servant of Elisha (2 Kgs 9:1-13). Killed Joram and Ahaziah (2 Kgs 9:14-29; 2 Chr 22:7-9), Jezebel (2 Kgs 9:30-37), relatives of Ahab (2 Kgs 10:1-17; Hos 1:4), ministers of Baal (2 Kgs 10:18-29). Death (2 Kgs 10:30-36).

JEPHTHAH
Judge from Gilead who delivered Israel from Ammon (Jgs 10:6–12:7). Made rash vow concerning his daughter (Jgs 11:30-40).

JEREMIAH
Prophet to Judah (Jer 1:1-3). Called by the LORD (Jer 1). Put in stocks (Jer 20:1-3). Threatened for prophesying (Jer 11:18-23; 26). Opposed by Hananiah (Jer 28). Scroll burned (Jer 36). Imprisoned (Jer 37). Thrown into cistern (Jer 38). Forced to Egypt with those fleeing Babylonians (Jer 43).

JERICHO
Nm 22: 1 other side of the Jordan opposite J.
Dt 34: 3 the plain (the valley of J, the City
Jos 3:16 the people crossed over opposite J.
Jos 5:10 at Gilgal on the plains of J,
Jos 6: 2 I have delivered J, its king, and its
Jos 6:26 who attempts to rebuild this city, J.
1 Kgs 16:34 his reign, Hiel from Bethel rebuilt J.
2 Kgs 25: 5 overtook him in the desert near J,
Lk 10:30 he went down from Jerusalem to J.
Lk 18:35 as he approached J a blind man was
Lk 19: 1 He came to J and intended to pass
Heb 11:30 faith the walls of J fell after being

JEROBOAM
1. Official of Solomon; rebelled to become first king of Israel (1 Kgs 11:26-40; 12:1-20; 2 Chr 10). Idolatry (1 Kgs 12:25-33; Tb 1:5; Sir 47:23-25); judgment for (1 Kgs 13–14; 2 Chr 13).
2. Son of Jehoash; king of Israel (1 Kgs 14:23-29).

JERUBBAAL → =GIDEON
Jgs 6:32 So on that day Gideon was called J,
1 Sm 12:11 The LORD sent J, Barak,

JERUSALEM → =JEBUS, JERUSALEM'S, =SALEM
Jos 10: 1 king of J, heard that Joshua had
Jos 15: 8 flank of the Jebusites (that is, J),
Jgs 1: 8 The Judahites fought against J,
1 Sm 17:54 of the Philistine and brought it to J;
2 Sm 5: 5 J he was king thirty-three years over
2 Sm 9:13 But Meribbaal lived in J.
2 Sm 11: 1 David himself remained in J.
2 Sm 15:29 took the ark of God back to J
2 Sm 24:16 stretched forth his hand toward J
1 Kgs 3: 1 the LORD, and the wall around J.
1 Kgs 9:15 house, Millo, the wall of J, Hazor,
1 Kgs 9:19 Solomon desired to build in J,
1 Kgs 10:26 cities and to the king's service in J.
1 Kgs 10:27 silver as common in J as stones,
1 Kgs 11: 7 on the mountain opposite J.
1 Kgs 11:13 my servant and for the sake of J,

1 Kgs 11:36 have a holding before me in J,
1 Kgs 14:25 Shishak, king of Egypt, attacked J.
2 Kgs 12:18 Hazael resolved to go on to attack J.
2 Kgs 14:13 came to J Joash tore down the wall of J,
2 Kgs 18:17 a great army to King Hezekiah at J.
2 Kgs 18:35 then rescue J from my power?"
2 Kgs 19:31 For out of J shall come a remnant,
2 Kgs 21: 4 In J I will set my name.
2 Kgs 21:12 I am about to bring such evil on J
2 Kgs 23:27 I will reject this city, J, which I
2 Kgs 24:10 attacked J, and the city came under
2 Kgs 24:14 He deported all J: all the officers
2 Kgs 24:20 This befell J and Judah because
2 Kgs 25: 1 his whole army advanced against J,
2 Kgs 25:10 down the walls that surrounded J,
1 Chr 11: 4 Then David and all Israel went to J,
1 Chr 21:16 in hand stretched out against J.
2 Chr 1: 4 ark of God from Kiriath-jearim to J,
2 Chr 3: 1 the LORD in J on Mount Moriah,
2 Chr 6: 6 but now I have chosen J, that my
2 Chr 9: 1 came to J to test him with subtle
2 Chr 20:15 of Judah, inhabitants of J, and King
2 Chr 20:27 at their head, returned to J with joy;
2 Chr 29: 8 has come upon Judah and J;
2 Chr 36:19 God, tore down the walls of J,
Ezr 1: 2 me to build him a house in J,
Ezr 2: 1 and who came back to J and Judah,
Ezr 3: 1 the people gathered as one in J.
Ezr 4:12 up from you to us have arrived at J
Ezr 4:24 on the house of God in J ceased.
Ezr 6:12 or to destroy this house of God in J.
Ezr 7: 8 Ezra came to J in the fifth month
Ezr 9: 9 us a protective wall in Judah and J.
Ezr 10: 7 exiles should gather together in J,
Neh 1: 2 after the captivity, and about J.
Neh 1: 3 The wall of J has been breached,
Neh 2:17 how J lies in ruins and its gates
Neh 2:17 let us rebuild the wall of J,
Neh 2:20 share nor claim nor memorial in J."
Neh 3: 8 They restored J as far as the Broad
Neh 4: 2 fight against J and to throw us
Neh 11: 1 bring one man in ten to reside in J,
Neh 12:27 At the dedication of the wall of J,
Neh 12:43 and the rejoicing at J could be heard
Tb 1: 6 to go often to J for the festivals,
Jdt 4: 2 greatly alarmed for J and the temple
Jdt 15: 9 "You are the glory of J!
1 Mc 1:14 built a gymnasium in J according
1 Mc 1:29 he came to J with a strong force.
1 Mc 6: 7 he had built upon the altar in J;
Ps 51:20 build up the walls of J.
Ps 79: 1 they have laid J in ruins.
Ps 122: 2 are standing within your gates, J.
Ps 122: 6 For the peace of J pray:
Ps 125: 2 As mountains surround J,
Ps 137: 5 If I forget you, J, may my right
Ps 147: 2 The LORD rebuilds J, and gathers
Ps 147:12 Glorify the LORD, J;
Eccl 1:12 Qoheleth, was king over Israel in J,
Sg 6: 4 fair as J, fearsome as celestial
Is 1: 1 Judah and J in the days of Uzziah,
Is 2: 1 Amoz, saw concerning Judah and J.
Is 3: 1 will take away from J
Is 3: 8 J has stumbled, Judah has fallen;
Is 4: 3 left in J Will be called holy:
Is 4: 3 everyone inscribed for life in J.
Is 8:14 and a snare to those who dwell in J;
Is 27:13 LORD on the holy mountain, in J.
Is 31: 5 the LORD of hosts shall shield J,
Is 33:20 your eyes shall see J as a quiet
Is 40: 2 Speak to the heart of J,
Is 40: 9 Cry out at the top of your voice, J,
Is 52: 1 Put on your glorious garments, J,
Is 52: 2 shake off the dust, sit enthroned, J;
Is 62: 6 Upon your walls, J, I have stationed
Is 62: 7 until he re-establishes J And makes

Is   65:18 I am creating J to be a joy and its
Is   66:13 in J you shall find your comfort.
Jer   2: 2 cry out this message for J to hear!
Jer   3:17 honor the name of the LORD at J,
Jer   4: 5 it in Judah, in J announce it;
Jer   4:14 Cleanse your heart of evil, J,
Jer   5: 1 Roam the streets of J,
Jer   6: 6 throw up a siege mound against J.
Jer   9:10 I will turn J into a heap of ruins,
Jer   13:27 Woe to you, J! How long will it be
Jer   26:18 Zion shall be plowed as a field, J,
Jer   32: 2 king of Babylon was besieging J,
Jer   33:10 in the streets of J now deserted,
Jer   39: 1 all his army marched against J
Jer   51:50 from far away, let J come to mind.
Jer   52:14 all the walls that surrounded J.
Lam   1: 8 J has sinned grievously,
Ez   8: 3 in divine vision to J to the entrance
Ez   14:21 though I send against J my four evil
Ez   16: 2 make known to J her abominations.
Ez   21: 7 of man, turn your face toward J:
Ez   23: 4 Samaria was Oholah and J,
Dn   5: 3 the house of God in J, had been
Dn   6:11 with the windows open toward J.
Dn   9: 2 J was to lie in ruins for seventy
Dn   9:12 under heaven as happened in J.
Dn   9:25 of the word that J was to be rebuilt
Jl   4: 1 I restore the fortunes of Judah and J,
Jl   4:16 and from J raises his voice,
Jl   4:17 J will be holy, and strangers will
Am   2: 5 it will devour the strongholds of J.
Mi   1: 5 of the house of Judah? Is it not J?
Mi   4: 2 and the word of the LORD from J.
Zep   3:16 On that day, it shall be said to J:
Zec   1:14 I am jealous for J and for Zion
Zec   1:17 Zion, and will again choose J.
Zec   2: 6 And he said, "To measure J—
Zec   2: 8 J will be unwalled,
Zec   8: 3 to Zion, and I will dwell within J;
Zec   8: 8 bring them back to dwell within J.
Zec   8:15 in these days I intend to favor J
Zec   8:22 to seek the LORD of hosts in J
Zec   9: 9 Shout for joy, O daughter J!
Zec   9:10 Ephraim, and the horse from J;
Zec   12: 3 day I will make J a heavy stone
Zec   12:10 the inhabitants of J a spirit of mercy
Zec   14: 2 I will gather all the nations against J
Zec   14: 8 fresh water will flow from J,
Zec   14:16 nations that came against J will go
Mt   2: 1 magi from the east arrived in J,
Mt   16:21 his disciples that he must go to J
Mt   20:18 we are going up to J, and the Son
Mt   21:10 he entered J the whole city was
Mt   23:37 "J, J, you who kill the prophets
Mk   10:33 we are going up to J, and the Son
Mk   15:41 who had come up with him to J.
Lk   2:22 they took him up to J to present him
Lk   2:41 Each year his parents went to J
Lk   2:43 the boy Jesus remained behind in J,
Lk   4: 9 Then he led him to J, made him
Lk   9:31 he was going to accomplish in J.
Lk   9:51 determined to journey to J,
Lk   18:31 we are going up to J and everything
Lk   21:20 you see J surrounded by armies,
Lk   21:24 J will be trampled underfoot
Lk   23:28 "Daughters of J, do not weep
Lk   24:47 to all the nations, beginning from J.
Jn   1:19 When the Jews from J sent priests
Jn   4:20 that the place to worship is in J."
Jn   5: 1 of the Jews, and Jesus went up to J.
Jn   10:22 was then taking place in J.
Acts   1: 4 enjoined them not to depart from J,
Acts   1: 8 and you will be my witnesses in J,
Acts   6: 7 the disciples in J increased greatly;
Acts   9:13 he has done to your holy ones in J.
Acts   9:28 moved about freely with them in J,

Acts   11:27 some prophets came down from J
Acts   15: 2 should go up to J to the apostles
Acts   20:22 by the Spirit, I am going to J.
Acts   21: 4 the Spirit not to embark for J.
Acts   23:11 borne witness to my cause in J,
Rom   15:19 so that from J all the way around
Gal   4:25 it corresponds to the present J,
Heb   12:22 the heavenly J, and countless angels
Rev   3:12 the new J, which comes down
Rev   21: 2 city, a new J, coming down
Rev   21:10 me the holy city J coming down

JERUSALEM'S → JERUSALEM
Is   62: 1 for J sake I will not keep still,

JESHUA → =JOSHUA
Ezr   4: 3 But Zerubbabel, J, and the rest
Ezr   10:18 Of the descendants of J,
Neh   12: 1 Zerubbabel, son of Shealtiel, and J:
Sir   49:12 And J, Jozadak's son? In their time

JESSE
   Father of David (Ru 4:17-22; 1 Sm 16; 1 Chr 2:12-17).

JESUS → =JUSTUS
   1. Jesus the Messiah.
   LIFE: Genealogy (Mt 1:1-17; Lk 3:21-37). Birth announced (Mt 1:18-25; Lk 1:26-45). Birth (Mt 2:1-12; Lk 2:1-40). Escape to Egypt (Mt 2:13-23). As a boy in the temple (Lk 2:41-52). Baptism (Mt 3:13-17; Mk 1:9-11; Lk 3:21-22; Jn 1:32-34). Temptation (Mt 4:1-11; Mk 1:12-13; Lk 4:1-13). Ministry in Galilee (Mt 4:12–18:35; Mk 1:14—9:50; Lk 4:14—13:9; Jn 1:35—2:11; 4; 6), Transfiguration (Mt 17:1-8; Mk 9:2-8; Lk 9:28-36), on the way to Jerusalem (Mt 19–20; Mk 10; Lk 13:10—19:27), in Jerusalem (Mt 21–25; Mk 11–13; Lk 19:28—21:38; Jn 2:12—3:36; 5; 7–12). Last supper (Mt 26:17-35; Mk 14:12-31; Lk 22:1-38; Jn 13–17). Arrest and trial (Mt 26:36—27:31; Mk 14:43—15:20; Lk 22:39—23:25; Jn 18:1—19:16). Crucifixion (Mt 27:32-66; Mk 15:21-47; Lk 23:26-55; Jn 19:28-42). Resurrection and appearances (Mt 28; Mk 16; Lk 24; Jn 20–21; Acts 1:1-11; 7:56; 9:3-6; 1 Cor 15:1-8; Rev 1:1-20).
   MIRACLES. *Healings:* official's son (Jn 4:43-54), demoniac in Capernaum (Mk 1:23-26; Lk 4:33-35), Peter's mother-in-law (Mt 8:14-17; Mk 1:29-31; Lk 4:38-39), leper (Mt 8:2-4; Mk 1:40-45; Lk 5:12-16), paralytic (Mt 9:1-8; Mk 2:1-12; Lk 5:17-26), cripple (Jn 5:1-9), shriveled hand (Mt 12:10-13; Mk 3:1-5; Lk 6:6-11), centurion's servant (Mt 8:5-13; Lk 7:1-10), widow's son raised (Lk 7:11-17), demoniac (Mt 12:22-23; Lk 11:14), Gadarene demoniacs (Mt 8:28-34; Mk 5:1-20; Lk 8:26-39), woman's bleeding and Jairus' daughter (Mt 9:18-26; Mk 5:21-43; Lk 8:40-56), blind man (Mt 9:27-31), mute man (Mt 9:32-33), Canaanite woman's daughter (Mt 15:21-28; Mk 7:24-30), deaf man (Mk 7:31-37), blind man (Mk 8:22-26), demoniac boy (Mt 17:14-18; Mk 9:14-29; Lk 9:37-43), ten lepers (Lk 17:11-19), man born blind (Jn 9:1-7), Lazarus raised (Jn 11), crippled woman (Lk 13:11-17), man with dropsy (Lk 14:1-6), two blind men (Mt 20:29-34; Mk 10:46-52; Lk 18:35-43), Malchus' ear (Lk 22:50-51). *Other Miracles:* water to wine (Jn 2:1-11), catch of fish (Lk 5:1-11), storm stilled (Mt 8:23-27; Mk 4:37-41; Lk 8:22-25), 5,000 fed (Mt 14:15-21; Mk 6:35-44; Lk 9:10-17; Jn 6:1-14), walking on water (Mt 14:25-33; Mk 6:48-52; Jn 6:15-21), 4,000 fed (Mt 15:32-39; Mk 8:1-9), money from fish (Mt 17:24-27), fig tree cursed (Mt 21:18-22; Mk 11:12-14), catch of fish (Jn 21:1-14).
   MAJOR TEACHING: Sermon on the Mount (Mt 5–7; Lk 6:17-49), to Nicodemus (Jn 3), to Samaritan woman (Jn 4), Bread of Life (Jn 6:22-59), at Feast of Tabernacles (Jn 7–8), woes to Pharisees (Mt 23; Lk 11:37-54), Good Shepherd (Jn 10:1-18), Olivet Discourse (Mt 24–25; Mk 13; Lk 21:5-36), Upper Room Discourse (Jn 13–16).
   PARABLES: Sower (Mt 13:3-23; Mk 4:3-25; Lk 8:5-18), seed's growth (Mk 4:26-29), wheat and weeds (Mt 13:24-30, 36-43), mustard seed (Mt 13:31-32; Mk 4:30-32), yeast (Mt 13:33; Lk 13:20-21), hidden treasure (Mt 13:44), valuable pearl (Mt 13:45-46), net (Mt 13:47-51), house owner (Mt 13:52), good Samaritan (Lk 10:25-37), unmerciful servant (Mt 18:15-35), lost sheep (Mt 18:10-14; Lk 15:4-7), lost coin (Lk 15:8-10), prodigal son (Lk 15:11-32), dishonest manager (Lk 16:1-13), rich man and Lazarus (Lk 16:19-31), persistent widow (Lk 18:1-8), Pharisee and tax collector (Lk 18:9-14), payment of workers (Mt 20:1-16), tenants and the vineyard (Mt 21:28-46; Mt 12:1-12; Lk 20:9-19), wedding banquet (Mt 22:1-14), faithful servant (Mt 24:45-51), ten virgins (Mt 25:1-13), talents (Mt 25:1-30; Lk 19:12-27).
   DISCIPLES see APOSTLES. Call (Jn 1:35-51; Mt 4:18-22; 9:9; Mk

1:16-20; 2:13-14; Lk 5:1-11, 27-28). Named Apostles (Mk 3:13-19; Lk 6:12-16). Twelve sent out (Mt 10; Mk 6:7-11; Lk 9:1-5). Seventy sent out (Lk 10:1-24). Defection of (Jn 6:60-71; Mt 26:56; Mk 14:50-52). Final commission (Mt 28:16-20; Jn 21:15-23; Acts 1:3-8).

Acts	2:32	God raised this J; of this we are all
Acts	9: 5	"I am J, whom you are persecuting.
Acts	9:34	him, "Aeneas, J Christ heals you.
Acts	15:11	through the grace of the Lord J,
Acts	16:31	"Believe in the Lord J and you
Acts	20:24	that I received from the Lord J,
Rom	3:24	through the redemption in Christ J,
Rom	5:17	life through the one person J Christ.
Rom	8: 1	for those who are in Christ J.
1 Cor	1: 7	the revelation of our Lord J Christ.
1 Cor	2: 2	I was with you except J Christ,
1 Cor	6:11	in the name of the Lord J Christ
1 Cor	8: 6	and one Lord, J Christ,
1 Cor	12: 3	spirit of God says, "J be accursed."
1 Cor	12: 3	And no one can say, "J is Lord,"
2 Cor	4: 5	ourselves but J Christ as Lord,
2 Cor	4: 5	as your slaves for the sake of J.
2 Cor	13: 5	Do you not realize that J Christ is
Eph	1: 5	to himself through J Christ,
Eph	2:10	in Christ J for the good works
Eph	2:20	Christ J himself as the capstone.
Phil	1: 6	complete it until the day of Christ J.
Phil	2: 5	that is also yours in Christ J,
Phil	2:10	name of J every knee should bend,
Col	3:17	in the name of the Lord J,
1 Thes	1:10	whom he raised from [the] dead, J,
1 Thes	4:14	For if we believe that J died
1 Thes	5:23	for the coming of our Lord J Christ.
2 Thes	1: 7	of the Lord J from heaven with his
2 Thes	2: 1	to the coming of our Lord J Christ
1 Tm	1:15	Christ J came into the world to save
2 Tm	1:10	appearance of our savior Christ J,
2 Tm	2: 3	me like a good soldier of Christ J.
2 Tm	3:12	in Christ J will be persecuted.
Ti	2:13	God and of our savior J Christ,
Heb	2: 9	we do see J "crowned with glory
Heb	3: 1	reflect on J, the apostle and high
Heb	4:14	has passed through the heavens, J,
Heb	6:20	where J has entered on our behalf as
Heb	7:22	to that same degree has J
Heb	12: 2	while keeping our eyes fixed on J,
Heb	12:24	and J, the mediator of a new
Heb	13: 8	J Christ is the same yesterday,
1 Pt	1: 3	through the resurrection of J Christ
2 Pt	1:16	and coming of our Lord J Christ,
1 Jn	1: 7	the blood of his Son J cleanses us
1 Jn	2: 1	Father, J Christ the righteous one.
1 Jn	4:15	acknowledges that J is the Son
Rev	1: 1	The revelation of J Christ,
Rev	12:17	and bear witness to J.
Rev	17: 6	on the blood of the witnesses to J.
Rev	22:16	"I, J, sent my angel to give you this
Rev	22:20	Amen! Come, Lord J!"

2. Disciple, also called Justus (Col 4:11).
3. Writer of Sirach or Ecclesiasticus (Sir Pr:1; 50:27; 51:1).

JETHRO
Father-in-law and adviser of Moses (Ex 3:1; 4:18; 18). Also known as Reuel (Ex 2:18).

JEW → JEWISH, JEWS, JUDAISM
Est	2: 5	of Susa a certain J named Mordecai,
Est	10: 3	The J Mordecai was next in rank
Dn	14:28	"The king has become a J,"
Jn	4: 9	him, "How can you, a J, ask me,
Jn	18:35	answered, "I am not a J, am I?
Acts	21:39	"I am a J, of Tarsus in Cilicia,
Rom	1:16	for J first, and then Greek.
Rom	2: 9	does evil, J first and then Greek.
Rom	2:29	Rather, one is a J inwardly,
Rom	10:12	For there is no distinction between J
1 Cor	9:20	To the Jews I became like a J to win
Col	3:11	Here there is not Greek and J,

JEWELS
Is	61:10	as a bride adorns herself with her j.

JEWISH → JEW
Est	6:13	is of J ancestry, you will not prevail
1 Mc	8:29	an agreement with the J people.
Jn	2: 6	there for J ceremonial washings,
Acts	13: 6	who was a J false prophet.
Acts	24:24	with his wife Drusilla, who was J.
Ti	1:14	of paying attention to J myths

JEWS → JEW
Ezr	5: 5	God was upon the elders of the J,
Neh	3:33	He ridiculed the J,
Est	3:13	kill and annihilate all the J,
Est	4:14	come to the J from another source;
Est	8:17	banqueting and feasting for the J.
Est	10: 3	in high standing among the J,
Dn	3: 8	Chaldeans came and accused the J
Mt	2: 2	is the newborn king of the J?
Mt	27:11	him, "Are you the king of the J?"
Mt	27:37	This is Jesus, the King of the J.
Lk	23: 3	him, "Are you the king of the J?"
Jn	4: 9	(For J use nothing in common
Jn	4:22	because salvation is from the J.
Jn	7:13	because they were afraid of the J.
Jn	9:22	because they were afraid of the J.
Jn	19: 3	and said, "Hail, King of the J!"
Jn	19:21	"Do not write 'The King of the J,'
Jn	19:21	he said, 'I am the King of the J.' "
Acts	20:21	I earnestly bore witness for both J
Acts	21:20	there are from among the J,
Rom	3:29	Does God belong to J alone?
Rom	9:24	not only from the J
1 Cor	1:22	For J demand signs and Greeks look
1 Cor	9:20	To the J I became like a Jew to win over J;
1 Cor	12:13	into one body, whether J or Greeks,
1 Thes	2:14	compatriots as they did from the J,
Rev	2: 9	slander of those who claim to be J
Rev	3: 9	of Satan who claim to be J and are

JEZEBEL
Sidonian wife of Ahab (1 Kgs 16:31). Promoted Baal worship (1 Kgs 16:32-33). Killed prophets of the LORD (1 Kgs 18:4, 13). Opposed Elijah (1 Kgs 19:1-2). Had Naboth killed (1 Kgs 21). Death prophesied (1 Kgs 21:17-24). Killed by Jehu (2 Kgs 9:30-37). Metaphor of immorality (Rev 2:20).

JEZREEL → JEZREELITE
1 Kgs	21:23	devour Jezebel in the confines of J.
2 Kgs	9:36	of J the dogs shall devour the flesh
2 Kgs	10: 7	baskets, and sent them to Jehu in J.
Hos	1: 4	house of Jehu for the bloodshed at J
Hos	2: 2	great indeed shall be the day of J!
Hos	2:24	and oil, and these will respond to J.

JEZREELITE → JEZREEL
1 Kgs	21: 1	Naboth the J had a vineyard
2 Kgs	9:25	ground in the field of Naboth the J.

JOAB
Nephew of David (1 Chr 2:16). Commander of his army (2 Sm 8:16). Victorious over Ammon (2 Sm 10; 1 Chr 19), Rabbah (2 Sm 11; 1 Chr 20), Jerusalem (1 Chr 11:6), Absalom (2 Sm 18), Sheba (2 Sm 20). Killed Abner (2 Sm 3:22-39), Amasa (2 Sm 20:1-13). Numbered David's army (2 Sm 24; 1 Chr 21). Sided with Adonijah (1 Kgs 1:17, 19). Killed by Benaiah (1 Kgs 2:5-6, 28-35).

JOANNA
Lk	8: 3	J, the wife of Herod's steward
Lk	24:10	women were Mary Magdalene, J,

JOASH → =JEHOASH
1. Son of Ahaziah; king of Judah. Sheltered from Athaliah by Jehoiada (2 Kgs 11; 2 Chr 22:10–23:21). Repaired temple (2 Chr 24). See Jehoash, 1.
2. Son of Jehoahaz, king of Israel (2 Kgs 13; 2 Chr 25:17-25). See Jehoash, 2.

JOB
Wealthy man from Uz; feared God (Jb 1:1-5). Integrity tested by

disaster (Jb 1:6-22), personal affliction (Jb 2). Maintained innocence in debate with three friends (Jb 3–31), Elihu (Jb 32–37). Rebuked by the LORD (Jb 38–41). Vindicated and restored to greater stature by the LORD (Jb 42). Example of righteousness (Sir 49:9; Ez 14:14, 20).

JOCHEBED
Mother of Moses, Aaron and Miriam (Ex 6:20; Nm 26:59).

JOEL
1. Son of Samuel (1 Sm 8:2; 1 Chr 6:13).
2. Prophet (Jl 1:1; Acts 2:16).

JOHANAN
1. First high priest in Solomon's temple (1 Chr 5:36-37).
2. Jewish leader who tried to save Gedaliah from assassination (Jer 40:13-14); took Jews, including Jeremiah, to Egypt (Jer 40–43).

JOHN
1. Son of Zechariah and Elizabeth (Lk 1). Called the Baptist (Mt 3:1-12; Mk 1:2-8). Witness to Jesus (Mt 3:11-12; Mk 1:7-8; Lk 3:15-18; Jn 1:6-35; 3:27-30; 5:33-36). Doubts about Jesus (Mt 11:2-6; Lk 7:18-23). Arrest (Mt 4:12; Mk 1:14). Execution (Mt 14:1-12; Mk 6:14-29; Lk 9:7-9). Ministry compared to Elijah (Mt 11:7-19; Mk 9:11-13; Lk 7:24-35).
2. Apostle; brother of James (Mt 4:21-22; 10:2; Mk 3:17; Lk 5:1-10). At transfiguration (Mt 17:1-13; Mk 9:1-13; Lk 9:28-36). Desire to be greatest (Mk 10:35-45). Leader of church at Jerusalem (Acts 4:1-3; Gal 2:9). Elder who wrote epistles (2 Jn 1; 3 Jn 1). Prophet who wrote Revelation (Rev 1:1; 22:8).
3. Cousin of Barnabas, co-worker with Paul, (Acts 12:12–13:13; 15:37; see Mark).
4. Son of Simon Maccabeus; a high priest (1 Mc 13:53; 16).

JOIN → JOINED
Ex	1:10	war they too may j our enemies
Neh	10:30	j their influential kindred,
Ez	37:17	J the two sticks together so they
Dn	11:34	many shall j them,
Acts	5:13	None of the others dared to j them,
Acts	9:26	Jerusalem he tried to j the disciples,
Rom	15:30	to j me in the struggle by your

JOINED → JOIN
Mt	19: 6	what God has j together, no human
Mk	10: 9	Therefore what God has j together,
Eph	4:16	body, j and held together by every

JOINT → JOINTS
Rom	8:17	heirs of God and j heirs with Christ,

JOINTS → JOINT
Heb	4:12	soul and spirit, j and marrow,

JOKING
Prv	26:19	and then say, "I was only j."

JONADAB
2 Sm	13: 3	Now Amnon had a friend named J,
Jer	35: 8	We have obeyed J, Rechab's son,

JONAH
Prophet in days of Jeroboam II (2 Kgs 14:25). Called to Nineveh; fled to Tarshish (Jon 1:1-3). Cause of storm; thrown into sea (Jon 1:4-16). Swallowed by fish (Jon 2:1). Prayer (Jon 2). Preached to Nineveh (Jon 3). Attitude reproved by the LORD (Jon 4). Sign of (Mt 12:39-41; Lk 11:29-32).

JONATHAN
1. Son of Saul (1 Sm 13:16; 1 Chr 8:33). Valiant warrior (1 Sm 13–14). Relation to David (1 Sm 18:1-4; 19–20; 23:16-18). Killed at Gilboa (1 Sm 31). Mourned by David (2 Sm 1).
2. Brother and successor of Judas Maccabeus (1 Mc 2:5; 9:28-31).

JOPPA
2 Chr	2:15	down to you in rafts to the port of J,
Ezr	3: 7	from the Lebanon to the port of J,
Jon	1: 3	He went down to J, found a ship
Acts	9:43	And he stayed a long time in J

JORAM → =JEHORAM
1. Son of Jehoshaphat; king of Judah (2 Kgs 8:16-24). See Jehoram, 1.
2. Son of Ahab; king of Israel. Killed with Ahaziah by Jehu (2 Kgs 8:25-29; 9:14-26; 2 Chr 22:5-9). See Jehoram, 2.

JORDAN
Gn	13:10	watered the whole J Plain was as far
Nm	22: 1	other side of the J opposite Jericho.
Nm	34:12	boundary will descend along the J
Dt	1: 1	to all Israel beyond the J
Dt	3:27	well, for you shall not cross this J.
Jos	1: 2	prepare to cross the J to the land
Jos	3:11	earth will cross the J before you.
Jos	3:17	had completed the crossing of the J.
Jos	4: 8	the J riverbed as the LORD had
Jos	4:22	'Israel crossed the J here on dry
Jos	23: 4	between the J and the Great Sea
2 Kgs	2: 7	the two of them stood next to the J.
2 Kgs	2:13	back and stood at the bank of the J.
2 Kgs	5:10	"Go and wash seven times in the J,
2 Kgs	6: 4	they arrived at the J they began
Ps	114: 3	sea saw and fled; the J turned back.
Is	8:23	the land across the J,
Jer	12: 5	will you do in the jungle of the J?
Mt	3: 6	in the J River as they acknowledged
Mt	4:15	the sea, beyond the J,
Mk	1: 9	and was baptized in the J by John.
Jn	1:28	happened in Bethany across the J,

JOSEPH → =BARNABAS, =BARSABBAS
1. Son of Jacob by Rachel (Gn 30:24; 1 Chr 2:2). Favored by Jacob, hated by brothers (Gn 37:3-4). Dreams (Gn 37:5-11). Sold by brothers (Gn 37:12-36). Served Potiphar; imprisoned by false accusation (Gn 39). Interpreted dreams of Pharaoh's servants (Gn 40), of Pharaoh (Gn 41:4-40). Made greatest in Egypt (Gn 41:41-57). Sold grain to brothers (Gn 42–45). Brought Jacob and sons to Egypt (Gn 46–47). Sons Ephraim and Manasseh blessed (Gn 48). Blessed (Gn 49:22-26; Dt 33:13-17). Death (Gn 50:22-26; Ex 13:19; Heb 11:22). 12,000 from (Rev 7:8).
2. Husband of Mary mother of Jesus (Mt 1:16-24; 2:13-19; Lk 1:27; 2; Jn 1:45).
3. Disciple from Arimathea; buried Jesus in his tomb (Mt 27:57-61; Mk 15:43-47; Lk 24:50-52).
4. Original name of Barnabas (Acts 4:36).

JOSHUA → =HOSHEA, =JESHUA
1. Son of Nun; name changed from Hoshea (Nm 13:8, 16; 1 Chr 7:27). Fought Amalekites under Moses (Ex 17:9-14). Servant of Moses on Sinai (Ex 24:13; 32:17). Spied Canaan (Nm 13). With Caleb, allowed to enter land (Nm 14:6, 30). Succeeded Moses (Dt 1:38; 31:1-8; 34:9).
Charged Israel to conquer Canaan (Jos 1). Crossed Jordan (Jos 3–4). Circumcised sons of wilderness wanderings (Jos 5). Conquered Jericho (Jos 6), Ai (Jos 7–8), five kings at Gibeon (Jos 10:1-28), southern Canaan (Jos 10:29-43), northern Canaan (Jos 11–12). Defeated at Ai (Jos 7). Deceived by Gibeonites (Jos 9). Renewed covenant (Jos 8:30-35; 24:1-27). Divided land among tribes (Jos 13–22). Last words (Jos 23). Death (Jos 24:28-31).
2. High priest during rebuilding of temple (Hg 1–2; Zec 3:1-9; 6:11). See Jeshua.

JOSIAH
Son of Amon; king of Judah (2 Kgs 21:26; 1 Chr 3:14). Prophesied (1 Kgs 13:2). Book of the Law discovered during his reign (2 Kgs 22; 2 Chr 34:14-31). Reforms (2 Kgs 23:1-25; 2 Chr 34:1-13; 35:1-19; Sir 49:1-4). Killed by Pharaoh Neco (2 Kgs 23:29-30; 2 Chr 35:20-26).

JOTHAM
1. Son of Gideon (Jgs 9).
2. Son of Azariah (Uzziah); king of Judah (2 Kgs 15:32-38; 2 Chr 26:21–27:9).

JOURNEY
Ex	3:18	now, let us go a three days' j
Ezr	8:21	seek from him a safe j for ourselves,
Am	3: 3	Do two j together unless they have agreed?
Mt	25:14	a man who was going on a j called
Lk	9: 3	"Take nothing for the j,

JOY → JOYFULLY, OVERJOYED
Ezr	3:12	lifted up their voices in shouts of j.
Ezr	6:16	of this house of God with j.
Ezr	6:22	the LORD had filled them with j
Est	9:22	was turned for them from sorrow into j,
1 Mc	3:45	J had disappeared from Jacob,

1 Mc	4:58	There was great j among the people
Jb	20: 5	is short and the j of the impious
Jb	38: 7	all the sons of God shouted for j?
Ps	5:12	will be glad and forever shout for j.
Ps	16:11	life, abounding j in your presence,
Ps	20: 6	May we shout for j at your victory,
Ps	21: 7	gladden him with the j of your face.
Ps	27: 6	his tent sacrifices with shouts of j;
Ps	35:27	who favor my just cause shout for j
Ps	43: 4	of God, to God, my j, my delight.
Ps	48: 3	of heights, the j of all the earth,
Ps	51:10	You will let me hear gladness and j;
Ps	65: 9	evening you make resound with j.
Ps	65:14	they cheer and sing for j.
Ps	71:23	will shout for j as I sing your praise;
Ps	92: 5	works of your hands I shout for j.
Ps	98: 8	the mountains shout with them for j,
Ps	105:43	He brought his people out with j,
Ps	107:22	recount his works with shouts of j.
Ps	119:111	they are the j of my heart.
Ps	126: 2	our tongues sang for j.
Ps	126: 5	sow in tears will reap with cries of j.
Ps	126: 6	Will return with cries of j,
Ps	132: 9	your devout will shout for j."
Ps	132:16	its devout shall shout for j.
Ps	135: 3	Sing to his name, for it brings j!
Ps	149: 5	glory, cry out for j on their couches,
Prv	10: 1	A wise son gives his father j,
Prv	12:20	but those who counsel peace have j.
Prv	14:10	and its j no stranger shares.
Prv	14:13	sad, and the end of j may be sorrow.
Prv	15:20	A wise son gives his father j,
Prv	15:23	One has j from an apt response;
Prv	17:21	the father of a numskull has no j.
Prv	21:15	justice is done it is a j for the just,
Prv	29: 3	Whoever loves wisdom gives j to his father,
Eccl	10:19	merriment and wine gives j to the living,
Sir	26: 2	A loyal wife brings j to her
Is	9: 2	You have brought them abundant j
Is	12: 3	With j you will draw water
Is	16:10	there is no singing, no shout of j;
Is	24:11	all j has grown dim, cheer is exiled
Is	35:10	singing, crowned with everlasting j;
Is	48:20	With shouts of j declare this,
Is	51: 3	J and gladness shall be found in her,
Is	51:11	singing, crowned with everlasting j;
Is	52: 8	together they shout for j, For they
Is	55:12	in j you shall go forth, in peace you
Is	60:15	a j from generation to generation.
Is	61: 7	everlasting j shall be theirs.
Is	65:18	I am creating Jerusalem to be a j
Is	66: 5	his glory, that we may see your j";
Jer	15:16	your words were my j,
Jer	31:13	I will turn their mourning into j,
Jer	33: 9	this city shall become j for me,
Jer	48:33	J and gladness are taken away
Jer	51:48	shall shout over Babylon with j,
Lam	2:15	in beauty and j of all the earth?"
Lam	5:15	The j of our hearts has ceased,
Bar	5: 9	For God is leading Israel in j
Ez	24:25	their glorious j, the delight of their
Jl	1:12	J itself has dried up among
Jl	1:16	house of our God, j and gladness?
Zec	8:19	will become occasions of j and gladness,
Zec	9: 9	Shout for j, O daughter Jerusalem!
Mt	13:20	word and receives it at once with j.
Mt	13:44	out of j goes and sells all that he has
Mk	4:16	the word, receive it at once with j.
Lk	1:14	And you will have j and gladness,
Lk	1:44	the infant in my womb leaped for j.
Lk	2:10	good news of great j that will be
Lk	6:23	Rejoice and leap for j on that day!
Lk	8:13	receive the word with j, but they
Lk	24:41	they were still incredulous for j
Lk	24:52	returned to Jerusalem with great j,
Jn	3:29	So this j of mine has been made

Jn	15:11	told you this so that my j may be
Jn	16:20	grieve, but your grief will become j.
Jn	16:22	no one will take your j away
Jn	16:24	so that your j may be complete.
Jn	17:13	they may share my j completely.
Acts	8: 8	There was great j in that city.
Acts	13:52	The disciples were filled with j
Rom	14:17	peace, and j in the holy Spirit;
Rom	15:13	the God of hope fill you with all j
Rom	15:32	I may come to you with j by the will
2 Cor	1:24	we work together for your j, for you
2 Cor	2: 3	all of you that my j is that of all
Gal	5:22	the fruit of the Spirit is love, j,
Phil	1: 4	praying always with j in my every
Phil	1:25	for your progress and j in the faith,
Phil	2: 2	complete my j by being of the same
Phil	4: 1	I love and long for, my j and crown,
1 Thes	1: 6	with j from the holy Spirit,
1 Thes	2:19	For what is our hope or j or crown
1 Thes	2:20	For you are our glory and j.
1 Thes	3: 9	for all the j we feel on your account
2 Tm	1: 4	tears, so that I may be filled with j,
Phlm	1: 7	For I have experienced much j
Heb	12: 2	the j that lay before him he endured
Heb	13:17	that they may fulfill their task with j
Jas	1: 2	Consider it all j, my brothers,
Jas	4: 9	mourning and your j into dejection.
1 Pt	1: 8	with an indescribable and glorious j,
1 Jn	1: 4	this so that our j may be complete.
2 Jn	1:12	face so that our j may be complete.
3 Jn	1: 4	Nothing gives me greater j than

JOYFULLY → JOY

1 Mc	4:56	altar and j offered burnt offerings

JUBILANT → JUBILATION

Is	24: 8	ended the shouts of the j,

JUBILATION → JUBILANT

Prv	11:10	when the wicked perish, there is j.

JUBILEE

Lv	25:10	It shall be a j for you, when each
Nm	36: 4	the Israelites celebrate the j year,

JUDAH → JUDAHITE, JUDEA

1. Son of Jacob by Leah (Gn 29:35; 35:23; 1 Chr 2:1). Did not want to kill Joseph (Gn 37:26-27). Among Canaanites, fathered Perez by Tamar (Gn 38). Tribe of blessed as ruling tribe (Gn 49:8-12; Dt 33:7), numbered (Nm 1:27; 26:22), allotted land (Jos 15; Ez 48:7), failed to fully possess (Jos 15:63; Jgs 1:1-20).

2. Name used for people and land of Southern Kingdom.

Ru	1: 7	On the road back to the land of J,
2 Sm	2: 4	David king over the house of J.
2 Sm	5: 5	he was king over J seven years
2 Sm	24: 1	"Go, take a census of Israel and J."
1 Chr	28: 4	For he chose J as leader, then one
Neh	6: 7	to proclaim you king of J.
1 Mc	2: 6	that were being committed in J
1 Mc	7:50	a few days the land of J was at rest.
1 Mc	9:57	and the land of J was at rest for two
Sir	49: 4	these kings of J, right to the very
Is	1: 1	saw concerning J and Jerusalem
Is	3: 8	has stumbled, J has fallen;
Jer	2:28	as your cities are your gods, O J!
Jer	13:19	J is taken into exile—
Jer	30: 3	fortunes of my people Israel and J—
Jer	31:31	house of Israel and the house of J.
Lam	1: 3	J has gone into exile,
Hos	1: 7	for the house of J I will feel pity;
Jl	4: 1	when I restore the fortunes of J
Mi	5: 1	least among the clans of J,
Zec	2: 2	are the horns that scattered J, Israel,
Zec	8:15	favor Jerusalem and the house of J;
Zec	11:14	breaking the kinship between J
Mal	2:11	J has broken faith;
Mal	2:11	J has profaned the Lord's holy
Mt	2: 6	means least among the rulers of J;
Heb	7:14	is clear that our Lord arose from J,

Heb   8: 8   house of Israel and the house of J.
Rev   5: 5   The lion of the tribe of J, the root

JUDAHITE → JUDAH
Zec   8:23   take hold of the cloak of every J and say,

JUDAISM → JEW
Acts   13:43 were converts to J followed Paul
Gal   1:13   heard of my former way of life in J,

JUDAS → =BARSABBAS, =JUDE , MACCABEUS, =THADDAEUS
     1. Apostle; son of James (Lk 6:16; Jn 14:22; Acts 1:13). Probably also called Thaddaeus (Mt 10:3; Mk 3:18).
     2. Brother of James and Jesus (Mt 13:55; Mk 6:3), also called Jude (Jude 1).
     3. Christian prophet (Acts 15:22-32).
     4. Apostle, also called Iscariot, who betrayed Jesus (Mt 10:4; 26:14-56; Mk 3:19; 14:10-50; Lk 6:16; 22:3-53; Jn 6:71; 12:4; 13:2-30; 18:2-11). Suicide of (Mt 27:3-5; Acts 1:16-25).
     5. Leader of the Maccabean revolt (1 Mc 2:4, 66). Recaptured Jerusalem and rededicated the temple and altar (1 Mc 4:36-61). Death of (1 Mc 9).

JUDE → =JUDAS
Jude   1: 1   J, a slave of Jesus Christ

JUDEA → JUDAH, JUDEAN
Jdt   4: 7   since these offered access to J.
1 Mc   5:23   and brought them to J with great
Dn   14:33 The prophet Habakkuk was in J.
Mt   2: 1   Jesus was born in Bethlehem of J,
Mt   3: 1   preaching in the desert of J
Mt   24:16 then those in J must flee
Lk   1: 5   King of J, there was a priest named
Lk   3: 1   Pontius Pilate was governor of J,
Lk   7:17   him spread through the whole of J
Acts   1: 8   throughout J and Samaria,
Acts   8: 1   throughout the countryside of J
Acts   9:31   The church throughout all J,
1 Thes 2:14   of God that are in J in Christ Jesus.

JUDEAN → JUDEA
Mk   1: 5   People of the whole J countryside

JUDGE → JUDGE'S, JUDGED, JUDGES, JUDGING, JUDGMENT, JUDGMENTS
Gn   18:25 Should not the j of all the world do
Ex   2:14   appointed you ruler and j over us?
Dt   17: 9 to the j who is in office at that time.
Jgs   2:18   he would be with the j and save
Jgs   2:18   their enemies as long as the j lived.
Jgs   11:27 who is j, decide this day between
1 Sm   24:13 May the LORD j between me
1 Kgs   3: 9   a listening heart to j your people
Tb   3: 2   you are j of the world.
Ps   7: 9   J me, LORD, according to my
Ps   7:12   God is a just j, powerful and patient,
Ps   50: 6 for God himself is the j.
Ps   75: 3 will choose the time; I will j fairly.
Ps   82: 8 O God, j the earth, for yours are all
Ps   94: 2 Rise up, O j of the earth;
Sir   7: 6   to become a j if you do not have
Is   2: 4   He shall j between the nations,
Is   11: 3 Not by appearance shall he j,
Is   33:22 For the LORD is our j, the LORD
Jer   11:20 just J, searcher of mind and heart,
Ez   7: 3   you, j you according to your ways,
Ez   7:27   to their judgments I will j them.
Ez   18:30 Therefore I will j you,
Ez   22: 2 You, son of man, will you j?
Ez   33:20 I will j each of you according
Ez   34:17 I will j between one sheep
Mi   4: 3   He shall j between many peoples
Lk   12:14 who appointed me as your j
Lk   18: 2 "There was a j in a certain town
Jn   5:30   I j as I hear, and my judgment is
Jn   7:24   by appearances, but j justly."
Jn   8:15   You j by appearances, but I do not j
Jn   8:16   And even if I should j, my judgment
Jn   12:48 my words has something to j him:

Jn   18:31 and j him according to your law."
Acts   7:27   appointed you ruler and j over us?
Acts   10:42 appointed by God as j of the living
Rom   2: 1   you, the j, do the very same things.
Rom   2:16   God will j people's hidden works
Rom   3: 6   For how else is God to j the world?
1 Cor   5:12   not your business to j those within?
1 Cor   6: 2   that the holy ones will j the world?
1 Cor   6: 3   you not know that we will j angels?
2 Tm   4: 1   who will j the living and the dead,
2 Tm   4: 8   the just j, will award to me
Heb   10:30 "The Lord will j his people."
Heb   12:23 and God the j of all, and the spirits
Heb   13: 4 for God will j the immoral
Jas   4:12   lawgiver and j who is able to save
Jas   4:12   then are you to j your neighbor?
Jas   5: 9   the J is standing before the gates.
1 Pt   4: 5   him who stands ready to j the living

JUDGE'S → JUDGE
Jn   19:13 and seated him on the j bench

JUDGED → JUDGE
1 Sm   7:15   Samuel j Israel as long as he lived.
Ps   9:20   let the nations be j in your presence.
Mt   7: 1   judging, that you may not be j.
Rom   2:12   all who sin under the law will be j
1 Cor   4: 3   me in the least that I be j by you
Jas   2:12   so act as people who will be j
Jas   3: 1   that we will be j more strictly,
Jas   5: 9   one another, that you may not be j.
Rev   20:12 The dead were j according to their

JUDGES → JUDGE
Dt   1:16   I charged your j at that time,
Jgs   2:16   the LORD raised up j to save them
Ru   1: 1   the time of the j there was a famine
1 Sm   2:10   the LORD j the ends of the earth.
1 Sm   8: 1   appointed his sons j over Israel.
Jb   9:24   he covers the faces of its j.
Sir   16:12 he j people, each according to their
Lk   11:19 Therefore they will be your j.
Acts   4:19   you rather than God, you be the j.
1 Cor   4: 4   the one who j me is the Lord.
Jas   4:11   j his brother speaks evil of the law and j the law.
1 Pt   1:17   him who j impartially according
1 Pt   2:23   himself over to the one who j justly.
Rev   18: 8 mighty is the Lord God who j her."
Rev   19:11 He j and wages war

JUDGING → JUDGE
Mt   19:28 thrones, j the twelve tribes of Israel.

JUDGMENT → JUDGE
Ex   6: 6   arm and with mighty acts of j.
Dt   1:17   fearing no one, for the j is God's.
Jdt   9: 6   your j is made with foreknowledge.
Ps   1: 5   the wicked will not arise at the j,
Ps   9: 8   forever, has set up his throne for j.
Ps   82: 1 gives j in the midst of the gods.
Ps   119:121 I have fulfilled your righteous j;
Ps   143: 2 Do not enter into j with your
Eccl   11: 9 all this that God will bring you to j.
Eccl   12:14 God will bring to j every work,
Is   3:14   The Lord enters into j
Is   28: 6 A spirit of j for the one who sits in j,
Jer   25:31 he enters into j against all flesh:
Ez   20:35 enter into j with you face to face.
Dn   7:22   j was pronounced in favor
Jl   4: 2   There I will enter into j with them
Hb   1:12   you have appointed them for j,
Zep   3: 5   morning rendering j unfailingly,
Mal   3: 5   I will draw near to you for j, and I
Mt   5:21   whoever kills will be liable to j.'
Mt   5:22   with his brother will be liable to j,
Mt   10:15 Gomorrah on the day of j than
Mt   11:24 on the day of j than for you."
Mt   12:36 of j people will render an account
Mt   12:41 At the j, the men of Nineveh will

Jn	5:22	but he has given all j to his Son,
Jn	5:30	and my j is just, because I do not
Jn	9:39	"I came into this world for j,
Jn	12:31	Now is the time of j on this world;
Acts	24:25	and self-restraint and the coming j,
Rom	2: 1	every one of you who passes j.
Rom	2: 2	We know that the j of God on those
Rom	5:16	one sin there was the j that brought
Rom	14:10	we shall all stand before the j seat
1 Cor	11:29	body, eats and drinks j on himself.
2 Cor	5:10	we must all appear before the j seat
2 Thes	1: 5	This is evidence of the just j of God,
Heb	6: 2	of the dead and eternal j.
Heb	9:27	beings die once, and after this the j,
Heb	10:27	a fearful prospect of j and a flaming
Jas	2:13	For the j is merciless to one who has
Jas	2:13	mercy triumphs over j.
1 Pt	4:17	it is time for the j to begin
2 Pt	2: 4	handed them over to be kept for j;
2 Pt	2: 9	under punishment for the day of j,
2 Pt	3: 7	for fire, kept for the day of j
1 Jn	4:17	on the day of j because as he is,
Jude	1: 6	in gloom, for the j of the great day.
Rev	14: 7	for his time has come to sit in j.
Rev	17: 1	I will show you the j on the great
Rev	18:10	In one hour your j has come."

JUDGMENTS → JUDGE

Tb	3: 5	your many j are right in dealing
Wis	17: 1	For great are your j, and hard
Rom	11:33	How inscrutable are his j and how
Rev	16: 7	almighty, your j are true and just."
Rev	19: 2	for true and just are his j.

JUDITH

Virtuous widow and heroine of the book of Judith (Jdt 8–16).

JUG

1 Kgs	17:12	in my jar and a little oil in my j.

JUICE

Nm	6: 3	or any kind of grape j, nor eat either

JUMPED → JUMPING

Jn	21: 7	was lightly clad, and j into the sea.

JUMPING → JUMPED

Acts	3: 8	walking and j and praising God.

JUST → JUSTICE, JUSTIFICATION, JUSTIFIED, JUSTIFIES, JUSTIFY, JUSTLY

Dt	32: 4	without deceit, j and upright is he!
Neh	9:33	has come upon us you have been j,
Tb	3: 2	Lord, and all your deeds are j;
Ps	51: 6	So that you are j in your word,
Ps	145:17	The LORD is j in all his ways,
Prv	12: 5	The plans of the j are right;
Is	26: 7	The way of the j is smooth;
Is	26: 7	the path of the j you make level.
Ez	45: 9	and do what is j and right!
Jn	5:30	and my judgment is j, because I do
2 Thes	1: 6	For it is surely j on God's part
Heb	2: 2	received its j recompense,
1 Jn	1: 9	he is faithful and j and will forgive
Rev	15: 3	J and true are your ways, O king
Rev	16: 5	"You are j, O Holy One, who are
Rev	16: 7	your judgments are true and j."
Rev	19: 2	for true and j are his judgments.

JUSTICE → JUST

Ex	23: 2	not follow the crowd in perverting j.
Dt	16:19	You must not distort j: you shall not
Dt	16:20	J, j alone shall you pursue,
1 Sm	8: 3	accepting bribes and perverting j.
2 Sm	15: 4	to me and I would render him j."
1 Kgs	10: 9	king to carry out judgment and j."
2 Chr	9: 8	them to carry out judgment and j."
Jb	8: 3	does the Almighty pervert j?
Jb	29:14	j was my robe and my turban.
Jb	34:12	the Almighty cannot pervert j.
Jb	34:17	Can an enemy of j be in control,

Jb	37:23	abundant in j, who never oppresses.
Ps	33: 5	He loves j and right. The earth is
Ps	72: 2	to the king; your j to the king's son;
Ps	72: 2	he may govern your people with j,
Ps	82: 3	render j to the afflicted and needy.
Ps	89:15	J and judgment are the foundation
Ps	99: 4	lover of j, you have established
Ps	101: 1	I sing of mercy and j;
Ps	103: 6	deeds, brings j to all the oppressed.
Ps	112: 5	who conducts his affairs with j.
Ps	140:13	cause of the needy, j for the poor.
Prv	8:20	I walk, along the paths of j,
Prv	16:12	to kings, for by j the throne endures.
Prv	17:23	thus perverting the course of j.
Prv	19:28	An unprincipled witness scoffs at j,
Prv	21:15	When j is done it is a joy
Prv	28: 5	The evil understand nothing of j,
Prv	29: 4	By a king builds up the land;
Eccl	3:16	and wickedness also in the seat of j.
Eccl	5: 7	of rights and j in the realm, do not
Is	1:17	Make j your aim:
Is	1:21	J used to lodge within her, but now,
Is	1:27	Zion shall be redeemed by j, and her
Is	5: 7	for j, but hark, the outcry!
Is	5:16	by j the Holy God shown holy.
Is	9: 6	and sustains By judgment and j,
Is	16: 5	upholding right, prompt to do j.
Is	28:17	a measuring line, and j a level.—
Is	30:18	For the LORD is a God of j:
Is	32:16	and j abide in the garden land.
Is	33: 5	he fills Zion with right and j.
Is	42: 1	he shall bring forth j to the nations.
Is	42: 4	be bruised until he establishes j
Is	56: 1	to come, my j, about to be revealed.
Is	59: 9	far from us and j does not reach us.
Is	59:14	is turned away, and j stands far off;
Jer	9:23	act with fidelity, j, and integrity
Jer	21:12	Each morning dispense j,
Lam	3:35	denies j to anyone in the very sight
Hos	2:21	I will betroth you to me with j
Am	5: 7	to those who turn j into wormwood
Am	5:15	good, and let j prevail at the gate;
Am	5:24	Rather let j surge like waters,
Am	6:12	Yet you have turned j into gall,
Mt	12:18	he will proclaim j to the Gentiles.
Mt	12:20	quench, until he brings j to victory.
Lk	18: 8	to it that j is done for them speedily.
Acts	8:33	[his] humiliation j was denied him.
Acts	28: 4	sea, J has not let him remain alive."

JUSTIFICATION → JUST

Rom	4:25	and was raised for our j.
Rom	5:21	might reign through j for eternal life
Gal	2:21	for if j comes through the law,

JUSTIFIED → JUST

Jb	40: 8	you condemn me that you may be j?
Lk	18:14	you, the latter went home j,
Rom	2:13	those who observe the law will be j.
Rom	3: 4	"That you may be j in your words,
Rom	3:20	since no human being will be j
Rom	3:24	They are j freely by his grace
Rom	3:28	that a person is j by faith apart
Rom	4: 2	if Abraham was j on the basis of his
Rom	5: 1	since we have been j by faith,
Rom	5: 9	since we are now j by his blood,
Rom	8:30	and those he called he also j; and those he j he also glorified.
Rom	10:10	believes with the heart and so is j,
1 Cor	6:11	you were j in the name of the Lord
Gal	2:16	know that a person is not j by works
Gal	2:16	Jesus that we may be j by faith
Gal	2:16	works of the law no one will be j.
Gal	2:17	if, in seeking to be j in Christ,
Gal	3:11	no one is j before God by the law is
Gal	3:24	Christ, that we might be j by faith.
Gal	5: 4	you who are trying to be j by law;

Ti	3: 7	so that we might be **j** by his grace
Jas	2:21	Was not Abraham our father **j**
Jas	2:24	See how a person is **j** by works
Jas	2:25	**j** by works when she welcomed

JUSTIFIES → JUST

Rom	4: 5	in the one who **j** the ungodly,

JUSTIFY → JUST

Lk	10:29	But because he wished to **j** himself,
Lk	16:15	"You **j** yourselves in the sight
Rom	3:30	will **j** the circumcised on the basis
Gal	3: 8	that God would **j** the Gentiles

JUSTLY → JUST

Wis	9:12	I will judge your people **j** and be
Jer	7: 5	of you deals **j** with your neighbor;
Lk	23:41	we have been condemned **j**,
1 Pt	2:23	over to the one who judges **j**.

JUSTUS → =BARSABBAS, =JESUS

Acts	1:23	who was also known as **J**,
Acts	18: 7	belonging to a man named Titus **J**,
Col	4:11	who is called **J**, who are

K

KADESH → KADESH-BARNEA

Nm	20: 1	month, and the people stayed at **K**.
Dt	1:46	had to stay as long as you did at **K**.

KADESH-BARNEA → KADESH

Nm	32: 8	I sent them from **K** to reconnoiter

KEDESH

Jos	12:22	the king of **K**, one; the king
Jgs	4: 6	summoned from **K** of Naphtali.

KEEP → KEEPER, KEEPING, KEEPS, KEPT

Gn	6:19	to **k** them alive along with you.
Gn	17: 9	you must **k** my covenant throughout
Ex	15:26	and **k** all his statutes, I will not
Ex	19: 5	me completely and **k** my covenant,
Ex	20: 6	love me and **k** my commandments.
Nm	6:24	The LORD bless you and **k** you!
Dt	5:10	love me and **k** my commandments.
Dt	6:17	But **k** the commandments
Dt	7: 9	love him and **k** his commandments,
Jos	22: 5	all his ways, **k** his commandments,
1 Kgs	8:25	your descendants **k** to their way,
1 Kgs	8:58	in his ways and **k** the commands,
2 Kgs	17:19	Judah did not **k** the commandments
1 Chr	29:18	**k** such thoughts in the hearts
Neh	1: 5	you and **k** your commandments.
Jb	14:16	steps, and not **k** watch for sin in me.
Ps	37:34	for the LORD, and **k** his way;
Ps	78:10	They did not **k** God's covenant;
Ps	119: 9	the young **k** his way without fault?
Prv	4:21	sight, **k** them within your heart;
Prv	7: 2	**K** my commands and live, and my
Prv	7: 5	they may **k** you from a stranger,
Eccl	3: 6	a time to **k**, and a time to cast away.
Eccl	12:13	Fear God and **k** his commandments,
Sir	1:26	wisdom, **k** the commandments,
Sir	21:11	who **k** the Law control their thoughts;
Mt	19:17	into life, **k** the commandments."
Jn	10:24	"How long are you going to **k** us
2 Cor	12: 7	me, to **k** me from being too elated.
1 Tm	5:22	in another's sins. **K** yourself pure.
1 Pt	3:10	see good days must **k** the tongue
2 Pt	1: 8	they will **k** you from being idle
Jude	1: 6	who did not **k** to their own domain
Jude	1:21	**K** yourselves in the love of God
Jude	1:24	the one who is able to **k** you
Rev	3:10	I will **k** you safe in the time of trial
Rev	22: 9	of those who **k** the message of this

KEEPER → KEEP

Gn	4: 9	Am I my brother's **k**?"

KEEPING → KEEP

Nm	17:25	for safe **k** as a sign to the rebellious,

Dt	13:19	your God, **k** all his commandments,
Prv	15: 3	**k** watch on the evil and the good.
Is	56: 2	**K** the sabbath without profaning it, **k** one's hand from doing any evil.
Lk	2: 8	**k** the night watch over their flock.

KEEPS → KEEP

Prv	11:13	a trustworthy person **k** a confidence.
Is	26: 2	nation may enter, one that **k** faith.
Jn	7:19	Yet none of you **k** the law.
Jn	8:51	whoever **k** my word will never see
Jas	2:10	For whoever **k** the whole law,
Rev	22: 7	is the one who **k** the prophetic

KEILAH

1 Sm	23: 5	So David went with his men to **K**
1 Sm	23: 5	them, and freed the inhabitants of **K**.

KENITE

Jgs	1:16	The descendants of Hobab the **K**,
Jgs	4:17	wife of Heber the **K**, for there was

KEPT → KEEP

2 Sm	22:22	For I **k** the ways of the LORD;
Jn	17: 6	to me, and they have **k** your word.
2 Tm	4: 7	finished the race; I have **k** the faith.
Heb	13: 4	and the marriage bed be **k** undefiled,
1 Pt	1: 4	and unfading, **k** in heaven for you
2 Pt	3: 7	**k** for the day of judgment
Rev	3: 8	yet you have **k** my word and have
Rev	3:10	Because you have **k** my message

KETTLES

Mk	7: 4	of cups and jugs and **k** [and beds].)

KETURAH

Wife of Abraham (Gn 25:1-4; 1 Chr 1:32-33).

KEY → KEYS

Is	22:22	I will place the **k** of the House
Lk	11:52	You have taken away the **k**
Rev	3: 7	the true, who holds the **k** of David,
Rev	9: 1	It was given the **k** for the passage
Rev	20: 1	in his hand the **k** to the abyss

KEYS → KEY

Mt	16:19	I will give you the **k** to the kingdom
Rev	1:18	I hold the **k** to death

KICK

Acts	26:14	hard for you to **k** against the goad.'

KIDNAPPER → KIDNAPPING

Ex	21:16	A **k**, whether he sells the person

KIDNAPPING → KIDNAPPER

Dt	24: 7	If anyone is caught **k** a fellow Israelite,

KIDRON

2 Sm	15:23	the king crossed the Wadi **K** with all
Jn	18: 1	his disciples across the **K** valley

KILL → KILLED, KILLS

Gn	4:14	Anyone may **k** me at sight."
Gn	12:12	then they will **k** me, but let you live.
Gn	20:11	so they would **k** me on account
Gn	26: 7	of the place would **k** him on account
Gn	37:18	reached them, they plotted to **k** him.
Ex	4:23	to let him go, I will **k** your son,
Eccl	3: 3	A time to **k**, and a time to heal;
Mt	10:28	be afraid of those who **k** the body but cannot **k** the soul;
Mt	17:23	and they will **k** him, and he will be
Mk	9:31	over to men and they will **k** him,
Jn	7:19	Why are you trying to **k** me?"
Rev	11: 7	them and conquer them and **k** them.

KILLED → KILL

Gn	4: 8	attacked his brother Abel and **k** him.
Ex	13:15	the LORD **k** every firstborn
1 Kgs	11:40	Solomon tried to have Jeroboam **k**,
1 Mc	2:24	forward and **k** him upon the altar.
Dn	14:28	has destroyed Bel, **k** the dragon,
Mk	8:31	and be **k**, and rise after three days.
Lk	11:48	for they **k** them and you do
Acts	23:12	to eat or drink until they had **k** Paul.

Rom	11: 3	"Lord, they have **k** your prophets,
Rev	9:18	a third of the human race was **k**.
Rev	19:21	The rest were **k** by the sword

KILLS → KILL

Gn	4:15	If anyone **k** Cain, Cain shall be
Prv	1:32	For the straying of the naive **k** them,

KIND → KINDNESS, KINDS

Gn	1:11	every **k** of plant that bears seed
Gn	1:11	every **k** of fruit tree on earth
Gn	1:24	bring forth every **k** of living creature:
Gn	6:20	Of every **k** of bird, of every **k** of animal, and of every **k** of thing that crawls
Prv	14:21	happy the one who is **k** to the poor!
Prv	14:31	those who are **k** to the needy honor
Lk	6:35	for he himself is **k** to the ungrateful
Jn	18:32	he said indicating the **k** of death he
Jn	21:19	by what **k** of death he would glorify
1 Cor	13: 4	Love is patient, love is **k**. It is not
1 Cor	15:35	With what **k** of body will they come
Eph	4:32	[And] be **k** to one another,

KINDNESS → KIND

2 Sm	9: 3	to whom I may show God's **k**?"
Prv	21:21	pursues justice and **k** will find life
Sir	3:14	**K** to a father will not be forgotten;
Rom	2: 4	that the **k** of God would lead you
Rom	11:22	See, then, the **k** and severity of God:
Rom	11:22	but God's **k** to you, provided you remain in his **k**;
2 Cor	6: 6	patience, **k**, in a holy spirit,
Gal	5:22	joy, peace, patience, **k**, generosity,
Eph	2: 7	of his grace in his **k** to us in Christ
Col	3:12	heartfelt compassion, **k**, humility,
Ti	3: 4	when the **k** and generous love

KINDRED → KINSMAN

Lv	25:48	they still may be redeemed by one of their **k**,

KINDS → KIND

Lv	19:19	yours with two different **k** of seed;
Lv	19:19	with two different **k** of thread.
Sir	25: 2	Three **k** of people I hate, and I
Jer	15: 3	Four **k** of scourge I have decreed

KING → KING'S, KINGDOM, KINGDOMS, KINGS, KINGSHIP

Gn	14:18	Melchizedek, **k** of Salem,
Gn	20: 2	So Abimelech, **k** of Gerar,
Gn	26: 8	Abimelech, **k** of the Philistines,
Ex	1: 8	Then a new **k**, who knew nothing
Nm	21:26	the city of Sihon, **k** of the Amorites,
Nm	21:33	But Og, **k** of Bashan,
Nm	22:10	son of Zippor, **k** of Moab, sent me
Nm	23:21	them is the war-cry of their **K**.
Dt	17:14	"I will set a **k** over me, like all
Jgs	9: 8	out to anoint a **k** over themselves.
Jgs	17: 6	those days there was no **k** in Israel;
Jgs	18: 1	those days there was no **k** in Israel.
Jgs	19: 1	when there was no **k** in Israel,
Jgs	21:25	those days there was no **k** in Israel;
1 Sm	8: 5	your example, appoint a **k** over us,
1 Sm	8: 7	They are rejecting me as their **k**.
1 Sm	11:15	and there they made Saul **k**
1 Sm	12:12	saw Nahash, **k** of the Ammonites,
1 Sm	12:12	the LORD your God is your **k**.
1 Sm	15:11	I regret having made Saul **k**, for he
1 Sm	16: 1	whom I have rejected as **k** of Israel?
1 Sm	16: 1	his sons I have decided on a **k**.
2 Sm	2: 4	anointed David **k** over the house
Tb	10:13	Lord of heaven and earth, the **K** of all,
Jdt	9:12	waters, **K** of all you have created,
Ps	2: 6	"I myself have installed my **k**
Ps	10:16	The LORD is **k** forever;
Ps	24: 7	that the **k** of glory may enter.
Ps	33:16	A **k** is not saved by a great army,
Ps	44: 5	You are my **k** and my God,
Ps	47: 8	For God is **k** over all the earth;
Ps	48: 3	of Zaphon, the city of the great **k**.
Is	6: 5	and my eyes have seen the **K**,
Is	32: 1	a **k** will reign justly and princes will

Is	43:15	One, the creator of Israel, your **K**.
Jer	10:10	the eternal **K**, Before whose anger
Jer	30: 9	their **k**, whom I will raise
Hos	3: 5	their God, and David, their **k**;
Mi	2:13	Their **k** shall go through before
Zep	3:15	The **K** of Israel, the LORD,
Zec	9: 9	your **k** is coming to you, a just
Zec	14: 9	LORD will be **k** over the whole
Mal	1:14	For a great **k** am I, says the LORD
Mt	2: 2	"Where is the newborn **k**
Mt	21: 5	'Behold, your **k** comes to you,
Mt	27:11	him, "Are you the **k** of the Jews?"
Mt	27:37	This is Jesus, the **K** of the Jews.
Mk	15:32	Let the Messiah, the **K** of Israel,
Lk	19:38	"Blessed is the **k** who comes
Lk	23: 3	him, "Are you the **k** of the Jews?"
Jn	1:49	you are the **K** of Israel."
Jn	12:13	of the Lord, [even] the **k** of Israel."
Jn	18:37	said to him, "Then you are a **k**?"
Jn	18:37	Jesus answered, "You say I am a **k**.
Jn	19:15	to them, "Shall I crucify your **k**?"
Jn	19:15	"We have no **k** but Caesar."
Jn	19:21	"Do not write 'The **K** of the Jews,'
Jn	19:21	said, 'I am the **K** of the Jews.' "
Acts	17: 7	claim instead that there is another **k**,
1 Tm	1:17	To the **k** of ages, incorruptible,
1 Tm	6:15	the **K** of kings and Lord of lords,
Heb	7: 1	**k** of Salem and priest of God Most
Rev	15: 3	are your ways, O **k** of the nations.
Rev	17:14	he is Lord of lords and **k** of kings,
Rev	19:16	"**K** of kings and Lord of lords."

KING'S → KING

2 Sm	9:13	because he always ate at the **k** table.
Prv	21: 1	A **k** heart is channeled water
Jer	52:33	ate at the **k** table as long as he lived.
Heb	11:23	they were not afraid of the **k** edict.

KINGDOM → KING

Ex	19: 6	You will be to me a **k** of priests,
1 Sm	28:17	he has torn the **k** from your hand
2 Sm	7:12	your loins, and I will establish his **k**.
1 Kgs	11:31	to tear the **k** out of Solomon's hand
1 Chr	17:11	own sons, and I will establish his **k**.
Wis	10:10	Showed him the **k** of God and gave
Is	9: 6	and over his **k**, which he confirms
Jer	18: 7	a nation or **k** that I will uproot
Dn	2:39	Another **k** shall take your place,
Dn	2:44	up a **k** that shall never be destroyed
Dn	5:28	your **k** has been divided and given
Mt	3: 2	for the **k** of heaven is at hand!"
Mt	4:17	for the **k** of heaven is at hand."
Mt	4:23	proclaiming the gospel of the **k**,
Mt	5: 3	spirit, for theirs is the **k** of heaven.
Mt	5:10	for theirs is the **k** of heaven.
Mt	5:19	be called least in the **k** of heaven.
Mt	5:19	be called greatest in the **k** of heaven.
Mt	5:20	will not enter into the **k** of heaven.
Mt	6:10	your **k** come, your will be done,
Mt	6:33	But seek first the **k** [of God] and his
Mt	7:21	Lord,' will enter the **k** of heaven,
Mt	8:12	the children of the **k** will be driven
Mt	9:35	proclaiming the gospel of the **k**,
Mt	10: 7	'The **k** of heaven is at hand.'
Mt	11:11	in the **k** of heaven is greater than he.
Mt	11:12	the **k** of heaven suffers violence,
Mt	12:25	"Every **k** divided against itself will
Mt	12:28	the **k** of God has come upon you.
Mt	13:11	of the **k** of heaven has been granted
Mt	13:19	of the **k** without understanding it,
Mt	13:24	"The **k** of heaven may be likened
Mt	13:31	"The **k** of heaven is like a mustard
Mt	13:33	"The **k** of heaven is like yeast
Mt	13:38	the good seed the children of the **k**.
Mt	13:44	"The **k** of heaven is like a treasure
Mt	13:45	the **k** of heaven is like a merchant
Mt	13:47	the **k** of heaven is like a net thrown

Mt	13:52	in the k of heaven is like the head
Mt	16:19	you the keys to the k of heaven.
Mt	16:28	the Son of Man coming in his k."
Mt	18: 1	is the greatest in the k of heaven?"
Mt	18: 3	you will not enter the k of heaven.
Mt	18: 4	is the greatest in the k of heaven.
Mt	18:23	That is why the k of heaven may be
Mt	19:12	for the sake of the k of heaven.
Mt	19:14	for the k of heaven belongs to such
Mt	19:23	who is rich to enter the k of heaven.
Mt	20: 1	"The k of heaven is like
Mt	20:21	the other at your left, in your k."
Mt	21:31	prostitutes are entering the k of God
Mt	21:43	the k of God will be taken away
Mt	22: 2	"The k of heaven may be likened
Mt	23:13	You lock the k of heaven before
Mt	24:14	of the k will be preached throughout
Mt	25: 1	the k of heaven will be like ten
Mt	25:34	Inherit the k prepared for you
Mt	26:29	you new in the k of my Father."
Mk	1:15	The k of God is at hand.
Mk	3:24	If a k is divided against itself, that k cannot stand.
Mk	4:11	of the k of God has been granted
Mk	4:26	"This is how it is with the k of God;
Mk	6:23	ask of me, even to half of my k."
Mk	9: 1	they see that the k of God has come
Mk	9:47	enter into the k of God with one eye
Mk	10:14	for the k of God belongs to such as
Mk	10:15	whoever does not accept the k
Mk	10:23	have wealth to enter the k of God!"
Mk	10:24	how hard it is to enter the k of God!
Mk	11:10	Blessed is the k of our father David
Mk	12:34	are not far from the k of God."
Mk	13: 8	rise against nation and k against k.
Mk	14:25	I drink it new in the k of God."
Mk	15:43	who was himself awaiting the k
Lk	1:33	and of his k there will be no end."
Lk	4:43	the good news of the k of God,
Lk	6:20	are poor, for the k of God is yours.
Lk	7:28	in the k of God is greater than he."
Lk	8: 1	the good news of the k of God.
Lk	8:10	of the k of God has been granted
Lk	9: 2	sent them to proclaim the k of God
Lk	9:11	spoke to them about the k of God,
Lk	9:27	not taste death until they see the k
Lk	9:60	go and proclaim the k of God."
Lk	9:62	left behind is fit for the k of God."
Lk	10: 9	'The k of God is at hand for you.'
Lk	10:11	the k of God is at hand.
Lk	11: 2	be your name, your k come.
Lk	11:20	the k of God has come upon you.
Lk	12:31	seek his k, and these other things
Lk	12:32	Father is pleased to give you the k.
Lk	13:18	he said, "What is the k of God like?
Lk	13:29	will recline at table in the k of God.
Lk	14:15	one who will dine in the k of God."
Lk	16:16	then on the k of God is proclaimed;
Lk	17:20	of the k of God cannot be observed,
Lk	17:21	the k of God is among you."
Lk	18:16	for the k of God belongs to such as
Lk	18:24	have wealth to enter the k of God!
Lk	18:29	children for the sake of the k of God
Lk	19:11	the k of God would appear there
Lk	21:31	know that the k of God is near.
Lk	22:16	there is fulfillment in the k of God."
Lk	22:18	the vine until the k of God comes."
Lk	22:29	and I confer a k on you, just as my
Lk	22:30	eat and drink at my table in my k;
Lk	23:42	me when you come into your k."
Lk	23:51	and was awaiting the k
Jn	3: 3	no one can see the k of God without
Jn	3: 5	you, no one can enter the k of God
Jn	18:36	"My k does not belong to this
Acts	1: 3	and speaking about the k of God.
Acts	1: 6	going to restore the k to Israel?"
Acts	8:12	the good news about the k of God

Acts	14:22	hardships to enter the k of God."
Acts	19: 8	arguments about the k of God.
Acts	20:25	I preached the k during my travels
Acts	28:23	bearing witness to the k of God
Acts	28:31	hindrance he proclaimed the k
Rom	14:17	For the k of God is not a matter
1 Cor	4:20	For the k of God is not a matter
1 Cor	6: 9	the unjust will not inherit the k
1 Cor	15:24	when he hands over the k to his God
1 Cor	15:50	blood cannot inherit the k of God,
Eph	5: 5	any inheritance in the k of Christ
Col	1:13	us to the k of his beloved Son,
Col	4:11	are my co-workers for the k of God,
1 Thes	2:12	of the God who calls you into his k
2 Thes	1: 5	considered worthy of the k of God
2 Tm	4:18	will bring me safe to his heavenly k.
Heb	1: 8	scepter is the scepter of your k.
Heb	12:28	the unshakable k should have
Jas	2: 5	heirs of the k that he promised
2 Pt	1:11	entry into the eternal k of our Lord
Rev	1: 6	who has made us into a k,
Rev	1: 9	the k, and the endurance we have
Rev	5:10	You made them a k and priests
Rev	11:15	"The k of the world now belongs
Rev	12:10	come, and the k of our God
Rev	16:10	Its k was plunged into darkness,

KINGDOMS → KING

Dt	3:21	will the LORD do to all the k
1 Kgs	5: 1	Solomon ruled over all the k
2 Kgs	19:15	You alone are God over all the k
2 Kgs	19:19	that all the k of the earth may know
2 Chr	20: 6	do you not rule over all the k
Ps	68:33	You k of the earth, sing to God;
Dn	7:27	all the k under the heavens shall be
Ez	37:22	never again be divided into two k.
Dn	2:44	it shall break in pieces all these k
Zep	3: 8	to assemble k, In order to pour
Lk	4: 5	showed him all the k of the world
Heb	11:33	who by faith conquered k, did what

KINGS → KING

Gn	14: 9	king of Ellasar—four k against five.
Gn	17: 6	k will stem from you.
Jos	12: 1	These are the k of the land whom
2 Sm	11: 1	the year, the time when k go to war,
1 Kgs	10:23	King Solomon surpassed all the k
1 Mc	2:48	of the k and did not let the sinner
Ps	2: 2	K on earth rise up and princes plot
Ps	68:30	that k may bring you tribute.
Ps	72:11	May all k bow before him,
Ps	89:28	Most High over the k of the earth.
Ps	110: 5	who crushes k on the day of his
Ps	138: 4	All the k of earth will praise you,
Ps	149: 8	To bind their k in shackles,
Prv	8:15	By me k reign, and rulers enact
Prv	16:12	Wrongdoing is an abomination to k,
Prv	31: 4	It is not for k, Lemuel, not for k
Is	24:21	and the k of the earth on the earth.
Is	52:15	nations, k shall stand speechless;
Is	60:11	with their k in the vanguard.
Dn	2:21	establishes k and deposes them.
Dn	2:47	gods and Lord of k and a revealer
Dn	7:24	The ten horns shall be ten k rising
Lk	10:24	and k desired to see what you see,
Lk	21:12	they will have you led before k
Acts	4:26	The k of the earth took their stand
1 Cor	4: 8	you have become k without us!
1 Cor	4: 8	I wish that you had become k,
1 Tm	2: 2	for k and for all in authority, that we
1 Tm	6:15	the King of k and Lord of lords,
Rev	1: 5	dead and ruler of the k of the earth.
Rev	17: 2	The k of the earth have had
Rev	17:12	saw represent ten k who have not
Rev	17:14	for he is Lord of lords and king of k,
Rev	19:16	"King of k and Lord of lords."
Rev	19:19	I saw the beast and the k of the earth

Rev   21:24 it the k of the earth will bring their

KINGSHIP → KING
1 Sm   13:14 but now your k shall not endure.
Dn   3:100 his k is an everlasting k,
Dn   7:14 received dominion, splendor, and k;
Dn   7:14 that shall not pass away, his k,

KINSMAN → KINDRED
Gn   14:14 Abram heard that his k had been captured,
Tb   5:14 It turns out that you are a k,

KISH
1 Sm   10:21 finally Saul, son of K, was chosen.

KISHON
Jgs   5:21 The Wadi K swept them away;
1 Kgs 18:40 brought them down to the Wadi K
Ps   83:10 with Sisera and Jabin at the wadi K,

KISLEV
Neh   1: 1 In the month K of the twentieth year,
1 Mc   1:54 On the fifteenth day of the month K,
1 Mc   4:59 from the twenty-fifth day of the month K,
Zec   7: 1 on the fourth day of the ninth month, K.

KISS → KISSED, KISSES, KISSING
Gn   27:26 "Come closer, my son, and k me."
Gn   27:27 As Jacob went up to k him, Isaac smelled
Gn   31:28 did not even allow me a parting k
2 Sm   15: 5 his hand, hold him, and k him.
2 Sm   20: 9 held Amasa's beard as if to k him.
1 Kgs 19:20 let me k my father and mother
Ps   85:11 justice and peace will k.
Prv   24:26 An honest reply—a k on the lips.
Sg   1: 2 Let him k me with kisses of his
Sg   8: 1 I would k you and none would
Mt   26:48 "The man I shall k is the one;
Mk   14:44 "The man I shall k is the one;
Lk   7:45 You did not give me a k, but she has
Lk   22:47 He went up to Jesus to k him.
Lk   22:48 the Son of Man with a k?"
Rom   16:16 Greet one another with a holy k.
1 Cor 16:20 Greet one another with a holy k.
2 Cor 13:12 Greet one another with a holy k.
1 Thes 5:26 Greet all the brothers with a holy k.
1 Pt   5:14 Greet one another with a loving k.

KISSED → KISS
Gn   29:11 Then Jacob k Rachel and wept
Gn   32: 1 Laban k his grandchildren and his
Gn   33: 4 on his neck, k him as he wept.
Gn   45:15 Joseph then k all his brothers
Gn   48:10 to him, he k and embraced them.
Gn   50: 1 and wept over him as he k him.
Ex   4:27 at the mountain of God, he k him.
Ex   18: 7 bowed down, and then k him.
Ru   1: 9 She k them good-bye, but they wept
1 Sm   10: 1 oil on Saul's head and k him,
1 Sm   20:41 They k each other and wept aloud
2 Sm   14:33 Then the king k Absalom.
2 Sm   19:40 he k Barzillai and bade him farewell
1 Kgs 19:18 every mouth that has not k him.
Tb   5:17 and he k his father and mother.
Tb   7: 6 Raguel jumped up, k him, and broke
Tb   10:12 She k them both and saw them safely
Est   C: 6 I would have gladly k the soles
Mt   26:49 said, "Hail, Rabbi!" and he k him.
Mk   14:45 and said, "Rabbi." And he k him.
Lk   15:20 to his son, embraced him and k him.
Acts   20:37 their arms around Paul and k him,

KISSES → KISS
Prv   7:13 Then she grabs him, k him,
Sg   1: 2 Let him kiss me with k of his
Sir   29: 5 he k the lender's hand and speaks

KISSING → KISS
Lk   7:45 she has not ceased k my feet since

KNEADING
Dt   28: 5 your grain basket and your k bowl!

Dt   28:17 your grain basket and your k bowl!

KNEE → KNEES
Is   45:23 To me every k shall bend;
Rom   14:11 Lord, every k shall bend before me,
Phil   2:10 name of Jesus every k should bend,

KNEEL → KNELT
Ps   95: 6 let us k before the LORD who

KNEES → KNEE
Is   35: 3 feeble, make firm k that are weak,
Lk   5: 8 he fell at the k of Jesus and said,
Heb   12:12 drooping hands and your weak k.

KNELT → KNEEL
2 Chr 6:13 it, Solomon k in the presence
Mt   9:18 came forward, k down before him,
Mt   17:14 approached, k down before him,
Acts   20:36 he had finished speaking he k down

KNEW → KNOW
Dt   34:10 whom the LORD k face to face,
Jer   1: 5 I formed you in the womb I k you,
Jon   4: 2 I k that you are a gracious
Mt   7:23 to them solemnly, 'I never k you.
Mt   12:25 But he k what they were thinking
Lk   4:41 speak because they k that he was
Jn   2:24 to them because he k them all,
Jn   4:10 "If you k the gift of God and who is
Jn   8:19 If you k me, you would know my
Jn   13: 1 Jesus k that his hour had come
Jn   13:11 For he k who would betray him;
Rom   1:21 for although they k God they did not

KNIFE → KNIVES
Gn   22:10 and took the k to slaughter his son.
Prv   23: 2 Stick the k in your gullet if you have

KNIT
Jb   10:11 bones and sinews k me together.
Ps   139:13 you k me in my mother's womb.

KNIVES → KNIFE
Jos   5: 2 Make flint k and circumcise Israel
Prv   30:14 their teeth are k,
Jl   4:10 swords, and your pruning k into spears;

KNOCK → KNOCKING, KNOCKS
Mt   7: 7 k and the door will be opened
Lk   11: 9 k and the door will be opened
Rev   3:20 I stand at the door and k.

KNOCKING → KNOCK
Sg   5: 2 The sound of my lover k!
Lk   13:25 will you stand outside k and saying,

KNOCKS → KNOCK
Mt   7: 8 and to the one who k, the door will
Lk   12:36 immediately when he comes and k.

KNOW → FOREKNEW, FOREKNOWLEDGE, KNEW, KNOWING, KNOWLEDGE, KNOWN, KNOWS
Gn   15: 8 "how will I k that I will possess
Gn   22:12 For now I k that you fear God,
Ex   3:19 Yet I k that the king of Egypt will
Ex   6: 7 and you will k that I, the LORD,
Ex   14: 4 the Egyptians will k that I am
Ex   18:11 Now I k that the LORD is greater
Ex   33:12 have not let me k whom you will
Ex   33:13 please let me k your ways so that,
Nm   16:28 "This is how you shall k
Jos   3: 7 that they may k that, as I was
1 Kgs 8:39 for it is you alone who k the heart
Est   C: 5 You k all things. You k, Lord, that it
Jb   19:25 for me, I k that my vindicator lives,
Jb   42: 2 I k that you can do all things,
Jb   42: 3 marvelous for me, which I did not k.
Ps   100: 3 K that the LORD is God, he made
Ps   139:23 Probe me, God, my heart;
Prv   27: 1 for you do not k what any day may
Eccl   8:16 I applied my heart to k wisdom
Is   1: 3 But Israel does not k, my people has

Jer	4:22	people are fools, they do not k me;
Jer	4:22	but they do not k how to do good.
Jer	6:15	they do not k how to blush.
Jer	31:34	and relatives, "K the LORD!"
Jer	31:34	from least to greatest, shall k me—
Ez	2: 5	they shall k that a prophet has been
Ez	6:10	they shall k that I the LORD did
Ez	39: 7	the nations shall k that I am the LORD,
Mt	6: 3	let your left hand k what your right
Mt	7:11	k how to give good gifts to your
Mt	9: 6	that you may k that the Son of Man
Mt	22:29	because you do not k the scriptures
Mt	24:42	For you do not k on which day your
Mt	26:74	and to swear, "I do not k the man."
Mk	12:24	because you do not k the scriptures
Lk	11:13	k how to give good gifts to your
Lk	13:25	'I do not k where you are from.'
Lk	18:20	You k the commandments,
Lk	21:31	k that the kingdom of God is near.
Lk	22:34	deny three times that you k me."
Lk	23:34	[them, they k not what they do."]
Jn	3:11	you, we speak of what we k and we
Jn	4:42	we k that this is truly the savior
Jn	7:28	"You k me and also k where I am
Jn	7:28	sent me, whom you do not k, is true.
Jn	8:14	But you do not k where I come
Jn	8:19	"You k neither me nor my Father.
Jn	8:32	and you will k the truth,
Jn	8:55	You do not k him, but I k him.
Jn	8:55	But I do k him and I keep his word.
Jn	9:25	"If he is a sinner, I do not k.
Jn	9:25	One thing I do k is that I was blind
Jn	10:14	and I k mine and mine k me,
Jn	10:27	I k them, and they follow me.
Jn	12:35	in the dark does not k where he is
Jn	13:35	This is how all will k that you are
Jn	14:17	But you k it, because it remains
Jn	15:21	because they do not k the one who
Jn	16:30	we realize that you k everything
Jn	17: 3	that they should k you, the only true
Jn	17:23	the world may k that you sent me,
Jn	21:15	"Yes, Lord, you k that I love you."
Jn	21:24	and we k that his testimony is true.
Acts	1: 7	"It is not for you to k the times
Acts	1:24	Lord, who k the hearts of all,
Rom	6: 6	We k that our old self was crucified
Rom	6:16	Do you not k that if you present
Rom	7:14	We k that the law is spiritual;
Rom	7:18	For I k that good does not dwell
Rom	8:26	for we do not k how to pray as we
Rom	8:28	We k that all things work for good
1 Cor	1:21	not come to k God through wisdom,
1 Cor	2: 2	I resolved to k nothing while I was
1 Cor	3:16	Do you not k that you are the temple
1 Cor	5: 6	Do you not k that a little yeast
1 Cor	6: 2	Do you not k that the holy ones will
1 Cor	6:15	Do you not k that your bodies are
1 Cor	6:16	do you not k that anyone who joins
1 Cor	6:19	Do you not k that your body is
1 Cor	8: 2	he does not yet k as he ought to k.
1 Cor	8: 4	we k that "there is no idol
1 Cor	9:13	Do you not k that those who
1 Cor	9:24	Do you not k that the runners
1 Cor	12: 2	You k how, when you were pagans,
1 Cor	13: 9	For we k partially and we prophesy
1 Cor	13:12	At present I k partially; then I shall k fully,
1 Cor	14: 9	how will anyone k what is being
2 Cor	5: 1	For we k that if our earthly
2 Cor	5: 6	although we k that while we are
2 Cor	8: 9	For you k the gracious act of our
2 Cor	12: 2	body or out of the body I do not k,
Eph	1:18	that you may k what is the hope
Eph	3:19	to k the love of Christ that surpasses
Phil	3:10	to k him and the power of his
Phil	4:12	I k indeed how to live in humble
Phil	4:12	I k also how to live with abundance.

Col	4: 6	that you k how you should respond
1 Thes	3: 3	For you yourselves k that we are
1 Thes	5: 2	For you yourselves k very well
2 Thes	2: 6	And now you k what is restraining,
1 Tm	3: 5	a man does not k how to manage his
1 Tm	3:15	you should k how to behave
2 Tm	1:12	for I k him in whom I have believed
2 Tm	2:23	for you k that they breed quarrels.
Ti	1:16	They claim to k God, but by their
Heb	8:11	saying, 'K the Lord,' for all shall k me,
Jas	1: 3	for you k that the testing of your
Jas	4: 4	Do you not k that to be a lover
2 Pt	1:12	even though you already k them
1 Jn	2: 3	we may be sure that we k him is
1 Jn	2: 4	Whoever says, "I k him," but does
1 Jn	2:11	and does not k where he is going
1 Jn	2:18	Thus we k this is the last hour.
1 Jn	2:29	you also k that everyone who acts
1 Jn	3: 1	reason the world does not k us is that it did not k him.
1 Jn	3: 2	We do k that when it is revealed we
1 Jn	3:14	We k that we have passed
1 Jn	3:16	The way we came to k love was
1 Jn	3:19	[Now] this is how we shall k that we
1 Jn	3:24	the way we k that he remains in us
1 Jn	4: 8	is without love does not k God,
1 Jn	4:13	This is how we k that we remain
1 Jn	5: 2	In this way we k that we love
1 Jn	5:13	you may k that you have eternal life,
1 Jn	5:15	we k that what we have asked him
1 Jn	5:18	We k that no one begotten by God
1 Jn	5:20	also k that the Son of God has come
2 Jn	1: 1	only I but also all who k the truth—
3 Jn	1:12	and you k our testimony is true.
Rev	2: 2	"I k your works, your labor,
Rev	2: 9	"I k your tribulation and poverty,
Rev	2:13	"I k that you live where Satan's
Rev	2:19	"I k your works, your love, faith,
Rev	3: 3	you will never k at what hour I will
Rev	3: 8	" " "I k your works (behold,
Rev	3:15	"I k your works; I k that you are neither cold nor hot.

KNOWING → KNOW

Gn	3:22	like one of us, k good and evil!
Jn	18: 4	k everything that was going
1 Cor	15:58	k that in the Lord your labor is not
2 Cor	4:14	k that the one who raised the Lord
Phil	3: 8	good of k Christ Jesus my Lord.
Phlm	1:21	k that you will do even more than I
2 Pt	2:21	righteousness than after k it to turn

KNOWLEDGE → KNOW

Gn	2: 9	the tree of the k of good and evil.
Gn	2:17	except the tree of k of good and
2 Chr	1:10	wisdom and k to govern this people,
Jb	21:22	Can anyone teach God k,
Ps	19: 3	night unto night whispers k.
Ps	73:11	"Does the Most High have any k?"
Ps	94:10	one who teaches man not have k?
Ps	119:66	Teach me wisdom and k, for in your
Ps	139: 6	Such k is too wonderful for me,
Prv	1: 4	naive, k and discretion to the young.
Prv	1: 7	of the LORD is the beginning of k;
Prv	1:29	Because they hated k, and the fear
Prv	2: 5	the k of God you will find;
Prv	2: 6	from his mouth come k
Prv	2:10	k will be at home in your soul,
Prv	3:20	By his k the depths are split,
Prv	8:10	silver, and k rather than choice gold.
Prv	8:12	with prudence, and useful k I have.
Prv	9:10	k of the Holy One is understanding.
Prv	10:14	The wise store up k, but the mouth
Prv	11: 9	through their k the just are rescued.
Prv	12: 1	Whoever loves discipline loves k,
Prv	12:23	The shrewd conceal k, but the hearts
Prv	14: 6	vain, but k is easy for the intelligent.
Prv	15: 7	The lips of the wise spread k,
Prv	15:14	The discerning heart seeks k,

Prv	18:15	heart of the intelligent acquires **k**, and the ear of the wise seeks **k**.
Prv	19: 2	Desire without **k** is not good;
Prv	19:25	the intelligent and they gain **k**.
Prv	23:12	and your ear to words of **k**.
Prv	24: 4	by **k** its rooms are filled with every
Eccl	1:18	whoever increases **k** increases grief.
Eccl	2:26	he gives wisdom and **k** and joy;
Eccl	7:12	and **k** is profitable because wisdom
Is	11: 2	a spirit of **k** and of fear
Is	11: 9	the earth shall be filled with **k**
Is	40:14	Whom did he consult to gain **k**?
Dn	1:17	these four young men God gave **k**
Hos	4: 6	My people are ruined for lack of **k**! Since you have rejected **k**,
Hb	2:14	with the **k** of the LORD's glory,
Mal	2: 7	For a priest's lips preserve **k**,
Lk	1:77	to give his people **k** of salvation
Lk	11:52	You have taken away the key of **k**.
Rom	2:20	law you have the formulation of **k**
Rom	11:33	riches and wisdom and **k** of God!
Rom	15:14	filled with all **k**, and able
1 Cor	8: 1	we realize that "all of us have **k**";
1 Cor	8:10	with your **k**, reclining at table
1 Cor	8:11	Thus through your **k**, the weak
1 Cor	12: 8	the expression of **k** according
1 Cor	13: 2	comprehend all mysteries and all **k**;
1 Cor	13: 8	if **k**, it will be brought to nothing.
2 Cor	4: 6	to bring to light the **k** of the glory
2 Cor	8: 7	faith, discourse, **k**, all earnestness,
2 Cor	10: 5	raising itself against the **k** of God,
2 Cor	11: 6	in speaking, I am not so in **k**;
Eph	3:19	the love of Christ that surpasses **k**,
Eph	4:13	of faith and **k** of the Son of God,
Phil	1: 9	and more in **k** and every kind
Col	1:10	fruit and growing in the **k** of God,
Col	2: 3	all the treasures of wisdom and **k**.
Col	3:10	for **k**, in the image of its creator.
1 Tm	2: 4	saved and to come to **k** of the truth.
1 Tm	6:20	and the absurdities of so-called **k**.
Heb	10:26	after receiving **k** of the truth,
2 Pt	1: 3	through the **k** of him who called us
2 Pt	1: 5	your faith with virtue, virtue with **k**,
2 Pt	3:18	in the **k** of our Lord and savior Jesus
1 Jn	2:20	the holy one, and you all have **k**.

KNOWN → KNOW

Ex	6: 3	I did not make myself **k** to them.
Dt	13: 3	whom you have not **k**, "and let us
Ps	67: 3	So shall your way be **k**
Ps	98: 2	The LORD has made his victory **k**;
Ps	105: 1	make **k** among the peoples his
Sir	4:24	wisdom becomes **k** through speech,
Is	12: 4	the nations make **k** his deeds,
Ez	38:23	make myself **k** in the sight of many
Zec	14: 7	it is **k** to the LORD—
Mt	10:26	nor secret that will not be **k**.
Mt	24:43	of the house had **k** the hour of night
Lk	6:44	For every tree is **k** by its own fruit.
Jn	17:26	I made **k** to them your name and I will make it **k**,
Acts	2:28	You have made **k** to me the paths
Rom	1:19	what can be **k** about God is evident
Rom	9:22	his wrath and make **k** his power,
Rom	11:34	"For who has **k** the mind
Rom	16:26	made **k** to all nations to bring
1 Cor	2:16	For "who has **k** the mind
1 Cor	8: 3	if one loves God, one is **k** by him.
1 Cor	13:12	I shall know fully, as I am fully **k**.
2 Cor	3: 2	on our hearts, **k** and read by all,
Eph	1: 9	he has made **k** to us the mystery
Eph	3: 3	[that] the mystery was made **k** to me
Eph	6:19	to make **k** with boldness the mystery
2 Tm	3:15	infancy you have **k** [the] sacred
2 Pt	2:21	for them not to have **k** the way
Rev	1: 1	He made it **k** by sending his angel

KNOWS → KNOW

Gn	3: 5	God **k** well that when you eat of it
Est	4:14	Who **k**—perhaps it was for a time
Jb	23:10	Yet he **k** my way; if he tested me,
Ps	1: 6	the LORD **k** the way of the just,
Ps	44:22	God who **k** the secrets of the heart?
Ps	103:14	For he **k** how we are formed,
Prv	14:10	The heart **k** its own bitterness,
Eccl	2:19	who **k** whether that one will be wise
Eccl	8: 5	observes a command **k** no harm, and the wise heart **k** times
Wis	9:11	For she **k** and understands all things,
Jon	3: 9	Who **k**? God may again repent
Mt	6: 8	Your Father **k** what you need before
Mt	11:27	No one **k** the Son except the Father,
Mt	11:27	no one **k** the Father except the Son
Mt	24:36	"But of that day and hour no one **k**,
Lk	12:30	your Father **k** that you need them.
Lk	16:15	of others, but God **k** your hearts;
Acts	15: 8	And God, who **k** the heart,
Rom	8:27	who searches hearts **k** what is
1 Cor	2:11	who **k** what pertains to a person
1 Cor	2:11	no one **k** what pertains to God
1 Cor	3:20	"The Lord **k** the thoughts
2 Tm	2:19	"The Lord **k** those who are his";
Jas	4:17	So for one who **k** the right thing
2 Pt	2: 9	the Lord **k** how to rescue the devout
1 Jn	4: 6	and anyone who **k** God listens to us,
1 Jn	4: 7	loves is begotten by God and **k** God.
Rev	2:17	which no one **k** except the one who
Rev	19:12	that no one **k** except himself.

KOHATH → KOHATHITES

Gn	46:11	Gershon, **K**, and Merari.
Nm	26:58	Now **K** begot Amram,
1 Chr	23: 6	Gershon, **K**, and Merari.

KOHATHITES → KOHATH

Nm	4:15	can the **K** enter to carry them.
2 Chr	34:12	of the **K**, who directed them.

KORAH → KORAHITES

1. Levite who led rebellion against Moses and Aaron (Nm 16; Jude 11).

2. Psalms of the sons of Korah: See Korahites.

KORAHITES → KORAH

Psalms of the Korahites: Pss 42; 44–49; 84; 85; 87; 88.

L

LABAN

Brother of Rebekah (Gn 24:29), father of Rachel and Leah (Gn 29:16). Received Abraham's servant (Gn 24:29-51). Provided daughters as wives for Jacob in exchange for Jacob's service (Gn 29:1-30). Provided flocks for Jacob's service (Gn 30:25-43). After Jacob's departure, pursued and covenanted with him (Gn 31).

LABOR → LABORER, LABORERS

Ex	1:11	to oppress them with forced **l**.
Ex	20: 9	Six days you may **l** and do all your
Dt	5:13	Six days you may **l** and do all your
Ps	48: 7	there, anguish, like a woman's **l**,
Ps	127: 1	the house, they **l** in vain who build.
Is	54: 1	you who have never been in **l**,
1 Cor	3: 8	receive wages in proportion to his **l**.
1 Cor	15:58	that in the Lord your **l** is not in vain.
Phil	2:16	that I did not run in vain or **l** in vain.
1 Thes	1: 3	your work of faith and **l** of love

LABORER → LABOR

Lv	19:13	overnight the wages of your **l**.
Lk	10: 7	you, for the **l** deserves his payment.

LABORERS → LABOR

Lk	10: 2	is abundant but the **l** are few;
Lk	10: 2	harvest to send out **l** for his harvest.

LACHISH

Jos	10:32	The LORD delivered **L** into the power
2 Chr	25:27	But he was pursued to **L** and killed

LACK → LACKING, LACKS

Dt	8: 9	bread and where you will l nothing,
Ps	34:11	seek the Lord l no good thing.
Prv	5:23	They will die from l of discipline,
1 Cor	7: 5	may not tempt you through your l

LACKING → LACK

Col	1:24	filling up what is l in the afflictions
Jas	1: 4	perfect and complete, l in nothing.

LACKS → LACK

Jas	1: 5	But if any of you l wisdom,
2 Pt	1: 9	Anyone who l them is blind

LADY

2 Jn	1: 1	The Presbyter to the chosen L
2 Jn	1: 5	But now, L, I ask you, not as though

LAID → LAY

Nm	27:23	he l his hands on him
Dt	34: 9	since Moses had l his hands
1 Kgs	6:37	of the Lord's house were l
Ezr	3:11	of the Lord's house had been l.
1 Mc	2:12	We see our sanctuary l waste,
Ps	102:26	Of old you l the earth's foundations;
Is	14: 8	"Now that you are l to rest, no one
Is	53: 6	the Lord l upon him the guilt
Zec	4: 9	Zerubbabel have l the foundations
Mk	6:29	and took his body and l it in a tomb.
Mk	16: 6	Behold the place where they l him.
Lk	6:48	deeply and l the foundation on rock;
Jn	19:42	So they l Jesus there because
Acts	6: 6	who prayed and l hands on them.
Acts	7:58	The witnesses l down their cloaks
1 Jn	3:16	love was that he l down his life

LAKE

Lk	8:33	down the steep bank into the l

LAMB → LAMB'S, LAMBS

2 Sm	12: 6	for the l because he has done this
Is	11: 6	the wolf shall be a guest of the l,
Is	53: 7	Like a l led to slaughter or a sheep
Is	65:25	wolf and the l shall pasture together,
Jer	11:19	Yet I was like a trusting l led
Mk	14:12	when they sacrificed the Passover l,
Jn	1:29	"Behold, the L of God, who takes
Acts	8:32	and as a l before its shearer is silent,
1 Cor	5: 7	For our paschal l, Christ, has been
1 Pt	1:19	as of a spotless unblemished l.
Rev	5:12	"Worthy is the L that was slain
Rev	6: 1	watched while the L broke open
Rev	7:14	them white in the blood of the L.
Rev	12:11	conquered him by the blood of the L
Rev	13: 8	belongs to the L who was slain.
Rev	14: 1	there was the L standing on Mount
Rev	15: 3	of God, and the song of the L:
Rev	17:14	They will fight with the L, but the L will conquer them,
Rev	19: 7	the wedding day of the L has come,
Rev	21: 9	you the bride, the wife of the L."
Rev	21:14	of the twelve apostles of the L.
Rev	21:23	gave it light, and its lamp was the L.
Rev	22: 1	from the throne of God and of the L

LAMB'S → LAMB

Rev	21:27	names are written in the L book

LAMBS → LAMB

Ex	12:21	and procure l for your families,
Ex	29:38	two yearling l as the sacrifice
Ps	114: 4	skipped like rams; the hills, like l.
Is	40:11	in his arms he gathers the l,
Lk	10: 3	sending you like l among wolves.
Jn	21:15	He said to him, "Feed my l."

LAME

2 Sm	4: 4	hasty flight, he fell and became l.
2 Sm	5: 6	and the l will drive you away!"
Is	33:23	and the l will carry off the loot.
Is	35: 6	Then the l shall leap like a stag,
Mi	4: 6	I will gather the l, And I will

Zep	3:19	I will save the l, and assemble
Mt	11: 5	blind regain their sight, the l walk,
Mt	15:31	made whole, the l walking,
Lk	14:13	poor, the crippled, the l, the blind;
Jn	5: 3	number of ill, blind, l, and crippled.

LAMECH

Gn	4:19	L took two wives; the name

LAMENT

2 Sm	1:17	Then David chanted this l for Saul

LAMP → LAMPS, LAMPSTAND, LAMPSTANDS

1 Sm	3: 3	The l of God was not yet
2 Sm	22:29	You are my l, O Lord!
Ps	18:29	For you, Lord, give light to my l;
Ps	119:105	Your word is a l for my feet, a light
Ps	132:17	I will set a l for my anointed.
Prv	6:23	For the command is a l,
Prv	20:27	A l from the Lord is human
Prv	31:18	her l is never extinguished at night.
Mt	5:15	Nor do they light a l and then put it
Mt	6:22	"The l of the body is the eye.
Lk	8:16	"No one who lights a l conceals it
Jn	5:35	He was a burning and shining l,
Rev	21:23	gave it light, and its l was the Lamb.
Rev	22: 5	nor will they need light from l

LAMPS → LAMP

Ex	25:37	You shall then make seven l for it
Ex	25:37	set up the l that they give their light
1 Mc	4:50	and lighted the l on the lampstand,
2 Mc	1: 8	we lighted the l and set
Mt	25: 1	be like ten virgins who took their l
Lk	12:35	"Gird your loins and light your l

LAMPSTAND → LAMP

1 Mc	4:50	altar and lighted the lamps on the l,
Zec	4: 2	I replied, "I see a l all of gold,
Zec	4:11	on the right of the l and on its left?"
Heb	9: 2	one, in which were the l, the table,
Rev	2: 5	and remove your l from its place,

LAMPSTANDS → LAMP

Rev	1:12	when I turned, I saw seven gold l
Rev	1:20	right hand, and of the seven gold l:
Rev	1:20	the seven l are the seven churches.
Rev	11: 4	the two l that stand before the Lord

LAND → COASTLANDS, HOMELAND, LANDMARK, LANDOWNER, LANDS

Gn	1:10	God called the dry l "earth,"
Gn	7:22	Everything on dry l with the breath
Gn	12: 1	Go forth from your l, your relatives,
Gn	12: 1	house to a l that I will show you.
Gn	12: 7	your descendants I will give this l.
Gn	12:10	since the famine in the l was severe.
Gn	13:15	all the l that you see I will give
Gn	15:18	To your descendants I give this l,
Gn	17: 8	as aliens, the whole l of Canaan,
Gn	24: 7	to me, 'I will give this l to your
Gn	26: 1	There was a famine in the l,
Gn	28:15	you go, and bring you back to this l.
Gn	31:13	Leave this l and return to the l
Gn	40:15	from the l of the Hebrews, and I
Gn	41:30	the famine has exhausted the l,
Gn	50:24	from this l to the l that he promised
Ex	1: 7	very numerous that the l was filled
Ex	3: 8	lead them up from that l into a good and spacious l,
Ex	6: 8	bring you into the l which I swore
Ex	8:18	the Lord am in the midst of the l.
Ex	20: 2	brought you out of the l of Egypt,
Ex	20:12	the l the Lord your God is giving
Ex	34:12	the inhabitants of the l that you are
Nm	13: 2	men to reconnoiter the l of Canaan,
Nm	14: 9	not be afraid of the people of the l,
Nm	14:30	shall enter the l where I solemnly
Nm	26:55	But the l shall be divided by lot,
Nm	35:33	For bloodshed pollutes the l,
Nm	35:33	the l can have no expiation

Dt	1: 8	possess the l that the LORD swore
Dt	8: 7	country, a l with streams of water,
Dt	11:10	The l you are to enter and possess is
Dt	28:21	of you from the l you are entering
Dt	29:23	the LORD dealt thus with this l?
Jos	1: 6	people possession of the l I swore
Jos	2: 1	reconnoiter the l and Jericho."
Jos	5:12	ate of the yield of the l of Canaan.
Jos	11:23	Thus Joshua took the whole l,
Jos	11:23	And the l had rest from war.
Jos	13: 2	This is the remaining l:
Jos	14: 4	given no share of the l except cities
Jos	14: 9	'The l where you have set foot shall
Ru	1: 1	judges there was a famine in the l;
2 Sm	21:14	God granted relief to the l.
1 Kgs	8:34	to the l you gave their ancestors.
1 Kgs	17: 7	because no rain had fallen in the l.
2 Kgs	17: 5	of Assyria occupied the whole l
2 Kgs	25:21	death in Riblah, in the l of Hamath.
2 Chr	7:14	pardon their sins and heal their l.
2 Chr	7:20	uproot the people from the l I gave
2 Chr	36:21	Until the l has retrieved its lost
Ezr	9:11	The l which you are entering to take
Neh	9:36	the l which you gave our ancestors
Tb	14: 7	dwell forever in the l of Abraham,
Tb	14: 7	will disappear completely from the l.
1 Mc	1:44	to follow customs foreign to their l;
1 Mc	14:11	He brought peace to the l, and Israel
Ps	25:13	his descendants will inherit the l.
Ps	44: 4	own swords did they conquer the l,
Ps	142: 6	my portion in the l of the living.
Prv	2:21	For the upright will dwell in the l,
Prv	12:11	Those who till their own l have food
Sir	46: 8	the l flowing with milk and honey.
Is	2: 8	Their l is full of idols;
Is	9: 1	in a l of gloom a light has shone.
Is	36:18	of the nations rescued his l
Is	53: 8	was cut off from the l of the living,
Jer	2: 7	into the garden l to eat its fine fruits,
Jer	2: 7	But you entered and defiled my l,
Jer	22:29	O l, l, l, hear the word
Ez	7:23	for the l is filled with bloodshed
Ez	39:28	will gather them back to their l,
Dn	11:41	He shall enter the glorious l
Hos	2:25	I will sow her for myself in the l,
Zec	3: 9	away the guilt of that l in one day.
Mal	3:24	strike the l with utter destruction.
Mk	15:33	came over the whole l until three
Heb	11: 9	in the promised l as in a foreign
Rev	10: 2	on the sea and his left foot on the l,

LANDMARK → LAND

Prv	22:28	Do not remove the ancient l

LANDOWNER → LAND, OWN

Mt	20: 1	of heaven is like a l who went
Mt	20:11	it they grumbled against the l,
Mt	21:33	There was a l who planted

LANDS → LAND

Gn	26: 3	descendants I will give all these l,
Ps	105:44	He gave them the l of the nations,
Ps	106:27	nations, disperse them in foreign l.
Ps	107: 3	Those gathered from foreign l,
Ps	136:21	And made their l a heritage, for his
Ez	11:16	the nations, scattered them over the l,
Ez	20: 6	milk and honey, a jewel among all l.
Ez	36:24	gather you from all the l, and bring

LANGUAGE

Gn	11: 1	The whole world had the same l
Neh	13:24	children, half spoke the l of Ashdod,
Jer	5:15	a people whose l you do not know,
Acts	2: 6	heard them speaking in his own l.
Col	3: 8	and obscene l out of your mouths.

LANTERNS

Jn	18: 3	the Pharisees and went there with l,

LAODICEA

Col	4:16	you yourselves read the one from L.
Rev	3:14	"To the angel of the church in L,

LAP

Lk	6:38	will be poured into your l.

LARGE → ENLARGE, ENLARGES

Dt	6:10	fine, l cities that you did not build,
Gal	6:11	See with what l letters I am writing

LASHES

2 Cor	11:24	Jews I received forty l minus one.

LAST → EVERLASTING, LASTING, LASTS

2 Sm	23: 1	These are the l words of David:
Is	41: 4	am the first, and at the l I am he.
Is	44: 6	I am the first, I am the l; there is no
Is	48:12	is I who am the first, and am I the l.
Mt	19:30	But many who are first will be l, and the l will be first.
Mt	20: 8	beginning with the l and ending
Mt	27:64	This l imposture would be worse
Mk	9:35	first, he shall be the l of all
Mk	15:37	gave a loud cry and breathed his l.
Jn	6:40	I shall raise him [on] the l day."
Jn	7:37	On the l and greatest day
Jn	11:24	in the resurrection on the l day."
Acts	2:17	'It will come to pass in the l days,'
1 Cor	15: 8	L of all, as to one born abnormally,
1 Cor	15:26	The l enemy to be destroyed is
1 Cor	15:45	the l Adam a life-giving spirit.
1 Cor	15:52	the blink of an eye, at the l trumpet.
1 Tm	4: 1	in the l times some will turn away
2 Tm	3: 1	will be terrifying times in the l days.
Heb	1: 2	in these l days, he spoke to us
2 Pt	2:20	their l condition is worse than their
2 Pt	3: 3	in the l days scoffers will come
1 Jn	2:18	Children, it is the l hour; and just as
Jude	1:18	[the] l time there will be scoffers
Rev	1:17	I am the first and the l,
Rev	2: 8	" 'The first and the l, who once
Rev	15: 1	angels with the seven l plagues,
Rev	21: 9	filled with the seven l plagues came
Rev	22:13	the first and the l, the beginning

LASTING → LAST

Heb	10:34	you had a better and l possession.

LASTS → LAST

Tb	13: 1	because his kingship l for all ages.

LATE → LATER

Jas	5: 7	it receives the early and the l rains.

LATER → LATE

Jb	42:12	Thus the LORD blessed the l days of Job
Jn	13: 7	now, but you will understand l."

LATIN

Jn	19:20	and it was written in Hebrew, L,

LAUGH → LAUGHED, LAUGHINGSTOCK, LAUGHS, LAUGHTER

Gn	18:13	"Why did Sarah l and say, 'Will I
Gn	21: 6	"God has given me cause to l,
Ps	59: 9	But you, LORD, l at them;
Eccl	3: 4	A time to weep, and a time to l;
Lk	6:21	are now weeping, for you will l.

LAUGHED → LAUGH

Gn	17:17	down and l as he said to himself,
Gn	18:12	So Sarah l to herself and said,

LAUGHINGSTOCK → LAUGH

Sir	13:12	Mercilessly they will make you a l,
Lam	3:14	I have become a l to all my people,

LAUGHS → LAUGH

Ps	2: 4	The one enthroned in heaven l;
Ps	37:13	But my Lord l at them, because he

LAUGHTER → LAUGH

Ps	126: 2	Then our mouths were filled with l;
Prv	14:13	Even in l the heart may be sad,
Eccl	7: 3	Sorrow is better than l;

Jas   4: 9 Let your l be turned into mourning

LAVISHED
Eph   1: 8 that he l upon us. In all wisdom

LAW → LAWFUL, LAWGIVER, LAWLESS, LAWLESSNESS, LAWS,
        LAWSUIT, LAWSUITS
Dt   1: 5 Moses undertook to explain this l:
Dt   17:18 write a copy of this l upon a scroll
Dt   27:26 do not uphold the words of this l!"
Dt   31: 9 Moses had written down this l,
Dt   31:11 you shall read this l aloud
Dt   31:26 Take this book of the l and put it
Jos   1: 7 to observe the entire l which Moses
Jos   1: 8 Do not let this book of the l depart
Jos   8:32 the stones a copy of the l written
2 Kgs   22: 8 found the book of the l in the temple
2 Chr   6:16 way, walking by my l, as you have.
2 Chr   17: 9 the book of the l of the LORD;
2 Chr   34:14 the l of the LORD given through
Ezr   7: 6 well-versed in the l of Moses given
Neh   8: 2 the priest brought the l before
Neh   8: 8 from the book of the l of God,
1 Mc   1:56 of the l that they found they tore
1 Mc   2:21 forbid that we should forsake the l
1 Mc   2:48 They saved the l from the hands
Ps   1: 2 the l of the LORD is his joy;
Ps   1: 2 on his l he meditates day and night.
Ps   19: 8 The l of the LORD is perfect,
Ps   40: 9 your l is in my inner being!"
Sir   2:16 who love him are filled with his l.
Sir   33: 2 Whoever hates the l is without
Jer   2: 8 experts in the l did not know me:
Jer   8: 8 we have the l of the LORD"?
Jer   31:33 I will place my l within them,
Bar   4: 1 of God, the l that endures forever;
Dn   9:11 the oath written in the l of Moses,
Dn   9:11 all Israel transgressed your l
Hos   4: 6 Since you have forgotten the l
Hb   1: 4 This is why the l is numb
Mt   5:17 that I have come to abolish the l
Mt   7:12 This is the l and the prophets.
Mt   22:36 in the l is the greatest?"
Mt   22:40 The whole l and the prophets
Mt   23:23 the weightier things of the l:
Lk   2:23 as it is written in the l of the Lord,
Lk   2:39 prescriptions of the l of the Lord,
Lk   10:25 was a scholar of the l who stood
Lk   10:26 to him, "What is written in the l?
Lk   11:46 "Woe also to you scholars of the l!
Lk   16:17 of a letter of the l to become invalid.
Lk   24:44 written about me in the l of Moses
Jn   1:17 because while the l was given
Jn   7:19 Did not Moses give you the l? Yet none of you keeps
                the l.
Jn   18:31 and judge him according to your l."
Acts   6:13 against [this] holy place and the l.
Acts   15: 5 them to observe the Mosaic l."
Acts   28:23 about Jesus from the l of Moses
Rom   2:12 All who sin outside the l will
Rom   2:12 who sin under the l will be judged
Rom   2:13 who observe the l will be justified.
Rom   2:15 the demands of the l are written
Rom   2:20 in the l you have the formulation
Rom   2:25 has value if you observe the l; but if you break the l,
Rom   3:19 what the l says is addressed to those under the l,
Rom   3:20 in his sight by observing the l;
Rom   3:20 through the l comes consciousness
Rom   3:21 been manifested apart from the l,
Rom   3:28 by faith apart from works of the l.
Rom   3:31 then annulling the l by this faith?
Rom   3:31 contrary, we are supporting the l.
Rom   4:13 It was not through the l
Rom   4:15 For the l produces wrath;
Rom   5:13 is not accounted when there is no l.
Rom   5:20 The l entered in so
Rom   6:14 since you are not under the l

Rom   6:15 sin because we are not under the l
Rom   7: 1 the l has jurisdiction over one as
Rom   7: 4 to death to the l through the body
Rom   7: 5 awakened by the l, worked in our
Rom   7: 6 But now we are released from the l,
Rom   7: 7 That the l is sin? Of course not!
Rom   7: 8 Apart from the l sin is dead.
Rom   7: 9 I once lived outside the l,
Rom   7:12 So then the l is holy,
Rom   7:14 We know that the l is spiritual;
Rom   7:22 For I take delight in the l of God,
Rom   7:25 my mind, serve the l of God but, with my flesh, the l of
                sin.
Rom   8: 2 Jesus has freed you from the l of sin
Rom   8: 3 For what the l,
Rom   8: 4 decree of the l might be fulfilled
Rom   8: 7 it does not submit to the l of God,
Rom   9: 4 the giving of the l, the worship,
Rom   9:31 who pursued the l of righteousness,
Rom   10: 4 the end of the l for the justification
Rom   13: 8 loves another has fulfilled the l.
Rom   13:10 love is the fulfillment of the l.
1 Cor   9: 9 It is written in the l of Moses,
1 Cor   9:20 those under the l I became like one under the l—
1 Cor   9:20 though I myself am not under the l—
1 Cor   9:21 those outside the l I became like one outside the l—
1 Cor   9:21 though I am not outside God's l but within the l of
                Christ—
1 Cor   15:56 is sin, and the power of sin is the l.
Gal   2:19 For through the l I died to the l,
Gal   3:11 before God by the l is clear,
Gal   3:19 Why, then, the l? It was added
Gal   4: 4 born of a woman, born under the l,
Gal   5: 4 who are trying to be justified by l;
Gal   5:23 Against such there is no l.
Gal   6: 2 so you will fulfill the l of Christ.
Eph   2:15 abolishing the l with its
Phil   3: 5 in observance of the l a Pharisee,
Phil   3: 9 of my own based on the l
1 Tm   1: 8 We know that the l is good, provided that one uses it
                as l,
Ti   3: 9 and quarrels about the l, for they are
Heb   7:12 is necessarily a change of l as well.
Heb   7:19 for the l brought nothing
Heb   10: 1 Since the l has only a shadow
Jas   1:25 peers into the perfect l of freedom
Jas   2: 8 if you fulfill the royal l according
Jas   2:10 For whoever keeps the whole l,
Jas   4:11 his brother speaks evil of the l and judges the l.
Jas   4:11 If you judge the l, you are not a doer of the l

LAWFUL → LAW
Mt   12:12 So it is l to do good
Mt   19: 3 "Is it l for a man to divorce his wife
Lk   14: 3 "Is it l to cure on the sabbath
1 Cor   6:12 "Everything is l for me," but not
1 Cor   10:23 "Everything is l," but not

LAWGIVER → GIVE, LAW
Jas   4:12 There is one l and judge who is able

LAWLESS → LAW
2 Thes   2: 8 And then the l one will be revealed,

LAWLESSNESS → LAW
Wis   5:23 Thus l will lay waste the whole
2 Cor   6:14 do righteousness and l have?
2 Thes   2: 7 the mystery of l is already at work.
1 Jn   3: 4 commits sin commits l, for sin is l.

LAWS → LAW
Neh   9:13 ordinances, true l, good statutes
1 Mc   3:21 are fighting for our lives and our l.
Heb   8:10 I will put my l in their minds and I
Heb   10:16 'I will put my l in their hearts, and I

LAWSUIT → LAW
Ex   23: 2 When testifying in a l, you shall not

LAWSUITS → LAW
1 Cor   6: 7   that you have l against one another.

LAY → LAID, LAYING, LAYS
Gn   22:12   "Do not l your hand on the boy,"
Ex   7: 4   Therefore I will l my hand on Egypt
Ex   29:10   his sons shall l their hands on its
Nm   8:10   the Israelites shall l their hands
Nm   27:18   of spirit, and l your hand upon him.
Dt   9:25   I l prostrate before the LORD,
Is   44:28   of the temple, "L its foundations."
Mt   28: 6   Come and see the place where he l.
Jn   10:15   I will l down my life for the sheep.
Jn   10:18   from me, but I l it down on my own.
Jn   13:37   I will l down my life for you."
Jn   15:13   this, to l down one's life for one's
Acts   8:19   whom I l my hands may receive
1 Cor   3:11   no one can l a foundation other than
1 Jn   3:16   so we ought to l down our lives

LAYING → LAY
Is   28:16   See, I am l a stone in Zion, a stone
Acts   8:18   the Spirit was conferred by the l
Heb   6: 1   without l the foundation all over
Heb   6: 2   about baptisms and l on of hands,
1 Pt   2: 6   "Behold, I am l a stone in Zion,

LAYS → LAY
Jn   10:11   A good shepherd l down his life

LAZARUS
   1. Poor man in Jesus' parable (Lk 16:19-31).
   2. Brother of Mary and Martha whom Jesus raised from the dead (Jn 11:1–12:19).

LAZINESS → LAZY
Prv   19:15   L brings on deep sleep,

LAZY → LAZINESS
Ex   5: 8   They are l; that is why they are
Ex   5:17   He answered, "L! You are l!
Mt   25:26   in reply, 'You wicked, l servant!
Ti   1:12   vicious beasts, and l gluttons."

LEAD → LEADER, LEADERS, LEADS, LED
Ex   15:10   like l they sank in the mighty
Ex   32:34   l the people where I have told you.
Ps   27:11   l me on a level path because of my
Ps   139:24   l me along an ancient path.
Jer   31: 9   I will l them to streams of water,
Dn   12: 3   those who l the many to justice shall
Rom   2: 4   of God would l you to repentance?

LEADER → LEAD
1 Chr   28: 4   For he chose Judah as l, then one

LEADERS → LEAD
Is   3:12   My people, your l deceive you,
Lk   19:47   and the l of the people, meanwhile,
Heb   13: 7   Remember your l who spoke
Heb   13:17   Obey your l and defer to them,

LEADS → LEAD
Ps   23: 2   lie down; to still waters he l me;
Ps   68: 7   who l prisoners out to prosperity,
Prv   12:26   the way of the wicked l them astray.
Prv   16:17   The path of the upright l away from
Is   49:10   For he who pities them l them
Mt   7:14   constricted the road that l to life.
Jn   10: 3   own sheep by name and l them out.
Rom   6:16   either of sin, which l to death,
Rom   6:16   obedience, which l to righteousness?
2 Cor   2:14   who always l us in triumph in Christ

LEAF → LEAVES
Gn   8:11   in its bill was a plucked-off olive l!

LEAH
   Wife of Jacob (Gn 29:16-30); bore six sons and one daughter (Gn 29:31–30:21; 34:1; 35:23; Ru 4:11).

LEAP → LEAPED, LEAPING, LEAPS
2 Sm   22:30   with my God to help I can l a wall.
Is   35: 6   Then the lame shall l like a stag,

Lk   6:23   Rejoice and l for joy on that day!

LEAPED → LEAP
Lk   1:41   greeting, the infant l in her womb,

LEAPING → LEAP
1 Chr   15:29   and when she saw King David l

LEAPS → LEAP
Jb   37: 1   heart trembles and l out of its place.

LEARN → LEARNED, LEARNING
Dt   4:10   that they may l to fear me as long as
Dt   5: 1   that you may l them and take care
Dt   18: 9   you, you shall not l to imitate
Dt   31:12   hear and so l to fear the LORD,
Prv   19:25   a scoffer and the naive l a lesson;
Is   1:17   l to do good. Make justice your aim:
Is   26: 9   the world's inhabitants l justice.
Mt   11:29   my yoke upon you and l from me,
Mk   13:28   "L a lesson from the fig tree.
1 Tm   5: 4   let these first l to perform their
Ti   3:14   too, l to devote themselves to good
Rev   14: 3   No one could l this hymn except

LEARNED → LEARN
Prv   24: 5   than the strong, and the l, than the mighty,
Eph   4:20   That is not how you l Christ,
Phil   4: 9   Keep on doing what you have l
Phil   4:11   for I have l, in whatever situation I
2 Tm   3:14   remain faithful to what you have l
2 Tm   3:14   you know from whom you l it,
Heb   5: 8   he was, he l obedience from what he

LEARNING → LEARN
Prv   1: 5   by hearing them will advance in l,
Prv   9: 9   teach the just, and they advance in l.
Acts   26:24   much l is driving you mad."

LEAST → LESS
1 Sm   9:21   is not my clan the l among the clans
Mt   2: 6   are by no means l among the rulers
Mt   5:19   one of the l of these commandments
Mt   5:19   do so will be called l in the kingdom
Mt   25:40   for one of these l brothers of mine,
Lk   7:28   yet the l in the kingdom of God is
Lk   9:48   the one who is l among all of you is
1 Cor   15: 9   For I am the l of the apostles, not fit
Eph   3: 8   me, the very l of all the holy ones,

LEATHER
2 Kgs   1: 8   with a l belt around his waist."
Mt   3: 4   and had a l belt around his waist.

LEAVE → LEAVES, LEFT
Ex   11: 8   L, you and all your followers!
Nm   11:20   'Why did we ever l Egypt?' "
Jl   2:14   again relent and l behind a blessing,
Mt   5:24   l your gift there at the altar, go first
Mk   10: 7   this reason a man shall l his father
Jn   14:18   I will not l you orphans; I will come
Jn   14:27   Peace I l with you; my peace I give
Eph   5:31   this reason a man shall l [his] father

LEAVEN → LEAVENED, LEAVENS
Ex   12:15   will have your houses clear of all l.
Dt   16: 4   No l is to be found with you in all
Mt   16: 6   beware of the l of the Pharisees

LEAVENED → LEAVEN
Ex   12:20   You shall eat nothing l;
Mt   13:33   flour until the whole batch was l."

LEAVENS → LEAVEN
1 Cor   5: 6   that a little yeast l all the dough?
Gal   5: 9   A little yeast l the whole batch

LEAVES → LEAF, LEAVE
Gn   3: 7   so they sewed fig l together
Ps   1: 3   its fruit in season; Its l never wither;
Jer   17: 8   heat when it comes, its l stay green;
Ez   47:12   their l will not wither, nor will their
Ez   47:12   for food, and their l for healing."
Mk   11:13   he reached it he found nothing but l;

Rev 22: 2 the l of the trees serve as medicine

LEBANON
Dt 11:24 from the wilderness and the L,
1 Kgs 5:13 from the cedar on L to the hyssop
2 Kgs 14: 9 "A thistle of L sent word to a cedar of L,
Ps 29: 6 Makes L leap like a calf, and Sirion
Ps 92:13 tree, shall grow like a cedar of L.
Is 40:16 L would not suffice for fuel, nor its
Hb 2:17 violence done to L shall cover you,

LECTURE
Acts 19: 9 hold daily discussions in the l hall

LED → LEAD
Neh 9:12 column of cloud you l them by day,
2 Kgs 18:11 Israelites to Assyria and l them off
Ps 78:52 God l forth his people like sheep,
Is 53: 7 Like a lamb l to slaughter or a sheep
Jer 11:19 Yet I was like a trusting lamb l
Am 2:10 and who l you through the desert
Mt 4: 1 Jesus was l by the Spirit
Mt 27:31 and l him off to crucify him.
Acts 8:32 "Like a sheep he was l
Rom 8:14 For those who are l by the Spirit

LEECH
Prv 30:15 The l has two daughters:

LEEKS
Nm 11: 5 the melons, the l, the onions,

LEFT → LEAVE, LEFT-HANDED
Gn 7:23 those with him in the ark were l.
Gn 13: 9 If you prefer the l, I will go
Gn 13: 9 prefer the right, I will go to the l."
Nm 26:65 not one of them was l except Caleb,
Dt 28:14 either to the right or to the l,
Jos 1: 7 from it either to the right or to the l,
Prv 4:27 Turn neither to right nor to l,
Is 30:21 you would turn to the right or the l.
Mt 6: 3 do not let your l hand know what
Mt 25:33 on his right and the goats on his l.
Mk 8: 8 picked up the fragments l over—
Mk 10:40 right or at my l is not mine to give
Lk 17:34 one will be taken, the other l.
1 Thes 4:15 who are l until the coming
Rev 10: 2 on the sea and his l foot on the land,

LEFT-HANDED → HAND, LEFT
Jgs 3:15 of Gera, a Benjaminite who was l.
Jgs 20:16 who were l, every one of them able

LEGION → LEGIONS
Lk 8:30 He replied, "L," because many

LEGIONS → LEGION
Mt 26:53 with more than twelve l of angels?

LEGS
Dn 2:33 its l iron, its feet partly iron
Jn 19:33 dead, they did not break his l,

LEMA
Mt 27:46 voice, "Eli, Eli, l sabachthani?"
Mk 15:34 "Eloi, Eloi, l sabachthani?"

LEMUEL
Prv 31: 1 The words of L, king of Massa,
Prv 31: 4 It is not for kings, L, not for kings

LEND → LENDER, LENDS
Dt 28:12 You will l to many nations
Dt 28:44 They will l to you, not you to them.
Sir 8:12 Do not l to one more powerful than
Sir 8:12 or if you l, count it as lost.
Sir 29: 2 L to your neighbor in his time of need,
Lk 6:34 If you l money to those from whom
Lk 6:34 Even sinners l to sinners, and get

LENDER → LEND
Prv 22: 7 the borrower is the slave of the l.
Is 24: 2 buyer and seller, L and borrower,

LENDS → LEND
Prv 19:17 cares for the poor l to the LORD,

LENGTH → LONG
Gn 13:17 the land, across its l and breadth,
Ps 21: 5 you gave it to him, l of days forever.

LEOPARD → LEOPARDS
Is 11: 6 the l shall lie down with the young
Dn 7: 6 and saw another beast, like a l;
Rev 13: 2 The beast I saw was like a l, but it

LEOPARDS → LEOPARD
Jer 13:23 change their skin, l their spots?

LEPER → LEPROSY
2 Kgs 5: 1 valiant as he was, the man was a l.
Mt 8: 2 And then a l approached, did him
Mt 26: 6 Bethany in the house of Simon the l,

LEPERS → LEPROSY
Lk 7:22 the lame walk, l are cleansed,

LEPROSY → LEPER, LEPERS, LEPROUS
Mt 8: 3 His l was cleansed immediately.

LEPROUS → LEPROSY
2 Chr 26:20 they saw that his forehead was l,

LESS → LEAST
Ex 30:15 nor shall the poor give l,
2 Chr 6:18 how much l this house which I have
2 Chr 32:15 how much the l shall your god
Ezr 9:13 have made l of our sinfulness than it

LESSON
Mk 13:28 "Learn a l from the fig tree.

LET
Gn 1: 3 L there be light, and there was light.
Gn 1: 6 L there be a dome in the middle
Gn 1: 9 L the water under the sky be
Gn 1:11 L the earth bring forth vegetation:
Gn 1:14 L there be lights in the dome
Gn 1:14 L them mark the seasons, the days
Gn 1:20 L the water teem with an abundance
Gn 1:20 on the earth l birds fly beneath
Gn 1:24 L the earth bring forth every kind
Gn 1:26 L us make human beings in our
Gn 1:26 L them have dominion over the fish
Gn 11: 7 l us go down and there confuse their
Ex 5: 1 L my people go, that they may hold
Ex 5: 2 I should obey him and l Israel go?
Ex 5: 2 LORD, and I will not l Israel go."
Ex 13:17 when Pharaoh l the people go,
1 Mc 4:36 l us go up to purify the sanctuary
Ps 22: 9 if he loves him, l him rescue him."
Ps 25: 2 do not l me be disgraced;
Ps 25: 2 do not l my enemies gloat over me.
Ps 33: 8 L all the earth fear the LORD;
Ps 95: 1 l us sing joyfully to the LORD;
Ps 118:24 l us rejoice in it and be glad.
Jer 9:23 But rather, l those who boast,
Lam 3:40 L us search and examine our ways,
Dn 3:74 L the earth bless the Lord,
Jl 4:10 l the weakling boast, "I am
Mt 5:37 L your 'Yes' mean 'Yes,' and your
Mt 27:43 l him deliver him now if he wants
Jn 7:37 "L anyone who thirsts come to me
Jn 14: 1 "Do not l your hearts be troubled.
Eph 4:26 do not l the sun set on your anger,
Col 3:15 l the peace of Christ control your
Col 3:16 L the word of Christ dwell in you
Heb 10:22 l us approach with a sincere heart
Jas 5:12 but l your "Yes" mean "Yes"
1 Jn 4: 7 Beloved, l us love one another,
Rev 22:17 L the hearer say, "Come."

LETTER → LETTERS
Mt 5:18 not the smallest l or the smallest part of a l will pass
Acts 15:23 This is the l delivered by them:
2 Cor 3: 2 You are our l, written on our hearts,

2 Cor   3: 6   new covenant, not of l but of spirit;
2 Cor   3: 6   for the l brings death, but the Spirit
2 Thes   3:14   obey our word as expressed in this l,

LETTERS → LETTER
2 Chr   32:17   for he had written l to deride
2 Cor   3: 7   of death, carved in l on stone,
2 Cor   10:10   say, "His l are severe and forceful,
2 Pt   3:16   these things as he does in all his l.

LEVEL
Ps   143:10   spirit guide me on ground that is l.
Is   26: 7   the path of the just you make l.
Is   45: 2   go before you and l the mountains;
Lk   6:17   and stood on a stretch of l ground.

LEVI → LEVITE, LEVITES, LEVITICAL, =MATTHEW
1. Son of Jacob by Leah (Gn 29:34; 46:11; 1 Chr 2:1). With Simeon avenged rape of Dinah (Gn 34). Tribe of blessed (Gn 49:5-7; Dt 33:8-11), chosen as priests (Nm 3–4), numbered (Nm 3:39; 26:62), given cities, but not land (Nm 18; 35; Dt 10:9; Jos 13:14; 21), land (Ez 48:8-22), 12,000 from (Rev 7:7).
2. See Matthew.

LEVIATHAN
Jb   3: 8   Sea, those skilled at disturbing L!
Jb   40:25   Can you lead L about with a hook,
Ps   74:14   You crushed the heads of L,
Ps   104:26   There ships ply their course and L,
Is   27: 1   and strong, L the fleeing serpent,

LEVITE → LEVI
Ex   4:14   Aaron the L, who is a good speaker;
Jgs   19: 1   there was a L residing in remote
Acts   4:36   a L, a Cypriot by birth,

LEVITES → LEVI
Nm   1:53   but the L shall camp around
Nm   1:53   The L shall keep guard over
Nm   3:12   The L, therefore, are mine,
Nm   8: 6   Take the L from among
Nm   16: 7   is the holy one. You L go too far!"
Nm   18:21   To the L, however, I hereby assign
Nm   35: 7   which you will assign to the L.
Jos   14: 4   But the L were given no share
1 Chr   15: 2   carry the ark of God except the L,
2 Chr   31: 2   and the L according to their former
Ezr   6:18   and the L in their divisions
Neh   8: 9   and the L who were instructing

LEVITICAL → LEVI
Heb   7:11   came through the l priesthood,

LIABLE
Mt   5:22   his brother will be l to judgment,
Mt   5:22   fool,' will be l to fiery Gehenna.

LIAR → LIE
Prv   19:22   rather be poor than a l.
Jn   8:44   because he is a l and the father
Jn   8:55   know him, I would be like you a l.
Rom   3: 4   though every human being is a l,
1 Jn   1:10   we make him a l, and his word is
1 Jn   2: 4   not keep his commandments is a l,
1 Jn   2:22   Who is the l? Whoever denies
1 Jn   5:10   not believe God has made him a l

LIARS → LIE
Ps   63:12   but the mouths of l will be shut!
Sir   15: 8   l never think of her.
1 Tm   1:10   sodomites, kidnapers, l, perjurers,
1 Tm   4: 2   through the hypocrisy of l
Ti   1:12   said, "Cretans have always been l,

LIBATION → LIBATIONS
Phil   2:17   out as a l upon the sacrificial service
2 Tm   4: 6   already being poured out like a l,

LIBATIONS → LIBATION
Jer   19:13   and poured out l to other gods.

LIBERTY
Lv   25:10   You shall proclaim l in the land
Is   61: 1   To proclaim l to the captives,

1 Cor   8: 9   make sure that this l of yours in no

LICENTIOUS → LICENTIOUSNESS
2 Pt   2: 2   Many will follow their l ways,

LICENTIOUSNESS → LICENTIOUS
Mk   7:22   malice, deceit, l, envy, blasphemy,
Rom   13:13   not in promiscuity and l,
2 Cor   12:21   immorality, and l they practiced.
Gal   5:19   immorality, impurity, l,
Eph   4:19   have handed themselves over to l
Jude   1: 4   pervert the grace of our God into l

LICK
Ps   72: 9   before him, his enemies l the dust.
Is   49:23   you and l the dust at your feet.
Mi   7:17   They will l the dust like a snake,

LIE → LIAR, LIARS, LIES, LYING
Gn   19:32   with wine and then l with him,
Gn   39: 7   longing and said, "L with me."
Lv   18:22   You shall not l with a male as
Ru   3: 4   a place at his feet and you l down.
Ps   4: 9   In peace I will l down and fall
Prv   3:24   When you l down, you will not be
Prv   14: 5   A trustworthy witness does not l,
Sir   7:13   Refuse to tell l after l, for it never
Is   11: 6   the leopard shall l down
Ez   34:14   There they will l down on good
Dn   13:20   give in to our desire, and l with us.
Rom   1:25   exchanged the truth of God for a l
1 Jn   1: 6   we l and do not act in truth.
1 Jn   2:21   because every l is alien to the truth.

LIES → LIE
Ex   22:18   Anyone who l with an animal shall
Lv   20:13   If a man l with a male as
Ps   12: 3   They tell l to one another,
Jer   14:14   These prophets utter l in my name,
Jer   27:10   For they prophesy l to you, so as
Hos   12: 1   Ephraim has surrounded me with l,
Zep   3:13   shall do no wrong and speak no l;
Jn   8:44   he is a liar and the father of l.
Phil   3:13   forgetting what l behind
Phil   3:13   straining forward to what l ahead,

LIFE → LIVE
Gn   2: 7   blew into his nostrils the breath of l,
Gn   2: 9   with the tree of l in the middle
Gn   6:17   sky in which there is the breath of l;
Gn   9: 5   demand an accounting for human l.
Ex   21:23   injury ensues, you shall give l for l,
Nm   35:31   of the l of a murderer who deserves
Dt   12:23   for blood is l; you shall not eat that l with the flesh.
Dt   19:21   L for l, eye for eye, tooth for tooth,
Dt   30:15   I have today set before you l
Dt   30:19   I have set before you l and death,
Dt   30:19   Choose l, then, that you and your
Dt   32:47   this word you will enjoy a long l
1 Sm   19: 5   When he took his l in his hands
Neh   9: 6   To all of them you give l,
Jdt   13:20   because you risked your l when our
Jb   2: 6   is in your power; only spare his l."
Jb   10: 1   I loathe my l. I will give myself
Ps   16:11   You will show me the path to l,
Ps   23: 6   will pursue me all the days of my l;
Ps   34:13   Who is the man who delights in l,
Ps   36:10   For with you is the fountain of l,
Ps   63: 4   For your love is better than l;
Ps   119:50   your promise that gives me l.
Prv   3: 2   days, and years of l, and peace,
Prv   3:16   Long l is in her right hand, in her
Prv   3:18   She is a tree of l to those who grasp
Prv   4:23   heart, for in it are the sources of l.
Prv   6:23   and a way to l are the reproofs
Prv   6:26   woman is a trap for your precious l.
Prv   7:23   snare, unaware that his l is at stake.
Prv   8:35   For whoever finds me finds l,
Prv   10:11   mouth of the just is a fountain of l,
Prv   10:27   Fear of the LORD prolongs l,

Prv	11:30	The fruit of justice is a tree of l,
Prv	13:12	but a wish fulfilled is a tree of l.
Prv	13:14	of the wise is a fountain of l,
Prv	14:27	of the LORD is a fountain of l,
Prv	15: 4	A soothing tongue is a tree of l,
Prv	16:22	Good sense is a fountain of l
Prv	18:21	and l are in the power of the tongue;
Prv	19:23	The fear of the LORD leads to l;
Prv	21:21	and kindness will find l and honor.
Eccl	2:17	Therefore I detested l, since for me
Eccl	7:12	is profitable because wisdom gives l
Eccl	9: 9	Enjoy l with the wife you love,
Eccl	9: 9	This is your lot in l, for the toil
Sir	4:12	Those who love her love l;
Sir	30:22	of heart is the very l of a person,
Sir	31:27	Wine is very l to anyone, if taken
Is	53:10	By making his l as a reparation
Lam	3:58	my case, Lord, you redeemed my l.
Jon	2: 7	you brought my l up from the pit,
Mal	2: 5	My covenant with him was the l
Mt	6:25	do not worry about your l, what you
Mt	6:25	Is not l more than food and the body
Mt	7:14	constricted the road that leads to l.
Mt	10:39	Whoever finds his l will lose it,
Mt	10:39	whoever loses his l for my sake will
Mt	16:25	wishes to save his l will lose it,
Mt	16:25	whoever loses his l for my sake will
Mt	19:16	good must I do to gain eternal l?"
Mt	19:29	more, and will inherit eternal l.
Mt	20:28	to give his l as a ransom for many."
Mt	25:46	but the righteous to eternal l."
Mk	3: 4	to save l rather than to destroy it?"
Mk	9:43	to enter into l maimed than with two
Mk	10:30	and eternal l in the age to come.
Mk	10:45	to give his l as a ransom for many."
Lk	6: 9	to save l rather than to destroy it?"
Lk	12:15	be rich, one's l does not consist
Lk	12:22	do not worry about your l and what
Jn	1: 4	through him was l, and this l was the light
Jn	3:15	in him may have eternal l."
Jn	3:36	believes in the Son has eternal l,
Jn	3:36	disobeys the Son will not see l,
Jn	4:14	of water welling up to eternal l."
Jn	5:21	Father raises the dead and gives l,
Jn	5:21	does the Son give l to whomever he
Jn	5:24	in the one who sent me has eternal l
Jn	5:24	but has passed from death to l.
Jn	5:39	you have eternal l through them;
Jn	5:40	do not want to come to me to have l.
Jn	6:27	the food that endures for eternal l,
Jn	6:35	said to them, "I am the bread of l;
Jn	6:47	you, whoever believes has eternal l.
Jn	6:48	I am the bread of l.
Jn	6:51	is my flesh for the l of the world."
Jn	6:63	It is the spirit that gives l,
Jn	6:63	I have spoken to you are spirit and l.
Jn	6:68	You have the words of eternal l.
Jn	8:12	but will have the light of l."
Jn	10:10	I came so that they might have l
Jn	10:11	A good shepherd lays down his l
Jn	10:28	I give them eternal l, and they shall
Jn	11:25	"I am the resurrection and the l;
Jn	12:25	Whoever loves his l loses it,
Jn	12:25	whoever hates his l in this world
Jn	12:50	that his commandment is eternal l.
Jn	13:37	I will lay down my l for you."
Jn	14: 6	am the way and the truth and the l.
Jn	15:13	lay down one's l for one's friends.
Jn	17: 3	Now this is eternal l, that they
Jn	20:31	through this belief you may have l
Acts	2:28	made known to me the paths of l;
Acts	3:15	The author of l you put to death,
Acts	13:48	were destined for eternal l came
Rom	2: 7	eternal l to those who seek glory,
Rom	5:10	will we be saved by his l.
Rom	5:18	act acquittal and l came to all.

Rom	5:21	eternal l through Jesus Christ our
Rom	6: 4	we too might live in newness of l.
Rom	6:13	to God as raised from the dead to l
Rom	6:22	and its end is eternal l.
Rom	6:23	God is eternal l in Christ Jesus our
Rom	7:10	that was for l turned out to be death
Rom	8: 2	of the spirit of l in Christ Jesus has
Rom	8: 6	but the concern of the spirit is l
Rom	8:11	the dead will give l to your mortal
Rom	8:38	that neither death, nor l, nor angels,
1 Cor	15:19	If for this l only we have hoped
1 Cor	15:36	is not brought to l unless it dies.
2 Cor	2:16	former an odor of l that leads to l.
2 Cor	3: 6	brings death, but the Spirit gives l.
2 Cor	4:10	so that the l of Jesus may also be
2 Cor	5: 4	is mortal may be swallowed up by l.
Gal	6: 8	the spirit will reap eternal l
Phil	1:20	my body, whether by l or by death.
Phil	2:16	as you hold on to the word of l,
Phil	4: 3	whose names are in the book of l.
Col	3: 3	your l is hidden with Christ in God.
1 Tm	1:16	to believe in him for everlasting l.
1 Tm	4: 8	since it holds a promise of l both
1 Tm	6:12	Lay hold of eternal l, to which you
1 Tm	6:19	so as to win the l that is true l.
2 Tm	1:10	brought l and immortality to light
Ti	1: 2	in the hope of eternal l that God,
Ti	3: 7	become heirs in hope of eternal l.
Heb	7:16	of a l that cannot be destroyed.
Jas	1:12	he will receive the crown of l
Jas	3:13	works by a good l in the humility
1 Pt	3: 7	we are joint heirs of the gift of l,
1 Pt	3:10	"Whoever would love l and see
1 Pt	4: 2	what remains of one's l in the flesh
2 Pt	1: 3	on us everything that makes for l
1 Jn	1: 1	our hands concerns the Word of l—
1 Jn	2:25	promise that he made us: eternal l.
1 Jn	3:14	to l because we love our brothers.
1 Jn	3:16	was that he laid down his l for us;
1 Jn	5:11	God gave us eternal l, and this l is
1 Jn	5:20	He is the true God and eternal l.
Jude	1:21	Jesus Christ that leads to eternal l.
Rev	2: 7	to eat from the tree of l that is
Rev	2: 8	who once died but came to l,
Rev	2:10	and I will give you the crown of l.
Rev	3: 5	erase his name from the book of l
Rev	11:11	days, a breath of l from God entered
Rev	13: 8	of the world in the book of l,
Rev	17: 8	in the book of l from the foundation
Rev	20: 4	They came to l and they reigned
Rev	20:12	scroll was opened, the book of l.
Rev	20:15	in the book of l was thrown
Rev	21:27	are written in the Lamb's book of l.
Rev	22: 2	of the river grew the tree of l
Rev	22:14	so as to have the right to the tree of l
Rev	22:19	take away his share in the tree of l

LIFE-GIVING → GIVE, LIVE

1 Cor	15:45	being," the last Adam a l spirit.

LIFETIME → LIVE

Ps	30: 6	lasts but a moment; his favor a l.
Lk	16:25	good during your l while Lazarus

LIFT → LIFTED, LIFTING, LIFTS

Ps	24: 7	L up your heads, O gates;
Ps	25: 1	To you, O LORD, I l up my soul,
Ps	28: 2	I l up my hands toward your holy place.
Ps	63: 5	I will l up my hands, calling on your
Ps	119:28	depressed; l me up acccording to your word.
Ps	134: 2	L up your hands toward
Is	40:26	L up your eyes on high and see who
Lam	2:19	L up your hands to him for the lives
Lk	11:46	you yourselves do not l one finger

LIFTED → LIFT

Nm	9:21	Whether the cloud l during the day
Ez	3:12	Then the spirit l me up, and I heard
Ez	8: 3	The spirit l me up between earth

Ez	11: 1	The spirit l me up and brought me
Mt	21:21	'Be l up and thrown into the sea,'
Jn	3:14	just as Moses l up the serpent
Jn	3:14	so must the Son of Man be l up,
Jn	12:34	that the Son of Man must be l up?

LIFTING → LIFT

1 Tm	2: 8	men should pray, l up holy hands,

LIFTS → LIFT

1 Sm	2: 8	from the ash heap l up the poor,
Ps	113: 7	dust, l the poor from the ash heap,

LIGAMENT → LIGAMENTS

Eph	4:16	held together by every supporting l,

LIGAMENTS → LIGAMENT

Col	2:19	and held together by its l and bonds,

LIGHT → DAYLIGHT, ENLIGHTENED, ENLIGHTENING, ENLIGHTENS, LIGHTED, LIGHTEN, LIGHTENED, LIGHTS

Gn	1: 3	Let there be l, and there was l.
Gn	1: 5	God called the l "day,"
Ex	13:21	of a column of fire to give them l.
Ex	25:37	that they give their l on the space
Jb	3:20	Why is l given to the toilers,
Jb	38:19	What is the way to the dwelling of l,
Ps	4: 7	show us the l of your face!"
Ps	18:29	you, LORD, give l to my lamp;
Ps	27: 1	The LORD is my l and my
Ps	36:10	of life, and in your l we see l.
Ps	56:14	before God in the l of the living.
Ps	104: 2	robed in l as with a cloak.
Ps	119:105	a lamp for my feet, a l for my path.
Ps	119:130	revelation of your words sheds l,
Ps	139:12	Darkness and l are but one.
Prv	4:18	the path of the just is like shining l,
Prv	13: 9	The l of the just gives joy,
Eccl	2:13	over folly as l has over darkness.
Wis	7:26	For she is the reflection of eternal l,
Is	2: 5	let us walk in the l of the LORD!
Is	9: 1	in darkness have seen a great l;
Is	9: 1	in a land of gloom a l has shone.
Is	42: 6	for the people, a l for the nations,
Is	45: 7	I form the l, and create the darkness,
Is	49: 6	I will make you a l to the nations,
Is	53:11	of his anguish he shall see the l;
Is	58:10	your l shall rise in the darkness,
Is	60: 1	for your l has come, the glory
Is	60:19	No longer shall the sun be your l
Is	60:19	the LORD will be your l forever,
Bar	5: 9	Israel in joy by the l of his glory,
Am	5:18	It will be darkness, not l!
Mi	7: 8	sit in darkness, the LORD is my l.
Mt	4:16	sit in darkness have seen a great l,
Mt	5:14	You are the l of the world.
Mt	5:16	so, your l must shine before others,
Mt	6:22	whole body will be filled with l;
Mt	11:30	my yoke is easy, and my burden l."
Mk	13:24	and the moon will not give its l,
Lk	2:32	a l for revelation to the Gentiles,
Lk	8:16	that those who enter may see the l.
Lk	11:33	that those who enter might see the l.
Jn	1: 4	this life was the l of the human race;
Jn	1: 5	the l shines in the darkness,
Jn	1: 7	to testify to the l, so that all might
Jn	1: 9	The true l, which enlightens
Jn	3:19	that the l came into the world,
Jn	3:19	but people preferred darkness to l,
Jn	5:35	you were content to rejoice in his l.
Jn	8:12	saying, "I am the l of the world.
Jn	8:12	but will have the l of life."
Jn	9: 5	the world, I am the l of the world."
Jn	12:35	"The l will be among you only
Jn	12:35	Walk while you have the l,
Jn	12:46	I came into the world as l,
Acts	9: 3	a l from the sky suddenly flashed
Acts	13:47	'I have made you a l to the Gentiles,
Rom	13:12	[and] put on the armor of l;

2 Cor	4: 6	said, "Let l shine out of darkness,"
2 Cor	4: 6	to bring to l the knowledge
2 Cor	6:14	Or what fellowship does l have
2 Cor	11:14	Satan masquerades as an angel of l.
Eph	5: 8	but now you are l in the Lord. Live as children of l,
Eph	5: 9	for l produces every kind
Col	1:12	the inheritance of the holy ones in l.
1 Thes	5: 5	For all of you are children of the l
1 Tm	6:16	who dwells in unapproachable l,
1 Pt	2: 9	out of darkness into his wonderful l.
1 Jn	1: 5	God is l, and in him there is no
1 Jn	1: 7	if we walk in the l as he is in the l,
1 Jn	2: 8	and the true l is already shining.
1 Jn	2: 9	Whoever says he is in the l,
Rev	8:12	The day lost its l for a third
Rev	21:23	it, for the glory of God gave it l,
Rev	22: 5	nor will they need l from lamp
Rev	22: 5	for the Lord God shall give them l,

LIGHTED → LIGHT

1 Mc	4:50	and l the lamps on the lampstand,

LIGHTEN → LIGHT

2 Chr	10: 9	'L the yoke your father imposed
Jon	1: 5	To l the ship for themselves,

LIGHTENED → LIGHT

Acts	27:38	they l the ship by throwing

LIGHTNING → LIGHTNINGS

Ex	19:16	there were peals of thunder and l,
Ex	20:18	people witnessed the thunder and l,
2 Sm	22:15	l, and dispersed them.
Ez	1:13	intensely, and from it l flashed.
Dn	10: 6	his face shone like l, his eyes were
Mt	24:27	For just as l comes from the east
Mt	28: 3	His appearance was like l and his
Lk	10:18	"I have observed Satan fall like l
Rev	4: 5	From the throne came flashes of l,
Rev	8: 5	flashes of l, and an earthquake.
Rev	11:19	There were flashes of l, rumblings,
Rev	16:18	Then there were l flashes,

LIGHTNINGS → LIGHTNING

Dn	3:73	L and clouds, bless the Lord;

LIGHTS → LIGHT

Gn	1:14	Let there be l in the dome
Gn	1:16	God made the two great l,
Ps	136: 7	Who made the great l, for his mercy
Jas	1:17	coming down from the Father of l,

LIKE → ALIKE, LIKENESS

Gn	3: 5	be opened and you will be l gods,
Gn	3:22	The man has become l one of us,
Gn	13:16	make your descendants l the dust
Ex	8: 6	that there is none l the LORD,
Ex	15:11	Who is l you among the gods,
Ex	34: 1	"Cut two stone tablets l the former,
Nm	11: 7	Manna was l coriander seed and had
Nm	13:33	we seemed l mere grasshoppers,
Dt	8:20	L the nations which the LORD
Dt	18:15	A prophet l me will the LORD,
Dt	32:31	their "rock" is not l our Rock;
1 Sm	2: 2	There is no Holy One l the LORD;
2 Sm	7:22	there is no God l you in heaven
1 Kgs	14: 8	have not been l my servant David,
1 Chr	17:21	"Is there, l your people Israel,
Jb	1: 8	There is no one on earth l him,
Jb	40: 9	Have you an arm l that of God,
Jb	40: 9	can you thunder with a voice l his?
Ps	1: 3	He is l a tree planted near streams
Ps	1: 4	They are l chaff driven by the wind.
Ps	22:15	L water my life drains away;
Ps	22:15	My heart has become l wax, it melts
Ps	35:10	who is l you, Who rescue
Ps	48:11	L your name, O God, so is your
Ps	103:15	As for man, his days are l the grass;
Ps	113: 5	Who is l the LORD our God,
Ps	114: 4	The mountains skipped l rams; the hills, l lambs.

Ps	144: 4	his days are l a passing shadow.
Prv	7:22	l an ox that goes to slaughter;
Prv	11:22	L a golden ring in a swine's snout is
Eccl	12:11	The sayings of the wise are l goads;
Eccl	12:11	l fixed spikes are the collected
Sir	9:10	A new friend is l new wine—
Sir	21:14	A fool's mind is l a broken jar:
Is	1:18	Though your sins be l scarlet,
Is	11: 7	the lion shall eat hay l the ox.
Is	40: 6	all their loyalty l the flower
Is	46: 9	I am God, there is none l me.
Is	53: 2	He grew up l a sapling before him,
Is	53: 6	We had all gone astray l sheep,
Is	64: 5	all become l something unclean,
Is	64: 5	all our just deeds are l polluted rags;
Jer	10: 6	No one is l you, LORD, you are
Jer	23:29	Is not my word l fire—
Lam	1:12	Is there any pain l my pain,
Ez	1: 4	something l polished metal gleamed
Ez	1:26	figure that looked l a human being.
Dn	7: 4	The first was l a lion,
Dn	7: 4	stand on two feet l a human being,
Dn	7:13	the clouds of heaven One l a son
Dn	10: 6	his face shone l lightning, his eyes were l fiery torches,
Hos	2: 1	of the Israelites will be l the sand
Hos	6: 4	Your loyalty is l morning mist,
Hos	14: 6	I will be l the dew for Israel:
Mi	7:18	Who is a God l you, who removes
Na	1: 6	His fury is poured out l fire,
Zec	1: 4	Do not be l your ancestors to whom
Mt	9:36	l sheep without a shepherd.
Mt	10:16	I am sending you l sheep
Lk	6:48	one is l a person building a house,
Lk	13:18	"What is the kingdom of God l?
Acts	3:22	'A prophet l me will the Lord,
Rom	5:15	the gift is not l the transgression.
Rom	9:29	we would have become l Sodom
Jas	1:24	promptly forgets what he looked l.
1 Pt	1:24	for: "All flesh is l grass, and all its glory l the flower of the field;
2 Pt	3: 8	Lord one day is l a thousand years
2 Pt	3: 8	and a thousand years l one day.
2 Pt	3:10	day of the Lord will come l a thief,
Rev	1:13	the lampstands one l a son of man,
Rev	2:18	whose eyes are l a fiery flame
Rev	3: 3	I will come l a thief, and you will
Rev	4: 7	the second was l a calf,
Rev	10: 1	his face was l the sun and his feet
Rev	16:15	("Behold, I am coming l a thief."
Rev	19:12	His eyes were [l] a fiery flame,

LIKENESS → LIKE

Gn	1:26	beings in our image, after our l.
Gn	5: 1	he made them in the l of God;
Ez	1: 5	figures in the l of four living creatures
Ez	1:28	the appearance of the l of the glory
Rom	8: 3	his own Son in the l of sinful flesh
Phil	2: 7	form of a slave, coming in human l;
Jas	3: 9	who are made in the l of God.

LILIES → LILY

Sg	2:16	and l to him; he feeds among the l.

LILITH

Is	34:14	There shall the l repose, and find

LILY → LILIES

Sg	2: 1	flower of Sharon, a l of the valleys.
Sg	2: 2	Like a l among thorns, so is my
Hos	14: 6	he will blossom like the l;

LIMITS

Ex	19:23	Set l around the mountain to make it
2 Cor	10:13	to the l God has apportioned us,

LIMPED

Gn	32:32	Jacob l along because of his hip.

LINE

Is	28:17	I will make judgment a measuring l,

LINEN

Ex	26: 1	of ten sheets woven of fine l twined
Ex	28:39	tunic of fine l shall be brocaded.
Ex	28:39	The turban shall be made of fine l.
Prv	31:22	fine l and purple are her clothing.
Jer	13: 1	Go buy yourself a l loincloth;
Ez	9: 2	their midst was a man dressed in l,
Dn	10: 5	I saw a man dressed in l with a belt
Mk	15:46	wrapped him in the l cloth and laid
Rev	15: 6	They were dressed in clean white l,
Rev	19: 8	to wear a bright, clean l garment."
Rev	19: 8	(The l represents the righteous

LINGER

Prv	23:30	Whoever l long over wine,

LION → LION'S, LIONS, LIONS'

Gn	49: 9	lies down like a l, like a lioness—
Jgs	14: 6	and he tore the l apart barehanded,
1 Sm	17:34	whenever a l or bear came to carry
Ps	91:13	viper, trample the l and the dragon.
Eccl	9: 4	live dog is better off than a dead l."
Sir	27:28	lies in wait for them like a l.
Is	11: 7	the l shall eat hay like the ox.
Is	65:25	and the l shall eat hay like the ox—
Jer	4: 7	Up comes the l from its lair,
Jer	25:38	Like a l he leaves his lair, and their
Ez	1:10	and on the right the face of a l,
Ez	10:14	the third a l, the fourth an eagle.
Dn	7: 4	The first was like a l,
Hos	13: 7	So, I will be like a l to them,
1 Pt	5: 8	around like a roaring l looking
Rev	4: 7	The first creature resembled a l,
Rev	5: 5	The l of the tribe of Judah, the root

LION'S → LION

Gn	49: 9	Judah is a l cub, you have grown
2 Tm	4:17	I was rescued from the l mouth.

LIONS → LION

Dn	6:21	been able to save you from the l?"

LIONS' → LION

Dn	14:31	They threw Daniel into a l den,
Na	2:12	the lionesses' den, the young l cave,
Rev	9: 8	Their teeth were like l teeth,

LIPS

Jb	27: 4	My l shall not speak falsehood,
Ps	12: 4	the LORD cut off all deceiving l,
Ps	40:10	See, I do not restrain my l;
Ps	63: 4	my l shall ever praise you!
Ps	119:171	May my l pour forth your praise,
Ps	140: 4	serpent, venom of asps upon their l.
Ps	141: 3	keep watch over the door of my l.
Prv	4:24	from you, deceitful l put far from you.
Prv	5: 3	the l of the stranger drip honey,
Prv	10:13	On the l of the intelligent is found
Prv	10:18	conceals hatred has lying l,
Prv	10:21	The l of the just nourish many,
Prv	10:32	The l of the just know favor,
Prv	12:22	Lying l are an abomination
Prv	13: 3	who open wide their l bring ruin.
Prv	15: 7	The l of the wise spread knowledge,
Prv	24:26	An honest reply—a kiss on the l.
Prv	26:23	finish on earthenware are smooth l
Prv	27: 2	a stranger, not your own l.
Eccl	10:12	but the l of fools consume them.
Sg	4:11	Your l drip honey, my bride,
Sir	12:16	With their l enemies speak sweetly,
Is	6: 5	For I am a man of unclean l,
Is	29:13	and honors me with their l alone,
Mal	2: 7	For a priest's l preserve knowledge,
Mt	15: 8	'This people honors me with their l,
Rom	3:13	the venom of asps is on their l;
1 Cor	14:21	by the l of foreigners I will speak
Heb	13:15	the fruit of l that confess his name.
1 Pt	3:10	evil and the l from speaking deceit,

LIST

1 Chr	27: 1	This is the l of the Israelite family

LISTEN → LISTENED, LISTENING, LISTENS

Ex	4: 1	they do not believe me or l to me?
Ex	6:30	possible that Pharaoh will l to me?"
Ex	7:13	his heart and would not l to them,
Ex	15:26	If you l closely to the voice
Dt	21:18	rebellious son who will not l to his
Jos	24:24	our God, and will l to his voice."
Jgs	2:17	they did not l to their judges either,
2 Kgs	17:40	But they did not l; they continued
2 Kgs	21: 9	But they did not l.
Ps	34:12	Come, children, l to me; I will teach
Ps	81: 9	'L, my people, I will testify against
Sir	6:33	If you are willing to l, you can
Is	1:10	L to the instruction of our God,
Mk	9: 7	is my beloved Son. L to him."
Lk	16:31	'If they will not l to Moses
Acts	3:22	to him you shall l in all that he may

LISTENED → LISTEN

Gn	3:17	Because you l to your wife and ate
Dt	9:19	Yet once again the Lord l to me.

LISTENING → LISTEN

1 Sm	3:10	"Speak, for your servant is l."

LISTENS → LISTEN

Lk	10:16	Whoever l to you l to me.
Jn	18:37	belongs to the truth l to my voice."
1 Jn	4: 6	and anyone who knows God l to us,

LITTLE

Ex	16:18	a small amount did not have too l.
Ex	23:30	L by l I will drive them out before
1 Kgs	17:12	flour in my jar and a l oil in my jug.
Ps	8: 6	Yet you have made him l less than
Prv	6:10	A l sleep, a l slumber, a l folding
Prv	13:11	away, but gathered l by l, it grows.
Prv	15:16	Better a l with fear of the Lord
Prv	16: 8	Better a l with justice, than a large
Eccl	10: 1	than wisdom or wealth is a l folly!
Sir	29:23	Whether l or much, be content
Sir	51:28	Acquire but a l instruction, and you
Is	11: 6	with a l child to guide them.
Mt	6:30	provide for you, O you of l faith?
Mt	8:26	are you terrified, O you of l faith?"
Mt	14:31	him, "O you of l faith, why did you
Mt	16: 8	he said, "You of l faith, why do you
Mt	17:20	to them, "Because of your l faith.
Lk	7:47	But the one to whom l is forgiven, loves l."
1 Cor	5: 6	that a l yeast leavens all the dough?
2 Cor	8:15	whoever had l did not have less."
Gal	5: 9	A l yeast leavens the whole batch
1 Tm	5:23	have a l wine for the sake of your
Heb	2: 7	for a l while lower than the angels;
1 Pt	5:10	you after you have suffered a l.

LIVE → ALIVE, LIFE, LIFE-GIVING, LIFETIME, LIVED, LIVES, LIVING

Gn	12:12	then they will kill me, but let you l."
Ex	1:16	but if it is a girl, she may l."
Ex	33:20	my face, for no one can see me and l.
Dt	4: 1	that you may l, and may enter
Dt	5:24	a mortal and that person may still l.
Dt	8: 3	it is not by bread alone that people l,
Dt	30: 6	being, in order that you may l.
Jos	6:25	Joshua let her l, along with her father's
Jb	14:14	die, and l again, all the days of my
Ps	63: 5	I will bless you as long as I l;
Ps	119:175	Let my soul l to praise you;
Prv	4: 4	keep my commands, and l!
Prv	15:27	but those who hate bribes will l.
Wis	5:15	But the righteous l forever,
Is	26:19	But your dead shall l, their corpses
Ez	18: 9	he shall surely l—oracle of the Lord
Ez	18:32	of the Lord God. Turn back and l!
Am	5: 6	that you may l, lest he flare
Jon	4: 3	it is better for me to die than to l."
Hb	2: 4	is righteous because of faith shall l.

Mt	4: 4	'One does not l by bread alone,
Lk	4: 4	'One does not l by bread alone.' "
Lk	10:28	do this and you will l."
Jn	6:51	eats this bread will l forever;
Jn	11:25	in me, even if he dies, will l,
Jn	14:19	see me, because I l and you will l.
Acts	17:28	For 'In him we l and move and have
Rom	1:17	who is righteous by faith will l."
Rom	6: 8	that we shall also l with him.
Rom	14: 8	For if we l, we l for the Lord,
Rom	14: 8	so then, whether we l or die, we are
2 Cor	5:15	that those who l might no longer l for themselves
2 Cor	6:16	"I will l with them and move
Gal	2:20	yet I l, no longer I, but Christ lives
Gal	3:12	one who does these things will l
Gal	5:25	If we l in the Spirit, let us
Eph	4:17	you must no longer l as the Gentiles
Eph	5: 8	in the Lord. L as children of light,
2 Tm	3:12	fact, all who want to l religiously
Ti	2:12	worldly desires and to l temperately,
Heb	10:38	But my just one shall l by faith,

LIVED → LIVE

Dt	26: 5	and l there as a resident alien.
Mt	1:18	but before they l together, she was

LIVES → LIVE

Gn	3:22	of life, and eats of it and l forever?
Ex	30:16	of the ransom paid for their l.
Dt	17:19	and he shall read it as long as he l,
Tb	13: 1	Blessed be God who l forever,
Jb	19:25	I know that my vindicator l,
Ps	18:47	The Lord l! Blessed be my rock!
Prv	14:25	The truthful witness saves l,
Is	65:20	shall there be in it an infant who l
Ez	18:27	right and just, they save their l;
Dn	12: 7	him who l forever that it should be
Jn	11:26	everyone who l and believes in me
Rom	6:10	as to his life, he l for God.
Gal	2:20	live, no longer I, but Christ l in me;
Heb	7:25	him, since he l forever to make
1 Jn	3:16	to lay down our l for our brothers.
Rev	4:10	him, who l forever and ever.
Rev	10: 6	swore by the one who l forever
Rev	15: 7	fury of God, who l forever and ever.

LIVESTOCK

Ex	34:19	opens the womb among all your l,

LIVING → LIVE

Gn	2: 7	life, and the man became a l being.
Gn	3:20	she was the mother of all the l.
Gn	6:19	all l creatures you shall bring two
Gn	8:21	again strike down every l being, as I
Dt	5:26	the voice of the l God speaking
Jos	3:10	that there is a l God in your midst:
1 Sm	17:26	insult the armies of the l God?"
2 Kgs	19: 4	sent to taunt the l God, and will
Ps	84: 3	heart and flesh cry out for the l God.
Ps	142: 6	my portion in the land of the l.
Eccl	9: 4	is chosen among all the l has hope:
Is	53: 8	he was cut off from the land of the l,
Jer	2:13	forsaken me, the source of l waters;
Jer	10:10	he is the l God, the eternal King,
Jer	17:13	the Lord, source of l waters.
Ez	1: 5	of four l creatures appeared.
Ez	10:17	the spirit of the l creatures was
Dn	6:27	"For he is the l God,
Hos	2: 1	be called, "Children of the l God."
Mt	16:16	the Messiah, the Son of the l God."
Mt	22:32	the God of the dead but of the l."
Jn	4:10	he would have given you l water."
Jn	6:51	I am the l bread that came down
Jn	7:38	'Rivers of l water will flow
Rom	9:26	be called children of the l God."
Rom	12: 1	to offer your bodies as a l sacrifice,
Rom	14: 9	be Lord of both the dead and the l.
2 Cor	6:16	For we are the temple of the l God;
1 Tm	4:10	we have set our hope on the l God,

2 Tm	4: 1	who will judge the l and the dead,
Heb	4:12	the word of God is l and effective,
Heb	10:20	l way he opened for us through
Heb	10:31	to fall into the hands of the l God.
1 Pt	1:23	through the l and abiding word
1 Pt	2: 4	Come to him, a l stone,
Rev	4: 6	there were four l creatures covered

LOAD
Gal	6: 5	for each will bear his own l.

LOAF → LOAVES
Prv	6:26	of a harlot may be scarcely a l
Mk	8:14	they had only one l with them

LOAN
Dt	24:10	When you make a l of any kind

LOAVES → LOAF
Nm	11: 8	cook it in a pot and make it into l,
Mk	6:41	taking the five l and the two fish
Mk	6:41	broke the l, and gave them to [his]
Mk	8: 6	taking the seven l he gave thanks,
Mk	8:19	when I broke the five l for the five
Lk	11: 5	'Friend, lend me three l of bread,

LOCK → LOCKED, LOCKS
Mt	23:13	You l the kingdom of heaven before

LOCKED → LOCK
Jn	20:19	when the doors were l,
Acts	5:23	"We found the jail securely l
Rev	20: 3	abyss, which he l over it and sealed,

LOCKS → LOCK
Jgs	16:19	a man who shaved off the seven l

LOCUST → LOCUSTS
Jl	2:25	what the swarming l has eaten,
Mal	3:11	I will rebuke the l for you so that it

LOCUSTS → LOCUST
Ex	10: 4	go, tomorrow I will bring l into your
2 Chr	6:28	mildew, or l swarm, or caterpillars;
Am	4: 9	l devoured your gardens
Mt	3: 4	His food was l and wild honey.
Rev	9: 3	L came out of the smoke onto

LODGE
Ru	1:16	go I will go, wherever you l I will l.

LOFTY
Is	26: 5	on high, the l city he brings down,

LOINS
Ex	12:11	with your l girt, sandals on your feet
Heb	7:10	his father's l when Melchizedek met

LOIS
Godly grandmother of Timothy (2 Tm 1:5).

LONG → LENGTH, LONGED, LONGER, LONGING, LONGS
Ex	20:12	you may have a l life in the land
Nm	14:11	How l will this people spurn me?
Nm	14:11	How l will they not trust me,
Dt	6: 2	I enjoin on you, and thus have l life.
1 Kgs	18:21	"How l will you straddle the issue?
2 Chr	1:11	or even for a l life for yourself,
Ps	13: 2	How l will you hide your face
Ps	63: 5	I will bless you as l as I live;
Ps	119:97	your law, Lord! I study it all day l.
Ps	119:174	I l for your salvation, LORD;
Prv	3:16	L life is in her right hand, in her left
Is	6:11	"How l, O Lord?" I asked.
Is	48: 3	Things of the past I declared l ago,
Lk	10:13	they would l ago have repented,
1 Cor	11:14	man wears his hair l it is a disgrace
1 Cor	11:15	if a woman has l hair it is her glory,
Phil	1: 8	how I l for all of you
1 Pt	2: 2	l for pure spiritual milk so
Rev	6:10	in a loud voice, "How l will it be,

LONGED → LONG
Mt	13:17	righteous people l to see what you
2 Tm	4: 8	to all who have l for his appearance.

1 Pt	1:12	things into which angels l to look.

LONGER → LONG
Gn	17: 5	No l will you be called Abram;
Gn	32:29	"You shall no l be named Jacob,
Jer	31:34	and no l remember their sin.
Ez	14:11	of Israel may no l stray from me,
Ez	14:11	no l defile themselves by all their
Mt	5:13	It is no l good for anything but to be
Mk	10: 8	So they are no l two but one flesh.
Jn	13:33	will be with you only a little while l.
Jn	15:15	I no l call you slaves,
Rom	6: 6	that we might no l be in slavery
Gal	2:20	yet I live, no l I, but Christ lives
Eph	2:19	So then you are no l strangers
Eph	4:14	so that we may no l be infants,

LONGING → LONG
Ps	119:20	all times my soul is stirred with l
2 Cor	5: 2	l to be further clothed with our

LONGS → LONG
Ps	42: 2	As the deer l for streams of water, so my soul l for you,

LOOK → LOOKED, LOOKING, LOOKS
Gn	15: 5	L up at the sky and count the stars,
Gn	19:17	Do not l back or stop anywhere
Ex	3: 6	face, for he was afraid to l at God.
Nm	21: 8	has been bitten will l at it and recover.
Dt	3:27	L well, for you shall not cross this
Dt	26:15	L down, then, from heaven,
Ps	34: 6	L to him and be radiant, and your
Ps	80:15	l down from heaven and see;
Prv	4:25	Let your eyes l straight ahead
Is	3: 9	Their very l bears witness against
Is	17: 7	their eyes shall l to the Holy One
Is	31: 1	l not to the Holy One of Israel nor
Is	42:18	listen, you blind ones, l and see!
Hb	1:13	Your eyes are too pure to l
Zec	12:10	when they l on him whom they have
Mt	6:26	L at the birds in the sky; they do not
Mk	13:21	If anyone says to you then, 'L,
Lk	24:39	L at my hands and my feet, that it is
Jn	4:35	l up and see the fields ripe
Jn	13:33	You will l for me, and as I told
Jn	19:37	"They will l upon him whom they
1 Pt	1:12	things into which angels longed to l.

LOOKED → LOOK
Gn	19:26	But Lot's wife l back, and she was
Ps	102:20	"The LORD l down from the holy
Sir	16:29	Then the Lord l upon the earth,
Ez	10: 1	something that l like a throne.
Dn	8: 3	I l up and saw standing by the river
Dn	10: 5	As I l up, I saw a man dressed
Dn	13:35	As she wept she l up to heaven,
Zec	2: 1	I raised my eyes and l and there
Zec	2: 5	I raised my eyes and l, and there
Lk	22:61	and the Lord turned and l at Peter;
1 Jn	1: 1	what we l upon and touched
Rev	5:11	I l again and heard the voices
Rev	6: 2	I l, and there was a white horse,
Rev	14: 1	I l and there was the Lamb standing

LOOKING → LOOK
Mk	1:37	him said, "Everyone is l for you."
Mk	8:24	L up he replied, "I see people l like
Lk	2:49	to them, "Why were you l for me?
Acts	1:11	why are you standing there l
Phil	2: 4	each l out not for his own interests,
Heb	11:26	for he was l to the recompense.
1 Pt	5: 8	prowling around like a roaring lion l

LOOKS → LOOK
1 Sm	16: 7	The LORD l into the heart.
Ps	14: 2	The LORD l down from heaven
Ps	33:13	From heaven the LORD l down
Sir	11: 2	Do not praise anyone for good l;
Mt	5:28	everyone who l at a woman
Lk	9:62	l to what was left behind is fit

LOOSE

Mt	16:19	and whatever you l on earth shall be
Mt	18:18	and whatever you l on earth shall be

LORD → LORD'S, LORDS

Gn	18:27	I am presuming to speak to my L,
Gn	45: 8	to Pharaoh, l of all his household,
Ex	4:10	said to the LORD, "If you please, my L,
Nm	12:11	he said to Moses, "Ah, my l!
Nm	16:13	that now you must also l it over us?
Dt	10:17	is the God of gods, the L of lords,
Tb	4:19	At all times bless the L, your God,
Tb	4:19	it is the L who gives all good things.
Jdt	6: 4	Nebuchadnezzar, l of all the earth.
Ps	16: 2	I say to the LORD, you are my L,
Ps	35:23	in my cause, my God and my L.
Ps	38:23	to help me, my L and my salvation!
Ps	40:18	and poor, my L keeps me in mind.
Ps	54: 6	as my helper; the L sustains my life.
Ps	57:10	praise you among the peoples, L;
Ps	62:13	so too, my L, does mercy, For you
Ps	73:28	to make the L GOD my refuge.
Ps	86: 5	L, you are good and forgiving,
Ps	86: 8	among the gods can equal you, O L;
Ps	97: 5	before the L of all the earth.
Ps	110: 1	The LORD says to my l: "Sit at my
Ps	110: 5	At your right hand is the L,
Ps	130: 3	If you, LORD, keep account of sins, L,
Ps	135: 5	that our L is greater than all gods.
Ps	136: 3	Praise the L of lords; for his mercy
Ps	147: 5	Great is our L, vast in power,
Is	6: 1	I saw the L seated on a high
Is	7:14	Therefore the L himself will give
Is	25: 8	The L GOD will wipe away
Is	40:10	comes with power the L GOD,
Is	49:14	my L has forgotten me."
Is	61: 1	The spirit of the L GOD is
Jer	2:19	oracle of the L, the GOD of hosts.
Jer	46:10	Today belongs to the L GOD
Ez	4:14	"Oh no, L GOD," I protested.
Dn	2:47	is the God of gods and L of kings
Dn	3:57	Bless the L, all you works of the L,
Dn	5:23	you have rebelled against the L
Dn	9: 3	I turned to the L God, to seek help,
Dn	9: 7	Justice, O L, is on your side;
Dn	9: 9	But to the L, our God,
Dn	9:19	L, hear! L, pardon! L, be attentive
Am	8:11	oracle of the L GOD—when I will
Am	9: 5	The L GOD of hosts, Who melts
Zep	1: 7	in the presence of the L GOD!
Mt	1:20	the angel of the L appeared to him
Mt	3: 3	'Prepare the way of the L,
Mt	4: 7	'You shall not put the L, your God,
Mt	4:10	'The L, your God, shall you worship
Mt	7:22	'L, L, did we not prophesy in your
Mt	12: 8	Son of Man is L of the sabbath."
Mt	20:25	rulers of the Gentiles l it over them,
Mt	21: 9	he who comes in the name of the L;
Mt	22:37	"You shall love the L, your God,
Mt	22:44	'The L said to my l, "Sit at my right
Mt	23:39	comes in the name of the L.' "
Mk	1: 3	'Prepare the way of the L,
Mk	5:19	all that the L in his pity has done
Mk	12:29	The L our God is L alone!
Mk	12:30	You shall love the L your God
Mk	12:11	by the L has this been done, and it is
Mk	12:37	David himself calls him 'l';
Lk	1:11	the angel of the L appeared to him,
Lk	1:32	the L God will give him the throne
Lk	1:46	proclaims the greatness of the L;
Lk	2: 9	The angel of the L appeared to them
Lk	2: 9	glory of the L shone around them,
Lk	2:11	born for you who is Messiah and L.
Lk	4:18	"The Spirit of the L is upon me,
Lk	4:19	a year acceptable to the L."
Lk	5:12	with him, and said, "L, if you wish,
Lk	5:17	the power of the L was with him

Lk	6: 5	Son of Man is l of the sabbath."
Lk	6:46	"Why do you call me, 'L, L,'
Lk	10:21	Father, L of heaven and earth,
Lk	10:27	"You shall love the L, your God,
Lk	10:39	named Mary [who] sat beside the L
Lk	19:38	who comes in the name of the L.
Lk	24:34	"The L has truly been raised
Jn	1:23	straight the way of the L," '
Jn	9:38	He said, "I do believe, L," and he
Jn	20:18	"I have seen the L," and what he
Jn	20:28	said to him, "My L and my God!"
Jn	21:17	and he said to him, "L, you know
Acts	2:21	who calls on the name of the L.'
Acts	2:34	'The L said to my L, "Sit at my
Acts	2:36	that God has made him both L
Acts	4:26	gathered together against the L
Acts	5:19	the angel of the L opened the doors
Acts	7:59	he called out, "L Jesus, receive my
Acts	8:16	baptized in the name of the L Jesus.
Acts	9:31	up and walked in the fear of the L,
Acts	10:36	Jesus Christ, who is L of all,
Acts	11:23	remain faithful to the L in firmness
Acts	16:31	"Believe in the L Jesus and you
Acts	22:10	The L answered me, 'Get up and go
Rom	4:24	the one who raised Jesus our L
Rom	5: 1	God through our L Jesus Christ,
Rom	6:23	is eternal life in Christ Jesus our L.
Rom	8:39	love of God in Christ Jesus our L.
Rom	10: 9	with your mouth that Jesus is L
Rom	10:12	the same L is L of all, enriching all
Rom	10:13	the name of the L will be saved."
Rom	12:11	zeal, be fervent in spirit, serve the L.
Rom	13:14	But put on the L Jesus Christ,
Rom	14: 4	for the L is able to make him stand.
Rom	14: 8	For if we live, we live for the L,
Rom	14: 8	and if we die, we die for the L;
Rom	14: 9	that he might be L of both the dead
1 Cor	1:31	boasts, should boast in the L."
1 Cor	2: 8	they would not have crucified the L
1 Cor	2:16	"who has known the mind of the L,
1 Cor	3: 5	just as the L assigned each one.
1 Cor	4: 4	the one who judges me is the L.
1 Cor	6:13	but for the L, and the L is for the body;
1 Cor	6:14	God raised the L and will also raise
1 Cor	7:10	this instruction (not I, but the L):
1 Cor	7:12	To the rest I say (not the L):
1 Cor	7:25	have no commandment from the L,
1 Cor	7:32	is anxious about the things of the L, how he may please the L.
1 Cor	7:39	wishes, provided that it be in the L.
1 Cor	8: 6	we exist, and one L, Jesus Christ,
1 Cor	10:21	You cannot drink the cup of the L
1 Cor	10:21	cannot partake of the table of the L
1 Cor	11:23	For I received from the L what I
1 Cor	11:23	that the L Jesus, on the night he was
1 Cor	11:27	cup of the L unworthily will have
1 Cor	11:27	for the body and blood of the L.
1 Cor	12: 3	"Jesus is L," except by the holy
1 Cor	15:57	victory through our L Jesus Christ.
1 Cor	15:58	fully devoted to the work of the L,
1 Cor	15:58	in the L your labor is not in vain.
1 Cor	16:22	If anyone does not love the L,
2 Cor	1:24	Not that we l it over your faith;
2 Cor	2:12	a door was opened for me in the L,
2 Cor	3:17	Now the L is the Spirit, and where the Spirit of the L is,
2 Cor	4: 5	ourselves but Jesus Christ as L,
2 Cor	5: 8	the body and go home to the L.
2 Cor	8: 5	they gave themselves first to the L
2 Cor	10:17	boasts, should boast in the L."
2 Cor	10:18	the one whom the L recommends.
2 Cor	13:10	authority that the L has given me
Gal	6:14	in the cross of our L Jesus Christ,
Eph	2:21	grows into a temple sacred in the L;
Eph	4: 5	one L, one faith, one baptism;
Eph	5: 8	but now you are light in the L.
Eph	5:10	to learn what is pleasing to the L.

Eph	5:19	and playing to the L in your hearts,
Eph	5:22	to their husbands as to the L.
Eph	6: 1	obey your parents [in the L], for this
Eph	6: 8	the L for whatever good he does,
Eph	6:10	draw your strength from the L
Phil	2:11	confess that Jesus Christ is L,
Phil	3: 1	my brothers, rejoice in the L.
Phil	3: 8	good of knowing Christ Jesus my L.
Phil	4: 1	in this way stand firm in the L,
Phil	4: 4	Rejoice in the L always. I shall say
Phil	4: 5	be known to all. The L is near.
Col	1:10	to live in a manner worthy of the L,
Col	2: 6	as you received Christ Jesus the L,
Col	3:13	as the L has forgiven you, so must
Col	3:17	in the name of the L Jesus,
Col	3:18	your husbands, as is proper in the L.
Col	3:20	for this is pleasing to the L.
Col	3:24	receive from the L the due payment
Col	3:24	be slaves of the L Christ.
Col	4:17	that you received in the L."
1 Thes	1: 6	became imitators of us and of the L,
1 Thes	3: 8	now live, if you stand firm in the L.
1 Thes	3:12	and may the L make you increase
1 Thes	4: 1	and exhort you in the L Jesus that,
1 Thes	4: 6	for the L is an avenger in all these
1 Thes	4:15	are left until the coming of the L,
1 Thes	4:17	the clouds to meet the L in the air.
1 Thes	4:17	Thus we shall always be with the L.
1 Thes	5: 2	day of the L will come like a thief
1 Thes	5:23	the coming of our L Jesus Christ.
2 Thes	1: 7	at the revelation of the L Jesus
2 Thes	2: 1	to the coming of our L Jesus Christ
2 Thes	2: 8	whom the L [Jesus] will kill
2 Thes	3: 3	But the L is faithful;
2 Thes	3: 5	May the L direct your hearts
1 Tm	1:14	grace of our L has been abundant,
1 Tm	6:14	the appearance of our L Jesus Christ
1 Tm	6:15	the King of kings and L of lords,
2 Tm	1: 8	ashamed of your testimony to our L,
2 Tm	2:19	"The L knows those who are his";
2 Tm	2:19	upon the name of the L avoid evil."
2 Tm	4: 8	me, which the L, the just judge,
2 Tm	4:17	But the L stood by me and gave me
Phlm	1:25	The grace of the L Jesus Christ be
Heb	1:10	O L, you established the earth,
Heb	8: 2	and of the true tabernacle that the L,
Heb	8:11	'Know the L,' for all shall know
Heb	10:30	"The L will judge his people."
Heb	12: 6	for whom the L loves,
Heb	12:14	without which no one will see the L.
Heb	13: 6	"The L is my helper, [and] I will
Jas	1: 7	he will receive anything from the L,
Jas	3: 9	With it we bless the L and Father,
Jas	4:10	Humble yourselves before the L
Jas	5:11	because "the L is compassionate
Jas	5:15	person, and the L will raise him up.
1 Pt	1:25	the word of the L remains forever."
1 Pt	2: 3	you have tasted that the L is good.
1 Pt	3:12	face of the L is against evildoers."
1 Pt	3:15	sanctify Christ as L in your hearts.
2 Pt	1:11	into the eternal kingdom of our L
2 Pt	1:16	and coming of our L Jesus Christ,
2 Pt	2: 9	then the L knows how to rescue
2 Pt	3: 9	The L does not delay his promise,
2 Pt	3:10	day of the L will come like a thief,
2 Pt	3:18	and in the knowledge of our L
Jude	1: 4	who deny our only Master and L,
Jude	1:14	the L has come with his countless
Rev	4: 8	holy is the L God almighty,
Rev	11: 8	where indeed their L was crucified.
Rev	11:15	of the world now belongs to our L
Rev	11:17	give thanks to you, L God almighty,
Rev	14:13	who die in the L from now on."
Rev	15: 4	Who will not fear you, L, or glorify
Rev	17:14	for he is L of lords and king
Rev	19: 6	The L has established his reign,
Rev	19:16	"King of kings and L of lords."
Rev	21:22	for its temple is the L God almighty
Rev	22: 5	for the L God shall give them light,
Rev	22:20	Amen! Come, L Jesus!

*LORD → *GOD, *LORD'S [This is the proper name of God, *Yahweh*, and is LORD in the NAB]

Gn	2: 4	When the L God made the earth
Gn	2: 7	the L God formed the man
Gn	2:16	The L God gave the man this
Gn	2:22	The L God then built the rib
Gn	3: 9	The L God then called to the man
Gn	3:13	The L God then asked the woman:
Gn	3:14	Then the L God said to the snake:
Gn	3:23	The L God therefore banished him
Gn	4: 4	The L looked with favor on Abel
Gn	4:15	So the L put a mark on Cain,
Gn	4:26	began to invoke the L by name.
Gn	6: 8	But Noah found favor with the L.
Gn	8:20	Then Noah built an altar to the L,
Gn	10: 9	mighty hunter in the eyes of the L;
Gn	11: 9	because there the L confused
Gn	12: 1	The L said to Abram:
Gn	12: 7	The L appeared to Abram and said:
Gn	13: 4	and there Abram invoked the L
Gn	15: 6	Abram put his faith in the L,
Gn	15:18	On that day the L made a covenant
Gn	17: 1	the L appeared to Abram and said:
Gn	18: 1	The L appeared to Abraham
Gn	18:14	too marvelous for the L to do?
Gn	18:19	way of the L by doing what is right
Gn	19:14	"the L is about to destroy
Gn	21: 1	The L took note of Sarah as he had
Gn	22:14	the mountain the L will provide."
Gn	24: 1	and the L had blessed him in every
Gn	25:21	Isaac entreated the L on behalf
Gn	25:21	The L heard his entreaty, and his
Gn	26: 2	The L appeared to him and said:
Gn	26:25	there and invoked the L by name.
Gn	28:16	the L is in this place and I did not
Gn	31:49	"May the L keep watch between
Gn	39: 2	The L was with Joseph and he
Gn	39:23	since the L was with him and was
Ex	3: 2	There the angel of the L appeared
Ex	3:15	The L, the God of your ancestors,
Ex	4:11	seeing or blind? Is it not I, the L?
Ex	4:31	the L had observed the Israelites
Ex	5: 2	I do not know the L, and I will not
Ex	6: 2	Moses, and said to him: I am the L.
Ex	6: 7	the L, am your God who has freed
Ex	8: 6	know that there is none like the L,
Ex	9:12	the L hardened Pharaoh's heart,
Ex	9:29	may know that the earth belongs to the L.
Ex	9:30	you do not yet fear the L God."
Ex	10:16	"I have sinned against the L,
Ex	12:27	is the Passover sacrifice for the L,
Ex	12:29	midnight the L struck down every
Ex	13: 9	a strong hand the L brought you
Ex	13:12	dedicate to the L every newborn
Ex	13:12	your animals will belong to the L.
Ex	14:13	see the victory the L will win
Ex	14:30	Thus the L saved Israel on that day
Ex	15: 3	The L is a warrior, L is his name!
Ex	15:11	is like you among the gods, O L?
Ex	15:26	listen closely to the voice of the L,
Ex	15:26	for I, the L, am your healer.
Ex	16:12	know that I, the L, am your God.
Ex	16:29	The L has given you the sabbath.
Ex	17: 7	quarreled there and tested the L,
Ex	17: 7	"Is the L in our midst or not?"
Ex	18:10	"Blessed be the L," he said,
Ex	19: 8	"Everything the L has said,
Ex	19:20	the L summoned Moses to the top
Ex	20: 2	I am the L your God, who brought
Ex	20: 5	For I, the L, am your God.
Ex	20: 7	shall not invoke the name of the L,
Ex	20:10	day is a sabbath of the L your God.

Ex	20:11	in six days the L made the heavens
Ex	20:11	That is why the L has blessed
Ex	23:25	You shall serve the L, your God;
Ex	24: 3	everything that the L has told us."
Ex	28:36	seal engraving, "Sacred to the L."
Ex	30:11	The L also told Moses:
Ex	32:11	O L, should your anger burn
Ex	33: 9	its entrance while the L spoke
Ex	34: 5	The L came down in a cloud
Ex	34: 5	and proclaimed the name, "L."
Ex	34: 6	The L, the L, a God gracious
Ex	34:14	down to any other god, for the L—
Ex	40:34	glory of the L filled the tabernacle.
Ex	40:38	of the L was over the tabernacle
Lv	1: 2	an offering of livestock to the L,
Lv	1: 9	a sweet-smelling oblation to the L.
Lv	8:36	that the L had commanded through
Lv	9:23	the glory of the L appeared to all
Lv	19: 2	for I, the L your God, am holy.
Lv	20: 8	I, the L, make you holy.
Lv	20:26	for I, the L, am holy, and I have set
Lv	23:40	you shall make merry before the L,
Lv	24:16	of the L in a curse shall be put
Nm	6:24	The L bless you and keep you!
Nm	8: 5	The L said to Moses:
Nm	10:29	for the L has promised prosperity
Nm	11: 1	bitterly in the hearing of the L;
Nm	14:14	you, L, who directly revealed
Nm	14:18	'The L is slow to anger
Nm	20:13	the Israelites quarreled with the L,
Nm	21: 6	So the L sent among the people
Nm	21:14	the "Book of the Wars of the L":
Nm	22:31	Then the L opened Balaam's eyes,
Nm	22:31	he saw the angel of the L standing
Nm	23:12	"Is it not what the L puts in my
Nm	30: 3	When a man makes a vow to the L
Nm	32:12	have followed the L unreservedly.
Dt	1:21	See, the L, your God, has given
Dt	2: 7	It is now forty years that the L,
Dt	4:29	Yet when you seek the L,
Dt	4:39	that the L is God in the heavens
Dt	5: 6	I am the L your God, who brought
Dt	5: 9	For I, the L, your God,
Dt	5:11	shall not invoke the name of the L,
Dt	5:14	day is a sabbath of the L your God.
Dt	6: 4	The L is our God, the L alone!
Dt	6: 5	you shall love the L, your God,
Dt	6:16	You shall not put the L, your God,
Dt	7: 6	For you are a people holy to the L,
Dt	7: 8	It was because the L loved you
Dt	7: 9	then, that the L, your God, is God:
Dt	8: 5	his son, so the L, your God,
Dt	9:10	The L gave me the two stone
Dt	10:12	Israel, what does the L, your God,
Dt	10:12	to love and serve the L, your God,
Dt	10:17	For the L, your God, is the God
Dt	10:20	The L, your God, shall you fear,
Dt	11: 1	Love the L, your God, therefore,
Dt	11:13	loving and serving the L,
Dt	13: 4	whether you really love the L,
Dt	14: 1	You are children of the L,
Dt	17:15	set over you a king whom the L,
Dt	18: 2	the L himself is their heritage,
Dt	18:15	A prophet like me will the L,
Dt	28: 1	diligently obey the voice of the L,
Dt	28:15	you do not obey the voice of the L,
Dt	28:69	which the L commanded Moses
Dt	30: 4	even from there will the L,
Dt	30: 6	The L, your God, will circumcise
Dt	30: 6	so that you will love the L,
Dt	30:10	you will obey the voice of the L,
Dt	30:10	when you return to the L,
Dt	30:16	obey the commandments of the L,
Dt	30:16	you today, loving the L, your God,
Dt	30:20	by loving the L, your God,
Dt	30:20	the land which the L swore to your
Dt	31: 6	of them, for it is the L, your God,
Jos	1:13	the servant of the L,
Jos	2:11	of you, since the L, your God,
Jos	7:20	have indeed sinned against the L,
Jos	10:14	when the L obeyed the voice
Jos	10:14	for the L fought for Israel.
Jos	21:44	the L gave them peace on every
Jos	22: 5	love the L, your God, follow him
Jos	22:22	"The L is the God of gods.
Jos	22:22	or treachery against the L,
Jos	22:34	among them that the L is God.
Jos	23:11	take great care to love the L,
Jos	24:15	household, we will serve the L."
Jos	24:18	Therefore we also will serve the L,
Jgs	2:12	and abandoned the L, the God
Jgs	2:12	down to them, and provoked the L.
Jgs	3: 9	the Israelites cried out to the L,
Ru	1: 8	May the L show you the same
Ru	4:13	the L enabled her to conceive
1 Sm	1:11	"O L of hosts, if you look
1 Sm	1:19	they worshiped before the L,
1 Sm	1:19	and the L remembered her.
1 Sm	1:28	Now I, in turn, give him to the L;
1 Sm	1:28	he shall be dedicated to the L."
1 Sm	2: 2	There is no Holy One like the L;
1 Sm	2:25	intercede for the sinner with the L;
1 Sm	2:25	but if anyone sins against the L,
1 Sm	2:26	in worth in the estimation of the L
1 Sm	3: 1	was minister to the L under Eli,
1 Sm	3: 1	the word of the L was scarce
1 Sm	3: 8	The L called Samuel again,
1 Sm	3:19	up, and the L was with him,
1 Sm	4: 3	fetch the ark of the L from Shiloh
1 Sm	5: 3	the ground before the ark of the L.
1 Sm	7:12	far as this place the L has been our
1 Sm	10: 1	"The L anoints you ruler over his
1 Sm	11:15	offerings there before the L,
1 Sm	12: 5	"The L is witness against you this
1 Sm	12:18	Samuel called upon the L,
1 Sm	12:18	all the people feared the L
1 Sm	12:22	great name the L will not abandon
1 Sm	12:24	you must fear the L and serve him
1 Sm	13:14	The L has sought out a man
1 Sm	14: 6	Perhaps the L will help us,
1 Sm	14: 6	difficult for the L to grant victory
1 Sm	15:22	"Does the L delight in burnt
1 Sm	15:28	"The L has torn the kingdom
1 Sm	16:13	on, the spirit of the L rushed
1 Sm	17:47	For the battle belongs to the L,
1 Sm	17:45	you in the name of the L of hosts,
2 Sm	6:14	David came dancing before the L
2 Sm	8: 6	The L brought David victory in all
2 Sm	12:13	"I have sinned against the L."
2 Sm	12:13	part, the L has removed your sin.
2 Sm	19:22	He cursed the anointed of the L."
2 Sm	22: 2	O L, my rock, my fortress,
2 Sm	22:29	You are my lamp, O L!
1 Kgs	3: 3	Although Solomon loved the L,
1 Kgs	5:19	a house for the name of the L,
1 Kgs	5:26	The L gave Solomon wisdom as he
1 Kgs	8:11	glory of the L had filled the house of the L.
1 Kgs	8:61	must be wholly devoted to the L,
1 Kgs	10: 9	Blessed be the L, your God,
1 Kgs	10: 9	the L has made you king to carry
1 Kgs	11: 4	heart was not entirely with the L,
1 Kgs	18:21	If the L is God, follow him;
1 Kgs	18:37	Answer me, L! Answer me,
1 Kgs	18:39	"The L is God! The L is God!"
1 Kgs	19:11	on the mountain before the L; the L will pass by.
1 Kgs	19:11	but the L was not in the wind;
1 Kgs	19:11	the L was not in the earthquake;
1 Kgs	22: 5	"Seek the word of the L at once."
2 Kgs	3:18	since the L does not consider this
2 Kgs	13:23	But the L was gracious with Israel

2 Kgs	17:20	So the L rejected the entire people
2 Kgs	18: 6	Hezekiah held fast to the L
2 Kgs	19:31	zeal of the L of hosts shall do this.
2 Kgs	22: 8	of the law in the temple of the L."
2 Kgs	23: 3	presence of the L to follow the L
2 Kgs	23:25	king who turned to the L as he did,
2 Kgs	24: 4	and the L would not forgive.
2 Kgs	25: 9	He burned the house of the L,
1 Chr	10:13	of his treason against the L
1 Chr	11: 9	for the L of hosts was with him.
1 Chr	13: 6	the name "L enthroned
1 Chr	16:11	Rely on the mighty L;
1 Chr	17: 1	of the L is under tentcloth."
1 Chr	17:20	L, there is no one like you, no God
1 Chr	21:24	not take what is yours for the L,
1 Chr	22:11	my son, the L be with you,
1 Chr	25: 7	were trained in singing to the L,
1 Chr	28: 9	for the L searches all hearts
1 Chr	29:11	Yours, L, are greatness and might,
2 Chr	1: 1	on the kingdom, for the L, his God,
2 Chr	2:10	"Because the L loves his people,
2 Chr	6:17	Now, L, God of Israel,
2 Chr	7: 1	the glory of the L filled the house.
2 Chr	7:12	The L appeared to Solomon during
2 Chr	9: 8	you on his throne as king for the L,
2 Chr	13:12	do not fight against the L, the God
2 Chr	14: 5	because the L had given him rest.
2 Chr	15:15	The L was found by them,
2 Chr	16: 9	of the L roam over the whole earth,
2 Chr	17: 9	them the book of the law of the L;
2 Chr	19: 9	in the fear of the L, with fidelity
2 Chr	20:20	Let your faith in the L, your God,
2 Chr	21: 7	the L was unwilling to destroy
2 Chr	26: 5	and as long as he sought the L,
2 Chr	30: 9	The L, your God, is gracious
2 Chr	32: 8	flesh, but we have the L, our God,
2 Chr	33:13	The L let himself be won over:
2 Chr	33:13	knew that the L is indeed God.
2 Chr	36:22	the L roused the spirit of Cyrus,
Ezr	3:10	to praise the L in the manner laid
Ezr	7: 6	because the hand of the L, his God,
Ezr	7:10	practice of the law of the L
Neh	4: 8	Keep in mind the L, who is great
Neh	8: 1	which the L had commanded
Neh	8:10	for today is holy to our L.
Neh	8:10	in the L is your strength!"
Neh	9: 6	"You are the L, you alone;
Jb	1: 6	to present themselves before the L,
Jb	1:21	The L gave and the L has taken
Jb	1:21	blessed be the name of the L!"
Jb	38: 1	Then the L answered Job
Jb	42:12	Thus the L blessed the later days
Ps	1: 2	Rather, the law of the L is his joy;
Ps	2: 2	princes plot together against the L
Ps	3: 9	Salvation is from the L!
Ps	4: 7	L, show us the light of your face!"
Ps	6: 2	not reprove me in your anger, L,
Ps	7: 2	L my God, in you I trusted;
Ps	8:10	O L, our Lord, how awesome is
Ps	9:10	The L is a stronghold
Ps	9:20	Arise, L, let no mortal prevail;
Ps	10:16	The L is king forever;
Ps	11: 5	The L tests the righteous
Ps	12: 7	The promises of the L are sure,
Ps	13: 2	How long, L? Will you utterly
Ps	14: 6	the poor have the L as their refuge.
Ps	15: 4	but honors those who fear the L;
Ps	16: 2	I say to the L, you are my Lord,
Ps	16: 8	I keep the L always before me;
Ps	17: 1	Hear, L, my plea for justice.
Ps	18: 2	I love you, L, my strength,
Ps	18:32	Truly, who is God except the L?
Ps	19: 8	The law of the L is perfect,
Ps	19:15	of my heart before you, L, my rock
Ps	20: 6	The L grant your every petition!
Ps	21:14	Arise, L, in your power!
Ps	23: 1	The L is my shepherd;
Ps	23: 6	the house of the L for endless days.
Ps	24: 3	may go up the mountain of the L?
Ps	25: 4	Make known to me your ways, L;
Ps	25:10	All the paths of the L are mercy
Ps	27: 1	The L is my light and my
Ps	27: 1	The L is my life's refuge;
Ps	27: 4	One thing I ask of the L;
Ps	28: 7	The L is my strength and my
Ps	29: 4	The voice of the L is power;
Ps	29: 4	the voice of the L is splendor.
Ps	30: 5	Sing praise to the L, you faithful;
Ps	31: 6	you will redeem me, L,
Ps	32: 2	to whom the L imputes no guilt,
Ps	33:12	is the nation whose God is the L,
Ps	34: 2	I will bless the L at all times;
Ps	34: 8	the L encamps around those who
Ps	34: 9	Taste and see that the L is good;
Ps	35:10	shall say, "O L, who is like you,
Ps	36: 7	being and beast you sustain, L.
Ps	37: 4	in the L who will give you your
Ps	37: 5	Commit your way to the L;
Ps	38:22	Do not forsake me, O L;
Ps	40: 2	Surely, I wait for the L.
Ps	40:14	Come quickly to help me, L!
Ps	41:11	"But you, L, take note of me
Ps	46: 8	The L of hosts is with us;
Ps	47: 3	For the L, the Most High, is to be
Ps	48: 2	Great is the L and highly praised
Ps	50: 1	the L, has spoken and summoned
Ps	55:23	Cast your care upon the L,
Ps	59: 9	But you, L, laugh at them;
Ps	68: 5	before him whose name is the L.
Ps	69:32	will please the L more than oxen,
Ps	70: 6	help and deliverer. L, do not delay!
Ps	71: 1	In you, L, I take refuge;
Ps	78: 4	The praiseworthy deeds of the L
Ps	81:11	"I am the L your God,
Ps	83:17	shame, till they seek your name, L.
Ps	84:12	For a sun and shield is the L God,
Ps	84:12	The L withholds no good thing
Ps	85: 8	Show us, L, your mercy;
Ps	86:11	Teach me, L, your way that I may
Ps	88: 2	L, the God of my salvation, I call
Ps	89: 7	Who in the skies ranks with the L?
Ps	89: 7	Who is like the L among the sons
Ps	91: 9	Because you have the L for your
Ps	92: 2	It is good to give thanks to the L,
Ps	92: 5	For you make me jubilant, L;
Ps	93: 1	The L is king, robed with majesty;
Ps	94: 1	L, avenging God, avenging God,
Ps	94:12	the one whom you guide, L,
Ps	95: 3	For the L is the great God,
Ps	96: 1	Sing to the L a new song;
Ps	96: 5	idols, but the L made the heavens.
Ps	97: 1	The L is king; let the earth rejoice;
Ps	97:10	You who love the L, hate evil,
Ps	98: 2	The L has made his victory known;
Ps	99: 1	The L is king, the peoples tremble;
Ps	100: 2	serve the L with gladness;
Ps	101: 1	to you, L, I sing praise.
Ps	102:13	But you, L, are enthroned forever;
Ps	103: 1	Bless the L, my soul; all my being,
Ps	103: 8	Merciful and gracious is the L,
Ps	104:24	How varied are your works, L!
Ps	104:33	I will sing to the L all my life;
Ps	105: 4	Seek out the L and his might;
Ps	106:47	Save us, L, our God;
Ps	107: 8	Let them thank the L for his
Ps	108: 4	praise you among the peoples, L;
Ps	109:26	Help me, L, my God; save me
Ps	110: 1	The L says to my lord: "Sit at my
Ps	110: 4	The L has sworn and will not
Ps	111: 2	Great are the works of the L,
Ps	111: 4	gracious and merciful is the L.
Ps	112: 1	Blessed the man who fears the L,

Ps	113: 1	praise the name of the L.
Ps	113: 5	Who is like the L our God,
Ps	115: 1	Not to us, L, not to us but to your
Ps	115:18	It is we who bless the L, both now
Ps	116: 5	Gracious is the L and righteous;
Ps	116:12	How can I repay the L for all
Ps	116:15	the eyes of the L is the death of his
Ps	117: 1	Praise the L, all you nations!
Ps	118: 7	The L is with me as my helper;
Ps	118:18	The L chastised me harshly,
Ps	118:24	This is the day the L has made;
Ps	118:26	who comes in the name of the L.
Ps	119: 1	who walk by the law of the L.
Ps	119:64	The earth, L, is filled with your
Ps	119:89	Your word, L, stands forever;
Ps	119:126	It is time for the L to act;
Ps	120: 1	The L answered me when I called
Ps	121: 2	My help comes from the L,
Ps	121: 5	The L is your guardian; the L is
Ps	122: 1	"Let us go to the house of the L."
Ps	123: 2	So our eyes are on the L our God,
Ps	124: 1	Had not the L been with us,
Ps	124: 8	Our help is in the name of the L,
Ps	125: 2	the L surrounds his people both
Ps	126: 3	The L has done great things for us;
Ps	127: 1	Unless the L build the house,
Ps	127: 1	Unless the L guard the city, in vain
Ps	128: 1	Blessed are all who fear the L,
Ps	129: 4	But the just L cut me free
Ps	130: 5	I wait for the L, my soul waits
Ps	131: 3	hope in the L, now and forever.
Ps	132: 1	O L, for David all his hardships;
Ps	132:13	Yes, the L has chosen Zion,
Ps	133: 3	There the L has decreed a blessing,
Ps	134: 3	May the L bless you from Zion,
Ps	135: 3	Praise the L, for the L is good!
Ps	135: 6	Whatever the L desires he does
Ps	136: 1	Praise the L, for he is good;
Ps	138: 8	The L is with me to the end.
Ps	139: 1	L, you have probed me, you know
Ps	140: 2	Deliver me, L, from the wicked;
Ps	141: 3	Set a guard, L, before my mouth,
Ps	142: 6	I cry out to you, L, I say, You are
Ps	143: 9	Rescue me, L, from my foes, for I
Ps	144: 3	L, what is man that you take notice
Ps	145: 8	The L is gracious and merciful,
Ps	145: 9	The L is good to all,
Ps	145:17	The L is just in all his ways,
Ps	145:18	The L is near to all who call
Ps	146: 5	whose hope is in the L, his God,
Ps	146: 7	The L sets prisoners free;
Ps	147: 2	The L rebuilds Jerusalem.
Ps	148: 1	Praise the L from the heavens;
Ps	148: 7	Praise the L from the earth,
Ps	149: 4	For the L takes delight in his
Ps	150: 6	that has breath give praise to the L!
Prv	1: 7	Fear of the L is the beginning
Prv	1:29	fear of the L they did not choose.
Prv	2: 5	you understand the fear of the L,
Prv	2: 6	For the L gives wisdom, from his
Prv	3: 5	Trust in the L with all your heart,
Prv	3: 7	fear the L and turn away from evil;
Prv	3: 9	Honor the L with your wealth,
Prv	3:12	For whom the L loves he reproves,
Prv	3:19	The L by wisdom founded
Prv	6:16	There are six things the L hates,
Prv	8:13	[The fear of the L is hatred]
Prv	8:35	life, and wins favor from the L;
Prv	9:10	of wisdom is fear of the L,
Prv	10:27	Fear of the L prolongs life,
Prv	11:20	heart are an abomination to the L,
Prv	12: 2	person wins favor from the L,
Prv	12:22	lips are an abomination to the L,
Prv	14: 2	who walk uprightly fear the L,
Prv	14:26	fear of the L is a strong defense,
Prv	14:27	The fear of the L is a fountain
Prv	15: 3	The eyes of the L are in every
Prv	15:16	fear of the L than a great fortune
Prv	15:29	The L is far from the wicked,
Prv	15:33	The fear of the L is training
Prv	16: 1	the L comes the tongue's response.
Prv	16: 2	the measurer of motives is the L.
Prv	16: 3	Entrust your works to the L,
Prv	16: 9	the way, but the L directs the steps.
Prv	17: 3	but the tester of hearts is the L.
Prv	18:10	name of the L is a strong tower;
Prv	18:22	a favor granted by the L.
Prv	19:14	but a prudent wife is from the L.
Prv	19:17	cares for the poor lends to the L,
Prv	19:23	The fear of the L leads to life;
Prv	20:12	the L has made them both.
Prv	20:22	Wait for the L, who will help you.
Prv	20:24	Our steps are from the L;
Prv	21: 2	but it is the L who weighs hearts.
Prv	21: 3	acceptable to the L than sacrifice.
Prv	21:30	no counsel prevail against the L.
Prv	22: 2	the L is the maker of them all.
Prv	22:19	That your trust may be in the L,
Prv	23:17	only those who always fear the L;
Prv	24:21	My son, fear the L and the king;
Prv	25:22	and the L will vindicate you.
Prv	28: 5	seek the L understand everything.
Prv	29:25	the one who trusts in the L is safe.
Prv	31:30	the woman who fears the L is to be
Sir	4:28	and the L will do battle for you.
Is	1: 4	They have forsaken the L,
Is	1:18	let us set things right, says the L:
Is	2: 3	the word of the L from Jerusalem.
Is	2:11	and the L alone will be exalted,
Is	3:13	The L rises to accuse, stands to try
Is	4: 2	The branch of the L will be beauty
Is	5: 7	of the L of hosts is the house
Is	5:16	the L of hosts shall be exalted
Is	6: 3	holy, holy is the L of hosts!
Is	7:11	Ask for a sign from the L,
Is	9: 6	zeal of the L of hosts will do this!
Is	11: 2	The spirit of the L shall rest
Is	11: 9	be filled with knowledge of the L,
Is	12: 2	For the L is my strength and my
Is	13: 9	the day of the L comes, cruel,
Is	24: 1	The L is about to empty the earth
Is	25: 1	O L, you are my God, I extol you,
Is	26: 4	Trust in the L forever! For the L
Is	26: 8	The course of your judgments, L,
Is	26:13	L, our God, lords other than you
Is	27: 3	I, the L, am its keeper, I water it
Is	28: 5	On that day the L of hosts will be
Is	29: 6	shall be visited by the L of hosts,
Is	29:19	lowly shall again find joy in the L,
Is	30:18	the L is waiting to be gracious
Is	30:18	For the L is a God of justice;
Is	30:26	the day the L binds up the wounds
Is	33: 2	L, be gracious to us; for you we
Is	33: 6	is the fear of the L, her treasure.
Is	33:22	For the L is our judge, the L is our lawgiver, the L is our king;
Is	34: 2	The L is angry with all the nations,
Is	35: 2	They will see the glory of the L,
Is	35:10	the ransomed of the L shall return,
Is	37:15	Hezekiah prayed to the L:
Is	38: 7	from the L that the L will carry
Is	40: 3	prepare the way of the L!
Is	40: 5	glory of the L shall be revealed,
Is	40:27	"My way is hidden from the L,
Is	40:28	The L is God from of old,
Is	40:31	in the L will renew their strength,
Is	41:14	oracle of the L; the Holy One
Is	41:20	the hand of the L has done this,
Is	42: 8	I am the L, L is my name;
Is	42:10	Sing to the L a new song,
Is	43: 3	For I, the L, am your God,
Is	43:11	I, I am the L; there is no savior

Is	44: 6	king, its redeemer, the L of hosts:
Is	44:23	For the L has redeemed Jacob,
Is	45: 5	I am the L, there is no other,
Is	45: 7	I, the L, do all these things.
Is	45:17	Israel has been saved by the L,
Is	49:14	said, "The L has forsaken me;
Is	51: 1	pursue justice, who seek the L;
Is	51:11	Those whom the L has ransomed
Is	51:15	For I am the L, your God,
Is	51:15	the L of hosts by name.
Is	52:10	The L has bared his holy arm
Is	53: 1	the arm of the L been revealed?
Is	53: 6	the L laid upon him the guilt of us
Is	54: 5	the L of hosts is his name,
Is	55: 6	Seek the L while he may be found,
Is	55: 7	them turn to the L to find mercy;
Is	56: 6	who join themselves to the L,
Is	56: 6	To love the name of the L,
Is	58: 5	a fast, a day acceptable to the L?
Is	58:11	Then the L will guide you always
Is	60: 2	Upon you the L will dawn,
Is	60:19	the L will be your light forever,
Is	61: 1	because the L has anointed me;
Is	61: 3	planting of the L to show his glory.
Is	61: 8	For I, the L, love justice, I hate
Is	62: 4	For the L delights in you, and your
Is	63: 7	loving deeds of the L I will recall,
Is	64: 7	Yet, L, you are our father;
Is	65:23	shall be a people blessed by the L
Is	66:15	For see, the L will come in fire,
Jer	2:19	and bitter is your forsaking the L,
Jer	3:12	oracle of the L—I will not remain
Jer	4: 4	Be circumcised for the L,
Jer	6:10	the word of the L has become
Jer	8: 7	do not know the order of the L.
Jer	9:23	that I, the L, act with fidelity,
Jer	10: 6	No one is like you, L, you are
Jer	10:10	The L is truly God, he is the living
Jer	10:21	The L they have not sought;
Jer	12: 1	O L, if I should dispute with you;
Jer	14:20	We recognize our wickedness, L,
Jer	16:19	L, my strength, my fortress,
Jer	17: 7	are those who trust in the L; the L
Jer	17:10	the L, explore the mind and test
Jer	17:13	O Hope of Israel, L!
Jer	17:13	they have forsaken the L,
Jer	23: 6	"The L our justice."
Jer	24: 7	heart to know me, that I am the L.
Jer	28: 9	prophet whom the L has truly sent
Jer	31:11	The L shall ransom Jacob, he shall
Jer	31:22	The L has created a new thing
Jer	31:34	and relatives, "Know the L!"
Jer	32:27	I am the L, the God of all
Jer	33:16	shall call her: "The L our justice."
Jer	40: 3	because you sinned against the L
Jer	42: 4	whatever the L answers, I will tell
Jer	50: 4	come, to seek the L, their God;
Lam	1: 5	Because the L has afflicted her
Lam	3:24	The L is my portion, I tell myself,
Lam	3:25	The L is good to those who trust
Lam	3:40	our ways, and return to the L!
Ez	1: 3	There the hand of the L came
Ez	1:28	the likeness of the glory of the L.
Ez	3:23	of the L was standing there like
Ez	10: 4	brilliant with the glory of the L.
Ez	10:18	the glory of the L left the threshold
Ez	15: 7	You shall know that I am the L,
Ez	34:24	I, the L, will be their God,
Ez	36:23	shall know that I am the L—
Ez	37: 4	Dry bones, hear the word of the L!
Ez	43: 4	glory of the L entered the temple
Ez	44: 4	of the L filled the LORD's house!
Ez	48:35	of the city is "The L is there."
Dn	9: 2	number of years the L had decreed
Dn	9:14	so the L kept watch over the evil
Dn	9:14	The L, our God, is just in all
Hos	1: 7	I will save them by the L,
Hos	2:15	but me she forgot—oracle of the L.
Hos	2:22	fidelity, and you shall know the L.
Hos	3: 1	Just as the L loves the Israelites,
Hos	3: 5	will turn back and seek the L,
Hos	3: 5	They will come trembling to the L
Hos	4: 1	Hear the word of the L, Israelites,
Hos	4: 1	for the L has a dispute
Hos	6: 1	let us return to the L, For it is he
Hos	6: 3	know, let us strive to know the L;
Hos	10:12	for it is time to seek the L, till he
Hos	12: 6	The L is the God of hosts, the L is
Hos	14: 2	Return, Israel, to the L, your God;
Jl	1:15	For near is the day of the L,
Jl	2:11	How great is the day of the L!
Jl	2:13	and return to the L, your God,
Jl	2:21	for the L has done great things!
Jl	3: 4	Before the day of the L arrives,
Jl	3: 5	name of the L will escape harm.
Jl	4:14	is the day of the L in the Valley
Jl	4:16	The L roars from Zion,
Jl	4:16	but the L will be a shelter for his
Am	1: 2	The L roars from Zion, and raises
Am	4:13	the earth, the L, the God of hosts,
Am	5: 6	Seek the L, that you may live,
Am	5:18	who yearn for the day of the L!
Am	5:18	What will the day of the L mean
Am	7:15	flock, and the L said to me, 'Go,
Am	8:11	but for hearing the word of the L.
Ob	1:15	day of the L against all the nations!
Jon	1: 3	flee to Tarshish, away from the L.
Jon	2:10	deliverance is from the L.
Mi	4: 2	the word of the L from Jerusalem.
Mi	5: 3	shepherd by the strength of the L,
Mi	6: 2	the L has a case against his people;
Mi	6: 8	and what the L requires of you:
Mi	7: 7	I will look to the L, I will wait
Na	1: 2	jealous and avenging God is the L,
Na	1: 3	The L is slow to anger, yet great
Na	1: 3	the L will not leave the guilty
Hb	1:12	L, you have appointed them
Hb	2:20	But the L is in his holy temple;
Zep	1: 7	for near is the day of the L, Yes,
Zep	1:14	Near is the great day of the L,
Zep	3:17	The L, your God, is in your midst,
Hg	1:12	the people obeyed the L their God,
Hg	1:12	thus the people feared the L.
Zec	1: 2	The L was very angry with your
Zec	1:17	the L will again comfort Zion,
Zec	3: 1	standing before the angel of the L,
Zec	3: 2	And the angel of the L said
Zec	3: 2	"May the L rebuke you,
Zec	6:12	he will build the temple of the L.
Zec	8:21	go to implore the favor of the L and to seek the L of hosts.
Zec	9:16	the L their God will save them:
Zec	14: 5	Then the L, my God, will come,
Zec	14: 7	it is known to the L—not day
Zec	14: 9	The L will be king over the whole
Zec	14: 9	that day the L will be the only one,
Zec	14:20	"Holy to the L" will be written
Mal	1: 2	I love you, says the L; but you say,
Mal	3: 6	For I, the L, do not change,
Mal	3:23	Before the day of the L comes,

LORD'S → LORD

Sir	11:17	The L gift remains with the devout;
Acts	21:14	rest, saying, "The L will be done."
Rom	14: 8	whether we live or die, we are the L.
1 Cor	10:26	earth and its fullness are the L."
1 Cor	11:20	then, it is not to eat the L supper,
1 Pt	2:13	human institution for the L sake,
Rev	1:10	was caught up in spirit on the L day

*LORD'S → *LORD [This is the proper name of God, *Yahweh*, and is LORD's in the NAB]

Nm	11:23	Is this beyond the L reach?
Dt	32: 9	But the L portion was his people;
1 Sm	24:11	master, for he is the L anointed.'
2 Sm	1:16	'I put the L anointed to death.'"
2 Sm	22:31	the L promise is tried and true;
Ps	11: 4	the L throne is in heaven.
Ps	24: 1	The earth is the L and all it holds,
Is	2: 2	the L house shall be established as
Is	53:10	the L will to crush him with pain.
Jer	13:17	will run with tears for the L flock,
Lam	3:26	to hope in silence for the L deliverance.
Ob	1:21	and the kingship shall be the L.
Hb	2:16	the L right hand shall come around
Zep	2: 3	sheltered on the day of the L anger.
Mal	1:12	saying that the L table is defiled,

LORDS → LORD

Dt	10:17	gods, the Lord of l, the great God,
Ps	136: 3	Praise the Lord of l; for his mercy
Is	26:13	God, l other than you have ruled us;
1 Cor	8: 5	sure, many "gods" and many "l"),
1 Tm	6:15	the King of kings and Lord of l,
Rev	17:14	for he is Lord of l and king of kings,
Rev	19:16	"King of kings and Lord of l."

LOSE → LOSES, LOSS, LOST

Mk	8:35	wishes to save his life will l it,
Lk	9:25	for one to gain the whole world yet l
Jn	6:39	I should not l anything of what he
Heb	12: 3	may not grow weary and l heart.
Heb	12: 5	or l heart when reproved by him;
2 Jn	1: 8	that you do not l what we worked

LOSES → LOSE

Jn	12:25	Whoever loves his life l it,

LOSS → LOSE

1 Cor	3:15	is burned up, that one will suffer l;
Phil	3: 8	consider everything as a l because
Phil	3: 8	his sake I have accepted the l of all

LOST → LOSE

Nm	17:27	we are l, we are all l!
Ps	119:176	I have wandered like a l sheep;
Jer	50: 6	L sheep were my people,
Ez	34: 4	or seek the l but ruled them harshly
Ez	34:16	The l I will search out, the strays I
Mt	10: 6	Go rather to the l sheep of the house
Mt	15:24	"I was sent only to the l sheep
Mt	18:14	that one of these little ones be l.
Lk	15: 4	go after the l one until he finds it?
Lk	15: 6	because I have found my l sheep.'
Lk	15: 9	I have found the coin that I l.'
Lk	15:24	he was l, and has been found.'
Lk	19:10	to seek and to save what was l."
Jn	17:12	none of them was l except the son

LOT → LOT'S, LOTS

1. Nephew of Abraham (Gn 11:27; 12:5). Chose to live in Sodom (Gn 13). Rescued from four kings (Gn 14). Rescued from Sodom (Gn 19:1-29; 2 Pt 2:7). Fathered Moab and Ammon by his daughters (Gn 19:30-38).

2. Object cast to make decisions.

Nm	33:54	the land among yourselves by l,
Est	3: 7	or l, was cast in Haman's presence
Est	9:24	or l, for the time of their defeat
Prv	16:33	Into the bag the l is cast,
Prv	18:18	The l puts an end to disputes,
Eccl	3:22	in their work; for this is their l.
Eccl	5:18	so that they receive their l and find
Eccl	9: 3	the worst, that there is one l for all.
Wis	2: 9	for this is our portion, and this our l.
Lk	17:32	Remember the wife of L.
Acts	1:26	and the l fell upon Matthias, and he

LOT'S → LOT

Gn	19:26	But L wife looked back, and she

LOTS → LOT

Jos	18:10	cast l for them before the LORD
1 Sm	14:42	"Cast l between me and my son
1 Chr	25: 8	They cast l for their functions
Est	F: 7	For this purpose he arranged two l:
Ps	22:19	for my clothing they cast l.
Jl	4: 3	For my people they cast l,
Jon	1: 7	let us cast l to discover on whose
Jon	1: 7	So they cast l, and the lot fell
Mt	27:35	divided his garments by casting l;
Acts	1:26	Then they gave l to them,

LOUD → ALOUD

Ex	12:30	and there was l wailing throughout
Ex	19:16	and a very l blast of the shofar,
Prv	27:14	greet their neighbor with a l voice
Mk	15:34	o'clock Jesus cried out in a l voice,
Jn	11:43	he cried out in a l voice, "Lazarus,
Rev	1:10	behind me a voice as l as a trumpet,
Rev	21: 3	I heard a l voice from the throne

LOVE → BELOVED, LOVED, LOVER, LOVERS, LOVES, LOVING

Gn	22: 2	whom you l, and go to the land
Gn	29:20	a few days because of his l for her.
Gn	29:32	now my husband will l me.'"
Ex	20: 6	showing l down to the thousandth generation of those who l me
Lv	19:18	You shall l your neighbor as
Lv	19:34	you shall l the alien as yourself;
Dt	5:10	showing l down to the thousandth generation of those who l me
Dt	6: 5	Therefore, you shall l the LORD,
Dt	7: 9	generation toward those who l him
Dt	7:13	He will l and bless and multiply
Dt	10:12	his ways, to l and serve the LORD,
Dt	10:15	the LORD set his heart to l them.
Dt	11: 1	L the LORD, your God, therefore,
Dt	13: 4	whether you really l the LORD,
Dt	30: 6	so that you will l the LORD,
Jos	22: 5	l the LORD, your God, follow him
Jos	23:11	you, take great care to l the LORD,
Jgs	14:16	You do not l me! You proposed
Jgs	16: 4	that he fell in l with a woman
Jgs	16:15	"How can you say 'I l you'
1 Sm	18:22	you, and all his officers l you.
1 Sm	20:17	And in his l for David,
2 Sm	1:26	More wondrous your l to me than the l of women.
2 Sm	13: 4	said to him, "I am in l with Tamar,
2 Sm	19: 7	you and hating those who l you.
2 Chr	9: 8	In the l your God has for Israel,
2 Chr	19: 2	and l those who hate the LORD?
Neh	1: 5	of mercy with those who l you
Tb	4:13	Therefore, son, l your kindred.
Tb	14: 7	Those who l God sincerely will
1 Mc	4:33	by the sword of those who l you,
2 Mc	6:20	unlawful to taste even for l of life.
Ps	4: 3	Why do you l what is worthless,
Ps	5:12	will rejoice in you who l your name.
Ps	18: 2	I l you, LORD, my strength,
Ps	26: 8	Lord, I l the refuge of your house,
Ps	31:24	L the LORD, all you who are
Ps	45: 1	*maskil* of the Korahites. A l song.
Ps	45: 8	You l justice and hate wrongdoing;
Ps	52: 5	You l evil more than good,
Ps	52: 6	You l all the words that create
Ps	61: 8	send your l and fidelity to preserve
Ps	63: 4	For your l is better than life;
Ps	69:17	me, LORD, in your generous l;
Ps	69:37	those who l God's name will dwell
Ps	85:11	L and truth will meet;
Ps	92: 3	To proclaim your l at daybreak,
Ps	97:10	You who l the LORD, hate evil,
Ps	109: 4	In return for my l they slander me,
Ps	109: 5	me evil for good, hatred for my l.
Ps	116: 1	I l the LORD, who listened to my
Ps	119:47	commandments, which I dearly l.
Ps	119:48	I study your statutes, which I l.

Ps	119:97	How I l your law, Lord! I study it
Ps	119:113	I hate every hypocrite; your law I l.
Ps	119:119	therefore I l your testimonies.
Ps	119:127	Truly I l your commandments more
Ps	119:159	See how I l your precepts, LORD;
Ps	119:163	I hate and abhor; your law I l.
Ps	119:167	I l them very much.
Ps	122: 6	"May those who l you prosper!
Ps	145:20	LORD watches over all who l him,
Prv	1:22	you naive ones, will you l naivete,
Prv	4: 6	l her, and she will safeguard you;
Prv	5:19	whose l you will ever have your fill,
Prv	7:18	Come, let us drink our fill of l, until morning, let us feast on l!
Prv	8:17	Those who l me I also l, and those
Prv	8:21	Granting wealth to those who l me,
Prv	8:36	all who hate me l death."
Prv	9: 8	the wise, and they will l you.
Prv	10:12	disputes, but l covers all offenses.
Prv	15:17	of herbs where l is than a fatted ox
Prv	17:19	Those who l an offense l a fight;
Prv	20:13	Do not l sleep lest you be reduced
Prv	27: 5	Better is an open rebuke than a l
Eccl	3: 8	A time to l, and a time to hate;
Eccl	9: 1	L from hatred mortals cannot tell;
Eccl	9: 6	l and hatred and rivalry have long
Eccl	9: 9	Enjoy life with the wife you l,
Sg	1: 2	for your l is better than wine,
Sg	1: 3	therefore young women l you.
Sg	1: 4	Rightly do they l you!
Sg	2: 4	hall and his glance at me signaled l.
Sg	2: 5	me with apples, for I am sick with l.
Sg	2: 7	awaken, or stir up l until it is ready.
Sg	3: 5	awaken or stir up l until it is ready.
Sg	4:10	How beautiful is your l, my sister,
Sg	4:10	much better is your l than wine,
Sg	5: 8	you tell him? that I am sick with l.
Sg	7:13	There will I give you my l.
Sg	8: 4	awaken or stir up l until it is ready!
Sg	8: 6	For L is strong as Death, longing is
Sg	8: 7	Deep waters cannot quench l,
Sg	8: 7	all the wealth of his house for l,
Wis	1: 1	L righteousness, you who judge
Wis	3: 9	faithful shall abide with him in l:
Wis	6:12	perceived by those who l her,
Wis	6:18	care for discipline is l of her;
Wis	11:24	For you l all things that are
Sir	Pr: 1	to use their l of learning in speech
Sir	2:15	those who l him keep his ways.
Sir	2:16	those who l him are filled with his
Sir	4:12	Those who l her l life;
Sir	4:14	those who l her the Lord loves.
Sir	7:30	With all your strength l your Maker
Sir	34:19	of the Lord are upon those who l him;
Sir	40: 2	but better than either, l of friends.
Is	43: 4	and I l you, I give people in return
Is	54: 8	with enduring l I take pity on you,
Is	54:10	My l shall never fall away from you
Is	61: 8	the LORD, l justice, I hate robbery
Is	63: 9	Because of his l and pity
Is	66:10	because of her, all you who l her;
Jer	31: 3	With age-old l I have loved you;
Ez	16: 8	that you were now old enough for l.
Ez	23:17	came to her, to her l couch;
Dn	9: 4	show mercy toward those who l you
Dn	14:38	not forsaken those who l you."
Hos	3: 1	Go, l a woman who is loved by her
Hos	4:18	they l shame more than their honor.
Hos	9:15	I will l them no longer;
Hos	11: 4	with human cords, with bands of l;
Hos	14: 5	their apostasy, I will l them freely;
Am	4: 5	For so you l to do, Israelites—
Am	5:15	Hate evil and l good, and let justice
Mi	3: 2	who hate what is good, and l evil?
Mi	6: 8	Only to do justice and to l goodness,

Zep	3:17	and renew you in his l, Who will
Zec	8:17	in your heart, nor l a false oath.
Zec	8:19	So l faithfulness and peace!
Mal	1: 2	I l you, says the LORD; but you say, "How do you l us?"
Mt	5:43	'You shall l your neighbor and hate
Mt	5:44	But I say to you, l your enemies,
Mt	5:46	For if you l those who l you,
Mt	6: 5	who l to stand and pray
Mt	6:24	will either hate one and l the other,
Mt	19:19	and 'you shall l your neighbor as
Mt	22:37	said to him, "You shall l the Lord,
Mt	22:39	You shall l your neighbor as
Mt	23: 6	They l places of honor at banquets,
Mt	24:12	the l of many will grow cold.
Mk	12:30	You shall l the Lord your God
Mk	12:31	'You shall l your neighbor as
Mk	12:33	And 'to l him with all your heart,
Mk	12:33	l your neighbor as yourself' is worth
Lk	6:27	you who hear I say, l your enemies,
Lk	6:32	For if you l those who l you,
Lk	6:32	Even sinners l those who l them.
Lk	6:35	l your enemies and do good to them,
Lk	7:42	Which of them will l him more?"
Lk	7:47	hence, she has shown great l.
Lk	10:27	said in reply, "You shall l the Lord,
Lk	11:42	to judgment and to l for God.
Lk	11:43	You l the seat of honor
Lk	16:13	will either hate one and l the other,
Lk	20:46	and l greetings in marketplaces,
Jn	5:42	that you do not have the l of God
Jn	8:42	you would l me, for I came
Jn	11: 3	"Master, the one you l is ill."
Jn	13:34	a new commandment: l one another.
Jn	13:35	if you have l for one another."
Jn	14:15	"If you l me, you will keep my
Jn	14:21	and I will l him and reveal myself
Jn	14:23	and my Father will l him, and we
Jn	14:24	Whoever does not l me does not
Jn	14:31	world must know that I l the Father
Jn	15: 9	so I also l you. Remain in my l.
Jn	15:10	commandments and remain in his l.
Jn	15:12	l one another as I l you.
Jn	15:13	No one has greater l than this, to lay
Jn	15:17	This I command you: l one another.
Jn	15:19	world, the world would l its own;
Jn	17:26	that the l with which you loved me
Jn	21:15	do you l me more than these?"
Jn	21:15	Lord, you know that I l you."
Jn	21:16	son of John, do you l me?"
Jn	21:16	Lord, you know that I l you."
Jn	21:17	son of John, do you l me?"
Jn	21:17	him a third time, "Do you l me?"
Rom	5: 5	because the l of God has been
Rom	5: 8	God proves his l for us in that while
Rom	8:28	work for good for those who l God,
Rom	8:35	separate us from the l of Christ?
Rom	8:39	to separate us from the l of God
Rom	12: 9	Let l be sincere; hate what is evil,
Rom	12:10	l one another with mutual affection;
Rom	13: 8	to anyone, except to l one another;
Rom	13: 9	"You shall l your neighbor as
Rom	13:10	L does no evil to the neighbor;
Rom	13:10	hence, l is the fulfillment of the law.
Rom	14:15	is no longer in accord with l.
Rom	15:30	Christ and by the l of the Spirit,
1 Cor	2: 9	has prepared for those who l him,"
1 Cor	4:21	a rod, or with l and a gentle spirit?
1 Cor	8: 1	inflates with pride, but l builds up.
1 Cor	13: 1	angelic tongues but do not have l,
1 Cor	13: 2	move mountains but do not have l,
1 Cor	13: 3	that I may boast but do not have l,
1 Cor	13: 4	L is patient, l is kind.
1 Cor	13: 4	It is not jealous, [l] is not pompous,
1 Cor	13: 8	L never fails. If there are
1 Cor	13:13	So faith, hope, l remain, these three;
1 Cor	13:13	but the greatest of these is l.

1 Cor	14: 1	Pursue l, but strive eagerly
1 Cor	16:14	every act should be done with l.
1 Cor	16:22	If anyone does not l the Lord,
1 Cor	16:24	My l to all of you in Christ Jesus.
2 Cor	2: 4	might know the abundant l I have
2 Cor	2: 8	urge you to reaffirm your l for him.
2 Cor	5:14	For the l of Christ impels us,
2 Cor	6: 6	in a holy spirit, in unfeigned l,
2 Cor	8: 7	and in the l we have for you,
2 Cor	8: 8	of your l by your concern for others.
2 Cor	8:24	proof before the churches of your l
2 Cor	11:11	Because I do not l you?
2 Cor	12:15	If I l you more, am I to be loved
2 Cor	13:11	the God of l and peace will be
2 Cor	13:13	Lord Jesus Christ and the l of God
Gal	5: 6	but only faith working through l.
Gal	5:13	rather, serve one another through l.
Gal	5:14	"You shall l your neighbor as
Gal	5:22	the fruit of the Spirit is l, joy, peace,
Eph	1: 4	without blemish before him. In l
Eph	1:15	and of your l for all the holy ones,
Eph	2: 4	because of the great l he had for us,
Eph	3:17	that you, rooted and grounded in l,
Eph	3:19	and to know the l of Christ
Eph	4: 2	bearing with one another through l,
Eph	4:15	living the truth in l, we should grow
Eph	4:16	growth and builds itself up in l.
Eph	5: 2	and live in l, as Christ loved us
Eph	5:25	Husbands, l your wives, even as
Eph	5:28	husbands should l their wives as
Eph	5:33	of you should l his wife as himself,
Eph	6:23	and l with faith, from God
Eph	6:24	with all who l our Lord Jesus Christ
Phil	1: 9	that your l may increase ever more
Phil	1:16	The latter act out of l, aware that I
Phil	2: 1	any solace in l, any participation
Phil	2: 2	with the same l, united in heart,
Phil	4: 1	my brothers, whom I l and long for,
Col	1: 4	the l that you have for all the holy
Col	1: 8	also told us of your l in the Spirit.
Col	2: 2	as they are brought together in l,
Col	3:14	And over all these put on l, that is,
Col	3:19	Husbands, l your wives, and avoid
1 Thes	1: 3	labor of l and endurance in hope
1 Thes	3: 6	the good news of your faith and l,
1 Thes	3:12	and abound in l for one another
1 Thes	4: 9	been taught by God to l one another.
1 Thes	5: 8	on the breastplate of faith and l
1 Thes	5:13	them with special l on account
2 Thes	1: 3	the l of every one of you for one
2 Thes	2:10	because they have not accepted the l
2 Thes	3: 5	direct your hearts to the l of God
1 Tm	1: 5	of this instruction is l from a pure
1 Tm	1:14	faith and l that are in Christ Jesus.
1 Tm	2:15	women persevere in faith and l
1 Tm	4:12	in speech, conduct, l, faith,
1 Tm	6:10	For the l of money is the root of all
1 Tm	6:11	devotion, faith, l, patience,
2 Tm	1: 7	but rather of power and l
2 Tm	1:13	faith and l that are in Christ Jesus.
2 Tm	2:22	righteousness, faith, l, and peace,
2 Tm	3:10	faith, patience, l, endurance,
Ti	2: 2	sound in faith, l, and endurance.
Ti	2: 4	younger women to l their husbands
Ti	3:15	Greet those who l us in the faith.
Phlm	1: 5	as I hear of the l and the faith you
Phlm	1: 7	joy and encouragement from your l,
Phlm	1: 9	I rather urge you out of l, being as I
Heb	6:10	the l you have demonstrated for his
Heb	10:24	how to rouse one another to l
Heb	13: 1	Let mutual l continue.
Heb	13: 5	Let your life be free from l
Jas	1:12	that he promised to those who l him.
Jas	2: 5	he promised to those who l him?
Jas	2: 8	"You shall l your neighbor as
1 Pt	1: 8	you have not seen him you l him;

1 Pt	1:22	to the truth for sincere mutual l,
1 Pt	2:17	Give honor to all, l the community,
1 Pt	4: 8	let your l for one another be intense,
1 Pt	4: 8	because l covers a multitude of sins.
2 Pt	1: 7	affection, mutual affection with l.
1 Jn	2: 5	the l of God is truly perfected
1 Jn	2:15	Do not l the world or the things
1 Jn	2:15	the l of the Father is not in him.
1 Jn	3: 1	See what l the Father has bestowed
1 Jn	3:10	anyone who does not l his brother.
1 Jn	3:11	we should l one another,
1 Jn	3:14	to life because we l our brothers.
1 Jn	3:14	Whoever does not l remains
1 Jn	3:16	The way we came to know l was
1 Jn	3:17	how can the l of God remain
1 Jn	3:18	let us l not in word or speech
1 Jn	3:23	l one another just as he commanded
1 Jn	4: 7	Beloved, let us l one another, because l is of God;
1 Jn	4: 8	Whoever is without l does not know God, for God is l.
1 Jn	4: 9	this way the l of God was revealed
1 Jn	4:10	In this is l: not that we have loved
1 Jn	4:11	us, we also must l one another.
1 Jn	4:12	if we l one another, God remains
1 Jn	4:12	his l is brought to perfection in us.
1 Jn	4:16	to believe in the l God has for us.
1 Jn	4:16	God is l, and whoever remains in l
1 Jn	4:17	this is l brought to perfection among
1 Jn	4:18	There is no fear in l, but perfect l drives out fear
1 Jn	4:18	one who fears is not yet perfect in l.
1 Jn	4:19	We l because he first loved us.
1 Jn	4:20	If anyone says, "I l God," but hates
1 Jn	4:20	whoever does not l a brother whom he has seen cannot l God whom he
1 Jn	4:21	loves God must also l his brother.
1 Jn	5: 2	way we know that we l the children of God when we l God
1 Jn	5: 3	For the l of God is this, that we keep
2 Jn	1: 1	to her children whom I l in truth—
2 Jn	1: 3	the Father's Son in truth and l.
2 Jn	1: 5	let us l one another.
2 Jn	1: 6	For this is l, that we walk according
3 Jn	1: 1	the beloved Gaius whom I l in truth.
3 Jn	1: 6	testified to your l before the church.
Jude	1: 2	peace, and l be yours in abundance.
Jude	1:12	are blemishes on your l feasts,
Jude	1:21	Keep yourselves in the l of God
Rev	2: 4	you have lost the l you had at first.
Rev	2:19	"I know your works, your l, faith,
Rev	3:19	Those whom I l, I reprove

LOVED → LOVE

Gn	29:30	also, and he l her more than Leah.
Gn	37: 3	Israel l Joseph best of all his sons,
Gn	37: 4	saw that their father l him best of all
Dt	7: 8	It was because the LORD l you
1 Sm	1: 5	portion to Hannah because he l her,
1 Sm	18: 1	he l him as his very self.
1 Sm	18: 3	because Jonathan l him as his very
1 Sm	18:16	But all Israel and Judah l David,
1 Sm	18:20	Saul's daughter Michal l David.
1 Sm	18:28	his own daughter Michal l David.
1 Sm	20:17	because he l him as he l himself.
2 Sm	12:24	The LORD l him
1 Kgs	3: 3	Although Solomon l the LORD,
1 Kgs	11: 1	King Solomon l many foreign
2 Chr	11:21	Rehoboam l Maacah,
Est	2:17	The king l Esther more than all
Jb	19:19	those whom I l have turned against
Ps	109:17	He l cursing; may it come
Wis	4:10	The one who pleased God was l,
Wis	7:10	Beyond health and beauty I l her,
Wis	8: 2	Her I l and sought after from my
Wis	16:26	children whom you l might learn,
Sir	3:17	you will be l more than a giver
Sir	7:35	for such things you will be l.
Sir	47: 8	With his whole heart he l his Maker
Jer	8: 2	of heaven, which they l and served,

Jer	31: 3	With age-old love I have l you;
Ez	16:37	both those you l and those you
Hos	9:10	as abhorrent as the thing they l.
Hos	11: 1	When Israel was a child I l him,
Mk	10:21	at him, l him and said to him,
Jn	3:16	For God so l the world that he gave
Jn	11: 5	Now Jesus l Martha and her sister
Jn	11:36	the Jews said, "See how he l him."
Jn	13: 1	He l his own in the world and he l them to the end.
Jn	13:23	the one whom Jesus l, was reclining
Jn	13:34	As I have l you, so you also should
Jn	14:21	whoever loves me will be l by my
Jn	14:28	If you l me, you would rejoice that I
Jn	16:27	because you have l me and have
Jn	17:23	that you l them even as you l me.
Jn	17:24	me, because you l me before
Jn	17:26	which you l me may be in them
Jn	19:26	and the disciple there whom he l,
Jn	20: 2	to the other disciple whom Jesus l,
Jn	21: 7	So the disciple whom Jesus l said
Jn	21:20	the disciple following whom Jesus l,
Rom	8:37	through him who l us.
Rom	9:13	"I l Jacob but hated Esau."
2 Cor	12:15	If I love you more, am I to be l less?
Gal	2:20	in the Son of God who has l me
Eph	5: 2	as Christ l us and handed himself
Eph	5:25	even as Christ l the church
2 Thes	2:16	Father, who has l us and given us
Heb	1: 9	You l justice and hated wickedness;
2 Pt	2:15	who l payment for wrongdoing,
1 Jn	4:10	not that we have l God, but that he l us
1 Jn	4:11	if God so l us, we also must love
1 Jn	4:19	We love because he first l us.

LOVELY

Gn	49:21	loose, which brings forth l fawns.
Jdt	8: 7	in appearance and very l to behold.
Ps	84: 2	How l your dwelling, O LORD
Prv	5:19	your l hind, your graceful doe.
Sg	2:14	voice is sweet, and your face is l."
Sg	4: 3	your lips, and your mouth—l!
Jer	6: 2	L and delicate daughter Zion,

LOVER → LOVE

Ps	99: 4	O mighty king, l of justice,
Prv	21:17	The l of pleasure will suffer want;
Sg	2:10	My l speaks and says to me, "Arise,
Sg	5: 2	The sound of my l knocking! "Open to me,
1 Tm	3: 3	not contentious, not a l of money.
Ti	1: 8	but hospitable, a l of goodness,

LOVERS → LOVE

Eccl	5: 9	nor l of wealth with their gain;
Sg	5: 1	Eat, friends; drink! Drink deeply, l!
Wis	15: 6	L of evil things, and worthy of such
Jer	3: 1	played the prostitute with many l,
Jer	4:30	Your l reject you, they seek your
Jer	22:20	Abarim, for all your l are crushed.
Jer	22:22	shepherds, your l shall go into exile.
Jer	30:14	All your l have forgotten you,
Lam	1:19	I cried out to my l, but they failed
Ez	16:33	But you bestowed gifts on all your l,
Ez	16:36	in your prostitution with your l
Ez	16:37	I will now gather together all your l
Ez	23: 5	married to me and lusted after her l,
Ez	23: 9	Therefore I handed her over to her l,
Ez	23:22	I will now stir up your l against you,
Hos	2: 7	"I will go after my l, who give me
Hos	2: 9	If she runs after her l, she will not
Hos	2:12	bare her shame in full view of her l,
Hos	2:14	are the fees my l have given me";
Hos	2:15	her jewelry, and went after her l—
Hos	8: 9	Ephraim bargained for l.
2 Tm	3: 2	be self-centered and l of money,
2 Tm	3: 4	l of pleasure rather than l of God,

LOVES → LOVE

Ru	4:15	is the daughter-in-law who l you.
2 Chr	2:10	"Because the LORD l his people,

2 Mc	15:14	is a man who l his fellow Jews
Ps	11: 7	The LORD is just and l just deeds;
Ps	33: 5	He l justice and right. The earth is
Ps	37:28	For the LORD l justice and does
Ps	87: 2	The LORD l the gates of Zion
Ps	119:140	Your servant l your promise;
Ps	146: 8	the LORD l the righteous.
Prv	3:12	whom the LORD l he reproves,
Prv	12: 1	Whoever l discipline l knowledge,
Prv	13: 1	A wise son l correction,
Prv	13:24	but whoever l will apply discipline.
Prv	15: 9	but he l one who pursues justice.
Prv	16:13	whoever speaks what is right he l.
Prv	22:11	The LORD l the pure of heart;
Prv	29: 3	Whoever l wisdom gives joy to his
Sg	1: 7	you whom my soul l, where you
Sg	3: 1	I sought him whom my soul l—
Sg	3: 2	Let me seek him whom my soul l."
Sg	3: 3	"Him whom my soul l—
Sg	3: 4	when I found him whom my soul l.
Wis	7:28	God l nothing so much as the one
Wis	8: 7	Or if one l righteousness,
Sir	4:14	those who love her the Lord l.
Sir	30: 1	Whoever l a son will chastise him
Is	1:23	Each one of them l a bribe
Hos	3: 1	Just as the LORD l the Israelites,
Hos	12: 8	holds a false balance, he l to extort!
Mal	2:11	place, which he l, and has married
Mt	10:37	"Whoever l father or mother more
Mt	10:37	and whoever l son or daughter more
Lk	7: 5	for he l our nation and he built
Lk	7:47	to whom little is forgiven, l little."
Jn	3:35	The Father l the Son and has given
Jn	5:20	For the Father l his Son and shows
Jn	10:17	This is why the Father l me,
Jn	12:25	Whoever l his life loses it,
Jn	16:27	For the Father himself l you,
Rom	13: 8	the one who l another has fulfilled
1 Cor	8: 3	But if one l God, one is known
2 Cor	9: 7	for God l a cheerful giver.
Eph	5:28	He who l his wife l himself.
Heb	12: 6	for whom the Lord l, he disciplines;
1 Jn	2:10	Whoever l his brother remains
1 Jn	4: 7	everyone who l is begotten by God
1 Jn	5: 1	and everyone who l the father l [also] the one begotten
Rev	1: 5	To him who l us and has freed us

LOVING → LOVE

Dt	11:13	today, l and serving the LORD,
Dt	11:22	I am giving you, l the LORD,
Dt	19: 9	I give you today, l the LORD,
Dt	30:16	am giving you today, l the LORD,
Dt	30:20	by l the LORD, your God,
Wis	7:22	Never harmful, l the good, keen,
Is	56:10	Dreaming, reclining, l their sleep.

LOW → LOWER, LOWERED, LOWEST, LOWING, LOWLY

Jb	22:29	For when they are brought l, you will say,
Is	40: 4	up, every mountain and hill made l;
Lk	3: 5	mountain and hill shall be made l.

LOWER → LOW

Dt	28:43	and higher, while you sink l and l.
Eph	4: 9	descended into the l [regions]
Heb	2: 7	for a little while l than the angels;

LOWERED → LOW

Acts	10:11	l to the ground by its four corners.

LOWEST → LOW

Gn	9:25	The l of slaves shall he be to his
Lk	14:10	and take the l place so

LOWING → LOW

1 Sm	15:14	my ears, the l of oxen that I hear?"

LOWLY → LOW

Jdt	9:11	You are God of the l,
Jb	5:11	He sets up the l on high, and those
Ps	138: 6	cares for the l and knows the proud

Prv   3:34   scoff, he scoffs at, but the l he favors.
Lk   1:52   from their thrones but lifted up the l.
Rom 12:16   be haughty but associate with the l;

LOYAL → LOYALTY
Ps   32: 6   every l person should pray to you in time
Ps   50: 5   "Gather my l ones to me, those who made
Dn   11:32   but those who remain l to their God

LOYALTY → LOYAL
Hos   6: 6   For it is l that I desire, not sacrifice,

LUKE
      Associate of Paul (Col 4:14; 2 Tm 4:11; Phlm 24).

LUKEWARM → WARM
Rev   3:16   because you are l, neither hot nor

LUMP
Rom   9:21   of the same l one vessel for a noble

LUNATIC → LUNATICS
Mt   17:15   for he is a l and suffers severely;

LUNATICS → LUNATIC
Mt   4:24   those who were possessed, l,

LURE
Mt   13:22   and the l of riches choke the word

LUST → LUSTED, LUSTFUL, LUSTS
Sir   23: 6   Let neither gluttony nor l overcome me;
Dn   13: 8   for her walk, they began to l for her.
Mt   5:28   l has already committed adultery

LUSTED → LUST
Ez   23: 5   married to me and l after her lovers,

LUSTFUL → LUST
Sir   19: 2   Wine and women make the heart l,
1 Thes 4: 5   l passion as do the Gentiles who do

LUSTS → LUST
Rom   1:24   impurity through the l of their hearts

LUXURY
Prv   19:10   L is not befitting a fool;
Jas   5: 5   You have lived on earth in l

LUZ → =BETHEL
Gn   28:19   name of the town had been L.
Gn   48: 3   appeared to me at L in the land

LYDDA
Acts 9:32   down to the holy ones living in L.

LYDIA → LYDIA'S
Acts 16:14   them, a woman named L, a dealer

LYDIA'S → LYDIA
Acts 16:40   went to L house where they saw

LYING → LIE
Ru   3: 8   only to find a woman l at his feet.
1 Sm   5: 4   broken off and l on the threshold,
1 Kgs 22:23   the LORD has put a l spirit
Ps   31:19   Strike dumb their l lips,
Ps   120: 2   deliver my soul from l lips,
Prv   6:17   Haughty eyes, a l tongue,
Prv   12:19   lips endure forever, the l tongue,
Prv   12:22   L lips are an abomination
Prv   21: 6   by l is chasing a bubble over deadly
Prv   26:28   The l tongue is its owner's enemy,
Wis   1:11   and a l mouth destroys the soul.
Hos   4: 2   Swearing, l, murder,
Mt   8:14   saw his mother-in-law l in bed
Mk   7:30   she found the child l in bed
Lk   2:12   clothes and l in a manger."
Jn   5: 6   When Jesus saw him l there

LYRE → LYRES
Gn   4:21   the ancestor of all who play the l
Ps   33: 2   on the ten-stringed l offer praise.
Ps   57: 9   Awake, my soul; awake, l and harp!

LYRES → LYRE
1 Chr 15:16   instruments, harps, l, and cymbals,
1 Chr 25: 6   harps and l, serving in the house

Neh   12:27   the music of cymbals, harps, and l.

LYSIAS
1 Mc   3:32   He left L, a noble of royal descent,
Acts 23:26   "Claudius L to his excellency

LYSTRA
Acts 14: 8   At L there was a crippled man,
2 Tm   3:11   and L, persecutions that I endured.

M

MACCABEUS → JUDAS
1 Mc   2: 4   Judas, who was called M;
1 Mc   2:66   And Judas M, a mighty warrior

MACEDONIA
Acts 16: 9   "Come over to M and help us."
Acts 18: 5   and Timothy came down from M,
Acts 20: 3   he decided to return by way of M.

MACHPELAH
Gn   23: 9   he will sell me the cave of M that he
Gn   49:30   the cave in the field of M,
Gn   50:13   him in the cave in the field of M,

MAD → MADMEN, MADNESS
Dt   28:34   until you are driven m by what your
Jer   51: 7   its wine, thus they have gone m.

MADE → MAKE
Gn   1: 7   God m the dome, and it separated
Gn   1:16   God m the two great lights,
Gn   1:25   God m every kind of wild animal,
Gn   1:31   God looked at everything he had m,
Gn   3:21   The LORD God m for the man
Gn   9: 6   of God have human beings been m.
Gn   15:18   day the LORD m a covenant
Gn   24:21   not the LORD had m his journey
Gn   45: 9   God has m me lord of all Egypt;
Ex   7: 1   I have m you a god to Pharaoh,
Ex   20:11   six days the LORD m the heavens
Ex   20:11   the sabbath day and m it holy.
Ex   24: 8   which the LORD has m with you
Ex   36: 8   doing the work m the tabernacle
Ex   37: 1   Bezalel m the ark of acacia wood,
Ex   37:10   The table was m of acacia wood,
Ex   37:17   The menorah was m of pure beaten
Ex   37:25   of incense was m of acacia wood,
Ex   38: 9   The court was m as follows.
Nm   21: 2   then m this vow to the LORD:
Nm   21: 9   Accordingly Moses m a bronze
Dt   1:28   Our men have m our hearts melt
Dt   5: 2   m a covenant with us at Horeb;
Dt   32: 6   the one who m and established you?
Jos   24:25   So Joshua m a covenant
Jgs   11:30   Jephthah m a vow to the LORD.
1 Sm   1:11   and m this vow: "O LORD
1 Sm   15:11   I regret having m Saul king, for he
2 Sm   23: 5   He has m an eternal covenant
1 Kgs 12:28   took counsel, m two calves of gold,
2 Kgs 17:38   The covenant I m with you,
2 Kgs 18: 4   the bronze serpent Moses had m,
2 Kgs 19:15   It is you who m the heavens
2 Chr 2:11   of Israel, who m heaven and earth,
2 Chr 3:10   holy of holies he m two cherubim
2 Chr 4:19   Solomon m all the articles that were
Neh   9: 6   You m the heavens, the highest
Neh   9:10   thus you m for yourself a name even
Tb   8: 6   You m Adam, and you m his wife
1 Mc   4:49   They m new sacred vessels
Jb   31: 1   I m a covenant with my eyes not
Jb   33: 4   For the spirit of God m me,
Ps   8: 6   Yet you have m him little less than
Ps   33: 6   word the heavens were m;
Ps   95: 5   land belong to God, who m them,
Ps   96: 5   but the LORD m the heavens.
Ps   98: 2   The LORD has m his victory
Ps   118:24   This is the day the LORD has m;

Ps	136: 7	Who **m** the great lights, for his
Ps	139:14	you, because I am wonderfully **m**;
Prv	8:26	earth and the fields were not yet **m**,
Eccl	3:11	God has **m** everything appropriate
Eccl	7:13	straight what God has **m** crooked?
Is	43: 7	I formed them, **m** them.
Is	45:12	It was I who **m** the earth and created
Is	66: 2	My hand **m** all these things when all
Jer	10:12	The one who **m** the earth by his
Jer	27: 5	It was I who **m** the earth,
Jer	31:32	It will not be like the covenant I **m**
Jer	33: 2	says the LORD who **m** the earth,
Jer	51:15	He **m** the earth by his power,
Dn	3: 1	had a golden statue **m**, sixty cubits
Am	5: 8	The one who **m** the Pleiades
Jon	1: 9	who **m** the sea and the dry land."
Mk	2:27	them, "The sabbath was **m** for man,
Lk	19:46	you have **m** it a den of thieves.' "
Jn	9: 6	ground and **m** clay with the saliva,
Acts	2:36	that God has **m** him both Lord
Acts	10:15	"What God has **m** clean, you are
Acts	17:24	The God who **m** the world and all
Acts	17:24	in sanctuaries **m** by human hands,
1 Cor	1:20	Has not God **m** the wisdom
2 Cor	5:21	our sake he **m** him to be sin who did
2 Cor	12: 9	power is **m** perfect in weakness."
Eph	2:14	he who **m** both one and broke down
Heb	2: 7	You **m** him for a little while lower
Heb	8: 9	It will not be like the covenant I **m**
Jas	3: 9	it we curse human beings who are **m**
Rev	5:10	You **m** them a kingdom and priests
Rev	14: 7	Worship him who **m** heaven
Rev	19: 7	come, his bride has **m** herself ready.

MADMEN → MAD, MAN

1 Sm	21:16	Do I not have enough **m**, that you

MADNESS → MAD

Dt	28:28	the LORD will strike you with **m**,
Eccl	7:25	is foolishness and folly is **m**.
Eccl	9: 3	and **m** is in their hearts during life;
2 Pt	2:16	and restrained the prophet's **m**.

MAGDALENE

Mt	27:56	Among them were Mary **M**
Mk	16: 1	sabbath was over, Mary **M**, Mary,
Lk	8: 2	called **M**, from whom seven demons

MAGIC → MAGICIAN, MAGICIANS

Acts	8:11	them by his **m** for a long time,

MAGICIAN → MAGIC

Dn	2:10	asked such a thing of any **m**,
Acts	13: 6	they met a **m** named Bar-Jesus who

MAGICIANS → MAGIC

Gn	41: 8	So Pharaoh had all the **m** and sages
Ex	7:11	and they also, the **m** of Egypt,
Ex	7:22	But the Egyptian **m** did the same
Ex	8: 3	the **m** did the same by their magic
Ex	8:14	Though the **m** did the same thing
Ex	9:11	of the boils the **m** could not stand
Ex	9:11	there were boils on the **m** as well as
Dn	2: 2	So he ordered that the **m**,
Dn	5:11	father, made him chief of the **m**,

MAGNIFY

Ps	34: 4	**M** the LORD with me; and let us

MAGOG

Ez	38: 2	face against Gog of the land of **M**,
Ez	39: 6	I will send fire against **M**
Rev	20: 8	Gog and **M**, to gather them

MAHANAIM

Gn	32: 3	So he named that place **M**.
2 Sm	17:24	at **M** while Absalom crossed

MAHER-SHALAL-HASH-BAZ

Is	8: 3	LORD said to me: Name him **M**,

MAHLON

Ru	1: 5	both **M** and Chilion died also,

MAID → MAIDS

Ps	123: 2	Like the eyes of a **m** on the hand
Is	24: 2	servant and master, **M** and mistress,

MAIDS → MAID

1 Sm	25:42	with her five **m** attending her.
Est	2: 9	choosing seven **m** for her
Est	2: 9	her **m** to the best place in the harem.

MAIMED

Mk	9:43	to enter into life **m** than with two

MAJESTIC → MAJESTY

Jb	37: 4	voice roars, his **m** voice thunders;
2 Pt	1:17	came to him from the **m** glory,

MAJESTY → MAJESTIC

Ex	15: 7	In your great **m** you overthrew your
1 Chr	16:27	Splendor and **m** go before him;
1 Chr	29:11	are greatness and might, **m**, victory,
Jb	37:22	surrounding God's awesome **m**!
Jb	40:10	yourself with grandeur and **m**,
Ps	21: 6	**m** and splendor you confer
Ps	45: 4	splendor and **m** ride on triumphant!
Ps	68:35	of God, whose **m** protects Israel,
Ps	93: 1	The LORD is king, robed with **m**;
Ps	104: 1	You are clothed with **m**
Is	2:10	LORD and the splendor of his **m**!
Is	2:19	LORD and the splendor of his **m**,
Is	2:21	LORD and the splendor of his **m**,
Is	24:14	sing for joy in the **m** of the LORD,
Is	26:10	and do not see the **m** of the LORD.
Heb	1: 3	at the right hand of the **M** on high,
Heb	8: 1	of the throne of the **M** in heaven,
2 Pt	1:16	we had been eyewitnesses of his **m**.
Jude	1:25	Jesus Christ our Lord be glory, **m**,

MAKE → MADE, MAKER, MAKES, MAKING, TENTMAKERS

Gn	1:26	Let us **m** human beings in our
Gn	2:18	I will **m** a helper suited to him.
Gn	6:14	**M** yourself an ark of gopherwood,
Gn	11: 4	sky, and so **m** a name for ourselves;
Gn	12: 2	I will **m** of you a great nation, and I
Gn	12: 2	I will **m** your name great,
Gn	13:16	I will **m** your descendants like
Gn	17: 6	I will **m** nations of you;
Gn	21:18	for I will **m** of him a great nation."
Gn	22:17	**m** your descendants as countless as
Gn	24:40	you and **m** your journey successful,
Gn	26: 4	I will **m** your descendants as
Gn	28: 3	bless you and **m** you fertile,
Gn	46: 3	for there I will **m** you a great nation.
Gn	48: 4	'I will **m** you fertile and multiply
Ex	6: 3	I did not **m** myself known to them.
Ex	20:23	nor shall you **m** for yourselves gods
Ex	25: 9	of its furnishings, so you are to **m** it.
Ex	25:10	You shall **m** an ark of acacia wood,
Ex	25:23	shall also **m** a table of acacia wood,
Ex	25:31	You shall **m** a menorah of pure
Ex	25:40	See that you **m** them according
Ex	32: 1	**m** us a god who will go before us;
Ex	32:10	Then I will **m** of you a great nation.
Nm	21: 8	**M** a seraph and mount it on a pole,
Dt	7: 2	**M** no covenant with them and do
Jos	9: 7	can we **m** a covenant with you?"
2 Sm	7: 9	I will **m** your name like
1 Mc	1:11	**m** a covenant with the Gentiles all
Jb	7:17	beings, that you **m** much of them,
Ps	4: 9	you alone, LORD, **m** me secure.
Ps	110: 1	hand, while I **m** your enemies your
Prv	3: 6	and he will **m** straight your paths.
Eccl	5: 3	When you **m** a vow to God,
Sir	2: 6	**m** your ways straight and hope
Is	6:10	**M** the heart of this people sluggish,
Is	40: 3	**M** straight in the wasteland
Is	61: 8	an everlasting covenant I will **m**
Jer	10:11	The gods that did not **m** heaven
Jer	16:20	Can human beings **m** for themselves
Jer	31:31	when I will **m** a new covenant

Jer	32:40	With them I will **m** an everlasting
Ez	34:25	I will **m** a covenant of peace
Ez	37:26	I will **m** a covenant of peace
Hos	2:20	I will **m** a covenant for them
Mt	3: 3	the Lord, **m** straight his paths.' "
Mt	28:19	and **m** disciples of all nations,
Mk	1:17	and I will **m** you fishers of men."
Jn	1:23	desert, "**M** straight the way
Acts	2:35	until I **m** your enemies your
Rom	14: 4	for the Lord is able to **m** him stand.
Heb	1:13	hand until I **m** your enemies your
2 Pt	1: 5	**m** every effort to supplement your
1 Jn	1:10	have not sinned," we **m** him a liar,

MAKER → MAKE

Jb	4:17	be more blameless than their **M**?
Jb	32:22	my **M** would soon take me away.
Jb	35:10	my **M**, who gives songs in the night,
Jb	36: 3	my **m** I will establish what is right.
Ps	149: 2	Let Israel be glad in its **m**,
Prv	14:31	who oppress the poor revile their **M**,
Prv	17: 5	mocks the poor reviles their **M**;
Prv	22: 2	the Lord is the **m** of them all.
Sir	38:15	a sinner before his **M** will be defiant
Is	17: 7	that day people shall turn to their **m**,
Is	29:16	what is made should say of its **m**,
Is	45: 9	anyone who contends with their **M**;
Is	45:11	the Holy One of Israel, his **m**:
Is	51:13	your **m**, who stretched
Is	54: 5	For your husband is your **M**;
Hos	8:14	Israel has forgotten his **m** and has
Hb	2:18	image, that its **m** should carve it?
Hb	2:18	that its very **m** should trust in it,

MAKES → MAKE

Ex	4:11	Who **m** another mute or deaf,
Prv	13:12	Hope deferred **m** the heart sick,
Mk	7:37	He **m** the deaf hear and [the] mute

MAKING → MAKE

Gn	6: 6	the Lord regretted **m** human beings
Eccl	12:12	Of the **m** of many books there is no
Is	66:22	heavens and the new earth which I am **m**
Mt	21:13	but you are **m** it a den of thieves."
Jn	5:18	own father, **m** himself equal to God.
Eph	5:16	**m** the most of the opportunity,
Col	1:20	**m** peace by the blood of his cross

MALACHI
Postexilic prophet (Mal 1:1).

MALE → MALES

Gn	1:27	**m** and female he created them.
Gn	5: 2	he created them **m** and female.
Gn	6:19	into the ark, one **m** and one female ,
Gn	17:10	every **m** among you you shall be
Lv	20:13	If a man lies with a **m** as
Mt	19: 4	the Creator 'made them **m**
Lk	2:23	"Every **m** that opens the womb
Rev	12: 5	She gave birth to a son, a **m** child,

MALES → MALE

Ex	12:48	all his **m** must be circumcised,

MALICE → MALICIOUS

Rom	1:29	of wickedness, evil, greed, and **m**;
1 Cor	5: 8	the yeast of **m** and wickedness,
Eph	4:31	from you, along with all **m**.
Col	3: 8	anger, fury, **m**, slander, and obscene
Ti	3: 3	and pleasures, living in **m** and envy,
1 Pt	2: 1	Rid yourselves of all **m** and all

MALICIOUS → MALICE

Ps	35:11	**M** witnesses rise up, accuse me

MALIGNED

1 Pt	3:16	when you are **m**, those who defame

MAMRE → =HEBRON

Gn	13:18	went on to settle near the oak of **M**,
Gn	25: 9	of Zohar the Hittite, which faces **M**,

MAN → FISHERMEN, HORSEMEN, MADMEN, MAN'S, MEN

Gn	2: 7	the Lord God formed the **m**
Gn	2: 7	and the **m** became a living being.
Gn	2:15	took the **m** and settled him
Gn	2:18	It is not good for the **m** to be alone.
Gn	2:20	The **m** gave names to all the tame
Gn	2:20	to be a helper suited to the **m**.
Gn	2:23	the **m** said: "This one, at last,
Gn	2:23	out of **m** this one has been taken."
Gn	2:25	The **m** and his wife were both
Gn	3: 9	then called to the **m** and asked him:
Gn	3:22	The **m** has become like one of us,
Gn	4: 1	The **m** had intercourse with his wife
Gn	32:25	a **m** wrestled with him until
Lv	20:10	If a **m** commits adultery with his
Lv	20:13	If a **m** lies with a male as
Dt	22: 5	nor shall a **m** put on a woman's
Jgs	8:21	for as a **m** is, so is his strength."
1 Sm	13:14	sought out a **m** after his own heart
Est	6: 7	"For the **m** whom the king wishes
Jb	38: 3	Gird up your loins now, like a **m**;
Jb	40: 7	Gird up your loins now, like a **m**.
Ps	8: 5	What is **m** that you are mindful of him, and a son of **m** that
Ps	22: 7	I am a worm, not a **m**, scorned by men,
Ps	56:12	I do not fear. What can **m** do to me?
Ps	90: 1	A prayer of Moses, the **m** of God.
Prv	30:19	and the way of a **m** with a woman.
Is	53: 3	avoided by men, a **m** of suffering,
Ez	8: 2	was a figure that looked like a **m**.
Dn	7:13	of heaven One like a son of **m**.
Zec	6:12	There is a **m** whose name is
Mt	9: 6	the Son of **M** has authority on earth
Mt	19: 5	this reason a **m** shall leave his father
Mk	2:27	"The sabbath was made for **m**, not **m** for the sabbath.
Mk	9:12	is it written regarding the Son of **M**
Lk	6: 5	them, "The Son of **M** is lord
Jn	3:14	so must the Son of **M** be lifted up,
Jn	9:35	"Do you believe in the Son of **M**?"
Acts	7:56	the Son of **M** standing at the right
1 Cor	7: 1	"It is a good thing for a **m** not
1 Cor	7: 2	immorality every **m** should have his
1 Cor	11: 3	that Christ is the head of every **m**,
1 Cor	11: 7	God, but woman is the glory of **m**.
1 Cor	11:14	that if a **m** wears his hair long it is
1 Cor	13:11	when I became a **m**, I put aside
1 Cor	15:47	The first **m** was from the earth,
1 Cor	15:47	the second **m**, from heaven.
Eph	5:31	this reason a **m** shall leave [his]
Rev	1:13	the lampstands one like a son of **m**,
Rev	14:14	one who looked like a son of **m**,

MAN'S → MAN

Nm	17:17	Write each **m** name on his staff;

MANAGE

1 Tm	3: 4	He must **m** his own household well,
1 Tm	3: 5	know how to **m** his own household,
1 Tm	3:12	only once and must **m** their children
1 Tm	5:14	and **m** a home, so as to give

MANASSEH
1. Firstborn of Joseph (Gn 41:51; 46:20). Blessed by Jacob but not as firstborn (Gn 48). Tribe of blessed (Dt 33:17), numbered (Nm 1:35; 26:34), half allotted land east of Jordan (Nm 32; Jos 13:8-33), half west (Jos 16; Ez 48:4), failed to fully possess (Jos 17:12-13; Jgs 1:27), 12,000 from (Rev 7:6).
2. Son of Hezekiah; king of Judah (2 Kgs 21:1-18; 2 Chr 33:1-20). Judah exiled for his detestable sins (2 Kgs 21:10-15). Repentance (2 Chr 33:12-19).

MANDRAKES

Gn	30:14	and came upon some **m** in the field
Gn	30:14	give me some of your son's **m**."
Sg	7:14	The **m** give forth fragrance,

MANGER

Lk	2:12	clothes and lying in a **m**."

MANIFESTATION
1 Cor 12: 7 each individual the **m** of the Spirit is
2 Thes 2: 8 powerless by the **m** of his coming,

MANNA
Ex   16:31 house of Israel named this food **m**.
Nm   11: 6 to look forward to but this **m**."
Dt   8:16 fed you in the wilderness with **m**,
Jos   5:12 produce of the land, the **m** ceased.
Jos   5:12 No longer was there **m**
Ps   78:24 God rained **m** upon them for food;
Jn   6:49 Your ancestors ate the **m**
Heb   9: 4 were the gold jar containing the **m**,
Rev   2:17 I shall give some of the hidden **m**;

MANOAH
Father of Samson (Jgs 13:2-21; 16:31).

MANTLE
Gn   25:25 his whole body was like a hairy **m**;
Jos   7:21 I saw a beautiful Babylonian **m**,
2 Kgs   2: 8 Elijah took his **m**, rolled it
2 Kgs   2:13 picked up the **m** which had fallen
Zec   13: 4 not put on the hairy **m** to mislead,

MANY
Dt   15: 6 you will lend to **m** nations,
Dt   15: 6 you will rule over **m** nations,
1 Kgs   8: 5 sheep and oxen too **m** to number
1 Kgs   11: 1 Solomon loved **m** foreign women
1 Mc   1:62 But **m** in Israel were determined
Ps   32:10 **M** are the sorrows of the wicked
Ps   106:43 **M** times did he rescue them,
Prv   10:19 Where words are **m**, sin is not
Prv   15:22 they succeed when advisers are **m**.
Prv   31:29 "**M** are the women of proven worth,
Eccl   5: 2 dreams come along with **m** cares,
Eccl   12:12 making of **m** books there is no end,
Sir   27: 1 For the sake of profit **m** sin,
Is   52:15 So shall he startle **m** nations,
Is   53:11 shall justify the **m**, their iniquity he
Is   53:12 Bore the sins of **m**, and interceded
Jer   11:13 as **m** as your cities are your gods,
Dn   9:27 make a firm covenant with the **m**;
Dn   12: 3 those who lead the **m** to justice shall
Mt   6: 7 be heard because of their **m** words.
Mt   10:31 are worth more than **m** sparrows.
Mt   18:21 As **m** as seven times?"
Mt   22:14 **M** are invited, but few are chosen."
Mt   24: 5 For **m** will come in my name,
Mt   24: 5 Messiah,' and they will deceive **m**.
Mt   26:28 on behalf of **m** for the forgiveness
Mk   10:31 But **m** that are first will be last,
Mk   10:45 to give his life as a ransom for **m**."
Lk   2:34 for the fall and rise of **m** in Israel,
Lk   10:41 anxious and worried about **m** things.
Jn   2:23 **m** began to believe in his name
Jn   20:30 Now Jesus did **m** other signs
Jn   21:25 also **m** other things that Jesus did,
Acts   1: 3 to them by **m** proofs after he had
Acts   5:12 **M** signs and wonders were done
Acts   14:22 us to undergo **m** hardships to enter
Rom   5:19 of one the **m** will be made righteous.
Rom   12: 5 though **m**, are one body in Christ
1 Cor   1:26 Not **m** of you were wise by human
1 Cor   1:26 powerful, not **m** were of noble birth.
1 Cor   12:12 a body is one though it has **m** parts,
1 Cor   12:12 the body, though **m**, are one body,
Heb   2:10 in bringing **m** children to glory,
Heb   9:28 once to take away the sins of **m**,
Jas   3: 1 Not **m** of you should become
1 Jn   2:18 so now **m** antichrists have appeared.
2 Jn   1: 7 **M** deceivers have gone
Rev   5:11 **m** angels who surrounded the throne
Rev   19:12 and on his head were **m** diadems.

MAON
1 Sm   23:24 were in the wilderness below **M**,

MARA → =NAOMI
Ru   1:20 Call me **M** ['Bitter'],

MARAH
Ex   15:23 they arrived at **M**, where they could
Ex   15:23 Hence this place was called **M**.

MARCH → MARCHING
Jos   6: 4 the seventh day **m** around the city

MARCHING → MARCH
2 Sm   5:24 you hear the sound of **m** in the tops

MARK → MARKED, MARKS
1. Cousin of Barnabas (Acts 12:12; 15:37-39; Col 4:10; 2 Tm 4:11;
Phlm 24; 1 Pt 5:13), see John.
2. Brand or symbol:
Gn   4:15 So the LORD put a **m** on Cain,
Rev   14: 9 or accepts its **m** on forehead
Rev   16: 2 on those who had the **m** of the beast
Rev   19:20 astray those who had accepted the **m**
Rev   20: 4 its image nor had accepted its **m**

MARKED → MARK
Jer   43:11 with death, those **m** for death; with exile, those **m** for
             exile;
Ez   9: 6 do not touch anyone **m** with the X.

MARKET → MARKETPLACE, MARKETPLACES
1 Cor   10:25 Eat anything sold in the **m**,

MARKETPLACE → MARKET
Lk   7:32 are like children who sit in the **m**
Jn   2:16 making my Father's house a **m**."

MARKETPLACES → MARKET
Mt   23: 7 greetings in **m**, and the salutation

MARKS → MARK
Gal   6:17 for I bear the **m** of Jesus on my

MARRED
Is   52:14 so **m** were his features,

MARRIAGE → MARRY
Sir   23:18 man who dishonors his **m** bed says
Mt   22:30 neither marry nor are given in **m**
Mt   24:38 marrying and giving in **m**,
Heb   13: 4 Let **m** be honored among all and the **m** bed be kept
             undefiled,

MARRIED → MARRY
Dt   24: 5 to bring joy to the wife he has **m**.
Mal   2:11 has **m** a daughter of a foreign god.
Mk   12:23 For all seven had been **m** to her."
Rom   7: 2 Thus a **m** woman is bound by law
1 Cor   7:10 To the **m**, however, I give this
1 Cor   7:33 a **m** man is anxious about the things
1 Tm   3: 2 be irreproachable, **m** only once,
1 Tm   3:12 Deacons may be **m** only once
1 Tm   5: 9 than sixty years old, **m** only once,
Ti   1: 6 a man be blameless, **m** only once,

MARRIES → MARRY
Mt   5:32 and whoever **m** a divorced woman
Mt   19: 9 and **m** another commits adultery."
Mk   10:11 **m** another commits adultery against
Lk   16:18 and **m** another commits adultery,
Lk   16:18 the one who **m** a woman divorced
1 Cor   7:28 an unmarried woman sin if she **m**;
1 Cor   7:38 the one who **m** his virgin does well;

MARROW
Heb   4:12 joints and **m**, and able to discern

MARRY → INTERMARRY, INTERMARRYING, MARRIAGE, MARRIED,
         MARRIES, MARRYING
Mt   19:10 with his wife, it is better not to **m**."
Mt   22:30 resurrection they neither **m** nor are
1 Cor   7: 9 exercise self-control they should **m**, for it is better to **m**
             than to be
1 Cor   7:28 If you **m**, however, you do not sin,
1 Tm   5:14 I would like younger widows to **m**,

MARRYING → MARRY
Neh   13:27 our God by **m** foreign women?"

Mt	24:38	drinking, **m** and giving in marriage,
Lk	17:27	**m** and giving in marriage

MARTHA
Sister of Mary and Lazarus (Lk 10:38-42; Jn 11; 12:2).

MARVELED → MARVELOUS

Jdt	10:19	They **m** at her beauty,
Jdt	11:20	They **m** at her wisdom
2 Thes	1:10	and to be **m** at on that day among all

MARVELOUS → MARVELED, MARVELS

Jb	9:10	things **m** and innumerable.
Jb	42: 3	not understand; things too **m** for me,
Ps	96: 3	among all peoples, his **m** deeds.
Ps	98: 1	LORD, for he has done **m** deeds.

MARVELS → MARVELOUS

Ex	34:10	I will perform **m** never before done

MARY
1. Mother of Jesus (Mt 1:16-25; Lk 1:27-56; 2:1-40). With Jesus at temple (Lk 2:41-52), at the wedding in Cana (Jn 2:1-5), questioning his sanity (Mk 3:21), at the cross (Jn 19:25-27). Among disciples after Ascension (Acts 1:14).
2. Magdalene; former demoniac (Lk 8:2). Helped support Jesus' ministry (Lk 8:1-3). At the cross (Mt 27:56; Mk 15:40; Jn 19:25), burial (Mt 27:61; Mk 15:47). Saw angel after resurrection (Mt 28:1-10; Mk 16:1-9; Lk 24:1-12); also Jesus (Jn 20:1-18).
3. Sister of Martha and Lazarus (Jn 11). Washed Jesus' feet (Jn 12:1-8).
4. Mother of James and Joses; witnessed crucifixion (Mt 27:56; Mk 15:40) and empty tomb (Mk 16:1; Lk 24:10).

MASONS

1 Chr	22:15	workers, stonecutters, **m**, carpenters,
2 Chr	24:12	who hired **m** and carpenters

MASSAH

Ex	17: 7	The place was named **M**
Dt	33: 8	Him you tested at **M**,
Ps	95: 8	as on the day of **M** in the desert.

MASTER → MASTER'S, MASTERS

Gn	24:12	God of my **m** Abraham, let it turn
Ex	21: 5	'I love my **m** and my wife
Sir	23: 1	Father and **M** of my life, do not
Mal	1: 6	his father, and a servant fears his **m**;
Mal	1: 6	And if I am a **m**, where is the fear
Mt	10:24	his teacher, no slave above his **m**.
Mt	24:46	servant whom his **m** on his arrival
Mt	25:21	His **m** said to him, 'Well done,
Mt	25:23	His **m** said to him, 'Well done,
Jn	13:16	slave is greater than his **m** nor any
Jn	15:20	'No slave is greater than his **m**.'
Eph	6: 9	they and you have a **M** in heaven
Col	4: 1	that you too have a **M** in heaven.
2 Pt	2: 1	and even deny the **M** who ransomed

MASTER'S → MASTER

Gn	39: 7	time, his **m** wife looked at him

MASTERS → MASTER

Mt	6:24	"No one can serve two **m**.
Lk	16:13	No servant can serve two **m**.
Eph	6: 5	obedient to your human **m** with fear
Eph	6: 9	**M**, act in the same way toward
Col	3:22	obey your human **m** in everything,
Col	4: 1	**M**, treat your slaves justly
1 Tm	6: 1	must regard their **m** as worthy
1 Tm	6: 2	Those whose **m** are believers must
Ti	2: 9	the control of their **m** in all respects,
1 Pt	2:18	subject to your **m** with all reverence,

MAT → MATS

Mk	2: 9	'Rise, pick up your **m** and walk'?
Jn	5: 8	"Rise, take up your **m**, and walk."

MATCH → MATCHED

Lk	5:36	from it will not **m** the old cloak.

MATCHED → MATCH

2 Cor	8:11	your eager willingness may be **m**

MATERIAL

Rom	15:27	also to serve them in **m** blessings.
1 Cor	9:11	that we reap a **m** harvest from you?

MATS → MAT

Mk	6:55	in the sick on **m** to wherever they
Acts	5:15	and **m** so that when Peter came by,

MATTANIAH → =ZEDEKIAH
Original name of King Zedekiah (2 Kgs 24:17).

MATTATHIAS
Priest who started the Maccabean revolt (1 Mc 2).

MATTHEW → =LEVI
Apostle; former tax collector (Mt 9:9-13; 10:3; Mk 3:18; Lk 6:15; Acts 1:13). Also called Levi (Mk 2:14-17; Lk 5:27-32).

MATTHIAS
Disciple chosen to replace Judas (Acts 1:23-26).

MATURE

Lk	8:14	life, and they fail to produce **m** fruit.
1 Cor	2: 6	speak a wisdom to those who are **m**,
Phil	3:15	who are "perfectly **m**" adopt this
Heb	5:14	But solid food is for the **m**, for those

MEAL

Heb	12:16	sold his birthright for a single **m**.

MEAN → MEANING, MEANINGLESS, MEANS

Ex	12:26	'What does this rite of yours **m**?'
Jos	4: 6	'What do these stones **m** to you?'

MEANING → MEAN

Gn	40: 5	and each dream with its own **m**.

MEANINGLESS → MEAN

1 Tm	1: 6	from these and turned to **m** talk,

MEANS → MEAN

Sir	8:13	not give collateral beyond your **m**;

MEASURE → MEASURED, MEASURES, MEASURING

Ps	147: 5	in power, with wisdom beyond **m**.
Ez	45: 3	also **m** off a length of twenty-five
Zec	2: 6	And he said, "To **m** Jerusalem—
Mk	4:24	The **m** with which you **m** will be
Lk	6:38	a good **m**, packed together,
Lk	6:38	For the **m** with which you **m** will
Rev	11: 1	"Come and **m** the temple of God

MEASURED → MEASURE

Jer	31:37	If the heavens on high could be **m**,

MEASURES → MEASURE

Prv	20:10	varying **m**, are both an abomination

MEASURING → MEASURE

Ez	40: 3	in his hand a linen cord and a **m** rod.
Zec	2: 5	there was a man with a **m** cord
Rev	11: 1	I was given a **m** rod like a staff
Rev	21:15	me held a gold **m** rod to measure

MEAT

Ex	16: 3	Egypt, as we sat by our kettles of **m**
Lv	11: 8	You shall not eat their **m**, and you
Nm	11:13	Where can I get **m** to give to all this
Prv	23:20	those who glut themselves on **m**.
Ez	11: 3	city is the pot, and we are the **m**."
Rom	14:21	it is good not to eat **m** or drink wine
1 Cor	8:13	I will never eat **m** again, so that I

MEDAD

Nm	11:27	**M** are prophesying in the camp,"

MEDDLES

Prv	26:17	Whoever **m** in the quarrel of another

MEDE → MEDIA

Dn	6: 1	And Darius the **M** succeeded

MEDES → MEDIA

Dn	5:28	and given to the **M** and Persians."
Dn	6: 9	according to the law of the **M**
Dn	8:20	saw represents the kings of the **M**
Acts	2: 9	We are Parthians, **M**, and Elamites,

MEDIA → MEDE, MEDES
Ezr 6: 2 the stronghold in the province of M,
Tb 1:14 lived at Rages, in the land of M.

MEDIATOR
Jb 33:23 a m, one out of a thousand, to show
Gal 3:19 by angels at the hand of a m.
1 Tm 2: 5 There is also one m between God
Heb 8: 6 more excellent a ministry as he is m
Heb 9:15 For this reason he is m of a new
Heb 12:24 and Jesus, the m of a new covenant,

MEDITATE → MEDITATES
Ps 77: 7 and as I m, my spirit probes:
Ps 119:148 eyes greet the night watches as I m
Sir 14:20 Happy those who m on Wisdom,

MEDITATES → MEDITATE
Ps 1: 2 on his law he m day and night.
Sir 39: 7 as he m upon God's mysteries.

MEDIUM → MEDIUMS
Lv 20:27 man or a woman who acts as a m
1 Sm 28: 7 "Find me a m through whom I can
1 Sm 28: 7 is a woman in Endor who is a m."

MEDIUMS → MEDIUM
1 Sm 28: 3 Meanwhile Saul had driven m

MEEK
Mt 5: 5 Blessed are the m, for they will

MEET → MEETING, MET
Ex 19:17 people out of the camp to m God,
Ex 30:36 tent of meeting where I will m you.
Ps 85:11 Love and truth will m;
Prv 29:13 The poor and the oppressor m: the LORD
Am 4:12 prepare to m your God, O Israel!
1 Thes 4:17 the clouds to m the Lord in the air.

MEETING → MEET
Ex 27:21 before the LORD in the tent of m,
Ex 29:44 Thus I will consecrate the tent of m
Ex 33: 7 It was called the tent of m.
Ex 40:34 the cloud covered the tent of m,
Jos 18: 1 where they set up the tent of m;

MEGIDDO
Jos 12:21 of Taanach, one; the king of M, one;
Jgs 1:27 towns, or those of M and its towns.

MELCHIZEDEK
Gn 14:18 M, king of Salem, brought out bread
Ps 110: 4 priest forever in the manner of M."
Heb 5:10 priest according to the order of M.
Heb 6:20 forever according to the order of M.
Heb 7: 1 This "M, king of Salem and priest
Heb 7:11 to arise according to the order of M,

MELONS
Nm 11: 5 and the cucumbers, the m, the leeks,

MELT → MELTED, MELTS
Ps 97: 5 The mountains m like wax before
Mi 1: 4 The mountains m under him

MELTED → MELT
2 Pt 3:12 flames and the elements m by fire.

MELTS → MELT
Ps 22:15 like wax, it m away within me.
Ps 147:18 he issues his command, it m them;

MEMBER → MEMBERS
Mk 15:43 a distinguished m of the council,

MEMBERS → MEMBER
Rom 7:23 I see in my m another principle
Rom 7:23 the law of sin that dwells in my m.
1 Cor 6:15 that your bodies are m of Christ?
1 Cor 6:15 make them the m of a prostitute?
Eph 2:19 and m of the household of God,
Eph 3: 6 are coheirs, m of the same body,
Eph 4:25 for we are m one of another.
Eph 5:30 because we are m of his body.

MEMORIAL → MEMORY
Jos 4: 7 are to serve as a perpetual m

MEMORY → MEMORIAL
Jb 18:17 His m perishes from the earth,
Prv 10: 7 The m of the just serves as blessing,
Sir 10:17 erasing their m from the world.

MEN → MAN
Gn 18: 2 he saw three m standing near him.
Nm 13: 2 Send m to reconnoiter the land
Jgs 15:15 it, and with it killed a thousand m.
1 Kgs 12:10 The young m who had grown
Ps 148:12 Young m and women too,
Dn 1:17 To these four young m God gave
Dn 3:92 "I see four m unbound and unhurt,
Mk 6:44 [the loaves] were five thousand m.
Lk 9:30 two m were conversing with him,
Acts 4:13 ordinary m, they were amazed,
1 Tm 2: 8 in every place the m should pray,
Ti 2: 2 that older m should be temperate,
Ti 2: 6 Urge the younger m, similarly,

MENAHEM
King of Israel (2 Kgs 15:14-23).

MENE
Dn 5:25 M, TEKEL, and PERES.
Dn 5:26 M, God has numbered your

MENORAH → MENORAHS
Ex 25:31 shall make a m of pure beaten gold—
Nm 3:31 the ark, the table, the m, the altars,

MENORAHS → MENORAH
2 Chr 4: 7 He made the m of gold, ten of them

MENTION → MENTIONED
Am 6:10 for no one must m the name
Eph 5:12 shameful even to m the things done

MENTIONED → MENTION
Eph 5: 3 must not even be m among you,

MEPHIBOSHETH
Son of Jonathan shown kindness by David (2 Sm 4:4; 9; 21:7). Accused of siding with Absalom (2 Sm 16:1-4; 19:24-30).

MERAB
Daughter of Saul (1 Sm 14:49; 18:17-19; 2 Sm 21:8).

MERARI
Gn 46:11 Gershon, Kohath, and M.
1 Chr 6: 4 The sons of M were Mahli
2 Chr 34:12 Levites of the line of M,

MERCHANDISE → MERCHANT
Neh 10:32 the local inhabitants bring in m

MERCHANT → MERCHANDISE, MERCHANTS
Prv 31:14 Like a m fleet, she secures her
Mt 13:45 heaven is like a m searching for fine

MERCHANTS → MERCHANT
Rev 18:11 The m of the earth will weep

MERCIES → MERCY
Ps 89:50 Where are your former m, Lord,
Rom 12: 1 by the m of God, to offer your bodies

MERCIFUL → MERCY
Dt 4:31 is a m God, he will not abandon
1 Kgs 20:31 of the house of Israel are m kings.
Neh 9:31 for you are a gracious and m God.
Ps 111: 4 gracious and m is the LORD.
Ps 145: 8 The LORD is gracious and m,
Sir 2:11 the Lord is compassionate and m;
Jer 3:12 For I am m, oracle of the LORD,
Mt 5: 7 Blessed are the m, for they will be
Lk 6:36 Be m, just as [also] your Father is m.
Lk 18:13 'O God, be m to me a sinner.'
Heb 2:17 that he might be a m and faithful

MERCY → MERCIES, MERCIFUL
Ex 33:19 will, I who grant m to whom I will.
Jos 11:20 be put under the ban without m,

1 Chr	21:13	the LORD, whose **m** is very great,
Tb	3: 2	All your ways are **m** and fidelity;
Jdt	13:14	who has not withdrawn his **m**
Ps	5: 8	through the abundance of your **m**,
Ps	17: 7	Show your wonderful **m**, you who deliver
Ps	21: 8	stands firm through the **m** of the Most High.
Ps	25: 6	Remember your compassion and your **m**,
Ps	25: 7	remember me according to your **m**,
Ps	25:10	All the paths of the LORD are **m** and truth
Ps	26: 3	Your **m** is before my eyes;
Ps	31: 8	I will rejoice and be glad in your **m**,
Ps	31:22	marvelously he showed to me his **m**
Ps	32:10	**m** surrounds the one who trusts in the LORD.
Ps	36: 6	LORD, your **m** reaches to heaven;
Ps	36: 8	How precious is your **m**, O God!
Ps	36:11	Show **m** on those who know you,
Ps	42: 9	By day may the LORD send his **m**,
Ps	44:27	help us! Redeem us in your **m**.
Ps	48:10	O God, your **m** within your temple
Ps	51: 3	Have **m** on me, God, in accord
Ps	52:10	I trust in God's **m** forever and ever.
Ps	57: 4	May God send fidelity and **m**.
Ps	57:11	For your **m** towers to the heavens;
Ps	59:17	of your strength, extol your **m** at dawn,
Ps	69:17	in your great **m** turn to me.
Ps	77: 9	Has God's **m** ceased forever?
Ps	85: 8	Show us, LORD, your **m**; grant us
Ps	86:13	Your **m** to me is great; you have
Ps	88:12	Is your **m** proclaimed in the grave,
Ps	89: 3	I said, "My **m** is established forever;
Ps	89:15	**m** and faithfulness march before you.
Ps	89:25	My faithfulness and **m** will be with him;
Ps	89:29	Forever I will maintain my **m** for him;
Ps	89:34	But I will not take my **m** from him,
Ps	90:14	Fill us at daybreak with your **m**,
Ps	94:18	your **m**, LORD, holds me up.
Ps	98: 3	He has remembered his **m** and
Ps	100: 5	His **m** endures forever, his faithfulness
Ps	103: 4	and crowns you with **m** and compassion,
Ps	103:11	so his **m** towers over those who fear him.
Ps	106: 1	who is good, whose **m** endures forever.
Ps	106: 7	They did not remember your manifold **m**;
Ps	106:45	covenant and relented in his abundant **m**,
Ps	107: 1	for he is good, his **m** endures forever!"
Ps	108: 5	For your **m** is greater than the heavens;
Ps	115: 1	glory because of your **m** and faithfulness.
Ps	117: 2	His **m** for us is strong; the faithfulness
Ps	118: 1	for he is good, his **m** endures forever.
Ps	118: 2	Let Israel say: his **m** endures forever.
Ps	118: 3	house of Aaron say, his **m** endures forever.
Ps	118: 4	fear the LORD say, his **m** endures forever.
Ps	118:29	for he is good, his **m** endures forever.
Ps	119:41	Let your **m** come to me, LORD, salvation
Ps	119:64	The earth, LORD, is filled with your **m**;
Ps	119:76	May your **m** comfort me in accord with
Ps	119:149	Hear my voice in your **m**, O LORD;
Ps	136: 1	is good; for his **m** endures forever;
Ps	136: 2	is good; for his **m** endures forever;
Ps	136: 3	is good; for his **m** endures forever;
Ps	136: 4	is good; for his **m** endures forever;
Ps	136: 5	is good; for his **m** endures forever;
Ps	136: 6	is good; for his **m** endures forever;
Ps	136: 7	is good; for his **m** endures forever;
Ps	136: 8	is good; for his **m** endures forever;
Ps	136: 9	is good; for his **m** endures forever;
Ps	136:10	is good; for his **m** endures forever;
Ps	136:11	is good; for his **m** endures forever;
Ps	136:12	is good; for his **m** endures forever;
Ps	136:13	is good; for his **m** endures forever;
Ps	136:14	is good; for his **m** endures forever;
Ps	136:15	is good; for his **m** endures forever;
Ps	136:16	is good; for his **m** endures forever;
Ps	136:17	is good; for his **m** endures forever;
Ps	136:18	is good; for his **m** endures forever;
Ps	136:19	is good; for his **m** endures forever;
Ps	136:20	is good; for his **m** endures forever;
Ps	136:21	is good; for his **m** endures forever;
Ps	136:22	is good; for his **m** endures forever;
Ps	136:23	is good; for his **m** endures forever;
Ps	136:24	is good; for his **m** endures forever;
Ps	136:25	is good; for his **m** endures forever;
Ps	136:26	is good; for his **m** endures forever;
Ps	138: 2	I praise your name for your **m** and
Ps	138: 8	LORD, your **m** endures forever.
Ps	145: 8	slow to anger and abounding in **m**.
Prv	28:13	confess and forsake them obtain **m**.
Wis	3: 9	grace and **m** are with his holy ones,
Sir	2: 7	wait for his **m**, do not stray lest you
Sir	17:29	How great is the **m** of the Lord,
Is	47: 6	but you showed them no **m**;
Is	55: 7	them turn to the LORD to find **m**;
Lam	3:22	The LORD's acts of **m** are not exhausted,
Dn	2:18	that they might implore the **m**
Hb	1:17	to slaughter nations without **m**?
Zec	1:12	how long will you be without **m**
Mt	5: 7	merciful, for they will be shown **m**.
Mt	9:13	words, 'I desire **m**, not sacrifice.'
Mt	12: 7	meant, 'I desire **m**, not sacrifice,'
Mt	23:23	judgment and **m** and fidelity.
Lk	1:50	His **m** is from age to age to those
Lk	1:58	had shown his great **m** toward her,
Lk	1:72	to show **m** to our fathers and to be
Lk	1:78	because of the tender **m** of our God
Lk	10:37	"The one who treated him with **m**."
Rom	9:15	"I will show **m** to whom I will,
Rom	9:18	he has **m** upon whom he wills,
Rom	9:23	of his glory to the vessels of **m**,
Rom	11:30	but have now received **m** because
Rom	11:31	by virtue of the **m** shown to you,
Rom	11:31	you, they too may [now] receive **m**.
Rom	15: 9	might glorify God for his **m**. As it is
1 Cor	7:25	who by the Lord's **m** is trustworthy.
2 Cor	4: 1	ministry through the **m** shown us,
Eph	2: 4	who is rich in **m**,
Phil	2:27	but God had **m** on him, not just
1 Tm	1: 2	grace, **m**, and peace from God
2 Tm	1: 2	grace, **m**, and peace from God
2 Tm	1:16	May the Lord grant **m** to the family
2 Tm	1:18	grant him to find **m** from the Lord
Ti	3: 5	we had done but because of his **m**,
Heb	4:16	the throne of grace to receive **m**
Jas	2:13	to one who has not shown **m**;
Jas	3:17	compliant, full of **m** and good fruits,
1 Pt	1: 3	in his great **m** gave us a new birth
1 Pt	2:10	you "had not received **m**" but now you have received **m**.
2 Jn	1: 3	Grace, **m**, and peace will be with us
Jude	1:21	for the **m** of our Lord Jesus Christ
Jude	1:23	on others have **m** with fear,

MERIBAH

Ex	17: 7	place was named Massah and **M**,
Nm	20:13	These are the waters of **M**.
Dt	33: 8	against him at the waters of **M**.
Ps	95: 8	Do not harden your hearts as at **M**,
Ps	106:32	the waters of **M** they angered God,

MERRY

Eccl	9: 7	and drink your wine with a **m** heart,
Lk	12:19	years, rest, eat, drink, be **m**!" '

MESHACH → =MISHAEL

Hebrew exiled to Babylon; name changed from Mishael (Dn 1:6-7). Refused defilement by food (Dn 1:8-20). Refused to worship idol (Dn 3:1-18); saved from furnace (Dn 3:19-97).

MESHECH

Ps	120: 5	I am a foreigner in **M**, I live among
Ez	38: 3	Gog, chief prince of **M** and Tubal.
Ez	39: 1	at you, chief prince of **M** and Tubal.

MESOPOTAMIA

Acts	2: 9	inhabitants of **M**,
Acts	7: 2	father Abraham while he was in **M**,

MESSAGE → MESSENGER, MESSENGERS

Is	28: 9	To whom would he convey the **m**?

Acts 2:41 who accepted his **m** were baptized,
1 Cor 1:18 The **m** of the cross is foolishness
2 Cor 5:19 to us the **m** of reconciliation.
1 Jn 1: 5 Now this is the **m** that we have
1 Jn 3:11 For this is the **m** you have heard

MESSENGER → MESSAGE
Jgs 2: 1 A **m** of the LORD went up from Gilgal
Jgs 6:12 and the **m** of the LORD appeared to him
Jgs 6:22 I have seen the **m** of the LORD face to face!"
1 Kgs 19: 5 suddenly a **m** touched him and said, "Get up
2 Kgs 1: 3 the **m** of the LORD said to Elijah the Tishbite:
Jb 33:23 If then there be a divine **m**, a mediator,
Is 42:19 servant, or deaf like the **m** I send?
Is 63: 9 or a **m**, but his presence that saved them.
Hg 1:13 Then Haggai, the **m** of the LORD,
Mal 2: 7 because he is the **m** of the LORD
Mal 3: 1 Now I am sending my **m**—
Mal 3: 1 The **m** of the covenant whom you
Mt 11:10 I am sending my **m** ahead of you;

MESSENGERS → MESSAGE
2 Chr 36:15 their ancestors, sent his **m** to them,
Jb 4:18 and even with his **m** he finds fault.
Ps 104: 4 You make the winds your **m**;
Is 44:26 carry out the plan my **m** announce.

MESSIAH → CHRIST, MESSIAHS
Mt 16:16 "You are the **M**, the Son
Mt 26:63 living God whether you are the **M**,
Mk 13:21 to you then, 'Look, here is the **M**!
Lk 2:11 has been born for you who is **M**
Lk 23:35 is the chosen one, the **M** of God."
Jn 1:20 it, but admitted, "I am not the **M**."
Jn 1:41 "We have found the **M**" (which is
Jn 4:25 "I know that the **M** is coming,
Jn 10:24 If you are the **M**, tell us plainly."
Acts 2:36 has made him both Lord and **M**,
Acts 3:20 send you the **M** already appointed
Rom 9: 5 according to the flesh, is the **M**.

MESSIAHS → MESSIAH
Mt 24:24 False **m** and false prophets will
Mk 13:22 False **m** and false prophets will arise

MET → MEET
Mt 28: 9 Jesus **m** them on their way
Jn 18: 2 because Jesus had often **m** there

METHUSELAH
Gn 5:27 lifetime of **M** was nine hundred

MICAH
1. Idolater from Ephraim (Jgs 17–18).
2. Prophet from Moresheth (Jer 26:18-19; Mi 1:1).

MICAIAH
Prophet of the LORD who spoke against Ahab (1 Kgs 22:1-28; 2 Chr 18:1-27).

MICHAEL
Archangel (Jude 9); warrior in angelic realm, protector of Israel (Dn 10:13, 21; 12:1; Rev 12:7).

MICHAL
Daughter of Saul, wife of David (1 Sm 14:49; 18:20-28). Warned David of Saul's plot (1 Sm 19). Saul gave her to Palti (1 Sm 25:43); David retrieved her (2 Sm 3:13-16). Criticized David for dancing before the ark (2 Sm 6:16-23; 1 Chr 15:29).

MIDDLE → MIDST
Gn 3: 3 the tree in the **m** of the garden
Acts 1:18 he burst open in the **m**, and all his
Rev 22: 2 down the **m** of its street.

MIDIAN → MIDIANITE, MIDIANITES
Ex 2:15 Pharaoh and went to the land of **M**.
Ex 18: 1 the priest of **M**, heard of all
Ps 83:10 Deal with them as with **M**;

MIDIANITE → MIDIAN
Gn 37:28 **M** traders passed by, and they
Nm 25: 6 and brought in a **M** woman to his

MIDIANITES → MIDIAN
Gn 37:36 The **M**, meanwhile, sold Joseph
Nm 31: 2 Avenge the Israelites on the **M**,

MIDNIGHT → NIGHT
Ex 11: 4 **m** I will go forth through Egypt.
Ex 12:29 at **m** the LORD struck down every
Ps 119:62 At **m** I rise to praise you because
Acts 16:25 About **m**, while Paul and Silas were

MIDST → MIDDLE
Dt 13: 6 you purge the evil from your **m**.
Mt 10:16 you like sheep in the **m** of wolves;

MIDWIVES
Ex 1:17 The **m**, however, feared God;

MIGHT → ALMIGHTY, MIGHTY
Dt 5:29 Would that they **m** always be
2 Sm 22:33 This God who girded me with **m**,
1 Chr 29:11 Yours, LORD, are greatness and **m**,
2 Chr 20: 6 In your hand is power and **m**,
Is 63:15 is your zealous care and your **m**,
Mi 3: 8 LORD, with justice and with **m**;
Zec 4: 6 Not by **m**, and not by power,
Mk 14:35 it were possible the hour **m** pass
Jn 1: 7 so that all **m** believe through him.
2 Cor 8: 9 by his poverty you **m** become rich.
1 Pt 2:24 sin, we **m** live for righteousness.
1 Jn 4: 9 so that we **m** have life through him.

MIGHTY → MIGHT
Gn 10: 9 He was a **m** hunter in the eyes
Gn 49:24 the power of the **M** One of Jacob.
Dt 3:24 your greatness and your **m** hand.
Dt 10:17 the great God, **m** and awesome,
1 Chr 16:11 Rely on the **m** LORD; constantly
Neh 9:32 God, great, **m**, and awesome God,
Ps 24: 8 strong and **m**, the LORD, **m** in war.
Ps 45: 4 sword upon your hip, **m** warrior!
Ps 68:34 sends forth his voice as a **m** voice?
Ps 71:16 I will speak of the **m** works
Ps 89: 9 **M** LORD, your faithfulness
Ps 99: 4 O **m** king, lover of justice, you have
Ps 106: 2 Who can recount the **m** deeds
Ps 145: 4 next and proclaims your **m** works.
Ps 150: 1 give praise in the **m** dome
Sir 15:18 **m** in power, he sees all things.
Is 49:26 your redeemer, the **M** One of Jacob.
Is 60:16 your redeemer, the **M** One of Jacob.
Is 63: 1 announce vindication, **m** to save."
Jer 32:19 great in counsel, **m** in deed,
Ez 20:33 with **m** hand and outstretched arm,
Dn 3:100 are his signs, how **m** his wonders;
Lk 1:49 The **M** One has done great things
1 Pt 5: 6 yourselves under the **m** hand
Rev 18: 8 **m** is the Lord God who judges her."

MILCAH
Gn 11:29 the name of Nahor's wife was **M**,

MILCOM → =MOLECH
1 Kgs 11:33 and **M**, god of the Ammonites.
Jer 49: 3 For **M** is going into exile,
Zep 1: 5 to the LORD but swear by **M**;

MILDEW
2 Chr 6:28 comes, or **m**, or locusts swarm,

MILE
Mt 5:41 press you into service for one **m**,

MILETUS
2 Tm 4:20 while I left Trophimus sick at **M**.

MILK
Ex 3: 8 a land flowing with **m** and honey,
Ex 23:19 boil a young goat in its mother's **m**.
Prv 30:33 the churning of **m** produces curds,
Sg 4:11 honey and **m** are under your tongue;
Is 55: 1 money, wine and **m** without cost!
Jl 4:18 and the hills flow with **m**,
1 Cor 3: 2 I fed you **m**, not solid food,

Heb 5:12 You need **m**, [and] not solid food.
1 Pt 2: 2 pure spiritual **m** so that through it

MILLSTONE → STONE

Jgs 9:53 cast the upper part of a **m** down
Lk 17: 2 him if a **m** were put around his neck

MIND → MINDFUL, MINDS

Ps 26: 2 and test me; search my heart and **m**.
Eccl 2: 3 I probed with my **m** how to beguile
Sir 21:14 A fool's **m** is like a broken jar:
Jer 17:10 explore the **m** and test the heart,
Lam 3:21 But this I will call to **m**;
Mt 22:37 all your soul, and with all your **m**.
Mk 3:21 for they said, "He is out of his **m**."
Mk 5:15 there clothed and in his right **m**.
Mk 12:30 with all your **m**, and with all your
Lk 10:27 and with all your **m**, and your
Rom 1:28 their undiscerning **m** to do what is
Rom 7:25 with my **m**, serve the law of God
Rom 11:34 who has known the **m** of the Lord
1 Cor 1:10 but that you be united in the same **m**
1 Cor 2:16 "who has known the **m** of the Lord,
1 Cor 2:16 But we have the **m** of Christ.
1 Cor 14:14 at prayer but my **m** is unproductive.
1 Thes 4:11 to **m** your own affairs, and to work
2 Tm 3: 8 people of depraved **m**,

MINDFUL → MIND

Ps 8: 5 What is man that you are **m** of him,
Heb 2: 6 is man that you are **m** of him,

MINDS → MIND

Ps 7:10 O just God, who tries hearts and **m**.
Lk 24:45 he opened their **m** to understand
2 Cor 4: 4 of this age has blinded the **m**
2 Cor 5:13 For if we are out of our **m**, it is
Eph 4:23 be renewed in the spirit of your **m**,
Phil 4: 7 your hearts and **m** in Christ Jesus.
Heb 8:10 I will put my laws in their **m** and I
Heb 10:16 I will write them upon their **m**,' "
Rev 2:23 I am the searcher of hearts and **m**

MINGLED

Ps 106:35 But **m** with the nations and imitated

MINISTER → MINISTERS, MINISTRY

Ex 28:43 or approach the altar to **m**
Dt 10: 8 to stand before the Lord to **m**
1 Chr 15: 2 Lord and to **m** to him forever."
Rom 15:16 to be a **m** of Christ Jesus
Rom 16: 1 a **m** of the church at Cenchreae,

MINISTERS → MINISTER

Ps 103:21 hosts, his **m** who carry out his will.
2 Cor 3: 6 who has indeed qualified us as **m**
2 Cor 11:15 masquerade as **m** of righteousness.
Phil 1: 1 Philippi, with the overseers and **m**;

MINISTRY → MINISTER

Acts 1:17 and was allotted a share in this **m**.
Rom 11:13 to the Gentiles, I glory in my **m**
Rom 12: 7 if **m**, in ministering; if one is
2 Cor 3: 7 Now if the **m** of death,
2 Cor 4: 1 we have this **m** through the mercy
2 Cor 5:18 and given us the **m** of reconciliation,
2 Cor 6: 3 no fault may be found with our **m**;
Eph 4:12 the holy ones for the work of **m**,
2 Tm 4: 5 of an evangelist; fulfill your **m**.
Heb 8: 6 so much more excellent a **m** as he is

MIRE

Ps 69:15 Rescue me from the **m**, and do not

MIRIAM

Sister of Moses and Aaron (Nm 26:59). Led dancing at Red Sea (Ex 15:20-21). Struck with leprosy for criticizing Moses (Nm 12). Death (Nm 20:1).

MIRROR

Jb 37:18 of the skies, hard as a molten **m**?
1 Cor 13:12 as in a **m**, but then face to face.
Jas 1:23 who looks at his own face in a **m**.

MISCARRIAGE → MISCARRY

Ex 21:22 so that she suffers a **m**, but no

MISCARRY → MISCARRIAGE

Ex 23:26 in your land will be barren or **m**;

MISERY

Rom 3:16 ruin and **m** are in their ways,

MISFORTUNE

Nm 23:21 **M** I do not see in Jacob, nor do I see
Prv 13:21 **M** pursues sinners, but the just shall

MISHAEL → =MESHACH

Original name of Meshach (Dn 1:6-19; 2:17; 3:88).

MISLEAD → MISLEADS, MISLED

Mk 13:22 to **m**, if that were possible, the elect.

MISLEADS → MISLEAD

Dt 27:18 "Cursed be anyone who **m** the blind

MISLED → MISLEAD

2 Kgs 21: 9 Manasseh **m** them into doing even

MISSING

Jgs 20:16 to sling a stone at a hair without **m**.
Is 40:26 of his power not one of them is **m**!

MISSION

Acts 12:25 and Saul completed their relief **m**,

MIST → MISTS

Is 44:22 like a cloud, your sins like a **m**;
Hos 6: 4 Your loyalty is like morning **m**,
Acts 13:11 Immediately a dark **m** fell

MISTAKE

Eccl 5: 5 his representative, "It was a **m**."

MISTRESS

Gn 16: 4 her **m** lost stature in her eyes.
Ps 123: 2 eyes of a maid on the hand of her **m**,
Is 47: 7 always, a sovereign **m** forever!"
Na 3: 4 a charming **m** of witchcraft,

MISTS → MIST

2 Pt 2:17 springs and **m** driven by a gale;

MIXED → MIXING

Ex 29: 2 flour make unleavened cakes **m**
Prv 9: 5 and drink of the wine I have **m**!
Dn 2:41 As you saw the iron **m** with clay
Rev 8: 7 came hail and fire **m** with blood,

MIXING → MIXED

Is 5:22 drinking wine, masters at **m** drink!

MIZPAH

Gn 31:49 and also **M**, for he said:
1 Sm 7: 6 It was at **M** that Samuel began
1 Mc 3:46 and went to **M** near Jerusalem,
1 Mc 3:46 formerly at **M** there was a place
Jer 41: 1 to Gedaliah, son of Ahikam, at **M**.

MOAB → MOABITE, MOABITES

Gn 19:37 birth to a son whom she named **M**,
Nm 22: 3 and **M** feared the Israelites greatly
Dt 34: 5 So there, in the land of **M**, Moses,
Jgs 3:12 king of **M**, against Israel because
Ru 1: 1 sons to reside on the plateau of **M**.
1 Sm 22: 4 He left them with the king of **M**;
2 Kgs 1: 1 death, **M** rebelled against Israel.
Is 15: 1 Oracle on **M**: Laid waste in a night,
Jer 48: 1 Concerning **M**. Thus says
Ez 25:11 I will execute judgment upon **M**
Am 2: 1 For three crimes of **M**, and now
Zep 2: 9 Israel, **M** shall become like Sodom,

MOABITE → MOAB

Dt 23: 4 **M** may ever come into the assembly
Ru 1:22 with her **M** daughter-in-law Ruth,
Ru 4:10 I also acquire Ruth the **M**,
Neh 13: 1 or **M** may ever be admitted

MOABITES → MOAB

Gn 19:37 He is the ancestor of the **M** of today.

MOAN

Is 59:11 like doves we **m** without ceasing.

MOCK → MOCKED, MOCKS

Ps 22: 8 All who see me **m** me;
Prv 1:26 will **m** when terror overtakes you;
Mk 10:34 who will **m** him, spit upon him,

MOCKED → MOCK

Neh 2:19 Geshem the Arab **m** and ridiculed
Mt 27:29 kneeling before him, they **m** him,
Lk 23:11 him contemptuously and **m** him,
Gal 6: 7 God is not **m**, for a person will reap

MOCKS → MOCK

Prv 30:17 The eye that **m** a father, or scorns

MODEIN

1 Mc 2:23 on the altar in **M** according

MODEL

Ti 2: 7 showing yourself as a **m** of good

MODERATE → MODERATION

Sir 31:22 do, be **m**, and no sickness will befall

MODERATION → MODERATE

Sir 31:27 is very life to anyone, if taken in **m**.

MODEST

Sir 26:15 A **m** wife is a supreme blessing;

MOLDED

Wis 7: 1 in my mother's womb I was **m**
Sir 33:13 to be **m** according to his pleasure,

MOLECH → =MILCOM

Lv 18:21 your offspring for immolation to **M**,
2 Kgs 23:10 or daughters by fire in honor of **M**.
Jer 32:35 their sons and daughters to **M**;

MOMENT → MOMENTARY

Ex 33: 5 up in your company even for a **m**,
Jb 20: 5 the joy of the impious but for a **m**?
Ps 30: 6 For his anger lasts but a **m**;
Prv 12:19 the lying tongue, for only a **m**.
Is 54: 7 For a brief **m** I abandoned you,
Is 66: 8 or a nation be born in a single **m**?

MOMENTARY → MOMENT

2 Cor 4:17 this **m** light affliction is producing

MONEY

Ex 22:24 If you lend **m** to my people,
Ex 30:16 you receive this ransom **m**
2 Kgs 12: 5 census tax, personal redemption **m**—
Tb 5:19 Do not heap **m** upon **m**!
Ps 15: 5 lends no **m** at interest, accepts no
Eccl 5: 9 covetous are never satisfied with **m**,
Eccl 7:12 of wisdom is as the protection of **m**;
Eccl 10:19 but **m** answers for everything.
Sir 7:18 Do not barter a friend for **m**,
Is 55: 1 buy grain without **m**, wine and milk
Mi 3:11 the prophets divine for **m**,
Mk 11:15 the tables of the **m** changers
Lk 9: 3 nor **m**, and let no one take a second
1 Tm 3: 3 not contentious, not a lover of **m**,
1 Tm 6:10 the love of **m** is the root of all evils,
2 Tm 3: 2 be self-centered and lovers of **m**,
Heb 13: 5 Let your life be free from love of **m**

MONSTERS

Gn 1:21 God created the great sea **m** and all
Ps 148: 7 you sea **m** and all the deeps

MONTH → MONTHS

Ex 12: 2 you will reckon it the first **m**
Ex 40:12 first day of the first **m** you shall set
Nm 3:15 enrolling every male of a **m**
Nm 11:21 them meat to eat for a whole **m**.'
Ezr 6:19 on the fourteenth day of the first **m**.
Neh 8: 2 On the first day of the seventh **m**,
Est 9:21 and the fifteenth of the **m** of Adar
1 Mc 1:59 day of each **m** they sacrificed
1 Mc 4:59 the twenty-fifth day of the **m** Kislev,

Ez 47:12 Every **m** they will bear fresh fruit
Rev 9:15 day, **m**, and year to kill a third
Rev 22: 2 twelve times a year, once each **m**;

MONTHS → MONTH

Ex 2: 2 he was, she hid him for three **m**.
Jgs 11:37 Do nothing for two **m**, that I and my
1 Sm 6: 1 the land of the Philistines seven **m**
1 Chr 13:14 with his family for three **m**,
Jn 4:35 'In four **m** the harvest will be here'?
Rev 9: 5 but only to torment them for five **m**;
Rev 11: 2 the holy city for forty-two **m**.
Rev 13: 5 authority to act for forty-two **m**.

MOON → MOONS

Gn 37: 9 the **m** and eleven stars were bowing
Dt 17: 3 the **m** or any of the host of heaven,
Jos 10:13 The sun stood still, the **m** stayed,
Ps 8: 4 the **m** and stars that you set
Ps 72: 7 great bounty, till the **m** be no more.
Ps 89:38 Like the **m** it will stand eternal,
Ps 104:19 You made the **m** to mark
Ps 121: 6 not strike you, nor the **m** by night.
Ps 136: 9 The **m** and stars to rule the night,
Ps 148: 3 Praise him, sun and **m**;
Sg 6:10 beautiful as the white **m**, pure as
Sir 27:11 but the fool changes like the **m**.
Is 13:10 and the **m** will not give its light.
Jer 31:35 day, **m** and stars to light the night;
Ez 32: 7 the **m** will not give light.
Dn 3:62 Sun and **m**, bless the Lord;
Jl 3: 4 will darken, the **m** turn blood-red,
Hb 3:11 the **m** left its lofty station,
Mt 24:29 and the **m** will not give its light,
Acts 2:20 and the **m** to blood,
1 Cor 15:41 the brightness of the **m** another,
Rev 6:12 and the whole **m** became like blood.
Rev 8:12 a third of the **m**, and a third
Rev 12: 1 with the **m** under her feet,
Rev 21:23 no need of sun or **m** to shine on it,

MOONS → MOON

2 Chr 8:13 at the new **m**, and on the fixed
2 Chr 31: 3 on sabbaths, new **m**, and festivals,

MORALS

1 Cor 15:33 "Bad company corrupts good **m**."

MORDECAI

Benjamite exile who raised Esther (Est 2:5-15). Exposed plot to kill Ahasuerus (Est 2:19-23). Refused to honor Haman (Est 3:1-6; 5:9-14). Charged Esther to foil Haman's plot against the Jews (Est 4). Ahasuerus forced Haman to honor Mordecai (Est 6). Mordecai exalted (Est 8–10). Established Purim (Est 9:18-32).

MORE → MOST

Ex 1:12 Yet the **m** they were oppressed,
Ex 1:12 the **m** they multiplied and spread,
Jos 10:11 **M** died from these hailstones than
Jgs 16:30 his dying were **m** than those he had
2 Sm 18: 8 the forest consumed **m** combatants
1 Kgs 16:33 Ahab did **m** to provoke the LORD,
Jb 42:12 days of Job **m** than his earlier ones.
Ps 19:11 **M** desirable than gold, than a hoard
Ps 37:10 a little, and the wicked will be no **m**;
Ps 69:32 please the LORD **m** than oxen,
Ps 119:127 your commandments **m** than gold,
Ps 130: 6 looks for the Lord **m** than sentinels
Prv 21: 3 just is **m** acceptable to the LORD
Is 54: 1 For **m** numerous are the children
Lam 5: 7 ancestors, who sinned, are no **m**;
Jon 3: 4 "Forty days **m** and Nineveh shall be
Mt 2:18 be consoled, since they were no **m**."
Mk 4:25 the one who has, **m** will be given;
Mk 12:43 in **m** than all the other contributors
Lk 12:23 For life is **m** than food and the body **m** than clothing.
Jn 21:15 do you love me **m** than these?"
Acts 17:11 Jews were **m** fair-minded than those
Rom 5: 9 How much **m** then, since we are
1 Cor 12:31 show you a still **m** excellent way.

2 Cor	3: 9	righteousness will abound much **m**
Heb	8:12	and remember their sins no **m**."
Heb	10:17	evildoing I will remember no **m**."
Rev	10: 6	them, "There shall be no **m** delay.
Rev	21: 4	and there shall be no **m** death
Rev	22: 5	Night will be no **m**, nor will they

MORIAH

Gn	22: 2	you love, and go to the land of **M**.
2 Chr	3: 1	LORD in Jerusalem on Mount **M**,

MORNING → MORNINGS

Gn	1: 5	Evening came, and **m** followed—
Ex	12:10	not keep any of it beyond the **m**;
Ex	12:10	over in the **m** must be burned up.
Ex	16:12	in the **m** you will have your fill
Ex	29:39	one lamb in the **m** and the other
Dt	28:67	In the **m** you will say, "Would that it were **m**!"
2 Sm	23: 4	the light at sunrise on a cloudless **m**,
Ezr	3: 3	LORD on it, both **m** and evening.
Jb	38: 7	While the **m** stars sang together
Prv	27:14	with a loud voice in the early **m**,
Eccl	11: 6	In the **m** sow your seed,
Is	50: 4	**M** after **m** he wakens my ear to hear
Lam	3:23	They are renewed each **m**—
Hos	6: 4	Your loyalty is like **m** mist,
Hos	13: 3	they will be like a **m** cloud or like
Zep	3: 5	**M** after **m** rendering judgment
Lk	24:22	they were at the tomb early in the **m**
Acts	2:15	for it is only nine o'clock in the **m**.
2 Pt	1:19	and the **m** star rises in your hearts.
Rev	2:28	And to him I will give the **m** star.
Rev	22:16	of David, the bright **m** star."

MORNINGS → MORNING

Dn	8:14	three hundred evenings and **m**;
Dn	8:26	vision of the evenings and the **m**,

MORTAL → MORTALS

Rom	1:23	the likeness of an image of **m** man
Rom	6:12	not reign over your **m** bodies so
Rom	8:11	will give life to your **m** bodies also,
1 Cor	15:53	which is **m** must clothe itself
2 Cor	5: 4	so that what is **m** may be swallowed
Rev	13: 3	but this **m** wound was healed.

MORTALS → MORTAL

Ps	118: 6	what can **m** do against me?
Is	51:12	Can you then fear **m** who die,
Is	52:14	beyond that of **m** his appearance,

MOSES

Levite; brother of Aaron (Ex 6:20; 1 Chr 5:29). Put in basket into Nile; discovered and raised by Pharaoh's daughter (Ex 2:1-10). Fled to Midian after killing Egyptian (Ex 2:11-15). Married to Zipporah, fathered Gershom (Ex 2:16-22).

Called by the LORD to deliver Israel (Ex 3–4). Pharaoh's resistance (Ex 5). Ten plagues (Ex 7–11). Passover and Exodus (Ex 12–13). Led Israel through Red Sea (Ex 14). Song of deliverance (Ex 15:1-21). Brought water from rock (Ex 17:1-7). Raised hands to defeat Amalekites (Ex 17:8-16). Delegated judges (Ex 18; Dt 1:9-18).

Received Law at Sinai (Ex 19–23; 25–31; Jn 1:17). Announced Law to Israel (Ex 19:7-8; 24; 35). Broke tablets because of golden calf (Ex 32; Dt 9). Saw glory of the LORD (Ex 33–34). Supervised building of tabernacle (Ex 36–40). Set apart Aaron and priests (Lv 8–9). Numbered tribes (Nm 1–4; 26). Opposed by Aaron and Miriam (Nm 12). Sent spies into Canaan (Nm 13). Announced forty years of wandering for failure to enter land (Nm 14). Opposed by Korah (Nm 16). Forbidden to enter land for striking rock (Nm 20:1-13; Dt 1:37). Lifted bronze snake for healing (Nm 21:4-9; Jn 3:14). Final address to Israel (Dt 1–33). Succeeded by Joshua (Nm 27:12-23; Dt 34). Death and burial by God (Dt 34:5-12). Praise of (Sir 45).

"Law of Moses" (1 Kgs 2:3; Ezr 3:2; Mk 12:26; Lk 24:44). "Book of Moses" (2 Chr 25:12; Neh 13:1). "Song of Moses" (Ex 15:1-21; Rev 15:3). "Prayer of Moses" (Ps 90).

MOST → MORE

Gn	14:18	He was a priest of God **M** High.
Nm	4: 4	the **m** sacred objects.
Nm	24:16	and knows what the **M** High knows,

Ps	46: 5	the holy dwelling of the **M** High.
Ps	78:35	God was their rock, God **M** High,
Ps	91: 1	dwell in the shelter of the **M** High,
Wis	5:15	thought of them is with the **M** High.
Is	14:14	I will be like the **M** High!"
Jer	3:19	the **m** beautiful heritage among
Dn	7:25	He shall speak against the **M** High
Dn	7:25	down the holy ones of the **M** High,
Mk	5: 7	me, Jesus, Son of the **M** High God?
Lk	1:32	will be called Son of the **M** High,
Lk	1:76	be called prophet of the **M** High,
1 Cor	10: 5	Yet God was not pleased with **m**
Eph	5:16	making the **m** of the opportunity,
Col	4: 5	making the **m** of the opportunity.
Jude	1:20	yourselves up in your **m** holy faith;

MOTH → MOTHS

Mt	6:19	earth, where **m** and decay destroy,

MOTHER → GRANDMOTHER, MOTHER'S, MOTHER-IN-LAW, MOTHERHOOD, MOTHERS

Gn	2:24	why a man leaves his father and **m**
Gn	3:20	because she was the **m** of all
Ex	20:12	Honor your father and your **m**,
Ex	21:15	father or **m** shall be put to death.
Ex	21:17	father or **m** shall be put to death.
Dt	5:16	Honor your father and your **m**,
Dt	21:18	will not listen to his father or **m**,
Dt	22: 6	and the **m** bird is sitting on them,
Dt	22: 6	shall not take away the **m** bird along
Dt	27:16	who dishonors father or **m**!"
Jgs	5: 7	arose, when I arose, a **m** in Israel.
1 Sm	2:19	His **m** used to make a little garment
2 Sm	20:19	down a city that is a **m** in Israel.
1 Kgs	19:20	me kiss my father and **m** good-bye,
Tb	4: 3	Honor your **m**, and do not abandon
Ps	27:10	Even if my father and **m** forsake me,
Ps	51: 7	in guilt, in sin my **m** conceived me.
Ps	113: 9	a home, the joyful **m** of children.
Prv	20:20	Those who curse father or **m**—
Prv	23:22	do not despise your **m** when she is
Prv	23:25	Let your father and **m** rejoice;
Prv	30:17	or scorns the homage due a **m**,
Prv	31: 1	the instruction his **m** taught him:
Sir	3: 6	who obey the Lord honor their **m**.
Is	8: 4	my **m**," the wealth of Damascus
Is	66:13	As a **m** comforts her child, so I will
Jer	20:17	my **m** would have been my grave,
Hos	2: 4	Accuse your **m**, accuse! for she is
Mi	7: 6	the daughter rises up against her **m**,
Mt	2:11	they saw the child with Mary his **m**.
Mt	10:35	a daughter against her **m**,
Mt	10:37	or **m** more than me is not worthy
Mt	12:48	one who told him, "Who is my **m**?
Mt	19: 5	a man shall leave his father and **m**
Mt	19:19	honor your father and your **m**';
Mk	7:10	'Honor your father and your **m**,'
Mk	7:10	curses father or **m** shall die.'
Mk	10:19	honor your father and your **m**.' "
Lk	12:53	a **m** against her daughter and a daughter against her **m**,
Lk	14:26	me without hating his father and **m**,
Lk	18:20	honor your father and your **m**.' "
Jn	19:27	to the disciple, "Behold, your **m**."
Eph	5:31	[his] **m** and be joined to his wife,
Eph	6: 2	"Honor your father and **m**."
2 Tm	1: 5	and in your **m** Eunice and that I am
Heb	7: 3	Without father, **m**, or ancestry,
Rev	17: 5	the great, the **m** of harlots

MOTHER'S → MOTHER

Ex	23:19	not boil a young goat in its **m** milk.
Jb	1:21	I came forth from my **m** womb,
Prv	1: 8	and reject not your **m** teaching;
Prv	6:20	and do not reject your **m** teaching;
Eccl	5:14	they came forth from their **m** womb,
Eccl	11: 5	the human frame in the **m** womb,
Jn	3: 4	he cannot reenter his **m** womb

MOTHER-IN-LAW → MOTHER

Dt	27:23	who has relations with his m!"
Ru	2:11	your m after your husband's death;
Tb	10:12	your father-in-law and your m,
Mi	7: 6	The daughter-in-law against her m,
Mt	10:35	a daughter-in-law against her m;
Mk	1:30	Simon's m lay sick with a fever.

MOTHERHOOD → MOTHER

1 Tm	2:15	But she will be saved through m,

MOTHERS → MOTHER

Prv	29:15	youths disgrace their m.
Hos	10:14	of war, smashing m along with their
Mk	10:30	and sisters and m and children
1 Tm	5: 2	older women as m, and younger

MOTHS → MOTH

Is	51: 8	shall be like a garment eaten by m,

MOTIONED

Acts	12:17	He m to them with his hand to be

MOTIVES

1 Thes	2: 3	was not from delusion or impure m,

MOUNT → MOUNTAIN, MOUNTAINS

Ex	19:20	LORD came down upon M Sinai,
Ex	34:29	As Moses came down from M Sinai
Nm	33:39	years old when he died on M Hor.
Dt	11:29	M Gerizim you shall pronounce the blessing, on M Ebal, the curse.
Dt	34: 1	from the plains of Moab to M Nebo,
Jos	8:30	Later, on M Ebal, Joshua built
1 Chr	10: 8	and his sons fallen on M Gilboa.
2 Chr	3: 1	LORD in Jerusalem on M Moriah,
Ps	74: 2	heritage, M Zion where you dwell.
Ps	78:68	of Judah, M Zion which he loved.
Is	14:13	take my seat on the M of Assembly,
Mi	4: 1	days to come the m of the LORD's house
Mi	4: 7	shall be king over them on M Zion,
Zec	14: 4	feet will stand on the M of Olives,
Zec	14: 4	The M of Olives will be split in two
Mk	13: 3	the M of Olives opposite the temple
Heb	12:22	you have approached M Zion
Rev	14: 1	was the Lamb standing on M Zion,

MOUNTAIN → MOUNT

Ex	3: 1	he came to the m of God, Horeb.
Ex	19: 2	encamped there in front of the m,
Ex	19:20	Moses to the top of the m,
Ex	24:18	He was on the m for forty days
Ex	32:19	broke them on the base of the m.
Dt	5: 4	you on the m from the midst
1 Kgs	16:24	bought the m of Samaria from Shemer
Ps	48: 2	in the city of our God: His holy m,
Ps	68:17	at the m where God has chosen
Is	2: 2	The m of the LORD's house shall be established as the highest m
Is	11: 9	harm or destroy on all my holy m;
Is	40: 4	up, every m and hill made low;
Is	65:25	harm or destroy on all my holy m,
Dn	2:45	from the m without a hand being put
Mt	4: 8	devil took him up to a very high m,
Mt	17:20	you will say to this m,
Mk	9: 2	up a high m apart by themselves.
Lk	3: 5	every m and hill shall be made low.
Jn	4:21	the Father neither on this m nor
2 Pt	1:18	we were with him on the holy m.
Rev	6:14	every m and island was moved
Rev	8: 8	like a large burning m was hurled
Rev	21:10	high m and showed me the holy city

MOUNTAINS → MOUNT

Gn	7:20	cubits higher than the submerged m.
Gn	8: 4	ark came to rest on the m of Ararat.
Jb	14:18	M fall and crumble, rocks move
Ps	36: 7	Your justice is like the highest m,
Ps	46: 3	m quake to the depths of the sea,
Ps	90: 2	Before the m were born, the earth
Ps	97: 5	The m melt like wax before

Ps	125: 2	As m surround Jerusalem,
Sir	43:16	by his power he shakes the m.
Is	52: 7	beautiful upon the m are the feet
Is	54:10	Though the m fall away
Is	55:12	M and hills shall break out in song
Ez	34: 6	wandered over all the m and high
Ez	39: 4	Upon the m of Israel you shall fall,
Dn	3:75	M and hills, bless the Lord;
Hos	10: 8	Then they will cry out to the m,
Na	2: 1	this moment on the m the footsteps
Mk	13:14	those in Judea must flee to the m,
Lk	23:30	that time people will say to the m,
1 Cor	13: 2	if I have all faith so as to move m
Rev	6:16	They cried out to the m
Rev	16:20	island fled, and m disappeared.

MOURN → MOURNING, MOURNS

Gn	23: 2	Abraham proceeded to m and weep for her.
Eccl	3: 4	a time to m, and a time to dance.
Sir	7:34	who weep, but m with those who m.
Is	61: 2	by our God; To comfort all who m;
Zec	12:10	they will m for him as one mourns
Mt	5: 4	Blessed are they who m, for they
Mt	9:15	the wedding guests m as long as

MOURNING → MOURN

Est	4: 3	the Jews went into deep m,
Est	9:22	into joy, from m into celebration.
1 Mc	1:39	her feasts were turned into m,
Ps	30:12	You changed my m into dancing;
Eccl	7: 2	to the house of m than to the house
Is	61: 3	them oil of gladness instead of m,
Jer	31:13	I will turn their m into joy, I will
Lam	5:15	ceased, dancing has turned into m;
Rev	21: 4	there shall be no more death or m,

MOURNS → MOURN

Zec	12:10	for him as one m for an only child,

MOUTH → MOUTHS

Ex	4:15	to him and put the words in his m.
Nm	16:30	and the ground opens its m
Nm	22:38	only what God puts in my m."
Dt	8: 3	forth from the m of the LORD.
Dt	18:18	my words into the m of the prophet;
Dt	30:14	in your m and in your heart, to do it.
2 Kgs	4:34	placing his m upon the child's m,
Jb	23:12	the words of his m I have treasured
Jb	40: 4	I put my hand over my m.
Ps	17: 3	My m has not transgressed
Ps	19:15	the words of my m be acceptable,
Ps	40: 4	And puts a new song in my m,
Ps	71: 8	My m shall be filled with your
Ps	78: 2	I will open my m in a parable,
Ps	119:103	sweeter than honey to my m!
Ps	141: 3	before my m, keep watch over
Prv	2: 6	from his m come knowledge
Prv	8: 7	Indeed, my m utters truth, and my
Prv	10:11	The m of the just is a fountain
Prv	10:11	but the m of the wicked conceals
Prv	10:31	The m of the just yields wisdom,
Prv	26:28	and the flattering m works ruin.
Prv	27: 2	another praise you, not your own m;
Eccl	6: 7	All human toil is for the m,
Sg	1: 2	him kiss me with kisses of his m,
Wis	1:11	and a lying m destroys the soul.
Is	40: 5	for the m of the LORD has spoken.
Is	48: 3	ago, they went forth from my m,
Is	51:16	I have put my words into your m,
Is	53: 7	submitted and did not open his m,
Is	55:11	word be that goes forth from my m;
Is	59:21	have put in your m Shall not depart
Jer	1: 9	his hand and touched my m,
Jer	1: 9	See, I place my words in your m!
Ez	3: 2	So I opened my m, and he gave me
Dn	7: 8	eyes, and a m that spoke arrogantly.
Hos	6: 5	I killed them by the words of my m;
Mal	2: 7	is to be sought from his m,
Mt	4: 4	comes forth from the m of God.' "

Mt	12:34	fullness of the heart the **m** speaks.
Mt	15:11	It is not what enters one's **m**
Mt	15:11	out of the **m** is what defiles one."
Lk	6:45	fullness of the heart the **m** speaks.
Acts	8:32	is silent, so he opened not his **m**.
2 Thes	2: 8	will kill with the breath of his **m**
Jas	3:10	From the same **m** come blessing
1 Pt	2:22	and no deceit was found in his **m**."
Rev	1:16	two-edged sword came out of his **m**,
Rev	2:16	them with the sword of my **m**.
Rev	3:16	cold, I will spit you out of my **m**.
Rev	10:10	In my **m** it was like sweet honey,
Rev	13: 6	It opened its **m** to utter blasphemies
Rev	19:15	Out of his **m** came a sharp sword

MOUTHS → MOUTH

Ps	73: 9	They set their **m** against
Ps	78:36	But they deceived him with their **m**,
Ps	115: 5	They have **m** but do not speak,
Ps	135:17	nor is there breath in their **m**.
Sir	21:26	The mind of fools is in their **m**,
Dn	6:23	closed the lions' **m** so that they have
Rom	3:14	their **m** are full of bitter cursing.
Eph	4:29	should come out of your **m**, but only
Heb	11:33	they closed the **m** of lions,
Jas	3: 3	If we put bits into the **m** of horses
Rev	9:17	and out of their **m** came fire, smoke,

MOVE → MOVED, MOVES

Dt	19:14	You shall not **m** your neighbor's
Is	46: 7	and does not **m** from the place.
Mt	17:20	mountain, 'M from here to there,' and it will **m**.
Acts	17:28	For 'In him we live and **m** and have

MOVED → MOVE

1 Chr	16:30	will surely stand fast, never to be **m**.
Ps	93: 1	surely stand in place, never to be **m**.
Ez	1:19	When the living creatures **m**, the wheels **m** with them;

MOVES → MOVE

Dt	27:17	be anyone who **m** a neighbor's

MUCH

Ex	16:18	They gathered as **m** as each needed
1 Kgs	8:27	how **m** less this house which I have
Jb	7:17	that you make **m** of them, or pay
Jb	42:10	to Job twice as **m** as he had before.
Prv	16:16	How **m** better to get wisdom than
Eccl	1:18	For in **m** wisdom there is **m** sorrow;
Eccl	9:18	but one bungler destroys **m** good.
Eccl	12:12	in **m** study there is weariness
Hg	1: 9	You expected **m**, but it came
Mt	12:12	How **m** more valuable a person is
Mt	23:15	Gehenna twice as **m** as yourselves.
Lk	12:48	**M** will be required of the person entrusted with **m**,
Jn	8:26	I have **m** to say about you
Jn	12:24	but if it dies, it produces **m** fruit.
Jn	15: 5	in me and I in him will bear **m** fruit,
2 Cor	3:11	how **m** more will what endures be
2 Cor	8:15	"Whoever had **m** did not have
Heb	9:14	how **m** more will the blood

MUD

Is	57:20	still, Its waters cast up mire and **m**.
Jer	38: 6	and Jeremiah sank down into the **m**.

MULBERRY

Lk	17: 6	you would say to [this] **m** tree,

MULE

2 Sm	18: 9	as the **m** passed under the branches
1 Kgs	1:38	Solomon on King David's **m**,

MULTIPLIED → MULTIPLY

Ex	11: 9	my wonders may be **m** in the land

MULTIPLIES → MULTIPLY

Sir	6: 5	Pleasant speech **m** friends,

MULTIPLY → MULTIPLIED, MULTIPLIES

Gn	1:28	Be fertile and **m**; fill the earth
Gn	9: 7	Be fertile, then, and **m**;

MULTITUDE

Dn	10: 6	of his voice was like the roar of a **m**.
Jas	5:20	death and will cover a **m** of sins.
1 Pt	4: 8	because love covers a **m** of sins.
Rev	7: 9	this I had a vision of a great **m**,
Rev	19: 6	like the sound of a great **m**

MURDER → MURDERED, MURDERER, MURDERERS, MURDERS

Hos	4: 2	lying, **m**, stealing and adultery break
Mt	15:19	the heart come evil thoughts, **m**,
Lk	23:25	imprisoned for rebellion and **m**,
Rom	1:29	full of envy, **m**, rivalry, treachery,

MURDERED → MURDER

Mt	23:31	of those who **m** the prophets;

MURDERER → MURDER

Nm	35:16	that person is a **m**, and the **m** must
Nm	35:31	the life of a **m** who deserves to die,
Jn	8:44	He was a **m** from the beginning
Acts	3:14	asked that a **m** be released to you.

MURDERERS → MURDER

1 Tm	1: 9	who kill their fathers or mothers, **m**,
Rev	21: 8	the depraved, **m**, the unchaste,
Rev	22:15	the **m**, the idol-worshipers, and all

MURDERS → MURDER

Rev	9:21	Nor did they repent of their **m**,

MUSIC → MUSICAL

Ps	105: 2	Sing praise to him, play **m**;
Lam	5:14	the gate, the young men their **m**.
Lk	15:25	house, he heard the sound of **m**

MUSICAL → MUSIC

1 Chr	15:16	and to play on **m** instruments, harps,
2 Chr	23:13	their **m** instruments were leading
Neh	12:36	with the **m** instruments of David,

MUST

Dt	18:13	You **m** be altogether sincere
Mt	16:21	to show his disciples that he **m** go
Mt	17:10	say that Elijah **m** come first?"
Mk	10:17	what **m** I do to inherit eternal life?"
Mk	13: 7	such things **m** happen, but it will not
Lk	9:22	"The Son of Man **m** suffer greatly
Jn	3: 7	you, 'You **m** be born from above.'
Jn	3:14	so **m** the Son of Man be lifted up,
Jn	3:30	He **m** increase; I **m** decrease."
Jn	4:24	those who worship him **m** worship
2 Cor	5:10	we **m** all appear before the judgment
Gal	6: 4	Each one **m** examine his own work,
1 Tm	3: 2	a bishop **m** be irreproachable,
1 Tm	3: 8	Similarly, deacons **m** be dignified,
Heb	11: 6	who approaches God **m** believe
Rev	4: 1	you what **m** happen afterwards."
Rev	22: 6	his servants what **m** happen soon."

MUSTARD

Mt	13:31	heaven is like a **m** seed that a person
Mt	17:20	you have faith the size of a **m** seed,
Mk	4:31	It is like a **m** seed that, when it is
Lk	13:19	It is like a **m** seed that a person took
Lk	17: 6	you have faith the size of a **m** seed,

MUTE

Mt	9:33	was driven out the **m** person spoke.
Mk	7:37	the deaf hear and [the] **m** speak."

MUTILATION

Phil	3: 2	the evil workers! Beware of the **m**!

MUTTER

Is	8:19	and soothsayers who chirp and **m**;

MUTUAL → MUTUALLY

Rom	12:10	love one another with **m** affection;
Heb	13: 1	Let **m** love continue.
2 Pt	1: 7	devotion with **m** affection,

MUTUALLY → MUTUAL

Rom	1:12	and I may be **m** encouraged by one

MUZZLE

Dt 25: 4 You shall not **m** an ox when it
1 Cor 9: 9 "You shall not **m** an ox while it is
1 Tm 5:18 "You shall not **m** an ox when it is

MYRRH

Ps 45: 9 With **m**, aloes, and cassia your robes
Sg 1:13 My lover is to me a sachet of **m**;
Mt 2:11 gifts of gold, frankincense, and **m**.
Mk 15:23 gave him wine drugged with **m**,
Jn 19:39 came bringing a mixture of **m**
Rev 18:13 spice, incense, **m**, and frankincense;

MYRTLE

Is 55:13 shall grow, instead of nettles, the **m**.
Zec 1: 8 in the shadows among **m** trees;

MYSTERIES → MYSTERY

Wis 14:23 either child sacrifices or occult **m**,
Sir 39: 7 as he meditates upon God's **m**,
Dn 2:28 is a God in heaven who reveals **m**,
Dn 2:29 he who reveals **m** showed you what
Dn 2:47 Lord of kings and a revealer of **m**;
1 Cor 13: 2 and comprehend all **m** and all
1 Cor 14: 2 no one listens; he utters **m** in spirit.

MYSTERY → MYSTERIES

Dn 2:18 God of heaven in regard to this **m**,
Dn 2:19 During the night the **m** was revealed
Dn 2:27 "The **m** about which the king has
Dn 2:30 me also this **m** has been revealed;
Dn 2:47 you were able to reveal this **m**."
Rom 11:25 want you to be unaware of this **m**,
Rom 16:25 to the revelation of the **m** kept secret
1 Cor 2: 1 brothers, proclaiming the **m** of God,
1 Cor 15:51 Behold, I tell you a **m**. We shall not
Eph 1: 9 made known to us the **m** of his will
Eph 3: 3 [that] the **m** was made known to me
Eph 3: 4 my insight into the **m** of Christ,
Eph 3: 9 [all] what is the plan of the **m** hidden
Eph 5:32 This is a great **m**, but I speak
Eph 6:19 with boldness the **m** of the gospel
Col 1:26 the **m** hidden from ages
Col 1:27 glory of this **m** among the Gentiles;
Col 2: 2 for the knowledge of the **m** of God,
Col 4: 3 to speak of the **m** of Christ,
2 Thes 2: 7 For the **m** of lawlessness is already
1 Tm 3: 9 holding fast to the **m** of the faith
1 Tm 3:16 Undeniably great is the **m**
Rev 17: 5 which is a **m**, "Babylon the great,
Rev 17: 7 explain to you the **m** of the woman

MYTHS

1 Tm 1: 4 to concern themselves with **m**
1 Tm 4: 7 Avoid profane and silly **m**.
2 Tm 4: 4 the truth and will be diverted to **m**.
Ti 1:14 of paying attention to Jewish **m**
2 Pt 1:16 did not follow cleverly devised **m**

N

NAAMAN

Aramean general whose leprosy was cleansed by Elisha (2 Kgs 5; Lk 4:27).

NABAL

Wealthy Carmelite the Lord killed for refusing to help David (1 Sm 25). David married Abigail, his widow (1 Sm 25:39-43).

NABOTH

Jezreelite killed by Jezebel for his vineyard (1 Kgs 21). Ahab's family destroyed for this (1 Kgs 21:17-24; 2 Kgs 9:21-37).

NADAB

1. Firstborn of Aaron (Ex 6:23); killed with Abihu for offering unauthorized fire (Lv 10; Nm 3:4).
2. Son of Jeroboam I; king of Israel (1 Kgs 15:25-32).

NAHASH

1 Sm 11: 1 later, **N** the Ammonite went
1 Sm 11: 1 All the people of Jabesh begged **N**,

NAHOR

Gn 11:26 old, he begot Abram, **N** and Haran.
Gn 22:23 These eight Milcah bore to **N**,
Gn 24:15 the wife of Abraham's brother **N**—

NAHUM

Prophet against Nineveh (Tb 14:4; Na 1:1).

NAILING → NAILS

Col 2:14 it from our midst, **n** it to the cross;

NAILS → NAILING

Is 41: 7 it with **n** so it will not totter.
Jn 20:25 I see the mark of the **n** in his hands

NAIVE

Prv 1:22 "How long, you **n** ones, will you love naivete,
Prv 8: 5 You **n** ones, gain prudence, you fools,

NAKED → NAKEDNESS

Gn 2:25 The man and his wife were both **n**,
Jb 1:21 "**N** I came forth from my mother's womb, and **n** shall I go back there.
Eccl 5:14 shall they return, **n** as they came,
Is 58: 7 Clothing the **n** when you see them,
Mk 14:52 left the cloth behind and ran off **n**.
2 Cor 5: 3 taken it off, we shall not be found **n**.
Rev 3:17 pitiable, poor, blind, and **n**.

NAKEDNESS → NAKED

Gn 9:22 saw his father's **n**, and he told his
Ez 16: 8 my cloak over you to cover your **n**;
Rom 8:35 or famine, or **n**, or peril,
Rev 3:18 so that your shameful **n** may not be

NAME → NAME'S, NAMED, NAMES

Gn 2:19 each living creature was then its **n**.
Gn 4:26 began to invoke the Lord by **n**.
Gn 11: 4 sky, and so make a **n** for ourselves;
Gn 12: 2 I will make your **n** great, so that you
Gn 12: 8 and invoked the Lord by **n**.
Gn 13: 4 Abram invoked the Lord by **n**.
Gn 17: 5 your **n** will be Abraham, for I am
Gn 21:33 there he invoked by **n** the Lord,
Gn 26:25 there and invoked the Lord by **n**.
Gn 32:30 asked him, "Please tell me your **n**."
Gn 32:30 "Why do you ask for my **n**?"
Ex 3:15 This is my **n** forever; this is my title
Ex 6: 3 and Jacob, but by my **n**, Lord,
Ex 20: 7 You shall not invoke the **n**
Ex 20: 7 anyone who invokes his **n** in vain.
Ex 33:19 you, and I will proclaim my **n**,
Ex 34: 5 him there and proclaimed the **n**,
Nm 17:17 Write each man's **n** on his staff;
Dt 5:11 You shall not invoke the **n**
Dt 5:11 anyone who invokes his **n** in vain.
Dt 10: 8 and to bless in his **n**, as they have
Dt 12:11 place for his **n** you shall bring all
Dt 18: 5 to minister in the **n** of the Lord,
Dt 25: 6 that his **n** may not be blotted
Dt 28:58 to fear this glorious and awesome **n**,
Jos 7: 9 us and efface our **n** from the earth.
Jos 7: 9 What will you do for your great **n**?"
Jgs 13:17 "What is your **n**, that we may honor
1 Sm 17:45 against you in the **n** of the Lord
1 Sm 25:25 Nabal, for he is just like his **n**. His **n** means fool,
2 Sm 6: 2 which bears the **n** "the Lord
1 Chr 17: 8 I will make your **n** like
2 Chr 7:14 whom my **n** has been pronounced,
Ezr 6:12 may the God who causes his **n**
Neh 9:10 for yourself a **n** even to this day.
Tb 11:14 blessed be his great **n**, and blessed
Tb 11:14 May his great **n** be with us,
Jdt 16: 1 a new song, exalt and acclaim his **n**.
Ps 5:12 will rejoice in you who love your **n**.
Ps 8: 2 awesome is your **n** through all
Ps 9: 6 their **n** you blotted out for all time.
Ps 9:11 Those who know your **n** trust
Ps 20: 8 we on the **n** of the Lord our God.
Ps 23: 3 right paths for the sake of his **n**.

Ps	29: 2	to the Lord the glory due his n.
Ps	34: 4	and let us exalt his n together.
Ps	44:21	we had forgotten the n of our God,
Ps	54: 3	O God, by your n save me.
Ps	66: 2	sing of his glorious n;
Ps	68: 5	Sing to God, praise his n;
Ps	68: 5	before him whose n is the Lord.
Ps	74:10	the enemy revile your n forever?
Ps	74:21	the poor and needy praise your n.
Ps	79: 9	on account of the glory of your n.
Ps	96: 8	to the Lord the glory due his n!
Ps	103: 1	all my being, bless his holy n!
Ps	113: 1	Lord, praise the n of the Lord.
Ps	115: 1	to your n give glory because of your
Ps	124: 8	Our help is in the n of the Lord,
Ps	138: 2	I praise your n for your mercy
Ps	138: 2	For you have exalted over all your n
Ps	145: 1	I will bless your n forever and ever.
Ps	149: 3	Let them praise his n in dance,
Prv	10: 7	but the n of the wicked will rot.
Prv	18:10	The n of the Lord is a strong
Prv	22: 1	A good n is more desirable than
Prv	30: 4	What is that person's n, or the n of his son?"
Eccl	7: 1	A good n is better than good
Sg	1: 3	Your n is a flowing perfume—
Sir	41:13	days, but a good n, for days without
Is	12: 4	to the Lord, acclaim his n;
Is	12: 4	proclaim how exalted is his n.
Is	26: 8	your n and your memory are
Is	40:26	them, calling them all by n.
Is	42: 8	I am the Lord, Lord is my n;
Is	50:10	Yet trust in the n of the Lord
Is	56: 5	an eternal n, which shall not be cut
Is	57:15	dwells forever, whose n is holy:
Is	63:14	to make for yourself a glorious n.
Jer	7:11	bears my n become in your eyes
Jer	10: 6	great, great and mighty is your n.
Jer	15:16	Because I bear your n, Lord,
Jer	27:15	but they prophesy falsely in my n.
Ez	20:44	with you thus, for the sake of my n,
Ez	36:22	but for the sake of my holy n,
Ez	48:35	the n of the city is "The Lord is
Dn	2:20	"Blessed be the n of God forever
Hos	12: 6	God of hosts, the Lord is his n!
Jl	3: 5	the n of the Lord will escape
Am	9:12	and all nations claimed in my n—
Mi	5: 3	by the majestic n of the Lord,
Mi	6: 9	city (It is prudent to fear your n!):
Zep	3: 9	may call upon the n of the Lord,
Zec	6:12	There is a man whose n is Branch—
Zec	13: 9	They will call upon my n, and I will
Zec	14: 9	and the Lord's n the only one.
Mal	1: 6	to you, O priests, who disdain my n.
Mal	3:20	a son and you are to n him Jesus,
Mt	6: 9	in heaven, hallowed be your n,
Mt	7:22	did we not prophesy in your n?
Mt	7:22	we not drive out demons in your n?
Mt	7:22	we not do mighty deeds in your n?'
Mt	12:21	in his n the Gentiles will hope."
Mt	18:20	three are gathered together in my n,
Mt	24: 5	For many will come in my n,
Mt	28:19	them in the n of the Father,
Mk	11: 9	he who comes in the n of the Lord!
Lk	1:31	a son, and you shall n him Jesus.
Lk	11: 2	hallowed be your n, your kingdom
Lk	19:38	who comes in the n of the Lord.
Jn	1:12	God, to those who believe in his n,
Jn	5:43	I came in the n of my Father,
Jn	5:43	yet if another comes in his own n,
Jn	10: 3	as he calls his own sheep by n
Jn	12:28	Father, glorify your n."
Jn	14:13	And whatever you ask in my n,
Jn	15:16	the Father in my n he may give you.
Jn	16:23	the Father in my n he will give you.
Jn	16:24	have not asked anything in my n;
Jn	17:11	in your n that you have given me,

Jn	20:31	belief you may have life in his n.
Acts	2:21	who calls on the n of the Lord.'
Acts	3:16	And by faith in his n, this man,
Acts	3:16	and know, his n has made strong,
Acts	4:12	is there any other n under heaven
Acts	4:17	again to speak to anyone in this n."
Acts	5:40	to stop speaking in the n of Jesus,
Acts	15:17	Gentiles on whom my n is invoked.
Rom	10:13	on the n of the Lord will be saved."
1 Cor	6:11	in the n of the Lord Jesus Christ
Phil	2: 9	bestowed on him the n that is above every n,
Phil	2:10	at the n of Jesus every knee should
Col	3:17	in the n of the Lord Jesus,
2 Tm	2:19	upon the n of the Lord avoid evil."
Heb	1: 4	the angels as the n he has inherited
Heb	13:15	is, the fruit of lips that confess his n.
Jas	5:14	[him] with oil in the n of the Lord,
1 Pt	4:16	but glorify God because of the n.
1 Jn	3:23	should believe in the n of his Son,
1 Jn	5:13	you who believe in the n of the Son
Rev	2: 3	and have suffered for my n, and you
Rev	2:13	yet you hold fast to my n and have
Rev	2:17	upon which is inscribed a new n,
Rev	3: 5	and I will never erase his n
Rev	3: 5	but will acknowledge his n
Rev	3: 8	my word and have not denied my n.
Rev	3:12	him I will inscribe the n of my God
Rev	3:12	and the n of the city of my God,
Rev	3:12	from my God, as well as my new n.
Rev	11:18	ones and those who fear your n,
Rev	13:17	the stamped image of the beast's n or the number that stood for its n.
Rev	14: 1	forty-four thousand who had his n and his Father's n written on their
Rev	16: 9	blasphemed the n of God who had
Rev	19:12	He had a n inscribed that no one
Rev	19:13	his n was called the Word of God.
Rev	19:16	He has a n written on his cloak
Rev	20:15	Anyone whose n was not found
Rev	22: 4	and his n will be on their foreheads.

NAME'S → NAME

Ps	79: 9	us, pardon our sins for your n sake.
Ps	106: 8	Yet he saved them for his n sake

NAMED → NAME

Gn	5:29	and n him Noah, saying, "This one
Gn	27:36	"He is well n Jacob, is he not!
Gn	35:10	You will no longer be n Jacob, but Israel
Ex	16:31	The house of Israel n this food manna.
1 Sm	4:21	She n the child Ichabod, saying,
1 Sm	7:12	he n it Ebenezer, explaining,

NAMES → NAME

Gn	2:20	The man gave n to all the tame
Ex	28: 9	engrave on them the n of the sons
Hos	2:19	from her mouth the n of the Baals;
Mt	10: 2	The n of the twelve apostles are
Lk	10:20	rejoice because your n are written
Phil	4: 3	whose n are in the book of life.
Rev	17: 3	was covered with blasphemous n,
Rev	17: 8	of the earth whose n have not been
Rev	21:12	and on which n were inscribed,
Rev	21:12	[the n] of the twelve tribes
Rev	21:14	were inscribed the twelve n

NAOMI → =MARA

Wife of Elimelech, mother-in-law of Ruth (Ru 1:2, 4). Left Bethlehem for Moab during famine (Ru 1:1). Returned a widow, with Ruth (Ru 1:6-22). Advised Ruth to seek marriage with Boaz (Ru 2:17–3:4). Cared for Ruth's son Obed (Ru 4:13-17).

NAPHTALI

Son of Jacob by Bilhah (Gn 30:8; 35:25; 1 Chr 2:2). Tribe of blessed (Gn 49:21; Dt 33:23), numbered (Nm 1:43; 26:50), allotted land (Jos 19:32-39; Ez 48:3), failed to fully possess (Jgs 1:33), supported Deborah (Jgs 4:10; 5:18), David (1 Chr 12:35), 12,000 from (Rev 7:6).

NARD
Jn   12: 3 oil made from genuine aromatic n

NARROW
Nm   22:24 stood in a n lane between vineyards
Mt   7:13 "Enter through the n gate;
Lk   13:24 "Strive to enter through the n door,

NATHAN
Prophet and chronicler of Israel's history (1 Chr 29:29; 2 Chr 9:29). Announced the Davidic covenant (2 Sm 7; 1 Chr 17). Denounced David's sin with Bathsheba (2 Sm 12). Supported Solomon (1 Kgs 1).

NATHANAEL → =BARTHOLOMEW?
Apostle (Jn 1:45-49; 21:2). Probably also called Bartholomew (Mt 10:3).

NATION → NATIONS
Gn   12: 2 I will make of you a great n, and I
Gn   15:14 judgment on the n they must serve,
Gn   35:11 A n, indeed an assembly of nations,
Ex   19: 6 me a kingdom of priests, a holy n.
Ex   32:10 Then I will make of you a great n.
Nm   14:12 I will make of you a n greater
Dt   4: 7 For what great n is there that has
Jos   4: 1 After the entire n had completed
Jos   5: 8 of the entire n was complete,
2 Sm   7:23 What other n on earth is there like
2 Sm   7:23 What god has ever led a n,
1 Chr 16:20 Wandering from n to n, from one
Ps   33:12 Blessed is the n whose God is
Ps 147:20 He has not done this for any other n;
Prv 14:34 Justice exalts a n, but sin is
Is   2: 4 One n shall not raise the sword
Is   26: 2 gates that a righteous n may enter,
Is   65: 1 To a n that did not invoke my name.
Is   66: 8 or a n be born in a single moment?
Jer   2:11 Does any other n change its gods?—
Jer   18: 8 that n against whom I have decreed
Ez   37:22 I will make them one n in the land,
Mi   4: 3 One n shall not raise the sword
Mal   3: 9 for you, the whole n, rob me.
Mt   24: 7 N will rise against n, and kingdom
Jn   11:50 that the whole n may not perish."
1 Pt   2: 9 a holy n, a people of his own,
Rev   5: 9 tribe and tongue, people and n.
Rev   7: 9 one could count, from every n, race,
Rev   14: 6 dwell on earth, to every n, tribe,

NATIONS → NATION
Gn   17: 4 the father of a multitude of n.
Gn   18:18 and all the n of the earth are to find
Gn   22:18 in your descendants all the n
Gn   25:23 Two n are in your womb,
Ex   34:24 I will drive out the n before you
Dt   7: 1 and removes many n before you—
Dt   7: 1 seven n more numerous and powerful
Dt   15: 6 you will lend to many n, and borrow
Dt   15: 6 you will rule over many n, and none
Jos   23: 7 these n that survive among you.
Jgs   3: 1 These are the n the LORD allowed
1 Sm   8:20 We too must be like all the n,
1 Kgs 5:14 People from all n came to hear
2 Kgs 17:15 the surrounding n whom
2 Chr 20: 6 rule over all the kingdoms of the n?
Ps   2: 1 Why do the n protest
Ps   2: 8 give you the n as your inheritance,
Ps   9: 6 You rebuked the n, you destroyed
Ps   22:29 to the LORD, the ruler over the n.
Ps   33:10 The LORD foils the plan of n,
Ps   46:11 I am exalted among the n,
Ps   47: 9 God rules over the n; God sits
Ps   66: 7 His eyes are fixed upon the n.
Ps   67: 3 earth, your victory among all the n.
Ps   72:17 may all the n regard him as favored.
Ps 106:35 But mingled with the n and imitated
Ps 110: 6 Who judges n, heaps up corpses,
Ps 113: 4 High above all n is the LORD;
Sir 44:21 bless the n through his descendants,

Is   2: 2 All n shall stream toward it.
Is   11:10 Him the n will seek out;
Is   12: 4 Among the n make known his
Is   40:15 the n count as a drop in the bucket,
Is   42: 1 he shall bring forth justice to the n.
Is   52:15 So shall he startle many n,
Is   60: 3 N shall walk by your light,
Is   60:12 such n shall be utterly destroyed!
Is   66:18 I am coming to gather all n
Jer   1: 5 a prophet to the n I appointed you.
Jer   3:17 All n will gather together there
Jer   31:10 you n, proclaim it on distant coasts,
Jer   33: 9 pride, before all the n of the earth,
Jer   46:28 I will make an end of all the n
Lam   1: 1 was great among the n is now like
Ez   22: 4 you an object of scorn for the n
Ez   36:23 desecrated among the n, in whose
Ez   36:23 Then the n shall know that I am
Ez   37:22 They shall never again be two n,
Ez   39:21 I will display my glory among the n,
Ez   39:21 and all the n will see the judgment I
Jl   2:17 a disgrace, a byword among the n!
Jl   4: 2 I will gather all the n and bring
Jl   4: 2 they scattered them among the n,
Am   9:12 and all n claimed in my name—
Zep   3: 8 For it is my decision to gather n,
Hg   2: 7 I will shake all the n,
Hg   2: 7 treasures of all the n will come in.
Zec   8:13 as you became a curse among the n,
Zec   9:10 and he will proclaim peace to the n.
Zec   14: 2 gather all the n against Jerusalem
Mal   1:11 For my name is great among the n,
Mal   3:12 All the n will call you blessed,
Mt   24:   You will be hated by all n because
Mt   24:14 the world as a witness to all n,
Mt   25:32 all the n will be assembled before
Mt   28:19 and make disciples of all n,
Rom 4:18 become "the father of many n,"
Rev   2:26 end, I will give authority over the n.
Rev   12: 5 to rule all the n with an iron rod.
Rev   15: 4 All the n will come and worship
Rev   18:23 all n were led astray by your magic
Rev   19:15 came a sharp sword to strike the n.
Rev   20: 8 to deceive the n at the four corners
Rev   21:24 The n will walk by its light, and to it
Rev   22: 2 the trees serve as medicine for the n.

NATIVE
Ex   12:49 There will be one law for the n
Acts   2: 8 us hear them in his own n language?

NATURAL → NATURE
Rom 1:26 Their females exchanged n relations
Rom 11:21 if God did not spare the n branches,

NATURE → NATURAL
1 Cor 11:14 Does not n itself teach you
Eph   2: 3 and we were by n children of wrath,
2 Pt   1: 4 may come to share in the divine n,

NAZARETH
Mt   2:23 went and dwelt in a town called N,
Mk   1:24 have you to do with us, Jesus of N?
Lk   1:26 God to a town of Galilee called N,
Lk   4:16 He came to N, where he had grown
Jn   1:46 anything good come from N?"
Acts 10:38 how God anointed Jesus of N

NAZIRITE → NAZIRITES
Nm   6: 2 women solemnly take the n vow

NAZIRITES → NAZIRITE
Am   2:12 But you made the n drink wine,

NAZOREAN
Mt   2:23 fulfilled, "He shall be called a N."

NEAR → NEARER
Dt   30:14 No, it is something very n to you,
Ps   73:28 to be n God is my good, to make
Ps 145:18 The LORD is n to all who call

Is   55: 6 found, call upon him while he is **n**.
Ez   7: 7 The time has come, **n** is the day:
Jl   1:15 For **n** is the day of the LORD,
Zep   1:14 **N** is the great day of the LORD,
Mal   3: 5 I will draw **n** to you for judgment,
Rom   10: 8 "The word is **n** you, in your mouth
Phil   4: 5 be known to all. The Lord is **n**.
Jas   4: 8 Draw **n** to God, and he will draw **n**
Rev   1: 3 in it, for the appointed time is **n**.
Rev   22:10 book, for the appointed time is **n**.

NEARER → NEAR
Rom   13:11 our salvation is **n** now than

NEBO
Dt   34: 1 the plains of Moab to Mount **N**,
Is   46: 1 Bel bows down, **N** stoops,

NEBUCHADNEZZAR
    Babylonian king, also spelled Nebuchadrezzar. Subdued and exiled
Judah (2 Kgs 24–25; 2 Chr 36; Jer 39). Dreams interpreted by Daniel
(Dn 2; 4). Worshiped God (Dn 3:98-100; 4:34-37).

NEBUZARADAN
2 Kgs   25: 8 king of Babylon), **N**,
Jer   52:12 king of Babylon, **N**,

NECESSARY
Lk   24:26 Was it not **n** that the Messiah should
Acts   15: 5 said, "It is **n** to circumcise them
2 Cor   9: 5 So I thought it **n** to encourage
Phil   1:24 the flesh is more **n** for your benefit.
Heb   9:23 it was **n** for the copies

NECK → NECKS, STIFF-NECKED
Gn   27:16 hands and the hairless part of his **n**.
Prv   1: 9 for your head; a pendant for your **n**.
Prv   3:22 soul, and an adornment for your **n**.
Prv   6:21 always, tie them around your **n**.
Sg   7: 5 Your **n** like a tower of ivory;
Sir   51:26 Take her yoke upon your **n**;
Jer   28:10 from the **n** of Jeremiah the prophet
Hos   10:11 laid a yoke upon her beautiful **n**;
Mt   18: 6 a great millstone hung around his **n**

NECKS → NECK
Jos   10:24 your feet on the **n** of these kings."
Is   3:16 and walk with **n** outstretched,
Jer   7:26 they have stiffened their **n** and done

NECO
    Pharaoh who killed Josiah (2 Kgs 23:29-30; 2 Chr 35:20-24), de-
posed Jehoahaz (2 Kgs 23:33-35; 2 Chr 36:3-4).

NEED → NEEDS, NEEDY
Mt   3:14 saying, "I **n** to be baptized by you,
Mt   6: 8 knows what you **n** before you ask
Mt   21: 3 reply, 'The master has **n** of them.'
Mk   2:17 who are well do not **n** a physician,
Lk   12:30 your Father knows that you **n** them.
Lk   15:14 and he found himself in dire **n**.
Acts   2:45 all according to each one's **n**.
Acts   4:35 distributed to each according to **n**.
1 Cor   12:21 "I do not **n** you," nor again
1 Cor   12:21 head to the feet, "I do not **n** you."
1 Thes   5: 1 you have no **n** for anything to be
1 Jn   2:27 you do not **n** anyone to teach you.
1 Jn   3:17 worldly means sees a brother in **n**
Rev   21:23 The city had no **n** of sun or moon
Rev   22: 5 nor will they **n** light from lamp

NEEDLE
Lk   18:25 pass through the eye of a **n** than

NEEDS → NEED
2 Cor   8:14 present time should supply their **n**,
2 Cor   8:14 surplus may also supply your **n**,

NEEDY → NEED
Dt   15:11 land will never lack for **n** persons;
Dt   15:11 and to your **n** kin in your land."
1 Sm   2: 8 He raises the **n** from the dust;
Ps   9:19 For the **n** will never be forgotten,

Ps   35:10 afflicted and **n** from the despoiler?"
Ps   74:21 the poor and **n** praise your name.
Ps   113: 7 He raises the **n** from the dust,
Ps   140:13 will take up the cause of the **n**,
Prv   14:31 who are kind to the **n** honor him.
Prv   31: 9 justly, defend the **n** and the poor!
Prv   31:20 poor, and extends her arms to the **n**.
Sir   4: 3 angry, nor delay giving to the **n**.
Am   8: 4 you who trample upon the **n**

NEGEB
Gn   13: 1 went up to the **N** with his wife
Gn   24:62 was living in the region of the **N**.
Jos   11:16 the entire **N**, all the land of Goshen,
Ps   126: 4 like the dry stream beds of the **N**.

NEGLECT → NEGLECTED
Dt   12:19 you do not **n** the Levite as long as
Dt   14:27 But do not **n** the Levite within your
Neh   10:40 We will not **n** the house of our God.
Sir   7:10 impatient in prayer or **n** almsgiving.
Acts   6: 2 not right for us to **n** the word of God
1 Tm   4:14 Do not **n** the gift you have,

NEGLECTED → NEGLECT
Mt   23:23 have **n** the weightier things

NEHEMIAH
    Cupbearer of Artaxerxes (Neh 2:1); governor of Israel (Neh 8:9).
Returned to Jerusalem to rebuild walls (Neh 2–6). With Ezra, reestab-
lished worship (Neh 8). Prayer confessing nation's sin (Neh 9). Dedicated wall (Neh 12). Story of the miraculous fire (2 Mc 1).

NEHUSHTAN
2 Kgs   18: 4 incense to it. (It was called **N**.)

NEIGHBOR → NEIGHBOR'S, NEIGHBORS
Ex   3:22 Every woman will ask her **n**
Ex   20:16 bear false witness against your **n**.
Lv   19:18 You shall love your **n** as yourself.
Dt   5:20 dishonest witness against your **n**.
Prv   24:28 Do not testify falsely against your **n**
Prv   25:18 who bears false witness against a **n**.
Prv   27:10 Better a **n** near than kin far away.
Prv   27:14 Those who greet their **n** with a loud
Prv   29: 5 speak flattery to their **n** cast a net
Sir   29:20 Help your **n** according to your
Is   19: 2 war against brother, **N** against **n**,
Mt   5:43 'You shall love your **n** and hate
Mt   19:19 shall love your **n** as yourself.' "
Mk   12:31 'You shall love your **n** as yourself.'
Lk   10:27 your mind, and your **n** as yourself."
Lk   10:29 said to Jesus, "And who is my **n**?"
Rom   13: 9 shall love your **n** as yourself."
Rom   13:10 Love does no evil to the **n**;
Rom   15: 2 each of us please our **n** for the good,
Jas   2: 8 shall love your **n** as yourself,"

NEIGHBOR'S → NEIGHBOR
Ex   20:17 You shall not covet your **n** house.
Ex   20:17 You shall not covet your **n** wife,
Ex   22:25 If you take your **n** cloak as a pledge,
Dt   5:21 You shall not covet your **n** wife.
Dt   5:21 You shall not desire your **n** house
Dt   19:14 not move your **n** boundary markers
Dt   27:17 who moves a **n** boundary markers!"

NEIGHBORS → NEIGHBOR
2 Kgs   4: 3 borrow vessels from all your **n**—
Ezr   1: 6 All their **n** gave them help in every
Ps   79: 4 have become the reproach of our **n**,
Ps   80: 7 left us to be fought over by our **n**;
Prv   3:29 Do not plot evil against your **n**,

NEPHEW
Tb   1:22 in fact, my **n**, of my father's house,

NEPHILIM
Gn   6: 4 The **N** appeared on earth in those

NEST → NESTS
Dt   22: 6 you come across a bird's **n**
Ob   1: 4 and your **n** is set among the stars,

Hb   2: 9 setting your **n** on high to escape

NESTS → NEST

Mt   8:20 dens and birds of the sky have **n**,

NET → NETS

Prv   1:17 In vain a **n** is spread right under
Prv   29: 5 flattery to their neighbor cast a **n**
Lam   1:13 He spread out a **n** for my feet,
Hb   1:15 He gathers them in his fishing **n**,
Mt   13:47 of heaven is like a **n** thrown
Jn   21: 6 "Cast the **n** over the right side

NETS → NET

Ps   141:10 Let the wicked fall into their own **n**,
Mt   4:20 At once they left their **n**
Mk   1:16 his brother Andrew casting their **n**
Lk   5: 4 and lower your **n** for a catch."

NEVER

Gn   8:21 **N** again will I curse the ground
Dt   32:17 to gods they had **n** known,
Ps   15: 5 acts like this shall **n** be shaken.
Ps   30: 7 I once said, "I shall **n** be shaken."
Ps   119:93 I will **n** forget your precepts;
Prv   10:30 The just will **n** be disturbed,
Prv   27:20 and Abaddon can **n** be satisfied;
Prv   27:20 eyes of mortals can **n** be satisfied.
Prv   30:15 Three things **n** get their fill, four **n**
Sir   4:25 **N** speak against the truth,
Jer   33:17 David shall **n** lack a successor
Dn   2:44 a kingdom that shall **n** be destroyed
Mt   7:23 to them solemnly, 'I **n** knew you.
Mk   3:29 holy Spirit will **n** have forgiveness,
Jn   4:14 the water I shall give will **n** thirst;
Jn   6:35 whoever comes to me will **n** hunger,
Jn   6:35 whoever believes in me will **n** thirst.
Jn   8:51 keeps my word will **n** see death."
Jn   10:28 eternal life, and they shall **n** perish.
Jn   11:26 lives and believes in me will **n** die.
1 Cor   13: 8 Love **n** fails. If there are prophecies,
Heb   13: 5 "I will **n** forsake you or abandon
2 Pt   1:10 for, in doing so, you will **n** stumble.

NEW → ANEW, NEWBORN, NEWNESS

Ex   1: 8 Then a **n** king, who knew nothing
Jgs   5: 8 **N** gods were their choice;
Ezr   9: 9 Thus he has given us **n** life to raise
Jdt   16: 1 Improvise for him a **n** song,
1 Mc   4:47 built a **n** altar like the former one.
Ps   33: 3 Sing to him a **n** song;
Ps   40: 4 And puts a **n** song in my mouth,
Ps   98: 1 Sing a **n** song to the LORD, for he
Eccl   1: 9 Nothing is **n** under the sun!
Sir   9:10 **n** ones cannot equal them.
Sir   9:10 A **n** friend is like **n** wine—
Is   42: 9 come to pass, **n** ones I now declare;
Is   42:10 Sing to the LORD a **n** song,
Is   43:19 See, I am doing something **n**!
Is   62: 2 be called by a **n** name bestowed
Is   65:17 See, I am creating **n** heavens and a **n** earth;
Is   66:22 Just as the **n** heavens and the **n** earth
Jer   31:31 I will make a **n** covenant
Ez   11:19 and a **n** spirit I will put within them.
Ez   18:31 make for yourselves a **n** heart and a **n** spirit.
Ez   36:26 I will give you a **n** heart, and a **n** spirit I will put
Mt   9:17 People do not put **n** wine into old
Mt   9:17 Rather, they pour **n** wine into fresh
Mt   13:52 from his storeroom both the **n**
Mk   1:27 A **n** teaching with authority.
Lk   5:39 been drinking old wine desires **n**,
Lk   22:20 "This cup is the **n** covenant in my
Jn   13:34 I give you a **n** commandment:
Acts   17:19 we learn what this **n** teaching is
1 Cor   11:25 "This cup is the **n** covenant in my
2 Cor   3: 6 us as ministers of a **n** covenant,
2 Cor   5:17 whoever is in Christ is a **n** creation:
2 Cor   5:17 behold, **n** things have come.
Gal   6:15 but only a **n** creation.

Eph   2:15 in himself one **n** person in place
Eph   4:24 and put on the **n** self,
Col   3:10 and have put on the **n** self, which is
Heb   8: 8 I will conclude a **n** covenant
Heb   9:15 he is mediator of a **n** covenant:
Heb   10:20 by the **n** and living way he opened
Heb   12:24 the mediator of a **n** covenant,
1 Pt   1: 3 his great mercy gave us a **n** birth
2 Pt   3:13 we await **n** heavens and a **n** earth in which righteousness
1 Jn   2: 7 I am writing no **n** commandment
2 Jn   1: 5 I were writing a **n** commandment
Rev   2:17 upon which is inscribed a **n** name,
Rev   3:12 the city of my God, the **n** Jerusalem,
Rev   3:12 my God, as well as my **n** name.
Rev   5: 9 They sang a **n** hymn:
Rev   14: 3 [to be] a **n** hymn before the throne,
Rev   21: 1 Then I saw a **n** heaven and a **n** earth.
Rev   21: 2 saw the holy city, a **n** Jerusalem,
Rev   21: 5 said, "Behold, I make all things **n**."

NEWBORN → BEAR, NEW

1 Pt   2: 2 like **n** infants, long for pure spiritual

NEWNESS → NEW

Rom   6: 4 we too might live in **n** of life.

NEWS

2 Kgs   7: 9 This is a day of good **n**, and we are
Prv   15:30 good **n** invigorates the bones.
Prv   25:25 thirst is good **n** from a far country.
Is   40: 9 a high mountain, Zion, herald of good **n**!
Is   41:27 will give Jerusalem a herald of good **n**."
Is   52: 7 the feet of the one bringing good **n**,
Mt   11: 5 poor have the good **n** proclaimed
Lk   1:19 and to announce to you this good **n**.
Lk   2:10 proclaim to you good **n** of great joy
Lk   3:18 he preached good **n** to the people.
Lk   4:43 I must proclaim the good **n**
Lk   8: 1 and proclaiming the good **n**
Acts   14: 7 continued to proclaim the good **n**.
Acts   14:21 they had proclaimed the good **n**
Rom   10:15 of those who bring [the] good **n**!"

NICANOR'S

1 Mc   7:43 **N** army was crushed, and he himself
2 Mc   15:37 Since **N** doings ended in this way,

NICODEMUS

Pharisee who visted Jesus at night (Jn 3). Argued for fair treatment of Jesus (Jn 7:50-52). With Joseph, prepared Jesus for burial (Jn 19:38-42).

NICOLAITANS

Rev   2: 6 you hate the works of the **N**, which I
Rev   2:15 who hold to the teaching of [the] **N**.

NIGER

Acts   13: 1 Symeon who was called **N**,

NIGHT → MIDNIGHT, NIGHTS

Gn   1: 5 and the darkness he called "**n**."
Gn   1:16 and the lesser one to govern the **n**,
Gn   8:22 and day and **n** shall not cease.
Ex   13:21 at **n** by means of a column of fire
Ex   13:21 they could travel both day and **n**.
Ex   40:38 day, and fire in the cloud at **n**,
Dt   28:66 will stand in dread both day and **n**,
Jos   1: 8 Recite it by day and by **n**, that you
Jb   35:10 Maker, who gives songs in the **n**,
Ps   1: 2 on his law he meditates day and **n**.
Ps   16: 7 even at **n** my heart exhorts me.
Ps   19: 3 **n** unto **n** whispers knowledge.
Ps   42: 9 by **n** may his righteousness be
Ps   63: 7 you through the watches of the **n**
Ps   74:16 Yours the day and yours the **n** too;
Ps   77: 7 At **n** I ponder in my heart; and as I
Ps   91: 5 fear the terror of the **n** nor the arrow
Ps   119:55 Even at **n** I remember your name
Ps   121: 6 not strike you, nor the moon by **n**.
Ps   136: 9 The moon and stars to rule the **n**,
Prv   31:18 her lamp is never extinguished at **n**.

Eccl	2:23	even at **n** their hearts are not at rest.
Is	21:11	how much longer the **n**?
Jer	33:20	and my covenant with **n** so that day
Mt	24:43	the house had known the hour of **n**
Lk	2: 8	and keeping the **n** watch over their
Lk	6:12	and he spent the **n** in prayer to God.
Jn	3: 2	He came to Jesus at **n** and said
Jn	9: 4	**N** is coming when no one can work.
Jn	11:10	But if one walks at **n**, he stumbles,
1 Cor	11:23	on the **n** he was handed over,
1 Thes	5: 2	the Lord will come like a thief at **n**.
1 Thes	5: 5	We are not of the **n** or of darkness.
Rev	8:12	for a third of the time, as did the **n**.
Rev	20:10	will be tormented day and **n** forever
Rev	21:25	be shut, and there will be no **n** there.
Rev	22: 5	**N** will be no more, nor will they

NIGHTS → NIGHT

Gn	7:12	forty **n** heavy rain poured down
Ex	24:18	mountain for forty days and forty **n**.
1 Kgs	19: 8	and forty **n** to the mountain of God,
Jon	2: 1	of the fish three days and three **n**.
Mt	4: 2	He fasted for forty days and forty **n**,
Mt	12:40	of the whale three days and three **n**,
Mt	12:40	of the earth three days and three **n**.

NILE

Gn	41: 2	up out of the **N** came seven cows,

NIMROD

Gn	10: 9	"Like **N**, a mighty hunter

NINE

Nm	34:13	has commanded to be given to the **n**
Jos	13: 7	apportion among the **n** tribes
Mk	15:25	It was **n** o'clock in the morning
Acts	2:15	it is only **n** o'clock in the morning.

NINETY

Gn	17:17	Can Sarah give birth at **n**?"

NINETY-NINE

Gn	17: 1	When Abram was **n** years old,
Lk	15: 4	of them would not leave the **n**

NINEVEH

Tb	1:10	and came as a captive to **N**, all my
Jon	1: 2	Set out for the great city of **N**,
Na	1: 1	Oracle concerning **N**. The book
Mt	12:41	the men of **N** will arise with this

NOAH

Righteous man (Ez 14:14, 20) called to build ark (Gn 6–8; Heb 11:7; 1 Pt 3:20; 2 Pt 2:5). God's covenant with (Gn 9:1-17). Drunkenness of (Gn 9:18-23). Blessed sons, cursed Canaan (Gn 9:24-27). Praised (Sir 44:17-18).

NOB

1 Sm	21: 2	the priest of **N**, who came trembling

NOBLE → NOBLES

Is	32: 8	But the **n** plan **n** deeds, and in **n** deeds they persist.
Lam	4: 1	lost its luster, the **n** metal changed;
1 Cor	1:26	powerful, not many were of **n** birth.
1 Tm	3: 1	the office of bishop desires a **n** task.

NOBLES → NOBLE

Prv	8:16	and **n**, all the judges of the earth.

NOISE

Ex	32:17	Joshua heard the **n** of the people
Is	29: 6	earthquake, and great **n**, whirlwind,

NONE

Nm	14:23	**N** of those who have spurned me
Ps	86: 8	**N** among the gods can equal you,

NOON → AFTERNOON

Mk	15:33	At **n** darkness came over the whole

NORTH

Is	41:25	I have stirred up one from the **n**,
Jer	4: 6	Disaster I bring from the **n**,
Ez	1: 4	a great stormwind came from the **N**,
Dn	11: 6	to the king of the **n** to carry

Zec	2:10	Flee from the land of the **n**—

NOSE → NOSES

2 Kgs	19:28	I will put my hook in your **n** and my

NOSES → NOSE

Ps	115: 6	but do not hear, **n** but do not smell.

NOSTRILS

Gn	2: 7	blew into his **n** the breath of life,
Gn	7:22	with the breath of life in its **n** died.
Ps	18:16	at the storming breath of your **n**.
Is	2:22	mortals, in whose **n** is but a breath;

NOTHING

2 Sm	24:24	burnt offerings that cost me **n**."
2 Chr	9: 2	and there was **n** so obscure
Jb	1: 9	"Is it for **n** that Job is God-fearing?
Eccl	1: 9	**N** is new under the sun!
Eccl	3:22	that there is **n** better for mortals than
Eccl	8:15	because there is **n** better for mortals
Sir	32:19	Do **n** without deliberation;
Sir	39:20	To him, **n** is small or insignificant,
Sir	39:20	and **n** too wonderful or hard
Is	44: 9	Those who fashion idols are all **n**;
Jer	32:17	**n** is too difficult for you.
Mt	17:20	**N** will be impossible for you."
Lk	1:37	for **n** will be impossible for God."
Lk	8:17	For there is **n** hidden that will not
Lk	8:17	and **n** secret that will not be known
Lk	12: 2	"There is **n** concealed that will not
Jn	15: 5	because without me you can do **n**.
1 Cor	2: 2	I resolved to know **n** while I was
1 Cor	13: 2	but do not have love, I am **n**.
1 Tm	6: 7	For we brought **n** into the world,
Heb	7:19	for the law brought **n** to perfection;

NOTORIOUS

Mt	27:16	they had a **n** prisoner called [Jesus]

NOW

Gn	22:12	For **n** I know that you fear God,
Ezr	9: 8	"And **n**, only a short time ago,
Ps	20: 7	**N** I know the LORD gives victory
Lk	1:48	from **n** on will all ages call me
Jn	2:10	have kept the good wine until **n**."
Jn	5:25	is **n** here when the dead will hear
Jn	9:25	is that I was blind and **n** I see."
Jn	13:19	From **n** on I am telling you before it
Jn	13:36	you cannot follow me **n**, though you
Jn	16:12	to tell you, but you cannot bear it **n**.
Rom	3:21	**n** the righteousness of God has been
Rom	5: 9	then, since we are **n** justified by his
Rom	8: 1	**n** there is no condemnation for those
Rom	13:11	it is the hour **n** for you to awake
Rom	13:11	our salvation is nearer **n** than
2 Cor	6: 2	Behold, **n** is a very acceptable time;
2 Cor	6: 2	behold, **n** is the day of salvation.
Eph	2: 2	air, the spirit that is **n** at work
Eph	3: 5	generations as it has **n** been revealed
Col	1:26	**n** it has been manifested to his holy
1 Pt	1: 8	you do not see him **n** yet believe
1 Pt	2:10	but **n** you are God's people;
1 Pt	2:10	but **n** you have received mercy.
1 Jn	2:18	coming, so **n** many antichrists have

NOWHERE → WHERE

Lk	9:58	Son of Man has **n** to rest his head."

NULLIFY

Rom	3: 3	Will their infidelity **n** the fidelity
Gal	2:21	I do not **n** the grace of God;

NUMBER → NUMBERED, NUMBERS, NUMEROUS

Dt	32: 8	after the **n** of the divine beings;
Ps	105:12	When they were few in **n**, a handful,
Acts	2:47	their **n** those who were being saved.
Acts	6: 1	as the **n** of disciples continued
Acts	11:21	a great **n** who believed turned
Rom	11:25	part, until the full **n** of the Gentiles
Rev	6:11	while longer until the **n** was filled
Rev	7: 4	I heard the **n** of those who had been

Rev 13:18 who understands can calculate the **n**
Rev 13:18 for it is a **n** that stands for a person.
Rev 13:18 His **n** is six hundred and sixty-six.

NUMBERED → NUMBER
2 Sm 24:10 David regretted having **n** the people.
Dn 5:26 God has **n** your kingdom and put

NUMBERS → NUMBER
Ps 147: 4 He **n** the stars, and gives to all
Acts 9:31 of the holy Spirit it grew in **n**.

NUMEROUS → NUMBER
Ex 1: 9 and become more **n** than we are!
Zec 10: 8 and they will be as **n** as before.

NURSE → NURSED, NURSING
Gn 21: 7 "that Sarah would **n** children!
Ex 2: 7 a Hebrew woman to **n** the child
Is 66:11 So that you may **n** and be satisfied

NURSED → NURSE
Ex 2: 9 woman took the child and **n** him.
Lk 11:27 and the breasts at which you **n**."
Lk 23:29 bore and the breasts that never **n**.'

NURSING → NURSE
Lk 21:23 women and **n** mothers in those days,

O

OAK
Ez 6:13 every green tree and leafy **o**—

OATH
Gn 21:31 the two of them took an **o** there.
Gn 26: 3 in fulfillment of the **o** that I swore
Nm 30: 3 binds himself under **o** to a pledge,
Dt 7: 8 his fidelity to the **o** he had sworn
Jos 2:17 free of this **o** that you made us take,
1 Sm 14:24 that day, Saul laid an **o** on them,
Ps 15: 4 Who keeps an **o** despite the cost,
Ps 132:11 The LORD swore an **o** to David
Eccl 8: 2 the king, in view of your **o** to God.
Mt 26:72 Again he denied it with an **o**, "I do
Heb 7:20 others became priests without an **o**,

OBADIAH
1. Believer who sheltered 100 prophets from Jezebel (1 Kgs 18:1-16).
2. Prophet against Edom (Ob 1).

OBED
Ru 4:22 **O** was the father of Jesse, and Jesse
Lk 3:32 Jesse, the son of **O**, the son of Boaz,

OBED-EDOM
2 Sm 6:12 had blessed the household of **O**
1 Chr 13:13 instead at the house of **O** the Gittite.

OBEDIENCE → OBEY
Rom 1: 5 to bring about the **o** of faith,
Rom 5:19 so through the **o** of one the many
Rom 6:16 to death, or of **o**, which leads
Rom 15:18 me to lead the Gentiles to **o** by word
Rom 16:19 For while your **o** is known to all,
Rom 16:26 nations to bring about the **o** of faith,
2 Cor 7:15 as he remembers the **o** of all of you,
2 Cor 10: 6 once your **o** is complete.
Heb 5: 8 he learned **o** from what he suffered;
1 Pt 1:22 you have purified yourselves by **o**

OBEDIENT → OBEY
Ps 103:20 at his behest, **o** to his command.
Lk 2:51 to Nazareth, and was **o** to them;
Acts 6: 7 priests were becoming **o** to the faith.
Rom 6:16 yourselves to someone as **o** slaves,
Rom 6:17 you have become **o** from the heart
2 Cor 2: 9 whether you were **o** in everything,
Phil 2: 8 himself, becoming **o** to death,
Ti 3: 1 to be **o**, to be open to every good
1 Pt 1:14 Like **o** children, do not act

OBEY → OBEDIENCE, OBEDIENT, OBEYED, OBEYING
Jgs 3: 4 they would **o** the commandments
Ezr 7:26 All who will not **o** the law of your
1 Mc 2:22 We will not **o** the words of the king
Sir 3: 6 those who **o** the Lord honor their mother.
Jer 11: 7 Egypt even to this day: **o** my voice.
Jer 42: 6 not, we will **o** the command
Mt 8:27 even the winds and the sea **o**?"
Acts 5:29 "We must **o** God rather than men.
Acts 5:32 God has given to those who **o** him."
Rom 6:12 bodies so that you **o** their desires.
Rom 6:16 you are slaves of the one you **o**,
Eph 6: 1 **o** your parents [in the Lord], for this
Col 3:20 **o** your parents in everything,
Col 3:22 Slaves, **o** your human masters
2 Thes 3:14 If anyone does not **o** our word as
Heb 5: 9 eternal salvation for all who **o** him,
Heb 13:17 **O** your leaders and defer to them,
1 Pt 4:17 for those who fail to **o** the gospel

OBEYED → OBEY
Gn 22:18 because you **o** my command."
Gn 26: 5 this because Abraham **o** me,
Heb 11: 8 faith Abraham **o** when he was called
1 Pt 3: 6 thus Sarah **o** Abraham, calling him

OBEYING → OBEY
Dt 11:27 a blessing for **o** the commandments

OBSCENITY
Eph 5: 4 no **o** or silly or suggestive talk,

OBSERVE → OBSERVING
Lv 20: 8 careful, therefore, to **o** my statutes.
Nm 24:17 I **o** him, though not near: A star
Dt 4: 6 **O** them carefully, for this is your
Dt 11:22 to **o** this entire commandment I am
Dt 26:16 commanding you to **o** these statutes
Dt 26:16 to **o** them with your whole heart
1 Mc 2:67 Gather about you all who **o** the law,

OBSERVING → OBSERVE
Gal 4:10 You are **o** days, months, seasons,

OBSOLETE
Heb 8:13 covenant, he declares the first one **o**.
Heb 8:13 what has become **o** and has grown

OBSTACLE
1 Cor 9:12 so as not to place an **o** to the gospel

OBTAIN → OBTAINED, OBTAINING
2 Tm 2:10 they too may **o** the salvation that is

OBTAINED → OBTAIN
Heb 8: 6 Now he has **o** so much more

OBTAINING → OBTAIN
Heb 9:12 blood, thus **o** eternal redemption.

OBVIOUS
Gal 5:19 Now the works of the flesh are **o**:

OCCUPY
Neh 2: 8 wall and the house that I will **o**."

ODED
2 Chr 28: 9 of the LORD by the name of **O**.

ODOR
Gn 8:21 the LORD smelled the sweet **o**,
Tb 8: 3 The **o** of the fish repulsed

OFFEND → OFFENSE, OFFENSES
Jb 34:31 I will **o** no more;

OFFENSE → OFFEND
Dt 19:15 crime or any **o** that may have been
Prv 19:11 and an honor to overlook an **o**.
Mt 11: 6 blessed is the one who takes no **o**
Mk 6: 3 And they took **o** at him.

OFFENSES → OFFEND
Prv 10:12 up disputes, but love covers all **o**.

OFFER → OFFERED, OFFERING, OFFERINGS
Gn 22: 2 There **o** him up as a burnt offering

Ex	29:38	this is what you shall regularly **o**
Dt	12:14	but **o** them in the place
1 Mc	2:23	sight of all to **o** sacrifice on the altar
Ps	4: 6	**O** fitting sacrifices and trust
Sir	38:11	**O** your sweet-smelling oblation
Mt	5:24	and then come and **o** your gift.
Heb	9:25	that he might **o** himself repeatedly,
Heb	13:15	let us continually **o** God a sacrifice

OFFERED → OFFER

Gn	22:13	**o** it up as a burnt offering in place
1 Mc	4:53	**o** sacrifice according to the law
Heb	5: 7	he **o** prayers and supplications
Heb	7:27	that once for all when he **o** himself.
Heb	9:14	eternal spirit **o** himself unblemished
Heb	11: 4	By faith Abel **o** to God a sacrifice
Heb	11:17	when put to the test, **o** up Isaac,

OFFERING → OFFER

Gn	4: 4	with favor on Abel and his **o**,
Ex	29:14	camp, since this is a purification **o**.
Ex	29:24	as an elevated **o** before the LORD.
Ps	40: 7	Sacrifice and **o** you do not want;
Ps	51:18	a burnt **o** you would not accept.
Ps	141: 2	my uplifted hands an evening **o**.
Sir	30:19	What good is an **o** to an idol
Is	53:10	By making his life as a reparation **o**,
Eph	5: 2	over for us as a sacrificial **o** to God
Heb	10:14	one **o** he has made perfect forever

OFFERINGS → OFFER

1 Sm	13: 9	burnt offering and communion **o**!"
1 Chr	21:26	sacrificed burnt **o** and communion **o**.
Sir	35: 1	To keep the law is to make many **o**;
Is	1:13	To bring **o** is useless; incense is
Mk	12:33	is worth more than all burnt **o**
Heb	10: 6	and sin **o** you took no delight in.

OFFICERS

Ex	15: 4	the elite of his **o** were drowned

OFFSPRING

Gn	3:15	and between your **o** and hers;
Gn	15: 4	your own **o** will be your heir.
Nm	32:14	And now here you are, **o** of sinful stock,
Ps	37:25	abandoned or his **o** begging for bread.
Is	44: 3	will pour out my spirit upon your **o**,
Dn	13:56	"**O** of Canaan, not of Judah,"
Mal	2:15	Godly **o**! You should be on guard,
Acts	17:29	Since therefore we are the **o** of God,

OFTEN

Jn	18: 2	because Jesus had **o** met there

OG

Nm	21:33	But **O**, king of Bashan,
Dt	31: 4	just as he dealt with Sihon and **O**,
Ps	136:20	**O**, king of Bashan, for his mercy

OHOLIAB

Craftsman who worked on the tabernacle (Ex 31:6; 35:34; 36:1-2; 38:23).

OIL

Gn	28:18	pillar, and poured **o** on top of it.
Gn	35:14	he made a libation and poured out **o**.
Ex	25: 6	**o** for the light;
Ex	25: 6	spices for the anointing **o**
Ex	29: 7	take the anointing **o** and pour it
Ex	30:25	blend them into sacred anointing **o**,
Dt	14:23	wine and **o**, as well as the firstlings
1 Sm	10: 1	Samuel poured **o** on Saul's head
1 Sm	16:13	with the horn of **o** in hand,
1 Kgs	17:16	nor the jug of **o** run dry,
2 Kgs	4: 6	And then the **o** stopped.
Ps	23: 5	You anoint my head with **o**;
Ps	45: 8	anointed you with the **o** of gladness
Ps	104:15	hearts, **o** to make their faces shine,
Prv	5: 3	and her mouth is smoother than **o**;
Is	61: 3	To give them **o** of gladness instead
Jl	2:24	spilling over with new wine and **o**.

Mt	25: 3	their lamps, brought no **o** with them,
Heb	1: 9	anointed you with the **o** of gladness
Jas	5:14	anoint [him] with **o** in the name

OLD → OLDER

Gn	17:12	when he is eight days **o**, shall be
Gn	17:17	to a man who is a hundred years **o**?
Gn	21: 7	have borne him a son in his **o** age."
Dt	32: 7	Remember the days of **o**,
Ps	71: 9	Do not cast me aside in my **o** age;
Ps	74:12	are my king from of **o**,
Prv	22: 6	even when **o**, they will not swerve
Sir	8: 6	Do not insult one who is **o**, for some of us will also grow **o**.
Sir	9:10	Do not abandon **o** friends;
Lam	5:21	renew our days as of **o**.
Dn	13:61	They rose up against the two **o** men,
Jl	3: 1	your **o** men will dream dreams,
Mi	5: 1	Whose origin is from of **o**,
Mk	2:22	pours new wine into **o** wineskins.
Jn	3: 4	person once grown **o** be born again?
Acts	2:17	your **o** men shall dream dreams.
Rom	4:19	he was almost a hundred years **o**)
1 Cor	5: 7	Clear out the **o** yeast, so that you
2 Cor	5:17	the **o** things have passed away;
Eph	4:22	you should put away the **o** self
1 Jn	2: 7	but an **o** commandment that you had
1 Jn	2: 7	The **o** commandment is the word

OLDER → OLD

1 Tm	5: 1	Do not rebuke an **o** man, but appeal
1 Tm	5: 2	**o** women as mothers, and younger
Ti	2: 2	that **o** men should be temperate,
Ti	2: 3	**o** women should be reverent in their

OLIVE → OLIVES

Gn	8:11	in its bill was a plucked-off **o** leaf!
Jgs	9: 8	So they said to the **o** tree,
Ps	52:10	I, like an **o** tree flourishing
Jer	11:16	has named you "a spreading **o** tree,
Hb	3:17	Though the yield of the **o** fails
Zec	4: 3	And beside it are two **o** trees,
Rom	11:17	a wild **o** shoot, were grafted in their
Rom	11:17	to share in the rich root of the **o** tree,
Rom	11:24	from what is by nature a wild **o** tree,
Rom	11:24	grafted back into their own **o** tree.
Rev	11: 4	These are the two **o** trees

OLIVES → OLIVE

Zec	14: 4	feet will stand on the Mount of **O**,
Zec	14: 4	The Mount of **O** will be split in two
Mt	24: 3	he was sitting on the Mount of **O**,
Jas	3:12	produce **o**, or a grapevine figs?

OMEGA

Rev	1: 8	"I am the Alpha and the **O**,"
Rev	21: 6	I [am] the Alpha and the **O**,
Rev	22:13	I am the Alpha and the **O**, the first

OMENS

Sir	34: 5	Divination, **o**, and dreams are

OMRI

King of Israel (1 Kgs 16:21-26).

ONAN

Gn	38: 8	Then Judah said to **O**,
Gn	46:12	**O** had died in the land of Canaan;

ONCE → ONE

Ex	30:10	**O** a year Aaron shall purge its
Jb	40: 5	I have spoken **o**, I will not reply;
Lam	1: 1	sits the city, **o** filled with people.
Rom	6:10	death, he died to sin **o** and for all;
Rom	7: 9	I **o** lived outside the law,
Eph	5: 8	For you were **o** darkness, but now
Heb	7:27	he did that **o** for all when he offered
Heb	9:12	he entered **o** for all
Heb	9:27	appointed that human beings die **o**,
1 Pt	2:10	**O** you were "no people" but now
1 Pt	3:18	For Christ also suffered for sins **o**,

ONE → EVERYONE, FIRST, ONCE, ONES
Gn   2:24 and the two of them become o body.
Jos   23:10 O of you puts to flight a thousand,
Ps   14: 3 Not o does what is good, not even o.
Eccl   4: 9 Two are better than o: They get
Eccl   7:27 adding o to o to find the sum.
Is   30:17 shall tremble at the threat of o—
Ez   34:23 I will appoint o shepherd over them
Ez   37:22 I will make them o nation
Ez   37:22 there shall be o king for them all.
Zec   14: 9 day the LORD will be the only o,
Zec   14: 9 and the LORD's name the only o.
Mal   2:10 Have we not all o father? Has not o God created us?
Mk   10: 8 and the two shall become o flesh.'
Mk   10: 8 they are no longer two but o flesh.
Mk   10:21 to him, "You are lacking in o thing.
Lk   10:42 There is need of only o thing.
Jn   1:18 No o has ever seen God.
Jn   10:16 voice, and there will be o flock,
Jn   10:30 The Father and I are o."
Jn   17:22 so that they may be o, as we are o,
Rom   3:10 "There is no o just, not o,
Rom   5:15 o person's transgression the many
Rom   5:15 the o person Jesus Christ overflow
1 Cor   6:16 to a prostitute becomes o body
1 Cor   6:16 it says, "will become o flesh."
1 Cor   8: 4 and that "there is no God but o."
1 Cor 10:17 Because the loaf of bread is o, we, though many, are o
               body, for we all partake of the o loaf.
1 Cor 12:13 in o Spirit we were all baptized
1 Cor 12:13 we were all baptized into o body,
1 Cor 12:13 were all given to drink of o Spirit.
Eph   4: 5 o Lord, o faith, o baptism;
1 Tm   2: 5 For there is o God. There is also o mediator
2 Pt   3: 8 the Lord o day is like a thousand
2 Pt   3: 8 and a thousand years like o day.

ONES → ONE
Dt   33: 3 all the holy o are at your side;
1 Chr 16:13 offspring of Jacob, the chosen o!
Mt   18: 6 one of these little o who believe
Jude   1:14 has come with his countless holy o

ONESIMUS
Col   4: 9 together with O, a trustworthy
Phlm   1:10 I urge you on behalf of my child O,

ONIAS
1 Mc   12: 7 sent to the high priest O from Arius,
2 Mc   3: 1 of the piety of the high priest O
2 Mc   4:36 to see him about the murder of O.

ONIONS
Nm   11: 5 the leeks, the o, and the garlic.

ONLY
Gn   7:23 O Noah and those with him
Gn   22: 2 Take your son Isaac, your o one,
1 Kgs 18:22 "I am the o remaining prophet
Ps   37: 8 not be provoked; it brings o harm.
Mk   13:32 nor the Son, but o the Father.
Jn   1:14 the glory as of the Father's o Son,
Jn   1:18 The o Son, God, who is
Jn   3:16 the world that he gave his o Son,
1 Tm   1:17 invisible, the o God,
1 Jn   4: 9 God sent his o Son into the world so

ONYX
Ex   28: 9 Get two o stones and engrave

OPEN → OPENED, OPENLY, OPENS
Dt   28:12 The LORD will o up for you his
Ps   51:17 Lord, you will o my lips;
Ps   78: 2 I will o my mouth in a parable,
Ps   118:19 O the gates of righteousness;
Ps   145:16 You o wide your hand and satisfy
Prv   15:11 Abaddon lie o before the LORD;
Prv   27: 5 Better is an o rebuke than a love
Sg   5: 2 "O to me, my sister, my friend,
Is   42: 7 To o the eyes of the blind, to bring

Is   53: 7 he submitted and did not o his mouth;
Mal   3:10 I do not o the floodgates of heaven
Mt   13:35 "I will o my mouth in parables,
Mt   17:27 O its mouth and you will find a coin
Rev   3: 8 I have left an o door before you,
Rev   4: 1 this I had a vision of an o door
Rev   5: 2 "Who is worthy to o the scroll

OPENED → OPEN
Gn   3: 7 the eyes of both of them were o,
Nm   16:32 and the earth o its mouth
Neh   8: 5 Ezra o the scroll so that all
Neh   8: 5 When he o it, all the people stood.
Is   35: 5 see, and the ears of the deaf be o;
Dn   7:10 convened, and the books were o.
Mt   3:16 the heavens were o [for him],
Lk   11: 9 knock and the door will be o to you.
Lk   24:45 he o their minds to understand
Acts   10:11 He saw heaven o and something
Heb   10:20 living way he o for us through
Rev   11:19 God's temple in heaven was o,
Rev   20:12 the throne, and scrolls were o.
Rev   20:12 Then another scroll was o, the book

OPENLY → OPEN
Jn   7:26 look, he is speaking o and they say

OPENS → OPEN
Rev   3: 7 who o and no one shall close,

OPHIR
1 Kgs 10:11 which used to bring gold from O,
Is   13:12 human beings, than the gold of O.

OPPONENTS
2 Tm   2:25 correcting o with kindness.

OPPORTUNITY
Mt   26:16 he looked for an o to hand him over.
Rom   7: 8 finding an o in the commandment,
2 Cor   5:12 but giving you an o to boast of us,
Gal   5:13 do not use this freedom as an o
Phil   4:10 about me but lacked an o.
Heb   11:15 they would have had o to return.

OPPOSE → OPPOSED, OPPOSES
2 Tm   3: 8 Moses, so they also o the truth—

OPPOSED → OPPOSE
Gal   3:21 then o to the promises [of God]?
Gal   5:17 these are o to each other, so that you
2 Tm   3: 8 as Jannes and Jambres o Moses,

OPPOSES → OPPOSE
2 Thes 2: 4 who o and exalts himself
1 Pt   5: 5 "God o the proud but bestows favor

OPPRESS → OPPRESSED, OPPRESSES, OPPRESSING, OPPRESSION,
               OPPRESSOR, OPPRESSORS
Ex   1:11 over the Israelites to o them
Ex   22:20 You shall not o or afflict a resident
2 Sm   7:10 nor shall the wicked ever again o them,
Ps   105:14 He let no one o them; for their sake
Zec   7:10 Do not o the widow or the orphan,

OPPRESSED → OPPRESS
Gn   15:13 and o for four hundred years.
Ex   1:12 Yet the more they were o, the more
Ps   9:10 LORD is a stronghold for the o,
Ps   103: 6 deeds, brings justice to all the o.
Ps   146: 7 secures justice for the o, who gives
Sir   4: 9 Deliver the o from their oppressors;
Lk   4:18 to the blind, to let the o go free,

OPPRESSES → OPPRESS
Jb   37:23 abundant in justice, who never o.
Ez   18:12 o the poor and needy,

OPPRESSING → OPPRESS
Jas   2: 6 Are not the rich o you? And do they

OPPRESSION → OPPRESS
Dt   26: 7 our affliction, our toil and our o.
Ps   119:134 Free me from human o, that I may
Ez   45: 9 Put away violence and o, and do

OPPRESSOR → OPPRESS
Ps   72: 4 children of the poor and crush the o.
Is   51:13 of the o When he prepares himself

OPPRESSORS → OPPRESS
Jer   22: 3 the victims from the hand of their o.

ORACLE
Nm   24: 3 The o of Balaam, son of Beor,
2 Sm 23: 1 The o of David, son of Jesse;
Am   9:12 o of the LORD, the one who does this.
Mal   1: 1 An o. The word of the LORD to Israel

ORDAINED
Nm   3: 3 the anointed priests whom he o

ORDER → ORDERLY, ORDERS
Mk   7: 9 God in o to uphold your tradition!
Jn   10:17 because I lay down my life in o
Rom   7: 4 the dead in o that we might bear
Heb   5:10 according to the o of Melchizedek.
Heb   7:11 according to the o of Melchizedek,
Heb   7:11 according to the o of Aaron?

ORDERLY → ORDER
Lk   1: 3 write it down in an o sequence

ORDERS → ORDER
Acts   5:28 "We gave you strict o [did we not?]

ORDINARY
Acts   4:13 them to be uneducated, o men,

OREB
Jgs   7:25 two princes of Midian, O and Zeeb,
Jgs   7:25 they had the heads of O and Zeeb
Ps   83:12 Make their nobles like O and Zeeb,

ORIGIN
Mt   21:26 'Of human o,' we fear the crowd,
Acts   5:38 or this activity is of human o, it will

ORNAMENTS
Ex   33: 6 the Israelites stripped off their o.

ORNAN → =ARAUNAH
1 Chr 21:15 threshing floor of O the Jebusite.
2 Chr 3: 1 threshing floor of O the Jebusite.

ORPAH
Ru   1: 4 one named O, the other Ruth.

ORPHAN → ORPHANS
Ex   22:21 shall not wrong any widow or o.
Hos   14: 4 for in you the o finds compassion."

ORPHANS → ORPHAN
Jn   14:18 I will not leave you o; I will come
Jas   1:27 to care for o and widows in their

OTHER → OTHERS
Ex   20: 3 shall not have o gods beside me.
Ex   23:13 not mention the name of any o god;
Dt   4:35 the LORD is God; there is no o.
Jgs   2:19 their ancestors, following o gods,
2 Kgs 17: 7 They venerated o gods,
2 Chr 2: 4 our God is greater than all o gods.
Ps   147:20 has not done this for any o nation;
Is   45: 5 there is no o, there is no God
Dn   3:96 there is no o God who can rescue
Mt   6:24 will either hate one and love the o,
Mt   6:24 be devoted to one and despise the o.
Lk   17:34 one will be taken, the o left.
Jn   20:30 Now Jesus did many o signs
Jn   21:25 also many o things that Jesus did,
1 Cor 3:11 can lay a foundation o than the one
2 Pt   3:16 just as they do the o scriptures.

OTHERS → OTHER
Mt   7:12 o whatever you would have them do
Lk   6:31 Do to o as you would have them do
Phil   2: 3 humbly regard o as more important

OTHNIEL
   Nephew of Caleb (Jos 15:15-19; Jgs 1:12-15). Judge who freed Israel
from Aram (Jgs 3:7-11).

OUGHT
Rom   8:26 do not know how to pray as we o,
Rom   12: 3 himself more highly than one o
2 Pt   3:11 what sort of persons o [you] to be,
1 Jn   3:16 so we o to lay down our lives
3 Jn   1: 8 we o to support such persons,

OUTCOME → COME
Is   41:22 reflect on them and know their o;
Heb   13: 7 Consider the o of their way of life

OUTSIDE → OUTSIDERS
Prv   22:13 The sluggard says, "A lion is o;
Dn   14: 7 "it is only clay inside and bronze o;
Lk   11:39 Although you cleanse the o
Lk   13:33 that a prophet should die o
1 Cor 5:13 God will judge those o.
Heb   13:12 Jesus also suffered o the gate,
Rev   22:15 O are the dogs, the sorcerers,

OUTSIDERS → OUTSIDE
Prv   5:17 yours alone, not shared with o;
Col   4: 5 yourselves wisely toward o,
1 Thes 4:12 yourselves properly toward o
1 Tm   3: 7 have a good reputation among o,

OUTSTRETCHED → STRETCH
Ex   6: 6 I will redeem you by my o arm
Dt   4:34 with strong hand and o arm,
1 Kgs 8:42 your mighty hand and your o arm),
Ps   136:12 With mighty hand and o arm, for his
Is   3:16 and walk with necks o,
Jer   27: 5 by my great power, with my o arm;
Jer   32:17 your great power and your o arm;
Ez   20:33 with mighty hand and o arm,

OUTWARDLY
Rom   2:28 One is not a Jew o.

OVER
Ex   12:13 Seeing the blood, I will pass o you;
Ex   12:23 the LORD will pass o that door
Ps   8: 7 have given him rule o the works
Ps   145:20 The LORD watches o all who love
Mk   15:15 handed him o to be crucified.

OVERCOME
Jn   1: 5 and the darkness has not o it.

OVERFLOWS
Ps   23: 5 anoint my head with oil; my cup o.

OVERJOYED → JOY
Acts 12:14 She was so o when she recognized

OVERLOOK → OVERLOOKED
Prv   19:11 anger, and an honor to o an offense.
Heb   6:10 is not unjust so as to o your work

OVERLOOKED → OVERLOOK
Acts 17:30 God has o the times of ignorance,

OVERSEERS
Acts 20:28 the holy Spirit has appointed you o,
Phil   1: 1 in Philippi, with the o and ministers:

OVERSHADOW → OVERSHADOWING
Lk   1:35 power of the Most High will o you.

OVERSHADOWING → OVERSHADOW
Heb   9: 5 the cherubim of glory o the place

OVERTAKE → OVERTAKEN
Sir   7: 1 Do no evil, and evil will not o you;

OVERTAKEN → OVERTAKE
Jer   44:23 therefore this evil has o you,

OVERTHREW
Gn   19:25 He o those cities and the whole

OVERTURNED
Mk   11:15 He o the tables of the money

OVERWHELMED → OVERWHELMING
2 Cor 2: 7 or else the person may be o

OVERWHELMING → OVERWHELMED
Prv   27: 4 and wrath o, but before jealousy

OWE → OWES
Mt   18:28 demanding, 'Pay back what you o.'
Rom 13: 8 O nothing to anyone, except to love

OWES → OWE
Phlm   1:18 you any injustice or o you anything,

OWN → LANDOWNER, OWNER
Gn   15: 4 your o offspring will be your heir.
Ex   32:13 you swore to them by your o self,
Dt   18:15 for you from among your o kindred;
Dt   24:16 one's o crime shall a person be put
1 Sm 13:14 a man after his o heart to appoint as
Ps 141:10 Let the wicked fall into their o nets,
Prv   3: 7 Do not be wise in your o eyes,
Prv 26:12 those who are wise in their o eyes?
Is   48:11 my sake, for my o sake, I do this;
Is   53: 6 like sheep, all following our o way;
Jer 31:30 shall die because of their o iniquity:
Ez   33: 4 their blood will be on their o heads.
Lk   6:42 the wooden beam in your o eye?
Jn   1:11 He came to what was his o, but his o people did not accept him.
Jn 10:18 from me, but I lay it down on my o.
Rom 8:32 He who did not spare his o Son
1 Cor 6:19 God, and that you are not your o?
Phil   2: 4 looking out not for his o interests,

OWNER → OWN
Mt 21:40 What will the o of the vineyard do

OX → OXEN
Ex 20:17 or female slave, his o or donkey,
Dt 22:10 You shall not plow with an o
Dt 25: 4 You shall not muzzle an o when it
Prv   7:22 like an o that goes to slaughter;
Is 11: 7 the lion shall eat hay like the o.
Is 65:25 and the lion shall eat hay like the o—
Ez   1:10 the face of an o, and each had
Lk 13:15 of you on the sabbath untie his o
1 Cor 9: 9 shall not muzzle an o while it is
1 Tm 5:18 "You shall not muzzle an o when it

OXEN → OX
1 Kgs 19:20 Elisha left the o, ran after Elijah,
Lk 14:19 'I have purchased five yoke of o
1 Cor 9: 9 Is God concerned about o,

P

PAGAN → PAGANS
1 Kgs 14:24 There were also p priests in the land.
1 Kgs 15:12 banishing the p priests from the land

PAGANS → PAGAN
Mt   6:32 All these things the p seek.
1 Cor 12: 2 how, when you were p, you were

PAID → PAY
Mt 26:15 They p him thirty pieces of silver,

PAIN → PAINFUL, PAINS
Gn   3:16 in p you shall bring forth children.
Jb   6:10 could exult through unremitting p,
Jb 33:19 Or he is chastened on a bed of p,
Is 53: 4 Yet it was our p that he bore,
Jer 15:18 Why is my p continuous, my wound
Jn 16:21 no longer remembers the p because
1 Pt 2:19 For whenever anyone bears the p
Rev 21: 4 wailing or p, [for] the old order has

PAINFUL → PAIN
2 Cor 2: 1 to you again in p circumstances.

PAINS → PAIN
Rom 8:22 groaning in labor p even until now;
1 Thes 5: 3 them, like labor p upon a pregnant

PAIRS
Gn   7: 2 take with you seven p, a male

PALACES
2 Chr 36:19 burnt down all its p, and destroyed
Hos   8:14 forgotten his maker and has built p.
Lk   7:25 sumptuously are found in royal p.

PALE
Is 29:22 no longer shall his face grow p.
Rev   6: 8 and there was a p green horse.

PALM → PALMS
Ex 15:27 springs of water and seventy p trees,
Jgs   4: 5 used to sit under Deborah's p tree,
1 Kgs 6:29 carved figures of cherubim, p trees,
Ps 92:13 just shall flourish like the p tree,
Is 40:12 Who has measured with his p the waters,
Jn 12:13 they took p branches and went
Rev   7: 9 holding p branches in their hands.

PALMS → PALM
Is 49:16 the p of my hands I have engraved

PANELED
Hg   1: 4 your p houses while this house lies

PANGS
Is 13: 8 P and sorrows take hold of them,

PANIC
Ex 14:24 the Egyptian army and threw it into a p;
Dt 28:20 The LORD will send on you a curse, p,
Jdt 14: 3 do not find him, p will seize them,

PAPER
2 Jn   1:12 I do not intend to use p and ink.

PAPYRUS
Ex   2: 3 she took a p basket, daubed it

PARABLE → PARABLES
Mt 13:18 "Hear then the p of the sower.
Mt 15:15 in reply, "Explain [this] p to us."
Mt 21:33 "Hear another p. There was
Lk 20:19 that he had addressed this p to them.

PARABLES → PARABLE; See also JESUS: PARABLES
Mt 13:35 "I will open my mouth in p, I will
Lk   8:10 they are made known through p so

PARADISE
Lk 23:43 today you will be with me in P."
2 Cor 12: 4 was caught up into P and heard

PARALYTIC → PARALYZED
Mt   9: 2 to him a p lying on a stretcher.
Mt   9: 2 Jesus saw their faith, he said to the p,

PARALYZED → PARALYTIC
Acts 8: 7 many p and crippled people were

PARAN
Gn 21:21 He lived in the wilderness of P.
Nm 10:12 came to rest in the wilderness of P.
Hb   3: 3 the Holy One from Mount P.

PARCHED
Ps 143: 6 you, my soul to you like a p land.

PARCHMENTS
2 Tm 4:13 papyrus rolls, and especially the p.

PARDON
Ex 34: 9 yet p our wickedness and sins,
Nm 14:19 P, then, the iniquity of this people
Dt 29:19 will never consent to p them.
2 Chr 30:18 "May the good LORD grant p
Jb   7:21 Why do you not p my offense,

PARENTS
Prv 19:14 are an inheritance from p,
Mk 13:12 children will rise up against p
Lk   2:27 and when the p brought in the child
Lk 18:29 or brothers or p or children
Lk 21:16 You will even be handed over by p,
Jn   9: 3 "Neither he nor his p sinned; it is so
Rom 1:30 and rebellious toward their p.
2 Cor 12:14 ought not to save for their p, but p for their children.
Eph   6: 1 Children, obey your p [in the Lord],

Col	3:20	Children, obey your **p** in everything,
1 Tm	5: 4	and to make recompense to their **p**,
2 Tm	3: 2	disobedient to their **p**, ungrateful,

PARTAKE
1 Cor	10:17	body, for we all **p** of the one loaf.

PARTIAL → PARTIALITY, PARTLY, PARTS
1 Cor	13:10	perfect comes, the **p** will pass away.
Heb	1: 1	past, God spoke in **p** and various ways

PARTIALITY → PARTIAL
2 Chr	19: 7	no injustice, no **p**, no bribe-taking."
Jb	13: 8	Is it for him that you show **p**?
Jb	13:10	rebuke you if in secret you show **p**.
Prv	24:23	To show **p** in judgment is not good.
Prv	28:21	To show **p** is never good: for even
Wis	6: 7	For the Ruler of all shows no **p**,
Mal	2: 9	but show **p** in your instruction.
Rom	2:11	There is no **p** with God.
Gal	2: 6	God shows no **p**)—those of repute
Eph	6: 9	and that with him there is no **p**.
Jas	2: 1	show no **p** as you adhere to the faith

PARTLY → PART
Dn	2:33	legs iron, its feet **p** iron and **p** clay.

PARTNERSHIP
2 Cor	6:14	For what **p** do righteousness

PARTS → PARTIAL
Nm	18:29	from their best **p**, that is the part

PASHHUR
Priest; opponent of Jeremiah (Jer 20:1-6).

PASS → PASSED, PASSING
Ex	12:13	Seeing the blood, I will **p** over you;
Ex	12:23	the LORD will **p** over that door
Ex	33:19	make all my goodness **p** before you,
Nm	20:17	Please let us **p** through your land.
Nm	21:22	"Let us **p** through your land.
Nm	23:19	not act, to decree and not bring it to **p**?
1 Kgs	19:11	before the LORD; the LORD will **p** by.
Ps	105:19	Till his prediction came to **p**,
Is	43: 2	When you **p** through waters, I will
Jer	22: 8	Many nations will **p** by this city
Lam	1:12	Come, all who **p** by the way,
Am	5:17	when I **p** through your midst,
Mt	24:35	Heaven and earth will **p** away,
Mt	24:35	but my words will not **p** away.
Mk	14:35	it were possible the hour might **p**
2 Pt	3:10	then the heavens will **p** away

PASSED → PASS
Gn	15:17	which **p** between those pieces.
Ex	12:27	who **p** over the houses
Ex	33:22	you with my hand until I have **p** by.
Ex	34: 6	So the LORD **p** before him
Ps	37:36	When I **p** by again, he was gone;
Lk	10:32	him, he **p** by on the opposite side.
1 Cor	10: 1	the cloud and all **p** through the sea,
2 Cor	5:17	the old things have **p** away;
1 Jn	3:14	We know that we have **p** from death
Rev	21: 1	and the former earth had **p** away,
Rev	21: 4	[for] the old order has **p** away."

PASSING → PASS
Wis	2: 5	our lifetime is the **p** of a shadow;
1 Cor	7:31	world in its present form is **p** away.
1 Jn	2: 8	for the darkness is **p** away,
1 Jn	2:17	and its enticement are **p** away.

PASSION → PASSIONATE, PASSIONS
Col	3: 5	immorality, impurity, **p**, evil desire,

PASSIONATE → PASSION
Dt	6:15	who is in your midst, is a **p** God—
Jos	24:19	he is a holy God; he is a **p** God

PASSIONS → PASSION
Rom	7: 5	our sinful **p**, awakened by the law,
Gal	5:24	have crucified their flesh with its **p**

PASSOVER
Ex	12:11	it in a hurry. It is the LORD's **P**.
Nm	9: 2	to celebrate the **P** at the prescribed
Dt	16: 1	by keeping the **P** of the LORD,
Jos	5:10	they celebrated the **P** on the evening
2 Kgs	23:21	"Observe the **P** of the LORD,
2 Chr	30: 1	to celebrate the **P** to the LORD,
Ezr	6:19	The returned exiles kept the **P**
Mk	14:12	when they sacrificed the **P** lamb,
Mk	14:12	and prepare for you to eat the **P**?"
Lk	22: 8	preparations for us to eat the **P**."
Heb	11:28	By faith he kept the **P** and sprinkled

PAST
Acts	14:16	In **p** generations he allowed all
2 Pt	1: 9	of the cleansing of his **p** sins.

PASTORS
Eph	4:11	others as **p** and teachers,

PASTURE → PASTURES
Ps	79:13	the sheep of your **p**, will give thanks
Jer	23: 1	and scatter the flock of my **p**—
Jn	10: 9	will come in and go out and find **p**.

PASTURES → PASTURE
Ps	23: 2	In green **p** he makes me lie down;

PATH → PATHS
Ps	16:11	You will show me the **p** to life,
Ps	27:11	on a level **p** because of my enemies.
Ps	119:105	a lamp for my feet, a light for my **p**.
Ps	139:24	See if there is a wicked **p** in me; lead me along an ancient **p**.
Prv	2: 9	and just, what is fair, every good **p**;
Prv	12:28	In the **p** of justice is life,
Prv	15:19	the **p** of the diligent is a highway.
Prv	15:24	The **p** of life leads upward
Is	26: 7	the **p** of the just you make level.
Mt	13: 4	some seed fell on the **p**, and birds

PATHS → PATH
Ps	17: 5	My steps have kept to your **p**;
Ps	25: 4	teach me your **p**.
Prv	2:13	those who have left the straight **p**
Prv	3: 6	and he will make straight your **p**.
Prv	4:11	I direct you, I lead you on straight **p**.
Prv	5:21	all their **p** he surveys;
Prv	8:20	I walk, along the **p** of justice,
Is	2: 3	ways, and we may walk in his **p**."
Mi	4: 2	ways, that we may walk in his **p**."
Mt	3: 3	the Lord, make straight his **p**.' "
Heb	12:13	Make straight **p** for your feet,

PATIENCE → PATIENT
Prv	25:15	By **p** is a ruler persuaded, and a soft
Mi	2: 7	of Jacob, "Is the LORD short of **p**;
Rom	2: 4	and **p** in low esteem,
Rom	9:22	has endured with much **p** the vessels
2 Cor	6: 6	by purity, knowledge, **p**, kindness,
Gal	5:22	joy, peace, **p**, kindness, generosity,
Col	1:11	for all endurance and **p**, with joy
Col	3:12	humility, gentleness, and **p**,
1 Tm	1:16	display all his **p** as an example
2 Tm	3:10	purpose, faith, **p**, love, endurance,
2 Tm	4: 2	encourage through all **p**
Heb	6:12	through faith and **p**, are inheriting
Jas	5:10	as an example of hardship and **p**,
2 Pt	3:15	And consider the **p** of our Lord as

PATIENT → PATIENCE, PATIENTLY
Neh	9:30	You were **p** with them for many
Jb	6:11	what is my limit that I should be **p**?
Eccl	7: 8	better is a **p** spirit than a lofty one.
1 Cor	13: 4	Love is **p**, love is kind. It is not
1 Thes	5:14	support the weak, be **p** with all.
Jas	5: 7	Be **p**, therefore, brothers,
Jas	5: 7	being **p** with it until it receives
Jas	5: 8	You too must be **p**.
2 Pt	3: 9	but he is **p** with you, not wishing

PATIENTLY → PATIENT
2 Mc   6:14 the Sovereign Lord **p** waits until
Acts   26: 3 And therefore I beg you to listen **p**.
1 Pt   3:20 disobedient while God **p** waited

PATMOS
Rev   1: 9 on the island called **P** because I

PATRIARCH → PATRIARCHS
Heb   7: 4 to whom the **p** "Abraham [indeed]

PATRIARCHS → PATRIARCH
Acts   7: 9 "And the **p**, jealous of Joseph,
Rom   9: 5 theirs the **p**, and from them,
Rom   15: 8 to confirm the promises to the **p**,

PATTERN
Ex   25:40 them according to the **p** shown you
Nm   8: 4 the **p** which the Lord had shown
Heb   8: 5 according to the **p** shown you

PAUL → =SAUL
Also called Saul (Acts 13:9). Pharisee from Tarsus (Acts 9:11; Phil 3:5). Apostle (Gal 1). At stoning of Stephen (Acts 8:1). Persecuted Church (Acts 9:1-2; Gal 1:13). Vision of Jesus on road to Damascus (Acts 9:4-9; 26:12-18). In Arabia (Gal 1:17). Preached in Damascus; escaped death through the wall in a basket (Acts 9:19-25). In Jerusalem; sent back to Tarsus (Acts 9:26-30).

Brought to Antioch by Barnabas (Acts 11:22-26). First missionary journey to Cyprus and Galatia (Acts 13–14). Stoned at Lystra (Acts 14:19-20). At Jerusalem council (Acts 15). Split with Barnabas over Mark (Acts 15:36-41).

Second missionary journey with Silas (Acts 16–20). Called to Macedonia (Acts 16:6-10). Freed from prison in Philippi (Acts 16:16-40). In Thessalonica (Acts 17:1-9). Speech in Athens (Acts 17:16-33). In Corinth (Acts 18). In Ephesus (Acts 19). Return to Jerusalem (Acts 20). Farewell to Ephesian elders (Acts 20:13-38). Arrival in Jerusalem (Acts 21:1-26). Arrested (Acts 21:27-36). Addressed crowds (Acts 22), Sanhedrin (Acts 23:1-11). Sent to Caesarea (Acts 23:12-35). Trial before Felix (Acts 24), Festus (Acts 25:1-12). Before Agrippa (Acts 25:13–26:32). Voyage to Rome; shipwreck (Acts 27). Arrival in Rome (Acts 28).

Letters: Romans, 1 and 2 Corinthians, Galatians, Ephesians, Philippians, Colossians, 1 and 2 Thessalonians, 1 and 2 Timothy, Titus, Philemon.

PAVEMENT
Jn   19:13 bench in the place called Stone **P**,

PAY → PAID, PAYS, REPAID, REPAY, REPAYS
Dt   24:15 day you shall **p** the servant's wages
1 Mc   2:68 **P** back the Gentiles what they
Prv   6:31 caught they must **p** back sevenfold,
Sir   35:10 generous spirit **p** homage to the Lord,
Mt   22:17 Is it lawful to **p** the census tax
Rom   13: 6 This is why you also **p** taxes,
Rom   13: 7 **P** to all their dues, taxes to whom

PAYS → PAY
Ps   137: 8 blessed the one who **p** you back

PEACE → PEACEABLE, PEACEFUL, PEACEMAKERS
Lv   26: 6 I will establish **p** in the land,
Nm   6:26 upon you kindly and give you **p**!
Dt   20:10 a city to attack it, offer it terms of **p**.
Jos   11:19 no city made **p** with the Israelites;
1 Sm   1:17 "Go in **p**, and may the God of Israel
1 Sm   7:14 There was also **p** between Israel
2 Sm   10:19 they made **p** with the Israelites
1 Kgs   2:33 there shall be **p** forever
1 Chr   19:19 they made **p** with David and became
1 Chr   22: 9 and in his time I will bestow **p**
Tb   7: 1 You have come in **p**! Now enter in **p**!"
1 Mc   14:11 He brought **p** to the land, and Israel
Jb   22:21 Settle with him and have **p**.
Ps   29:11 the Lord bless his people with **p**!
Ps   34:15 and do good; seek **p** and pursue it.
Ps   85: 9 surely he will speak of **p** To his
Ps   85:11 justice and **p** will kiss.
Ps   119:165 Lovers of your law have much **p**;
Ps   120: 7 When I speak of **p**, they are for war.
Ps   122: 6 For the **p** of Jerusalem pray:

Ps   147:14 He brings **p** to your borders,
Prv   3:17 ways, and all her paths are **p**;
Prv   12:20 but those who counsel **p** have joy.
Prv   16: 7 he makes even enemies be at **p**
Eccl   3: 8 a time of war, and a time of **p**.
Is   9: 5 Father-Forever, Prince of **P**.
Is   26: 3 With firm purpose you maintain **p**; in **p**, because of our trust
Is   32:17 The work of justice will be **p**;
Is   48:22 There is no **p** for the wicked,
Is   52: 7 Announcing **p**, bearing good news,
Is   54:10 nor my covenant of **p** be shaken,
Is   55:12 in **p** you shall be brought home;
Is   57: 2 and enter into **p**; They rest
Is   57:19 creating words of comfort. **P**!
Is   57:21 There is no **p** for the wicked!
Is   59: 8 The way of **p** they know not,
Is   59: 8 no one who walks in them knows **p**.
Jer   6:14 the injury to my people: "**P**, **p**!" they say, though there is no **p**.
Jer   8:11 the daughter of my people: "**P**, **p**!" they say, though there is no **p**.
Lam   3:17 My life is deprived of **p**, I have
Ez   13:10 led my people astray, saying, "**P**!" when there is no **p**,
Ez   34:25 I will make a covenant of **p**
Ez   37:26 I will make a covenant of **p**
Mi   5: 4 he shall be **p**. If Assyria invades our
Na   2: 1 good news, of one announcing **p**!
Zec   8:19 So love faithfulness and **p**!
Zec   9:10 he will proclaim **p** to the nations.
Mt   10:13 is worthy, let your **p** come upon it;
Mt   10:34 I have come to bring not **p**
Mt   10:34 come to bring **p** upon the earth.
Mk   9:50 to guide our feet into the path of **p**."
Lk   2:14 and on earth **p** to those on whom his
Lk   7:50 faith has saved you; go in **p**."
Lk   19:38 **P** in heaven and glory
Jn   14:27 **P** I leave with you; my **p** I give
Jn   16:33 this so that you might have **p** in me.
Acts   10:36 as he proclaimed **p** through Jesus
Rom   2:10 and **p** for everyone who does good,
Rom   3:17 and the way of **p** they know not.
Rom   5: 1 we have **p** with God through our
Rom   8: 6 concern of the spirit is life and **p**.
Rom   14:19 then pursue what leads to **p**
Rom   16:20 of **p** will quickly crush Satan under
1 Cor   7:15 God has called you to **p**.
1 Cor   14:33 is not the God of disorder but of **p**.
2 Cor   13:11 live in **p**, and the God of love and **p**
Gal   5:22 of the Spirit is love, joy, **p**, patience,
Eph   2:14 For he is our **p**, he who made both
Eph   2:15 place of the two, thus establishing **p**,
Eph   2:17 preached **p** to you who were far off and **p** to those who were near,
Eph   4: 3 of the spirit through the bond of **p**:
Eph   6:15 in readiness for the gospel of **p**.
Phil   4: 7 Then the **p** of God that surpasses all
Col   1:20 making **p** by the blood of his cross
Col   3:15 And let the **p** of Christ control your
Col   3:15 the **p** into which you were also called
1 Thes   5: 3 are saying, "**P** and security,"
1 Thes   5:13 Be at **p** among yourselves.
1 Thes   5:23 **p** himself make you perfectly holy
2 Thes   3:16 the Lord of **p** himself give you **p**
2 Tm   2:22 and **p**, along with those who call
Heb   7: 2 "king of Salem," that is, king of **p**.
Heb   12:14 Strive for **p** with everyone,
Heb   13:20 May the God of **p**, who brought
Jas   3:18 righteousness is sown in **p** for those who cultivate **p**.
1 Pt   3:11 do good, seek **p** and follow after it.
2 Pt   3:14 spot or blemish before him, at **p**.
Rev   6: 4 was given power to take **p** away

PEACEABLE → PEACE
Jas   3:17 is first of all pure, then **p**, gentle,

PEACEFUL → PEACE
Heb   12:11 pain, yet later it brings the **p** fruit

PEACEMAKERS → PEACE
Mt   5: 9 Blessed are the **p**, for they will be

PEARL → PEARLS
Mt   13:46 When he finds a **p** of great price,
Rev   21:21 of the gates made from a single **p**;

PEARLS → PEARL
Jb   28:18 the value of wisdom surpasses **p**.
Mt   7: 6 or throw your **p** before swine,
Mt   13:45 like a merchant searching for fine **p**.
1 Tm   2: 9 or **p**, or expensive clothes,
Rev   21:21 The twelve gates were twelve **p**,

PEBBLE
Am   9: 9 sieve, letting no **p** fall to the ground.

PEG
Jgs   4:21 got a tent **p** and took a mallet in her
Jgs   4:21 and drove the **p** through his temple
Is   22:23 I will fix him as a **p** in a firm place,

PEKAH
       King of Israel (2 Kgs 15:25-31; 2 Chr 28:6; Is 7:1).

PEKAHIAH
       Son of Menahem; king of Israel (2 Kgs 15:22-26).

PELETHITES
2 Sm   20: 7 the Cherethites and **P** and all
1 Chr 18:17 of the Cherethites and the **P**;

PEN
Ps   45: 2 My tongue is the **p** of a nimble
3 Jn   1:13 but I do not wish to write with **p**

PENALTY
Prv   19:19 A wrathful person bears the **p**;
Ez   23:49 on you the **p** of your depravity,
Rom   1:27 their own persons the due **p** for their

PENIEL
Gn   32:31 Jacob named the place **P**,

PENINNAH
1 Sm   1: 2 one named Hannah, the other **P**;

PENNY
Mt   5:26 until you have paid the last **p**.
Lk   12:59 until you have paid the last **p**."

PENTECOST
2 Mc   12:32 also called **P**, they lost no time
Acts   2: 1 When the time for **P** was fulfilled,
Acts   20:16 if at all possible, for the day of **P**.
1 Cor 16: 8 I shall stay in Ephesus until **P**,

PEOPLE → PEOPLE'S, PEOPLES
Gn   11: 6 while they are one **p** and all have
Ex   3:10 you to Pharaoh to bring my **p**,
Ex   5: 1 Let my **p** go, that they may hold
Ex   6: 7 I will take you as my own **p**, and I
Ex   8:19 make a distinction between my **p** and your **p**.
Ex   13:17 when Pharaoh let the **p** go, God did
Ex   15:13 love you led the **p** you redeemed,
Ex   15:24 As the **p** grumbled against Moses,
Ex   19: 8 all the **p** answered together,
Ex   24: 3 When Moses came to the **p**
Ex   32: 1 When the **p** saw that Moses was
Ex   32: 9 I have seen this **p**, how stiff-necked
Ex   32:12 your mind about punishing your **p**.
Ex   33:13 this nation is indeed your own **p**.
Nm   11:11 that you burden me with all this **p**?
Nm   14:11 How long will this **p** spurn me?
Nm   14:19 the iniquity of this **p** in keeping
Nm   21: 7 Then the **p** came to Moses and said,
Nm   21: 7 So Moses prayed for the **p**,
Nm   22: 5 "A **p** has come out of Egypt!
Dt   4: 6 is truly a wise and discerning **p**."
Dt   4:20 that you might be his **p**, his heritage,
Dt   5:28 the words these **p** have spoken
Dt   7: 6 For you are a **p** holy to the LORD,

Dt   7: 6 the earth to be a **p** specially his own.
Dt   26:18 you will be a **p** specially his own,
Dt   31: 7 you shall bring this **p** into the land
Dt   31:16 this **p** will prostitute themselves
Jos   1: 6 you may give this **p** possession
Jos   3:16 Thus the **p** crossed over opposite
Jos   24:25 made a covenant with the **p** that day
Jgs   2: 7 The **p** served the LORD during
Ru   1:16 Your **p** shall be my **p** and your God,
1 Sm   10:24 Then Samuel addressed all the **p**,
1 Sm   10:24 is no one like him among all the **p**!"
1 Sm   12:22 the LORD will not abandon his **p**,
1 Sm   12:22 has decided to make you his **p**.
2 Sm   5: 2 You shall shepherd my **p** Israel;
2 Sm   7:10 I will assign a place for my **p** Israel
2 Sm   7:23 on earth is there like your **p** Israel?
2 Sm   7:23 redeeming it as his **p** and making
2 Sm   24:17 the angel who was striking the **p**,
1 Kgs 3: 8 among the **p** you have chosen, a **p** so vast
1 Kgs 8:30 of your **p** Israel which they offer
1 Kgs 8:56 who has given rest to his **p** Israel,
1 Kgs 18:39 this, all the **p** fell prostrate and said,
2 Kgs 23: 3 And all the **p** stood by the covenant.
1 Chr 29:17 joy I have seen your **p** here present
2 Chr 2:10 "Because the LORD loves his **p**,
2 Chr 7:14 if then my **p**, upon whom my name
2 Chr 7:20 I will uproot the **p** from the land
2 Chr 36:16 LORD's anger against his **p** blazed
Ezr   3: 1 the **p** gathered as one in Jerusalem.
Neh   1:10 your **p**, whom you freed by your
Neh   3:38 The **p** worked enthusiastically.
Neh   8: 1 the whole **p** gathered as one
Jdt   13:17 All the **p** were greatly astonished.
Jdt   13:17 humiliated the enemies of your **p**."
Est   3: 6 Mordecai's **p**, throughout the realm
Est   7: 3 beg that you spare the lives of my **p**.
1 Mc   3:43 "Let us raise our **p** from their ruin
1 Mc   3:43 "Let us raise our **p** from their ruin
Ps   3: 9 May your blessing be upon your **p**!
Ps   29:11 the LORD give might to his **p**; may the LORD bless his **p**
Ps   33:12 the **p** chosen as his inheritance.
Ps   50: 4 and to the earth to judge his **p**:
Ps   53: 7 captivity of his **p** Jacob will rejoice
Ps   81:14 O that my **p** would listen to me,
Ps   94:14 the LORD will not forsake his **p**,
Ps   95: 7 we are the **p** he shepherds, the sheep
Ps   125: 2 LORD surrounds his **p** both now
Ps   135:14 For the LORD defends his **p**,
Ps   144:15 Blessed the **p** so fortunate;
Ps   144:15 blessed the **p** whose God is the LORD.
Ps   149: 4 the LORD takes delight in his **p**,
Prv   29: 2 the just flourish, the **p** rejoice;
Prv   29: 2 when the wicked rule, the **p** groan.
Prv   29:18 Without a vision the **p** lose restraint;
Sir   33:10 Likewise, all **p** are of clay,
Is   1: 3 not know, my **p** has not understood.
Is   1: 4 nation, **p** laden with wickedness,
Is   5:13 Therefore my **p** go into exile
Is   6:10 Make the heart of this **p** sluggish,
Is   9: 1 The **p** who walked in darkness have
Is   19:25 "Blessed be my **p** Egypt,
Is   25: 8 reproach of his **p** he will remove
Is   29:13 Since this **p** draws near with words
Is   40: 1 give comfort to my **p**, says your
Is   40: 7 "Yes, the **p** is grass!
Is   42: 6 and set you as a covenant for the **p**,
Is   49:13 For the LORD comforts his **p**
Is   51: 4 Be attentive to me, my **p**;
Is   52: 6 Therefore my **p** shall know my
Is   53: 8 living, struck for the sins of his **p**.
Is   60:21 Your **p** will all be just; for all time
Is   62:12 They shall be called "The Holy **P**,"
Is   65: 2 my hands all day to a rebellious **p**,
Jer   2:11 my **p** have changed their glory
Jer   2:13 Two evils my **p** have done:
Jer   2:32 Yet my **p** have forgotten me days

Jer	4:22	My **p** are fools, they do not know
Jer	5:14	And this **p** the wood that it shall
Jer	5:31	Yet my **p** like it this way;
Jer	6:27	for my **p** I have appointed you,
Jer	7:16	now, must not intercede for this **p**!
Jer	7:23	be your God and you shall be my **p**.
Jer	18:15	Yet my **p** have forgotten me:
Jer	23: 2	the shepherds who shepherd my **p**:
Jer	30: 3	restore the fortunes of my **p** Israel
Jer	31:33	their God, and they shall be my **p**.
Jer	50: 6	Lost sheep were my **p**,
Ez	13:23	I will deliver my **p** from your hand.
Ez	36: 8	and bear fruit for my **p** Israel,
Ez	36:28	you will be my **p**, and I will be your
Ez	37:13	you come up out of them, my **p**!
Ez	38:14	when my **p** Israel dwell securely,
Ez	39: 7	my holy name among my **p** Israel,
Dn	7:27	be given to the **p** of the holy ones
Dn	9:19	upon your city and your **p**!"
Dn	9:24	weeks are decreed for your **p**
Dn	10:14	happen to your **p** in the last days;
Dn	12: 1	the great prince, guardian of your **p**;
Dn	12: 1	At that time your **p** shall escape,
Hos	2: 3	Say to your brothers, "My **P**," and to
Hos	2:25	say to Not-My-People, "You are my **p**,"
Hos	4:14	Thus a **p** without understanding
Jl	2:18	for his land and took pity on his **p**.
Jl	4:16	LORD will be a shelter for his **p**, a fortress for the **p** of Israel.
Am	9:14	I will restore my **p** Israel, they shall
Mi	3: 5	O you who lead my **p** astray,
Mi	6: 2	the LORD has a case against his **p**;
Mi	7:14	Shepherd your **p** with your staff,
Zep	2: 9	remnant of my **p** shall plunder them,
Hg	1:12	the **p** obeyed the LORD their God,
Hg	1:12	thus the **p** feared the LORD.
Zec	2:15	They will be my **p**, and I will dwell
Zec	8: 7	going to rescue my **p** from the land
Zec	13: 9	"They are my **p**," and they will
Mt	1:21	because he will save his **p**
Mt	2: 6	who is to shepherd my **p** Israel.' "
Mt	4:16	the **p** who sit in darkness have seen
Mk	7: 6	'This **p** honors me with their lips,
Mk	8:27	"Who do **p** say that I am?"
Lk	1:17	to prepare a **p** fit for the Lord."
Lk	1:68	and brought redemption to his **p**.
Lk	2:10	of great joy that will be for all the **p**.
Lk	21:23	a wrathful judgment upon this **p**.
Jn	11:50	one man should die instead of the **p**,
Jn	18:14	man should die rather than the **p**.
Acts	2:47	and enjoying favor with all the **p**.
Acts	5:13	join them, but the **p** esteemed them.
Acts	15:14	from among the Gentiles a **p** for his
Acts	18:10	you, for I have many **p** in this city."
Rom	9:25	who were not my **p** I will call 'my **p**,'
Rom	11: 1	I ask, then, has God rejected his **p**?
Rom	15:10	"Rejoice, O Gentiles, with his **p**."
2 Cor	6:16	be their God and they shall be my **p**.
Ti	2:14	cleanse for himself a **p** as his own,
Heb	2:17	God to expiate the sins of the **p**.
Heb	4: 9	rest still remains for the **p** of God.
Heb	5: 3	for himself as well as for the **p**.
Heb	8:10	their God, and they shall be my **p**.
Heb	10:30	"The Lord will judge his **p**."
Heb	13:12	consecrate the **p** by his own blood.
1 Pt	2: 9	a holy nation, a **p** of his own,
1 Pt	2:10	Once you were "no **p**" but now you are God's **p**;
2 Pt	2: 1	also false prophets among the **p**,
Rev	18: 4	my **p**, so as not to take part in her

PEOPLE'S → PEOPLE

2 Chr 25:15 "Why have you sought this **p** gods

PEOPLES → PEOPLE

Gn	17:16	and rulers of **p** will issue from her.
Gn	25:23	two **p** are separating while still
Gn	27:29	May **p** serve you, and nations bow

Gn	28: 3	you may become an assembly of **p**.
Jos	4:24	that all the **p** of the earth may know
1 Kgs	8:43	all the **p** of the earth may know your
Ezr	3: 3	lived in fear of the **p** of the lands,
Ezr	10: 2	foreign women of the **p** of the land.
Ps	2: 1	protest and the **p** conspire in vain?
Ps	9: 9	who judges the **p** with fairness.
Ps	67: 4	May the **p** praise you, God;
Ps	87: 6	notes in the register of the **p**:
Ps	96:10	He rules the **p** with fairness.
Ps	117: 1	Extol him, all you **p**!
Is	2: 4	nations, and set terms for many **p**.
Is	17:12	the roaring of many **p**—a roar like
Is	25: 6	hosts will provide for all **p** A feast
Is	34: 1	be attentive, you **p**!
Is	49:22	and to the **p** raise my signal;
Is	55: 4	As I made him a witness to **p**, a leader and commander of **p**,
Dn	7:14	**p** and tongues will serve him.
Dn	8:24	He shall destroy powerful **p**;
Mi	4: 1	the hills, And **p** shall stream to it:
Mi	5: 6	shall be in the midst of many **p**,
Zep	3: 9	I will make pure the speech of the **p**,
Zep	3:20	praise, among all the **p** of the earth,
Zec	8:20	There will yet come **p**
Zec	12: 2	cup of reeling for all **p** round about.
Acts	4:25	rage and the **p** entertain folly?
Rev	10:11	must prophesy again about many **p**,

PEOR

Nm	25: 3	attached itself to the Baal of **P**,
Dt	4: 3	who followed the Baal of **P**;
Jos	22:17	Is the iniquity of **P** not enough,

PERES

Dn	5:25	MENE, TEKEL, and **P**.
Dn	5:28	**P**, your kingdom has been divided

PEREZ

Gn	38:29	So he was called **P**.
Ru	4:12	house become like the house of **P**,
Mt	1: 3	Judah became the father of **P**

PERFECT → PERFECTER, PERFECTION

Jb	36: 4	one **p** in knowledge is before you.
Jb	37:16	of him who is **p** in knowledge?
Ps	19: 8	The law of the LORD is **p**,
Sg	6: 9	One alone is my dove, my **p** one,
Ez	27: 3	you said, "I am a ship, **p** in beauty;
Ez	28:12	full of wisdom, **p** in beauty.
Mt	5:48	So be **p**, just as your heavenly Father is **p**.
Mt	19:21	to him, "If you wish to be **p**, go,
Rom	12: 2	what is good and pleasing and **p**.
2 Cor	7: 1	making holiness **p** in the fear
2 Cor	12: 9	for power is made **p** in weakness."
Heb	2:10	their salvation **p** through suffering.
Heb	5: 9	and when he was made **p**,
Heb	7:28	a son, who has been made **p** forever.
Heb	9: 9	offered that cannot **p** the worshiper
Heb	9:11	and more **p** tabernacle not made
Heb	10: 1	it can never make **p** those who come
Heb	10:14	he has made **p** forever those who
Heb	11:40	us they should not be made **p**.
Heb	12:23	and the spirits of the just made **p**,
Jas	1:17	and every **p** gift is from above,
Jas	1:25	the one who peers into the **p** law
Jas	3: 2	he is a **p** man, able to bridle his
1 Jn	4:18	**p** love drives out fear because fear
1 Jn	4:18	and so one who fears is not yet **p**

PERFECTER → PERFECT

Heb 12: 2 on Jesus, the leader and **p** of faith.

PERFECTION → PERFECT

Ps	119:96	I have seen the limits of all **p**,
Ez	28:12	You were a seal of **p**,
Heb	7:11	If, then, **p** came through the levitical
1 Jn	4:12	and his love is brought to **p** in us.

PERFORMED
Ex   4:30   and he **p** the signs before the people.
Ps   78:43   When he **p** his signs in Egypt,
Jn   10:41   to him and said, "John **p** no sign,
Rev   19:20   it the false prophet who had **p** in its

PERFUME
Sg   1: 3   Your name is a flowing **p**—

PERGAMUM
Rev   1:11   to Ephesus, Smyrna, **P**, Thyatira,
Rev   2:12   "To the angel of the church in **P**,

PERIL
Rom   8:35   or nakedness, or **p**, or the sword?

PERISH → PERISHABLE, PERISHED, PERISHES, PERISHING
Jos   23:13   until you **p** from this good land
Est   4:16   contrary to the law. If I **p**, I **p**!"
Ps   37:20   The wicked **p**,
Ps   73:27   But those who are far from you **p**;
Ps   102:27   They **p**, but you remain;
Prv   11:10   when the wicked **p**, there is
Prv   19: 9   and whoever utters lies will **p**.
Prv   21:28   The false witness will **p**, but one
Is   29:14   The wisdom of the wise shall **p**,
Is   60:12   that will not serve you shall **p**;
Jer   51:18   work, that will **p** at the time
Jon   1: 6   of us so that we will not **p**."
Jon   3: 9   wrath, so that we will not **p**."
Lk   13: 3   repent, you will all **p** as they did!
Jn   3:16   who believes in him might not **p**
Jn   10:28   eternal life, and they shall never **p**.
Acts   8:20   him, "May your money **p** with you,
Rom   2:12   will also **p** without reference to it,
Col   2:22   These are all things destined to **p**
Heb   1:11   They will **p**, but you remain;
2 Pt   3: 9   not wishing that any should **p**

PERISHABLE → PERISH
1 Cor   9:25   They do it to win a **p** crown, but we
1 Pt   1:18   not with **p** things like silver or gold
1 Pt   1:23   not from **p** but from imperishable

PERISHED → PERISH
Dt   2:14   of soldiers had **p** from the camp,
Ps   119:92   I would have **p** in my affliction.

PERISHES → PERISH
Jn   6:27   Do not work for food that **p**

PERISHING → PERISH
1 Cor   1:18   is foolishness to those who are **p**,
2 Cor   2:15   saved and among those who are **p**,
2 Cor   4: 3   it is veiled for those who are **p**,

PERIZZITES
Gn   13: 7   and the **P** were living in the land.
Ex   3: 8   the Amorites, the **P**, the Girgashites,

PERJURERS
1 Tm   1:10   liars, **p**, and whatever else is

PERMIT
1 Tm   2:12   I do not **p** a woman to teach

PERPETUAL
Ex   29: 9   priesthood be theirs by a **p** statute,

PERPLEXED
2 Cor   4: 8   **p**, but not driven to despair;

PERSECUTE → PERSECUTED, PERSECUTING, PERSECUTION, PERSECUTIONS
Mt   5:11   you when they insult you and **p** you
Mt   5:44   and pray for those who **p** you,
Lk   11:49   some of them they will kill and **p**'
Lk   21:12   they will seize and **p** you, they will
Jn   15:20   persecuted me, they will also **p** you.
Rom   12:14   Bless those who **p** [you],

PERSECUTED → PERSECUTE
Mt   5:10   Blessed are they who are **p**
Mt   5:12   Thus they **p** the prophets who were
Jn   15:20   If they **p** me, they will

Acts   22: 4   I **p** this Way to death, binding both
1 Cor   4:12   when **p**, we endure;
1 Cor 15: 9   because I **p** the church of God.
2 Cor   4: 9   **p**, but not abandoned;
Phil   3: 6   in zeal I **p** the church,
2 Tm   3:12   religiously in Christ Jesus will be **p**.

PERSECUTING → PERSECUTE
Acts   9: 5   "I am Jesus, whom you are **p**.
Acts   22: 8   the Nazorean whom you are **p**.'
Acts   26:15   'I am Jesus whom you are **p**.

PERSECUTION → PERSECUTE
Mt   13:21   or **p** comes because of the word,
Acts   8: 1   broke out a severe **p** of the church
Rom   8:35   or distress, or **p**, or famine,

PERSECUTIONS → PERSECUTE
Mk   10:30   with **p**, and eternal life in the age
2 Cor 12:10   hardships, **p**, and constraints,
2 Thes 1: 4   faith in all your **p** and the afflictions
2 Tm   3:11   **p**, and sufferings, such as happened
2 Tm   3:11   and Lystra, **p** that I endured.

PERSEVERE → PERSEVERED, PERSEVERES
Dn   12:12   patience and **p** for the one thousand three
Rom   12:12   endure in affliction, **p** in prayer.

PERSEVERED → PERSEVERE
Sir   2:10   Has anyone **p** in his fear and been
Heb   11:27   for he **p** as if seeing the one who is

PERSEVERES → PERSEVERE
Mt   24:13   one who **p** to the end will be saved.

PERSIA → PERSIANS
Ezr   1: 1   king of **P**, in order to fulfill
Ezr   1: 1   spirit of Cyrus king of **P** to issue
Dn   10:20   I must fight the prince of **P** again.

PERSIANS → PERSIA
Jdt   16:10   "The **P** trembled at her boldness,

PERSISTENCE → PERSISTENT
Lk   11: 8   whatever he needs because of his **p**.

PERSISTENT → PERSISTENCE
2 Tm   4: 2   be **p** whether it is convenient

PERSUADE → PERSUADED
Acts   26:28   "You will soon **p** me to play
2 Cor   5:11   fear of the Lord, we try to **p** others;

PERSUADED → PERSUADE
Prv   25:15   By patience is a ruler **p**, and a soft
Mt   27:20   the elders **p** the crowds to ask

PERVERSE → PERVERT, PERVERTED, PERVERTING
2 Sm   22:27   but to the **p** you are devious.
Prv   17:20   The **p** in heart come to no good,
Wis   1: 3   For **p** counsels separate people
Lk   9:41   "O faithless and **p** generation,

PERVERT → PERVERSE
Jb   8: 3   Does God **p** judgment,
Gal   1: 7   and wish to **p** the gospel of Christ.

PERVERTED → PERVERSE
Jer   3:21   Because they have **p** their way,

PERVERTING → PERVERSE
Ex   23: 2   not follow the crowd in **p** justice.
1 Sm   8: 3   gain, accepting bribes and **p** justice.
Prv   17:23   pocket, thus **p** the course of justice.

PESTILENCE
Dt   32:24   and consuming fever and bitter **p**,
Ps   91: 6   Nor the **p** that roams in darkness,
Rev   18: 8   her plagues will come in one day, **p**,

PETER → =CEPHAS, =SIMON
Apostle, brother of Andrew, also called Simon (Mt 10:2; Mk 3:16; Lk 6:14; Acts 1:13), and Cephas (Jn 1:42). Confession of Christ (Mt 16:13-20; Mk 8:27-30; Lk 9:18-27). At transfiguration (Mt 17:1-8; Mk 9:2-8; Lk 9:28-36; 2 Pt 1:16-18). Caught fish with coin (Mt 17:24-27). Denial of Jesus predicted (Mt 26:31-35; Mk 14:27-31; Lk 22:31-34; Jn 13:31-38).

Denied Jesus (Mt 26:69-75; Mk 14:66-72; Lk 22:54-62; Jn 18:15-27). Commissioned by Jesus to shepherd his flock (Jn 21:15-23).

Speech at Pentecost (Acts 2). Healed beggar (Acts 3:1-10). Speech at temple (Acts 3:11-26), before Sanhedrin (Acts 4:1-22). In Samaria (Acts 8:14-25). Sent by vision to Cornelius (Acts 10). Announced salvation of Gentiles in Jerusalem (Acts 11; 15). Freed from prison (Acts 12). Inconsistency at Antioch (Gal 2:11-21). At Jerusalem Council (Acts 15).

Letters: 1 and 2 Peter.

PHARAOH → PHARAOH'S
Gn	12:15	saw her they praised her to P,
Gn	41:14	P therefore had Joseph summoned,
Gn	47:10	Jacob blessed P and withdrew
Ex	1:22	P then commanded all his people,
Ex	2:15	Moses fled from P and went
Ex	3:11	"Who am I that I should go to P
Ex	5: 2	P answered, "Who is the Lord,
Ex	11: 1	more plague I will bring upon P
Ex	14:17	I will receive glory through P
Dt	7: 8	from the hand of P, king of Egypt.
Is	36: 6	That is what P, king of Egypt,
Rom	9:17	For the scripture says to P, "This is

PHARAOH'S → PHARAOH
Ex	11:10	all these wonders in P presence,
Ex	11:10	the Lord hardened P heart,
Heb	11:24	be known as the son of P daughter;

PHARISEE → PHARISEES
Lk	11:37	a P invited him to dine at his home.
Jn	3: 1	there was a P named Nicodemus,
Acts	5:34	But a P in the Sanhedrin named
Acts	23: 6	I am a P, the son of Pharisees;
Phil	3: 5	in observance of the law a P,

PHARISEES → PHARISEE
Mt	5:20	surpasses that of the scribes and P,
Mt	16: 6	beware of the leaven of the P
Mt	23:13	you, scribes and P, you hypocrites.
Mk	2:18	John and the disciples of the P fast,
Lk	11:42	Woe to you P! You pay tithes
Acts	23: 7	a dispute broke out between the P

PHILADELPHIA
Rev	1:11	Thyatira, Sardis, P, and Laodicea."
Rev	3: 7	"To the angel of the church in P,

PHILEMON
Phlm	1: 1	brother, to P, our beloved and our

PHILIP
1. Apostle (Mt 10:3; Mk 3:18; Lk 6:14; Jn 1:43-48; 14:8; Acts 1:13).
2. Deacon (Acts 6:1-7); evangelist in Samaria (Acts 8:4-25), to Ethiopian (Acts 8:26-40).
3. Herod Philip I (Mt 14:3; Mk 6:17).
4. Herod Philip II (Lk 3:1).

PHILIPPI
Mt	16:13	Caesarea P he asked his disciples,
Acts	16:12	and from there to P, a leading city
Phil	1: 1	ones in Christ Jesus who are in P,

PHILISTIA → PHILISTINE, PHILISTINES
Ex	15:14	anguish gripped the dwellers in P.
Ps	60:10	I will triumph over P."

PHILISTINE → PHILISTIA
1 Sm	14: 1	let us go over to the P outpost
1 Sm	17:23	talking with them, the P champion,
1 Sm	17:37	me from the hand of this P."

PHILISTINES → PHILISTIA
Gn	21:34	in the land of the P for a long time.
Gn	26: 1	Abimelech, king of the P in Gerar.
Ex	23:31	the Red Sea to the sea of the P,
Jgs	10: 7	he sold them into the power of the P
Jgs	13: 1	the power of the P for forty years.
Jgs	16: 5	The lords of the P came up to her
Jgs	16:30	saying, "Let me die with the P!"
1 Sm	4: 1	time, the P gathered for an attack
1 Sm	5: 1	The P, having captured the ark
1 Sm	13:20	to the P to sharpen their plowshares,

1 Sm	17: 1	The P rallied their forces for battle
1 Sm	17:51	When the P saw that their hero was
1 Sm	23: 1	that the P were attacking Keilah
1 Sm	27: 1	but to escape to the land of the P;
2 Sm	5:17	When the P had heard that David
2 Sm	8: 1	David defeated the P and subdued
2 Sm	21:15	was another battle between the P
2 Kgs	18: 8	he who struck the P as far as Gaza,
Jer	47: 4	the Lord is destroying the P,
Ez	25:16	out my hand against the P, and I
Am	1: 8	and the last of the P shall perish,

PHILOSOPHERS → PHILOSOPHY
Acts	17:18	Stoic p engaged him in discussion.

PHILOSOPHY → PHILOSOPHERS
Col	2: 8	seductive p according to human

PHINEHAS
1. Grandson of Aaron (Ex 6:25; Jos 22:30-32). Zeal for the Lord stopped plague (Nm 25:7-13; Ps 106:30).
2. Son of Eli; a wicked priest (1 Sm 1:3; 2:12-17; 4:1-19).

PHOEBE
Rom	16: 1	I commend to you P our sister,

PHYLACTERIES
Mt	23: 5	They widen their p and lengthen

PHYSICAL
1 Tm	4: 8	while p training is of limited value,

PHYSICIAN
Mt	9:12	who are well do not need a p,
Lk	4:23	you will quote me this proverb, 'P,
Col	4:14	Luke the beloved p sends greetings,

PIECE → BREASTPIECE, PIECES
Ex	15:25	who pointed out to him a p of wood.
Mk	2:21	No one sews a p of unshrunken
Jn	19:23	woven in one p from the top down.

PIECES → PIECE
Gn	15:17	which passed between those p.
1 Kgs	11:30	his new cloak, tore it into twelve p,
Mi	1: 7	carved figures shall be broken to p,
Lk	20:18	on that stone will be dashed to p;

PIERCE → PIERCED
Ex	21: 6	he shall p his ear with an awl,
Lk	2:35	you yourself a sword will p) so

PIERCED → PIERCE
Nm	25: 8	the tent where he p the two of them,
Jn	19:37	look upon him whom they have p."
1 Tm	6:10	have p themselves with many pains.
Rev	1: 7	will see him, even those who p him.

PIETY
Acts	3:12	him walk by our own power or p?

PIG
Dt	14: 8	And the p, which indeed has

PIGEON → PIGEONS
Lv	12: 6	a p or a turtledove for a purification

PIGEONS → PIGEON
Lk	2:24	pair of turtledoves or two young p,"

PILATE
Governor of Judea. Questioned Jesus (Mt 27:1-26; Mk 15:15; Lk 22:66–23:25; Jn 18:28–19:16); sent him to Herod (Lk 23:6-12); consented to his crucifixion when crowds chose Barabbas (Mt 27:15-26; Mk 15:6-15; Lk 23:13-25; Jn 19:1-10).

PILLAR → PILLARS
Gn	19:26	and she was turned into a p of salt.
Wis	10: 7	soul, a standing p of salt.
1 Tm	3:15	God, the p and foundation of truth.
Rev	3:12	I will make into a p in the temple

PILLARS → PILLAR
Ps	75: 4	quake, I make steady its p."
Rev	10: 1	sun and his feet were like p of fire.

PINIONS
Dt 32:11 took them, bore them upon his **p**.
Ps 91: 4 He will shelter you with his **p**,

PISGAH
Dt 3:27 Go up to the top of **P** and look

PIT
Ps 7:16 but he falls into the **p** he has made.
Ps 40: 3 me up from the **p** of destruction,
Ps 103: 4 Who redeems your life from the **p**,
Prv 23:27 For the harlot is a deep **p**,
Prv 26:27 Whoever digs a **p** falls into it;
Is 24:17 Terror, **p**, and trap for you,
Is 38:17 my life from the **p** of destruction;
Ez 19: 4 in their **p** he was caught;
Jon 2: 7 you brought my life up from the **p**,
Mt 15:14 person, both will fall into a **p**."

PITCH
Gn 6:14 and cover it inside and out with **p**.
Ex 2: 3 daubed it with bitumen and **p**,
Dn 14:27 Then Daniel took some **p**, fat,

PITY
Dt 7:16 You are not to look on them with **p**,
Jb 19:21 **P** me, **p** me, you my friends,
Ps 72:13 He shows **p** to the needy
Ez 7: 4 will not spare you, nor will I have **p**;
Hos 1: 6 I will no longer feel **p** for the house
Hos 2:25 and I will have **p** on Not-Pitied.
Jl 2:18 his land and took **p** on his people.

PLACE → PLACES
Gn 50:19 Can I take the **p** of God?
Ex 3: 5 for the **p** where you stand is holy
Ex 26:33 divides the holy **p** from the holy
Dt 12: 5 seek out the **p** which the LORD,
Jos 5:15 for the **p** on which you are standing
2 Chr 6:21 from the **p** of your enthronement,
Ezr 9: 8 and gave us a stake in his holy **p**;
Jb 22:22 and **p** his words in your heart.
Ps 24: 3 Who can stand in his holy **p**?
Ps 132:14 "This is my resting **p** forever;
Eccl 6: 6 do not both go to the same **p**?
Hg 2: 9 And in this **p** I will give you peace—
Mt 27:33 they came to a **p** called Golgotha
Mt 27:33 (which means **P** of the Skull),
Jn 14: 3 And if I go and prepare a **p** for you,
2 Pt 1:19 it, as to a lamp shining in a dark **p**,
Rev 20:11 and there was no **p** for them.

PLACES → PLACE
Lv 26:30 I will demolish your high **p**,
1 Kgs 3: 2 were sacrificing on the high **p**,
2 Kgs 18: 4 It was he who removed the high **p**,
Ps 78:58 They enraged him with their high **p**,
Jer 19: 5 building high **p** for Baal to burn
Jn 14: 2 house there are many dwelling **p**.

PLAGUE → PLAGUES
Ex 11: 1 One more **p** I will bring
Nm 11:33 struck them with a very great **p**.
2 Chr 6:28 whatever **p** or sickness there may
Zec 14:12 this will be the **p**
Rev 11: 6 with any **p** as often as they wish.
Rev 16:21 the **p** of hail because this **p** was so

PLAGUES → PLAGUE
Hos 13:14 Where are your **p**, O death!
Rev 9:18 By these three **p** of fire, smoke,
Rev 15: 1 seven angels with the seven last **p**,
Rev 21: 9 filled with the seven last **p** came
Rev 22:18 to him the **p** described in this book,

PLAIN
Gn 13:12 settled among the cities of the **P**,
Gn 19:29 God destroyed the cities of the **P**,
Is 40: 4 The rugged land shall be a **p**,

PLAN → PLANNED, PLANS
Is 46:10 I say that my **p** shall stand,

PLANNED → PLAN
Is 23: 9 The LORD of hosts has **p** it,
Is 46:11 I have **p** it, and I will do it.

PLANS → PLAN
Tb 4:19 your endeavors and **p** may prosper.
Prv 15:22 **P** fail when there is no counsel,
Prv 16: 3 LORD, and your **p** will succeed.
Prv 19:21 Many are the **p** of the human heart,
Prv 20:18 **P** made with advice succeed;
Jer 29:11 I know well the **p** I have in mind
Jer 29:11 **p** for your welfare and not for woe,
2 Cor 1:17 do I make my **p** according to human

PLANT → PLANTED, PLANTS, REPLANTED
Gn 1:29 I give you every seed-bearing **p**
Gn 9:20 soil, was the first to **p** a vineyard.
Eccl 3: 2 a time to **p**, and a time to uproot the **p**.
Am 9:15 I will **p** them upon their own
Mt 15:13 "Every **p** that my heavenly Father

PLANTED → PLANT
Gn 2: 8 The LORD God **p** a garden
Ps 1: 3 He is like a tree **p** near streams
Ps 92:14 **P** in the house of the LORD,
Jer 17: 8 are like a tree **p** beside the waters
Mt 15:13 Father has not **p** will be uprooted.
Mt 21:33 was a landowner who **p** a vineyard,
Lk 13: 6 was a person who had a fig tree **p**
1 Cor 3: 6 I **p**, Apollos watered, but God

PLANTS → PLANT
Gn 9: 3 them all to you as I did the green **p**.
Ps 144:12 our sons be like **p** well nurtured
Prv 31:16 from her earnings she **p** a vineyard.
1 Cor 3: 7 neither the one who **p** nor the one
1 Cor 9: 7 Who **p** a vineyard without eating its

PLASTER
Dt 27: 2 large stones and coat them with **p**.
Dn 5: 5 writing on the **p** of the wall

PLATES
Ex 25:29 You shall make its **p** and cups,

PLATFORM
2 Chr 6:13 made a bronze **p** five cubits long,
Neh 8: 4 on a wooden **p** that had been made

PLATTER
Mk 6:25 at once on a **p** the head of John

PLAY → PLAYED, PLAYING
Ps 33: 3 skillfully **p** with joyful chant.
Is 11: 8 The baby shall **p** by the viper's den,

PLAYED → PLAY
Mt 11:17 'We **p** the flute for you, but you did
1 Cor 14: 7 how will what is being **p** on flute

PLAYING → PLAY
1 Sm 18:10 **p** the harp as at other times,
1 Sm 19: 9 while David was **p** the harp nearby.
Zec 8: 5 with boys and girls **p** in its streets.
Rev 14: 2 like that of harpists **p** their harps.

PLEASANT
Gn 49:15 and how **p** the land, He bent his
Ps 16: 6 **P** places were measured out for me;
Ps 133: 1 How good and how **p** it is,

PLEASE → PLEASED, PLEASES, PLEASING, PLEASURE, PLEASURES
Ps 69:32 will **p** the LORD more than oxen,
Sir 2:16 who fear the Lord seek to **p** him;
Rom 8: 8 who are in the flesh cannot **p** God.
Rom 15: 1 of the weak and not to **p** ourselves;
Rom 15: 3 For Christ did not **p** himself;
1 Cor 7:32 of the Lord, how he may **p** the Lord.
1 Cor 7:33 the world, how he may **p** his wife,
1 Cor 10:33 just as I try to **p** everyone in every
2 Cor 5: 9 we aspire to **p** him, whether we are
1 Thes 2: 4 not as trying to **p** human beings,
1 Thes 4: 1 conduct yourselves to **p** God—
Heb 11: 6 faith it is impossible to **p** him,

PLEASED → PLEASE

Nm	14: 8	If the LORD is p with us, he will
Nm	24: 1	the LORD was p to bless Israel,
1 Kgs	3:10	The Lord was p by Solomon's
Ez	43:27	Then I will be p with you—oracle
Dn	8: 4	it did what it p and grew powerful.
Mi	6: 7	Will the LORD be p
Hg	1: 8	build the house that I may be p with it,
Mt	3:17	Son, with whom I am well p."
Mt	17: 5	Son, with whom I am well p;
Mk	1:11	with you I am well p."
Lk	3:22	with you I am well p."
1 Cor	10: 5	Yet God was not p with most
Col	1:19	him all the fullness was p to dwell,
Heb	11: 5	up, he was attested to have p God.
2 Pt	1:17	beloved, with whom I am well p."

PLEASES → PLEASE

1 Jn	3:22	commandments and do what p him.

PLEASING → PLEASE

Ezr	6:10	offer sacrifices of p odor to the God
Ps	104:34	May my meditation be p to him;
Eph	5:10	Try to learn what is p to the Lord.
Phil	4:18	an acceptable sacrifice, p to God.
1 Tm	5: 4	to their parents, for this is p to God.
Heb	13:21	you what is p to him through Jesus

PLEASURE → PLEASE

Gn	18:12	is old, am I still to have sexual p?"
Ps	147:10	horses, no p in the runner's stride.
Prv	21:17	The lover of p will suffer want;
Ez	18:32	For I find no p in the death
Ez	33:11	I swear I take no p in the death
2 Tm	3: 4	lovers of p rather than lovers

PLEASURES → PLEASE

Lk	8:14	anxieties and riches and p of life,
Ti	3: 3	slaves to various desires and p,

PLEDGE

Gn	38:17	you leave me a p until you send it."
Nm	30: 3	or binds himself under oath to a p,
Dt	24: 6	even its upper stone as a p for debt,
Dt	24: 6	be taking as a p the debtor's life.
Dt	24:17	take the clothing of a widow as p.
Prv	6: 1	given your hand in p to another,
Ez	18: 7	gives back the p received for a debt,

PLENTY

Prv	12:11	till their own land have food in p,

PLOW → PLOWED, PLOWSHARES

Dt	22:10	You shall not p with an ox
Prv	20: 4	In seedtime sluggards do not p;
Lk	9:62	"No one who sets a hand to the p

PLOWED → PLOW

Jgs	14:18	"If you had not p with my heifer,
Ps	129: 3	Upon my back the plowers p,

PLOWSHARES → PLOW

Is	2: 4	They shall beat their swords into p
Jl	4:10	Beat your p into swords, and your
Mi	4: 3	They shall beat their swords into p,

PLUCK

Dt	23:26	you may p some of the ears

PLUNDER → PLUNDERED

Dt	1:39	little ones, who you said would become p,
Jer	30:16	All who p you shall become p,
Zep	2: 9	remnant of my people shall p them,

PLUNDERED → PLUNDER

Ez	39:10	plundering those who p them,

PLUNGE

1 Tm	6: 9	desires, which p them into ruin

PODS

Lk	15:16	to eat his fill of the p

POETS

Acts	17:28	as even some of your p have said,

POINT

Heb	12: 4	resisted to the p of shedding blood.

POISON

Ps	64: 4	like swords, bend their bows of p words.
Jas	3: 8	It is a restless evil, full of deadly p.

POLE → POLES

Nm	21: 8	Make a seraph and mount it on a p,

POLES → POLE

Ex	25:13	Then make p of acacia wood

POLISHED

Ez	1: 7	hooves of a bull, gleaming like p brass.

POLLUTED

Prv	25:26	A trampled fountain or a p spring—

POMEGRANATES

Ex	28:33	hem at the bottom you shall make p,
Dt	8: 8	of vines and fig trees and p, of olive
1 Kgs	7:18	He also cast p, two rows around

PONDER

Ps	48:10	We p, O God, your mercy within
Ps	64:10	proclaims God's actions, they p his deeds.

PONTIUS

Lk	3: 1	when P Pilate was governor

POOL → POOLS

2 Sm	2:13	them at the p of Gibeon.
1 Kgs	22:38	out the chariot at the p of Samaria,
Jn	5: 2	at the Sheep [Gate] a p called
Jn	9: 7	him, "Go wash in the P of Siloam"
Rev	19:20	into the fiery p burning with sulfur.
Rev	20:10	astray was thrown into the p of fire
Rev	20:14	were thrown into the p of fire.
Rev	20:14	(This p of fire is the second death.

POOLS → POOL

Ps	107:35	He changed the desert into p
Ps	114: 8	Who turned the rock into p of water,

POOR → POVERTY

Ex	23: 3	You shall not favor the p
Dt	15:11	"Open your hand freely to your p
Dt	24:12	If the person is p, you shall not
Dt	24:14	You shall not exploit a p and needy
1 Sm	2: 8	from the ash heap lifts up the p,
2 Sm	12: 1	were two men, one rich, the other p.
Jb	24: 4	all the p of the land are driven
Jb	29:16	I was a father to the p;
Ps	14: 6	would crush the hopes of the p,
Ps	14: 6	but the p have the LORD as their
Ps	40:18	Though I am afflicted and p,
Ps	112: 9	Lavishly he gives to the p;
Ps	113: 7	dust, lifts the p from the ash heap,
Ps	140:13	cause of the needy, justice for the p.
Prv	13: 7	another acts p but has great wealth.
Prv	14:20	their neighbors the p are despised,
Prv	14:31	Those who oppress the p revile their
Prv	17: 5	Whoever mocks the p reviles their
Prv	19: 1	Better to be p and walk in integrity
Prv	19:17	Whoever cares for the p lends
Prv	19:22	rather be p than a liar.
Prv	21:13	the cry of the p will themselves call
Prv	22: 2	Rich and p have a common bond:
Prv	22: 9	for they share their food with the p.
Prv	22:22	Do not rob the p because they are p,
Prv	28: 6	Better to be p and walk in integrity
Prv	28:27	who give to the p have no lack,
Prv	29: 7	The just care for the cause of the p;
Prv	31: 9	justly, defend the needy and the p!
Prv	31:20	She reaches out her hands to the p,
Eccl	4:13	Better is a p but wise youth than
Sir	4: 8	Give a hearing to the p, and return
Sir	7:32	To the p also extend your hand,
Is	3:14	the loot wrested from the p is
Is	10: 2	robbing my people's p of justice,
Is	14:30	In my pastures the p shall graze,
Is	25: 4	For you have been a refuge to the p,

Is   32: 7   To ruin the **p** with lies,
Jer   22:16   justice to the weak and the **p**,
Ez   18:12   oppresses the **p** and needy,
Zec   7:10   orphan, the resident alien or the **p**;
Mt   5: 3   "Blessed are the **p** in spirit,
Mt   11: 5   and the **p** have the good news
Mk   10:21   give to [the] **p** and you will have
Mk   12:42   A **p** widow also came and put
Mk   14: 7   The **p** you will always have
Lk   4:18   me to bring glad tidings to the **p**.
Lk   6:20   "Blessed are you who are **p**,
Lk   14:13   a banquet, invite the **p**, the crippled,
Lk   19: 8   I shall give to the **p**, and if I have
Lk   21: 2   he noticed a **p** widow putting in two
Jn   12: 8   You always have the **p** with you,
Rom   15:26   for the **p** among the holy ones
2 Cor   6:10   as **p** yet enriching many;
2 Cor   8: 9   sake he became **p** although he was
2 Cor   9: 9   scatters abroad, he gives to the **p**;
Jas   2: 2   and a **p** person in shabby clothes
Jas   2: 5   Did not God choose those who are **p**
Rev   3:17   you are wretched, pitiable, **p**, blind,

PORCIUS
Acts   24:27   Felix was succeeded by **P** Festus.

PORTENT
Ps   71: 7   I have become a **p** to many, but you
Is   20: 3   years as a sign and **p** against Egypt

PORTION → APPORTION
Dt   32: 9   But the LORD's **p** was his people;
1 Sm   1: 5   he would give a double **p** to Hannah
Ps   16: 5   LORD, my allotted **p** and my cup,
Ps   73:26   the rock of my heart, my **p** forever.
Ps   119:57   My **p** is the LORD; I promise
Ps   142: 6   my **p** in the land of the living.
Sir   17:17   but Israel is the Lord's own **p**.
Is   53:12   give him his **p** among the many,
Is   61: 7   disgrace was proclaimed their **p**,
Jer   10:16   Jacob's **p** is nothing like them:
Lam   3:24   The LORD is my **p**, I tell myself,
Zec   2:16   LORD will inherit Judah as his **p**

POSSESS → POSSESSED, POSSESSING, POSSESSION, POSSESSIONS
Dt   11:31   the Jordan to enter and **p** the land
Prv   3:35   The wise will **p** glory, but fools
Is   14: 2   house of Israel will **p** them as male
Is   60:21   for all time they will **p** the land;
Dn   7:18   kingship, to **p** it forever and ever."

POSSESSED → POSSESS
Mt   8:16   they brought him many who were **p**

POSSESSING → POSSESS
2 Cor   6:10   having nothing and yet **p** all things.

POSSESSION → POSSESS
Ex   19: 5   will be my treasured **p** among all
Jos   1:11   your God, is giving as your **p**.' "
Ps   2: 8   and, as your **p**, the ends of the earth.
Ps   135: 4   for himself, Israel as his treasured **p**.
Mal   3:17   my own special **p**, on the day

POSSESSIONS → POSSESS
Lk   12:15   one's life does not consist of **p**."
Lk   19: 8   "Behold, half of my **p**, Lord, I shall
Acts   4:32   that any of his **p** was his own,

POSSIBLE
Mt   19:26   but for God all things are **p**."
Mt   26:39   if it is **p**, let this cup pass from me;
Mk   10:27   All things are **p** for God."
Mk   14:35   if it were **p** the hour might pass
Lk   18:27   for human beings is **p** for God."

POSTERITY
Tb   4:12   that their **p** would inherit the land.

POT → POTSHERD, POTTER, POTTER'S
2 Kgs   4:40   of God, there is death in the **p**!"

POTIPHAR
Egyptian who bought Joseph (Gn 37:36), set him over his house (Gn 39:1-6), sent him to prison (Gn 39:7-30).

POTSHERD → POT
Jb   2: 8   He took a **p** to scrape himself, as he
Ps   22:16   As dry as a **p** is my throat;

POTTER → POT
Sir   33:13   Like clay in the hands of a **p**, to be
Is   29:16   is as though the **p** were taken to be
Is   29:16   Or the vessel should say of the **p**,
Is   64: 7   we are the clay and you our **p**:
Jer   18: 6   house of Israel, as this **p** has done?—
Jer   18: 6   like clay in the hand of the **p**, so are
Rom   9:21   does not the **p** have a right over

POTTER'S → POT
Jer   18: 2   Arise and go down to the **p** house;
Mt   27: 7   it to buy the **p** field as a burial place

POUR → POURED, POURING
Dt   12:16   but must **p** it out on the ground like
Ps   62: 9   P out your hearts to God our refuge!
Ps   79: 6   P out your wrath on nations that do
Is   44: 3   I will **p** out water upon the thirsty
Is   44: 3   I will **p** out my spirit upon your
Ez   39:29   once I **p** out my spirit upon the house
Jl   3: 1   come to pass I will **p** out my spirit
Zec   12:10   I will **p** out on the house of David
Mal   3:10   **p** down upon you blessing without
Acts   2:17   'that I will **p** out a portion of my
Rev   16: 1   **p** out the seven bowls of God's fury

POURED → POUR
Gn   28:18   a sacred pillar, and **p** oil on top of it.
Gn   35:14   it he made a libation and **p** out oil.
2 Sm   23:16   and instead **p** it out to the LORD,
Is   32:15   spirit from on high is **p** out on us.
Lam   4:11   his anger, **p** out his blazing wrath;
Mk   14: 3   alabaster jar and **p** it on his head.
Acts   2:33   Spirit from the Father and **p** it forth,
Acts   10:45   the holy Spirit should have been **p**
Rom   5: 5   the love of God has been **p**
Phil   2:17   even if I am **p** out as a libation
2 Tm   4: 6   For I am already being **p** out like
Ti   3: 6   whom he richly **p** out on us through
Rev   14:10   **p** full strength into the cup of his
Rev   16: 2   and **p** out his bowl on the earth.

POURING → POUR
1 Sm   1:15   I was only **p** out my heart
Ez   20: 8   Then I considered **p** out my fury

POVERTY → POOR
Prv   6:11   **p** will come upon you like a robber,
Prv   10:15   the ruin of the poor is their **p**.
Prv   13:18   P and shame befall those who let go
Prv   24:34   **p** will come upon you like a robber,
Prv   30: 8   give me neither **p** nor riches;
Sir   10:31   Honored in **p**, how much more so in wealth!
Sir   11:14   evil, life and death, **p** and riches—
Mk   12:44   from her **p**, has contributed all she
Lk   21: 4   from her **p**, has offered her whole
2 Cor   8: 2   their profound **p** overflowed
2 Cor   8: 9   by his **p** you might become rich.
Rev   2: 9   "I know your tribulation and **p**,

POWDER
Ex   32:20   fire and then ground it down to **p**,

POWER → POWERFUL, POWERS
Ex   9:16   to show you my **p** and to make my
Ex   15: 6   magnificent in **p**, your right hand,
Ex   32:11   out of the land of Egypt with great **p**
Dt   8:17   "It is my own **p** and the strength
Dt   34:12   and the awesome **p** that Moses
2 Chr   20: 6   In your hand is **p** and might, and no
Jdt   9:14   are God, the God of all **p** and might,
Jb   36:22   Look, God is exalted in his **p**.
Jb   37:23   him, preeminent in **p** and judgment,

Ps	63: 3	to you in the sanctuary to see your **p**
Ps	68:35	Confess the **p** of God,
Ps	68:35	Israel, whose **p** is in the sky.
Ps	147: 5	vast in **p**, with wisdom beyond
Prv	3:27	owner when it is in your **p** to act.
Prv	18:21	and life are in the **p** of the tongue;
Is	40:26	the strength of his **p** not one of them
Jer	10:12	one who made the earth by his **p**,
Jer	27: 5	by my great **p**, with my outstretched
Dn	2:20	and ever, for wisdom and **p** are his.
Dn	6:28	saved Daniel from the lions' **p**."
Hos	13:14	I deliver them from the **p** of Sheol?
Mi	3: 8	I am filled with **p**, with the spirit
Na	1: 3	is slow to anger, yet great in **p**;
Mt	22:29	know the scriptures or the **p** of God.
Mt	24:30	upon the clouds of heaven with **p**
Mk	9: 1	kingdom of God has come in **p**."
Mk	13:26	coming in the clouds' with great **p**
Lk	1:17	and **p** of Elijah to turn the hearts
Lk	1:35	you, and the **p** of the Most High will
Lk	4:14	to Galilee in the **p** of the Spirit,
Lk	6:19	to touch him because **p** came forth
Lk	8:46	for I know that **p** has gone
Lk	9: 1	gave them **p** and authority over all
Lk	10:19	I have given you the **p** 'to tread
Lk	21:27	of Man coming in a cloud with **p**
Lk	24:49	the city until you are clothed with **p**
Jn	19:11	"You would have no **p** over me if it
Acts	1: 8	you will receive **p** when the holy
Acts	4:33	great **p** the apostles bore witness
Acts	8:10	"This man is the 'P of God' that is
Acts	10:38	Nazareth with the holy Spirit and **p**.
Acts	26:18	and from the **p** of Satan to God,
Rom	1:16	It is the **p** of God for the salvation
Rom	1:20	his invisible attributes of eternal **p**
Rom	9:17	to show my **p** through you that my
Rom	15:13	in hope by the **p** of the holy Spirit.
Rom	15:19	by the **p** of signs and wonders,
Rom	15:19	by the **p** of the Spirit [of God],
1 Cor	1:18	us who are being saved it is the **p**
1 Cor	1:24	Christ the **p** of God and the wisdom
1 Cor	2: 4	with a demonstration of spirit and **p**,
1 Cor	6:14	Lord and will also raise us by his **p**.
1 Cor	15:24	and every authority and **p**.
1 Cor	15:56	is sin, and the **p** of sin is the law.
2 Cor	4: 7	that the surpassing **p** may be of God
2 Cor	6: 7	in truthful speech, in the **p** of God;
2 Cor	12: 9	for **p** is made perfect in weakness."
2 Cor	12: 9	order that the **p** of Christ may dwell
2 Cor	13: 4	but he lives by the **p** of God.
2 Cor	13: 4	shall live with him by the **p** of God.
Gal	3:22	confined all things under the **p**
Eph	1:19	of his **p** for us who believe,
Eph	1:21	authority, **p**, and dominion,
Eph	3:16	with **p** through his Spirit in the inner
Eph	3:20	imagine, by the **p** at work within us,
Eph	6:10	the Lord and from his mighty **p**.
Phil	3:10	him and the **p** of his resurrection
Phil	3:21	body by the **p** that enables him
Col	1:11	strengthened with every **p**, in accord
1 Thes	1: 5	also in **p** and in the holy Spirit
2 Tm	1: 7	cowardice but rather of **p** and love
2 Tm	3: 5	a pretense of religion but deny its **p**.
Heb	2:14	might destroy the one who has the **p**
Heb	7:16	but by the **p** of a life that cannot be
1 Pt	1: 5	by the **p** of God are safeguarded
2 Pt	1: 3	His divine **p** has bestowed on us
2 Pt	1: 3	called us by his own glory and **p**.
2 Pt	1:16	when we made known to you the **p**
Jude	1:25	majesty, **p**, and authority from ages
Rev	4:11	to receive glory and honor and **p**,
Rev	5:12	the Lamb that was slain to receive **p**
Rev	7: 2	the four angels who were given **p**
Rev	11:17	For you have assumed your great **p**
Rev	12:10	"Now have salvation and **p** come,
Rev	13: 2	To it the dragon gave its own **p**
Rev	20: 6	second death has no **p** over these;

POWERFUL → POWER

Est	9: 4	Mordecai was **p** in the royal palace,
1 Cor	1:26	not many were **p**, not many were
Jas	5:16	of a righteous person is very **p**.

POWERS → POWER

Mt	14: 2	that is why mighty **p** are at work
Rom	8:38	things, nor future things, nor **p**,
Eph	6:12	with the **p**, with the world rulers
Col	1:16	or dominions or principalities or **p**;
Heb	6: 5	of God and the **p** of the age to come,
1 Pt	3:22	authorities, and **p** subject to him.

PRACTICE → PRACTICED, PRACTICES

Sir	50:29	If they put them into **p**, they can
Ez	13:23	false visions or **p** divination again.
Mt	23: 3	For they preach but they do not **p**.

PRACTICED → PRACTICE

Acts	19:19	of those who had **p** magic collected

PRACTICES → PRACTICE

Jgs	2:19	relinquishing none of their evil **p**
Ps	101: 7	No one who **p** deceit can remain
Col	3: 9	have taken off the old self with its **p**

PRAISE → PRAISED, PRAISES, PRAISING

Ex	15: 2	This is my God, I **p** him; the God
Dt	26:19	he will set you high in **p** and renown
1 Chr	23: 5	four thousand were to **p** the LORD
2 Chr	20:21	**p** the holy Splendor as it went forth
Ezr	3:10	with cymbals to **p** the LORD
Neh	9: 5	is exalted above all blessing and **p**."
Jdt	15:14	people loudly sang this hymn of **p**:
Ps	22:24	"You who fear the LORD, give **p**!
Ps	33: 1	**p** from the upright is fitting.
Ps	34: 2	his **p** shall be always in my mouth.
Ps	42: 6	for I shall again **p** him, my savior
Ps	43: 5	for I shall again **p** him, my savior
Ps	45:18	thus nations shall **p** you forever.
Ps	51:17	and my mouth will proclaim your **p**.
Ps	56: 5	I **p** the word of God; I trust in God,
Ps	65: 2	To you we owe our hymn of **p**,
Ps	66: 2	give him glorious **p**.
Ps	66: 8	loudly sound his **p**,
Ps	69:31	That I may **p** God's name in song
Ps	69:35	Let the heaven and the earth **p** him,
Ps	71: 8	mouth shall be filled with your **p**,
Ps	71:14	hope in you and add to all your **p**.
Ps	71:22	That I may **p** you with the lyre
Ps	74:21	the poor and needy **p** your name.
Ps	89: 6	The heavens **p** your marvels,
Ps	100: 4	with thanksgiving, his courts with **p**.
Ps	102:19	born, that they may **p** the LORD:
Ps	106: 2	LORD, proclaim in full God's **p**?
Ps	111:10	His **p** endures forever.
Ps	113: 1	**P**, you servants of the LORD,
Ps	117: 1	**P** the LORD, all you nations!
Ps	119:175	Let my soul live to **p** you;
Ps	135: 1	**P** the name of the LORD! **P**,
Ps	139:14	I **p** you, because I am wonderfully
Ps	147: 1	How good to sing **p** to our God;
Ps	147: 1	how pleasant to give fitting **p**.
Ps	148: 1	**P** the LORD from the heavens;
Ps	148:13	Let them all **p** the LORD's name,
Ps	150: 2	Give **p** for his mighty deeds, **p** him
Ps	150: 6	has breath give **p** to the LORD!
Prv	27: 2	Let another **p** you, not your own
Prv	31:31	let her deeds **p** her at the city gates.
Sir	11: 2	Do not **p** anyone for good looks;
Sir	39:14	Raise your voices in a chorus of **p**;
Sir	44: 1	I will now **p** the godly,
Is	42:10	his **p** from the ends of the earth:
Jer	33: 9	joy for me, a name of **p** and pride,
Dn	3:57	**p** and exalt him above all forever.
Hb	3: 3	heavens, and his **p** filled the earth;
Mt	21:16	you have brought forth **p**'?"

Lk	19:37	his disciples began to **p** God aloud
Rom	2:29	his **p** is not from human beings
Rom	15:11	"**P** the Lord, all you Gentiles,
Rom	15:11	and let all the peoples **p** him."
1 Cor	14:15	I will sing **p** with the spirit, but I will also sing **p** with the mind.
Eph	1: 6	for the **p** of the glory of his grace
Eph	1:12	might exist for the **p** of his glory,
Eph	1:14	possession, to the **p** of his glory.
1 Thes	2: 6	nor did we seek **p** from human
Heb	13:15	offer God a sacrifice of **p**, that is,
Jas	5:13	in good spirits? He should sing **p**.
Rev	19: 5	"**P** our God, all you his servants,

PRAISED → PRAISE

Gn	12:15	officials saw her they **p** her
Jgs	16:24	people saw him, they **p** their god.
2 Sm	14:25	all Israel there was no man more **p**
Ps	18: 4	**P** be the Lord, I exclaim!
Ps	48: 2	and highly **p** in the city of our God:
Prv	31:30	who fears the Lord is to be **p**.
Eccl	8:15	Therefore I **p** joy, because there is nothing
Dn	5: 4	they **p** their gods of gold and silver,

PRAISES → PRAISE

2 Chr	29:30	Levites to sing the **p** of the Lord
2 Chr	29:30	They sang **p** till their joy was full,
Ps	9:15	Then I will declare all your **p**,
Ps	18:50	I will sing **p** to your name.
Ps	145:21	My mouth will speak the **p**
Sir	24: 1	Wisdom sings her own **p**,
Is	38:18	you thanks, nor death that **p** you;

PRAISING → PRAISE

Lk	2:13	with the angel, **p** God and saying:
Lk	2:20	and **p** God for all they had heard
Acts	2:47	**p** God and enjoying favor with all
Acts	3: 8	walking and jumping and **p** God.

PRAY → PRAYED, PRAYER, PRAYERS, PRAYING, PRAYS

Ex	8: 5	me the time when I am to **p** for you
Nm	21: 7	**P** to the Lord to take the serpents
1 Sm	12:23	the Lord by ceasing to **p** for you
2 Chr	6:38	**p** toward their land which you gave
2 Chr	7:14	humble themselves and **p**, and seek
Ezr	6:10	heaven and **p** for the life of the king
Jb	42: 8	and let my servant Job **p** for you.
Ps	5: 3	For to you I will **p**, Lord;
Ps	122: 6	For the peace of Jerusalem **p**:
Sir	3: 5	and when they **p** they are heard.
Sir	37:15	**p** to God to make your steps firm
Jer	29: 7	**p** for it to the Lord, for upon its
Jer	29:12	and come and **p** to me, I will listen
Mt	5:44	and **p** for those who persecute you,
Mt	6: 5	"When you **p**, do not be like
Mt	6: 5	to stand and **p** in the synagogues
Mt	6: 9	"This is how you are to **p**:
Mt	14:23	up on the mountain by himself to **p**.
Mt	19:13	might lay his hands on them and **p**.
Mt	26:36	here while I go over there and **p**."
Lk	6:28	you, **p** for those who mistreat you.
Lk	11: 1	**p** just as John taught his disciples."
Lk	18: 1	**p** always without becoming weary.
Lk	18:10	went up to the temple area to **p**;
Lk	22:40	"**P** that you may not undergo
Rom	8:26	do not know how to **p** as we ought,
1 Cor	11:13	is it proper for a woman to **p** to God
1 Cor	14:13	in a tongue should **p** to be able
1 Cor	14:15	I will **p** with the spirit, but I will also **p** with the mind.
Eph	6:18	**p** at every opportunity in the Spirit.
1 Thes	5:17	**P** without ceasing.
2 Thes	1:11	To this end, we always **p** for you,
Jas	5:13	He should **p**. Is anyone in good
Jas	5:16	one another and **p** for one another,
1 Jn	5:16	he should **p** to God and he will give
1 Jn	5:16	I do not say that you should **p**.
Jude	1:20	most holy faith; **p** in the holy Spirit.

PRAYED → PRAY

Nm	11: 2	he **p** to the Lord and the fire died
Nm	21: 7	So Moses **p** for the people,
1 Sm	1:27	I **p** for this child, and the Lord
2 Kgs	6:17	Then he **p**, "O Lord, open his
2 Chr	30:18	because Hezekiah **p** for them,
Neh	4: 3	We **p** to our God and posted a watch
Jb	42:10	of Job, after he had **p** for his friends;
Dn	9: 4	I **p** to the Lord, my God,
Mk	1:35	off to a deserted place, where he **p**.
Mk	14:35	**p** that if it were possible the hour
Lk	22:41	throw from them and kneeling, he **p**,
Acts	4:31	As they **p**, the place where they
Acts	6: 6	these men to the apostles who **p**
Acts	8:15	who went down and **p** for them,
Jas	5:17	yet he **p** earnestly that it might not

PRAYER → PRAY

2 Chr	7:12	I have heard your **p**, and I have
2 Chr	30:27	heard and their **p** reached heaven,
2 Chr	33:19	His **p** and how his supplication was
1 Mc	3:46	at Mizpah there was a place of **p**
Ps	4: 2	take pity on me, hear my **p**.
Ps	6:10	the Lord will receive my **p**.
Ps	17: 1	A **p** of David. Hear, Lord,
Ps	17: 1	to my **p** from lips without guile.
Ps	55: 2	Listen, God, to my **p**; do not hide
Ps	66:20	who did not reject my **p** and refuse
Prv	15: 8	the **p** of the upright is his delight.
Prv	15:29	wicked, but hears the **p** of the just.
Is	56: 7	make them joyful in my house of **p**;
Is	56: 7	house shall be called a house of **p**
Hb	3: 1	**P** of Habakkuk, the prophet.
Mt	21:13	'My house shall be a house of **p**,'
Mt	21:22	you ask for in **p** with faith, you will
Mk	9:29	kind can only come out through **p**."
Mk	11:24	all that you ask for in **p**,
Acts	1:14	themselves with one accord to **p**,
Acts	6: 4	we shall devote ourselves to **p**
Acts	10:31	your **p** has been heard and your
Acts	16:13	thought there would be a place of **p**.
Rom	10: 1	and **p** to God on their behalf is
Rom	12:12	endure in affliction, persevere in **p**.
1 Cor	7: 5	to be free for **p**, but then return
Phil	1: 9	And this is my **p**: that your love
Phil	4: 6	but in everything, by **p** and petition,
Col	4: 2	Persevere in **p**, being watchful in it
1 Tm	4: 5	holy by the invocation of God in **p**.
Jas	5:15	and the **p** of faith will save the sick
Jas	5:16	The fervent **p** of a righteous person
1 Pt	3:12	and his ears turned to their **p**,

PRAYERS → PRAY

Ps	65: 3	you who hear our **p**. To you all flesh
Mk	12:40	and, as a pretext, recite lengthy **p**.
Acts	2:42	breaking of the bread and to the **p**.
2 Cor	1:11	the gift granted us through the **p**
1 Tm	2: 1	I ask that supplications, **p**, petitions,
Heb	5: 7	he offered **p** and supplications
1 Pt	3: 7	so that your **p** may not be hindered.
Rev	5: 8	which are the **p** of the holy ones.
Rev	8: 3	with the **p** of all the holy ones,

PRAYING → PRAY

1 Sm	1:13	for Hannah was **p** silently;
Dn	6:12	found Daniel **p** and pleading before
Lk	3:21	also had been baptized and was **p**,
Lk	9:29	While he was **p** his face changed
Acts	9:11	Tarsus named Saul. He is there **p**,
Acts	16:25	Silas were **p** and singing hymns

PRAYS → PRAY

Sir	34:29	If one **p** and another curses, whose voice
1 Cor	11: 4	Any man who **p** or prophesies

PREACHING

1 Tm	5:17	especially those who toil in **p**

PRECEDE

1 Thes	4:15	will surely not **p** those who have

PRECEPTS
Ps	19: 9	The p of the LORD are right,
Ps	119: 4	to observe your p with care.
Ps	119:15	I will ponder your p and consider
Ps	119:27	me understand the way of your p;
Ps	119:40	See how I long for your p;
Ps	119:45	space because I cherish your p.
Ps	119:56	good fortune, for I have kept your p.
Ps	119:63	fear you, of all who observe your p.
Ps	119:69	but I keep your p with all my heart.
Ps	119:87	earth, but I do not forsake your p.
Ps	119:93	I will never forget your p;
Ps	119:94	save me, for I cherish your p.
Ps	119: 100	my elders, because I keep your p.
Ps	119:104	Through your p I gain
Ps	119:110	me, but from your p I do not stray.
Ps	119:128	Thus, I follow all your p;
Ps	119:134	that I may observe your p.
Ps	119:141	and despised, I do not forget your p.
Ps	119:159	See how I love your p, LORD;
Ps	119:168	I observe your p and testimonies;
Ps	119:173	help me, for I have chosen your p.
Mt	15: 9	teaching as doctrines human p.' "
Mk	7: 7	me, teaching as doctrines human p.'

PRECIOUS
1 Sm	26:21	you considered my life p today even
2 Chr	3: 6	covered the house with p stones
Ps	72:14	for p is their blood in his sight.
Prv	3:15	She is more p than corals, and no
Is	28:16	tested, A p cornerstone as a sure
Ez	28:13	p stones of every kind were your
1 Pt	1:19	with the p blood of Christ as
1 Pt	2: 4	chosen and p in the sight of God,
1 Pt	2: 6	chosen and p, and whoever believes
2 Pt	1: 4	he has bestowed on us the p

PREDESTINED
Rom	8:29	p to be conformed to the image
Rom	8:30	And those he p he also called;

PREDICTED
Acts	11:28	p by the Spirit that there would be

PREGNANT
Gn	19:36	of Lot became p by their father.
Ex	21:22	have a fight and hurt a p woman,
Ps	7:15	is p with mischief, and gives birth
Mt	24:19	Woe to p women and nursing
1 Thes	5: 3	like labor pains upon a p woman,

PREPARATION → PREPARE
Mt	27:62	the one following the day of p,
Jn	19:14	It was p day for Passover, and it

PREPARE → PREPARATION, PREPARED
Is	40: 3	In the wilderness p the way
Am	4:12	thus with you, p to meet your God,
Mal	3: 1	he will p the way before me;
Mt	3: 3	the desert, 'P the way of the Lord,
Mt	11:10	he will p your way before you.'
Jn	14: 2	that I am going to p a place for you?

PREPARED → PREPARE
Ex	23:20	and bring you to the place I have p.
1 Chr	15: 1	and p a place for the ark of God,
Mt	20:23	whom it has been p by my Father."
Mt	25:34	Inherit the kingdom p for you
Rom	9:23	which he has p previously for glory,
1 Cor	2: 9	what God has p for those who love
Eph	2:10	works that God has p in advance,
Heb	10: 5	not desire, but a body you p for me;
Heb	11:16	God, for he has p a city for them.
Rev	12: 6	the desert where she had a place p
Rev	21: 2	God, p as a bride adorned for her

PRESBYTER → PRESBYTERS
1 Tm	5:19	an accusation against a p unless it is
1 Pt	5: 1	you, as a fellow p and witness
2 Jn	1: 1	The P to the chosen Lady and to her
3 Jn	1: 1	The P to the beloved Gaius whom I

PRESBYTERS → PRESBYTER
Acts	11:30	did, sending it to the p in care
Acts	14:23	They appointed p for them in each
Acts	15: 2	apostles and p about this question.
Acts	15: 6	the p met together to see about this
Acts	15:23	"The apostles and the p,
Acts	16: 4	by the apostles and p in Jerusalem.
Acts	20:17	Miletus he had the p of the church
Acts	21:18	to James, and all the p were present.
1 Tm	5:17	P who preside well deserve double
Ti	1: 5	done and appoint p in every town,
Jas	5:14	He should summon the p
1 Pt	5: 1	So I exhort the p among you,
1 Pt	5: 5	members, be subject to the p.

PRESCRIBED
Ezr	3: 4	the feast of Booths in the manner p,
Mt	8: 4	and offer the gift that Moses p;

PRESENCE → PRESENT
Nm	4: 7	the P they shall spread a violet cloth
Jb	1:12	forth from the p of the LORD.
Jb	2: 7	went forth from the p of the LORD
Ps	16:11	to life, abounding joy in your p,
Ps	31:21	hide them in the shelter of your p,
Ps	41:13	and let me stand in your p forever.
Ps	139: 7	From your p, where can I flee?
Jn	8:38	what I have seen in the Father's p;
Acts	2:28	you will fill me with joy in your p.'
2 Thes	1: 9	separated from the p of the Lord
Jude	1:24	and exultant, in the p of his glory,
Rev	20:11	the sky fled from his p and there

PRESENT → PRESENCE, PRESENTED
Jb	1: 6	to p themselves before the LORD,
Jb	2: 1	to p themselves before the LORD,
Lk	2:22	to Jerusalem to p him to the Lord,
Rom	6:13	do not p the parts of your bodies
Rom	6:13	p yourselves to God as raised
Rom	8:18	this p time are as nothing compared
Rom	8:38	nor principalities, nor p things,
1 Cor	3:22	life or death, or the p or the future:
1 Cor	7:31	world in its p form is passing away.
2 Cor	11: 2	husband to p you as a chaste virgin
Eph	5:27	he might p to himself the church
Col	1:22	to p you holy, without blemish,
1 Tm	4: 8	a promise of life both for the p
2 Tm	2:15	Be eager to p yourself as acceptable
2 Pt	3: 7	The p heavens and earth have been

PRESENTED → PRESENT
Acts	1: 3	He p himself alive to them by many

PRESERVE → PRESERVES
Prv	14: 3	but the lips of the wise p them.

PRESERVES → PRESERVE
Sir	32:24	Whoever keeps the law p himself;

PRESS → PRESSURE
Rev	14:20	The wine p was trodden outside
Rev	19:15	in the wine p the wine of the fury

PRESSURE → PRESS
2 Cor	11:28	there is the daily p upon me of my

PRESUMES → PRESUMPTUOUSLY
Dt	18:20	if a prophet p to speak a word in my

PRESUMPTUOUSLY → PRESUMES
Dt	18:22	The prophet has spoken it p;

PRETEXT
1 Thes	2: 5	as you know, or with a p for greed—
1 Pt	2:16	yet without using freedom as a p

PREVAIL → PREVAILED
Gn	32:26	saw that he could not p over him,
1 Sm	2: 9	for not by strength does one p.
2 Chr	14:10	do not let men p against you."
Jdt	11:10	nor does the sword p against them,
Wis	7:30	wickedness does not p over Wisdom.

PREVAILED → PREVAIL
Gn   32:29 and human beings and have p."

PREY
Gn   15:11 Birds of p swooped down

PRICE
Gn   23: 9 at its full p for a burial place."
1 Chr 21:22 Sell it to me at its full p,
Sir   6:15 Faithful friends are beyond p,
Zec 11:13 the handsome p at which they
Mt   13:46 When he finds a pearl of great p,
Mt   27: 9 value of a man with a p on his head,
Mt   27: 9 a p set by some of the Israelites,
1 Cor 6:20 For you have been purchased at a p.
1 Cor 7:23 You have been purchased at a p.

PRIDE → PROUD
Prv   8:13 P, arrogance, the evil way,
Prv 11: 2 When p comes, disgrace comes;
Prv 16:18 P goes before disaster,
Sir 10: 7 Odious to the Lord and to mortals is p,
Is   25:11 His p will be brought low despite
Am   8: 7 has sworn by the p of Jacob:
2 Cor 7: 4 in you, I have great p in you;

PRIEST → PRIESTHOOD, PRIESTS
Gn   14:18 He was a p of God Most High.
Ex   2:16 Now the p of Midian had seven
Ex   18: 1 Jethro, the p of Midian, heard of all
Nm   5:10 what is given to a p shall be his.
Jgs 17:10 "Be father and p to me, and I will
1 Sm 2:11 of the LORD under the p Eli.
1 Sm 2:35 will choose a faithful p who shall do
1 Sm 21: 7 So the p gave him holy bread,
2 Chr 13: 9 seven rams becomes a p of no-gods.
Ps 110: 4 "You are a p forever in the manner
Sir   7:31 Honor God and respect the p;
Jer 23:11 Both prophet and p are godless!
Ez   1: 3 the LORD came to the p Ezekiel,
Zec   6:13 The p will be at his right hand,
Mk   14:63 At that the high p tore his garments
Heb   2:17 and faithful high p before God
Heb   3: 1 and high p of our confession,
Heb   4:14 have a great high p who has passed
Heb   4:15 do not have a high p who is unable
Heb   5: 6 "You are a p forever according
Heb   6:20 becoming high p forever according
Heb   7: 3 Son of God, he remains a p forever.
Heb   7:15 more obvious if another p is raised
Heb   7:26 that we should have such a high p:
Heb   8: 1 we have such a high p, who has
Heb   9:11 Christ came as high p of the good
Heb 10:21 we have "a great p over the house
Heb 13:11 whose blood the high p brings

PRIESTHOOD → PRIEST
Ex   29: 9 Thus shall the p be theirs
Nm   16:10 him, and yet you seek the p too.
Nm   25:13 the covenant of an everlasting p,
Ezr   2:62 and they were excluded from the p.
2 Mc 11: 3 to put the high p up for sale every
Heb   7:24 has a p that does not pass away.
1 Pt   2: 5 to be a holy p to offer spiritual
1 Pt   2: 9 race, a royal p, a holy nation,

PRIESTS → PRIEST
Ex   19: 6 You will be to me a kingdom of p,
Ex   28: 1 Israelites, that they may be my p:
Ex   40:15 father, anoint them also as my p.
Dt   31: 9 it to the levitical p who carry the ark
Jos   6: 4 seven p carrying ram's horns ahead
Jos   6: 4 and have the p blow the horns.
1 Sm 22:17 "Turn and kill the p of the LORD,
2 Chr 5: 7 The p brought the ark
2 Chr 31: 1 re-established the divisions of the p
2 Chr 34: 5 the bones of the p he burned
Ezr   6:20 for their colleagues the p,
Ezr 10: 5 an oath from the leaders of the p,
Neh   3:28 the Horse Gate the p carried

Neh 13:30 the various functions for the p
1 Mc 4:42 He chose blameless p,
Ps   99: 6 and Aaron were among his p,
Jer   5:31 the p teach on their own authority;
Ez   22:26 Her p violate my law and desecrate
Dn   14:28 the dragon, and put the p to death."
Mi   3:11 for a bribe, the p teach for pay,
Mal   1: 6 to you, O p, who disdain my name.
Mt   20:18 will be handed over to the chief p
Mt   27: 3 thirty pieces of silver to the chief p
Mk   2:26 that only the p could lawfully eat,
Mk   15: 3 The chief p accused him of many
Jn   19:15 The chief p answered, "We have no
Acts 6: 7 group of p were becoming obedient
Heb   7:27 as did the high p, to offer sacrifice
Rev   1: 6 kingdom, p for his God and Father,
Rev   5:10 them a kingdom and p for our God,
Rev 20: 6 they will be p of God and of Christ,

PRINCE → PRINCES
Dt   33:16 brow of the p among his brothers.
Is   9: 5 Father-Forever, P of Peace.
Ez   34:24 my servant David will be p in their
Ez   37:25 David my servant as their p forever.
Ez   45:17 of the p to provide burnt offerings,
Ez   46: 8 When the p enters, he shall always
Dn   8:11 It grew even to the P of the host,
Dn   8:25 he rises against the P of princes,
Dn   10:20 Soon I must fight the p of Persia
Dn   10:20 I leave, the p of Greece will come;
Dn   10:21 these except Michael, your p,
Dn   11:22 crushed, even the p of the covenant.
Dn   12: 1 the great p, guardian of your people;

PRINCES → PRINCE
Ps   2: 2 p plot together against the LORD
Ps 113: 8 Seats them with p, the p of the people,
Ps 118: 9 LORD than to put one's trust in p.
Ps 146: 3 Put no trust in p, in children
Ps 148:11 p and all who govern on earth;
Prv 31: 4 strong drink is not for p,
Is   40:23 Who brings p to nought and makes
Dn   8:25 he rises against the Prince of p,
Dn   10:13 one of the chief p, came to help me.

PRISCA → See PRISCILLA

PRISCILLA
    Wife of Aquila, also called Prisca; co-worker with Paul (Acts 18; Rom
16:3; 1 Cor 16:19; 2 Tm 4:19); instructor of Apollos (Acts 18:24-28).

PRISON → IMPRISONMENT, IMPRISONMENTS, PRISONER,
    PRISONERS
Jgs 16:25 So they called Samson from the p,
2 Kgs 25:29 Jehoiachin took off his p garb;
Ps 142: 8 Lead my soul from p, that I may
Mt   14:10 and he had John beheaded in the p.
Mt   25:36 for me, in p and you visited me.'
Lk   22:33 I am prepared to go to p and to die
Acts 12: 5 Peter thus was being kept in p,
1 Pt   3:19 went to preach to the spirits in p,
Rev   2:10 devil will throw some of you into p,
Rev 20: 7 Satan will be released from his p.

PRISONER → PRISON
Mk   15: 6 to them one p whom they requested.
Eph   3: 1 I, Paul, a p of Christ [Jesus] for you

PRISONERS → PRISON
Ps   68: 7 who leads p out to prosperity,
Ps 146: 7 The LORD sets p free;
Is   42: 7 to bring out p from confinement,
Is   61: 1 to the captives, release to the p,
Zec   9:12 Return to a fortress, O p of hope;
Heb 13: 3 Be mindful of p as if sharing their

PRIVATE → PRIVATELY
Mk   4:34 he explained everything in p.
Mk   9:28 his disciples asked him in p,

PRIVATELY → PRIVATE
Mk   13: 3   John, and Andrew asked him **p**,

PRIZE
1 Cor   9:24   in the race, but only one wins the **p**?
Phil   3:14   goal, the **p** of God's upward calling,

PROCESSION
Ps   118:27   Join in **p** with leafy branches

PROCLAIM → PROCLAIMED, PROCLAIMING, PROCLAIMS, PROCLAMATION
Dt   32: 3   For I will **p** the name
Ps   22:32   they may **p** to a people yet unborn
Ps   97: 6   The heavens **p** his justice;
Is   12: 4   deeds, **p** how exalted is his name.
Is   40: 6   A voice says, "P!" I answer, "What shall I **p**?"
Is   61: 1   To **p** liberty to the captives,
Jer   7: 2   LORD and **p** this message there:
Mt   10:27   hear whispered, **p** on the housetops.
Mt   12:18   and he will **p** justice to the Gentiles.
Lk   4:19   to **p** a year acceptable to the Lord."
Lk   9:60   go and **p** the kingdom of God."
Acts   17:23   unknowingly worship, I **p** to you.
1 Cor   11:26   you **p** the death of the Lord until he
Col   1:28   It is he whom we **p**,

PROCLAIMED → PROCLAIM
Ex   34: 5   with him there and **p** the name,
Lk   16:16   then on the kingdom of God is **p**,
Rom   9:17   my name may be **p** throughout

PROCLAIMING → PROCLAIM
Mk   1:14   Jesus came to Galilee **p** the gospel
Acts   4: 2   **p** in Jesus the resurrection

PROCLAIMS → PROCLAIM
Ps   19: 2   the firmament **p** the works of his

PROCLAMATION → PROCLAIM
Rom   16:25   my gospel and the **p** of Jesus Christ,

PROCONSUL
Acts   13:12   the **p** saw what had happened,

PRODUCE → PRODUCED, PRODUCES
Jos   5:11   they ate of the **p** of the land
Prv   3: 9   wealth, with first fruits of all your **p**;

PRODUCED → PRODUCE
Rom   7: 8   **p** in me every kind of covetousness.

PRODUCES → PRODUCE
Lk   6:45   of goodness in his heart **p** good,
Lk   6:45   person out of a store of evil **p** evil;
Rom   5: 3   knowing that affliction **p** endurance,
2 Cor   7:10   For godly sorrow **p** a salutary
2 Cor   7:10   regret, but worldly sorrow **p** death.
Heb   6: 8   But if it **p** thorns and thistles, it is
Jas   1: 3   testing of your faith **p** perseverance.

PROFANE → PROFANED
Lv   22:32   Do not **p** my holy name,
1 Mc   1:45   to **p** the sabbaths and feast days,

PROFANED → PROFANE
Jdt   4:12   or the sanctuary to be **p** and mocked
1 Mc   1:43   sacrificed to idols and **p** the sabbath.
Jer   34:16   then you again **p** my name by taking

PROFESS → PROFESSES, PROFESSING
1 Tm   2:10   as befits women who **p** reverence

PROFESSES → PROFESS
Wis   2:13   He **p** to have knowledge of God

PROFESSING → PROFESS
1 Tm   6:21   By **p** it, some people have deviated

PROFIT → PROFITABLE
Prv   14:23   In all labor there is **p**, but mere talk
Prv   31:12   She brings him **p**, not loss, all
Eccl   2:11   after wind. There is no **p** under the sun.
Eccl   6: 8   What **p** have the wise compared to fools, or what **p** have the lowly
Sir   29:11   that will **p** you more than the gold.

Mt   16:26   What **p** would there be for one

PROFITABLE → PROFIT
Eccl   7:12   knowledge is **p** because wisdom gives life

PROGRESS
Phil   1:25   the service of all of you for your **p**
1 Tm   4:15   so that your **p** may be evident

PROMISE → PROMISED, PROMISES
Neh   5:13   every man who fails to keep this **p**,
Ps   106:24   they did not believe the **p**.
Ps   119:41   salvation in accord with your **p**.
Ps   119:50   affliction, your **p** that gives me life.
Ps   119:58   mercy on me in accord with your **p**.
Ps   119:172   May my tongue sing of your **p**,
Acts   2:39   For the **p** is made to you and to your
Acts   26: 7   **p** as they fervently worship God day
Rom   4:13   through the law that the **p** was made
Rom   4:20   He did not doubt God's **p**
Rom   9: 8   of the **p** are counted as descendants.
Gal   3:18   the law, it is no longer from a **p**;
Gal   3:18   it on Abraham through a **p**.
Gal   4:28   like Isaac, are children of the **p**.
Eph   2:12   and strangers to the covenants of **p**,
Eph   6: 2   is the first commandment with a **p**,
1 Tm   4: 8   since it holds a **p** of life both
2 Tm   1: 1   God for the **p** of life in Christ Jesus,
Heb   4: 1   on our guard while the **p** of entering
Heb   6:13   When God made the **p** to Abraham,
2 Pt   2:19   They **p** them freedom, though they
2 Pt   3: 9   The Lord does not delay his **p**,
2 Pt   3:13   to his **p** we await new heavens

PROMISED → PROMISE
Gn   21: 1   the LORD did for her as he had **p**.
Gn   28:15   you until I have done what I **p** you.
Ex   32:13   and all this land that I **p**, I will give
Nm   10:29   for the LORD has **p** prosperity
Dt   1:11   times over, and bless you as he **p**!
Dt   15: 6   will bless you as he **p**, you will lend
Dt   26:18   as he **p** you, you will keep all his
Jos   23: 5   as the LORD, your God, **p** you.
1 Kgs   9: 5   forever, as I **p** David your father:
Acts   13:32   you that what God **p** our ancestors
Rom   4:21   that what he had **p** he was also able
Eph   1:13   were sealed with the **p** holy Spirit,
Ti   1: 2   does not lie, **p** before time began,
Heb   10:36   of God and receive what he has **p**.
Jas   1:12   life that he **p** to those who love him.
Jas   2: 5   that he **p** to those who love him?

PROMISES → PROMISE
Neh   9: 8   You fulfilled your **p**, for you are
Ps   12: 7   The **p** of the LORD are sure,
Wis   12:21   the sworn covenants of goodly **p**!
Rom   9: 4   of the law, the worship, and the **p**;
Rom   15: 8   to confirm the **p** to the patriarchs,
2 Cor   1:20   For however many are the **p** of God,
2 Cor   7: 1   Since we have these **p**, beloved,
Gal   3:21   law then opposed to the **p** [of God]?
Heb   8: 6   better covenant, enacted on better **p**.
2 Pt   1: 4   on us the precious and very great **p**,

PROMPT → PROMPTED
Ex   25: 2   that their hearts **p** them to give me.

PROMPTED → PROMPT
Mt   14: 8   P by her mother, she said,

PROOF → PROVE
2 Cor   8:24   So give **p** before the churches

PROOFS → PROVE
Acts   1: 3   by many **p** after he had suffered,

PROPER
Sir   31:28   is wine enough, drunk at the **p** time.
1 Cor   11:13   is it **p** for a woman to pray to God
Jude   1: 6   but deserted their **p** dwelling, he has

PROPERTY

Lv	25:10	of you shall return to your own **p**,
Mt	12:29	strong man's house and steal his **p**,
Lk	15:12	father divided the **p** between them.
Acts	5: 1	his wife Sapphira, sold a piece of **p**.

PROPHECIES → PROPHESY

Tb	14: 4	not a single word of the **p** will fail.
1 Cor	13: 8	If there are **p**, they will be brought

PROPHECY → PROPHESY

Acts	21: 9	four virgin daughters gifted with **p**.
1 Cor	12:10	to another **p**; to another discernment
1 Cor	14: 6	or knowledge, or **p**, or instruction?
1 Cor	14:22	whereas **p** is not for unbelievers
2 Pt	1:20	that there is no **p** of scripture that is
Rev	19:10	Witness to Jesus is the spirit of **p**."

PROPHESIED → PROPHESY

Nm	11:25	them, they **p** but did not continue.
Jer	2: 8	The prophets **p** by Baal, and went
Jer	26:11	He has **p** against this city!
Mt	11:13	and the law **p** up to the time of John.
Jn	11:51	he **p** that Jesus was going to die
Acts	19: 6	and they spoke in tongues and **p**.
Jude	1:14	**p** also about them when he said,

PROPHESIES → PROPHESY

2 Chr	18: 7	because he **p** not good but always
Jer	28: 9	But the prophet who **p** peace is
Ez	12:27	he **p** for distant times!"
1 Cor	11: 4	or **p** with his head covered brings
1 Cor	14: 5	One who **p** is greater than one who

PROPHESY → PROPHECIES, PROPHECY, PROPHESIED, PROPHESIES, PROPHESYING, PROPHET, PROPHET'S, PROPHETESS, PROPHETIC, PROPHETS

Jer	5:31	The prophets **p** falsely,
Ez	13: 2	**p** against the prophets of Israel, **p**!
Ez	13: 2	to those who **p** their own thoughts:
Ez	13:17	own thoughts, and **p** against them.
Ez	34: 2	**p** against the shepherds of Israel.
Ez	37: 4	**P** over these bones, and say to them:
Jl	3: 1	Your sons and daughters will **p**,
Am	2:12	the prophets, "Do not **p**!"
Am	7:16	'Do not **p** against Israel, do not
Mt	7:22	Lord, did we not **p** in your name?
Lk	22:64	and questioned him, saying, "**P**!
Acts	2:17	sons and your daughters shall **p**,
1 Cor	13: 9	know partially and we **p** partially,
1 Cor	14: 5	in tongues, but even more to **p**.
1 Cor	14:39	strive eagerly to **p**, and do not forbid
Rev	11: 3	commission my two witnesses to **p**

PROPHESYING → PROPHESY

Nm	11:27	and Medad are **p** in the camp,"
Rev	11: 6	can fall during the time of their **p**.

PROPHET → PROPHESY

Ex	7: 1	Aaron your brother will be your **p**.
Dt	18:18	for them a **p** like you from among
Dt	18:18	my words into the mouth of the **p**; the **p** shall tell them all
Dt	18:22	did not speak. The **p** has spoken it
Dt	34:10	no **p** has arisen in Israel like Moses,
Jgs	4: 4	At that time the **p** Deborah, wife of
1 Sm	3:20	Samuel was a trustworthy **p**
1 Sm	9: 9	is now called **p** was formerly called
1 Sm	19:23	he continued on, acting like a **p**
1 Kgs	1: 8	Nathan the **p**, Shimei and Rei,
1 Kgs	18:36	Elijah the **p** came forward and said,
1 Kgs	22: 7	"Is there no other **p** of the LORD
2 Kgs	5: 8	find out that there is a **p** in Israel."
2 Kgs	6:12	"The Israelite **p** Elisha can tell
2 Kgs	20: 1	was mortally ill, the **p** Isaiah,
2 Kgs	22:14	went to Huldah the **p**, wife of Shallum,
2 Chr	35:18	since the time of Samuel the **p**;
2 Chr	36:12	himself before Jeremiah the **p**,
Neh	6:14	in mind as well Noadiah the woman **p**

1 Mc	4:46	of a **p** who could determine what
1 Mc	14:41	forever until a trustworthy **p** arises.
Jer	1: 5	a **p** to the nations I appointed you.
Jer	23:11	Both **p** and priest are godless!
Jer	28: 1	year, Hananiah the **p**, son of Azzur,
Ez	2: 5	know that a **p** has been among them.
Ez	33:33	that there was a **p** among them.
Dn	3:38	We have in our day no prince, **p**,
Dn	9: 2	had decreed to the **p** Jeremiah:
Hos	9: 7	"The **p** is a fool, the man
Am	7:14	"I am not a **p**, nor do I belong
Hb	1: 1	which Habakkuk the **p** received
Hg	1: 1	LORD came through Haggai the **p**
Zec	1: 1	LORD came to the **p** Zechariah,
Mal	3:23	I am sending to you Elijah the **p**,
Mt	10:41	Whoever receives a **p** because he is a **p** will receive
Mt	11: 9	To see a **p**? Yes, I tell you, and more than a **p**.
Mt	12:39	it except the sign of Jonah the **p**.
Lk	1:76	will be called **p** of the Most High,
Lk	4:24	no **p** is accepted in his own native
Lk	7:16	"A great **p** has arisen in our midst,"
Lk	20: 6	are convinced that John was a **p**."
Lk	24:19	who was a **p** mighty in deed
Jn	1:21	"Are you the **P**?"
Jn	7:40	words said, "This is truly the **P**."
Acts	7:37	your own kinsfolk, a **p** like me.'
Acts	13: 6	Bar-Jesus who was a Jewish false **p**.
Acts	21:10	a **p** named Agabus came down
1 Cor	14:37	If anyone thinks that he is a **p**
Rev	16:13	and from the mouth of the false **p**.
Rev	19:20	it the false **p** who had performed
Rev	20:10	the beast and the false **p** were.

PROPHET'S → PROPHESY

Mt	10:41	is a prophet will receive a **p** reward,

PROPHETESS → PROPHESY

Is	8: 3	I went to the **p** and she conceived

PROPHETIC → PROPHESY

1 Sm	10:10	he joined them in their **p** ecstasy.
1 Sm	19:20	presided over by Samuel in a **p** state,
2 Pt	1:19	we possess the **p** message that is

PROPHETS → PROPHESY

Nm	11:29	the people of the LORD were **p**!
1 Sm	10:11	in a prophetic state among the **p**,
1 Sm	10:11	Is Saul also among the **p**?"
1 Sm	19:24	say, "Is Saul also among the **p**?"
1 Sm	28: 6	dreams nor by Urim nor through **p**.
1 Kgs	18: 4	Jezebel was slaughtering the **p**
1 Kgs	18: 4	Obadiah took a hundred **p**, hid them
1 Kgs	18:40	said to them, "Seize the **p** of Baal.
1 Kgs	19:10	and murdered your **p** by the sword.
2 Kgs	17:23	through all his servants, the **p**.
1 Chr	16:22	my anointed, to my **p** do no harm."
2 Chr	18:22	in the mouths of these **p** of yours;
Ezr	6:14	supported by the message of the **p**,
Neh	9:30	your spirit, by means of your **p**;
1 Mc	9:27	had not been since the time **p** ceased
Ps	105:15	ones, to my **p** do no harm."
Jer	5:13	The **p** are wind, and the word is not
Jer	14:14	These **p** utter lies in my name,
Jer	23: 9	Concerning the **p**: My heart is
Jer	23:30	Therefore I am against the **p**—
Lam	2: 9	Even her **p** do not obtain any vision
Ez	13: 2	prophesy against the **p** of Israel,
Hos	6: 5	I struck them down through the **p**,
Mi	3: 6	The sun shall go down upon the **p**,
Zep	3: 4	Its **p** are reckless,
Zec	1: 5	And the **p**, can they live forever?
Mt	5:17	come to abolish the law or the **p**.
Mt	7:12	do to you. This is the law and the **p**.
Mt	7:15	"Beware of false **p**, who come
Mt	22:40	law and the **p** depend on these two
Mt	24:24	messiahs and false **p** will arise,
Lk	6:23	their ancestors treated the **p**
Lk	10:24	many **p** and kings desired to see
Lk	11:49	'I will send to them **p** and apostles;

Lk 16:29 'They have Moses and the **p**.
Lk 24:25 heart to believe all that the **p** spoke!
Lk 24:44 and in the **p** and psalms must be
Acts 3:24 Moreover, all the **p** who spoke,
Acts 10:43 To him all the **p** bear witness,
Acts 13: 1 were in the church at Antioch **p**
Acts 26:22 nothing different from what the **p**
Acts 28:23 from the law of Moses and the **p**.
Rom 1: 2 promised previously through his **p**
Rom 3:21 testified to by the law and the **p**,
Rom 11: 3 they have killed your **p**, they have
1 Cor 12:28 second, p; third, teachers;
1 Cor 12:29 Are all **p**? Are all teachers?
1 Cor 14:32 spirits of **p** are under the prophets' control,
Eph 2:20 the foundation of the apostles and **p**,
Eph 3: 5 his holy apostles and **p** by the Spirit,
Eph 4:11 others as **p**, others as evangelists,
1 Thes 2:15 Jesus and the **p** and persecuted us;
Heb 1: 1 ways to our ancestors through the **p**;
1 Pt 1:10 **p** who prophesied about the grace
2 Pt 2: 1 were also false **p** among the people,
2 Pt 3: 2 previously spoken by the holy **p**
1 Jn 4: 1 because many false **p** have gone
Rev 11:10 because these two **p** tormented
Rev 16: 6 the blood of the holy ones and the **p**,
Rev 18:20 you holy ones, apostles, and **p**.

PROPORTION
Dt 16:10 you will give shall be in **p**
Rom 12: 6 if prophecy, in **p** to the faith;

PROPOSED
Acts 1:23 So they **p** two, Joseph called

PROSPER → PROSPERED, PROSPERITY, PROSPERS
Dt 4:40 you and your children after you may **p**,
Tb 4: 6 righteousness, will **p** in their affairs.
Prv 28:13 who conceal their sins do not **p**,
Jer 12: 1 Why does the way of the wicked **p**,

PROSPERED → PROSPER
1 Chr 29:23 he **p**, and all Israel obeyed him.
2 Chr 14: 6 on every side." So they built and **p**.
2 Chr 31:21 did this with all his heart, and he **p**.

PROSPERITY → PROSPER
Dt 30: 9 will again take delight in your **p**,
Jb 36:11 they spend their days in **p**,
Ps 25:13 He will abide in **p**, and his
Ps 73: 3 when I saw the **p** of the wicked.
Sir 12: 8 In **p** we cannot know our friends;

PROSPERS → PROSPER
Ps 1: 3 never wither; whatever he does **p**.

PROSTITUTE → PROSTITUTES, PROSTITUTION
Dt 23:18 be no temple **p** among the Israelite
1 Cor 6:15 and make them the members of a **p**?
1 Cor 6:16 himself to a **p** becomes one body

PROSTITUTES → PROSTITUTE
Mt 21:31 **p** are entering the kingdom of God
Lk 15:30 swallowed up your property with **p**,
1 Cor 6: 9 adulterers nor boy **p** nor sodomites

PROSTITUTION → PROSTITUTE
Hos 1: 2 to Hosea: Go, get for yourself a woman of **p** and children
of **p**,

PROSTRATE
Dt 9:18 I lay **p** before the LORD for forty
Dn 8:17 I was standing, I fell **p** in terror.

PROTECT → PROTECTED, PROTECTION, PROTECTS
Ps 12: 8 You, O LORD, **p** us always;

PROTECTED → PROTECT
Jos 24:17 and **p** us along our entire journey
Jn 17:12 with them I **p** them in your name

PROTECTION → PROTECT
Eccl 7:12 For the **p** of wisdom is as the **p** of money;

PROTECTS → PROTECT
Ps 116: 6 The LORD **p** the simple;

1 Jn 5:18 but the one begotten by God he **p**,

PROTEST
Acts 13:51 from their feet in **p** against them

PROUD → PRIDE
Ps 94: 2 give the **p** what they deserve!
Prv 16:19 than to share plunder with the **p**.
Prv 21: 4 Haughty eyes and a **p** heart—
Sir 10: 9 Why are dust and ashes **p**?
Is 2:12 will have his day against all that is **p**
Hos 13: 6 they became **p**, therefore they forgot
Jas 4: 6 "God resists the **p**, but gives grace
1 Pt 5: 5 "God opposes the **p** but bestows

PROVE → PROOF, PROOFS, PROVING
Ezr 2:59 Immer were unable to **p** that their

PROVERB → PROVERBS
Prv 26: 7 A **p** in the mouth of a fool hangs
Prv 26: 9 of a drunkard is a **p** in the mouth
Ez 18: 3 you will ever repeat this **p** in Israel.
Lk 4:23 "Surely you will quote me this **p**,

PROVERBS → PROVERB
1 Kgs 5:12 also uttered three thousand **p**,
Prv 1: 1 The **p** of Solomon, the son
Prv 10: 1 The **P** of Solomon: A wise son
Prv 25: 1 These also are **p** of Solomon.
Eccl 12: 9 scrutinized and arranged many **p**.

PROVIDE → PROVIDED, PROVIDES, PROVISION
Gn 22: 8 "God will **p** the sheep for the burnt
1 Cor 10:13 the trial he will also **p** a way out,
1 Tm 5: 8 whoever does not **p** for relatives

PROVIDED → PROVIDE
1 Kgs 8:21 I have **p** there a place for the ark
Rom 11:22 you, **p** you remain in his kindness;

PROVIDES → PROVIDE
1 Tm 6:17 who richly **p** us with all things

PROVING → PROVE
Acts 9:22 **p** that this is the Messiah.

PROVISION → PROVIDE
Rom 13:14 and make no **p** for the desires

PROVOCATION → PROVOKE
Prv 27: 3 but a fool's **p** is heavier than both.

PROVOKE → PROVOCATION, PROVOKED
Dt 32:21 with a foolish nation I will **p** them.
Jer 25: 6 do not **p** me with the works of your

PROVOKED → PROVOKE
Jgs 2:12 down to them, and **p** the LORD.
Ps 78:41 God, **p** the Holy One of Israel.
Bar 4: 7 For you **p** your Maker

PROWLING
1 Pt 5: 8 opponent the devil is **p** around like

PRUDENCE → PRUDENT
Wis 8: 7 She teaches moderation and **p**,

PRUDENT → PRUDENCE
Prv 19:14 but a **p** wife is from the LORD.
Jer 49: 7 has counsel perished from the **p**,
Mi 6: 9 the city (It is **p** to fear your name!):

PRUNES → PRUNING
Jn 15: 2 does he **p** so that it bears more fruit.

PRUNING → PRUNES
Is 2: 4 and their spears into **p** hooks;
Jl 4:10 and your **p** knives into spears;
Mi 4: 3 and their spears into **p** hooks;

PSALM → PSALMS
Acts 13:33 as it is written in the second **p**,

PSALMS → PSALM
Lk 20:42 himself in the Book of **P** says:
Lk 24:44 prophets and **p** must be fulfilled."
Acts 1:20 For it is written in the Book of **P**:
Eph 5:19 addressing one another [in] **p**

Col 3:16 one another, singing **p**, hymns,

PTOLEMY
1 Mc 1:18 to make war on **P**, king of Egypt.
1 Mc 10:51 Alexander sent ambassadors to **P**,

PUBLIC → PUBLICLY
Col 2:15 he made a **p** spectacle of them,

PUBLICLY → PUBLIC
Gal 3: 1 eyes Jesus Christ was **p** portrayed as
Heb 10:33 times you were **p** exposed to abuse

PUL → =TIGLATH-PILESER
2 Kgs 15:19 **P**, king of Assyria, came against

PULLED → PULLS
Neh 13:25 of their men and **p** out their hair;
Jer 38:13 **p** him up by rope out of the cistern.

PULLS → PULLED
Mt 9:16 its fullness **p** away from the cloak

PUNISH → PUNISHMENT
Ex 32:34 When it is time for me to **p**, I will **p**
Is 13:11 Thus I will **p** the world for its evil
Jer 2:19 you, your own infidelities **p** you.
Jer 21:14 I will **p** you—
Zep 1:12 I will **p** the people who settle like
Acts 4:21 them, finding no way to **p** them,

PUNISHMENT → PUNISH
Gn 4:13 "My **p** is too great to bear.
Ps 91: 8 the **p** of the wicked you will see.
Lam 4: 6 The **p** of the daughter of my people
Hos 9: 7 They have come, the days of **p**!
Mt 25:46 And these will go off to eternal **p**,
2 Pt 2: 9 keep the unrighteous under **p**
1 Jn 4:18 fear because fear has to do with **p**,
Jude 1: 7 by undergoing a **p** of eternal fire.

PUR → PURIM
Est 3: 7 of King Ahasuerus, the **p**, or lot,

PURCHASE
Jer 32: 7 with the offer: "**P** my field in Anathoth,

PURE → PURIFICATION, PURIFIED, PURIFY, PURITY
Ex 25:11 it inside and outside with **p** gold,
Ex 25:31 make a menorah of **p** beaten gold—
Ex 37: 6 The cover was made of **p** gold,
1 Kgs 6:21 the interior of the house with **p** gold,
Tb 8:15 are you, God, with every **p** blessing!
Ps 19:10 The fear of the LORD is **p**,
Ps 24: 4 "The clean of hand and **p** of heart,
Ps 73:13 in vain that I have kept my heart **p**,
Prv 15:26 LORD, but gracious words are **p**.
Wis 7:25 a **p** emanation of the glory
Hb 1:13 Your eyes are too **p** to look
Phil 1:10 so that you may be **p** and blameless
Phil 4: 8 whatever is **p**, whatever is lovely,
1 Tm 1: 5 instruction is love from a **p** heart,
1 Tm 5:22 in another's sins. Keep yourself **p**.
Heb 10:22 and our bodies washed in **p** water.
Jas 1:27 Religion that is **p** and undefiled
Jas 3:17 wisdom from above is first of all **p**,
1 Jn 3: 3 hope based on him makes himself **p**, as he is **p**.
Rev 21:18 while the city was **p** gold, clear as

PURGE
Ex 30:10 Once a year Aaron shall **p** its horns.
Dt 13: 6 Thus shall you **p** the evil from your
Dt 19:19 Thus shall you **p** the evil from your

PURIFICATION → PURE
2 Mc 1:18 Since we shall be celebrating the **p**
Lk 2:22 completed for their **p** according
Heb 1: 3 he had accomplished **p** from sins,

PURIFIED → PURE
Ezr 6:20 one of whom had **p** himself
Neh 12:30 and Levites first **p** themselves,
Neh 12:30 then they **p** the people, the gates,
Ps 12: 7 in a crucible, silver **p** seven times.
Dn 12:10 Many shall be refined, **p**, and tested,

1 Pt 1:22 Since you have **p** yourselves

PURIFY → PURE
Nm 19:12 they shall **p** themselves
Nm 19:12 if they fail to **p** themselves
Jer 33: 8 I will **p** them of all the guilt they
Mal 3: 3 and he will **p** the Levites,
Jas 4: 8 and **p** your hearts, you of two

PURIM → PUR
Est 9:26 so these days have been named **P**

PURITY → PURE
2 Cor 6: 6 by **p**, knowledge, patience,
1 Tm 4:12 speech, conduct, love, faith, and **p**.
1 Tm 5: 2 women as sisters with complete **p**.

PURPLE
Ex 25: 4 violet, **p**, and scarlet yarn;
Prv 31:22 fine linen and **p** are her clothing.
Dn 5:29 Belshazzar they clothed Daniel in **p**,
Mk 15:17 They clothed him in **p** and,
Rev 17: 4 The woman was wearing **p**
Rev 18:16 wearing fine linen, **p** and scarlet,

PURPOSE
Rom 8:28 who are called according to his **p**.
Eph 1:11 the **p** of the One who accomplishes
Eph 3:11 the eternal **p** that he accomplished
Heb 6:17 of the immutability of his **p**,
Rev 17:17 it into their minds to carry out his **p**

PURSUE → PURSUED, PURSUES, PURSUIT
Dt 19: 6 of blood might in hot anger **p**,
Ps 34:15 and do good; seek peace and **p** it.
Prv 28: 1 The wicked flee though none **p**;
Is 51: 1 me, you who **p** justice, who seek
Rom 14:19 Let us then **p** what leads to peace
1 Cor 14: 1 **P** love, but strive eagerly
1 Tm 6:11 Instead, **p** righteousness, devotion,
2 Tm 2:22 desires and **p** righteousness, faith,

PURSUED → PURSUE
Ps 18:38 I **p** my enemies and overtook them;

PURSUES → PURSUE
Lv 26:17 You will flee though no one **p** you.
Prv 13:21 Misfortune **p** sinners, but the just
Prv 21:21 Whoever **p** justice and kindness will
Sir 31: 5 whoever **p** money will be led astray

PURSUIT → PURSUE
Prv 11:19 life, but **p** of evil, toward death.

PUT → PUTS, PUTTING
Gn 3:15 I will **p** enmity between you
Gn 4:15 So the LORD **p** a mark on Cain,
Gn 24: 2 "**P** your hand under my thigh,
Gn 47:29 **p** your hand under my thigh as
Ex 4: 6 **P** your hand into the fold of your
Ex 4: 6 So he **p** his hand into the fold of his
Nm 17:25 **P** back Aaron's staff in front
2 Chr 22:11 and **p** him and his nurse in a bedroom.
Is 42: 1 Upon him I have **p** my spirit;
Is 59:17 He **p** on justice as his breastplate,
Jer 32:14 and **p** them in an earthenware jar,
Ez 36:27 I will **p** my spirit within you so
Ez 37:14 I will **p** my spirit in you that you
Mt 4: 7 'You shall not **p** the Lord,
Jn 20:25 and **p** my finger into the nailmarks
Jn 20:25 and **p** my hand into his side, I will
Rom 8:13 the spirit you **p** to death the deeds
Rom 9:33 in him shall not be **p** to shame."
Rom 10:11 believes in him will be **p** to shame."
1 Cor 13:11 a man, I **p** aside childish things.
1 Cor 15:25 reign until he has **p** all his enemies
Eph 6:11 **P** on the armor of God so that you
Heb 8:10 I will **p** my laws in their minds and I
1 Pt 3:18 **P** to death in the flesh, he was

PUTS → PUT
Nm 23:12 "Is it not what the LORD **p** in my
Ps 40: 4 And **p** a new song in my mouth,

PUTTING → PUT
Eph   4:25   Therefore, p away falsehood,

Q

QUAIL
Ex   16:13   q came up and covered the camp.
Nm   11:31   LORD that drove in q from the sea
Ps   105:40   They asked and he brought them q;
Wis   16: 2   by providing q for their food,

QUAKE → EARTHQUAKE, EARTHQUAKES, QUAKED
Na   1: 5   The mountains q before him,

QUAKED → QUAKE
Ps   68: 9   The earth q, the heavens poured,
Mt   27:51   The earth q, rocks were split,

QUARREL → QUARRELED, QUARRELS
Prv   17:14   check a q before it bursts forth!
Prv   20: 3   strife, while every fool starts a q.
Prv   26:17   the q of another is one who grabs
Sir   28:11   and a hasty q provokes bloodshed.

QUARRELED → QUARREL
Ex   17: 7   because the Israelites q there

QUARRELS → QUARREL
2 Tm   2:23   for you know that they breed q.
Ti   3: 9   and q about the law, for they are

QUEEN
1 Kgs   10: 1   The q of Sheba, having heard
2 Chr   15:16   her position as q mother because
Est   1:12   But Q Vashti refused to come
Est   2:17   and made her q in place of Vashti.
Est   4:14   a time like this that you became q?"
Jer   7:18   to make cakes for the Q of Heaven,
Mt   12:42   the judgment the q of the south will
Acts   8:27   that is, the q of the Ethiopians,
Rev   18: 7   said to herself, 'I sit enthroned as q;

QUENCH → QUENCHED
Sg   8: 7   Deep waters cannot q love,
Is   1:31   and there shall be none to q them.
Jer   4: 4   and burn so that no one can q it,

QUENCHED → QUENCH
Jer   7:20   it will burn and not be q.
Mk   9:48   does not die, and the fire is not q.'

QUESTION → QUESTIONS
Jb   38: 3   I will q you, and you tell me
Jb   40: 7   I will q you, and you tell me
Mk   11:29   said to them, "I shall ask you one q.

QUESTIONS → QUESTION
2 Chr   9: 1   Jerusalem to test him with subtle q,
Mt   22:46   anyone dare to ask him any more q.

QUICK → QUICK-TEMPERED, QUICKLY
Eccl   5: 1   and let not your heart be q to utter
Jas   1:19   everyone should be q to hear,

QUICK-TEMPERED → QUICK, TEMPER
Prv   14:17   The q make fools of themselves,
Sir   8:16   Do not defy the q, or ride with them

QUICKLY → QUICK
Jos   23:16   and you will q perish from the good
Ps   22:20   my strength, come q to help me.
Prv   25: 8   do not bring forth too q against an opponent;
Mt   28: 7   Then go q and tell his disciples,
Jn   13:27   "What you are going to do, do q."
Rom   9:28   q will the Lord execute sentence
Gal   1: 6   you are so q forsaking the one who

QUIET → QUIETLY
Eccl   9:17   The q words of the wise are better
1 Tm   2: 2   that we may lead a q and tranquil

QUIETLY → QUIET
Mt   1:19   to shame, decided to divorce her q.

QUIRINIUS
Lk   2: 2   when Q was governor of Syria.

QUIVER
Ps   127: 5   Blessed is the man who has filled his q
Is   49: 2   sharpened arrow, in his q he hid me.

QUOTE
Lk   4:23   "Surely you will q me this proverb,

R

RAAMSES
Ex   1:11   the garrison cities of Pithom and R.

RABBI → RABBOUNI
Mt   23: 8   As for you, do not be called 'R.'
Mt   26:49   over to Jesus and said, "Hail, R!"
Jn   1:38   him, "R" (which translated means

RABBOUNI → RABBI
Jn   20:16   and said to him in Hebrew, "R,"

RACE
Eccl   9:11   under the sun that the r is not won
1 Cor   9:24   in the stadium all run in the r,
2 Tm   4: 7   I have finished the r; I have kept
Heb   12: 1   in running the r that lies before us
1 Pt   2: 9   But you are "a chosen r, a royal

RACHEL
Daughter of Laban (Gn 29:16); wife of Jacob (Gn 29:28); bore two sons (Gn 30:22-24; 35:16-24; 46:19). Stole Laban's gods (Gn 31:19, 32-35). Death (Gn 35:19-20).

RADIANCE → RADIANT
Rev   21:11   Its r was like that of a precious

RADIANT → RADIANCE
Ps   34: 6   Look to him and be r, and your
Sg   5:10   My lover is r and ruddy;
Is   60: 5   Then you shall see and be r,

RAGE → RAGING
Acts   4:25   'Why did the Gentiles r

RAGING → RAGE
Is   28:15   When the r flood passes through,
Jon   1:15   into the sea, and the sea stopped r.

RAGS
Jer   38:12   tattered r between your armpits

RAGUEL'S
Tb   3:17   R daughter Sarah came down
Tb   14:13   he inherited R estate as well as

RAHAB
Prostitute of Jericho who hid Israelite spies (Jos 2; 6:22-25; Heb 11:31; Jas 2:25). Mother of Boaz (Mt 1:5).

RAIN → RAINED, RAINS
Gn   2: 5   the LORD God had sent no r
Gn   7: 4   now I will bring r down on the earth
Ex   16: 4   I am going to r down bread
Dt   11:14   I will give the seasonal r to your land, the early r and the late r,
1 Kgs   17: 1   be no dew or r except at my word."
1 Kgs   18: 1   that I may send r upon the earth.
2 Chr   6:26   are closed so that there is no r,
Jb   38:28   Has the r a father?
Ps   147: 8   with clouds, provides r for the earth,
Is   45: 8   like gentle r let the clouds drop it
Jer   14:22   the nations are there any that give r?
Zec   14:17   then there will be no r for them.
Mt   5:45   and causes r to fall on the just
Mt   7:25   The r fell, the floods came,
Jas   5:17   prayed earnestly that it might not r,
Jas   5:17   and six months it did not r
Rev   11: 6   so that no r can fall during the time

RAINBOW → BOW, RAIN
Ez   1:28   like the appearance of the r in the clouds

RAINED → RAIN
Gn   19:24   and the LORD r down sulfur
Ex   9:23   the LORD r down hail
Ps   78:24   God r manna upon them for food;
Ps   78:27   He r meat upon them like dust,

Lk   17:29 brimstone r from the sky to destroy

RAINS → RAIN
Lv   26: 4 I will give you your r in due season,
Jas   5: 7 it receives the early and the late r.

RAISE → RISE
Dt   18:15 r up for you from among your own
Dt   32:40 For I r my hand to the heavens and will
Prv   8: 1 call, and Understanding r her voice?
Is   11:12 He shall r a signal to the nations
Mt   3: 9 God can r up children to Abraham
Jn   2:19 and in three days I will r it up."
Jn   6:39 that I should r it [on] the last day.
Acts   3:22 r up for you from among your own
1 Cor   6:14 and will also r us by his power.
2 Cor   4:14 who raised the Lord Jesus will r us
Heb   11:19 God was able to r even

RAISED → RISE
Jgs   2:18 When the LORD r up judges
Mt   17:23 and he will be r on the third day."
Lk   7:22 the dead are r, the poor have
Lk   24:34 "The Lord has truly been r and has
Acts   2:24 But God r him up, releasing him
Acts   10:40 This man God r [on] the third day
Acts   13:30 But God r him from the dead,
Rom   4:25 and was r for our justification.
Rom   6: 4 just as Christ was r from the dead
Rom   8:11 the one who r Jesus from the dead
Rom   9:17 "This is why I have r you up,
Rom   10: 9 your heart that God r him
1 Cor   15: 4 that he was r on the third day
1 Cor   15:20 But now Christ has been r
2 Cor   5:15 who for their sake died and was r.
Eph   2: 6 r us up with him, and seated us
Col   2:12 also r with him through faith
Col   2:12 of God, who r him from the dead.

RAISES → RISE
1 Sm   2: 8 He r the needy from the dust;
Ps   113: 7 He r the needy from the dust,
Jn   5:21 For just as the Father r the dead

RAM → RAM'S, RAMS, RAMS'
Gn   22:13 saw a single r caught by its horns
Gn   22:13 and took the r and offered it up as
Ex   29:22 since this is the r for installation;
Dn   8: 3 the river a r with two great horns,

RAM'S → RAM
Jos   6: 4 with seven priests carrying r horns

RAMAH
Jer   31:15 In R is heard the sound of sobbing,
Mt   2:18 "A voice was heard in R,

RAMPARTS
Ps   48:14 Consider the r, examine its citadels,

RAMS → RAM
1 Sm   15:22 to listen, better than the fat of r.
Ps   114: 4 The mountains skipped like r;
Mi   6: 7 be pleased with thousands of r,

RAMS' → RAM
Ex   25: 5 r skins dyed red, and tahash skins;

RAN → RUN
Gn   39:12 her hand, he escaped and r outside.
1 Kgs   18:46 and r before Ahab as far as
Lk   24:12 But Peter got up and r to the tomb,

RANGE
Zec   4:10 that r over the whole earth."

RANK → RANKS
Est   10: 3 The Jew Mordecai was next in r

RANKS → RANK
1 Sm   17:10 "I defy the r of Israel today.
Jn   1:15 one who is coming after me r ahead

RANSOM → RANSOMED
Ex   13:13 firstborn of a donkey you will r with

Ex   13:13 human firstborn of your sons you must r.
Mt   20:28 to give his life as a r for many."
Mk   10:45 to give his life as a r for many."
Gal   4: 5 to r those under the law, so that we
1 Tm   2: 6 who gave himself as r for all.

RANSOMED → RANSOM
Is   35:10 the r of the LORD shall return,
Is   51:11 whom the LORD has r will return

RAPHAEL
Tb   3:17 So R was sent to heal them both:
Tb   5: 4 found the angel R standing before
Tb   12:15 I am R, one of the seven angels who

RASH → RASHLY
Ps   106:33 spirit that r words crossed his lips.

RASHLY → RASH
Prv   20:25 It is a trap to pledge r a sacred gift,

RATHER
Jb   32: 2 for considering himself r than God
Mt   10: 6 Go r to the lost sheep of the house
Acts   5:29 "We must obey God r than men.
1 Cor   14:19 church I would r speak five words

RAVEN → RAVENS
Gn   8: 7 and he released a r. It flew back
Jb   38:41 Who provides nourishment for the r

RAVENS → RAVEN
1 Kgs   17: 6 R brought him bread and meat
Ps   147: 9 food and young r what they cry for.
Lk   12:24 Notice the r: they do not sow

RAW
Ex   12: 9 Do not eat any of it r or even boiled
1 Sm   2:15 meat from you, only r meat."

RAZOR
Jgs   16:17 said, "No r has touched my head,
1 Sm   1:11 No r shall ever touch his head."

REACHED → REACHES
Ps   18:17 He r down from on high and seized

REACHES → REACHED
Prv   31:20 She r out her hands to the poor,

READ → READER, READING, READS
Ex   24: 7 he r it aloud to the people,
Dt   17:19 and he shall r it as long as he lives,
Jos   8:34 were r aloud all the words
2 Kgs   23: 2 He r aloud to them all the words
Neh   8: 8 Ezra r clearly from the book
Neh   8: 8 all could understand what was r.
Is   34:16 the book of the LORD and r:
Jer   36: 6 r the words of the LORD
Dn   5:16 if you are able to r the writing
Mk   12:10 Have you not r this scripture
Lk   4:16 on the sabbath day. He stood up to r
2 Cor   3: 2 on our hearts, known and r by all,
2 Cor   3:15 whenever Moses is r, a veil lies

READER → READ
Mt   24:15 the holy place (let the r understand),
Mk   13:14 he should not (let the r understand),

READING → READ
Jer   36:23 Each time Jehudi finished r three
Acts   8:30 and heard him r Isaiah the prophet
Acts   8:30 you understand what you are r?"
1 Tm   4:13 I arrive, attend to the r, exhortation,

READS → READ
Rev   1: 3 Blessed is the one who r aloud

READY
Ps   119:173 Keep your hand r to help me, for I
Mt   25:10 and those who were r went
1 Pt   1: 5 a salvation that is r to be revealed
1 Pt   3:15 Always be r to give an explanation
Rev   19: 7 come, his bride has made herself r.

REAFFIRM
2 Cor   2: 8   I urge you to r your love for him.

REAP → REAPER, REAPS
Lv   19: 9   be so thorough that you r the field
Jb   4: 8   and sow trouble will r them.
Ps   126: 5   who sow in tears will r with cries
Hos   8: 7   the wind, they will r the whirlwind;
Hos   10:12   justice, r the reward of loyalty;
Lk   12:24   they do not sow or r;
Jn   4:38   to r what you have not worked for;
1 Cor   9:11   thing that we r a material harvest
2 Cor   9: 6   sows sparingly will also r sparingly,
2 Cor   9: 6   bountifully will also r bountifully.
Gal   6: 7   a person will r only what he sows,
Rev   14:15   "Use your sickle and r the harvest,
Rev   14:15   for the time to r has come,

REAPER → REAP
Jn   4:36   The r is already receiving his
Jn   4:36   the sower and r can rejoice together.

REAPS → REAP
Am   9:13   who plows shall overtake the one who r
Jn   4:37   that 'One sows and another r.'

REAR
Nm   10:25   Finally, as r guard for all the camps,
Is   52:12   your r guard is the God of Israel.

REASON
Mt   19: 5   this r a man shall leave his father
Rom   4:16   For this r, it depends on faith,
Heb   9:15   For this r he is mediator of a new
2 Pt   1: 5   For this very r, make every effort

REBEKAH
   Sister of Laban, secured as bride for Isaac (Gn 24). Mother of Esau and Jacob (Gn 25:19-26). Taken by Abimelech as sister of Isaac; returned (Gn 26:1-11). Encouraged Jacob to trick Isaac out of blessing (Gn 27:1-17).

REBEL → REBELLED, REBELLION, REBELLIOUS, REBELS
Ex   23:21   Do not r against him, for he will not
Nm   14: 9   Only do not r against the LORD!
1 Sm   12:14   and do not r against the LORD's

REBELLED → REBEL
Nm   20:24   because you both r against my
Ps   78:56   tested and r against God Most High,
Is   63:10   they r and grieved his holy spirit;

REBELLION → REBEL
1 Sm   15:23   For a sin of divination is r,
Heb   3: 8   not your hearts as at the r in the day

REBELLIOUS → REBEL
Ps   78: 8   a r and defiant generation,
Ez   2: 5   they are a r house—they shall know

REBELS → REBEL
Jos   1:18   Anyone who r against your orders

REBIRTH → BEAR
Ti   3: 5   he saved us through the bath of r

REBUILD → BUILD
Neh   2:17   let us r the wall of Jerusalem,
Tb   14: 5   and they will r Jerusalem with due
Am   9:14   they shall r and inhabit their ruined
Acts   15:16   return and r the fallen hut of David;
Acts   15:16   from its ruins I shall r it and raise it

REBUILT → BUILD
Ezr   6: 3   the house is to be r as a place
Ez   36:36   have r what was destroyed

REBUKE → REBUKED, REBUKES
Ps   50: 8   Not for your sacrifices do I r you,
Ps   119:21   a curse you r the proud who stray
Prv   27: 5   Better is an open r than a love
Eccl   7: 5   to listen to the r of the wise than
Is   54: 9   to be angry with you, or to r you.
Zec   3: 2   "May the LORD r you,

Zec   3: 2   who has chosen Jerusalem r you!
Mk   8:32   took him aside and began to r him.
Lk   17: 3   If your brother sins, r him; and if he
Jude   1: 9   but said, "May the Lord r you!"

REBUKED → REBUKE
Mt   8:26   he got up, r the winds and the sea,
Mt   17:18   Jesus r him and the demon came
Lk   4:39   He stood over her, r the fever, and it

REBUKES → REBUKE
Prv   28:23   Whoever r another wins more favor

RECALL
Ps   77:12   I will r the deeds of the LORD; yes, r your wonders of old.

RECEDED
Gn   8: 3   Gradually the waters r

RECEIVE → RECEIVED, RECEIVES
Gn   4:11   its mouth to r your brother's blood
Dt   9: 9   the mountain to r the stone tablets
Ps   24: 5   He will r blessings
Mt   10:41   a prophet will r a prophet's reward,
Mt   10:41   is righteous will r a righteous man's
Mk   10:30   who will not r a hundred times
Jn   16:24   ask and you will r, so that your joy
Jn   20:22   and said to them, "R the holy Spirit.
Acts   1: 8   But you will r power when the holy
Acts   2:38   you will r the gift of the holy Spirit.
Acts   19: 2   "Did you r the holy Spirit
Acts   20:35   more blessed to give than to r.'"
Rom   11:31   to you, they too may [now] r mercy.
1 Cor   4: 5   everyone will r praise from God.
Heb   4:16   the throne of grace to r mercy
Jas   1: 7   he will r anything from the Lord,
Jas   1:12   has been proved he will r the crown
1 Jn   3:22   and r from him whatever we ask,
Rev   4:11   to r glory and honor and power,
Rev   5:12   the Lamb that was slain to r power

RECEIVED → RECEIVE
Jos   14: 1   which the Israelites r as heritage
Ps   68:19   took captives, r slaves as tribute,
Mt   6: 2   say to you, they have r their reward.
Mt   10: 8   Without cost you have r;
Jn   1:16   From his fullness we have all r,
Acts   8:17   on them and they r the holy Spirit.
Acts   10:47   who have r the holy Spirit even as
Rom   8:15   fear, but you r a spirit of adoption,
Rom   11:30   have now r mercy because of their
1 Cor   2:12   We have not r the spirit of the world
1 Cor 11:23   For I r from the Lord what I
Col   2: 6   So, as you r Christ Jesus the Lord,
Col   4:17   the ministry that you r in the Lord."
1 Tm   4: 4   is to be rejected when r
1 Pt   2:10   you "had not r mercy" but now you have r mercy.
1 Pt   4:10   As each one has r a gift, use it
2 Pt   1: 1   to those who have r a faith of equal
2 Pt   1:17   For he r honor and glory from God

RECEIVES → RECEIVE
Lk   11:10   For everyone who asks, r;
Jn   13:20   you, whoever r the one I send r me,
Jn   13:20   whoever r me r the one who sent

RECENT
1 Tm   3: 6   He should not be a r convert,

RECHABITES
Jer   35: 5   I set before the R bowls full

RECITE → RECITED
Ex   17:14   be remembered, and r it to Joshua:

RECITED → RECITE
Dt   31:30   Moses r the words of this song

RECKLESS
2 Tm   3: 4   traitors, r, conceited,

RECLINING
Est   7: 8   on the couch on which Esther was r;

Jn   13:23 Jesus loved, was **r** at Jesus' side.

RECOGNITION → RECOGNIZE
1 Cor 16:18 So give **r** to such people.

RECOGNIZE → RECOGNITION, RECOGNIZED, RECOGNIZING
Gn   42: 8 although they did not **r** him,
Jb   2:12 up their eyes and did not **r** him,
Lk   19:44 you because you did not **r** the time

RECOGNIZED → RECOGNIZE
Gn   42: 8 When Joseph **r** his brothers,
Lk   24:31 eyes were opened and they **r** him,

RECOGNIZING → RECOGNIZE
Lk   24:16 eyes were prevented from **r** him.

RECOILED
Ez   23:17 as they had defiled her, she **r** from them.

RECOMMENDATION
2 Cor   3: 1 do, letters of **r** to you or from you?

RECOMPENSE
Is   40:10 reward with him, his **r** before him.
Is   49: 4 the LORD, my **r** is with my God.
Is   62:11 is with him, his **r** before him."

RECONCILE → RECONCILED, RECONCILIATION, RECONCILING
Acts   7:26 and tried to **r** them peacefully,
Eph   2:16 and might **r** both with God, in one
Col   1:20 through him to **r** all things for him,

RECONCILED → RECONCILE
Mt   5:24 go first and be **r** with your brother,
Rom   5:10 we were **r** to God through the death
Rom   5:10 once **r**, will we be saved by his life.
1 Cor   7:11 single or become **r** to her husband—
2 Cor   5:18 who has **r** us to himself through
2 Cor   5:20 you on behalf of Christ, be **r** to God.
Col   1:22 he has now **r** in his fleshly body

RECONCILIATION → RECONCILE
Rom   5:11 whom we have now received **r**.
Rom 11:15 their rejection is the **r** of the world,
2 Cor   5:18 and given us the ministry of **r**,
2 Cor   5:19 entrusting to us the message of **r**.

RECONCILING → RECONCILE
2 Cor   5:19 God was **r** the world to himself

RECORDED → RECORDS
Est   9:20 Mordecai **r** these events and sent
Ps   56: 9 stored in your flask, **r** in your book?

RECORDS → RECORDED
Ezr   2:62 These searched their family **r**,

RECOVER
Is   38: 1 are about to die; you shall not **r**."
Jn   4:52 He asked them when he began to **r**.

RED
Ex   15: 4 officers were drowned in the **R** Sea.
Nm   19: 2 for you a **r** heifer without defect
2 Kgs   3:22 saw the water as **r** as blood,
1 Mc   4: 9 ancestors were saved in the **R** Sea,
Ps 106: 9 He roared at the **R** Sea and it dried
Prv 23:31 not look on the wine when it is **r**,
Is   1:18 Though they be **r** like crimson,
Zec   1: 8 man mounted on a **r** horse standing
Zec   6: 2 The first chariot had **r** horses,
Mt   16: 3 for the sky is **r** and threatening.'
Heb 11:29 faith they crossed the **R** Sea as if it
Rev   6: 4 Another horse came out, a **r** one.
Rev   12: 3 it was a huge **r** dragon, with seven

REDEEM → REDEEMED, REDEEMER, REDEEMS, REDEMPTION
Lv   25:25 who has the duty to **r** it, shall come
Ps   26:11 **r** me, be gracious to me!
Ps   44:27 up, help us! **R** us in your mercy.
Ps 130: 8 And he will **r** Israel from all its sins.
Hos 13:14 shall I **r** them from death?
Lk   24:21 that he would be the one to **r** Israel;

REDEEMED → REDEEM
Ex   15:13 your love you led the people you **r**;
2 Sm   7:23 whom you **r** for yourself
Ps 107: 2 that be the prayer of the LORD's **r**, those **r** from the hand of the foe,
Is   1:27 Zion shall be **r** by justice, and her
Is   35: 9 But there the **r** shall walk,
Is   44:22 return to me, for I have **r** you.
Is   63: 9 love and pity the LORD **r** them,

REDEEMER → REDEEM
Ps   19:15 you, LORD, my rock and my **r**.
Ps   34:23 The LORD is the **r** of the souls
Ps   78:35 their rock, God Most High, their **r**.
Is   44: 6 king, its **r**, the LORD of hosts:
Is   48:17 your **r**, the Holy One of Israel:
Is   59:20 Then for Zion shall come a **r**,

REDEEMS → REDEEM
1 Mc   4:11 shall know that there is One who **r**

REDEMPTION → REDEEM
Lk   2:38 to all who were awaiting the **r**
Lk   21:28 raise your heads because your **r** is
Rom   3:24 by his grace through the **r** in Christ
Rom   8:23 for adoption, the **r** of our bodies.
1 Cor   1:30 righteousness, sanctification, and **r**,
Eph   1: 7 In him we have **r** by his blood,
Eph   1:14 of our inheritance toward **r** as God's
Eph   4:30 you were sealed for the day of **r**.
Col   1:14 in whom we have **r**, the forgiveness
Heb   9:12 own blood, thus obtaining eternal **r**.

REED → REEDS
2 Kgs 18:21 that broken **r** of a staff,
Is   42: 3 A bruised **r** he will not break,
Mt   12:20 A bruised **r** he will not break,
Lk   7:24 a **r** swayed by the wind?

REEDS → REED
Ex   2: 3 placed it among the **r** on the bank

REELED
Ps 107:27 They **r**, staggered like drunkards;

REFINE → REFINED, REFINING
Zec   13: 9 I will **r** them as one refines silver,

REFINED → REFINE
Ps   12: 7 are sure, silver **r** in a crucible,
Is   48:10 See, I **r** you, but not like silver;
Dn   12:10 Many shall be **r**, purified,

REFINING → REFINE
Mal   3: 3 Levites, **R** them like gold or silver,

REFLECT → REFLECTING, REFLECTION
Sir   6:37 **R** on the law of the Most High,

REFLECTING → REFLECT
Lk   2:19 these things, **r** on them in her heart.

REFLECTION → REFLECT
Wis   7:26 For she is the **r** of eternal light,

REFRESH → REFRESHMENT
Phlm   1:20 in the Lord. **R** my heart in Christ.

REFRESHMENT → REFRESH
Acts   3:20 the Lord may grant you times of **r**

REFUGE
Ru   2:12 whose wings you have come for **r**."
2 Sm 22: 3 my God, my rock of **r**!
2 Sm 22: 3 my stronghold, my **r**, my savior,
Ps   2:11 Blessed are all who take **r** in him!
Ps   11: 1 In the LORD I take **r**; how can you
Ps   16: 1 me safe, O God; in you I take **r**.
Ps   17: 7 your right arm those who seek **r**
Ps   31: 3 Be my rock of **r**, a stronghold
Ps   34: 9 is the stalwart one who takes **r**
Ps   36: 8 of Adam take **r** in the shadow
Ps   46: 2 God is our **r** and our strength,
Ps   59:17 my fortress, my **r** in time of trouble.
Ps   62: 9 Pour out your hearts to God our **r**!

Ps 71: 1 In you, Lord, I take r;
Ps 91: 2 to the Lord, "My r and fortress,
Ps 118: 8 Better to take r in the Lord than
Prv 14:26 defense, a r even for one's children.
Prv 14:32 the just find a r in their integrity.
Prv 30: 5 a shield to those who take r in him.
Is 25: 4 For you have been a r to the poor,
Jer 16:19 fortress, my r in the day of distress!
Na 1: 7 for him, a r on the day of distress,

REFULGENCE
Heb 1: 3 who is the r of his glory, the very

REFUSE → REFUSED
Ex 7:27 If you r to let them go, then I will
Jer 13:10 wicked people who r to obey my words,

REFUSED → REFUSE
Ex 13:15 Pharaoh stubbornly r to let us go,
Jer 5: 3 laid them low, but they r correction;
Jer 5: 3 harder than stone, and r to return.
Heb 12:25 they r the one who warned them

REFUTE → REFUTED
Ti 1: 9 sound doctrine and to r opponents.

REFUTED → REFUTE
Acts 18:28 He vigorously r the Jews in public,

REGAIN → REGAINED
Acts 9:17 that you may r your sight and be

REGAINED → REGAIN
Acts 22:13 at that very moment I r my sight

REGARD
Phil 2: 6 of God, did not r equality with God

REGRET → REGRETS
Nm 23:19 speaks falsely, nor a mortal, who feels r.
1 Sm 15:11 I r having made Saul king, for he
2 Cor 7:10 a salutary repentance without r,

REGRETS → REGRET
Jer 8: 6 No one r wickedness, saying, "What have I

REGULATIONS
Col 2:20 why do you submit to r as if you
Heb 9:10 r concerning the flesh,

REHOBOAM
   Son of Solomon (1 Kgs 11:43; 1 Chr 3:10). Harsh treatment of subjects caused divided kingdom (1 Kgs 12:1-24; 14:21-31; 2 Chr 10–12).

REIGN → REIGNED
Ex 15:18 May the Lord r forever and ever!
Dt 17:20 and his descendants may r long
Ps 146:10 The Lord shall r forever,
Prv 8:15 By me kings r, and rulers enact
Is 24:23 of hosts will r on Mount Zion
Is 32: 1 a king will r justly and princes will
Jer 23: 5 As king he shall r and govern
1 Cor 15:25 For he must r until he has put all his
2 Tm 2:12 persevere we shall also r with him.
Rev 5:10 our God, and they will r on earth."
Rev 11:15 and he will r forever and ever."
Rev 11:17 power and have established your r.
Rev 20: 6 and they will r with him
Rev 22: 5 and they shall r forever and ever.

REIGNED → REIGN
Rev 20: 4 they r with Christ for a thousand

REJECT → REJECTED, REJECTION, REJECTS
Sir 7:19 Do not r a sensible wife; a gracious wife
Is 30:12 Because you r this word, And put
Jer 14:21 Do not r us, for your name's sake,
Hos 4: 6 I will r you from serving as my

REJECTED → REJECT
1 Sm 15:23 Because you have r the word
1 Sm 15:23 Lord in turn has r you as king."
2 Kgs 17:20 So the Lord r the entire people
Ps 60: 3 O God, you r us, broke our
Ps 118:22 stone the builders r has become
Jer 8: 9 Since they have r the word

Mal 1: 3 I loved Jacob, but r Esau;
Mt 21:42 that the builders r has become
Acts 4:11 He is 'the stone r by you,
1 Tm 4: 4 and nothing is to be r when received
1 Pt 2: 4 r by human beings but chosen
1 Pt 2: 7 which the builders r has become

REJECTION → REJECT
Rom 11:15 if their r is the reconciliation

REJECTS → REJECT
Lk 10:16 listens to me. Whoever r you r me.
Lk 10:16 whoever r me r the one who sent
Jn 12:48 Whoever r me and does not accept

REJOICE → REJOICED, REJOICES, REJOICING
1 Chr 16:10 r, O hearts that seek the Lord!
1 Chr 16:31 the heavens be glad and the earth r;
2 Chr 6:41 your faithful ones r in good things.
Ps 14: 7 Jacob would r, and Israel be glad
Ps 31: 8 I will r and be glad in your mercy,
Ps 51:10 the bones you have crushed will r.
Ps 63:12 But the king shall r in God;
Ps 67: 5 May the nations be glad and r;
Ps 97: 1 let the earth r; let the many islands
Ps 105: 3 let hearts that seek the Lord r!
Ps 118:24 let us r in it and be glad.
Ps 119:162 I r at your promise, as one who has
Ps 149: 2 the people of Zion r in their king.
Prv 24:17 Do not r when your enemies fall,
Prv 29: 2 When the just flourish, the people r;
Sir 8: 7 Do not r when someone dies;
Is 9: 2 They r before you as people r
Is 35: 1 the Arabah will r and bloom;
Is 62: 5 his bride so shall your God r in you.
Lam 4:21 R and gloat, daughter Edom, dwelling in
Hb 3:18 Yet I will r in the Lord and exult
Zep 3:17 Who will r over you with gladness,
Zec 10: 7 Their children will see and r—
Lk 6:23 R and leap for joy on that day!
Lk 10:20 do not r because the spirits are
Lk 10:20 r because your names are written
Lk 15: 6 'R with me because I have found
Lk 15: 9 'R with me because I have found
Rom 12:15 R with those who r, weep with those
Phil 2:17 I r and share my joy with all of you.
Phil 3: 1 Finally, my brothers, r in the Lord.
Phil 4: 4 R in the Lord always. I shall say it again: r!
1 Thes 5:16 R always.
1 Pt 4:13 r to the extent that you share
1 Pt 4:13 revealed you may also r exultantly.
Rev 18:20 R over her, heaven, you holy ones,
Rev 19: 7 Let us r and be glad and give him

REJOICED → REJOICE
Ex 18: 9 Jethro r over all the goodness
1 Chr 29: 9 The people r over these free-will
1 Chr 29: 9 King David also r greatly.
Jb 31:25 Or had I r that my wealth was great,
Jn 8:56 Abraham your father r to see my

REJOICES → REJOICE
Ps 16: 9 my heart is glad, my soul r;
Ps 64:11 The righteous r and takes refuge
Prv 11:10 When the just prosper, the city r;
Prv 17: 5 whoever r in their misfortune will not go
Is 62: 5 as a bridegroom r in his bride so
Lk 1:47 my spirit r in God my savior.
1 Cor 13: 6 wrongdoing but r with the truth.

REJOICING → REJOICE
1 Chr 16:27 power and r are in his holy place.
2 Cor 6:10 as sorrowful yet always r;

RELATIONS → RELATIVE
Lv 18:20 You shall not have sexual r
Lv 20:15 a man has sexual r with an animal,
Mt 1:25 He had no r with her until she bore

RELATIVE → RELATIONS, RELATIVES
Ru 2:20 "This man is a near r of ours,

RELATIVES → RELATIVE
Lk   21:16 by parents, brothers, r, and friends,
1 Tm   5: 8 whoever does not provide for r

RELEASE → RELEASED
Is   61: 1 to the captives, r to the prisoners,
Mt   27:15 the governor was accustomed to r
Rev   9:14 "R the four angels who are bound

RELEASED → RELEASE
Gn   8: 8 Then he r a dove, to see if the waters
Mk   15:15 the crowd, r Barabbas to them and,
Rev   20: 7 Satan will be r from his prison.

RELENT → RELENTED, RELENTING
Ez   24:14 hold back! I will not have pity or r.
Jl   2:14 Perhaps he will again r and leave
Zec   8:14 Lord of hosts—and I did not r,

RELENTED → RELENT
Am   7: 3 The Lord r concerning this. "This shall
Am   7: 6 The Lord r concerning this. "This also

RELENTING → RELENT
Jl   2:13 steadfast love, and r in punishment.

RELIED → RELY
2 Chr   13:18 were victorious because they r
2 Chr   16: 8 yet, because you r on the Lord,

RELIEF
Est   4:14 r and deliverance will come

RELIGION → RELIGIOUS
1 Mc   1:43 many Israelites delighted in his r;
1 Mc   2:19 they forsake the r of their ancestors
Acts   25:19 issues with him about their own r
Acts   26: 5 Pharisee, the strictest party of our r.
Jas   1:26 but deceives his heart, his r is vain.
Jas   1:27 R that is pure and undefiled before

RELIGIOUS → RELIGION
Acts   17:22 that in every respect you are very r.
1 Tm   5: 4 to perform their r duty to their own
Jas   1:26 If anyone thinks he is r and does not

RELY → RELIED
2 Chr   14:10 for we r on you, and in your name
Prv   3: 5 on your own intelligence do not r;
Sir   5: 1 Do not r on your wealth, or say,
Rom   2:17 call yourself a Jew and r on the law

REMAIN → REMAINED, REMAINS
Gn   6: 3 My spirit shall not r in human
Nm   33:55 you allow to r will become barbs
Mk   14:34 R here and keep watch."
Jn   15: 4 R in me, as I in you.
Jn   15: 7 If you r in me and my words r in you,
1 Cor   7:20 Everyone should r in the state
1 Cor   13:13 So faith, hope, love r, these three;
Heb   1:11 They will perish, but you r;
1 Jn   2:28 children, r in him, so that when he
1 Jn   3:24 who keep his commandments r
2 Jn   1: 9 who is so "progressive" as not to r

REMAINED → REMAIN
2 Sm   11: 1 David himself r in Jerusalem.
1 Jn   2:19 been, they would have r with us.

REMAINS → REMAIN
2 Tm   2:13 If we are unfaithful he r faithful,
Heb   4: 9 a sabbath rest still r for the people
Heb   7: 3 Son of God, he r a priest forever.
Heb   10:26 there no longer r sacrifice for sins

REMEDY
2 Chr   36:16 his people blazed up beyond r.

REMEMBER → REMEMBERED, REMEMBERS, REMEMBRANCE
Ex   20: 8 R the sabbath day—keep it holy.
Dt   5:15 R that you too were once slaves
Dt   8:18 R then the Lord, your God,
Jos   1:13 "R what Moses, the servant
Neh   13:31 R this in my favor, my God!

1 Mc   4:10 r the covenant with our ancestors,
Jb   10: 9 r that you fashioned me from clay!
Jb   36:24 R, you should extol his work,
Ps   74: 2 R your people, whom you acquired
Eccl   12: 1 R your Creator in the days of your
Is   46: 8 R this and be firm, take it to heart,
Jer   31:34 iniquity and no longer r their sin.
Lam   5: 1 R, Lord, what has happened
Ez   36:31 Then you will r your evil behavior
Hos   7: 2 to mind that I r all their wickedness.
Hb   3: 2 in your wrath r compassion!
Mk   8:18 and not hear? And do you not r,
Lk   17:32 R the wife of Lot.
Lk   23:42 r me when you come into your
2 Tm   2: 8 R Jesus Christ, raised from the dead,
Heb   8:12 evildoing and r their sins no more."
Jude   1:17 r the words spoken beforehand
Rev   3: 3 R then how you accepted and heard;

REMEMBERED → REMEMBER
Gn   8: 1 God r Noah and all the animals,
Gn   30:22 Then God r Rachel. God listened
1 Sm   1:19 wife Hannah, and the Lord r her.
Ps   78:35 They r that God was their rock,
Ps   98: 3 He has r his mercy and faithfulness
Ps   106:45 For their sake he r his covenant
Ps   136:23 The Lord r us in our low estate,
Is   17:10 Rock, your refuge, you have not r.
Is   65:17 things shall not be r nor come
Ez   18:22 committed shall be r against him;
Ez   33:13 none of their just deeds shall be r;
Mt   26:75 Then Peter r the word that Jesus had
Rev   16:19 But God r great Babylon, giving it

REMEMBERS → REMEMBER
Ps   103:14 we are formed, r that we are dust.
Ps   111: 5 fear him, he r his covenant forever.

REMEMBRANCE → REMEMBER
1 Cor   11:24 that is for you. Do this in r of me."
Heb   10: 3 sacrifices there is only a yearly r

REMIND → REMINDER
Jn   14:26 and r you of all that [I] told you.

REMINDER → REMIND
Ex   13: 9 your hand and a r on your forehead,

REMNANT
Gn   45: 7 of you to ensure for you a r on earth
2 Kgs   19:31 For out of Jerusalem shall come a r,
Ezr   9: 8 who left us a r and gave us a stake
Is   10:21 A r will return, the r of Jacob,
Is   11:11 hand to reclaim the r of his people
Jer   23: 3 I myself will gather the r of my
Jer   50:20 for I will forgive the r I preserve.
Zep   3:13 the r of Israel. They shall do no
Zec   8:12 these things to the r of this people
Rom   9:27 of the sea, only a r will be saved;
Rom   11: 5 also at the present time there is a r,

REMOVAL → REMOVED
1 Pt   3:21 It is not a r of dirt from the body

REMOVED → REMOVAL
Jn   20: 1 and saw the stone r from the tomb.

REND
Jl   2:13 R your hearts, not your garments,

RENEW → RENEWAL, RENEWED
Is   40:31 in the Lord will r their strength,
Zep   3:17 and r you in his love, Who will sing

RENEWAL → RENEW
Rom   12: 2 transformed by the r of your mind,
Ti   3: 5 of rebirth and r by the holy Spirit,

RENEWED → RENEW
Ps   103: 5 so your youth is r like the eagle's.
2 Cor   4:16 our inner self is being r day by day.
Eph   4:23 and be r in the spirit of your minds,

Col   3:10 which is being r, for knowledge,

RENOUNCED
Ps   89:40 You r the covenant with your
2 Cor   4: 2 we have r shameful, hidden things;

RENOWN
Gn   6: 4 were the heroes of old, the men of r.
Ps   135:13 forever, your r, from generation

REPAID → PAY
Lk   14:14 For you will be r at the resurrection

REPAIR → REPAIRED, REPAIRER, REPARATION
2 Chr   24: 5 all Israel that you may r the house

REPAIRED → REPAIR
2 Chr   29: 3 of the LORD's house and r them.

REPAIRER → REPAIR
Is   58:12 "R of the breach," they shall call

REPARATION → REPAIR
Lv   5:15 as r an unblemished ram from the flock,
Lv   5:25 as r to the LORD an unblemished ram
1 Sm   6: 4 "What r offering should be our amends
Hos   5:15 until they make r and seek my presence.

REPAY → PAY
Ps   28: 4 R them for their deeds, for the evil
Ps   35:12 They r me evil for good; my soul is
Jer   25:14 thus I will r them according to their
Jer   51:56 of recompense, he will surely r.
Jl   2:25 I will r you double what
Rom   12:17 Do not r anyone evil for evil;
Rom   12:19 is mine, I will r, says the Lord."
Heb   10:30 I will r," and again:

REPAYS → PAY
1 Sm   26:23 The LORD r everyone's righteousness
Is   59:18 to their deeds he r his enemies

REPENT → REPENTANCE, REPENTED, REPENTS
Jb   42: 6 I have said, and r in dust and ashes.
Jon   3: 9 Who knows? God may again r and turn
Mt   3: 2 [and] saying, "R, for the kingdom
Mt   4:17 Jesus began to preach and say, "R,
Lk   13: 3 if you do not r, you will all perish as
Acts   2:38 [said] to them, "R and be baptized,
Acts   3:19 R, therefore, and be converted,
Acts   17:30 that all people everywhere r
Acts   26:20 I preached the need to r and turn
Rev   2: 5 R, and do the works you did at first.
Rev   2:21 I have given her time to r, but she refuses to r of her
                 harlotry.
Rev   9:20 did not r of the works of their
Rev   16: 9 but they did not r or give him glory.

REPENTANCE → REPENT
Mt   3: 8 good fruit as evidence of your r.
Mk   1: 4 desert proclaiming a baptism of r
Mk   6:12 So they went off and preached r.
Lk   3: 8 good fruits as evidence of your r.
Lk   5:32 not come to call the righteous to r
Lk   24:47 and that r, for the forgiveness
Acts   5:31 and savior to grant Israel r
Acts   11:18 granted life-giving r to the Gentiles
Acts   20:21 Greeks to r before God and to faith
Acts   26:20 to do works giving evidence of r.
Rom   2: 4 of God would lead you to r?
2 Cor   7:10 produces a salutary r without regret,
Heb   6: 1 r from dead works and faith in God,
2 Pt   3: 9 perish but that all should come to r.

REPENTED → REPENT
Zec   1: 6 Then they r and admitted:
Mt   11:21 they would long ago have r
Lk   11:32 at the preaching of Jonah they r,

REPENTS → REPENT
1 Sm   15:29 The Glory of Israel neither deceives nor r, for he is not a
                 mortal who r."
Lk   15: 7 over one sinner who r than over
Lk   15:10 of God over one sinner who r."

REPHAIM
Gn   15:20 the Hittites, the Perizzites, the R,
Jos   12: 4 a survivor of the R, who lived

REPLANTED → PLANT
Ez   36:36 destroyed and r what was desolate.

REPORT → REPORTS
1 Kgs   10: 7 "I did not believe the r until I came
1 Kgs   10: 7 and prosperity surpass the r I heard.

REPORTS → REPORT
Gn   37: 2 Joseph brought their father bad r
Nm   13:32 spread discouraging r among

REPROACH
Jb   27: 6 my heart does not r me for any
Is   51: 7 Do not fear the r of others;
Jer   20: 8 of the LORD has brought me r

REPROOF → REPROVE
Prv   3:11 do not spurn; do not disdain his r;
Prv   13:18 who hold on to r receive honor.

REPROVE → REPROOF, REPROVES
Rev   3:19 Those whom I love, I r and chastise.

REPROVES → REPROVE
Jb   5:17 Happy the one whom God r!
Prv   3:12 For whom the LORD loves he r,

REQUESTS
Phil   4: 6 make your r known to God.

REQUIRE → REQUIRED, REQUIRES
Mal   2:15 what does the One r? Godly offspring!

REQUIRED → REQUIRE
1 Cor   4: 2 Now it is of course r of stewards

REQUIRES → REQUIRE
Mi   6: 8 and what the LORD r of you:

RESCUE → RESCUED, RESCUES
Ps   22: 9 if he loves him, let him r him."
Ps   31: 3 your ear to me; make haste to r me!
Ps   69:15 R me from those who hate me
Ps   82: 4 R the lowly and poor;
Is   31: 5 shield and deliver, to spare and r.
2 Cor   1:10 death, and he will continue to r us;
2 Cor   1:10 hope [that] he will also r us again,
2 Pt   2: 9 the Lord knows how to r the devout

RESCUED → RESCUE
Ps   81: 8 In distress you called and I r you;
Prv   11: 8 The just are r from a tight spot, but
Acts   12:11 and r me from the hand of Herod
2 Pt   2: 7 and if he r Lot, a righteous man

RESCUES → RESCUE
Ps   37:40 The LORD helps and r them,
Sir   40:24 but better than either, charity that r.

RESERVED
2 Pt   2:17 the gloom of darkness has been r.
2 Pt   3: 7 earth have been r by the same word

RESIST → RESISTED, RESISTS
Jas   4: 7 R the devil, and he will flee
1 Pt   5: 9 R him, steadfast in faith,

RESISTED → RESIST
Heb   12: 4 against sin you have not yet r

RESISTS → RESIST
Rom   13: 2 whoever r authority opposes what

RESOLVED
1 Mc   1:62 r in their hearts not to eat anything
Dn   1: 8 Daniel was r not to defile himself

RESPECT → RESPECTED
Mk   12: 6 all, thinking, 'They will r my son.'
Rom   13: 7 toll is due, r to whom r is due,
Eph   5:33 and the wife should r her husband.
1 Thes   5:12 r those who are laboring among you

RESPECTED → RESPECT
Acts   5:34 of the law, r by all the people,

Heb 12: 9 to discipline us, and we **r** them.

RESPOND
Ps 38:16 I wait; O Lord, my God, you **r**.
Hos 2:17 There she will **r** as in the days

REST → RESTED, RESTING
Gn 8: 4 the ark came to **r** on the mountains
Ex 16:23 Tomorrow is a day of **r**, a holy
Ex 31:15 day is the sabbath of complete **r**,
Ex 33:14 myself will go along, to give you **r**.
Lv 25: 4 shall have a sabbath of complete **r**,
Nm 10:36 And when it came to **r**, he would
Dt 12:10 he has given you **r** from all your
2 Sm 7:11 I will give you **r** from all your
Jb 3:17 troubling, there the weary are at **r**.
Ps 95:11 "They shall never enter my **r**."
Prv 6:10 a little folding of the arms to **r**—
Is 11: 2 of the LORD shall **r** upon him:
Jer 6:16 thus you will find **r** for yourselves.
Jer 47: 6 When will you find **r**?
Mt 11:28 are burdened, and I will give you **r**.
Mk 6:31 to a deserted place and **r** a while."
1 Cor 2: 5 your faith might **r** not on human
Heb 3:11 shall not enter into my **r**." ' "
Heb 4: 3 we who believed enter into [that] **r**,
Heb 4: 3 'They shall not enter into my **r**,' "
Heb 4:10 And whoever enters into God's **r**,
Rev 14:13 "let them find **r** from their labors,

RESTED → REST
Gn 2: 2 he **r** on the seventh day from all
Ex 16:30 that the people **r** on the seventh day.
Ex 20:11 but on the seventh day he **r**.
Heb 4: 4 God **r** on the seventh day from all

RESTING → REST
Ps 132:14 "This is my **r** place forever;

RESTITUTION
Ex 21:36 it, he must make full **r**, an ox

RESTLESS
Jas 3: 8 It is a **r** evil, full of deadly poison.

RESTORE → RESTORED, RESTORES
2 Chr 24: 4 Joash decided to **r** the house
Ps 51:14 **R** to me the gladness of your
Ps 80: 4 O God, **r** us; light up your face
Ps 126: 4 **R** our captives, LORD, like the dry
Is 49: 6 Jacob, and **r** the survivors of Israel;
Mt 17:11 will indeed come and **r** all things;
Acts 1: 6 this time going to **r** the kingdom
1 Pt 5:10 Christ [Jesus] will himself **r**,

RESTORED → RESTORE
Ps 85: 2 your land, **r** the captives of Jacob.
Mk 3: 5 stretched it out and his hand was **r**.
Mk 8:25 his sight was **r** and he could see

RESTORES → RESTORE
Ps 14: 7 glad when the LORD **r** his people!

RESTRAIN → RESTRAINED, RESTRAINING
Gn 45: 1 Joseph could no longer **r** himself
Ps 19:14 from arrogant ones **r** your servant;

RESTRAINED → RESTRAIN
2 Pt 2:16 voice and **r** the prophet's madness.

RESTRAINING → RESTRAIN
2 Thes 2: 6 And now you know what is **r**,

RESURRECTION
2 Mc 7:14 for you, there will be no **r** to life."
2 Mc 12:43 inasmuch as he had the **r** in mind;
Mt 22:23 him, saying that there is no **r**.
Mt 22:28 Now at the **r**, of the seven,
Mt 22:30 At the **r** they neither marry nor are
Mt 22:31 And concerning the **r** of the dead,
Mt 27:53 forth from their tombs after his **r**,
Mk 12:18 who say there is no **r**, came to him
Mk 12:23 the **r** [when they arise] whose wife
Lk 14:14 be repaid at the **r** of the righteous."

Lk 20:27 those who deny that there is a **r**,
Lk 20:33 Now at the **r** whose wife will
Lk 20:35 the **r** of the dead neither marry nor
Jn 5:29 done good deeds to the **r** of life,
Jn 5:29 deeds to the **r** of condemnation.
Jn 11:24 will rise, in the **r** on the last day."
Jn 11:25 told her, "I am the **r** and the life;
Acts 1:22 become with us a witness to his **r**."
Acts 2:31 and spoke of the **r** of the Messiah,
Acts 4: 2 in Jesus the **r** of the dead.
Acts 4:33 witness to the **r** of the Lord Jesus,
Acts 17:18 preaching about 'Jesus' and '**R**.'
Acts 17:32 they heard about **r** of the dead,
Acts 23: 6 trial for hope in the **r** of the dead."
Acts 23: 8 the Sadducees say that there is no **r**
Acts 24:15 that there will be a **r** of the righteous
Acts 24:21 you today for the **r** of the dead.' "
Rom 1: 4 of holiness through **r** from the dead,
Rom 6: 5 also be united with him in the **r**.
1 Cor 15:12 some among you say there is no **r**
1 Cor 15:13 If there is no **r** of the dead,
1 Cor 15:21 the **r** of the dead came also through
1 Cor 15:42 So also is the **r** of the dead.
Phil 3:10 the power of his **r** and [the] sharing
Phil 3:11 if somehow I may attain the **r**
2 Tm 2:18 that [the] **r** has already taken place
Heb 6: 2 **r** of the dead and eternal judgment.
Heb 11:35 received back their dead through **r**.
Heb 11:35 in order to obtain a better **r**.
1 Pt 1: 3 a living hope through the **r** of Jesus
1 Pt 3:21 through the **r** of Jesus Christ,
Rev 20: 5 years were over. This is the first **r**.
Rev 20: 6 is the one who shares in the first **r**.

RETAIN
Nm 36: 7 but all the Israelites will **r** their own
Jn 20:23 and whose sins you **r** are retained."

RETIRE
Nm 8:25 on up shall **r** from the work force

RETRIBUTION
Jer 50:15 This is **r** from the LORD! Take **r** on her,
Rom 11: 9 a stumbling block and a **r** for them;

RETURN → RETURNED, RETURNS
Gn 3:19 eat bread, Until you **r** to the ground,
Gn 3:19 you are dust, and to dust you shall **r**.
Gn 18:10 "I will **r** to you about this time next
Gn 15:16 fourth generation your descendants will **r** here,
Dt 30: 2 and **r** to the LORD, your God,
2 Sm 12:23 go to him, but he will not **r** to me."
2 Chr 30: 9 If you **r** to the LORD, your kinfolk
2 Chr 30: 9 his face from you if you **r** to him."
Neh 1: 9 if you **r** to me and carefully keep
Jb 10:21 Before I go whence I shall not **r**,
Jb 16:22 numbered, and I go the road of no **r**.
Jb 22:23 If you **r** to the Almighty, you will
Ps 51:15 ways, that sinners may **r** to you.
Ps 104:29 breath, they perish and **r** to the dust.
Prv 26:11 As dogs **r** to their vomit, so fools
Is 10:21 A remnant will **r**, the remnant
Is 35:10 the ransomed of the LORD shall **r**,
Is 44:22 **r** to me, for I have redeemed you.
Is 55:11 It shall not **r** to me empty, but shall
Jer 3:12 the north, and say: **R**, rebel Israel—
Jer 4: 1 If you **r**, Israel—oracle of the LORD—**r** to me.
Jer 24: 7 for they shall **r** to me with their
Jer 31: 8 an immense throng—they shall **r**.
Lam 3:40 our ways, and **r** to the LORD!
Hos 5: 4 Their deeds do not allow them to **r**
Hos 6: 1 "Come, let us **r** to the LORD,
Hos 12: 7 You must **r** to your God.
Hos 14: 2 **R**, Israel, to the LORD, your God;
Jl 2:12 **r** to me with your whole heart,
Am 4: 6 Yet you did not **r** to me—oracle of
Zec 1: 3 says the LORD of hosts, **R** to me—
Zec 1: 3 and I will **r** to you, says the LORD
Zec 10: 9 they will bear their children and **r**.

Mal	3: 7	**R** to me, that I may **r** to you,
Mal	3: 7	But you say, "Why should we **r**?"
Rom	9: 9	"About this time I shall **r** and Sarah

RETURNED → RETURN

Gn	8: 9	and it **r** to him in the ark, for there
Nm	13:25	They **r** from reconnoitering the land
Ezr	2: 1	of the province who **r**
Neh	7: 6	of the province who **r**
Jdt	4: 3	they had only recently **r** from exile,
1 Pt	2:25	but you have now **r** to the shepherd

RETURNS → RETURN

Eccl	12: 7	the dust **r** to the earth as it once was,
Eccl	12: 7	the life breath **r** to God who gave it.
Sir	40:11	All that is of earth **r** to earth,
Sir	40:11	and what is from above **r** above.
1 Thes	5:15	See that no one **r** evil for evil;

REUBEN → REUBENITES

Firstborn of Jacob by Leah (Gn 29:32; 46:8; 1 Chr 2:1). Attempted to rescue Joseph (Gn 37:21-30). Lost birthright for sleeping with Bilhah (Gn 35:22; 49:4). Tribe of blessed (Gn 49:3-4; Dt 33:6), numbered (Nm 1:21; 26:7), allotted land east of Jordan (Nm 32; 34:14; Jos 13:15), west (Ez 48:6), failed to help Deborah (Jgs 5:15-16), supported David (1 Chr 12:38), 12,000 from (Rev 7:5).

REUBENITES → REUBEN

Nm	32: 1	Now the **R** and Gadites had a very
Dt	29: 7	and gave it as a heritage to the **R**,
Jos	13: 8	as well as the **R** and Gadites,

REVEAL → REVEALED, REVEALS, REVELATION, REVELATIONS

Est	2:10	Esther did not **r** her nationality
Sir	1:30	the Lord will **r** your secrets and cast
Ez	39: 7	I will **r** my holy name among my people
Mt	11:27	to whom the Son wishes to **r** him.

REVEALED → REVEAL

Dt	29:28	but the **r** things are for us
2 Sm	7:27	God of Israel, have **r** to your servant,
Is	40: 5	the glory of the LORD shall be **r**,
Is	53: 1	has the arm of the LORD been **r**?
Dn	2:19	During the night the mystery was **r**
Mt	11:25	the learned you have **r** them
Mt	16:17	and blood has not **r** this to you,
Lk	17:30	be on the day the Son of Man is **r**.
Jn	2:11	Cana in Galilee and so **r** his glory,
Jn	12:38	has the might of the Lord been **r**?"
Rom	1:17	in it is **r** the righteousness of God
Rom	8:18	with the glory to be **r** for us.
1 Cor	2:10	this God has **r** to us through
1 Cor	3:13	It will be **r** with fire, and the fire
Eph	3: 5	generations as it has now been **r**
2 Thes	2: 3	comes first and the lawless one is **r**,
1 Pt	1:20	world but **r** in the final time for you,
1 Pt	4:13	so that when his glory is **r** you may
1 Jn	3: 2	what we shall be has not yet been **r**.
1 Jn	3: 2	when it is **r** we shall be like him,
Rev	15: 4	your righteous acts have been **r**."

REVEALS → REVEAL

Dn	2:22	He **r** deep and hidden things
Dn	2:28	is a God in heaven who **r** mysteries,

REVELATION → REVEAL

Lk	2:32	a light for **r** to the Gentiles,
Rom	16:25	to the **r** of the mystery kept secret
1 Cor	14: 6	if I do not speak to you by way of **r**,
1 Cor	14:26	another an instruction, a **r**, a tongue,
1 Cor	14:30	But if a **r** is given to another person
Gal	1:12	it came through a **r** of Jesus Christ.
Gal	2: 2	I went up in accord with a **r**, and I
Eph	1:17	**r** resulting in knowledge of him.
Eph	3: 3	was made known to me by **r**, as I
Rev	1: 1	The **r** of Jesus Christ, which God

REVELATIONS → REVEAL

2 Cor	12: 1	go on to visions and **r** of the Lord.
2 Cor	12: 7	because of the abundance of the **r**.

REVELRY

2 Pt	2:13	Thinking daytime **r** a delight,

REVERE → REVERENCE, REVERENT

1 Kgs	8:43	may **r** you as do your people Israel,
Neh	1:11	servants who willingly **r** your name.

REVERENCE → REVERE

Tb	14: 6	the world will turn and **r** God in truth;
Eph	5:21	to one another out of **r** for Christ.
Heb	5: 7	and he was heard because of his **r**.
1 Pt	1:17	yourselves with **r** during the time

REVERENT → REVERE

Ti	2: 3	older women should be **r** in their
1 Pt	3: 2	when they observe your **r**

REVILE

Ps	74:10	Will the enemy **r** your name

REVIVE

Is	57:15	To **r** the spirit of the lowly, to **r** the heart of the crushed.
Hos	6: 2	He will **r** us after two days;

REVOKED

Est	8: 8	the royal signet ring cannot be **r**.

REWARD → REWARDED, REWARDS

Gn	15: 1	I will make your **r** very great.
1 Sm	24:20	may the LORD **r** you graciously
2 Chr	15: 7	there shall be a **r** for what you do."
Ps	19:12	obeying them brings much **r**.
Ps	127: 3	LORD, the fruit of the womb, a **r**.
Prv	11:18	those who sow justice have a sure **r**.
Is	40:10	Here is his **r** with him,
Is	62:11	See, his **r** is with him,
Mt	5:12	for your **r** will be great in heaven.
Mt	6: 5	to you, they have received their **r**.
Mt	10:41	a prophet will receive a prophet's **r**,
Mt	10:41	will receive a righteous man's **r**.
Lk	6:23	your **r** will be great in heaven.
Lk	6:35	then your **r** will be great and you

REWARDED → REWARD

2 Sm	22:21	righteousness; **r** my clean hands.
Prv	13:13	reveres the command will be **r**.

REWARDS → REWARD

Heb	11: 6	and that he **r** those who seek him.

REZIN

Is	7: 1	son of Uzziah, **R**, king of Aram,

RHODA

Acts	12:13	a maid named **R** came to answer it.

RIB → RIBS

Gn	2:22	built the **r** that he had taken

RIBLAH

2 Kgs	25: 6	brought to **R** to the king of Babylon,

RIBS → RIB

Gn	2:21	he took out one of his **r** and closed

RICH → ENRICHED, RICHES, RICHLY

2 Sm	12: 1	were two men, one **r**, the other poor.
Jb	34:19	nor respects the **r** more than
Ps	49:17	Do not fear when a man becomes **r**,
Prv	13: 7	One acts **r** but has nothing;
Prv	21:17	wine and perfume will never be **r**.
Prv	22: 2	**R** and poor have a common bond:
Prv	28:20	to be **r** will not go unpunished.
Eccl	5:11	of the **r** allows them no sleep.
Sir	8: 2	Do not quarrel with the **r**, lest they
Ez	34:14	in **r** pastures they will be pastured
Mt	19:23	one who is **r** to enter the kingdom
Lk	1:53	the **r** he has sent away empty.
Lk	6:24	But woe to you who are **r**, for you
Lk	12:21	is not **r** in what matters to God."
Lk	16: 1	"A **r** man had a steward who was
Lk	16:19	"There was a **r** man who dressed
2 Cor	8: 9	he became poor although he was **r**,
2 Cor	8: 9	by his poverty you might become **r**.
Eph	2: 4	But God, who is **r** in mercy,

1 Tm	6: 9	Those who want to be r are falling
1 Tm	6:17	Tell the r in the present age not
1 Tm	6:18	good, to be r in good works, to be
Jas	1:10	and the r one in his lowliness, for he
Jas	2: 5	are poor in the world to be r in faith
Jas	5: 1	you r, weep and wail over your
Rev	2: 9	and poverty, but you are r.
Rev	3:17	'I am r and affluent and have no
Rev	3:18	refined by fire so that you may be r,

RICHES → RICH

1 Kgs	3:13	I give you such r and glory
1 Kgs	10:23	all the kings of the earth in r
Ps	49: 7	and boast of their abundant r?
Ps	119:14	your testimonies more than in all r.
Prv	3:16	hand, in her left are r and honor;
Prv	8:18	With me are r and honor, wealth
Prv	10: 4	but the busy hand brings r.
Prv	11:28	Those who trust in their r will fall,
Prv	22: 1	name is more desirable than great r,
Prv	30: 8	me, give me neither poverty nor r;
Lk	8:14	are choked by the anxieties and r
Rom	9:23	to make known the r of his glory
Rom	11:33	the depth of the r and wisdom
Eph	2: 7	he might show the immeasurable r
Eph	3: 8	to the Gentiles the inscrutable r
Col	1:27	to make known the r of the glory

RICHLY → RICH

Col	3:16	the word of Christ dwell in you r,
1 Tm	6:17	who r provides us with all things
Ti	3: 6	whom he r poured out on us

RID

1 Pt	2: 1	R yourselves of all malice and all

RIDDLE → RIDDLES

Jgs	14:12	them, "Let me propose a r to you.
Ez	17: 2	propose a r, and tell this proverb

RIDDLES → RIDDLE

Nm	12: 8	I speak to him, plainly and not in r.
Prv	1: 6	the words of the wise and their r.

RIDE → RIDER, RIDERS, RIDES, RIDING

Ps	45: 4	and majesty r on triumphant!

RIDER → RIDE

Ps	68: 5	exalt the r of the clouds.
Rev	6: 2	a white horse, and its r had a bow.
Rev	19:11	its r was [called] "Faithful

RIDERS → RIDE

Rev	9:17	is how I saw the horses and their r.

RIDES → RIDE

Dt	33:26	who r the heavens in his power,
Dt	33:26	who r the clouds in his majesty;

RIDING → RIDE

Zec	9: 9	and r on a donkey, on a colt,

RIGGING

Is	33:23	The r hangs slack; it cannot hold

RIGHT → BIRTHRIGHT, RIGHTLY, RIGHTS

Gn	13: 9	you prefer the left, I will go to the r; if you prefer the r,
Gn	48:13	Ephraim with his r hand, to Israel's r, and brought them
Ex	14:22	with the water as a wall to their r
Ex	15: 6	magnificent in power, your r hand,
Ex	15:26	God, and do what is r in his eyes:
Dt	5:32	not turning aside to the r
Dt	6:18	Do what is r and good in the sight
Dt	13:19	doing what is r in the sight
Dt	28:14	aside, either to the r or to the left,
Jos	1: 7	Do not swerve from it either to the r
1 Sm	12:23	to teach you the good and r way.
Jb	4:17	"Can anyone be more in the r than God?
Jb	35: 2	Do you think it r to say, "I am in the r, not God"?
Jb	40:14	for your own r hand can save you.
Ps	16: 8	with him at my r hand, I shall never
Ps	16:11	the delights at your r hand forever.
Ps	17: 7	your r arm those who seek refuge

Ps	18:36	your r hand has upheld me;
Ps	19: 9	The precepts of the LORD are r,
Ps	44: 4	It was your r hand, your own arm,
Ps	45: 5	justice may your r hand show your
Ps	63: 9	fast to you; your r hand upholds me.
Ps	73:23	you take hold of my r hand.
Ps	80:18	hand be with the man on your r,
Ps	89:14	your r hand is ever exalted.
Ps	91: 7	ten thousand at your r hand,
Ps	110: 1	"Sit at my r hand, while I make
Ps	110: 5	At your r hand is the Lord,
Ps	118:15	"The LORD's r hand works
Ps	137: 5	Jerusalem, may my r hand forget.
Ps	139:10	me, your r hand holds me fast.
Prv	3:16	Long life is in her r hand, in her left
Prv	4:27	Turn neither to r nor to left,
Prv	12:15	way of fools is r in their own eyes,
Prv	14:12	Sometimes a way seems r,
Prv	16:25	Sometimes a way seems r,
Prv	18:17	the case first seem to be in the r;
Is	30:21	when you would turn to the r
Is	41:10	you with my victorious r hand.
Is	41:13	your God, who grasp your r hand;
Is	48:13	my r hand spread out the heavens.
Is	64: 4	that you might meet us doing r,
Ez	1:10	and on the r the face of a lion,
Ez	18: 5	a man is just—if he does what is r,
Ez	18:21	statutes and does what is just and r,
Ez	33:14	from sin and do what is just and r—
Am	3:10	do not know how to do what is r—
Jon	4:11	who cannot know their r hand
Zec	3: 1	the adversary stood at his r side
Mt	5:29	If your r eye causes you to sin,
Mt	6: 3	left hand know what your r is doing,
Mt	22:44	"Sit at my r hand until I place your
Mt	25:33	He will place the sheep on his r
Mk	14:62	of Man seated at the r hand
Acts	2:34	said to my Lord, "Sit at my r hand
Acts	7:55	Jesus standing at the r hand of God,
Rom	8:34	who also is at the r hand of God,
Rom	9:21	not the potter have a r over the clay,
1 Cor	9: 4	Do we not have the r to eat
Eph	1:20	and seating him at his r hand
Eph	6: 1	parents [in the Lord], for this is r.
Col	3: 1	where Christ is seated at the r hand
Heb	1: 3	he took his seat at the r hand
Heb	1:13	"Sit at my r hand until I make your
Heb	10:12	took his seat forever at the r hand
1 Pt	3:22	heaven and is at the r hand of God,
Rev	1:16	In his r hand he held seven stars.
Rev	22:11	The righteous must still do r,
Rev	22:14	robes so as to have the r to the tree

RIGHTEOUS → RIGHTEOUSNESS

Tb	3: 2	"You are r, Lord, and all your
Ps	55:23	He will never allow the r
Ps	119:137	You are r, LORD, and just are
Ps	146: 8	the LORD loves the r.
Jer	23: 5	I will raise up a r branch for David;
Mt	13:43	the r will shine like the sun
Mt	13:49	and separate the wicked from the r
Mt	25:37	Then the r will answer him and say,
Mt	25:46	but the r to eternal life."
Mk	2:17	I did not come to call the r
Acts	3:14	You denied the Holy and R One
Acts	24:15	there will be a resurrection of the r
Rom	1:17	"The one who is r by faith will
Rom	5:19	of one the many will be made r.
Jas	5:16	of a r person is very powerful.
1 Pt	3:12	For the eyes of the Lord are on the r
1 Pt	3:18	the r for the sake of the unrighteous,
1 Pt	4:18	"And if the r one is barely saved,
2 Pt	2: 7	a r man oppressed by the licentious
1 Jn	2: 1	the Father, Jesus Christ the r one.
1 Jn	3: 7	who acts in righteousness is r, just as he is r.
Rev	19: 8	(The linen represents the r deeds

RIGHTEOUSNESS → RIGHTEOUS

Gn	15: 6	attributed it to him as an act of r.
Tb	12: 8	with r is better than wealth
Ps	18:21	The LORD acknowledged my r,
Mt	3:15	it is fitting for us to fulfill all r."
Mt	5: 6	are they who hunger and thirst for r,
Mt	5:10	who are persecuted for the sake of r,
Mt	5:20	unless your r surpasses
Mt	6:33	first the kingdom [of God] and his r,
Jn	16: 8	the world in regard to sin and r
Rom	1:17	in it is revealed the r of God
Rom	3:22	the r of God through faith in Jesus
Rom	4: 3	and it was credited to him as r."
Rom	4: 5	ungodly, his faith is credited as r.
Rom	4: 6	to whom God credits r apart
Rom	4: 9	was credited to Abraham as r."
Rom	4:13	through the r that comes from faith.
Rom	4:22	why "it was credited to him as r."
Rom	6:13	bodies to God as weapons for r.
Rom	6:16	or of obedience, which leads to r?
Rom	6:18	sin, you have become slaves of r.
Rom	6:19	so now present them as slaves to r
Rom	8:10	sin, the spirit is alive because of r.
Rom	9:30	who did not pursue r, have achieved it, that is, r that comes from faith;
Rom	10: 3	unawareness of the r that comes
Rom	10: 3	they did not submit to the r of God.
Rom	14:17	of food and drink, but of r, peace,
1 Cor	1:30	God, as well as r, sanctification,
2 Cor	5:21	that we might become the r of God
2 Cor	6: 7	with weapons of r at the right
2 Cor	6:14	For what partnership do r
2 Cor	9: 9	to the poor; his r endures forever."
2 Cor	9:10	and increase the harvest of your r.
2 Cor	11:15	also masquerade as ministers of r.
Gal	3: 6	and it was credited to him as r."
Eph	4:24	self, created in God's way in r
Eph	6:14	truth, clothed with r as a breastplate,
Phil	1:11	the fruit of r that comes through
Phil	3: 6	church, in r based on the law I was
Phil	3: 9	not having any r of my own based
Phil	3: 9	faith in Christ, the r from God,
1 Tm	6:11	Instead, pursue r, devotion, faith,
2 Tm	2:22	from youthful desires and pursue r,
2 Tm	3:16	for correction, and for training in r,
2 Tm	4: 8	now on the crown of r awaits me,
Heb	5:13	lacks experience of the word of r,
Heb	11: 7	inherited the r that comes through
Heb	12:11	later it brings the peaceful fruit of r
Jas	2:23	and it was credited to him as r,"
Jas	3:18	the fruit of r is sown in peace
1 Pt	2:24	free from sin, we might live for r.
2 Pt	2:21	have known the way of r than
2 Pt	3:13	and a new earth in which r dwells.
Rev	19:11	He judges and wages war in r.

RIGHTLY → RIGHT

Gn	4: 7	If you act r, you will be accepted;
Lk	7:43	said to him, "You have judged r."

RIGHTS → RIGHT

Ex	21:10	food, her clothing, or her conjugal r.
Prv	31: 8	mute, and for the r of the destitute;
1 Cor	9:15	I have not used any of these r,

RING → EARRINGS

Gn	41:42	Pharaoh took off his signet r
Est	3:12	and sealed with the royal signet r.
Est	8:10	and sealed with the royal signet r,
Prv	11:22	Like a golden r in a swine's snout is
Jer	22:24	were a signet r on my right hand,
Hg	2:23	and I will make you like a signet r,
Lk	15:22	put a r on his finger and sandals

RIOT → RIOTS

Mk	14: 2	may be a r among the people."

RIOTS → RIOT

2 Cor	6: 5	beatings, imprisonments, r, labors,

RIPE

Jl	4:13	Wield the sickle, for the harvest is r;
Mk	4:29	And when the grain is r, he wields
Jn	4:35	and see the fields r for the harvest.
Rev	14:15	the earth's harvest is fully r."

RISE → ARISE, ARISEN, ARISES, RAISE, RAISED, RAISES, RISES, RISING, ROSE

Nm	24:17	and a scepter shall r from Israel,
Ps	7: 7	R up, LORD, in your anger;
Ps	94: 2	R up, O judge of the earth;
Is	26:19	dead shall live, their corpses shall r!
Dn	12:13	you shall r for your reward
Am	8:14	They shall fall, never to r again.
Mt	5:45	for he makes his sun r on the bad
Mk	8:31	and be killed, and r after three days.
Mk	13: 8	Nation will r against nation
Lk	18:33	him, but on the third day he will r."
Jn	20: 9	that he had to r from the dead.
Acts	17: 3	had to suffer and r from the dead,
1 Thes	4:16	and the dead in Christ will r first.

RISES → RISE

Eccl	1: 5	The sun r and the sun sets;
2 Pt	*1:19	the morning star r in your hearts.

RISING → RISE

Ps	113: 3	From the r of the sun to its setting
Mt	2: 2	We saw his star at its r and have
Mk	9:10	questioning what r from the dead

RIVALRY

Phil	1:15	preach Christ from envy and r,

RIVER → RIVERS

Gn	2:10	A r rises in Eden to water
Gn	15:18	the Wadi of Egypt to the Great R,
Dt	1: 7	the Lebanon as far as the Great R,
Dt	11:24	the Euphrates R to the Western Sea,
Ps	46: 5	Streams of the r gladden the city
Is	48:18	your peace would be like a r,
Is	66:12	spread prosperity over her like a r,
Ez	47:12	Along each bank of the r every kind
Mt	3: 6	the Jordan R as they acknowledged
Rev	22: 1	Then the angel showed me the r

RIVERS → RIVER

Ps	78:16	caused r of water to flow down.
Ps	78:44	God turned their r to blood;
Ps	137: 1	By the r of Babylon there we sat
Sg	8: 7	cannot quench love, nor r sweep it away.
Rev	8:10	It fell on a third of the r
Rev	16: 4	angel poured out his bowl on the r

ROAD → CROSSROADS

Nm	22:22	a position on the r as his adversary.
Mt	7:13	the r broad that leads to destruction,
Mk	11: 8	people spread their cloaks on the r,

ROAR → ROARING, ROARS

Ps	76: 7	At your r, O God of Jacob,
2 Pt	3:10	heavens will pass away with a mighty r

ROARING → ROAR

Ps	65: 8	You still the r of the seas, the r of their waves,
1 Pt	5: 8	around like a r lion looking

ROARS → ROAR

Jer	25:30	The LORD r from on high,
Jer	25:30	Mightily he r over his sheepfold,
Hos	11:10	the LORD, who r like a lion;
Hos	11:10	When he r, his children shall come
Jl	4:16	The LORD r from Zion,
Am	1: 2	The LORD r from Zion, and raises

ROASTED

Ex	12: 8	eating it r with unleavened bread

ROB → ROBBER, ROBBERS, ROBBERY

Mal	3: 8	Can anyone r God? But you are

Rom   2:22 who detest idols, do you r temples?

ROBBER → ROB
1 Cor   5:11 or a r, not even to eat with such

ROBBERS → ROB
Lk   10:30 fell victim to r as he went down
1 Cor   6:10 nor slanderers nor r will inherit

ROBBERY → ROB
Is   61: 8 justice, I hate r and wrongdoing;
Ez   22:29 practice extortion and commit r;

ROBE → ROBED, ROBES
Ex   28: 4 an ephod, a r, a brocade tunic,
Is   61:10 and wrapped me in a r of justice,
Lk   15:22 'Quickly bring the finest r and put it
Rev   1:13 wearing an ankle-length r,
Rev   6:11 Each of them was given a white r,

ROBED → ROBE
Ps   93: 1 The LORD is king, r with majesty;
Ps   93: 1 the LORD is r, girded with might.

ROBES → ROBE
Ps   45: 9 aloes, and cassia your r are fragrant.
Zec   3: 4 and I am clothing you in stately r."
Mk   12:38 who like to go around in long r
Rev   22:14 are they who wash their r so as

ROCK → ROCKS, ROCKY
Gn   49:24 of the Shepherd, the R of Israel,
Ex   17: 6 in front of you on the r in Horeb.
Ex   17: 6 Strike the r, and the water will flow
Ex   33:22 I will set you in the cleft of the r
Nm   20: 8 forth water from the r for them,
Dt   32: 4 the R—how faultless are his deeds,
Dt   32:15 and scorned the R of their salvation.
Dt   32:31 Indeed, their "r" is not like our R;
1 Sm   2: 2 there is no R like our God.
2 Sm   22: 2 O LORD, my r, my fortress,
Ps   18: 3 LORD, my r, my fortress,
Ps   18: 3 My God, my r of refuge, my shield,
Ps   19:15 LORD, my r and my redeemer.
Ps   27: 5 and set me high upon a r.
Ps   40: 3 Sets my feet upon r, steadies my
Ps   61: 3 Raise me up, set me on a r,
Ps   62: 3 God alone is my r and salvation,
Ps   92:16 my r, in whom there is no wrong."
Wis   11: 4 was given them from the sheer r,
Sir   4: 6 their R will hear the sound of their cry.
Is   26: 4 For the LORD is an eternal R.
Is   44: 8 There is no other R, I know of none!
Is   48:21 Water from the r he set flowing
Is   48:21 he cleft the r, and waters welled
Is   51: 1 Look to the r from which you were
Mt   7:24 wise man who built his house on r.
Mt   16:18 upon this r I will build my church,
Mk   15:46 that had been hewn out of the r.
Rom   9:33 and a r that will make them fall,
1 Cor   10: 4 a spiritual r that followed them, and the r was the
                  Christ.
1 Pt   2: 8 and a r that will make them fall."

ROCKS → ROCK
Ps   78:15 He split r in the desert, gave water
Is   2:19 People will go into caves in the r
Mt   27:51 The earth quaked, r were split,
Jn   10:31 Jews again picked up r to stone him.

ROCKY → ROCK
Mk   4: 5 on r ground where it had little soil.

ROD → RODS
2 Sm   7:14 I will reprove him with a human r
Ps   2: 9 an iron r you will shepherd them,
Ps   23: 4 your r and your staff comfort me.
Prv   13:24 Whoever spares the r hates
Prv   14: 3 mouth of the fool is a r for pride,
Prv   22:15 the r of discipline will drive it out.
Prv   23:13 if you beat them with the r,
Prv   29:15 The r of correction gives wisdom,

Is   11: 4 the ruthless with the r of his mouth,
Rev   2:27 He will rule them with an iron r.
Rev   19:15 He will rule them with an iron r,

RODS → ROD
2 Cor   11:25 Three times I was beaten with r,

ROLL → ROLLED
Mk   16: 3 "Who will r back the stone for us
Heb   1:12 You will r them up like a cloak,

ROLLED → ROLL
Lk   24: 2 They found the stone r away

ROMAN → ROME
Acts   16:37 even though we are R citizens
Acts   22:25 to scourge a man who is a R citizen

ROMANS → ROME
1 Mc   8: 1 had heard of the reputation of the R.
1 Mc   14:24 to confirm the alliance with the R.
Jn   11:48 and the R will come and take away

ROME → ROMAN, ROMANS
Acts   18: 2 had ordered all the Jews to leave R.
Acts   28:14 And thus we came to R.
Rom   1:15 preach the gospel also to you in R.

ROOF
Gn   19: 8 come under the shelter of my r."
Jos   2: 6 Now, she had led them to the r,
2 Sm   11: 2 about on the r of the king's house.
2 Sm   11: 2 the r he saw a woman bathing;
Mt   8: 8 to have you enter under my r;
Mk   2: 4 they opened up the r above him.
Acts   10: 9 went up to the r terrace to pray

ROOM → ROOMS
Mt   6: 6 go to your inner r, close the door,
Mk   14:15 show you a large upper r furnished
Rom   12:19 revenge but leave r for the wrath;
2 Cor   7: 2 Make r for us; we have not wronged
Eph   4:27 and do not leave r for the devil.

ROOMS → ROOM
Mt   24:26 'He is in the inner r,' do not believe

ROOT → ROOTED, ROOTS
Prv   12:12 the r of the righteous will bear fruit.
Sir   47:22 to David a r from his own family.
Is   11:10 On that day, The r of Jesse,
Mt   3:10 now the ax lies at the r of the trees.
Mt   13:21 he has no r and lasts only for a time.
Rom   11:18 you do not support the r; the r supports you.
Rom   15:12 "The r of Jesse shall come,
1 Tm   6:10 love of money is the r of all evils,
Rev   5: 5 of the tribe of Judah, the r of David,
Rev   22:16 I am the r and offspring of David,

ROOTED → ROOT
Eph   3:17 that you, r and grounded in love,
Col   2: 7 r in him and built upon him

ROOTS → ROOT
Is   11: 1 and from his r a bud shall blossom.
Jer   17: 8 that stretches out its r to the stream:
Ez   17: 9 Will he not tear up its r and strip its

ROSE → RISE
Acts   10:41 with him after he r from the dead.
1 Thes 4:14 if we believe that Jesus died and r,

ROT → ROTTED
Prv   10: 7 but the name of the wicked will r.
Zec   14:12 their flesh will r while they stand
Zec   14:12 and their eyes will r in their sockets,

ROTTED → ROT
Jas   5: 2 Your wealth has r away,

ROUGH
Is   40: 4 land shall be a plain, the r country,
Bar   4:26 children have trodden r roads,
Lk   3: 5 and the r ways made smooth,

ROYAL

2 Chr 22:10 to kill off the whole r family
Is 62: 3 a r diadem in the hand of your God.
Jas 2: 8 you fulfill the r law according
1 Pt 2: 9 are "a chosen race, a r priesthood,

RUBBISH

1 Cor 4:13 We have become like the world's r,
Phil 3: 8 and I consider them so much r,

RUDDER

Jas 3: 4 a very small r wherever the pilot's

RUDDY

1 Sm 16:12 He was r, a youth with beautiful
Sg 5:10 My lover is radiant and r;

RUDE

1 Cor 13: 5 it is not r, it does not seek its own

RUIN → RUINS

Prv 10:14 the mouth of a fool is imminent r.
Prv 19:13 The foolish son is r to his father,
Prv 26:28 and the flattering mouth works r.
Is 25: 2 the fortified city a r, The castle
Hos 4:14 without understanding comes to r.
1 Tm 6: 9 which plunge them into r

RUINS → RUIN

Ezr 9: 9 house of our God and restore its r,
Neh 2:17 how Jerusalem lies in r and its gates
Jer 9:10 will turn Jerusalem into a heap of r,
Am 9:11 raise up its r, and rebuild it as
Acts 15:16 from its r I shall rebuild it and raise

RULE → RULER, RULERS, RULES

Gn 4: 7 urge is for you, yet you can r over it.
Dt 15: 6 you will r over many nations, and none will r over you.
Jgs 8:22 then said to Gideon, "R over us—
Prv 17: 2 A wise servant will r over
Is 32: 1 justly and princes will r rightly.
Rom 15:12 come, raised up to r the Gentiles;
Rev 2:27 He will r them with an iron rod.
Rev 12: 5 destined to r all the nations
Rev 19:15 He will r them with an iron rod,

RULER → RULE

Ex 2:14 "Who has appointed you r
Prv 23: 1 When you sit down to dine with a r,
Prv 25:15 By patience is a r persuaded,
Prv 29:26 Many curry favor with a r, but it is
Eccl 9:17 than the shout of a r of fools.
Mt 2: 6 since from you shall come a r,
Acts 7:27 'Who appointed you r and judge
Eph 2: 2 following the r of the power
Rev 1: 5 dead and r of the kings of the earth.

RULERS → RULE

Prv 29:12 If r listen to lying words,
Sir 4:27 do not refuse to do so before r.
Is 40:23 makes the r of the earth as nothing.
Mt 2: 6 by no means least among the r
Mt 20:25 that the r of the Gentiles lord it over
Rom 13: 3 For r are not a cause of fear to good
1 Cor 2: 6 of the r of this age who are passing
Eph 6:12 the world r of this present darkness,

RULES → RULE

2 Sm 23: 3 justice, who r in the fear of God,
Ps 66: 7 who r by his might forever,
Is 40:10 GOD, who r by his strong arm;
2 Tm 2: 5 by competing according to the r.

RUMOR → RUMORS

Ez 7:26 Disaster after disaster, r upon r.

RUMORS → RUMOR

Jer 51:46 when r spread through the land;

RUN → FORERUNNER, RAN, RUNNERS, RUNNING, RUNS

Ps 119:32 I will r the way of your
Prv 4:12 and should you r, you will not
Prv 18:10 tower; the just r to it and are safe.
Is 40:31 They will r and not grow weary,

1 Cor 9:24 in the stadium all r in the race,
1 Cor 9:24 one wins the prize? R so as to win.
Gal 2: 2 not be running, or have r, in vain.
Phil 2:16 may be that I did not r in vain

RUNNERS → RUN

1 Cor 9:24 that the r in the stadium all run

RUNNING → RUN

Ps 133: 2 on the head, r down upon the beard,
Gal 5: 7 You were r well; who hindered you
Heb 12: 1 and persevere in r the race that lies

RUNS → RUN

Jn 10:12 and leaves the sheep and r away,

RUTH

Moabitess; widow who went to Bethlehem with mother-in-law Naomi (Ru 1). Gleaned in field of Boaz; shown favor (Ru 2). Proposed marriage to Boaz (Ru 3). Married (Ru 4:1-12); bore Obed, ancestor of David (Ru 4:13-22), Jesus (Mt 1:5).

RUTHLESS

Rom 1:31 are senseless, faithless, heartless, r.

S

SABACHTHANI

Mt 27:46 a loud voice, "*Eli, Eli, lema s?*"
Mk 15:34 loud voice, "*Eloi, Eloi, lema s?*"

SABBATH → SABBATHS

Ex 16:23 day of rest, a holy s of the LORD.
Ex 20: 8 Remember the s day—keep it holy.
Ex 31:14 you must keep the s for it is holiness
Nm 15:32 gathering wood on the s day.
Dt 5:12 Observe the s day—keep it holy,
Neh 13:17 you are doing, profaning the s day?
1 Mc 1:43 to idols and profaned the s.
1 Mc 2:38 and soldiers attacked them on the s,
Is 56: 2 Keeping the s without profaning it,
Is 58:13 If you refrain from trampling the s,
Is 58:13 If you call the s a delight,
Jer 17:21 care not to carry burdens on the s,
Mt 12: 1 through a field of grain on the s.
Mk 2:28 Son of Man is lord even of the s."
Lk 6: 9 to do good on the s rather than to do
Lk 13:10 teaching in a synagogue on the s.
Lk 14: 3 "Is it lawful to cure on the s

SABBATHS → SABBATH

Ex 31:13 Keep my s, for that is to be the sign
2 Chr 36:21 the land has retrieved its lost s,
1 Mc 1:45 to profane the s and feast days,
Ez 20:12 I also gave them my s to be a sign

SACKCLOTH → CLOTH

1 Chr 21:16 elders, clothed in s, fell face down,
Jdt 4:10 slave, girded themselves with s.
Jdt 8: 5 of her house, put s about her waist,
1 Mc 2:14 put on s, and mourned bitterly.
Ps 30:12 you took off my s and clothed me
Dn 9: 3 petition, with fasting, s, and ashes.
Jl 1:13 spend the night in s, ministers of my
Jon 3: 5 of them, great and small, put on s.
Mt 11:21 would long ago have repented in s
Rev 6:12 the sun turned as black as dark s

SACRED

Ex 28: 2 you shall have s vestments made.
Ex 34:13 smash their s stones, and cut down

SACRIFICE → SACRIFICED, SACRIFICES

Ex 5:17 us go and offer s to the LORD.'
Ex 12:27 'It is the Passover s for the LORD,
1 Sm 2:13 When someone offered a s,
1 Sm 15:22 Obedience is better than s, to listen,
1 Mc 1:47 to s swine and unclean animals,
1 Mc 4:53 offered s according to the law
Ps 40: 7 S and offering you do not want;
Ps 50:14 Offer praise as your s to God;
Ps 51:18 For you do not desire s or I would
Ps 54: 8 I will offer you generous s and give

Prv	15: 8	The s of the wicked is
Prv	21: 3	acceptable to the LORD than s.
Prv	21:27	The s of the wicked is
Dn	8:11	whom the daily s was removed,
Dn	9:27	Half the week he shall abolish s
Dn	11:31	abolishing the daily s and setting
Dn	12:11	the time that the daily s is abolished
Hos	6: 6	not s, and knowledge of God rather
Mt	9:13	of the words, 'I desire mercy, not s.'
1 Cor	10:20	I mean that what they s, [they s] to demons,
Phil	4:18	an acceptable s, pleasing to God.
Heb	9:26	of the ages to take away sin by his s.
Heb	11: 4	to God a s greater than Cain's.
Heb	13:15	let us continually offer God a s

SACRIFICED → SACRIFICE

Ex	40:29	s burnt offerings and grain offerings on it,
1 Sm	13: 9	Then he s the burnt offering.
Acts	15:29	to abstain from meat s to idols,
1 Cor	5: 7	paschal lamb, Christ, has been s.
1 Cor	8: 1	Now in regard to meat s to idols:
Rev	2:14	to eat food s to idols and to play
Rev	2:20	the harlot and to eat food s to idols.

SACRIFICES → SACRIFICE

Ex	22:19	Whoever s to any god,
2 Chr	7: 1	the burnt offerings and the s,
Ezr	6: 3	to be rebuilt as a place for offering s
Ps	50: 8	Not for your s do I rebuke you,
Sir	35: 2	the commandments s a peace
Is	1:11	I care for the multitude of your s?
Is	56: 7	and their s will be acceptable on my
Jer	6:20	with me, your s do not please me.
Am	5:25	Did you bring me s and grain
Mk	12:33	than all burnt offerings and s."
Heb	9:23	themselves by better s than these.
Heb	13:16	God is pleased by s of that kind.
1 Pt	2: 5	to offer spiritual s acceptable to God

SAD

Neh	2: 1	Because I had never before been s
Lk	18:23	he heard this he became quite s,

SADDUCEES

Mt	16: 1	The Pharisees and S came and,
Mt	16: 6	the leaven of the Pharisees and S."
Mt	22:34	heard that he had silenced the S,
Mk	12:18	Some S, who say there is no
Acts	23: 7	out between the Pharisees and S,

SAFE → SAFEGUARD, SAFETY

Ezr	8:21	from him a s journey for ourselves,
Prv	18:10	the just run to it and are s.
Prv	28:18	Whoever walks blamelessly is s,

SAFEGUARD → GUARD, SAFE

Phil	3: 1	no burden for me but is a s for you.

SAFETY → SAFE

Is	14:30	graze, and the needy lie down in s;

SAKE

1 Sm	12:22	For the s of his own great name
1 Kgs	11:12	for the s of David your father;
Ps	23: 3	right paths for the s of his name.
Ps	25:11	For the s of your name, LORD,
Ps	106: 8	for his name's s to make his power
Ps	109:21	kindly with me for your name's s;
Ps	132:10	For the s of David your servant,
Is	43:25	out, for my own s, your offenses;
Is	48: 9	For the s of my name I restrain my
Is	48: 9	the s of my renown I hold it back
Is	48:11	For my s, for my own s, I do this;
Is	62: 1	For Zion's s I will not be silent,
Is	62: 1	Jerusalem's s I will not keep still,
Jer	14:21	for your name's s, do not disgrace
Bar	2:14	and deliver us for your own s:
Ez	20: 9	I acted for the s of my name, that it
Ez	20:14	but I acted for the s of my name,
Ez	20:22	acting for the s of my name, lest it
Ez	36:32	Not for your s do I act—oracle of

Dn	3:34	For your name's s, do not deliver us
Dn	9:17	and for your own s, Lord, let your
Mt	10:39	loses his life for my s will find it.
Mt	19:29	for the s of my name will receive
Mk	13:20	the s of the elect whom he chose,
Rom	8:36	your s we are being slain all
Rom	9: 3	from Christ for the s of my brothers,
Rom	14:20	For the s of food, do not destroy
1 Cor	9:23	All this I do for the s of the gospel,
2 Cor	4:11	given up to death for the s of Jesus,
2 Cor	12:10	and constraints, for the s of Christ;
1 Pt	2:13	human institution for the Lord's s,
3 Jn	1: 7	have set out for the s of the Name

SALE → SELL

Dt	28:68	there you will offer yourselves for s

SALEM → =JERUSALEM

Gn	14:18	king of S, brought out bread
Heb	7: 2	and he was also "king of S,"

SALIVA

Jn	9: 6	ground and made clay with the s,

SALT → SALTED

Gn	19:26	and she was turned into a pillar of s.
2 Kgs	2:20	me a new bowl and put s into it."
Mt	5:13	"You are the s of the earth. But if s loses its taste,
Mk	9:50	S is good, but if s becomes insipid,
Mk	9:50	Keep s in yourselves and you will
Lk	14:34	"S is good, but if s itself loses its taste,
Col	4: 6	seasoned with s, so that you know

SALTED → SALT

Mk	9:49	"Everyone will be s with fire.

SALVATION → SAVE

2 Sm	22:47	Exalted be God, the rock of my s.
1 Chr	16:23	earth, announce his s, day after day.
2 Chr	6:41	will be clothed with s, your faithful
Jb	13:16	This shall be my s: no impious man
Ps	27: 1	The LORD is my light and my s;
Ps	35: 3	Say to my soul, "I am your s."
Ps	37:39	The s of the righteous is
Ps	38:23	to help me, my Lord and my s!
Ps	50:23	steadfast look upon the s of God."
Ps	51:14	to me the gladness of your s;
Ps	53: 7	bring forth from Zion the s of Israel?
Ps	62: 2	God alone, from whom comes my s.
Ps	62: 3	God alone is my rock and s,
Ps	62: 7	God alone is my rock and my s,
Ps	68:20	by day, God, our s, who carries us.
Ps	85: 8	grant us your s.
Ps	85:10	Near indeed is his s for those who
Ps	95: 1	cry out to the rock of our s.
Ps	96: 2	proclaim his s day after day.
Ps	116:13	I will raise the cup of s and call
Ps	119:41	s in accord with your promise.
Ps	119:81	My soul longs for your s; I put my
Ps	119:123	My eyes long to see your s
Ps	119:155	S is far from sinners because they
Ps	119:166	I look for your s, LORD, and I
Ps	119:174	I long for your s, LORD;
Wis	5: 2	and be amazed at the unexpected s.
Is	12: 3	draw water from the fountains of s,
Is	33: 2	morning, our s in time of trouble!
Is	45: 8	Let the earth open and s bud forth;
Is	46:13	it is not far off, my s shall not tarry;
Is	46:13	I will put s within Zion,
Is	49: 6	that my s may reach to the ends
Is	49: 8	you, on the day of s I help you;
Is	51: 5	my s shall go forth and my arm
Is	51: 6	My s shall remain forever and my
Is	51: 8	forever, my s, for all generations.
Is	52: 7	news, announcing s, saying to Zion,
Is	52:10	the earth can see the s of our God.
Is	56: 1	is just, for my s is about to come,
Is	59:11	for s, but it is far from us.
Is	60:18	You shall call your walls "S"
Is	61:10	has clothed me with garments of s,

Jer	3:23	in the LORD our God is Israel's s.
Bar	4:24	so shall they soon see God's s come
Mk	16: S	[proclamation of eternal s. Amen.]
Lk	1:77	of s through the forgiveness of their
Lk	2:30	for my eyes have seen your s,
Lk	3: 6	all flesh shall see the s of God.' "
Lk	19: 9	"Today s has come to this house
Jn	4:22	because s is from the Jews.
Acts	4:12	There is no s through anyone else,
Acts	13:26	to us this word of s has been sent.
Acts	13:47	you may be an instrument of s
Acts	16:17	who proclaim to you a way of s."
Acts	28:28	you that this s of God has been sent
Rom	1:16	for the s of everyone who believes:
Rom	11:11	their transgression s has come
Rom	13:11	For our s is nearer now than
2 Cor	1: 6	it is for your encouragement and s;
2 Cor	6: 2	and on the day of s I helped you."
2 Cor	6: 2	behold, now is the day of s.
Eph	1:13	truth, the gospel of your s, and have
Eph	6:17	take the helmet of s and the sword
Phil	1:28	them of destruction, but of your s.
Phil	2:12	work out your s with fear
1 Thes	5: 8	and the helmet that is hope for s.
1 Thes	5: 9	but to gain s through our Lord Jesus
2 Thes	2:13	for s through sanctification
2 Tm	2:10	that they too may obtain the s that is
2 Tm	3:15	you wisdom for s through faith
Heb	1:14	sake of those who are to inherit s?
Heb	2: 3	we escape if we ignore so great a s?
Heb	2:10	to their s perfect through suffering.
Heb	5: 9	of eternal s for all who obey him,
Heb	6: 9	of better things related to s,
1 Pt	1: 5	to a s that is ready to be revealed
1 Pt	1: 9	of [your] faith, the s of your souls.
1 Pt	1:10	Concerning this s, prophets who
1 Pt	2: 2	that through it you may grow into s,
2 Pt	3:15	the patience of our Lord as s, as our
Jude	1: 3	to write to you about our common s,
Rev	7:10	"S comes from our God, who is
Rev	12:10	"Now have s and power come,
Rev	19: 1	S, glory, and might belong to our

SAMARIA → SAMARITAN, SAMARITANS, SHEMER

1 Kgs	16:24	then bought the mountain of S
1 Kgs	16:24	the mountain the city he named S,
1 Kgs	16:32	house of Baal which he built in S,
1 Kgs	20:43	set off for home and entered S.
2 Kgs	17: 6	the king of Assyria took S,
Is	36:19	Where are the gods of S?
Is	36:19	Have they saved S from my power?
Ez	23: 4	S was Oholah and Jerusalem,
Hos	8: 5	He has rejected your calf, S!
Am	6: 1	secure on the mount of S,
Mi	1: 6	So I will make S a ruin in the field,
Jn	4: 4	He had to pass through S.
Acts	1: 8	throughout Judea and S,
Acts	8: 1	the countryside of Judea and S,
Acts	8:14	heard that S had accepted the word

SAMARITAN → SAMARIA

Lk	10:33	But a S traveler who came upon him
Lk	17:16	Jesus and thanked him. He was a S.
Jn	8:48	not right in saying that you are a S
Acts	8:25	the good news to many S villages.

SAMARITANS → SAMARIA

Jn	4: 9	use nothing in common with S.)

SAME

Ex	5: 8	them the s quota of bricks as they
Ex	7:22	the Egyptian magicians did the s
Ex	8: 3	But the magicians did the s by their
Dt	7:19	The s also will he do to all
1 Sm	2:34	Both of them will die on the s day.
Ps	102:28	but you are the s, your years have
Sir	42:21	he is from all eternity one and the s,
Acts	1:11	in the s way as you have seen him
Acts	11:17	God gave them the s gift he gave

Rom	2: 1	you, the judge, do the very s things.
Rom	10:12	the s Lord is Lord of all,
Rom	12: 4	the parts do not have the s function,
1 Cor	10: 3	All ate the s spiritual food,
1 Cor	12: 4	of spiritual gifts but the s Spirit;
1 Cor	12: 5	forms of service but the s Lord;
Phil	2: 5	among yourselves the s attitude
Heb	1:12	But you are the s, and your years
Heb	13: 8	Jesus Christ is the s yesterday,

SAMSON

Danite judge. Birth promised (Jgs 13). Married a Philistine, but his wife given away (Jgs 14). Vengeance on the Philistines (Jgs 15). Betrayed by Delilah (Jgs 16:1-22). Death (Jgs 16:23-31). Feats of strength: killed lion (Jgs 14:6), 30 Philistines (Jgs 14:19), 1, 000 Philistines with jawbone (Jgs 15:13-17), carried off gates of Gaza (Jgs 16:3), pushed down temple of Dagon (Jgs 16:25-30; Heb 11:32).

SAMUEL

Ephraimite judge and prophet (Heb 11:32). Birth prayed for (1 Sm 1:10-18). Dedicated to temple by Hannah (1 Sm 1:21-28). Raised by Eli (1 Sm 2:11, 18-26). Called as prophet (1 Sm 3). Led Israel to victory over Philistines (1 Sm 7). Asked by Israel for a king (1 Sm 8). Anointed Saul as king (1 Sm 9–10). Farewell speech (1 Sm 12). Rebuked Saul for sacrifice (1 Sm 13). Announced rejection of Saul (1 Sm 15). Anointed David as king (1 Sm 16). Protected David from Saul (1 Sm 19:18-24). Death (1 Sm 25:1). Returned from dead to condemn Saul (1 Sm 28).

SANBALLAT

Led opposition to Nehemiah's rebuilding of Jerusalem (Neh 2:10, 19; 4; 6).

SANCTIFICATION → SANCTIFY

Rom	6:19	as slaves to righteousness for s.
Rom	6:22	the benefit that you have leads to s,
1 Cor	1:30	as well as righteousness, s,
2 Thes	2:13	for salvation through s by the Spirit

SANCTIFIED → SANCTIFY

1 Chr	15:14	the Levites s themselves to bring
Rom	15:16	be acceptable, s by the holy Spirit.
1 Cor	1: 2	to you who have been s in Christ
1 Cor	6:11	you were s, you were justified

SANCTIFY → SANCTIFICATION, SANCTIFIED

1 Pt	3:15	but s Christ as Lord in your hearts.

SANCTUARIES → SANCTUARY

Lv	26:31	your cities and desolate your s,
Am	7: 9	and the s of Israel made desolate;

SANCTUARY → SANCTUARIES

Ex	15:17	LORD, the s, LORD, your hands
Ex	25: 8	They are to make a s for me, that I
Nm	3:28	who performed the duties of the s.
Nm	18: 1	for any sin with respect to the s;
1 Kgs	6:19	he set up the inner s to house the ark
1 Chr	22:19	to build the s of the LORD God,
1 Mc	1:21	He insolently entered the s and took
1 Mc	4:36	let us go up to purify the s
Ps	60: 8	In the s God promised:
Ps	63: 3	to you in the s to see your power
Ps	73:17	Till I entered the s of God and came
Ps	74: 7	They set your s on fire,
Ps	150: 1	Praise God in his holy s;
Lam	1:10	She has seen the nations enter her s,
Ez	5:11	because you have defiled my s
Ez	37:26	and put my s among them forever.
Dn	8:11	and whose s was cast down.
Dn	9:26	shall destroy the city and the s.
Heb	8: 2	a minister of the s and of the true
Heb	8: 5	copy and shadow of the heavenly s,
Heb	9:24	Christ did not enter into a s made

SAND → SANDS

Ex	2:12	the Egyptian and hid him in the s.
Hos	2: 1	the Israelites will be like the s
Mt	7:26	like a fool who built his house on s.
Rom	9:27	the Israelites were like the s

SANDS → SAND

Gn	22:17	of the sky and the s of the seashore;

Gn	32:13	make your descendants like the s
Gn	41:49	Joseph collected grain like the s
1 Kgs	4:20	Israel were as numerous as the s
Heb	11:12	sky and as countless as the s

SANDAL → SANDALS

Dt	25: 9	to him and strip his s from his foot
Ru	4: 7	one party would take off a s
Jn	1:27	whose s strap I am not worthy

SANDALS → SANDAL

Ex	3: 5	Remove your s from your feet,
Ex	12:11	girt, s on your feet and your staff
Dt	29: 4	in tatters nor your s from your feet;
Jos	5:15	"Remove your s from your feet,
Mt	3:11	I am not worthy to carry his s.

SANG → SING

Ex	15: 1	and the Israelites s this song
Nm	21:17	Then Israel s this song:
Jgs	5: 1	On that day Deborah s this song—
1 Sm	18: 7	The women played and s:
2 Chr	29:30	They s praises till their joy was full,
Jb	38: 7	While the morning stars s together
Ps	106:12	believed his words and s his praise.

SANK → SINK

Jer	38: 6	and Jeremiah s down into the mud.

SAPPHIRA

Acts	5: 1	with his wife S, sold a piece

SAPPHIRE

Ex	24:10	feet there appeared to be s tilework,
Ex	28:18	row, a garnet, a s, and a beryl;
Ez	1:26	of a throne that looked like s;
Ez	10: 1	cherubim was something like a s,
Rev	21:19	the second s, the third chalcedony,

SARAH → =SARAI

Wife of Abraham, originally named Sarai; barren (Gn 11:29-31; 1 Pt 3:6). Taken by Pharaoh as Abraham's sister; returned (Gn 12:10-20). Gave Hagar to Abraham; sent her away in pregnancy (Gn 16). Name changed; Isaac promised (Gn 17:15-21; 18:10-15; Heb 11:11). Taken by Abimelech as Abraham's sister; returned (Gn 20). Isaac born; Hagar and Ishmael sent away (Gn 21:1-21; Gal 4:21-31). Death (Gn 23).

SARAI → =SARAH

Gn	17:15	As for S your wife, do not call her S;

SARDIS

Rev	3: 1	"To the angel of the church in S,

SASH

Ex	28: 4	a brocade tunic, a turban, and a s.
Rev	1:13	robe, with a gold s around his chest.

SAT → SIT

Gn	48: 2	rallied his strength and s up in bed.
1 Kgs	19: 4	solitary broom tree and s beneath it.
Ps	137: 1	Babylon there we s weeping
Mt	5: 1	and after he had s down,
Mt	13: 2	that he got into a boat and s down,
Mt	28: 2	rolled back the stone, and s upon it.
Lk	7:15	The dead man s up and began
Lk	10:39	named Mary [who] s beside
Jn	12:14	Jesus found an ass and s upon it,

SATAN

1 Chr	21: 1	A s rose up against Israel, and he
Jb	1: 6	the s also came among them.
Jb	2: 1	LORD, the s also came with them.
Mt	4:10	Jesus said to him, "Get away, S!
Mt	12:26	And if S drives out S, he is divided
Mt	16:23	said to Peter, "Get behind me, S!
Mk	4:15	S comes at once and takes away
Lk	10:18	said, "I have observed S fall like
Lk	22: 3	Then S entered into Judas, the one
Jn	13:27	he took the morsel, S entered him.
Acts	5: 3	why has S filled your heart so
Acts	26:18	and from the power of S to God,
Rom	16:20	will quickly crush S under your feet.
1 Cor	5: 5	are to deliver this man to S

1 Cor	7: 5	S may not tempt you through your
2 Cor	2:11	not be taken advantage of by S,
2 Cor	11:14	for even S masquerades as an angel
2 Cor	12: 7	to me, an angel of S, to beat me,
2 Thes	2: 9	the power of S in every mighty deed
1 Tm	1:20	whom I have handed over to S to be
1 Tm	5:15	already turned away to follow S.
Rev	2: 9	are members of the assembly of S.
Rev	2:13	martyred among you, where S lives.
Rev	2:24	of the so-called deep secrets of S:
Rev	3: 9	the assembly of S who claim to be
Rev	12: 9	who is called the Devil and S,
Rev	20: 2	which is the Devil or S, and tied it
Rev	20: 7	S will be released from his prison.

SATISFACTION → SATISFY

Ti	2: 9	giving them s, not talking back

SATISFIED → SATISFY

Dt	31:20	eaten and are s and have grown fat,
Ps	107: 9	For he s the thirsty,
Prv	27:20	Sheol and Abaddon can never be s;
Prv	27:20	the eyes of mortals can never be s.
Eccl	5: 9	The covetous are never s
Mi	6:14	without being s, food that will leave

SATISFY → SATISFACTION, SATISFIED

Ps	91:16	With length of days I will s him,
Prv	6:30	hunger they steal to s their appetite.
Is	55: 2	your wages for what does not s?
Is	58:10	on the hungry and s the afflicted;
Mk	15:15	wishing to s the crowd,

SATRAPS

Est	3:12	Haman, an order to the royal s,
Dn	6: 2	kingdom one hundred and twenty s.

SAUL → =PAUL

1. Benjamite; anointed by Samuel as first king of Israel (1 Sm 9–10). Defeated Ammonites (1 Sm 11). Rebuked for offering sacrifice (1 Sm 13:1-15). Defeated Philistines (1 Sm 14). Rejected as king for failing to annihilate Amalekites (1 Sm 15). Soothed from evil spirit by David (1 Sm 16:14-23). Sent David against Goliath (1 Sm 17). Jealousy and attempted murder of David (1 Sm 18:1-11). Gave David Michal as wife (1 Sm 18:12-30). Second attempt to kill David (1 Sm 19). Anger at Jonathan (1 Sm 20:26-34). Pursued David: killed priests at Nob (1 Sm 22), went to Keilah and Ziph (1 Sm 23), life spared by David at En Gedi (1 Sm 24) and in his tent (1 Sm 26). Rebuked by Samuel for consulting witch at Endor (1 Sm 28). Wounded by Philistines; took his own life (1 Sm 31; 1 Chr 10). Lamented by David (2 Sm 1:17-27). Children (1 Sm 14:49-51; 1 Chr 8).

2. See Paul.

SAVAGE

Acts	20:29	my departure s wolves will come

SAVE → SALVATION, SAVED, SAVES, SAVING, SAVIOR, SAVIORS

1 Chr	16:35	And say, "S us, O God, our savior,
Jdt	6: 2	Their God will not s them;
Ps	6: 5	s me because of your mercy.
Ps	28: 9	S your people, bless your
Ps	31:17	s me in your mercy.
Ps	54: 3	O God, by your name s me.
Ps	71: 2	listen to me and s me!
Ps	86: 2	s your servant who trusts in you.
Ps	119:94	s me, for I cherish your precepts.
Is	33:22	is our king; he it is who will s us.
Is	35: 4	recompense he comes to s you.
Is	36:20	that the LORD should s Jerusalem
Is	45:20	idols and pray to gods that cannot s.
Is	59: 1	of the LORD is not too short to s,
Is	63: 1	announce vindication, mighty to s."
Jer	17:14	s me, that I may be saved, for you
Lam	4:17	watched for a nation unable to s.
Ez	7:19	gold cannot s them on the day
Ez	14:14	they could only s themselves
Ez	33:12	the just cannot s their lives
Ez	34:22	I will s my flock so they can no
Hos	1: 7	I will s them by the LORD,
Hos	1: 7	but I will not s them by bow

Zep	1:18	nor their gold will be able to s them.
Mt	1:21	because he will s his people
Mt	16:25	wishes to s his life will lose it,
Mt	27:42	he cannot s himself.
Lk	6: 9	to s life rather than to destroy it?"
Lk	19:10	to seek and to s what was lost."
Lk	23:37	are King of the Jews, s yourself."
Jn	12:27	'Father, s me from this hour'?
Jn	12:47	the world but to s the world.
Acts	2:40	"S yourselves from this corrupt
Rom	11:14	jealous and thus s some of them.
1 Cor	7:16	whether you will s your husband;
1 Cor	7:16	whether you will s your wife?
1 Cor	9:22	all things to all, to s at least some.
1 Tm	1:15	came into the world to s sinners.
Heb	7:25	s those who approach God through
Jas	2:14	Can that faith s him?
Jas	5:20	of his way will s his soul from death
Jude	1:23	s others by snatching them

SAVED → SAVE

Ex	14:30	Thus the LORD s Israel
2 Chr	32:22	Thus the LORD s Hezekiah
Est	F: 6	Israel, who cried to God and was s. "The Lord s his people
1 Mc	2:59	for their faith, were s from the fire.
Ps	33:16	A king is not s by a great army,
Ps	34: 7	and from all his distress he s him.
Ps	106: 8	Yet he s them for his name's sake
Ps	116: 6	I was helpless, but he s me.
Is	45:17	Israel has been s by the LORD,
Jer	4:14	evil, Jerusalem, that you may be s.
Jer	17:14	me, that I may be s, for you are my
Dn	3:88	and s us from the power of death;
Mt	10:22	endures to the end will be s.
Mt	19:25	and said, "Who then can be s?"
Mt	24:13	who perseveres to the end will be s.
Mk	15:31	themselves and said, "He s others;
Lk	7:50	the woman, "Your faith has s you;
Lk	13:23	will only a few people be s?"
Jn	10: 9	enters through me will be s, and will
Acts	2:21	everyone shall be s who calls
Acts	2:47	number those who were being s.
Acts	4:12	race by which we are to be s."
Acts	15:11	that we are s through the grace
Acts	16:30	"Sirs, what must I do to be s?"
Rom	5: 9	will we be s through him
Rom	8:24	For in hope we were s.
Rom	9:27	of the sea, only a remnant will be s;
Rom	10: 9	him from the dead, you will be s.
Rom	10:13	on the name of the Lord will be s."
Rom	11:26	and thus all Israel will be s, as it is
1 Cor	1:18	to us who are being s it is the power
1 Cor	3:15	the person will be s, but only as
1 Cor	5: 5	so that his spirit may be s on the day
1 Cor	10:33	that of the many, that they may be s.
1 Cor	15: 2	Through it you are also being s,
Eph	2: 5	Christ (by grace you have been s),
Eph	2: 8	grace you have been s through faith,
2 Thes	2:10	love of truth so that they may be s.
1 Tm	2: 4	who wills everyone to be s
1 Tm	2:15	she will be s through motherhood,
2 Tm	1: 9	He s us and called us to a holy life,
Ti	3: 5	he s us through the bath of rebirth
1 Pt	4:18	if the righteous one is barely s,

SAVES → SAVE

Ps	34:19	s those whose spirit is crushed.
Prv	14:25	The truthful witness s lives,
Sir	2:11	sins and s in time of trouble.
Sir	51: 8	For he s those who take refuge
Dn	13:60	blessing God who s those who hope
1 Pt	3:21	baptism, which s you now. It is not

SAVING → SAVE

2 Sm	22: 3	My shield, my s horn, my stronghold,
Ps	7:11	a shield above me s the upright of heart.
Ps	78:22	in God, did not trust in his s power.

SAVIOR → SAVE

2 Sm	22: 3	my s, from violence you keep me
2 Kgs	13: 5	So the LORD gave Israel a s,
Jdt	9:11	in despair, s of those without hope.
Est	D: 2	invoking the all-seeing God and s,
Est	E:13	our s and constant benefactor,
1 Mc	4:30	"Blessed are you, S of Israel,
1 Mc	9:21	one has fallen, the s of Israel!"
Wis	16: 7	was seen, but by you, the s of all.
Sir	46: 1	the great s of God's chosen ones,
Sir	51: 1	and King, I praise you, God my s!
Is	19:20	he will send them a s to defend
Is	43: 3	God, the Holy One of Israel, your s.
Is	43:11	there is no s but me.
Is	45:15	is hidden, the God of Israel, the s!
Is	49:26	LORD, am your s, your redeemer,
Is	60:16	LORD, am your s, your redeemer,
Is	63: 8	So he became their s
Jer	14: 8	LORD, our s in time of need!
Bar	4:22	reach you from your eternal S.
Hos	13: 4	do not know; there is no s but me.
Lk	1:47	my spirit rejoices in God my s.
Lk	2:11	the city of David a s has been born
Jn	4:42	that this is truly the s of the world."
Acts	5:31	and s to grant Israel repentance
Acts	13:23	has brought to Israel a s, Jesus.
Eph	5:23	church, he himself the s of the body.
Phil	3:20	and from it we also await a s,
1 Tm	1: 1	Jesus by command of God our s
1 Tm	2: 3	is good and pleasing to God our s,
1 Tm	4:10	the living God, who is the s of all,
2 Tm	1:10	the appearance of our s Christ Jesus,
Ti	1: 3	by the command of God our s,
Ti	1: 4	the Father and Christ Jesus our s.
Ti	2:10	doctrine of God our s in every way.
Ti	2:13	great God and of our s Jesus Christ,
Ti	3: 4	love of God our s appeared,
Ti	3: 6	out on us through Jesus Christ our s,
2 Pt	1: 1	of our God and s Jesus Christ:
2 Pt	1:11	and s Jesus Christ will be richly
2 Pt	2:20	of [our] Lord and s Jesus Christ,
2 Pt	3: 2	Lord and s through your apostles.
2 Pt	3:18	of our Lord and s Jesus Christ.
1 Jn	4:14	the Father sent his Son as s
Jude	1:25	our s, through Jesus Christ our Lord

SAVIORS → SAVE

Neh	9:27	to your great mercy give them s

SAW → SEE

Gn	1: 4	God s that the light was good.
Gn	3: 6	The woman s that the tree was good
Gn	6: 2	God s how beautiful the daughters
Gn	6:12	God s how corrupt the earth had
Ex	2:11	he s an Egyptian striking a Hebrew,
Nm	22:23	the donkey s the angel
Dt	4:15	Because you s no form at all
Dt	32:19	The LORD s and was filled
2 Sm	11: 2	the roof he s a woman bathing;
Ps	73: 3	the arrogant when I s the prosperity
Eccl	2:13	I s that wisdom has as much profit
Is	6: 1	I s the Lord seated on a high
Ez	1: 1	opened, and I s divine visions.—
Dn	8: 2	my vision I s myself in the fortress
Dn	10: 7	I alone, Daniel, s the vision;
Am	9: 1	I s the Lord standing beside
Mt	3:16	he s the Spirit of God descending
Mt	9: 2	When Jesus s their faith, he said
Mk	1:10	of the water he s the heavens being
Mk	3:11	whenever unclean spirits s him they
Lk	9:32	they s his glory and the two men
Jn	1:29	next day he s Jesus coming toward
Jn	20: 1	s the stone removed from the tomb.
Jn	20: 8	tomb first, and he s and believed.
Acts	7:55	to heaven and s the glory of God
Acts	10:11	He s heaven opened and something
Rev	1: 2	Jesus Christ by reporting what he s.

Rev 1:12 I turned, I **s** seven gold lampstands
Rev 5: 6 Then I **s** standing in the midst
Rev 21: 1 Then I **s** a new heaven and a new
Rev 21:22 I **s** no temple in the city, for its
Rev 22: 8 who heard and **s** these things,
Rev 22: 8 **s** them I fell down to worship

SAWED
Heb 11:37 They were stoned, **s** in two,

SAY → SAYING, SAYINGS, SAYS
Gn 12:19 Why did you **s**, 'She is my sister,'
Gn 18:13 "Why did Sarah laugh and **s**,
Sir 11:23 Do not **s**: "What do I need?
Mt 10:19 are to speak or what you are to **s**.
Mt 10:19 at that moment what you are to **s**.
Mt 16:15 "But who do you **s** that I am?"
Mk 2: 9 Which is easier, to **s** to the paralytic,
Mk 2: 9 sins are forgiven,' or to **s**, 'Rise,
Mk 8:27 "Who do people **s** that I am?"
Lk 11:54 catch him at something he might **s**.
Jn 8:26 I have much to **s** about you
Jn 12:49 sent me commanded me what to **s**
1 Cor 15:12 can some among you **s** there is no
Rev 22:17 The Spirit and the bride **s**, "Come."
Rev 22:17 Let the hearer **s**, "Come."

SAYING → SAY
Jn 8:43 do you not understand what I am **s**?
1 Tm 1:15 This **s** is trustworthy and deserves
1 Tm 3: 1 This **s** is trustworthy:
1 Tm 4: 9 This **s** is trustworthy and deserves
2 Tm 2:11 This **s** is trustworthy: If we have
Ti 3: 8 This **s** is trustworthy. I want you

SAYINGS → SAY
Eccl 12:11 The **s** of the wise are like goads;

SAYS → SAY
1 Sm 9: 6 everything he **s** comes true.
Ps 110: 1 The LORD **s** to my lord:
Eccl 1: 2 Vanity of vanities, **s** Qoheleth,
Eccl 12: 8 Vanity of vanities, **s** Qoheleth,
Rom 3:19 what the law **s** is addressed to those
1 Tm 4: 1 Now the Spirit explicitly **s**

SCABBARD
Jer 47: 6 Return to your **s**; stop, be still!

SCALES
Ex 4: 6 his hand covered with **s**, like snowflakes.
Tb 2:10 in my eyes, causing white **s** on them.
Tb 11:13 used both hands to peel the white **s** from
Prv 16:11 and **s** belong to the LORD;
Dn 5:27 you have been weighed on the **s**
Acts 9:18 Immediately things like **s** fell

SCARLET
Is 1:18 Though your sins be like **s**,
Mt 27:28 threw a **s** military cloak about him.
Rev 17: 3 I saw a woman seated on a **s** beast

SCATTER → SCATTERED, SCATTERS
Dt 4:27 The LORD will **s** you among
Neh 1: 8 I will **s** you among the peoples;
Ps 89:11 with your strong arm you **s** your foes.
Jer 9:15 I will **s** them among nations whom
Bar 2:29 the nations to which I will **s** them.

SCATTERED → SCATTER
Gn 11: 4 otherwise we shall be **s** all over
Nm 10:35 may your enemies be **s**, and may
Dt 30: 3 the LORD, your God, has **s** you.
2 Chr 18:16 "I see all Israel **s** on the mountains,
Tb 13: 5 among whom you have been **s**.
Jer 31:10 The One who **s** Israel, now gathers
Ez 34:12 he himself is among his **s** sheep,
Ez 34:12 every place where they were **s**
Zec 2: 2 "Those are the horns that **s** Judah,
Acts 8: 1 and all were **s** throughout
Acts 8: 4 Now those who had been **s** went

SCATTERS → SCATTER
Mt 12:30 whoever does not gather with me **s**.
Jn 10:12 and the wolf catches and **s** them.

SCEPTER
Gn 49:10 The **s** shall never depart from Judah,
Est 4:11 extends the golden **s** will such
Ps 45: 7 your royal **s** is a **s** for justice.
Ps 125: 3 The **s** of the wicked will not prevail
Heb 1: 8 and a righteous **s** is the **s** of your kingdom.

SCHEMES → SCHEMING
Ps 10: 2 they trap them by their cunning **s**.

SCHEMING → SCHEMES
Eph 4:14 in the interests of deceitful **s**.

SCOFFER → SCOFFERS
Prv 21:24 Proud, boastful—**s** is the name:

SCOFFERS → SCOFFER
Ps 1: 1 sinners, nor sit in company with **s**.
2 Pt 3: 3 the last days **s** will come [to] scoff,

SCORCHED → SCORCHING
Mk 4: 6 it was **s** and it withered for lack

SCORCHING → SCORCHED
Jas 1:11 For the sun comes up with its **s** heat

SCORNED
Ps 22: 7 not a man, **s** by men,

SCORPION → SCORPIONS
Lk 11:12 Or hand him a **s** when he asks
Rev 9: 5 that of a **s** when it stings a person.

SCORPIONS → SCORPION
1 Kgs 12:11 but I will beat you with **s**.' "
Rev 9:10 They had tails like **s**, with stingers;

SCOUNDRELS
1 Kgs 21:10 set two **s** opposite him to accuse

SCOURGE → SCOURGED
Mt 10:17 and **s** you in their synagogues,
Mk 10:34 spit upon him, **s** him, and put him
Acts 22:25 to **s** a man who is a Roman citizen

SCOURGED → SCOURGE
Jn 19: 1 Pilate took Jesus and had him **s**.

SCRIBE → SCRIBES
Neh 8: 1 Ezra the **s** to bring forth the book
Neh 12:36 Ezra the **s** was at their head.
Mk 12:32 The **s** said to him, "Well said,

SCRIBES → SCRIBE
Mt 7:29 having authority, and not as their **s**.
Mt 23:13 "Woe to you, **s** and Pharisees,
Mk 12:38 "Beware of the **s**, who like to go
Acts 4: 5 and **s** were assembled in Jerusalem,

SCRIPTURE → SCRIPTURES
Mk 12:10 Have you not read this **s** passage:
Lk 4:21 "Today this **s** passage is fulfilled
Jn 2:22 they came to believe the **s**
Jn 7:42 Does not **s** say that the Messiah will
Jn 10:35 came, and **s** cannot be set aside,
Acts 1:16 the **s** had to be fulfilled
Acts 8:32 This was the **s** passage he was
2 Tm 3:16 All **s** is inspired by God and is
2 Pt 1:20 there is no prophecy of **s** that is

SCRIPTURES → SCRIPTURE
Mt 22:29 because you do not know the **s**
Mk 14:49 but that the **s** may be fulfilled."
Lk 24:27 what referred to him in all the **s**.
Lk 24:45 their minds to understand the **s**.
Jn 5:39 You search the **s**, because you think
Acts 17:11 examined the **s** daily to determine
Acts 18:28 from the **s** that the Messiah is Jesus.
1 Cor 15: 3 our sins in accordance with the **s**;
1 Cor 15: 4 third day in accordance with the **s**;
2 Pt 3:16 just as they do the other **s**.

SCROLL

Dt	31:24	out on a **s** the words of this law
1 Mc	1:57	was found with a **s** of the covenant,
Ps	40: 8	with an inscribed **s** written upon me.
Is	34: 4	heavens shall be rolled up like a **s**.
Jer	36: 4	down on a **s** what Jeremiah said,
Bar	1:14	the LORD this **s** that we send you:
Ez	3: 1	eat this **s**, then go,
Zec	5: 1	my eyes again and saw a flying **s**.
Lk	4:17	and was handed a **s** of the prophet
Lk	4:17	He unrolled the **s** and found
Heb	10: 7	I said, 'As is written of me in the **s**,
Rev	1:11	"Write on a **s** what you see
Rev	5: 2	"Who is worthy to open the **s**
Rev	6:14	was divided like a torn **s** curling up,
Rev	10: 8	take the **s** that lies open in the hand

SEA → SEAS, SEASHORE

Gn	1:26	dominion over the fish of the **s**,
Gn	32:13	descendants like the sands of the **s**,
Gn	41:49	grain like the sands of the **s**,
Ex	14:16	the Israelites may pass through the **s**
Ex	14:27	stretched out his hand over the **s**,
Ex	14:27	Egyptians into the midst of the **s**.
Ex	15: 1	and chariot he has cast into the **s**.
Nm	11:31	that drove in quail from the **s**
Nm	34: 6	boundary you will have the Great **S**
Dt	11:24	Euphrates River to the Western **S**,
Dt	30:13	Nor is it across the **s**, that you
Dt	30:13	"Who will cross the **s** to get it
1 Kgs	7:23	Then he made the molten **s**;
2 Kgs	25:13	and the bronze **s** in the house
Neh	9:11	The **s** you divided before them,
Neh	9:11	passed through the midst of the **s**;
Jb	11: 9	in measure, and broader than the **s**.
Ps	46: 3	quake to the depths of the **s**,
Ps	74:13	You stirred up the **s** by your might;
Ps	93: 4	powerful than the breakers of the **s**,
Ps	95: 5	The **s** and dry land belong to God,
Ps	106: 7	defied the Most High at the Red **S**.
Ps	139: 9	of dawn and dwell beyond the **s**,
Eccl	1: 7	All rivers flow to the **s**, yet never does the **s** become full.
Is	10:22	were like the sand of the **s**,
Is	48:18	vindication like the waves of the **s**,
Is	57:20	But the wicked are like the tossing **s**
Bar	3:30	Who has crossed the **s** and found
Jon	1: 4	hurled a great wind upon the **s**,
Jon	2: 4	into the heart of the **s**, and the flood
Mi	7:19	into the depths of the **s** all our sins;
Hb	2:14	glory, just as the water covers the **s**.
Zec	9:10	His dominion will be from **s** to **s**,
Mt	18: 6	to be drowned in the depths of the **s**.
Mk	11:23	'Be lifted up and thrown into the **s**,'
1 Cor	10: 1	cloud and all passed through the **s**,
Heb	11:29	faith they crossed the Red **S** as if it
Jas	1: 6	is like a wave of the **s** that is driven
Jude	1:13	They are like wild waves of the **s**,
Rev	4: 6	resembled a **s** of glass like crystal.
Rev	8: 8	mountain was hurled into the **s**. A third of the **s** turned to blood,
Rev	10: 2	He placed his right foot on the **s**
Rev	12:18	its position on the sand of the **s**,
Rev	13: 1	come out of the **s** with ten horns
Rev	15: 2	I saw something like a **s** of glass
Rev	15: 2	the **s** of glass were standing those
Rev	20:13	The **s** gave up its dead;
Rev	21: 1	away, and the **s** was no more.

SEAL → SEALED, SEALS

Est	8: 8	and **s** the letter with the royal signet
Sg	8: 6	Set me as a **s** upon your heart, as a **s**
Sir	22:27	mouth, an effective **s** on my lips,
Is	8:16	**s** the instruction with my disciples.
Mt	27:66	the tomb by fixing a **s** to the stone
Jn	6:27	him the Father, God, has set his **s**."
1 Cor	9: 2	for you are the **s** of my apostleship
2 Cor	1:22	he has also put his **s** upon us

Rev	6: 3	When he broke open the second **s**,
Rev	6: 5	When he broke open the third **s**,
Rev	6: 7	When he broke open the fourth **s**,
Rev	6: 9	When he broke open the fifth **s**,
Rev	6:12	while he broke open the sixth **s**,
Rev	7: 2	holding the **s** of the living God.
Rev	7: 3	or the trees until we put the **s**
Rev	8: 1	When he broke open the seventh **s**,
Rev	9: 4	those people who did not have the **s**
Rev	10: 4	"**S** up what the seven thunders have
Rev	22:10	"Do not **s** up the prophetic words

SEALED → SEAL

Is	29:11	become like the words of a **s** scroll.
Is	29:11	reply is, "I cannot, because it is **s**."
Dn	6:18	the king **s** with his own ring
Dn	12: 9	kept secret and **s** until the end time.
Eph	1:13	him, were **s** with the promised holy
Rev	5: 1	sides and was **s** with seven seals.
Rev	20: 3	which he locked over it and **s**,

SEALS → SEAL

Rev	5: 2	to open the scroll and break its **s**?"
Rev	6: 1	broke open the first of the seven **s**,

SEAMLESS

Jn	19:23	but the tunic was **s**, woven in one

SEARCH → SEARCHED, SEARCHER, SEARCHES, SEARCHING

Dt	4:29	indeed find him if you **s** after him
1 Chr	28: 9	If you **s** for him, he will be found;
Ezr	5:17	let a **s** be made in the royal archives
Prv	2: 4	and like hidden treasures **s** her out,
Mt	2: 8	"Go and **s** diligently for the child.

SEARCHED → SEARCH

Jb	5:27	See, this we have **s** out; so it is!

SEARCHER → SEARCH

Prv	24:12	Surely, the **S** of hearts knows and

SEARCHES → SEARCH

1 Chr	28: 9	soul, for the LORD **s** all hearts
Rom	8:27	the one who **s** hearts knows what is

SEARCHING → SEARCH

Lk	15: 8	house, **s** carefully until she finds it?

SEAS → SEA

Ps	65: 8	You still the roaring of the **s**,

SEASHORE → SEA, SHORE

Gn	22:17	of the sky and the sands of the **s**;
Jos	11: 4	numerous as the sands on the **s**,
1 Kgs	5: 9	as vast as the sand on the **s**.
Heb	11:12	as countless as the sands on the **s**.

SEASON → SEASONED, SEASONS

Dt	28:12	to give your land rain in due **s**
Ps	1: 3	of water, that yields its fruit in **s**;

SEASONED → SEASON

Col	4: 6	always be gracious, **s** with salt,

SEASONS → SEASON

Ps	104:19	You made the moon to mark the **s**,
Gal	4:10	days, months, **s**, and years.
1 Thes	5: 1	Concerning times and **s**, brothers,

SEAT → SEATED

Mt	23: 2	the Pharisees have taken their **s**
Rom	14:10	shall all stand before the judgment **s**
2 Cor	5:10	all appear before the judgment **s**

SEATED → SEAT

Lk	22:69	of Man will be **s** at the right hand
Eph	2: 6	and **s** us with him in the heavens
Col	3: 1	where Christ is **s** at the right hand

SECLUSION

Lk	1:24	and she went into **s** for five months,

SECOND → TWO

Ex	4: 8	believe the message of the **s** sign.
Nm	9:11	you shall celebrate it in the **s** month,
1 Kgs	9: 2	appeared to Solomon a **s** time, as he

Ez	10:14	first a cherub, the **s** a human being,
Dn	7: 5	The **s** beast was like a bear;
Jon	3: 1	the LORD came to Jonah a **s** time:
Hg	2:20	the LORD came a **s** time to Haggai
Mt	22:39	The **s** is like it: You shall love your
1 Cor	12:28	to be, first, apostles; **s**, prophets;
1 Cor	15:47	the **s** man, from heaven.
Ti	3:10	After a first and **s** warning,
Heb	9:28	will appear a **s** time, not to take
Rev	2:11	not be harmed by the **s** death." '
Rev	4: 7	a lion, the **s** was like a calf, the third
Rev	6: 3	When he broke open the **s** seal,
Rev	6: 3	I heard the **s** living creature cry out,
Rev	8: 8	When the **s** angel blew his trumpet,
Rev	11:14	The **s** woe has passed, but the third
Rev	16: 3	The **s** angel poured out his bowl
Rev	20: 6	The **s** death has no power over
Rev	20:14	(This pool of fire is the **s** death.
Rev	21: 8	and sulfur, which is the **s** death."

SECRET → SECRETLY, SECRETS

Ps	139:15	you, When I was being made in **s**,
Prv	21:14	A **s** gift allays anger, and a present
Jer	23:24	hide in **s** without my seeing them?—
Mt	6: 4	so that your almsgiving may be **s**.
Mt	6: 4	Father who sees in **s** will repay you.
Mt	6: 6	door, and pray to your Father in **s**.
Mt	6: 6	Father who sees in **s** will repay you.
Jn	18:20	gather, and in **s** I have said nothing.
Phil	4:12	in all things I have learned the **s**

SECRETLY → SECRET

Dt	13: 7	your intimate friend entices you **s**,
Ps	51: 8	true sincerity; and **s** you teach me wisdom.
Mt	2: 7	Then Herod called the magi **s**

SECRETS → SECRET

Ps	44:22	God who knows the **s** of the heart?
Prv	11:13	One who slanders reveals **s**,
1 Cor	14:25	the **s** of his heart will be disclosed,

SECT

Acts	24: 5	ringleader of the **s** of the Nazoreans.

SECURE → SECURELY, SECURITY

Ps	16: 9	my body also dwells **s**,

SECURELY → SECURE

Prv	10: 9	Whoever walks honestly walks **s**,

SECURITY → SECURE

Ps	40: 5	Blessed the man who sets his **s** in the LORD,
1 Thes	5: 3	"Peace and **s**," then sudden disaster

SEDUCES

Ex	22:15	When a man **s** a virgin who is not

SEE → FORESAW, SAW, SEEING, SEEN, SEER, SEERS, SEES, SIGHT

Gn	2:19	man to **s** what he would call them;
Gn	8: 8	to **s** if the waters had lessened
Gn	9:16	clouds, I will **s** it and remember
Gn	13:15	all the land that you **s** I will give
Ex	14:13	**s** the victory the LORD will win
Ex	14:13	Egyptians whom you **s** today you **s** today you will never **s** again.
Ex	33:20	But you cannot **s** my face, for no one can **s** me and live.
Nm	14:23	not one shall **s** the land which I
Nm	14:23	who have spurned me shall **s** it.
Tb	2:10	For four years I was unable to **s**,
Tb	11: 8	again and will **s** the light of day."
Jb	19:26	off, and from my flesh I will **s** God:
Ps	16:10	nor let your devout one **s** the pit.
Ps	115: 5	but do not speak, eyes but do not **s**.
Is	40: 5	and all flesh shall **s** it together;
Is	53:10	offering, he shall **s** his offspring,
Is	53:11	of his anguish he shall **s** the light;
Ez	8:12	"The LORD cannot **s** us;
Dn	3:92	"I **s** four men unbound and unhurt,
Jl	3: 1	your young men will **s** visions.
Mi	7: 9	I will **s** his righteousness.
Mt	5: 8	clean of heart, for they will **s** God.

Mt	7: 5	you will **s** clearly to remove
Mt	13:16	eyes, because they **s**, and your ears,
Mk	8:18	Do you have eyes and not **s**,
Mk	14:62	'you will **s** the Son of Man seated
Lk	3: 6	and all flesh shall **s** the salvation
Jn	9:25	is that I was blind and now I **s**."
Jn	14:19	while the world will no longer **s** me,
Jn	14:19	but you will **s** me, because I live
Jn	16:16	while and you will no longer **s** me,
Jn	16:16	little while later and you will **s** me."
Acts	2:17	your young men shall **s** visions,
1 Cor	13:12	At present we **s** indistinctly,
2 Cor	13: 5	to **s** whether you are living in faith.
Heb	12:14	which no one will **s** the Lord.
1 Jn	3: 2	like him, for we shall **s** him as he is.
Rev	1: 7	and every eye will **s** him, even those

SEED → SEEDS, SEEDTIME

Gn	1:11	every kind of plant that bears **s**
Gn	1:11	earth that bears fruit with its **s** in it.
Eccl	11: 6	In the morning sow your **s**,
Is	55:10	Giving **s** to the one who sows
Mt	13:31	of heaven is like a mustard **s**
Mt	17:20	have faith the size of a mustard **s**,
Mk	4:31	It is like a mustard **s** that, when it is
Lk	8:11	The **s** is the word of God.
2 Cor	9:10	The one who supplies **s** to the sower
2 Cor	9:10	and multiply your **s** and increase
1 Pt	1:23	perishable but from imperishable **s**,
1 Jn	3: 9	because God's **s** remains in him;

SEEDS → SEED

Mk	4:31	the smallest of all the **s** on the earth.

SEEDTIME → SEED

Gn	8:22	the days of the earth, **s** and harvest,

SEEING → SEE

Ex	12:13	**S** the blood, I will pass over you;

SEEK → SEEKING, SEEKS, SOUGHT

Dt	4:29	Yet when you **s** the LORD,
2 Chr	7:14	and **s** my face and turn from their
2 Chr	15: 2	and if you **s** him he will be found;
Ps	9:11	you never forsake those who **s** you,
Ps	34:11	but those who **s** the LORD lack no
Ps	105: 3	let hearts that **s** the LORD rejoice!
Ps	105: 4	**S** out the LORD and his might; constantly **s** his face.
Ps	119: 2	who **s** him with all their heart.
Ps	119:10	With all my heart I **s** you; do not let
Ps	119:176	**s** out your servant, for I do not
Prv	8:17	love, and those who **s** me find me.
Prv	11:27	Those who **s** the good **s** favor,
Prv	25:27	nor to **s** honor after honor.
Prv	28: 5	those who **s** the LORD understand
Sir	2:16	Those who fear the Lord **s** to please
Sir	51:26	she is close to those who **s** her,
Is	55: 6	**S** the LORD while he may be
Jer	29:13	when you **s** me with all your heart,
Hos	10:12	for it is time to **s** the LORD, till he
Am	5: 6	**S** the LORD, that you may live,
Zep	2: 3	**S** the LORD, all you humble
Zep	2: 3	**S** justice, **s** humility;
Lk	19:10	For the Son of Man has come to **s**
Jn	5:30	because I do not **s** my own will
Acts	15:17	rest of humanity may **s** out the Lord,
1 Cor	7:27	to a wife? Do not **s** a separation.
1 Cor	10:24	No one should **s** his own advantage,
Heb	11: 6	that he rewards those who **s** him.
1 Pt	3:11	do good, **s** peace and follow after it.

SEEKING → SEEK

Rom	10:20	[by] those who were not **s** me;
1 Cor	10:33	not **s** my own benefit

SEEKS → SEEK

Ps	24: 6	Such is the generation that **s** him,
Prv	14: 6	The scoffer **s** wisdom in vain,
Prv	15:14	The discerning heart **s** knowledge,
Jn	4:23	indeed the Father **s** such people

Rom   3:11   there is no one who s God.

SEEM → SEEMED, SEEMS
Zec   8: 6   should it s impossible in my eyes

SEEMED → SEEM
Gn   29:20 yet they s to him like a few days
Nm   13:33 in our own eyes we s like mere
Lk   24:11 but their story s like nonsense
Rev   13: 3 of its heads s to have been mortally

SEEMS → SEEM
Prv   14:12 Sometimes a way s right,
Prv   16:25 Sometimes a way s right,
Heb   12:11 all discipline s a cause not for joy

SEEN → SEE
Gn   16:13 "Have I really s God and remained
Ex   33:23 but my face may not be s.
Dt   4: 9 the things your own eyes have s,
Jos   23: 3 You have s all that the LORD,
Jgs   6:22 that I have s the messenger
Jgs   13:22 certainly die, for we have s God."
Ezr   3:12 enough to have s the former house,
Ps   37:25 in old age have I s the righteous one
Ps   37:35 I have s a ruthless scoundrel,
Ps   98: 3 of the earth have s the victory of our
Is   6: 5 and my eyes have s the King,
Is   9: 1 in darkness have s a great light;
Is   64: 3 no eye ever s, any God but you
Mt   2: 9 that they had s at its rising preceded
Mt   4:16 sit in darkness have s a great light,
Lk   2:30 for my eyes have s your salvation,
Jn   1:18 No one has ever s God.
Jn   6:46 anyone has s the Father except
Jn   6:46 is from God; he has s the Father.
Jn   14: 9 Whoever has s me has s the Father.
Jn   20:25 said to him, "We have s the Lord."
Jn   20:29 to believe because you have s me?
Jn   20:29 Blessed are those who have not s
1 Cor   2: 9 "What eye has not s, and ear has
Phil   4: 9 and received and heard and s in me.
1 Tm   3:16 vindicated in the spirit, s by angels,
1 Pt   1: 8 you have not s him you love him;
1 Jn   1: 3 what we have s and heard we
1 Jn   4:12 No one has ever s God. Yet, if we
3 Jn   1:11 does what is evil has never s God.
Rev   1:19 what you have s, and what is

SEER → SEE
1 Sm   9: 9 to say, "Come, let us go to the s."
1 Sm   9: 9 prophet was formerly called s.)
2 Sm   24:11 the prophet Gad, David's s, saying:
1 Chr   29:29 in the history of Samuel the s,
1 Chr   29:29 and the history of Gad the s,
2 Chr   9:29 of Iddo the s concerning Jeroboam,
2 Chr   29:30 words of David and of Asaph the s.

SEERS → SEE
2 Chr   33:19 recorded in the chronicles of his s.
Mi   3: 7 Then the s shall be put to shame,

SEES → SEE
Is   47:10 you said, "No one s me."
Mt   6: 4 your Father who s in secret will
Mt   6: 6 your Father who s in secret will
Mt   6:18 your Father who s what is hidden
Jn   5:19 but only what he s his father doing;
1 Jn   3:17 who has worldly means s a brother

SEIR
Gn   32: 4 to his brother Esau in the land of S,
Dt   2: 4 descendants of Esau, who live in S.
Ez   35: 2 set your face against Mount S

SELECT
Acts   6: 3 s from among you seven reputable

SELF → SELFISH, SELFISHNESS
Jos   22: 5 your whole heart and your whole s."
Rom   6: 6 know that our old s was crucified
Eph   4:22 you should put away the old s

Col   3:10 and have put on the new s, which is

SELF-ABASEMENT
Col   2:18 you, delighting in s and worship

SELF-CONDEMNED → CONDEMN
Ti   3:11 is perverted and sinful and stands s.

SELF-CONTROL → CONTROL
1 Cor   7: 5 tempt you through your lack of s.
2 Pt   1: 6 knowledge with s, s with endurance,

SELF-CONTROLLED → CONTROL
Ti   1: 8 temperate, just, holy, and s,
Ti   2: 5 to be s, chaste, good homemakers,

SELF-INDULGENCE → INDULGE
Mt   23:25 inside they are full of plunder and s.

SELFISH → SELF
Phil   1:17 proclaim Christ out of s ambition,
Jas   3:14 and s ambition in your hearts,
Jas   3:16 where jealousy and s ambition exist,

SELFISHNESS → SELF
2 Cor   12:20 jealousy, fury, s, slander, gossip,

SELL → SALE, SELLING, SELLS, SOLD
Prv   23:23 Buy truth and do not s:
Mk   10:21 Go, s what you have, and give
Acts   2:45 they would s their property
Rev   13:17 s except one who had the stamped

SELLING → SELL
Mk   11:15 area he began to drive out those s
Lk   17:28 eating, drinking, buying, s, planting,

SELLS → SELL
Prv   31:24 She makes garments and s them,
Mt   13:44 out of joy goes and s all that he has

SEND → SENDING, SENT
Ex   33: 2 I will s an angel before you
1 Sm   5:11 "S away the ark of the God
Ps   43: 3 S your light and your fidelity,
Ps   57: 4 May God s help from heaven
Ps   57: 4 May God s fidelity and mercy.
Ps   104:30 S forth your spirit, they are created
Is   6: 8 the Lord saying, "Whom shall I s?
Is   6: 8 "Here I am," I said; "s me!"
Mt   9:38 of the harvest to s out laborers
Mt   24:31 And he will s out his angels
Lk   11:49 said, 'I will s to them prophets
Lk   20:13 I shall s my beloved son;
Jn   3:17 God did not s his Son into the world
Jn   14:26 that the Father will s in my name—
Jn   15:26 Advocate comes whom I will s you
Jn   16: 7 But if I go, I will s him to you.
Acts   3:20 s you the Messiah already appointed
1 Cor   1:17 For Christ did not s me to baptize

SENDING → SEND
Mal   3:23 Now I am s to you Elijah
Mt   10:16 I am s you like sheep in the midst
Rom   8: 3 by s his own Son in the likeness
Rev   1: 1 He made it known by s his angel

SENNACHERIB
Assyrian king whose siege of Jerusalem was overthrown by the LORD following prayer of Hezekiah and Isaiah (2 Kgs 18:13–19:37; 2 Chr 32:1-21; Is 36–37).

SENSELESS
Rom   1:21 and their s minds were darkened.

SENSIBLE
Sir   25: 8 the man who lives with a s woman,

SENSUALITY
1 Tm   5:11 when their s estranges them from Christ,

SENT → SEND
Gn   45: 5 lives that God s me here ahead
Ex   3:14 I AM has s me to you.
Nm   16:29 humanity, the LORD has not s me.
Nm   21: 6 So the LORD s among the people

Jos	2: 1	Nun, secretly **s** out two spies
Jos	24:12	I **s** the hornets ahead of you
2 Sm	24:15	The LORD **s** plague over Israel
2 Kgs	14: 9	of Israel, **s** this reply to Amaziah,
2 Kgs	14: 9	"A thistle of Lebanon **s** word
Ps	107:20	S forth his word to heal them,
Is	55:11	achieving the end for which I **s** it.
Is	61: 1	He has **s** me to bring good news
Jer	28: 9	whom the LORD has truly **s** only
Dn	3:95	who **s** his angel to deliver
Dn	6:23	My God **s** his angel and closed
Mt	10:40	me receives the one who **s** me.
Lk	1:26	the angel Gabriel was **s** from God
Lk	4:18	He has **s** me to proclaim liberty
Lk	9: 2	he **s** them to proclaim the kingdom
Lk	10:16	me rejects the one who **s** me."
Lk	13:34	prophets and stone those **s** to you,
Jn	1: 6	A man named John was **s** from God.
Jn	3:28	but that I was **s** before him.
Jn	4:34	is to do the will of the one who **s** me
Jn	5:24	in the one who **s** me has eternal life
Jn	8:16	but it is I and the Father who **s** me.
Jn	9: 4	of the one who **s** me while it is day.
Jn	16: 5	I am going to the one who **s** me,
Jn	17: 3	God, and the one whom you **s**,
Jn	17:18	As you **s** me into the world, so I **s** them into the world.
Jn	20:21	As the Father has **s** me, so I send
Rom	10:15	can people preach unless they are **s**?
Gal	4: 4	of time had come, God **s** his Son,
Gal	4: 6	God **s** the spirit of his Son into our
1 Jn	4:10	**s** his Son as expiation for our sins.
Rev	22:16	Jesus, **s** my angel to give you this

SENTENCE → SENTENCED

Eccl	8:11	Because the **s** against an evil deed is
Acts	13:28	they found no grounds for a death **s**,
2 Cor	1: 9	had accepted within ourselves the **s**

SENTENCED → SENTENCE

1 Cor	4: 9	the last of all, like people **s** to death,

SEPARATE → SEPARATED, SEPARATES

Mt	19: 6	together, no human being must **s**."
Rom	8:35	What will **s** us from the love
1 Cor	7:10	A wife should not **s** from her
2 Cor	6:17	come forth from them and be **s**,"

SEPARATED → SEPARATE

Gn	1: 4	then **s** the light from the darkness.
Gn	1: 7	it **s** the water below the dome
Neh	13: 3	they **s** all those of mixed descent
Heb	7:26	undefiled, **s** from sinners,

SEPARATES → SEPARATE

Prv	16:28	and talebearing **s** bosom friends.
Mt	25:32	as a shepherd **s** the sheep
1 Cor	7:15	If the unbeliever **s**, however, let him

SERAPHIM

Is	6: 2	S were stationed above;
Is	6: 6	Then one of the **s** flew to me,

SERIOUS

1 Pt	4: 7	be **s** and sober for prayers.

SERPENT → SERPENTS

Ex	7:10	his servants, and it turned into a **s**.
Nm	21: 9	Accordingly Moses made a bronze **s**
Nm	21: 9	and whenever the **s** bit someone,
2 Kgs	18: 4	smashed the bronze **s** Moses had
Is	27: 1	Leviathan the fleeing **s**, Leviathan the coiled **s**;
2 Cor	11: 3	that, as the **s** deceived Eve by his
Rev	12: 9	the ancient **s**, who is called
Rev	20: 2	the ancient **s**, which is the Devil

SERPENTS → SERPENT

Nm	21: 6	sent among the people seraph **s**,
Mt	10:16	so be shrewd as **s** and simple as
1 Cor	10: 9	them did, and suffered death by **s**.

SERVANT → SERVANT'S, SERVANTS

Ex	14:31	in the LORD and in Moses his **s**.

Nm	12: 7	Not so with my **s** Moses!
1 Sm	3:10	"Speak, for your **s** is listening."
1 Kgs	3: 7	your **s**, king to succeed David my
1 Kgs	8:56	he made through Moses his **s**.
1 Kgs	8:66	LORD had given to David his **s**
1 Kgs	20:40	But while your **s** was occupied here
Jb	1: 8	satan, "Have you noticed my **s** Job?
Jb	2: 3	satan, "Have you noticed my **s** Job?
Jb	42: 8	and go to my **s** Job, and sacrifice
Jb	42: 8	and let my **s** Job pray for you.
Ps	19:12	By them your **s** is warned;
Ps	19:14	from arrogant ones restrain your **s**;
Ps	31:17	Let your face shine on your **s**;
Ps	78:70	He chose David his **s**, took him
Ps	89: 4	I have sworn to David my **s**:
Ps	105:26	He sent his **s** Moses, and Aaron
Ps	119:135	Let your face shine upon your **s**;
Ps	136:22	his **s**, for his mercy endures forever.
Prv	14:35	The king favors the skillful **s**,
Is	41: 8	Israel, my **s**, Jacob, whom I have
Is	42: 1	Here is my **s** whom I uphold,
Is	43:10	of the LORD—my **s** whom I have chosen
Is	44: 1	Jacob, my **s**, Israel, whom I have
Is	45: 4	my **s**, of Israel my chosen one,
Is	48:20	LORD has redeemed his **s** Jacob.
Is	49: 3	said to me, You are my **s**, in you,
Is	52:13	See, my **s** shall prosper, he shall be
Is	53:11	My **s**, the just one, shall justify
Jer	30:10	But you, my **s** Jacob, do not fear!—
Jer	33:21	with my **s** David be broken,
Ez	34:24	my **s** David will be prince in their
Zec	3: 8	I will surely bring my **s** the Branch.
Mt	8:13	at that very hour [his] **s** was healed.
Mt	20:26	be great among you shall be your **s**;
Lk	1:54	He has helped Israel his **s**,
Lk	1:69	within the house of David his **s**,
Jn	12:26	where I am, there also will my **s** be.
Acts	3:13	has glorified his **s** Jesus whom you
Rom	13: 4	for it is a **s** of God for your good.
Rom	13: 4	it is the **s** of God to inflict wrath
Heb	3: 5	in all his house" as a "**s**" to testify
Rev	15: 3	the song of Moses, the **s** of God,
Rev	19:10	I am a fellow **s** of yours and of your

SERVANT'S → SERVANT

Ps	119:122	Guarantee your **s** welfare; do not let

SERVANTS → SERVANT

Dt	32:36	on his **s** he will have pity.
2 Kgs	17:23	as he had declared through all his **s**,
Ezr	5:11	'We are the **s** of the God of heaven
Jb	4:18	he puts no trust in his **s**, and even
Ps	34:23	is the redeemer of the souls of his **s**;
Ps	90:13	How long? Have pity on your **s**!
Ps	113: 1	Praise, you **s** of the LORD,
Is	65: 8	So will I do for the sake of my **s**:
Is	65:14	My **s** shall shout for joy of heart,
Jer	7:25	on sending all my **s** the prophets
Dn	3:33	upon us, your **s**, who revere you.
Dn	9: 6	not obeyed your **s** the prophets,
Acts	4:29	enable your **s** to speak your word
Rev	7: 3	the foreheads of the **s** of our God."
Rev	19: 2	avenged on her the blood of his **s**."
Rev	22: 3	be in it, and his **s** will worship him.

SERVE → SERVED, SERVES, SERVICE, SERVING

Gn	15:14	judgment on the nation they must **s**,
Gn	25:23	and the older will **s** the younger.
Ex	20: 5	not bow down before them or **s** them.
Nm	8:25	retire from the work force and **s** no more.
Dt	6:13	him shall you **s**, and by his name
Dt	10:12	to love and **s** the LORD, your God,
Dt	28:47	Since you would not **s** the LORD,
Jos	22: 5	and **s** him with your whole heart
Jos	24:14	the LORD and **s** him completely
Jos	24:14	and in Egypt, and **s** the LORD.
Jos	24:15	choose today whom you will **s**,
Jos	24:15	household, we will **s** the LORD."

Jos	24:18	we also will s the Lord, for he is
2 Kgs	17:35	nor bow down to them, nor s them,
Neh	9:35	They did not s you nor turn away
Jb	36:11	If they listen and s him, they spend
Ps	2:11	S the Lord with fear;
Ps	100: 2	s the Lord with gladness;
Is	60:12	that will not s you shall perish;
Jer	2:20	You said, "I will not s."
Jer	25: 6	Do not follow other gods to s
Dn	3:17	whom we s, can save us
Mt	4:10	and him alone shall you s.' "
Mt	6:24	"No one can s two masters.
Mt	6:24	You cannot s God and mammon.
Mk	10:45	to s and to give his life as a ransom
Lk	16:13	No servant can s two masters.
Lk	16:13	You cannot s God and mammon."
Rom	12:11	zeal, be fervent in spirit, s the Lord.
1 Thes	1: 9	to God from idols to s the living
1 Pt	4:10	it to s one another as good stewards

SERVED → SERVE

Gn	29:20	So Jacob s seven years for Rachel,
Jos	24:15	gods your ancestors s beyond
Mt	20:28	the Son of Man did not come to be s
Jn	12: 2	and Martha s, while Lazarus was
Acts	17:25	nor is he s by human hands because

SERVES → SERVE

Jn	12:26	Whoever s me must follow me,
Jn	12:26	Father will honor whoever s me.
Rom	14:18	whoever s Christ in this way is
1 Pt	4:11	whoever s, let it be with the strength

SERVICE → SERVE

1 Cor	16:15	to the s of the holy ones—
Rev	2:19	your love, faith, s, and endurance,

SERVING → SERVE

1 Pt	1:12	that they were s not themselves

SET → SETS

Gn	9:13	I s my bow in the clouds to serve as
Gn	28:18	his head, s it up as a sacred pillar,
Gn	31:45	a stone and s it up as a sacred pillar.
Gn	35:14	with him, Jacob s up a sacred pillar,
Ex	26:30	You shall s up the tabernacle according
Ex	40:18	It was Moses who s up the tabernacle.
Dt	27: 2	you, s up some large stones and coat
Dt	30:15	I have today s before you life
Jos	4: 9	Joshua s up the twelve stones
1 Kgs	16:32	Ahab s up an altar to Baal in the house
2 Kgs	21: 3	He s up altars to Baal and also made
Is	50: 7	Therefore I have s my face like
Dn	11:28	riches, his mind s against the holy
Rom	1: 1	and s apart for the gospel of God,
1 Pt	1:13	and s your hopes completely

SETH

Gn	4:25	birth to a son whom she called S.
1 Chr	1: 1	Adam, S, Enosh,

SETS → SET

Jb	5:11	He s up the lowly on high,
Ps	146: 7	The Lord s prisoners free;

SETTLE → SETTLED

Gn	47: 4	So now please let your servants s
Nm	33:53	possession of the land and s in it,

SETTLED → SETTLE

Ex	24:16	of the Lord s upon Mount Sinai.
Ex	40:35	because the cloud s down upon it
Dt	19: 1	them and s in their cities

SEVEN → SEVENFOLD, SEVENTH

Gn	4:15	kills Cain, Cain shall be avenged s times.
Gn	4:24	If Cain is avenged s times, then Lamech
Gn	7: 2	take with you s pairs, a male and its
Gn	21:28	set apart s ewe lambs of the flock,
Gn	29:18	"I will serve you s years for your
Gn	41: 2	up out of the Nile came s cows,
Gn	41: 5	He saw s ears of grain,

Ex	2:16	priest of Midian had s daughters,
Ex	12:15	For s days you must eat unleavened
Ex	25:37	You shall then make s lamps for it
Ex	29:35	S days you shall spend installing
Nm	23: 1	to Balak, "Build me s altars here,
Nm	23: 1	here prepare s bulls and s rams
Dt	7: 1	s nations more numerous
Jos	6: 4	s priests carrying ram's horns ahead
Jos	6: 4	day march around the city s times,
Jgs	16:13	you weave the s locks of my hair
1 Sm	2: 5	The barren wife bears s sons,
1 Kgs	19:18	I will spare s thousand in Israel—
2 Kgs	5:10	"Go and wash s times in the Jordan,
Tb	3: 8	given in marriage to s husbands,
Ps	119: 164	S times a day I praise you because
Prv	6:16	yes, s are an abomination to him;
Prv	9: 1	house, she has set up her s columns;
Prv	24:16	Though the just fall s times,
Prv	26:25	them, for s abominations are in their
Sir	40: 8	beast, but for sinners s times more,
Is	4: 1	S women will take hold of one man
Dn	3:19	to be heated s times more than usual
Dn	9:25	ruler, there shall be s weeks.
Zec	3: 9	stone with s facets I will engrave its
Zec	4: 2	There are s lamps on it, with s spouts on each of the lamps
Mt	18:22	not s times but seventy-seven times.
Mk	12:20	Now there were s brothers.
Mk	16: 9	of whom he had driven s demons.
Lk	11:26	and brings back s other spirits more
Rom	11: 4	myself s thousand men who have
Rev	1: 4	John, to the s churches in Asia:
Rev	1: 4	from the s spirits before his throne,
Rev	1:12	I turned, I saw s gold lampstands
Rev	1:16	In his right hand he held s stars.
Rev	3: 1	" 'The one who has the s spirits
Rev	3: 1	of God and the s stars says this:
Rev	4: 5	S flaming torches burned in front
Rev	4: 5	which are the s spirits of God.
Rev	5: 1	sides and was sealed with s seals.
Rev	6: 1	broke open the first of the s seals,
Rev	8: 2	the s angels who stood before God
Rev	8: 2	before God were given s trumpets.
Rev	10: 4	When the s thunders had spoken,
Rev	12: 3	dragon, with s heads and ten horns,
Rev	12: 3	and on its heads were s diadems.
Rev	15: 1	s angels with the s last plagues,
Rev	15: 7	creatures gave the s angels s gold
Rev	16: 1	from the temple to the s angels,
Rev	16: 1	pour out the s bowls of God's fury
Rev	17: 9	The s heads represent s hills
Rev	17: 9	They also represent s kings:

SEVENFOLD → SEVEN

Lv	26:18	the chastisement for your sins s,
Prv	6:31	Yet if caught they must pay back s,

SEVENTH → SEVEN

Gn	2: 2	the s day God completed the work
Gn	2: 2	he rested on the s day from all
Ex	16:30	that the people rested on the s day.
Ex	20:10	the s day is a sabbath of the Lord
Ex	23:11	the s year you shall let the land lie
Ex	23:12	but on the s day you must rest,
Jos	6:16	The s time around, the priests blew
1 Mc	6:53	because it was the s year,
Heb	4: 4	spoken somewhere about the s day
Heb	4: 4	God rested on the s day from all his
Jude	1:14	of the s generation from Adam,
Rev	8: 1	When he broke open the s seal,
Rev	11:15	Then the s angel blew his trumpet.
Rev	16:17	The s angel poured out his bowl

SEVENTY → SEVENTY-SEVEN

Gn	46:27	Egypt amounted to s persons in all.
Ex	24: 1	Abihu, and s of the elders of Israel.
Nm	11:25	he bestowed it on the s elders;
2 Chr	36:21	have rest while s years are fulfilled.

Ps   90:10 S is the sum of our years, or eighty,
Jer   25:12 but when the s years have elapsed,
Dn   9: 2   was to lie in ruins for s years.
Dn   9:24   "S weeks are decreed for your

SEVENTY-SEVEN → SEVENTY
Gn   4:24   seven times, then Lamech s times."
Mt   18:22 to you, not seven times but s times.

SEVERE
Gn   12:10 since the famine in the land was s.
Lk   4:25   a s famine spread over the entire
Lk   15:14 a s famine struck that country,
Acts   11:28 there would be a s famine all over
2 Cor   8: 2   for in a s test of affliction,

SEWED
Gn   3: 7   so they s fig leaves together

SEX → SEXUAL
1 Pt   3: 7   honor to the weaker female s,

SEXUAL → SEX
Jude   1: 7   they, indulged in s promiscuity

SHADE
Ps   91: 1 who abide in the s of the Almighty,
Ps   121: 5 the LORD is your s at your right
Is   25: 4 from the rain, s from the heat.
Ez   31: 6 in its s dwelt all the mighty nations.
Jon   4: 6   giving s that relieved him of any
Mk   4:32   birds of the sky can dwell in its s."

SHADOW → SHADOWS
2 Kgs   20:11 He made the s go back the ten steps
1 Chr   29:15 Our days on earth are like a s,
Jb   14: 2 swift as a s that does not abide.
Ps   17: 8 hide me in the s of your wings
Ps   36: 8 take refuge in the s of your wings.
Ps   57: 2 the s of your wings I seek refuge till
Ps   63: 8 in the s of your wings I shout
Lk   1:79   who sit in darkness and death's s,
Acts   5:15   by, at least his s might fall on one
Heb   8: 5   and s of the heavenly sanctuary,
Heb   10: 1 Since the law has only a s

SHADOWS → SHADOW
Col   2:17   These are s of things to come;

SHADRACH → =HANANIAH
     Hebrew exiled to Babylon; name changed from Hananiah (Dn 1:6-
7). Refused defilement by food (Dn 1:8-20). Refused to worship idol
(Dn 3:1-18); saved from furnace (Dn 3:19-97).

SHAKE → SHAKEN, SHAKING, SHOOK
Hg   2: 6   I will s the heavens and the earth,
Hg   2:21   I will s the heavens and the earth;
Mk   6:11   s the dust off your feet in testimony
Heb   12:26 "I will once more s not only earth

SHAKEN → SHAKE
Mt   24:29 the powers of the heavens will be s.
Lk   6:38   packed together, s down,

SHAKING → SHAKE
Mt   27:39 passing by reviled him, s their heads
Mk   15:29 him, s their heads and saying,

SHALLUM
     King of Israel (2 Kgs 15:10-16).

SHALMANESER
     King of Assyria; conquered and deported Israel (2 Kgs 17:3-4; 18:9;
Tb 1:2).

SHAME → ASHAMED, SHAMEFUL, SHAMELESS
Jdt   14:18 One Hebrew woman has brought s on the house
Ps   97: 7 All who serve idols are put to s,
Prv   6:33   and their s will not be wiped away;
Prv   18:13 before listening, theirs is folly and s.
Is   30: 5 nor benefit, but only s and reproach.
Is   45:17 You shall never be put to s
Is   61: 7 Because their s was twofold
Dn   3:40   who trust in you cannot be put to s.
Hos   4: 7   me, I will change their glory into s.

Jl   2:26   people will never again be put to s.
Rom   9:33   in him shall not be put to s."
Rom   10:11 believes in him will be put to s."
1 Cor   1:27   foolish of the world to s the wise,
1 Cor   1:27   weak of the world to s the strong,
Phil   3:19   their glory is in their "s."
Heb   12: 2 despising its s, and has taken his
1 Pt   2: 6   believes in it shall not be put to s."
1 Jn   2:28   not be put to s by him at his coming.

SHAMEFUL → SHAME
2 Cor   4: 2   we have renounced s, hidden things;
Eph   5:12   for it is s even to mention the things

SHAMELESS → SHAME
Sir   23: 6 do not give me up to s desires.
Jer   13:27 your neighings, your s prostitutions:

SHAMGAR
     Judge; killed 600 Philistines (Jgs 3:31; 5:6).

SHAPHAN
2 Kgs   22: 8 priest Hilkiah informed the scribe S,
2 Kgs   22: 8 Hilkiah gave the book to S,

SHARE → SHARED, SHARING
2 Sm   20: 1 cried out, "We have no s in David,
2 Chr   10:16 "What s have we in David?
Neh   2:20   but you have neither s nor claim nor
Lk   3:11   "Whoever has two tunics should s
Lk   15:12 give me the s of your estate
Acts   8:21   You have no s or lot in this matter,
Rom   1:11   I may s with you some spiritual gift
Rom   15:27 the Gentiles have come to s in their
2 Cor   1: 7   know that as you s in the sufferings,
2 Cor   1: 7   you also s in the encouragement.
Eph   4:28   he may have something to s
Col   1:12   who has made you fit to s
1 Tm   6:18   works, to be generous, ready to s,
2 Tm   2: 6   ought to have the first s of the crop.
Heb   12:10 in order that we may s his holiness.
Heb   13:16 to do good and to s what you have;
Rev   18: 4 sins and receive a s in her plagues,
Rev   22:19 God will take away his s in the tree

SHARED → SHARE
Heb   2:14   and flesh, he likewise s in them,
Heb   6: 4   heavenly gift and s in the holy Spirit

SHARING → SHARE
Phil   3:10   [the] s of his sufferings by being

SHARON
Sg   2: 1   I am a flower of S, a lily

SHARP → SHARPENED, SHARPENS, SHARPER
Prv   5: 4   as s as a two-edged sword.
Is   5:28   Their arrows are s, and all their
Acts   15:39 So s was their disagreement
Rev   1:16   A s two-edged sword came
Rev   2:12   the s two-edged sword says this:
Rev   14:14 his head and a s sickle in his hand.
Rev   19:15 his mouth came a s sword to strike

SHARPENED → SHARP
Is   49: 2 He made me a s arrow, in his quiver
Ez   21:14 sword, a sword has been s, a sword,

SHARPENS → SHARP
Prv   27:17 one person s another.

SHARPER → SHARP
Heb   4:12   s than any two-edged sword,

SHATTERED
Ex   15: 6 right hand, O LORD, s the enemy.
1 Sm   2:10   The LORD's foes shall be s;

SHAVE → SHAVED
Nm   6:18   of meeting the nazirite shall s his
Dt   14: 1 not gash yourselves nor s the hair

SHAVED → SHAVE
Nm   6:19   the nazirite has s off the dedicated
Jgs   16:17 If I am s, my strength will leave me,

1 Cor 11: 5 thing as if she had had her head s.

SHEAF → SHEAVES
Gn   37: 7 suddenly my s rose to an upright
Gn   37: 7 sheaves formed a ring around my s
Lv   23:11 who shall elevate the s before
Dt   24:19 field and overlook a s in the field,

SHEAR → SHEARER, SHEARERS
Dt   15:19 nor s the firstlings of your flock.

SHEARER → SHEAR
Acts   8:32 and as a lamb before its s is silent,

SHEARERS → SHEAR
Is   53: 7 slaughter or a sheep silent before s,

SHEAVES → SHEAF
Gn   37: 7 we were, binding s in the field,
Gn   37: 7 and your s formed a ring around my
Ru   2:15 among the s themselves without
Ps   126: 6 of joy, carrying their bundled s.

SHEBA
    1. Benjamite; rebelled against David (2 Sm 20).
    2. Queen of Sheba (1 Kgs 10; 2 Chr 9). Queen of the South (Mt 12:42; Lk 11:31).

SHECHEM
    1. Raped Jacob's daughter Dinah; killed by Simeon and Levi (Gn 34).
    2. City where Joshua renewed the covenant (Jos 24). Abimelech as king (Jgs 9).

SHED → BLOODSHED, SHEDDING, SHEDS
Gn   9: 6 being shall that one's blood be s;
Nm   35:33 the blood s on it except through
Dt   19:10 innocent blood will not be s and you
1 Mc   1:24 He s much blood and spoke
Prv   6:17 tongue, hands that s innocent blood,
Is   59: 7 and they hasten to s innocent blood;
Ez   22:12 in you who take bribes to s blood.
Mt   23:35 you all the righteous blood s
Rom   3:15 Their feet are quick to s blood;
Rev   16: 6 For they have s the blood

SHEDDING → SHED
Heb   9:22 without the s of blood there is no
Heb   12: 4 yet resisted to the point of s blood.

SHEDS → SHED
Gn   9: 6 Anyone who s the blood of a human

SHEEP → SHEEP'S
Nm   27:17 not be like s without a shepherd."
1 Sm   15:14 is this bleating of s that comes
1 Kgs   22:17 like s without a shepherd,
Ps   44:23 day long, considered only as s to be
Ps   74: 1 does your anger burn against the s
Ps   78:52 God led forth his people like s,
Ps   119:176 I have wandered like a lost s;
Is   53: 6 We had all gone astray like s,
Is   53: 7 or a s silent before shearers, he did
Jer   50: 6 Lost s were my people,
Ez   34:15 I myself will pasture my s;
Zec   13: 7 that the s may be scattered;
Mt   9:36 like s without a shepherd.
Mt   10: 6 Go rather to the lost s of the house
Mt   10:16 I am sending you like s in the midst
Mt   12:11 one of you who has a s that falls
Mt   25:32 as a shepherd separates the s
Lk   15: 4 man among you having a hundred s
Jn   10: 3 and the s hear his voice, as he calls
Jn   10: 3 as he calls his own s by name
Jn   10: 7 I say to you, I am the gate for the s.
Jn   10:11 lays down his life for the s.
Jn   10:15 I will lay down my life for the s.
Jn   10:27 My s hear my voice; I know them,
Jn   21:17 [Jesus] said to him, "Feed my s.
Acts   8:32 "Like a s he was led
Rom   8:36 upon as s to be slaughtered."
Heb   13:20 great shepherd of the s by the blood
1 Pt   2:25 For you had gone astray like s,

SHEEP'S → SHEEP
Mt   7:15 who come to you in s clothing,

SHEET
Acts   10:11 resembling a large s coming down,
Acts   11: 5 resembling a large s coming down,

SHEKEL → SHEKELS
Ex   30:13 to the standard of the sanctuary s—twenty gerahs to the s—

SHEKELS → SHEKEL
1 Chr   21:25 So David paid Ornan six hundred s

SHELAH
Gn   38:11 for he feared that S also might die
Gn   46:12 Er, Onan, S, Perez, and Zerah—

SHELTER
Ps   27: 5 God will hide me in his s in time
Ps   31:21 hide them in the s of your presence,
Ps   55: 9 "I would soon find a s Selah
Ps   61: 5 take refuge in the s of your wings.
Ps   91: 1 dwell in the s of the Most High,
Sir   6:14 Faithful friends are a sturdy s;
Is   4: 6 his glory will be s and protection:
Is   25: 4 S from the rain, shade from the heat.
Rev   7:15 who sits on the throne will s them,

SHEM
    Son of Noah (Gn 5:32; 6:10). Blessed (Gn 9:26). Descendants (Gn 10:21-31; 11:10-32; Lk 3:36).

SHEMAIAH
1 Kgs   12:22 the word of God came to S, a man
2 Chr   12: 5 S the prophet came to Rehoboam
Jer   29:31 Thus says the LORD concerning S,
Jer   29:31 Because S prophesies to you,

SHEMER → SAMARIA
1 Kgs   16:24 Samaria, after S, the former owner.

SHEOL
Ps   6: 6 Who praises you in S?
Ps   16:10 you will not abandon my soul to S,
Ps   55:16 let them go down alive to S, for evil
Ps   139: 8 if I lie down in S, there you are.

SHEPHERD → SHEPHERDS
Gn   48:15 The God who has been my s
Gn   49:24 because of the S, the Rock of Israel,
Nm   27:17 may not be like sheep without a s."
1 Kgs   22:17 like sheep without a s,
1 Chr   11: 2 You shall s my people Israel;
Ps   23: 1 The LORD is my s;
Ps   78:71 brought him, to s Jacob, his people,
Ps   80: 2 O S of Israel, lend an ear, you who
Is   40:11 Like a s he feeds his flock;
Jer   31:10 he guards them as a s his flock.
Ez   34: 5 they were scattered for lack of a s,
Mi   5: 3 as s by the strength of the LORD,
Zec   10: 2 sheep, wretched, for they have no s.
Zec   11:17 my worthless s who forsakes
Zec   13: 7 against my s, against the one who is
Zec   13: 7 Strike the s that the sheep may be
Mt   2: 6 who is to s my people Israel.' "
Mt   25:32 as a s separates the sheep
Mt   26:31 'I will strike the s, and the sheep
Mk   6:34 for they were like sheep without a s;
Jn   10:11 I am the good s. A good s lays down
Jn   10:14 I am the good s, and I know mine
Jn   10:16 and there will be one flock, one s.
Heb   13:20 the dead the great s of the sheep
1 Pt   2:25 you have now returned to the s
1 Pt   5: 4 And when the chief S is revealed,
Rev   7:17 the center of the throne will s them

SHEPHERDS → SHEPHERD
Gn   46:34 since all s are abhorrent
Ex   2:19 Egyptian delivered us from the s.
Is   56:11 S who have no understanding;
Jer   3:15 for you s after my own heart,
Jer   23: 1 Woe to the s who destroy

Jer 50: 6 my people, their **s** misled them,
Ez 34: 2 prophesy against the **s** of Israel.
Ez 34: 2 Should not **s** pasture the flock?
Zec 10: 3 My wrath is kindled against the **s**,
Lk 2: 8 Now there were **s** in that region

SHESHBAZZAR

Ezr 1: 8 who counted them out to **S**,
Ezr 5:16 Then this same **S** came and laid

SHIBBOLETH → SIBBOLETH

Jgs 12: 6 they would ask him to say "**S**."

SHIELD → SHIELDED

Gn 15: 1 I am your **s**; I will make your
Dt 33:29 Your help and **s**, and the sword
2 Sm 22:31 he is a **s** for all who trust in him.
2 Sm 22:36 have given me your protecting **s**,
Ps 3: 4 you, LORD, are a **s** around me;
Ps 5:13 surround him with favor like a **s**.
Ps 7:11 God is a **s** above me saving
Ps 18: 3 of refuge, my **s**, my saving horn,
Ps 28: 7 LORD is my strength and my **s**,
Ps 33:20 for the LORD, he is our help and **s**.
Ps 84:12 For a sun and **s** is the LORD God,
Ps 91: 4 his faithfulness is a protecting **s**.
Ps 115: 9 the LORD, who is their help and **s**.
Ps 119:114 You are my refuge and **s**;
Ps 144: 2 My **s**, in whom I take refuge,
Prv 2: 7 is the **s** of those who walk honestly,
Prv 30: 5 he is a **s** to those who take refuge
Zec 12: 8 the LORD will **s** the inhabitants
Eph 6:16 hold faith as a **s**, to quench all

SHIELDED → SHIELD

Dt 32:10 He **s** them, cared for them,
Is 49: 2 sword, concealed me, **s** by his hand.
Is 51:16 mouth, I covered you, **s** by my hand,

SHIFTING

Col 1:23 not **s** from the hope of the gospel

SHILOH

Jos 18: 1 of the Israelites assembled at **S**,
1 Sm 1:24 at the house of the LORD in **S**.
1 Sm 3:21 LORD continued to appear at **S**,
1 Sm 3:21 to Samuel at **S** through his word.
Ps 78:60 He forsook the shrine at **S**, the tent

SHIMEI

Cursed David (2 Sm 16:5-14); spared (2 Sm 19:17-24). Killed by Solomon (1 Kgs 2:8-9, 36-46).

SHINAR

Gn 11: 2 came to a valley in the land of **S**
Dn 1: 2 which he carried off to the land of **S**

SHINE → SHINES, SHINING, SHONE

Nm 6:25 The LORD let his face **s** upon you,
Ps 37: 6 make your righteousness **s** like
Ps 67: 2 may his face **s** upon us.
Ps 94: 1 God, avenging God, **s** forth!
Ps 132:18 with shame, but on him his crown shall **s**."
Is 60: 1 Arise! **S**, for your light has come,
Dn 12: 3 with insight shall **s** brightly like
Mt 5:16 your light must **s** before others,
Mt 13:43 the righteous will **s** like the sun
2 Cor 4: 6 said, "Let light **s** out of darkness,"
Phil 2:15 among whom you **s** like lights
Rev 21:23 no need of sun or moon to **s** on it,

SHINES → SHINE

Ps 50: 2 perfection of beauty, God **s** forth.
Is 62: 1 Until her vindication **s** forth like
Jn 1: 5 the light **s** in the darkness,

SHINING → SHINE

Jn 5:35 He was a burning and **s** lamp,
2 Pt 1:19 as to a lamp **s** in a dark place,
1 Jn 2: 8 away, and the true light is already **s**.

SHIP → SHIPS, SHIPWRECK, SHIPWRECKED

Jon 1: 4 the storm was so great that the **s** was

Acts 27:22 one of you will be lost, only the **s**.

SHIPS → SHIP

1 Kgs 22:49 Jehoshaphat made Tarshish **s** to go
1 Kgs 22:49 but in fact the **s** did not go,
Ps 107:23 Some went off to sea in **s**,
Jas 3: 4 It is the same with **s**:
Rev 8: 9 and a third of the **s** were wrecked.

SHIPWRECK → SHIP

1 Tm 1:19 have made a **s** of their faith,

SHIPWRECKED → SHIP

2 Cor 11:25 three times I was **s**, I passed a night

SHISHAK

2 Chr 12: 2 the fifth year of King Rehoboam, **S**,

SHONE → SHINE

Mt 17: 2 his face **s** like the sun and his
Lk 2: 9 the glory of the Lord **s** around them,
2 Cor 4: 6 has **s** in our hearts to bring to light

SHOOK → SHAKE

2 Sm 22: 8 The earth rocked and **s**; the foundations
Is 6: 4 cry, the frame of the door **s**
Acts 13:51 So they **s** the dust from their feet
Acts 18: 6 he **s** out his garments and said
Heb 12:26 His voice **s** the earth at that time,

SHOOT → SHOOTS

Is 11: 1 a **s** shall sprout from the stump
Rom 11:17 a wild olive, were grafted in their

SHOOTS → SHOOT

Hos 14: 7 and his **s** will go forth.

SHORE → SEASHORE

Lk 5: 3 put out a short distance from the **s**.

SHORT

Is 59: 1 of the LORD is not too **s** to save,
Lk 19: 3 of the crowd, for he was **s** in stature.
Rev 12:12 for he knows he has but a **s** time."

SHOULDER → SHOULDERS

Is 22:22 key of the House of David on his **s**;

SHOULDERS → SHOULDER

Ex 28:12 on his **s** as a reminder before
Mt 23: 4 [to carry] and lay them on people's **s**,
Lk 15: 5 it, he sets it on his **s** with great joy

SHOUT → SHOUTED, SHOUTS

Jos 6:16 "Now **s**, for the LORD has given
Ezr 3:11 all the people raised a great **s** of joy,
Ps 20: 6 May we **s** for joy at your victory,
Ps 35:27 let those who favor my just cause **s**
Ps 47: 2 **s** to God with joyful cries.
Is 12: 6 **S** with exultation, City of Zion,
Is 44:23 **S**, you depths of the earth.
Zec 9: 9 for joy, O daughter Jerusalem!

SHOUTED → SHOUT

1 Sm 17: 8 stood and **s** to the ranks of Israel:
Jb 38: 7 and all the sons of God **s** for joy?
Mk 15:13 They **s** again, "Crucify him."

SHOUTS → SHOUT

Ps 27: 6 in his tent sacrifices with **s** of joy;

SHOW → SHOWBREAD, SHOWED, SHOWING, SHOWN, SHOWS

Gn 12: 1 house to a land that I will **s** you.
Ex 9:16 to **s** you my power and to make my
Ex 25: 9 all that I **s** you regarding the pattern
1 Sm 20:14 may you **s** me the kindness
2 Sm 9: 1 whom I may **s** kindness for the sake
Ps 17: 7 **S** your wonderful mercy, you who
Ps 85: 8 **S** us, LORD, your mercy;
Prv 12:16 Fools immediately **s** their anger,
Prv 28:21 To **s** partiality is never good:
Is 30:18 truly, he shall rise to **s** you mercy;
Mi 7:20 You will **s** faithfulness to Jacob,
Zec 7: 9 and **s** kindness and compassion
Mt 22:19 **S** me the coin that pays the census
Jn 2:18 "What sign can you **s** us for doing

Jn	14: 8	"Master, **s** us the Father,
1 Cor	12:31	I shall **s** you a still more excellent
2 Cor	11:30	of the things that **s** my weakness.
Eph	2: 7	come he might **s** the immeasurable
Rev	1: 1	to **s** his servants what must happen
Rev	4: 1	and I will **s** you what must happen
Rev	17: 1	I will **s** you the judgment
Rev	21: 9	I will **s** you the bride, the wife

SHOWBREAD → BREAD, SHOW

Ex	25:30	On the table you shall always keep **s**
1 Sm	21: 7	no other bread was on hand except the **s**

SHOWED → SHOW

Gn	39:21	**s** him kindness by making the chief
Dt	34: 1	and the LORD **s** him all the land—
Mt	4: 8	**s** him all the kingdoms of the world
Lk	24:40	he **s** them his hands and his feet.
Jn	20:20	he **s** them his hands and his side.
Rev	21:10	**s** me the holy city Jerusalem coming
Rev	22: 1	Then the angel **s** me the river

SHOWERS

Jer	3: 3	Therefore the **s** were withheld,

SHOWING → SHOW

Ex	20: 6	**s** love down to the thousandth generation
Dt	5:10	**s** love down to the thousandth generation
Ti	2: 7	**s** yourself as a model of good deeds

SHOWN → SHOW

Ex	25:40	the pattern **s** you on the mountain.
1 Kgs	3: 6	"You have **s** great kindness to your
Ps	78:11	the wonders that he had **s** them.
Jn	10:32	"I have **s** you many good works

SHOWS → SHOW

Rom	9:16	but upon God, who **s** mercy.

SHREWDLY

Ex	1:10	let us deal **s** with them to stop their

SHUDDER

Ez	32:10	their kings will **s** at you, when I

SHUH

Jb	2:11	Bildad from **S**, and Zophar

SHULAMMITE

Sg	7: 1	Turn, turn, O **S**! turn, turn that we
Sg	7: 1	How can you gaze upon the **S** as

SHUNAMITE

1 Kgs	1: 3	of Israel, and found Abishag the **S**.

SHUNAMMITE

2 Kgs	4:12	Gehazi, "Call this **S** woman."

SHUT

Gn	7:16	Then the LORD **s** him in.
Gn	19: 6	When he had **s** the door behind him,
Is	22:22	opens, no one will **s**, what he shuts,
Rev	21:25	the day its gates will never be **s**,

SIBBOLETH → SHIBBOLETH

Jgs	12: 6	If he said "**S**," not pronouncing it

SICK → SICKBED, SICKNESS

Prv	13:12	Hope deferred makes the heart **s**,
Sg	2: 5	with apples, for I am **s** with love.
Sir	7:35	Do not hesitate to visit the **s**,
Ez	34: 4	the weak nor heal the **s** nor bind
Mt	8:16	spirits by a word and cured all the **s**,
Mt	9:12	not need a physician, but the **s** do.
Mt	10: 8	Cure the **s**, raise the dead,
Acts	19:12	his skin were applied to the **s**,
2 Tm	4:20	while I left Trophimus **s** at Miletus.
Jas	5:14	Is anyone among you **s**?

SICKBED → BED, SICK

Ps	41: 4	The LORD sustains him on his **s**,

SICKLE

Jl	4:13	Wield the **s**, for the harvest is ripe;
Mk	4:29	grain is ripe, he wields the **s** at once,
Rev	14:14	his head and a sharp **s** in his hand.

SICKNESS → SICK

Ex	23:25	I will remove **s** from your midst;

SIDE → ASIDE, SIDES

1 Chr	22: 9	rest from all his enemies on every **s**.
Ps	91: 7	Though a thousand fall at your **s**,
Ez	4: 4	Then lie down on your left **s**,
Jn	19:18	one on either **s**, with Jesus
Jn	19:34	soldier thrust his lance into his **s**,
Jn	20:20	he showed them his hands and his **s**.
Rev	22: 2	On either **s** of the river grew the tree

SIDES → SIDE

Ex	29:16	and splash on all the **s** of the altar.
Nm	33:55	in your eyes and thorns in your **s**,
Jos	23:13	a scourge for your **s** and thorns

SIDON

Jgs	1:31	inhabitants of Acco or those of **S**,
1 Kgs	17: 9	go to Zarephath of **S** and stay there.
Mt	11:21	midst had been done in Tyre and **S**,
Mk	7:31	and went by way of **S** to the Sea
Lk	4:26	widow in Zarephath in the land of **S**.

SIEGE → BESIEGED

2 Kgs	25: 1	it, and built **s** walls on every side.
Ez	4: 2	Lay **s** to it: build up **s** works,

SIEVE

Sir	27: 4	When a **s** is shaken, the husks
Am	9: 9	As one sifts with a **s**, letting no

SIFT

Lk	22:31	behold Satan has demanded to **s** all

SIGHED → SIGHING

Mk	8:12	He **s** from the depth of his spirit

SIGHING → SIGHED

Ps	5: 2	words, O LORD; understand my **s**.

SIGHT → SEE

Ex	3: 3	aside to look at this remarkable **s**.
2 Kgs	24:20	so angry that he cast them out of his **s**.
Ps	72:14	for precious is their blood in his **s**.
Mt	11: 5	the blind regain their **s**, the lame
Acts	1: 9	and a cloud took him from their **s**.
Acts	4:19	"Whether it is right in the **s** of God
2 Cor	5: 7	for we walk by faith, not by **s**.
1 Pt	3: 4	which is precious in the **s** of God.

SIGN → SIGNS

Gn	9:12	This is the **s** of the covenant that I
Ex	13:16	It will be like a **s** on your hand
Nm	17: 3	In this way they shall serve as a **s**
Jgs	6:17	give me a **s** that you are the one
1 Kgs	13: 3	He also gave a **s** that same day
1 Kgs	13: 3	"This is the **s** that the LORD has
Is	7:14	the Lord himself will give you a **s**;
Is	55:13	as an everlasting **s** that shall not fail.
Ez	20:12	my sabbaths to be a **s** between me
Ez	24:24	Ezekiel shall be a **s** for you:
Mt	12:38	we wish to see a **s** from you."
Mt	16: 1	him to show them a **s** from heaven.
Mt	24: 3	what **s** will there be of your coming,
Mt	24:30	the **s** of the Son of Man will appear
Mk	8:12	does this generation seek a **s**?
Mk	8:12	say to you, no **s** will be given to this
Lk	2:12	And this will be a **s** for you:
Lk	11:29	it seeks a **s**, but no **s** will be given it, except the **s** of Jonah.
Jn	2:18	"What **s** can you show us for doing
Rom	4:11	he received the **s** of circumcision as
1 Cor	11:10	this reason a woman should have a **s**
1 Cor	14:22	tongues are a **s** not for those who

SIGNET

Gn	41:42	Pharaoh took off his **s** ring and put
Est	3:10	The king took the **s** ring from his
Est	8: 2	The king removed his **s** ring that he
Jer	22:24	were a **s** ring on my right hand,
Hg	2:23	and I will make you like a **s** ring,

SIGNS → SIGN

Ex	4: 9	they do not believe even these two **s**
Ex	7: 3	despite the many **s** and wonders
Ps	105:27	They worked his **s** in Egypt
Sir	45: 3	At his words God performed **s** and
Is	8:18	we are **s** and portents in Israel
Dn	6:28	working **s** and wonders in heaven
Mt	16: 3	[you cannot judge the **s** of the times.]
Mt	24:24	they will perform **s** and wonders so
Mk	13:22	will perform **s** and wonders in order
Jn	3: 2	no one can do these **s** that you are
Jn	7:31	he perform more **s** than this man has
Jn	9:16	"How can a sinful man do such **s**?"
Jn	20:30	Now Jesus did many other **s**
Acts	2:19	above and **s** on the earth below:
Acts	5:12	Many **s** and wonders were done
1 Cor	1:22	For Jews demand **s** and Greeks look
2 Cor	12:12	The **s** of an apostle were performed
2 Cor	12:12	with all endurance, **s** and wonders,
2 Thes	2: 9	deed and in **s** and wonders that lie,
Heb	2: 4	God added his testimony by **s**,
Rev	13:13	It performed great **s**, even making
Rev	16:14	demonic spirits who performed **s**.
Rev	19:20	had performed in its sight the **s**

SIHON

Nm	21:21	Now Israel sent messengers to **S**,
Dt	31: 4	with them just as he dealt with **S**
Ps	136:19	**S**, king of the Amorites, for his

SILAS

Prophet (Acts 15:22-32); co-worker with Paul on second missionary journey (Acts 16–18; 2 Cor 1:19). Co-writer with Paul (1 Thes 1:1; 2 Thes 1:1); Peter (1 Pt 5:12).

SILENCE → SILENCED, SILENT

Ps	8: 3	your foes, to **s** enemy and avenger.
1 Pt	2:15	doing good you may **s** the ignorance
Rev	8: 1	there was **s** in heaven for about half

SILENCED → SILENCE

Mt	22:34	heard that he had **s** the Sadducees,
Rom	3:19	so that every mouth may be **s**

SILENT → SILENCE

Ps	39: 3	Mute and **s** before the wicked,
Ps	83: 2	God, do not be **s**; God, do not be deaf
Prv	17:28	keeping **s**, are considered wise;
Is	53: 7	or a sheep **s** before shearers, he did
Is	62: 1	For Zion's sake I will not be **s**,
Mk	14:61	But he was **s** and answered nothing.
Acts	8:32	and as a lamb before its shearer is **s**,
1 Cor	14:34	women should keep **s**

SILOAM

Jn	9: 7	the Pool of **S**" (which means Sent).

SILVER → SILVERSMITH

Gn	37:28	Joseph for twenty pieces of **s**
Ex	11: 2	for **s** and gold articles
Ex	20:23	not make alongside of me gods of **s**,
Ex	25: 3	gold, **s**, and bronze;
Dt	17:17	he accumulate a vast amount of **s**
Jos	7:21	two hundred shekels of **s**, and a bar
2 Chr	1:15	The king made **s** and gold as
1 Mc	1:23	And he took away the **s** and gold
Ps	12: 7	are sure, **s** refined in a crucible,
Ps	66:10	us, O God, tried us as **s** tried by fire.
Ps	115: 4	Their idols are **s** and gold, the work
Prv	2: 4	If you seek her like **s**, and like
Prv	3:14	Her profit is better than profit in **s**,
Prv	8:10	Take my instruction instead of **s**,
Prv	22: 1	and high esteem, than gold and **s**.
Prv	25: 4	Remove the dross from **s**, and it
Prv	25:11	in **s** settings are words spoken
Is	48:10	See, I refined you, but not like **s**;
Ez	22:18	they have become the dross from **s**.
Dn	2:32	its chest and arms were **s**, its belly
Dn	5: 4	praised their gods of gold and **s**,

Hg	2: 8	Mine is the **s** and mine the gold—
Zec	11:12	out my wages, thirty pieces of **s**.
Zec	13: 9	I will refine them as one refines **s**,
Mal	3: 3	He will sit refining and purifying **s**,
Mal	3: 3	Refining them like gold or **s**,
Mt	26:15	They paid him thirty pieces of **s**,
Acts	3: 6	"I have neither **s** nor gold, but what
1 Cor	3:12	on this foundation with gold, **s**,
2 Tm	2:20	are vessels not only of gold and **s**
1 Pt	1:18	not with perishable things like **s**

SILVERSMITH → SILVER

Acts	19:24	There was a **s** named Demetrius

SIMEON → =SIMON

1. Son of Jacob by Leah (Gn 29:33; 35:23; 1 Chr 2:1). With Levi killed Shechem for rape of Dinah (Gn 34:25-29). Held hostage by Joseph in Egypt (Gn 42:24–43:23). Tribe of blessed (Gn 49:5-7), numbered (Nm 1:23; 26:14), allotted land (Jos 19:1-9; Ez 48:24), 12,000 from (Rev 7:7).
2. Godly Jew who blessed the infant Jesus (2:25-35).
3. See Peter (Acts 15:14; 2 Pt 1:1).

SIMON → =PETER, =SIMEON

1. See Peter.
2. Apostle, called the Zealot (Mt 10:4; Mk 3:18; Lk 6:15; Acts 1:13).
3. Samaritan sorcerer (Acts 8:9-24).

SIMPLE

Ps	19: 8	trustworthy, giving wisdom to the **s**.
Ps	119:130	light, gives understanding to the **s**.

SIN → SINFUL, SINNED, SINNER, SINNERS, SINS

Gn	4: 7	but if not, **s** lies in wait at the door:
Ex	32:32	if you would only forgive their **s**!
Ex	34: 7	wickedness, rebellion, and **s**;
Nm	32:23	of your **s** will overtake you.
1 Sm	12:23	from me to **s** against the LORD
1 Sm	15:23	For a **s** of divination is rebellion,
1 Kgs	8:46	"When they **s** against you (for there is no one who does not **s**),
1 Kgs	13:34	is the account of the **s** of the house
Neh	13:26	king of Israel, **s** because of them?
Neh	13:26	Israel, yet even he was led into **s**
Tb	12:10	those who commit **s** and do evil are
Jb	1:22	In all this Job did not **s**, nor did he
Ps	4: 5	Tremble and **s** no more;
Ps	32: 5	Then I declared my **s** to you;
Ps	32: 5	you took away the guilt of my **s**.
Ps	38:19	my guilt and grieve over my **s**.
Ps	39: 2	my ways, lest I **s** with my tongue;
Ps	51: 4	and from my **s** cleanse me.
Ps	51: 7	in guilt, in **s** my mother conceived me.
Ps	119:11	that I may not **s** against you.
Prv	5:22	of their own **s** they will be held fast;
Prv	20: 9	clean, I am cleansed of my **s**"?
Wis	10:13	was sold, but rescued him from **s**.
Sir	7: 8	Do not plot to repeat a **s**;
Sir	42: 1	be ashamed, lest you **s** to save face:
Is	3: 9	they boast of their **s** like Sodom,
Is	6: 7	is removed, your **s** purged."
Jer	16:18	their **s** because they profaned my
Dn	9:20	confessing my **s** and the **s** of my people Israel,
Mi	6: 7	of my body for the **s** of my soul?
Mt	5:29	If your right eye causes you to **s**,
Mk	3:29	but is guilty of an everlasting **s**."
Jn	1:29	who takes away the **s** of the world.
Jn	8: 7	you who is without **s** be the first
Jn	8:34	everyone who commits **s** is a slave of **s**.
Jn	8:46	Can any of you charge me with **s**?
Jn	16: 9	**s**, because they do not believe
Acts	7:60	do not hold this **s** against them";
Rom	4: 8	is the man whose **s** the Lord does
Rom	5:12	as through one person **s** entered the world, and through **s**, death,
Rom	5:20	increase but, where **s** increased,
Rom	6: 2	How can we who died to **s** yet live
Rom	6:11	of yourselves as [being] dead to **s**
Rom	6:14	For **s** is not to have any power over

Rom 6:23 For the wages of s is death,
Rom 7: 7 That the law is s? Of course not!
Rom 7: 7 I did not know s except through
Rom 7:25 but, with my flesh, the law of s.
Rom 8: 2 has freed you from the law of s
Rom 14:23 for whatever is not from faith is s.
1 Cor 8:12 When you s in this way against your
1 Cor 15:56 The sting of death is s, and the power of s is the law.
2 Cor 5:21 him to be s who did not know s,
Eph 4:26 Be angry but do not s; do not let
1 Tm 5:20 Reprimand publicly those who do s,
Heb 4:15 tested in every way, yet without s.
Heb 9:26 ages to take away s by his sacrifice.
Heb 10:18 there is no longer offering for s.
Heb 11:25 than enjoy the fleeting pleasure of s.
Heb 12: 1 every burden and s that clings to us
Jas 1:15 desire conceives and brings forth s,
Jas 1:15 s reaches maturity it gives birth
1 Pt 2:22 "He committed no s, and no deceit
1 Jn 1: 7 his Son Jesus cleanses us from all s.
1 Jn 1: 8 "We are without s," we deceive
1 Jn 2: 1 you so that you may not commit s. But if anyone does s,
1 Jn 3: 4 Everyone who commits s commits lawlessness, for s is lawlessness.
1 Jn 3: 5 away sins, and in him there is no s.
1 Jn 3: 9 who is begotten by God commits s,
1 Jn 3: 9 he cannot s because he is begotten
1 Jn 5:16 if the s is not deadly, he should pray
1 Jn 5:16 only for those whose s is not deadly.
1 Jn 5:16 There is such a thing as deadly s,
1 Jn 5:17 All wrongdoing is s, but there is s that is not deadly.

SINAI → =HOREB
Ex 19: 1 they came to the wilderness of S.
Ex 19:20 Lord came down upon Mount S,
Ex 31:18 speaking to Moses on Mount S,
Nm 1:19 them in the wilderness of S.
Ps 68:18 S the Lord entered the holy place.
Gal 4:25 Hagar represents S, a mountain

SINCERE → SINCERELY, SINCERITY
2 Cor 11: 3 thoughts may be corrupted from a s
1 Tm 1: 5 a good conscience, and a s faith.
2 Tm 1: 5 as I recall your s faith that first lived

SINCERELY → SINCERE
Jos 24:14 fear the Lord and serve him completely and s.

SINCERITY → SINCERE
1 Cor 5: 8 with the unleavened bread of s
2 Cor 1:12 with the simplicity and s of God,
2 Cor 2:17 but as out of s, indeed as from God

SINEWS
Ez 37: 6 I will put s on you, make flesh grow

SINFUL → SIN
1 Mc 1:10 sprang from these a s offshoot,
Is 1: 4 Ah! S nation, people laden
Lk 5: 8 from me, Lord, for I am a s man."
Rom 7: 5 we were in the flesh, our s passions,
Rom 8: 3 own Son in the likeness of s flesh

SING → SANG, SINGER, SINGERS, SINGING, SONG, SONGS
Ex 15: 1 I will s to the Lord, for he is
1 Sm 21:12 that during their dances they s out,
Jdt 16:13 "I will s a new song to my God.
Ps 8: 2 I will s of your majesty above the heavens
Ps 13: 6 salvation, I will s to the Lord,
Ps 30: 5 S praise to the Lord, you faithful;
Ps 33: 3 S to him a new song;
Ps 47: 7 S praise to God, s praise; s praise
Ps 57: 8 I will s and chant praise.
Ps 59:17 But I shall s of your strength,
Ps 66: 2 all the earth; s of his glorious name;
Ps 68: 5 S to God, praise his name;
Ps 89: 2 I will s of your mercy forever,
Ps 95: 1 let us s joyfully to the Lord;
Ps 96: 1 S to the Lord a new song;

Ps 98: 1 S a new song to the Lord, for he
Ps 101: 1 I s of mercy and justice;
Ps 108: 2 Let me s and chant praise.
Ps 119:172 May my tongue s of your promise,
Ps 137: 3 "S for us a song of Zion!"
Ps 149: 1 S to the Lord a new song,
Is 5: 1 Now let me s of my friend,
Is 27: 2 The pleasant vineyard, s about it!
1 Cor 14:15 I will s praise with the spirit, but I will also s praise with the mind.
Jas 5:13 in good spirits? He should s praise.

SINGED
Dn 3:94 not a hair of their heads had been s,

SINGER → SING
Ez 33:32 them you are only a s of love songs,

SINGERS → SING
Ezr 2:70 the s, the gatekeepers,
Ps 68:26 The s go first, the harpists follow;

SINGING → SING
Is 35:10 and enter Zion s,
Is 51:11 will return and enter Zion s,
Acts 16:25 and s hymns to God as the prisoners
Eph 5:19 s and playing to the Lord in your
Col 3:16 admonish one another, s psalms,

SINGLE
Nm 13:23 cut down a branch with a s cluster
Mt 6:27 by worrying add a s moment to your
Heb 12:16 who sold his birthright for a s meal.
Rev 21:21 of the gates made from a s pearl;

SINK → SANK
Jer 51:64 and say: Thus Babylon shall s.

SINNED → SIN
1 Sm 15:24 "I have s, for I have transgressed
2 Sm 12:13 "I have s against the Lord."
2 Sm 24:10 "I have s grievously in what I have
2 Chr 6:37 say, 'We have s and done wrong;
Jb 1: 5 "It may be that my children have s
Jb 33:27 all and say, "I s and did wrong,
Ps 51: 6 Against you, you alone have I s;
Jer 2:35 that word of yours, "I have not s."
Jer 14:20 we have s against you.
Lam 5: 7 Our ancestors, who s, are no more;
Dn 9: 5 We have s, been wicked and done
Mi 7: 9 because I have s against him,
Mt 27: 4 "I have s in betraying innocent
Lk 15:18 I have s against heaven and against
Jn 9: 2 who s, this man or his parents,
Rom 3:23 all have s and are deprived
Rom 5:12 came to all, inasmuch as all s—
2 Pt 2: 4 not spare the angels when they s,
1 Jn 1:10 "We have not s," we make him

SINNER → SIN
Lk 15: 7 heaven over one s who repents than
Lk 18:13 'O God, be merciful to me a s.'
Jas 5:20 whoever brings back a s

SINNERS → SIN
Ps 1: 1 Nor stand in the way of s, nor sit
Ps 25: 8 therefore he shows s the way,
Ps 51:15 your ways, that s may return to you.
Prv 1:10 My son, should s entice you,
Prv 23:17 Do not let your heart envy s,
Is 1:28 and s together shall be crushed,
Mt 9:13 come to call the righteous but s."
Mk 14:41 of Man is to be handed over to s.
Lk 6:33 is that to you? Even s do the same.
Lk 15: 2 "This man welcomes s and eats
Rom 5: 8 while we were still s Christ died
1 Tm 1:15 Jesus came into the world to save s.
Heb 7:26 separated from s, higher than
Heb 12: 3 he endured such opposition from s,

SINS → SIN
1 Sm 2:25 If someone s against another,

1 Sm	2:25	but if anyone s against the LORD,
2 Kgs	17:22	Jeroboam in all the s he committed;
2 Chr	7:14	pardon their s and heal their land.
Ps	19:13	Cleanse me from my inadvertent s.
Ps	51:11	Turn away your face from my s;
Ps	79: 9	pardon our s for your name's sake.
Ps	103:10	has not dealt with us as our s merit,
Sir	2:11	forgives s and saves in time
Sir	3: 3	who honor their father atone for s;
Sir	34:31	So one who fasts for s, but goes
Is	1:18	Though your s be like scarlet,
Is	38:17	Behind your back you cast all my s.
Is	40: 2	of the LORD double for all her s.
Is	43:25	your s I remember no more.
Is	53:12	transgressors, Bore the s of many,
Is	59: 2	It is your s that make him hide his
Lam	3:39	about their s!
Ez	18: 4	Only the one who s shall die!
Ez	33:10	crimes and our s weigh us down;
Mi	7:19	into the depths of the sea all our s;
Mt	1:21	will save his people from their s."
Mt	9: 6	authority on earth to forgive s"—
Mt	18:15	"If your brother s [against you],
Mt	26:28	of many for the forgiveness of s.
Mk	1: 5	River as they acknowledged their s.
Lk	5:24	authority on earth to forgive s"—
Lk	11: 4	forgive us our s for we ourselves
Lk	17: 3	If your brother s, rebuke him;
Jn	8:24	told you that you will die in your s.
Jn	8:24	that I AM, you will die in your s."
Jn	20:23	Whose s you forgive are forgiven
Jn	20:23	whose s you retain are retained."
Acts	2:38	Christ for the forgiveness of your s;
Acts	3:19	that your s may be wiped away,
Acts	10:43	forgiveness of s through his name."
Acts	22:16	baptized and your s washed away,
Acts	26:18	they may obtain forgiveness of s
Rom	4: 7	forgiven and whose s are covered.
1 Cor	6:18	but the immoral person s against his
1 Cor	15: 3	Christ died for our s in accordance
Eph	2: 1	dead in your transgressions and s
1 Tm	5:22	and do not share in another's s.
Heb	1: 3	accomplished purification from s,
Heb	2:17	God to expiate the s of the people.
Heb	7:27	first for his own s and then for those
Heb	8:12	and remember their s no more."
Heb	9:28	once to take away the s of many,
Heb	10: 4	of bulls and goats take away s.
Heb	10:12	this one offered one sacrifice for s,
Heb	10:26	no longer remains sacrifice for s
Jas	5:16	confess your s to one another
Jas	5:20	and will cover a multitude of s.
1 Pt	2:24	He himself bore our s in his body
1 Pt	3:18	For Christ also suffered for s once,
1 Pt	4: 8	love covers a multitude of s.
1 Jn	1: 9	If we acknowledge our s, he is
1 Jn	1: 9	will forgive our s and cleanse us
1 Jn	2: 2	He is expiation for our s, and not for our s only but for those
1 Jn	3: 5	that he was revealed to take away s,
1 Jn	4:10	sent his Son as expiation for our s.
Rev	1: 5	freed us from our s by his blood,

SISERA

Jgs	4: 2	The general of his army was S,
Jgs	5:26	She hammered S, crushed his head;

SISTER → SISTERS

Gn	12:13	that you are my s, so that I may fare
Gn	20: 2	of his wife Sarah, "She is my s."
Gn	26: 7	wife, he answered, "She is my s."
Tb	10:12	I am your mother, and Sarah is your s.
Prv	7: 4	Say to Wisdom, "You are my s!"
Sg	4: 9	ravished my heart, my s, my bride;
Jer	3: 7	even though that traitor her s Judah,
Ez	16:46	Your elder s was Samaria with her
Ez	16:46	and your younger s was Sodom

Mk	3:35	the will of God is my brother and s
Lk	10:40	you not care that my s has left me
Jn	11: 5	loved Martha and her s and Lazarus.
Rom	16: 1	I commend to you Phoebe our s,
2 Jn	1:13	of your chosen s send you greetings.

SISTERS → SISTER

Mt	19:29	up houses or brothers or s or father
Mk	6: 3	And are not his s here with us?"
1 Tm	5: 2	younger women as s with complete

SIT → SAT, SITS, SITTING

Ex	18:14	Why do you s alone while all
1 Kgs	8:25	from your line to s before me
Ps	1: 1	nor s in company with scoffers.
Ps	26: 5	with the wicked I do not s.
Ps	139: 2	you know when I s and stand;
Is	16: 5	and on it shall s in fidelity,
Mi	4: 4	They shall all s under their own
Mal	3: 3	He will s refining and purifying
Mt	20:23	but to s at my right and at my left
Mt	22:44	"S at my right hand until I place
Mk	14:32	his disciples, "S here while I pray."
Lk	22:30	you will s on thrones judging
Acts	2:34	to my Lord, "S at my right hand
Heb	1:13	"S at my right hand until I make

SITS → SIT

Ps	29:10	The LORD s enthroned
Is	28: 6	for the one who s in judgment,

SITTING → SIT

Lk	8:35	whom the demons had come out s

SIX → SIXTH

Ex	20: 9	S days you may labor and do all
1 Chr	20: 6	who had s fingers to each hand and s toes to each foot;
Prv	6:16	There are s things the LORD
Is	6: 2	each of them had s wings:
Rev	4: 8	each of them with s wings,
Rev	13:18	His number is s hundred and sixty-six.

SIXTH → SIX

Rev	6:12	while he broke open the s seal,
Rev	16:12	The s angel emptied his bowl

SIXTY

Mt	13: 8	fruit, a hundred or s or thirtyfold.

SIXTY-SIX

Rev	13:18	His number is six hundred and s.

SIZE

Mt	17:20	if you have faith the s of a mustard

SKIES → SKY

Ps	89: 7	Who in the s ranks

SKILL → SKILLFULLY

Ex	28: 3	whom I have endowed with s
2 Chr	2:12	a craftsman of great s, Huram-abi,

SKILLFULLY → SKILL

Ps	33: 3	s play with joyful chant.

SKIN → SKINS, WINESKINS

Ex	34:30	noticed how radiant the s of his face
Jb	2: 4	the LORD and said, "S for s!
Jb	19:20	My bones cling to my s, and I have escaped by the s of my teeth.
Jer	13:23	Can Ethiopians change their s,
Ez	37: 6	cover you with s, and put breath

SKINS → SKIN

Ex	25: 5	rams' dyed red, and tahash s;
Lk	5:37	the new wine will burst the s, and it
Lk	5:37	be spilled, and the s will be ruined.

SKIRT

Lam	1: 9	Her uncleanness is on her s;

SKULL

2 Kgs	9:35	they found nothing of her but the s,
Mt	27:33	(which means Place of the S),

SKY → SKIES
Gn	1: 8	God called the dome "s."
Mt	16: 3	for the s is red and threatening.'
Mt	16: 3	to judge the appearance of the s,
Rev	6:13	The stars in the s fell to the earth
Rev	6:14	the s was divided like a torn scroll
Rev	11: 6	close up the s so that no rain can fall

SLACK
Prv	18: 9	Those s in their work are kin

SLAIN
1 Chr	10: 1	and they fell, s on Mount Gilboa.
Ez	37: 9	into these s that they may come

SLANDER → SLANDERED, SLANDERERS, SLANDERS
Ps	15: 3	Who does not s with his tongue,
2 Cor	12:20	fury, selfishness, s, gossip, conceit,
Col	3: 8	malice, s, and obscene language
1 Pt	2: 1	deceit, insincerity, envy, and all s;

SLANDERED → SLANDER
1 Cor	4:13	when s, we respond gently.

SLANDERERS → SLANDER
1 Tm	3:11	not s, but temperate and faithful
Ti	2: 3	not s, not addicted to drink,

SLANDERS → SLANDER
Ps	101: 5	Whoever s a neighbor in secret I

SLAPPED
Mt	26:67	and struck him, while some s him,

SLAUGHTER → SLAUGHTERED
Ex	29:11	Then s the bull before the LORD,
Dt	12:15	any of your communities you may s
Prv	7:22	like an ox that goes to s; Like a stag
Is	53: 7	Like a lamb led to s or a sheep
Jer	11:19	I was like a trusting lamb led to s,
Acts	8:32	"Like a sheep he was led to the s,

SLAUGHTERED → SLAUGHTER
Ex	12: 6	it will be s during the evening
Nm	14:16	is why he s them in the wilderness.'
Zec	11: 4	Shepherd the flock to be s.
Rom	8:36	are looked upon as sheep to be s."
Rev	6: 9	those who had been s because

SLAVE → ENSLAVE, SLAVERY, SLAVES
Gn	9:26	God of Shem! Let Canaan be his s.
Gn	21:10	"Drive out that s and her son!
Mk	10:44	be first among you will be the s
Jn	8:34	everyone who commits sin is a s
1 Cor	7:21	Were you a s when you were
1 Cor	9:19	I have made myself a s to all so as
Gal	3:28	there is neither s nor free person,
Gal	4:30	"Drive out the s woman and her
Gal	4:30	of the s woman shall not share
Phil	2: 7	taking the form of a s,
Col	3:11	barbarian, Scythian, s, free;
Phlm	1:16	no longer as a s but more than a s,
Rev	13:16	free and s, to be given a stamped

SLAVERY → SLAVE
Ex	20: 2	land of Egypt, out of the house of s.
Dt	7: 8	redeemed you from the house of s.
Rom	7:14	but I am carnal, sold into s to sin.
Gal	5: 1	do not submit again to the yoke of s.
1 Tm	6: 1	of s must regard their masters as

SLAVES → SLAVE
Gn	9:25	The lowest of s shall he be to his
Eccl	10: 7	I have seen s on horseback,
Eccl	10: 7	while princes went on foot like s.
Jer	34: 9	Everyone must free their Hebrew s,
Rom	6:16	as obedient s, you are s of the one you obey,
1 Cor	7:23	Do not become s to human beings.
1 Cor	12:13	Jews or Greeks, s or free persons,
Eph	6: 5	S, be obedient to your human
Col	3:22	S, obey your human masters
Col	4: 1	treat your s justly and fairly,
Ti	2: 9	S are to be under the control of their

2 Pt	2:19	though they themselves are s

SLAYS
Jb	5: 2	and indignation s the simpleton.

SLEEP → ASLEEP, SLEEPER, SLEEPING, SLEEPLESS, SLEEPS
Gn	2:21	So the LORD God cast a deep s
Ex	22:26	What will he s in? If he cries
Dt	24:13	your neighbor may s in the garment
Ps	13: 4	light to my eyes lest I s in death,
Ps	76: 6	they sank into s; the hands of all
Ps	78:65	Then the Lord awoke as from s,
Ps	121: 3	foot to slip; or your guardian to s.
Ps	127: 2	this God gives to his beloved in s.
Ps	132: 4	I will give my eyes no s, my eyelids
Prv	6: 9	when will you rise from your s?
Prv	6:10	A little s, a little slumber, a little
Eccl	5:11	S is sweet to the laborer,
Eccl	5:11	of the rich allows them no s.
Is	29:10	poured out on you a spirit of deep s.
Dn	12: 2	Many of those who s in the dust
Acts	20: 9	sinking into a deep s as Paul talked
Acts	20: 9	Once overcome by s, he fell down
1 Thes	5: 7	Those who s go to s at night,

SLEEPER → SLEEP
Eph	5:14	O s, and arise from the dead,

SLEEPING → SLEEP
Mt	9:24	The girl is not dead but s."

SLEEPLESS → SLEEP
2 Cor	11:27	through many s nights,

SLEEPS → SLEEP
Ps	121: 4	of Israel never slumbers nor s.

SLING
Jgs	20:16	of them able to s a stone at a hair
1 Sm	17:50	triumphed over the Philistine with s
Prv	26: 8	is like entangling a stone in the s.

SLIP → SLIPPED, SLIPPERY, SLIPPING
Dt	4: 9	nor let them s from your heart as

SLIPPED → SLIP
Ps	73: 2	my steps had nearly s,

SLIPPERY → SLIP
Ps	35: 6	Make their way s and dark,
Ps	73:18	You set them, indeed, on a s road;
Jer	23:12	shall become for them s ground.

SLIPPING → SLIP
Ps	94:18	I say, "My foot is s," your mercy,

SLOW
Ex	4:10	but I am s of speech and tongue."
Ex	34: 6	s to anger and abounding in love
Nm	14:18	'The LORD is s to anger
Neh	9:17	s to anger and rich in mercy;
Ps	86:15	and gracious God, s to anger,
Ps	103: 8	gracious is the LORD, s to anger,
Ps	145: 8	s to anger and abounding in mercy.
Prv	19:11	It is good sense to be s to anger,
Jl	2:13	is gracious and merciful, s to anger,
Jon	4: 2	and merciful God, s to anger,
Na	1: 3	The LORD is s to anger, yet great
Lk	24:25	How s of heart to believe all
Jas	1:19	should be quick to hear, s to speak, s to wrath,

SLUGGISH
Heb	6:12	so that you may not become s,

SLUMBER → SLUMBERS
Prv	6:10	a little s, a little folding of the arms

SLUMBERS → SLUMBER
Ps	121: 4	of Israel never s nor sleeps.
Prv	10: 5	a son who s during harvest,

SMALL → SMALLEST
Nm	26:54	to a s tribe a s heritage,
Mk	12:42	in two s coins worth a few cents.
Lk	19:17	been faithful in this very s matter;
Jas	3: 5	same way the tongue is a s member

Jas   3: 5 Consider how **s** a fire can set a huge

SMALLEST → SMALL
Mk   4:31 is the **s** of all the seeds on the earth.

SMASH
Dt   12: 3 their altars, **s** their sacred pillars,

SMEAR
Ps   119:69 The arrogant **s** me with lies, but I

SMELL
Dt   4:28 see nor hear, neither eat nor **s.**
Ps   115: 6 but do not hear, noses but do not **s.**
Dn   3:94 there was not even a **s** of fire

SMOKE → SMOKING
Gn   19:28 he saw **s** over the land rising like the **s** from a kiln.
Ex   19:18 was completely enveloped in **s,**
Ps   68: 3 As the **s** is dispersed, disperse them;
Ps   104:32 touches the mountains and they **s!**
Is   6: 4 and the house was filled with **s.**
Jl   3: 3 earth, blood, fire, and columns of **s;**
Rev   8: 4 The **s** of the incense along
Rev   9: 2 **s** came up out of the passage like
Rev   9: 2 darkened by the **s** from the passage.
Rev   15: 8 filled with the **s** from God's glory

SMOKING → SMOKE
Gn   15:17 there appeared a **s** fire pot
Ex   20:18 of the shofar and the mountain **s,**

SMOLDERING
Mt   12:20 break, a **s** wick he will not quench,

SMOOTH → SMOOTHER
1 Sm   17:40 David selected five **s** stones
Prv   6:24 from the **s** tongue of the foreign
Prv   7:21 with her **s** lips she leads him astray.
Lk   3: 5 straight, and the rough ways made **s,**

SMOOTHER → SMOOTH
Ps   55:22 **S** than oil are his words, but they are
Prv   5: 3 honey, and her mouth is **s** than oil;

SMYRNA
Rev   2: 8 "To the angel of the church in **S,**

SNAKE
Gn   3: 1 Now the **s** was the most cunning of all
Gn   3:13 The woman answered, "The **s** tricked me,
Gn   3:14 Then the Lord God said to the **s:**
Lk   11:11 among you would hand his son a **s**

SNARE → ENSNARED, SNARES
Jgs   2: 3 for you, and their gods a **s** for you.
Ps   69:23 May their own table be a **s** for them,
Ps   91: 3 will rescue you from the fowler's **s,**
Prv   29:25 Fear of others becomes a **s,**
Rom   11: 9 "Let their table become a **s**

SNARES → SNARE
Ps   18: 6 the **s** of death lay in wait for me.
Prv   13:14 life, turning one from the **s** of death.

SNATCHED
Acts   8:39 the Spirit of the Lord **s** Philip away,

SNEEZED
2 Kgs   4:35 him, and the boy **s** seven times

SNOUT
Prv   11:22 in a swine's **s** is a beautiful woman

SNOW
2 Kgs   5:27 went out, a leper with skin like **s.**
Ps   51: 9 me, and I will be whiter than **s.**
Is   1:18 they may become white as **s;**
Dn   7: 9 His clothing was white as **s,** the hair
Mt   28: 3 and his clothing was white as **s.**
Rev   1:14 was as white as white wool or as **s,**

SO-CALLED → CALL
1 Cor   8: 5 even though there are **s** gods
2 Thes   2: 4 exalts himself above every **s** god

SOAP
Jer   2:22 and use much **s,** The stain of your

SOBER
1 Thes   5: 6 rest do, but let us stay alert and **s.**

SOCKET
Gn   32:26 he struck Jacob's hip at its **s,**
Gn   32:26 that Jacob's **s** was dislocated as he

SODOM
Gn   13:12 the Plain, pitching his tents near **S.**
Gn   13:13 the inhabitants of **S** were wicked,
Gn   18:20 The outcry against **S** and Gomorrah
Gn   19:24 Lord rained down sulfur upon **S**
Is   1: 9 We would have become as **S,**
Ez   16:49 look at the guilt of your sister **S:**
Lk   10:12 it will be more tolerable for **S**
Rom   9:29 we would have become like **S**
Jude   1: 7 Likewise, **S,** Gomorrah,
Rev   11: 8 which has the symbolic names "**S**"

SOFT
Prv   25:15 and a **s** tongue can break a bone.

SOIL → SOILED
Gn   9:20 a man of the **s,** was the first to plant
Mt   13:23 rich **s** is the one who hears the word

SOILED → SOIL
Rev   3: 4 who have not **s** their garments;

SOLD → SELL
Gn   37:28 They **s** Joseph for twenty pieces
Dt   32:30 it was because their Rock **s** them,
1 Mc   1:15 and **s** themselves to wrongdoing.
Mt   10:29 Are not two sparrows **s** for a small
Acts   5: 1 wife Sapphira, **s** a piece of property.
Rom   7:14 but I am carnal, **s** into slavery to sin.
1 Cor   10:25 Eat anything **s** in the market,
Heb   12:16 who **s** his birthright for a single

SOLDIER → SOLDIERS
2 Tm   2: 3 me like a good **s** of Christ Jesus.

SOLDIERS → SOLDIER
Mt   27:27 the **s** of the governor took Jesus
Mt   28:12 gave a large sum of money to the **s,**
Jn   19:23 When the **s** had crucified Jesus,

SOLE
Is   1: 6 From the **s** of the foot to the head

SOLID
1 Cor   3: 2 I fed you milk, not **s** food,
Heb   5:14 But **s** food is for the mature,

SOLITARY
Lam   1: 1 How **s** sits the city, once filled

SOLOMON → =JEDIDIAH
Son of David by Bathsheba; king of Judah (2 Sm 12:24; 1 Chr 3:5, 10). Appointed king by David (1 Kgs 1); adversaries Adonijah, Joab, Shimei killed by Benaiah (1 Kgs 2). Asked for wisdom (1 Kgs 3; 2 Chr 1). Judged between two prostitutes (1 Kgs 3:16-28). Built temple (1 Kgs 5–7; 2 Chr 2–5); prayer of dedication (1 Kgs 8; 2 Chr 6). Visited by Queen of Sheba (1 Kgs 10; 2 Chr 9). Wives turned his heart from God (1 Kgs 11:1-13). Jeroboam rebelled against (1 Kgs 11:26-40). Death (1 Kgs 11:41-43; 2 Chr 9:29-31).
Proverbs of (1 Kgs 5:12; Prv 1:1; 10:1; 25:1); psalms of (Ps 72; 127); song of (Sg 1:1).

SOLVE
Dn   5:16 give interpretations and **s** problems;

SOME
Gn   3: 6 So she took **s** of its fruit and ate it;
Gn   3: 6 and she also gave **s** to her husband,
1 Cor   9:22 all things to all, to save at least **s.**
Eph   4:11 And he gave **s** as apostles, others as
Phil   1:15 **s** preach Christ from envy
1 Tm   4: 1 in the last times **s** will turn away
2 Tm   2:20 **s** for lofty and others for humble
2 Pt   3:16 In them there are **s** things hard

SOMEONE
Ex   4:13 you please, my Lord, send **s** else!"
Lk   16:31 they be persuaded if **s** should rise

Rom 10:14 And how can they hear without s

SOMETHING

Acts 3: 5 expecting to receive s from them.
Phil 2: 6 equality with God s to be grasped.
Rev 8: 8 s like a large burning mountain was

SON → SONS

Gn 5: 3 when he begot a s in his likeness,
Gn 17:19 your wife Sarah is to bear you a s,
Gn 21: 2 bore Abraham a s in his old age,
Gn 21:10 "Drive out that slave and her s!
Gn 21:10 No s of that slave is going to share
Gn 22: 2 Take your s Isaac, your only one,
Gn 22:12 did not withhold from me your s,
Gn 25:11 God blessed his s Isaac, who lived
Ex 4:23 Let my s go, that he may serve me.
Ex 4:23 I will kill your s, your firstborn.
Dt 18:10 you anyone who causes their s
Dt 21:18 rebellious s who will not listen
2 Sm 7:14 to him, and he shall be a s to me.
1 Kgs 8:19 but your s, who comes from your
2 Kgs 6:29 So we boiled my s and ate him.
2 Kgs 6:29 up your s that we may eat him.'
1 Chr 22:10 he shall be a s to me, and I will be
Prv 1: 8 my s, your father's instruction,
Prv 2: 1 My s, if you receive my words
Ps 2: 7 he said to me, "You are my s;
Prv 3: 1 My s, do not forget my teaching,
Prv 3:12 reproves, as a father, the s he favors.
Prv 4:10 Hear, my s, and receive my words,
Prv 5: 1 My s, to my wisdom be attentive,
Prv 7: 1 My s, keep my words, and treasure
Prv 10: 1 A wise s gives his father joy,
Prv 10: 1 a foolish s is a grief to his mother.
Prv 13: 1 A wise s loves correction,
Prv 23:26 My s, give me your heart, and let
Is 7:14 pregnant and about to bear a s,
Is 8: 3 and she conceived and bore a s.
Is 9: 5 child is born to us, a s is given to us;
Jer 31:20 Is Ephraim not my favored s,
Hos 11: 1 him, out of Egypt I called my s.
Mal 1: 6 A s honors his father, and a servant
Mt 1: 1 of Jesus Christ, the s of David, the s of Abraham.
Mt 1:23 shall be with child and bear a s,
Mt 2:15 "Out of Egypt I called my s."
Mt 3:17 "This is my beloved S, with whom
Mt 4: 3 "If you are the S of God,
Mt 8:20 the S of Man has nowhere to rest his
Mt 11:27 one knows the S except the Father,
Mt 11:27 one knows the Father except the S
Mt 11:27 to whom the S wishes to reveal him.
Mt 12: 8 For the S of Man is Lord
Mt 12:32 speaks a word against the S of Man
Mt 12:40 so will the S of Man be in the heart
Mt 13:55 Is he not the carpenter's s? Is not his
Mt 14:33 "Truly, you are the S of God."
Mt 16:16 Messiah, the S of the living God."
Mt 16:27 For the S of Man will come with his
Mt 17: 5 "This is my beloved S, with whom
Mt 19:28 when the S of Man is seated on his
Mt 20:18 the S of Man will be handed over
Mt 20:28 so, the S of Man did not come to be
Mt 21: 9 "Hosanna to the S of David;
Mt 22:42 about the Messiah? Whose s is he?"
Mt 24:27 will the coming of the S of Man be.
Mt 24:30 the sign of the S of Man will appear
Mt 24:30 they will see the S of Man coming
Mt 24:44 not expect, the S of Man will come.
Mt 25:31 "When the S of Man comes in his
Mt 26:63 you are the Messiah, the S of God."
Mt 27:54 "Truly, this was the S of God!"
Mt 28:19 and of the S, and of the holy Spirit,
Mk 1:11 heavens, "You are my beloved S;
Mk 2:28 is why the S of Man is lord even
Mk 8:38 the S of Man will be ashamed
Mk 9: 7 a voice, "This is my beloved S.

Mk 10:45 For the S of Man did not come to be
Mk 13:32 nor the S, but only the Father.
Mk 14:62 'you will see the S of Man seated
Mk 15:39 said, "Truly this man was the S
Lk 1:32 will be called S of the Most High,
Lk 1:35 will be called holy, the S of God.
Lk 2: 7 and she gave birth to her firstborn s.
Lk 3:22 heaven, "You are my beloved S;
Lk 9:35 that said, "This is my chosen S;
Lk 9:58 the S of Man has nowhere to rest his
Lk 12: 8 me before others the S of Man will
Lk 15:21 His s said to him, 'Father, I have
Lk 15:21 longer deserve to be called your s.'
Lk 18: 8 But when the S of Man comes,
Lk 18:31 about the S of Man will be fulfilled.
Lk 19:10 For the S of Man has come to seek
Lk 20:44 him 'lord,' how can he be his s?"
Jn 1:34 testified that he is the S of God."
Jn 1:49 him, "Rabbi, you are the S of God;
Jn 3:14 so must the S of Man be lifted up,
Jn 3:16 the world that he gave his only S,
Jn 3:36 believes in the S has eternal life,
Jn 3:36 whoever disobeys the S will not see
Jn 5:19 a s cannot do anything on his own,
Jn 5:19 for what he does, his s will do also.
Jn 6:40 that everyone who sees the S
Jn 11: 4 that the S of God may be glorified
Jn 12:34 that the S of Man must be lifted up?
Jn 13:31 "Now is the S of Man glorified,
Jn 17: 1 Give glory to your s, so that your s may glorify you,
Acts 7:56 the S of Man standing at the right
Acts 13:33 in the second psalm, 'You are my s;
Rom 1: 4 established as S of God in power
Rom 5:10 to God through the death of his S,
Rom 8: 3 by sending his own S in the likeness
Rom 8:29 be conformed to the image of his S,
Rom 8:32 He who did not spare his own S
1 Cor 15:28 then the S himself will [also] be
Col 1:13 us to the kingdom of his beloved S,
1 Thes 1:10 and to await his S from heaven,
Heb 1: 2 he spoke to us through a s, whom he
Heb 1: 5 "You are my s; this day I have
Heb 1: 5 to him, and he shall be a s to me"?
Heb 4:14 Jesus, the S of God, let us hold fast
Heb 5: 5 "You are my s; this day I have
Heb 7:28 appoints a s, who has been made
Heb 10:29 who has contempt for the S of God,
Heb 12: 6 he scourges every s he
Jas 2:21 when he offered his s Isaac
2 Pt 1:17 glory, "This is my S, my beloved,
1 Jn 1: 3 is with the Father and with his S,
1 Jn 1: 7 the blood of his S Jesus cleanses us
1 Jn 2:23 one who denies the S has the Father,
1 Jn 2:23 but whoever confesses the S has
1 Jn 3: 8 the S of God was revealed
1 Jn 4: 9 God sent his only S into the world
1 Jn 4:14 the Father sent his S as savior
1 Jn 5: 5 believes that Jesus is the S of God?
1 Jn 5:11 eternal life, and this life is in his S.
Rev 1:13 the lampstands one like a s of man,
Rev 2:18 " "The S of God, whose eyes are
Rev 12: 5 She gave birth to a s, a male child,
Rev 14:14 the cloud one who looked like a s

SONG → SING

Ex 15: 1 and the Israelites sang this s
Dt 31:21 them, this s will speak to them as
Dt 32:44 all the words of this s in the hearing
Ps 33: 3 Sing to him a new s;
Ps 40: 4 And puts a new s in my mouth,
Ps 69:31 That I may praise God's name in s
Ps 96: 1 Sing to the LORD a new s;
Ps 98: 4 break into s; sing praise.
Ps 149: 1 Sing to the LORD a new s,
Is 5: 1 my beloved's s about his vineyard.
Is 54: 1 break forth in jubilant s, you who
Is 55:12 hills shall break out in s before you,

Rev	15: 3	and they sang the s of Moses,
Rev	15: 3	of God, and the s of the Lamb:

SONGS → SING

1 Kgs	5:12	and his s numbered a thousand
Jdt	15:13	wearing garlands and singing s of praise.
1 Mc	4:54	very day it was rededicated with s,
Eph	5:19	psalms and hymns and spiritual s,
Col	3:16	and spiritual s with gratitude in your

SONS → SON

Gn	6: 2	the s of God saw how beautiful
Gn	9: 1	Noah and his s and said to them:
Gn	10:32	These are the clans of Noah's s,
Gn	35:22	The s of Jacob were now twelve.
Ex	13:15	I ransom every firstborn of my s.'
Ex	28: 9	on them the names of the s of Israel:
Nm	18: 8	to you and to your s as a perquisite.
Dt	7: 3	your daughters to their s nor taking their daughters for your s.
Ru	4:15	is worth more to you than seven s!"
1 Sm	1: 8	Am I not better for you than ten s?"
1 Mc	1:48	to leave their s uncircumcised,
1 Mc	2: 2	He had five s: John, who was called
Ps	132:12	If your s observe my covenant,
Ps	132:12	I shall teach them, Their s, in turn,
Jl	3: 1	Your s and daughters will prophesy,
Mal	3:24	turn the heart of fathers to their s, and the heart of s to their fathers,
Acts	2:17	Your s and your daughters shall
2 Cor	6:18	you shall be s and daughters to me,

SOON

Ps	106:13	But they s forgot all he had done;
Rev	1: 1	his servants what must happen s.
Rev	22: 7	"Behold, I am coming s."
Rev	22:12	"Behold, I am coming s.
Rev	22:20	says, "Yes, I am coming s." Amen!

SOOTHSAYER → SOOTHSAYERS

Dt	18:10	practices divination, or is a s, augur,

SOOTHSAYERS → SOOTHSAYER

Is	2: 6	diviners, and s, like the Philistines;
Mi	5:11	shall no longer be s among you.

SORCERERS → SORCERY

Ex	7:11	summoned the wise men and the s,
Jer	27: 9	to your soothsayers and s, who say
Dn	2: 2	enchanters, s, and Chaldeans be
Rev	21: 8	the unchaste, s, idol-worshipers,
Rev	22:15	are the dogs, the s, the unchaste,

SORCERIES → SORCERY

Is	47: 9	upon you Despite your many s

SORCERY → SORCERERS, SORCERIES

Gal	5:20	idolatry, s, hatreds, rivalry,

SORDID

Ti	1:11	for s gain what they should not.

SOREK

Jgs	16: 4	in the Wadi S whose name was

SORES

Lk	16:20	named Lazarus, covered with s,

SORROW → SORROWFUL, SORROWS

Est	9:22	was turned for them from s into joy,
Eccl	1:18	in much wisdom there is much s;
Is	35:10	gladness, s and mourning flee away.
Is	51:11	gladness, s and mourning will flee.
Rom	9: 2	that I have great s and constant

SORROWFUL → SORROW

2 Cor	6:10	as s yet always rejoicing;

SORROWS → SORROW

Ps	16: 4	They multiply their s who court

SOUGHT → SEEK

1 Sm	13:14	The LORD has s out a man
2 Chr	26: 5	and as long as he s the LORD,
Ps	34: 5	I s the LORD, and he answered

Sir	51:13	young and innocent, I s wisdom.

SOUL → SOULS

Ps	16: 9	my heart is glad, my s rejoices;
Ps	19: 8	LORD is perfect, refreshing the s.
Ps	25: 1	To you, O LORD, I lift up my s,
Ps	33:20	Our s waits for the LORD, he is
Ps	34: 3	My s will glory in the LORD;
Ps	42: 2	of water, so my s longs for you,
Ps	42:12	my s, why do you groan within me?
Ps	49: 9	The redemption of his s is costly;
Ps	62: 6	My s, be at rest in God alone,
Ps	63: 9	My s clings fast to you;
Ps	103: 1	Bless the LORD, my s;
Ps	116: 7	Return, my s, to your rest;
Ps	130: 5	my s waits and I hope for his word.
Prv	13:19	Desire fulfilled delights the s,
Prv	24:14	must know, is wisdom to your s.
Sir	7:29	With all your s fear God and revere
Lam	3:20	it over and over, my s is downcast.
Mi	6: 7	fruit of my body for the sin of my s?
Mt	10:28	kill the body but cannot kill the s;
Mt	10:28	of the one who can destroy both s
Mt	22:37	with all your s, and with all your
Lk	1:46	"My s proclaims the greatness
1 Thes	5:23	you entirely, spirit, s, and body,
Heb	4:12	penetrating even between s
Heb	6:19	This we have as an anchor of the s,
Jas	5:20	his way will save his s from death
1 Pt	2:11	desires that wage war against the s.
3 Jn	1: 2	health, just as your s is prospering.

SOULS → SOUL

1 Pt	1: 9	[your] faith, the salvation of your s.
1 Pt	2:25	the shepherd and guardian of your s.
Rev	6: 9	I saw underneath the altar the s
Rev	20: 4	saw the s of those who had been

SOUND

Gn	3: 8	they heard the s of the LORD God
Ex	32:18	the s I hear is singing."
Dt	4:12	You heard the s of the words,
Ps	66: 8	loudly s his praise,
Ps	115: 7	they produce no s from their throats.
Ez	1:24	Then I heard the s of their wings,
Jl	2: 1	s the alarm on my holy mountain!
Jn	3: 8	and you can hear the s it makes,
1 Cor	14: 8	if the bugle gives an indistinct s,
1 Cor	15:52	For the trumpet will s, the dead will
1 Tm	1:10	else is opposed to s teaching,
1 Tm	6: 3	does not agree with the s words
2 Tm	1:13	Take as your norm the s words
2 Tm	4: 3	will not tolerate s doctrine but,
Ti	1: 9	able both to exhort with s doctrine
Ti	2: 1	what is consistent with s doctrine,
Rev	1:15	his voice was like the s of rushing
Rev	19: 6	multitude or the s of rushing water

SOURCE

Heb	5: 9	he became the s of eternal salvation

SOUTH

Dn	11: 5	king of the s shall grow strong,
Mt	12:42	the queen of the s will arise

SOVEREIGN

Acts	4:24	with one accord and said, "S Lord,

SOW → SOWED, SOWER, SOWN, SOWS

Ex	23:10	For six years you may s your land
Jb	4: 8	and s trouble will reap them.
Ps	126: 5	Those who s in tears will reap
Prv	22: 8	Those who s iniquity reap calamity,
Eccl	11: 6	In the morning s your seed,
Hos	8: 7	When they s the wind, they will
Hos	10:12	"S for yourselves justice,
Mt	6:26	they do not s or reap, they gather
Mt	13: 3	"A sower went out to s.
1 Cor	15:36	What you s is not brought to life

2 Pt   2:22 "A bathed s returns to wallowing

SOWED → SOW
Mt   13:24 a man who s good seed in his field.

SOWER → SOW
Mt   13:18 "Hear then the parable of the s.
Jn   4:36 so that the s and reaper can rejoice
2 Cor   9:10 The one who supplies seed to the s

SOWN → SOW
Mk   4:15 on the path where the word is s.
Mk   4:15 and takes away the word s in them.
1 Cor   9:11 If we have s spiritual seed for you,
1 Cor   15:42 It is s corruptible; it is raised

SOWS → SOW
Mk   4:14 The sower s the word.
Jn   4:37 the saying is verified that 'One s
2 Cor   9: 6 whoever s sparingly will also reap
2 Cor   9: 6 and whoever s bountifully will

SPAN
Is   40:12 marked off the heavens with a s,

SPARE → SPARED, SPARINGLY
Ps   78:50 he did not s them from death,
Rom   11:21 God did not s the natural branches,
Rom   11:21 [perhaps] he will not s you either.
2 Pt   2: 4 God did not s the angels when they

SPARED → SPARE
Gn   12:13 my life may be s for your sake."

SPARINGLY → SPARE
2 Cor   9: 6 whoever sows s will also reap s,

SPARROW → SPARROWS
Ps   84: 4 As the s finds a home

SPARROWS → SPARROW
Mt   10:29 Are not two s sold for a small coin?
Lk   12: 7 You are worth more than many s.

SPAT → SPIT
Lk   18:32 be mocked and insulted and s upon;
Jn   9: 6 he s on the ground and made clay

SPEAK → SPEAKER, SPEAKING, SPEAKS, SPEECH, SPOKE, SPOKEN
Gn   18:27 "See how I am presuming to s
Ex   33:11 The LORD used to s to Moses face
Nm   12: 8 face to face I s to him,
Nm   12: 8 fear to s against my servant Moses?
Dt   18:20 if a prophet presumes to s a word
1 Sm   3: 9 if you are called, reply, 'S, LORD,
2 Kgs   18:26 Do not s to us in the language
Jb   13: 3 But I would s with the Almighty;
Ps   49: 4 My mouth shall s words of wisdom,
Ps   135:16 They have mouths but do not s;
Prv   23: 9 Do not s in the hearing of fools;
Eccl   3: 7 a time to be silent, and a time to s.
Is   28:11 a strange language he will s to this
Is   40: 2 S to the heart of Jerusalem,
Jer   10: 5 field are they, they cannot s;
Ez   3:18 or s out to dissuade the wicked
Dn   7:25 He shall s against the Most High
Mt   13:13 This is why I s to them in parables,
Mk   7:37 the deaf hear and [the] mute s."
Jn   12:49 because I did not s on my own,
Jn   12:49 commanded me what to say and s.
Acts   2: 4 and began to s in different tongues,
Acts   4:18 ordered them not to s or teach at all
1 Cor   12:30 Do all s in tongues?
1 Cor   13: 1 If I s in human and angelic tongues
1 Cor   14: 2 a tongue does not s to human beings
1 Cor   14:19 church I would rather s five words
Eph   4:25 putting away falsehood, s the truth,
Jas   1:19 to hear, slow to s, slow to wrath,

SPEAKER → SPEAK
Ex   6:30 "Since I am a poor s, how is it

SPEAKING → SPEAK
Ex   4:12 I will assist you in s and teach you

Dt   5:26 of the living God s from the midst
Mt   10:20 Spirit of your Father s through you.
Acts   2: 6 because each one heard them s
Acts   10:46 they could hear them s in tongues
1 Cor   14:39 and do not forbid s in tongues,

SPEAKS → SPEAK
Ex   33:11 to face, as a person s to a friend.
Mt   12:32 whoever s a word against the Son
Mt   12:32 whoever s against the holy Spirit
Lk   6:45 the fullness of the heart the mouth s.
1 Cor   14: 5 prophesies is greater than one who s
Heb   11: 4 through this, though dead, he still s.

SPEAR → SPEARS
1 Sm   19:10 to pin David to the wall with the s,
1 Sm   19:10 and the s struck only the wall,
1 Sm   20:33 this Saul brandished his s to strike
Ps   46:10 splinters the s, and burns the shields

SPEARS → SPEAR
Is   2: 4 and their s into pruning hooks;
Jl   4:10 and your pruning knives into s;
Mi   4: 3 and their s into pruning hooks;

SPECTACLE
1 Cor   4: 9 since we have become a s

SPEECH → SPEAK
Ex   4:10 but I am slow of s and tongue."
Sir   4:29 Do not be haughty in your s, or lazy
Jn   10: 6 Although Jesus used this figure of s,
1 Tm   4:12 for those who believe, in s, conduct,
1 Jn   3:18 let us love not in word or s

SPELLS
Dt   18:11 or who casts s, consults ghosts

SPEND → SPENT
Jgs   19:20 but do not s the night in the public
Is   55: 2 Why s your money for what is not
2 Cor   12:15 I will most gladly s and be utterly

SPENT → SPEND
Mk   5:26 doctors and had s all that she had.
Lk   6:12 and he s the night in prayer to God.
Lk   15:14 When he had freely s everything,

SPICES
Ex   25: 6 s for the anointing oil
1 Kgs   10:10 a very large quantity of s,
1 Kgs   10:10 such an abundance of s as the queen
Jn   19:40 with burial cloths along with the s,

SPIED → SPYING
Jos   6:22 the two men who had s out the land,

SPIES → SPYING
Gn   42: 9 He said to them: "You are s.
Jos   2: 1 secretly sent out two s from Shittim,
Heb   11:31 for she had received the s in peace.

SPIN
Mt   6:28 They do not work or s.

SPIRIT → SPIRITS, SPIRITUAL, SPIRITUALLY
Gn   6: 3 My s shall not remain in human
Ex   31: 3 filled him with a divine s of skill
Nm   11:25 Taking some of the s that was
Nm   11:25 and as the s came to rest on them,
Nm   24: 2 tribe, the s of God came upon him,
Dt   34: 9 was filled with the s of wisdom,
Jgs   6:34 clothed with the s of the LORD,
Jgs   11:29 The s of the LORD came
Jgs   13:25 The s of the LORD came
Jgs   14: 6 the s of the LORD rushed
Jgs   15:14 the s of the LORD rushed
1 Sm   10: 6 The s of the LORD will rush
1 Sm   16:13 on, the s of the LORD rushed
1 Sm   16:14 The s of the LORD had departed
1 Sm   16:14 by an evil s from the LORD.
1 Sm   16:15 An evil s from God is tormenting
2 Sm   23: 2 The s of the LORD spoke through
2 Kgs   2: 9 receive a double portion of your s."

2 Kgs 2:15 "The s of Elijah rests on Elisha."
2 Chr 18:21 become a lying s in the mouths
Neh   9:20 Your good s you bestowed on them,
Jb   33: 4 For the s of God made me,
Ps   31: 6 Into your hands I commend my s;
Ps   34:19 saves those whose s is crushed.
Ps   51:12 renew within me a steadfast s.
Ps   51:13 face, nor take from me your holy s.
Ps   51:19 My sacrifice, O God, is a contrite s;
Ps   106:33 They so embittered his s that rash
Ps   139: 7 Where can I go from your s?
Ps   143:10 May your kind s guide me
Prv   16:18 and a haughty s before a fall.
Prv   29:23 but the humble of s acquire honor.
Wis   1: 6 For wisdom is a kindly s, yet she
Is   11: 2 The s of the LORD shall rest
Is   11: 2 a s of wisdom and of understanding,
Is   11: 2 A s of counsel and of strength,
Is   32:15 Until the s from on high is poured
Is   42: 1 Upon him I have put my s;
Is   44: 3 pour out my s upon your offspring,
Is   48:16 GOD has sent me, and his s."
Is   57:15 also with the contrite and lowly of s,
Is   57:15 To revive the s of the lowly,
Is   59:21 My s which is upon you and my
Is   61: 1 The s of the Lord GOD is
Is   63:10 they rebelled and grieved his holy s;
Ez   3:12 Then the s lifted me up, and I heard
Ez   11:19 and a new s I will put within them.
Ez   13: 3 the fools who follow their own s
Ez   36:26 and a new s I will put within you.
Jl   3: 1 I will pour out my s upon all flesh.
Zec   4: 6 but by my s, says the LORD
Mt   1:18 found with child through the holy S.
Mt   3:11 He will baptize you with the holy S
Mt   3:16 he saw the S of God descending like
Mt   4: 1 was led by the S into the desert
Mt   5: 3 "Blessed are the poor in s, for theirs
Mt   10:20 but the S of your Father speaking
Mt   12:31 blasphemy against the S will not be
Mt   26:41 The s is willing, but the flesh is
Mt   28:19 and of the Son, and of the holy S,
Mk   1: 8 will baptize you with the holy S."
Lk   1:15 the holy S even from his mother's
Lk   1:35 "The holy S will come upon you,
Lk   1:80 child grew and became strong in s,
Lk   3:16 He will baptize you with the holy S
Lk   4: 1 Filled with the holy S,
Lk   4: 1 and was led by the S into the desert
Lk   4:18 "The S of the Lord is upon me,
Lk   11:13 heaven give the holy S to those who
Lk   23:46 into your hands I commend my s";
Jn   1:33 whomever you see the S come down
Jn   1:33 who will baptize with the holy S.'
Jn   3: 5 without being born of water and S.
Jn   3: 6 is flesh and what is born of s is s.
Jn   3:34 He does not ration his gift of the S.
Jn   4:24 God is S, and those who worship him must worship in S
Jn   6:63 It is the s that gives life,
Jn   6:63 words I have spoken to you are s
Jn   7:39 to the S that those who came
Jn   7:39 of course, no S yet, because Jesus
Jn   14:17 the S of truth, which the world
Jn   14:26 the holy S that the Father will send
Jn   15:26 the S of truth that proceeds
Jn   16:13 But when he comes, the S of truth,
Jn   20:22 said to them, "Receive the holy S.
Acts   1: 5 will be baptized with the holy S."
Acts   1: 8 when the holy S comes upon you,
Acts   2: 4 they were all filled with the holy S
Acts   2: 4 as the S enabled them to proclaim.
Acts   2:17 out a portion of my s upon all flesh.
Acts   2:38 will receive the gift of the holy S.
Acts   4:31 they were all filled with the holy S
Acts   5: 3 heart so that you lied to the holy S
Acts   6: 3 men, filled with the S and wisdom,

Acts   7:51 ears, you always oppose the holy S;
Acts   8:15 that they might receive the holy S,
Acts   9:17 sight and be filled with the holy S."
Acts 11:16 will be baptized with the holy S.'
Acts 13: 2 the holy S said, "Set apart for me
Acts 19: 2 "Did you receive the holy S
Acts 19: 2 even heard that there is a holy S."
Rom   7: 6 may serve in the newness of the s
Rom   8: 4 to the flesh but according to the s.
Rom   8: 5 according to the s with the things of the s.
Rom   8: 9 you are in the s, if only the S of God
Rom   8: 9 Whoever does not have the S
Rom   8:13 by the s you put to death the deeds
Rom   8:15 you did not receive a s of slavery
Rom   8:15 but you received a s of adoption,
Rom   8:16 The S itself bears witness with our s
Rom   8:23 who have the firstfruits of the S,
Rom   8:26 the S too comes to the aid of our
Rom   8:26 but the S itself intercedes
1 Cor 2:10 has revealed to us through the S. For the S scrutinizes everything,
1 Cor 2:14 what pertains to the S of God,
1 Cor 5: 3 absent in body but present in s,
1 Cor 6:17 to the Lord becomes one s with him.
1 Cor 6:19 is a temple of the holy S within you,
1 Cor 12: 4 of spiritual gifts but the same S;
1 Cor 12:13 in one S we were all baptized
1 Cor 12:13 we were all given to drink of one S.
2 Cor 1:22 given the S in our hearts as a first
2 Cor 3: 3 ink but by the S of the living God,
2 Cor 3: 6 new covenant, not of letter but of s;
2 Cor 3: 6 brings death, but the S gives life.
2 Cor 3:17 Now the Lord is the S, and where the S of the Lord is,
2 Cor 5: 5 who has given us the S as a first
2 Cor 7: 1 every defilement of flesh and s,
Gal   3: 2 did you receive the S from works
Gal   3:14 the promise of the S through faith.
Gal   5:16 live by the S and you will certainly
Gal   5:22 the fruit of the S is love, joy, peace,
Gal   5:25 If we live in the S, let us also follow the S.
Gal   6: 8 sows for the s will reap eternal life from the s.
Eph   1:13 sealed with the promised holy S,
Eph   2:18 have access in one S to the Father.
Eph   4: 3 the unity of the s through the bond
Eph   4: 4 one body and one S, as you were
Eph   4:30 do not grieve the holy S of God,
Eph   5:18 debauchery, but be filled with the S,
Eph   6:17 of salvation and the sword of the S,
Col   2: 5 yet I am with you in s, rejoicing as I
1 Thes 5:19 Do not quench the S.
1 Thes 5:23 holy and may you entirely, s, soul,
2 Thes 2:13 through sanctification by the S
1 Tm   3:16 vindicated in the s, seen by angels,
2 Tm   1: 7 For God did not give us a s
2 Tm   4:22 The Lord be with your s.
Heb   2: 4 of the holy S according to his will.
Heb   4:12 even between soul and s,
Heb   6: 4 gift and shared in the holy S
Heb   10:29 and insults the s of grace?
1 Pt   1: 2 through sanctification by the S,
2 Pt   1:21 the holy S spoke under the influence
1 Jn   3:24 in us is from the S that he gave us.
1 Jn   4: 1 do not trust every s but test
1 Jn   4:13 in us, that he has given us of his S.
Jude   1:20 most holy faith; pray in the holy S.
Rev   1:10 caught up in s on the Lord's day
Rev   2: 7 ought to hear what the S says
Rev   4: 2 At once I was caught up in s.

SPIRITS → SPIRIT

Lv   19:31 Do not turn to ghosts or consult s,
Nm   16:22 God of the s of all living creatures,
Nm   27:16 the God of the s of all humanity,
Dt   18:11 consults ghosts and s, or seeks
Mt   12:45 itself seven other s more evil than
Lk   4:36 power he commands the unclean s,
Acts   8: 7 For unclean s, crying out in a loud

1 Cor	12:10	to another discernment of s;
1 Cor	14:32	the s of prophets are under
Heb	12: 9	all the more to the Father of s
1 Pt	3:19	went to preach to the s in prison,
1 Jn	4: 1	test the s to see whether they belong
Rev	1: 4	from the seven s before his throne,
Rev	16:13	saw three unclean s like frogs come
Rev	22: 6	the God of prophetic s, sent his

SPIRITUAL → SPIRIT
Rom	1:11	I may share with you some s gift so
Rom	7:14	We know that the law is s; but I am
Rom	12: 1	pleasing to God, your s worship.
Rom	15:27	come to share in their s blessings,
1 Cor	2:13	describing s realities in s terms.
1 Cor	3: 1	I could not talk to you as s people,
1 Cor	9:11	If we have sown s seed for you, is it
1 Cor	10: 3	All ate the same s food,
1 Cor	12: 1	Now in regard to s gifts, brothers,
1 Cor	14: 1	but strive eagerly for the s gifts,
1 Cor	15:44	a natural body; it is raised a s body.
1 Cor	15:46	But the s was not first;
1 Cor	15:46	rather the natural and then the s.
Eph	1: 3	Christ with every s blessing
Eph	5:19	[in] psalms and hymns and s songs,
Col	1: 9	of his will through all s wisdom
Col	3:16	s songs with gratitude in your hearts
1 Pt	2: 2	long for pure s milk so that through
1 Pt	2: 5	let yourselves be built into a s house
1 Pt	2: 5	to offer s sacrifices acceptable

SPIRITUALLY → SPIRIT
1 Cor	2:14	understand it, because it is judged s.

SPIT → SPAT
Dt	25: 9	from his foot and s in his face,
Mk	14:65	Some began to s on him.
Rev	3:16	cold, I will s you out of my mouth.

SPLENDOR
1 Chr	29:11	and might, majesty, victory, and s.
Jb	37:22	From Zaphon the golden s comes,
Ps	21: 6	majesty and s you confer upon him.
Ps	29: 2	down before the LORD's holy s!
Ps	145: 5	of the s of your majestic glory,
Dn	7:14	He received dominion, s, and kingship;
Eph	5:27	present to himself the church in s,

SPLIT
Ex	14:21	sea into dry ground. The waters were s,
Nm	16:31	the ground beneath them s open,
Mt	27:51	The earth quaked, rocks were s,
Rev	16:19	The great city was s into three parts,

SPOIL → SPOILS
Nm	14: 3	Our wives and little ones will be taken as s.
Nm	14:31	you said would be taken as s, I will bring in,
Ps	119:162	as one who has found rich s.

SPOILS → SPOIL
Ex	15: 9	I will divide the s and have my fill

SPOKE → SPEAK
Gn	16:13	the LORD who s to her she gave
Dt	4:12	the LORD s to you from the midst
Dt	5: 4	face, the LORD s with you
Ps	99: 7	the pillar of cloud he s to them;
Mt	9:33	was driven out the mute person s.
Mk	4:33	many such parables he s the word
2 Cor	4:13	therefore I s," we too believe
Heb	1: 1	God s in partial and various ways
Heb	13: 7	your leaders who s the word of God
2 Pt	1:21	the holy Spirit s under the influence

SPOKEN → SPEAK
Dt	18:22	prophet has s it presumptuously;
Jb	42: 7	the LORD had s these words
Jb	42: 7	You have not s rightly concerning
Prv	25:11	in silver settings are words s

SPONGE
Jn	19:29	So they put a s soaked in wine

SPOT → SPOTS, SPOTTED
Eph	5:27	without s or wrinkle or any such
2 Pt	3:14	be eager to be found without s

SPOTS → SPOT
Jer	13:23	change their skin, leopards their s?

SPOTTED → SPOT
Gn	30:32	every s or speckled one among

SPRANG → SPRING
Mt	13: 5	It s up at once because the soil was
Mk	4: 5	It s up at once because the soil was

SPREAD → SPREADING
Ex	37: 9	The cherubim had their wings s
Ps	78:19	and said, "Can God s a table
Is	48:13	my right hand s out the heavens.
Ez	1:11	Their wings were s out above.
Mk	11: 8	Many people s their cloaks
Mk	11: 8	others s leafy branches that they had
Jn	21:23	So the word s among the brothers
Acts	6: 7	The word of God continued to s,
Acts	13:49	to s through the whole region.
2 Tm	2:17	their teaching will s like gangrene.

SPREADING → SPREAD
Lv	19:16	go about s slander among your people;
1 Sm	2:24	the LORD's people s is not good.

SPRING → SPRANG, SPRINGS
Gn	16: 7	found her by a s in the wilderness,
Ps	85:12	Truth will s from the earth;
Is	45: 8	let righteousness s up with them!
Is	58:11	like a flowing s whose waters never
Jer	8:23	that my head were a s of water,
Jl	4:18	A s will rise from the house of the LORD,
Jn	4:14	become in him a s of water welling
Rev	21: 6	gift from the s of life-giving water.

SPRINGS → SPRING
Is	49:10	and guides them beside s of water.
2 Pt	2:17	These people are waterless s
Rev	7:17	lead them to s of life-giving water,

SPRINKLE → SPRINKLED
Nm	8: 7	S them with the water
2 Mc	1:21	ordered the priests to s the wood
Ez	36:25	I will s clean water over you

SPRINKLED → SPRINKLE
Lv	8:11	he s some of the oil seven times
Heb	10:22	with our hearts s clean from an evil
Heb	11:28	kept the Passover and s the blood,

SPROUT
Nm	17:20	of the man whom I choose shall s.

SPURN
Nm	14:11	Moses: How long will this people s me?
Ps	43: 2	my strength. Why then do you s me?

SPYING → SPIED, SPIES
Gn	42:30	grounds that we were s on the land.

SQUANDERED
Lk	15:13	country where he s his inheritance

SQUARE → SQUARES
Gn	19: 2	will pass the night in the town s."
Ex	27: 1	on a s, five cubits long and five
Ex	28:16	It is to be s when folded double,
Ex	30: 2	with a s surface, a cubit long,
Jgs	19:20	not spend the night in the public s."

SQUARES → SQUARE
Prv	1:20	in the open s she raises her voice;

STAFF → STAFFS
Gn	38:25	seal and cord and s these are."
Ex	4: 4	of it, and it became a s in his hand.
Ex	7:12	Each one threw down his s,
Ex	7:12	Aaron's s swallowed their staffs.
Ex	14:16	lift up your s and stretch out your
Nm	17:21	and Aaron's s was among them.
Nm	20:11	struck the rock twice with his s,

Ps 23: 4 your rod and your **s** comfort me.
Mi 7:14 Shepherd your people with your **s**,
Zec 11:10 I took my **s** Delight and snapped it

STAFFS → STAFF
Nm 17:22 Moses deposited the **s** before

STAGES
Nm 33: 1 The following are the **s**

STAGGER → STAGGERED
Is 28: 7 these also **s** from wine and stumble
Is 28: 7 and prophet **s** from strong drink, they **s** in their visions,
Is 29: 9 who **s**, but not from strong drink!

STAGGERED → STAGGER
Ps 107:27 They reeled, **s** like drunkards;

STAIN
Jer 2:22 The **s** of your guilt is still before

STAIRWAY
Gn 28:12 a **s** rested on the ground, with its top

STALK → STALKS
Gn 41: 5 and healthy, growing on a single **s**.

STALKS → STALK
Jos 2: 6 hidden them among her **s** of flax

STALL → STALLS
Mal 3:20 go out leaping like calves from the **s**

STALLS → STALL
1 Kgs 5: 6 Solomon had forty thousand **s**
Hb 3:17 the fold and there is no herd in the **s**,

STAND → STANDING, STANDS, STOOD
Ex 9:11 the boils the magicians could not **s**
Ex 14:13 **S** your ground and see the victory
Dt 11:25 None shall **s** up against you;
Jos 10:12 Sun, **s** still at Gibeon, Moon,
2 Chr 20:17 Take your places, **s** firm, and see
Jb 19:25 he will at last **s** forth upon the dust.
Ps 10: 1 do you **s** afar and pay no heed
Ps 24: 3 Who can **s** in his holy place?
Ps 76: 8 who can **s** before you and your great
Ps 130: 3 account of sins, Lord, who can **s**?
Ez 22:30 or **s** in the breach before me to keep
Mal 3: 2 Who can **s** firm when he appears?
Mt 12:25 house divided against itself will **s**.
Rom 5: 2 [faith] to this grace in which we **s**,
Rom 14: 4 for the Lord is able to make him **s**.
Rom 14:10 we shall all **s** before the judgment
1 Cor 16:13 on your guard, **s** firm in the faith,
2 Cor 1:24 your joy, for you **s** firm in the faith.
Eph 6:11 be able to **s** firm against the tactics
2 Thes 2:15 **s** firm and hold fast to the traditions

STANDARDS
1 Cor 1:26 many of you were wise by human **s**,

STANDING → STAND
Gn 18:22 Abraham remained **s** before
Nm 22:23 angel of the LORD **s** in the road
2 Chr 18:18 whole host of heaven **s** to his right
Am 7: 7 He was **s**, plummet in hand,
Am 9: 1 I saw the Lord **s** beside the altar.
Zec 1: 8 a red horse **s** in the shadows among
Zec 3: 1 the high priest **s** before the angel
Acts 7:55 and Jesus **s** at the right hand of God,
1 Cor 10:12 thinks he is **s** secure should take
1 Tm 3:13 serve well as deacons gain good **s**
Jas 5: 9 the Judge is **s** before the gates.
Rev 20:12 and the lowly, **s** before the throne,

STANDS → STAND
1 Kgs 7:27 He also made ten **s** of bronze,
Ps 26:12 My foot **s** on level ground;
2 Tm 2:19 God's solid foundation **s**,

STAR → STARS
Nm 24:17 A **s** shall advance from Jacob,
Sir 50: 6 Like a **s** shining among the clouds,
Is 14:12 O Morning **S**, son of the dawn!

Mt 2: 2 We saw his **s** at its rising and have
2 Pt 1:19 the morning **s** rises in your hearts.
Rev 2:28 to him I will give the morning **s**.
Rev 8:11 The **s** was called "Wormwood,"
Rev 9: 1 I saw a **s** that had fallen
Rev 22:16 of David, the bright morning **s**."

STARS → STAR
Gn 1:16 one to govern the night, and the **s**.
Gn 15: 5 Look up at the sky and count the **s**,
Gn 37: 9 eleven **s** were bowing down to me."
Dt 1:10 now you are as numerous as the **s**
Jb 38: 7 While the morning **s** sang together
Ps 148: 3 praise him, all shining **s**.
Is 14:13 Above the **s** of God I will set up my
Dn 3:63 **S** of heaven, bless the Lord;
Dn 12: 3 to justice shall be like the **s** forever.
Jl 2:10 and the **s** withhold their brightness.
Mk 13:25 the **s** will be falling from the sky,
Rev 1:16 In his right hand he held seven **s**.
Rev 6:13 The **s** in the sky fell to the earth like
Rev 8:12 and a third of the **s** were struck,
Rev 12: 1 on her head a crown of twelve **s**.
Rev 12: 4 away a third of the **s** in the sky

STATE
1 Cor 7:20 Everyone should remain in the **s**

STATUE
Dn 2:31 O king, you saw a **s**, very large
Dn 3: 1 had a golden **s** made, sixty cubits

STATURE
1 Sm 2:26 young Samuel was growing in **s**

STATUTES
Dt 4: 1 hear the **s** and ordinances I am
Dt 11: 1 and keep his charge, **s**, ordinances,
Dt 30:16 keeping his commandments, **s** and ordinances,
1 Kgs 3: 3 walking in the **s** of David his father,
1 Kgs 11:33 my eyes, according to my **s** and my
Neh 9:13 laws, good **s** and commandments;
Is 24: 5 laws, violated **s**, broken the ancient

STAY
Ex 16:29 Each of you **s** where you are and let

STEADFAST
Ps 57: 8 My heart is **s**, God, my heart is **s**.
Ps 108: 2 My heart is **s**, God; my heart is **s**.
Is 57: 1 The **s** are swept away, while no one understands.
1 Pt 5: 9 Resist him, **s** in faith,

STEADY
Ex 17:12 his hands remained **s** until sunset.

STEAL → STEALING, STOLE, STOLEN
Gn 31:30 house, why did you **s** my gods?"
Ex 20:15 You shall not **s**.
Dt 5:19 You shall not **s**.
Jer 23:30 those who **s** my words from each
Mt 6:19 destroy, and thieves break in and **s**.
Mt 19:18 you shall not **s**; you shall not bear
Jn 10:10 A thief comes only to **s**
Rom 2:21 preach against stealing, do you **s**?
Rom 13: 9 You shall not **s**; you shall not

STEALING → STEAL
Rom 2:21 You who preach against **s**, do you

STEPHEN
Early church leader (Acts 6:5). Arrested (Acts 6:8-15). Speech to Sanhedrin (Acts 7). Stoned (Acts 7:54-60; 8:2; 11:19; 22:20).

STEPS
Ex 20:26 shall not ascend to my altar by **s**,
Ps 37:23 The valiant one whose **s** are guided
Prv 5: 5 go down to death, her **s** reach Sheol;
Prv 14:15 but the shrewd watch their **s**.
Prv 16: 9 way, but the LORD directs the **s**.
Prv 20:24 Our **s** are from the LORD;

STEW
Gn 25:29 when Jacob was cooking a **s**,

2 Kgs 4:39 of vegetable s without anybody's

STEWARD → STEWARDS, STEWARDSHIP
Ti   1: 7 For a bishop as God's s must be

STEWARDS → STEWARD
1 Cor 4: 2 of course required of s that they be
1 Pt   4:10 it to serve one another as good s

STEWARDSHIP → STEWARD
1 Cor 9:17 then I have been entrusted with a s.
Eph   3: 2 have heard of the s of God's grace
Col   1:25 in accordance with God's s given

STICK
2 Kgs 6: 6 Elisha cut off a s, threw it
Ez   37:16 of man, take one s and write on it,
Ez   37:16 Ephraim's s, and the whole house

STIFF-NECKED → NECK
Ex   32: 9 seen this people, how s they are,
Ex   34: 9 This is indeed a s people;
Bar   2:30 to me, because they are a s people.
Acts   7:51 "You s people,

STILL → STILLBORN
Ex   14:14 you have only to keep s."
Jos   10:13 The sun stood s, the moon stayed,
Ps   37: 7 Be s before the LORD;
Ps   46:11 "Be s and know that I am God!
Ps   89:10 you s its swelling waves.
Dn   11:35 the end time which is s appointed
Mk   4:39 Be s!" The wind ceased and there
Rom   5: 8 while we were s sinners Christ died
Heb   11: 4 this, though dead, he s speaks.
Rev   22:11 Let the wicked s act wickedly, and the filthy s be filthy.
Rev   22:11 The righteous must s do right, and the holy s be holy."

STILLBORN → BEAR, STILL
Nm   12:12 Do not let her be like the s baby

STING
1 Cor 15:55 Where, O death, is your s?"

STIR → STIRRED, STIRS
Ps   80: 3 S up your power, and come to save
Prv   29:22 The ill-tempered s up strife,
Sg   2: 7 or s up love until it is ready.

STIRRED → STIR
Sir   51:21 My whole being was s to seek her;
Hg   1:14 so the LORD s up the spirit
Acts   13:50 s up a persecution against Paul

STIRS → STIR
Prv   10:12 Hatred s up disputes, but love
Prv   15: 1 wrath, but a harsh word s up anger.
Prv   28:25 The greedy person s up strife,

STOIC
Acts   17:18 and S philosophers engaged him

STOLE → STEAL
Mt   28:13 and s him while we were asleep.'

STOLEN → STEAL
Prv   9:17 S water is sweet, and bread taken

STOMACH
Ez   3: 3 feed your s and fill your belly
Mk   7:19 but the s and passes
1 Cor   6:13 "Food for the s and the s for food,"
1 Tm   5:23 a little wine for the sake of your s
Rev   10: 9 It will turn your s sour, but in your

STONE → CORNERSTONE, MILLSTONE, STONED, STONES, STONING
Gn   28:18 the next morning Jacob took the s
Gn   31:45 Jacob took a s and set it up as
Gn   35:14 set up a sacred pillar, a s pillar,
Ex   17: 4 A little more and they will s me!"
Ex   28:10 six of their names on one s,
Ex   31:18 the s tablets inscribed by God's own
Ex   34: 1 "Cut two s tablets like the former,
Dt   4:13 which he wrote on two s tablets.
Dt   28:36 serve other gods, of wood and s,

1 Sm   7:12 then took a s and placed it between
1 Sm   17:50 over the Philistine with sling and s;
Ps   91:12 lest you strike your foot against a s.
Ps   118:22 The s the builders rejected has
Is   8:14 He shall be a snare, a s for injury,
Is   28:16 See, I am laying a s in Zion, a s that has been tested,
Jer   3: 9 committing adultery with s
Zec   3: 9 at the s that I have placed before
Zec   3: 9 this one s with seven facets I will
Mt   4: 6 you dash your foot against a s.'
Mt   7: 9 you would hand his son a s when he
Mt   24: 2 there will not be left here a s upon another s that will not
Mk   12:10 'The s that the builders rejected has
Mk   16: 3 "Who will roll back the s for us
Lk   4: 3 command this s to become bread."
Lk   20:18 on that s will be dashed to pieces;
Jn   8: 7 sin be the first to throw a s at her."
Jn   10:32 of these are you trying to s me?"
Jn   19:13 in the place called S Pavement,
Acts   4:11 He is 'the s rejected by you,
Rom   9:32 They stumbled over the s
2 Cor   3: 3 not on tablets of s but on tablets
1 Pt   2: 4 a living s, rejected by human beings
1 Pt   2: 6 "Behold, I am laying a s in Zion,

STONED → STONE
Nm   15:36 outside the camp and s him to death,
Jos   7:25 And all Israel s him to death.
1 Kgs 21:13 out of the city and s him to death.
2 Chr 24:21 at the king's command they s him
Acts   14:19 They s Paul and dragged him
Heb   11:37 They were s, sawed in two,

STONES → STONE
Ex   24: 4 an altar and twelve sacred s for
Ex   28: 9 Get two onyx s and engrave
Dt   27: 2 set up some large s and coat them
Jos   4: 3 "Take up twelve s from this spot
1 Sm   17:40 David selected five smooth s
1 Kgs 18:31 He took twelve s, for the number
Ps   102:15 Its s are dear to your servants;
Eccl   3: 5 A time to scatter s, and a time
Sir   21:10 The path of sinners is smooth s,
Mt   3: 9 children to Abraham from these s.
Mt   4: 3 that these s become loaves
Mk   13: 1 what s and what buildings!"
Lk   19:40 they keep silent, the s will cry out!"
1 Cor   3:12 gold, silver, precious s, wood, hay,
1 Pt   2: 5 like living s, let yourselves be built

STONING → STONE
1 Sm   30: 6 for the soldiers spoke of s him,
Acts   7:59 As they were s Stephen, he called

STOOD → STAND
Ex   15: 8 the flowing waters s like a mound,
Jos   10:13 The sun s still, the moon stayed,
Lk   10:25 was a scholar of the law who s
Lk   22:28 It is you who have s by me in my
Jn   20:19 Jesus came and s in their midst
2 Tm   4:17 But the Lord s by me and gave me

STOOP
Mk   1: 7 I am not worthy to s and loosen

STOP → STOPPED
Gn   19:17 back or s anywhere on the Plain.

STOPPED → STOP
2 Kgs   4: 6 is none left." And then the oil s.

STORE → STOREHOUSE, STORING
Sir   29:12 S up almsgiving in your treasury,
Mt   6:19 "Do not s up for yourselves
Lk   12:17 do not have space to s my harvest?'

STOREHOUSE → HOUSE, STORE
Mal   3:10 Bring the whole tithe into the s,

STORING → STORE
Rom   2: 5 you are s up wrath for yourself

STORM
Ps	107:29	He hushed the s to silence,
Jer	30:23	Look! The s of the LORD!
Jer	30:23	In a whirling s that bursts
Jon	1:12	I know that this great s has come

STRAIGHT
Prv	3: 6	him, and he will make s your paths.
Prv	4:25	Let your eyes look s ahead and your
Prv	11: 5	of the honest makes their way s,
Prv	15:21	of understanding goes the s way.
Prv	21: 2	All your ways may be s in your own eyes,
Sir	2: 6	make your ways s and hope in him.
Is	40: 3	Make s in the wasteland a highway
Mt	3: 3	of the Lord, make s his paths.' "
Lk	3: 5	The winding roads shall be made s,
Jn	1:23	"Make s the way of the Lord," '
Acts	9:11	go to the street called S and ask
2 Pt	2:15	Abandoning the s road, they have

STRAIN → STRAINING
Mt	23:24	who s out the gnat and swallow

STRAINING → STRAIN
Phil	3:13	but s forward to what lies ahead,

STRANGE → STRANGER, STRANGERS
Dt	32:16	With s gods they incited him,
1 Cor	14:21	"By people speaking s tongues
Heb	13: 9	away by all kinds of s teaching.
1 Pt	4:12	as if something s were happening

STRANGER → STRANGE
Mt	25:35	drink, a s and you welcomed me,
Jn	10: 5	But they will not follow a s;

STRANGERS → STRANGE
1 Chr	16:19	in number, a handful, and s there,
1 Mc	1:38	away, she became the abode of s.
Eph	2:12	and s to the covenants of promise,
Heb	11:13	acknowledged themselves to be s
3 Jn	1: 5	do for the brothers, especially for s;

STRAW
Ex	5:10	'I will not provide you with s.
1 Cor	3:12	precious stones, wood, hay, or s,

STRAY → ASTRAY, STRAYED
Ps	119:10	do not let me s from your

STRAYED → STRAY
Wis	5: 6	then, have s from the way of truth,
Hos	7:13	to them, for they have s from me!

STREAM → STREAMS
Is	2: 2	All nations shall s toward it.
Am	5:24	righteousness like an unfailing s.
Mi	4: 1	the hills, And peoples shall s to it:

STREAMS → STREAM
Ps	1: 3	He is like a tree planted near s
Ps	42: 2	As the deer longs for s of water,
Ps	46: 5	S of the river gladden the city
Is	35: 6	the wilderness, and s in the Arabah.
Jer	31: 9	I will lead them to s of water,

STREET → STREETS
Prv	1:20	Wisdom cries aloud in the s,
Mt	6: 5	on s corners so that others may see
Acts	9:11	go to the s called Straight and ask
Rev	21:21	the s of the city was of pure gold,
Rev	22: 2	down the middle of its s.

STREETS → STREET
Ps	144:14	walls, no exile, no outcry in our s.
Zec	8: 5	with boys and girls playing in its s.
Mt	12:19	will anyone hear his voice in the s.

STRENGTH → STRONG
Ex	15: 2	My s and my refuge is the LORD,
Dt	33:25	may your s endure through all your
Jgs	16:15	me where you get your great s!"
1 Sm	2: 9	for not by s does one prevail.
1 Chr	29:12	yours to give greatness and s to all.

Neh	8:10	rejoicing in the LORD is your s!"
Jdt	9:11	"Your s is not in numbers, nor does
1 Mc	3:19	but on s that comes from Heaven.
Ps	18: 2	He said: I love you, LORD, my s,
Ps	28: 7	The LORD is my s and my shield,
Ps	46: 2	God is our refuge and our s,
Ps	59:10	My s, for you I watch;
Ps	59:18	My s, your praise I will sing;
Ps	118:14	The LORD, my s and might,
Ps	147:10	takes no delight in the s of horses,
Prv	31:25	She is clothed with s and dignity,
Is	12: 2	For the LORD is my s and my
Is	40:26	the s of his power not one of them is
Is	40:31	in the LORD will renew their s,
Mi	5: 3	as shepherd by the s of the LORD,
Hb	3:19	GOD, my Lord, is my s;
Mk	12:30	all your mind, and with all your s.'
Lk	10:27	with all your s, and with all your
1 Cor	1:25	of God is stronger than human s.
2 Tm	4:17	Lord stood by me and gave me s,
1 Pt	4:11	it be with the s that God supplies,

STRENGTHEN → STRONG
Jgs	16:28	S me only this once that I may
Is	35: 3	S hands that are feeble, make firm
Is	41:10	I will s you, I will help you, I will
Lk	22:32	back, you must s your brothers."
1 Thes	3:13	so as to s your hearts, to be
2 Thes	2:17	and s them in every good deed
Heb	12:12	So s your drooping hands and your
1 Pt	5:10	confirm, s, and establish you

STRENGTHENED → STRONG
Acts	15:32	and s the brothers with many words.
Heb	13: 9	is good to have our hearts s by grace

STRETCH → OUTSTRETCHED, STRETCHED
Ex	3:20	So I will s out my hand and strike
Ps	138: 7	You s out your hand;
Zep	1: 4	I will s out my hand against Judah,
Mk	3: 5	said to the man, "S out your hand."
Acts	4:30	as you s forth [your] hand to heal,

STRETCHED → STRETCH
Ex	14:21	Moses s out his hand over the sea;
2 Sm	24:16	the angel s forth his hand toward
1 Kgs	13: 4	Jeroboam s forth his hand
1 Kgs	13: 4	But the hand he s forth against him
Is	45:12	It was my hands that s
Jer	10:12	and by his skill s out the heavens.
Mt	12:13	He s it out, and it was restored as

STRICKEN → STRIKE
Is	53: 4	We thought of him as s,

STRICT → STRICTEST
Acts	5:28	"We gave you s orders [did we not?]

STRICTEST → STRICT
Acts	26: 5	Pharisee, the s party of our religion.

STRIFE
Prv	17: 1	than a house full of feasting with s.
Prv	20: 3	A person gains honor by avoiding s,
Prv	22:10	discord goes too; s and insult cease.
Prv	23:29	Who have s? Who have anxiety?

STRIKE → STRICKEN, STRIKES, STRUCK
Gn	3:15	They will s at your head, while you s at their heel.
Ex	17: 6	S the rock, and the water will flow
Is	11: 4	He shall s the ruthless with the rod
Zec	13: 7	S the shepherd that the sheep may
Mal	3:24	and s the land with utter destruction.
Mk	14:27	'I will s the shepherd, and the sheep
Rev	19:15	came a sharp sword to s the nations.

STRIKES → STRIKE
Ex	21:12	Whoever s someone a mortal blow
Zec	2:12	Whoever s you s me directly in the eye.
Mt	5:39	When someone s you on [your]

STRIPPED
Gn	37:23	his brothers, they s him of his tunic,

Mt 27:28 They **s** off his clothes and threw
Acts 16:22 and the magistrates had them **s**

STRIVE
1 Cor 12:31 S eagerly for the greatest spiritual

STRONG → STRENGTH, STRENGTHEN, STRENGTHENED, STRONGER, STRONGHOLD
Ex 6: 1 For by a **s** hand, he will let them go;
Ps 140: 8 my master, my **s** deliverer,
Prv 18:10 name of the LORD is a **s** tower;
Is 35: 4 fearful of heart: Be **s**, do not fear!
Jer 50:34 S is their Redeemer, whose name is
Bar 2:11 out of the land of Egypt with a **s** hand,
Dn 2:40 shall be a fourth kingdom, **s** as iron;
Hg 2: 4 be **s**, Zerubbabel—oracle of the LORD—
Hg 2: 4 Be **s**, all you people of the land—
Zec 8: 9 Let your hands be **s**, you who now
Mt 12:29 can anyone enter a **s** man's house
Mt 12:29 unless he first ties up the **s** man?
Lk 1:80 child grew and became **s** in spirit,
Lk 2:40 The child grew and became **s**,
Rom 15: 1 We who are **s** ought to put
1 Cor 1:27 weak of the world to shame the **s**,
1 Cor 16:13 in the faith, be courageous, be **s**.
2 Cor 12:10 for when I am weak, then I am **s**.
2 Tm 2: 1 be **s** in the grace that is in Christ

STRONGER → STRONG
2 Sm 3: 1 in which David grew ever **s**,
1 Cor 1:25 of God is **s** than human strength.

STRONGHOLD → STRONG
Ps 9:10 The LORD is a **s** for the oppressed, a **s** in times of trouble.
Ps 18: 3 my shield, my saving horn, my **s**!
Ps 144: 2 and my fortress, my **s**, my deliverer,

STRUCK → STRIKE
Gn 32:26 him, he **s** Jacob's hip at its socket,
Nm 20:11 Moses **s** the rock twice with his
1 Sm 17:49 and **s** the Philistine on the forehead.
2 Chr 18:23 came up and **s** Micaiah on the cheek,
Ps 78:20 when he **s** the rock, water gushed
Dn 2:34 to it, and it **s** its iron and clay feet,
Acts 23: 3 of the law order me to be **s**?"

STRUGGLE
Eph 6:12 For our **s** is not with flesh and blood
Heb 12: 4 your **s** against sin you have not yet

STUBBLE
Ex 15: 7 your wrath to consume them like **s**.
Is 33:11 conceive dry grass, bring forth **s**;
Mal 3:19 arrogant and all evildoers will be **s**,

STUBBORN → STUBBORNLY, STUBBORNNESS
Jer 19:15 they have become **s** and have not obeyed
Hos 4:16 For like a **s** cow, Israel is **s**;

STUBBORNLY → STUBBORN
Ex 13:15 When Pharaoh **s** refused to let us

STUBBORNNESS → STUBBORN
Dt 9:27 look upon the **s** of this people nor

STUDY
Ezr 7:10 Ezra had set his heart on the **s**
Eccl 12:12 in much **s** there is weariness

STUMBLE → STUMBLED, STUMBLING
Ps 37:24 May **s**, but he will never fall,
Prv 3:23 your foot will never **s**;
Prv 4:12 and should you run, you will not **s**.
Jer 13:16 Before your feet **s** on mountains
Dn 11:35 Some of those with insight shall **s** so
Hos 14:10 walk in them, but sinners **s** in them.
Jn 11: 9 he does not **s**, because he sees
Rom 9:33 in Zion that will make people **s**
1 Pt 2: 8 "A stone that will make people **s**,
1 Pt 2: 8 They **s** by disobeying the word, as is

STUMBLED → STUMBLE
Rom 9:32 They **s** over the stone that causes

STUMBLING → STUMBLE
Rom 9:32 over the stone that causes **s**,
Rom 11: 9 a **s** block and a retribution for them;
Rom 14:13 rather resolve never to put a **s** block
1 Cor 1:23 a **s** block to Jews and foolishness
1 Cor 8: 9 in no way becomes a **s** block

STUMP
Is 11: 1 shall sprout from the **s** of Jesse,

STUPID
Prv 12: 1 but whoever hates reproof is **s**.

SUBDUE
Gn 1:28 fill the earth and **s** it.
1 Chr 17:10 And I will **s** all your enemies.

SUBJECTED
Rom 8:20 but because of the one who **s** it,
1 Cor 15:28 When everything is **s** to him,
1 Cor 15:28 be **s** to the one who **s** everything

SUBMIT
Rom 8: 7 it does not **s** to the law of God,
Gal 5: 1 and do not **s** again to the yoke
Col 2:20 why do you **s** to regulations as
Jas 4: 7 So **s** yourselves to God.

SUCCEED → SUCCESS, SUCCESSFUL
1 Kgs 2: 3 that you may **s** in whatever you do,
1 Kgs 22:22 You shall **s** in deceiving him.
Prv 15:22 but they **s** when advisers are many.
Prv 21:11 when the wise **s**, they gain knowledge.

SUCCESS → SUCCEED
Gn 39: 3 brought him **s** in whatever he did,
Gn 39:23 was bringing **s** to whatever he was
Neh 2:20 God of heaven who will grant us **s**.
1 Mc 4:55 Heaven, who had given them **s**.

SUCCESSFUL → SUCCEED
Gn 24:56 the LORD has made my journey **s**;

SUCCOTH
Gn 33:17 and Jacob broke camp for S.
Gn 33:17 That is why the place was named S.
Jgs 8:16 briers he thrashed the people of S.

SUCH
Ps 139: 6 S knowledge is too wonderful
Mt 8:10 no one in Israel have I found **s** faith.
Jn 9:16 can a sinful man do **s** signs?"
2 Cor 3: 4 S confidence we have through
Gal 5:23 Against **s** there is no law.
Heb 7:26 that we should have **s** a high priest:
Heb 12: 3 how he endured **s** opposition
2 Jn 1: 7 **s** is the deceitful one
3 Jn 1: 8 we ought to support **s** persons,

SUDDEN → SUDDENLY
Prv 3:25 Do not be afraid of **s** terror,
1 Thes 5: 3 then **s** disaster comes upon them,

SUDDENLY → SUDDEN
Mal 3: 1 the lord whom you seek will come **s**
Mk 13:36 May he not come **s** and find you
Acts 9: 3 from the sky **s** flashed around him.

SUFFER → SUFFERED, SUFFERING, SUFFERINGS, SUFFERS
Lk 22:15 this Passover with you before I **s**,
Lk 24:26 the Messiah should **s** these things
Lk 24:46 is written that the Messiah would **s**
Acts 3:18 prophets, that his Messiah would **s**.
1 Cor 3:15 is burned up, that one will **s** loss;
Heb 9:26 he would have had to **s** repeatedly
1 Pt 3:17 For it is better to **s** for doing good,
1 Pt 4:16 to **s** as a Christian should not be
Rev 2:10 of anything that you are going to **s**.

SUFFERED → SUFFER
Heb 2:18 was tested through what he **s**, he is
Heb 5: 8 learned obedience from what he **s**;
1 Pt 2:21 because Christ also **s** for you,
1 Pt 4: 1 since Christ **s** in the flesh,

SUFFERING → SUFFER
Jb   2:13 for they saw how great was his **s**.
Is   53: 3 by men, a man of **s**, knowing pain,

SUFFERINGS → SUFFER
Rom   8:18 that the **s** of this present time are as
2 Cor   1: 5 For as Christ's **s** overflow to us,
2 Cor   1: 7 we know that as you share in the **s**,
Phil   3:10 sharing of his **s** by being conformed
1 Pt   1:11 advance to the **s** destined for Christ
1 Pt   4:13 that you share in the **s** of Christ,

SUFFERS → SUFFER
1 Cor 12:26 If [one] part **s**, all the parts suffer

SUFFICIENT
2 Cor 12: 9 said to me, "My grace is **s** for you,

SULFUR
Rev   9:17 mouths came fire, smoke, and **s**.
Rev   14:10 in burning **s** before the holy angels
Rev   19:20 into the fiery pool burning with **s**.
Rev   20:10 thrown into the pool of fire and **s**,
Rev   21: 8 is in the burning pool of fire and **s**,

SUMMED
Rom   13: 9 there may be, are **s** up in this saying,

SUMMER
Prv   6: 8 She procures her food in the **s**,
Mk   13:28 leaves, you know that **s** is near.

SUMMON
Ps   68:29 **S** again, O God, your power,

SUN
Jos   10:13 The **s** stood still, the moon stayed,
Jos   10:13 The **s** halted halfway across
Jgs   5:31 who love you be like the **s** rising
Ps   72: 5 May they fear you with the **s**,
Ps   84:12 For a **s** and shield is the LORD
Ps   113: 3 of the **s** to its setting let the name
Ps   121: 6 By day the **s** will not strike you,
Ps   136: 8 The **s** to rule the day, for his mercy
Ps   148: 3 Praise him, **s** and moon;
Eccl   1: 9 Nothing is new under the **s**!
Sg   6:10 pure as the blazing **s**, fearsome as
Is   60:19 No longer shall the **s** be your light
Dn   3:62 **S** and moon, bless the Lord;
Jl   3: 4 The **s** will darken, the moon turn
Jl   4:15 **S** and moon are darkened,
Mi   3: 6 The **s** shall go down
Mal   3:20 name, the **s** of justice will arise
Mt   5:45 for he makes his **s** rise on the bad
Mt   13:43 the righteous will shine like the **s**
Mt   17: 2 his face shone like the **s** and his
Mk   13:24 tribulation the **s** will be darkened,
Acts   2:20 The **s** shall be turned to darkness,
Eph   4:26 do not let the **s** set on your anger,
Rev   1:16 and his face shone like the **s** at its
Rev   8:12 a third of the **s**, a third of the moon,
Rev   9: 2 The **s** and the air were darkened
Rev   10: 1 his face was like the **s** and his feet
Rev   12: 1 a woman clothed with the **s**,
Rev   19:17 I saw an angel standing on the **s**.
Rev   21:23 The city had no need of **s** or moon
Rev   22: 5 will they need light from lamp or **s**,

SUPERAPOSTLES → APOSTLE
2 Cor 11: 5 in any way inferior to these "**s**."
2 Cor 12:11 am in no way inferior to these "**s**,"

SUPERIOR
Heb   1: 4 as far **s** to the angels as the name he

SUPPER
1 Cor 11:25 way also the cup, after **s**, saying,

SUPPLICATION → SUPPLICATIONS
Eph   6:18 With all prayer and **s**, pray at every
Eph   6:18 and **s** for all the holy ones

SUPPLICATIONS → SUPPLICATION
1 Tm   2: 1 then, I ask that **s**, prayers, petitions,

Heb   5: 7 offered prayers and **s** with loud cries

SUPPLIES
2 Cor   9:10 The one who **s** seed to the sower

SUPPORT → SUPPORTS
Ps   18:19 distress, but the LORD was my **s**.
Mk   7:11 "Any **s** you might have had
Rom   11:18 consider that you do not **s** the root;

SUPPORTS → SUPPORT
Rom   11:18 not support the root; the root **s** you.

SUPPRESS
Rom   1:18 wickedness of those who **s** the truth

SURE → SURELY, SURETY
Nm   32:23 you can be **s** that the consequences
Prv   4:26 feet, and all your ways will be **s**.
Is   28:16 cornerstone as a **s** foundation;
Eph   5: 5 Be **s** of this, that no immoral
Heb   6:19 as an anchor of the soul, **s** and firm,
1 Jn   2: 3 The way we may be **s** that we know

SURELY → SURE
Gn   50:24 God will **s** take care of you and lead
Prv   23:18 For you will **s** have a future,
Ez   33:15 they shall **s** live; they shall not die.
Mk   14:19 to him, one by one, "**S** it is not I?"

SURETY → SURE
Prv   17:18 becoming **s** for their neighbors.
Sir   29:14 A good person will be **s** for a neighbor,
Sir   29:18 Going **s** has ruined many who were prosperous

SURPASSES → SURPASSING
Sir   25:11 Fear of the Lord **s** all else.
Eph   3:19 the love of Christ that **s** knowledge,
Phil   4: 7 **s** all understanding will guard your

SURPASSING → SURPASSES
2 Cor   9:14 because of the **s** grace of God

SURPRISED
1 Pt   4:12 do not be **s** that a trial by fire is

SURROUND → SURROUNDED, SURROUNDS
Ps   22:13 Many bulls **s** me; fierce bulls
Ps   125: 2 As mountains **s** Jerusalem,

SURROUNDED → SURROUND
Jgs   19:22 **s** the house and beat on the door.
Ps   118:11 They **s** me on every side;
Lk   21:20 you see Jerusalem **s** by armies,
Heb   12: 1 since we are **s** by so great a cloud
Rev   20: 9 and **s** the camp of the holy ones

SURROUNDS → SURROUND
Ps   32:10 mercy **s** the one who trusts
Ps   125: 2 the LORD **s** his people both now

SURVIVORS
Ez   14:22 there will still be some **s** in it who

SUSA
Neh   1: 1 year, I was in the citadel of **S**
Est   1: 2 throne in the royal precinct of **S**,

SUSANNA
    Righteous woman wrongly accused of immorality (Dn 13:1-44); vindicated by Daniel (Dn 13:45-64).

SUSPENSE
Jn   10:24 long are you going to keep us in **s**?

SUSPICIONS
1 Tm   6: 4 come envy, rivalry, insults, evil **s**,

SUSTAIN → SUSTAINED, SUSTAINS
Ps   36: 7 human being and beast you **s**, LORD.

SUSTAINED → SUSTAIN
Neh   9:21 Forty years in the desert you **s** them:

SUSTAINS → SUSTAIN
Heb   1: 3 who **s** all things by his mighty word.

SWALLOW → SWALLOWED
Nm   16:34 saying, "The earth might **s** us too!"

Ps	84: 4	and the s a nest to settle her young,
Jon	2: 1	the LORD sent a great fish to s Jonah,
Mt	23:24	strain out the gnat and s the camel!

SWALLOWED → SWALLOW

Gn	41: 7	and the thin ears s up the seven fat,
Nm	16:32	earth opened its mouth and s them
Ps	106:17	The earth opened and s Dathan,
1 Cor	15:54	"Death is s up in victory.
2 Cor	5: 4	so that what is mortal may be s

SWEAR → SWEARING, SWEARS, SWORE, SWORN

Dt	10:20	fast and by his name shall you s.
Jos	2:12	then, s to me by the LORD that,
Jos	23: 7	name, or s by them, or serve them,
Sir	23:11	who s many oaths heap up offenses;
Sir	23:11	If they s in error, guilt is incurred;
Sir	23:11	If they s without reason they cannot be
Is	45:23	By myself I s, uttering my just
Is	45:23	by me every tongue shall s,
Mt	5:34	But I say to you, do not s at all;
Heb	6:13	he had no one greater by whom to s,
Jas	5:12	do not s, either by heaven

SWEARING → SWEAR

Hos	4: 2	S, lying, murder,

SWEARS → SWEAR

Mt	23:20	One who s by the altar s by it

SWEAT

Gn	3:19	By the s of your brow you shall eat
Lk	22:44	that his s became like drops

SWEEP → SWEPT

Gn	18:23	"Will you really s away
Lk	15: 8	not light a lamp and s the house,

SWEET → SWEETER

Jb	20:12	Though wickedness is s in his
Ps	119:103	How s to my tongue is your
Prv	9:17	Stolen water is s, and bread taken
Prv	20:17	Bread earned by deceit is s,
Eccl	5:11	Sleep is s to the laborer,
Is	5:20	who change bitter to s, and s into bitter!
Ez	3: 3	it was as s as honey in my mouth.
Rev	10:10	In my mouth it was like s honey,

SWEETER → SWEET

Jgs	14:18	said to him, "What is s than honey,
Ps	19:11	S also than honey or drippings
Ps	119:103	promise, s than honey to my mouth!

SWELL

Dt	8: 4	nor did your feet s these forty years.

SWEPT → SWEEP

Ps	88:17	Your wrath has s over me;
Mt	12:44	it finds it empty, s clean, and put
Rev	12: 4	Its tail s away a third of the stars

SWIFT → SWIFTLY

Eccl	9:11	sun that the race is not won by the s,
Jer	46: 6	The s cannot flee, nor the warrior
2 Pt	2: 1	them, bringing s destruction

SWIFTLY → SWIFT

Ps	147:15	command to earth; his word runs s!

SWINE

1 Mc	1:47	to sacrifice s and unclean animals,
Mt	7: 6	or throw your pearls before s,
Mk	5:12	with him, "Send us into the s.

SWORD → SWORDS

Gn	3:24	and the fiery revolving s east
Ex	18: 4	has rescued me from Pharaoh's s."
Nm	14: 3	land only to have us fall by the s?
Dt	32:41	When I sharpen my flashing s,
Jos	5:13	stood facing him, drawn s in hand.
1 Sm	17:45	"You come against me with s
1 Sm	17:47	shall learn that it is not by s or spear
1 Sm	31: 4	"Draw your s and run me through;
1 Sm	31: 4	so Saul took his own s and fell
2 Sm	12:10	the s shall never depart from your

1 Chr	21:30	he was fearful of the s of the angel
Neh	4:12	working, had a s tied at his side.
Ps	22:21	Deliver my soul from the s, my life
Ps	44: 7	nor does my s bring me victory.
Ps	45: 4	Gird your s upon your hip,
Ps	57: 5	their tongue, a sharpened s.
Prv	5: 4	as sharp as a two-edged s.
Prv	12:18	of some people is like s thrusts,
Sir	21: 3	lawlessness is like a two-edged s;
Is	2: 4	shall not raise the s against another,
Is	49: 2	my mouth like a sharp-edged s,
Jer	15: 2	whoever is marked for the s, to the s;
Lam	1:20	Outside the s bereaves—
Ez	5: 2	the city and strike it with the s;
Ez	5: 2	and then unsheathe the s after it.
Hos	2:20	Bow and s and warfare I will
Mi	4: 3	shall not raise the s against another,
Mt	10:34	come to bring not peace but the s.
Mt	26:52	all who take the s will perish by the s.
Lk	2:35	you yourself a s will pierce) so
Acts	12: 2	the brother of John, killed by the s,
Rom	13: 4	does not bear the s without purpose;
Eph	6:17	of salvation and the s of the Spirit,
Heb	4:12	sharper than any two-edged s,
Heb	11:34	fires, escaped the devouring s;
Rev	1:16	A sharp two-edged s came
Rev	6: 4	And he was given a huge s.
Rev	13:14	who had been wounded by the s
Rev	19:15	his mouth came a sharp s to strike

SWORDS → SWORD

Ps	44: 4	their own s did they conquer
Ps	64: 4	They sharpen their tongues like s,
Is	2: 4	They shall beat their s
Jl	4:10	Beat your plowshares into s,
Mi	4: 3	They shall beat their s
Mk	14:48	against a robber, with s and clubs,

SWORE → SWEAR

Gn	26: 3	oath that I s to your father Abraham,
Ex	6: 8	into the land which I s to give
Ex	32:13	and how you s to them by your own
Nm	14:30	enter the land where I solemnly s
Dt	6:10	land which he s to your ancestors,
Ps	132:11	The LORD s an oath to David
Lk	1:73	the oath he s to Abraham our father,
Heb	3:11	As I s in my wrath, "They shall not
Heb	6:13	whom to swear, "he s by himself,"
Rev	10: 6	and s by the one who lives forever

SWORN → SWEAR

Ps	110: 4	The LORD has s and will not
Am	4: 2	The Lord GOD has s by his
Heb	7:21	"The Lord has s, and he will not

SYCAMORE

Lk	19: 4	and climbed a s tree in order to see

SYCHAR

Jn	4: 5	came to a town of Samaria called S,

SYMBOL

Heb	11:19	and he received Isaac back as a s.

SYMPATHIZE

Heb	4:15	have a high priest who is unable to s

SYNAGOGUE → SYNAGOGUES

Mt	13:54	and taught the people in their s.
Lk	4:16	into the s on the sabbath day.
Lk	8:41	an official of the s, came forward.
Acts	13:14	the sabbath they entered [into] the s
Acts	14: 1	they entered the Jewish s together
Acts	18: 4	he entered into discussions in the s,
Acts	18:26	He began to speak boldly in the s;

SYNAGOGUES → SYNAGOGUE

Mt	4:23	teaching in their s,
Mt	6: 2	as the hypocrites do in the s
Mt	10:17	to courts and scourge you in their s,
Lk	12:11	When they take you before s
Acts	13: 5	the word of God in the Jewish s.

SYNTYCHE
Phil   4: 2   and I urge S to come to a mutual

SYRIA → SYRIAN, SYROPHOENICIAN
Mt   4:24   His fame spread to all of S, and they

SYRIAN → SYRIA
Lk   4:27   cleansed, but only Naaman the S."

SYROPHOENICIAN → SYRIA
Mk   7:26   woman was a Greek, a S by birth,

T

TABERNACLE → TABERNACLES
Ex   25: 9   regarding the pattern of the t and
Ex   38:21   the various amounts used on the t, the t of the covenant,
Ex   40:18   It was Moses who set up the t.
Ex   40:34   and the glory of the LORD filled the t.
Lv   8:10   Moses anointed and consecrated the t
Lv   26:11   I will set my t in your midst,
Nm   1:50   give the Levites charge of the t
1 Chr   6:33   services of the t of the house of God.
Heb   9:11   more perfect t not made by hands,

TABERNACLES → TABERNACLE
Jn   7: 2   But the Jewish feast of T was near.

TABITHA → =DORCAS
Disciple, also known as Dorcas, whom Peter raised from the dead (Acts 9:36-42).

TABLE → TABLES
Ex   25:23   shall also make a t of acacia wood,
Nm   3:31   was the ark, the t, the menorah,
Ps   23: 5   You set a t before me in front of my
Ps   78:19   said, "Can God spread a t
1 Cor   10:21   cannot partake of the t of the Lord and of the t of demons.

TABLES → TABLE
Mk   11:15   He overturned the t of the money
Jn   2:15   and overturned their t,

TABLET → TABLETS
Prv   7: 3   write them on the t of your heart.
Is   30: 8   come, write it on a t they can keep,
Lk   1:63   He asked for a t and wrote, "John is

TABLETS → TABLET
Ex   31:18   Sinai, he gave him the two t
Ex   31:18   the stone t inscribed by God's own
Ex   32:19   he threw the t down and broke them
Dt   10: 5   placed the t in the ark I had made.
2 Cor   3: 3   not on t of stone but on t that are

TAIL → TAILS
Dt   28:13   will make you the head not the t,
Jgs   15: 4   and turning them t to t, he took
Rev   12: 4   Its t swept away a third of the stars

TAILS → TAIL
Rev   9:10   They had t like scorpions,
Rev   9:10   with their t they had power to harm
Rev   9:19   is in their mouths and in their t; for their t are like snakes,

TAKE → TAKEN, TAKES, TAKING, TOOK
Gn   22: 2   T your son Isaac, your only one,
Ex   6: 7   I will t you as my own people, and I
Nm   1: 2   T a census of the whole community
Dt   31:26   T this book of the law and put it
1 Sm   8:11   He will t your sons and assign them
1 Kgs   11:34   Yet I will not t any of the kingdom
1 Kgs   19: 4   T my life, for I am no better than
Ps   2:11   Blessed are all who t refuge in him!
Ps   27:14   Wait for the LORD, t courage;
Ps   31:25   Be strong and t heart, all who hope
Ps   51:13   face, nor t from me your holy spirit.
Ps   118: 8   Better to t refuge in the LORD
Hos   14: 3   T with you words, and return
Mt   1:20   do not be afraid to t Mary your wife
Mt   2:13   "Rise, t the child and his mother,
Mt   2:20   t the child and his mother and go

Mt   11:29   T my yoke upon you and learn
Mt   16:24   must deny himself, t up his cross,
Mt   17:27   and t the first fish that comes up.
Mt   26:26   it to his disciples said, "T and eat;
Mk   8:34   must deny himself, t up his cross,
Acts   1:20   And: 'May another t his office.'
1 Tm   3: 5   how can he t care of the church

TAKEN → TAKE
Gn   2:23   for out of man this one has been t."
Gn   27:36   now he has t away my blessing."
Nm   8:16   I have t them for myself in place
Jos   7:11   They have t goods subject
Sir   44:16   walked with the LORD and was t,
Jer   38:28   guard until the day Jerusalem was t.
Dn   5: 2   had t from the temple in Jerusalem,
Mt   13:12   even what he has will be t away.
Mt   24:40   one will be t, and one will be left.
Jn   20:13   to them, "They have t my Lord,
1 Tm   3:16   throughout the world, t up in glory.
Heb   11: 5   By faith Enoch was t up so that he
Heb   11: 5   no more because God had t him."

TAKES → TAKE
Ps   149: 4   the LORD t delight in his people,
Mk   4:15   and t away the word sown in them.
Lk   6:30   the one who t what is yours do not
Jn   1:29   who t away the sin of the world.
Jn   10:18   No one t it from me, but I lay it
Rev   22:19   if anyone t away from the words

TAKING → TAKE
Phil   2: 7   himself, t the form of a slave,

TALENT → TALENTS
Mt   25:25   off and buried your t in the ground.

TALENTS → TALENT
Mt   25:15   To one he gave five t;

TALITHA
Mk   5:41   hand and said to her, "*T koum*,"

TALK
1 Cor   4:20   kingdom of God is not a matter of t

TALL → TALLER
1 Chr   11:23   Egyptian, a huge man five cubits t.

TALLER → TALL
Dt   1:28   people are bigger and t than we,

TAMAR
1. Wife of Judah's sons Er and Onan (Gn 38:1-10). Tricked Judah into fathering children when he refused her his third son (Gn 38:11-30; Mt 1:3).
2. Daughter of David, raped by Amnon (2 Sm 13).

TAMARISK
Gn   21:33   Abraham planted a t at Beer-sheba,

TAMBOURINE → TAMBOURINES
Ex   15:20   Aaron's sister, took a t in her hand,

TAMBOURINES → TAMBOURINE
Ps   150: 4   Give praise with t and dance,
Jer   31: 4   Carrying your festive t, you shall go

TAME
Gn   1:25   wild animal, every kind of t animal,
Gn   2:20   The man gave names to all the t animals,
Gn   7:14   of wild animal, every kind of t animal,
Jas   3: 8   no human being can t the tongue.

TANNER
Acts   9:43   long time in Joppa with Simon, a t.

TARGET
Jb   16:12   He has set me up for a t;

TARSHISH
Ps   48: 8   the east wind wrecks the ships of T!
Is   60: 9   with the ships of T in the lead,
Jon   1: 3   But Jonah made ready to flee to T,
Jon   4: 2   This is why I fled at first toward T.

TARSUS
Acts   9:11 Judas for a man from T named Saul.
Acts 11:25 Then he went to T to look for Saul,

TASK
Ex   18:18 The t is too heavy for you;
Acts   6: 3 whom we shall appoint to this t,
1 Tm   3: 1 office of bishop desires a noble t.

TASTE → TASTED
Prv 24:13 if pure honey is sweet to your t,
Mt   16:28 here who will not t death until they
Col   2:21 Do not t! Do not touch!"
Heb   2: 9 God he might t death for everyone.

TASTED → TASTE
Heb   6: 4 enlightened and t the heavenly gift
1 Pt   2: 3 for you have t that the Lord is good.

TATTOO
Lv   19:28 the dead, and do not t yourselves.

TAUGHT → TEACH
Dt   31:22 day, and he t it to the Israelites.
2 Chr 17: 9 They t in Judah, having with them
2 Chr 17: 9 of Judah and t among the people.
Prv   4: 4 He t me and said to me:
Is   40:14 Who t him the path of judgment,
Is   54:13 All your children shall be t
Hos 11: 3 Yet it was I who t Ephraim to walk,
Mt   7:29 he t them as one having authority,
Jn   6:45 'They shall all be t by God.'
1 Cor 2:13 not with words t by human wisdom,
1 Cor 2:13 but with words t by the Spirit,
1 Jn   2:27 just as it t you, remain in him.

TAUNT
Ps 102: 9 All day long my enemies t me;
Jer   24: 9 and a byword, a t and a curse, in all

TAX → TAXES
2 Chr 24: 6 Jerusalem the t levied by Moses,
Mt   5:46 Do not the t collectors do the same?
Mt 11:19 a friend of t collectors and sinners.'
Mt 17:24 of the temple t approached Peter
Mt 17:24 your teacher pay the temple t?"
Mt 22:17 lawful to pay the census t to Caesar
Lk 18:10 and the other was a t collector.

TAXES → TAX
Rom 13: 7 all their dues, t to whom t are due,

TEACH → TAUGHT, TEACHER, TEACHERS, TEACHES, TEACHING, TEACHINGS
Ex   4:12 and t you what you are to say.
Dt   11:19 T them to your children,
1 Kgs 8:36 (for you t them the good way in which they
2 Kgs 17:28 began to t them how to venerate the Lord.
Jb   6:24 T me, and I will be silent;
Jb   21:22 Can anyone t God knowledge,
Ps   25: 4 t me your paths.
Ps   34:12 I will t you fear of the Lord.
Ps   51:15 I will t the wicked your ways,
Ps   78: 5 they were to t their children;
Ps   90:12 T us to count our days aright,
Ps 143:10 T me to do your will, for you are my
Prv   9: 9 t the just, and they advance
Jer 31:34 They will no longer t their friends
Lk 11: 1 t us to pray just as John taught his
Lk 12:12 For the holy Spirit will t you
Jn 14:26 he will t you everything and remind
Rom 2:21 then you who t another, are you failing to t yourself?
1 Cor 11:14 Does not nature itself t you
Col   3:16 richly, as in all wisdom you t
1 Tm 1: 3 people not to t false doctrines
1 Tm 2:12 I do not permit a woman to t
2 Tm 2: 2 have the ability to t others as well.
Heb   5:12 have someone t you again the basic
Heb   8:11 And they shall not t, each one his
1 Jn   2:27 you do not need anyone to t you.

TEACHER → TEACH
Mt 10:24 No disciple is above his t, no slave
Mt 22:36 "T, which commandment in the law
Lk   6:40 No disciple is superior to the t;
Lk   6:40 every disciple will be like his t.
Jn   1:38 (which translated means T),
Jn   3: 2 know that you are a t who has come
Jn 13:14 the master and t, have washed your
Rom 12: 7 if one is a t, in teaching;
2 Tm 1:11 preacher and apostle and t.

TEACHERS → TEACH
Ps 119:99 I have more insight than all my t,
Prv   5:13 did I not listen to the voice of my t,
1 Cor 12:28 third, t; then, mighty deeds;
Eph   4:11 evangelists, others as pastors and t,
2 Tm 4: 3 curiosity, will accumulate t
Heb   5:12 Although you should be t by this
Jas   3: 1 Not many of you should become t,
2 Pt   2: 1 as there will be false t among you,

TEACHES → TEACH
Ps 25: 9 and t the humble his way.
Ps 94:10 The one who t man not have
Mt   5:19 t others to do so will be called least
1 Tm 6: 3 Whoever t something different
1 Jn   2:27 his anointing t you about everything

TEACHING → TEACH
Ps 78: 1 Attend, my people, to my t;
Ps 89:31 If his descendants forsake my t,
Prv   1: 8 and reject not your mother's t;
Prv   3: 1 do not forget my t, take to heart my
Prv   6:23 and the t a light, and a way to life
Prv 13:14 The t of the wise is a fountain
Mt 28:20 t them to observe all that I have
Mk   1:27 A new t with authority.
Mk 11:18 crowd was astonished at his t.
Lk 19:47 every day he was t in the temple
Jn   7:17 his will shall know whether my t is
Acts 2:42 themselves to the t of the apostles
Acts 5:28 [did we not?] to stop t in that name.
Acts 5:28 have filled Jerusalem with your t
Rom 12: 7 if one is a teacher, in t;
Col   1:28 and t everyone with all wisdom,
1 Tm 4:13 to the reading, exhortation, and t.
1 Tm 5:17 those who toil in preaching and t
1 Tm 6: 3 Lord Jesus Christ and the religious t
2 Tm 3:16 inspired by God and is useful for t,
Ti   1:11 are upsetting whole families by t
Ti   2: 7 with integrity in your t, dignity,
2 Jn 1: 9 in the t of the Christ does not have
2 Jn 1: 9 remains in the t has the Father

TEACHINGS → TEACH
Ps 105:45 keep his statutes and observe his t.
Col   2:22 accord with human precepts and t.

TEAR → TEARS, TORE, TORN
Mk   2:21 from the old, and the t gets worse.
Rev 7:17 God will wipe away every t
Rev 21: 4 He will wipe every t from their

TEARS → TEAR
Ps 42: 4 My t have been my bread day
Ps 126: 5 Those who sow in t will reap
Is   25: 8 Lord God will wipe away the t
Jer   8:23 my eyes a fountain of t, That I
Jer 31:16 cries of weeping, hold back your t!
Lam 1:16 They stream with t! How far
Lk   7:38 began to bathe his feet with her t.
2 Cor 2: 4 of heart I wrote to you with many t,
Phil 3:18 told you and now tell you even in t,
Heb 5: 7 t to the one who was able to save

TEETH → TOOTH
Nm 11:33 the meat was still between their t,
Jb 19:20 I have escaped by the skin of my t.
Ps   3: 8 you break the t of the wicked.
Ps 35:16 me, gnashed their t against me.

Sir	21: 2	Its *t*, lion's *t*, destroying human
Jer	31:29	the children's *t* are set on edge,"
Dn	7: 7	it had great iron *t* with which it
Jl	1: 6	With *t* like a lion's, fangs like those
Mt	8:12	will be wailing and grinding of *t*."
Acts	7:54	and they ground their *t* at him.
Rev	9: 8	Their *t* were like lions' *t*,

TEKEL

Dn	5:25	MENE, T, and PERES.
Dn	5:27	T, you have been weighed

TEKOA

2 Sm	14: 4	So the woman of T went to the king
Am	1: 1	one of the sheepbreeders from T,

TELL → FORETOLD, FORTUNE-TELLING, TOLD

Ex	6:11	Go, *t* Pharaoh, king of Egypt, to let
Nm	22:35	but you may say only what I *t* you."
Ru	3: 4	He will then *t* you what to do."
1 Sm	3:15	He was afraid to *t* Eli the vision,
2 Chr	18:15	must I adjure you to *t* me nothing
Ps	50:12	I would not *t* you, for mine is
Dn	2: 4	T your servants the dream and we
Jn	20:15	him away, *t* me where you laid him,
1 Cor	15:51	Behold, I *t* you a mystery.

TEMAN

Jb	2:11	Eliphaz from T, Bildad from Shuh,

TEMPER → QUICK-TEMPERED, TEMPERATE

Prv	14:29	great wisdom; a short *t* raises folly high.
Prv	16:32	and those who rule their *t*,

TEMPERATE → TEMPER

1 Tm	3: 2	irreproachable, married only once, *t*,
1 Tm	3:11	but *t* and faithful in everything.
Ti	2: 2	that older men should be *t*,

TEMPLE → TEMPLES

Jgs	4:21	and drove the peg through his *t*
1 Sm	3: 3	in the *t* of the LORD where the ark
Ezr	3:10	the foundation of the LORD's *t*,
1 Mc	2: 8	Her *t* has become like a man
1 Mc	4:48	the interior of the *t* and consecrated
Ps	11: 4	The LORD is in his holy *t*;
Ps	27: 4	the LORD's beauty, to visit his *t*.
Ps	30: 1	A song for the dedication of the T.
Is	6: 1	the train of his garment filling the *t*.
Jer	7: 4	"The *t* of the LORD! The *t* of the LORD!"
Ez	8:16	There at the door of the LORD's *t*,
Ez	43: 4	of the LORD entered the *t* by way
Dn	5: 2	had taken from the *t* in Jerusalem,
Mi	1: 2	you, the Lord from his holy *t*!
Hb	2:20	But the LORD is in his holy *t*;
Mt	4: 5	him stand on the parapet of the *t*,
Mt	12: 6	something greater than the *t* is here.
Mt	26:61	said, 'I can destroy the *t* of God
Lk	21: 5	about how the *t* was adorned
Jn	2:14	in the *t* area those who sold oxen,
Jn	2:21	speaking about the *t* of his body.
Acts	2:46	to meeting together in the *t* area
Acts	5:42	both at the *t* and in their homes,
1 Cor	3:16	not know that you are the *t* of God,
1 Cor	6:19	your body is a *t* of the holy Spirit
2 Cor	6:16	What agreement has the *t* of God
2 Cor	6:16	For we are the *t* of the living God;
Eph	2:21	grows into a *t* sacred in the Lord;
2 Thes	2: 4	so as to seat himself in the *t* of God,
Rev	3:12	into a pillar in the *t* of my God,
Rev	11:19	Then God's *t* in heaven was opened,
Rev	11:19	his covenant could be seen in the *t*.
Rev	21:22	I saw no *t* in the city, for its *t* is the Lord God almighty

TEMPLES → TEMPLE

Rom	2:22	You who detest idols, do you rob *t*?

TEMPT → TEMPTATION, TEMPTED, TEMPTER, TEMPTS

1 Cor	7: 5	Satan may not *t* you through your

TEMPTATION → TEMPT

1 Tm	6: 9	who want to be rich are falling into *t*

Jas	1:12	is the man who perseveres in *t*,

TEMPTED → TEMPT

Mt	4: 1	into the desert to be *t* by the devil.
Mk	1:13	the desert for forty days, *t* by Satan.
Lk	4: 2	for forty days, to be *t* by the devil.
Gal	6: 1	so that you also may not be *t*.
Jas	1:13	should say, "I am being *t* by God";
Jas	1:14	each person is *t* when he is lured

TEMPTER → TEMPT

Mt	4: 3	The *t* approached and said to him,
1 Thes	3: 5	fear that somehow the *t* had put you

TEMPTS → TEMPT

Jas	1:13	to evil, and he himself *t* no one.

TEN → TENTH

Gn	18:32	What if *t* are found there?"
Gn	18:32	For the sake of the *t*, he replied,
Ex	34:28	words of the covenant, the *t* words.
Dt	4:13	the *t* words, which he wrote on two
Dt	10: 4	the *t* words that the LORD had
1 Sm	1: 8	I not better for you than *t* sons?"
2 Kgs	20: 9	go forward or back *t* steps?"
Ps	91: 7	side, *t* thousand at your right hand,
Dn	1:12	test your servants for *t* days.
Dn	7:24	The *t* horns shall be *t* kings rising
Mt	25: 1	will be like *t* virgins who took their
Mt	25:28	him and give it to the one with *t*.
Lk	15: 8	what woman having *t* coins
Rev	12: 3	with seven heads and *t* horns,
Rev	17:12	The *t* horns that you saw represent *t* kings

TENANTS

Mt	21:34	to the *t* to obtain his produce.

TEND

Jn	21:16	He said to him, "T my sheep."

TENDER

Lk	1:78	because of the *t* mercy of our God

TENT → TENTMAKERS, TENTS

Ex	27:21	the LORD in the *t* of meeting,
Ex	33: 7	used to pitch a *t* outside the camp
Ex	33: 7	the tabernacle of the *t* of meeting.
2 Sm	7: 2	but the ark of God dwells in a *t*!"
Ps	61: 5	Let me dwell in your *t* forever,
Is	33:20	as a quiet abode, a *t* not to be struck,
Is	54: 2	Enlarge the space for your *t*,
Is	54: 2	out your *t* cloths unsparingly;
2 Cor	5: 1	dwelling, a *t*, should be destroyed,

TENTH → TEN

Gn	14:20	Abram gave him a *t* of everything.
Is	6:13	If there remain a *t* part in it,
Heb	7: 4	"Abraham [indeed] gave a *t*" of his

TENTMAKERS → MAKE, TENT

Acts	18: 3	worked, for they were *t* by trade.

TENTS → TENT

Ps	84:11	than a home in the *t* of the wicked.

TERAH

Gn	11:27	These are the descendants of T.

TEREBINTH

Is	6:13	As with a *t* or an oak whose trunk

TERRIFIED → TERROR

1 Sm	17:11	Philistine, they were stunned and *t*.
Ez	19: 7	were *t* at the sound of his roar.
Mt	14:26	him walking on the sea they were *t*.
Heb	12:21	said, "I am *t* and trembling."
Rev	11:13	the rest were *t* and gave glory

TERRIFYING → TERROR

Dt	26: 8	with *t* power, with signs and wonders,
Dn	7: 7	I saw a fourth beast, *t*, horrible,
2 Tm	3: 1	will be *t* times in the last days.

TERROR → TERRIFIED, TERRIFYING, TERRORS

1 Sm	14:15	Then *t* spread through the camp
Ps	91: 5	You shall not fear the *t* of the night

Is   2:19 At the t of the LORD
Is   24:17 T, pit, and trap for you,
Jer   20:10 "T on every side!

TERRORS → TERROR
Jb   6: 4 the t of God are arrayed against me.
Ps   31:14 of the crowd; t are all around me.
Ps   55: 5 death's t fall upon me.

TERTIUS
Rom   16:22 I, T, the writer of this letter,

TEST → TESTED, TESTER, TESTING
Ex   16: 4 thus will I t them, to see whether
Dt   6:16 God, to the t, as you did at Massah.
1 Kgs 10: 1 came to t him with subtle questions.
Jdt   8:12 are you to put God to the t today,
Ps   26: 2 Examine me, Lord, and t me;
Jer   9: 6 I will refine them and t them;
Lk   4:12 the Lord, your God, to the t.' "
Lk   10:25 of the law who stood up to t him
Acts   5: 9 "Why did you agree to t the Spirit
1 Cor   3:13 the fire [itself] will t the quality
1 Cor 10: 9 Let us not t Christ as some of them
2 Cor 13: 5 you are living in faith. T yourselves.
2 Cor 13: 5 unless, of course, you fail the t.
1 Thes 5:21 T everything; retain what is good.
Heb   11:17 when put to the t, offered up Isaac,
1 Jn   4: 1 but t the spirits to see whether they
Rev   3:10 the whole world to t the inhabitants

TESTED → TEST
Ex   17: 7 quarreled there and t the LORD,
Ps   66:10 You t us, O God, tried us as silver
Ps   78:41 Again and again they t God,
Prv   30: 5 Every word of God is t; he is a shield
Sir   44:20 and when t was found loyal.
Is   28:16 a stone that has been t, A precious
Is   48:10 I t you in the furnace of affliction.
Dn   1:14 this request, and t them for ten days;
1 Tm   3:10 Moreover, they should be t first;
Heb   2:18 he himself was t through what he
Heb   2:18 able to help those who are being t.
Heb   3: 9 where your ancestors t and tried me
Heb   4:15 but one who has similarly been t

TESTER → TEST
Jer   6:27 A t for my people I have appointed

TESTIFIED → TESTIFY
Jn   1:15 John t to him and cried out, saying,
Jn   5:37 the Father who sent me has t on my
1 Pt   1:11 them indicated when it t in advance

TESTIFIES → TESTIFY
Jn   5:32 there is another who t on my behalf,
1 Jn   5: 6 The Spirit is the one that t,

TESTIFY → TESTIFIED, TESTIFIES, TESTIMONIES, TESTIMONY
Jn   1: 7 came for testimony, to t to the light,
Jn   5:39 even they t on my behalf.
Jn   7: 7 because I t to it that its works are
Jn   15:26 from the Father, he will t to me.
1 Jn   4:14 and t that the Father sent his Son as
1 Jn   5: 7 So there are three that t,

TESTIMONIES → TESTIFY
Ps   119: 2 Blessed those who keep his t,
Ps   119:24 Your t are my delight; they are my counselors.
Ps   119:78 with falsehood, that I may study your t.
Ps   119:99 my teachers, because I ponder your t.

TESTIMONY → TESTIFY
Mk   14:59 Even so their t did not agree.
Lk   22:71 "What further need have we for t?
Jn   8:17 the t of two men can be verified.
Jn   21:24 them, and we know that his t is true.
Heb   2: 4 God added his t by signs, wonders,
1 Jn   5: 9 If we accept human t, the t of God is
1 Jn   5: 9 Now the t of God is this, that he has
Rev   1: 9 God's word and gave t to Jesus.
Rev   12:11 the Lamb and by the word of their t;

TESTING → TEST
Dt   13: 4 is t you to know whether you really
Heb   3: 8 in the day of t in the desert,
Jas   1: 3 that the t of your faith produces

THADDAEUS → =JUDAS
Apostle (Mt 10:3; Mk 3:18); probably also known as Judas son of James (Lk 6:16; Acts 1:13).

THANK → THANKFULLY, THANKS, THANKSGIVING
2 Chr 29:31 and t offerings for the house
Ps   107: 8 Let them t the LORD for his
Lk   18:11 I t you that I am not like the rest
Jn   11:41 "Father, I t you for hearing me.

THANKFULLY → THANK
1 Cor 10:30 If I partake t, why am I reviled

THANKS → THANK
1 Chr 16: 8 Give t to the LORD, invoke his
Ps   30:13 my God, forever will I give you t.
Ps   75: 2 We thank you, God, we give t;
Ps   107: 1 "Give t to the LORD for he is
Ps   118:28 You are my God, I give you t;
Sir   51: 1 I give you t, LORD and King,
Is   38:18 For it is not Sheol that gives you t,
Is   38:19 the living give you t, as I do today.
Dn   3:89 Give t to the Lord, who is good,
Rom   1:21 him glory as God or give him t.
Rom   14: 6 the Lord, since he gives t to God;
1 Cor 11:24 t be to God who gives us the victory
2 Cor   2:14 But t be to God, who always leads
2 Cor   9:15 T be to God for his indescribable
Phil   1: 3 I give t to my God at every
1 Thes 5:18 In all circumstances give t, for this
Rev   4: 9 t to the one who sits on the throne,
Rev   11:17 "We give t to you, Lord God

THANKSGIVING → THANK
Lv   7:12 If someone offers it for t,
Jdt   15:14 Judith led all Israel in this song of t,
Ps   100: 1 A psalm of t. Shout joyfully
Ps   100: 4 Enter his gates with t, his courts
Ps   147: 7 Sing to the LORD with t;
2 Cor   9:11 which through us produces t to God,
Phil   4: 6 with t, make your requests known
1 Tm   4: 3 to be received with t by those who
Rev   7:12 and glory, wisdom and t, honor,

THEFT → THIEF
Mt   15:19 adultery, unchastity, t, false witness,
Mk   7:21 evil thoughts, unchastity, t, murder,

THEME
Ps   45: 2 My heart is stirred by a noble t, as I

THEOPHILUS
Lk   1: 3 sequence for you, most excellent T,
Acts   1: 1 In the first book, T, I dealt with all

THESSALONICA
Acts   17: 1 they reached T, where there was
Phil   4:16 I was at T you sent me something

THICK
Zep   1:15 and gloom, a day of t black clouds,

THICKET
Gn   22:13 ram caught by its horns in the t.

THIEF → THEFT, THIEVES
Lk   12:39 the hour when the t was coming,
Jn   10:10 A t comes only to steal
1 Thes 5: 2 the Lord will come like a t at night.
1 Pt   4:15 as a murderer, a t, an evildoer, or as
Rev   16:15 ("Behold, I am coming like a t."

THIEVES → THIEF
Mt   6:19 destroy, and t break in and steal.
Jn   10: 8 All who came [before me] are t
1 Cor   6:10 nor t nor the greedy nor drunkards

THIGH → THIGHS
Gn   24: 2 "Put your hand under my t,
Gn   47:29 put your hand under my t as a sign
Rev   19:16 written on his cloak and on his t,

THIGHS → THIGH
Dn   2:32 were silver, its belly and t bronze,

THIN
Gn   41: 7 the t ears swallowed up the seven

THING → ANYTHING, EVERYTHING, THINGS
Gn   18:25 Far be it from you to do such a t,
Ps   27: 4 One t I ask of the LORD;
Ps   84:12 The LORD withholds no good t
Jer   31:22 The LORD has created a new t
Mk   10:21 to him, "You are lacking in one t.
Lk   10:42 There is need of only one t.
Jn   9:25 One t I do know is that I was blind
Phil   3:13 Just one t: forgetting what lies

THINGS → THING
Ps   71:19 You have done great t; O God,
Ps   87: 3 Glorious t are said of you, O city
Prv   6:16 There are six t the LORD hates,
Is   42: 9 See, the earlier t have come to pass,
Is   66: 2 My hand made all these t when all
Jl   2:21 for the LORD has done great t!
Mt   19:26 but for God all t are possible."
Mk   11:33 you by what authority I do these t."
Jn   1: 3 All t came to be through him,
Jn   1:50 You will see greater t than this."
Jn   21:25 are also many other t that Jesus did,
Eph   1:22 And he put all t beneath his feet
Eph   1:22 gave him as head over all t
Col   1:17 He is before all t, and in him all t
Heb   1: 3 and who sustains all t by his mighty
1 Pt   4: 7 The end of all t is at hand.
Rev   4:11 and power, for you created all t;

THINK → THINKING, THINKS, THOUGHT, THOUGHTS
Ps   63: 7 I t of you upon my bed, I remember
Jn   5:39 because you t you have eternal life
Rom   12: 3 not to t more highly than one ought to t, but to t soberly,
Phil   4: 8 of praise, t about these things.

THINKING → THINK
Dn   13: 9 They perverted their t; they would not
Mt   12:25 he knew what they were t and said
1 Cor 14:20 stop being childish in your t.
1 Cor 14:20 like infants, but in your t be mature.

THINKS → THINK
1 Cor 10:12 whoever t he is standing secure

THIRD → THREE
Ez   5:12 A t of your people shall die
Ez   5:12 another t shall fall by the sword all
Ez   5:12 a t I will scatter to the winds
Ez   10:14 second a human being, the t a lion,
Dn   5: 7 be t in governing the kingdom."
Hos   6: 2 on the t day he will raise us up,
Mt   26:44 withdrew again and prayed a t time,
Mk   14:41 He returned a t time and said
Lk   18:33 him, but on the t day he will rise."
Jn   21:17 He said to him the t time, "Simon,
Jn   21:17 that he had said to him a t time,
2 Cor 12: 2 was caught up to the t heaven.
Rev   4: 7 the t had a face like that of a human
Rev   6: 5 When he broke open the t seal,
Rev   6: 5 I heard the t living creature cry out,
Rev   8:10 When the t angel blew his trumpet,
Rev   8:10 It fell on a t of the rivers
Rev   12: 4 Its tail swept away a t of the stars

THIRST → THIRSTS, THIRSTY
Ex   17: 3 To have us die of t with our children
Dt   28:48 in hunger and t, in nakedness
Ps   69:22 and for my t they gave me vinegar.
Mt   5: 6 who hunger and t for righteousness,
Rev   7:16 They will not hunger or t anymore,

THIRSTS → THIRST
Ps   42: 3 My soul t for God, the living God.
Ps   63: 2 for you my soul t, In a land parched,

THIRSTY → THIRST
Ps   107: 9 For he satisfied the t,
Prv   25:21 to eat, if t, give something to drink;
Mt   25:35 I was t and you gave me drink,
Rom   12:20 if he is t, give him something
Rev   21: 6 To the t I will give a gift

THIRTY
Gn   41:46 Joseph was t years old when he
2 Sm 23:24 brother of Joab, was among the T;
Prv   22:20 Have I not written for you t sayings,
Mk   4:20 accept it and bear fruit t and sixty
Lk   3:23 his ministry he was about t years

THISTLE → THISTLES
2 Kgs 14: 9 "A t of Lebanon sent word

THISTLES → THISTLE
Gn   3:18 Thorns and t it shall bear for you,
Hos   10: 8 and t will overgrow their altars.
Heb   6: 8 But if it produces thorns and t, it is

THOMAS
     Apostle (Mt 10:3; Mk 3:18; Lk 6:15; Jn 11:16; 14:5; 21:2; Acts 1:13).
Doubted resurrection (Jn 20:24-28).

THONGS
Lk   3:16 to loosen the t of his sandals.

THORN → THORNBUSH, THORNS
Mi   7: 4 brier, the most honest like a t hedge.
2 Cor 12: 7 a t in the flesh was given to me,

THORNBUSH → BUSH, THORN
Is   55:13 In place of the t, the cypress shall

THORNS → THORN
Gn   3:18 T and thistles it shall bear for you,
Nm   33:55 in your eyes and t in your sides,
Jer   12:13 They have sown wheat and reaped t,
Mt   13: 7 Some seed fell among t, and the t grew up
Jn   19: 2 the soldiers wove a crown out of t
Heb   6: 8 But if it produces t and thistles, it is

THOUGH
Is   1:18 T your sins be like scarlet, they may
Hb   3:17 For t the fig tree does not blossom,
Hb   3:17 T the yield of the olive fails
Hb   3:17 T the flocks disappear from the fold

THOUGHT → THINK
Gn   39: 8 my master does not give a t to anything
2 Cor 10: 5 take every t captive in obedience

THOUGHTS → THINK
Is   55: 8 For my t are not your t, nor are your
Mt   9: 4 said, "Why do you harbor evil t?
Rom   2:15 their conflicting t accuse or even
1 Cor 3:20 "The Lord knows the t of the wise,
Heb   4:12 reflections and t of the heart.

THOUSAND → THOUSANDS
Dt   32:30 "How could one rout a t, or two put ten t to flight,
Jos   23:10 One of you puts to flight a t,
Jgs   15:16 of an ass I have slain a t men."
Ps   84:11 in your courts than a t elsewhere.
Ps   90: 4 A t years in your eyes are merely
Ps   91: 7 Though a t fall at your side, ten t
Ps   105: 8 he commanded for a t generations,
Mt   14:21 who ate were about five t men,
Mt   15:38 Those who ate were four t men,
2 Pt   3: 8 the Lord one day is like a t years and a t years like one day.
Rev   20: 4 reigned with Christ for a t years.

THOUSANDS → THOUSAND
1 Sm 18: 7 "Saul has slain his t, David his tens of t."
Ps   50:10 beasts by the t on my mountains.
Ps   68:18 chariots were myriad, t upon t;
Sg   5:10 outstanding among t.

Dn	7:10	T upon t were ministering to him,
Mi	6: 7	Will the Lord be pleased with t

THREAT → THREATEN, THREATS

Is	30:17	shall tremble at the t of one—
Lam	2:17	He has fulfilled the t Decreed

THREATEN → THREAT

1 Pt	2:23	when he suffered, he did not t;

THREATS → THREAT

Bar	2:24	out the t you had made through your
Acts	9: 1	breathing murderous t against

THREE → THIRD

Gn	6:10	Noah begot t sons: Shem, Ham,
Gn	18: 2	up, he saw t men standing near him.
Ex	23:14	T times a year you shall celebrate
Dt	19:15	the testimony of two or t witnesses.
1 Sm	31: 8	his t sons fallen on Mount Gilboa.
2 Sm	23: 9	one of the T warriors with David
Jb	2:11	Now when t of Job's friends heard
Prv	30:15	T things never get their fill,
Prv	30:18	T things are too wonderful for me,
Prv	30:21	Under t things the earth trembles,
Prv	30:29	T things are stately in their stride,
Sir	25: 1	With t things I am delighted,
Sir	25: 2	T kinds of people I hate, and I
Dn	3:91	"Did we not cast t men bound
Dn	7: 5	the teeth in its mouth were t tusks.
Am	1: 3	For t crimes of Damascus, and now
Jon	2: 1	in the belly of the fish t days and t nights.
Zec	11: 8	I did away with the t shepherds,
Mt	12:40	was in the belly of the whale t days and t nights,
Mt	12:40	in the heart of the earth t days and t nights.
Mt	17: 4	I will make t tents here, one for you,
Mt	18:20	t are gathered together in my name,
Mt	26:34	crows, you will deny me t times."
Mt	26:75	crows you will deny me t times."
Mt	27:63	'After t days I will be raised up.'
Mk	8:31	and be killed, and rise after t days.
Mk	14:30	twice you will deny me t times."
Jn	2:19	and in t days I will raise it up."
1 Cor	13:13	So faith, hope, love remain, these t;
1 Cor	14:27	let it be two or at most t, and each
2 Cor	12: 8	T times I begged the Lord
2 Cor	13: 1	of two or t witnesses a fact shall be
1 Jn	5: 7	So there are t that testify,

THRESH → THRESHING

Mi	4:13	Arise and t, O daughter Zion;

THRESHING → THRESH

Ru	3: 3	attire and go down to the t floor.
2 Sm	24:18	altar to the Lord on the t floor
Hos	9: 1	a prostitute's fee upon every t floor.
Lk	3:17	fan is in his hand to clear his t floor
1 Tm	5:18	shall not muzzle an ox when it is t,"

THRESHOLD

1 Sm	5: 4	hands broken off and lying on the t,
Ez	10:18	the Lord left the t of the temple
Ez	47: 1	under the t of the temple toward

THREW → THROW

Ex	7:10	Aaron t his staff down before
Ex	15:25	When he t it into the water,
Ex	32:19	and he t the tablets down and broke
2 Kgs	6: 6	cut off a stick, t into the water,
Rev	20: 3	and t it into the abyss, which he

THROAT → THROATS

Ps	5:10	Their t is an open grave;

THROATS → THROAT

Ps	115: 7	they produce no sound from their t.
Rom	3:13	Their t are open graves;

THRONE → ENTHRONED, THRONES

Dt	17:18	When he is sitting upon his royal t,
2 Sm	7:13	I will establish his royal t forever.
1 Chr	17:12	and I will establish his t forever.
Ps	11: 4	the Lord's t is in heaven.

Ps	45: 7	Your t, O God, stands forever;
Ps	47: 9	God sits upon his holy t.
Ps	89:15	are the foundation of your t;
Prv	20:28	and he upholds his t by justice.
Is	6: 1	Lord seated on a high and lofty t,
Is	66: 1	The heavens are my t, the earth,
Jer	33:21	descendant to act as king upon his t,
Ez	1:26	of a t that looked like sapphire;
Dn	7: 9	and the Ancient of Days took his t.
Dn	7: 9	His t was flames of fire,
Mt	5:34	not by heaven, for it is God's t;
Mt	19:28	of Man is seated on his t of glory,
Lk	1:32	the Lord God will give him the t
Acts	7:49	'The heavens are my t, the earth is
Heb	1: 8	"Your t, O God, stands forever
Heb	4:16	So let us confidently approach the t
Heb	12: 2	his seat at the right of the t of God.
Rev	2:13	that you live where Satan's t is,
Rev	3:21	the right to sit with me on my t, as I
Rev	3:21	and sit with my Father on his t.
Rev	4: 2	A t was there in heaven, and on the t sat
Rev	4:10	before the one who sits on the t
Rev	4:10	down their crowns before the t,
Rev	5:13	"To the one who sits on the t
Rev	20:11	Next I saw a large white t
Rev	22: 1	flowing from the t of God
Rev	22: 3	The t of God and of the Lamb will

THRONES → THRONE

Ps	122: 5	There are the t of justice, the t of the house of David.
Dn	7: 9	T were set up and the Ancient
Mt	19:28	will yourselves sit on twelve t,
Col	1:16	invisible, whether t or dominions
Rev	4: 4	the throne I saw twenty-four other t
Rev	20: 4	Then I saw t; those who sat on them

THRONG

Ps	35:18	will praise you before the mighty t.

THROUGH

Gn	21:12	for it is t Isaac that descendants will
Ex	15:19	walked on dry land t the midst
Is	43: 2	When you pass t waters, I will be
Is	43: 2	When you walk t fire, you shall not
Jn	14: 6	comes to the Father except t me.
Rom	5: 1	with God t our Lord Jesus Christ,
1 Cor	8: 6	t whom all things are and t whom
Gal	2:19	For t the law I died to the law, that I
Eph	2: 8	grace you have been saved t faith,
Col	1:16	all things were created t him
Heb	1: 2	he spoke to us t a son, whom he
Heb	1: 2	and t whom he created the universe,

THROW → THREW, THROWN

Ex	1:22	"T into the Nile every boy that is
Ex	4: 3	God said: T it on the ground.
Zec	11:13	said to me, T it in the treasury—
Mt	5:30	you to sin, cut it off and t it away.
Mt	7: 6	or t your pearls before swine,
Jn	8: 7	is without sin be the first to t a stone

THROWN → THROW

Mk	11:23	'Be lifted up and t into the sea,'
Rev	12: 9	whole world, was t down to earth,
Rev	12: 9	and its angels were t down with it.
Rev	19:20	The two were t alive into the fiery
Rev	20:10	Devil who had led them astray was t
Rev	20:14	Hades were t into the pool of fire.

THUMMIM

Ex	28:30	you shall put the Urim and T,
Ezr	2:63	a priest to consult the Urim and T.

THUNDER → THUNDERED, THUNDERS

Ex	9:23	the Lord sent forth peals of t
Ex	20:18	as all the people witnessed the t
Jb	40: 9	or can you t with a voice like his?
Mk	3:17	named Boanerges, that is, sons of t;
Rev	4: 5	lightning, rumblings, and peals of t.
Rev	6: 1	creatures cry out in a voice like t,

Rev 16:18 and peals of t, and a great

THUNDERED → THUNDER
Ps 18:14 The LORD t from heaven;

THUNDERS → THUNDER
Ps 29: 3 the God of glory t, the LORD,
Rev 10: 3 out, the seven t raised their voices,
Rev 10: 4 When the seven t had spoken, I was
Rev 10: 4 up what the seven t have spoken,

THYATIRA
Acts 16:14 from the city of T, a worshiper
Rev 2:18 "To the angel of the church in T,

TIBERIAS
Jn 6: 1 across the Sea of Galilee [of T].

TIBERIUS
Lk 3: 1 year of the reign of T Caesar,

TIBNI
King of Israel (1 Kgs 16:21-22).

TIE → TIED
Mt 23: 4 They t up heavy burdens [hard]

TIED → TIE
Jos 2:21 she t the scarlet cord in the window.
Jn 13: 4 a towel and t it around his waist.

TIGLATH-PILESER → =PUL
2 Kgs 16: 7 Ahaz sent messengers to T,

TIGRIS
Gn 2:14 The name of the third river is the T;
Dn 10: 4 on the bank of the great river, the T.

TILES
Lk 5:19 the stretcher through the t

TILL
Gn 4:12 If you t the ground, it shall no

TIME → TIMES
Gn 4:26 At that t people began to invoke
Dt 32:35 for the t they lose their footing;
Est 4:14 perhaps it was for a t like this
Ps 119:126 It is t for the LORD to act;
Eccl 3: 1 There is an appointed t
Eccl 3: 1 and a t for every affair under
Eccl 3:11 made everything appropriate to its t,
Dn 12: 1 "At that t there shall arise Michael,
Dn 12: 1 It shall be a t unsurpassed in distress
Hos 10:12 for it is t to seek the LORD, till he
Lk 21: 8 'I am he,' and 'The t has come.'
Rom 5: 6 at the appointed t for the ungodly.
1 Cor 4: 5 judgment before the appointed t,
1 Cor 7:29 you, brothers, the t is running out.
2 Cor 6: 2 "In an acceptable t I heard you,
2 Cor 6: 2 Behold, now is a very acceptable t;
Gal 4: 4 when the fullness of t had come,
Heb 9:28 will appear a second t, not to take
1 Pt 4:17 For it is t for the judgment to begin
Rev 1: 3 in it, for the appointed t is near.
Rev 2:21 I have given her t to repent, but she
Rev 22:10 book, for the appointed t is near.

TIMES → TIME
Ex 23:14 Three t a year you shall celebrate
Jos 6: 4 day march around the city seven t,
Ps 9:10 a stronghold in t of trouble.
Ps 62: 9 Trust God at all t, my people!
Prv 24:16 Though the just fall seven t,
Eccl 8: 5 and the wise heart knows t
Mt 16: 3 [you cannot judge the signs of the t.]
Mt 18:22 not seven t but seventy-seven t.
Mk 14:30 twice you will deny me three t."
Lk 17: 4 if he wrongs you seven t in one day
Lk 17: 4 and returns to you seven t saying,
Acts 1: 7 "It is not for you to know the t
1 Tm 4: 1 that in the last t some will turn away
2 Tm 3: 1 there will be terrifying t in the last

TIMOTHY
Believer from Lystra (Acts 16:1). Joined Paul on second missionary journey (Acts 16–20). Sent to settle problems at Corinth (1 Cor 4:17; 16:10). Led church at Ephesus (1 Tm 1:3). Co-writer with Paul (1 Thes 1:1; 2 Thes 1:1; Phlm 1).

TIP
Jgs 6:21 out the t of the staff he held.

TIRED
Jn 4: 6 Jesus, t from his journey, sat down

TIRZAH
1 Kgs 15:33 all Israel in T for twenty-four years.

TISHBITE
1 Kgs 17: 1 Elijah the T, from Tishbe in Gilead,
2 Kgs 1: 8 "It is Elijah the T!" he exclaimed.

TITHE → TITHES
Nm 18:26 them to the LORD, a t of the t;
Dt 12:17 partake of your t of grain or wine
Mal 3: 8 we robbed you?" Of t and contributions!
Mal 3:10 Bring the whole t

TITHES → TITHE
Mal 3: 8 Of t and contributions!
Mt 23:23 You pay t of mint and dill

TITUS
Gentile co-worker of Paul (Gal 2:1-3; 2 Tm 4:10); sent to Corinth (2 Cor 2:13; 7–8; 12:18), Crete (Ti 1:4-5).

TOBIAH
Enemy of Nehemiah and the exiles (Neh 2:10-19; 4; 6; 13:4-9). Son of Tobit:
Tb 1: 9 By her I had a son whom I named T.
Tb 3:17 as a wife to T, the son of Tobit,

TOBIJAH
Zec 6:14 as a gracious reminder to Heldai, T,

TOBIT
Tb 1: 1 This book tells the story of T,
Tb 1: 3 I, T, have walked all the days of my
Tb 3:17 the son of T, and to rid her
Tb 7: 4 "Do you know our kinsman T?"
Tb 11:16 T went out to the gate of Nineveh

TODAY
Ex 14:13 the LORD will win for you t.
Ex 14:13 whom you see t you will never see
Ex 34:11 what I am commanding you t.
Dt 30:15 See, I have t set before you life
Ps 2: 7 are my son; t I have begotten you.
Ps 95: 7 Oh, that t you would hear his voice:
Lk 4:21 "T this scripture passage is fulfilled
Lk 19: 9 "T salvation has come to this house
Lk 23:43 t you will be with me in Paradise."
Heb 3: 7 that t you would hear his voice,
Heb 3:13 yourselves daily while it is still "t,"
Heb 4: 7 he once more set a day, "t,"
Heb 4: 7 that t you would hear his voice:
Heb 13: 8 Jesus Christ is the same yesterday, t,

TOES
Dn 2:42 and the t partly iron and partly clay,

TOGETHER
Gn 3: 7 so they sewed fig leaves t and made
Dt 22:10 an ox and a donkey harnessed t.
Ps 2: 2 princes plot t against the LORD
Ps 34: 4 and let us exalt his name t.
Is 11: 6 and the young lion shall browse t,
Ez 37: 7 The bones came t, bone joining
Mt 19: 6 what God has joined t, no human
Acts 2:44 All who believed were t and had all
Acts 4:26 the princes gathered t against
Acts 5:12 They were all t in Solomon's

TOIL
Gn 3:16 I will intensify your t in childbearing;
Gn 3:17 t you shall eat its yield all the days
Gn 5:29 our work and the t of our hands,

TOLA
A judge of Israel (Jgs 10:1-2).

TOLD → TELL
Gn	3:11	Who t you that you were naked?
Jgs	16:17	So he t her all that was in his heart
Ps	44: 2	our ancestors have t us The deeds
Lk	2:20	seen, just as it had been t to them.
Jn	14:29	And now I have t you this before it

TOLERABLE → TOLERATE
Lk	10:12	it will be more t for Sodom
Lk	10:14	But it will be more t for Tyre

TOLERATE → TOLERABLE
Rev	2: 2	and that you cannot t the wicked;

TOMB → TOMBS
Mk	15:46	laid him in a t that had been hewn
Mk	15:46	a stone against the entrance to the t.
Lk	24: 2	the stone rolled away from the t;

TOMBS → TOMB
Mt	23:29	You build the t of the prophets
Mt	27:52	t were opened, and the bodies

TOMORROW
Prv	27: 1	Do not boast about t, for you do not
Is	22:13	"Eat and drink, for t we die!"
Mt	6:34	Do not worry about t; t will take care of itself.
1 Cor	15:32	"Let us eat and drink, for t we die."
Jas	4:14	no idea what your life will be like t.

TONGUE → DOUBLE-TONGUED, TONGUES
Ex	4:10	but I am slow of speech and t."
Jb	33: 2	my t and voice form words.
Ps	34:14	Keep your t from evil, your lips
Ps	39: 2	watch my ways, lest I sin with my t;
Ps	51:16	and my t will sing joyfully of your
Ps	52: 6	create confusion, you deceitful t.
Ps	71:24	my t shall recount your justice day
Ps	119:172	May my t sing of your promise,
Ps	137: 6	May my t stick to my palate if I do
Ps	139: 4	Even before a word is on my t,
Prv	6:17	a lying t, hands that shed innocent
Prv	12:18	but the t of the wise is healing.
Prv	15: 4	A soothing t is a tree of life,
Prv	18:21	and life are in the power of the t;
Prv	25:15	and a soft t can break a bone.
Prv	26:28	The lying t is its owner's enemy,
Prv	28:23	than one who flatters with the t.
Prv	31:26	kindly instruction is on her t.
Sg	4:11	honey and milk are under your t;
Is	45:23	by me every t shall swear,
Is	50: 4	has given me a well-trained t, That I
Is	59: 3	falsehood, and your t utters deceit.
Mk	7:33	ears and, spitting, touched his t;
Lk	16:24	of his finger in water and cool my t,
Rom	14:11	every t shall give praise to God."
1 Cor	14: 2	who speaks in a t does not speak
1 Cor	14: 4	speaks in a t builds himself up,
1 Cor	14:13	one who speaks in a t should pray
1 Cor	14:19	also, than ten thousand words in a t.
1 Cor	14:26	a revelation, a t, or an interpretation.
1 Cor	14:27	If anyone speaks in a t, let it be two
Phil	2:11	every t confess that Jesus Christ is
Jas	3: 5	In the same way the t is a small
Jas	3: 8	but no human being can tame the t.

TONGUES → TONGUE
Ps	12: 5	who say, "By our t we prevail;
Acts	2: 3	there appeared to them t as of fire,
Acts	10:46	they could hear them speaking in t
Acts	19: 6	and they spoke in t and prophesied.
Rom	3:13	they deceive with their t;
1 Cor	12:10	to another varieties of t; to another interpretation of t.
1 Cor	12:28	administration, and varieties of t.
1 Cor	12:30	Do all speak in t? Do all interpret?
1 Cor	13: 1	and angelic t but do not have love,
1 Cor	13: 8	if t, they will cease;
1 Cor	14: 5	I should like all of you to speak in t,

1 Cor	14: 5	is greater than one who speaks in t,
1 Cor	14: 9	because of speaking in t, do not
1 Cor	14:18	I speak in t more than any of you,
1 Cor	14:21	"By people speaking strange t
1 Cor	14:22	Thus, t are a sign not for those who
1 Cor	14:39	and do not forbid speaking in t,

TOOK → TAKE
Gn	2:21	he t out one of his ribs and closed
Gn	3: 6	So she t some of its fruit and ate it;
Gn	5:24	was no longer here, for God t him.
Ex	4:20	Moses t the staff of God with him.
1 Mc	1:23	And he t away the silver and gold
1 Mc	1:23	t all the hidden treasures he could
1 Mc	4:47	Then they t uncut stones,
Ps	78:70	servant, t him from the sheepfolds.
Dn	7: 9	the Ancient of Days t his throne.
Mt	4: 5	the devil t him to the holy city,
Mt	4: 8	the devil t him up to a very high
Mt	8:17	"He t away our infirmities and bore
Mt	26:26	they were eating, Jesus t bread,
Mt	26:27	Then he t a cup, gave thanks,
1 Cor	11:23	night he was handed over, t bread,

TOOTH → TEETH
Ex	21:24	eye for eye, t for t, hand for hand,
Mt	5:38	'An eye for an eye and a t for a t.'

TOP → TOPS
Gn	28:12	with its t reaching to the heavens;
Ex	19:20	to the t of the mountain, the LORD
Ex	19:20	Moses to the t of the mountain,
Mt	27:51	was torn in two from t to bottom.
Jn	19:23	in one piece from the t down.

TOPHETH
2 Kgs	23:10	king also defiled T in the Valley
Jer	19:12	I will make this city like T.

TOPS → TOP
Gn	8: 5	day of the tenth month the t

TORCH → TORCHES
Gn	15:17	a smoking fire pot and a flaming t,
Is	62: 1	and her salvation like a burning t.
Rev	8:10	a large star burning like a t fell

TORCHES → TORCH
Ez	1:13	indeed like t moved back and forth
Dn	10: 6	his eyes were like fiery t, his arms
Rev	4: 5	Seven flaming t burned in front

TORE → TEAR
1 Mc	1:56	of the law that they found they t
1 Mc	4:45	so they t down the altar.
Mt	26:65	the high priest t his robes and said,

TORMENT → TORMENTED, TORMENTORS
Lk	16:28	lest they too come to this place of t.'

TORMENTED → TORMENT
1 Sm	16:14	he was t by an evil spirit
Rev	20:10	There they will be t day and night

TORMENTORS → TORMENT
Ps	137: 3	the words of a song; Our t, for joy:
Is	51:23	I will put it into the hands of your t,

TORN → TEAR
Gn	37:33	Joseph has been t to pieces!"
1 Sm	28:17	he has t the kingdom from your
Mk	1:10	he saw the heavens being t open
Lk	23:45	the temple was t down the middle.
Gal	4:15	you would have t out your eyes

TORTURED
Heb	11:35	Some were t and would not accept

TOSSED → TOSSING
Eph	4:14	no longer be infants, t by waves
Jas	1: 6	is driven and t about by the wind.

TOSSING → TOSSED
Is	57:20	the wicked are like the t sea

TOUCH → TOUCHED, TOUCHES
Gn   3: 3   'You shall not eat it or even t it,
Ex   19:12 All who t the mountain must be put
Nm   4:15 they shall not t the sacred objects;
Ps   105:15 "Do not t my anointed ones, to my
Wis   3: 1 of God, and no torment shall t them.
Is   52:11 out from there, t nothing unclean!
Ez   9: 6 do not t anyone marked with the X.
Mt   9:21 "If only I can t his cloak, I shall be
Lk   18:15 infants to him that he might t them,
Lk   24:39 T me and see, because a ghost does
2 Cor   6:17 the Lord, "and t nothing unclean;
Col   2:21 Do not taste! Do not t!"
Heb   11:28 of the firstborn might not t them.

TOUCHED → TOUCH
1 Sm   10:26 whose hearts the LORD had t.
Is   6: 7 He t my mouth with it.
Is   6: 7 "now that this has t your lips,
Jer   1: 9 extended his hand and t my mouth,
Dn   10:16 something like a hand t my lips;
Mt   8: 3 He stretched out his hand, t him,
Mt   14:36 and as many as t it were healed.
Mk   5:30 asked, "Who has t my clothes?"
Acts   19:12 aprons that t his skin were applied
1 Jn   1: 1 t with our hands concerns the Word

TOUCHES → TOUCH
Ps   104:32 t the mountains and they smoke!
Heb   12:20 "If even an animal t the mountain,

TOWER → TOWERS, WATCHTOWER
Gn   11: 4 a city and a t with its top in the sky,
Ps   61: 4 a t of strength against the foe.
Prv   18:10 name of the LORD is a strong t;
Lk   14:28 construct a t does not first sit down

TOWERS → TOWER
Ps   48:13 around it, note the number of its t.
Ps   122: 7 ramparts, prosperity within your t."

TOWN
Mt   2:23 and dwelt in a t called Nazareth,
Mt   10:11 Whatever t or village you enter,
Lk   2: 3 to be enrolled, each to his own t.

TRADE
Rev   18:22 in any t will ever be found in you

TRADITION
Mt   15: 2 "Why do your disciples break the t
Mk   7:13 of your t that you have handed on.
Col   2: 8 philosophy according to human t,

TRAIN → TRAINED, TRAINING, TRAINS
Prv   22: 6 T the young in the way they should
1 Tm   4: 7 T yourself for devotion,

TRAINED → TRAIN
Heb   5:14 for those whose faculties are t
Heb   12:11 to those who are t by it.

TRAINING → TRAIN
1 Tm   4: 8 while physical t is of limited value,
2 Tm   3:16 and for t in righteousness,
Ti   2:12 and t us to reject godless ways

TRAINS → TRAIN
Ps   144: 1 my rock, who t my hands for battle,

TRAITOR → TREASON
Lk   6:16 and Judas Iscariot, who became a t.

TRAMPLE → TRAMPLED
Ps   91:13 the viper, t the lion and the dragon.
Am   2: 7 They t the heads of the destitute
Am   8: 4 this, you who t upon the needy
Mt   7: 6 swine, lest they t them underfoot,
Rev   11: 2 Gentiles, who will t the holy city

TRAMPLED → TRAMPLE
1 Mc   3:45 The sanctuary was t on,
Is   63: 6 I t down the peoples in my anger,
Dn   8: 7 the ram to the ground and t upon it.

Dn   8:10 and some of the stars and t on them.
Mt   5:13 to be thrown out and t underfoot.
Lk   21:24 Jerusalem will be t underfoot

TRANCE
Acts   10:10 making preparations he fell into a t.
Acts   11: 5 of Joppa when in a t I had a vision,
Acts   22:17 praying in the temple, I fell into a t

TRANSFIGURED
Mt   17: 2 And he was t before them;
Mk   9: 2 And he was t before them,

TRANSFORMED
Rom   12: 2 be t by the renewal of your mind,
2 Cor   3:18 are being t into the same image

TRANSGRESS → TRANSGRESSED, TRANSGRESSION,
          TRANSGRESSIONS, TRANSGRESSOR
Jos   23:16 If you t the covenant of the LORD,

TRANSGRESSED → TRANSGRESS
Dn   9:11 because all Israel t your law

TRANSGRESSION → TRANSGRESS
Dn   9:24 Then t will stop and sin will end,
Gal   6: 1 even if a person is caught in some t,

TRANSGRESSIONS → TRANSGRESS
Gal   3:19 It was added for t,

TRANSGRESSOR → TRANSGRESS
Gal   2:18 down, then I show myself to be a t.
Jas   2:11 kill, you have become a t of the law.

TRANSPARENT
Rev   21:21 the city was of pure gold, t as glass.

TRAP → ENTRAP
Jos   23:13 they will be a snare and a t for you,
Ps   69:23 and their communion offerings a t.
Is   8:14 A t and a snare to those who dwell
Lk   20:20 to be righteous who were to t him
Rom   11: 9 their table become a snare and a t,

TRAVEL → TRAVELER
Ex   13:21 Thus they could t both day

TRAVELER → TRAVEL
Jer   14: 8 like a t stopping only for a night?

TREAD → TREADING, TREADS
Ps   91:13 You can t upon the asp
Lk   10:19 I have given you the power 'to t
Rev   19:15 and he himself will t out in the wine

TREADING → TREAD
Mi   7:19 on us, t underfoot our iniquities?
1 Cor   9: 9 shall not muzzle an ox while it is t

TREADS → TREAD
Dt   25: 4 not muzzle an ox when it t out grain.

TREASON → TRAITOR
2 Kgs   11:14 tore her garments and cried out, "T, t!"

TREASURE → TREASURED, TREASURES, TREASURIES, TREASURY
Ps   119:11 In my heart I t your promise, that I
Is   33: 6 is the fear of the LORD, her t.
Mt   6:21 For where your t is, there also will
Mt   13:44 heaven is like a t buried in a field,
Mt   19:21 poor, and you will have t in heaven.
Lk   12:33 an inexhaustible t in heaven that no
2 Cor   4: 7 we hold this t in earthen vessels,
1 Tm   6:19 thus accumulating as t a good

TREASURED → TREASURE
Jb   23:12 of his mouth I have t in my heart.

TREASURES → TREASURE
Dt   33:19 seas and the hidden t of the sand.
2 Kgs   24:13 He carried off all the t of the house
Prv   10: 2 Ill-gotten t profit nothing,
Is   45: 3 I will give you t of darkness,
Mt   6:19 store up for yourselves t on earth,
Col   2: 3 in whom are hidden all the t
Heb   11:26 Anointed greater wealth than the t

TREASURIES → TREASURE
Prv   8:21 who love me, and filling their t.

TREASURY → TREASURE
Sir   29:12 Store up almsgiving in your t,
Mt   27: 6 to deposit this in the temple t, for it
Mk   12:43 all the other contributors to the t.

TREE → TREES
Gn   1:29 every t that has seed-bearing fruit
Gn   2: 9 the LORD God made grow every t
Gn   2: 9 with the t of life in the middle
Gn   2: 9 and the t of the knowledge of good
Gn   3:24 to guard the way to the t of life.
Dt   21:23 shall not remain on the t overnight.
1 Kgs   14:23 high hill and under every green t
1 Kgs   19: 4 until he came to a solitary broom t
Ps   52:10 I, like an olive t flourishing
Ps   92:13 just shall flourish like the palm t,
Prv   3:18 She is a t of life to those who grasp
Prv   11:30 The fruit of justice is a t of life,
Prv   27:18 Those who tend a fig t eat its fruit;
Is   65:22 As the years of a t, so the years
Jer   17: 8 They are like a t planted beside
Ez   17:24 I bring low the high t, lift high the lowly t,
Ez   17:24 Wither up the green t, and make the dry t bloom.
Ez   47:12 the river every kind of fruit t will grow;
Hos   9:10 Like the first fruits of the fig t,
Hos   14: 7 His splendor will be like the olive t
Hb   3:17 though the fig t does not blossom,
Mt   3:10 Therefore every t that does not bear
Mt   12:33 "Either declare the t good and its
Mt   12:33 or declare the t rotten and its fruit is
Mt   12:33 for a t is known by its fruit.
Mk   11:13 from a distance a fig t in leaf,
Lk   19: 4 climbed a sycamore t in order to see
Acts   5:30 him killed by hanging him on a t.
Rom   11:24 what is by nature a wild olive t,
Rom   11:24 grafted back into their own olive t.
Jas   3:12 Can a fig t, my brothers,
Rev   2: 7 right to eat from the t of life that is
Rev   22: 2 side of the river grew the t of life
Rev   22:14 so as to have the right to the t of life
Rev   22:19 take away his share in the t of life

TREES → TREE
Gn   3: 1 from any of the t in the garden'?"
Gn   3: 2 eat of the fruit of the t in the garden;
Dt   20:19 you shall not destroy its t by putting
Dt   20:19 Are the t of the field human beings,
Jgs   9: 8 One day the t went out to anoint
1 Chr   14:15 marching in the tops of the balsam t,
Ps   96:12 Then let all the t of the forest rejoice
Is   55:12 you, all t of the field shall clap their
Zec   3:10 another under your vines and fig t."
Zec   4:11 "What are these two olive t,
Mt   3:10 now the ax lies at the root of the t.
Mk   8:24 "I see people looking like t
Jude   1:12 by winds, fruitless t in late autumn,
Rev   8: 7 up, along with a third of the t and all
Rev   11: 4 These are the two olive t

TREMBLE → TREMBLED, TREMBLES, TREMBLING
1 Chr   16:30 T before him, all the earth;
Ps   99: 1 The LORD is king, the peoples t;
Ps   114: 7 T, earth, before the Lord,
Jer   5:22 should you not t before me?
Jl   2: 1 Let all the inhabitants of the land t,
Hb   3: 6 he looked and made the nations t.

TREMBLED → TREMBLE
Ex   19:16 so that all the people in the camp t.
Ex   20:18 smoking, they became afraid and t.
2 Sm   22: 8 the foundations of the heavens t;

TREMBLES → TREMBLE
Ps   97: 4 the earth sees and t.
Ps   104:32 Who looks at the earth and it t,
Is   66: 2 crushed in spirit, who t at my word.

TREMBLING → TREMBLE
Ps   2:11 exult with t, Accept correction lest
Phil   2:12 out your salvation with fear and t.

TRENCH
1 Kgs   18:38 and lapped up the water in the t.

TRESPASSES
2 Cor   5:19 not counting their t against them

TRIAL → TRIALS
2 Pt   2: 9 how to rescue the devout from t
Rev   3:10 safe in the time of t that is going

TRIALS → TRIAL
Lk   22:28 you who have stood by me in my t;
Jas   1: 2 when you encounter various t,
1 Pt   1: 6 have to suffer through various t,

TRIBE → HALF-TRIBE, TRIBES
Nm   1: 4 there shall be a man from each t,
Nm   36: 9 will pass from one t to another,
Jos   13:14 no heritage to the t of Levi;
Jgs   21: 6 "Today one t has been cut off from Israel.
1 Kgs   11:13 I will give your son one t
Ps   78:68 God chose the t of Judah,
Heb   7:13 are said belonged to a different t,
Rev   5: 5 The lion of the t of Judah, the root
Rev   5: 9 for God those from every t
Rev   14: 6 on earth, to every nation, t, tongue,

TRIBES → TRIBE
Gn   49:28 All these are the twelve t of Israel,
Ex   24: 4 stones for the twelve t of Israel.
Ex   39:14 the name of one of the twelve t.
1 Kgs   11:31 hand and will give you ten of the t.
1 Kgs   18:31 for the number of t of the sons
Ps   122: 4 There the t go up, the t of the LORD,
Is   49: 6 to raise up the t of Jacob,
Mt   19:28 judging the twelve t of Israel.
Jas   1: 1 to the twelve t in the dispersion,
Rev   21:12 of the twelve t of the Israelites.

TRIBUTE
1 Kgs   5: 1 they paid Solomon t and served him

TRIED → TRY
Ps   66:10 O God, t us as silver t by fire.
Jn   19:12 Pilate t to release him; but the Jews
Gal   1:23 now preaching the faith he once t to

TRIMMED
Mt   25: 7 virgins got up and t their lamps.

TRIUMPH → TRIUMPHS
Ps   118: 7 I shall look in t on my foes.
2 Cor   2:14 who always leads us in t in Christ
Col   2:15 them, leading them away in t by it.

TRIUMPHS → TRIUMPH
Jas   2:13 mercy t over judgment.

TROPHIMUS
2 Tm   4:20 while I left T sick at Miletus.

TROUBLE → TROUBLED, TROUBLES
Jb   14: 1 woman is short-lived and full of t,
Ps   9:10 a stronghold in times of t.
Ps   22:12 for t is near, and there is no one
Ps   27: 5 hide me in his shelter in time of t,
Prv   25:19 a trust betrayed in time of t.
Sir   51:10 Do not abandon me in time of t,
Is   33: 2 morning, our salvation in time of t!

TROUBLED → TROUBLE
Jn   14: 1 "Do not let your hearts be t.
Jn   14:27 Do not let your hearts be t or afraid.

TROUBLES → TROUBLE
Jb   5:19 Out of six t he will deliver you,
Ps   25:17 Relieve the t of my heart;

TRUE → TRULY, TRUTH
Jos   23:15 your God, made to you has come t for you,
1 Sm   9: 6 everything he says comes t.
1 Kgs   10: 6 your deeds and your wisdom is t,"

2 Chr 15: 3 time Israel was without a t God,
Ps   51: 8 Behold, you desire t sincerity;
Lk   16:11 who will trust you with t wealth?
Jn   1: 9 The t light, which enlightens
Jn   4:23 t worshipers will worship the Father
Jn   6:32 my Father gives you the t bread
Jn   7:28 me, whom you do not know, is t.
Jn   15: 1 "I am the t vine, and my Father is
Jn   17: 3 the only t God, and the one whom
Jn   19:35 has testified, and his testimony is t;
Jn   21:24 and we know that his testimony is t.
Rom   3: 4 God must be t, though every human
Phil   4: 8 brothers, whatever is t, whatever is
1 Thes 1: 9 idols to serve the living and t God
1 Jn   2: 8 which holds t in him and among
1 Jn   2: 8 and the t light is already shining.
1 Jn   5:20 to know the one who is t. And we are in the one who
             is t,
1 Jn   5:20 He is the t God and eternal life.
3 Jn   1:12 and you know our testimony is t.
Rev   3: 7 the t, who holds the key of David,
Rev   3:14 the faithful and t witness, the source
Rev   6:10 holy and t master, before you sit
Rev   15: 3 Just and t are your ways, O king
Rev   16: 7 your judgments are t and just."
Rev   19: 2 for t and just are his judgments.
Rev   19: 9 he said to me, "These words are t;
Rev   19:11 rider was [called] "Faithful and T."
Rev   21: 5 for they are trustworthy and t."
Rev   22: 6 "These words are trustworthy and t,

TRULY → TRUE
Jer   10:10 The LORD is t God, he is the living God,
Mt   27:54 "T, this was the Son of God!"
1 Tm   5: 3 Honor widows who are t widows.

TRUMPET → TRUMPETERS, TRUMPETS
Nm   29: 1 be a day on which you sound the t.
Is   27:13 On that day, A great t shall blow,
Ez   33: 5 They heard the t blast but ignored
Mt   24:31 send out his angels with a t blast,
1 Cor 15:52 in the blink of an eye, at the last t. For the t will sound,
1 Thes 4:16 an archangel and with the t of God,
Rev   1:10 behind me a voice as loud as a t,
Rev   8: 7 When the first one blew his t,

TRUMPETERS → TRUMPET
2 Chr 5:13 When the t and singers were heard

TRUMPETS → TRUMPET
Nm   10: 2 Make two t of silver, making them
Rev   8: 2 before God were given seven t.

TRUST → ENTRUST, ENTRUSTED, TRUSTED, TRUSTS, TRUSTWORTHY
Nm   14:11 How long will they not t me,
Dt   1:32 you would not t the LORD,
2 Kgs 18:19 On what do you base this t of yours?
1 Chr 9:22 them in their position of t.
Jb   4:18 Look, he puts no t in his servants,
Jb   31:24 Had I put my t in gold or called fine
Ps   4: 6 sacrifices and t in the LORD.
Ps   5:12 Then all who t in you will be glad
Ps   9:11 Those who know your name t
Ps   25: 2 my God, in you I t; do not let me be
Ps   26: 1 In the LORD I t; I do not falter.
Ps   31: 7 idols, but I t in the LORD.
Ps   31:15 But I t in you, LORD; I say,
Ps   33:21 in his holy name we t.
Ps   37: 3 T in the LORD and do good
Ps   37: 5 t in him and he will act
Ps   40: 4 fear and they shall t in the LORD.
Ps   44: 7 Not in my bow do I t, nor does my
Ps   49: 7 Of those who t in their wealth
Ps   52:10 I t in God's mercy forever and ever.
Ps   55:24 their days, but I put my t in you.
Ps   56: 4 I am afraid, in you I place my t.
Ps   56: 5 I t in God, I do not fear.
Ps   56:12 In God I t, I do not fear.
Ps   62: 9 T God at all times, my people!

Ps   71: 5 my t, GOD, from my youth.
Ps   78:22 God, did not t in his saving power.
Ps   91: 2 and fortress, my God in whom I t."
Ps   115:11 Those who fear the LORD t
Ps   119:42 with a word, for I t in your word.
Ps   143: 8 hear of your mercy, for in you I t.
Ps   146: 3 Put no t in princes, in children
Prv   3: 5 T in the LORD with all your heart,
Prv   22:19 That your t may be in the LORD,
Sir   2: 6 T in God, and he will help you;
Is   26: 4 T in the LORD forever!
Is   30:15 quiet and in t shall be your strength.
Is   31: 1 Who put their t in chariots because
Is   36: 4 On what do you base this t of yours?
Is   42:17 back in utter shame who t in idols;
Jer   2:37 has rejected those in whom you t,
Jer   5:17 the fortified cities in which you t.
Jer   7: 4 Do not put your t in these deceptive
Jer   7: 8 You put your t in deceptive words
Jer   7:14 in which you t, and to the place
Jer   9: 3 put no t in any brother.
Jer   17: 7 Blessed are those who t in the LORD; the LORD will be
             their t.
Jer   49:11 your widows, let them t in me.
Mi   7: 5 in a friend, do not t a companion;
Heb   2:13 and again: "I will put my t in him";

TRUSTED → TRUST
1 Sm 27:12 Achish t David, thinking,
Jb   12:20 He silences the t adviser,
Ps   22: 5 In you our fathers t; they t and you
Ps   22: 6 in you they t and were not
Ps   52: 9 he t in the abundance of his wealth,
Jer   13:25 forgotten me, and t in deception,
Dn   3:95 to deliver the servants that t in him;
Dn   6:24 to be unharmed because he t in his
Dn   13:35 she t in the Lord wholeheartedly.
Zep   3: 2 In the LORD it has not t,

TRUSTS → TRUST
Ps   21: 8 For the king t in the LORD,
Ps   32:10 mercy surrounds the one who t
Ps   84:13 hosts, blessed the man who t in you!
Ps   86: 2 save your servant who t in you.
Ps   115: 8 them, and anyone who t in them.
Ps   115: 9 The house of Israel t in the LORD,
Ps   115:10 house of Aaron t in the LORD,
Ps   135:18 them, and anyone who t in them.
Prv   16:20 happy the one who t in the LORD!
Prv   28:25 the one who t in the LORD will
Prv   29:25 the one who t in the LORD is safe.

TRUSTWORTHY → TRUST
Ex   18:21 men, t men who hate dishonest gain,
Tb   5: 3 find yourself a t person who will
Tb   5: 9 and whether he is t enough to travel
Tb   10: 6 man who is traveling with him is t
Ps   145:13 The LORD is t in all his words,
Prv   11:13 but a t person keeps a confidence.
Prv   14: 5 A t witness does not lie, but one
Sir   46:15 As a t prophet he was sought
1 Cor 4: 2 of stewards that they be found t.
1 Cor 7:25 as one who by the Lord's mercy is t.
Rev   21: 5 down, for they are t and true."
Rev   22: 6 to me, "These words are t and true,

TRUTH → TRUE, TRUTHFUL
Gn   42:16 will your words be tested for their t;
1 Kgs 22:16 the t in the name of the LORD?"
2 Chr 18:15 the t in the name of the LORD?"
Ps   15: 2 is right, speaking t from the heart;
Ps   31: 6 you will redeem me, LORD, God of t.
Ps   45: 5 In the cause of t, meekness,
Ps   86:11 your way that I may walk in your t,
Ps   119:43 Do not take the word of t from my
Ps   145:18 him, to all who call upon him in t.
Prv   23:23 Buy t and do not sell:
Sir   4:25 Never speak against the t,
Is   30:10 prophets, "Do not prophesy t for us;

Is	59:14	For t stumbles in the public square,
Jer	9: 2	and not with t, they are powerful
Jer	9: 4	the other, no one speaks the t.
Jer	26:15	in t it was the LORD who sent me
Dn	8:12	It cast t to the ground, and was
Zec	8:16	Speak the t to one another;
Mk	5:33	Jesus and told him the whole t.
Lk	20:21	of God in accordance with the t.
Jn	1:14	only Son, full of grace and t.
Jn	1:17	and t came through Jesus Christ.
Jn	4:23	worship the Father in Spirit and t;
Jn	4:24	him must worship in Spirit and t."
Jn	5:33	to John, and he testified to the t.
Jn	8:32	and you will know the t, and the t will set you free."
Jn	8:40	a man who has told you the t that I
Jn	8:44	and does not stand in t, because there is no t in him.
Jn	8:45	But because I speak the t, you do
Jn	14: 6	"I am the way and the t and the life.
Jn	14:17	the Spirit of t, which the world
Jn	15:26	the Spirit of t that proceeds
Jn	16:13	the Spirit of t, he will guide you to all t.
Jn	17:17	Consecrate them in the t. Your word is t.
Jn	18:37	into the world, to testify to the t.
Jn	18:37	who belongs to the t listens to my
Jn	18:38	Pilate said to him, "What is t?"
Jn	19:35	he knows that he is speaking the t,
Acts	20:30	will come forward perverting the t
Rom	1:18	of those who suppress the t by their
Rom	1:25	They exchanged the t of God
Rom	2: 8	to those who selfishly disobey the t
Rom	2:20	formulation of knowledge and t—
Rom	9: 1	I speak the t in Christ, I do not lie;
1 Cor	5: 8	unleavened bread of sincerity and t.
1 Cor	13: 6	wrongdoing but rejoices with the t.
2 Cor	4: 2	of the t we commend ourselves
2 Cor	11:10	By the t of Christ in me, this boast
2 Cor	12: 6	foolish, for I would be telling the t.
2 Cor	13: 8	we cannot do anything against the t, but only for the t.
Gal	5: 7	you from following [the] t?
Eph	1:13	who have heard the word of t,
Eph	4:15	Rather, living the t in love,
Eph	4:21	were taught in him, as t is in Jesus,
Eph	6:14	fast with your loins girded in t,
Col	1: 5	already heard through the word of t,
2 Thes	2:10	have not accepted the love of t so
2 Thes	2:13	by the Spirit and belief in t.
1 Tm	2: 4	and to come to knowledge of the t.
1 Tm	2: 7	and apostle (I am speaking the t,
1 Tm	2: 7	teacher of the Gentiles in faith and t.
1 Tm	3:15	God, the pillar and foundation of t.
1 Tm	4: 3	those who believe and know the t.
1 Tm	6: 5	who are deprived of the t,
2 Tm	2:15	the word of t without deviation.
2 Tm	2:18	have deviated from the t by saying
2 Tm	2:25	that leads to knowledge of the t,
2 Tm	3: 7	able to reach a knowledge of the t.
2 Tm	4: 4	will stop listening to the t and will
Ti	1: 1	and the recognition of religious t,
Ti	1:14	of people who have repudiated the t.
Heb	10:26	after receiving knowledge of the t,
Jas	1:18	the word of t that we may be a kind
Jas	3:14	do not boast and be false to the t.
Jas	5:19	among you should stray from the t
1 Pt	1:22	to the t for sincere mutual love,
2 Pt	1:12	are established in the t you have.
2 Pt	2: 2	of them the way of t will be reviled.
1 Jn	1: 8	ourselves, and the t is not in us.
1 Jn	2: 4	is a liar, and the t is not in him.
1 Jn	2:21	not because you do not know the t
1 Jn	2:21	because every lie is alien to the t.
1 Jn	3:18	in word or speech but in deed and t.
1 Jn	3:19	shall know that we belong to the t
1 Jn	4: 6	This is how we know the spirit of t
1 Jn	5: 6	one that testifies, and the Spirit is t.
2 Jn	1: 1	to her children whom I love in t—
2 Jn	1: 1	but also all who know the t—
2 Jn	1: 2	because of the t that dwells in us
2 Jn	1: 3	Jesus Christ the Father's Son in t
2 Jn	1: 4	in the t just as we were commanded
3 Jn	1: 1	the beloved Gaius whom I love in t.
3 Jn	1: 3	to how truly you walk in the t.
3 Jn	1: 4	my children are walking in the t.
3 Jn	1: 8	that we may be co-workers in the t.
3 Jn	1:12	from all, even from the t itself.

TRUTHFUL → TRUTH

Prv	12:19	T lips endure forever, the lying
Prv	14:25	The t witness saves lives,
2 Cor	6: 7	in t speech, in the power of God;

TRY → TRIED

1 Cor	10:33	just as I t to please everyone
2 Cor	5:11	of the Lord, we t to persuade others;
Eph	5:10	T to learn what is pleasing

TRYPHO

1 Mc	11:39	When a certain T, who had
1 Mc	13:31	T dealt treacherously

TUNIC → TUNICS

Ex	28: 4	a robe, a brocade t, a turban,
Lk	9: 3	and let no one take a second t.
Jn	19:23	They also took his t, but the t was seamless,

TUNICS → TUNIC

Ex	28:40	of Aaron's sons you shall have t

TURN → TURNED, TURNING, TURNS

Ex	23:27	I will make all your enemies t
Nm	32:15	If you t away from following him,
2 Chr	7:14	my face and t from their evil ways,
2 Chr	30: 9	he will not t away his face from you
Ps	6: 5	T back, LORD, rescue my soul;
Ps	119:132	T to me and be gracious,
Prv	7:25	Do not let your heart t to her ways,
Is	6:10	and they t and be healed.
Is	28: 6	for those who t back the battle
Is	30:21	when you would t to the right
Is	45:22	T to me and be safe, all you ends
Is	53: 3	Like one from whom you t your face,
Jer	31:13	I will t their mourning into joy,
Ez	33: 9	you warn the wicked to t from their
Ez	33:11	T, t from your evil ways!
Jl	3: 4	The sun will darken, the moon t blood-red,
Mal	3:24	He will t the heart of fathers to their
Mt	5:39	t the other one to him as well.
Lk	1:17	of Elijah to t the hearts of fathers
Acts	26:18	eyes that they may t from darkness
Gal	4: 9	how can you t back again
1 Pt	3:11	must t from evil and do good,

TURNED → TURN

Dt	23: 6	t this curse into a blessing for you,
1 Kgs	11: 4	was old his wives had t his heart
2 Chr	15: 4	their distress they t to the LORD,
Est	9:22	as the month which was t for them
Ps	114: 3	sea saw and fled; the Jordan t back.
Is	9:11	his wrath is not t back, and his hand
Jon	3:10	their actions how they t from their
Zec	7:11	they stubbornly t their backs
Lk	22:32	and once you have t back, you must

TURNING → TURN

Dt	5:32	not t aside to the right or to the left,
Dt	28:14	not t aside, either to the right

TURNS → TURN

2 Cor	3:16	whenever a person t to the Lord

TURTLEDOVES

Lv	5: 7	for the wrong committed two t
Lv	12: 8	she may take two t or two pigeons,
Lk	2:24	to offer the sacrifice of "a pair of t

TWELVE

Gn	35:22	The sons of Jacob were now t.
Gn	49:28	All these are the t tribes of Israel,
Ex	24: 4	and t sacred stones for the t tribes
Ex	28:21	t of them to match the names

Ex	28:21	with the name of one of the t tribes.
Jos	4: 3	"Take up t stones from this spot
1 Kgs	11:30	his new cloak, tore it into t pieces,
1 Kgs	18:31	He took t stones, for the number
Mt	10: 1	he summoned his t disciples
Lk	9:17	up, they filled t wicker baskets.
Jas	1: 1	to the t tribes in the dispersion,
Rev	12: 1	and on her head a crown of t stars.
Rev	21:12	with t gates where t angels were
Rev	21:12	[the names] of the t tribes
Rev	21:14	the city had t courses of stones as its
Rev	21:14	were inscribed the t names of the t apostles
Rev	21:21	The t gates were t pearls,
Rev	22: 2	that produces fruit t times a year,

TWENTY

Nm	1: 3	all the men in Israel of t years

TWICE → TWO

Ex	16: 5	let it be t as much as they gather
Nm	20:11	Moses struck the rock t with his
1 Sm	18:11	But t David escaped him.
1 Kgs	11: 9	of Israel, who had appeared to him t
Jb	42:10	to Job t as much as he had before.
Mk	14:30	the cock crows t you will deny me

TWILIGHT

Ex	12: 6	be slaughtered during the evening t.
Ex	16:12	In the evening t you will eat meat,

TWINS

Gn	25:24	came, there were t in her womb.

TWO → SECOND, TWICE, TWO-EDGED, TWOFOLD

Gn	1:16	God made the t great lights,
Gn	4:19	Lamech took t wives; the name
Gn	6:19	all living creatures you shall bring t
Ex	31:18	he gave him the t tablets
Ex	34: 1	"Cut t stone tablets like the former,
Dt	4:13	which he wrote on t stone tablets.
Dt	17: 6	Only on the testimony of t or three
Dt	25:13	shall not keep t differing weights
1 Kgs	3:16	t prostitutes came to the king
Prv	30: 7	T things I ask of you, do not deny
Prv	30:15	The leech has t daughters:
Eccl	4: 9	T are better than one: They get
Is	6: 2	with t they covered their faces, with t they covered their feet, and with t they hovered.
Ez	1:11	one, t wings touched one another,
Ez	1:11	the other t wings covered the body.
Dn	8: 3	the river a ram with t great horns,
Zec	4:11	"What are these t olive trees,
Zec	14: 4	of Olives will be split in t from east
Mt	6:24	"No one can serve t masters.
Mt	18:16	take one or t others along with you,
Mt	18:16	be established on the testimony of t
Mt	19: 5	and the t shall become one flesh'?
Mk	6: 7	began to send them out t by t
Mk	12:42	in t small coins worth a few cents.
Mk	15:27	him they crucified t revolutionaries,
Lk	9:30	t men were conversing with him,
Lk	17:35	there will be t women grinding meal
Lk	18:10	"T people went up to the temple
1 Cor	6:16	For "the t," it says, "will become
Gal	4:24	These women represent t covenants.
Eph	5:31	and the t shall become one flesh."
Rev	11: 3	I will commission my t witnesses
Rev	19:20	The t were thrown alive

TWO-EDGED → EDGE, TWO

Sir	21: 3	All lawlessness is like a t sword;
Heb	4:12	effective, sharper than any t sword,
Rev	1:16	A sharp t sword came out of his
Rev	2:12	one with the sharp t sword says this:

TWOFOLD → TWO

Is	61: 7	Because their shame was t and disgrace
Is	61: 7	They will possess t in their own land;

TYCHICUS

Companion of Paul (Acts 20:4; Eph 6:21; Col 4:7; 2 Tm 4:12; Ti 3:12).

TYPE

Rom	5:14	who is the t of the one who was

TYRANNUS

Acts	19: 9	discussions in the lecture hall of T.

TYRE

1 Kgs	5:15	king of T, heard that Solomon had
Ps	45:13	honor him, daughter of T.
Is	23: 1	Oracle on T: Wail,
Ez	27: 2	son of man, raise a lament over T,
Ez	28:12	raise a lament over the king of T,
Mt	11:22	it will be more tolerable for T

U

UNAPPROACHABLE

1 Tm	6:16	who dwells in u light, and whom no

UNBELIEF → UNBELIEVER, UNBELIEVERS, UNBELIEVING

Mk	9:24	out, "I do believe, help my u!"
Rom	11:20	They were broken off because of u,
Rom	11:23	if they do not remain in u, will be
1 Tm	1:13	I acted out of ignorance in my u.

UNBELIEVER → UNBELIEF

1 Cor	7:12	any brother has a wife who is an u,
1 Cor	7:13	woman has a husband who is an u,
1 Cor	10:27	If an u invites you and you want
1 Cor	14:24	an u or uninstructed person should
2 Cor	6:15	a believer in common with an u?
1 Tm	5: 8	the faith and is worse than an u.

UNBELIEVERS → UNBELIEF

1 Cor	6: 6	against brother, and that before u?
1 Cor	14:22	not for those who believe but for u, whereas prophecy is not for u
1 Cor	14:23	people or u should come in,
2 Cor	4: 4	age has blinded the minds of the u,
2 Cor	6:14	with those who are different, with u.

UNBELIEVING → UNBELIEF

1 Cor	7:14	the u husband is made holy through
1 Cor	7:14	the u wife is made holy through
Ti	1:15	are defiled and u nothing is clean;

UNCIRCUMCISED → UNCIRCUMCISION

Ex	12:48	But no one who is u may eat of it.
1 Sm	17:26	Who is this u Philistine that he
1 Mc	1:48	to leave their sons u, and to defile
Jer	9:25	For all the nations are u,
Jer	9:25	whole house of Israel is u at heart.
Acts	7:51	people, u in heart and ears,
Rom	3:30	of faith and the u through faith.
Rom	4:11	through faith while he was u.
Rom	4:11	the father of all the u who believe,
1 Cor	7:18	Was an u person called?
Gal	2: 7	entrusted with the gospel to the u,

UNCIRCUMCISION → UNCIRCUMCISED

Rom	2:25	your circumcision has become u.
1 Cor	7:19	nothing, and u means nothing;
Gal	5: 6	neither circumcision nor u counts
Gal	6:15	nor does u, but only a new creation.
Col	2:13	and the u of your flesh, he brought
Col	3:11	Jew, circumcision and u, barbarian,

UNCLEAN → UNCLEANNESS

Lv	5: 2	touches any u thing, such as
1 Mc	1:47	to sacrifice swine and u animals,
Is	6: 5	For I am a man of u lips,
Is	6: 5	living among a people of u lips,
Is	52:11	go out from there, touch nothing u!
Mk	3:11	whenever u spirits saw him they
Mk	6: 7	gave them authority over u spirits.
Acts	10:14	I eaten anything profane and u."
Rom	14:14	Lord Jesus that nothing is u in itself;
Rom	14:14	it is u for someone who thinks it u.
2 Cor	6:17	the Lord, "and touch nothing u;

Rev   21:27 but nothing **u** will enter it,

UNCLEANNESS → UNCLEAN
Lv   5: 3 it, touches some human **u**,
Lv   5: 3 whatever kind of **u** this may be,

UNCLOTHED
2 Cor   5: 4 because we do not wish to be **u**

UNCOVER → UNCOVERED
Ru   3: 4 then go **u** a place at his feet and you

UNCOVERED → UNCOVER
Ru   3: 7 She crept up, **u** a place at his feet,

UNDER
Gn   24: 2 "Put your hand **u** my thigh,
Gn   47:29 put your hand **u** my thigh as a sign
1 Kgs   5: 5 everyone **u** their own vine and fig
Jer   3:13 there to strangers **u** every green tree
Mi   4: 4 They shall all sit **u** their own vines, **u** their own fig trees,
Mt   5:15 and then put it **u** a bushel basket;
Mt   22:44 your enemies **u** your feet" '?
Lk   13:34 a hen gathers her brood **u** her wings,
Acts   4:12 any other name **u** heaven given
Rom   6:14 since you are not **u** the law but **u** grace?
1 Cor 15:27 subjected everything **u** his feet."
Gal   3:10 on works of the law are **u** a curse;
Gal   4: 4 born of a woman, born **u** the law,

UNDERSTAND → UNDERSTANDING, UNDERSTANDS,
                UNDERSTOOD
Gn   11: 7 no one will **u** the speech of another.
Jb   42: 3 I have spoken but did not **u**;
Ps   73:16 Though I tried to **u** all this, it was
Ps   119:27 Make me **u** the way of your
Prv   2: 5 will you **u** the fear of the LORD;
Prv   2: 9 Then you will **u** what is right
Prv   30:18 for me, yes, four I cannot **u**:
Is   44:18 They do not know, do not **u**;
Jer   17: 9 heart, beyond remedy; who can **u** it?
Dn   9:25 Know and **u**: From the utterance
Hos   14:10 is wise enough to **u** these things?
Mt   13:15 with their ears and **u** with their heart
Mt   24:15 in the holy place (let the reader **u**),
Mk   4:13 them, "Do you not **u** this parable?
Mk   4:13 how will you **u** any of the parables?
Lk   24:45 their minds to **u** the scriptures.
Jn   13: 7 you do not **u** now, but you will **u** later."
Acts   8:30 "Do you **u** what you are reading?"
Rom   7:15 What I do, I do not **u**. For I do not
Rom   15:21 have never heard of him shall **u**."
1 Cor   2:12 we may **u** the things freely given us
1 Cor   2:14 and he cannot **u** it, because it is
Eph   5:17 try to **u** what is the will of the Lord.
Heb   11: 3 By faith we **u** that the universe was
2 Pt   3:16 them there are some things hard to **u**

UNDERSTANDING → UNDERSTAND
Ex   36: 1 **u** in knowing how to do all the work
Dt   32:28 devoid of reason, having no **u**.
1 Kgs   5: 9 exceptional **u**, and knowledge,
Jb   12:12 wisdom, and with length of days **u**.
Jb   28:12 Where is the place of **u**?
Jb   28:28 and avoiding evil is **u**.
Jb   32: 8 of the Almighty, that gives them **u**.
Ps   119:130 sheds light, gives **u** to the simple.
Prv   2: 2 wisdom, inclining your heart to **u**;
Prv   2: 6 his mouth come knowledge and **u**;
Prv   3:13 finds wisdom, the one who gains **u**!
Prv   15:21 person of **u** goes the straight way.
Prv   15:32 those who heed reproof acquire **u**.
Prv   16:16 To get **u** is preferable to silver.
Prv   18: 2 Fools take no delight in **u**, but only
Prv   19: 8 those who preserve **u** will find
Prv   23:23 do not sell: wisdom, instruction, **u**!
Is   11: 2 a spirit of wisdom and of **u**, A spirit
Is   40:14 or showed him the way of **u**?
Dn   10:12 you made up your mind to acquire **u**
Hos   4:11 wine and new wine take away **u**.

Mk   12:33 heart, with all your **u**, with all your
Lk   2:47 heard him were astounded at his **u**
Phil   4: 7 that surpasses all **u** will guard your
Col   1: 9 through all spiritual wisdom and **u**
Col   2: 2 all the richness of fully assured **u**,
2 Tm   2: 7 for the Lord will give you **u**
Jas   3:13 Who among you is wise and **u**?

UNDERSTANDS → UNDERSTAND
1 Chr 28: 9 hearts and **u** all the mind's thoughts.
Mt   13:23 the one who hears the word and **u** it,

UNDERSTOOD → UNDERSTAND
Neh   8:12 for they **u** the words that had been
Is   40:21 Have you not **u** from the founding
Rom   1:20 divinity have been able to be **u**

UNDERTAKEN
Lk   1: 1 Since many have **u** to compile
1 Mc   4:51 finished all the work they had **u**.

UNFAIR
Ez   18:25 Is it my way that is **u**? Are not your ways **u**?

UNFAITHFUL
Nm   5:12 goes astray and becomes **u** to him
Rom   3: 3 What if some were **u**?

UNGODLINESS → UNGODLY
Jer   23:15 Jerusalem's prophets **u** has gone

UNGODLY → UNGODLINESS
Rom   5: 6 died at the appointed time for the **u**.

UNGRATEFUL
Lk   6:35 for he himself is kind to the **u**
2 Tm   3: 2 disobedient to their parents, **u**,

UNHOLY
1 Tm   1: 9 and sinful, the **u** and profane,

UNITED → UNITY
Rom   6: 5 be **u** with him in the resurrection.
1 Cor   1:10 that you be **u** in the same mind

UNITY → UNITED
Eph   4: 3 preserve the **u** of the spirit through
Eph   4:13 until we all attain to the **u** of faith

UNJUST
Rom   3: 5 Is God **u**, humanly speaking,
Heb   6:10 God is not **u** so as to overlook your

UNKNOWN
Acts   17:23 an altar inscribed, 'To an **U** God.'

UNLEAVENED
Ex   12:17 the custom of the **u** bread, since it
Dt   16:16 at the feast of **U** Bread, at the feast
Mt   26:17 first day of the Feast of **U** Bread,

UNLESS
Ps   127: 1 **U** the LORD build the house,
Ps   127: 1 **U** the LORD guard the city,
Jn   4:48 him, "**U** you people see signs
Jn   12:24 you, **u** a grain of wheat falls
Acts   8:31 can I, **u** someone instructs me?"

UNMARRIED
1 Cor   7: 8 Now to the **u** and to widows, I say:
1 Cor   7:32 An **u** man is anxious

UNNATURAL
Rom   1:26 exchanged natural relations for **u**,
Jude   1: 7 promiscuity and practiced **u** vice,

UNPRODUCTIVE
1 Cor 14:14 spirit is at prayer but my mind is **u**.
Ti   3:14 needs, so that they may not be **u**.

UNPUNISHED
Prv   6:29 none who touches her shall go **u**.
Prv   11:21 the wicked shall not go **u**,
Prv   19: 5 The false witness will not go **u**,
Prv   28:20 hastens to be rich will not go **u**.

UNQUENCHABLE
Lk   3:17 the chaff he will burn with **u** fire."

UNRIGHTEOUS
1 Pt   3:18 the righteous for the sake of the **u**,
2 Pt   2: 9 to keep the **u** under punishment

UNSEARCHABLE
Rom 11:33 his judgments and how **u** his ways!

UNSHRUNKEN
Mt   9:16 an old cloak with a piece of **u** cloth,

UNSPIRITUAL
Jas   3:15 down from above but is earthly, **u**,

UNSTABLE
2 Pt   3:16 **u** distort to their own destruction,

UNTIE
Lk   13:15 one of you on the sabbath **u** his ox
Lk   19:30 has ever sat. **U** it and bring it here.

UNVEILED
1 Cor 11: 5 with her head **u** brings shame
2 Cor   3:18 gazing with **u** face on the glory

UNWASHED
Mt 15:20 to eat with **u** hands does not defile."
Mk   7: 2 with unclean, that is, **u**, hands.

UNWILLING
2 Thes 3:10 you that if anyone was **u** to work,

UNWORTHILY
1 Cor 11:27 the cup of the Lord **u** will have

UPHELD → UPHOLD
Rom 14: 4 And he will be **u**, for the Lord is

UPHOLD → UPHELD, UPHOLDS
Ps 51:14 your salvation; **u** me with a willing spirit.
Is   41:10 I will **u** you with my victorious right
Is   42: 1 Here is my servant whom I **u**,

UPHOLDS → UPHOLD
Ps 63: 9 fast to you; your right hand **u** me.

UPRIGHT → UPRIGHTLY
Gn 37: 7 my sheaf rose to an **u** position,
Dt 32: 4 without deceit, just and **u** is he!
Jb   1: 1 a blameless and **u** man named Job,
Jb   1: 8 blameless and **u**, fearing God
Jb   2: 3 blameless and **u**, fearing God
Ps 11: 7 the **u** will see his face.
Ps 25: 8 Good and **u** is the LORD,
Ps 33: 1 praise from the **u** is fitting.
Ps 64:11 in the LORD; all the **u** give praise.
Ps 112: 4 through the darkness for the **u**;
Prv 2: 7 He has success in store for the **u**,
Prv 2:21 For the **u** will dwell in the land,
Prv 3:32 but the **u** are close to him.
Prv 11: 3 The honesty of the **u** guides them;
Prv 15: 8 but the prayer of the **u** is his delight.
Prv 21:29 the **u** maintains a straight course.

UPRIGHTLY → UPRIGHT
Prv 14: 2 Those who walk **u** fear the LORD,

UPROOTED
Lk 17: 6 tree, 'Be **u** and planted in the sea,'
Jude 1:12 in late autumn, twice dead and **u**.

UR
Gn 15: 7 LORD who brought you from **U**
Neh 9: 7 Who brought him from **U**

URGED
Gn 19:15 was breaking, the angels **u** Lot on,
Ex 12:33 from the land, **u** the people on,

URIAH
Hittite husband of Bathsheba, killed at David's order (2 Sm 11).

URIM
Ex 28:30 of decision you shall put the **U**
1 Sm 28: 6 nor by **U** nor through prophets.
Ezr 2:63 should be a priest to consult the **U**

USE → USED, USEFUL, USELESS, USES
Sir 14: 3 to misers, what **u** is gold?

Gal 5:13 But do not **u** this freedom as
2 Tm 2:20 for lofty and others for humble **u**.

USED → USE
Jn 10: 6 Although Jesus **u** this figure
1 Cor 6:11 That is what some of you **u** to be;

USEFUL → USE
2 Tm 3:16 by God and is **u** for teaching,
Phlm 1:11 to you but is now **u** to [both] you
Heb 6: 7 and brings forth crops **u** to those

USELESS → USE
Phlm 1:11 who was once **u** to you but is now

USES → USE
1 Tm 1: 8 good, provided that one **u** it as law,

UTTER → UTTERANCE, UTTERING, UTTERS
Mt 5:11 and **u** every kind of evil against you
Rev 13: 6 to **u** blasphemies against God,

UTTERANCE → UTTER
Prv 6: 2 been snared by the **u** of your lips,

UTTERING → UTTER
Rev 13: 5 was given a mouth **u** proud boasts

UTTERS → UTTER
Lv 5: 4 rashly **u** an oath with bad or good

UZ
Jb 1: 1 the land of **U** there was a blameless

UZZAH
2 Sm 6: 6 **U** stretched out his hand to the ark
1 Chr 13: 9 **U** stretched out his hand to steady

UZZIAH → =AZARIAH
Son of Amaziah; king of Judah also known as Azariah (2 Kgs 15:1-7; 2 Chr 26). Struck with leprosy because of pride (2 Chr 26:16-23).

V

VAIN → VANITIES, VANITY
Lv 26:16 You will sow your seed in **v**,
Ps 2: 1 and the peoples conspire in **v**?
Ps 73:13 Is it in **v** that I have kept my heart
Ps 127: 1 the house, they labor in **v** who build.
Ps 127: 1 city, in **v** does the guard keep watch.
Is 65:23 They shall not toil in **v**, nor beget
Ez 6:10 I the LORD did not threaten in **v**
Mt 15: 9 in **v** do they worship me, teaching as
1 Cor 15: 2 to you, unless you believed in **v**.
1 Cor 15:58 in the Lord your labor is not in **v**.
2 Cor 6: 1 not to receive the grace of God in **v**.
Gal 2: 2 not be running, or have run, in **v**.
Phil 2:16 Christ may be that I did not run in **v** or labor in **v**.

VALLEY → VALLEYS
Jos 7:26 is why the place is called the **V**
Jos 10:12 Gibeon, Moon, in the **v** of Aijalon!
1 Sm 17: 3 hill, with a **v** between them.
2 Kgs 23:10 Topheth in the **V** of Ben-hinnom,
2 Chr 33: 6 by fire in the **V** of Ben-hinnom.
Ps 23: 4 Even though I walk through the **v**
Is 22: 1 Oracle on the **V** of Vision:
Is 40: 4 Every **v** shall be lifted up,
Is 40: 4 plain, the rough country, a broad **v**.
Hos 2:17 the **v** of Achor as a door of hope.
Jl 4:14 of the LORD in the **V** of Decision.
Lk 3: 5 Every **v** shall be filled and every

VALLEYS → VALLEY
Dt 8: 7 welling up in the hills and **v**,
Sg 2: 1 a flower of Sharon, a lily of the **v**.

VALUE
Rom 3: 1 Or what is the **v** of circumcision?
1 Tm 4: 8 physical training is of limited **v**,

VANISH → VANISHED
Is 2:18 The idols will **v** completely.

VANISHED → VANISH
Lk 24:31 him, but he **v** from their sight.

VANITIES → VAIN
Eccl   1: 2   Vanity of v, says Qoheleth, vanity of v!
Eccl   12: 8   Vanity of v, says Qoheleth,

VANITY → VAIN
Eccl   1: 2   V of vanities, says Qoheleth, v of vanities! All things
                   are v!
Eccl   12: 8   V of vanities, says Qoheleth, all things are v!

VARIOUS
Mk   1:34   who were sick with v diseases,
Heb   1: 1   v ways to our ancestors through
1 Pt   1: 6   may have to suffer through v trials,

VASHTI
        Queen of Persia replaced by Esther (Est 1–2).

VAST
Ps   139:17   how v the sum of them!

VATS
Prv   3:10   with new wine your v will overflow.
Jl   2:24   the v spilling over with new wine

VEGETABLES
Dn   1:12   Let us be given v to eat and water
Rom   14: 2   while the weak person eats only v.

VEGETATION
Gn   1:11   Let the earth bring forth v:

VEIL → VEILED
Ex   26:31   You shall make a v woven of violet,
Ex   34:33   with them, he put a v over his face.
Lv   4:17   before the LORD, toward the v.
2 Chr   3:14   He made the v of violet, purple,
Is   40:22   stretches out the heavens like a v
Mt   27:51   the v of the sanctuary was torn
Mk   15:38   The v of the sanctuary was torn
Lk   23:45   the v of the temple was torn down
2 Cor   3:13   who put a v over his face so
2 Cor   3:15   is read, a v lies over their hearts,
Heb   6:19   into the interior behind the v,
Heb   9: 3   Behind the second v was
Heb   10:20   way he opened for us through the v,

VEILED → VEIL
2 Cor   4: 3   And even though our gospel is v, it is v for those who
                   are perishing,

VENGEANCE → AVENGE, AVENGED, AVENGER, AVENGING
Nm   31: 3   execute the LORD's v on Midian.
Sir   28: 1   The vengeful will face the Lord's v;
Is   34: 8   For the LORD has a day of v,
Na   1: 2   The LORD takes v on his

VENOM
Dt   32:33   Their wine is the v of serpents,

VENT
Prv   29:11   Fools give v to all their anger;

VERDICT
Lk   23:24   The v of Pilate was that their

VERY
Gn   1:31   he had made, and found it v good.
Gn   15: 1   I will make your reward v great.
Dt   30:14   No, it is something v near to you,
Mt   4: 8   took him up to a v high mountain,

VICTORIES → VICTORY
Ps   44: 5   my God, who bestows v on Jacob.

VICTORY → VICTORIES
1 Sm   2: 1   up my enemies; I rejoice in your v.
2 Sm   8: 6   The LORD brought David v in all
Prv   21:31   day of battle, but v is the LORD's.
Prv   24: 6   and v depends on many counselors.
Is   59:17   breastplate, v as a helmet on his head;
1 Cor 15:54   "Death is swallowed up in v.
1 Cor 15:57   who gives us the v through our Lord
1 Jn   5: 4   the v that conquers the world is our

VIEW
Dt   32:49   and v the land of Canaan, which I

VILLAGE
Mt   10:11   Whatever town or v you enter,

VINDICATED → VINDICATION
Mt   11:19   But wisdom is v by her works."
1 Tm   3:16   in the flesh, v in the spirit,

VINDICATION → VINDICATED
Is   54:17   of the LORD, their v from me—

VINE → GRAPEVINE, VINES, VINEYARD, VINEYARDS
Ps   80: 9   You brought a v out of Egypt;
Ps   128: 3   like a fruitful v within your home,
Is   36:16   from your v, each from your own
Jer   2:21   But I had planted you as a choice v,
Jer   2:21   so obnoxious to me, a spurious v?
Ez   17: 6   it might sprout and become a v,
Hos   10: 1   is a luxuriant v whose fruit matches
Hb   3:17   not blossom, and no fruit appears on the v,
Mk   14:25   again the fruit of the v until the day
Jn   15: 1   "I am the true v, and my Father is the v grower.

VINEGAR
Nm   6: 3   they may neither drink wine v,
Nm   6: 3   other v, or any kind of grape juice,
Ps   69:22   and for my thirst they gave me v.
Prv   10:26   As v to the teeth, and smoke

VINES → VINE
Mi   4: 4   They shall all sit under their own v,
Rev   14:18   cut the clusters from the earth's v,

VINEYARD → VINE
Gn   9:20   of the soil, was the first to plant a v.
Dt   22: 9   You shall not sow your v with two
1 Kgs 21: 1   Naboth the Jezreelite had a v
Prv   31:16   from her earnings she plants a v.
Sg   1: 6   my own v I did not take care of.
Is   5: 1   my beloved's song about his v. My friend had a v on a
                   fertile
Is   27: 2   The pleasant v, sing about it!
Mt   21:33   was a landowner who planted a v,
1 Cor   9: 7   Who plants a v without eating its

VINEYARDS → VINE
Nm   22:24   in a narrow lane between v
Dt   6:11   with v and olive groves that you did
Sg   2:15   the little foxes that damage the v; for our v are in bloom!

VIOLENCE → VIOLENT, VIOLENTLY
Ps   7:17   his v falls on his own skull.
Ps   73: 6   v clothes them as a robe.
Is   60:18   No longer shall v be heard
Ez   45: 9   Put away v and oppression, and do
Jl   4:19   Because of v done to the Judahites,
Jon   3: 8   way and from the v of their hands.
Hb   2:17   For the v done to Lebanon shall
Hb   2:17   and v done to the land, to the city
Zep   3: 4   what is holy, and do v to the law.

VIOLENT → VIOLENCE
Mt   11:12   and the v are taking it by force.

VIOLENTLY → VIOLENCE
Ex   19:18   and the whole mountain trembled v.

VIOLET
Ex   25: 4   v, purple, and scarlet yarn;
Ex   26:31   You shall make a veil woven of v,
Ex   28:31   shall make entirely of v material.
2 Chr   3:14   He made the veil of v, purple,

VIPER → VIPERS
Acts   28: 3   was putting it on the fire when a v,

VIPERS → VIPER
Mt   12:34   You brood of v, how can you say
Mt   23:33   you brood of v, how can you flee
Lk   3: 7   baptized by him, "You brood of v!

VIRGIN → VIRGINS
1 Kgs   1: 2   "Let a young v be sought to attend
Sir   9: 5   not entertain any thoughts about a v,
Jer   31:21   Turn back, v Israel, turn back

Lam	2:13	to comfort you, **v** daughter Zion?
Mt	1:23	the **v** shall be with child and bear
1 Cor	7:36	behaving improperly toward his **v**,
2 Cor	11: 2	present you as a chaste **v** to Christ.

VIRGINS → VIRGIN

Est	2: 2	"Let beautiful young **v** be sought
1 Cor	7:25	Now in regard to **v**, I have no

VISIBLE

Eph	5:13	exposed by the light becomes **v**,
Col	1:16	and on earth, the **v** and the invisible,
Heb	11: 3	what is **v** came into being through

VISION → VISIONS

Gn	15: 1	the Lord came to Abram in a **v**:
1 Sm	3:15	He was afraid to tell Eli the **v**,
Ps	89:20	Then you spoke in **v**;
Prv	29:18	Without a **v** the people lose restraint;
Is	22: 1	Oracle on the Valley of **V**:
Dn	7: 2	In the **v** I saw during the night,
Dn	8: 1	After this first **v**, I, Daniel,
Dn	8:26	As for the **v** of the evenings
Dn	8:26	But you, keep this **v** secret: it is
Dn	9:24	introduced, **v** and prophecy ratified,
Dn	10: 7	I alone, Daniel, saw the **v**;
Dn	10: 7	although they did not see the **v**.
Lk	1:22	he had seen a **v** in the sanctuary.
Acts	9:10	and the Lord said to him in a **v**,
Acts	10:17	the meaning of the **v** he had seen,
Acts	16: 9	During [the] night Paul had a **v**.
Acts	26:19	not disobedient to the heavenly **v**.
Rev	9:17	in my **v** this is how I saw the horses

VISIONS → VISION

Nm	12: 6	you, in **v** I reveal myself to them,
Is	30:10	smooth things to us, see **v** that deceive!
Jer	23:16	They speak **v** from their own fancy,
Lam	2:14	Your prophets provided you **v**
Ez	1: 1	opened, and I saw divine **v**.—
Dn	1:17	to Daniel the understanding of all **v**
Jl	3: 1	dreams, your young men will see **v**.
Acts	2:17	your young men shall see **v**,

VOICE → VOICES

Dt	4:33	Did a people ever hear the **v** of God
Jb	40: 9	or can you thunder with a **v** like his?
Ps	29: 3	The **v** of the Lord is over
Ps	95: 7	Oh, that today you would hear his **v**:
Prv	1:20	in the open squares she raises her **v**;
Prv	8: 1	call, and Understanding raise her **v**?
Is	40: 3	A **v** proclaims: In the wilderness
Dn	9:14	we did not listen to his **v**.
Mt	2:18	"A **v** was heard in Ramah,
Mt	3:17	And a **v** came from the heavens,
Mk	1: 3	A **v** of one crying out in the desert:
Jn	1:23	"I am 'the **v** of one crying
Jn	5:25	the dead will hear the **v** of the Son
Jn	10: 3	and the sheep hear his **v**, as he calls
Jn	12:28	Then a **v** came from heaven,
Rom	10:18	for "Their **v** has gone forth to all
Heb	3: 7	that today you would hear his **v**,
Rev	3:20	If anyone hears my **v** and opens

VOICES → VOICE

Rev	11:15	There were loud **v** in heaven,

VOID

Rom	4:14	faith is null and the promise is **v**.

VOMIT

Lv	18:28	otherwise the land will **v** you
Prv	26:11	As dogs return to their **v**, so fools
Is	28: 8	all the tables are covered with **v**,
2 Pt	2:22	"The dog returns to its own **v**,"

VOTIVE

Lv	7:16	if the sacrifice offered is a **v**
Dt	12: 6	your **v** and voluntary offerings,
1 Kgs	7:51	the **v** offerings of his father David,

VOW → VOWED, VOWS

Gn	28:20	Jacob then made this **v**:
Nm	6: 2	women solemnly take the nazirite **v**
Nm	21: 2	then made this **v** to the Lord:
Nm	30: 3	a man makes a **v** to the Lord
Dt	23:22	When you make a **v** to the Lord,
Jgs	11:30	Jephthah made a **v** to the Lord.
1 Sm	1:11	and made this **v**: "O Lord
Eccl	5: 3	When you make a **v** to God,
Sir	18:23	Before making a **v** prepare yourself;
Acts	18:18	hair cut because he had taken a **v**.

VOWED → VOW

Jon	2:10	What I have **v** I will pay:

VOWS → VOW

Ps	22:26	my **v** I will fulfill before those who
Ps	50:14	fulfill your **v** to the Most High.
Ps	116:14	I will pay my **v** to the Lord
Jon	1:16	sacrifice to the Lord and made **v**.

VULTURE → VULTURES

Dt	14:12	any of the following: the griffon **v**,

VULTURES → VULTURE

Mt	24:28	the corpse is, there the **v** will gather.

W

WADI

Nm	34: 5	turn from Azmon to the **W** of Egypt
2 Kgs	24: 7	of Egypt from the **w** of Egypt

WAFERS

Ex	16:31	it tasted like **w** made with honey.

WAGE → WAGES

Rom	4: 4	A worker's **w** is credited not as

WAGES → WAGE

Mi	1: 7	all its **w** shall be burned in the fire,
Mi	1: 7	As the **w** of a prostitute it gathered
Mal	3: 5	those who deprive a laborer of **w**,
Jn	6: 7	"Two hundred days' **w** worth
Rom	6:23	For the **w** of sin is death, but the gift

WAIL → WAILING

Jl	1: 8	**W** like a young woman dressed in sackcloth
Mi	1: 8	For this I will lament and **w**,

WAILING → WAIL

Mt	8:12	where there will be **w** and grinding
Mt	13:42	where there will be **w** and grinding
Mt	22:13	where there will be **w** and grinding
Mt	24:51	where there will be **w** and grinding
Mt	25:30	where there will be **w** and grinding

WAIST

Is	11: 5	shall be the band around his **w**,
Mt	3: 4	and had a leather belt around his **w**.

WAIT → WAITED

Ps	27:14	**W** for the Lord, take courage;
Ps	27:14	be stouthearted, **w** for the Lord!
Ps	37:34	**W** eagerly for the Lord, and keep
Ps	40: 2	Surely, I **w** for the Lord; who bends
Ps	130: 5	I **w** for the Lord, my soul waits
Prv	1:18	They lie in **w** for their own blood,
Sir	2: 7	that fear the Lord, **w** for his mercy,
Is	30:18	happy are all who **w** for him!
Hb	2: 3	If it delays, **w** for it, it will surely
Acts	1: 4	to **w** for "the promise of the Father
Rom	8:23	groan within ourselves as we **w**

WAITED → WAIT

Mt	8:15	and she rose and **w** on him.
1 Pt	3:20	while God patiently **w** in the days

WALK → WALKED, WALKING, WALKS

Gn	17: 1	**W** in my presence and be blameless.
Dt	26:17	and you will **w** in his ways,
Dt	28: 9	your God, and **w** in his ways.
Ps	23: 4	Even though I **w** through the valley
Ps	84:12	from those who **w** without reproach.

Ps	89:16	who w in the radiance of your face,
Ps	115: 7	but do not feel, feet but do not w;
Ps	119:45	I will w freely in an open space
Prv	4:12	When you w, your step will not be
Prv	13:20	W with the wise and you become
Is	2: 3	ways, and we may w in his paths."
Is	2: 5	let us w in the light of the LORD!
Is	30:21	w in it," when you would turn
Is	40:31	grow weary, w and not grow faint.
Is	43: 2	When you w through fire, you shall
Jer	6:16	and w it; thus you will find rest
Jer	6:16	But they said, "We will not w it."
Ez	36:27	within you so that you w in my statutes,
Mi	4: 5	We will w in the name of the LORD,
Mi	6: 8	and to w humbly with your God.
Zec	10:12	in whose name they will w—
Mk	2: 9	'Rise, pick up your mat and w'?
Jn	8:12	Whoever follows me will not w
2 Cor	5: 7	for we w by faith, not by sight.
1 Jn	1: 7	if we w in the light as he is
2 Jn	1: 6	is love, that we w according to his
2 Jn	1: 6	beginning, in which you should w.
3 Jn	1: 3	to how truly you w in the truth.
Rev	9:20	which cannot see or hear or w.
Rev	21:24	The nations will w by its light,

WALKED → WALK

Gn	5:24	Enoch w with God, and he was no
Acts	3: 8	and w around, and went

WALKING → WALK

Dt	8: 6	by w in his ways and fearing him.
Dn	3:92	unbound and unhurt, w in the fire,
Mt	14:26	the disciples saw him w on the sea
Acts	3: 8	w and jumping and praising God.
2 Jn	1: 4	your children w in the truth just as
3 Jn	1: 4	that my children are w in the truth.

WALKS → WALK

Ps	15: 2	Whoever w without blame,
Prv	10: 9	Whoever w honestly w securely,

WALL → WALLS

Ex	14:22	with the water as a w to their right
Jos	2:15	lived in a house built into the city w.
Jos	6:20	The w collapsed, and the people
Neh	1: 3	The w of Jerusalem has been
Neh	2:17	let us rebuild the w of Jerusalem,
Neh	12:27	dedication of the w of Jerusalem,
Dn	5: 5	plaster of the w in the king's palace.
Zec	2: 9	I will be an encircling w of fire
Acts	9:25	down through an opening in the w,
2 Cor	11:33	a basket through a window in the w
Eph	2:14	and broke down the dividing w
Rev	21:12	high w, with twelve gates where

WALLOWING

2 Pt	2:22	"A bathed sow returns to w

WALLS → WALL

2 Kgs	25: 4	the city w were breached.
Neh	2:13	observing how the w of Jerusalem
Ps	51:20	build up the w of Jerusalem.
Is	26: 1	he sets up victory as our w
Is	60:18	You shall call your w "Salvation"
Jer	52:14	of the guard tore down all the w
Heb	11:30	By faith the w of Jericho fell

WANDER → WANDERED, WANDERER, WANDERING

Nm	32:13	he made them w in the wilderness

WANDERED → WANDER

Ez	34: 6	and w over all the mountains

WANDERER → WANDER

Gn	4:12	You shall become a constant w

WANDERING → WANDER

1 Chr	16:20	W from nation to nation, from one

WANT → WANTED, WANTING, WANTS

1 Sm	9:20	Whom should Israel w if not you and
Ps	40: 7	Sacrifice and offering you do not w;

Prv	28:19	in idle pursuits will have plenty of w.
Lk	18:41	"What do you w me to do
Lk	19:14	'We do not w this man to be our
Rom	7:15	For I do not do what I w, but I do
2 Cor	12:14	for I w not what is yours, but you.

WANTED → WANT

Mt	14: 5	Although he w to kill him, he feared

WANTING → WANT

Dn	5:27	weighed on the scales and found w;

WANTS → WANT

Mt	5:42	your back on one who w to borrow.
Mt	27:43	him deliver him now if he w him.

WAR → WARRIOR, WARRIORS, WARS

Ex	17:16	LORD has a w against Amalek
Ps	24: 8	strong and mighty, the LORD, mighty in w.
Ps	68:31	scatter the peoples that delight in w.
Ps	120: 7	I speak of peace, they are for w.
Ps	144: 1	hands for battle, my fingers for w;
Eccl	3: 8	a time of w, and a time of peace.
Is	2: 4	nor shall they train for w again.
Dn	7:21	horn made w against the holy ones
Dn	9:26	until the end of the w, which is
Rom	7:23	my members another principle at w
1 Pt	2:11	desires that wage w against the soul.
Rev	12: 7	Then w broke out in heaven;
Rev	19:11	and wages w in righteousness.

WARM → LUKEWARM, WARMED, WARMING, WARMS

Eccl	4:11	together, they keep each other w. How can one alone keep w?
Jas	2:16	in peace, keep w, and eat well,"

WARMED → WARM

Hg	1: 6	yourselves, but have not been w;

WARMING → WARM

Mk	14:67	Seeing Peter w himself, she looked

WARMS → WARM

Is	44:15	some of the wood he w himself,

WARN → FOREWARNED, WARNED, WARNING, WARNINGS, WARNS

Ex	19:21	w the people not to break through
Ez	3:18	you do not w them or speak
Ez	3:19	If, however, you w the wicked and they
Ez	3:21	other hand, you w the just to avoid sin,
Ez	33: 9	you w the wicked to turn from their
Lk	16:28	so that he may w them, lest they too
Rev	22:18	I w everyone who hears

WARNED → WARN

2 Kgs	17:13	The LORD w Israel and Judah
Mt	2:12	having been w in a dream not
Mt	2:22	because he had been w in a dream,
Mt	3: 7	Who w you to flee from the coming
Heb	11: 7	w about what was not yet seen,
Heb	12:25	they refused the one who w them

WARNING → WARN

1 Sm	8: 9	give them a solemn w and inform
Ez	33: 5	the trumpet blast but ignored the w;
Ez	33: 5	If they had heeded the w, they could
Acts	4:17	us give them a stern w never again

WARNS → WARN

Heb	12:25	from the one who w from heaven.

WARRIOR → WAR

Ex	15: 3	The LORD is a w, LORD is his
1 Mc	2:66	a mighty w from his youth, shall be

WARRIORS → WAR

2 Sm	23:22	he made a name among the Thirty w

WARS → WAR

Nm	21:14	"Book of the W of the LORD":
Ps	46:10	Who stops w to the ends
Mt	24: 6	You will hear of w and reports of w;

WASH → WASHED, WASHING

2 Kgs	5:10	and w seven times in the Jordan,
Ps	51: 9	w me, and I will be whiter than

Jn 9: 7 him, "Go w in the Pool of Siloam"
Jn 13: 5 began to w the disciples' feet
Rev 22:14 are they who w their robes so as

WASHED → WASH
Ps 73:13 pure, w my hands in innocence?
Jn 9:11 So I went there and w and was able
1 Cor 6:11 but now you have had yourselves w,
Heb 10:22 and our bodies w in pure water.
Rev 7:14 they have w their robes and made

WASHING → WASH
Lk 11:38 observe the prescribed w before

WASTE → WASTING
Lv 26:31 I will lay w your cities and desolate
1 Mc 2:12 We see our sanctuary laid w,
Is 6:11 people, and the land is a desolate w.
Jer 2:15 They have turned his land into a w;
Ez 4:17 every one will w away because

WASTING → WASTE
2 Cor 4:16 although our outer self is w away,

WATCH → WATCHER, WATCHES, WATCHING, WATCHTOWER
Gn 31:49 the LORD keep w between you
Ps 59:10 My strength, for you I w;
Prv 6:22 you lie down they will w over you,
Zec 12: 4 over the house of Judah I will keep w,
Lk 2: 8 keeping the night w over their flock.
Heb 13:17 for they keep w over you and will

WATCHER → WATCH
Jb 7:20 do I do to you, O w of mortals?

WATCHES → WATCH
Ps 63: 7 I remember you through the w

WATCHING → WATCH
Jer 1:12 for I am w over my word to carry it

WATCHTOWER → TOWER, WATCH
Is 5: 2 Within it he built a w, and hewed

WATER → WATERED, WATERLESS, WATERS
Ex 7:20 all the w in the Nile was changed
Ex 15:25 When he threw it into the w, the w became fresh.
Ex 17: 1 But there was no w for the people
Nm 5:19 be immune to this w of bitterness
Nm 20: 2 Since the community had no w,
Nm 21: 5 where there is no food or w?
2 Kgs 2: 8 rolled it up and struck the w:
2 Kgs 6: 5 the iron ax blade slipped into the w.
Ps 1: 3 a tree planted near streams of w,
Ps 22:15 Like w my life drains away;
Ps 107:35 changed the desert into pools of w,
Prv 5:15 Drink w from your own cistern,
Prv 5:15 running w from your own well.
Prv 9:17 Stolen w is sweet, and bread taken
Sir 15: 3 give him the w of understanding
Is 12: 3 With joy you will draw w
Is 30:20 in adversity and w in affliction.
Is 32: 2 They will be like streams of w
Is 49:10 guides them beside springs of w.
Jer 2:13 broken cisterns that cannot hold w.
Jer 31: 9 I will lead them to streams of w,
Ez 36:25 I will sprinkle clean w over you
Mt 14:29 to walk on the w toward Jesus.
Mk 1: 8 I have baptized you with w;
Mk 9:41 Anyone who gives you a cup of w
Lk 5: 4 "Put out into deep w and lower
Jn 2: 9 the headwaiter tasted the w that had
Jn 2: 9 who had drawn the w knew),
Jn 3: 5 of God without being born of w
Jn 4:10 he would have given you living w."
Jn 7:38 'Rivers of living w will flow
Jn 19:34 blood and w flowed out.
Eph 5:26 her by the bath of w with the word,
Heb 10:22 and our bodies washed in pure w.
Jas 3:11 opening both pure and brackish w?
1 Jn 5: 6 This is the one who came through w
1 Jn 5: 6 not by w alone, but by w and blood.

Rev 7:17 them to springs of life-giving w,
Rev 21: 6 gift from the spring of life-giving w.
Rev 22: 1 me the river of life-giving w,
Rev 22:17 it receive the gift of life-giving w.

WATERED → WATER
1 Cor 3: 6 Apollos w, but God caused

WATERLESS → WATER
2 Pt 2:17 These people are w springs
Jude 1:12 They are w clouds blown

WATERS → WATER
Gn 1: 2 mighty wind sweeping over the w—
Gn 7: 7 ark because of the w of the flood.
Jos 4: 7 'The w of the Jordan ceased to flow
Ps 18:17 drew me out of the deep w.
Ps 23: 2 me lie down; to still w he leads me;
Ps 106:32 the w of Meribah they angered God,
Eccl 11: 1 your bread upon the face of the w;
Sg 8: 7 Deep w cannot quench love,
Jer 17: 8 are like a tree planted beside the w
1 Cor 3: 7 nor the one who w is anything,

WAVE → WAVES
Jas 1: 6 for the one who doubts is like a w

WAVER
Jude 1:22 On those who w, have mercy;

WAVES → WAVE
Ps 89:10 you still its swelling w.
Jude 1:13 They are like wild w of the sea,

WAX
Ps 22:15 My heart has become like w,
Ps 97: 5 mountains melt like w before

WAY → HIGHWAY, WAYS
Gn 3:24 to guard the w to the tree of life.
Ex 13:21 of cloud to show them the w,
Dt 1:33 the cloud, to show you the w to go.
1 Sm 12:23 to teach you the good and right w.
2 Sm 22:31 God's w is unerring;
1 Kgs 8:36 (for you teach them the good w
2 Chr 6:27 (For you teach them the good w
Jb 23:10 Yet he knows my w; if he tested me,
Ps 1: 6 Because the LORD knows the w
Ps 1: 6 the w of the wicked leads to ruin.
Ps 18:31 God's w is unerring;
Ps 32: 8 show you the w you should walk,
Ps 37: 5 Commit your w to the LORD;
Ps 86:11 your w that I may walk in your
Prv 4:11 On the w of wisdom I direct you,
Prv 12:15 The w of fools is right in their own
Prv 14:12 Sometimes a w seems right,
Prv 16:17 attend to their w guard their lives.
Prv 22: 6 the young in the w they should go;
Prv 30:19 and the w of a man with a woman.
Is 30:21 "This is the w; walk in it,"
Is 35: 8 will be there, called the holy w;
Is 40: 3 the wilderness prepare the w
Is 48:17 leading you on the w you should go.
Is 53: 6 like sheep, all following our own w;
Is 55: 7 Let the wicked forsake their w,
Mal 3: 1 he will prepare the w before me;
Mt 3: 3 desert, 'Prepare the w of the Lord,
Lk 7:27 he will prepare your w before you.'
Jn 14: 6 "I am the w and the truth
Acts 1:11 in the same w as you have seen him
Acts 9: 2 or women who belonged to the W,
Acts 19: 9 disparaged the W before
Acts 22: 4 I persecuted this W to death,
Acts 24:14 that according to the W, which they
1 Cor 10:13 trial he will also provide a w out,
1 Cor 12:31 show you a still more excellent w.
Heb 9: 8 In this w the holy Spirit shows
Heb 9: 8 the w into the sanctuary had not yet
Heb 10:20 living w he opened for us through
2 Pt 2:21 have known the w of righteousness

WAYS → WAY

Ex	33:13	please let me know your **w** so that,
Dt	10:12	to follow in all his **w**, to love
Dt	26:17	and you will walk in his **w**,
Dt	30:16	and walking in his **w**, and keeping
Dt	32: 4	are his deeds, how right all his **w**!
2 Kgs	17:13	Give up your evil **w** and keep my
Jb	34:21	For his eyes are upon our **w**, and all
Ps	25: 4	Make known to me your **w**,
Ps	51:15	I will teach the wicked your **w**,
Ps	119:59	I have examined my **w** and turned
Ps	139: 3	with all my **w** you are familiar.
Ps	145:17	The LORD is just in all his **w**,
Prv	3: 6	In all your **w** be mindful of him,
Prv	3:17	Her **w** are pleasant **w**, and all her
Prv	4:26	feet, and all your **w** will be sure.
Prv	5:21	the **w** of each person are plain
Prv	6: 6	study her **w** and learn wisdom;
Prv	7:25	Do not let your heart turn to her **w**,
Prv	16: 2	All one's **w** are pure in one's own
Prv	16: 7	is pleased with someone's **w**,
Sir	2:15	those who love him keep his **w**.
Is	2: 3	That he may instruct us in his **w**,
Is	42:24	In his **w** they refused to walk,
Is	55: 8	thoughts, nor are your **w** my **w**—
Jer	18:11	reform your **w** and your deeds.
Ez	16:47	Not only did you walk in their **w**
Ez	16:47	corrupt in all your **w** than they were.
Ez	22:31	bringing down their **w** upon their heads—
Lk	3: 5	and the rough **w** made smooth,
Rev	15: 3	Just and true are your **w**, O king

WEAK → WEAKENED, WEAKER, WEAKLING, WEAKNESS, WEAKNESSES

Jdt	9:11	supporter of the **w**, protector of those
Ez	34: 4	did not strengthen the **w** nor heal
Mt	26:41	spirit is willing, but the flesh is **w**."
Acts	20:35	of that sort we must help the **w**,
Rom	14: 1	Welcome anyone who is **w** in faith,
Rom	15: 1	to put up with the failings of the **w**
1 Cor	1:27	and God chose the **w** of the world
1 Cor	8: 9	becomes a stumbling block to the **w**.
1 Cor	9:22	To the **w** I became **w**, to win over the **w**.
2 Cor	12:10	for when I am **w**, then I am strong.
Gal	4: 9	can you turn back again to the **w**
1 Thes	5:14	support the **w**, be patient with all.
Heb	12:12	drooping hands and your **w** knees.

WEAKENED → WEAK

Rom	8: 3	For what the law, **w** by the flesh,

WEAKER → WEAK

Jgs	16: 7	Samson answered her, "I shall grow **w**
2 Sm	3: 1	but the house of Saul ever **w**.
1 Cor	12:22	to be **w** are all the more necessary,
1 Pt	3: 7	showing honor to the **w** female sex,

WEAKLING → WEAK

Jl	4:10	let the **w** boast, "I am a warrior!"

WEAKNESS → WEAK

Rom	8:26	Spirit too comes to the aid of our **w**;
1 Cor	1:25	the **w** of God is stronger than human
1 Cor	2: 3	I came to you in **w** and fear
2 Cor	11:30	boast of the things that show my **w**.
2 Cor	12: 9	for power is made perfect in **w**."
2 Cor	13: 4	indeed he was crucified out of **w**,
Heb	5: 2	erring, for he himself is beset by **w**
Heb	7:28	the law appoints men subject to **w**
Heb	11:34	out of **w** they were made powerful,

WEAKNESSES → WEAK

2 Cor	12: 5	I will not boast, except about my **w**.
2 Cor	12: 9	rather boast most gladly of my **w**,
2 Cor	12:10	I am content with **w**, insults,
Heb	4:15	is unable to sympathize with our **w**,

WEALTH

Dt	8:18	who gives you the power to get **w**,
Ps	49: 7	Of those who trust in their **w**

Ps	49:11	and they leave their **w** to others.
Ps	112: 3	**W** and riches shall be in his house;
Prv	13: 7	another acts poor but has great **w**.
Prv	13:11	**W** won quickly dwindles away,
Prv	13:22	the **w** of the sinner is stored
Prv	19: 4	**W** adds many friends, but the poor
Eccl	5: 9	nor lovers of **w** with their gain;
Sir	5: 1	Do not rely on your **w**, or say,
Lk	16:11	not trustworthy with dishonest **w**, who will trust you with true **w**?

WEANED

1 Sm	1:22	"Once the child is **w**, I will take
Ps	131: 2	soul, Like a **w** child to its mother,

WEAPON → WEAPONS

Neh	4:11	hand and held a **w** with the other.
Is	54:17	Every **w** fashioned against you shall

WEAPONS → WEAPON

Jn	18: 3	there with lanterns, torches, and **w**.
2 Cor	6: 7	with **w** of righteousness at the right
2 Cor	10: 4	for the **w** of our battle are not

WEAR → WEARING

Dt	22: 5	A woman shall not **w** a man's
Ps	102:27	they all **w** out like a garment;
Is	51: 6	the earth **w** out like a garment
Mt	6:31	or 'What are we to **w**?'

WEARIED → WEARY

Is	43:24	your sins, **w** me with your crimes.
Mal	2:17	You have **w** the LORD with your
Mal	2:17	you say, "How have we **w** him?"

WEARING → WEAR

1 Sm	18: 4	took off the cloak he was **w**
Jn	19: 5	out, **w** the crown of thorns
Jas	2: 3	to the one **w** the fine clothes
1 Pt	3: 3	braiding the hair, **w** gold jewelry,

WEARY → WEARIED

Is	40:28	He does not faint or grow **w**, and his
Is	40:31	They will run and not grow **w**,
Is	50: 4	know how to answer the **w** a word
Heb	12: 3	in order that you may not grow **w**
Rev	2: 3	name, and you have not grown **w**.

WEDDING

Mt	22: 2	to a king who gave a **w** feast for his
Mt	22:11	there not dressed in a **w** garment.
Jn	2: 1	the third day there was a **w** in Cana

WEEDS

Mt	13:25	and sowed **w** all through the wheat,

WEEK → WEEKS

Mt	28: 1	the first day of the **w** was dawning,
Lk	18:12	I fast twice a **w**, and I pay tithes
1 Cor	16: 2	the first day of the **w** each of you

WEEKS → WEEK

Ex	34:22	You shall keep the feast of **W**
Lv	23:15	you shall count seven full **w**;
Lv	25: 8	You shall count seven **w** of years—
Dn	9:24	"Seventy **w** are decreed for your

WEEP → WEEPING, WEPT

Eccl	3: 4	A time to **w**, and a time to laugh;
Lam	1:16	For these things I **w**—My eyes!
Lk	23:28	of Jerusalem, do not **w** for me;
Rom	12:15	who rejoice, **w** with those who **w**.

WEEPING → WEEP

Ps	6: 9	has heard the sound of my **w**.
Ps	30: 6	At dusk **w** comes for the night;
Ps	126: 6	Those who go forth **w**,
Jer	31:15	the sound of sobbing, bitter **w**!
Mt	2:18	Rachel **w** for her children, and she
Lk	6:21	Blessed are you who are now **w**,

WEIGHED → WEIGHT

Dn	5:27	you have been **w** on the scales

WEIGHT → WEIGHED, WEIGHTS
Dt 25:15 But use a full and just **w**, a full

WEIGHTS → WEIGHT
Dt 25:13 You shall not keep two differing **w**
Prv 20:23 Varying **w** are an abomination

WELL
Gn 12:16 Abram fared **w** on her account,
2 Kgs 18:31 Drink water, each from your own **w**,
2 Chr 6: 8 a house for my name, you did **w**.
Prv 5:15 running water from your own **w**.
Mt 3:17 Son, with whom I am **w** pleased."
Mt 17: 5 Son, with whom I am **w** pleased;
Mt 25:21 His master said to him, '**W** done,
Jn 4: 6 Jacob's **w** was there.
Eph 6: 3 "that it may go **w** with you
2 Pt 1:17 with whom I am **w** pleased."

WEPT → WEEP
Is 38: 3 And Hezekiah **w** bitterly.
Dn 13:35 As she **w** she looked up to heaven,
Lk 19:41 near, he saw the city and **w** over it,

WEST → WESTERN
Ps 103:12 As far as the east is from the **w**,
Ps 107: 3 from east and **w**, from north
Is 43: 5 from the **w** I will gather you.
Zec 14: 4 east to **w** by a very deep valley,

WESTERN → WEST
Nm 34: 6 this will be your **w** boundary.
Dt 11:24 the Euphrates River to the **W** Sea,
Zec 14: 8 eastern sea, and half to the **w** sea.

WHATEVER
Ps 135: 6 **W** the LORD desires he does
Mt 16:19 **W** you bind on earth shall be bound
Mt 16:19 **w** you loose on earth shall be loosed
Mt 18:18 **w** you bind on earth shall be bound
Mt 18:18 **w** you loose on earth shall be loosed
Jn 14:13 And **w** you ask in my name, I will
Jn 15:16 so that **w** you ask the Father in my
Phil 4: 8 brothers, **w** is true, **w** is honorable, **w** is just, **w** is pure, **w** is lovely, **w** is gracious,
Phil 4:11 in **w** situation I find myself, to be
1 Jn 5:15 he hears us in regard to **w** we ask,

WHEAT
Ex 34:22 with the first fruits of the **w** harvest,
Mt 3:12 floor and gather his **w** into his barn,
Mt 13:25 and sowed weeds all through the **w**,
Lk 22:31 demanded to sift all of you like **w**,
Jn 12:24 you, unless a grain of **w** falls
Jn 12:24 dies, it remains just a grain of **w**;

WHEEL → WHEELS
Ez 1:16 as though one **w** was inside

WHEELS → WHEEL
Ex 14:25 he so clogged their chariot **w**
Ez 1:16 The **w** and their construction
Dn 7: 9 of fire, with **w** of burning fire.

WHENEVER
Dt 4: 7 God, is to us **w** we call upon him?

WHERE → EVERYWHERE, NOWHERE, WHEREVER
Dt 32:37 He will say, **W** are their gods,
Jb 28:12 **W** is the place of understanding?
Ps 42: 4 me every day, "**W** is your God?"
Ps 139: 7 **W** can I go from your spirit?
Ps 139: 7 From your presence, **w** can I flee?
Hos 13:14 **W** are your plagues, O death!
Hos 13:14 **w** is your sting, Sheol!
Mal 1: 6 a father, **w** is the honor due to me?
Mal 1: 6 a master, **w** is the fear due to me?
Mt 6:21 For **w** your treasure is,
Mt 28: 6 Come and see the place **w** he lay.
Jn 3: 8 The wind blows **w** it wills, and you do not know **w** it comes from or **w** it goes;
Jn 13:33 the Jews, '**W** I go you cannot come,'
1 Cor 15:55 **W**, O death, is your victory? **W**, O death, is your sting?"
Col 3: 1 **w** Christ is seated at the right hand
2 Pt 3: 4 "**W** is the promise of his coming?

WHEREVER → WHERE
Jos 1: 7 that you may succeed **w** you go.
Mk 14: 9 **w** the gospel is proclaimed
Lk 9:57 him, "I will follow you **w** you go."
Rev 14: 4 who follow the Lamb **w** he goes.

WHETHER
Rom 14: 8 so then, **w** we live or die, we are
1 Jn 4: 1 test the spirits to see **w** they belong

WHILE
Is 55: 6 Seek the LORD **w** he may be found, call upon him **w** he is near.
Is 65:24 **w** they are yet speaking, I will hear.
Jn 12:35 will be among you only a little **w**.
Jn 12:35 Walk **w** you have the light,
Jn 16:16 "A little **w** and you will no longer
Jn 16:16 again a little **w** later and you will
Rom 5: 8 **w** we were still sinners Christ died
2 Cor 5: 4 For **w** we are in this tent we groan

WHIP
Jn 2:15 He made a **w** out of cords and drove

WHIRLWIND → WIND
2 Kgs 2:11 and Elijah went up to heaven in a **w**,
Sir 48:12 Elijah was enveloped in the **w**,
Hos 8: 7 sow the wind, they will reap the **w**;

WHISPERED
Mt 10:27 what you hear **w**,

WHITE → WHITER, WHITEWASH, WHITEWASHED
Nm 12:10 stricken with a scaly infection, **w** as snow!
Dn 7: 9 His clothing was **w** as snow, the hair
Zec 1: 8 him were red, sorrel, and **w** horses.
Zec 6: 3 the third chariot **w** horses,
Mt 5:36 for you cannot make a single hair **w**
Mt 28: 3 and his clothing was **w** as snow.
Acts 1:10 in **w** garments stood beside them.
Rev 1:14 hair of his head was as **w** as **w** wool
Rev 2:17 also give a **w** amulet upon which is
Rev 3: 4 will walk with me dressed in **w**,
Rev 6: 2 and there was a **w** horse, and its
Rev 7:13 "Who are these wearing **w** robes,
Rev 14:14 I looked and there was a **w** cloud,
Rev 19:11 opened, and there was a **w** horse;
Rev 20:11 Next I saw a large **w** throne

WHITER → WHITE
Ps 51: 9 wash me, and I will be **w** than snow.

WHITEWASH → WHITE
Ez 13:10 a wall is built, they cover it with **w**,
Ez 22:28 her prophets cover them with **w**,

WHITEWASHED → WHITE
Mt 23:27 You are like **w** tombs, which appear
Acts 23: 3 "God will strike you, you **w** wall.

WHOEVER
Mt 12:50 For **w** does the will of my heavenly
Mk 3:29 But **w** blasphemes against the holy
Mk 9:40 For **w** is not against us is for us.
Jn 3:36 **W** believes in the Son has eternal
Jn 3:36 **w** disobeys the Son will not see life,

WHOLE → WHOLEHEARTED
Gn 11: 1 The **w** world had the same language
Gn 18:28 Will you destroy the **w** city because
Ex 12:47 The **w** community of Israel must
Dt 6: 5 love the LORD, your God, with your **w** heart, and with your **w** being, and with your **w** strength.
Dt 11:13 loving and serving the LORD, your God, with your **w** heart and your **w** being,
Dt 13:17 all its spoils as a **w** burnt offering
1 Kgs 10:24 the **w** world sought audience
Is 1: 5 The **w** head is sick, the **w** heart faint.
Is 14:26 is the plan proposed for the **w** earth,
Ez 37:11 man, these bones are the **w** house

Dn	2:35	mountain and filled the w earth.
Mt	5:29	than to have your w body thrown
Mt	6:22	your w body will be filled
Mt	16:26	there be for one to gain the w world
Mk	15:33	came over the w land until three
Acts	17:26	made from one the w human race
Rom	3:19	the w world stand accountable
1 Cor	12:17	If the w body were an eye,
1 Cor	12:17	If the w body were hearing,
Gal	5: 9	A little yeast leavens the w batch
Gal	5:14	For the w law is fulfilled in one
Eph	2:21	Through him the w structure is held
Ti	1:11	as they are upsetting w families
Jas	2:10	For whoever keeps the w law,
1 Jn	2: 2	only but for those of the w world.
1 Jn	5:19	the w world is under the power
Rev	3:10	to come to the w world to test
Rev	12: 9	who deceived the w world,
Rev	13: 3	the w world followed

WHOLEHEARTED → HEART, WHOLE

Ps	119:80	May I be w toward your statutes,

WHY

Gn	4: 6	said to Cain: W are you angry?
Gn	12:19	W did you say, 'She is my sister,'
Gn	32:30	"W do you ask for my name?"
Jgs	13:18	W do you ask my name?
Jb	24: 1	W are times not set
Ps	2: 1	W do the nations protest
Ps	10: 1	W, LORD, do you stand afar
Ps	22: 2	God, w have you abandoned me?
Ps	42: 6	W are you downcast, my soul; w do
Ps	79:10	W should the nations say,
Is	40:27	W, O Jacob, do you say,
Lam	5:20	W have you utterly forgotten us,
Mt	9:11	"W does your teacher eat with tax
Mt	17:19	"W could we not drive it out?"
Mt	27:46	my God, w have you forsaken me?"
Mk	10:18	him, "W do you call me good?
Acts	9: 4	Saul, w are you persecuting me?"

WICK

Is	42: 3	and a dimly burning w he will not
Mt	12:20	a smoldering w he will not quench,

WICKED → WICKEDNESS

Gn	13:13	the inhabitants of Sodom were w,
Ex	23: 1	the w to be a witness supporting
Nm	14:35	this to this entire w community
2 Chr	19: 2	"Should you help the w and love
Jb	15:20	The w is in torment all his days,
Jb	20:29	This is the portion of the w,
Jb	27:13	is the portion of the w with God,
Ps	1: 1	not walk in the counsel of the w,
Ps	1: 5	Therefore the w will not arise
Ps	7:10	Let the malice of the w end.
Ps	10:13	Why should the w scorn God,
Ps	11: 6	rains upon the w fiery coals
Ps	12: 9	On every side the w roam;
Ps	26: 5	with the w I do not sit.
Ps	32:10	Many are the sorrows of the w one,
Ps	36: 2	Sin directs the heart of the w man;
Ps	37:40	rescues and saves them from the w,
Ps	50:16	But to the w God says:
Ps	58: 4	The w have been corrupt since birth;
Ps	73: 3	when I saw the prosperity of the w.
Ps	82: 2	and favor the cause of the w?
Ps	112:10	The w sees and is angry;
Ps	112:10	the desire of the w come to nothing.
Ps	119:61	the snares of the w surround me,
Ps	140: 9	not grant the desires of the w one;
Ps	141:10	Let the w fall into their own nets,
Ps	146: 9	but thwarts the way of the w.
Prv	4:14	The path of the w do not enter,
Prv	5:22	own iniquities the w will be caught,
Prv	6:18	A heart that plots w schemes,
Prv	9: 7	reproves the w incurs opprobrium.
Prv	10:20	the heart of the w is of little worth.

Prv	10:28	the expectation of the w perishes.
Prv	11: 5	but by their wickedness the w fall.
Prv	11:10	when the w perish, there is
Prv	12: 5	the designs of the w are deceit.
Prv	12:10	but the compassion of the w is cruel.
Prv	14:19	and the w, at the gates of the just.
Prv	21:10	The soul of the w desires evil;
Prv	21:29	The face of the w hardens,
Prv	28: 1	The w flee though none pursue;
Prv	28: 4	abandon instruction praise the w,
Prv	29: 7	the w do not understand such care.
Prv	29:16	When the w increase,
Prv	29:27	an abomination to the w, one whose
Eccl	7:15	and the w living long in their
Eccl	8:14	those who are w but are treated as
Is	11: 4	breath of his lips he shall slay the w.
Is	13:11	for its evil and the w for their guilt.
Is	26:10	The w, when spared, do not learn
Is	48:22	There is no peace for the w,
Is	53: 9	He was given a grave among the w,
Is	55: 7	Let the w forsake their way,
Is	57:20	the w are like the tossing sea
Ez	3:18	If I say to the w, You shall surely
Ez	3:18	out to dissuade the w from their evil
Ez	13:22	encourage the w so they do not turn
Ez	18:21	if the w man turns away from all
Ez	18:23	find pleasure in the death of the w—
Ez	21:30	depraved and w prince of Israel,
Ez	33: 8	When I say to the w, "You w,
Ez	33: 8	up to warn the w about their ways,
Ez	33:11	no pleasure in the death of the w,
Ez	33:19	When the w turn away
Dn	12:10	and tested, but the w shall prove w;
Dn	12:10	the w shall have no understanding,
Lk	6:35	is kind to the ungrateful and the w.

WICKEDNESS → WICKED

Gn	6: 5	the LORD saw how great the w
Dt	9: 4	the w of these nations the LORD is
Prv	11: 5	but by their w the wicked fall.
Eccl	3:16	sun in the judgment place I saw w, and w also in the seat of justice.
Wis	2:21	for their w blinded them,
Jer	8: 6	No one regrets w, saying,
Jer	14:20	We recognize our w, LORD,
Ez	18:20	to the just, and w to the wicked.
Ez	33:19	When the wicked turn away from w
Jon	1: 2	for their w has come before me.
Rom	1:18	w of those who suppress the truth by their w.
Heb	1: 9	You loved justice and hated w;

WIDE

Ps	81:11	Open w your mouth that I may fill
Mt	7:13	for the gate is w and the road broad

WIDOW → WIDOW'S, WIDOWHOOD, WIDOWS

Ex	22:21	You shall not wrong any w
Dt	10:18	justice for the orphan and the w,
Ru	4: 5	the Moabite, the w of the late heir,
Jdt	8: 4	Judith was living as a w in her home
Ps	146: 9	to the aid of the orphan and the w,
Is	1:17	the orphan's plea, defend the w.
Lam	1: 1	great among the nations is now like a w.
Lk	2:37	as a w until she was eighty-four.
Lk	18: 3	a w in that town used to come
Lk	21: 3	this poor w put in more than all
1 Tm	5: 4	if a w has children or grandchildren,
Rev	18: 7	I am no w, and I will never know

WIDOW'S → WIDOW

Gn	38:14	So she took off her w garments,
Jdt	8: 5	her waist, and wore w clothing.
Prv	15:25	but preserves intact the w landmark.

WIDOWHOOD → WIDOW

Is	54: 4	of your w no longer remember.

WIDOWS → WIDOW

Ps	68: 6	of the fatherless, defender of w—

Lk	4:25	there were many **w** in Israel
Acts	6: 1	because their **w** were being
1 Cor	7: 8	Now to the unmarried and to **w**,
1 Tm	5: 3	Honor **w** who are truly **w**.
Jas	1:27	for orphans and **w** in their affliction

WIFE → WIVES

Gn	2:24	and mother and clings to his **w**,
Gn	3:20	man gave his **w** the name "Eve,"
Gn	12:18	did you not tell me she was your **w**?
Gn	19:26	But Lot's **w** looked back, and she
Gn	20:11	would kill me on account of my **w**.
Gn	24:67	He took Rebekah as his **w**.
Ex	20:17	shall not covet your neighbor's **w**,
Nm	5:12	If a man's **w** goes astray
Dt	5:21	shall not covet your neighbor's **w**.
Dt	24: 5	to bring joy to the **w** he has married.
Ru	4:13	came together as husband and **w**,
2 Sm	12:10	have taken the **w** of Uriah the Hittite to be your **w**.
Tb	8: 6	you made his **w** Eve to be his helper
Ps	128: 3	Your **w** will be like a fruitful vine
Prv	5:18	and have joy of the **w** of your youth,
Prv	6:24	Keeping you from another's **w**,
Prv	18:22	To find a **w** is to find happiness,
Prv	19:14	but a prudent **w** is from the LORD.
Eccl	9: 9	Enjoy life with the **w** you love,
Sir	7:19	Do not reject a sensible **w**;
Sir	26: 1	Happy the husband of a good **w**;
Sir	26: 3	A good **w** is a generous gift
Mal	2:14	the **w** of your youth With whom you
Mal	2:14	companion, your covenanted **w**.
Mt	1:20	take Mary your **w** into your home.
Mt	5:32	whoever divorces his **w** (unless
Mt	19: 3	a man to divorce his **w** for any cause
Mk	6:18	for you to have your brother's **w**."
Mk	10: 2	for a husband to divorce his **w**?"
Mk	12:23	[they arise] whose **w** will she be?
Lk	17:32	Remember the **w** of Lot.
Lk	18:29	no one who has given up house or **w**
1 Cor	7: 2	every man should have his own **w**,
1 Cor	7:11	a husband should not divorce his **w**.
1 Cor	7:33	the world, how he may please his **w**,
Eph	5:23	head of his **w** just as Christ is head
Eph	5:28	He who loves his **w** loves himself.
Eph	5:33	of you should love his **w** as himself,
Eph	5:33	the **w** should respect her husband.
Rev	21: 9	you the bride, the **w** of the Lamb."

WILD → WILDERNESS

Gn	1:25	God made every kind of **w** animal,
Gn	8: 1	and all the animals, **w** and tame,
Ex	32:25	were running **w** because Aaron had
Ps	50:11	whatever moves in the **w** is mine.
Mk	1: 6	He fed on locusts and **w** honey.
Mk	1:13	He was among **w** beasts,
Rom	11:17	off, and you, a **w** olive shoot,
Jude	1:13	They are like **w** waves of the sea,

WILDERNESS → WILD

Is	35: 6	For waters will burst forth in the **w**,
Is	40: 3	In the **w** prepare the way of the LORD!

WILL → WILLING, WILLS

Ezr	10:11	of your ancestors, and do his **w**:
Tb	12:18	favor on my part, but by God's **w**.
Est	C: 2	you when it is your **w** to save Israel.
2 Mc	1: 3	to do his **w** wholeheartedly
2 Mc	12:16	Capturing the city by the **w** of God,
Ps	40: 9	I delight to do your **w**, my God;
Ps	103:21	his ministers who carry out his **w**.
Ps	143:10	Teach me to do your **w**, for you are
Wis	14: 5	But you **w** that the products of your
Sir	42:15	he accepts the one who does his **w**.
Is	42:21	the LORD's **w** for the sake of his justice
Is	53:10	it was the LORD's **w** to crush him
Mt	6:10	kingdom come, your **w** be done,
Mt	7:21	only the one who does the **w** of my
Mt	11:26	such has been your gracious **w**.
Mt	12:50	whoever does the **w** of my heavenly

Mt	18:14	way, it is not the **w** of your heavenly
Mt	21:31	of the two did his father's **w**?"
Mt	26:42	my drinking it, your **w** be done!"
Mk	3:35	whoever does the **w** of God is my
Lk	10:21	such has been your gracious **w**.
Lk	22:42	still, not my **w** but yours be done."
Jn	4:34	to do the **w** of the one who sent me
Jn	5:30	because I do not seek my own **w** but the **w** of the one who sent me.
Jn	6:38	from heaven not to do my own **w** but the **w** of the one who sent me.
Jn	6:39	this is the **w** of the one who sent me,
Jn	6:40	For this is the **w** of my Father,
Jn	7:17	to do his **w** shall know whether my
Jn	9:31	but if one is devout and does his **w**,
Acts	21:14	saying, "The Lord's **w** be done."
Acts	22:14	designated you to know his **w**,
Rom	2:18	know his **w** and are able to discern
Rom	8:27	the holy ones according to God's **w**.
Rom	9:16	So it depends not upon a person's **w**
Rom	9:19	For who can oppose his **w**?"
Rom	12: 2	you may discern what is the **w**
Rom	15:32	to you with joy by the **w** of God.
1 Cor	1: 1	of Christ Jesus by the **w** of God,
2 Cor	1: 1	of Christ Jesus by the **w** of God,
Gal	1: 4	age in accord with the **w** of our God
Gal	3:15	even a human **w** once ratified.
Eph	1: 5	in accord with the favor of his **w**,
Eph	1: 9	to us the mystery of his **w** in accord
Eph	1:11	according to the intention of his **w**,
Eph	5:17	to understand what is the **w**
Eph	6: 6	doing the **w** of God from the heart,
Col	1: 9	his **w** through all spiritual wisdom
1 Thes	4: 3	This is the **w** of God, your holiness:
1 Thes	5:18	for this is the **w** of God for you
2 Tm	2:26	are entrapped by him, for his **w**.
Heb	2: 4	of the holy Spirit according to his **w**.
Heb	9:16	Now where there is a **w**, the death
Heb	9:17	For a **w** takes effect only at death;
Heb	10: 7	I come to do your **w**, O God.' "
Heb	10: 9	"Behold, I come to do your **w**."
Heb	10:10	By this "**w**," we have been
Heb	10:36	need endurance to do the **w** of God
Heb	13:21	that is good, that you may do his **w**.
1 Pt	2:15	For it is the **w** of God that by doing
1 Pt	3:17	if that be the **w** of God,
1 Pt	4: 2	human desires, but on the **w** of God.
1 Pt	4:19	with God's **w** their souls over
2 Pt	1:21	ever came through human **w**;
1 Jn	2:17	whoever does the **w** of God remains
1 Jn	5:14	we ask anything according to his **w**,
Rev	4:11	because of your **w** they came to be

WILLING → WILL

1 Chr	28: 9	with a whole heart and a **w** soul,
Ps	51:14	uphold me with a **w** spirit.
Mt	26:41	The spirit is **w**, but the flesh is
Lk	22:42	if you are **w**, take this cup away

WILLS → WILL

Ezr	7:18	the silver and gold, as your God **w**.
Dn	11: 3	rule with great might, doing as he **w**.
Dn	11:36	"The king shall do as he **w**, exalting himself

WIN → WON

1 Cor	9:19	so as to **w** over as many as possible.

WIND → WHIRLWIND, WINDS

Gn	1: 2	and a mighty **w** sweeping over
1 Kgs	19:11	and violent **w** rending the mountains
1 Kgs	19:11	but the LORD was not in the **w**;
Ps	1: 4	They are like chaff driven by the **w**.
Ps	18:11	borne along on the wings of the **w**.
Ps	104: 3	traveling on the wings of the **w**,
Prv	30: 4	who has cupped the **w** in the hollow
Eccl	1:14	all is vanity and a chase after **w**.
Ez	5: 2	the final third scatter to the **w**
Hos	8: 7	When they sow the **w**, they will reap
Jon	1: 4	hurled a great **w** upon the sea,

Jon	4: 8	God provided a scorching east w;
Mk	4:41	then is this whom even w and sea
Jn	3: 8	The w blows where it wills, and you
Acts	2: 2	sky a noise like a strong driving w,
Eph	4:14	along by every w of teaching arising
Jas	1: 6	is driven and tossed about by the w.

WINDOW → WINDOWS

Jos	2:21	she tied the scarlet cord in the w.
1 Sm	19:12	Michal let David down through a w,
Acts	20: 9	was sitting on the w sill was sinking
2 Cor	11:33	in a basket through a w in the wall

WINDOWS → WINDOW

2 Kgs	7: 2	LORD were to make w in heaven,

WINDS → WIND

Ps	104: 4	You make the w your messengers;
Dn	3:65	All you w, bless the Lord;
Mt	7:25	and the w blew and buffeted
Mt	8:27	is this, whom even the w and the sea
Mt	24:31	will gather his elect from the four w,
Heb	1: 7	"He makes his angels w and his

WINE → WINESKINS

Gn	9:21	He drank some of the w,
Gn	19:32	let us ply our father with w
Nm	6: 3	they shall abstain from w and strong
Nm	6: 3	they may neither drink w vinegar,
Dt	7:13	your soil, your grain and w and oil,
Jgs	13: 4	be careful to drink no w or beer
1 Sm	1:15	I have had neither w nor liquor;
Neh	13:12	brought in the tithes of grain, w,
2 Mc	15:39	as it is unpleasant to drink w by itself
Ps	4: 8	have when grain and w abound.
Ps	75: 9	hand, foaming w, fully spiced.
Ps	104:15	w to gladden their hearts,
Prv	3:10	with new w your vats will overflow.
Prv	9: 2	her meat, mixed her w, yes, she has
Prv	20: 1	W is arrogant, strong drink is
Prv	23:31	Do not look on the w when it is red,
Prv	31: 4	Lemuel, not for kings to drink w;
Prv	31: 6	perishing, and w to the embittered;
Eccl	2: 3	how to beguile my senses with w
Eccl	9: 7	drink your w with a merry heart,
Eccl	10:19	and w gives joy to the living,
Sg	1: 2	for your love is better than w,
Sg	7:10	And your mouth like the best w—
Sir	9:10	A new friend is like new w—
Sir	31:28	and delight is w enough,
Sir	31:29	and disgrace is w drunk amid anger
Sir	40:30	W and strong drink delight the soul,
Is	5:22	who are champions at drinking w,
Is	28: 7	stagger from w and stumble
Is	28: 7	strong drink, overpowered by w;
Is	29: 9	drunk, but not from w, who stagger,
Is	51:21	afflicted one, drunk, but not with w,
Is	55: 1	money, w and milk without cost!
Dn	1: 8	himself with the king's food or w;
Jl	2:24	the vats spilling over with new w
Jl	4:18	day the mountains will drip new w,
Am	2:12	But you made the nazirites drink w,
Mi	2:11	"I will preach to you w and strong
Mt	9:17	People do not put new w into old
Mt	9:17	the skins burst, the w spills out,
Mt	9:17	Rather, they pour new w into fresh
Mt	27:34	they gave Jesus w to drink mixed
Lk	23:36	As they approached to offer him w
Jn	2: 3	When the w ran short, the mother
Jn	2: 3	said to him, "They have no w."
Jn	2: 9	tasted the water that had become w,
Acts	2:13	"They have had too much new w."
Rom	14:21	drink w or do anything that causes
Eph	5:18	And do not get drunk on w,
1 Tm	5:23	have a little w for the sake of your
Rev	14: 8	made all the nations drink the w
Rev	14:10	will also drink the w of God's fury,
Rev	18: 3	all the nations have drunk the w

WINESKINS → SKIN, WINE

Mt	9:17	do not put new wine into old w.
Mt	9:17	they pour new wine into fresh w,

WINGED → WINGS

Gn	1:21	teems, and all kinds of w birds.

WINGS → WINGED

Ex	19: 4	how I bore you up on eagles' w
Ex	37: 9	The cherubim had their w spread
Ru	2:12	under whose w you have come
1 Kgs	8: 7	The cherubim had their w spread
2 Chr	3:11	The w of the cherubim spanned
Ps	17: 8	hide me in the shadow of your w
Ps	91: 4	under his w you may take refuge;
Is	6: 2	each of them had six w:
Is	40:31	they will soar on eagles' w;
Ez	1: 6	but each had four faces and four w,
Ez	1:11	Their w were spread out above.
Ez	1:11	two w touched one another,
Ez	1:11	the other two w covered the body.
Ez	10:21	of them had four faces and four w,
Ez	10:21	like human hands under their w.
Zec	5: 9	they had w like the w of a stork—
Lk	13:34	a hen gathers her brood under her w,
Rev	4: 8	each of them with six w,

WINNOW → WINNOWING, WINNOWS

Is	41:16	When you w them, the wind shall

WINNOWING → WINNOW

Jer	15: 7	I winnowed them with a w fork
Mt	3:12	His w fan is in his hand.

WINNOWS → WINNOW

Prv	20:26	A wise king w the wicked,

WINTER

Gn	8:22	Summer and w, and day and night
Ps	74:17	summer and w you made.
Mk	13:18	Pray that this does not happen in w.

WIPE → WIPED

Is	25: 8	Lord GOD will w away the tears
Rev	7:17	God will w away every tear
Rev	21: 4	He will w every tear from their

WIPED → WIPE

Acts	3:19	that your sins may be w away,

WISDOM → WISE

Dt	4: 6	for this is your w and discernment
1 Kgs	5: 9	God gave Solomon w,
1 Kgs	10: 6	your deeds and your w is true,"
2 Chr	1:10	w and knowledge to govern this
Jb	11: 6	And tell you the secrets of w,
Jb	12:13	With him are w and might;
Jb	28:12	As for w—where can she be found?
Jb	28:28	See: the fear of the Lord is w;
Ps	37:30	The mouth of the righteous utters w;
Ps	51: 8	and secretly you teach me w.
Ps	111:10	the LORD is the beginning of w;
Prv	1: 7	fools despise w and discipline.
Prv	1:20	W cries aloud in the street,
Prv	2: 6	For the LORD gives w, from his
Prv	3:13	Happy the one who finds w, the one
Prv	4: 5	Get w, get understanding!
Prv	4: 7	The beginning of w is: get w;
Prv	8:11	[For W is better than corals, and no]
Prv	9: 1	W has built her house, she has set
Prv	9:10	The beginning of w is fear
Prv	11: 2	but with the humble is w.
Prv	13:10	w is with those who take counsel.
Prv	15:33	fear of the LORD is training for w,
Prv	23:23	w, instruction, understanding!
Prv	29: 3	Whoever loves w gives joy to his
Prv	29:15	The rod of correction gives w,
Prv	31:26	She opens her mouth in w;
Eccl	1:13	investigate in w all things that are
Eccl	2: 3	Guided by w, I probed with my
Eccl	2:13	w has as much profit over folly as

Eccl	7:12	protection of **w** is as the protection
Eccl	7:12	is profitable because **w** gives life
Eccl	10: 1	more weighty than **w** or wealth is
Wis	6:12	Resplendent and unfading is **W**,
Wis	7: 7	and the spirit of **W** came to me.
Sir	1: 1	All **w** is from the Lord and remains
Sir	24: 1	**W** sings her own praises, among her
Is	11: 2	a spirit of **w** and of understanding,
Is	28:29	is his counsel and great his **w**.
Jer	9:22	Let not the wise boast of his **w**,
Jer	10:12	established the world by his **w**,
Bar	3:12	have forsaken the fountain of **w**!
Ez	28:12	full of **w**, perfect in beauty.
Dn	5:14	insight and extraordinary **w**.
Mt	11:19	But **w** is vindicated by her works."
Mt	12:42	the earth to hear the **w** of Solomon;
Mt	13:54	"Where did this man get such **w**
Lk	2:40	and became strong, filled with **w**;
Lk	2:52	And Jesus advanced [in] **w** and age
Acts	6: 3	filled with the Spirit and **w**,
Rom	11:33	the depth of the riches and **w**
1 Cor	1:17	not with the **w** of human eloquence,
1 Cor	1:19	"I will destroy the **w** of the wise,
1 Cor	1:20	Has not God made the **w**
1 Cor	1:30	who became for us **w** from God,
1 Cor	2: 7	we speak God's **w**, mysterious,
1 Cor	3:19	the **w** of this world is foolishness
1 Cor	12: 8	the Spirit the expression of **w**;
Eph	1:17	may give you a spirit of **w**
Col	1: 9	of his will through all spiritual **w**
Col	1:28	and teaching everyone with all **w**,
Col	2: 3	are hidden all the treasures of **w**
Col	2:23	While they have a semblance of **w**
Jas	1: 5	But if any of you lacks **w**, he should
Jas	3:13	in the humility that comes from **w**.
Jas	3:17	the **w** from above is first of all pure,
Rev	5:12	power and riches, **w** and strength,
Rev	7:12	and glory, **w** and thanksgiving,
Rev	13:18	**W** is needed here;
Rev	17: 9	Here is a clue for one who has **w**.

WISE → WISDOM, WISELY, WISER

Gn	41:39	one as discerning and **w** as you are.
Ex	7:11	turn, summoned the **w** men
Dt	4: 6	"This great nation is truly a **w**
Dt	16:19	a bribe blinds the eyes even of the **w**
1 Kgs	3:12	I give you a heart so **w**
Tb	6:12	The girl is **w**, courageous, and very beautiful;
Jb	5:13	He catches the **w** in their own ruses,
Jb	32: 9	not those of many days who are **w**,
Ps	94: 8	You fools, when will you be **w**?
Ps	107:43	Whoever is **w** will take note of these
Prv	3: 7	Do not be **w** in your own eyes,
Prv	9: 9	Instruct the **w**, and they become still
Prv	10: 1	A **w** son gives his father joy,
Prv	13: 1	A **w** son loves correction,
Prv	13:20	Walk with the **w** and you become **w**,
Prv	16:23	The heart of the **w** makes
Prv	17:28	keeping silent, are considered **w**;
Prv	20: 1	none who are intoxicated by them are **w**.
Prv	23:15	if your heart is **w**, my heart also will
Prv	24: 5	The **w** are more powerful than
Prv	26: 5	lest they become **w** in their own
Prv	29:11	but the **w**, biding their time,
Eccl	2:14	**W** people have eyes in their heads,
Eccl	7:19	defense for the **w** than ten princes
Eccl	9:17	of the **w** are better heeded than
Eccl	12:11	The sayings of the **w** are like goads;
Is	29:14	The wisdom of the **w** shall perish,
Jer	8: 9	The **w** are put to shame, terrified,
Jer	9:22	Let not the **w** boast of his wisdom,
Dn	2:21	He gives wisdom to the **w**
Am	5:13	at this time the **w** are struck dumb
Mt	11:25	have hidden these things from the **w**
Mt	25: 2	them were foolish and five were **w**.
Rom	1:22	While claiming to be **w**,
Rom	16:27	to the only **w** God, through Jesus

1 Cor	1:19	"I will destroy the wisdom of the **w**,
1 Cor	1:26	of you were **w** by human standards,
1 Cor	3:18	one among you considers himself **w**
1 Cor	3:18	become a fool so as to become **w**.
1 Cor	3:19	"He catches the **w** in their own
Eph	5:15	live, not as foolish persons but as **w**,
Jas	3:13	Who among you is **w**

WISELY → WISE

Jer	23: 5	king he shall reign and govern **w**,
Col	4: 5	Conduct yourselves **w** toward

WISER → WISE

1 Kgs	5:11	He was **w** than anyone else—**w** than
Prv	9: 9	the wise, and they become still **w**;
Prv	26:16	eyes sluggards are **w** than seven
1 Cor	1:25	of God is **w** than human wisdom,

WISH → WISHES

Rom	9: 3	For I could **w** that I myself were
Rev	3:15	I **w** you were either cold or hot.

WISHES → WISH

Est	6: 6	for the man whom the king **w**

WITHER → WITHERED, WITHERS

Ps	1: 3	Its leaves never **w**; whatever he does

WITHERED → WITHER

Mt	13: 6	scorched, and it **w** for lack of roots.
Mt	21:19	And immediately the fig tree **w**.

WITHERS → WITHER

Is	40: 7	The grass **w**, the flower wilts,
1 Pt	1:24	the grass **w**, and the flower wilts;

WITHHELD → WITHHOLD

Am	4: 7	And I **w** the rain from you
Hg	1:10	Therefore, the heavens **w** the dew,

WITHHOLD → WITHHELD, WITHHOLDS

Neh	9:20	Your manna you did not **w**
Ps	40:12	may you not **w** your compassion
Prv	23:13	Do not **w** discipline from youths;

WITHHOLDS → WITHHOLD

Ps	84:12	The LORD **w** no good thing

WITHIN

Ps	42: 6	why do you groan **w** me?
Ps	122: 7	May peace be **w** your ramparts,
Ps	122: 7	prosperity **w** your towers."
Prv	4:21	your sight, keep them **w** your heart;
Jer	31:33	I will place my law **w** them,
Zec	12: 1	and fashions the human spirit **w**:
Mk	7:21	From **w** people, from their hearts,
1 Cor	2:11	the spirit of the person that is **w**?

WITHOUT

Nm	27:17	not be like sheep **w** a shepherd."
2 Chr	18:16	mountains, like sheep **w** a shepherd,
Ps	69: 5	are those who hate me **w** cause.
Prv	19: 2	Desire **w** knowledge is not good;
Is	52: 3	**w** money you shall be redeemed.
Is	55: 1	buy grain **w** money, wine and milk **w** cost!
Mt	9:36	abandoned, like sheep **w** a shepherd.
Mt	23:23	have done, **w** neglecting the others.
Jn	8: 7	among you who is **w** sin be the first
Eph	2:12	were at that time **w** Christ,
Eph	2:12	**w** hope and **w** God in the world.
Phil	2:14	Do everything **w** grumbling
Heb	4:15	been tested in every way, yet **w** sin.
Heb	9:22	**w** the shedding of blood there is no

WITHSTAND

2 Chr	20: 6	and might, and no one can **w** you.
Est	9: 2	and no one could **w** them, for fear

WITNESS → EYEWITNESSES, WITNESSES

Nm	35:30	A single **w** does not suffice
Dt	19:15	One **w** alone shall not stand against
Jgs	11:10	"The LORD is **w** between us
1 Sm	12: 5	"The LORD is **w** against you this
1 Sm	12: 5	and the LORD's anointed is **w**,
Jb	16:19	Even now my **w** is in heaven,

Prv	14:25	The truthful w saves lives,
Prv	19: 9	The false w will not go unpunished,
Prv	21:28	The false w will perish, but one who
Rom	2:15	also bears w and their conflicting
1 Pt	5: 1	and w to the sufferings of Christ
Rev	1: 5	the faithful w, the firstborn
Rev	2:13	my faithful w, who was martyred
Rev	3:14	the faithful and true w, the source

WITNESSES → WITNESS

Dt	17: 6	or three w shall a person be put
Dt	19:15	on the testimony of two or three w.
Jos	24:22	"You are w against yourselves
Jos	24:22	They replied, "We are w!"
Ps	27:12	and lying w have risen against me.
Prv	12:17	but the deceitful make lying w.
Is	43:10	You are my w—
Mt	18:16	on the testimony of two or three w.'
Mt	26:60	though many false w came forward.
Mk	14:63	"What further need have we of w?
Acts	1: 8	and you will be my w in Jerusalem,
Acts	2:32	of this we are all w.
Acts	6:13	presented false w who testified,
Heb	12: 1	surrounded by so great a cloud of w,
Rev	11: 3	I will commission my two w

WIVES → WIFE

Gn	6:18	wife and your sons' w with you.
Dt	17:17	shall he have a great number of w,
Dt	21:15	If a man has two w, one loved
1 Kgs	11: 3	He had as w seven hundred
1 Chr	14: 3	David took other w in Jerusalem
Mt	19: 8	allowed you to divorce your w,
Eph	5:22	W should be subordinate to their
Eph	5:25	love your w, even as Christ loved
Col	3:18	W, be subordinate to your husbands,
1 Pt	3: 1	you w should be subordinate to your

WOE

Is	3:11	W to the wicked! It will go ill
Is	6: 5	Then I said, "W is me, I am
Jer	13:27	W to you, Jerusalem!
Jer	23: 1	W to the shepherds who destroy
Lam	5:16	w to us that we sinned!
Hos	9:12	w to them when I turn away
Mt	18: 7	W to the world because of things
Mt	18: 7	but w to the one through whom they
Mt	23:13	"W to you, scribes and Pharisees,
Mt	23:16	"W to you, blind guides, who say,
Mk	14:21	w to that man by whom the Son
Lk	6:24	But w to you who are rich, for you
Lk	11:42	W to you Pharisees! You pay tithes
Lk	11:52	W to you, scholars of the law!
1 Cor	9:16	and w to me if I do not preach it!
Jude	1:11	W to them! They followed the way
Rev	8:13	cry out in a loud voice, "W! W!

WOLF → WOLVES

Is	11: 6	the w shall be a guest of the lamb,
Is	65:25	The w and the lamb shall pasture
Jn	10:12	sees a w coming and leaves
Jn	10:12	and the w catches and scatters them.

WOLVES → WOLF

Ez	22:27	her officials are like w tearing prey,
Zep	3: 3	Its judges are desert w that have no
Mt	7:15	but underneath are ravenous w.
Mt	10:16	you like sheep in the midst of w;
Acts	20:29	my departure savage w will come

WOMAN → WOMAN'S, WOMEN, WOMEN'S

Gn	2:22	he had taken from the man into a w.
Gn	2:23	This one shall be called 'w,'
Gn	3: 6	The w saw that the tree was good
Gn	3:12	"The w whom you put here
Gn	3:15	put enmity between you and the w,
Gn	3:16	To the w he said: I will intensify
Gn	12:11	"I know that you are a beautiful w.
Gn	20: 3	because of the w you have taken,

Ex	3:22	Every w will ask her neighbor
Ex	21:22	have a fight and hurt a pregnant w,
Nm	30: 4	"When a w makes a vow
Dt	20: 7	there anyone who has betrothed a w
Dt	21:11	if you see a beautiful w among
Dt	22: 5	A w shall not wear a man's
Dt	24: 1	a man, after marrying a w, is later
Jgs	9:54	say about me, 'A w killed him.' "
Jgs	14: 2	"I saw in Timnah a w, a Philistine.
Jgs	16: 4	a w in the Wadi Sorek whose name
Ru	3:11	know you to be a worthy w.
1 Sm	1:15	"I am an unhappy w. I have had
1 Sm	25: 3	The w was intelligent and attractive,
1 Sm	28: 7	"There is a w in Endor who is
2 Sm	11: 2	From the roof he saw a w bathing;
2 Sm	14: 2	and brought from there a wise w,
2 Sm	20:16	a wise w from the city called out,
1 Kgs	17:24	The w said to Elijah, "Now indeed I
2 Kgs	4: 8	where there was a w of influence,
2 Kgs	8: 1	to the w whose son he had restored
2 Kgs	9:34	"Attend to that accursed w and bury
Jdt	8:31	since you are a devout w,
Jb	14: 1	Man born of w is short-lived
Prv	9:13	W Folly is raucous, utterly foolish;
Prv	11:16	A gracious w gains esteem,
Prv	11:22	is a beautiful w without judgment.
Prv	12: 4	A w of worth is the crown of her husband,
Prv	30:23	Under an unloved w who is wed,
Prv	31:10	Who can find a w of worth?
Prv	31:30	the w who fears the LORD is to be
Sir	9: 3	Do not go near a strange w, lest you
Dn	13: 2	a very beautiful and God-fearing w,
Hos	1: 2	Go, get for yourself a w of prostitution
Mt	5:28	a w with lust has already committed
Mt	9:20	A w suffering hemorrhages
Mt	15:22	a Canaanite w of that district came
Mt	26: 7	a w came up to him
Mk	7:25	Soon a w whose daughter had
Lk	7:37	Now there was a sinful w in the city
Lk	10:38	village where a w whose name was
Lk	13:12	he called to her and said, "W,
Lk	15: 8	"Or what w having ten coins
Jn	2: 4	[And] Jesus said to her, "W,
Jn	4: 7	A w of Samaria came to draw water.
Jn	8: 4	this w was caught in the very act
Jn	19:26	he said to his mother, "W, behold,
Jn	20:15	Jesus said to her, "W, why are you
Acts	16:14	One of them, a w named Lydia,
Acts	17:34	the Areopagus, a w named Damaris,
Rom	7: 2	Thus a married w is bound by law
1 Cor	7: 2	wife, and every w her own husband.
1 Cor	7:34	An unmarried w or a virgin is
1 Cor	7:34	A married w, on the other hand,
1 Cor	11: 6	if a w does not have her head veiled,
1 Cor	11: 6	for a w to have her hair cut off
1 Cor	11: 7	of God, but w is the glory of man.
1 Cor	11:12	For just as w came from man, so man is born of w;
Gal	4: 4	born of a w, born under the law,
1 Tm	2:11	A w must receive instruction
1 Tm	5:16	If any w believer has widowed
Rev	2:20	that you tolerate the w Jezebel,
Rev	12: 1	in the sky, a w clothed with the sun,
Rev	12: 4	the dragon stood before the w
Rev	12:13	it pursued the w who had given
Rev	17: 3	place where I saw a w seated
Rev	17:18	The w whom you saw represents

WOMAN'S → WOMAN

Dt	22: 5	nor shall a man put on a w clothing;
Jgs	4: 9	into a w power that the LORD is going to

WOMB

Gn	25:23	Two nations are in your w,
Ex	13: 2	whatever opens the w among
Dt	7:13	he will bless the fruit of your w
Jb	1:21	I came forth from my mother's w,

Ps	22:10	For you drew me forth from the **w**,
Ps	139:13	you knit me in my mother's **w**.
Prv	31: 2	what are you doing, son of my **w**;
Eccl	11: 5	the human frame in the mother's **w**,
Jer	1: 5	I formed you in the **w** I knew you,
Lk	1:44	the infant in my **w** leaped for joy.
Jn	3: 4	he cannot reenter his mother's **w**
Rom	4:19	years old) and the dead **w** of Sarah.

WOMEN → WOMAN

Nm	25: 1	themselves with the Moabite **w**.
Jgs	5:24	Most blessed of **w** is Jael, the wife
Jgs	5:24	blessed among tent-dwelling **w**!
Ezr	10: 2	by taking as wives foreign **w**
Neh	13:26	he was led into sin by foreign **w**.
Jdt	15:13	and the other **w** crowned themselves
Jdt	15:13	people, she led the **w** in the dance,
Sg	1: 8	most beautiful among **w**,
Sir	19: 2	Wine and **w** make the heart lustful,
Is	3:12	oppress them, **w** rule over them!
Zec	5: 9	saw two **w** coming forth with wind
Mt	11:11	**w** there has been none greater than
Mt	24:41	Two **w** will be grinding at the mill;
Mt	28: 5	the angel said to the **w** in reply,
Mk	15:41	These **w** had followed him when he
Mk	15:41	many other **w** who had come
Lk	1:42	"Most blessed are you among **w**,
Lk	8: 2	some **w** who had been cured of evil
Lk	23:27	including many **w** who mourned
Lk	23:55	The **w** who had come from Galilee
Acts	1:14	together with some **w**, and Mary
Acts	8:12	men and **w** alike were baptized.
Acts	16:13	with the **w** who had gathered there.
Acts	17: 4	and not a few of the prominent **w**.
1 Cor	14:34	**w** should keep silent
1 Tm	2: 9	**w** should adorn themselves
1 Tm	5: 2	older **w** as mothers, and younger **w** as sisters
2 Tm	3: 6	make captives of **w** weighed down
Ti	2: 3	older **w** should be reverent in their
Ti	2: 4	they may train younger **w** to love
Heb	11:35	**W** received back their dead through
1 Pt	3: 5	how the holy **w** who hoped in God

WOMEN'S → WOMAN

Rev	9: 8	and they had hair like **w** hair.

WON → WIN

Est	2: 9	pleased him and **w** his favor.
1 Pt	3: 1	they may be **w** over without a word

WONDER → WONDERFUL, WONDERFULLY, WONDERS, WONDROUS

Ex	7: 9	"Produce a sign or **w**," you will say

WONDERFUL → WONDER

Ps	119:129	**W** are your testimonies;
Ps	139:14	**w** are your works!
Is	28:29	**w** is his counsel and great his

WONDERFULLY → WONDER

Ps	139:14	I praise you, because I am **w** made;

WONDERS → WONDER

Ex	11:10	and Aaron performed all these **w**
Ex	15:11	in deeds of renown, worker of **w**,
Ps	78:32	they did not believe in his **w**.
Ps	136: 4	Who alone has done great **w**, for his
Dn	3:100	are his signs, how mighty his **w**;
Jn	4:48	you people see signs and **w**,
2 Cor	12:12	signs and **w**, and mighty deeds.
2 Thes	2: 9	deed and in signs and **w** that lie,
Heb	2: 4	added his testimony by signs, **w**,

WONDROUS → WONDER

Ps	26: 7	and recount all your **w** deeds.

WOOD → WOODEN, WOODS, WOODWORKER

Gn	22: 9	altar there and arranged the **w** on it.
Gn	22: 9	put him on top of the **w** on the altar.
Ex	15:25	pointed out to him a piece of **w**.
Ex	25:10	You shall make an ark of acacia **w**,
Ex	25:13	make poles of acacia **w** and plate

Ex	25:23	shall also make a table of acacia **w**,
Ex	27: 1	You shall make an altar of acacia **w**,
Dt	28:64	serve other gods, of **w** and stone,
1 Kgs	18:23	and place it on the **w**, but start no
1 Kgs	18:23	the other and place it on the **w**,
Is	44:19	"Half the **w** I burned in the fire,
Is	44:19	Shall I worship a block of **w**?"
Is	60:17	Instead of **w**, bronze;
Ez	20:32	foreign lands, serving **w** and stone."
Hos	4:12	My people consult their piece of **w**,
Hb	2:19	Ah! you who say to **w**, "Awake!"
1 Cor	3:12	silver, precious stones, **w**, hay,

WOODEN → WOOD

Neh	8: 4	the scribe stood on a **w** platform

WOODS → WOOD

2 Kgs	2:24	two she-bears came out of the **w**

WOODWORKER → WOOD, WORK

Is	44:13	The **w** stretches a line, and marks out

WOOL

Dt	22:11	shall not wear cloth made from **w**
Prv	31:13	She seeks out **w** and flax
Is	1:18	they may become white as **w**.
Dn	7: 9	the hair on his head like pure **w**;
Rev	1:14	of his head was as white as white **w**

WORD → BYWORD, WORDS

Gn	15: 1	the **w** of the LORD came to Abram
Nm	30: 3	he shall not violate his **w**, but must
Jgs	3:20	Ehud said, "I have a **w** from God for you."
1 Kgs	6:12	will fulfill toward you my **w** which I spoke
1 Kgs	8:20	Now the LORD has fulfilled the **w** he spoke:
1 Kgs	8:56	Not a single **w** has gone unfulfilled
1 Chr	17: 3	that same night the **w** of God came
2 Chr	36:22	realize the **w** of the LORD spoken
2 Chr	36:22	both by **w** of mouth and in writing:
Ps	33: 4	For the LORD's **w** is upright;
Ps	107:20	Sent forth his **w** to heal them,
Ps	119:42	answer my taunters with a **w**, for I trust in your **w**.
Ps	119:74	to see me, because I hope in your **w**.
Ps	119:89	Your **w**, LORD, stands forever;
Ps	119:105	Your **w** is a lamp for my feet, a light
Ps	139: 4	Even before a **w** is on my tongue,
Prv	12:25	the heart, but a kind **w** gives it joy.
Prv	15: 1	wrath, but a harsh **w** stirs up anger.
Prv	15:23	a **w** in season, how good it is!
Prv	30: 5	Every **w** of God is tested; he is
Sir	3: 8	In **w** and deed honor your father,
Sir	18:16	So a **w** can be better than a gift.
Is	1:10	Hear the **w** of the LORD,
Is	40: 8	the **w** of our God stands forever."
Is	55:11	So shall my **w** be that goes forth
Jer	5:13	wind, and the **w** is not with them.
Jer	23:29	Is not my **w** like fire—
Mt	4: 4	by every **w** that comes forth
Mt	12:36	for every careless **w** they speak.
Mt	15: 6	You have nullified the **w** of God
Mk	4:14	The sower sows the **w**.
Lk	1: 2	of the **w** have handed them down
Jn	1: 1	In the beginning was the **W**, and the **W** was with God, and the **W** was God.
Jn	1:14	And the **W** became flesh and made
Jn	8:37	because my **w** has no room among
Jn	17:17	them in the truth. Your **w** is truth.
Acts	4:31	continued to speak the **w** of God
Acts	6: 4	and to the ministry of the **w**."
Rom	9: 6	it is not that the **w** of God has failed.
Rom	10: 8	"The **w** is near you, in your mouth
Rom	10: 8	is, the **w** of faith that we preach),
2 Cor	2:17	many who trade on the **w** of God;
2 Cor	4: 2	or falsifying the **w** of God,
Gal	6: 6	the **w** should share all good things
Eph	6:17	of the Spirit, which is the **w** of God.
Phil	2:16	as you hold on to the **w** of life,
Col	3:16	Let the **w** of Christ dwell in you
2 Tm	2:15	imparting the **w** of truth without

Heb	1: 3	sustains all things by his mighty w.
Heb	4:12	the w of God is living and effective,
Heb	6: 5	and tasted the good w of God
Jas	1:21	and humbly welcome the w that has
Jas	1:22	Be doers of the w and not hearers
1 Pt	1:23	the living and abiding w of God,
2 Pt	3: 5	and through water by the w of God;
1 Jn	1: 1	our hands concerns the W of life—
1 Jn	2: 5	But whoever keeps his w, the love
Rev	3: 8	yet you have kept my w and have
Rev	12:11	and by the w of their testimony;
Rev	19:13	his name was called the W of God.
Rev	20: 4	to Jesus and for the w of God,

WORDS → WORD

Ex	24: 3	related all the w and ordinances
Ex	34:28	on the tablets the w of the covenant, the ten w.
Dt	4:13	he commanded you to keep: the ten w,
Dt	10: 4	the ten w that the LORD had spoken
Dt	11:18	take these w of mine into your heart
Dt	13: 4	do not listen to the w of that prophet
Dt	18:19	to my w which the prophet speaks
Dt	31:24	on a scroll the w of this law in their
Dt	32:45	had finished speaking all these w
Jos	8:34	were read aloud all the w of the law,
2 Sm	7:28	are truly God and your w are truth
2 Sm	23: 1	These are the last w of David:
Ps	5: 2	Give ear to my w, O LORD;
Ps	19:15	Let the w of my mouth be
Ps	64: 4	bend their bows of poison w.
Ps	119: 9	Only by observing your w.
Ps	119:130	revelation of your w sheds light,
Prv	2: 1	if you receive my w and treasure my
Prv	2:16	foreign woman with her smooth w,
Prv	10:19	Where w are many, sin is not
Prv	16:24	Pleasing w are a honeycomb,
Prv	25:11	in silver settings are w spoken
Prv	26:22	The w of a talebearer are like dainty
Prv	30: 6	Add nothing to his w, lest he
Eccl	5: 1	therefore let your w be few.
Sir	32: 8	Be brief, say much in few w;
Jer	15:16	When I found your w, I devoured
Jer	15:16	your w were my joy, the happiness
Hos	6: 5	I killed them by the w of my mouth;
Zec	1: 6	But my w and my statutes,
Mt	7:24	who listens to these w of mine
Mt	12:37	By your w you will be acquitted,
Mt	12:37	by your w you will be condemned."
Mt	24:35	away, but my w will not pass away.
Lk	6:47	listens to my w, and acts on them.
Jn	6:68	You have the w of eternal life.
Jn	15: 7	in me and my w remain in you,
1 Cor	2:13	them not with w taught by human
1 Cor	2:13	but with w taught by the Spirit,
1 Cor	14:19	church I would rather speak five w
1 Cor	14:19	than ten thousand w in a tongue.
Rev	19: 9	he said to me, "These w are true;
Rev	22: 6	"These w are trustworthy and true,
Rev	22:19	from the w in this prophetic book,

WORK → CO-WORKER, CO-WORKERS, WOODWORKER, WORKED, WORKING, WORKMAN, WORKS

Gn	2: 2	God completed the w he had been
Gn	2: 2	from all the w he had undertaken.
Ex	20:10	You shall not do any w, either you,
Ex	23:12	For six days you may do your w,
Ex	40:33	Thus Moses finished all the w.
Dt	5:14	You shall not do any w, either you,
1 Chr	22:16	Set to w, therefore, and the LORD
2 Chr	2: 6	send me men skilled at w in gold,
2 Chr	2: 6	who know how to do engraved w,
2 Chr	8:16	All of Solomon's w was carried
Ezr	4:24	w on the house of God in Jerusalem
Ezr	6: 7	elders of the Jews continue the w
Neh	2:18	And they undertook the w with vigor.
Jb	1:10	You have blessed the w of his
Ps	8: 4	your heavens, the w of your fingers,

Ps	90:17	Prosper the w of our hands!
Prv	31:31	Acclaim her for the w of her hands,
Eccl	11: 5	So you do not know the w of God,
Is	64: 7	we are all the w of your hand.
Jer	48:10	who do the LORD's w carelessly,
Lk	13:14	are six days when w should be done.
Jn	5:17	"My Father is at w until now, so I am at w."
Jn	6:27	Do not w for food that perishes
Jn	6:29	said to them, "This is the w of God,
Jn	9: 4	Night is coming when no one can w.
Jn	17: 4	accomplishing the w that you gave
Acts	13: 2	and Saul for the w to which I have
Rom	14:20	food, do not destroy the w of God.
1 Cor	3:13	the w of each will come to light,
1 Cor	3:13	will test the quality of each one's w.
Gal	6: 4	Each one must examine his own w,
Eph	3:20	by the power at w within us,
Phil	1: 6	the one who began a good w in you
Phil	2:12	w out your salvation with fear
1 Thes	4:11	and to w with your [own] hands,
2 Thes	2: 7	of lawlessness is already at w.
2 Thes	3:10	that if anyone was unwilling to w,
2 Tm	2:21	the house, ready for every good w.
2 Tm	3:17	equipped for every good w.
Heb	6:10	not unjust so as to overlook your w

WORKED → WORK

2 Thes	3: 8	night and day we w, so as not
2 Jn	1: 8	that you do not lose what we w

WORKING → WORK

1 Cor	4:12	and we toil, w with our own hands.
Gal	5: 6	but only faith w through love.

WORKMAN → WORK

2 Tm	2:15	to God, a w who causes no disgrace,

WORKS → WORK

Ps	8: 7	You have given him rule over the w
Ps	46: 9	Come and see the w of the LORD,
Ps	77:13	I will ponder all your w;
Ps	92: 6	How great are your w, LORD!
Is	2: 8	bow down to the w of their hands,
Rom	4: 6	credits righteousness apart from w:
Gal	2:16	a person is not justified by w
Gal	2:16	in Christ and not by w of the law,
Gal	2:16	because by w of the law no one will
Gal	5:19	Now the w of the flesh are obvious:
Eph	2: 9	it is not from w, so no one may
Eph	2:10	the good w that God has prepared
1 Tm	6:18	to be rich in good w, to be generous,

WORLD → WORLDLY

1 Chr	16:30	the w will surely stand fast,
Ps	9: 9	It is he who judges the w
Ps	19: 5	their messages, to the ends of the w.
Ps	50:12	for mine is the w and all that fills it.
Ps	96:13	To govern the w with justice
Is	13:11	Thus I will punish the w for its evil
Mt	4: 8	of the w in their magnificence,
Mt	5:14	You are the light of the w. A city set
Mt	16:26	there be for one to gain the whole w
Jn	1:10	He was in the w, and the w came
Jn	1:10	him, but the w did not know him.
Jn	1:29	who takes away the sin of the w.
Jn	3:16	God so loved the w that he gave his
Jn	3:17	Son into the w to condemn the w,
Jn	3:17	the w might be saved through him.
Jn	8:12	saying, "I am the light of the w.
Jn	9: 5	While I am in the w, I am the light of the w."
Jn	15:19	If you belonged to the w,
Jn	15:19	because you do not belong to the w,
Jn	15:19	and I have chosen you out of the w,
Jn	16:33	In the w you will have trouble,
Jn	16:33	courage, I have conquered the w."
Jn	17:18	As you sent me into the w, so I sent them into the w.
Jn	18:36	kingdom does not belong to this w
Jn	18:36	If my kingdom did belong to this w,
Acts	17:31	he will 'judge the w with justice'

Rom   3:19 the whole **w** stand accountable
Rom   5:12 one person sin entered the **w,**
Rom 10:18 their words to the ends of the **w.**"
1 Cor 1:27 foolish of the **w** to shame the wise,
1 Cor 1:27 weak of the **w** to shame the strong,
1 Cor 3:19 the wisdom of this **w** is foolishness
1 Cor 6: 2 that the holy ones will judge the **w?**
1 Cor 6: 2 If the **w** is to be judged by you,
2 Cor 5:19 God was reconciling the **w**
Gal   6:14 which the **w** has been crucified to me, and I to the **w.**
1 Tm 1:15 came into the **w** to save sinners.
1 Tm 6: 7 For we brought nothing into the **w,**
Heb   1: 6 he leads the first-born into the **w,**
Heb 11: 7 Through this he condemned the **w**
Heb 11:38 The **w** was not worthy of them.
Jas   1:27 to keep oneself unstained by the **w.**
Jas   4: 4 to be a lover of the **w** means enmity
Jas   4: 4 of the **w** makes himself an enemy
1 Pt 1:20 before the foundation of the **w**
1 Jn 2: 2 only but for those of the whole **w.**
1 Jn 2:15 Do not love the **w** or the things of the **w.**
1 Jn 2:15 If anyone loves the **w,** the love
1 Jn 5: 4 is begotten by God conquers the **w.**
1 Jn 5: 4 that conquers the **w** is our faith.
Rev 11:15 kingdom of the **w** now belongs
Rev 13: 8 the foundation of the **w** in the book

WORLDLY → WORLD
Ti   2:12 to reject godless ways and **w** desires

WORM → WORMS
Ps   22: 7 But I am a **w,** not a man,
Is   41:14 Do not fear, you **w** Jacob,
Mk   9:48 where 'their **w** does not die,

WORMS → WORM
Acts 12:23 he was eaten by **w** and breathed his

WORMWOOD
Am   5: 7 to those who turn justice into **w**
Rev   8:11 The star was called "**W,**"
Rev   8:11 a third of all the water turned to **w.**

WORRIED → WORRY
Lk 10:41 anxious and **w** about many things.

WORRY → WORRIED, WORRYING
Prv 12:25 **W** weighs down the heart, but a kind
Mt   6:25 I tell you, do not **w** about your life,
Mt   6:34 Do not **w** about tomorrow;
Mt 10:19 over, do not **w** about how you are

WORRYING → WORRY
Mt   6:27 of you by **w** add a single moment

WORSE → BAD
Mt 12:45 of that person is **w** than the first.
Jn   5:14 so that nothing **w** may happen
1 Tm 5: 8 faith and is **w** than an unbeliever.
2 Pt 2:20 last condition is **w** than their first.

WORSHIP → WORSHIPED, WORSHIPERS, WORSHIPING, WORSHIPS
Ps 95: 6 Enter, let us bow down in **w;**
Dn   3:95 or **w** any god except their own God.
Mt   4: 9 will prostrate yourself and **w** me."
Lk   4: 8 'You shall **w** the Lord, your God,
Jn   4:24 those who **w** him must **w** in Spirit
Rom 12: 1 pleasing to God, your spiritual **w.**
Rev   4:10 who sits on the throne and **w** him,
Rev 13:12 and its inhabitants **w** the first beast,
Rev 14: 7 **W** him who made heaven and earth
Rev 22: 3 be in it, and his servants will **w** him.

WORSHIPED → WORSHIP
Rev   5:14 and the elders fell down and **w.**
Rev 13: 4 They **w** the dragon because it gave
Rev 13: 4 they also **w** the beast and said,
Rev 20: 4 who had not **w** the beast or its image

WORSHIPERS → WORSHIP
Jn   4:23 when true **w** will worship the Father

WORSHIPING → WORSHIP
Acts 13: 2 While they were **w** the Lord

WORSHIPS → WORSHIP
Is 44:15 Yet he makes a god and **w** it, turns it

WORTHLESS → WORTHY
Ps 31: 7 You hate those who serve **w** idols,
Ps 60:13 aid against the foe; **w** is human help.
Rom 3:12 all alike are **w;** there is not one who

WORTHY → WORTHLESS
Mt 10:37 or mother more than me is not **w**
Mt 10:37 daughter more than me is not **w**
Mt 10:38 and follow after me is not **w** of me.
Lk   3:16 I am not **w** to loosen the thongs
Eph   4: 1 in a manner **w** of the call you have
Phil 1:27 yourselves in a way **w** of the gospel
Col   1:10 to live in a manner **w** of the Lord,
Heb   3: 3 But he is **w** of more "glory" than
Heb 11:38 The world was not **w** of them.
3 Jn 1: 6 Please help them in a way **w** of God
Rev   3: 4 in white, because they are **w.**
Rev   4:11 "**W** are you, Lord our God,
Rev   5: 2 "Who is **w** to open the scroll
Rev   5:12 "**W** is the Lamb that was slain

WOUND → WOUNDS
Ex 21:25 burn for burn, **w** for **w,**
Jer 10:19 undone, my **w** is beyond healing.
1 Cor 8:12 brothers and **w** their consciences,
Rev 13: 3 but this mortal **w** was healed.

WOUNDS → WOUND
Jb   5:18 For he **w,** but he binds up;
Ps 147: 3 and binding up their **w.**
Zec 13: 6 "What are these **w** on your chest?"
1 Pt 2:24 By his **w** you have been healed.

WOVEN
Jn 19:23 **w** in one piece from the top down.

WRAPPED
Mk 15:46 **w** him in the linen cloth and laid
Lk   2: 7 She **w** him in swaddling clothes

WRATH
Nm 17:11 for **w** has come forth
1 Chr 27:24 for because of it **w** fell upon Israel.
1 Mc 3: 8 He turned away **w** from Israel,
Ps   2: 5 his anger, in his **w** he terrifies them:
Ps   6: 2 Lord, nor punish in your **w.**
Ps 37: 8 abandon **w;** do not be provoked;
Prv 15: 1 A mild answer turns back **w,**
Sir 16:11 and forgives, but also pours out **w.**
Is 13:13 At the **w** of the Lord of hosts
Is 51:17 the Lord's hand the cup of his **w;**
Jer   6:11 But the **w** of the Lord brims
Lam   4:11 his anger, poured out his blazing **w;**
Zep   1:15 A day of **w** is that day, a day
Mt   3: 7 you to flee from the coming **w?**
Jn   3:36 but the **w** of God remains upon him.
Rom 1:18 The **w** of God is indeed being
Rom 2: 5 you are storing up **w** for yourself for the day of **w**
Rom 5: 9 be saved through him from the **w.**
Rom 9:22 wishing to show his **w** and make
Rom 9:22 patience the vessels of **w** made
Eph   2: 3 we were by nature children of **w,**
1 Thes 1:10 who delivers us from the coming **w.**
1 Thes 5: 9 For God did not destine us for **w,**
Rev   6:17 the great day of their **w** has come
Rev 19:15 the fury and **w** of God the almighty.

WRESTLED
Gn 32:25 a man **w** with him until the break

WRETCHED
Rev   3:17 yet do not realize that you are **w,**

WRINKLE
Eph   5:27 without spot or **w** or any such thing,

WRISTS

Acts   12: 7   The chains fell from his **w**.

WRITE → WRITES, WRITING, WRITTEN, WROTE

Ex	17:14	**W** this down in a book as something
Ex	34:27	**W** down these words,
Dt	6: 9	**W** them on the doorposts of your
Dt	10: 2	I will **w** upon the tablets the words
Prv	7: 3	**w** them on the tablet of your heart.
Jer	31:33	them, and **w** it upon their hearts;
Lk	1: 3	to **w** it down in an orderly sequence
Heb	8:10	and I will **w** them upon their hearts.
Rev	1:19	**W** down, therefore, what you have
Rev	21: 5	he said, "**W** these words down,

WRITES → WRITE

Dt   24: 1   and he **w** out a bill of divorce

WRITING → WRITE

Dt	31:24	When Moses had finished **w**
Dn	5: 7	"Whoever reads this **w** and tells me
1 Cor	14:37	that what I am **w** to you is
1 Jn	2: 7	I am **w** no new commandment
2 Jn	1: 5	you, not as though I were **w** a new

WRITTEN → WRITE

Ex	32:32	out of the book that you have **w**."
Dt	28:58	of this law which is **w** in this book,
Jos	1: 8	carefully observe all that is **w** in it;
Jos	23: 6	observe all that is **w** in the book
1 Kgs	2: 3	decrees as they are **w** in the law
Neh	8:14	They found it **w** in the law
Ps	40: 8	with an inscribed scroll **w** upon me.
Prv	22:20	Have I not **w** for you thirty sayings,
Dn	12: 1	everyone who is found **w**
Mal	3:16	A record book was **w** before him
Mt	26:24	Man indeed goes, as it is **w** of him,
Lk	10:20	rejoice because your names are **w**
Lk	24:44	that everything **w** about me
Jn	20:31	these are **w** that you may [come]
Jn	21:25	contain the books that would be **w**.
Rom	2:15	of the law are **w** in their hearts,
Rom	15: 4	whatever was **w** previously was **w**
1 Cor	4: 6	from us not to go beyond what is **w**,
1 Cor	10:11	and they have been **w** down as
2 Cor	3: 3	**w** not in ink but by the Spirit
Heb	10: 7	I said, 'As is **w** of me in the scroll,
Rev	13: 8	it, all whose names were not **w**
Rev	14: 1	and his Father's name **w** on their
Rev	17: 5	On her forehead was **w** a name,
Rev	20:12	deeds, by what was **w** in the scrolls.
Rev	20:15	whose name was not found **w**
Rev	21:27	those will enter whose names are **w**

WRONG → WRONGDOER, WRONGDOING, WRONGED

Nm	5: 7	person shall confess the **w** that has
1 Kgs	8:47	say, 'We have sinned and done **w**;
Zep	3: 5	in its midst is just, doing no **w**;
Zep	3:13	They shall do no **w** and speak no
Acts	23: 9	"We find nothing **w** with this man.
Col	3:25	recompense for the **w** he committed,

WRONGDOER → DO, WRONG

Col   3:25   For the **w** will receive recompense

WRONGDOING → DO, WRONG

1 Cor	13: 6	it does not rejoice over **w**
1 Jn	5:17	All **w** is sin, but there is sin that is

WRONGED → WRONG

Nm   5: 7   its value to the one that has been **w**.

WROTE → WRITE

Ex	24: 4	**w** down all the words of the Lord
Ex	34:28	he **w** on the tablets the words
Dt	10: 4	The Lord then **w** on the tablets,
Jer	36: 4	and he **w** down on a scroll what
Dn	5: 5	When the king saw the hand that **w**,
Jn	1:45	about whom Moses **w** in the law,
Jn	5:46	me, because he **w** about me.
Jn	8: 8	he bent down and **w** on the ground.

X

X

Ez	9: 4	mark an **X** on the foreheads of those who grieve
Ez	9: 6	do not touch anyone marked with the **X**.

Y

YARN

Ex	35:23	or scarlet **y**, fine linen or goat hair,
Lv	14: 4	scarlet **y**, and hyssop be obtained

YEAR → YEARS

Gn	17:21	shall bear to you by this time next **y**.
Ex	23:14	Three times a **y** you shall celebrate
Ex	34:23	Three times a **y** all your men shall
Nm	14:34	shall bear your punishment one **y**
Dt	1: 3	In the fortieth **y**, on the first day
Neh	10:32	In the seventh **y** we will forgo
Is	6: 1	In the **y** King Uzziah died, I saw
Is	34: 8	a **y** of requital for the cause of Zion.
Is	61: 2	To announce a **y** of favor
Is	63: 4	my **y** for redeeming had come.
Zec	14:16	came against Jerusalem will go up **y** after **y** to bow down
Lk	2:41	Each **y** his parents went
Lk	13: 8	leave it for this **y** also, and I shall
Jn	11:49	who was high priest that **y**,
Jn	18:13	who was high priest that **y**.
Heb	9: 7	goes into the inner one once a **y**,
Heb	10: 1	that they offer continually each **y**.

YEARNS

Is   26: 9   My soul **y** for you at night, yes,

YEARS → YEAR

Gn	1:14	the seasons, the days and the **y**,
Gn	41:26	The seven healthy cows are seven **y**,
Gn	41:26	the seven healthy ears are seven **y**—
Gn	41:30	seven **y** of famine will rise
Gn	47: 9	hard have been these **y** of my life,
Ex	12:40	was four hundred and thirty **y**.
Ex	16:35	Israelites ate the manna for forty **y**,
Nm	1: 3	all the men in Israel of twenty **y**
Nm	14:34	one year for each day: forty **y**.
Dt	2: 7	It is now forty **y** that the Lord,
Dt	8: 4	nor did your feet swell these forty **y**.
2 Sm	21: 1	time there was a famine for three **y**,
2 Chr	36:21	rest while seventy **y** are fulfilled.
Ezr	5:11	the house built here many **y** ago,
Neh	9:21	Forty **y** in the desert you sustained
Jb	36:26	number of his **y** past searching out.
Ps	90: 4	A thousand **y** in your eyes are
Ps	90:10	Seventy is the sum of our **y**,
Ps	95:10	Forty **y** I loathed that generation;
Prv	3: 2	many days, and **y** of life, and peace,
Prv	9:11	and the **y** of your life increased.
Prv	10:27	but the **y** of the wicked are cut short.
Eccl	6: 6	such a one live twice a thousand **y**
Jer	25:12	when the seventy **y** have elapsed,
Dn	9: 2	was to lie in ruins for seventy **y**.
Mt	2:16	and its vicinity two **y** old and under,
Mt	9:20	hemorrhages for twelve **y** came
Lk	3:23	he was about thirty **y** of age.
Lk	13:16	Satan has bound for eighteen **y** now,
Jn	2:20	under construction for forty-six **y**,
Gal	4:10	days, months, seasons, and **y**.
Heb	3:17	was he "provoked for forty **y**"?
2 Pt	3: 8	Lord one day is like a thousand **y** and a thousand **y** like one day.
Rev	20: 2	and tied it up for a thousand **y**

YEAST

1 Cor	5: 6	that a little **y** leavens all the dough?
Gal	5: 9	A little **y** leavens the whole batch

YES

Mt	5:37	Let your '**Y**' mean '**Y**,' and your
2 Cor	1:17	so that with me it is "**y**,
2 Cor	1:20	promises of God, their **Y** is in him;
Jas	5:12	but let your "**Y**" mean "**Y**"

YESTERDAY
Heb 13: 8 Jesus Christ is the same **y**, today,

YET
Am   4: 6 **Y** you did not return to me—
Mt   6:26 **y** your heavenly Father feeds them.
Jn   2: 4 My hour has not **y** come."
Jn   6:70 **Y** is not one of you a devil?"
Jn   7: 6 "My time is not **y** here, but the time
Jn   7: 8 my time has not **y** been fulfilled."
Jn   7:39 no Spirit **y**, because Jesus had not **y** been glorified.
Jn   8:20 because his hour had not **y** come.
Heb 12: 4 against sin you have not **y** resisted
Rev 17:10 and the last has not **y** come,

YIELDED
Is   5: 2 of grapes, but it **y** rotten grapes.

YOKE
Dt   28:48 He will put an iron **y** on your neck,
1 Kgs 12: 4 "Your father put a heavy **y** on us.
Sir   28:20 For its **y** is a **y** of iron, and its chains
Mt   11:30 For my **y** is easy, and my burden
Gal   5: 1 not submit again to the **y** of slavery.

YOUNG → YOUNGER, YOUNGEST, YOUTH, YOUTHFUL, YOUTHS
Gn   24:16 The **y** woman was very beautiful, a virgin,
Dt   22: 6 across a bird's nest with **y** birds
1 Sm   2:17 Thus the **y** men sinned grievously
2 Chr 10:14 to them as the **y** men had advised:
2 Chr 36:17 who killed their **y** men
2 Chr 36:17 for neither **y** men nor **y** women,
Est   2: 7 The **y** woman was beautifully formed
Ps   78:63 Fire consumed their **y** men; their **y** women heard no
              wedding songs.
Ps   119: 9 How can the **y** keep his way without
Prv   7: 7 I observed among the **y** men,
Prv   20:29 The glory of the **y** is their strength,
Eccl 11: 9 while you are **y** and let your heart be
Sg   1: 3 perfume—therefore **y** women love you.
Dn   1: 4 They should be **y** men without any
Dn   1:17 To these four **y** men God gave
Jl   3: 1 dreams, your **y** men will see visions.
Mk   14:51 Now a **y** man followed him wearing
Mk   16: 5 the tomb they saw a **y** man sitting
Lk   2:24 of turtledoves or two **y** pigeons,"
Acts   2:17 your **y** men shall see visions,
Acts   7:58 at the feet of a **y** man named Saul.
Acts 20: 9 a **y** man named Eutychus who was
1 Jn   2:13 I am writing to you, **y** men,

YOUNGER → YOUNG
Gn   19:35 then the **y** one went in and lay
Gn   25:23 other, and the older will serve the **y**.
Rom   9:12 told, "The older shall serve the **y**."
1 Tm   5: 1 as a father. Treat **y** men as brothers,
1 Tm   5: 2 **y** women as sisters with complete
1 Tm   5:14 So I would like **y** widows to marry,
1 Pt   5: 5 Likewise, you **y** members,

YOUNGEST → YOUNG
Gn   9:24 learned what his **y** son had done
Gn   42:20 you must bring me your **y** brother.
Jos   6:26 at the cost of his **y** son will he set
1 Sm 17:14 David was the **y**. While the three
1 Kgs 16:34 and at the cost of Segub, his **y** son,
Lk   22:26 the greatest among you be as the **y**,

YOUTH → YOUNG
1 Sm 17:33 for you are only a **y**, while he has been a warrior from
              his **y**.
Ps   71: 5 my trust, GOD, from my **y**.
Ps   103: 5 things, so your **y** is renewed like
Ps   144:12 plants well nurtured from their **y**,
Prv   2:17 forsakes the companion of her **y**
Prv   5:18 and have joy of the wife of your **y**,
Eccl   4:13 is a poor but wise **y** than an old
Eccl 11:10 for **y** and black hair are fleeting.
Eccl 12: 1 your Creator in the days of your **y**,
Is   65:20 years shall be considered a **y**,

Mal   2:14 your **y** With whom you have broken

YOUTHFUL → YOUNG
2 Tm   2:22 So turn from **y** desires and pursue

YOUTHS → YOUNG
Is   40:30 grow weary, and **y** stagger and fall,

Z

ZACCHAEUS
Lk   19: 2 Now a man there named **Z**, who was

ZADOK
2 Sm 15:27 The king also said to **Z** the priest:
1 Kgs 1:26 nor **Z** the priest, nor Benaiah,
Neh   13:13 Shelemiah the priest, **Z** the scribe,

ZALMON
Jgs   9:48 up Mount **Z** with all his soldiers,
Ps   68:15 it will be as when snow fell on **Z**.

ZALMUNNA
Jgs   8: 5 and I am pursuing Zebah and **Z**,
Ps   83:12 all their princes like Zebah and **Z**,

ZAPHON
Jos   13:27 Succoth, **Z**, the other part

ZAREPHATH
1 Kgs 17: 9 go to **Z** of Sidon and stay there.
Lk   4:26 only to a widow in **Z** in the land

ZEAL → ZEALOT, ZEALOUS
2 Kgs 10:16 me and see my **z** for the LORD."
2 Kgs 19:31 The **z** of the LORD of hosts shall
1 Mc   2:26 Thus he showed his **z** for the law,
Ps   69:10 Because **z** for your house has
Is   37:32 The **z** of the LORD of hosts shall
Jn   2:17 "**Z** for your house will consume
Rom   10: 2 to them that they have **z** for God,
Rom   12:11 Do not grow slack in **z**, be fervent
2 Cor 7:11 yearning, and **z**, and punishment.
Phil   3: 6 in **z** I persecuted the church,

ZEALOT → ZEAL
Lk   6:15 Simon who was called a **Z**,
Acts   1:13 Simon the **Z**, and Judas son
Gal   1:14 since I was even more a **z** for my

ZEALOUS → ZEAL
1 Kgs 19:10 "I have been most **z**
1 Kgs 19:14 replied, "I have been most **z**
1 Mc   2:27 "Let everyone who is **z** for the law
2 Mc   4: 2 and a **z** defender of the laws.
Ez   39:25 of Israel; I am **z** for my holy name.
Acts 21:20 they are all **z** observers of the law.

ZEBAH
Jgs   8: 5 and I am pursuing **Z** and Zalmunna,
Ps   83:12 Zeeb, all their princes like **Z**

ZEBEDEE
Mt   4:21 the son of **Z**, and his brother John.
Mt   4:21 with their father **Z**, mending their
Mt   26:37 along Peter and the two sons of **Z**,
Mk   1:20 So they left their father **Z** in the boat
Mk   10:35 the sons of **Z**, came to him and said
Lk   5:10 the sons of **Z**, who were partners

ZEBOIIM
Dt   29:22 Admah and **Z**, which the LORD
Hos   11: 8 you as Admah, or make you like **Z**?

ZEBUL
Jgs   9:30 When **Z**, the ruler of the city,

ZEBULUN
Son of Jacob by Leah (Gn 30:20; 35:23; 1 Chr 2:1). Tribe of blessed (Gn 49:13; Dt 33:18-19), numbered (Nm 1:31; 26:27), allotted land (Jos 19:10-16; Ez 48:26), failed to fully possess (Jgs 1:30), supported Deborah (Jgs 4:6-10; 5:14, 18), David (1 Chr 12:34), 12,000 from (Rev 7:8).

ZECHARIAH
1. Son of Jeroboam II; king of Israel (2 Kgs 15:8-12).

2. Postexilic prophet who encouraged rebuilding of temple (Ezr 5:1; 6:14; Zec 1:1).

ZEDEKIAH → =MATTANIAH

1. False prophet (1 Kgs 22:11-24; 2 Chr 18:10-23).
2. Mattaniah, son of Josiah (1 Chr 3:15), made king of Judah by Nebuchadnezzar (2 Kgs 24:17–25:7; 2 Chr 36:10-14; Jer 37–39; 52:1-11).

ZEEB

Jgs   7:25   Oreb and **Z**, killing Oreb at the rock
Ps   83:12 Make their nobles like Oreb and **Z**,

ZELOPHEHAD

Nm   26:33 of the daughters of **Z** were Mahlah,
Jos   17: 3 Furthermore, **Z**, son of Hepher,

ZEPHANIAH

Prophet; descendant of Hezekiah (Zep 1:1).

ZERUBBABEL

Descendant of David (1 Chr 3:19; Mt 1:3). Led return from exile (Ezr 2:2; Neh 7:7). Governor of Israel; helped rebuild altar and temple (Ezr 3; Hg 1–2; Zec 4).

ZERUIAH

2 Sm   2:18   The three sons of **Z** were there—

ZEUS

2 Mc   6: 2   and dedicate it to Olympian **Z**,
2 Mc   6: 2   on Mount Gerizim to **Z** the Host
Acts   14:12 They called Barnabas "**Z**" and Paul

ZIBA

2 Sm   9: 2   of the house of Saul named **Z**.
2 Sm   16: 1 went a little beyond the top and **Z**,

ZIKLAG

1 Sm   27: 6 That same day Achish gave him **Z**,
1 Sm   30: 1 They stormed **Z**, and set it on fire.
1 Sm   30:26 When David came to **Z**, he sent part

ZILPAH

Servant of Leah, mother of Jacob's sons Gad and Asher (Gn 30:9-12; 35:26, 46:16-18).

ZIMRI

King of Israel (1 Kgs 16:9-20).

ZIN

Nm   13:21 of **Z** as far as where Rehob adjoins

ZION

2 Sm   5: 7   captured the fortress of **Z**, which is
2 Kgs   19:31 and from Mount **Z**, survivors.
Ps   2: 6   myself have installed my king on **Z**,
Ps   9:12   to the LORD enthroned on **Z**;
Ps   14: 7 from **Z** might come the salvation
Ps   48: 3 Mount **Z**, the heights of Zaphon,
Ps   50: 2 From **Z**, the perfection of beauty,
Ps   65: 2 our hymn of praise, O God on **Z**;
Ps   74: 2 heritage, Mount **Z** where you dwell.
Ps   78:68 of Judah, Mount **Z** which he loved.
Ps   87: 2 gates of **Z** more than any dwelling

Ps   102:14 You will again show mercy to **Z**;
Ps   137: 3 "Sing for us a song of **Z**!"
Sir   24:10 him, and so I was established in **Z**.
Is   1:27   **Z** shall be redeemed by justice,
Is   2: 3   from **Z** shall go forth instruction,
Is   14:32 "The LORD has established **Z**,
Is   28:16 I am laying a stone in **Z**, a stone
Is   40: 9 Go up onto a high mountain, **Z**,
Is   51: 3 the LORD shall comfort **Z**,
Is   51:11 will return and enter **Z** singing,
Is   52: 1 Put on your strength, **Z**; Put on your
Is   52: 8 their eyes, the LORD's return to **Z**.
Jer   50: 5 They shall ask for **Z**,
Lam   2:13   to comfort you, virgin daughter **Z**?
Jl   2: 1   Blow the horn in **Z**, sound the alarm
Jl   4:16   The LORD roars from **Z**,
Jl   4:21   The LORD dwells in **Z**.
Am   1: 2   The LORD roars from **Z**,
Am   6: 1   to those who are complacent in **Z**,
Mi   3:12   you, **Z** shall be plowed like a field,
Mi   4: 2   from **Z** shall go forth instruction,
Zec   1:17   the LORD will again comfort **Z**,
Zec   9: 9   Exult greatly, O daughter **Z**!
Mt   21: 5 "Say to daughter **Z**, 'Behold,
Rom   9:33   I am laying a stone in **Z** that will
Rom   11:26 "The deliverer will come out of **Z**,
Heb   12:22 you have approached Mount **Z**
1 Pt   2: 6   "Behold, I am laying a stone in **Z**,
Rev   14: 1 was the Lamb standing on Mount **Z**,

ZIPH → ZIPHITES

1 Sm   23:14 or in the barren hill country near **Z**.
1 Sm   26: 1 Men from **Z** came to Saul

ZIPHITES → ZIPH

1 Sm   23:19 Some of the **Z** went up to Saul

ZIPPOR

Nm   22: 4 Balak, son of **Z**, was king of Moab;

ZIPPORAH

Daughter of Reuel; wife of Moses (Ex 2:21-22; 4:20-26; 18:1-6).

ZIV

1 Kgs   6: 1   the month of **Z** (the second month),

ZOAN

Ps   78:43 Egypt, his wonders in the plain of **Z**.

ZOAR

Gn   19:22 That is why the town is called **Z**.
Gn   19:30 Since Lot was afraid to stay in **Z**,

ZOBAH

1 Sm   14:47 the kings of **Z**, and the Philistines.
1 Chr   18: 3 king of **Z**, toward Hamath, who was

ZOPHAR

One of Job's friends (Jb 2:11; 11; 20; 42:9).

ZORAH

Jgs   13: 2 There was a certain man from **Z**,